Strategic Management Model

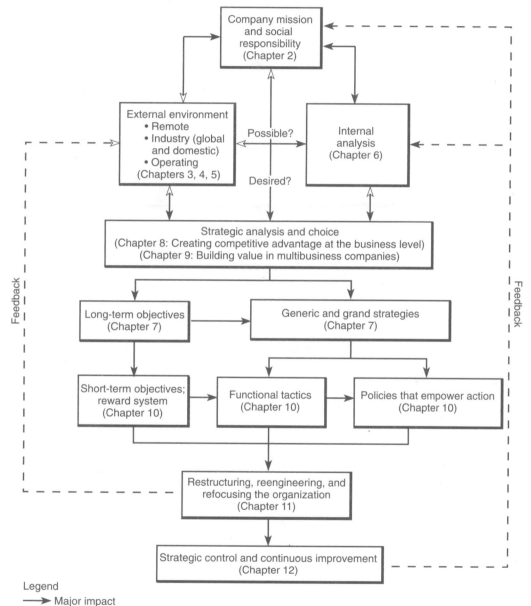

Company mission and social responsibility (Chapter 2)

External environment
• Remote
• Industry (global and domestic)
• Operating
(Chapters 3, 4, 5)

Possible?

Desired?

Internal analysis (Chapter 6)

Strategic analysis and choice
(Chapter 8: Creating competitive advantage at the business level)
(Chapter 9: Building value in multibusiness companies)

Long-term objectives (Chapter 7)

Generic and grand strategies (Chapter 7)

Short-term objectives; reward system (Chapter 10)

Functional tactics (Chapter 10)

Policies that empower action (Chapter 10)

Restructuring, reengineering, and refocusing the organization (Chapter 11)

Strategic control and continuous improvement (Chapter 12)

Feedback

Feedback

Legend
⟶ Major impact
⟶▷ Minor impact

STRATEGIC MANAGEMENT
FORMULATION, IMPLEMENTATION, AND CONTROL

JOHN A. PEARCE II

College of Commerce and Finance
Villanova University

RICHARD B. ROBINSON, JR.

The Darla Moore School of Business
University of South Carolina

Seventh Edition

Boston Burr Ridge, IL Dubuque, IA Madison, WI New York San Francisco St. Louis
Bangkok Bogotá Caracas Lisbon London Madrid
Mexico City Milan New Delhi Seoul Singapore Sydney Taipei Toronto

McGraw-Hill Higher Education 🪐
*A Division of The **McGraw-Hill** Companies*

STRATEGIC MANAGEMENT:
FORMULATION, IMPLEMENTATION, AND CONTROL

This book is printed on acid-free paper.

1 2 3 4 5 6 7 8 9 0 VNH/VNH 9 0 9 8 7 6 5 4 3 2 1 0 9

ISBN 0-07-229075-7

Vice president/Editor-in-chief: *Michael W. Junior*
Publisher: *Craig S. Beytien*
Development editor: *Sarah Reed*
Marketing manager: *Ellen Cleary*
Project manager: *Susanne Riedell*
Production supervisor: *Rose Hepburn*
Freelance design coordinator: *Gino Cieslik*
Front Cover Image: © *Super Stock*
Supplement coordinator: *Rose M. Range*
Compositor: *GAC Indianapolis*
Typeface: *10/12 Times Roman*
Printer: *Von Hoffmann Press, Inc.*

Library of Congress Cataloging-in-Publication Data

Pearce, John A.
    Strategic management : formulation, implementation, and control /
John A. Pearce II, Richard B. Robinson, Jr. -- 7th ed.
        p.   cm.
    Includes index.
    ISBN 0-07-229075-7
    1. Strategic planning.   I. Robinson, Richard B. (Richard Braden),
1947-   . II. Title.
HD30.28.P3395   2000
658.4'012--dc21   99-16363

http://www.mhhe.com

To Susan McCartney Pearce,
David Donham Pearce, Mark McCartney Pearce,
Josephine Elizabeth Robinson,
Katherine Elizabeth Robinson, John Braden Robinson—
for the love, joy, and vitality that they give to our lives.

PREFACE

This seventh edition of *Strategic Management: Formulation, Implementation, and Control* is both the culmination of over 20 years of work by many people and a major revision designed to accommodate the needs of strategy students in the 21st century. These are exciting times and we are excited about the many new developments in this book and the accompanying McGraw-Hill supplements. This preface describes what we have done to make the seventh edition uniquely effective in preparing students for strategic decisions in tomorrow's fast-paced global business arena. It also allows us the opportunity to recognize many outstanding contributors.

The seventh edition of *Strategic Management: Formulation, Implementation, and Control* is divided into 12 chapters that provide a thorough, state-of-the-art treatment of the critical business skills needed to plan and manage strategic activities. Each chapter has been filled with new, current real-world examples to illustrate concepts in companies students recognize and regularly read about in the news around the world. Strategic ramifications of topics like executive compensation, E-commerce, the Internet, entrepreneurship, ethics, continuous improvement, virtual organization, cultural diversity, outsourcing, strategic alliances, and the global economy can be found across several chapters in this seventh edition. While the text continues a solid academic connection, students will find the text material to be practical, skills oriented, and relevant to their jobs.

We are excited and honored to have been selected by *Business Week* to be their exclusive strategic partner among strategic management textbooks. Their editors were very comfortable with the framework we use to explain strategic management and our emphasis on practical, relevant coverage in our text. We were thrilled to have unlimited access to the world's best business publication to create examples, illustration modules, and various cases. The result is an extensively enhanced text and cases benefiting from hundreds of contemporary examples and illustrations provided by *Business Week* writers worldwide. You will see *Business Week*'s impact on our discussion case feature, our Strategy in Action modules, our cases, and our web site. Of course, we are also pleased with several hundred examples blended into the text material, which came from recent issues of *Business Week* or http://www.businessweek.com.

An Overview of Our Text Material

The seventh edition continues to use a model of the strategic management process as the basis for the organization of the text material. Previous adopters have identified that model as a key distinctive competence for our text because it offers a logical flow, distinct elements, and an easy-to-understand guide to strategic management. The model has been modestly refined to reflect strategic analysis at different organizational levels as well as the importance of internal analysis in the strategic management process. Adopters see quickly and feel comfortable that the model and subsequent structure continue to provide a student-friendly approach to the study of strategic management.

The text material is divided into 12 chapters. The first chapter provides an overview of the strategic management process and explains what students will find as they use this book. The remaining 11 chapters cover each part of the strategic management process and techniques that aid strategic analysis, forecasting, decision making, implementation, and control.

The literature and research in the strategic management area have developed at a rapid pace in recent years in both the academic and business press. This seventh edition includes several revisions designed to incorporate major developments from both these sources. While we have sought to include cutting-edge concepts, we have emphasized straightforward, logical, and simple presentation so that students can grasp these new ideas without additional reading. Some of the revisions that deserve particular note are:

Corporate Social Responsibility   This seventh edition overall, the integrative model for the book, and Chapter 2 on company mission and direction all give added emphasis to the issue of corporate social responsibility. Many collegiate business schools have decided that stand-alone courses in business ethics and social responsibility are no longer necessary. Such decisions make it important that all other business courses accept a greater role in discussing the relevant topics. Our revision helps professors fulfill this obligation by presenting a balanced discussion and useful guidelines to students and managers on key topics in corporate social responsibility.

Agency Theory   Of the recent approaches to corporate governance and strategic management, probably none has had a greater impact on managerial thinking than agency theory. While the breadth and measurement of its usefulness continue to be hotly debated, students of strategic management need to understand the role of agency in our free enterprise, capitalistic system. This seventh edition of *Strategic Management* presents agency theory in a coherent and practical manner. We believe that it arms students with a cutting-edge approach to increasing their understanding of the priorities of executive decision making and strategic control.

Resource-Based View of the Firm   One of the most significant conceptual frameworks to systematize and "measure" a firm's strategic capabilities is the resource-based view (RBV) of the firm. The RBV has received major academic and business press attention during the last decade helping to shape its value as a conceptual tool adding rigor during the internal analysis and strategic analysis phases of the strategic management process. We have made major changes in the seventh edition, particularly in Chapter 6, which presents the RBV in a logical and practical manner as an important underpinning of sound strategic thinking. Students will have a much better appreciation of tangible assets, intangible assets, and organization capabilities after reading this section. They will see different ways to answer the question "what makes a resource valuable?" and be able to determine when that resource creates a competitive advantage in a systematic, disciplined, creative manner.

Value Chain Analysis   Outsourcing has become standard business practice in virtually every facet of what business organizations undertake. This trend has enhanced the usefulness of the value chain approach in strategic analysis. We have simplified our treatment of this useful conceptual framework and added several contemporary examples to enable students to quickly and automatically incorporate the value chain perspective into their strategic thinking process.

Executive Compensation   While our text has led the field in its attempts to provide a practice-oriented approach to strategic management, we have redoubled our efforts to treat topics with an emphasis on application. Our new section on executive compensation in Chapter 10 is a clear example in the seventh edition. You will find an extended discussion of executive bonus options that provides a comparison of the relative merits of the five most popular approaches in use today.

Balanced Scoreboard   A recent evolution in the motivation that underpins strategic management is reflected in the widespread adoption of the Balanced Scoreboard approach to corporate performance evaluation. While the maximization of shareholder wealth retains the top spot in executive priorities, the guideline is now widely accepted that strategic initiatives must produce favorable outcomes over a range of stakeholder objectives. We try to help our readers gain an appreciation for this perspective in our seventh edition.

Bankruptcy   Many times our revisions are driven by changes in business trends. No where is that more evident in this edition than in our discussion of company bankruptcy. In the 1980s bankruptcy was treated as a last option that precluded any future for the firm. In the first decade of the 2000s the view has dramatically changed. Bankruptcy has been elevated to the status of a strategic option, and executives need to be well versed in its potentials and limitations, as you will see in Chapter 7.

Strategic Analysis and Choice   We have divided the discussion of strategic analysis and choice into two chapters. Chapter 8 examines the single business setting; Chapter 9 the multibusiness company and the diversification decision. We've added an interesting new section delineating the advantages of diversification and the case against it. *Business Week* has helped us add numerous outstanding examples to these two chapters from business writers around the world. DaimlerChrysler, Nokia, Caterpillar, and Amazon.com are just a few of the names your students will quickly recognize in coverage that illustrates and helps them more easily understand how strategic analysis is conducted and choices made.

Value of Simplicity in Implementation   We regularly conduct strategic management training programs with executives worldwide. We like to ask them about their current challenges running their companies. One refrain we always hear is the value of simplicity and specificity in implementing strategy. We have refined our discussion of functional tactics to incorporate this admonition from practicing managers, and to include an excellent example that will help your students understand this point in *Business Week* Strategy in Action 10–2.

Crossfunctional, Product-Team Structures   If there is one area in organizational structure that has become the mainstay of how newly global companies seek to implement strategies and build value in the process, it is in the use of often temporary product-team groups across functional areas, and corporate and national boundaries. We have given increased attention to this organizing approach to include several useful illustrations in Chapter 11.

Strategic Change: Structure, Leadership, and Culture in the 21st Century   The once unthinkable decline of many of the world's largest corporations has become all too common in the 21st century global economy. Hesitancy to change, clinging to outdated organizational structure, antiquated leadership, and change-resistant cultures have found many well-known companies losing sales and slipping into a survival crisis. And there is an even more critical danger: the inability to adapt to the speed and turbulence of technological change. After massive high-tech investments, managers are only beginning to make the organizational changes needed to transform information technology into the potent competitive weapon that it will need to be in the 21st century. We have added a major section in Chapter 11 that examines this 21st century environment of rapid, profound, constant strategic change. We benefited in the creation of this section from senior *Business Week* writer John Byrne and his work examining the "corporation of the future" for *Business Week*. The result is a very lively examination of the "playing field" your students will soon enter or already face. It includes a thorough look at Cisco, a company many feel is at the forefront of what the "new corporation" will look like.

General Electric and Jack Welch—A Classic Case for Strategic Management Principles   We have adapted the popular discussion case feature of our book, which is described more fully below. But it bears mentioning at this point that the discussion case modules at the ends of Chapters 11 and 12 take a comprehensive look at General Electric and the leadership of Jack Welch in order to provide your students with a comprehensive example of outstanding strategic management practices. Jack Welch and GE have become legends among business writers, investors, managers, and strategic management scholars because of the incredible success his leadership and the company have achieved over the last 20 years, building more value for shareholders than almost any other company in the history of the world. These two discussion cases make use of wonderful material and insights generated by senior *Business Week* writers who were given unprecedented access to GE, Welch, and their management team. The result is an exciting revelation and confirmation of all this book is about in a way that will interest, motivate, and educate your students with practical confirmation of what they have read and studied during the semester.

Our Strategic Alliance and Partnership with *Business Week*

Thanks to the insightful, determined leadership of Craig Beytien at McGraw-Hill and the staff at *Business Week*, we have realized a true dream that will in multiple ways benefit every teacher and student that uses this book. That dream is the selection of our book as *Business Week*'s exclusive strategic partner among strategic management textbooks provided to the collegiate market. We have long felt *Business Week* to be the unquestionable leader among business periodicals for its coverage of strategic issues in businesses, industries, and economies worldwide. Personal surveys of collegiate faculty teaching strategic management confirmed our intuition: While there are many outstanding business magazines and new publications, none match the consistent quality found in *Business Week* for the coverage of corporate strategies, case stories, and topics of interest to students and teachers of strategic management.

Through this partnership, we get unconditional access to *Business Week* material for this book and the insights of their writers and editorial staff in the use of their cutting-edge stories and topical coverage. *Business Week* gets to become more involved in the educational market as a supplements provider and they do so with the strategy book of their choosing to get increased exposure to strategic management teachers and students entering the business world. They plan to make their publication available on very favorable terms with the expectation that those initial users will roll over into long-term subscribers. From our point of view, this is a unique four-way win-win; teachers, students, authors and *Business Week* all stand to gain in many ways. We are most proud of their selection criteria: the strategy book that provides the most logical, proven framework to explain strategic management and that does so prioritizing practical, frequent illustrations. The most direct way you can see the impact of the *Business Week* alliance is in three book features: the discussion case, strategy in action modules, and short cases.

The Discussion Case Feature   We pioneered the cohesion case innovation several years ago and continue to be pleased by notes and comments from adopters that consider it very useful. The last two editions have used the Coca-Cola Company as the basis for discussion cases. *Business Week* writers liked the feature and suggested we consider using different companies and stories based on their extensively researched cover stories in recent domestic and international editions. After considerable discussion and adopter review, we decided to implement this new idea. The result has been the creation of a *Business Week* Discussion Case at the end of each chapter that illustrates key topics from that chapter in much the same way that the previous cohesion cases had done. Rather than every "story" covering the same company, we examine a variety of companies across the 12 stories. While they are still *cohesive* in that they help tie the text material together and comprehensively illustrate it, we think you will find the variety of exciting companies covered combined with the incredible depth of the *Business Week* research that underlies these stories make this feature a true pedagogical innovation once again. Amazon.com, Toyota-Japan, DaimlerChrysler, Caterpillar, and General Electric are just a few of the exciting situations examined in depth by *Business Week*'s senior staff and shared in detail with your students in a very readable fashion.

Strategy in Action Modules   Another pedagogical feature we pioneered, *strategy in action* modules, have become standard fare in most strategy books. While such affirmation is pleasing, we have long seen the need to obtain quality illustrations to be a difficult permissions and editorial task. No more. Our strategic alliance with *Business Week* lets us once again pioneer an innovation. We have worked with *Business Week* field correspondents worldwide to fill over 35 new *Business Week Strategy in Action* modules with short, hard-hitting current illustrations of key chapter topics. Your students will recognize the companies, for many are from the emerging E-commerce world while others sell products or provide services of interest to 20-something people. We are the only strategy book to have *Business Week*–derived illustration modules, and we are energized by the excitement, interest, and practical illustration value our students tell us they provide.

Short Cases   As professors of strategy management, we continually look for content or pedagogical developments or enhancements that make the strategy course more valuable. We have been concerned for some time about the length of cases typically available for classroom use. On the one hand, length often accommodates a breadth of information that in turn assures a class discussion that covers "all the bases." It even honors the professorial instruction we both experienced as students that "it is your job to extract the relevant information" from the lengthy case. The answer, we have long felt, is to have a blend of cases in terms of length—some long, to cover many issues within a company and allow for a truly comprehensive strategic analysis; but also some shorter cases that focus on one incident, or which allow for a case discussion of only 20 to 30 minutes in concert with other material, or which provide a springboard for discussion of truly current situations perhaps supplemented by web site and Internet-derived information. In brainstorming this issue in focus groups and with *Business Week*'s staff, we created the idea of short cases based on solidly developed *Business Week* articles. These short cases have generated useful class discussions while allowing coverage of other material during the case portion of the course or as a supplement and source of variety during the text portion of the course. We think you will find it useful. We have included 42 such cases in the book while continuing to include 21 more traditional cases.

Cases in the Seventh Edition

We are truly excited about the 63 cases and industry notes assembled in this seventh edition. Never before have we seen such an interesting, up-to-date collection of cases that offer such variety and yet name recognition appeal to 20-something readers. All of our cases involve current issues, or settings with current relevance. We place a major emphasis on strategy implementation issues versus offerings most commonly found in strategy texts. We have a good mixture of small and large firms, start-ups and industry legends, global and domestic market commitments, and service, retail, technology, and manufacturing activities. We have some cases that examine entrepreneurs and the companies they have pioneered into industry leaders based on unique, interesting strategies. And we have over 40 short cases from *Business Week*, which we described in the previous paragraph. They give you tremendous flexibility in the case portion of your strategy course, as well as the option to include short cases during earlier parts of a course where text material is primarily the topic of discussion.

Multiple industry situations may be examined using the cases assembled for this edition. The fast-food industry is set up for examination with a note on that industry along with cases about KFC, McDonald's, and Wendy's. A related case on Starbucks may also be examined in relationship to this industry. A second industry note about the U.S. airline industry accompanied by cases on Southwest, ValuJet, and a *Business Week* short case about Boeing make for an interesting series. Of particular interest in most classrooms is an industry note about the emerging U.S. education industry and an accompanying case about The Apollo Group [University of Phoenix]. It offers an exciting adventure into an industry in revolution and a company that has generated global excitement not to mention the largest private school in the United States in a few short years!

Our Web Site

We are pleased to offer a substantial web site designed to aid your use of this book. It includes areas accessible only to instructors and areas specifically designed to assist your students. The instructor section includes downloadable supplements, which keep your work area less cluttered and let you quickly obtain information you may not have at your fingertips. We include an interactive discussion feature for instructors so that you can share and use ideas about the course, the book, the cases, and the supplements. It functions much like a chat room and is available exclusively to instructors using our book. We also include a section that provides regular case updates to assist your teaching these cases. Similarly, *Business Week* provides regular updates relevant to companies, illustrations, and cases in our book. *Business Week* also provides access to the article archives through the instructor web site. We provide an elaborate array of linkages to company web sites and other sources that you might find useful in your course preparation. The student resources section of the web site provides interactive discussion groups where students and groups using the book may interact with other students around the world doing the same thing. Students are provided company and related business periodical (and other) web site linkages to aid and expedite their case research and preparation efforts. Practice quizzes and tests are provided that help your students prepare for tests on the text material and attempt to lower their anxiety in that regard. Access to *Business Week* articles that update the cases and key illustration modules in the book are provided. We expect your students will find the web site useful and interesting. Please visit us at www.mhhe.com/pearce.

Supplements

Components of our teaching package include a revised, comprehensive instructor's manual, test bank, PowerPoint presentation, and a computerized test bank. These are all available to qualified adopters of the text.

Professors can also choose between two simulation games as a possible package with this text: The Business Strategy Game (Thompson/Stappenbeck) or the International Business Management Decision Simulation (McDonald/Neelankavil).

- The Business Strategy Game provides an exercise to help students understand how the functional pieces of a business fit together. Students will work with the numbers, explore options, and try to unite production, marketing, finance, and human resource decisions into a coherent strategy.
- The International Business Management Decision Simulation is also a Windows based simulation that provides an international business analysis and plan simulation that allows students to create multinational business plans and compete with other student groups. Fifteen countries representing three regions of the world along with 4 product categories are included in the simulation. Students assess business plans by using the financial reports contained in the simulation.

Acknowledgments

We have benefited from the help of many people in the evolution of this project over seven editions. Students, adopters, colleagues, reviewers, and business contacts have provided hundreds of insightful comments, suggestions, and contributions that have progressively enhanced this book and its supplements. We are indebted to the researchers, writers, and practicing managers who have accelerated the development of the literature on strategic management.

We are particularly indebted to the talented case researchers who have produced the cases used in this book, as well as to case researchers dedicated to the revitalization of case research as an important academic endeavor. First-class case research is a major avenue through which top strategic management scholars should be recognized.

The following strategic management scholars have supported this project in its current edition through their case research efforts:

Anthony Akel
Long Island University, C. W. Post Campus

Abbas Ali
Indiana University of Pennsylvania

James Belohlav
DePaul University

Robert Birney
Alverno College

Mark Brodbeck
University of South Carolina

James W. Camerius
Northern Michigan University

Quentin Ciolfi
Brevard Community College

James W. Clinton
University of Northern Colorado

Emer Dooley
University of Washington

Cheryl Duval
Mercer University

Michele Gee
University of Wisconsin, Parkside

Mary Goldman
Empire State College

Gary Gray
Johnson and Wales University

Sue Greenfeld
California State University, San Bernardino

Bob Gulbro
Athens State

Carnella Hardin
Glendale College

Ted Helmer
Northern Arizona University

Cecil Horst
Keller Graduate School

W. Evans Howle
Coker College

Michael J. Keefe
Southwest Texas State University

Jeffrey A. Krug
University of Illinois

Suresh Kotha
University of Washington

Roger Lee
Salt Lake Community College

Gary Mahon
University of Arizona

Robert N. McGrath
Embry-Riddle Aeronautical University

Bill J. Middlebrook
Southwest Texas State University

Lydia Negron
Park College

Veleketa Redding
Mercer University

John K. Ross III
Southwest Texas State University

Jerry Rottman
Kentucky State University

Donald Schepers
University of Alabama, Huntsville

Melissa Schilling
University of Washington

Marian Schultz
University of West Florida

James Schultz
Embry-Riddle Aeronautical University

Leo Stevens
Louisiana Technical University

Johann Von Flue
Chapman University

Blaise P. Waguespack, Jr.
Embry-Riddle Aeronautical University

Ellen Weisbord
Pace University

George A. Wrigley
Embry-Riddle Aeronautical University

Abdall Yeusry
Bowie State University

We have personally made sure that the dean at each of the case author's respective institutions is aware of the value that their faculty member's case research provides the strategic management literature and field.

The development of this book through seven editions has benefited from the generous commitments of time, energy, and ideas from the following colleagues (we apologize if affiliations have changed):

Mary Ackenhusen
INSEAD

A. J. Almaney
DePaul University

James Almeida
Fairleigh Dickinson University

B. Alpert
San Francisco State University

Alan Amason
University of Georgia

Sonny Aries
University of Toledo

Katherine A. Auer
The Pennsylvania State University

Amy Vernberg Beekman
George Mason University

Patricia Bilafer
Bentley College

Robert Earl Bolick
Metropolitan State University

Bill Boulton
Auburn University

Charles Boyd
Southwest Missouri State University

Jeff Bracker
University of Louisville

Dorothy Brawley
Kennesaw State College

James W. Bronson
Washington State University

Eric Brown
George Mason University

Robert F. Bruner
INSEAD

William Burr
University of Oregon

Gene E. Burton
California State University–Fresno

Edgar T. Busch
Western Kentucky University

Charles M. Byles
Virginia Commonwealth University

Gerard A. Cahill

Jim Callahan
University of LaVerne

James W. Camerius
Northern Michigan University

Richard Castaldi
San Diego State University

Gary J. Castogiovanni
Louisiana State University

Jafor Chowdbury
University of Scranton

James J. Chrisman
University of Calgary

Neil Churchill
INSEAD

J. Carl Clamp
University of South Carolina

Earl D. Cooper
Florida Institute of Technology

Louis Coraggio
Troy State University

Jeff Covin
Indiana University

John P. Cragin
Oklahoma Baptist University

Larry Cummings
Northwestern University

Peter Davis
Memphis State University

William Davis
Auburn University

Julio DeCastro
University of Colorado

Philippe Demigne
INSEAD

D. Keith Denton
Southwest Missouri State University

F. Derakhshan
California State University–San Bernardino

Brook Dobni
University of Saskatchewan

Mark Dollinger
Indiana University

Jean–Christopher Donck
INSEAD

Max E. Douglas
Indiana State University

Yves Doz
INSEAD

Julie Driscoll
Bentley College

Derrick Dsouza
University of North Texas

Thomas J. Dudley
Pepperdine University

John Dunkelberg
Wake Forest University

Soumitra Dutta
INSEAD

Harold Dyck
California State University

Norbert Esser
Central Wesleyan College

Forest D. Etheredge
Aurora University

Liam Fahey

Mary Fandel
Bentley College

Mark Fiegener
Oregon State University

Calvin D. Fowler
Embry-Riddle Aeronautical University

Debbie Francis
Auburn University–Montgomery

Elizabeth Freeman
Southern Methodist University

Mahmound A. Gaballa
Mansfield University

Donna M. Gallo
Boston College

Diane Garsombke
University of Maine

Betsy Gatewood
Indiana University

Michael Geringer
Southern Methodist University

Bertrand George
INSEAD

Manton C. Gibbs
Indiana University of Pennsylvania

Nicholas A. Glaskowsky, Jr.
University of Miami

Tom Goho
Wake Forest University

Jon Goodman
University of Southern California

Pradeep Gopalakrishna
Hofstra University

R. H. Gordon
Hofstra University

Barbara Gottfried
Bentley College

Peter Goulet
University of Northern Iowa

Walter E. Greene
University of Texas–Pan American

Sue Greenfeld
California State University–San Bernardino

David W. Grigsby
Clemson University

Daniel E. Hallock
St. Edward's University

Don Hambrick
Columbia University

Barry Hand
Indiana State University

Jean M. Hanebury
Texas A&M University

Karen Hare
Bentley College

Earl Harper
Grand Valley State University

Samuel Hazen
Tarleton State University

W. Harvey Hegarty
Indiana University

Edward A. Hegner
California State University–Sacramento

Marilyn M. Helms
University of Tennessee–Chattanooga

Lanny Herron
University of Baltimore

D. Higginbothan
University of Missouri

Roger Higgs
Western Carolina University

William H. Hinkle
Johns Hopkins University

Charles T. Hofer
University of Georgia

Alan N. Hoffman
Bentley College

Richard Hoffman
College of William and Mary

Eileen Hogan
George Mason University

Phyllis G. Holland
Valdosta State University

Gary L. Holman
St. Martin's College

Don Hopkins
Temple University

Cecil Horst
Keller Graduate School of Management

Mel Horwitch
Theseus

Henry F. House
Auburn University–Montgomery

William C. House
University of Arkansas–Fayetteville

Frank Hoy
University of Texas–El Paso

Warren Huckabay

Eugene H. Hunt
Virginia Commonwealth University

Tammy G. Hunt
University of North Carolina–Wilmington

John W. Huonker
University of Arizona

Stephen R. Jenner
California State University

Shailendra Jha
Wilfrid Laurier University–Ontario

C. Boyd Johnson
California State University–Fresno

Troy Jones
University of Central Florida

Jon Kalinowski
Mankato State University

Al Kayloe
Lake Erie College

Michael J. Keefe
Southwest Texas State University

Kay Keels
Louisiana State University

James A. Kidney
Southern Connecticut State University

John D. King
Embry-Riddle Aeronautical University

Raymond M. Kinnunen
Northeastern University

John B. Knauff
University of St. Thomas

Rose Knotts
University of North Texas

Dan Kopp
Southwest Missouri State University

Michael Koshuta
Valparaiso University

Jeffrey A. Krug
The University of Illinois

Myroslaw Kyj
Widener University of Pennsylvania

Dick LaBarre
Ferris State University

Joseph Lampel
New York University

Ryan Lancaster
The University of Phoenix

Sharon Ungar Lane
Bentley College

Roland Larose
Bentley College

Anne T. Lawrence
San Jose State University

Joseph Leonard
Miami University–Ohio

Robert Letovsky
Saint Michael's College

Michael Levy
INSEAD

Benjamin Litt
Lehigh University

Frank S. Lockwood
University of Wisconsin

John Logan
University of South Carolina

Sandra Logan
Newberry College

Jean M. Lundin
Lake Superior State University

Rodney H. Mabry
Clemson University

Donald C. Malm
University of Missouri–St. Louis

Charles C. Manz
Arizona State University

John Maurer
Wayne State University

Denise Mazur
Aquinas College

Edward McClelland
Roanoke College

Bob McDonald
Central Wesleyan College

Patricia P. McDougall
Indiana University

S. Mehta
San Jose State University

Ralph Melaragno
Pepperdine University

Richard Merner
University of Delaware

Linda Merrill
Bentley College

Timothy Mescon
Kennesaw State College

Philip C. Micka
Park College

Bill J. Middlebrook
Southwest Texas State University

James F. Molly, Jr.
Northeastern University

Cynthia Montgomery
Harvard University

Robert Mockler
St. John's University

W. Kent Moore
Valdosta State University

Jaideep Motwani
Grand Valley State University

Karen Mullen
Bentley College

Gary W. Muller
Hofstra University

Terry Muson
Northern Montana College

Daniel Muzyka
INSEAD

Stephanie Newell
Bowling Green State University

Michael E. Nix
Trinity College of Vermont

Kenneth Olm
University of Texas–Austin

Benjamin M. Oviatt
Georgia State University

Joseph Paolillo
University of Mississippi

Gerald Parker
St. Louis University

Paul J. Patinka
University of Colorado

James W. Pearce
Western Carolina University

Michael W. Pitts
Virginia Commonwealth University

Douglas Polley
St. Cloud State University

Carlos de Pommes
Theseus

Valerie J. Porciello
Bentley College

Mark S. Poulous
St. Edward's University

John B. Pratt
Saint Joseph's College

Oliver Ray Price
West Coast University

John Primus
Golden Gate University

Norris Rath
Shepard College

Paula Rechner
University of Illinois

Richard Reed
Washington State University

J. Bruce Regan
University of St. Thomas

H. Lee Remmers
INSEAD

F. A. Ricci
Georgetown University

Linda Riesenman
Villanova University

Keith Robbins
Winthrop University

Gary Roberts
Kennesaw State College

Lloyd E. Roberts
Mississippi College

John K. Ross III
Southwest Texas State University

George C. Rubenson
Salisbury State University

Alison Rude
Bentley College

Les Rue
Georgia State University

Carol Rugg
Bentley College

J. A. Ruslyk
Memphis State University

Ronald J. Salazar
Idaho State University

Uri Savoray
INSEAD

Jack Scarborough
Barry University

Paul J. Schlachter
Florida International University

John Seeger
Bentley College

Martin Shapiro
Iona College

Arthur Sharplin
McNeese State University

Frank M. Shipper
Salisbury State University

Rodney C. Shrader
Georgia State University

Lois Shufeldt
Southwest Missouri State University

Bonnie Silvieria
Bentley College

F. Bruce Simmons III
The University of Akron

Mark Simon
Georgia State University

Michael Skipton
Memorial University

Fred Smith
Western Illinois University

Glenda Smith
Villanova University

Scott Snell
Michigan State University

Coral R. Snodgrass
Canisius College

Rudolph P. Snowadzky
University of Maine

Neil Snyder
University of Virginia

Melvin J. Stanford
Mankato State University

Romuald A. Stone
James Madison University

Warren S. Stone
Virginia Commonwealth University

Ram Subramanian
Grand Valley State University

Paul M. Swiercz
Georgia State University

Robert L. Swinth
Montana State University

Chris Taubman
INSEAD

Russell Teasley
University of South Carolina

James Teboul
INSEAD

George H. Tompson
University of New Zealand

Jody Tompson
University of New Zealand

Melanie Trevino
University of Texas–El Paso

Howard Tu
Memphis State University

Craig Tunwall
Ithaca College

Elaine M. Tweedy
University of Scranton

Arieh A. Ullmann
SUNY–Binghamton

P. Veglahn
James Madison University

George Vozikis
The Citadel

William Waddell
California State University–Los Angeles

Bill Warren
College of William and Mary

Kirby Warren
Columbia University

Steven J. Warren
Rutgers University

Michael White
University of Tulsa

Randy White
Auburn University

Sam E. White
Portland State University

Frank Winfrey
Kent State University

Joseph Wolfe
University of Tulsa

Robley Wood
Virginia Commonwealth University

Edward D. Writh, Jr.
Florida Institute of Technology

John Young
University of New Mexico

S. David Young
INSEAD

Jan Zahrly
Old Dominion University

Alan Zeiber
Portland State University

The valuable ideas, recommendations, and support from these outstanding scholars, teachers, and practitioners have added quality to this book.

We are affiliated with two separate universities, both of which provide wonderful environments that deserve unique praise and thanks.

As the Endowed Chairholder of the College of Commerce and Finance at Villanova University, Jack is able to combine his scholarly and teaching activities with his coauthorship of this text. He is grateful to Villanova University and his colleagues for the support and encouragement they provide.

Richard deeply appreciates the support of The Darla Moore School of Business colleagues Alan Bauerschmidt, Dean Kress, John Logan, Ken Robinson, Harry Sapeinza, Bill Sandberg, and David Schweiger; the logistical assistance provided by Cheryl Fowler and Susie Gorsage; and the visionary leadership provided by Program Director Hoyt Wheeler, Provost Jerry Odom, and President John Palms at the University of South Carolina.

Leadership from the Irwin company, now at the management list helm of McGraw-Hill, deserves our utmost thanks and appreciation. Gerald Saykes got us started some 25 years ago, and continues his support. John Black's background leadership through yet more strategic change has been a comfort. Craig Beytien's editorial leadership has enhanced our quality and success. Karen Mellon, no longer with McGraw-Hill, added value. Editorial and production assistance from Susanne Riedell and Rose Hepburn helped us meet deadlines and this to become a much better book. The Irwin/McGraw-Hill field organization deserves particular recognition and thanks for the previous and future success of this project. Sarah Reed has been a rock in this edition. She deserves additional thanks for shepherding and coordinating all our ancillaries. Ram Subramanian deserves recognition for his hard work on the instructor's guide. Ann Rogula helped create the best web site available for any strategy book. The quality you find in these items is a reflection of the commitment to quality Sarah and her team brought to the task!

We particularly want to thank *Business Week* editors and staff members that listened to the strategic alliance proposal, selected our book with which to do it, and have proven the ideal strategic partner every step of the way. Sharon Mulligan and Courtney Cashill deserve special appreciation for their trusting endorsement of the idea.

We hope that you will find our book and ancillaries all that you expect. We welcome your ideas and recommendations about our material. Please contact Jack or Richard at the following addresses:

Dr. John A. Pearce II	Dr. Richard Robinson
College of Commerce and Finance	College of Business Administration
Villanova University	University of South Carolina
Villanova, PA 19085-1678	Columbia, SC 29205
610-519-4332	803-777-5961
jpearce@cf-faculty.vill.edu	**Robinson@sc.edu.**

We wish you the utmost success teaching and studying strategic management.

Jack Pearce
Richard Robinson

ABOUT THE AUTHORS

John A. Pearce II, Ph.D., is the holder of the College of Commerce and Finance Endowed Chair in Strategic Management and Entrepreneurship at Villanova University. Previously, Dr. Pearce was holder of the Eakin Endowed Chair in Strategic Management at George Mason University and was a State of Virginia Eminent Scholar. In 1994, he received the Fulbright U.S. Professional Award for service in Malaysia. Professor Pearce has taught at Penn State, West Virginia University, the University of Malta where as a Fulbright Senior Professor in International Management he served as the Head of Business Faculties, and at the University of South Carolina where he was Director of Ph.D. Programs in Strategic Management. He received a Ph.D. degree in Business Administration from the Pennsylvania State University.

Professor Pearce is coauthor of 36 books that have been used to help educate more than 1,000,000 students and managers. He has also authored more than 200 articles and professional papers. These have been published in journals that include the *Academy of Management Journal, California Management Review, Journal of Applied Psychology, Journal of Business Venturing, Sloan Management Review,* and *Strategic Management Journal.* Several of these publications have resulted from Professor Pearce's work as a principal on research projects funded for more than $2 million. He is a recognized expert in the field of strategic management, with special accomplishments in the areas of strategy formulation, implementation, control, management during recessions, mission statement development, competitive assessment, industry analysis, joint ventures, and tools for strategy evaluation and design.

A frequent leader of executive development programs and an active consultant to business and industry, Dr. Pearce's client list includes domestic and multinational firms engaged in manufacturing, service, and nonprofit industries.

Richard B. Robinson, Jr., Ph.D., is Professor of Strategy and Entrepreneurship and Director of the Faber Entrepreneurship Center at The Darla Moore School of Business, University of South Carolina. He is an advisor to several growth companies and previously served as President and CEO of a regional environmental services company that was sold to Safety Kleen. Richard has published numerous articles and cases about strategic management issues.

BRIEF CONTENTS

CONTENTS

I

OVERVIEW OF STRATEGIC MANAGEMENT

The first chapter of this book introduces strategic management, the set of decisions and actions that result in the design and activation of strategies to achieve the objectives of an organization. The chapter provides an overview of the nature, benefits, and terminology of and the need for strategic management. Subsequent chapters provide greater detail.

The first major section of Chapter 1, "The Nature and Value of Strategic Management," emphasizes the practical value and benefits of strategic management for a firm. It also distinguishes between a firm's strategic decisions and its other planning tasks.

The section stresses the key point that strategic management activities are undertaken at three levels: corporate, business, and functional. The distinctive characteristics of strategic decision making at each of these levels affect the impact of activities at these levels on company operations. Other topics dealt with in this section are the value of formality in strategic management and the alignment of strategy makers in strategy formulation and implementation. The section concludes with a review of the planning research on business, which demonstrates that the use of strategic management processes yields financial and behavioral benefits that justify their costs.

The second major section of Chapter 1 presents a model of the strategic management process. The model, which will serve as an outline for the remainder of the text, describes approaches currently used by strategic planners. Its individual components are carefully defined and explained, as is the process for integrating them into the strategic management process. The section ends with a discussion of the model's practical limitations and the advisability of tailoring the recommendations made to actual business situations.

1 STRATEGIC MANAGEMENT

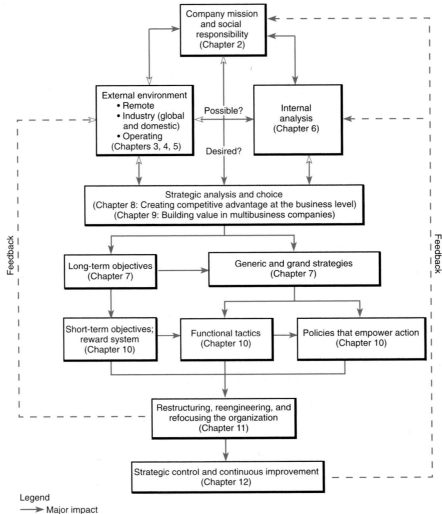

Legend
——→ Major impact
——▷ Minor impact

THE NATURE AND VALUE OF STRATEGIC MANAGEMENT

Managing activities internal to the firm is only part of the modern executive's responsibilities. The modern executive also must respond to the challenges posed by the firm's immediate and remote external environments. The immediate external environment includes competitors, suppliers, increasingly scarce resources, government agencies and their ever more numerous regulations, and customers whose preferences often shift inexplicably. The remote external environment comprises economic and social conditions, political priorities, and technological developments, all of which must be anticipated, monitored, assessed, and incorporated into the executive's decision making. However, the executive often is compelled to subordinate the demands of the firm's internal activities and external environment to the multiple and often inconsistent requirements of its stakeholders: owners, top managers, employees, communities, customers, and country. To deal effectively with everything that affects the growth and profitability of a firm, executives employ management processes that they feel will position it optimally in its competitive environment by maximizing the anticipation of environmental changes and of unexpected internal and competitive demands.

Broad-scope, large-scale management processes became dramatically more sophisticated after World War II. These processes responded to increases in the size and number of competing firms; to the expanded role of government as a buyer, seller, regulator, and competitor in the free enterprise system; and to greater business involvement in international trade. Perhaps the most significant improvement in management processes came in the 1970s, when "long-range planning," "new venture management," "planning, programming, budgeting," and "business policy" were blended. At the same time, increased emphasis was placed on environmental forecasting and external considerations in formulating and implementing plans. This all-encompassing approach is known as strategic management.

Strategic management is defined as the set of decisions and actions that result in the formulation and implementation of plans designed to achieve a company's objectives. It comprises nine critical tasks:

1. Formulate the company's mission, including broad statements about its purpose, philosophy, and goals.
2. Conduct an analysis that reflects the company's internal conditions and capabilities.
3. Assess the company's external environment, including both the competitive and general contextual factors.
4. Analyze the company's options by matching its resources with the external environment.
5. Identify the most desirable options by evaluating each option in light of the company's mission.
6. Select a set of long-term objectives and grand strategies that will achieve the most desirable options.
7. Develop annual objectives and short-term strategies that are compatible with the selected set of long-term objectives and grand strategies.
8. Implement the strategic choices by means of budgeted resource allocations in which the matching of tasks, people, structures, technologies, and reward systems is emphasized.
9. Evaluate the success of the strategic process as an input for future decision making.

As these nine tasks indicate, strategic management involves the planning, directing, organizing, and controlling of a company's strategy-related decisions and actions. By *strategy,* managers mean their large-scale, future-oriented plans for interacting with the competitive environment to achieve company objectives. A strategy is a company's game plan. Although that plan does not precisely detail all future deployments (of people, finances, and material), it does provide a framework for managerial decisions. A strategy reflects a company's awareness of how, when, and where it should compete; against whom it should compete; and for what purposes it should compete.

Dimensions of Strategic Decisions

What decisions facing a business are strategic and therefore deserve strategic management attention? Typically, strategic issues have the following dimensions.

Strategic Issues Require Top-Management Decisions   Since strategic decisions overarch several areas of a firm's operations, they require top-management involvement. Usually only top management has the perspective needed to understand the broad implications of such decisions and the power to authorize the necessary resource allocations. As top manager of Volvo GM Heavy Truck Corporation, Karl-Erling Trogen, president, wanted to push the company closer to the customer by overarching operations with service and customer relations empowering the work force closest to the customer with greater knowledge and authority. This strategy called for a major commitment to the parts and service end of the business where customer relations was first priority. Trogen's philosophy was to so empower the work force that more operating questions were handled on the line where workers worked directly with customers. He believed that the corporate headquarters should be more focused on strategic issues, such as engineering, production, quality, and marketing.

Strategic Issues Require Large Amounts of the Firm's Resources   Strategic decisions involve substantial allocations of people, physical assets, or moneys that either must be redirected from internal sources or secured from outside the firm. They also commit the firm to actions over an extended period. For these reasons, they require substantial resources. Whirlpool Corporation's "Quality Express" product delivery program exemplified a strategy that required a strong financial and personnel commitment from the company. The plan was to deliver products to customers when, where, and how they wanted them. This proprietary service uses contract logistics strategy to deliver Whirlpool, Kitchen Aid, Roper, and Estate brand appliances to 90 percent of the company's dealer and builder customers within 24 hours and to the other 10 percent within 48 hours. In highly competitive service-oriented businesses, achieving and maintaining customer satisfaction frequently involves a commitment from every facet of the organization.

Strategic Issues Often Affect the Firm's Long-Term Prosperity   Strategic decisions ostensibly commit the firm for a long time, typically five years; however, the impact of such decisions often lasts much longer. Once a firm has committed itself to a particular strategy, its image and competitive advantages usually are tied to that strategy. Firms become known in certain markets, for certain products, with certain technologies. They would jeopardize their previous gains if they shifted from these markets, products, or technologies by adopting a radically different strategy. Thus, strategic decisions have enduring effects on firms—for better or worse.

Strategic Issues Are Future Oriented   Strategic decisions are based on what managers forecast, rather than on what they know. In such decisions, emphasis is placed on the development of projections that will enable the firm to select the most promising strategic options. In the turbulent and competitive free enterprise environment, a firm will succeed only if it takes a proactive (anticipatory) stance toward change.

Strategic Issues Usually Have Multifunctional or Multibusiness Consequences   Strategic decisions have complex implications for most areas of the firm. Decisions about such matters as customer mix, competitive emphasis, or organizational structure necessarily involve a number of the firm's strategic business units (SBUs), divisions, or program units. All of these areas will be affected by allocations or reallocations of responsibilities and resources that result from these decisions.

Strategic Issues Require Considering the Firm's External Environment   All business firms exist in an open system. They affect and are affected by external conditions that are largely beyond their control. Therefore, to successfully position a firm in competitive situations, its strategic managers must look beyond its operations. They must consider what relevant others (e.g., competitors, customers, suppliers, creditors, government, and labor) are likely to do.

Three Levels of Strategy

The decision-making hierarchy of a firm typically contains three levels. At the top of this hierarchy is the corporate level, composed principally of a board of directors and the chief executive and administrative officers. They are responsible for the firm's financial performance and for the achievement of nonfinancial goals, such as enhancing the firm's image and fulfilling its social responsibilities. To a large extent, attitudes at the corporate level reflect the concerns of stockholders and society at large. In a multibusiness firm, corporate-level executives determine the businesses in which the firm should be involved. They also set objectives and formulate strategies that span the activities and functional areas of these businesses. Corporate-level strategic managers attempt to exploit their firm's distinctive competencies by adopting a portfolio approach to the management of its businesses and by developing long-term plans, typically for a five-year period. A key corporate strategy of Airborne Express's operations involved direct sale to high-volume corporate accounts and developing an expansive network in the international arena. Instead of setting up operations overseas, Airborne's long-term strategy was to form direct associations with national companies within foreign countries to expand and diversify their operations.

Another example of the portfolio approach involved a plan by state-owned Saudi Arabian Oil to spend $1.4 billion to build and operate an oil refinery in Korea with its partner, Ssangyong. To implement their program, the Saudis embarked on a new "cut-out-the-middleman" strategy to reduce the role of international oil companies in the processing and selling of Saudi crude oil.

In the middle of the decision-making hierarchy is the business level, composed principally of business and corporate managers. These managers must translate the statements of direction and intent generated at the corporate level into concrete objectives and strategies for individual business divisions, or SBUs. In essence, business-level strategic managers determine how the firm will compete in the selected product-market arena. They strive to identify and secure the most promising market segment within that arena. This segment is the piece of the total market that the firm can claim and defend because of its competitive advantages.

FIGURE 1–1
Alternative Strategic Management Structures

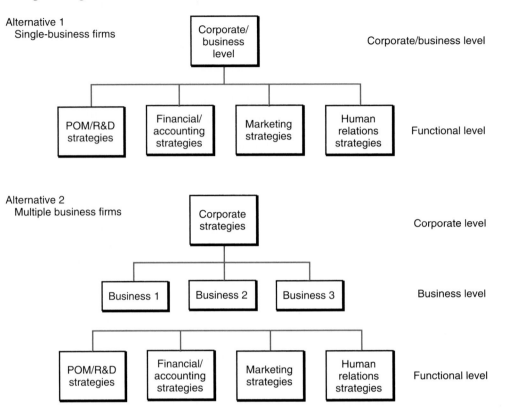

At the bottom of the decision-making hierarchy is the functional level, composed principally of managers of product, geographic, and functional areas. They develop annual objectives and short-term strategies in such areas as production, operations, research and development, finance and accounting, marketing, and human relations. However, their principal responsibility is to implement or execute the firm's strategic plans. Whereas corporate- and business-level managers center their attention on "doing the right things," managers at the functional level center their attention on "doing things right." Thus, they address such issues as the efficiency and effectiveness of production and marketing systems, the quality of customer service, and the success of particular products and services in increasing the firm's market shares.

Figure 1–1 depicts the three levels of strategic management as structured in practice. In alternative 1, the firm is engaged in only one business and the corporate- and business-level responsibilities are concentrated in a single group of directors, officers, and managers. This is the organizational format of most small businesses.

Alternative 2, the classical corporate structure, comprises three fully operative levels: the corporate level, the business level, and the functional level. The approach taken throughout this text assumes the use of alternative 2. Moreover, whenever appropriate, topics are covered from the perspective of each level of strategic management. In this way, the text presents a comprehensive discussion of the strategic management process.

FIGURE 1–2
Hierarchy of Objectives and Strategies

Ends (What is to be achieved?)	Means (How is it to be achieved?)	Strategic Decision Makers			
		Board of Directors	Corporate Managers	Business Managers	Functional Managers
Mission, including goals and philosophy		✓✓	✓✓	✓	
Long-term objectives	Grand strategy	✓	✓✓	✓✓	
Annual objectives	Short-term strategies and policies		✓	✓✓	✓✓

Note: ✓✓ indicates a principal responsibility; ✓ indicates a secondary responsibility.

Characteristics of Strategic Management Decisions

The characteristics of strategic management decisions vary with the level of strategic activity considered. As shown in Figure 1–2, decisions at the corporate level tend to be more value oriented, more conceptual, and less concrete than decisions at the business or functional level. For example, at Alcoa, the world's largest aluminum maker, chairman Paul O'Neill made Alcoa one of the nation's most centralized organizations by imposing a dramatic management reorganization that wiped out two layers of management. He found that this effort not only reduced costs but also enabled him to be closer to the front-line operations managers. Corporate-level decisions are often characterized by greater risk, cost, and profit potential; greater need for flexibility; and longer time horizons. Such decisions include the choice of businesses, dividend policies, sources of long-term financing, and priorities for growth.

Functional-level decisions implement the overall strategy formulated at the corporate and business levels. They involve action-oriented operational issues and are relatively short range and low risk. Functional-level decisions incur only modest costs, because they are dependent on available resources. They usually are adaptable to ongoing activities and, therefore, can be implemented with minimal cooperation. For example, the corporate headquarters of Sears, Roebuck & Company spent $60 million to automate 6,900 clerical jobs by installing 28,000 computerized cash registers at its 868 stores in the United States. Though this move eliminated many functional-level jobs, top management believed that reducing annual operating expenses by at least $50 million was crucial to competitive survival.

Because functional-level decisions are relatively concrete and quantifiable, they receive critical attention and analysis even though their comparative profit potential is low. Common functional-level decisions include decisions on generic versus brand-name labeling, basic versus applied research and development (R&D), high versus low inventory levels, general-purpose versus specific-purpose production equipment, and close versus loose supervision.

Business-level decisions help bridge decisions at the corporate and functional levels. Such decisions are less costly, risky, and potentially profitable than corporate-level decisions, but they are more costly, risky, and potentially profitable than functional-level decisions. Common business-level decisions include decisions on plant location, marketing segmentation and geographic coverage, and distribution channels.

Formality in Strategic Management

The formality of strategic management systems varies widely among companies. *Formality* refers to the degree to which participants, responsibilities, authority, and discretion in decision making are specified. It is an important consideration in the study of strategic management, because greater formality is usually positively correlated with the cost, comprehensiveness, accuracy, and success of planning.

A number of forces determine how much formality is needed in strategic management. The size of the organization, its predominant management styles, the complexity of its environment, its production process, its problems, and the purpose of its planning system all play a part in determining the appropriate degree of formality.[1]

In particular, formality is associated with the size of the firm and with its stage of development. Methods of evaluating strategic success also are linked to formality. Some firms, especially smaller ones, follow an *entrepreneurial* mode. They are basically under the control of a single individual, and they produce a limited number of products or services. In such firms, strategic evaluation is informal, intuitive, and limited. Very large firms, on the other hand, make strategic evaluation part of a comprehensive, formal planning system, an approach that Henry Mintzberg called the *planning mode*. Mintzberg also identified a third mode (the *adaptive mode*), which he associated with medium-sized firms in relatively stable environments.[2] For firms that follow the adaptive mode, the identification and evaluation of alternative strategies are closely related to existing strategy. It is not unusual to find different modes within the same organization. For example, Exxon might follow an entrepreneurial mode in developing and evaluating the strategy of its solar subsidiary but follow a planning mode in the rest of the company.

The Strategy Makers

The ideal strategic management team includes decision makers from all three company levels (the corporate, business, and functional)—for example, the chief executive officer (CEO), the product managers, and the heads of functional areas. In addition, the team obtains input from company planning staffs, when they exist, and from lower-level managers and supervisors. The latter provide data for strategic decision making and then implement strategies.

Because strategic decisions have a tremendous impact on a company and require large commitments of company resources, top managers must give final approval for strategic action. Figure 1–2 aligns levels of strategic decision makers with the kinds of objectives and strategies for which they are typically responsible.

Planning departments, often headed by a corporate vice president for planning, are common in large corporations. Medium-sized firms often employ at least one full-time staff member to spearhead strategic data-collection efforts. Even in small firms or less progressive larger firms, strategic planning often is spearheaded by an officer or by a group of officers designated as a planning committee.

Precisely what are managers' responsibilities in the strategic planning process at the corporate and business levels? Top management shoulders broad responsibility for all the major elements of strategic planning and management. It develops the major

[1]M. Goold and A. Campbell, "Managing the Diversified Corporation: The Tensions Facing the Chief Executive," *Long Range Planning,* August 1988, pp. 12–24.

[2]H. Mintzberg, "Strategy Making in Three Modes," *California Management Review* 16, no. 2 (1973), pp. 44–53.

portions of the strategic plan and reviews, and it evaluates and counsels on all other portions. General managers at the business level typically have principal responsibilities for developing environmental analysis and forecasting, establishing business objectives, and developing business plans prepared by staff groups.

A firm's president or CEO characteristically plays a dominant role in the strategic planning process. In many ways, this situation is desirable. The CEO's principal duty often is defined as giving long-term direction to the firm, and the CEO is ultimately responsible for the firm's success and, therefore, for the success of its strategy. In addition, CEOs are typically strong-willed, company-oriented individuals with high self-esteem. They often resist delegating authority to formulate or approve strategic decisions.

However, when the dominance of the CEO approaches autocracy, the effectiveness of the firm's strategic planning and management processes are likely to be diminished. For this reason, establishing a strategic management system implies that the CEO will allow managers at all levels to participate in the strategic posture of the company.

In implementing a company's strategy, the CEO must have an appreciation for the power and responsibility of the board, while retaining the power to lead the company with the guidance of informed directors. The interaction between the CEO and board is key to any corporation's strategy. Empowerment of the board has been a recent trend across major management teams. Strategy in Action 1–1 presents descriptions of the changes that companies have made in an attempt to monitor the relationships between the role of the board and the role of CEO.

Benefits of Strategic Management

Using the strategic management approach, managers at all levels of the firm interact in planning and implementing. As a result, the behavioral consequences of strategic management are similar to those of participative decision making. Therefore, an accurate assessment of the impact of strategy formulation on organizational performance requires not only financial evaluation criteria but also nonfinancial evaluation criteria—measures of behavior-based effects. In fact, promoting positive behavioral consequences also enables the firm to achieve its financial goals.[3] However, regardless of the profitability of strategic plans, several behavioral effects of strategic management improve the firm's welfare:

1. Strategy formulation activities enhance the firm's ability to prevent problems. Managers who encourage subordinates' attention to planning are aided in their monitoring and forecasting responsibilities by subordinates who are aware of the needs of strategic planning.

2. Group-based strategic decisions are likely to be drawn from the best available alternatives. The strategic management process results in better decisions because group interaction generates a greater variety of strategies and because forecasts based on the specialized perspectives of group members improve the screening of options.

3. The involvement of employees in strategy formulation improves their understanding of the productivity-reward relationship in every strategic plan and, thus, heightens their motivation.

4. Gaps and overlaps in activities among individuals and groups are reduced as participation in strategy formulation clarifies differences in roles.

---

[3]A. Langely, "The Roles of Formal Strategic Planning," *Long Range Planning,* June 1988, pp. 400–450.

STRATEGY IN ACTION 1–1

THE PROGRESS OF BOARD EMPOWERMENT

Company	Innovation
Dayton Hudson Corporation	Requires the inside directors to conduct an annual evaluation of the CEO.
Medtronic	Solicits opinions on board procedures by requiring all directors to complete a questionnaire; then the full board reviews the results at an annual meeting and tries to make improvements.
Stanhome	Developed a formal document that specifies the board's purpose, size, proportion of outside directors, annual calendar, and expectations of directors and management.
Mallinckrodt	Separated the roles of chair and CEO.
Lukens	Formed a committee of outside directors to study a major acquisition proposal, hold discussions with management, and recommend action to the full board.
Campbell Soup Company	Designated a lead director with the title of vice chairman.
Monsanto	Increased the proportion of the board's time that would be focused on strategic direction and considered specific capital proposals within that framework.
General Motors	Developed an explicit set of guidelines that outline how the board will function and be structured.

Source: Reprinted by permission of *Harvard Business Review.* An exhibit from "Empowering the Board," by Jay W. Lorsch, January–February 1995. Copyright © 1995 by the President and Fellows of Harvard University, all rights reserved.

5. Resistance to change is reduced. Though the participants in strategy formulation may be no more pleased with their own decisions than they would be with authoritarian decisions, their greater awareness of the parameters that limit the available options makes them more likely to accept those decisions.

Risks of Strategic Management

Managers must be trained to guard against three types of unintended negative consequences of involvement in strategy formulation.

First, the time that managers spend on the strategic management process may have a negative impact on operational responsibilities. Managers must be trained to minimize that impact by scheduling their duties to allow the necessary time for strategic activities.

Second, if the formulators of strategy are not intimately involved in its implementation, they may shirk their individual responsibility for the decisions reached. Thus, strategic managers must be trained to limit their promises to performance that the decision makers and their subordinates can deliver.

Third, strategic managers must be trained to anticipate and respond to the disappointment of participating subordinates over unattained expectations. Subordinates may expect their involvement in even minor phases of total strategy formulation to result in both acceptance of their proposals and an increase in their rewards, or they may expect a solicitation of their input on selected issues to extend to other areas of decision making.

Sensitizing managers to these possible negative consequences and preparing them with effective means of minimizing such consequences will greatly enhance the potential of strategic planning.

Executives' Views of Strategic Management

How do managers and corporate executives view the contribution of strategic management to the success of their firms? To answer this question, a survey was conducted that included over 200 executives from the Fortune 500, Fortune 500 Service, and INC 500 companies.[4] Their responses indicate that corporate America sees strategic management as instrumental to high performance, evolutionary and perhaps revolutionary in its ever-growing sophistication, action oriented, and cost effective. Clearly, the responding executives view strategic management as critical to their individual and organizational success.

THE STRATEGIC MANAGEMENT PROCESS

Businesses vary in the processes they use to formulate and direct their strategic management activities. Sophisticated planners, such as General Electric, Procter & Gamble, and IBM, have developed more detailed processes than less-formal planners of similar size. Small businesses that rely on the strategy formulation skills and limited time of an entrepreneur typically exhibit more basic planning concerns than those of larger firms in their industries. Understandably, firms with multiple products, markets, or technologies tend to use more complex strategic management systems. However, despite differences in detail and the degree of formalization, the basic components of the models used to analyze strategic management operations are very similar.

Because of the similarity among the general models of the strategic management process, it is possible to develop an eclectic model representative of the foremost thought in the strategic management area. This model is shown in Figure 1–3. It serves three major functions. First, it depicts the sequence and the relationships of the major components of the strategic management process. Second, it is the outline for this book. This chapter provides a general overview of the strategic management process, and the major components of the model will be the principal theme of subsequent chapters. Notice that the chapters of the text that discuss each of the strategic management process components are shown in each block. Finally, the model offers one approach for analyzing the case studies in this text and thus helps the analyst develop strategy formulation skills.

Components of the Strategic Management Model

This section will define and briefly describe the key components of the strategic management model. Each of these components will receive much greater attention in a later chapter. The intention here is simply to introduce them.

---

[4]V. Ramanujam, J. C. Camillus, and N. Venkatraman, "Trends in Strategic Planning," in *Strategic Planning and Management Handbook,* ed. W. R. King and D. I. Cleland (New York: Van Nostrand Reinhold, 1987), pp. 611–28.

FIGURE 1–3
Strategic Management Model

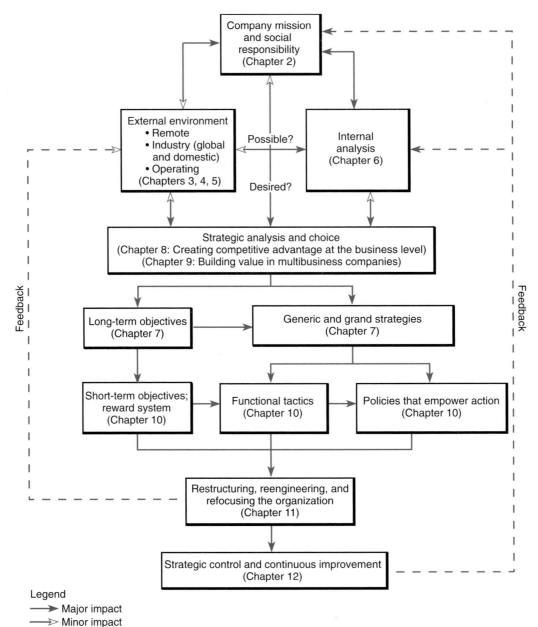

Company Mission

The mission of a company is the unique purpose that sets it apart from other companies of its type and identifies the scope of its operations. In short, the mission describes the company's product, market, and technological areas of emphasis in a way that reflects the values and priorities of the strategic decision makers. For example, Lee Hun-Hee, the new chairman of the Samsung Group, revamped the company mission by stamping his own brand of management on Samsung. Immediately, Samsung separated Chonju Paper Manufacturing and Shinsegae Department Store from other operations. This corporate act of downscaling reflected a revised management philosophy that favored specialization, thereby changing the direction and scope of the organization.

Social responsibility is a critical consideration for a company's strategic decision makers since the mission statement must express how the company intends to contribute to the societies that sustain it. A firm needs to set social responsibility aspirations for itself, just as it does in other areas of corporate performance.

Internal Analysis

The company analyzes the quantity and quality of the company's financial, human, and physical resources. It also assesses the strengths and weaknesses of the company's management and organizational structure. Finally, it contrasts the company's past successes and traditional concerns with the company's current capabilities in an attempt to identify the company's future capabilities.

External Environment

A firm's external environment consists of all the conditions and forces that affect its strategic options and define its competitive situation. The strategic management model shows the external environment as three interactive segments: the remote, industry, and operating environments.

Strategic Analysis and Choice

Simultaneous assessment of the external environment and the company profile enables a firm to identify a range of possibly attractive interactive opportunities. These opportunities are *possible* avenues for investment. However, they must be screened through the criterion of the company mission to generate a set of possible and *desired* opportunities. This screening process results in the selection of options from which a *strategic choice* is made. The process is meant to provide the combination of long-term objectives and generic and grand strategies that optimally position the firm in its external environment to achieve the company mission.

Strategic analysis and choice in single or dominant product/service businesses centers around identifying strategies that are most effective at building sustainable competitive advantage based on key value chain activities and capabilities—core competencies of the firm. Multibusiness companies find their managers focused on the question of which combination of businesses maximizes shareholder value as the guiding theme during their strategic analysis and choice.

Long-Term Objectives

The results that an organization seeks over a multiyear period are its *long-term objectives.* Such objectives typically involve some or all of the following areas: profitability, return on investment, competitive position, technological leadership, productivity, employee relations, public responsibility, and employee development.

Generic and Grand Strategies

Many businesses explicitly and all implicitly adopt one or more *generic strategies* characterizing their competitive orientation in the marketplace. Low cost, differentiation, or focus strategies define the three fundamental options. Enlightened managers seek to create ways their firm possesses both low cost and differentiation competitive advantages as part of their overall generic strategy. They usually combine these capabilities with a comprehensive, general plan of major actions through which their firm intends to achieve its long-term objectives in a dynamic environment. Called the *grand strategy,* this statement of means indicates how the objectives are to be achieved. Although every grand strategy is, in fact, a unique package of long-term strategies, 14 basic approaches can be identified: concentration, market development, product development, innovation, horizontal integration, vertical integration, joint venture, strategic alliances, consortia, concentric diversification, conglomerate diversification, turnaround, divestiture, and liquidation.

Each of these grand strategies will be covered in detail in Chapter 7.

Action Plans and Short-Term Objectives

Action plans translate generic and grand strategies into "action" by incorporating four elements. First, they identify specific functional *tactics and actions* to be undertaken in the next week, month, or quarter as part of the business's effort to build competitive advantage. The second element is a clear time frame for completion. Third, action plans create accountability by identifying who is responsible for each "action" in the plan. Fourth, each "action" in an action plan has one or more specific, immediate objectives that are identified as outcomes that action should generate.

Functional Tactics

Within the general framework created by the business's generic and grand strategies, each business function needs to identify and undertake activities unique to the function that help build a sustainable competitive advantage. Managers in each business function develop tactics that delineate the functional activities undertaken in their part of the business and usually include them as a core part of their action plan. *Functional tactics* are detailed statements of the "means" or activities that will be used to achieve short-term objectives and establish competitive advantage.

Policies that Empower Action

Speed is a critical necessity for success in today's competitive, global marketplace. One way to enhance speed and responsiveness is to force/allow decisions to be made whenever possible at the lowest level in organizations. *Policies* are broad, precedent-setting decisions that guide or substitute for repetitive or time-sensitive managerial decision making. Creating policies that guide and "preauthorize" the thinking, decisions, and actions of operating managers and their subordinates in implementing the business's strategy is essential for establishing and controlling the ongoing operating process of the firm in a manner consistent with the firm's strategic objectives. Policies often increase managerial effectiveness by standardizing routine decisions and empowering or expanding the discretion of managers and subordinates in implementing business strategies.

The following are examples of the nature and diversity of company policies:

A requirement that managers have purchase requests for items costing more than $5,000 cosigned by the controller.

The minimum equity position required for all new McDonald's franchises.

The standard formula used to calculate return on investment for the 43 strategic business units of General Electric.

A decision that Sears service and repair employees have the right to waive repair charges to appliance customers they feel have been poorly served by their Sears appliance.

Restructuring, Reengineering, and Refocusing the Organization

Until this point in the strategic management process, managers have maintained a decidedly market-oriented focus as they formulate strategies and begin implementation through action plans and functional tactics. Now the process takes an internal focus—getting the work of the business done efficiently and effectively so as to make the strategy successful. What is the best way to organize ourselves to accomplish the mission? Where should leadership come from? What values should guide our daily activities—what should the organization and its people be like? How can we shape rewards to encourage appropriate action? The intense competition in the global marketplace has made this tradition "internally focused" set of questions—how the activities within their business are conducted—recast themselves with unprecedented attentiveness to the marketplace. *Downsizing, restructuring,* and *reengineering* are terms that reflect the critical stage in strategy implementation wherein managers attempt to recast their organization. The company's structure, leadership, culture, and reward systems may all be changed to ensure cost competitiveness and quality demanded by unique requirements of its strategies.

Strategic Control and Continuous Improvement

Strategic control is concerned with tracking a strategy as it is being implemented, detecting problems or changes in its underlying premises, and making necessary adjustments. In contrast to postaction control, strategic control seeks to guide action on behalf of the generic and grand strategies as they are taking place and when the end results are still several years away. The rapid, accelerating change of the global marketplace of the last 10 years has made continuous improvement another aspect of strategic control in many organizations. *Continuous improvement* provides a way for managers to provide a form of strategic control that allows their organization to respond more proactively and timely to rapid developments in hundreds of areas that influence a business's success.

Strategic Management as a Process

A *process* is the flow of information through interrelated stages of analysis toward the achievement of an aim. Thus, the strategic management model in Figure 1–3 depicts a process. In the strategic management process, the flow of information involves historical, current, and forecast data on the operations and environment of the business. Managers evaluate these data in light of the values and priorities of influential individuals and groups—often called *stakeholders*—that are vitally interested in the actions of the business. The interrelated stages of the process are the 11 components discussed in the last section. Finally, the aim of the process is the formulation and implementation of strategies that work, achieving the company's long-term mission and near-term objectives.

Viewing strategic management as a process has several important implications. First, a change in any component will affect several or all of the other components. Most of the arrows in the model point two ways, suggesting that the flow of information usually is reciprocal. For example, forces in the external environment may influence the nature of a company's mission, and the company may in turn affect the external environment and heighten competition in its realm of operation. A specific example is a power company that is persuaded, in part by governmental incentives, to include a commitment to the development of energy alternatives in its mission statement. The company then might promise to extend its R&D efforts in the area of coal liquefaction. The external environment has affected the company's mission, and the revised mission signals a competitive condition in the environment.

A second implication of viewing strategic management as a process is that strategy formulation and implementation are sequential. The process begins with development or reevaluation of the company mission. This step is associated with, but essentially followed by, development of a company profile and assessment of the external environment. Then follow, in order, strategic choice, definition of long-term objectives, design of the grand strategy, definition of short-term objectives, design of operating strategies, institutionalization of the strategy, and review and evaluation.

The apparent rigidity of the process, however, must be qualified.

First, a firm's strategic posture may have to be reevaluated in response to changes in any of the principal factors that determine or affect its performance. Entry by a major new competitor, the death of a prominent board member, replacement of the chief executive officer, and a downturn in market responsiveness are among the thousands of changes that can prompt reassessment of a firm's strategic plan. However, no matter where the need for a reassessment originates, the strategic management process begins with the mission statement.

Second, not every component of the strategic management process deserves equal attention each time planning activity takes place. Firms in an extremely stable environment may find that an in-depth assessment is not required every five years. Companies often are satisfied with their original mission statements even after a decade of operation and spend only a minimal amount of time addressing this subject. In addition, while formal strategic planning may be undertaken only every five years, objectives and strategies usually are updated each year, and rigorous reassessment of the initial stages of strategic planning rarely is undertaken at these times.

A third implication of viewing strategic management as a process is the necessity of feedback from institutionalization, review, and evaluation to the early stages of the process. *Feedback* can be defined as the collection of postimplementation results to enhance future decision making. Therefore, as indicated in Figure 1–3, strategic managers should assess the impact of implemented strategies on external environments. Thus, future planning can reflect any changes precipitated by strategic actions. Strategic managers also should analyze the impact of strategies on the possible need for modifications in the company mission.

A fourth implication of viewing strategic management as a process is the need to regard it as a dynamic system. The term *dynamic* characterizes the constantly changing conditions that affect interrelated and interdependent strategic activities. Managers should recognize that the components of the strategic process are constantly evolving but that formal planning artificially freezes those components, much as an action photograph freezes the movement of a swimmer. Since change is continuous, the dynamic strategic planning process must be monitored constantly for significant shifts in any of its components as a precaution against implementing an obsolete strategy.

Changes in the Process

The strategic management process undergoes continual assessment and subtle updating. Although the elements of the basic strategic management model rarely change, the relative emphasis that each element receives will vary with the decision makers who use the model and with the environments of their companies.

A recent study describes general trends in strategic management, summarizing the responses of over 200 corporate executives.[5] This update shows there has been an increasing companywide emphasis on and appreciation for the value of strategic management activities. It also provides evidence that practicing managers have given increasing attention to the need for frequent and widespread involvement in the formulation and implementation phases of the strategic management process. Finally, it indicates that, as managers and their firms gain knowledge, experience, skill, and understanding in how to design and manage their planning activities, they become better able to avoid the potential negative consequences of instituting a vigorous strategic management process.

SUMMARY

Strategic management is the set of decisions and actions that result in the formulation and implementation of plans designed to achieve a company's objectives. Because it involves long-term, future-oriented, complex decision making and requires considerable resources, top-management participation is essential.

Strategic management is a three-tier process involving corporate-, business-, and functional-level planners, and support personnel. At each progressively lower level, strategic activities were shown to be more specific, narrow, short term, and action oriented, with lower risks but fewer opportunities for dramatic impact.

The strategic management model presented in this chapter will serve as the structure for understanding and integrating all the major phases of strategy formulation and implementation. The chapter provided a summary account of these phases, each of which is given extensive individual attention in subsequent chapters.

The chapter stressed that the strategic management process centers on the belief that a firm's mission can be best achieved through a systematic and comprehensive assessment of both its internal capabilities and its external environment. Subsequent evaluation of the firm's opportunities leads, in turn, to the choice of long-term objectives and grand strategies and, ultimately, to annual objectives and operating strategies, which must be implemented, monitored, and controlled.

QUESTIONS FOR DISCUSSION

1. Find a recent copy of *Business Week* and read the "Corporate Strategies" section. Was the main decision discussed strategic? At what level in the organization was the key decision made?

2. In what ways do you think the subject matter in this strategic management–business policy course will differ from that of previous courses you have taken?

3. After graduation, you are not likely to move directly to a top-level management position. In fact, few members of your class will ever reach the top-management level. Why, then, is it important for all business majors to study the field of strategic management?

4. Do you expect outstanding performance in this course to require a great deal of memorization? Why or why not?

[5]V. Ramanujam, J. C. Camillus, and N. Venkatraman, "Trends in Strategic Planning," in *Strategic Planning and Management Handbook,* ed. W. R. King and D. I. Cleland (New York: Van Nostrand Reinhold, 1987), p. 614.

5. You undoubtedly have read about individuals who seemingly have given singled-handed direction to their corporations. Is a participative strategic management approach likely to stifle or suppress the contributions of such individuals?

6. Think about the courses you have taken in functional areas, such as marketing, finance, production, personnel, and accounting. What is the importance of each of these areas to the strategic planning process?

7. Discuss with practicing business managers the strategic management models used in their firms. What are the similarities and differences between these models and the one in the text?

8. In what ways do you believe the strategic planning approach of not-for-profit organizations would differ from that of profit-oriented organizations?

9. How do you explain the success of firms that do not use a formal strategic planning process?

10. Think about your postgraduation job search as a strategic decision. How would the strategic management model be helpful to you in identifying and securing the most promising position?

BIBLIOGRAPHY

Adler, P. S.; D. W. McDonald; and F. MacDonald. "Strategic Management of Technical Functions." *Sloan Management Review* (Winter 1992), pp. 19–38.

Allen, M. G. "Strategic Management Hits Its Stride." *Planning Review* (September 1985), pp. 6–9.

Arkam, J. D., and S. S. Cowen. "Strategic Planning for Increased Profit in the Small Business." *Long Range Planning* (December 1990), pp. 63–70.

Baron, David P. "Integrated Strategy: Market and Nonmarket Components." *California Management Review* 37, no. 2 (Winter 1995), p. 47.

Blair, J. D., and K. B. Boal. "Strategy Formation Processes in Health Care Organizations: A Context-Specific Examination of Context-Free Strategy Issues." *Journal of Management* (June 1991), pp. 305–44.

Borch, Odd Jarl, and Michael B. Arthur. "Strategy Networks among Small Firms: Implications for Strategy Research Methodology." *Journal of Management Studies* 32, no. 4 (July 1995), p. 419.

Brandenburger, Adam M., and Barry J. Nalebuff. "The Right Game: Use Game Theory to Shape Strategy." *Harvard Business Review* 73, no. 4 (July–August 1995), p. 57.

Brooker, R. E., Jr. "Orchestrating the Planning Process." *The Journal of Business Strategy* (July–August 1991), pp. 4–9.

Carlson, F. P. "The Long and Short of Strategic Planning." *The Journal of Business Strategy* (May–June 1990), pp. 15–21.

Collins, James C., and Jerry I. Porras. "Building a Visionary Company." *California Management Review* 37, no. 2 (Winter 1995).

Goold, M., and A. Campbell. "Many Best Ways to Make Strategy." *Harvard Business Review* (November–December 1987), pp. 70–76.

Gopinath, C., and Richard C. Hoffman. "The Relevance of Strategy Research: Practitioner and Academic Viewpoints." *Journal of Management Studies* 32, no. 5 (September 1995), p. 575.

Hax, A. C. "Redefining the Concept of Strategy and the Strategy Formation Process." *Planning Review* (May–June 1990), pp. 34–41.

Hinterhuber, H. H., and W. Popp. "Are You a Strategist or Just a Manager." *Harvard Business Review* (January–February 1992), pp. 105–14.

Larwood, Laurie; Cecilia M. Falbe; Mark P. Krieger; and Paul Miesing. "Structure and Meaning of Organizational Vision." *The Academy of Management Journal* 38, no. 3 (June 1995), p. 740.

Meyer, A. D. "What Is Strategy's Distinctive Competence?" *Journal of Management* (December 1991), pp. 821–34.

Miles, Raymond E.; Henry J. Coleman, Jr.; and W. E. Dougles Creed. "Keys to Success in Corporate Redesign." *California Management Review* 37, no. 3 (Spring 1995), p. 128.

Pearce, J. A., II. "An Executive-Level Perspective on the Strategic Management Process." *California Management Review* (Spring 1982), pp. 39–48.

Peker, Peter, Jr., and Stan Abraham. "Is Strategic Management Living Up to Its Promise?" *Long Range Planning* 28, no. 5 (October 1995), p. 32.

Rappaport, A. "CFOs and Strategists: Forging a Common Framework." *Harvard Business Review* (May–June 1992), pp. 84–93.

Rouleau, Linda, and Francine Ségun. "Strategy and Organizational Theories: Common Forms of Discourse." *Journal of Management Studies* 32, no. 1 (January 1995), p. 101.

Schonberger, R. J. "Is Strategy Strategic? Impact of Total Quality Management on Strategy." *Academy of Management Executive* (August 1992), pp. 80–97.

Stalk, G.; P. Evans; and L. E. Shulman. "Competing on Capabilities: The New Rules of Corporate Strategy." *Harvard Business Review* (March–April 1992), pp. 57–69.

Taylor, Bernard. "The New Strategic Leadership—Driving Charge, Getting Results." *Long Range Planning* 28, no. 5 (October 1995), p. 71.

Veliyath, R. "Strategic Planning: Balancing Short-Run Performance and Longer Term Prospects." *Long Range Planning* (June 1992), pp. 86–97.

BusinessWeek

THE CORPORATION OF THE FUTURE

> As Chapter 1 has highlighted, three factors will characterize the team approach
> to strategic management in the 21st century: an unprecedented role for technol-
> ogy, globalization through strategic alliances, and constant change in how busi-
> nesses compete. Cisco Systems, Inc. exhibits a recognition of these factors in its
> strategic management activities. A study of its executives' decision making pro-
> vides an opportunity to tie together many of the concepts that are introduced in
> Chapter 1. Thus, a situational analysis of Cisco makes for an excellent first dis-
> cussion case.

Cisco is a good model. It reads the market well, responds quickly. And it knows
how to harness high tech.

The once unthinkable decline of many of the world's largest corporations has become all too common in recent years. Strategic blunders and oversights by management have pulled down such powerful and mighty giants as AT&T (*T*), Eastman Kodak
(*EK*), and General Motors (*GM*).

Yet there is a less visible but even more critical danger: the inability to adapt to the
speed and turbulence of technological change. After massive high-tech investments,
management is only beginning to make the organizational changes needed to transform
information technology into the potent competitive weapon that it will need to be in the
21st century.

THE IMPORTANCE OF TECHNOLOGY

Few companies have grasped the far-reaching importance of the new technology for
management better than Cisco Systems Inc. (*CSCO*). The San Jose (California) company has become the global leader in networking for the Internet, with annual revenues
of more than $8 billion. It's also a Wall Street darling, with a market cap approaching
$100 billion.

Cisco could well provide one of the best road maps to a new model of management.
Partly because it makes the tools to build the powerful networks that link businesses to
their customers and suppliers, Cisco itself has been at the forefront of using technology to transform management practices.

GLOBALIZATION THROUGH STRATEGIC ALLIANCES

Near-Religious

But it's not only the company's innovative use of technology that wins favorable
reviews. It's also the company's mind-set and culture, its willingness to team up with
outsiders to acquire and retain intellectual assets, its near-religious focus on the

Source: John A. Byrne in San Jose, California, "The Corporation of the Future," *Business Week:* August 13, 1998.

customer, and its progressive human resource policies. "Cisco is the quintessential outside-in company" says James F. Moore, chairman of consultants GeoPartners Research Inc. "They have mastered how to source talent, products, and momentum from outside their own walls. That's a powerful advantage."

This corporate adolescent—founded in 1984 by a group of computer scientists from Stanford University—is headed by a leader, John T. Chambers, who cut his teeth at successful companies that stumbled. At both IBM (*IBM*) and Wang Laboratories Inc. (*WANG*), the soft-spoken West Virginian got a firsthand glimpse of how arrogance and reluctance to change caused severe pain and dislocation.

CONSTANT CHANGE IN HOW BUSINESSES COMPETE

Those experiences, including a traumatic time when he survived five layoffs in 15 months at Wang—before resigning in 1990—colored his view of what a healthy organization should be. "It taught me how a company should be built in the first place and how to do things dramatically different the next time," says Chambers, 48, who joined Cisco in 1991 and became CEO in 1995. "Laying off people was the toughest thing I ever did. I'll move heaven and earth to avoid doing that again."

To hear Chambers tell it, his people and his organization are "in the sweet spot"— where technology and the future meet to transform not only business but all of life. His vision is simple: "We can change the way people live and work, play and learn." It is an idealistic phrase that falls out of his mouth repeatedly and unabashedly. It is also an inspiring and motivating declaration for each of Cisco's 13,000-plus employees.

Chambers aims to be the Jack Welch of the new millennium. Like General Electric Co.'s (*GE*) Chairman Welch, he has decided he wants to be No. 1 or No. 2 in every market, a condition that already exists in 14 of the 15 markets in which Cisco competes. Beyond that strategic goal, Chambers believes that the new rules of competition demand organizations built on change, not stability; organized around networks, not a rigid hierarchy; based on interdependencies of partners, not self-sufficiency; and constructed on technological advantage, not old-fashioned bricks and mortar.

The network structure has vast implications for managing in the next century. GM's Saturn Div. and Dell Computer Corp. (*DELL*) have shown how the network can eliminate inventory, by connecting with partners that deliver goods only when they are needed. In the new model that Chambers is creating at Cisco, however, the network is pervasive, central to nearly everything.

It seamlessly links Cisco to its customers, prospects, business partners, suppliers, and employees. This year, Cisco will sell more than $5 billion worth of goods—more than half its total—over the Internet, nearly three times the Internet sales booked by pioneer Dell. So successful has Cisco been in selling complex, expensive equipment over the Net that last year Cisco alone accounted for one-third of all electronic commerce.

Seven out of 10 customer requests for technical support are filled electronically— at satisfaction rates that eclipse those involving human interaction. Using the network for tech support allows Cisco to save more money than its nearest competitor spends on research and development. "It has saved me 1,000 engineers," gushes Chambers. "I take those 1,000 engineers, and instead of putting them into support, I put them into building new products. That gives you a gigantic competitive advantage."

The network also is the glue for the internal workings of the company. It swiftly connects Cisco with its web of partners, making the constellation of suppliers, contract manufacturers, and assemblers look like one company—Cisco—to the outside world.

Via the company's intranet, outside contractors directly monitor orders from Cisco customers and ship the assembled hardware to buyers later in the day—often without Cisco even touching the box. By outsourcing production of 70% of its products, Cisco has quadrupled output without building new plants and has cut the time it takes to get a new product to market by two-thirds, to just six months.

"Personal Touch"

The network also is Cisco's primary tool for recruiting talent, with half of all applications for jobs coming over the Net. When an employee wants information about a company event or health benefits, or needs to track an expense report, the network is the place to go at Cisco. The upshot: More than 1.7 million pages of information are accessible by employees who use the Cisco network thousands of times every day. "We are," says Chambers, "the best example of how the Internet is going to change everything."

Technology aids and abets this business model, but it does not completely displace human interaction. "The network works better when you've already had a personal touch," insists Chambers. That's why he does quarterly meetings with employees at a nearby convention center, why all employees in the month of their birth are invited to one of his 1 1/2-hour "birthday breakfasts," and why he works harder than most to encourage open and direct communication with all of Cisco's leaders.

Chambers also believes in partnering with other businesses. Plenty of companies forge links with others, but Cisco has a track record of making them work. "Partnerships are key to the new world strategies of the 21st century," says Donald J. Listwin, a Cisco senior vice-president. "Partners collapse time because they allow you to take on more things and bring them together quicker."

A good example is Cisco's partnership with Microsoft Corp. (*MSFT*), which last year resulted in a new technology to make networks more intelligent. The software lets networks know immediately a user's identity and location and to respond differently to each one. The partnership allows both companies to expand this market together more rapidly. "From initial discussion to technology, it took 18 months to get the product out," says Listwin. "It would have taken us four years to get to where we are [without such a partnership], and it's not clear we had the competence to get there alone."

Another theme—often heard but seldom exercised by corporate leaders—is the central importance of the customer. Nothing causes Chambers more restless nights than worry over how to serve customers better. That's why he spends as much as 55% of his time with customers and why he receives every night, 365 nights a year, voice mail updates on as many as 15 key clients.

"Arrogant"

In this new model, strategic direction is not formed by an insular group of top executives, but by the company's leading customers. It's an outside-in approach, as opposed to an inside-out. The customer is the strategy. "There is nothing more arrogant than telling a customer: 'Here is what you need to know,'" says Chambers. "Most of the time, you are not going to be right." Rather, Cisco's leading-edge customers are seen as partners in forming the company strategy. Example: After Boeing Co. (*BA*) and Ford Motor Co. (*F*) informed Chambers that their future network needs were unlikely to be satisfied by Cisco, Chambers went out to make his first acquisition to solve the problem. That deal, to acquire local-area-network switchmaker Crescendo Communications in 1993, put the company into a sector of the industry that now accounts for $2.8 billion in annual revenue.

Even such tactical moves as acquisitions and mergers are seen differently by a new-world company. Rather than acquire merely to speed growth or swell market share, Cisco routinely employs acquisitions to capture intellectual assets and next-generation products. "Most people forget that in a high-tech acquisition, you really are acquiring only people," says Chambers. "That's why so many of them fail. At what we pay, at $500,000 to $2 million an employee, we are not acquiring current market share. We are acquiring futures."

While most companies immediately cut costs and people from newly acquired outfits, Cisco adheres to what it calls the "Mario rule"—named after Senior Vice-President Mario Mazzola, who had been CEO of Crescendo when it was bought by Cisco. Before any employee in a newly acquired company can be terminated, both Chambers and the former CEO must give their consent. "It tells new employees that Cisco wants them, that Cisco cares about them, and that we're not just another big company," says Daniel Scheinman, vice-president for legal and government affairs. "It buys the trust of the people . . . and their passion is worth a lot more than any of the downside legal protection."

In talent-hungry Silicon Valley, Cisco measures the success of every acquisition first by employee retention, then by new product development, and finally return on investment. The company has been phenomenally successful at holding on to the intellectual assets it buys: Overall turnover among acquired employees is just 6% a year, two percentage points lower than Cisco's overall employee churn. The company works hard to embrace employees acquired in deals, often giving top talent key jobs in the new organization. Three of Cisco's main businesses are led by former CEOs of acquired companies.

Good Fit

Every acquisition, moreover, must meet Cisco guidelines. For years, Chambers watched IBM and other high-tech outfits acquire and then slowly smother any number of entrepreneurial companies. What he learned was that you never buy a company whose values and culture are much different from your own. Nor do you buy a company that is too far away from your central base of operation. The latter makes a cultural fit less likely and severely limits the speed a company needs to compete in the new economy.

Chambers also believes that each deal must boast both short-term and long-term wins for customers, shareholders, and employees. "If there are no results in three to six months, people begin to question the acquisition," says Charles H. Giancarlo, vice-president for global alliances. "If you have good short-term wins, it's a virtuous cycle."

Through it all, the emphasis is on doing it faster, cheaper, and better—an integral part of success in the new economy. At Cisco, wages are less important than ownership. Some 40% of the stock options at the company are held by "individual contributors" who on average boast more than $150,000 in option gains. Egalitarianism is critical to successful teamwork and to morale. "You never ask your team to do something you wouldn't do yourself," says Chambers, who flies coach and has no reserved parking space at headquarters.

There are other leaders, of course, besides Chambers, who hope to create an organization that may very well revolutionize the fundamental business models of major global companies. But he's surely in the "sweet spot," helping to write the new rules for managing.

II

STRATEGY FORMULATION

Strategy formulation guides executives in defining the business their firm is in, the ends it seeks, and the means it will use to accomplish those ends. The approach of strategy formulation is an improvement over that of traditional long-range planning. As discussed in the next eight chapters—about developing a firm's competitive plan of action—strategy formulation combines a future-oriented perspective with concern for the firm's internal and external environments.

The strategy formulation process begins with definition of the company mission, as discussed in Chapter 2. In that chapter, the purpose of business is defined to reflect the values of a wide variety of interested parties. Social responsibility is discussed as a critical consideration for a company's strategic decision makers since the mission statement must express how the company intends to contribute to the societies that sustain it.

Chapter 3 deals with the principal factors in a firm's external environment that strategic managers must assess so they can anticipate and take advantage of future business conditions. It emphasizes the importance to a firm's planning activities of factors in the firm's remote, industry, and operating environments. A key theme of the chapter is the problem of deciding whether to accept environmental constraints or to maneuver around them.

Chapter 4 describes the key differences in strategic planning and implementation among domestic, multinational, and global firms. It gives special attention to the new vision that a firm must communicate in a revised company mission when it multinationalizes.

Chapter 5 focuses on the environmental forecasting approaches currently used by strategic managers in assessing and anticipating changes in the external environment.

Chapter 6 shows how firms evaluate their company's strengths and weaknesses to produce an internal analysis. Strategic managers use such profiles to target competitive advantages they can emphasize and competitive disadvantages they should correct or minimize.

Chapter 7 examines the types of long-range objectives strategic managers set and specifies the qualities these objectives must have to provide a basis for direction and evaluation. The chapter also examines the generic and grand strategies that firms use to achieve long-range objectives.

Comprehensive approaches to the evaluation of strategic opportunities and to the final strategic decision are the focus of Chapter 8. The chapter shows how a firm's strategic options can be compared in a way that allows selection of the best available option. It also discusses how a company can create competitive advantages for each of its businesses.

Chapter 9 extends the attention on strategic analysis and choice by showing how managers can build value in multibusiness companies.

2

DEFINING THE COMPANY'S MISSION AND SOCIAL RESPONSIBILITY

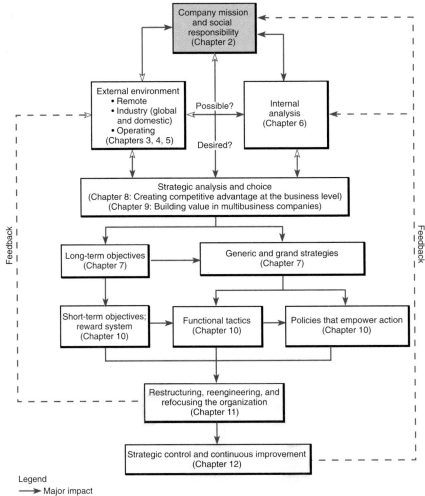

Legend

→ Major impact

⇢ Minor impact

WHAT IS A COMPANY MISSION?

Whether a firm is developing a new business or reformulating direction for an ongoing business, it must determine the basic goals and philosophies that will shape its strategic posture. This fundamental purpose that sets a firm apart from other firms of its type and identifies the scope of its operations in product and market terms is defined as the company mission. As discussed in Chapter 1, the company mission is a broadly framed but enduring statement of a firm's intent. It embodies the business philosophy of the firm's strategic decision makers, implies the image the firm seeks to project, reflects the firm's self-concept, and indicates the firm's principal product or service areas and the primary customer needs the firm will attempt to satisfy. In short, it describes the firm's product, market, and technological areas of emphasis, and it does so in a way that reflects the values and priorities of the firm's strategic decision makers. An excellent example is the company mission statement of Nicor, Inc., shown in Strategy in Action 2–1.

The Need for an Explicit Mission

No external body requires that the company mission be defined, and the process of defining it is time-consuming and tedious. Moreover, it contains broadly outlined or implied objectives and strategies rather than specific directives. Characteristically, it is a statement, not of measurable targets but of attitude, outlook, and orientation.

A company mission is designed to accomplish seven outcomes:
1. To ensure unanimity of purpose within the organization.
2. To provide a basis for motivating the use of the organization's resources.
3. To develop a basis, or standard, for allocating organizational resources.
4. To establish a general tone or organizational climate; for example, to suggest a businesslike operation.
5. To serve as a focal point for those who can identify with the organization's purpose and direction and to deter those who cannot do so from participating further in its activities.
6. To facilitate the translation of objectives and goals into a work structure involving the assignment of tasks to responsible elements within the organization.
7. To specify organizational purposes and the translation of these purposes into goals in such a way that cost, time, and performance parameters can be assessed and controlled.[1]

Noah Samara, the CEO of WorldSpace, Inc., has seen and satisfied the need for a mission for his company. As described in Global Strategy in Action 2–1, Samara's mission has inspired enthusiasm and financial backing for his fledgling firm.

FORMULATING A MISSION

The process of defining the company mission for a specific business can perhaps be best understood by thinking about the business at its inception. The typical business begins with the beliefs, desires, and aspirations of a single entrepreneur. Such an

Note: Portions of this chapter are adopted from John A. Pearce II, "The Company Mission as a Strategic Tool," *Sloan Management Review,* Spring 1992, pp. 15–24.

[1]William R. King and David I. Cleland, *Strategic Planning and Policy* (New York: Van Nostrand Reinhold, 1978), p. 124.

MISSION STATEMENT OF NICOR, INC.

PREAMBLE

We, the management of Nicor, Inc., here set forth our belief as to the purpose for which the company is established and the principles under which it should operate. We pledge our effort to the accomplishment of these purposes within these principles.

BASIC PURPOSE

The basic purpose of Nicor, Inc., is to perpetuate an investor-owned company engaging in various phases of the energy business, striving for balance among those phases so as to render needed satisfactory products and services and earn optimum, long-range profits.

WHAT WE DO

The principal business of the company, through its utility subsidiary, is the provision of energy through a pipe system to meet the needs of ultimate consumers. To accomplish its basic purpose, and to ensure its strength, the company will engage in other energy-related activities, directly or through subsidiaries or in participation with other persons, corporations, firms, or entities.

All activities of the company shall be consistent with its responsibilities to investors, customers, employees, and the public and its concern for the optimum development and utilization of natural resources and for environmental needs.

WHERE WE DO IT

The company's operations shall be primarily in the United States, but no self-imposed or regulatory geographical limitations are placed upon the acquisition, development, processing, transportation, or storage of energy resources, or upon other energy-related ventures in which the company may engage. The company will engage in such activities in any location where, after careful review, it has determined that such activity is in the best interest of its stockholders.

Utility service will be offered in the territory of the company's utility subsidiary to the best of its ability, in accordance with the requirements of regulatory agencies and pursuant to the subsidiary's purposes and principles.

owner-manager's sense of mission usually is based on the following fundamental beliefs:

1. The product or service of the business can provide benefits at least equal to its price.

2. The product or service can satisfy a customer need of specific market segments that is currently not being met adequately.

3. The technology that is to be used in production will provide a cost- and quality-competitive product or service.

4. With hard work and the support of others, the business can not only survive but also grow and be profitable.

BusinessWeek

MEDIA MOGUL FOR THE THIRD WORLD

GLOBAL STRATEGY IN ACTION 2–1

Noah Samara is the name. Radio is his game. Never heard of him? You will. This international man of mystery is about to launch a hugely ambitious, $850 million digital radio venture that's the talk of the telecommunications industry.

Samara is chief executive of Washington-based WorldSpace Inc. His privately held company has a *mission:* to use a novel satellite-broadcasting setup to bring "information affluence" to burgeoning markets in Asia, the Middle East, Africa, and Latin America. "The dream is ultimately to create a platform . . . so that these regions can hear themselves speak and sing," Samara says.

To get his business off the ground he's now focusing on middle-class city dwellers who can afford $100 digital radios and are eager to receive Western and regional news and entertainment. WorldSpace hopes to make its money by selling time on the satellites to various content providers. British Broadcasting Corp., Voice of America, and Bloomberg News acknowledge that they have had discussions with WorldSpace, and Samara says he has had exploratory talks with both Michael Jackson and Quincy Jones, as well as other artists, about entertainment content.

Samara, a soft-spoken Ethiopian-born lawyer, turns secretive when it comes to his backers. He will say only that they include investors from most of the major geographical areas to be served, as well as several wealthy individuals in the U.S. But Middle Eastern investment bankers say that the Bin Mahfouz family, which handles the Saudi royal family's finances, has invested in WorldSpace.

In June, the company announced agreements for Hitachi, JVC, Matsushita Electric Industrial, and Sanyo Technosound to make the custom radios for WorldSpace. France's Alcatel Alsthom and SGS-Thomson are developing satellites and microprocessors, respectively. "We have been captured by the spirit and *vision* of Mr. Samara," says SGS-Thomson Vice-President Sergio Garue.

Samara's enterprise has attracted high-powered executives as well. President John Cusick formerly headed PrimeStar Partners, a satellite-TV venture. McAdory Lipscomb, WorldSpace's senior vice-president for sales, marketing, and content, came from Showtime. And Pierre Madon, WorldSpace's senior vice-president for engineering and operations, is from Intelsat.

Source: Catherine Yang in Washington, with Marsha Johnston in Paris, "Media Mogul for the Third World," *Business Week:* June 30, 1997.

5. The management philosophy of the business will result in a favorable public image and will provide financial and psychological rewards for those who are willing to invest their labor and money in helping the business to succeed.

6. The entrepreneur's self-concept of the business can be communicated to and adopted by employees and stockholders.

As the business grows or is forced by competitive pressures to alter its product–market–technology, redefining the company mission may be necessary. If so, the revised mission statement will contain the same components as the original. It will state the basic type of product or service to be offered, the primary markets or customer groups to be served, and the technology to be used in production or delivery; the firm's fundamental concern for survival through growth and profitability; the firm's managerial philosophy; the public image the firm seeks; and the self-concept those affiliated with the firm should have of it. This chapter will discuss in detail these components.

STRATEGY IN ACTION 2–2

IDENTIFYING MISSION STATEMENT COMPONENTS: A COMPILATION OF EXCERPTS FROM ACTUAL CORPORATE MISSION STATEMENTS

1. Customer-market

We believe our first responsibility is to the doctors, nurses, and patients, to mothers and all others who use our products and services. (Johnson & Johnson)

To anticipate and meet market needs of farmers, ranchers, and rural communities within North America. (CENEX)

2. Product-service

AMAX's principal products are molybdenum, coal, iron ore, copper, lead, zinc, petroleum and natural gas, potash, phosphates, nickel, tungsten, silver, gold, and magnesium. (AMAX)

3. Geographic domain

We are dedicated to the total success of Corning Glass Works as a worldwide competitor. (Corning Glass)

4. Technology

Control Data is the business of applying microelectronics and computer technology in two general areas: computer-related hardware and computing-enhancing services, which include computation, information, education, and finance. (Control Data)

The common technology in these areas relates to discrete particle coatings. (NASHUA)

5. Concern for survival

In this respect, the company will conduct its operation prudently, and will provide the profits and growth which will assure Hoover's ultimate success. (Hoover Universal)

6. Philosophy

We are committed to improve health care throughout the world. (Baxter Travenol)

We believe human development to be the worthiest of the goals of civilization and independence to be the superior condition for nurturing growth in the capabilities of people. (Sun Company)

7. Self-concept

Hoover Universal is a diversified, multi-industry corporation with strong manufacturing capabilities, entrepreneurial policies, and individual business unit autonomy. (Hoover Universal)

8. Concern for public image

We are responsible to the communities in which we live and work and to the world community as well. (Johnson & Johnson)

Also, we must be responsive to the broader concerns of the public, including especially the general desire for improvement in the quality of life, equal opportunity for all, and the constructive use of natural resources. (Sun Company)

The examples shown in Strategy in Action 2–2 provide insights into how some major corporations handle them.

Basic Product or Service; Primary Market; Principal Technology

Three indispensable components of the mission statement are specification of the basic product or service, specification of the primary market, and specification of the principal technology for production or delivery. These components are discussed under one heading because only in combination do they describe the company's business activity. A good example of the three components is to be found in the business plan of ITT Barton, a division of ITT. Under the heading of business mission and area served, the following information is presented:

> The unit's mission is to serve industry and government with quality instruments used for the primary measurement, analysis, and local control of fluid flow, level, pressure, temperature, and fluid properties. This instrumentation includes flow meters, electronic readouts, indicators, recorders, switches, liquid level system, analytical instruments such as titrators, integrators, controllers, transmitters, and various instruments for the measurement of fluid properties (density, viscosity, gravity) used for processing variable sensing, data collecting, control, and transmission. The unit's mission includes fundamental loop-closing control and display devices, when economically justified, but excludes broadline central control room instrumentation, systems design, and turnkey responsibility.
>
> Markets served include instrumentation for oil and gas production, gas transportation, chemical and petrochemical processing, cryogenics, power generation, aerospace, government, and marine, as well as other instrument and equipment manufacturers.

In only 129 words, this segment of the mission statement clearly indicates to all readers—from company employees to casual observers—the basic products, primary markets, and principal technologies of ITT Barton.

Often the most referenced public statement of a company's selected products and markets appears in "silver bullet" form in the mission statement; for example, "Dayton-Hudson Corporation is a diversified retailing company whose business is to serve the American consumer through the retailing of fashion-oriented quality merchandise." Such an abstract of company direction is particularly helpful to outsiders who value condensed overviews.

Company Goals: Survival, Growth, Profitability

Three economic goals guide the strategic direction of almost every business organization. Whether or not the mission statement explicitly states these goals, it reflects the firm's intention to secure *survival* through *growth* and *profitability.*

A firm that is unable to survive will be incapable of satisfying the aims of any of its stakeholders. Unfortunately, the goal of survival, like the goals of growth and profitability, often is taken for granted to such an extent that it is neglected as a principal criterion in strategic decision making. When this happens, the firm may focus on short-term aims at the expense of the long run. Concerns for expediency, a quick fix, or a bargain may displace the assessment of long-term impact. Too often, the result is near-term economic failure owing to a lack of resource synergy and sound business practice. For example, Consolidated Foods, maker of Shasta soft drinks and L'eggs hosiery, sought growth through the acquisition of bargain businesses. However, the erratic sales patterns of its diverse holdings forced it to divest itself of more than four dozen companies. This process cost Consolidated Foods millions of dollars and hampered its growth.

Profitability is the mainstay goal of a business organization. No matter how profit is measured or defined, profit over the long term is the clearest indication of a firm's ability to satisfy the principal claims and desires of employees and stockholders. The key phrase here is "over the long term." Obviously, basing decisions on a short-term concern for profitability would lead to a strategic myopia. Overlooking the enduring concerns of customers, suppliers, creditors, ecologists, and regulatory agents may produce profit in the short term, but, over time, the financial consequences are likely to be detrimental.

The following excerpt from the Hewlett-Packard statement of mission ably expresses the importance of an orientation toward long-term profit:

> To achieve sufficient profit to finance our company growth and to provide the resources we need to achieve our other corporate objectives.

> In our economic system, the profit we generate from our operation is the ultimate source of the funds we need to prosper and grow. It is the one absolutely essential measure of our corporate performance over the long term. Only if we continue to meet our profit objective can we achieve our other corporate objectives.

A firm's growth is tied inextricably to its survival and profitability. In this context, the meaning of growth must be broadly defined. Although the product impact market studies (PIMS) have shown that growth in market share is correlated with profitability, other important forms of growth do exist. Growth in the number of markets served, in the variety of products offered, and in the technologies that are used to provide goods or services frequently lead to improvements in a firm's competitive ability. Growth means change, and proactive change is essential in a dynamic business environment.

Hewlett-Packard's mission statement provides an excellent example of corporate regard for growth:

> Objective: To let our growth be limited only by our profits and our ability to develop and produce technical products that satisfy real customer needs.
>
> We do not believe that large size is important for its own sake; however, for at least two basic reasons, continuous growth is essential for us to achieve our other objectives.
>
> In the first place, we serve a rapidly growing and expanding segment of our technological society. To remain static would be to lose ground. We cannot maintain a position of strength and leadership in our field without growth.
>
> In the second place, growth is important in order to attract and hold high-caliber people. These individuals will align their future only with a company that offers them considerable opportunity for personal progress. Opportunities are greater and more challenging in a growing company.

The issue of growth raises a concern about the definition of the company mission. How can a firm's product, market, and technology be specified sufficiently to provide direction without precluding the exercise of unanticipated strategic options? How can a firm so define its mission that it can consider opportunistic diversification while maintaining the parameters that guide its growth decision? Perhaps such questions are best addressed when a firm's mission statement outlines the conditions under which the firm might depart from ongoing operations. General Electric Company's extensive global mission provided the foundation for its GE Appliances (GEA) in Louisville, Kentucky. GEA did not see consumer preferences in the world market becoming Americanized. Instead, its expansion goals allowed for flexibility in examining the unique characteristics of individual foreign markets and tailoring strategies to fit them.

The growth philosophy of Dayton-Hudson also embodies this approach:

> The stability and quality of the corporation's financial performance will be developed through the profitable execution of our existing businesses, as well as through the acquisition or development of new businesses. Our growth priorities, in order, are as follows:
>
> 1. Development of the profitable market preeminence of existing companies in existing markets through new store development or new strategies within existing stores.
> 2. Expansion of our companies to feasible new markets.
> 3. Acquisition of other retailing companies that are strategically and financially compatible with Dayton-Hudson.
> 4. Internal development of new retailing strategies.

Capital allocations to fund the expansion of existing Dayton-Hudson operating companies will be based on each company's return on investment (ROI), in relationship to its ROI objective and its consistency in earnings growth and on the ability of its management to perform up to the forecasts contained in its capital requests. Expansion via acquisition or new venture will occur when the opportunity promises an acceptable

STRATEGY IN ACTION 2–3

SATURN'S STATEMENT OF PHILOSOPHY

We, the Saturn Team, in concert with the UAW and General Motors, believe that meeting the needs of customers, Saturn members, suppliers, dealers, and neighbors is fundamental to fulfilling our mission.

To meet our customers' needs . . .
- our products and services must be world leaders in value and satisfaction.

To meet our members' needs, we . . .
- will create a sense of belonging in an environment of mutual trust, respect, and dignity;
- believe that all people want to be involved in decisions that affect them, care about their jobs and each other, take pride in themselves and in their contributions, and want to share in the success of their efforts;
- will develop the tools, training, and education for each member, recognizing individual skills and knowledge;
- believe that creative, motivated, responsible team members who understand that change is critical to success are Saturn's most important asset.

To meet our suppliers' and dealers' needs, we . . .
- will strive to create real partnerships with them;
- will be open and fair in our dealings, reflecting trust, respect, and their importance to Saturn;
- want dealers and suppliers to feel ownership in Saturn's mission and philosophy as their own.

To meet the needs of our neighbors, the communities in which we live and operate, we . . .
- will be good citizens, protect the environment, and conserve natural resources;
- will seek to cooperate with government at all levels and strive to be sensitive, open, and candid in all our public statements.

rate of long-term growth and profitability, an acceptable degree of risk, and compatibility with Dayton-Hudson's long-term strategy.

Company Philosophy

The statement of a company's philosophy, often called the *company creed,* usually accompanies or appears within the mission statement. It reflects or specifies the basic beliefs, values, aspirations, and philosophical priorities to which strategic decision makers are committed in managing the company. Fortunately, the philosophies vary little from one firm to another. Owners and managers implicitly accept a general, unwritten, yet pervasive code of behavior that governs business actions and permits them to be largely self-regulated. Unfortunately, statements of company philosophy are often so similar and so platitudinous that they read more like public relations handouts than the commitment to values they are meant to be.

MANAGEMENT PHILOSOPHY OF DAYTON-HUDSON CORPORATION

The corporation will:

Set standards for return on investment (ROI) and earnings growth.
Approve strategic plans.
Allocate capital.
Approve goals.
Monitor, measure, and audit results.
Reward performance.
Allocate management resources.

The operating companies will be accorded the freedom and responsibility:

To manage their own business.
To develop strategic plans and goals that will optimize their growth.
To develop an organization that can ensure consistency of results and optimum growth.
To operate their businesses consistent with the corporation's statement of philosophy.

The corporate staff will provide only those services that are:

Essential to the protection of the corporation.
Needed for the growth of the corporation.
Wanted by operating companies and that provide a significant advantage in quality or cost.

The corporation will insist on:

Uniform accounting practices by type of business.
Prompt disclosure of operating results.
A systematic approach to training and developing people.
Adherence to appropriately high standards of business conduct and civic responsibility in accordance with the corporation's statement of philosophy.

Saturn's statement of philosophy, presented in Strategy in Action 2–3, indicates the company's clearly defined initiatives for satisfying the needs of its customers, employees, suppliers, and dealers.

Despite the similarity of these statements, the intentions of the strategic managers in developing them do not warrant cynicism. Company executives attempt to provide a distinctive and accurate picture of the firm's managerial outlook. One such statement of company philosophy is that of Dayton-Hudson Corporation. As Strategy in Action 2–4 shows, Dayton-Hudson's board of directors and executives have established especially clear directions for company decision making and action.

Perhaps most noteworthy in the Dayton-Hudson statement is its delineation of responsibility at both the corporate and business levels. In many ways, the statement could serve as a prototype for the three-tier approach to strategic management. This approach implies that the mission statement must address strategic concerns at the corporate, business, and functional levels of the organization. Dayton-Hudson's

GLOBAL STRATEGY IN ACTION 2–2

PRINCIPLES OF NISSAN MOTOR MANUFACTURING (UK) LTD.

People Principles
(All Other Objectives Can Only Be Achieved by People)

Selection	Hire the highest caliber people; look for technical capabilities and emphasize attitude.
Responsibility	Maximize the responsibility; staff by devolving decision making.
Teamwork	Recognize and encourage individual contributions, with everyone working toward the same objectives.
Flexibility	Expand the role of the individual: multiskilled, no job description, generic job titles.
Kaizen	Continuously seek 100.1 percent improvements; give "ownership of change."
Communications	"Every day, face to face."
Training	Establish individual "continuous development programs."
Supervisors	Regard as "the professionals at managing the production process"; give them much responsibility normally assumed by individual departments; make them the genuine leaders of their teams.
Single status	Treat everyone as a "first class" citizen; eliminate all illogical differences.
Trade unionism	Establish single union agreement with AEU emphasizing the common objective for a successful enterprise.

Key Corporate Principles

Quality	Building profitably the highest quality car sold in Europe.
Customers	Achieve target of no. 1 customer satisfaction in Europe.
Volume	Always achieve required volume.
New products	Deliver on time, at required quality, within cost.
Suppliers	Establish long-term relationships with single-source suppliers; aim for zero defects and just-in-time delivery; apply Nissan principles to suppliers.
Production	Use "most appropriate" technology; develop predictable "best method" of doing job; build in quality.
Engineering	Design "quality" and "ease of working" into the product and facilities; establish "simultaneous engineering" to reduce development time.

Source: Excerpted from Judith Kenner Thompson and Robert R. Rehder, "Nissan U.K.: A Worker's Paradox?" p. 51. Reprinted from *Business Horizons,* January–February 1995. Copyright 1995 by the Foundation for the School of Business at Indiana University. Used with permission.

management philosophy does this by balancing operating autonomy and flexibility on the one hand with corporate input and direction on the other.

As seen in Global Strategy in Action 2–2, the philosophy of Nissan Motor Manufacturing is expressed by the company's People Principles and Key Corporate Principles. These principles form the basis of the way the company operates on a daily basis. They address the principal concepts used in meeting the company's established goals. Nissan focuses on the distinction between the role of the individual and the corporation. In this way, employees can link their productivity and success to the productivity and success of the company. Given these principles, the company is able to concentrate on the issues most important to its survival, growth, and profitability.

Strategy in Action 2–5 provides an example of how General Motors uses a statement of company philosophy to clarify its environmental principles.

GENERAL MOTORS ENVIRONMENTAL PRINCIPLES

STRATEGY IN ACTION 2–5

As a responsible corporate citizen, General Motors is dedicated to protecting human health, natural resources, and the global environment. This dedication reaches further than compliance with the law to encompass the integration of sound environmental practices into our business decisions.

The following environmental principles provide guidance to General Motors personnel world-wide in the conduct of their daily business practices:

1. We are committed to actions to restore and preserve the environment.
2. We are committed to reducing waste and pollutants, conserving resources, and recycling materials at every stage of the product life cycle.
3. We will continue to participate actively in educating the public regarding environmental conservation.
4. We will continue to pursue vigorously the development and implementation of technologies for minimizing pollutant emissions.
5. We will continue to work with all governmental entities for the development of technically sound and financially responsible environmental laws and regulations.
6. We will continually assess the impact of our plants and products on the environment and the communities in which we live and operate with a goal of continuous improvement.

Source: 1991 General Motors Public Interest Report, p. 23.

Public Image

Both present and potential customers attribute certain qualities to particular businesses. Gerber and Johnson & Johnson make safe products; Cross Pen makes high-quality writing instruments; Étienne Aigner makes stylish but affordable leather products; Corvettes are power machines; and Izod Lacoste stands for the preppy look. Thus, mission statements should reflect the public's expectations, since this makes achievement of the firm's goals more likely. Gerber's mission statement should not open the possibility for diversification into pesticides, and Cross Pen's should not open the possibility for diversification into $0.59 brand-name disposables.

On the other hand, a negative public image often prompts firms to reemphasize the beneficial aspects of their mission. For example, in response to what it saw as a disturbing trend in public opinion, Dow Chemical undertook an aggressive promotional campaign to fortify its credibility, particularly among "employees and those who live and work in [their] plant communities." Dow described its approach in its annual report:

> All around the world today, Dow people are speaking up. People who care deeply about their company, what it stands for, and how it is viewed by others. People who are immensely proud of their company's performance, yet realistic enough to realize it is the public's perception of that performance that counts in the long run.

Firms seldom address the question of their public image in an intermittent fashion. Although public agitation often stimulates greater attention to this question, firms are concerned about their public image even in the absence of such agitation. The following excerpt from the mission statement of Intel Corporation is an example of this attitude:

STRATEGY IN ACTION 2–6

MISSION STATEMENTS FOR THE HIGH-END SHOE INDUSTRY

Allen-Edmonds

Allen-Edmonds provides high-quality shoes for the affluent consumer who appreciates a well-made, finely crafted, stylish dress shoe.

Bally

Bally shoes set you apart. They are the perfect shoe to complement your lifestyle. Bally shoes project an image of European style and elegance that ensures one is not just dressed, but well-dressed.

Bostonian

Bostonian shoes are for those successful individuals who are well-traveled, on the "go" and want a stylish dress shoe that can keep up with their variety of needs and activities. With Bostonian, you know you will always be well dressed whatever the situation.

Cole-Hahn

Cole-Hahn offers a line of contemporary shoes for the man who wants to go his own way. They are shoes for the urban, upscale, stylish man who wants to project an image of being one step ahead.

Florsheim

Florsheim shoes are the affordable classic men's dress shoes for those who want to experience the comfort and style of a solid dress shoe.

Johnston & Murphy

Johnston & Murphy is the quintessential business shoe for those affluent individuals who know and demand the best.

Source: "Thinking on Your Feet, the Johnston & Murphy Guerrilla Marketing Competition," (Johnston & Murphy, a GENESCO Company).

We are sensitive to our *image with our customers and the business community.* Commitments to customers are considered sacred, and we are upset with ourselves when we do not meet our commitments. We strive to demonstrate to the business world on a continuing basis that we are credible in describing the state of the corporation, and that we are well organized and in complete control of all things that determine the numbers.

Strategy in Action 2–6 presents a marketing translation of the essence of the mission statements of six high-end shoe companies. The impressive feature of the exhibit is that it shows dramatically how closely competing firms can incorporate subtle, yet meaningful, differences into their mission statements.

Company Self-Concept

A major determinant of a firm's success is the extent to which the firm can relate functionally to its external environment. To achieve its proper place in a competitive situation, the firm realistically must evaluate its competitive strengths and weaknesses. This idea—that the firm must know itself—is the essence of the company self-concept. The idea is not commonly integrated into theories of strategic management; its importance for individuals has been recognized since ancient times. As one scholar writes, "Man has struggled to understand himself, for how he thinks of himself will influence both what he chooses to do and what he expects from life. Knowing his identity connects him both with his past and with the potentiality of his future."[2]

Both individuals and firms have a crucial need to know themselves. The ability of either to survive in a dynamic and highly competitive environment would be severely limited if they did not understand their impact on others or of others on them.

In some senses, then, firms take on personalities of their own. Much behavior in firms is organizationally based; that is, a firm acts on its members in other ways than their individual interactions. Thus, firms are entities whose personality transcends the personalities of their members. As such, they can set decision-making parameters based on aims different and distinct from the aims of their members. These organizational considerations have pervasive effects.

> Organizations do have policies, do and do not condone violence, and may or may not greet you with a smile. They also manufacture goods, administer policies, and protect the citizenry. These are organizational actions and involve properties of organizations, not individuals. They are carried out by individuals, even in the case of computer-produced letters, which are programmed by individuals—but the genesis of the actions remains in the organization.[3]

The characteristics of the corporate self-concept have been summarized as follows:

1. It is based on management's perception of the way in which others (society) will respond to the company.
2. It directs the behavior of people employed by the company.
3. It is determined in part by the responses of others to the company.
4. It is incorporated into mission statements that are communicated to individuals inside and outside the company.[4]

Ordinarily, descriptions of the company self-concept per se do not appear in mission statements. Yet such statements often provide strong impressions of the company self-concept. For example, ARCO's environment, health, and safety (EHS) managers were adamant about emphasizing the company's position on safety and environmental performance as a part of the mission statement. The challenges facing the ARCO EHS managers included dealing with concerned environmental groups and a public that has become environmentally aware. They hoped to motivate employees toward safer behavior while reducing emissions and waste. They saw this as a reflection of the company's positive self-image.

The following excerpts from the Intel Corporation mission statement describe the corporate persona that its top management seeks to foster:

> Management is self-critical. The leaders must be capable of recognizing and accepting their mistakes and learning from them.
>
> Open (constructive) confrontation is encouraged at all levels of the corporation and is viewed as a method of problem solving and conflict resolution.
>
> Decision by consensus is the rule. Decisions once made are supported. Position in the organization is not the basis for quality of ideas.
>
> A highly communicative, open management is part of the style.

----

[2]J. Kelly, *Organizational Behavior* (Burr Ridge, IL: Irwin, 1974), p. 258.

[3]R. H. Hall, *Organizational Structure and Process* (Englewood Cliffs, NJ: Prentice Hall, 1972), p. 13.

[4]E. J. Kelley, *Marketing Planning and Competitive Strategy* (Englewood Cliffs, NJ: Prentice Hall, 1972), p. 5.

Management must be ethical. Managing by telling the truth and treating all employees equitably has established credibility that is ethical.

We strive to provide an opportunity for rapid development.

Intel is a results-oriented company. The focus is on substance versus form, quality versus quantity.

We believe in the principle that hard work, high productivity is something to be proud of.

The concept of assumed responsibility is accepted. (If a task needs to be done, assume you have the responsibility to get it done.)

Commitments are long term. If career problems occur at some point, reassignment is a better alternative than termination.

We desire to have all employees involved and participative in their relationship with Intel.

Newest Trends in Mission Components

Recently, two new issues have become so prominent in the strategic planning for organizations that they are increasingly becoming integral parts in the development and revisions of mission statements: sensitivity to consumer wants and concern for quality.

Customers

"The customer is our top priority" is a slogan that would be claimed by the majority of businesses in the United States and abroad. For companies including Caterpillar Tractor, General Electric, and Johnson & Johnson this means analyzing consumer needs before as well as after a sale. The bonus plan at Xerox allows for a 40 percent annual bonus, based on high customer reviews of the service that they receive, and a 20 percent penalty if the feedback is especially bad. For these firms and many others, the overriding concern for the company has become consumer satisfaction.

In addition many U.S. firms maintain extensive product safety programs to help assure consumer satisfaction. RCA, Sears, and 3M boast of such programs. Other firms including Calgon Corporation, Amoco, Mobil Oil, Whirlpool, and Zenith provide toll-free telephone lines to answer customer concerns and complaints.

The focus on customer satisfaction is demonstrated by retailer J. C. Penney in this excerpt from its statement of philosophy: "The Penney Idea is (1) To serve the public as nearly as we can to its complete satisfaction; (2) To expect for the service we render a fair remuneration, and not all the profit the traffic will bear; (3) To do all in our power to pack the customer's dollar full of value, quality, and satisfaction."

A focus on customer satisfaction causes managers to realize the importance of providing quality customer service. Strong customer service initiatives have led some firms to gain competitive advantages in the marketplace. Hence, many corporations have made the customer service initiative a key component of their corporate mission. Some key elements of customer service–driven organizations are listed in Figure 2–1.

Quality

"Quality is job one!" is a rallying point not only for Ford Motor Corporation but for many resurging U.S. businesses as well. Since the 1950s, two U.S. management experts have fostered a worldwide emphasis on quality in manufacturing. W. Edwards Deming and J. M. Juran's messages were first embraced by Japanese managers, whose quality consciousness led to global dominance in several industries including automobile, TV, audio equipment, and electronic components manufacturing. Deming summarizes his approach in 14 now well-known points:

1. Create constancy of purpose.
2. Adopt the new philosophy.

FIGURE 2–1
Key Elements of Customer Service–Driven Organizations

1. A mission statement or sense of mission makes customer service a priority.
2. Customer service goals are clearly defined.
3. Customer service standards are clearly defined.
4. Customer satisfaction with existing products and services is continuously measured.
5. Ongoing efforts are made to understand customers to determine where the organization should be headed.
6. Corrective action procedures are in place to remove barriers to servicing customers in a timely and effective fashion.
7. Customer service goals have an impact on organizational action.

Source: An excerpt from "Peters, 1987," p. 78. Reprinted from *Business Horizons,* July–August 1995. Copyright 1995 by the Foundation for the School of Business at Indiana University. Used with permission.

3. Cease dependence on mass inspection to achieve quality.
4. End the practice of awarding business on price tag alone. Instead, minimize total cost, often accomplished by working with a single supplier.
5. Improve constantly the system of production and service.
6. Institute training on the job.
7. Institute leadership.
8. Drive out fear.
9. Break down barriers between departments.
10. Eliminate slogans, exhortations, and numerical targets.
11. Eliminate work standards (quotas) and management by objective.
12. Remove barriers that rob workers, engineers, and managers of their right to pride of workmanship.
13. Institute a vigorous program of education and self-improvement.
14. Put everyone in the company to work to accomplish the transformation.

Beginning in the late 1980s, firms in the United States responded aggressively. The new philosophy is that quality should be the norm. For example, Motorola's production goal is 60 or fewer defects per every billion components that it manufactures. Managers who emphasize quality have even created their own jargon, as reviewed in Figure 2–2.

Strategy in Action 2–7 presents the integration of the quality initiative into the mission statements of three corporations. The emphasis on quality has received added emphasis in many corporate philosophies since the Congress created the Malcolm Baldrige Quality Award in 1987. Each year up to two Baldrige Awards can been given in three categories of a company's operations: manufacturing, services, and small businesses.

OVERSEEING THE STRATEGY MAKERS

Who is responsible for determining the firm's mission? Who is responsible for acquiring and allocating resources so the firm can thoughtfully develop and implement a strategic plan? Who is responsible for monitoring the firm's success in the competitive marketplace to determine whether that plan was well designed and activated? The answer to all of these questions is strategic decision makers. As you saw in Figure 1–3,

FIGURE 2–2
A Glossary of Quality-Speak

Acceptable Quality Level (AQL)

Minimum number of parts that must comply with quality standards, usually stated as a percentage.

Competitive Benchmarking

Rating a company's practices, processes, and products against the world's best, including those in other industries.

Continuous-Improvement Process (CIP)

Searching unceasingly for ever-higher levels of quality by isolating sources of defects. The goal: zero defects. The Japanese call it Kaizen.

Control Charts

Statistical plots derived from measuring factory processes, they help detect "process drift," or deviation, before it generates defects. Charts also help spot inherent variations in manufacturing processes that designers must account for to achieve "robust design" (below).

Just-in-Time (JIT)

When suppliers deliver materials and parts at the moment a factory needs them, thus eliminating costly inventories. Quality is paramount: A faulty part delivered at the last minute won't be detected.

Pareto Chart

A bar graph that ranks causes of process variation by the degree of impact on quality.

Poka-Yoke

Making the workplace mistake-proof. A machine fitted with guide rails permits a part to be worked on in just one way.

Quality Function Deployment (QFD)

A system that pays special attention to customer wants. Activities that don't contribute are considered wasteful.

Robust Design

A discipline for making designs "production-proof" by building in tolerances for manufacturing variables that are known to be unavoidable.

Six-Sigma Quality

A statistical measure expressing how close a product comes to its quality goal. One-sigma means 68% of products are acceptable; three-sigma means 99.7%. Six-sigma is 99.999997% perfect: 3.4 defects per million parts.

Statistical Process Control (SPC)

A method of analyzing deviations in production processes during manufacturing.

Statistical Quality Control (SQC)

A method of analyzing measured deviations in manufactured materials, parts, and products.

Taguchi Methods

Statistical techniques developed by Genichi Taguchi, a Japanese consultant, for optimizing design and production. These are used often on "robust design" projects.

Total Quality Control (TQC)

The application of quality principles to all company endeavors, including satisfying internal "customers." Manufacturing engineers, for instance, are customers of the design staff. Also known as total quality management (TQM).

STRATEGY IN ACTION 2–7

VISIONS OF QUALITY

CADILLAC

The Mission of the Cadillac Motor Company is to engineer, produce, and market the world's finest automobiles known for uncompromised levels of distinctiveness, comfort, convenience, and refined performance. Through its people, who are its strength, Cadillac will continuously improve the quality of its products and services to meet or exceed customer expectations and succeed as a profitable business.

MOTOROLA

Dedication to quality is a way of life at our company, so much so that it goes far beyond rhetorical slogans. Our ongoing program of continued improvement reaches out for change, refinement, and even revolution in our pursuit of quality excellence.

It is the objective of Motorola, Inc., to produce and provide products and services of the highest quality. In its activities, Motorola will pursue goals aimed at the achievement of quality excellence. These results will be derived from the dedicated efforts of each employee in conjunction with supportive participation from management at all levels of the corporation.

ZYTEC

Zytec is a company that competes on value; is market driven; provides superior quality and service; builds strong relationships with its customers; and provides technical excellence in its products.

most organizations have multiple levels of strategic decision makers; typically, the larger the firm, the more levels it will have. The strategic managers at the highest level are responsible for decisions that affect the entire firm, commit the firm and its resources for the longest periods, and declare the firm's sense of values. In other words, this group of strategic managers is responsible for overseeing the creation and accomplishment of the company mission. The term that describes the group is *board of directors.*

In overseeing the management of a firm, the board of directors operates as the representatives of the firm's stockholders. Elected by the stockholders, the board has these major responsibilities:

1. To establish and update the company mission.
2. To elect the company's top officers, the foremost of whom is the CEO.
3. To establish the compensation levels of the top officers, including their salaries and bonuses.
4. To determine the amount and timing of the dividends paid to stockholders.
5. To set broad company policy on such matters as labor–management relations, product or service lines of business, and employee benefit packages.
6. To set company objectives and to authorize managers to implement the long-term strategies that the top officers and the board have found agreeable.
7. To mandate company compliance with legal and ethical dictates.

In the current business environment, boards of directors are accepting the challenge of shareholders and other stakeholders to become active in establishing the strategic initiatives of the companies that they serve. A main mover in stimulating this invigorated role for board members is attorney Ira Millstein, whose activities are sketched in Strategy in Action 2–8.

This chapter considers the board of directors because the board's greatest impact on the behavior of a firm results from its determination of the company mission. The philosophy espoused in the mission statement sets the tone by which the firm and all of its employees will be judged. As logical extensions of the mission statement, the firm's objectives and strategies embody the board's view of proper business demeanor. Through its appointment of top executives and its decisions about their compensation, the board reveals its priorities for organizational achievement.

Board Success Factors

A review of writings and research on the behavior of boards discloses that they are judged to be most successful when:

1. They represent the interests of stockholders and carefully monitor the actions of senior executives to promote and protect those interests.[5]

2. They link the firm to influential stakeholders in its external environment, thereby promoting the company mission while ensuring attention to important societal concerns.[6]

3. They are composed of 8 to 12 highly qualified members.

4. They exercise independent and objective thinking in appraising the actions of senior executives and in introducing strategic changes.[7]

5. They pay special attention to their own composition to ensure an appropriate mix of inside and outside directors and the inclusion of minority representatives.[8]

6. They have a well-developed structure; that is, they are organized into appropriate committees to perform specialized tasks (e.g., to review executive compensation and to audit the company's financial transactions).[9]

7. They meet frequently to discuss progress in achieving organizational goals and to provide counsel to executives.[10]

8. They evaluate the CEO's performance at least annually to provide guidance on issues of leadership style.[11]

---

[5]P. L. Rechner and D. R. Dalton, "The Impact of CEO as Board Chairperson on Corporate Performance: Evidence vs. Rhetoric," *Academy of Management Executive* 3, no. 2 (1989), pp. 141–43.

[6]M. S. Mizruchi, "Who Controls Whom?: An Examination of the Relation between Management and Board of Directors in Large American Corporations," *Academy of Management Review,* August 1983, pp. 426–35.

[7]T. M. Jones and L. D. Goldberg, "Governing the Large Corporation: More Arguments for Public Directors," *Academy of Management Review* 7 (1982), pp. 603–11.

[8]I. F. Kesner, "Directors' Characteristics and Committee Membership: An Investigation of Type, Occupation, Tenure, and Gender," *Academy of Management Journal* 31 (1988), pp. 66–84; and J. A. Pearce II, "The Relationship of Internal versus External Orientations to Financial Measures of Strategic Performance," *Strategic Management Journal* 4 (1983), pp. 297–306.

[9]R. Molz, "Managerial Domination of Boards of Directors and Financial Performance," *Journal of Business Research* 16 (1988), pp. 235–50.

[10]A. Tashakori and W. Boulton, "A Look at the Board's Role Planning," *Journal of Business Strategy* 3, no. 3 (1985), pp. 64–70.

[11]R. Nader, "Reforming Corporate Governance," *California Management Review,* Winter 1984, pp. 126–32.

BusinessWeek

The Guru of Good Governance

STRATEGY IN ACTION 2–8

Like a caged animal, Ira M. Millstein is pacing his personal conference room at the New York law firm of Weil, Gotshal & Manges, on the 34th floor overlooking Central Park.

An eminence grise of corporate governance, he now spends well over half his time on *board* issues. He teaches governance at Yale University, lectures on it to lawyers, and advises clients that include Westinghouse Electric, Estee Lauder, Empire Blue Cross & Blue Shield, and LENS, the activist investor fund.

"Pet Rock"

Over nearly two decades, Millstein has helped transform the relationship between a company's *board* and its shareholders and management. Thanks in part to him, directors are more aware of their *responsibilities,* and shareholders are more likely to do something about poor performance. Along the way, Millstein has represented clients on every side of the issue: disgruntled investors, executives under attack by shareholders, and *boards* that want CEOs to resign.

Although he has long been a player in governance circles, it was his part in General Motors Corp.'s 1992 boardroom coup that made his name. Millstein tutored the *board* (once derided as "a pet rock" by departing director Ross Perot) to become more active, then guided the directors through their decision to oust Chairman and CEO Robert Stempel. GM Vice-Chairman Harry J. Pearce says Millstein "provided guidance on how to be a better company and to make sure we weren't reacting emotionally."

Millstein's involvement in governance began when he was hired in the late 1970s as outside counsel for the Business Roundtable, the assemblage of big company CEOs. In April 1982, the American Law Institute drafted a report urging changes that would make it harder for courts to dismiss shareholder suits. On the Roundtable's behalf, Millstein issued a counterargument, setting off a battle with attorneys and academics. "I was attacking the temple," says Millstein, "but I was convinced down to my toenails that litigation was not the way to increase corporate performance." The Institute took until 1994 to publish its final report, but in the end, Millstein prevailed, and the section on litigation was watered down.

Source: John A. Byrne in New York, with Keith Naughton in Detroit, "The Guru of Good Governance," *Business Week,* April 28, 1997.

9. They conduct strategy reviews to determine the fit between the firm's strategy and the requirements of its competitive environment.[12]

10. They formulate the ethical codes that are to govern the behavior of the firm's executives and employees.[13]

11. They promote a future-oriented outlook on the company mission by challenging executives to articulate their visions for the firm and for its interface with society.

---

[12]J. R. Harrison, "The Strategic Use of Corporate Board Committees," *California Management Review* 30 (1987), pp. 109–25; and J. W. Henke, Jr., "Involving the Board of Directors in Strategic Planning," *Journal of Business Strategy* 7, no. 2 (1986), pp. 87–95.

[13]K. R. Andrews, *The Concept of Corporate Strategy* (Burr Ridge, IL: Irwin, 1987).

BusinessWeek

continued

More important, the dispute led him to steep himself in the issue of how *boards* interact with management and shareholders. In 1987, he urged the new Council of Institutional Investors to focus on performance and *boards* rather than poison pills and social issues. In the audience was Dale Hanson, CEO of California Public Employees' Retirement System (CalPERS). "It was a turning point," says Richard H. Koppes, then CalPERS's general counsel. "Here was a spokesman for Corporate America who said you have a legitimate gripe if you focus on performance." Within two years, the fund became a strident, often effective activist shareholder.

WATERSHED

In 1989, participants in a governance seminar began questioning Millstein about the *board* of client GM. "They said the *board* ought to be doing something," he recalls. "That led to my thinking about being more forthcoming with everybody in Detroit." Today, he divides the history of governance into "pre-GM" and "post-GM." Says Millstein: "When General Motors went, the dominoes absolutely fell. After GM, American Express, Eastman Kodak, Westinghouse, and IBM all went. They did so because GM legitimized an active *board.*"

Millstein tends to view governance as a universal solution. Overseeing Drexel Burnham Lambert Inc.'s bankruptcy from 1990 to 1992, he won the trust of creditors by putting together a *board* of outsiders. He later did the same at Olympia & York Co. USA, staving off a potentially disastrous bankruptcy filing and permitting a less disruptive prepackaged bankruptcy. "Again, governance won the day," he asserts.

To help Elisabeth Goth pressure the *board* of lackluster Dow Jones, he made a list of independent directors and lobbied the company to hire them. Dow Jones added two outsiders, but not from his list. Driven by several factors—Millstein's hiring, news of Goth's campaign, and a large stake taken by hedge fund manager Michael Price—Dow Jones stock has risen 15% since late December.

Dow Jones's survival has never been at stake. It's merely a weak performer. The new challenge, says Millstein, is to squeeze better results from just such "middling, bumping-along, not-too-terrible" companies: "That would be where I would like to see *boards* become more active." No doubt, as that becomes the norm, Millstein will be on hand, helping to ratchet up the pressure—and advising the *boards* that respond.

These criteria can enable board members, CEOs, and stockholders to judge board behavior. The question "What should boards do?" can be answered largely by studying the criteria.

AGENCY THEORY

Whenever there is a separation of the owners (principals) and the managers (agents) of a firm, the potential exists for the wishes of the owners to be ignored. This fact, and the recognition that agents are expensive, established the basis for a set of complex but helpful ideas known as *agency theory.* Whenever owners (or managers) delegate decision-making authority to others, an agency relationship exists between the two parties. Agency relationships, such as those between stockholders and managers, can be very effective as long as managers make investment decisions in ways that are consistent with stockholders' interests. However, when the interests of managers diverge from those of owners, then managers' decisions are more likely to reflect the managers' preferences than the owners' preferences.

In general, owners seek stock value maximization. When managers hold important blocks of company stock, they too prefer strategies that result in stock appreciation. However, when managers better resemble "hired hands" than owner-partners, they often prefer strategies that increase their personal payoffs rather than those of shareholders. Such behavior can result in decreased stock performance (as when high executive bonuses reduce corporate earnings), and in strategic decisions that point the firm in the direction of outcomes that are suboptimal from a stockholder's perspective.

If, as agency theory argues, self-interested managers act in ways that increase their own welfare at the expense of the gain of corporate stockholders, then owners who delegate decision-making authority to their agents will incur both the loss of potential gain that would have resulted from owner-optimal strategies and/or the costs of monitoring and control systems that are designed to minimize the consequences of such self-centered management decisions. In combination, the cost of agency problems and the cost of actions taken to minimize agency problems, are called *agency costs*. These costs can often be identified by their direct benefit for the agents and their negative present value. Agency costs are found when there are differing self-interests between shareholders and managers, superiors and subordinates, or managers of competing departments or branch offices.

How Agency Problems Occur

Because owners have access to only a relatively small portion of the information that is available to executives about the performance of the firm and cannot afford to monitor every executive decision or action, executives are often free to pursue their own interests.[14] This condition is known as the *moral hazard problem* or *shirking*.[15]

As a result of moral hazards, executives may design strategies that provide the greatest possible benefits for themselves, with the welfare of the organization being given only secondary consideration. For example, executives may pre-sell products at year-end to trigger their annual bonuses even though the deep discounts that they must offer will threaten the price stability of their products for the upcoming year. Similarly, unchecked executives may advance their own self-interests by slacking on the job, altering forecasts to maximize their performance bonuses; unrealistically assessing acquisition targets' outlooks in order to increase the probability of increasing organizational size through their acquisition; or manipulating personnel records to keep or acquire key company personnel.

The second major reason that agency costs are incurred is known as *adverse selection*. This refers to the limited ability that stockholders have to precisely determine the competencies and priorities of executives at the time that they are hired. Because principals cannot initially verify an executive's appropriateness as an agent of the owners, unanticipated problems of nonoverlapping priorities between owners and agents are likely to occur.

The most popular solution to moral dilemma and adverse selection problems is for owners to attempt to more closely align their own best interests with those of their

---

[14]Substitute the terms *managers* for *owners* and *subordinates* for *executives* for another example of agency theory in operation.

[15]Shirking is described as "self-interest combined with guile."

agents through the use of executive bonus plans.[16] Foremost among these approaches are stock option plans, which enable executives to benefit directly from the appreciation of the company's stock just as other stockholders do. In most instances, executive bonus plans are unabashed attempts to align the interests of owners and executives and to thereby induce executives to support strategies that increase stockholder wealth. While such schemes are unlikely to eliminate self-interest as a major criterion in executive decision making, they help to reduce the costs associated with moral dilemmas and adverse selections.

Problems That Can Result from Agency

From a strategic management perspective there are five different kinds of problems that can arise because of the agency relationship between corporate stockholders and their company's executives:

1. Executives pursue growth in company size rather than in earnings. Shareholders generally want to maximize earnings, because earnings growth yields stock appreciation. However, because managers are typically more heavily compensated for increases in firm size than for earnings growth, they may recommend strategies that yield company growth such as mergers and acquisitions.

In addition, managers' stature in the business community is commonly associated with company size. Managers gain prominence by directing the growth of an organization, and they benefit in the forms of career advancement and job mobility that are associated with increases in company size.

Finally, executives need an enlarging set of advancement opportunities for subordinates whom they wish to motivate with nonfinancial inducements. Acquisitions can provide the needed positions.

2. Executives attempt to diversify their corporate risk. Whereas stockholders can vary their investment risks through management of their individual stock portfolios, managers' careers and stock incentives are tied to the performance of a single corporation, albeit the one that employs them. Consequently, executives are tempted to diversify their corporation's operation, businesses, and product lines to moderate the risk incurred in any single venture. While this approach serves the executives' personal agendas, it compromises the "pure play" quality of their firm as an investment. In other words, diversifying a corporation reduces the beta associated with the firm's return, which is an undesirable outcome for many stockholders.

3. Executives avoid risk. Even when, or perhaps especially when, executives are willing to restrict the diversification of their companies, they are tempted to minimize the risk that they face. Executives are often fired for failure, but rarely for mediocre corporate performance. Therefore, executives may avoid desirable levels of risk, if they anticipate little reward and opt for conservative strategies that minimize the risk of company failure. If they do, executives will rarely support plans for innovation, diversification, and rapid growth.

However, from an investor's perspective, risk taking is desirable when it is systematic. In other words, when investors can reasonably expect that their company will generate higher long-term returns from assuming greater risk, they may wish to pursue the greater payoff, especially when the company is positioned to perform better than its competitors that face the same nominal risks. Obviously, the agency relationship

---

[16]An in-depth discussion of executive bonus compensation is provided in Chapter 10.

creates a problem—should executives prioritize their job security or the company's financial returns to stockholders?

4. Managers act to optimize their personal payoffs. If executives can gain more from an annual performance bonus by achieving objective 1 than from stock appreciation resulting from the achievement of objective 2, then owners must anticipate that the executives will target objective 1 as their priority, even though objective 2 is clearly in the best interest of the shareholders. Similarly, executives may pursue a range of expensive perquisites that have a net negative effect on shareholder returns. Elegant comer offices, corporate jets, large staffs, golf club memberships, extravagant retirement programs, and limousines for executive benefit are rarely good investments for stockholders.

5. Executives act to protect their status. When their companies expand, executives want to assure that their knowledge, experience, and skills remain relevant and central to the strategic direction of the corporation. They favor doing more of what they already do well. In contrast, investors may prefer revolutionary advancement to incremental improvement. For example, when confronted with Amazon.com, competitor Barnes & Noble initiated a joint venture website with Bertelsmann. In addition, Barnes & Noble used vertical integration with the nation's largest book distributor, which supplies 60 percent of Amazon's books. This type of revolutionary strategy is most likely to occur when executives are given assurances that they will not make themselves obsolete within the changing company that they create.

Solutions to the Agency Problem

In addition to defining an agent's responsibilities in a contract, and including elements like bonus incentives that help align executives' and owners' interests, principals can take several other actions to minimize agency problems. The first is for the owners to pay executives a premium for their service. This premium helps executives to see their loyalty to the stockholders as the key to achieving their personal financial targets.

A second solution to agency problems is for executives to receive backloaded compensation. This means that executives are paid a handsome premium for superior future performance. Strategic actions taken in year one, which are to have an impact in year three, become the basis for executive bonuses in year three. This lag time between action and bonus more realistically rewards executives for the consequences of their decision making, ties the executive to the company for the long term, and properly focuses strategic management activities on the future.

Finally, creating teams of executives across different units of a corporation can help to focus performance measures on organizational rather than personal goals. Through the use of executive teams, owner interests often receive the priority that they deserve.

THE STAKEHOLDER APPROACH TO COMPANY RESPONSIBILITY

In defining or redefining the company mission, strategic managers must recognize the legitimate rights of the firm's claimant. These include not only stockholders and employees but also outsiders affected by the firm's actions. Such outsiders commonly include customers, suppliers, governments, unions, competitors, local communities, and the general public. Each of these interest groups has justifiable reasons for expecting (and often for demanding) that the firm satisfy their claims in a responsible manner. In general, stockholders claim appropriate returns on their investment; employees seek broadly defined job satisfactions; customers want what they pay for; suppliers seek dependable buyers; governments want adherence to legislation; unions seek benefits for their members; competitors want fair competition; local communities want the firm to be a responsible citizen; and the general public expects the firm's existence to improve the quality of life.

According to a recent survey of 2,361 directors in 291 of the largest southeastern U.S. companies:

1. Directors perceived the existence of distinct stakeholder groups.
2. Directors have high stakeholder orientations.
3. Directors view some stakeholders differently, depending on their occupation (CEO directors versus non-CEO directors) and type (inside versus outside directors).

The study also found that the perceived stakeholders were, in the order of their importance, customers and government, stockholders, employees, and society. The results clearly indicated that boards of directors no longer believe that the stockholder is the only constituency to whom they are responsible.

However, when a firm attempts to incorporate the interests of these groups into its mission statement, broad generalizations are insufficient. These steps need to be taken:

1. Identification of the stakeholders.
2. Understanding the stakeholders' specific claims vis-à-vis the firm.
3. Reconciliation of these claims and assignment of priorities to them.
4. Coordination of the claims with other elements of the company mission.

Identification   The left-hand column of Figure 2–3 lists the commonly encountered stakeholder groups, to which the executive officer group often is added. Obviously, though, every business faces a slightly different set of stakeholder groups, which vary in number, size, influence, and importance. In defining the company, strategic managers must identify all of the stakeholder groups and weigh their relative rights and their relative ability to affect the firm's success.

Understanding   The concerns of the principal stakeholder groups tend to center on the general claims listed in the right-hand column of Figure 2–3. However, strategic decision makers should understand the specific demands of each group. They then will be better able to initiate actions that satisfy these demands.

Reconciliation and Priorities   Unfortunately, the claims of various stakeholder groups often conflict. For example, the claims of governments and the general public tend to limit profitability, which is the central claim of most creditors and stockholders. Thus, claims must be reconciled in a mission statement that resolves the competing, conflicting, and contradicting claims of stakeholders. For objectives and strategies to be internally consistent and precisely focused, the statement must display a single-minded, though multidimensional, approach to the firm's aims.

There are hundreds, if not thousands, of claims on any firm—high wages, pure air, job security, product quality, community service, taxes, occupational health and safety regulations, equal employment opportunity regulations, product variety, wide markets, career opportunities, company growth, investment security, high ROI, and many, many more. Although most, perhaps all, of these claims may be desirable ends, they cannot be pursued with equal emphasis. They must be assigned priorities in accordance with the relative emphasis that the firm will give them. That emphasis is reflected in the criteria that the firm uses in its strategic decision making; in the firm's allocation of its human, financial, and physical resources; and in the firm's long-term objectives and strategies.

FIGURE 2–3
A Stakeholder View of Company Responsibility

Stakeholder	Nature of the Claim
Stockholders	Participation in distribution of profits, additional stock offerings, assets on liquidation; vote of stock; inspection of company books; transfer of stock; election of board of directors; and such additional rights as have been established in the contract with the corporation.
Creditors	Legal proportion of interest payments due and return of principal from the investment. Security of pledged assets; relative priority in event of liquidation. Management and owner prerogatives if certain conditions exist with the company (such as default of interest payments).
Employees	Economic, social, and psychological satisfaction in the place of employment. Freedom from arbitrary and capricious behavior on the part of company officials. Share in fringe benefits, freedom to join union and participate in collective bargaining, individual freedom in offering up their services through an employment contract. Adequate working conditions.
Customers	Service provided with the product; technical data to use the product; suitable warranties; spare parts to support the product during use; R&D leading to product improvement; facilitation of credit.
Suppliers	Continuing source of business; timely consummation of trade credit obligations; professional relationship in contracting for, purchasing, and receiving goods and services.
Governments	Taxes (income, property, and so on); adherence to the letter and intent of public policy dealing with the requirements of fair and free competition; discharge of legal obligations of businesspeople (and business organizations); adherence to antitrust laws.
Unions	Recognition as the negotiating agent for employees. Opportunity to perpetuate the union as a participant in the business organization.
Competitors	Observation of the norms for competitive conduct established by society and the industry. Business statesmanship on the part of peers.
Local communities	Place of productive and healthful employment in the community. Participation of company officials in community affairs, provision of regular employment, fair play, reasonable portion of purchases made in the local community, interest in and support of local government, support of cultural and charitable projects.
The general public	Participation in and contribution to society as a whole; creative communications between governmental and business units designed for reciprocal understanding; assumption of fair proportion of the burden of government and society. Fair price for products and advancement of the state-of-the-art technology that the product line involves.

Source : William R. King and David I. Cleland, *Strategic Planning and Policy.* ©1978 by Litton Educational Publishing, Inc., p. 153. Reprinted by permission of Van Nostrand Reinhold Company.

Coordination with Other Elements   The demands of stakeholder groups constitute only one principal set of inputs to the company mission. The other principal sets are the managerial operating philosophy and the determinants of the product-market offering. Those determinants constitute a reality test that the accepted claims must pass. The key question is: How can the firm satisfy its claimants and at the same time optimize its economic success in the marketplace?

Social Responsibility

As indicated in Figure 2–4, the various stakeholders of a firm can be divided into inside stakeholders and outside stakeholders. The insiders are the individuals or groups that are stockholders or employees of the firm. The outsiders are all the other individuals or groups that the firm's actions affect. The extremely large and often amorphous set of outsiders makes the general claim that the firm be socially responsible.[17]

[17]J. S. Bracker and A. J. Kinicki, "Strategic Management, Plant Closings and Social Responsibility: An Integrative Process Model," *Employee Responsibilities and Rights Journal* 1, no. 3 (1988), pp. 201–13.

FIGURE 2–4
Inputs to the Development of the Company Mission

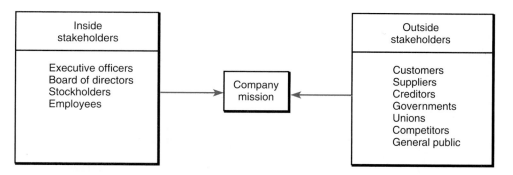

Perhaps the thorniest issues faced in defining a company mission are those that pertain to responsibility. The stakeholder approach offers the clearest perspective on such issues. Broadly stated, outsiders often demand that insiders' claims be subordinated to the greater good of the society; that is, to the greater good of outsiders. They believe that such issues as pollution, the disposal of solid and liquid wastes, and the conservation of natural resources should be principal considerations in strategic decision making. Also broadly stated, insiders tend to believe that the competing claims of outsiders should be balanced against one another in a way that protects the company mission. For example, they tend to believe that the need of consumers for a product should be balanced against the water pollution resulting from its production if the firm cannot eliminate that pollution entirely and still remain profitable. Some insiders also argue that the claims of society, as expressed in government regulation, provide tax money that can be used to eliminate water pollution and the like if the general public wants this to be done.

The issues are numerous, complex, and contingent on specific situations. Thus, rigid rules of business conduct cannot deal with them. Each firm *regardless of size* must decide how to meet its perceived social responsibility. While large, well-capitalized companies may have easy access to environmental consultants, this is not an affordable strategy for smaller companies. However, the experience of many small businesses demonstrates that it is feasible to accomplish significant pollution prevention and waste reduction without big expenditures and without hiring consultants. Once a problem area has been identified, a company's line employees frequently can develop a solution. Other important pollution prevention strategies include changing the materials used or redesigning how operations are bid out. Making pollution prevention a social responsibility can be beneficial to smaller companies. Publicly traded firms also can benefit directly from socially responsible strategies, as indicated in Global Strategy in Action 2–3.

Different approaches adopted by different firms reflect differences in competitive position, industry, country, environmental and ecological pressures, and a host of other factors. In other words, they will reflect both situational factors and differing priorities in the acknowledgment of claims. Obviously, winning the loyalty of the growing legions of consumers will require new marketing strategies and new alliances in the 21st century. Many marketers already have discovered these new marketing realities by adopting strategies called the "*4 E's*": (1) make it easy for the consumer to be green, (2) empower consumers with solutions, (3) enlist the

GLOBAL STRATEGY IN ACTION 2–3

SOCIAL INDEX LISTS RESPONSIBLE FIRMS

At one time, socially conscious investing was as simple as Just Say No—no investing in companies that produce alcohol, tobacco, or weapons, or are involved in gambling, nuclear energy, or South Africa.

But social investing has matured since arriving in the early 1970s, and it's no longer a cut-and-dried process. "In the past, it has primarily been a boycott movement with social change as a goal," says Amy Domini. "Newer criteria are more about corporate responsibility, and they're more difficult to apply."

Domini, with her husband, Peter Kinder, created the Domini Social Index of 400 socially responsible companies in May 1990. Their Cambridge, Massachusetts, firm screens more than 800 companies for product quality and consumer relations, environmental performance, corporate citizenship, and employee relations.

Companies on the Domini Social Index are not 1960s holdouts making tie-dye T-shirts or macramé plant hangers. The list includes Wal-Mart, Merck, Coca-Cola, PepsiCo, McDonald's, the Federal National Mortgage, and Sears.

The index should perform on a par with the Standard & Poor's 500 index over the long term, says Domini. But it can be more volatile short term, because it has more small companies than the S&P 500.

Source: Excerpted from Chris Wloszczyna, "Social Index Lists Responsible Firms," *USA Today,* March 30, 1992, Section 3B. Copyright 1992, USA TODAY. Reprinted with permission.

support of the consumer, and (4) establish credibility with all publics and help to avoid a backlash.

British Petroleum CEO, John Browne, faces the social responsibility questions asked of all leaders of global firms. Global Strategy in Action 2–4 presents Browne's view that for his global company to thrive, so must the communities in which his company does business.

Despite differences in their approaches, most American firms now try to assure outsiders that they attempt to conduct business in a socially responsible manner. Many firms, including Abt Associates, Dow Chemical, Eastern Gas and Fuel Associates, Exxon, and the Bank of America, conduct and publish annual social audits. Such audits attempt to evaluate a firm from the perspective of social responsibility. Private consultants often conduct them for the firm and offer minimally biased evaluations on what are inherently highly subjective issues.

Corporate Social Responsibility and Profitability

> Few trends could so thoroughly undermine the very foundations of our free society as the acceptance by corporate officials of a social responsibility other than to make as much money for their stockholders as possible.
>
> Milton Friedman, *Capitalism and Freedom,* 1962

In the four decades since Milton Friedman wrote these words, the issue of *corporate social responsibility* (CSR)—the idea that business has a duty to serve society as well as the financial interest of stockholders—has remained a highly contentious one. Yet managers recognize that deciding to what extent to embrace CSR is an important strategic decision.

There are three principal reasons why managers should be concerned about the socially responsible behavior of their firms. First, a company's right to exist depends on its responsiveness to the external environment. Second, federal, state, and local governments threaten increased regulation if business does not evolve to meet changing social standards. Third, a responsive corporate social policy may enhance a firm's long-term viability.[18] Underscoring the importance of these factors to the firm is the implicit belief that long-run profit maximization is inexorably linked to CSR.

The Debate

Should a company behave in a socially responsible manner? Coming down on one side of the question are those who, like Friedman, believe that a business bears a responsibility only for the financial well-being of its stockholders. Implicit in this statement is the idea that corporate actions motivated by anything other than shareholder wealth maximization threatens that well-being. On the other side, proponents of CSR assert that business does not function in a vacuum; it exists to serve, depends upon its environment, cannot be separated from it, and therefore has a responsibility to ensure its well-being. The environment is represented not only by stockholders/owners and employees, but also by such external stakeholders as customers, unions, suppliers, competitors, government agencies, local communities, and society in general.

The second argument for CSR suggests that stockholders' interests may transcend the financial. Many stockholders expect more from the companies in which they invest than simple appreciation in the economic value of the firm.

The third argument in favor of CSR is that the best way for a company to maximize shareholder wealth is to act in a socially responsible manner. It suggests that when a company behaves responsibly, benefits accrue directly to the bottom line. It also implies that when a company does not behave responsibly, the company and its shareholders suffer financially.

CSR and the Bottom Line[19]

The goal of every firm is to maintain viability through long-run profitability. Until all costs and benefits are accounted for, however, profits may not be claimed. In the case of CSR, costs and benefits are both economic and social. While economic costs and benefits are easily quantifiable, social costs and benefits are not. Managers therefore risk subordinating social consequences to other performance results that can be more straightforwardly measured.

The dynamic between CSR and success (profit) is complex. While one concept is clearly not mutually exclusive of the other, it is also clear that neither is a prerequisite of the other. Rather than viewing these two concepts as competing, it may be better to view CSR as a component in the decision-making process of business that must determine, among other objectives, how to maximize profits.

Attempts to undertake a cost-benefit analysis of CSR have not been very successful. The process is complicated by several factors. First, some CSR activities incur no

[18]Archie B. Carroll and Frank Hoy, "Integrating Corporate Social Policy into Strategic Management," *Journal of Business Strategy* 4 (Winter 1984), pp. 48–57.

[19]We wish to thank Professor Sebastian Rainone of Villanova University and Deborah Woodcock for their help in the development of this section.

BusinessWeek

GLOBALISM DOESN'T HAVE TO BE CRUEL

**GLOBAL
STRATEGY IN
ACTION
2–4**

In the twilight of the 20th century, making globalization work humanely is quickly becoming the dominant issue of our time. From Boston to Bangkok, trade, investment, and information technology are exploding across borders and overwhelming governments' ability to provide social safety nets and public services to cushion the impact on people. A political backlash is building in Asia, Europe, and Latin America. It could even happen in the U.S., once the current economic expansion comes to its inevitable end. Although international corporations cannot shoulder all the *responsibility,* no challenge is more central to global management than finding a balance between the relentless pressure for short-term profits and broader social *responsibilities.*

What's a chief executive to do? To what degree should companies take on the *responsibility* heretofore shouldered by governments? To what degree can they? One chief executive, John Browne of British Petroleum Co., has a clear philosophy and strategy. Browne believes that for BP to thrive, so must the communities in which it does business. To make that happen, Browne has insisted that the economic and social health of the villages, towns, and cities in which BP does business be a matter of central concern to the company's *board* of directors. He has also made social investment for the long term an important variable in compensating BP employees around the world.

AMBITIOUS GOALS

What to do and how to do it is left to local BP business units. But regular reviews of their activities are held by regional executives. In such areas as job training for local employees and building schools, ambitious goals are set, and performance is measured against them. Involved in the process along with BP employees and *board* directors are local residents whose views are regularly surveyed.

BP's community investments are extensive. In Vietnam, the company is providing computer-based technology to control the damage from recurrent flooding. In Turkey, BP recently financed the replanting of a forest around the Black Sea that had been destroyed by fire. In Zambia, it has supplied 200 solar-powered refrigerators to help doctors store antimalaria vaccines. In South

Source: Jeffrey E. Garten, "Globalism Doesn't Have to Be Cruel," *Business Week,* February 9, 1998.

dollar costs at all. For example, Second Harvest, the largest nongovernment, charitable food distributor in the nation, accepts donations from food manufacturers and food retailers of surplus food that would otherwise be thrown out due to overruns, warehouse damage, or labeling errors. In 10 years, Second Harvest has distributed more than 2 billion pounds of food. Gifts in Kind America is an organization that enables companies to reduce unsold or obsolete inventory by matching a corporation's donated products with a charity's or other nonprofit organization's needs. In addition, a tax break is realized by the company. In the past, corporate donations have included 130,000 pairs of shoes from Nike, 10,000 pairs of gloves from Aris Isotoner, and 480 computer systems from Apple Computer.

In addition, philanthropic activities of a corporation, which have been a traditional mainstay of CSR, are undertaken at a discounted cost to the firm since they are often tax deductible. The benefits of corporate philanthropy can be enormous as is shown by

Africa, it has supported the development of small business in urban areas such as Soweto. In Colombia, it is turning its own waste material into bricks for local homebuilding.

In addition, accidents in the workplace, noxious emissions, and oil spills are subject to monitoring and quantification. Ernst & Young verifies company recordkeeping. There is constant pressure to eliminate accidents.

NOT CHARITY

So far, the strategy has not impaired BP's bottom line. To the contrary. "These efforts have nothing to do with charity," says Browne, "and everything to do with our long-term self-interest. I see no trade-off between the short term and the long. Twenty years is just 80 quarters. And our shareholders want performance today, and tomorrow, and the day after."

So far, they've gotten it. Since the end of 1992, if an investor bought BP stock and reinvested the dividends, he or she would have earned a 33% annual return, outstripping by over 50% the comparable returns thrown off by the Dow Jones industrial average, the Standard & Poor's 500-stock index, or the S&P Energy Composite. In the past five years, the company's market capitalization has expanded nearly fourfold, to $77 billion. Meanwhile, profits have climbed nearly fivefold, to $4.7 billion. In the past year, BP's return on capital invested exceeded that of all other major energy companies.

Despite Browne's success in balancing the immediate needs of his shareholders with broader social *responsibilities,* he treads cautiously. "We have to be acutely conscious of our limitations. Companies can't substitute for governments." True enough. Even if governments shrink, they will have to become more effective in addressing everything from financial regulation to health care. But global companies do have a great stake in social stability and economic progress, and as governments recede, they will have to fill much more of the void.

Corporations would do well to take a page out of Browne's playbook: think long-term, invest heavily in the communities that you do business in, be obsessive about achieving profits, and fully integrate social *responsibility* into your policies on governance and compensation. The big question is whether Browne is part of the vanguard of a new breed of corporate leadership or just an admirable exception. The answer could help determine the magnitude of the backlash against globalization.

the many national social welfare causes that have been spurred by corporate giving. A few of these causes are described in Strategy in Action 2–9. While such acts of benevolence often help establish a general perception of the involved companies within society, some philanthropic acts bring specific credit to the firm. One good example is shown in Strategy in Action 2–10. It relates the experience of Malden Mills' CEO, Aaron Feuerstein, and the recognition that he received from the foundation established by actor Paul Newman.

Second, socially responsible behavior does not come at a prohibitive cost. One needs only to look at the problems of A. H. Robbins Company (Dalkon Shield), Beech-Nut Corporation (apple juice), Drexel Burnham (insider trading), and Exxon (*Valdez*) for stark answers on the "cost" of social responsibility (or its absence) in the business environment.

Third, socially responsible practices may create savings and, as a result, increase profits. SET Laboratories uses popcorn to ship software rather than polystyrene peanuts. It is

HOW CORPORATE PHILANTHROPY PROMOTES CAUSES

**STRATEGY IN
ACTION
2–9**

Now that U.S. companies are adopting strategic philanthropy, they are assuming an activist stance on social issues. As a result, many fringe causes, including the following, have become national movements.

HUNGER

Before the new approach to corporate philanthropy, the foundations of food companies gave cash donations to antihunger organizations. But when the ranks of the hungry increased tenfold in the 1980s, contributions managers in companies such as General Mills, Grand Metropolitan, Kraft General Foods, and Sara Lee decided to play a larger role *and* establish a rallying point around which disparate units of their companies could come together. Marketers arranged for a portion of product sales to be donated to antihunger programs, human resources staffs deployed volunteers, operating units provided free food, and CEOs joined the board of Chicago-based Second Harvest, the food industry's antihunger voice. As a result of those efforts, a complex infrastructure of food banks and soup kitchens was developed.

Now the trend is toward deeper political involvement. In 1993, Kraft General Foods became the first company to use its political capital to press for more funding for food stamps and other federal initiatives.

COMMUNITY AND ECONOMIC DEVELOPMENT

In the late 1980s, major banks such as Bank of America, Chase Manhattan, Citicorp, Morgan Guaranty, and Wells Fargo explored how philanthropy could be tied to marketing, human resources, government affairs, investment, and even trust management. Those banks had given mostly to the arts, but their business managers were concerned about the Community Reinvestment Act, which requires lenders to be responsive to low-income communities. Philanthropy managers used the act to gain internal support for positioning their companies as leaders in the antipoverty struggle. They pointed out that by going beyond the CRA requirements, they could develop positive relationships with regulators while scoring public relations points.

At least 60 banks in the United States have created community development corporations to assist run-down neighborhoods. An executive at Wells Fargo organized a national network of bankers who make low-interest loans to nonprofits working to bring enterprise to inner cities. About 20 percent of those banks' donations now go to those developers.

LITERACY

The effort to increase literacy in the United States is the favorite cause of the communications industry. Print media companies such as McGraw-Hill, Prentice Hall, the *Los Angeles Times,* the

continued

Washington Post, and the *New York Times* are trying to halt the drop in readership, and broadcasters and cable companies are compensating for their role in the decline of literacy. Those companies have mobilized their marketing, human resources, and lobbying power to establish workplace literacy programs. While human resources budgets fund such programs, philanthropy dollars go mostly to volunteer organizations.

SCHOOL REFORM

Under the old corporate philanthropy paradigm, elementary and secondary education received no more than 5 percent of the typical corporate philanthropy budget, and most of the institutions that received aid were private. Now about 15 percent of the country's cash gifts go to school reform, and a recent study estimated that at least one-third of U.S. school districts have partnership programs with business.

Even so, as a recent Conference Board report argues, those programs have not halted the decline of the public school system. The next step toward reform, promoted by the Business Roundtable, is for companies to mobilize their lobbying power at the state level to press for the overhaul of state educational agencies.

AIDS

AIDS is a top cause for insurance companies, who want to reduce claims; pharmaceutical companies, who want public support for the commercialization of AIDS drugs; and design-related companies, who want to support the large number of gays in their work force. Those industries put the first big money into AIDS prevention measures, and they've helped turn the American Foundation for AIDS Research into an advocate for more and better research by the National Institutes of Health.

ENVIRONMENTALISM

Until recently, corporate America feared environmentalism. But the new corporate philanthropy professionals consult their companies' environmental officers to find ways to link donations and volunteer programs to internal efforts at environmental stewardship. Environmental support varies across industries. In high-tech companies, environmentalism is largely a human resources issue because it's the favorite cause of many employees. Contribution managers in such companies typically conduct activities that elicit employee support for conservation. Among the makers of outdoor apparel, environmentalism is largely a marketing issue, so companies donate a portion of the purchase price to environmental nonprofits. In industries that pollute or extract natural resources, environmentalism is often a government affairs matter. Companies in those industries forge alliances with nonprofit adversaries in the hope of circumventing regulations.

BusinessWeek

MEET GEORGE, THE OSCAR FOR CORPORATE PHILANTHROPY

STRATEGY IN ACTION 2–10

*C*orporate philanthropy often means writing a check or buying a table at a charity ball. But for Aaron Feuerstein, owner of Malden Mills Industries Inc. in Lawrence, Massachusetts, it meant keeping workers on the payroll for months as he rebuilt his fire-razed plant.

Feuerstein is one of 10 corporate heroes who are in the running for the first annual Newman's Own/George Award. Actor Paul Newman, who founded the not-for-profit Newman's Own food company, and John F. Kennedy, Jr., president of *George* magazine, will present the award on April 13 for innovative and significant *corporate philanthropy*. A $250,000 check from Newman's foundation will go to the winner's favorite charity. Sony Electronics is giving $250,000 over the next two years to the awards.

Among those winnowed from 400 applicants are Norwest Corp., the Minneapolis bank that is providing $300 million in low-interest mortgages and giving Habitat for Humanity International $16.5 million to build 50,000 homes. EBSCO Industries Inc. in Birmingham, Alabama, made the list by raising $10 million to help revive the Alabama Symphony.

This celebration comes just when some politicians and investors are demanding more disclosure about corporate charity—a move that some in the philanthropic community claim could curtail giving. "[Philanthropy] has to succeed as part of a company's PR or marketing strategy, or the money should be paid out in dividends," says shareholder activist and investor Nell Minow, a principal in Lens Group.

The critics cut little ice with JFK Jr. and his leading givers. "It would be great if business competed for this award and didn't run afoul of shareholders," Kennedy said. Norwest Chairman Richard M. Kovacevich is vehemently opposed to disclosure. He says the 1.7% of pretax income that Norwest spends on such ventures as Habitat or low-interest mortgages is "an investment in our communities. Admittedly, it is hard to quantify [the payback], but so is marketing, advertising, even technology."

Source: Richard A. Melcher in Chicago, "Meet George, the Oscar for Corporate Philanthropy," *Business Week,* April 20, 1998.

environmentally safer and costs 60 percent less to use. Corporations that offer part-time and adjustable work schedules have realized that this can lead to reduced absenteeism, greater productivity and increased morale. DuPont opted for more flexible schedules for its employees after a survey revealed 50 percent of women and 25 percent of men considered working for another employer with more flexibility for family concerns.

Proponents argue that CSR costs are more than offset in the long run by an improved company image and increased community goodwill. These intangible assets can prove valuable in a crisis, as Johnson & Johnson discovered with the Tylenol cyanide scare in 1982. Because it had established a solid reputation as a socially responsible company before the incident, the public readily accepted the company's assurances of public safety. Consequently, financial damage to Johnson & Johnson was minimized, despite the company's $100 million voluntary recall of potentially tainted capsules. CSR may also head off new regulation, preventing increased compliance costs. It may even attract investors who are themselves socially responsible. Proponents believe that for these reasons, socially responsible behavior increases the financial value of the firm in the long run. The mission statement of Johnson & Johnson is provided as Strategy in Action 2–11.

Performance   To explore the relationship between socially responsible behavior and financial performance, an important question must first be answered: How do managers measure the financial impact of corporate social performance?

Critics of CSR believe that companies that behave in a socially responsible manner, and portfolios comprising these companies' securities, should perform more poorly financially than those that do not. The costs of CSR outweigh the benefits for individual firms, they suggest. In addition, traditional portfolio theory holds that investors minimize risk and maximize return by being able to choose from an infinite universe of investment opportunities. Portfolios based on social criteria should suffer, critics argue, because they are by definition restrictive in nature. This restriction should increase portfolio risk and reduce portfolio return.

Several research studies have attempted to determine the relationship between corporate social performance and financial performance.[20] Taken together, these studies fail to establish the nature of the relationship between social and financial performance. There are a number of possible explanations for the findings. One possibility is that there is no meaningful correlation between social and financial performance. A second possibility is that the benefits of CSR are offset by its negative consequences for the firm, thus producing a nondectectable net financial effect. Other explanations include methodological weaknesses and/or insufficient conceptual models or operational definitions used in the studies. However, among experts, a sense remains that a relationship between CSR and the bottom line does exist, although the exact nature of that relationship is unclear.[21]

CSR Today

A survey of 2,737 senior U.S. managers revealed that 92 percent believed that business should take primary responsibility for, or an active role in, solving environmental problems; 84 percent believed business should do the same for educational concerns.[22] Despite the uncertain impact of CSR on the corporate bottom line, CSR has become a priority with American business. Why? In addition to a commonsense belief that companies should be able to "do well by doing good," at least three broad trends are driving businesses to adopt CSR frameworks: the resurgence of environmentalism, increasing buyer power, and the globalization of business.

The Resurgence of Environmentalism   In March 1989, the Exxon *Valdez* ran aground in Prince William Sound, spilling 11 million gallons of oil, polluting miles of ocean and shore, and helping to revive worldwide concern for the ecological environment. Six

[20]Kenneth E. Aupperle, Archie B. Carroll, and John D. Hatfield, "An Empirical Examination of the Relationship Between Corporate Social Responsibility and Profitability," *Academy of Management Journal* 28, no. 2 (June 1985), pp. 446–63; Wallace N. Davidson III and Dan L. Worrell, "A Comparison and Test of the Use of Accounting and Stock Market Data in Relating Corporate Social Responsibility and Financial Performance," *Akron Business and Economic Review* 21, no. 3 (Fall 1990), pp. 7–19; Sally Hamilton, Hoje Jo, and Meir Statman, "Doing Well While Doing Good? The Investment Performance of Socially Responsible Mutual Funds," *Financial Analysts Journal* 49, no. 6 (November–December 1993), pp. 62–66; Jean B. McGuire, Alison Sundgren, and Thomas Schneeweis, "Corporate Social Responsibility and Firm Financial Performance," *Academy of Management Journal* 31, no. 4 (December 1988), pp. 854–72.

[21]Martin B. Meznar, James J. Chrisman, and Archie B. Carroll, "Social Responsibility and Strategic Management: Toward an Enterprise Strategy Classification," *Business and Professional Ethics Journal* 10, no. 1 (Spring 1991), pp. 47–66.

[22]Rosabeth Moss Kanter, "Transcending Business Boundaries: 12,000 World Managers View Change," *Harvard Business Review* 69, no. 3 (May–June 1991), pp. 151–64.

STRATEGY IN ACTION 2–11

MISSION STATEMENT: JOHNSON & JOHNSON

"We believe our first responsibility is to the doctors, nurses and patients, to mothers and fathers and all others who use our products and services. In meeting their needs everything we do must be of high quality. We must constantly strive to reduce our costs in order to maintain reasonable prices. Customers' orders must be serviced promptly and accurately. Our suppliers and distributors must have an opportunity to make a fair profit.

We are responsible to our employees, the men and women who work with us throughout the world. Everyone must be considered as an individual. We must respect their dignity and recognize their merit. They must have a sense of security in their jobs. Compensation must be fair and adequate, and working conditions clean, orderly and safe. Employees must feel free to make suggestions and complaints. There must be equal opportunity for employment, development and advancement for those qualified. We must provide competent management, and their actions must be just and ethical.

We are responsible to the communities in which we live and work and to the world community as well. We must be good citizens—support good works and charities and bear our fair share of taxes. We must encourage civic improvements and better health and education. We must maintain in good order the property we are privileged to use, protecting the environment and natural resources.

Our final responsibility is to our stockholders. Business must make a sound profit. We must experiment with new ideas. Research must be carried on, innovative programs developed and mistakes paid for. New equipment must be purchased, new facilities provided and new products launched. Reserves must be created to provide for adverse times. When we operate according to these principles, the stockholders should realize a fair return."

months after the *Valdez* incident, the Coalition for Environmentally Responsible Economies (CERES) was formed to establish new goals for environmentally responsible corporate behavior. The group drafted the CERES Principles to "establish an environmental ethic with criteria by which investors and others can assess the environmental performance of companies. Companies that sign these Principles pledge to go voluntarily beyond the requirements of the law."[23]

Increasing Buyer Power   The rise of the consumer movement has meant that buyers—consumers and investors—are increasingly flexing their economic muscle. Consumers are becoming more interested in buying products from socially responsible companies. Organizations such as the Council on Economic Priorities (CEP) help consumers make more informed buying decisions through such publications as *Shopping for a Better World,* which provides social performance information on 191 companies making more than 2,000 consumer products. CEP also sponsors the annual Corporate

[23]Alan J. Miller, *Socially Responsible Investing: How to Invest with Your Conscience* (New York: New York Institute of Finance, 1991).

Conscience Awards, which recognize socially responsible companies. One example of consumer power at work is the effective outcry over the deaths of dolphins in tuna fishermen's nets. "Consumers, environmentalists and shareholders convinced H. J. Heinz that the slaughter had to end, and the industry followed."[24]

Investors represent a second type of influential consumer. There has been a dramatic increase in the number of people interested in supporting socially responsible companies through their investments. Total assets "socially invested" grew at an average annual compound rate of 48 percent between 1984 and 1991; membership in the Social Investment Forum, a trade association serving social investing professionals, has been growing at a rate of about 50 percent annually. As baby boomers achieve their own financial success, the social investing movement has continued its rapid growth.

While social investing wields relatively low power as an individual private act (selling one's shares of Exxon does not affect the company), it can be very powerful as a collective public act. When investors vote their shares in behalf of pro-CSR issues, companies may be pressured to change their social behavior. The South African divestiture movement is one example of how effective this pressure can be.

The Vermont National Bank has added a Socially Responsible Banking Fund to its product line. Investors can designate any of their interest-bearing accounts with a $500 minimum balance to be used by the fund. This fund then lends these monies for purposes such as low income housing, the environment, education, farming, or small business development. Although it has had a "humble" beginning of approximately 800 people investing about $11 million, the bank has attracted out-of-state depositors and is growing faster than expected.

Social investors comprise both individuals and institutions. Much of the impetus for social investing originated with religious organizations that wanted their investments to mirror their beliefs. At present, the ranks of social investors have expanded to include educational institutions and large pension funds.

Large-scale social investing can be broken down into the two broad areas of guideline portfolio investing and shareholder activism. Guideline portfolio investing is the largest and fastest-growing segment of social investing. Individual and institutional guideline portfolio investors use ethical guidelines as screens to identify possible investments in stocks, bonds, and mutual funds. The investment instruments that survive the social screens are then layered over the investor's financial screens to create the investor's universe of possible investments.

Screens may be negative (e.g., excluding all tobacco companies) or they may combine negative and positive elements (e.g., eliminating companies with bad labor records while seeking out companies with good ones). Most investors rely on screens created by investment firms such as Kinder, Lydenberg Domini & Co. or by industry groups such as the Council on Economic Priorities. In addition to ecology, employee relations, and community development, corporations may be screened on their association with "sin" products (alcohol, tobacco, gambling), defense/weapons production, and nuclear power.

In contrast to guideline portfolio investors, who passively indicate their approval or disapproval of a company's social behavior by simply including or excluding it from their portfolios, shareholder activists seek to directly influence corporate social

---

[24]Peter D. Kinder, Steven D. Lydenberg, and Amy L. Domini, *Investing for Good: Making Money While Being Socially Responsible* (New York: HarperBusiness, HarperCollins Publishers, 1993).

behavior. Shareholder activists invest in a corporation hoping to improve specific aspects of the company's social performance, typically by seeking a dialogue with upper management. If this and successive actions fail to achieve the desired results, shareholder activists may introduce proxy resolutions to be voted upon at the corporation's annual meeting. The goal of these resolutions is to achieve change by gaining public exposure for the issue at hand. While the number of shareholder activists is relatively small, they are by no means small in achievement: Shareholder activists, led by such groups as the Interfaith Center on Corporate Responsibility, were the driving force behind the South African divestiture movement in the 1980s.[25]

In 1984, $40 billion was invested socially in the United States; by 1991, that aggregate capital investment had grown to $625 billion. While this represents only about 10 percent of the total assets invested in the United States, the proportion is growing. Currently, there are more than 35 socially screened mutual funds available in the United States alone.

The Globalization of Business   Management issues, including CSR, have become more complex as companies increasingly transcend national borders: It is difficult enough to come to a consensus on what constitutes socially responsible behavior within one culture, let alone determine common ethical values across cultures. In addition to different cultural views, the high barriers facing international CSR include differing corporate disclosure practices, inconsistent financial data and reporting methods, and the lack of CSR research organizations within countries. Despite these problems, CSR is growing abroad. The United Kingdom has 30 ethical mutual funds and Canada offers 6 socially responsible funds.[26]

CSR has evolved into an important strategic consideration for many companies. For long-run survival and growth, managers must learn to integrate CSR into company strategy. "Many businesses today feel that in order to respond effectively and efficiently to the major social issues and demands of the day, corporate social policy must be integrated into corporate strategy. Corporate executives will have to include social policy guidelines into the strategic plans from which the functional policies and operational plans will be derived."[27]

CSR's Effect on the Mission Statement

The mission statement not only identifies what product or service a company produces, how it produces it, and what market it serves, it also embodies what the company believes. As such, it is essential that the mission statement recognize the legitimate claims of its external stakeholders, which may include creditors, customers, suppliers, government, unions, competitors, local communities, and elements of the general public. This stakeholder approach has become widely accepted by U.S. business. For example, a survey of directors in 291 of the largest southeastern U.S. companies found

---

[25]Timothy Smith, Executive Director, Interfaith Center on Corporate Responsibility, interview with the author, New York City.

[26]Jack A. Brill and Alan Reder, *Investing from the Heart: The Guide to Socially Responsible Investments and Money Management* (New York: Crown Publishers, 1993).

[27]Jerry W. Anderson, *Corporate Social Responsibility: Guidelines for Top Management* (Westport, CT: Quorum Books, Greenwood Press, 1989).

that directors had high stakeholder orientations. Customers, government, stockholders, employees, and society, in that order, were the stakeholders these directors perceived as most important.

In developing mission statements, managers must identify all stakeholder groups and weigh their relative rights and abilities to affect the firm's success. Some companies are proactive in their approach to CSR, making it an integral part of their raison d'être (e.g., Ben & Jerry's ice cream); others are reactive, adopting socially responsible behavior only when they must (e.g., Exxon after the *Valdez* incident).

Social Audit

A *social audit* attempts to measure a company's actual social performance against the social objectives it has set for itself. A social audit may be conducted by the company itself. However, one conducted by an outside consultant who will impose minimal biases may prove more beneficial to the firm. As with a financial audit, an outside auditor brings credibility to the evaluation. This credibility is essential if management is to take the results seriously and if the general public is to believe the company's public relations pronouncements. "A comprehensive strategic management process that explicitly and formally assesses adverse social impacts is the key to truly effective corporate performance. Such an approach decreases the probability that unintended, socially disruptive outcomes will occur. Ultimately, this will lead to enhanced long-term viability for the firm."[28]

Careful, accurate monitoring and evaluation of a company's CSR actions are important not only because the company wants to be sure it is implementing CSR policy as planned, but also because CSR actions by their nature are open to intense public scrutiny. To make sure it is making good on its CSR promises, a company may conduct a social audit of its performance.

Once the social audit is complete, it may be distributed internally or both internally and externally, depending on the firm's goals and situation. Some firms include a section in their annual report devoted to social responsibility activities; others publish a separate periodic report on their social responsiveness. Companies publishing separate social audits include General Motors, Bank of America, Atlantic Richfield, Control Data, and Aetna Life and Casualty Company. By 1990, "the pressure for greater disclosure of social performance information has [sic] led 90 percent of the top 500 corporations to include [sic] about their social activities in the company's annual report."[29]

Large firms are not the only companies employing the social audit. Boutique ice cream maker Ben & Jerry's, a CSR pioneer, publishes a social audit in its annual report. The audit, conducted by an outside consultant, scores company performance in such areas as employee benefits, plant safety, ecology, community involvement, and customer service. The report is published unedited.

Despite negative marks in plant safety, employee ownership, and charitable activities in the company's 1992 social audit, Ben & Jerry's continues to use the social audit. The audit shows that the company "walks the talk," according to a company

---

[28]Gregory A. Daneke and David J. Lemak, "Integrating Strategic Management and Social Responsibility," *Business Forum* 10, no. 2–3 (Summer 1985), pp. 20–25.

[29]W. Frederick, J. Post, and K. Davis, *Business and Society* (New York: McGraw-Hill, 1992).

spokesperson. It also distinguishes the company from competitors, notes an outside observer.[30]

The social audit may be used for more than simply monitoring and evaluating firm social performance. Managers also use social audits to scan the external environment, determine firm vulnerabilities, and institutionalize CSR within the firm. In addition, companies themselves are not the only ones who conduct social audits; public interest groups and the media watch companies who claim to be socially responsible very closely to see if they practice what they preach. These organizations include consumer groups and socially responsible investing firms that construct their own guidelines for evaluating companies.

The Body Shop learned what can happen when a company's behavior falls short of its espoused mission and objectives. The 20-year-old manufacturer and retailer of naturally based hair and skin products had cultivated a socially responsible corporate image based on a reputation for socially responsible behavior. In late 1994, however, *Business Ethics* magazine published an exposé claiming that the company did not "walk the talk." It accused the Body Shop of using nonrenewable petrochemicals in its products, recycling far less than it claimed, using ingredients tested on animals, and making threats against investigative journalists. The Body Shop's contradictions were noteworthy because Anita Roddick, the company's founder, made CSR a centerpiece of the company's strategy.[31]

SUMMARY

Defining the company mission is one of the most often slighted tasks in strategic management. Emphasizing the operational aspects of long-range management activities comes much more easily for most executives. But the critical role of the mission statement repeatedly is demonstrated by failing firms whose short-run actions have been at odds with their long-run purposes.

The principal value of the mission statement is its specification of the firm's ultimate aims. A firm gains a heightened sense of purpose when its board of directors and its top executives address these issues: "What business are we in?" "What customers do we serve?" "Why does this organization exist?" However, the potential contribution of the company mission can be undermined if platitudes or ambiguous generalizations are accepted in response to these questions. It is not enough to say that Lever Brothers is in the business of "making anything that cleans anything" or that Polaroid is committed to businesses that deal with "the interaction of light and matter." Only if a firm clearly articulates its long-term intentions can its goals serve as a basis for shared expectations, planning, and performance evaluation.

A mission statement that is developed from this perspective provides managers with a unity of direction transcending individual, parochial, and temporary needs. It promotes a sense of shared expectations among all levels and generations of employees. It consolidates values over time and across individuals and interest groups. It projects a sense of worth and intent that can be identified and assimilated by outside stakeholders; that is, customers, suppliers, competitors, local committees, and the general

[30]Betsy Wiesendanger, "Ben & Jerry Scoop Up Credibility," *Public Relations Journal* 49, no. 8 (August 1993), p. 20.

[31]Jon Entine, "Shattered Image," *Business Ethics* 8, no. 5 (September/October 1994), pp. 23–28.

public. Finally, it asserts the firm's commitment to responsible action in symbiosis with the preservation and protection of the essential claims of insider stakeholders' survival, growth, and profitability.

QUESTIONS FOR DISCUSSION

1. Reread Nicor, Inc.'s mission statement in Strategy in Action 2–1. List five insights into Nicor that you feel you gained from knowing its mission.

2. Locate the mission statement of a company not mentioned in the chapter. Where did you find it? Was it presented as a consolidated statement, or were you forced to assemble it yourself from various publications of the firm? How many of the mission statement elements outlined in this chapter were discussed or revealed in the statement you found?

3. Prepare a two-page typewritten mission statement for your school of business or for a firm selected by your instructor.

4. List five potentially vulnerable areas of a firm without a stated company mission.

5. Define the term *social responsibility*. Find an example of a company action that was legal but not socially responsible. Defend your example on the basis of your definition.

6. Name five potentially valuable indicators of a firm's social responsibility and describe how company performance in each could be measured.

BIBLIOGRAPHY

Board of Directors

Bartlett, Christopher A., and Sumantha Ghoshal. "Changing the Role of Top Management: Beyond Systems to People." *Harvard Business Review* 73, no. 3 (May–June 1995), p. 132.

Donaldson, Gordon. "The New Task for Boards: The Strategic Audit." *Harvard Business Review* 73, no. 4 (July–August 1995), p. 99.

Hambrick, Donald C. "Fragmentation and the Other Problems CEOs Have with Their Top Management Teams." *California Management Review* 37, no. 3 (Spring 1995), p. 110.

Harrison, J. R. "The Strategic Use of Corporate Board Committees." *California Management Review* 30 (1987), pp. 109–25.

Henke, J. W., Jr. "Involving the Board of Directors in Strategic Planning." *Journal of Business Strategy* 7, no. 2 (1986), pp. 87–95.

Hout, Thomas M., and John C. Carter. "Getting It Done: New Roles for Senior Executives." *Harvard Business Review* 73, no. 6 (November–December 1995), p. 133.

Kerr, J., and R. A. Bettis. "Boards of Directors, Top Management Compensation, and Shareholder Returns." *Academy of Management Journal* 30 (1987), pp. 645–64.

Kesner, I. F. "Directors' Characteristics and Committee Membership: An Investigation of Type, Occupation Tenure, and Gender." *Academy of Management Journal* 31 (1988), pp. 66–84.

Lorsch, Jay W. "Empowering the Board." *Harvard Business Review* 73, no. 1 (January–February 1995), p. 107.

Molz, R. "Managerial Domination of Boards of Directors and Financial Performance." *Journal of Business Research* 16 (1988), pp. 235–50.

Park, Jae C. "Reengineering Boards of Directors." *Business Horizons* 38, no. 2 (March–April 1995), p. 63.

Pearce, J. A., II. "The Relationship of Internal versus External Orientations to Financial Measures of Strategic Performance." *Strategic Management Journal* 4 (1983), pp. 297–306.

Pound, John. "The Promise of the Governed Corporation." *Harvard Business Review* 73, no. 2 (March–April 1995), p. 89.

Rosenstein, J. "Why Don't U.S. Boards Get More Involved in Strategy?" *Long Range Planning* (June 1987), pp. 20–34.

Savage, G. T.; T. W. Nix; C. J. Whitehead; and J. D. Blair. "Strategies for Assessing and Managing Organizational Stakeholders." *Academy of Management Executive* (May 1991), pp. 61–75.

Smale, John G.; Alan J. Patricot; Denys Henderson; Bernard Marcus; and David N. Johnson. "Redraw the Line Between the Board and the CEO." *Harvard Business Review* 73, no. 2 (March–April 1995), p. 153.

Tichy, Noel M., and Ram Charan. "The CEO as Coach: An Interview with Allied Signal's Lawrence A. Bussidy." *Harvard Business Review* 73, no. 2 (March–April 1995), p. 68.

Zahra, S. A., and J. A. Pearce II. "Boards of Directors and Corporate Financial Performance: A Review and Integrative Model." *Journal of Management* 15 (1989), pp. 291–334.

Mission Statements

Bertodo, R. "Implementing a Strategic Vision." *Long Range Planning* (October 1990), pp. 22–30.

Campbell, A.; M. Gorld; and M. Alexander. "Corporate Strategy—The Quest for Parenting Advantage." *Harvard Business Review* 73, no. 2 (March–April 1995), p. 120.

Ireland, R. D., and M. A. Hitt. "Mission Statements; Importance, Challenge, and Recommendation for Development." *Business Horizons* (May–June 1992), pp. 34–42.

Klemm, M.; S. Sanderson; and G. Luffman. "Mission Statements: Selling Corporate Values to Employees." *Long Range Planning* (June 1991), pp. 73–78.

Osborne, R. L. "Core Value Statements: The Corporate Compass." *Business Horizons* (September–October 1991), pp. 28–34.

Pearce, J. A., II. "The Company Mission as a Strategic Tool." *Sloan Management Review* (Spring 1982), pp. 15–24.

Pearce, J. A., II, and F. R. David. "Corporate Mission Statements: The Bottom Line." *Academy of Management Executive* (May 1987), pp. 109–16.

Pearce, J. A., II; R. B. Robinson, Jr.; and Kendall Roth. "The Company Mission as a Guide to Strategic Action." In *Strategic Planning and Management Handbook,* ed. William R. King and David I. Cleland. New York: Van Nostrand Reinhold, 1987.

Rogers, J. E., Jr. "Adopting and Implementing a Corporate Environmental Charter." *Business Horizons* (March–April 1992), pp. 29–33.

Rothstein, Lawrence R. "The Empowerment Effort that Came Undone." *Harvard Business Review* 73, no. 1 (January–February 1995), p. 20.

Schmitt, Bernd H.; Alex Simonson; and Joshua Marcus. "Managing Corporate Image and Identity." *Long Range Planning* 28, no. 5 (October 1995), p. 82.

Tregoe, B. B.; J. W. Zimmerman; R. A. Smith; and P. M. Tobia. "The Driving Force." *Planning Review* (March–April 1990), pp. 4–17.

Social Responsibility and Business Ethics

Anderson, Jerry W. *Corporate Social Responsibility: Guidelines for Top Management.* (Westport, CT: Quorum Books, Greenwood Press, 1989).

Aupperle, K.; A. Carroll; and J. Hatfield. "An Empirical Examination of the Relationship between Corporate Social Responsibility and Profitability." *Academy of Management Journal* 28 (1985), pp. 446–63.

Badaracco, J. L., Jr. "Business Ethics: Four Spheres of Executive Responsibility." *California Management Review* (Spring 1992), pp. 64–79.

Bavaria, S. "Corporate Ethics Should Start in the Boardroom." *Business Horizons* (January–February 1991), pp. 9–12.

Bowie, N. "New Directions in Corporate Social Responsibility." *Business Horizons* (July–August 1991), pp. 56–65.

Brill, Jack A., and Alan Reder. *Investing from the Heart: The Guide to Socially Responsible Investments and Money Management* (New York: Crown Publishers, 1993).

Cadbury, A. "Ethical Managers Make Their Own Rules." *Harvard Business Review* (September–October 1987), pp. 69–73.

Carroll, A. B. "The Pyramid of Corporate Social Responsibility: Toward the Moral Management of Organizational Stakeholders." *Business Horizons* (July–August 1991), pp. 39–48.

Carroll, Archie B., and Frank Hoy. "Integrating Corporate Social Policy into Strategic Management." *Journal of Business Strategy* 4 (Winter 1984), pp. 48–57.

Dalton, D. R., and C. M. Daily. "The Constituents of Corporate Responsibility: Separate, But Not Separable, Interests?" *Business Horizons* (July–August 1991), pp. 74–78.

Daneke, Gregory A., and David J. Lemak. "Integrating Strategic Management and Social Responsibility." *Business Forum* 10, nos. 2–3 (Summer 1985), pp. 20–25.

Davidson, Wallace N., III, and Dan L. Worrell. "A Comparison and Test of the Use of Accounting and Stock Market Data in Relating Corporate Social Responsibility and Financial Performance." *Akron Business and Economic Review* 21, no. 3 (Fall 1990), pp. 7–19.

Day, G. S., and L. Fahey. "Putting Strategy into Shareholder Value Analysis." *Harvard Business Review* (March–April 1990), pp. 156–62.

Entine, Jon. "Shattered Image." *Business Ethics* 8, no. 5 (September/October 1994), pp. 23–38.

Frederick, W.; J. Post; and K. Davis. *Business and Society.* (New York: McGraw-Hill, 1992).

Freeman, R. E., and J. Liedtka. "Corporate Social Responsibility: A Critical Approach." *Business Horizons* (July–August 1991), pp. 92–98.

Friedman, Milton. *Capitalism and Freedom.* (Chicago: University of Chicago Press, 1962).

Hamilton, Sally; Hoje Jo; and Meir Statman. "Doing Well While Doing Good? The Investment Performance of Socially Responsible Mutual Funds." *Financial Analysts Journal* 49, no. 6 (November–December 1993), pp. 62–66.

Harrington, S. J. "What Corporate America Is Teaching about Ethics." *Academy of Management Executive* (February 1991), pp. 21–30.

Kanter, Rosabeth Moss. "Transcending Boundaries: 12,000 World Managers View Change." *Harvard Business Review* 69, no. 3 (May–June 1991), pp. 151–64.

Kinder, Peter D.; Steven D. Lydenberg; and Amy L. Domini. *Investing for Good: Making Money While Being Socially Responsible.* (New York: HarperBusiness, HarperCollins Publishers, 1993).

Litzinger, W. D., and T. E. Schaefer. "Business Ethics Bogeyman: The Perpetual Paradox." *Business Horizons* (March–April 1987), pp. 16–21.

McGuire, Jean B.; Alison Sundgren; and Thomas Schneeweis. "Corporate Social Responsibility and Firm Financial Performance." *Academy of Management Journal* 31, no. 4 (December 1988), pp. 854–72.

Meznar, Martin B.; James J. Chrisman; and Archie B. Carroll. "Social Responsibility and Strategic Management: Toward an Enterprise Strategy Classification." *Business and Professional Ethics Journal* 10, no. 1 (Spring 1991), pp. 47–66.

Miller, Alan J. *Socially Responsible Investing: How to Invest with Your Conscience.* (New York: New York Institute of Finance, 1991).

Smith, Timothy. Executive Director, Interfaith Center on Corporate Responsibility. Interview with the author, New York City, March 24, 1995.

Waddock, Sandra A., and Mary-Ellen Boyle. "The Dynamics of Change in Corporate Community Relations." *Management Review* 37, no. 4 (Summer 1995), p. 125.

Wiesendanger, Betsy. "Ben & Jerry Scoop Up Credibility." *Public Relations Journal* 49, no. 8 (August 1993), p. 20.

Wood, D. J. "Social Issues in Management: Theory and Research in Corporate Social Performance." *Journal of Management* (June 1991), pp. 383–406.

— —. "Toward Improving Corporate Social Performance." *Business Horizons* (July–August 1991), pp. 66–73.

CHAPTER 2 DISCUSSION CASE   BusinessWeek

THE TWO BOTTOM LINES: PROFITS AND PEOPLE

> A classic dilemma for strategic managers is how to weight profits for stockhold-
> ers against benefits for society as principal outcomes from the operation of a
> business. In this discussion case, Bagel Works, Inc., is finding that the two out-
> comes are not necessarily exclusive, and that it may be possible to become more
> profitable if managers can demonstrate to employees and customers that the firm
> really cares about benefiting society.

At Bagel Works Inc., a Keene (New Hampshire)-based chain of bagel stores, there's
an unusual December ritual. At all nine outlets, employees sift through local charities
that they think might deserve help, and come up with five nominees. The winners are
selected by secret ballots—cast in the stores by customers. For a year, the victors win
financial support, promotional space at Bagel Works, and often free bagels.

To co-founders Richard French, 34, and Jennifer Pearl, 31, the elections are a winner on several levels. They help with marketing and community relations, and boost
employee morale. But they also reflect the owners' commitment to running the business with an eye on values, not just the bottom line. At the 10-year-old, $5 million
company, the 140 employees benefit from "open book"-style management, and environmental concerns guide day-to-day operations. Most striking, for the past three
years, Bagel Works has donated 10% or more of pretax profits to charitable causes
such as homeless shelters.

Sounds nice, but does it make business sense? "Some could argue that we may be
able to make more money," concedes French. "But if we weren't doing some of those
things, we might have a lesser quality of employee or more turnover." And, he adds,
based on shoppers' responses, "it absolutely relates to customer loyalty."

French's instincts are well-intentioned, and they're also well-grounded. Consultants
cite growing evidence that socially conscious behavior brings tangible rewards far in
excess of forgone profits and time invested. The payoff can come in the form of higher
productivity, because employees want to stick around—a big bonus in a tight labor
market. It could show up in new business, because you've helped build a stronger, and
thus more economically vital, community. Or it could mean customers switching from
one of your rivals simply because they admire your efforts—a powerful competitive
edge, says Brian Lunde, senior vice-president of Walker Information, an Indianapolis
market-research firm. "A socially conscious company, all else being equal, is likely to
be viewed more favorably," he says, citing studies of consumer behavior.

At the very least, there is no evidence that socially conscious businesses are less profitable as a group, and considerable evidence that they gain a special advantage, says Al-
lan R. Cohen, a management professor at Babson College in Newton, Massachusetts.
"It doesn't subtract from the bottom line, it adds to the bottom line," says Robert W.
MacGregor, president of a Minnesota coalition of socially responsible businesses.

Source: Robin D. Schatz in New York, with Claire Poole in Houston, "The Two Bottom Lines: Profits and People," *Business Week:* December 7, 1998.

For some, being socially conscious is the basis of the business itself, such as companies that make environmentally sound products. For others, like Bagel Works, it's the way they conduct business and relate to their community. But what unites these owners is the old cliche about doing good and doing well. "I have two bottom lines to my activities," says Tim Joukowsky, one of the founders of AquaFuture Inc. in Turners Falls, Massachusetts. "Am I making money, and am I solving social problems?"

For the growing number of small companies that outsource production abroad, social consciousness can mean trying to influence and improve working conditions in foreign countries, says Marc J. Epstein, a business professor at Rice University in Houston. Take Mark Juarez, 41, owner of San Leandro (California)-based Tender Loving Things Inc., which markets bath products made in China. Juarez rejected several plants because of child labor and deplorable working conditions. But the ones he did select had problems, too. "You could almost fall over from the fumes," said Finance Director William L. Keyes. To help, the company set up a task force to improve processes and working conditions. The results so far: better sanitation, more safety equipment, and cutbacks in 16-hour days and 7-day weeks. Not by coincidence, product quality and productivity have improved, too.

Others see a direct marketing benefit. Hoboken (New Jersey)-based Cloud Nine, which makes natural chocolates and confections, advertises on its packaging that 10% of its profits go to protect the Brazilian rain forest—where most cocoa beans grow. President Joshua Taylor, an avid environmentalist, says the business has $10 million to $15 million in sales, thanks in part to customer support for its cause-based marketing. "It pays for itself," he says.

POPULAR CAUSE. Research supports Taylor's belief. In a 1996 survey of 2,000 people conducted by Roper Starch Worldwide Inc. and Cone Communications of Boston, 76% of the respondents said they'd switch from their current brand to one associated with a good cause if price and quality were equal. That's up from 66% in 1993, and new figures due out in January show the trend continuing.

Of course, linking your company to a cause can backfire if you pick one that isn't universally popular. Bagel Works' French remembers years ago when a local AIDS group they supported set up a table at one store for a day, where they distributed pamphlets, red ribbons—and condoms. One mother called French to protest that she hadn't planned to turn an errand with her child into a sex education lecture. French apologized. "Early on, we were just these idealistic kids. We have matured a little bit," he says.

How much should a company give? Groups like the Minneapolis Keystone Club ask members to start at 2% of pretax profits. Others choose to donate time and expertise to nonprofit groups—for instance, setting up a new purchasing system or designing new offices.

And martyrdom isn't required. Even the most ardent advocates say your first obligation to the community is to have a successful business. After all, it wouldn't be very socially conscious to throw everyone out of work. "There's an infinite amount of good to be done and only finite resources," says Cohen. "Think about issues that matter to people who work for you, the community you practice in, and your customers. What are appropriate causes that enhance your reputation with each of those constituents?" That's the difference between the new and the old idealists—they're crunching numbers along with their granola.

THE EXTERNAL ENVIRONMENT

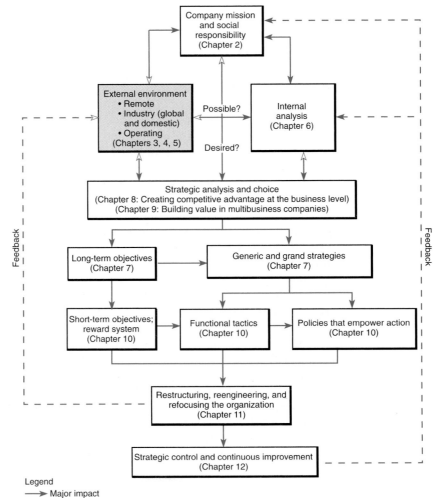

Legend
⟶ Major impact
—▷ Minor impact

A host of external factors influence a firm's choice of direction and action and, ultimately, its organizational structure and internal processes. These factors, which constitute the *external environment,* can be divided into three interrelated subcategories: factors in the *remote* environment, factors in the *industry* environment, and factors in the *operating* environment.[1] This chapter describes the complex necessities involved in formulating strategies that optimize a firm's market opportunities. Figure 3–1 suggests the interrelationship between the firm and its remote, its industry, and its operating environments. In combination, these factors form the basis of the opportunities and threats that a firm faces in its competitive environment.

REMOTE ENVIRONMENT

The remote environment comprises factors that originate beyond, and usually irrespective of, any single firm's operating situation: (1) economic, (2) social, (3) political, (4) technological, and (5) ecological factors. That environment presents firms with opportunities, threats, and constraints, but rarely does a single firm exert any meaningful reciprocal influence. For example, when the economy slows and construction starts to decrease, an individual contractor is likely to suffer a decline in business, but that contractor's success in stimulating local construction activities would be unable to reverse the overall decrease in construction starts. The trade agreements that resulted from improved relations between the United States and China and the United States and Russia are examples of the effects of political factors on individual firms. The agreements provided individual U.S. manufacturers with opportunities to broaden their international operations.

1. Economic Factors

Economic factors concern the nature and direction of the economy in which a firm operates. Because consumption patterns are affected by the relative affluence of various market segments, in its strategic planning each firm must consider economic trends in the segments that affect its industry. On both the national and international level, it must consider the general availability of credit, the level of disposable income, and the propensity of people to spend. Prime interest rates, inflation rates, and trends in the growth of the gross national product are other economic factors it must consider.

Until recently, the potential impact of international economic forces appeared to be severely restricted and was largely discounted. However, the emergence of new international power brokers has changed the focus of economic environmental forecasting. Among the most prominent of these power brokers are the European Economic Community (EEC, or Common Market), the Organization of Petroleum Exporting Countries (OPEC), and coalitions of developing countries.

The EEC, whose members include most of the West European countries, was established by the Treaty of Rome in 1957. It has eliminated quotas and established a tariff-free trade area for industrial products among its members. By fostering intra-European economic cooperation, it has helped its member countries compete more effectively in non-European international markets.

---

[1]Many authors refer to the operating environment as the *task* or *competitive* environment.

FIGURE 3–1
The Firm's External Environment

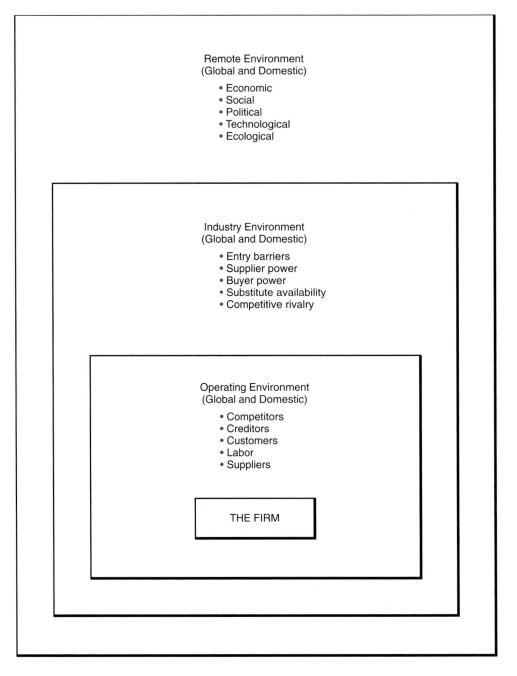

Remote Environment
(Global and Domestic)

• Economic
• Social
• Political
• Technological
• Ecological

Industry Environment
(Global and Domestic)

• Entry barriers
• Supplier power
• Buyer power
• Substitute availability
• Competitive rivalry

Operating Environment
(Global and Domestic)

• Competitors
• Creditors
• Customers
• Labor
• Suppliers

THE FIRM

2. Social Factors

The social factors that affect a firm involve the beliefs, values, attitudes, opinions, and lifestyles of persons in the firm's external environment, as developed from cultural, ecological, demographic, religious, educational, and ethnic conditioning. As social attitudes change, so too does the demand for various types of clothing, books, leisure activities, and so on. Like other forces in the remote external environment, social forces are dynamic, with constant change resulting from the efforts of individuals to satisfy their desires and needs by controlling and adapting to environmental factors. Teresa Iglesias-Soloman hoped to benefit from social changes with *Ninos,* a children's catalog written in both English and Spanish. The catalog featured books, videos, and Spanish cultural offerings for English-speaking children who wanted to learn Spanish and for Spanish-speaking children who wanted to learn English. *Ninos'* target market included middle-to-upper income Hispanic parents and a greater number of consumers, educators, bilingual schools, libraries, and purchasing agents. Iglesias-Solomon had reason to be optimistic about the future of *Ninos,* because the Hispanic population was growing five times faster than the general U.S. population.

One of the most profound social changes in recent years has been the entry of large numbers of women into the labor market. This has not only affected the hiring and compensation policies and the resource capabilities of their employers; it also has created or greatly expanded the demand for a wide range of products and services necessitated by their absence from the home. Firms that anticipated or reacted quickly to this social change offered such products and services as convenience foods, microwave ovens, and day care centers.

A second profound social change has been the accelerating interest of consumers and employees in quality-of-life issues. Evidence of this change is seen in recent contract negotiations. In addition to the traditional demand for increased salaries have been worker demands for such benefits as sabbaticals, flexible hours or four-day workweeks, lump-sum vacation plans, and opportunities for advanced training.

A third profound social change has been the shift in the age distribution of the population. Changing social values and a growing acceptance of improved birth control methods are expected to raise the mean age of the U.S. population, which was 27.9 in 1970, and 34.9 in the year 2000. This trend will have an increasingly unfavorable impact on most producers of predominantly youth-oriented goods and will necessitate a shift in their long-range marketing strategies. Producers of hair- and skin-care preparations already have begun to adjust their research and development to reflect anticipated changes in demand.

A consequence of the changing age distribution of the population has been a sharp increase in the demands made by a growing number of senior citizens. Constrained by fixed incomes, these citizens have demanded that arbitrary and rigid policies on retirement age be modified and have successfully lobbied for tax exemptions and increases in Social Security benefits. Such changes have significantly altered the opportunity-risk equations of many firms—often to the benefit of firms that anticipated the changes.

The problems of monitoring social changes are multiplied many times as businesses venture into international markets. One simple but poignant example is described in Strategy in Action 3–1.

Translating social change into forecasts of business effects is a difficult process, at best. Nevertheless, informed estimates of the impact of such alterations as geographic shifts in populations and changing work values, ethical standards, and religious orientation can only help a strategizing firm in its attempts to prosper.

3. Political Factors

The direction and stability of political factors is a major consideration for managers on formulating company strategy. Political factors define the legal and regulatory parameters within which firms must operate. Political constraints are placed on firms

BusinessWeek

IN INDIA, BEEF-FREE MICKEY D

**STRATEGY IN
ACTION
3–1**

India's sacred cows can stop fretting: McDonald's won't be requiring their services. The burger behemoth announced it will open its first franchises in India early next year—but without Big Macs. Deferring to the country's Hindu tradition, which prohibits the consumption of beef, the company instead will serve chicken and fish, as well as vegetable burgers. It's the first time the fast-food company has excluded beef from its menu. New Delhi consultant Dilip Cherian thinks other multinationals should follow McDonald's culturally sensitive lead: "It's not going to be one grand American burger that sweeps through India," he says.

Source: Keith H. Hammonds, ed., "In India, Beef-Free Mickey D," *Business Week:* April 17, 1995.

through fair-trade decisions, antitrust laws, tax programs, minimum wage legislation, pollution and pricing policies, administrative jawboning, and many other actions aimed at protecting employees, consumers, the general public, and the environment. Since such laws and regulations are most commonly restrictive, they tend to reduce the potential profits of firms. However, some political actions are designed to benefit and protect firms. Such actions include patent laws, government subsidies, and product research grants. Thus, political factors either may limit or benefit the firms they influence. For example, when Ethiopian Airlines organized in 1945, it received assistance from TWA and various Ethiopian governments. This support made Ethiopian Airlines one of the most successful members of the African air transport industry. The airline pioneered the hub concept in Africa and arranged its schedules to provide easy connections between many of the continent's countries, as well as between Africa and points in Europe and the Middle East and Asia. Without the political support of the Ethiopian governments, it would have been impossible for the airline to operate.[2]

Often, businesses work with the federal and state governments to resolve complaints brought by the public or their elected representatives. The recent settlement between states attorneys general and the "Big Tobacco" firms, described in Strategy in Action 3–2, is a prime example.

Political activity also has a significant impact on two governmental functions that influence the remote environment of firms: the supplier function and the customer function.

Supplier Function

Government decisions regarding the accessibility of private businesses to government-owned natural resources and national stockpiles of agricultural products will affect profoundly the viability of the strategies of some firms.

Customer Function

Government demand for products and services can create, sustain, enhance, or eliminate many market opportunities. For example, in the same way that the Kennedy

[2]*Air Transport World,* February 1992, pp. 110–12.

BusinessWeek

BIG TOBACCO MAKES A STINKY BEDFELLOW

STRATEGY IN ACTION

3–2

No sooner had the attorneys general of eight states inked their historic deal with Big Tobacco than antismoking activists were pleading with other fence-sitting states: Don't sign it. Smoking foes argued that the $206 billion settlement was riddled with loopholes.

No such luck. By Nov. 20, just one week after the deal was announced, the 46 states that hadn't already settled with tobacco signed—to meet a deadline pushed by the industry. "It's hard to say that getting $7 billion over 25 years isn't in the long-term interests of Massachusetts citizens," says George K. Weber, chief of tobacco litigation for the state.

He's right—if the goal is fattening state coffers. The governors can't wait to collect so they can enact popular tax cuts or education programs. Says University of Florida law professor Lars Noah: "This was the state AGs deciding to get as much as they can while the industry was still interested in making a deal."

On the other hand, if the goal is to reduce smoking and tobacco-related health-care costs, then it's not very successful. For example, Big Tobacco agrees not "to take any action the primary purpose of which is to initiate, maintain, or increase the incidence of youth smoking." But kids will still be able to get tobacco-branded clothes and gear from coupons in cigarette packs—and a survey in Massachusetts showed that kids with such merchandise were three times as likely to smoke. Large billboards advertising smoking are banned. But companies can coat neighborhoods with smaller signs.

Or consider the $1.45 billion to fund a national foundation to reduce smoking. Under the agreement, the money can't be used to tell consumers how the industry manipulates public opinion—even though studies have shown that's the most effective antismoking message for kids. When it comes to public health, the deal "is a complete sham," concludes cardiology professor and antismoking activist Stanton A. Glantz of the University of California, San Francisco.

The deal also closes off key lines of attack for antismoking litigators. Suppose a city wants to sue tobacco to recover the costs of smoking-related illnesses, much as the city of Chicago is now doing in suing gun manufacturers. The deal precludes such local suits—even though no city is party to the deal.

The deal's worst flaw, however, is that the money puts the states squarely into bed with industry. Big Tobacco added a provision that shrinks the payout to states if companies' market share drops or the federal government hikes cigarette taxes. That means that every dollar collected by new federal taxes would mean a dollar less for the states, and a 35¢ per pack tax hike would leave the states with nothing.

State lawyers say higher cigarette prices are a good thing, period. "Our true goal is reducing smoking. We are willing to give away state dollars to do that," says one AG aide. But imagine what will happen if Congress decides to raise cigarette taxes. Suddenly, 46 governors would risk losing much or all of the tobacco money they'd expected. The deal gives them a strong incentive to lobby against the move. No wonder Wall Street has bid up shares of Philip Morris Cos. and RJR Nabisco Inc. by 9.8% and 12.4%, respectively, since details of the deal began to surface Nov. 9.

This may be the best settlement anyone could have struck with the industry. And it's less frightening than the one proposed in June, 1997, which would have given companies immunity from private suits. Still, state AGs should have learned from the story of Dr. Faustus: Some deals are better not made at all.

Source: John Carey, "Big Tobacco Makes a Stinky Bedfellow," Commentary, *Business Week,* December 7, 1998.

administration's emphasis on landing a man on the moon spawned a demand for thousands of new products, the Carter administration's emphasis on developing synthetic fuels created a demand for new skills, technologies, and products; and the Reagan administration's strategic defense initiative (the "Star Wars" defense) sharply accelerated the development of laser technologies.

Entrepreneurial firms often feel such influences especially strongly. For example, in the six months following the August invasion of Kuwait, D. M. Offray & Son, a Chester, New Jersey, bow and ribbon manufacturer, sold about 28,409 miles of yellow ribbon in support of the armed forces. In order to keep up with the demand, the plant manager had to go to a triple-shift, six-day work week.[3]

4. Technological Factors

The fourth set of factors in the remote environment involves technological change. To avoid obsolescence and promote innovation, a firm must be aware of technological changes that might influence its industry. Creative technological adaptations can suggest possibilities for new products, for improvements in existing products, or in manufacturing and marketing techniques.

A technological breakthrough can have a sudden and dramatic effect on a firm's environment. It may spawn sophisticated new markets and products or significantly shorten the anticipated life of a manufacturing facility. Thus, all firms, and most particularly those in turbulent growth industries, must strive for an understanding both of the existing technological advances and the probable future advances that can affect their products and services. This quasi-science of attempting to foresee advancements and estimate their impact on an organization's operations is known as *technological forecasting.*

Technological forecasting can help protect and improve the profitability of firms in growing industries. It alerts strategic managers to both impending challenges and promising opportunities. As examples: (1) advances in xerography were a key to Xerox's success but caused major difficulties for carbon paper manufacturers, and (2) the perfection of transistors changed the nature of competition in the radio and television industry, helping such giants as RCA while seriously weakening smaller firms whose resource commitments required that they continue to base their products on vacuum tubes.

The key to beneficial forecasting of technological advancement lies in accurately predicting future technological capabilities and their probable impacts. A comprehensive analysis of the effect of technological change involves study of the expected impact of new technologies on the remote environment, on the competitive business situation, and on the business-society interface. In recent years, forecasting in the last area has warranted particular attention. For example, as a consequence of increased concern over the environment, firms must carefully investigate the probable effect of technological advances on quality-of-life factors, such as ecology and public safety.

5. Ecological Factors

The most prominent factor in the remote environment is often the reciprocal relationship between business and the ecology. The term *ecology* refers to the relationships

[3]*Fortune,* March 11, 1991, p. 14.

among human beings and other living things and the air, soil, and water that support them. Threats to our life-supporting ecology caused principally by human activities in an industrial society are commonly referred to as *pollution.* Specific concerns include global warming, loss of habitat and biodiversity, as well as air, water, and land pollution.

The global climate has been changing for ages; however, it is now evident that humanity's activities are accelerating this tremendously. A change in atmospheric radiation, due in part to ozone depletion, causes global warming. Solar radiation that is normally absorbed into the atmosphere reaches the earth's surface, heating the soil, water, and air.

Another area of great importance is the loss of habitat and biodiversity. Ecologists agree that the extinction of important flora and fauna is occurring at a rapid rate, and if this pace is continued, could constitute a global extinction on the scale of those found in fossil records. The earth's life forms are dependent on a well-functioning ecosystem. In addition, immeasurable advances in disease treatment can be attributed to research involving substances found in plants. As species become extinct, the life support system is irreparably harmed. The primary cause of extinction on this scale is a disturbance of natural habitat. For example, current data suggest that the earth's primary tropical forests, a prime source of oxygen and potential plant "cure," could be destroyed in only five decades.

Air pollution is created by dust particles and gaseous discharges that contaminate the air. Acid rain, or rain contaminated by sulfur dioxide, which can destroy aquatic and plant life, is believed to result from coal-burning factories in 70 percent of all cases. A health-threatening "thermal blanket" is created when the atmosphere traps carbon dioxide emitted from smokestacks in factories burning fossil fuels. This "greenhouse effect" can have disastrous consequences, making the climate unpredictable and raising temperatures.

Water pollution occurs principally when industrial toxic wastes are dumped or leak into the nation's waterways. Since fewer than 50 percent of all municipal sewer systems are in compliance with Environmental Protection Agency requirements for water safety, contaminated waters represent a substantial present threat to public welfare. Efforts to keep from contaminating the water supply are a major challenge to even the most conscientious of manufacturing firms. As described in Strategy in Action 3–3, highly reputed "green" supporter Patagonia has judged itself to be guilty of water pollution.

The Patagonia story is especially interesting because of the "green" fervor with which the company pursues its manufacturing objectives. Strategy in Action 3–4 provides some details on the difficulties that Patagonia faces in its attempts to do what many ecological activists believe should be a national mandate for all corporations.

Land pollution is caused by the need to dispose of ever-increasing amounts of waste. Routine, everyday packaging is a major contributor to this problem. Land pollution is more dauntingly caused by the disposal of industrial toxic wastes in underground sites. With approximately 90 percent of the annual U.S. output of 500 million metric tons of hazardous industrial wastes being placed in underground dumps, it is evident that land pollution and its resulting endangerment of the ecology have become a major item on the political agenda.

As a major contributor to ecological pollution, business now is being held responsible for eliminating the toxic by-products of its current manufacturing processes and for cleaning up the environmental damage that it did previously. Increasingly, managers are being required by the government or are being expected by the public to incorporate ecological concerns into their decision making. For example, between 1975 and 1992, 3M cut its pollution in half by reformulating products, modifying processes,

BusinessWeek

IT'S NOT EASY BEING GREEN

STRATEGY IN ACTION

3–3

Outdoor clothing company Patagonia Inc. has worked hard to be one of the greenest businesses around. It was the first apparel maker to sell synthetic fleece sweaters and warm-up pants made from recycled soda bottles. Last year, it switched to organic cotton for shirts and trousers—and ate half of the 20% markup that organic production added to the garments' cost. Its glossy catalog, printed on recycled paper that is 50% chlorine-free, uses pictures of adventurers in wild places to promote environmental causes.

But Patagonia still has a troubled conscience. In a surprisingly public mea culpa, the company's fall catalog opens with a letter to customers that is a stark critique of Patagonia's reliance on waterproof coatings such as Gore-Tex, which contains chemical toxins, and bright dyes based on strip-mined metals. It is only by using such "dirty" manufacturing processes, the company confesses, that it can offer the "bombproof" outdoor gear and striking colors that customers love. As the letter laments: "The production of our clothing takes a significant toll on the earth."

Turns out it's not easy being green. Patagonia and a handful of other companies that have made protection of the environment a central tenet of their businesses are running into a new wave of polluting problems that require tougher trade-offs than those of the past. Whether it's Ben & Jerry's Homemade coping with massive amounts of high-fat dairy waste, Stonyfield Farm searching for an affordable way to convert to organic fruit for its yogurt, or Orvis, the fishing-gear maker, trying to build a new headquarters that won't threaten bear habitats, green pioneers are struggling for ways to balance *environmental principles* with profit goals.

None are backing off their commitment to the environment. Instead, the greenest companies are testing the limits of what can be done cleanly. "We want it all," Yvon Chouinard, Patagonia's president, told a meeting of the company's suppliers last year. "The best quality and the lowest environmental impact." But it's getting tougher to push the green envelope without compromising business goals. "Our whole system of commerce is not designed to be ecologically sustainable," says Matthew Arnold, director of Washington-based Management Institute for Environment & Business. "These guys are showing the limits of the system to respond."

And customers have made it clear that quality comes first, even if it means passing up the chance to have less impact on the environment. Patagonia surveys show that just 20% of its customers buy from the company because they believe in its environmental mission.

Source: Paul C. Judge in Boston, "It's Not Easy Being Green," *Business Week:* November 24, 1997.

redesigning production equipment, and recycling by-products. Similarly, steel companies and public utilities have invested billions of dollars in costlier but cleaner-burning fuels and pollution control equipment. The automobile industry has been required to install expensive emission controls in cars. The gasoline industry has been forced to formulate new low-lead and no-lead products. And thousands of companies have found it necessary to direct their R&D resources into the search for ecologically superior products, such as Sears's phosphate-free laundry detergent and Pepsi-Cola's biodegradable plastic soft-drink bottle.

Environmental legislation impacts corporate strategies worldwide. Many companies fear the consequences of highly restrictive and costly environmental regulations. However, some manufacturers view these new controls as an opportunity, capturing markets with products that help customers satisfy their own regulatory standards. Other manufacturers contend that the costs of environmental spending inhibit the

PATAGONIA STICKS TO ITS KNITTING

STRATEGY IN ACTION 3–4

Patagonia. People love it or hate it. To some, it's "Patagucci," a high-priced, overexposed brand for the surfing and mountaineering set. To others, particularly those who embrace the company's devotion to protecting the environment, Patagonia is the outfitter of choice. "I would pay more to buy something from Patagonia," says Rick Gulley, 52, a climber and insurance executive in San Diego. "It's my experience with their clothing, but as important is the style of the company."

That style is a commitment to high-quality, no-frills outdoor goods, created with respect for the environment. And unlike rival North Face, Inc., privately held Patagonia is not reaching out to the masses. It's sticking to its knitting—a loyalty the Ventura (Calif.) outfitter learned when it grew too fast in the 1980s.

CACHET

With sales galloping along at a 30% annual growth rate, an expansion-minded Patagonia moved away from its outdoor enthusiasts. Products for which it was known—anoraks for subzero temperatures, say, or four weights of polyester underwear—gave way to casual wear designed for Middle America. By 1990, revenues, topped $100 million, but the brand was losing cachet.

Worse, when sales started to flatten, expenses didn't. In 1991, the company hit the wall. Facing a massive cash shortfall, its bankers demanded a reorganization that forced Patagonia to lay off one-fifth of its workforce. "It was the wake-up call," says Edward M. Schmults, a former Patagonia chief operating officer who is now president of rival Moonshine Mountaineering, owned by clothing maker Esprit.

For Patagonia, it was back to the basics. Refocusing on its core "technical" clothing that stresses function over fashion, the company dropped retailers and reduced its product offerings. It also launched an ambitious program to redesign its products to minimize the effect on the environment of making or using them.

To be sure, the company had always been environment-conscious. Founder and co-owner Yvon Chouinard was an early proponent of "clean climbing"—scaling rock walls without leaving behind any paraphernalia. Since 1985, he had been levying a 1% "earth tax" on sales—more than Patagonia spends on advertising—and devoting it to green causes.

But in a sobering essay in Patagonia's 1991 spring catalog, Chouinard took the company to task for the harmful materials at the heart of its high-performance gear. That led to the 1993 introduction of fleece shirts made of recycled plastic soda bottles, and in 1996, to using only organic cotton. The moves have clearly paid off: Sales and profits have grown steadily ever since, says Schmults. This year, sales should top $170 million. "I have a great deal of respect for Patagonia's ideals, and that makes me more passionate about selling it," says Christine Miller, who owns Sportago, an outdoor clothing store in St. Helens, Calif. With testimonials like that, Patagonia can afford to ignore fashion, discount stores, and its detractors.

Source: Larry Armstrong in Los Angeles, "Patagonia Sticks to Its Knitting," *Business Week:* December 7, 1998.

growth and productivity of their operations. Figure 3–2 takes a deeper look into the costs of environmental regulations.

The increasing attention by companies to protect the environment is evidenced in the attempts by firms to establish proecology policies. One such approach to environmental activism is described in Global Strategy in Action 3–1.

FIGURE 3–2
Environmental Costs and Competitiveness

Several recent efforts to quantify environmental spending have suggested that enormous costs are being incurred. A 1990 study by the U.S. EPA concluded that environmental spending was approaching 2 percent of GNP. Manufacturers then used this information to support their claim that regulation was harming industrial growth and putting the nation at a competitive disadvantage vis-à-vis foreign suppliers. The claims, however, simply did not hold up to closer inspection. First, only a small share of pollution abatement and control spending was incurred by industrial facilities. By one estimate (one used as a source for the EPA study), manufacturers incurred a total of $31.1 billion in environmental costs in 1990. This amounted to only 1.1 percent of product shipments. The costs identified by the EPA resulted from such areas as the requirement for catalytic converters on all automobiles ($14 billion in 1990), the construction and operation of public sewer systems ($20 billion), and the disposal of household wastes ($10 billion).

Even if environmental spending made up only 1 percent of costs, it would not be unreasonable for manufacturers to claim that these costs had a significant influence on competitiveness if international competitors were not required to meet similar requirements. Comparisons of international spending suggest, however, that manufacturers in important production areas around the world are experiencing costs similar to those faced by U.S. producers. Pollution control's share of capital expenditures in Germany was 12 percent in 1990, matching the costs incurred by American manufacturers. Similarly, recent environmental spending by U.S. pulp and paper manufacturers is closely matched by key competitors in Canada and Sweden.

These comparisons suggest that although pollution abatement expenditures are clearly a material part of total costs, the impact of these costs on competitiveness is mild. In fact, no clear link can be made between environmental regulation and measurably adverse effects on net exports, overall trade flows, or plant location decisions. It appear that little advantage has been gained by foreign firms based on the environmental requirements in the areas of their production.

Source: Excerpted from Benjamin C. Bonifant, Matthew R. Arnold, and Frederick J. Long, "Gaining Competitive Advantage through Environmental Investments," p. 39. Reprinted from *Business Horizons,* July–August 1995. Copyright 1995 by the Foundation for the School of Business at Indiana University. Used with permission.

Despite cleanup efforts to date, the job of protecting the ecology will continue to be a top strategic priority—usually because corporate stockholders and executives choose it, increasingly because the public and the government require it. As evidenced by Figure 3–3, the government has made numerous interventions into the conduct of business for the purpose of bettering the ecology.

Benefits of Eco-Efficiency

Many of the world's largest corporations are realizing that business activities must no longer ignore environmental concerns. Every activity is linked to thousands of other transactions and their environmental impact; therefore, corporate environmental responsibility must be taken seriously and environmental policy must be implemented to ensure a comprehensive organizational strategy. Because of increases in government regulations and consumer environmental concerns, the implementation of environmental policy has become a point of competitive advantage. Therefore, the rational goal of business should be to limit its impact on the environment, thus ensuring long-run benefits to both the firm and society. To neglect this responsibility is to ensure the demise of both the firm and our ecosystem.

Stephen Schmidheiny, chairman of the Business Council for Sustainable Development, has coined the term *eco-efficiency* to describe corporations that produce more-useful goods and services while continuously reducing resource consumption and pollution. He cites a number of reasons for corporations to implement environmental

With the special permission of Professor Porter and the *Harvard Business Review,* we present in this section of the chapter the major portion of his seminal article on the industry environment and its impact on strategic management.[4]

OVERVIEW

The nature and degree of competition in an industry hinge on five forces: the threat of new entrants, the bargaining power of customers, the bargaining power of suppliers, the threat of substitute products or services (where applicable), and the jockeying among current contestants. To establish a strategic agenda for dealing with these contending currents and to grow despite them, a company must understand how they work in its industry and how they affect the company in its particular situation. This chapter will detail how these forces operate and suggest ways of adjusting to them, and, where possible, of taking advantage of opportunities that they create.

HOW COMPETITIVE FORCES SHAPE STRATEGY

The essence of strategy formulation is coping with competition. Yet it is easy to view competition too narrowly and too pessimistically. While one sometimes hears executives complaining to the contrary, intense competition in an industry is neither coincidence nor bad luck.

Moreover, in the fight for market share, competition is not manifested only in the other players. Rather, competition in an industry is rooted in its underlying economics, and competitive forces exist that go well beyond the established combatants in a particular industry. Customers, suppliers, potential entrants, and substitute products are all competitors that may be more or less prominent or active depending on the industry.

The state of competition in an industry depends on five basic forces, which are diagrammed in Figure 3–4. The collective strength of these forces determines the ultimate profit potential of an industry. It ranges from intense in industries like tires, metal cans, and steel, where no company earns spectacular returns on investment, to mild in industries like oil-field services and equipment, soft drinks, and toiletries, where there is room for quite high returns.

In the economists' "perfectly competitive" industry, jockeying for position is unbridled and entry to the industry very easy. This kind of industry structure, of course, offers the worst prospect for long-run profitability. The weaker the forces collectively, however, the greater the opportunity for superior performance.

Whatever their collective strength, the corporate strategist's goal is to find a position in the industry where his or her company can best defend itself against these forces or can influence them in its favor. The collective strength of the forces may be painfully apparent to all the antagonists; but to cope with them, the strategist must delve below the surface and analyze the sources of competition. For example, what makes the industry vulnerable to entry? What determines the bargaining power of suppliers?

---

[4]M. E. Porter, "How Competitive Forces Shape Strategy," *Harvard Business Review,* March–April 1979, pp. 137–45.

FIGURE 3–4
Forces Driving Industry Competition

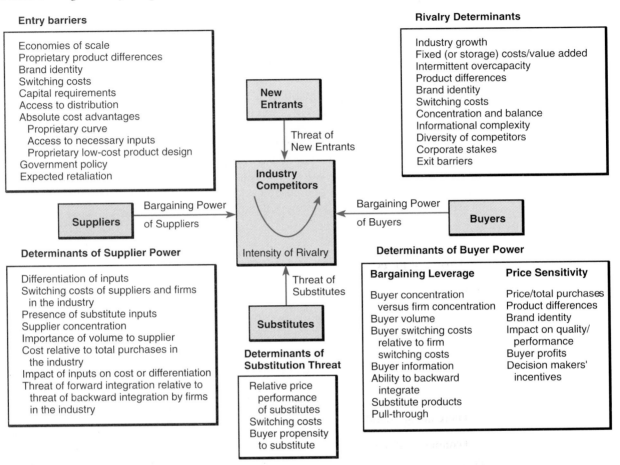

Knowledge of these underlying sources of competitive pressure provides the groundwork for a strategic agenda of action. They highlight the critical strengths and weaknesses of the company, animate the positioning of the company in its industry, clarify the areas where strategic changes may yield the greatest payoff, and highlight the places where industry trends promise to hold the greatest significance as either opportunities or threats.

Understanding these sources also proves to be of help in considering areas for diversification.

CONTENDING FORCES

The strongest competitive force or forces determine the profitability of an industry and so are of greatest importance in strategy formulation. For example, even a company with a strong position in an industry unthreatened by potential entrants will earn low returns if it faces a superior or a lower-cost substitute product—as the leading manufacturers of vacuum tubes and coffee percolators have learned to their sorrow. In such a situation, coping with the substitute product becomes the number one strategic priority.

Different forces take on prominence, of course, in shaping competition in each industry. In the oceangoing tanker industry, the key force is probably the buyers (the major oil companies), while in tires it is powerful OEM buyers coupled with tough competitors. In the steel industry the key forces are foreign competitors and substitute materials.

Every industry has an underlying structure, or a set of fundamental economic and technical characteristics, that gives rise to these competitive forces. The strategist, wanting to position his or her company to cope best with its industry environment or to influence that environment in the company's favor, must learn what makes the environment tick.

This view of competition pertains equally to industries dealing in services and to those selling products. To avoid monotony, I refer to both products and services as *products.* The same general principles apply to all types of business.

A few characteristics are critical to the strength of each competitive force. They will be discussed in this section.

A. Threat of Entry

New entrants to an industry bring new capacity, the desire to gain market share, and often substantial resources. Companies diversifying through acquisition into the industry from other markets often leverage their resources to cause a shake-up, as Philip Morris did with Miller beer.

The seriousness of the threat of entry depends on the barriers present and on the reaction from existing competitors that the entrant can expect. If barriers to entry are high and a newcomer can expect sharp retaliation from the entrenched competitors, he or she obviously will not pose a serious threat of entering.

There are six major sources of barriers to entry:

1. Economies of Scale

These economies deter entry by forcing the aspirant either to come in on a large scale or to accept a cost disadvantage. Scale economies in production, research, marketing, and service are probably the key barriers to entry in the mainframe computer industry, as Xerox and GE sadly discovered. Economies of scale also can act as hurdles in distribution, utilization of the sales force, financing, and nearly any other part of a business.

2. Product Differentiation

Brand identification creates a barrier by forcing entrants to spend heavily to overcome customer loyalty. Advertising, customer service, being first in the industry, and product differences are among the factors fostering brand identification. It is perhaps the most important entry barrier in soft drinks, over-the-counter drugs, cosmetics, investment banking, and public accounting. To create high fences around their business, brewers couple brand identification with economies of scale in production, distribution, and marketing.

3. Capital Requirements

The need to invest large financial resources in order to compete creates a barrier to entry, particularly if the capital is required for unrecoverable expenditures in up-front advertising or R&D. Capital is necessary not only for fixed facilities but also for customer credit, inventories, and absorbing start-up losses. While major corporations have the financial resources to invade almost any industry, the huge capital requirements in certain fields, such as computer manufacturing and mineral extraction, limit the pool of likely entrants.

4. Cost Disadvantages Independent of Size

Entrenched companies may have cost advantages not available to potential rivals, no matter what their size and attainable economies of scale. These advantages can stem from the effects of the learning curve (and of its first cousin, the experience curve), proprietary technology, access to the best raw materials sources, assets purchased at preinflation prices, government subsidies, or favorable locations. Sometimes cost advantages are enforceable legally, as they are through patents. (For analysis of the much-discussed experience curve as a barrier to entry, see Strategy in Action 3–5.)

5. Access to Distribution Channels

The new boy or girl on the block must, of course, secure distribution of his or her product or service. A new food product, for example, must displace others from the supermarket shelf via price breaks, promotions, intense selling efforts, or some other means. The more limited the wholesale or retail channels are and the more that existing competitors have these tied up, obviously the tougher that entry into the industry will be. Sometimes this barrier is so high that, to surmount it, a new contestant must create its own distribution channels, as Timex did in the watch industry in the 1950s.

6. Government Policy

The government can limit or even foreclose entry to industries, with such controls as license requirements and limits on access to raw materials. Regulated industries like trucking, liquor retailing, and freight forwarding are noticeable examples; more subtle government restrictions operate in fields like ski-area development and coal mining. The government also can play a major indirect role by affecting entry barriers through such controls as air and water pollution standards and safety regulations.

The potential rival's expectations about the reaction of existing competitors also will influence its decision on whether to enter. The company is likely to have second thoughts if incumbents have previously lashed out at new entrants, or if:

The incumbents possess substantial resources to fight back, including excess cash and unused borrowing power, productive capacity, or clout with distribution channels and customers.

The incumbents seem likely to cut prices because of a desire to keep market shares or because of industrywide excess capacity.

Industry growth is slow, affecting its ability to absorb the new arrival and probably causing the financial performance of all the parties involved to decline.

B. Powerful Suppliers

Suppliers can exert bargaining power on participants in an industry by raising prices or reducing the quality of purchased goods and services. Powerful suppliers, thereby, can squeeze profitability out of an industry unable to recover cost increases in its own prices. By raising their prices, soft-drink concentrate producers have contributed to the erosion of profitability of bottling companies because the bottlers—facing intense

THE EXPERIENCE CURVE AS AN ENTRY BARRIER

STRATEGY IN ACTION 3–5

In recent years, the experience curve has become widely discussed as a key element of industry structure. According to this concept, unit costs in many manufacturing industries (some dogmatic adherents say in all manufacturing industries) as well as in some service industries decline with "experience," or a particular company's cumulative volume of production. (The experience curve, which encompasses many factors, is a broader concept than the better-known learning curve, which refers to the efficiency achieved over time by workers through much repetition.)

The causes of the decline in unit costs are a combination of elements, including economies of scale, the learning curve for labor, and capital-labor substitution. The cost decline creates a barrier to entry because new competitors with no "experience" face higher costs than established ones, particularly the producer with the largest market share, and have difficulty catching up with the entrenched competitors.

Adherents of the experience curve concept stress the importance of achieving market leadership to maximize this barrier to entry, and they recommend aggressive action to achieve it, such as price cutting in anticipation of falling costs in order to build volume. For the combatant that cannot achieve a healthy market share, the prescription is usually, "Get out."

Is the experience curve an entry barrier on which strategies should be built? The answer is: not in every industry. In fact, in some industries, building a strategy on the experience curve can be potentially disastrous. That costs decline with experience in some industries is not news to corporate executives. The significance of the experience curve for strategy depends on what factors are causing the decline.

A new entrant may well be more efficient than the more experienced competitors; if it has built the newest plant, it will face no disadvantage in having to catch up. The strategic prescription, "You must have the largest, most efficient plant," is a lot different from "You must produce the greatest cumulative output of the item to get your costs down."

Whether a drop in costs with cumulative (not absolute) volume erects an entry barrier also depends on the sources of the decline. If costs go down because of technical advances known generally in the industry or because of the development of improved equipment that can be copied or purchased from equipment suppliers, the experience curve is not an entry barrier at all—in fact, new or less-experienced competitors may actually enjoy a cost advantage over the leaders. Free of the legacy of heavy past investments, the newcomer or less-experienced competitor can purchase or copy the newest and lowest-cost equipment and technology.

If, however, experience can be kept proprietary, the leaders will maintain a cost advantage. But new entrants may require less experience to reduce their costs than the leaders needed. All this suggests that the experience curve can be a shaky entry barrier on which to build a strategy.

While space does not permit a complete treatment here, I want to mention a few other crucial elements in determining the appropriateness of a strategy built on the entry barrier provided by the experience curve:

The height of the barrier depends on how important costs are to competition compared with other areas like marketing, selling, and innovation.

The barrier can be nullified by product or process innovations leading to a substantially new technology and, thereby, creating an entirely new experience curve. New entrants can leapfrog the industry leaders and alight on the new experience curve, to which those leaders may be poorly positioned to jump.

If more than one strong company is building its strategy on the experience curve, the consequences can be nearly fatal. By the time only one rival is left pursuing such a strategy, industry growth may have stopped and the prospects of reaping the spoils of victory may long since have evaporated.

competition from powdered mixes, fruit drinks, and other beverages—have limited freedom to raise their prices accordingly.

The power of each important supplier (or buyer) group depends on a number of characteristics of its market situation and on the relative importance of its sales or purchases to the industry compared with its overall business.

A *supplier* group is powerful if:

1. It is dominated by a few companies and is more concentrated than the industry it sells.

2. Its product is unique or at least differentiated, or if it has built-up switching costs. Switching costs are fixed costs that buyers face in changing suppliers. These arise because, among other things, a buyer's product specifications tie it to particular suppliers, it has invested heavily in specialized ancillary equipment or in learning how to operate a supplier's equipment (as in computer software), or its production lines are connected to the supplier's manufacturing facilities (as in some manufacturing of beverage containers).

3. It is not obliged to contend with other products for sale to the industry. For instance, the competition between the steel companies and the aluminum companies to sell to the can industry checks the power of each supplier.

4. It poses a credible threat of integrating forward into the industry's business. This provides a check against the industry's ability to improve the terms on which it purchases.

5. The industry is not an important customer of the supplier group. If the industry is an important customer, suppliers' fortunes will be tied closely to the industry, and they will want to protect the industry through reasonable pricing and assistance in activities like R&D and lobbying.

C. Powerful Buyers

Customers likewise can force down prices, demand higher quality or more service, and play competitors off against each other—all at the expense of industry profits.

A *buyer* group is powerful if:

1. It is concentrated or purchases in large volumes. Large-volume buyers are particularly potent forces if heavy fixed costs characterize the industry—as they do in metal containers, corn refining, and bulk chemicals, for example—which raise the stakes to keep capacity filled.

2. The products it purchases from the industry are standard or undifferentiated. The buyers, sure that they always can find alternative suppliers, may play one company against another, as they do in aluminum extrusion.

3. The products it purchases from the industry form a component of its product and represent a significant fraction of its cost. The buyers are likely to shop for a favorable price and purchase selectively. Where the product sold by the industry in question is a small fraction of buyers' costs, buyers are usually much less price sensitive.

4. It earns low profits, which create great incentive to lower its purchasing costs. Highly profitable buyers, however, are generally less price sensitive (i.e., of course, if the item does not represent a large fraction of their costs).

5. The industry's product is unimportant to the quality of the buyers' products or services. Where the quality of the buyers' products is very much affected by the industry's product, buyers are generally less price sensitive. Industries in which this situation exists include oil-field equipment, where a malfunction can lead to large losses and enclosures for electronic medical and test instruments, where the quality

of the enclosure can influence the user's impression about the quality of the equipment inside.

6. The industry's product does not save the buyer money. Where the industry's product or service can pay for itself many times over, the buyer is rarely price sensitive; rather, he or she is interested in quality. This is true in services like investment banking and public accounting, where errors in judgment can be costly and embarrassing, and in businesses like the mapping of oil wells, where an accurate survey can save thousands of dollars in drilling costs.

7. The buyers pose a credible threat of integrating backward to make the industry's product. The Big Three auto producers and major buyers of cars often have used the threat of self-manufacture as a bargaining lever. But sometimes an industry so engenders a threat to buyers that its members may integrate forward.

Most of these sources of buyer power can be attributed to consumers as a group as well as to industrial and commercial buyers; only a modification of the frame of reference is necessary. Consumers tend to be more price sensitive if they are purchasing products that are undifferentiated, expensive relative to their incomes, and of a sort where quality is not particularly important.

The buying power of retailers is determined by the same rules, with one important addition. Retailers can gain significant bargaining power over manufacturers when they can influence consumers' purchasing decisions, as they do in audio components, jewelry, appliances, sporting goods, and other goods.

D. Substitute Products

By placing a ceiling on the prices it can charge, substitute products or services limit the potential of an industry. Unless it can upgrade the quality of the product or differentiate it somehow (as via marketing), the industry will suffer in earnings and possibly in growth.

Manifestly, the more attractive the price-performance trade-off offered by substitute products, the firmer the lid placed on the industry's profit potential. Sugar producers confronted with the large-scale commercialization of high-fructose corn syrup, a sugar substitute, are learning this lesson today.

Substitutes not only limit profits in normal times but also reduce the bonanza an industry can reap in boom times. In 1978, the producers of fiberglass insulation enjoyed unprecedented demand as a result of high energy costs and severe winter weather. But the industry's ability to raise prices was tempered by the plethora of insulation substitutes, including cellulose, rock wool, and Styrofoam. These substitutes are bound to become an even stronger force once the current round of plant additions by fiberglass insulation producers has boosted capacity enough to meet demand (and then some).

Substitute products that deserve the most attention strategically are those that *(a)* are subject to trends improving their price-performance trade-off with the industry's product or *(b)* are produced by industries earning high profits. Substitutes often come rapidly into play if some development increases competition in their industries and causes price reduction or performance improvement.

E. Jockeying for Position

Rivalry among existing competitors takes the familiar form of jockeying for position—using tactics like price competition, product introduction, and advertising slugfests. This type of intense rivalry is related to the presence of a number of factors:

1. Competitors are numerous or are roughly equal in size and power. In many U.S. industries in recent years, foreign contenders, of course, have become part of the competitive picture.

2. Industry growth is slow, precipitating fights for market share that involve expansion-minded members.

3. The product or service lacks differentiation or switching costs, which lock in buyers and protect one combatant from raids on its customers by another.

4. Fixed costs are high or the product is perishable, creating strong temptation to cut prices. Many basic materials businesses, like paper and aluminum, suffer from this problem when demand slackens.

5. Capacity normally is augmented in large increments. Such additions, as in the chlorine and vinyl chloride businesses, disrupt the industry's supply-demand balance and often lead to periods of overcapacity and price cutting.

6. Exit barriers are high. Exit barriers, like very specialized assets or management's loyalty to a particular business, keep companies competing even though they may be earning low or even negative returns on investment. Excess capacity remains functioning, and the profitability of the healthy competitors suffers as the sick ones hang on. If the entire industry suffers from overcapacity, it may seek government help—particularly if foreign competition is present.

7. The rivals are diverse in strategies, origins, and "personalities." They have different ideas about how to compete and continually run head-on into each other in the process.

As an industry matures, its growth rate changes, resulting in declining profits and (often) a shakeout. In the booming recreational vehicle industry of the early 1970s, nearly every producer did well; but slow growth since then has eliminated the high returns, except for the strongest members, not to mention many of the weaker companies. The same profit story has been played out in industry after industry—snowmobiles, aerosol packaging, and sports equipment are just a few examples.

An acquisition can introduce a very different personality to an industry, as has been the case with Black & Decker's takeover of McCullough, the producer of chain saws. Technological innovation can boost the level of fixed costs in the production process, as it did in the shift from batch to continuous-line photo finishing in the 1960s.

While a company must live with many of these factors—because they are built into the industry economics—it may have some latitude for improving matters through strategic shifts. For example, it may try to raise buyers' switching costs or increase product differentiation. A focus on selling efforts in the fastest-growing segments of the industry or on market areas with the lowest fixed costs can reduce the impact of industry rivalry. If it is feasible, a company can try to avoid confrontation with competitors having high exit barriers and, thus, can sidestep involvement in bitter price cutting.

INDUSTRY ANALYSIS AND COMPETITIVE ANALYSIS

Designing viable strategies for a firm requires a thorough understanding of the firm's industry and competition. The firm's executives need to address four questions: (1) What are the boundaries of the industry? (2) What is the structure of the industry? (3) Which firms are our competitors? (4) What are the major determinants of competition? The answers to these questions provide a basis for thinking about the appropriate strategies that are open to the firm.

Industry Boundaries

An industry is a collection of firms that offer similar products or services. By "similar products," we mean products that customers perceive to be substitutable for one another. Consider, for example, the brands of personal computers (PCs) that are now being marketed. The firms that produce these PCs, such as AT&T, IBM, Apple, and Compaq, form the nucleus of the microcomputer industry.

Suppose a firm competes in the microcomputer industry. Where do the boundaries of this industry begin and end? Does the industry include desktops? Laptops? These are the kinds of questions that executives face in defining industry boundaries.

Why is a definition of industry boundaries important? First, it helps executives determine the arena in which their firm is competing. A firm competing in the microcomputer industry participates in an environment very different from that of the broader electronics business. The microcomputer industry comprises several related product families, including personal computers, inexpensive computers for home use, and workstations. The unifying characteristic of these product families is the use of a central processing unit (CPU) in a microchip. On the other hand, the electronics industry is far more extensive; it includes computers, radios, supercomputers, superconductors, and many other products.

The microcomputer and electronics industries differ in their volume of sales, their scope (some would consider microcomputers a segment of the electronics industry), their rate of growth, and their competitive makeup. The dominant issues faced by the two industries also are different. Witness, for example, the raging public debate being waged on the future of the "high-definition TV." U.S. policymakers are attempting to ensure domestic control of that segment of the electronics industry. They also are considering ways to stimulate "cutting-edge" research in superconductivity. These efforts are likely to spur innovation and stimulate progress in the electronics industry.

Second, a definition of industry boundaries focuses attention on the firm's competitors. Defining industry boundaries enables the firm to identify its competitors and producers of substitute products. This is critically important to the firm's design of its competitive strategy.

Third, a definition of industry boundaries helps executives determine key factors for success. Survival in the premier segment of the microcomputer industry requires skills that are considerably different from those required in the lower end of the industry. Firms that compete in the premier segment need to be on the cutting edge of technological development and to provide extensive customer support and education. On the other hand, firms that compete in the lower end need to excel in imitating the products introduced by the premier segment, to focus on customer convenience, and to maintain operational efficiency that permits them to charge the lowest market price. Defining industry boundaries enables executives to ask these questions: Do we have the skills it takes to succeed here? If not, what must we do to develop these skills?

Finally, a definition of industry boundaries gives executives another basis on which to evaluate their firm's goals. Executives use that definition to forecast demand for their firm's products and services. Armed with that forecast, they can determine whether those goals are realistic.

Problems in Defining Industry Boundaries

Defining industry boundaries requires both caution and imagination. Caution is necessary because there are no precise rules for this task and because a poor definition will lead to poor planning. Imagination is necessary because industries are dynamic—in every industry, important changes are under way in such key factors as competition, technology, and consumer demand.

Defining industry boundaries is a very difficult task. The difficulty stems from three sources:

1. The evolution of industries over time creates new opportunities and threats. Compare the financial services industry as we know it today with that of the 1990s, and then try to imagine how different the industry will be in the year 2020.

2. Industrial evolution creates industries within industries. The electronics industry of the 1960s has been transformed into many "industries"—TV sets, transistor radios, micro- and macrocomputers, supercomputers, superconductors, and so on. Such transformation allows some firms to specialize and others to compete in different, related industries.

3. Industries are becoming global in scope. Consider the civilian aircraft manufacturing industry. For nearly three decades, U.S. firms dominated world production in that industry. But small and large competitors were challenging their dominance by 1990. At that time, Airbus Industries (a consortium of European firms) and Brazilian, Korean, and Japanese firms were actively competing in the industry.

Developing a Realistic Industry Definition

Given the difficulties outlined above, how do executives draw accurate boundaries for an industry? The starting point is a definition of the industry in global terms; that is, in terms that consider the industry's international components as well as its domestic components.

Having developed a preliminary concept of the industry (e.g., computers), executives flesh out its current components. This can be done by defining its product segments. Executives need to select the scope of their firm's potential market from among these related but distinct areas.

To understand the makeup of the industry, executives adopt a longitudinal perspective. They examine the emergence and evolution of product families. Why did these product families arise? How and why did they change? The answers to such questions provide executives with clues about the factors that drive competition in the industry.

Executives also examine the companies that offer different product families, the overlapping or distinctiveness of customer segments, and the rate of substitutability among product families.

To realistically define their industry, executives need to examine five issues:

1. Which part of the industry corresponds to our firm's goals?
2. What are the key ingredients of success in that part of the industry?
3. Does our firm have the skills needed to compete in that part of the industry? If not, can we build those skills?
4. Will the skills enable us to seize emerging opportunities and deal with future threats?
5. Is our definition of the industry flexible enough to allow necessary adjustments to our business concept as the industry grows?

Industry Structure

Defining an industry's boundaries is incomplete without an understanding of its structural attributes. *Structural attributes* are the enduring characteristics that give an industry its distinctive character. Consider the cable television and financial services industries. Both industries are competitive, and both are important for our quality of life. But these industries have very different requirements for success. To succeed in the cable television industry, firms require vertical integration, which helps them lower their operating costs and ensures their access to quality programs; technological innovation, to enlarge the scope of their services and deliver them in new ways; and extensive marketing, using appropriate segmentation techniques to locate potentially viable niches. To succeed in the financial services industry, firms need to meet very different requirements, among which are extensive orientation of customers and an extensive capital base.

How can we explain such variations among industries? The answer lies in examining the four variables that industry comprises: (1) concentration, (2) economies of scale, (3) product differentiation, and (4) barriers to entry.

Concentration

This variable refers to the extent to which industry sales are dominated by only a few firms. In a highly concentrated industry (i.e., an industry whose sales are dominated by a handful of companies), the intensity of competition declines over time. High concentration serves as a barrier to entry into an industry, because it enables the firms that hold large market shares to achieve significant economies of scale (e.g., savings in production costs due to increased production quantities) and, thus, to lower their prices to stymie attempts of new firms to enter the market.

The U.S. aircraft manufacturing industry is highly concentrated. In 1998, its concentration ratio—the percent of market share held by the top four firms in the industry—was 67 percent. Competition in the industry has not been vigorous. Firms in the industry have been able to deter entry through proprietary technologies and the formation of strategic alliances (e.g., joint ventures).

Economies of Scale

This variable refers to the savings that companies within an industry achieve due to increased volume. Simply put, when the volume of production increases, the long-range average cost of a unit produced will decline.

Economies of scale result from technological and nontechnological sources. The technological sources are a higher level of mechanization or automation and a greater up-to-dateness of plant and facilities. The nontechnological sources include better managerial coordination of production functions and processes, long-term contractual agreements with suppliers, and enhanced employee performance arising from specialization.

Economies of scale are an important determinant of the intensity of competition in an industry. Firms that enjoy such economies can charge lower prices than their competitors. They also can create barriers to entry by reducing their prices temporarily or permanently to deter new firms from entering the industry.

Product Differentiation

This variable refers to the extent to which customers perceive products or services offered by firms in the industry as different.

The differentiation of products can be real or perceived. The differentiation between Apple's Macintosh and IBM's PS/2 Personal Computer was a prime example of real differentiation. These products differed significantly in their technology and performance. Similarly, the civilian aircraft models produced by Boeing differed markedly from those produced by Airbus. The differences resulted from the use of different design principles and different construction technologies. For example, the newer Airbus planes followed the principle of "fly by wire," whereas Boeing planes utilized the laws of hydraulics. Thus, in Boeing planes, wings were activated by mechanical handling of different parts of the plane, whereas in the Airbus planes, this was done almost automatically.

Perceived differentiation results from the way in which firms position their products and from their success in persuading customers that their products differ significantly from competing products. Marketing strategies provide the vehicles through which this is done. Witness, for example, the extensive advertising campaigns of the automakers, each of which attempts to convey an image of distinctiveness. BMW ads highlight the excellent engineering of the BMW and its symbolic value as a sign of achievement. Some automakers focus on roominess and durability, which are desirable attributes for the family segment of the automobile market.

Real and perceived differentiations often intensify competition among existing firms. On the other hand, successful differentiation poses a competitive disadvantage for firms that attempt to enter an industry.

Barriers to Entry

As Porter noted earlier in this chapter, barriers to entry are the obstacles that a firm must overcome to enter an industry. The barriers can be tangible or intangible. The tangible barriers include capital requirements, technological know-how, resources, and the laws regulating entry into an industry. The intangible barriers include the reputation of existing firms, the loyalty of consumers to existing brands, and access to the managerial skills required for successful operation in an industry.

Entry barriers both increase and reflect the level of concentration, economies of scale, and product differentiation in an industry, and such increases make it more difficult for new firms to enter the industry. Therefore, when high barriers exist in an industry, competition in that industry declines over time.

In summary, analysis of concentration, economies of scale, product differentiation, and barriers to entry in an industry enables a firm's executives to understand the forces that determine competition in an industry and sets the stage for identifying the firm's competitors and how they position themselves in the marketplace.

Industry regulations are a key element of industry structure and can constitute a significant barrier to entry for corporations. Escalating regulatory standards costs have been a serious concern for corporations for years. As legislative bodies continue their stronghold on corporate activities, businesses feel the impact on their bottom line. In-house counsel departments have been perhaps the most significant additions to corporate structure in the past decade. Legal fees have skyrocketed and managers have learned the hard way about the importance of adhering to regulatory standards. Figure 3–5 presents some key principles that enable corporations to abide by the ever-increasing regulations while keeping costs down, maintaining competitiveness, and enhancing creativity.

Competitive Analysis

How to Identify Competitors

In identifying their firm's current and potential competitors, executives consider several important variables:

   1. How do other firms define the scope of their market? The more similar the definitions of firms, the more likely the firms will view each other as competitors.

FIGURE 3–5
Innovation-Friendly Regulation

Regulation, properly conceived, need not drive up costs. The following principles of regulatory design will promote innovation, resource productivity, and competitiveness.

Focus on Outcomes, Not Technologies.

Past regulations have often prescribed particular remediation technologies, such as catalysts or scrubbers for air pollution. The phrases "best available technology" (BAT) and "best available control technology" (BACT) are deeply rooted in U.S. practice and imply that one technology is best, thus discouraging innovation.

Enact Strict Rather Than Lax Regulation.

Companies can handle lax regulation incrementally, often with end-of-pipe or secondary treatment solutions. Regulation, therefore, needs to be stringent enough to promote real innovation.

Regulate as Close to the End User as Practical, While Encouraging Upstream Solutions.

This will normally allow more flexibility for innovation in the end product and in all the production and distribution stages. Avoiding pollution entirely or, second best, mitigating it early in the value chain is almost always less costly than late-stage remediation or cleanup.

Employ Phase-In Periods.

Ample but well-defined phase-in periods tied to industry-capital-investment cycles will allow companies to develop innovative resource-saving technologies rather than force them to implement expensive solutions hastily, merely patching over problems.

Use Market Incentives.

Market incentives such as pollution charges and deposit-refund schemes draw attention to resource inefficiencies. In addition, tradable permits provide continuing incentives for innovation and encourage creative use of technologies that exceed current standards.

Harmonize or Converge Regulations in Associated Fields.

Liability exposure in the United States leads companies to stick to safe, BAT approaches, and inconsistent regulation on alternative technologies deters beneficial innovation. For example, one way to eliminate refrigerator cooling agents suspected of damaging the ozone layer involves replacing them with small amounts of propane and butane. But narrowly conceived safety regulations covering these gases seem to have impeded development of the new technology in the United States, while several leading European companies are already marketing the new products.

2. How similar are the benefits the customers derive from the products and services that other firms offer? The more similar the benefits of products or services, the higher the level of substitutability between them. High substitutability levels force firms to compete fiercely for customers.

3. How committed are other firms to the industry? Although this question may appear to be far removed from the identification of competitors, it is in fact one of the most important questions that competitive analysis must address, because it sheds light on the long-term intentions and goals. To size up the commitment of potential competitors to the industry, reliable intelligence data are needed. Such data may relate to potential resource commitments (e.g., planned facility expansions).

Common Mistakes in Identifying Competitors

Identifying competitors is a milestone in the development of strategy. But it is a process laden with uncertainty and risk, a process in which executives sometimes make costly mistakes. Examples of these mistakes are:

1. Overemphasizing current and known competitors while giving inadequate attention to potential entrants.
2. Overemphasizing large competitors while ignoring small competitors.
3. Overlooking potential international competitors.

FIGURE 3–5
(concluded)

Develop Regulations in Sync with Other Countries or Slightly Ahead of Them.

It is important to minimize possible competitive disadvantages relative to foreign companies that are not yet subject to the same standard. Developing regulations slightly ahead of other countries will also maximize export potential in the pollution-control sector by raising incentives for innovation.

Make the Regulatory Process More Stable and Predictable.

The regulatory process is as important as the standards. If standards and phase-in periods are set and accepted early enough and if regulators commit to keeping standards in place for, say, five years, industry can lock in and tackle root-cause solutions instead of government philosophy.

Require Industry Participation in Setting Standards from the Beginning.

U.S. regulation differs sharply from European regulation in its adversarial approach. Industry should help in designing phase-in periods, the content of regulations, and the most effective regulatory process.

Develop Strong Technical Capabilities among Regulators.

Regulators must understand an industry's economics and what drives its competitiveness. Better information exchange will help avoid costly gaming in which ill-informed companies use an array of lawyers and consultants to try to stall the poorly designed regulations of ill-informed regulators.

Minimize the Time and Resources Consumed in the Regulatory Process Itself.

Time delays in granting permits are usually costly for companies. Self-regulation with periodic inspections would be more efficient than requiring formal approvals. Potential and actual litigation creates uncertainty and consumes resources. Mandatory arbitration procedures or rigid arbitration steps before litigation would lower costs and encourage innovation.

Source: Reprinted by permission of *Harvard Business Review.* An excerpt from "Green and Competitive," by Michael E. Porter and Claas van der Linde, September–October 1995. Copyright © 1995 by the President and Fellows of Harvard University, all rights reserved.

4. Assuming that competitors will continue to behave in the same way they have behaved in the past.

5. Misreading signals that may indicate a shift in the focus of competitors or a refinement of their present strategies or tactics.

6. Overemphasizing competitors' financial resources, market position, and strategies while ignoring their intangible assets, such as a top-management team.

7. Assuming that all of the firms in the industry are subject to the same constraints or are open to the same opportunities.

8. Believing that the purpose of strategy is to outsmart the competition, rather than to satisfy customer needs and expectations.

OPERATING ENVIRONMENT

The operating environment, also called the *competitive* or *task environment,* comprises factors in the competitive situation that affect a firm's success in acquiring needed resources or in profitably marketing its goods and services. Among the most important of these factors are the firm's competitive position, the composition of its customers, its reputation among suppliers and creditors, and its ability to attract capable employees. The operating environment is typically much more subject to the firm's influence or control than the remote environment. Thus, firms can be much more proactive (as opposed to reactive) in dealing with the operating environment than in dealing with the remote environment.

FIGURE 3–6
Competitor Profile

Key Success Factors	Weight	Rating*	Weighted Score
Market share	0.30	4	1.20
Price competitiveness	0.20	3	0.60
Facilities location	0.20	5	1.00
Raw materials costs	0.10	3	0.30
Caliber of personnel	0.20	1	0.20
	1.00†		3.30

*The rating scale suggested is as follows: very strong competitive position (5 points), strong (4), average (3), weak (2), very weak (1).
†The total of the weights must always equal 1.00.

1. Competitive Position

Assessing its competitive position improves a firm's chances of designing strategies that optimize its environmental opportunities. Development of competitor profiles enables a firm to more accurately forecast both its short- and long-term growth and its profit potentials. Although the exact criteria used in constructing a competitor's profile are largely determined by situational factors, the following criteria are often included:

1. Market share.
2. Breadth of product line.
3. Effectiveness of sales distribution.
4. Proprietary and key-account advantages.
5. Price competitiveness.
6. Advertising and promotion effectiveness.
7. Location and age of facility.
8. Capacity and productivity.
9. Experience.
10. Raw materials costs.
11. Financial position.
12. Relative product quality.
13. R&D advantages position.
14. Caliber of personnel.
15. General images.
16. Customer profile.
17. Patents and copyrights.
18. Union relations.
19. Technological position.
20. Community reputation.

Once appropriate criteria have been selected, they are weighted to reflect their importance to a firm's success. Then the competitor being evaluated is rated on the criteria, the ratings are multiplied by the weight, and the weighted scores are summed to yield a numerical profile of the competitor, as shown in Figure 3–6.

This type of competitor profile is limited by the subjectivity of its criteria selection, weighting, and evaluation approaches. Nevertheless, the process of developing such profiles is of considerable help to a firm in defining its perception of its competitive position. Moreover, comparing the firm's profile with those of its competitors can aid its managers in identifying factors that might make the competitors vulnerable to the strategies the firm might choose to implement.

2. Customer Profiles

Perhaps the most vulnerable result of analyzing the operating environment is the understanding of a firm's customers that this provides. Developing a profile of a firm's present and prospective customers improves the ability of its managers to plan strategic operations, to anticipate changes in the size of markets, and to reallocate resources so as to support forecast shifts in demand patterns. The traditional approach to segmenting customers is based on customer profiles constructed from geographic, demographic, psychographic, and buyer behavior information, as illustrated in Figure 3–7.

Enterprising companies have quickly learned the importance of identifying target segments. In recent years, market research has increased tremendously as companies realize the benefits of demographic and psychographic segmentation. Research by American Express showed that competitors were stealing a prime segment of the company's business, affluent business travelers. AMEX's competing companies, including Visa and Mastercard, began offering high-spending business travelers frequent flier programs and other rewards including discounts on new cars. In turn, AMEX began to invest heavily in rewards programs, while also focusing on its strongest capabilities, assets, and competitive advantage. Unlike most credit card companies, AMEX cannot rely on charging interest to make money because its customers pay in full each month. Therefore, the company charges higher transaction fees to its merchants. In this way, increases in spending by AMEX customers who pay off their balances each month are more profitable to AMEX than to competing credit card companies. As Strategy in Action 3–6 shows, successful segmentation has paid off.

Assessing consumer behavior is a key element in the process of satisfying your target market needs. Many firms lose market share as a result of assumptions made about target segments. Market research and industry surveys can help to reduce a firm's chances of relying on illusive assumptions. Firms most vulnerable are those that have had success with one or more products in the marketplace and as a result try to base consumer behavior on past data and trends. Some dangerous implicit assumptions are listed in Figure 3–8.

Geographic

It is important to define the geographic area from which customers do or could come. Almost every product or service has some quality that makes it variably attractive to buyers from different locations. Obviously, a Wisconsin manufacturer of snow skis should think twice about investing in a wholesale distribution center in South Carolina. On the other hand, advertising in the *Milwaukee Sun-Times* could significantly expand the geographically defined customer market of a major Myrtle Beach hotel in South Carolina.

Demographic

Demographic variables most commonly are used to differentiate groups of present or potential customers. Demographic information (e.g., information on sex, age, marital status, income, and occupation) is comparatively easy to collect, quantify, and use in strategic forecasting, and such information is the minimum basis for a customer profile.

FIGURE 3–7
Major Segmentation Variables for Consumer Markets

Variable	Typical Breakdowns
Geographic	
Region	Pacific, Mountain, West North Central, West South Central, East North Central, East South Central, South Atlantic, Middle Atlantic, New England.
County size	A, B, C, D.
City or SMSA* size	Under 5,000; 5,000–20,000; 20,000–50,000; 50,000–100,000; 100,000–250,000; 250,000–500,000; 500,000–1,000,000; 1,000,000–4,000,000; 4,000,000 or over.
Density	Urban, suburban, rural.
Climate	Northern, southern.
Demographic	
Age	Under 6, 6–11, 12–19, 20–34, 35–49, 50–64, 65+.
Sex	Male, female.
Family size	1–2, 3–4, 5+.
Family life cycle	Young, single; young, married, no children; young, married, youngest child under 6; young, married, youngest child 6 or over; older, married, with children; older, married, no children under 18; older, single; other.
Income	Under $10,000; $10,000–$15,000; $15,000–$20,000; $20,000–$25,000; $25,000–$30,000; $30,000–$50,000; $50,000 and over.
Occupation	Professional and technical; managers, officials, and proprietors; clerical, sales; craftspeople, foremen; operatives; farmers; retired; students; housewives; unemployed.
Education	Grade school or less; some high school; high school graduate; some college; college graduate.
Religion	Catholic, Protestant, Jewish, other.
Race	White, Black, Oriental.
Nationality	American, British, French, German, Scandinavian, Italian, Latin American, Middle Eastern, Japanese.
Psychographic	
Social class	Lower lowers, upper lowers, working class, middle class, upper middles, lower uppers, upper uppers.
Lifestyle	Straights, swingers, longhairs.
Personality	Compulsive, gregarious, authoritarian, ambitious.
Behavioral	
Occasions	Regular occasion, special occasion.
Benefits	Quality, service, economy.
User status	Nonuser, ex-user, potential user, first-time user, regular user.
Usage rate	Light user, medium user, heavy user.
Loyalty status	None, medium, strong, absolute.
Readiness stage	Unaware, aware, informed, interested, desirous, intending to buy.
Attitude toward product	Enthusiastic, positive, indifferent, negative, hostile.

*SMSA stands for standard metropolitan statistical area.

Source: *Marketing Management,* 9/e by Kotler, © 1997. Adapted by permission of Prentice Hall, Inc., Upper Saddle River, NJ.

Psychographic

Personality and lifestyle variables often are better predictors of customer purchasing behavior than geographic or demographic variables. In such situations, a psychographic study is an important component of the customer profile. Advertising campaigns by soft-drink producers—Pepsi-Cola ("the Pepsi generation"), Coca-Cola ("the real

CUSTOMER SEGMENTATION AT AMEX

**STRATEGY IN
ACTION
3–6**

Self-selecting, individually correcting offers are new in customer segmentation. American Express is using the approach to reduce cost and shorten time-to-market when it tests new value propositions. One example is its recent *zero spender stimulation test.*

Zero spenders are customers who hold the American Express Card and pay the annual fee but rarely or never use the card. Since those customers not only generate lower profits but also are more likely to defect than an average AMEX customer, they are an obvious target for a loyalty program. However, not all customers in this segment are of equal potential value to American Express. Some are not using the card simply because they can't afford much discretionary spending, but others are using cash or a competitor's card instead. It is the zero spender in the second category that American Express wants to target. Easier said than done.

Although zero spenders consist of two different groups, the behavior of one is indistinguishable from that of the other. To identify the subsegments, AMEX has begun testing a series of self-selecting offers designed to attract the customers who have the highest potential value.

One such offer, high in value and likely to appeal only to those with significant discretionary spending ability, is two airline tickets for heavy card use during a six-month period. The cost of the offer is high, but the cost of losing potentially valuable customers and acquiring new ones would be higher. And trying to identify valuable customers through market research could be expensive and time consuming, given the size of the company's worldwide base of customers.

Customer rewards at AMEX are, in effect, a means of delivering mass-customized value. Most companies think of mass customization as it applies to packaging and delivery, but American Express is using reward to mass-customize the value proposition itself. The approach allows the company to test an unprecedented variety of offers and products while lowering costs and speeding time-to-market. All products and offers are designed not only to appeal to desired target segments but also to allow the customers to select the relevant propositions, thereby identifying themselves and making targeted marketing easier in the future. As a global company, AMEX can correlate lessons learned from one market with other markets—lessons showing which products and offers customers prefer and which behavior and profits each proposition generates.

Source: Reprinted by permission of *Harvard Business Review.* An excerpt from "Do Rewards Really Create Loyalty?" by Louise O'Brien and Charles Jones, May–June 1995. Copyright © by the President and Fellows of Harvard University, all rights reserved.

thing"), and 7UP ("America's turning 7UP")—reflect strategic management's attention to the psychographic characteristics of their largest customer segment—physically active, group-oriented nonprofessionals.

Buyer Behavior

Buyer behavior data also can be a component of the customer profile. Such data are used to explain or predict some aspect of customer behavior with regard to a product or service. As Figure 3–7 indicates, information on buyer behavior (e.g., usage rate, benefits sought, and brand loyalty) can provide significant aid in the design of more accurate and profitable strategies.

A second approach to identifying customer groups is by segmenting industrial markets. As shown in Figure 3–9, there is considerable overlap between the variables used

FIGURE 3–8
Some Dangerous Implicit Assumptions about Customer Behavior

1. Customers will buy our product because we think it's a good product.
2. Customers will buy our product because it's technically superior.
3. Customers will agree with our perception that the product is "great."
4. Customers run no risk in buying from us instead of continuing to buy from their past suppliers.
5. The product will sell itself.
6. Distributors are desperate to stock and service the product.
7. We can develop the product on time and on budget.
8. We will have no trouble attracting the right staff.
9. Competitors will respond rationally.
10. We can insulate our product from competition.
11. We will be able to hold down prices while gaining share rapidly.
12. The rest of our company will gladly support our strategy and provide help as needed.

Source: Reprinted by permission of *Harvard Business Review.* An excerpt from "Discovery-Driven Planning," by Rita Gunther McGrath and Ian C. MacMillan, July–August 1995. Copyright © by the President and Fellows of Harvard University, all rights reserved.

to segment individual and industrial consumers, but the definition of the customer differs.

3. Suppliers

Dependable relationships between a firm and its suppliers are essential to the firm's long-term survival and growth. A firm regularly relies on its suppliers for financial support, services, materials, and equipment. In addition, it occasionally is forced to make special requests for such favors as quick delivery, liberal credit terms, or broken-lot orders. Particularly at such times, it is essential for a firm to have had an ongoing relationship with its suppliers.

In assessing a firm's relationships with its suppliers, several factors, other than the strength of that relationship, should be considered. With regard to its competitive position with its suppliers, the firm should address the following questions:

Are the suppliers' prices competitive? Do the suppliers offer attractive quantity discounts?

How costly are their shipping charges? Are the suppliers competitive in terms of production standards?

In terms of deficiency rates, are the suppliers' abilities, reputations, and services competitive?

Are the suppliers reciprocally dependent on the firm?

4. Creditors

Because the quantity, quality, price, and accessibility of financial, human, and material resources are rarely ideal, assessment of suppliers and creditors is critical to an accurate evaluation of a firm's operating environment. With regard to its competitive position with its creditors, among the most important questions that the firm should address are the following:

FIGURE 3–9
Major Segmentation Variables for Industrial Markets

Demographic

Industry: Which industries that buy this product should we focus on?

Company size: What size companies should we focus on?

Location: What geographical areas should we focus on?

Operating Variables

Technology: What customer technologies should we focus on?

User-nonuser status: Should we focus on heavy, medium, light users or nonusers?

Customer capabilities: Should we focus on customers needing many services or few services?

Purchasing Approaches

Purchasing-function organization: Should we focus on companies with highly centralized or decentralized purchasing organizations?

Power structure: Should we focus on companies that are engineering dominated? Financially dominated? Other ways dominated?

Nature of existing relationships: Should we focus on companies with which we have strong existing relationships or simply go after the most desirable companies?

General purchase policies: Should we focus on companies that prefer leasing? Service contracts? Systems purchases? Sealed bidding?

Purchasing criteria: Should we focus on companies that are seeking quality? Service? Price?

Situational Factors

Urgency: Should we focus on companies that need quick and sudden delivery or service?

Specific application: Should we focus on certain applications of our product, rather than all applications?

Size of order: Should we focus on large or small orders?

Perfect Characteristics

Buyer-seller similarity: Should we focus on companies whose people and values are similar to ours?

Attitudes toward risk: Should we focus on risk-taking or risk-avoiding customers?

Loyalty: Should we focus on companies that show high loyalty to their suppliers?

Source: Adapted from Thomas V. Bonoma and Benson P. Shapiro, *Segmenting the Industrial Market* (Lexington, MA: Lexington Books, 1983).

Do the creditors fairly value and willingly accept the firm's stock as collateral?

Do the creditors perceive the firm as having an acceptable record of past payment? A strong working capital position? Little or no leverage?

Are the creditors' loan terms compatible with the firm's profitability objectives?

Are the creditors able to extend the necessary lines of credit?

The answers to these and related questions help a firm forecast the availability of the resources it will need to implement and sustain its competitive strategies.

5. Human Resources: Nature of the Labor Market

A firm's ability to attract and hold capable employees is essential to its success. However, a firm's personnel recruitment and selection alternatives often are influenced by the nature of its operating environment. A firm's access to needed personnel is affected primarily by three factors: the firm's reputation as an employer, local employment rates, and the ready availability of people with the needed skills.

Reputation

A firm's reputation within its operating environment is a major element of its ability to satisfy its personnel needs. A firm is more likely to attract and retain valuable employees if it is seen as permanent in the community, competitive in its compensation package, and concerned with the welfare of its employees, and if it is respected for its product or service and appreciated for its overall contribution to the general welfare.

Employment Rates

The readily available supply of skilled and experienced personnel may vary considerably with the stage of a community's growth. A new manufacturing firm would find it far more difficult to obtain skilled employees in a vigorous industrialized community than in an economically depressed community in which similar firms had recently cut back operations.

Availability

The skills of some people are so specialized that relocation may be necessary to secure the jobs and the compensation that those skills commonly command. People with such skills include oil drillers, chefs, technical specialists, and industry executives. A firm that seeks to hire such a person is said to have broad labor market boundaries; that is, the geographic area within which the firm might reasonably expect to attract qualified candidates is quite large. On the other hand, people with more common skills are less likely to relocate from a considerable distance to achieve modest economic or career advancements. Thus, the labor market boundaries are fairly limited for such occupational groups as unskilled laborers, clerical personnel, and retail clerks.

EMPHASIS ON ENVIRONMENTAL FACTORS

This chapter has described the remote, industry, and operating environments as encompassing five components each. While that description is generally accurate, it may give the false impression that the components are easily identified, mutually exclusive, and equally applicable in all situations. In fact, the forces in the external environment are so dynamic and interactive that the impact of any single element cannot be wholly disassociated from the impact of other elements. For example, are increases in OPEC oil prices the result of economic, political, social, or technological changes? Or are a manufacturer's surprisingly good relations with suppliers a result of competitors', customers', or creditors' activities or of the supplier's own activities? The answer to both questions is probably that a number of forces in the external environment have combined to create the situation. Such is the case in most studies of the environment.

Strategic managers are frequently frustrated in their attempts to anticipate the environment's changing influences. Different external elements affect different strategies at different times and with varying strengths. The only certainty is that the impact of the remote and operating environments will be uncertain until a strategy is implemented. This leads many managers, particularly in less-powerful or smaller firms to minimize long-term planning, which requires a commitment of resources. Instead, they favor allowing managers to adapt to new pressures from the environment. While such a decision has considerable merit for many firms, there is an associated trade-off, namely that absence of a strong resource and psychological commitment to a proactive strategy effectively bars a firm from assuming a leadership role in its competitive environment.

There is yet another difficulty in assessing the probable impact of remote, industry, and operating environments on the effectiveness of alternative strategies. Assessment of this kind involves collecting information that can be analyzed to disclose predictable effects. Except in rare instances, however, it is virtually impossible for any single firm to anticipate the consequences of a change in the environment; for example, what is the precise effect on alternative strategies of a 2 percent increase in the national inflation rate, a 1 percent decrease in statewide unemployment, or the entry of a new competitor in a regional market?

Still, assessing the potential impact of changes in the external environment offers a real advantage. It enables decision makers to narrow the range of the available options and to eliminate options that are clearly inconsistent with the forecast opportunities. Environmental assessment seldom identifies the best strategy, but it generally leads to the elimination of all but the most promising options.

SUMMARY

A firm's external environment consists of three interrelated sets of factors that play a principal role in determining the opportunities, threats, and constraints that the firm faces. The remote environment comprises factors originating beyond, and usually irrespective of, any single firm's operating situation—economic, social, political, technological, and ecological factors. Factors that more directly influence a firm's prospects originate in the environment of its industry, including entry barriers, competitor rivalry, the availability of substitutes, and the bargaining power of buyers and suppliers. The operating environment comprises factors that influence a firm's immediate competitive situation—competitive position, customer profiles, suppliers, creditors, and the labor market. These three sets of factors provide many of the challenges that a particular firm faces in its attempts to attract or acquire needed resources and to profitably market its goods and services. Environmental assessment is more complicated for multinational corporations (MNCs) than for domestic firms because multinationals must evaluate several environments simultaneously.

Thus, the design of business strategies is based on the conviction that a firm able to anticipate future business conditions will improve its performance and profitability. Despite the uncertainty and dynamic nature of the business environment, an assessment process that narrows, even if it does not precisely define, future expectations is of substantial value to strategic managers.

QUESTIONS FOR DISCUSSION

1. Briefly describe two important recent changes in the remote environment of U.S. business in each of the following areas:
   a. Economic.
   b. Social.
   c. Political.
   d. Technological.
   e. Ecological.
2. Describe two major environmental changes that you expect to have a major impact on the wholesale food industry in the next 10 years.

3. Develop a competitor profile for your college and for the college geographically closest to yours. Next, prepare a brief strategic plan to improve the competitive position of the weaker of the two colleges.

4. Assume the invention of a competitively priced synthetic fuel that could supply 25 percent of U.S. energy needs within 20 years. In what major ways might this change the external environment of U.S. business?

5. With your instructor's help, identify a local firm that has enjoyed great growth in recent years. To what degree and in what ways do you think this firm's success resulted from taking advantage of favorable conditions in its remote, industry, and operating environments?

6. Choose a specific industry and, relying solely on your impressions, evaluate the impact of the five forces that drive competition in that industry.

7. Choose an industry in which you would like to compete. Use the five-forces method of analysis to explain why you find that industry attractive.

8. Many firms neglect industry analysis. When does this hurt them? When does it not?

9. The model below depicts industry analysis as a funnel that focuses on remote-factor analysis to better understand the impact of factors in the operating environment. Do you find this model satisfactory? If not, how would you improve it?

10. Who in a firm should be responsible for industry analysis? Assume that the firm does not have a strategic planning department.

BIBLIOGRAPHY

Aaker, D. A. "Managing Assets and Skills: The Key to a Sustainable Competitive Advantage." *California Management Review* (Winter 1989), pp. 91–106.

Bonifant, Benjamin C., Matthew B. Arnold, and Frederick J. Long. "Gaining Competitive Advantage through Environmental Investments." *Business Horizons* 38, no. 1 (July–August 1995), p. 37.

Bylinsky, G. "Manufacturing for Reuse." *Fortune* (February 6, 1995), p. 102.

Fiesinger, E. G. "Dealing with Environmental Regulations and Agencies: An Industry Perspective." *Business Horizons* (March–April 1992), pp. 41–45.

Filho, P. V. "Environmental Analysis for Strategic Planning." *Managerial Planning* (January–February 1985), pp. 23–30.

Ginter, P. M., and W. J. Duncan. "Macroenvironmental Analysis for Strategic Management." *Long Range Planning* (December 1990), pp. 63–70.

Hooper, T. L., and B. T. Rocca. "Environmental Affairs: Now on the Strategic Agenda." *The Journal of Business Strategy* (May–June 1991), pp. 26–31.

Ilinitch, Anne Y., and Stefan C. Schaltegger. "Developing a Green Business Portfolio." *Long Range Planning* 28, no. 2 (April 1995), p. 79.

Ketelhöhn, Werner. "Re-engineering Strategic Management." *Long Range Planning* 28, no. 3 (June 1995), p. 68.

Lieberman, M. B. "The Learning Curve, Technology Barriers to Entry, and Competitive Survival in the Chemical Processing Industries." *Strategic Management Journal* (September–October 1989), pp. 431–47.

MacMillan, I. C. "Controlling Competitive Dynamics by Taking Strategic Initiative." *Academy of Management Executive* (May 1988), pp. 111–18.

Mascarenhas, B., and D. A. Aaker. "Mobility Barriers and Strategic Groups." *Strategic Management Journal* (September–October 1989), pp. 475–85.

Mayer, R. "Winning Strategies for Manufacturers in Mature Industries." *Journal of Business Strategy* (Fall 1987), pp. 23–31.

Miles, R. E. "Adapting to Technology and Competition: A New Industrial Relations System for the 21st Century." *California Management Review* (Winter 1989), pp. 9–28.

Ottman, J. A. "Industry's Response to Green Consumerism." *Journal of Business Strategy* (July–August 1992), pp. 3–7.

Porter, Michael E., and Claas van der Linde. "Toward a New Conception of the Environment-Competitiveness Relationship." *Journal of Economic Perspectives* (Fall 1995).

————. "Green and Competitive: Ending the Stalemate." *Harvard Business Review* 73, no. 5 (September–October 1995), p. 120.

Prescott, J. E., and J. H. Grant. "A Manager's Guide for Evaluating Competitive Analysis Techniques." *Interfaces* (May–June 1988), pp. 10–22.

Rafferty, J. "Exit Barriers and Strategic Position in Declining Markets." *Long Range Planning* (April 1987), pp. 86–91.

Reilly, W. K. "Environment, Inc." *Business Horizons* (March–April 1992), pp. 9–11.

Robertson, T. S., and H. Gatignon. "How Innovators Thwart New Entrants into Their Market." *Planning Review* (September–October 1991), pp. 4–11.

Sarkis, Joseph, and Abdul Rasheed. "Greening the Manufacturing Function." *Business Horizons* 38, no. 5 (September–October 1995), p. 17.

Schoemaker, Paul J. H., and Joyce A. Shoemaker. "Estimating Environmental Liability." *California Management Review* 37, no. 3 (Spring 1995), p. 29.

————. "Ecocentric Management in Industrial Ecosystems: Management Paradigm for a Risk Society." *Academy of Management Review* 20, no. 1 (1995), p. 118.

Thomas, L. M. "The Business Community and the Environment: An Important Partnership." *Business Horizons* (March–April 1992), pp. 21–24.

Ulrich, D., and F. Wiersema. "Gaining Strategic and Organizational Capability in a Turbulent Business Environment." *Academy of Management Executive* (May 1988), pp. 115–22.

Vesey, J. T. "The New Competitors: They Think in Terms of 'Speed to Market.'" *Academy of Management Executive* (May 1991), pp. 23–33.

Winsemius, P., and U. Guntram. "Responding to the Environmental Challenge." *Business Horizons* (March–April 1992), pp. 12–20.

Yoffie, D. B. "How an Industry Builds Political Advantage." *Harvard Business Review* (May–June 1988), pp. 82–89.

CHAPTER 3 DISCUSSION CASE   BusinessWeek

YAHOO!

> Few companies have prospered from the E-commerce frenzy as much as
> YAHOO!. In a competitive environment better characterized by chaos than or-
> der, YAHOO! has dashed ahead of real and potential competitors of staggering
> size and capabilities. This discussion case for Chapter 3 identifies how some of
> the factors in YAHOO!'s remote, industry, and operating environments defined
> opportunities that molded the company's direction.

On July 17, the top dogs at Warner Bros. Online gathered around a giant TV screen
in their offices high above the streets of Los Angeles. But instead of watching Bugs
Bunny, Daffy Duck, or some other famous Warner cartoon, they found themselves
transfixed by an internal slide presentation of a giant yellow Pac Man. His name:
Yahoo! His target: nearly everything.

The mesmerized executives watched as Yahoo ate his way through the best that the
Internet has to offer. First, he gobbled up the rights to news from such titans as CNN
and Reuters Holdings PLC. Then he moved on to electronic commerce, downing deals
with retailers such as bookseller Amazon.com Inc. and music outfit CDnow Inc. The
voracious little creature went on to munch his way through Internet staples E-mail and
chat rooms before finally coming to a stop just before entertainment. "Yahoo just gets
bigger and fatter and gets more and more revenue," said James Moloshok, senior vice-
president at Warner Bros. Online. But no more, he told his troops: Warner would fight
back.

How did little upstart Yahoo! Inc. make it onto the radar screen of Warner Bros., a division of media goliath Time Warner Inc.? In just three years, Yahoo has morphed from
an ordinary search service into the be-all, do-all of the Net, offering a dizzying array of
services and information. Need a daily fix of news, stock quotes, weather, and E-mail?
Head to Yahoo. Want to house-hunt, figure out a retirement plan, or research the Ebola
virus? Yep—Yahoo. It's even a Web hangout for those craving a little R&R of, say, online blackjack, shopping for premium handmade cigars, or Koi pond supplies.

Vast selection has catapulted Yahoo into the No. 1 spot on the Web, with 40 million
people who log on every month—more than the 30 million who tune in weekly to
NBC's top-rated TV show, ER. And Yahoo's stock? It has soared heavenward, to 23
times its 1996 IPO price: The market capitalization was $9.1 billion on Aug. 25. That
day the $97.50 stock price was 305 times projected 1998 earnings of 32 cents a
share—astonishing, considering that Microsoft Corp., the computer industry paceset-
ter, is valued at 52 times earnings. Yahoo CEO Timothy Koogle is unfazed by the valuation: "I'd be hard-pressed to say it's overhyped. We've set out to make Yahoo the
only place anyone needs to go to get connected to anything. There's nothing in the real
world to compare to that."

Source: Linda Himelstein in Santa Clara, California, with Heather Green and Richard Siklos in New York and Catherine Yang
in Washington, "Yahoo!" *Business Week:* September 7, 1998.

Little wonder, then, that media companies such as Warner Bros. and Walt Disney Co. are in such a stew over what to do about the Silicon Valley company. At stake is not only how to get the attention of today's 90 million cybersurfers. It's a digital land rush, with companies madly scrambling to stake a claim as an information giant in the next century. Already, more people are hopscotching across Web sites than the number of viewers TV could claim after a dozen years in existence. And there are no signs the Web's growth is slowing: By 2002, some 328 million people around the globe will be using this far-flung information pipeline, according to International Data Corp.

CHANGING REMOTE ENVIRONMENT

What's emerging faster than many imagined is a Net generation that rises not to its newspapers and TV news shows but to its coffee and glowing computer screens. Some 64% of cybersurfers watch less TV now than they did before their Web-cruising days, while 48% are not reading as much, according to market researchers Strategis Group. Suddenly, the prospect of being a media goliath without grabbing the eyes, minds, and pocketbooks of the Internet droves seems dicey indeed. "With Yahoo, you can't measure things like price to sales," says Abel Garcia, senior vice-president at investment firm Waddell & Reed Inc., one of Yahoo's largest shareholders. "You have to look at it as the new media company of the 21st century."

And that could be a mouth-watering prospect. Unlike traditional media, this new Internet breed will dish up not only information and entertainment but also a way to act on it. Like New Age general stores, new media companies stock news, staples, and all the hottest gossip. Consumers, for example, can get the latest information on long-term mortgage rates—and find a real estate broker, view their dream home, and apply for a home loan, all under one roof. When a deal is struck, the new media company collects a fee.

This lucrative, one-stop Web site approach is the most coveted business on the Net today. And, oddly enough, it goes by the drab name of "portals." These are glitzed up entrances to the Web that have so many goodies that their operators hope cyber-surfers congregate en masse and then rarely venture elsewhere. And like all high-rent districts, they can charge a premium for advertising, while also cashing in on consumer E-commerce. Online shopping alone is expected to balloon to $37.5 billion by 2002, says Jupiter Communications.

This has not escaped the giants of the media world, who are piling into the business like so many giddy teenagers squeezing into a Volkswagen Bug. In July, NBC spent $6 million for a 19% position in Snap!, the struggling portal operated by CNET Inc. Disney quickly ponied up $70 million and traded its majority stake in Starwave Corp. for 43% of rival Infoseek Corp. And insiders say that Excite Inc. has held talks with several media giants, including Time Warner. "The pitter-patter of competitive footsteps has turned into a clip-clop," says Internet analyst Mary G. Meeker of Morgan Stanley Dean Witter.

CHANGING INDUSTRY ENVIRONMENT

Almost overnight, the competition has gone from stiff to downright scary. Existing portals such as Infoseek have been beefed up with cash from media companies, while TV networks have signaled that they have no intention of being outnetworked by a cyberspace upstart. Technology bigwigs Microsoft and Netscape Communications Corp.

are joining in the scramble, too, bringing the powerful draw of their browsers with them. From America Online Inc. to General Electric Co./NBC, these giants are poised for combat. Enemy No. 1: Yahoo. "This is the first time since Yahoo started that it will be vulnerable," says Halsey M. Minor, CEO of rival CNET. "In the next nine months, things will be vastly different."

The firepower of new and invigorated rivals is worry enough for Yahoo. But the company may be facing a more fundamental threat: convincing Corporate America that it can get a big bang for its buck by advertising online. A small but growing number of companies are beginning to question the value portals bring to their marketing efforts, which could take the air out of worldwide ad spending forecast by Forrester Research Inc. to hit $15 billion by 2003.

Charles Schwab & Co., for example, no longer pays millions to AOL to be featured on its finance channel because it says less than 5% of its customers used AOL to get to Schwab's Web site. "Customers were looking at positions on portals a little like billboards on the side of the road," says Martha Deevy, Schwab's senior vice-president for electronic brokerage. "Over time, they just become part of the landscape."

Could it be? Is highflier Yahoo a mouse-click away from becoming a has-been? Already, analysts are predicting that no more than a handful of the more than a dozen already-declared players will survive the portal melee. They warn that the added competition—along with the ever-mushrooming number of Web sites—could spread crucial advertising revenues too thin. This year, portals are expected to attract 15% of Web traffic and 67% of North American ad dollars, or $870 million. By 2003, though, they will grab 20% of traffic but only 30% of ad dollars, or $3.2 billion, according to Forrester. "It's a real threat to Yahoo," says Forrester analyst Chris G. Charron.

Most experts are placing bets on AOL, with its 12.5 million subscribers—who account for 36% of the Web traffic that comes from households. And Microsoft gets a thumbs-up because, well, it's Microsoft. Although the software giant's online service Microsoft Network has been a huge disappointment, its new portal, MSN.COM, launched for the most part in late August, is expected to hit the mark with Netizens.

But it's tiny 600-person Yahoo that gets the most nods. It was first to market with a detailed search service, first to go public, first to turn an annual profit, and first to go mainstream by slapping its zany name on TV.

Now, Yahoo is promising to go where no portal has gone before—to telephones, televisions, pagers, handheld organizers, and the like. Koogle and his troops are working feverishly so that by early next year, Yahoo's zippy Web pages are accessible anywhere and from any device.

Even sooner, perhaps by year-end, the company plans to give its registered users the velvet-glove treatment by offering a so-called Yahoo wallet. This would allow users to register their credit cards and shipping addresses with Yahoo. Then, when they shop anywhere on the Web, they can take their virtual Yahoo wallet with them to make purchases instantly. As with credit cards, Yahoo will keep a tab and present a monthly online bill. "We want to build the biggest company we can," vows the 47-year-old Koogle. "We've taken the lid off."

The method in Yahoo's tactics is nothing short of madness. Indeed, the company's motto demands it: Do what's crazy, but not stupid. Nowhere has this principle been stronger than in Yahoo's branding campaigns. By conjuring up a cool California image—hip but not rad, easy-to-use but not simplistic—it has managed to create a cult-like following not unlike that of Apple Computer Inc.'s Macintosh.

Today, the Yahoo name is scrawled on seemingly every available surface. At the hockey rink of the San Jose Sharks, it's on the Zamboni ice-shaving machine. It's wrapped around tins of breath mints. It's on Slinkys, parachutes, skateboards, sailboats, surfboards, yo-yos, and kazoos. And the purple and yellow letters will soon appear on shoes, a music CD, the "ER" show, and the upcoming Ron Howard movie *Ed TV.* The best part: Yahoo has paid barely a whisper for all this publicity. In its early days, the company bartered for placement, but now—since gaining cachet—it gets much of this gratis.

Truth be told, the Yahoo brand may be the company's biggest asset. While rivals such as Excite or Infoseek may match Yahoo's information, services, and shopping, few have come close to its branding. Some 44% of the Internet users know Yahoo, according to Intelliquest Inc.—more than are familiar with Excite, Lycos, or even Microsoft. Only AOL and Netscape are better known. "The name contains the promise of the product," says Owen Shapiro, senior analyst at market and brand research firm Leo J. Shapiro & Associates. "It reinforces the idea that when I go to Yahoo, I'll be so pleased I'll be Yahooing afterwards."

CHANGING OPERATING ENVIRONMENTS

Although the company has helped define Internet branding, it must now keep redefining it to stay ahead of deep-pocketed rivals such as NBC. Yahoo was the first Net upstart to hit the airwaves with a series of humorous TV commercials in 1996 (Do you Yahoo!? remains a company tagline). But TV ads alone just won't cut it anymore. Now, Yahoo is trying to go one step further with product placements on TV's "Ally McBeal" and "Caroline in the City." And in an Aug. 27 announcement, Yahoo linked its brand with the likes of the Oakland Athletics baseball team and the popular Comedy Central cable channel by forming online clubs for their fans.

In a stab to get beyond T-shirts, of which it already has 20 different varieties, it licensed the logo to Gregory Mountain Sports, which is making computer bags to be sold in Staples Inc. and REI stores this fall. "We want a name that will stand the test of time," says Karen Edwards, vice-president for brand marketing, who joined Yahoo in January, 1996, after having done battle in the trenches at computer maker Apple's ad agency, BBDO Worldwide Inc. Edwards is so gung ho that she planted her Palo Alto (Calif.) garden this summer with purple petunias and yellow gladioli—the company's colors.

No doubt Yahoo's power brand will be one of its greatest weapons in fending off the coming assault. So, too, will be its healthy bank account. The company is sitting on almost $400 million in cash, thanks in part to a $250 million investment on July 8 by Softbank Corp., which now owns 31% of Yahoo. This is part of Softbank's strategy of Internet investments, including stakes in E*Trade and GeoCities. The Softbank money, not to mention Yahoo's stock, will come in handy as Koogle pursues a more aggressive acquisition strategy than in the past. Yahoo has made only four acquisitions so far, including the $49 million stock purchase of ViaWeb. But with greater competition and a need to keep expanding its services, Koogle says more are in the offing.

Apart from cold, hard cash, Yahoo has its stock price going for it—so long as it stays aloft. Compared with tech dynamo Microsoft, with a share price 2.7 times its projected 1999 earnings growth rate, Yahoo seems pricey at 4.1 times expected earnings growth. For Yahoo to be valued the same as Microsoft, it would have to hike earnings 66% next year—well above the 45% increase analysts are forecasting. Nonetheless, 14 out of 20 analysts rate the stock a buy. Why? Most say they expect the company will remain a leader in portals, cashing in handsomely in coming years. A big help: Yahoo boasts gross margins of 88%, just shy of Microsoft's 92%. "Yahoo has the potential to emerge as the first pure Internet giant," says analyst Paul Noglows of Hambrecht & Quist Inc.

But first, it will have to maintain its knack for giving Netizens what they want. That's why its executives have been in nonstop meetings (in sparsely furnished conference rooms bearing names such as Decent or Consistent—just so that people will be forced to say they are "in Decent" or "in Consistent") to discuss the company's tenuous future. "We are in the business of obsoleting Yahoo," says 29-year-old co-founder Jerry Yang, whose success has made him so popular in his parents' home country of Taiwan that he registers in hotels under an assumed name to avoid a crush of autograph-seekers.

It wasn't always that way. When Yang and David Filo were Stanford University graduate engineering students in late 1993, they were about as far away from Big Business as twentysomethings could be. Instead of writing dissertations, they spent most of their time surfing the Web and building lists of their favorite sites. On a whim, they decided to post their list, dubbed "Jerry's Guide to the World Wide Web." The reaction was explosive. So in 1995, the dissertations were chucked—and so was the list's name. Instead, Yahoo, which technically stands for Yet Another Hierarchical Officious Oracle, was born.

In the future, playing up this friendly neighborhood feel of Yahoo and downplaying its commercialization will be key to getting surfers to stick around. According to Media Metrix Inc., users hang out at Yahoo's site an average of nine minutes daily, versus about 42 for rival AOL's proprietary service. Yahoo is trying to increase that through its Hollywoodesque programming. On July 21, for instance, more than 18,000 people asked more than 100,000 questions during an online discussion with teen heartthrobs Hanson. And during the recent World Cup, Yahoo's multilingual site drew an estimated 13.5 million people—4 million from outside the U.S.

But with Netscape, Disney, and others on its heels, Yahoo will have to do more. Such as get personal. While all the major portals offer personalized services, Yahoo leads the pack with 18 million consumers registered on My Yahoo, a feature that stores personal data, such as ZIP codes and the occupations of people who choose to use it. That information, which is kept confidential, allows Yahoo to tailor advertisements, merchant's wares, and other services to consumers who would be most interested in them.

Yahoo plans to capitalize on knowing people's tastes by using push technology to tailor information and deliver Web material to the desktop. "I can picture Yahoo as a big depository for people's preferences and consumption patterns," explains Koogle, who is known as "T.K." around the office. "We'll have the ability to notify people of things they should tune into."

Or buy. At the moment, when it comes to E-commerce, the job of a portal is to send as much traffic to its partners' and advertisers' home pages as possible. But Yahoo hopes to do even more, including suggesting items for purchase based on an individual's preferences and past buying behavior. It also wants to launch an online billing and buying service. Yahoo already has a relationship with Visa International and is talking with Intuit Inc. and others about the venture. "We can be a central buying service," explains Chief Operating Officer Jeffrey Mallett, 34.

That's a shrewd move for Yahoo, which, like other portals, expects E-commerce to contribute a bigger piece of its revenue pie. Currently, E-commerce is expected to bring in some $42 million, or about 25% of Yahoo's projected 1998 revenue of $170 million. The rest comes from advertising. But Koogle expects that E-commerce will climb sharply within a year. Yahoo's popular finance site, for instance, where Media Metrix says 1.5 million users each month spend roughly 24 minutes of their time, may alone be worth $100 million in revenues from ads and other commerce within a year, says analysts.

And then there's expansion overseas. Yahoo is currently operating in nine different languages in 14 countries, including Australia, China, and Germany. Yahoo Japan is the most popular Web site in that country, where 10 million people are online. Overall, Yahoo estimates that 30% of its traffic comes from outside North America.

Will all this be enough? It's too early to tell—at least until Disney, Microsoft, and others play their hands. Rival Lycos, for one, nearly matches Yahoo's international record. It is in 11 countries in Europe alone. And archrival AOL shows no signs of slowing. It boasts a boatload of subscribers to its proprietary service and has plans to launch a new Web portal this month based on its recently acquired ICQ instant messaging service. ICQ (short for "I seek you") has nearly 7.5 million active users. Its wild popularity stems from its focus on a mix of E-mail and chat called instant messaging. The move is expected to appeal to hip young Netizens and to fill a void left by AOL's less-than-stellar Web site, AOL.com.

The Dulles (Virginia) company raked in $2.6 billion in revenues in 1998, 15 times Yahoo's expected revenues. Given that, AOL executives say that not even high-flying Yahoo will be able to threaten AOL's bright future. "Everyone is changing to be more like AOL," says President and Chief Operating Officer Robert W. Pittman. "But no one is going to out-AOL AOL." CEO Stephen M. Case takes a more measured approach: "We just need to make sure we're innovating rapidly. That's really the way to fend off any competitive threats."

That's what NBC thinks, too. But first, its focus will be on branding—an area that Yahoo has largely dominated. On July 27, NBC began airing a quirky ad campaign aimed at making Snap! a household name. NBC says the ads, with the tag line "Don't suffer from information overload. Snap! Out of It," should reach some 400 million viewers in the summer, and double that in the fourth quarter. "We think we can create a success with Snap! by bringing it to the attention of a much larger audience," says NBC President and CEO Robert C. Wright.

The Disney-Infoseek combo also is about to turbocharge its promotion efforts. In addition to TV, Disney will use its movies, theme parks, and cruise ships to raise Infoseek's profile. But it may not be known as Infoseek for long. By the end of the year, the alliance will unveil a new portal that will serve as an umbrella for Disney's roughly 25 Web properties. For its part, Excite is hot on Yahoo's trail, with a host of new services and promotional ventures of its own. Ditto for Netscape. Says Michael J. Homer, executive vice-president at Netscape's portal Netcenter: "It takes exactly one click for someone to never be a Yahoo user again."

Even before Yahoo feels the competitive heat, its fate depends largely on advertising. Today, the Internet is still an unruly frontier many are unwilling to bet on. The sugar daddy of all advertisers, Procter & Gamble Co., for instance, spends just $10 million on Net ads annually, out of its $3 billion ad budget. Executives from several major companies said at an Aug. 20 online ad conference that their puny Web spending wouldn't go up much until electronic ads become more consumer-friendly and interactive and until their effectiveness can be better measured.

Even an Internet startup is not convinced. Chris Larsen, CEO of Palo Alto's E-Loan Inc., an online mortgage business, says his company does better relying on traditional media for promotion than on the portals. In July, E-loan spent $250,000 on radio ads in California and Washington. The cost per customer: about $200, with about a 2% conversion rate on resulting loan applications. By contrast, Larsen's online deals cost him at least $300 a customer, with a conversion rate of just 0.5%. "Long-term, we think traditional media are the way to develop the brand," says Larsen. "I don't want to be too dependent on portals."

And as consumers get more Net-savvy, they may not need a helping portal hand. Jerry Kaplan, CEO of Internet auction house ONSALE Inc., says his company has seen its traffic from portals shrink faster than a cheap T-shirt in the past year. He figures the drop stems from an increased awareness of ONSALE's brand. "The next turn of the crank in Internet commerce will be that certain sites will emerge as destinations on their own, thereby eliminating the necessity to buy a broad presence on the portal sites," he says.

Koogle concedes that some businesses, particularly those with the best-known names, won't need to rely on Yahoo and other portals to attract online customers or build brand awareness. But he says most merchants will flock to them for their services, strong distribution, and loyal following. Media Metrix says 51% of Net surfers at work and 42% of those at home use Yahoo at least occasionally. That powerful presence is expected to keep the ad dollars rolling in. Forrester figures Yahoo will nab at least a quarter of all portal ad money in 2002.

That's why E*Trade Group Inc. CEO Christos M. Cotsakos, whose Internet brokerage put up millions of dollars on Aug. 6 for ads and access to Yahoo's finance channel customers, says that banking on Yahoo is a no-brainer. "It's like playing Double Jeopardy," says Cotsakos. "You place your biggest bets on the squares that will give you the best return. And Yahoo is the Double Jeopardy Square on the Internet."

Koogle had better hope so. Should the economic model for this emerging business start to fizzle, the coming competitive assault will be the least of Yahoo's worries. It could take years to turn the P&Gs of the world into Net believers, placing Yahoo squarely on the come line. For now, though, all hands at the company's spartan headquarters are focused on the bout before them. And they know that even one misstep will be seized upon by a legion of Yahoo wannabes. "There's a vast universe waiting for Yahoo to fall or stumble," says Michael Moritz, a Yahoo board member. If Yahoo doesn't gobble them up first.

4

THE GLOBAL ENVIRONMENT: STRATEGIC CONSIDERATIONS FOR MULTINATIONAL FIRMS

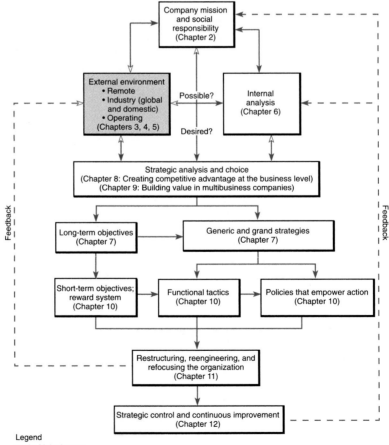

Special complications confront a firm involved in the globalization of its operations. *Globalization* refers to the strategy of approaching worldwide markets with standardized products. Such markets are most commonly created by end consumers that prefer lower-priced, standardized products over higher-priced, customized products and by global corporations that use their worldwide operations to compete in local markets.[1] Global corporations headquartered in one country with subsidiaries in other countries experience difficulties that are understandably associated with operating in several distinctly different competitive arenas.

Awareness of the strategic opportunities faced by global corporations and of the threats posed to them is important to planners in almost every domestic U.S. industry. Among corporations headquartered in the United States that receive more than 50 percent of their annual profits from foreign operations are Citicorp, Coca-Cola, Exxon, Gillette, IBM, Otis Elevator, and Texas Instruments. In fact, the 100 largest U.S. globals earn an average of 37 percent of their operating profits abroad. Equally impressive is the impact of foreign-based globals that operate in the United States. Their "direct foreign investment" in the United States now exceeds $90 billion, with Japanese, German, and French firms leading the way. As Global Strategy in Action 4–1 describes, Yamanouchi Pharmaceutical is a fast-growth company in the process of globalizing.

Understanding the myriad and sometimes subtle nuances of competing in global markets or against global corporations is rapidly becoming a required competence of strategic managers. For example, experts in the advertising community contend that Korean companies only recently recognized the importance of making their names known abroad. In the 1980s, there was very little advertising of Korean brands, and the country had very few recognizable brands abroad. Korean companies tended to emphasize sales and production more than marketing. The opening of the Korean advertising market in the 1990s indicated that Korean firms had acquired a new appreciation for the strategic competencies that are needed to compete globally and created an influx of global firms like Saatchi and Saatchi, J. W. Thompson, Ogilvy and Mather, and Bozell. Many of them established joint ventures or partnerships with Korean agencies. An excellent example of such a strategic approach to globalization by Philip Morris's KGFI is described in Global Strategy in Action 4–2. What is more, the opportunities for corporate growth often seem brightest in global markets. Figure 4–1 reports on the growth in national shares of the world's outputs and growth in national economies to the year 2020. While the United States had a commanding lead in the size of its economy in 1992, it will be caught by China in the year 2000 and far surpassed by 2020. Overall, in the next 20 years, rich industrial countries will be overshadowed by developing countries in their produced share of the world's output.

Because the growth in the number of global firms continues to overshadow other changes in the competitive environment, this section will focus on the nature, outlook, and operations of global corporations.

DEVELOPMENT OF A GLOBAL CORPORATION

The evolution of a global corporation often entails progressively involved strategy levels. The first level, which often entails export-import activity, has minimal effect on the existing management orientation or on existing product lines. The second level, which

---

[1]T. Levitt, "The Globalization of Markets," *Harvard Business Review,* September–October 1982, p. 91; and T. Hout, M. E. Porter, and E. Rudden, "How Global Companies Win Out," *Harvard Business Review,* September–October 1982, pp. 98–108.

YAMANOUCHI PHARMACEUTICAL READIES ITSELF FOR GLOBALIZATION

GLOBAL STRATEGY IN ACTION 4–1

The basic policy of the top management of Yamanouchi Pharmaceutical Co., Ltd., represented by Chairman Shigeo Morioka and President Masayoshi Onoda, is summarized by the concepts of big dual enterprise, three-pole tactics, and GBS (global big seven) 005. Big dual enterprise means the dual management diversification into pharmaceuticals and health foods. Three-pole tactics means concentrating activities in Asia (including Japan), America, and Europe, starting from Japan. The GSB 005 envisages the development of seven original new drugs acceptable to the world market until the year 2005, according to Managing Director Junichiro Matsumoto.

The company is actively engaged in project evolution aimed at the establishment of an integrated system covering research and development, and production and sales, as well as a strategy serving local communities. These steps are aimed at converting Yamanouchi into a global enterprise during the first decade of the 21st century.

Yamanouchi achieved excellent business results during fiscal 1994 (March 1995 term). Sales totaled ¥73,048 million, of which exports accounted for ¥12,770 million. Ordinary profit totaled ¥57,990 million. Sales and profit grew by 5.1 percent and 6.6 percent, respectively, from the previous year. The combined group including 54 subsidiaries (for example, Shaklee Corp. of the United States) showed sales of ¥384,323 million and ¥77,390 million, up 4.2 percent and 10.5 percent, respectively. The ordinary profit of the Yamanouchi Group thus achieved even higher growth than the parent company, reflecting the good performance of overseas subsidiaries.

In particular, Yamanouchi Ireland is playing a vital role as the production base of bulk famotidine (Gaster), an anti-ulcer drug agent, which is sold in over 100 countries and recorded annual sales surpassing $1,200 million worldwide. The globalization of Yamanouchi has thus entered a new stage.

Intensified activities related to Yamanouchi's globalization have been seen in the past decade. The firm established Yamanouchi Ireland and started the construction of a manufacturing plant in 1986. The construction was completed in 1988 and the plant moved into full-scale bulk production

Source: Excerpted from *Japan,* August 21, 1995, p. 30.

can involve foreign licensing and technology transfer, requires little change in management or operation. The third level typically is characterized by direct investment in overseas operations, including manufacturing plants. This level requires large capital outlays and the development of global management skills. Although the domestic operations of a firm at this level continue to dominate its policy, such a firm is commonly categorized as a true multinational corporation (MNC). The most involved strategy level is characterized by a substantial increase in foreign investment, with foreign assets comprising a significant portion of total assets. At this level, the firm begins to emerge as a global enterprise with global approaches to production, sales, finance, and control.

Some firms downplay their global nature (to never appear distracted from their domestic operations), whereas others highlight it. For example, General Electric's formal statement of mission and business philosophy includes the following commitment:

> To carry out a diversified, growing, and profitable worldwide manufacturing business in electrical apparatus, appliances, and supplies, and in related materials, products, systems, and services for industry, commerce, agriculture, government, the community, and the home.

A similar global orientation is evident at IBM, which operates in 125 countries, conducts business in 30 languages and more than 100 currencies, and has 23 major manufacturing facilities in 14 countries.

continued

of Gaster. Yamanouchi Research Institute (United Kingdom) was inaugurated at Oxford in 1990 as the firm's British research center mainly engaged in basic research centered on cell biology.

In 1991 Yamanouchi bought the pharmaceutical division of Royal Gist–Brocades (the Netherlands) and reorganized it as Brocades Pharma, a base for research and development, and production and sales of pharmaceuticals in Europe. The firm's name was again changed, to Yamanouchi Europe and Yamanouchi Pharma, in 1994 with the establishment of the head office in the Netherlands and sales branches in 12 countries including France, Germany, and Russia. A research center and two plants have been established to bolster development and production.

In the United States, Yamanouchi USA is engaged in clinical development and study. In addition, the firm carried out capital participation (29%) in Roberts, Inc., a middle-level pharmaceutical maker in the United States in 1992.

In the health food sector, in 1989 Yamanouchi bought San Francisco–based Shaklee Corp., a major producer of preparation-enriched foods, with a significant market share and Shaklee Japan, its Japanese subsidiary.

To consolidate its presence in Asia, Yamanouchi established Korea Yamanouchi Pharmaceutical in Seoul, ROK, and Shenyang Yamanouchi Pharmaceutical in Shenyang, China, in 1994. A new plant is slated to start operation in Shenyang in March 1997. The consolidation of the company's foundation in fast-growing Asia is thus making steady progress.

Matsumoto explains: "Our present state is compared to the Step in the Hop, Step, Jump. Jump, the last stage, is crucial. In fact, the next coming few years would be critically important. The structuring of the company's own sales network must be expedited." Overseas production is assisted by the plants of Shacklee and Yamanouchi Europe, but the sales network cannot be established so speedily. "The preparation of a more powerful sales system is essential in order to survive competition with European and American pharmaceutical firms," Matsumoto said. The company's strategy on this point is highly significant.

WHY FIRMS GLOBALIZE

The technological advantage once enjoyed by the United States has declined dramatically during the past 30 years. In the late 1950s, over 80 percent of the world's major technological innovations were first introduced in the United States. By 1990, the figure had declined to less than 50 percent. In contrast, France is making impressive advances in electric traction, nuclear power, and aviation. Germany leads in chemicals and pharmaceuticals, precision and heavy machinery, heavy electrical goods, metallurgy, and surface transport equipment. Japan leads in optics, solid-state physics, engineering, chemistry, and process metallurgy. Eastern Europe and the former Soviet Union, the so-called COMECON (Council for Mutual Economic Assistance) countries, generate 30 percent of annual worldwide patent applications. However, the United States has regained some of its lost technological advantage. Through globalization, U.S. firms often can reap benefits from industries and technologies developed abroad. Even a relatively small service firm that possesses a distinct competitive advantage can capitalize on large overseas operations. Some global opportunities require some social reorientation of the host country. An extraordinary example is provided by the experiences of Wackenhut Corrections Corporation, as described in Global Strategy in Action 4–3.

FIGURE 4–1
Projected Economic Growth

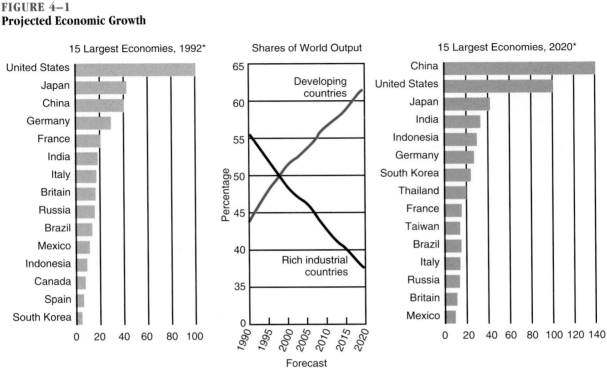

* United States = 100;
Other countries = percentage of U.S.'s GDP

Source: World Bank, *Global Economic Prospects and the Developing Countries,* 1998.

In many situations, global development makes sense as a competitive weapon. Direct penetration of foreign markets can drain vital cash flows from a foreign competitor's domestic operations. The resulting lost opportunities, reduced income, and limited production can impair the competitor's ability to invade U.S. markets. A case in point is IBM's move to establish a position of strength in the Japanese mainframe computer industry before two key competitors, Fiyitsue and Hitachi, could dominate it. Once IBM had achieved a substantial share of the Japanese market, it worked to deny its Japanese competitors the vital cash and production experience they needed to invade the U.S. market.

Firms that operate principally in the domestic environment have an important decision to make with regard to their globalization: Should they act before being forced to do so by competitive pressures or after? Should they: (1) be proactive by entering global markets in advance of other firms and thereby enjoy the first-mover advantages often accruing to risk-taker firms that introduce new products or services; or (2) be reactive by taking the more conservative approach and following other companies into global markets once customer demand has been proven and the high costs of new-product or -service introductions have been absorbed by competitors? Although the answers to these questions are determined by the specifics of the company and the context, the issues raised in Figure 4–2 are helpful to strategic decision makers faced with the dilemma.

GLOBAL STRATEGY IN ACTION 4–2

THE GLOBALIZATION OF PHILIP MORRIS'S KGFI

Outside of its core Western markets, Kraft General Foods International's (KGFI) food products have a growing presence in one of the most dynamic business environments in the world—the Asia-Pacific region. Its operations there are expanding rapidly, often aided by links with local manufacturers and distributors.

Japan and Korea, two of the world's fastest-growing economies in the last decade, are important examples. In both countries, local alliances can be crucial to market entry and success. Realizing this fact in the early 1970s, General Foods established joint ventures in both Japan and Korea. These joint ventures, combined with Kraft General Foods International's (KGFI) stand-alone operations, generate more than $1 billion in revenues. In the aggregate, their combined food operations in Japan and Korea are larger than many Fortune 500 companies.

Whereas soluble coffee accounts for just over 25 percent of the coffee consumed in U.S. homes, it fills over 70 percent of the cups consumed in the homes of convenience-minded Japan. Additionally, Japan is the origin of a unique form of packaged coffee—liquid—and a unique channel of distribution—vending machines. Japanese consumers have purchased packaged liquid coffee for years, and it amounts to a $5 billion category. Some 2 million vending machines dispense 9 billion cans of liquid coffee annually—an average of 75 cans per person.

Japan offers a culturally unique distribution channel for coffee products—the gift-set market. Many Japanese exchange specially packaged food or beverage assortments at least twice a year to commemorate holidays as well as special personal or business occasions. The gift-set business has helped Maxim products reinforce their quality image; it also will be a launching pad and support vehicle for Carte Noire coffees.

Outside the Ajinomoto General Foods joint venture, KGFI is developing a freestanding food business under the name Kraft Japan. It is building a cheese business with imported Philadelphia Brand cream cheese, the leading cream cheese in the Tokyo metropolitan market, as well as locally manufactured and licensed Kraft Milk Farm cheese slices. The cheese market is expected to grow approximately 5 percent per year. This is a rapid growth rate for a large food category. In addition to cheese, KGFI also imports Oscar Mayer prepared meats and Jocobs Suchard chocolates.

KGFI's joint venture in Korea, Doug Suh Foods Corporation, is one of the top 10 food companies in the country. Doug Suh manufactures coffees and cereals and has its own distribution network. One of Doug Suh's other businesses in Korea, Post Cereals, is also a strong number two, with a 42 percent category share.

Korea's $400 million coffee market is the fastest-growing major coffee market in the world, expanding at an average annual rate of 14 percent. Growing with the market, Maxim and Maxwell soluble coffees, in both traditional "agglomerate" and freeze-dried forms, account for more than 70 percent of the country's soluble coffee sales. The strength of these brands also brings the company a strong number one position in coffee mix, a mixture of soluble coffee, creamer, and sugar. In addition, its Frima brand leads the market in the nondairy creamer segment.

Beyond Australia, where it has a long-established, wholly owned business, and operations in Japan and Korea, KGFI is targeting many other countries for geographic expansion. In Indonesia, for instance, KGFI has established a rapidly growing cheese business through a licensee and introduced other KGFI products. In Taiwan, the joint venture company, PremierFoods Corporation, holds a 34 percent share of the soluble coffee market and is aggressively developing a Kraft cheese and Jocobs Suchard import business. KGF Philippines, a wholly owned subsidiary, has a leading position in the cheese and powdered soft-drink markets in its country. In the People's Republic of China, the company produces and markets Maxwell House coffees and Tang powdered soft drinks through two successful and rapidly growing joint ventures.

BusinessWeek

WACKENHUT GOES DIRECTLY TO JAIL

GLOBAL
STRATEGY IN
ACTION
4–3

When plans for a 600-bed minimum-security prison for Victoria, Australia, landed on the desk of George C. Zoley in the spring of 1996, the CEO of Palm Beach Gardens (Florida)-based Wackenhut Corrections Corp. wondered what his executives could be thinking. Included in Wackenhut's bid were three swimming pools, a meditation lake, and even a "town center" where inmates could shop and attend classes. Such amenities in a U.S. prison would be criticized as "coddling" offenders, and Zoley worried until his staff explained that they fit Victoria's progressive incarceration philosophy. Despite doubts, Zoley left them in the plan—and Wackenhut got the contract.

Such cultural sensitivity has helped turn what Zoley calls the exporting of "a sound low-tech business" into a moneymaker. It has also turned Wackenhut into a fast-moving up-and-comer in the private prison business. Second only to Corrections Corporation of America (CCA) in the U.S., Wackenhut is capitalizing on its international dominance and an expanded range of services to fuel breakout growth. A $62 million spin-off with scant earnings four years ago, analysts expect Wackenhut's revenues to climb 51%, to an estimated $208 million in 1997. Net income should rise 21%, to $11.7 million.

Even better, much of that growth has come at the expense of CCA. In July, Wackenhut beat out its bigger rival to win a $300 million, 10-year contract to run a federal prison in Taft, California—the first time the feds have turned a jail over to a private contractor. All told, with plans to add 11,000 prison beds in 1998—a 69% jump—analyst Brian W. Ruttenbur of Equitable Securities Corp. expects revenues to jump an additional 52%, to hit $317 million next year. Wackenhut also appears well-placed for a contract to be awarded in South Africa early next year, as well as planned contests in Jamaica and Canada. Boasts the hard-charging Zoley: "If we maintain our market share and growth rate, we will be a $1 billion company or more by 2004."

"GIGANTIC OPPORTUNITY"

Zoley has the tremendous overall growth in private prison contracts to thank for that. Beset by rising prison populations, governments are turning to private companies to build and operate their jails. Innovative facility design that uses fewer people and more technology to monitor inmates and lower labor costs have helped privatizers meet tough cost-savings goals.

Over the philosophical objections of unions and prisoner advocates, 25 states have privatized at least one prison. There's likely to be plenty more ahead: Today, private prisons house less than 3% of the 1.7 million U.S. prison population. But Charles W. Thomas, director of the Private Corrections Project at the Center for Studies in Criminology at the University of Florida, estimates average annual growth in private prisons of 25% over the next five years.

That has hardly gone unnoticed on Wall Street. Now trading at 28, Wackenhut's shares are up 32% this year. "There's a gigantic opportunity, and I expect both [CCA and Wackenhut] are going

Source: Gail DeGeorge in Miami, with Julia Flynn in London, "Wackenhut Goes Directly to Jail," *Business Week*, December 15, 1997.

Strategic Orientations of Global Firms

Multinational corporations typically display one of four orientations toward their overseas activities. They have a certain set of beliefs about how the management of foreign operations should be handled. A company with an *ethnocentric orientation* believes that the values and priorities of the parent organization should guide the strategic

continued

to flourish," says mutual-fund manager Ronald Baron, president of Baron Capital Management Inc. "It's not a bad thing to be second in an industry growing at this pace."

Indeed, Wackenhut is succeeding, in part, by being a smart follower. In the U.S. market, CCA took over the lead in 1994 by aggressively making acquisitions and providing capital to build prisons to cash-strapped inmates. It even built prisons on speculation, often to house out-of-state inmates. This year, CCA went even further, completing the first prison real estate investment trust and gaining $400 million to finance more building.

To catch up, Wackenhut is following suit—even as it goes its rival one further. Throughout the U.S., it's adding to the prisons it builds, finances, or owns, and it, too, is considering a prison REIT for 1998. But Zoley has also been quick to expand Wackenhut's skills into new areas of incarceration: In 1997, Wackenhut bought a Fort Lauderdale (Florida) psychiatric hospital, for example, and took on contracts to run a psychiatric prison in Mississippi and a juvenile maximum-security prison in Michigan. Unlike some rivals, Wackenhut will provide services a la carte for authorities who want to privatize only part of their prisons.

FOREIGN AFFAIRS

Moreover, Zoley's real ace is international. Although only one in 10 new private prison beds will come outside the U.S., Wackenhut dominates the lucrative overseas market. International now accounts for 20% of Wackenhut's revenues and 30% of its profits. Building on the reputation of parent and 55% owner Wackenhut Corp., which employs security guards in more than 50 countries, Wackenhut Corrections has succeeded abroad by building and running prisons and providing additional services such as prisoner transport and health services.

So far, the company has also successfully negotiated the risks of foreign markets. Hit by a rash of suicides in its Arthur Gorie (Australia) facility in its first 18 months and a year of violence in its Doncaster (England) prison, Wackenhut was forced to change its practices. It increased monitoring of high-risk inmates and guard training, and it has replaced American managers with local hires to help resolve cultural conflicts. The move has helped at Arthur Gorie, where outsiders say Wackenhut has become more sensitive to indigenous cultures. As it expands to less industrialized nations, business may be riskier, but that's a bet Zoley is willing to take to make Wackenhut itself a company worth following.

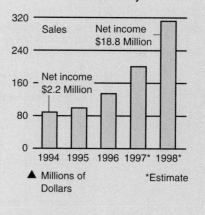

For Wackenhut, Crime Does Pay

Sales   Net income $18.8 Million

Net income $2.2 Million

1994 1995 1996 1997* 1998*

▲ Millions of Dollars   *Estimate

Data: Bloomberg Financial Markets, Equitable Securities Corp.

decision making of all its operations. If a corporation has a *polycentric orientation,* then the culture of the country in which a strategy is to be implemented is allowed to dominate the decision-making process. In contrast, a *regiocentric orientation* exists when the parent attempts to blend its own predispositions with those of the region under consideration, thereby arriving at a region-sensitive compromise. Finally, a corporation with a *geocentric orientation* adopts a global systems approach to strategic decision making, thereby emphasizing global integration.

FIGURE 4–2
Reasons for Going Global

	Proactive
Advantage/Opportunity	**Explanation of Action**
Additional resources	Various inputs—including natural resources, technologies, skilled personnel, and materials—may be obtained more readily outside the home country.
Lowered costs	Various costs—including labor, materials, transportation, and financing—may be lower outside the home country.
Incentives	Various incentives may be available from the host government or the home government to encourage foreign investment in specific locations.
New, expanded markets	New and different markets may be available outside the home country; excess resources—including management, skills, machinery, and money—can be utilized in foreign locations.
Exploitation of firm-specific advantages	Technologies, brands, and recognized names can all provide opportunities in foreign locations.
Taxes	Differing corporate tax rates and tax systems in different locations provide opportunities for companies to maximize their after-tax worldwide profits.
Economies of scale	National markets may be too small to support efficient production, while sales from several combined allow for larger-scale production.
Synergy	Operations in more than one national environment provide opportunities to combine benefits from one location with another, which is impossible without both of them.
Power and prestige	The image of being international may increase a company's power and prestige and improve its domestic sales and relations with various stakeholder groups.
Protect home market through offense in competitor's home	A strong offense in a competitor's market can put pressure on the competitor that results in a pull-back from foreign activities to protect itself at home.

	Reactive
Outside Occurrence	**Explanation of Reaction**
Trade barriers	Tariffs, quotas, buy-local policies, and other restrictive trade practices can make exports to foreign markets less attractive; local operations in foreign locations thus become attractive.
International customers	If a company's customer base becomes international, and the company wants to continue to serve it, then local operations in foreign locations may be necessary.
International competition	If a company's competitors become international, and the company wants to remain competitive, foreign operations may be necessary.
Regulations	Regulations and restrictions imposed by the home government may increase the cost of operating at home; it may be possible to avoid these costs by establishing foreign operations.
Chance	Chance occurrence results in a company deciding to enter foreign locations.

Source: Betty Jane Punnett and David A. Ricks, *International Business* (Boston: PWS-Kent, 1992), pp. 249–50.

Figure 4–3 shows the impacts of each of the four orientations on key activities of the firm. It is clear from the figure that the strategic orientation of a global firm plays a major role in determining the locus of control and corporate priorities of the firm's decision makers.

FIGURE 4–3
Orientation of a Global Firm

	Orientation of the Firm			
	Ethnocentric	**Polycentric**	**Regiocentric**	**Geocentric**
Mission	Profitability (viability)	Public acceptance (legitimacy)	Both profitability and public acceptance (viability and legitimacy)	Same as regiocentric
Governance	Top-down	Bottom-up (each subsidiary decides on local objectives)	Mutually negotiated between region and its subsidiaries	Mutually negotiated at all levels of the corporation
Strategy	Global integration	National responsiveness	Regional integration and national responsiveness	Global integration and national responsiveness
Structure	Hierarchical product divisions	Hierarchical area divisions, with autonomous national units	Product and regional organization tied through a matrix	A network of organizations (including some stakeholders and competitor organizations)
Culture	Home country	Host country	Regional	Global
Technology	Mass production	Batch production	Flexible manufacturing	Flexible manufacturing
Marketing	Product development determined primarily by the needs of home-country customers	Local product development based on local needs	Standardize within region, but not across regions	Global product, with local variations
Finance	Repatriation of profits to home country	Retention of profits in host country	Redistribution within region	Redistribution globally
Personnel practices	People of home country developed for key positions everywhere in the world	People of local nationality developed for key positions in their own country	Regional people developed for key positions anywhere in the region	Best people everywhere in the world developed for key positions everywhere in the world

Source: Adapted from Balaji S. Chakravarthy and Howard V. Perlmutter, "Strategic Planning for a Global Business," *Columbia Journal of World Business,* Summer 1985, pp. 5–6. Copyright 1985, Columbia Journal of World Business. Used with permission.

AT THE START OF GLOBALIZATION

To begin globalization, firms are advised to take four steps.[2]

Scan the Global Situation   Scanning includes reading journals and patent reports and checking other printed sources—as well as meeting people at scientific-technical conferences and in-house seminars.

Make Connections with Academia and Research Organizations   Firms active in overseas R&D often pursue work-related projects with foreign academics and sometimes enter into consulting agreements with them.

Increase the Firm's Global Visibility   Common methods that firms use to attract global attention include participating in trade fairs, circulating brochures on their products and inventions, and hiring technology acquisition consultants.

Undertake Cooperative Research Projects   Some firms engage in joint research projects with foreign firms to broaden their contacts, reduce expenses, diminish the risk for each partner, or forestall the entry of competitors into their markets.

[2]R. Rondstadt and R. Kramer, "Getting the Most out of Innovation Abroad," *Harvard Business Review,* March–April 1982, pp. 94–99.

In a similar vein, external and internal assessments may be conducted before a firm enters global markets. For example, Japanese investors conduct extensive assessments and analyses before selecting a U.S. site for a Japanese-owned firm. They prefer states with strong markets, low unionization rates, and low taxes. In addition, Japanese manufacturing plants prefer counties characterized by manufacturing conglomeration; low unemployment and poverty rates; and concentrations of educated, productive workers.

External assessment involves careful examination of critical features of the global environment, particular attention being paid to the status of the host nations in such areas as economic progress, political control, and nationalism. Expansion of industrial facilities, favorable balances of payments, and improvements in technological capabilities over the past decade are gauges of the host nation's economic progress. Political status can be gauged by the host nation's power in and impact on global affairs.

Internal assessment involves identification of the basic strengths of a firm's operations. These strengths are particularly important in global operations, because they are often the characteristics of a firm that the host nation values most and, thus, offer significant bargaining leverage. The firm's resource strengths and global capabilities must be analyzed. The resources that should be analyzed include, in particular, technical and managerial skills, capital, labor, and raw materials. The global capabilities that should be analyzed include the firm's product delivery and financial management systems.

A firm that gives serious consideration to internal and external assessment is Business International Corporation, which recommends that seven broad categories of factors be considered. As shown in Global Strategy in Action 4–4, these categories include economic, political, geographic, labor, tax, capital source, and business factors.

COMPLEXITY OF THE GLOBAL ENVIRONMENT

Global strategic planning is more complex than purely domestic planning. There are at least five factors that contribute to this increase in complexity:

1. Globals face multiple political, economic, legal, social, and cultural environments as well as various rates of changes within each of them.

2. Interactions between the national and foreign environments are complex, because of national sovereignty issues and widely differing economic and social conditions.

3. Geographic separation, cultural and national differences, and variations in business practices all tend to make communication and control efforts between headquarters and the overseas affiliates difficult.

4. Globals face extreme competition, because of differences in industry structures.

5. Globals are restricted in their selection of competitive strategies by various regional blocs and economic integrations, such as the European Economic Community, the European Free Trade Area, and the Latin American Free Trade Area. Indications of how these factors contribute to the increased complexity of global strategic management are provided in Figure 4–4.

CONTROL PROBLEMS OF THE GLOBAL FIRM

An inherent complicating factor for many global firms is that their financial policies typically are designed to further the goals of the parent company and pay minimal attention to the goals of the host countries. This built-in bias creates conflict between

GLOBAL STRATEGY IN ACTION

4-4

The following considerations were drawn from an 88-point checklist developed by Business International Corporation.

Economic factors:

1. Size of GNP and projected rate of growth.
2. Foreign exchange position.
3. Size of market for the firm's products; rate of growth.
4. Current or prospective membership in a customs union.

Political factors:

5. Form and stability of government.
6. Attitude toward private and foreign investment by government, customers, and competition.
7. Practice of favored versus neutral treatment for state industries.
8. Degree of antiforeign discrimination.

Geographic factors:

9. Efficiency of transport (railways, waterways, highways).
10. Proximity of site to export markets.
11. Availability of local raw materials.
12. Availability of power, water, gas.

Labor factors:

13. Availability of managerial, technical, and office personnel able to speak the language of the parent company.
14. Degree of skill and discipline at all levels.
15. Presence or absence of militant or Communist-dominated unions.
16. Degree and nature of labor voice in management.

Tax factors:

17. Tax-rate trends (corporate and personal income, capital, withholding, turnover, excise, payroll, capital gains, customs, and other indirect and local taxes).
18. Joint tax treaties with home country and others.
19. Duty and tax drawbacks when imported goods are exported.
20. Availability of tariff protection.

Capital source factors:

21. Cost of local borrowing.
22. Local availability of convertible currencies.
23. Modern banking systems.
24. Government credit aids to new businesses.

Business factors:

25. State of marketing and distribution system.
26. Normal profit margins in the firm's industry.
27. Competitive situation in the firm's industry: do cartels exist?
28. Availability of amenities for expatriate executives and their families.

FIGURE 4–4

Differences between Factors That Affect Strategic Management in the United States and Internationally

Factor	U.S. Operations	International Operations
Language	English used almost universally.	Use of local language required in many situations.
Culture	Relatively homogenous.	Quite diverse, both between countries and within countries.
Politics	Stable and relatively unimportant.	Often volatile and of decisive importance.
Economy	Relatively uniform.	Wide variations among countries and among regions within countries.
Government interference	Minimal and reasonably predictable.	Extensive and subject to rapid change.
Labor	Skilled labor available.	Skilled labor often scarce, requiring training or redesign of production methods.
Financing	Well-developed financial markets.	Poorly developed financial markets; capital flows subject to government control.
Media research	Data easy to collect.	Data difficult and expensive to collect.
Advertising	Many media available; few restrictions.	Media limited; many restrictions; low literacy rates rule out print media in some countries.
Money	U.S. dollar used universally.	Must change from one currency to another; problems created by changing exchange rates and government restrictions.
Transportation/ communication	Among the best in the world.	Often inadequate.
Control	Always a problem, but centralized control will work.	A worse problem—centralized control won't work; must walk a tightrope between overcentralizing and losing control through too much decentralizing.
Contracts	Once signed, are binding on both parties even if one party makes a bad deal.	Can be avoided and renegotiated if one party becomes dissatisfied.
Labor relations	Collective bargaining; layoff of workers easy.	Layoff of workers often not possible; may have mandatory worker participation in management; workers may seek change through political process rather than collective bargaining.

Source: Adapted from R. G. Murdick, R. C. Moor, R. H. Eckhouse, and T. W. Zimmerer, *Business Policy: A Framework for Analysis,* 4th ed. (Columbus, OH: Grid, 1984), p. 275.

the different parts of the global firm, between the whole firm and its home and host countries, and between the home country and host country themselves. The conflict is accentuated by the use of various schemes to shift earnings from one country to another in order to avoid taxes, minimize risk, or achieve other objectives.

Moreover, different financial environments make normal standards of company behavior concerning the disposition of earnings, sources of finance, and the structure of capital more problematic. Thus, it becomes increasingly difficult to measure the performance of international divisions.

In addition, important differences in measurement and control systems often exist. Fundamental to the concept of planning is a well-conceived, future-oriented approach to decision making that is based on accepted procedures and methods of analysis. Consistent approaches to planning throughout a firm are needed for effective review and evaluation by corporate headquarters. In the global firm, planning is complicated by differences in national attitudes toward work measurement, and by differences in government requirements about disclosure of information.

Although such problems are an aspect of the global environment, rather than a consequence of poor management, they are often most effectively reduced through increased attention to strategic planning. Such planning will aid in coordinating and integrating the firm's direction, objectives, and policies around the world. It enables the firm to anticipate and prepare for change. It facilitates the creation of programs to deal with worldwide development. Finally, it helps the management of overseas affiliates become more actively involved in setting goals and in developing means to more effectively utilize the firm's total resources.

An example of the need for coordination in global ventures and evidence that firms can successfully plan for global collaboration (e.g., through rationalized production) is the Ford Escort (Europe), the best-selling automobile in the world, which has a component manufacturing network that consists of plants in 15 countries.

GLOBAL STRATEGIC PLANNING

It should be evident from the previous sections that the strategic decisions of a firm competing in the global marketplace become increasingly complex. In such a firm, managers cannot view global operations as a set of independent decisions. These managers are faced with trade-off decisions in which multiple products, country environments, resource sourcing options, corporate and subsidiary capabilities, and strategic options must be considered.

A recent trend toward increased activism of stakeholders has added to the complexity of strategic planning for the global firm. *Stakeholder activism* refers to demands placed on the global firm by the foreign environments in which it operates, principally by foreign governments. This section provides a basic framework for the analysis of strategic decisions in this complex setting.

Multidomestic Industries and Global Industries

Michael E. Porter has developed a framework for analyzing the basic strategic alternatives of a firm that competes globally.[3] The starting point of the analysis is an understanding of the industry or industries in which the firm competes. International industries can be ranked along a continuum that ranges from multidomestic to global.

Multidomestic Industries

A multidomestic industry is one in which competition is essentially segmented from country to country. Thus, even if global corporations are in the industry, competition in one country is independent of competition in other countries. Examples of such industries include retailing, insurance, and consumer finance.

In a multidomestic industry, a global corporation's subsidiaries should be managed as distinct entities; that is, each subsidiary should be rather autonomous, having the authority to make independent decisions in response to local market conditions. Thus, the global strategy of such an industry is the sum of the strategies developed by subsidiaries operating in different countries. The primary difference between a domestic firm and a global firm competing in a multidomestic industry is that the latter

---

[3]Michael E. Porter, "Changing Patterns of International Competition," *California Management Review,* Winter 1986, pp. 9–40.

makes decisions related to the countries in which it competes and to how it conducts business abroad.

Factors that increase the degree to which an industry is multidomestic include:[4]

The need for customized products to meet the tastes or preferences of local customers.

Fragmentation of the industry, with many competitors in each national market.

A lack of economies of scale in the functional activities of firms in the industry.

Distribution channels unique to each country.

A low technological dependence of subsidiaries on R&D provided by the global firm.

Global Industries

A global industry is one in which competition crosses national borders. In fact, it occurs on a worldwide basis. In such an industry, a firm's strategic moves in one country can be significantly affected by its competitive position in another country. The very rapidly expanding list of global industries includes commercial aircraft, automobiles, mainframe computers, and electronic consumer equipment. Many authorities are convinced that almost all product-oriented industries soon will be global. As a result, strategic management planning must be global for at least six reasons:

1. *The increased scope of the global management task.* Growth in the size and complexity of global firms made management virtually impossible without a coordinated plan of action detailing what is expected of whom during a given period. The common practice of management by exception is impossible without such a plan.

2. *The increased globalization of firms.* Three aspects of global business make global planning necessary: (1) differences among the environmental forces in different countries, (2) greater distances, and (3) the interrelationships of global operations.

3. *The information explosion.* It has been estimated that the world's stock of knowledge is doubling every 10 years. Without the aid of a formal plan, executives can no longer know all that they must know to solve the complex problems they face. A global planning process provides an ordered means for assembling, analyzing, and distilling the information required for sound decisions.

4. *The increase in global competition.* Because of the rapid increase in global competition, firms must constantly adjust to changing conditions or lose markets to competitors. The increase in global competition also spurs managements to search for methods of increasing efficiency and economy.

5. *The rapid development of technology.* Rapid technological development has shortened product life cycles. Strategic management planning is necessary to ensure the replacement of products that are moving into the maturity stage, with fewer sales and declining profits. Planning gives management greater control of all aspects of new product introduction.

6. *Strategic management planning breeds managerial confidence.* Like the motorist with a road map, managers with a plan for reaching their objectives know where they are going. Such a plan breeds confidence, because it spells out every step along the way and assigns responsibility for every task. The plan simplifies the managerial job.

---

[4]Y. Doz and C. K. Prahalad, "Patterns of Strategic Control within Multinational Corporations," *Journal of International Business Studies,* Fall 1984, pp. 55–72.

A firm in a global industry must maximize its capabilities through a worldwide strategy. Such a strategy necessitates a high degree of centralized decision making in corporate headquarters so as to permit trade-off decisions across subsidiaries.

Among the factors that make for the creation of a global industry are:

Economies of scale in the functional activities of firms in the industry.

A high level of R&D expenditures on products that require more than one market to recover development costs.

The presence in the industry of predominantly global firms that expect consistency of products and services across markets.

The presence of homogeneous product needs across markets, which reduces the requirement of customizing the product for each market. The presence of a small group of global competitors.

A low level of trade regulation and of regulation regarding foreign direction investment.[5]

Six factors that drive the success of global companies are listed in Figure 4–5. They address key aspects of globalizing a business's operations and provide a framework within which companies can effectively pursue the global marketplace.

The Global Challenge

Although industries can be characterized as global or multidomestic, few "pure" cases of either type exist. A global firm competing in a global industry must be responsive, to some degree, to local market conditions. Similarly, a global firm competing in a multidomestic industry cannot totally ignore opportunities to utilize intracorporate resources in competitive positioning. Thus, each global firm must decide which of its corporate functional activities should be performed where and what degree of coordination should exist among them.

Location and Coordination of Functional Activities

Typical functional activities of a firm include purchases of input resources, operations, research and development, marketing and sales, and after-sales service. A multinational corporation has a wide range of possible location options for each of these activities and must decide which sets of activities will be performed in how many and which locations. A multinational corporation may have each location perform each activity, or it may center an activity in one location to serve the organization worldwide. For example, research and development centered in one facility may serve the entire organization.

A multinational corporation also must determine the degree to which functional activities are to be coordinated across locations. Such coordination can be extremely low, allowing each location to perform each activity autonomously, or extremely high, tightly linking the functional activities of different locations. Coca-Cola tightly links its R&D and marketing functions worldwide to offer a standardized brand name, concentrate formula, market positioning, and advertising theme. However, its operations function is more autonomous, with the artificial sweetener and packaging differing across locations.

---

[5]G. Harvel and C. K. Prahalad, "Managing Strategic Responsibility in the MNC," *Strategic Management Journal,* October–December 1983, pp. 341–51.

FIGURE 4–5
Factors That Drive Global Companies

1. **Global Management Team**
   Possesses global vision and culture.
   Includes foreign nationals.
   Leaves management of subsidiaries to foreign nationals.
   Frequently travels internationally.
   Has cross-cultural training.

2. **Global Strategy**
   Implement strategy as opposed to independent country strategies.
   Develop significant cross-country alliances.
   Select country targets strategically rather than opportunistically.
   Perform business functions where most efficient—no home-country bias.
   Emphasize participation in the triad—North America, Europe, and Japan.

3. **Global Operations and Products**
   Use common core operating processes worldwide to ensure quantity and uniformity.
   Product globally to obtain best cost and market advantage.

4. **Global Technology and R&D**
   Design global products but take regional differences into account.
   Manage development work centrally but carry out globally.
   Do not duplicate R&D and product development; gain economies of scale.

5. **Global Financing**
   Finance globally to obtain lowest cost.
   Hedge when necessary to protect currency risk.
   Price in local currencies.
   List shares on foreign exchanges.

6. **Global Marketing**
   Market global products but provide regional discretion if economies of scale are not affected.
   Develop global brands.
   Use core global marketing practices and themes.
   Simultaneously introduce new global products worldwide.

Source: Robert N. Lussier, Robert W. Baeder, and Joel Corman, "Measuring Global Practices: Global Strategic Planning through Company Situational Analysis," p. 57. Reprinted from *Business Horizons,* September–October 1994. Copyright 1994 by the Foundation for the School of Business at Indiana University. Used with permission.

Location and Coordination Issues

Figure 4–6 presents some of the issues related to the critical dimensions of location and coordination in multinational strategic planning. It also shows the functional activities that the firm performs with regard to each of these dimensions. For example, in connection with the service function, a firm must decide where to perform after-sale service and whether to standardize such service.

How a particular firm should address location and coordination issues depends on the nature of its industry and on the type of international strategy that the firm is pursuing. As discussed earlier, an industry can be ranked along a continuum that ranges between multidomestic at one extreme and global at the other. Little coordination of functional activities across countries may be necessary in a multidomestic industry, since competition occurs within each country in such an industry. However, as its industry becomes increasingly global, a firm must begin to coordinate an increasing number of functional activities to effectively compete across countries.

Going global impacts every aspect of a company's operations and structure. As firms redefine themselves as global competitors, work forces are becoming increasingly diversified. The most significant challenge for firms, therefore, is the ability to

FIGURE 4–6
Location and Coordination Issues of Functional Activities

Functional Activity	Location Issues	Coordination Issues
Operations	Location of production facilities for components.	Networking of international plants.
Marketing	Product line selection. Country (market) selection.	Commonality of brand name worldwide. Coordination of sales to multinational accounts. Similarity of channels and product positioning worldwide. Coordination of pricing in different countries.
Service	Location of service organization.	Similarity of service standards and procedures worldwide.
Research and development	Number and location of R&D centers.	Interchange among dispersed R&D centers. Developing products responsive to market needs in many countries. Sequence of product introductions around the world.
Purchasing	Location of the purchasing function.	Managing suppliers located in different countries. Transferring market knowledge. Coordinating purchases of common items.

Source: Adapted from Michael E. Porter, "Changing Patterns of International Competition," *California Management Review,* Winter 1986, p. 18.

adjust to a work force of varied cultures and lifestyles and the capacity to incorporate cultural differences to the benefit of the company's mission. Global Strategy in Action 4–5 illustrates Colgate-Palmolive's effort to become a truly global consumer products company, a vision that has impacted virtually every company function, including human resources.

Market Requirements and Product Characteristics

Businesses have discovered that being successful in foreign markets often demands much more than simply shipping their well-received domestic products overseas. Firms must assess two key dimensions of customer demand: customers' acceptance of standardized products and the rate of product innovation desired. As shown in the top figure of Global Strategy in Action 4–6, all markets can be arrayed along a continuum from markets in which products are standardized to markets in which products must be customized for customers from market to market. Standardized products in all markets include color film and petrochemicals, while dolls and toilets are good examples of customized products.

Similarly, products can be arrayed along a continuum from products that are not subject to frequent product innovations to products that are often upgraded. Products with a fast rate of change include computer chips and industrial machinery, while steel and chocolate bars are products that fit in the slow rate of change category.

The bottom figure of Global Strategy in Action 4–6 shows that the two dimensions can be combined to enable companies to simultaneously assess both customer need for

GLOBAL STRATEGY IN ACTION 4–5

Colgate Aligns HR with Its Global Vision

New York City–based Colgate-Palmolive Co. has a clear vision for its future: To become the best truly global consumer products company. This statement is telling. The few carefully chosen words demonstrate the commitment of this $7 billion firm to being more than a U.S.–based company that does business overseas. In the words of CEO Reuben Mark, taken from the company's 1992 annual report: "virtually every aspect of Colgate's business—from how we organize our operations to how we view new product development to how and where we manufacture—reflects our global orientation."

This global mindedness isn't a reaction to recent trends either. The company, which manages such internationally recognized brand-name products as Ajax, Fab, and Soft Soap, has been in 20 countries for more than 50 years, and in more than 50 countries for at least a decade. As far back as 30 years ago, Colgate created a global marketing training program to generate an international cadre of management.

Today, with operations in 75 countries and product distribution in at least 100 more, the company generates 64 percent of sales and 59 percent of operating profits overseas (Canada is included with the United States). As a consequence, two-thirds of the firm's employees now work outside of North America, providing strategic challenges for Colgate's human resources (HR) staff. More than ever before, they must ensure that the company attracts and retains *globalites*— those with the skills and interest to pursue international careers. And they must create systems for the fluid movement of workers across borders.

In 1991, HR met these challenges head on. Following an initiative by Mark to refocus the company's energies into five key business areas, the company formed a global human resources strategy team to better align HR with the business needs. The team was composed of senior line managers and senior HR leaders. "The objective of our global human resources strategy team was to work in partnership with management to build organizational excellence," says Brian Smith, director of global staffing and strategy. "We define organizational excellence here as the continuous alignment of Colgate people and business processes with vision, values, and strategies to become the best."

The year-long development process yielded: a set of international values that emphasize care for Colgate people, consumers, shareholders, and business partners; an order for all employees to work as part of a global team; and a commitment to continuous improvement. The team also developed strategic initiatives for generating, reinforcing, and sustaining organizational excellence. These initiatives' central feature was the development of recruitment, training, compensation, and recognition systems that reinforce the technical, managerial, and leadership competencies needed to support the global business.

The global human resources strategic team's work was unveiled at a week-long global HR conference in 1992. The conference was attended by the chairman, the president, the chief operating officer, each division's president, and more than 200 of Colgate's HR leaders representing 35 countries. Smith says that the senior leadership's commitment to this project was extraordinary, demonstrating HR's role as a key player in the company's global outlook.

Source: "Colgate Aligns HR with Its Global Vision," by Dawn Anfuso, copyright January 1995. Reprinted with the permission of *Personnel Journal*, ACC Communications Inc. (formerly known as ACC Croft, Inc.), Costa Mesa, CA, all rights reserved.

product standardization and rate of product innovation. The examples listed demonstrate the usefulness of the model in helping firms to determine the degree of customization that they must be willing to accept to become engaged in transnational operations.

GLOBAL STRATEGY IN ACTION 4–6

MARKET REQUIREMENTS AND PRODUCT CHARACTERISTICS

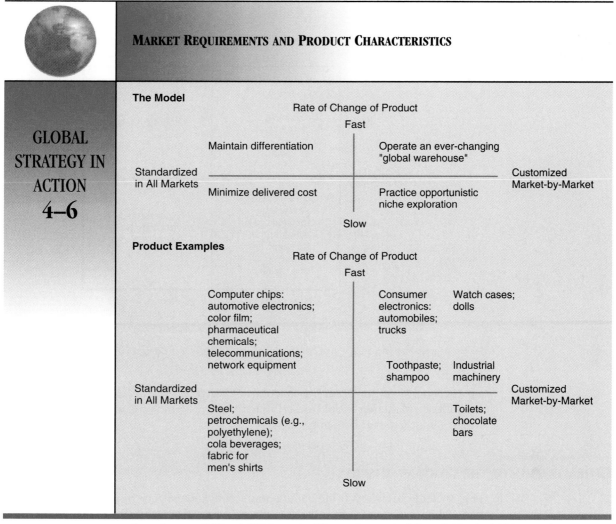

The Model

Rate of Change of Product

Fast

Maintain differentiation   Operate an ever-changing "global warehouse"

Standardized in All Markets   Customized Market-by-Market

Minimize delivered cost   Practice opportunistic niche exploration

Slow

Product Examples

Rate of Change of Product

Fast

Computer chips: automotive electronics; color film; pharmaceutical chemicals; telecommunications; network equipment

Consumer electronics: automobiles; trucks

Watch cases; dolls

Toothpaste; shampoo

Industrial machinery

Standardized in All Markets   Customized Market-by-Market

Steel; petrochemicals (e.g., polyethylene); cola beverages; fabric for men's shirts

Toilets; chocolate bars

Slow

Source: Lawrence H. Wortzel, *1989 International Business Resource Book* (Strategic Direction Publishers, 1989).

International Strategy Options

Figure 4–7 presents the basic multinational strategy options that have been derived from a consideration of the location and coordination dimensions. Low coordination and geographic dispersion of functional activities are implied if a firm is operating in a multidomestic industry and has chosen a country-centered strategy. This allows each subsidiary to closely monitor the local market conditions it faces and to respond freely to these conditions.

High coordination and geographic concentration of functional activities result from the choice of a pure global strategy. Although some functional activities, such as after-sale service, may need to be located in each market, tight control of those activities is necessary to ensure standardized performance worldwide. For example, IBM expects the same high level of marketing support and service for all of its customers, regardless of their location.

Two other strategy options are shown in Figure 4–7. High foreign investment with extensive coordination among subsidiaries would describe the choice of remaining at

FIGURE 4–7
International Strategy Options

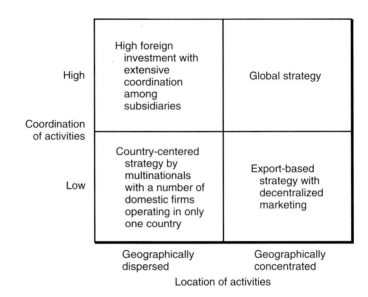

Source: Adapted from Michael E. Porter, "Changing Patterns of International Competition," *California Management Review,* Winter 1986, p. 19.

a particular growth stage, such as that of an exporter. An export-based strategy with decentralized marketing would describe the choice of moving toward globalization, which a multinational firm might make.

GLOBALIZATION OF THE COMPANY MISSION

Few strategic decisions bring about a more radical departure from the existing direction and operations of a firm than the decision to expand globally. Globalization subjects a firm to a radically different set of environmentally determined opportunities, constraints, and risks. To prevent these external factors from dictating the firm's direction, top management must reassess the firm's fundamental purpose, philosophy, and strategic intentions before globalization to ensure their continuation as decision criteria in proactive planning.

Expanding across national borders to secure new market or production opportunities initially may be viewed as consistent with the growth objectives outlined in a firm's existing mission statement. However, a firm's direction inherently is altered as globalization occurs. For example, as a firm expands overseas, its operations are physically relocated in foreign operating environments. Since strategic decisions are made in the context of some understanding of the environment, management will absorb information from new sources into its planning processes as the environment becomes pluralistic, with a revised corporate direction as a probable and desirable result. Thus, before reconsidering the firm's strategic choices, management must reassess its mission and institute the required changes as the appropriate environmental information is defined, collected, analyzed, and integrated into existing databases.

Management also must provide a mission that continues to serve as a basis for evaluating strategic alternatives as this information is incorporated into the firm's decision-making processes. Consider the financial component of Zale Corporation's mission statement from this standpoint:

> Our ultimate responsibility is to our shareholders. Our goal is to earn an optimum return on invested capital through steady profit growth and prudent, aggressive asset management. The attainment of this financial goal, coupled with a record of sound management, represents our approach toward influencing the value placed on our common stock in the market.

From a U.S. perspective, this component seems quite reasonable. In a global context, however, it could be unacceptable. Corporate financial goals vary in different countries. The clear preference of French, Japanese, and Dutch executives has been to maximize growth in after-tax earnings, and that of Norwegian executives has been to maximize earnings before interest and taxes. In contrast, these executives have assigned a low priority to the maximization of stockholder wealth. Thus, from a global perspective, a mission statement specifying that a firm's ultimate responsibility is to its stockholders may be an inappropriate basis for its financial operating philosophy. This example illustrates the critical need to review and revise the mission statement prior to global expansion so it will maintain its relevance in the new situations confronting the firm.

Components of the Company Mission Revisited

The mission statement must be revised to accommodate the changes in strategic decision making, corporate direction, and strategic alternatives mandated by globalization and must encompass the additional strategic capabilities that will result from globalizing operations. Therefore, each of its basic components needs to be analyzed in light of specific considerations that accompany globalization.

Product or Service, Market, and Technology

The mission statement defines the basic market need that the firm aims to satisfy. This definition is likely to remain essentially intact in the global corporation context, since competencies acquired in the firm's home country can be exploited as competitive advantages when they are transferred to other countries. However, confronted with a multiplicity of contexts, the firm must redefine its primary market to some extent.

The firm could define its market as global, which would necessitate standardization in product and company responses, or it could pursue a "market concept" orientation by focusing on the particular demands of each national market. The mission statement must provide a basis for strategic decision making in this trade-off situation. For example, the directive in Hewlett-Packard's mission statement, "HP customers must feel that they are dealing with one company with common policies and services," implies a standardized approach designed to provide comparable service to all customers. In contrast, Holiday Inn's mission statement reflects the marketing concept: "Basic to almost everything Holiday Inn, Inc., does is its interaction with its market, the consumer, and its consistent capacity to provide what the consumer wants, when, and where it is needed."

Company Goals: Survival, Growth, and Profitability

The mission statement specifies the firm's intention of securing its future through growth and profitability. In the United States, growth and profitability are considered essential to corporate survival. These goals also are acceptable in other countries supportive of the free enterprise system. Following global expansion, however, the firm may operate in countries that are not unequivocally committed to the profit motive. Many countries are committed to state ownership of industries that they view as critical to domestic prosperity. Austria, France, India, Italy, and Mexico are all good examples. A host country may view social welfare and development goals as taking precedence over the goals of free market capitalism. In developing countries, for example, employment and income distribution goals often take precedence over rapid economic growth.

Moreover, even countries that accept the profit motive may oppose the profit goals of global corporations. In such countries, the flow of global corporation profits often is viewed as unidirectional. At the extreme, the global is seen as a tool for exploiting the host country for the exclusive benefit of the parent company's home country, and its profits are regarded as evidence of corporate atrocities. This means that in a global context, a corporate commitment to profits may increase the risk of failure, rather than help secure survival.

Therefore, the mission statement of a global corporation must reflect the firm's intention of securing its survival through dimensions that extend beyond growth and profitability. A global corporation must develop a corporate philosophy that embodies its belief in a bidirectional flow of benefits among the firm and its multiple environments. The mission statement of Gulf & Western Americas Corporation expresses this view deftly: "We believe that in a developing country, revenue is inseparable from mandatory social responsibility and that a company is an integral part of the local and national community in which its activities are based." This statement maintains a commitment to profitability yet acknowledges the firm's responsibility to the host country.

The growth dimension of the mission statement remains closely tied to survival and profitability even in the global corporation context. Globalization disperses corporate resources and operations. This implies that strategic decision makers are no longer located exclusively at corporate headquarters, and that they are less accessible for participation in collective decision-making processes. To maintain the firm's cohesiveness in these circumstances, some mechanism is required to record its commitment to a unifying purpose. The mission statement can provide such a mechanism. It can provide the global corporation's decision makers with a common guiding thread of understanding and purpose.

Following the development of the mission statement, the firm's strategic managers will develop a set of time-specific performance objectives to guide the operations of the firm. Most of these objectives will be developed for the broad areas just discussed, namely products, services, markets, technologies, profitability, survival, and growth. Figure 4–8 lists five of the areas where objectives are commonly developed and indicates how globalization of a company alters their content.

Company Philosophy

Within the domestic setting, implicit understandings result in a general uniformity of corporate values and behavior even if a firm's philosophy goes unstated. Few domestic events challenge a firm to properly formulate and implement its implied or expressed philosophy. Globalization, however, is clearly such an event. A corporate philosophy developed from a singular perspective is inadequate for a firm that functions in variant cultures. A firm's values and beliefs are primarily culturally defined, reflecting the general philosophical perspective of the society in which the firm operates. Thus, when a firm extends its operations into another society, it encounters a new

FIGURE 4–8
Areas for Global Firm Objectives

Profitability

Level of profits

Return on assets, investment, equity, sales

Yearly profit growth

Yearly earnings per share growth

Marketing

Total sales volume

Market share—worldwide, region, country

Growth in sales volume

Growth in market share

Integration of country markets for marketing efficiency and effectiveness

Production

Ratio of foreign to domestic production volume

Economics of scale via international production integration

Quality and cost control

Introduction of cost-efficient production methods

Finance

Financing of foreign affiliates—retained earnings or local borrowing

Taxation—minimizing tax burden globally

Optimum capital structure

Foreign exchange management—minimizing losses from foreign fluctuations

Personnel/Human Resources

Development of managers with global orientation

Management development of host-country nationals

Source: Adapted from information found in Arvind V. Phatak, *International Dimensions of Management,* 2nd ed. (Boston: PWS-Kent Publishing, 1989), p. 72.

set of accepted corporate values and beliefs, which it must assimilate and incorporate into its own.

Self-Concept

The globalized self-concept of a firm is dependent on management's understanding of the firm's strengths and weaknesses as a competitor in each of its operating arenas. The firm's ability to survive in multiple dynamic and highly competitive environments is severely limited if its management does not understand the impact it has or can have on those environments, and vice versa.

Public Image

Domestically, a firm's public image often is shaped from a marketing viewpoint. That image is managed as a marketing tool whose objective is customer acceptance of the firm's product. Although this consideration remains critical in the global environment, in that environment it must be balanced with consideration of other organizational claimants than the customer. In many countries, the global corporation is a major user

FIGURE 4–9
International Strategy Options

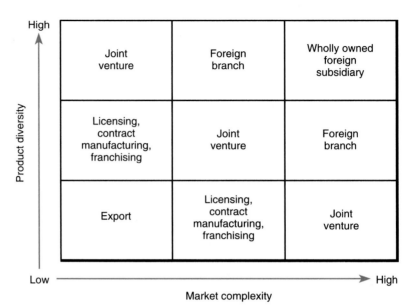

COMPETITIVE STRATEGIES FOR FIRMS IN FOREIGN MARKETS

of national resources and a major force in socialization processes. Thus, it must broaden its image so as to clearly convey its recognition of the additional internal and external claimants resulting from globalization. The following excerpt from Hewlett-Packard's mission statement exemplifies such an image: "As a corporation operating in many different communities throughout the world, we must assure ourselves that each of these communities is better for our presence . . . Each community has its particular set of social problems. Our company must help to solve these problems." These words convey an image of Hewlett-Packard's responsiveness to claimants throughout the world.

COMPETITIVE STRATEGIES FOR FIRMS IN FOREIGN MARKETS

Strategies for firms that are attempting to move toward globalization can be categorized by the degree of complexity of each foreign market being considered and by the diversity in a company's product line (see Figure 4–9). *Complexity* refers to the number of critical success factors that are required to prosper in a given competitive arena. When a firm must consider many such factors, the requirements of success increase in complexity. *Diversity,* the second variable, refers to the breadth of a firm's business lines. When a company offers many product lines, diversity is high.

Together, the complexity and diversity dimensions form a continuum of possible strategic choices. Combining these two dimensions highlights many possible actions.

Niche Market Exporting

The primary niche market approach for the company that wants to export is to modify select product performance or measurement characteristics to meet special foreign demands. Combining product criteria from both the U.S. and the foreign markets can be slow and tedious. There are, however, a number of expansion techniques that provide the U.S. firm with the know-how to exploit opportunities in the new environment. For example, copying product innovations in countries where patent protection is not emphasized and utilizing nonequity contractual arrangements with a foreign partner can assist in rapid product innovation. N. V. Philips and various Japanese competitors, such as Sony and Matsushita, now are working together for common global product standards within their markets. Siemens, with a centralized R&D in electronics, also has been very successful with this approach.

Exporting usually requires minimal capital investment. The organization maintains its quality control standards over production processes and finished goods inventory, and risk to the survival of the firm is typically minimal. Additionally, the U.S. Commerce Department through its Export Now Program and related government agencies lowers the risks to smaller companies by providing export information and marketing advice.

Licensing/Contract Manufacturing

Establishing a contractual arrangement is the next step for U.S. companies that want to venture beyond exporting but are not ready for an equity position on foreign soil. Licensing involves the transfer of some industrial property right from the U.S. licensor to a motivated licensee. Most tend to be patents, trademarks, or technical know-how that are granted to the licensee for a specified time in return for a royalty and for avoiding tariffs or import quotas. Bell South and U.S. West, with various marketing and service competitive advantages valuable to Europe, have extended a number of licenses to create personal computer networks in the United Kingdom.

Another licensing strategy open to U.S. firms is to contract the manufacturing of its product line to a foreign company to exploit local comparative advantages in technology, materials, or labor.

U.S. firms that use either licensing option will benefit from lowering the risk of entry into the foreign markets. Clearly, alliances of this type are not for everyone. They are used best in companies large enough to have a combination of international strategic activities and for firms with standardized products in narrow margin industries.

Two major problems exist with licensing. One is the possibility that the foreign partner will gain the experience and evolve into a major competitor after the contract expires. The experience of some U.S. electronics firms with Japanese companies shows that licensees gain the potential to become powerful rivals. The other potential problem stems from the control that the licensor forfeits on production, marketing, and general distribution of its products. This loss of control minimizes a company's degrees of freedom as it reevaluates its future options.

Franchising

A special form of licensing is franchising, which allows the franchisee to sell a highly publicized product or service, using the parent's brand name or trademark, carefully developed procedures, and marketing strategies. In exchange, the franchisee pays a fee to the parent company, typically based on the volume of sales of the franchisor in its defined market area. The franchise is operated by the local investor who must adhere to the strict policies of the parent.

Franchising is so popular that an estimated 500 U.S. businesses now franchise to over 50,000 local owners in foreign countries. Among the most active franchisees are

IS BRAZIL ANTITRUST—OR ANTI-FOREIGNER?

GLOBAL STRATEGY IN ACTION 4–7

Eager to get a foothold in Brazil's thirsty beer market, Miller Brewing Co. set up a joint venture with Cervejaria Brahma, the country's biggest brewer, in September, 1995, to produce and market Miller's Genuine Draft brand. Miller Chief Executive Jack MacDonough saw the country of 160 million as a springboard for expansion throughout South America. Brazil is "at the top of our list of opportunities," he said.

That strategy just went sour. In mid-June, Brazil's Administrative Council of Economic Defense (CADE), the country's antitrust watchdog agency, ordered Miller and Brahma, the world's no. 3 and no. 5 brewers, respectively, to disband their joint venture within two years. The enterprise could hurt competition, according to CADE members, who argued that Miller could produce beer in Brazil without Brahma's help. A few days later, CADE indicated that it would likely break up a rival partnership between Anheuser-Busch Cos., the world's biggest brewer, and Antarctica, Brazil's no. 2.

MIXED MESSAGE

CADE's beer verdicts, together with market restrictions it imposed earlier on Kolynos, a South American toothpaste producer bought by Colgate-Palmolive Co., are raising questions about Brazil's openness to investment from abroad. Privately, officials of President Fernando Henrique Cardoso's government have criticized the rulings, which are at odds with Cardoso's encouragement of foreign direct investment. This year, such investments have been flooding in at a $14 billion annual rate, economists say, up from $9 billion in 1996. Now, "people might refrain from joint ventures in other sectors," warns Nelio Weiss, a partner at accountants Coopers & Lybrand in Sao Paulo.

The Miller-Brahma ruling in particular has puzzled Brazil's business community. Unlike many Latin American countries where one beer company dominates, Brazil has three strong competitors: Brahma, with 47% of the market, Antarctica, with 26%, and Kaiser, no. 3 with 17%. No foreign brewer, analysts believe, could penetrate the vast Brazilian market without the help of a

Source: Ian Katz in Sao Paulo, with Richard A. Melcher in Chicago, "Is Brazil Antitrust or Anti-Foreigner?" *Business Week,* international ed.: July 21, 1997.

Avis, Burger King, Canada Dry, Coca-Cola, Hilton, Kentucky Fried Chicken, Manpower, Marriott, Midas, Muzak, Pepsi, and Service Master. However, the acknowledged global champion of franchising is McDonald's, which has 70 percent of its company-owned stores as franchisees in foreign nations.

Joint Ventures

As the multinational strategies of U.S. firms mature, most will include some form of joint venture (JV) with a target nation firm. AT&T followed this option in its strategy to produce its own personal computer by entering into several joint ventures with European producers to acquire the required technology and position itself for European expansion. Because JVs begin with a mutually agreeable pooling of capital, production or marketing equipment, patents, trademarks, or management expertise, they offer more permanent cooperative relationships than export or contract manufacturing.

BusinessWeek

continued

local partner. So far, Miller Genuine Draft has captured just a 0.2% share of the market, although it is a top seller in the premium-beer niche.

In the case of Colgate, which bought Kolynos for $1 billion in 1995, CADE ordered the company to take the high-profile Kolynos brand off Brazilian store shelves for four years. CADE expressed concern because Colgate, with its purchase of Kolynos from American Home Products Corp., raised its Brazilian market share to 78%, up from 22%.

Some critics accuse CADE of picking on foreigners. Council President Gesner Oliveira, a dissenter in the Miller-Brahma vote, said he saw "signs of xenophobia" among CADE's seven members. While some Brazilian sectors, from cement to broadcast TV, have long been dominated by a few players, beer "is one industry where there is competition," says Corrado Varoli, co-head of Latin American mergers for Morgan Stanley Dean Witter in New York.

CADE, long a do-nothing agency, was given greater independence in 1994 to safeguard competition in Brazil's newly opened economy. Now, business executives complain that it is attempting to impose an industrial policy. CADE argued that Miller could have opened its own brewery or used the distribution channels in Brazil of its parent company, Philip Morris Cos., instead of allying with Brahma—a quicker and cheaper route. The Miller-Brahma joint venture called for spending just $50 million on marketing over five years.

CADE defenders contend that the agency is not just targeting foreigners. It is expected to order Brazilian mining giant Vale do Rio Doce (CVRD), which was privatized in May, to sell its 7.7% stake in steel company Usiminas. That's because privatization left CVRD and its biggest corporate shareholder, steelmaker Siderurgica Nacional (CSN), in direct or indirect control of 80% of the nation's steel industry.

Miller and Brahma plan to appeal CADE's verdict, as does Anheuser-Busch. In addition to its joint venture to produce Budweiser beer, Anheuser bought a 5% stake in Antarctica with an option to purchase up to 30%. The hitch is that the appeals go back to CADE, so overturning the decisions will be difficult. In May, 1998, Cardoso will have the chance to replace five of CADE's seven members when their terms expire. Until then, foreign investors may have to beware of Brazilian antitrusters' sharp bite.

Compared to full ownership of the foreign entity, JVs provide a variety of benefits to each partner. U.S. firms without the managerial or financial assets to make a profitable independent impact on the integrated foreign markets can share management tasks and cash requirements often at exchange rates that favor the dollar. The coordination of manufacturing and marketing allows ready access to new markets, intelligence data, and reciprocal flows of technical information.

For example, Siemens, the German electronics firm, has a wide range of strategic alliances throughout Europe to share technology and research developments. For years, Siemens grew by acquisitions, but now, to support its horizontal expansion objectives, it is engaged in joint ventures with companies like Groupe Bull of France, International Computers of Britain, General Electric Company of Britain, IBM, Intel, Philips, and Rolm. Another example is Airbus Industries, which produces wide-body passenger planes for the world market as a direct result of JVs among many companies in Britain, France, Spain, and Germany.

Not all JVs produce such attractive results, however. Global Strategy in Action 4–7 describes the unpleasant experiences of Miller Brewing Company in Brazil.

JVs speed up the efforts of U.S. firms to integrate into the political, corporate, and cultural infrastructure of the foreign environment, often with a lower financial commitment than acquiring a foreign subsidiary. General Electric's (GE) 3 percent share in the European lighting market was very weak and below expectations. Significant increases in competition throughout many of their American markets by the European giant, Philips Lighting, forced GE to retaliate by expanding in Europe. GE's first strategy was an attempted joint venture with the Siemens lighting subsidiary, Osram, and with the British electronics firm, Thorn EMI. Negotiations failed over control issues. When recent events in Eastern Europe opened the opportunity for a JV with the Hungarian lighting manufacturer, Tungsram, which was receiving 70 percent of revenues from the West, GE capitalized on it.

Although joint ventures can address many of the requirements of complex markets and diverse product lines, U.S. firms considering either equity- or nonequity-based JVs face many challenges. For example, making full use of the native firm's comparative advantage may involve managerial relationships where no single authority exists to make strategic decisions or solve conflicts. Additionally, dealing with host-company management requires the disclosure of proprietary information and the potential loss of control over production and marketing quality standards. Addressing such challenges with well-defined covenants agreeable to all parties is difficult. Equally important is the compatibility of partners and their enduring commitments to mutually supportive goals. Without this compatibility and commitment, a joint venture is critically endangered.

Figure 4–10 provides an overview and summary of the benefits of an international joint venture. It shows that the ownership, location, and internalization advantages of international joint ventures promote technological innovation, the convergence of technologies, and globalization.

Foreign Branching

A foreign branch is an extension of the company in its foreign market—a separately located strategic business unit directly responsible for fulfilling the operational duties assigned to it by corporate management, including sales, customer service, and physical distribution. Host countries may require that the branch be "domesticated"; that is, have some local managers in middle and upper-level positions. The branch most likely will be outside any U.S. legal jurisdiction, liabilities may not be restricted to the assets of the given branch, and business licenses for operations may be of short duration, requiring the company to renew them during changing business regulations.

Wholly Owned Subsidiaries

Wholly owned foreign subsidiaries are considered by companies that are willing and able to make the highest investment commitment to the foreign market. These companies insist on full ownership for reasons of control and managerial efficiency. Policy decisions about local product lines, expansion, profits, and dividends typically remain with the U.S. senior managers.

Fully owned subsidiaries can be started either from scratch or by acquiring established firms in the host country. U.S. firms can benefit significantly if the acquired company has complementary product lines or an established distribution or service network.

FIGURE 4–10
Benefits of International Joint Ventures

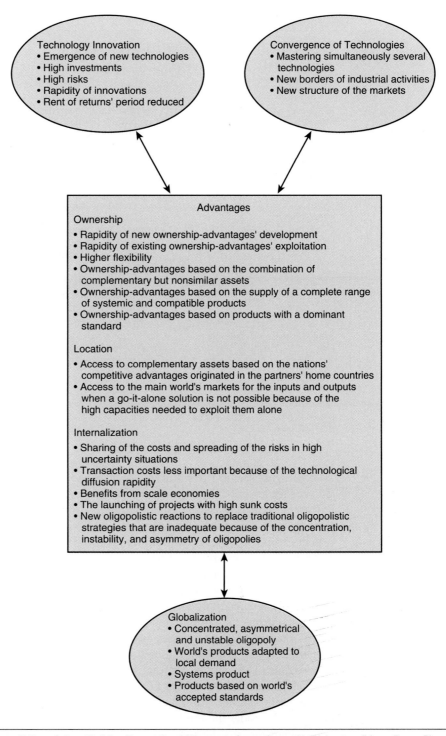

Technology Innovation
• Emergence of new technologies
• High investments
• High risks
• Rapidity of innovations
• Rent of returns' period reduced

Convergence of Technologies
• Mastering simultaneously several technologies
• New borders of industrial activities
• New structure of the markets

Advantages

Ownership

• Rapidity of new ownership-advantages' development
• Rapidity of existing ownership-advantages' exploitation
• Higher flexibility
• Ownership-advantages based on the combination of complementary but nonsimilar assets
• Ownership-advantages based on the supply of a complete range of systemic and compatible products
• Ownership-advantages based on products with a dominant standard

Location

• Access to complementary assets based on the nations' competitive advantages originated in the partners' home countries
• Access to the main world's markets for the inputs and outputs when a go-it-alone solution is not possible because of the high capacities needed to exploit them alone

Internalization

• Sharing of the costs and spreading of the risks in high uncertainty situations
• Transaction costs less important because of the technological diffusion rapidity
• Benefits from scale economies
• The launching of projects with high sunk costs
• New oligopolistic reactions to replace traditional oligopolistic strategies that are inadequate because of the concentration, instability, and asymmetry of oligopolies

Globalization
• Concentrated, asymmetrical and unstable oligopoly
• World's products adapted to local demand
• Systems product
• Products based on world's accepted standards

Source: Philippe Gulger, "Building Transnational Alliances to Create Competitive Advantage," *Long Range Planning* 25, no. 1 (1992), p. 92. Copyright 1992, with permission from Pergamon Press Ltd., Headington Hill Hall, Oxford OX3 OBW, U.K.

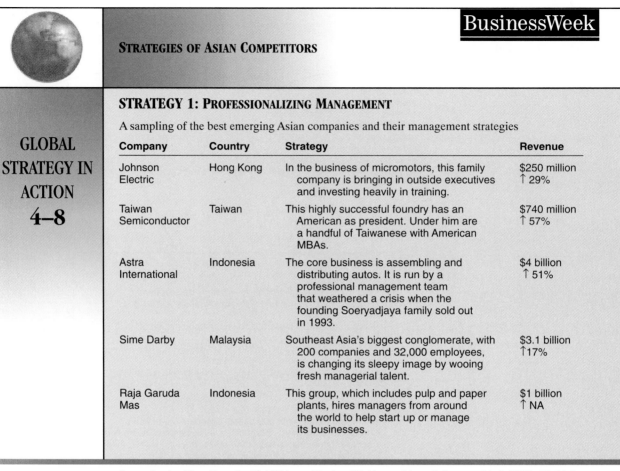

STRATEGIES OF ASIAN COMPETITORS

GLOBAL
STRATEGY IN
ACTION
4–8

STRATEGY 1: PROFESSIONALIZING MANAGEMENT

A sampling of the best emerging Asian companies and their management strategies

Company	Country	Strategy	Revenue
Johnson Electric	Hong Kong	In the business of micromotors, this family company is bringing in outside executives and investing heavily in training.	$250 million ↑ 29%
Taiwan Semiconductor	Taiwan	This highly successful foundry has an American as president. Under him are a handful of Taiwanese with American MBAs.	$740 million ↑ 57%
Astra International	Indonesia	The core business is assembling and distributing autos. It is run by a professional management team that weathered a crisis when the founding Soeryadjaya family sold out in 1993.	$4 billion ↑ 51%
Sime Darby	Malaysia	Southeast Asia's biggest conglomerate, with 200 companies and 32,000 employees, is changing its sleepy image by wooing fresh managerial talent.	$3.1 billion ↑17%
Raja Garuda Mas	Indonesia	This group, which includes pulp and paper plants, hires managers from around the world to help start up or manage its businesses.	$1 billion ↑ NA

Source: Reprinted from November 27, 1995 issue of *Business Week* by special permission, copyright © 1995 by The McGraw-Hill Companies, Inc.

U.S. firms seeking to improve their competitive postures through a foreign subsidiary face a number of risks to their normal mode of operations. First, if the high capital investment is to be rewarded, managers must attain extensive knowledge of the market, the host nation's language, and its business culture. Second, the host country expects both a long-term commitment from the U.S. enterprise and a portion of their nationals to be employed in positions of management or operations. Fortunately, hiring or training foreign managers for leadership positions is commonly a good policy, since they are close to both the market and contacts. This is especially important for smaller firms when markets are regional. Third, changing standards mandated by foreign regulations may eliminate a company's protected market niche. Product design and worker protection liabilities also may extend back to the home office.

The strategies shown in Figure 4–9 are not mutually exclusive. For example, a firm may engage in any number of joint ventures while maintaining an export business. Additionally, there are a number of other strategies that a firm should consider before deciding on its long-term approach to foreign markets. These will be discussed in detail in Chapter 7 under the topic of grand strategies. However, the strategies discussed in this chapter provide the most popular starting points for planning the globalization of a firm.

BusinessWeek

continued

STRATEGY 2: REMAINING ENTREPRENEURIAL

Company	Country	Strategy	Revenue
Acer	Taiwan	CEO Stan Shih has broken his PC-making company into small, decentralized units so that each can be highly responsive to the market.	$3.2 billion ↑71%
Li & Fung	Hong Kong	Run by the third generation of Fungs. Brothers William and Victor are both armed with Harvard degrees. They have created a global trading company that stays nimble because of its tightly run business units.	$792 million ↑14%
San Miguel Corp.	Philippines	This beer and food conglomerate is actively spinning off different divisions into separate companies as a way to gain market share and become more efficient.	$190 million ↑41%
VTech	Hong Kong	The territory's biggest electronics company is divided into small, snappy units, making it easier for its hands-on directors to manage successfully.	$650 million ↑18%
YTL Corp.	Malaysia	Run by the London-educated son of the founder, this construction company is determined not to become bureaucratic. There are no clock-in machines or set hours for senior staff.	$233 million ↑19.1%

(continued)

Sample Strategies of Global Competitors

It is interesting and informative to study the actual strategies of companies that have recently chosen to globalize their operations. Global Strategy in Action 4–8 provides examples of six different strategies that are being employed by Asian firms: professionalizing management, remaining entrepreneurial, sticking with the core business, bracing for more open markets, going public, and forging strategic alliances. As the details of their strategies make apparent, foreign firms must design plans that will enable them to generate the best mix of global operations and domestic market shares, exactly as U.S. firms are forced to do.

SUMMARY

To understand the strategic planning options available to a corporation, its managers need to recognize that different types of industry-based competition exist. Specifically, they must identify the position of their industry along the global versus multidomestic continuum and then consider the implications of that position for their firm.

The differences between global and multidomestic industries about the location and coordination of functional corporate activities necessitate differences in strategic

BusinessWeek

continued

STRATEGY 3: STICKING WITH THE CORE BUSINESS

Company	Country	Strategy	Revenue
Sun Hung Kai	Hong Kong	This property company is doing what it does best: real estate and infrastructure. Managed by the three Kwok brothers, each boasting Western degrees.	$2.56 billion ↑ 12%
Bukaka	Indonesia	Run by a team of skilled Indonesian engineers, this infrastructure company is winning major bids in Japan, Hong Kong, and throughout the region.	$74.2 million ↑ 10%
Formosa Plastics	Taiwan	Although the company has entered the integrated-circuit industry, it keeps a sharp emphasis on remaining the country's pacesetter in petrochemicals.	$9.1 billion ↑ 35%
Renong Bernad	Malaysia	This group of eight listed companies is now selling off assets to focus on infrastructure. Its leading executives want the company to specialize rather than be a hodgepodge of investments.	$1.3 billion ↑ 19%
Indofood	Indonesia	This Jakarta-based food company made it big at home with its near monopoly in flour milling. Now, it's exporting its noodles to China, Chile, and Poland with the goal of being a global player.	$6.0 billion ↑ 18.9%

STRATEGY 4: BRACING FOR MORE OPEN MARKETS

Company	Country	Strategy	Revenue
Chinatrust	Taiwan	The country's leading credit-card issuer is finding its niche by providing a wide range of services for Taiwanese executives working abroad and other overseas Chinese.	$12.6 billion* ↑ 20%
Philippines Long Distance	Philippines	Responding to new competition, PLDT has revamped management in a bid to boost sales through improved services and better marketing.	$240 million ↑ 40%
Thai Farmers Bank	Thailand	Catching up to Citibank in innovative products, the bank is undergoing a reengineering to become more responsive to customers.	$20 billion* ↑ 15.2%
President	Taiwan	Faced with tough rivals at home, this food company is rapidly expanding into China as a way to spur new growth.	$930 million ↑ 3%
Creative Technology	Singapore	Hit by clones in the market, the creator of the soundblaster is pumping big funds into R&D for new products.	$350 million ↑ 42%

*Assets.

continued

BusinessWeek

STRATEGY 5: GOING PUBLIC

Company	Country	Strategy	Revenue
Telkom Indonesia	Indonesia	This state-owned company is raising more than $1 billion of equity in Jakarta, New York, and London as part of the government's privatization drive.	$1.8 billion ↑ 30%
China Steel	Taiwan	Once a sleepy state enterprise, this well-run company has been privatized in a major bid to take on the global competition.	$2.9 billion ↑ 34%
Bimantara Citra	Indonesia	This company—with holdings ranging from a private TV station to a plastics maker—went public to prepare for competition.	$272 million ↑ 0.6%
Electricity Generating Co.	Thailand	Spun off from the state utility, EGCO expects to operate more efficiently because management has more flexibility than its parent.	$137 million ↑ NA
CDL	Singapore	This growing hotel and resort conglomerate is giving regional managers decision-making responsibility particularly in segments of the business that have gone public.	$351 million ↑ 72%

STRATEGY 6: FORGING STRATEGIC PARTNERSHIPS

Company	Country	Strategy	Revenue
Chraroen Pokphand	Thailand	The giant conglomerate is gaining depth by linking up with foreign players such as Nynex in the telecom market and Wal-Mart in retail.	$7.6 billion ↑ 26%
WYWY Group	Singapore	Y. Y. Wong, founder of this privately held Singapore distribution company, has had long working relations with Western and Japanese multinationals. Now, he's teaming up in telecom, entertainment, and restaurants.	$900 million ↑ 43%
UMC	Taiwan	The semiconductor manufacturer is expanding its reach by linking up with major U.S. partners, including Cirrus Logic and Xilinx.	$570 million ↑ 53%
Legend	China	This emerging computer distributor and manu-facturer in China is a marriage of a Hong Kong software house and Beijing's Academy of Sciences.	$480 million ↑ 50%
Mitac	Taiwan	The island's second-largest PC maker manu-factures for Compaq, Apple, and AT&T. It is jointly developing desktop computers with Compaq.	$570 million ↑ 50%

emphasis. As an industry becomes global, managers of firms within that industry must increase the coordination and concentration of functional activities.

The appendix at the end of this chapter lists many components of the environment with which global corporations must contend. This list is useful in understanding the issues that confront global corporations and in evaluating the thoroughness of global corporation strategies.

As a starting point for global expansion, the firm's mission statement needs to be reviewed and revised. As global operations fundamentally alter the direction and strategic capabilities of a firm, its mission statement, if originally developed from a domestic perspective, must be globalized.

The globalized mission statement provides the firm with a unity of direction that transcends the divergent perspectives of geographically dispersed managers. It provides a basis for strategic decisions in situations where strategic alternatives may appear to conflict. It promotes corporate values and commitments that extend beyond single cultures and satisfies the demands of the firm's internal and external claimants in different countries. Finally, it ensures the survival of the global corporation by asserting the global corporation's legitimacy with respect to support coalitions in a variety of operating environments.

Movement of a firm toward globalization often follows a systematic pattern of development. Commonly, businesses begin their foreign nation involvements progressively through niche market exporting, license-contract manufacturing, franchising, joint ventures, foreign branching, and foreign subsidiaries.

QUESTIONS FOR DISCUSSION

1. How does environmental analysis at the domestic level differ from global analysis?
2. Which factors complicate environmental analysis at the global level? Which factors are making such analysis easier?
3. Do you agree with the suggestion that soon all industries will need to evaluate global environments?
4. Which industries operate almost devoid of global competition? Which inherent immunities do they enjoy?

BIBLIOGRAPHY

Adler, N. J., and S. Bartholomew. "Managing Globally Competent People." *Academy of Management Executive* (August 1992), pp. 52–65.

Banks, Philip, and Ganesh Natarajan. "India: The New Asian Tiger." *Business Horizons* 38, no. 3 (May–June 1995), p. 47.

Beaver, William. "Levi's Is Leaving China." *Business Horizons* 38, no. 2 (March–April 1995), p. 35.

Calantone, R. J., and C. A. di Benedetto. "Defensive Marketing in Globally Competitive Industrial Markets." *Columbia Journal of World Business* (Fall 1988), pp. 3–14.

Chankin, W., and R. A. Mauborgne. "Becoming an Effective Global Competitor." *Journal of Business Strategy* (January–February 1988), pp. 33–37.

Chilton, Kenneth. "How American Manufacturers Are Facing the Global Marketplace." *Business Horizons* 38, no. 4 (July–August 1995), p. 10.

Cox, T., Jr. "The Multicultural Organization." *Academy of Management Executive* (May 1991), pp. 34–47.

Edmunds, John C. "The Multinational as an Engine of Value." *Business Horizons* 38, no. 4 (July–August 1995), p. 5.

Fagan, M. L. "A Guide to Global Sourcing." *The Journal of Business Strategy* (March–April 1991), pp. 21–25.

Franko, L. G. "Global Corporate Competition: Who's Winning, Who's Losing, and the R&D Factor as One Reason Why." *Strategic Management Journal* (September–October 1989), pp. 449–74.

Friedmann, R., and J. Kim. "Political Risk and International Marketing." *Columbia Journal of World Business* (Fall 1988), pp. 63–74.

Gomes-Casseres, B. "Joint Ventures in the Face of Global Competition." *Sloan Management Review* (Spring 1989), pp. 17–26.

Heenan, D. A. "Global Strategy: The End of Centralized Power." *The Journal of Business Strategy* (March–April 1991), pp. 46–49.

Hitt, Michael A.; Beverly B. Tyler; Camilla Hardel; and Daewoo Park. "Understanding Strategic Intent in the Global Marketplace." *The Academy of Management Executive* 9, no. 2 (May 1995), p. 12.

Hordes, Mark W.; J. Anthony Clancy; and Julie Baddaley. "A Primer for Global Start-Ups." *The Academy of Management Executive* 9, no. 2 (May 1995), p. 7.

Hu, Yao-Su. "The International Transferability of Competitive Advantage." *California Management Review* 37, no. 4 (Summer 1995), p. 73.

James, B. "Reducing the Risks of Globalization." *Long-Range Planning* (February 1990), pp. 80–88.

Johnston, W. B. "Global Work Force 2000: The New World Labor Market." *Harvard Business Review* (March–April 1991), pp. 115–29.

Kanter, Rosabeth Moss. "Thriving Locally in the Global Economy." *Harvard Business Review* 73, no. 5 (September–October 1995), p. 151.

Koepfler, E. R. "Strategic Options for Global Market Players." *Journal of Business Strategy* (July–August 1989), pp. 46–50.

Lasserre, Philippe. "Corporate Strategies for the Asia Pacific." *Long-Range Planning* 28, no. 1 (February 1995), p. 13.

Levy, B. "Korean and Taiwanese Firms as International Competitors." *Columbia Journal of World Business* (Spring 1988), pp. 43–51.

Maruyama, M. "Changing Dimensions in International Business." *Academy of Management Executive* (August 1992), pp. 88–96.

Ohmal, Kenschi. "Putting Global Logic First." *Harvard Business Review* 73, no. 1 (January–February 1995), p. 119.

O'Reilly, A. J. F. "Leading a Global Strategic Charge." *The Journal of Business Strategy* (July–August 1991), pp. 10–13.

Reilly, Tom. "The Harmonization of Standards in the European Union and the Impact on U.S. Business." *Business Horizons* 38, no. 2 (March–April 1995), p. 28.

Reynolds, A. "Competitiveness and the 'Global Capital Shortage.'" *Business Horizons* (November–December 1991), pp. 23–26.

Sera, K. "Corporate Globalization: A New Trend." *Academy of Management Executive* (February 1992), pp. 89–96.

Shama, Avraham. "Entry Strategies of U.S. Firms to the Former Soviet Bloc and Eastern Europe." *California Management Review* 37, no. 3 (Spring 1995), p. 90.

Shetty, Y. K. "Strategies for U.S. Competitiveness: A Survey of Business Leaders." *Business Horizons* (November–December 1991), pp. 43–48.

Sugiura, H. "How Honda Localizes Its Global Strategy." *Sloan Management Review* (Fall 1990), pp. 77–82.

Williamson, P. "Successful Strategies for Export." *Long-Range Planning* (February 1991), pp. 57–63.

APPENDIX

COMPONENTS OF THE MULTINATIONAL ENVIRONMENT

Multinational firms must operate within an environment that has numerous components. These components include:

I. Government, laws, regulations, and policies of home country (United States, for example).
  A. Monetary and fiscal policies and their effect on price trends, interest rates, economic growth, and stability.
  B. Balance-of-payments policies.
    1. Mandatory controls on direct investment.
    2. Interest equalization tax and other policies.
  C. Commercial policies, especially tariffs, quantitative import restrictions, and voluntary import controls.
  D. Export controls and other restrictions on trade.
  E. Tax policies and their impact on overseas business.
  F. Antitrust regulations, their administration, and their impact on international business.
  G. Investment guarantees, investment surveys, and other programs to encourage private investments in less-developed countries.
  H. Export-import and government export expansion programs.
  I. Other changes in government policy that affect international business.
II. Key political and legal parameters in foreign countries and their projection.
  A. Type of political and economic system, political philosophy, national ideology.
  B. Major political parties, their philosophies, and their policies.
  C. Stability of the government.
    1. Changes in political parties.
    2. Changes in governments.
  D. Assessment of nationalism and its possible impact on political environment and legislation.
  E. Assessment of political vulnerability.
    1. Possibilities of expropriation.
    2. Unfavorable and discriminatory national legislation and tax laws.
    3. Labor laws and problems.
  F. Favorable political aspects.
    1. Tax and other concessions to encourage foreign investments.
    2. Credit and other guarantees.
  G. Differences in legal system and commercial law.
  H. Jurisdiction in legal disputes.
  I. Antitrust laws and rules of competition.
  J. Arbitration clauses and their enforcement.
  K. Protection of patents, trademarks, brand names, and other industrial property rights.
III. Key economic parameters and their projection.

A. Population and its distribution by age groups, density, annual percentage increase, percentage of working age, percentage of total in agriculture, and percentage in urban centers.

B. Level of economic development and industrialization.

C. Gross national product, gross domestic product, or national income in real terms and also on a per capita basis in recent years and projections over future planning period.

D. Distribution of personal income.

E. Measures of price stability and inflation, wholesale price index, consumer price index, other price indexes.

F. Supply of labor, wage rates.

G. Balance-of-payments equilibrium or disequilibrium, level of international monetary reserves, and balance-of-payments policies.

H. Trends in exchange rates, currency stability, evaluation of possibility of depreciation of currency.

I. Tariffs, quantitative restrictions, export controls, border taxes, exchange controls, state trading, and other entry barriers to foreign trade.

J. Monetary, fiscal, and tax policies.

K. Exchange controls and other restrictions on capital movements, repatriation of capital, and remission of earnings.

IV. Business system and structure.

A. Prevailing business philosophy: mixed capitalism, planned economy, state socialism.

B. Major types of industry and economic activities.

C. Numbers, size, and types of firms, including legal forms of business.

D. Organization: proprietorship, partnerships, limited companies, corporations, cooperatives, state enterprises.

E. Local ownership patterns: public and privately held corporations, family-owned enterprises.

F. Domestic and foreign patterns of ownership in major industries.

G. Business managers available: their education, training, experience, career patterns, attitudes, and reputations.

H. Business associations and chambers of commerce and their influence.

I. Business codes, both formal and informal.

J. Marketing institutions: distributors, agents, wholesalers, retailers, advertising agencies, advertising media, marketing research, and other consultants.

K. Financial and other business institutions: commercial and investment banks, other financial institutions, capital markets, money markets, foreign exchange dealers, insurance firms, engineering companies.

L. Managerial processes and practices with respect to planning, administration, operations, accounting, budgeting, and control.

V. Social and cultural parameters and their projections.

A. Literacy and educational levels.

B. Business, economic, technical, and other specialized education available.

C. Language and cultural characteristics.

D. Class structure and mobility.

E. Religious, racial, and national characteristics.

F. Degree of urbanization and rural-urban shifts.

G. Strength of nationalistic sentiment.

H. Rate of social change.

I. Impact of nationalism on social and institutional change.

CHAPTER 4 DISCUSSION CASE   BusinessWeek

WHIRLPOOL: IN THE WRINGER

> The great frontiers for expanding sales and market shares are clearly in global-
> ization, especially when heavy involvement of developing nations is possible.
> These countries offer both burgeoning markets and relatively inexpensive sources
> of labor and material resources. However, as with all frontiers, nonestablished
> markets present many obstacles for new competitive entrants. The Chapter 4 Dis-
> cussion case presents such a situation; it is one of promise compromised by so-
> cial, economic, and political instability.

Whirlpool Corp.'s Brazilian operations have been caught in a veritable spin cycle over
the past year as the global financial crisis spread from Asia and Russia into Latin
America. To protect against a run on its currency, the real, Brazil doubled interest rates
in October, 1997, and again this fall after they had gradually fallen back. As a result,
Whirlpool's appliance sales in Brazil plummeted by about 25% this year, to $1 bil-
lion—or about 10% of the company's 1998 revenues, which analyst Nicholas P. Heymann of Prudential Securities pegs at $10.3 billion.

Now Whirlpool, based in Benton Harbor, Michigan, is battling to shore up Brazil—
the jewel of its global expansion strategy—even while it has stumbled over expansion
into Asia. The company has invested hundreds of millions of dollars to modernize and
cut costs in Brazil and solidify its position as the market leader in refrigerators, room
air-conditioners, and washers. The stakes are huge: Brazil is by far Whirlpool's biggest
emerging-market bet, and through much of the 90s, its most profitable foreign operation. Whirlpool's Brazilian affiliates contributed 1997 earnings of $78 million, com-
pared with a measly $11 million operating profit for the parent. Says Chairman and
Chief Executive Officer David R. Whitwam: "In Brazil, we've built a very commanding position in the market, and we'll see what kind of benefits that position can yield."

Things figure to get worse before they get better. Brazil is skidding into a recession
that could shrink gross domestic product by 3% next year. As a result, 1999 will likely
mark the third straight year appliance sales and profits decline at Brasmotor,
Whirlpool's local subsidiary. Prospects are so gloomy that it could be three years before sales return to 1996 levels.

That's quite a reversal. Sales at Brasmotor soared 28% from 1994 to 1995 and 15%
more in 1996. When Whirlpool spent $217 million last year to hike its stake in Bras-
motor from 33% to 66%, it looked brilliant for having persevered through Brazil's
idiosyncrasies.

TIRED TUNE

With recession now looming, though, Whirlpool's timing couldn't have been worse.
Still, executives are confident they can ride out the storm—and in any case, they don't
think they have any choice. Whitwam argues that growth in home appliances is most

Source: Ian Katz in Sao Paulo, "Whirlpool in the Wringer," *Business Week:* December 14, 1998.

likely to come in emerging markets, thanks to the low penetration rates for appliances: Only 15% of Brazil's households own microwave ovens, for instance, compared with 91% in the U.S. Whitwam estimates that once Brazil recovers, it should grow an average 5% to 6% a year, versus just 1% to 2% in North America and Europe.

But Whitwam has been singing that tune for years, and Wall Street has grown tired of waiting for his ambitious—and costly—global expansion plans to pay off. Whirlpool's problems in Brazil are a big reason why its stock price has risen less than 4% since the start of the year, to about 55, compared with a 21% gain for the Standard & Poor's 500-stock index. Moreover, analysts say Whirlpool also is being punished for the poor execution of a broader global strategy that relies too much on heavy capital investment. The company last year had to restructure its China operations, dropping out of one joint venture after refrigerator capacity in that country doubled over 30 months and drove prices down sharply. Prudential's Heymann expects Whirlpool to lose $16 million in Asia this year—better than a $62 million loss in 1997, but not the profit it had expected.

Competitors, meanwhile, have found better ways to expand. General Electric Co. pushed overseas with less costly licensing agreements and acquisitions. And Maytag Corp. is squeezing more money out of those "mature" markets, getting U.S. shoppers to pay more for its innovative Neptune front-loading washers. The result: Maytag will have margins next year of about 13%, Heymann says, compared with 7.5% for Whirlpool. "The companies that have stayed closer to the U.S. and Canada, such as Maytag, have done well," says Donald Bishop, an analyst for Van Deventer & Hoch, a Glendale (California) investment firm that holds 32,700 Whirlpool shares.

So far, though, Whirlpool continues to have an edge in Brazil. While profits have dwindled, it is the only major white-goods maker still making money there. Whirlpool reported $63 million in local profits through the first nine months of 1998, whereas competitor Electrolux of Sweden lost $13 million in Brazil. Whirlpool's advantage, which it lacks in Asia: 40 years of operating in Brazil have earned strong loyalty. Its Brastemp and Consul refrigerators have 60% of the market. "They have a great brand name that gives them a competitive advantage," says Eduardo de la Pena, an analyst with Brazilian investment bank Bozano Simonsen.

Old Hands

To keep that edge, Paulo Periquito, Whirlpool's executive vice-president for Latin America and CEO of its Brazilian operations, is attacking on several fronts. He has cut 3,500 jobs and links in the production chain to improve efficiency at its five plants in Brazil and one each in Argentina and Chile. But he's doing far more than just trimming costs. Whirlpool has invested $280 million in the past two years to renew plants and product lines. The company initiated a data-exchange system that links its computers with those of retailers to keep better track of stock—a rare level of connectedness for Brazil. And Brasmotor has launched a line of products with upgraded features, such as a microwave oven with a "crisp" setting to keep foods from getting soggy when reheated. Periquito, a Brazilian who came to Whirlpool in 1996 from Alcoa Inc., boasts that Whirlpool now can increase or decrease output by 50% in just 30 days. "We need that kind of flexibility and agility," he says.

No kidding. In Brazil's white-goods business, there's no such thing as "steady." Sales tend to either soar or crash. In 1994, demand for household appliances exploded after Brazil introduced an anti-inflation plan. Millions of low-income earners who had been waiting years to replace worn-out refrigerators and ranges rushed for stores. With price stability, a blue-collar worker could budget $75 a month for a year to buy a washing machine.

But then Asian currencies came under attack from speculators last year, and it wasn't long before traders shifted attention to other shaky markets like Brazil. The government of President Fernando Henrique Cardoso twice boosted interest rates to keep money from fleeing the country. Brazil avoided falling into an abyss but wreaked havoc on consumer spending. Until Brazil can cut its fiscal deficit, it will need high rates to avoid a devaluation.

Periquito is pinning his hopes on interest rates falling gradually in 1999, a prospect many economists consider possible under the International Monetary Fund's $42 billion bailout. The experience of surviving Brazil's many debt crises, bouts of hyperinflation, and military governments has given Whirlpool a been-there, done-that aura of confidence. But the current combination of declining growth and high interest rates is a particularly nasty mix. "If people aren't making money and interest rates are high, it's tough to force a demand for these products," Periquito admits. All he can do is get the company into shape for when the wild Brazilian roller-coaster starts to climb again.

5

ENVIRONMENTAL FORECASTING

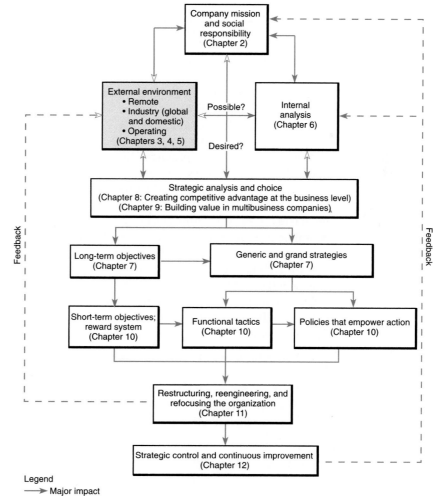

Company mission and social responsibility (Chapter 2)

External environment
• Remote
• Industry (global and domestic)
• Operating
(Chapters 3, 4, 5)

Possible?

Internal analysis (Chapter 6)

Desired?

Strategic analysis and choice
(Chapter 8: Creating competitive advantage at the business level)
(Chapter 9: Building value in multibusiness companies)

Long-term objectives (Chapter 7)

Generic and grand strategies (Chapter 7)

Short-term objectives; reward system (Chapter 10)

Functional tactics (Chapter 10)

Policies that empower action (Chapter 10)

Restructuring, reengineering, and refocusing the organization (Chapter 11)

Strategic control and continuous improvement (Chapter 12)

Feedback

Feedback

Legend
———▶ Major impact
———▷ Minor impact

IMPORTANCE OF FORECASTING

In a global marketplace characterized by accelerating change, the crucial responsibility for managers will be ensuring their firm's capacity for survival. This will be done by anticipating and adapting to environmental changes in ways that provide new opportunities for growth and profitability. The impact of changes in the remote industry and task environments must be understood and predicted.

Even large firms in established industries will be actively involved in transitions. The $5.5 billion loss in the U.S. auto industry in the early 1980s is a classic example of what can happen when firms fail to place a priority on environmental forecasting. The preceding decade saw a 20 percent penetration of the U.S. new car market by foreign competition, a nation-crippling oil embargo, rapidly climbing fuel prices, and uncertain future supplies of crude oil. Yet the long-range implications of these predictable factors on future auto sales were largely ignored by U.S. automakers. Because it was not open to changes in technology, Detroit was left without viable, fuel-efficient, quality alternatives for the American market. On the other hand, Japanese automakers anticipated the future need for fuel efficiency, quality, and service through careful market research and environmental forecasting. As a result, they gained additional market share at Detroit's expense.

In retaliation, American automakers spent $80 billion over a three-year period on product and capital-investment strategies that were meant to recapture their lost market share. They realized that success in strategic decisions rests not solely on dollar amounts but also on anticipation of and preparation for the future.

Accurate forecasting of changing elements in the environment is an essential part of strategic management. Forecasting the business environment for the 1990s led many firms to diversify. For example, USX Corporation (formerly U.S. Steel) purchased Marathon Oil so as to have a profit generator whose proceeds could be used to turn USX into a low-cost steel producer. Similarly, predicting future demand for new products is an arduous process. As Strategy in Action 5–1 suggests, the accuracy of new product forecasts can be critically important.

Other firms have forecast a need for massive retrenchment. One such firm is IBM, which laid off 40,000 employees in 1991–92 and another 25,000 employees in 1993 to streamline its cost of doing business. Still other firms have cut back in one area of operations to underwrite growth in another. For example, CBS sold its records division to Sony for $2 billion to raise the capital it needed for its planned expansion in television stations in the 1990s.

These and many other examples indicate that strategic managers need to develop skills in predicting significant environmental changes. To aid in the search for future opportunities and constraints, they should take the following steps:

1. Select the environmental variables that are critical to the firm.
2. Select the sources of significant environmental information.
3. Evaluate forecasting techniques.
4. Integrate forecast results into the strategic management process.
5. Monitor the critical aspects of managing forecasts.

SELECT CRITICAL ENVIRONMENTAL VARIABLES

Management experts have argued that an important cause of the turbulent business environment is the change in population structure and dynamics. This change, in turn, produced other major changes in the economic, social, and political environments.

FORECASTING DEMAND FOR NEW PRODUCTS ALWAYS DIFFICULT

STRATEGY IN ACTION 5–1

The major new project of the 90s, the so-called information superhighway, is developing rapidly. One sure sign is the increasing frequency of reported misuse for stock swindles, assorted sexual solicitations, slanderous communications, and other undesirable traffic.

When the Haloid company developed the dry-process copier in the later 1950s, it retained Stewart, Dougall & Associates, a now-defunct research and consulting firm, to estimate market potential and assist in developing market strategy. A common initial reaction to the product concept was that it seemed like a good idea that could replace some then-current methods like thermography because of the better appearance and durability of its plain-paper copies. The forecast seemed unbelievably high and turned out to be a serious underestimate.

It is difficult to project uses that go beyond replacements of current use and beyond the needs currently anticipated by potential users, even assuming that all potential users have been correctly identified. A little earlier, the same firm had forecast demand for another new product, polyethylene film; this forecast also turned out to be far short of reality.

The main obstacle to the prediction of demand is our limited vision. It is hard for us to realize how severely we are hemmed in by assumptions of the persistence of current patterns. Because early xerography equipment turned out relatively expensive copies compared to the mimeograph and multigraph, few analysts foresaw that it would virtually eliminate their use, and even affect traditional printing.

We tend to resist the notion of great supply-driven demand growth. It smacks of hucksterism that runs counter to the traditionally desirable posture of conservatism in forecasting and in research generally. This conservative posture has a severe downside, a risk of underestimation resulting in opportunity loss.

A closely related risk is failure to recognize problems that may arise, such as undesirable uses. In the last century, the great advantages offered by dynamite in mining and construction obscured realization of its destructive potential. Similarly, the information superhighway's potential for misuse, while realized by some, could not compete with the enthusiastic media hype of its benefits.

Anyone trying to forecast new-product demand should be well aware of the trade-off between the optimistic and the conservative views. That trade-off should be carefully modulated in accordance with the relative risks involved, an assessment that requires close cooperation of top management. After all, the company's future may depend on it.

There is no such thing as objectivity when we try to look into the future, except in data collection. The decision as to what data to collect, how to collect them, and how to interpret them cannot be objective, no matter how hard we try and it shouldn't be.

Source: "Forecasting Demand for New Products Always Difficult," by Thomas T. Semon, *Marketing News,* March 27, 1995, p. 10. Reprinted by permission of the American Marketing Association.

Historically, population shifts tended to occur over 40–50 year periods and, therefore, had little relevance to business decisions. During the second half of the 20th century, however, population changes have become radical, erratic, contradictory, and, therefore, of great importance.

For example, the U.S. baby boom between 1945 and the mid-1960s has had and will have a dramatic impact on all parts of society—from maternity wards and schools to the labor force and the marketplace. This population bulge is facing heavy competition for jobs, promotions, and housing, despite a highest-ever educational level.

Compounding the problem are the heightened expectations of women and of racial minorities. The lack of high-status jobs to fit these expectations poses a potential impetus for major social and economic changes. In addition, an increasingly aging labor force finds it difficult to give up status, power, and employment when retirement programs are either not financially attractive or not available at the traditional age of 65.

Obviously, the demands of these groups will have important effects on social and political changes in terms of lifestyle, consumption patterns, and political decisions. In economic terms, the size and potential affluence of these groups suggest increasing markets for housing, consumer products, and leisure goods and services.

Interestingly, the same shifts in population, life expectancy, and education have occurred in many developed nations. However, developing nations face the opposite population configurations. Although birthrates have declined, high survival rates resulting from medical improvements have created a large population of people who are reaching adulthood. Jobs and food are expected to be in short supply. Therefore, many developing countries will face severe social and political instability unless they can find appropriate work for their surplus labor.

The rates of population increase obviously can be of great importance, as indicated by the contrasting effects forecast above. If a growing population has sufficient purchasing power, new markets will be developed to satisfy its needs. However, too much growth in a country with a limited amount of resources or a drastic inequity in their distribution may result in major social and political upheavals that pose substantial risks for businesses.

If forecasting were as simple as predicting population trends, strategic managers would only need to examine census data to predict future markets. But economic interpretations are more complex. Population statistics are complicated by migration rates; mobility trends; birth, marriage, and death rates; and racial, ethnic, and religious structures. In addition, resource development and its political use in this interdependent world further confuse the problem—as evidenced by the actions of some of the oil states (e.g., Saudi Arabia, Iraq, Libya, and Kuwait). Changes in political situations, technology, or culture add further complications.

Domestically, the turbulence is no less severe. Continually changing products and services, changing competitors, uncertain government priorities, rapid social change, and major technological innovations all add to the complexity of planning for the future. To grow, to be profitable, and at times even to survive in this turbulent world, a firm needs sensitivity, commitment, and skill in recognizing and predicting these variables that will most profoundly affect its future.

Who Selects the Key Variables?

Although executives or committees in charge of planning may assist in obtaining the forecast data, the responsibility for environmental forecasting usually lies with top management. This is the case at the Sun (Oil) Company, where responsibility for the firm's long-range future is assigned to the chairman and vice chairman of the board of directors. A key duty of the vice chairman is environmental assessment. In this context, environment refers not to air, water, and land but rather to the general business setting created by the economic, technological, political, social, and ecological forces in which Sun plans to operate.

The environmental assessment group consists of Sun's chief economist, a specialist in technological assessment, and a public issues consultant—who all report to the vice president of environmental assessment. The chief economist evaluates and forecasts the state of the economy; the technological assessment specialist covers technology and science; and the public issues consultant concentrates on politics and society.

However, headquarters may lack the capability and proficiency needed to analyze political, economic, and social variables around the world. Therefore, on-the-spot personnel, outside consultants, or company task forces may be assigned to assist in forecasting.

What Variables Should Be Selected?

A list of the key variables that will have make-or-break consequences for the firm must be developed. Some of these variables may have been crucial in the past, and others may be expected to have future importance. This list can be kept manageable by limiting it in the following ways:

1.   Include all variables that would have a significant impact although their probability of occurrence is low. Also include highly probable variables regardless of their impact. Delete others with little impact and low probabilities.

2.   Disregard major disasters, such as nuclear war.

3.   When possible, aggregate variables into gross variables (e.g., a bank loan is based more on the dependability of a firm's cash flow than on the flow's component sources).

4.   If the value of one variable is based on the value of another, separate the dependent variable for future planning.

Limits of money, time, and forecasting skill prevent a firm from predicting many variables. The task of predicting even a dozen is substantial. Firms often try to select a set of key variables by analyzing the environmental factors in the industry that are most likely to foster sharp growth or decline in the marketplace. For the furniture, appliance, and textiles industries, housing starts are a key variable. Housing starts, in turn, are greatly affected by interest rates. Figure 5–1 identifies some issues that may have critical impacts on a firm's future success.

Another key consideration in attempting to forecast future performance is the amount of data needed. Data requirements are situation specific, but, as Figure 5–2 shows, depend on how quickly the data patterns change, the type of industry, the type of product, the analytical model selected, the forecast horizon, and ex-post forecast results.

SELECT SOURCES OF SIGNIFICANT ENVIRONMENTAL INFORMATION

Before formal forecasting can begin, appropriate sources of environmental information should be identified. Casual gathering of strategic information—through reading, interactions, and meetings—is part of the normal course of executive behavior but is subject to bias and must be balanced with alternative viewpoints. Although *The Wall Street Journal, Business Week, Fortune, Harvard Business Review, Forbes,* and other popular trade and scholarly journals are important sources of forecasting information, formal, deliberate, and structured searches are desirable. Appendix 5–A lists published sources that strategic managers can use to meet their specific forecasting needs. If the firm can afford the time and expense, it should also gather primary data in such areas as market factors, technological changes, and competitive and supplier strategies.

FIGURE 5–1
Strategic Forecasting Issues

Key Issues in the Remote Environment

Economy

What are the probable future directions of the economies in the firm's regional, national, and international markets? What changes in economic growth, inflation, interest rates, capital availability, credit availability, and consumer purchasing power can be expected? What income differences can be expected between the wealthy upper-middle class, the working class, and the underclass in various regions? What shifts in relative demand for different categories of goods and services can be expected?

Society and demographics

What effects will changes in social values and attitudes regarding childbearing, marriage, lifestyle, work, ethics, sex roles, racial equality, education, retirement, pollution, and energy have on the firm's development? What effects will population changes have on major social and political expectations— at home and abroad? What constraints or opportunities will develop? What pressure groups will increase in power?

Ecology

What natural or pollution-caused disasters threaten the firm's employees, customers, or facilities? How rigorously will existing environmental legislature be enforced? What new federal, state, and local laws will affect the firm, and in what ways?

Politics

What changes in government policy can be expected with regard to industry cooperation, antitrust activities, foreign trade, taxation, depreciation, environmental protection, deregulation, defense, foreign trade barriers, and other important parameters? What success will a new administration have in achieving its stated goals? What effect will that success have on the firm? Will specific international climates be hostile or favorable? Is there a tendency toward instability, corruption, or violence? What is the level of political risk in each foreign market? What other political or legal constraints or supports can be expected in international business (e.g., trade barriers, equity requirements, nationalism, patent protection)?

Technology

What is the current state of the art? How will it change? What pertinent new products or services are likely to become technically feasible in the foreseeable future? What future impact can be expected from technological breakthroughs in related product areas? How will those breakthroughs interface with the other remote considerations, such as economic issues, social values, public safety, regulations, and court interpretations?

Key Issues in the Industry Environment

New entrants

Will new technologies or market demands enable competitors to minimize the impact of traditional economies of scale in the industry? Will consumers accept our claims of product or service differentiation? Will potential new entrants be able to match the capital requirements that currently exist? How permanent are the cost disadvantages (independent of size) in our industry? Will conditions change so that all competitors have equal access to marketing channels? Is government policy toward competition in our industry likely to change?

Bargaining power of suppliers

How stable are the size and composition of our supplier group? Are any suppliers likely to attempt forward integration into our business level? How dependent will our suppliers be in the future? Are substitute suppliers likely to become available? Could we become our own supplier?

EVALUATE FORECASTING TECHNIQUES

Debate exists over the accuracy of quantitative versus qualitative approaches to forecasting (see Figure 5–3), with most research supporting quantitative models. However, the differences in the predictions derived from these approaches are often minimal. Moreover, subjective or judgmental approaches are often the only practical method of forecasting political, legal, social, and technological trends in the remote external

FIGURE 5–1
concluded

Substitute products or services

Are new substitutes likely? Will they be price competitive? Could we fight off substitutes by price competition? By advertising to sharpen product differentiation? What actions could we take to reduce the potential for having alternative products seen as legitimate substitutes?

Bargaining power of buyers

Can we break free of overcommitment to a few large buyers? How would our buyers react to attempts by us to differentiate our products? What possibilities exist that our buyers might vertically integrate backward? Should we consider forward integration? How can we make the value of our components greater in the products of our buyers?

Rivalry among existing firms

Are major competitors likely to undo the established balance of power in our industry? Is growth in our industry slowing such that competition will become fiercer? What excess capacity exists in our industry? How capable are our major competitors of withstanding intensified price competition? How unique are the objectives and strategies of our major competitors?

Key Issues in the Operating Environment

Competitive position

What strategic moves are expected by existing rivals—inside and outside the United States? What competitive advantage is necessary in selected foreign markets? What will be our competitors' priorities and ability to change? Is the behavior of our competitors predictable?

Customer profiles and market changes

What will our customer regard as needed value? Is marketing research done, or do managers talk to each other to discover what the customer wants? Which customer needs are not being met by existing products? Why? Are R&D activities under way to develop means for fulfilling these needs? What is the status of these activities? What marketing and distribution channels should we use? What do demographic and population changes portend for the size and sales potential of our market? What new market segments or products might develop as a result of these changes? What will be the buying power of our customer groups?

Supplier relationships

What is the likelihood of major cost increases because of dwindling supplies of a needed natural resource? Will sources of supply, especially of energy, be reliable? Are there reasons to expect major changes in the cost or availability of inputs as a result of money, people, or subassembly problems? Which suppliers can be expected to respond to emergency requests?

Creditors

What lines of credit are available to help finance our growth? What changes may occur in our creditworthiness? Are creditors likely to feel comfortable with our strategic plan and performance? What is the stock market likely to feel about our firm? What flexibility would our creditors show toward us during a downturn? Do we have sufficient cash reserves to protect our creditors and our credit rating?

Labor market

Are potential employees with desired skills and abilities available in the geographic areas in which our facilities are located? Are colleges and vocational-technical schools that can aid in meeting our training needs located near our plant or store sites? Are labor relations in our industry conducive to meeting our expanding needs for employees? Are workers whose skills we need shifting toward or away from the geographic location of our facilities?

environment. The same is true of several factors in the task environment, especially customer and competitive considerations.

Ultimately, the choice of technique depends not on the environmental factor under review but on such considerations as the nature of the forecast decision, the amount and accuracy of available information, the accuracy required, the time available, the importance of the forecast, the cost, and the competence and interpersonal relationships of the managers and forecasters involved. Frequently, assessment of such considerations leads to the selection of a combination of quantitative and qualitative techniques, thereby strengthening the accuracy of the ultimate forecast.

FIGURE 5–2
How Much Data Should You Use to Prepare Forecasts?

Sooner or later a decision has to be made as to how much data should be used to prepare the next period's forecast. Should you use all the data you have or a part of it? If you use part of the data, which part should be used? There is no simple answer to these questions; it depends on: (1) how quickly the data pattern changes, (2) the type of industry, (3) the type of product, (4) the model selected, (5) the forecast horizon, and (6) ex-post forecast results.

Data Pattern

As we know: Actual value = Pattern + Error. The best forecasting model is the one that most accurately captures the underlying pattern in a data set. The more a given model captures the pattern, the less will be the error. In a given company, the data pattern can change from one time to another because of a change in legislation, product mix, socio-demographic makeup, and the competitive environment. Technological developments and acquisitions and mergers can also change the data pattern. In that case, you need data from where the most recent data pattern starts. For example, if the most recent pattern starts in 1991, you should be using data starting 1991.

Type of Industry

The change in the data pattern is not the same in each and every industry. Some industries experience changes more rapidly than others. This may be because some industries are more prone to technological developments and/or mergers and acquisitions than others. In industries where the data pattern changes rapidly, forecasters often use data of a shorter period. In consumer product industries, for example, forecasters use data of the previous three years in preparing operations forecasts—forecasts of less than one year.

Type of Product

The type of product also makes a difference. Some products have a longer life than others. The life of essential products is generally much longer than that of fashion products. Other things being constant, the longer the life of a product the more data will be required and vice versa.

Forecast Horizon

How much data are needed also depends on whether we wish to prepare a short- or long-term forecast. Generally speaking, less data are needed for short-term forecasts and more data for long-term forecasts. If you wish to make a forecast for the next week or month, by and large, projecting the current trend adjusted for seasonal elements will be sufficient. This means a couple of years of data will be enough. However, if you wish to make a forecast for four or five years into the future, you will need much more data.

Model Selected

The data required also depends on the selected model because each model has its own requirement. For example, the "three-period moving average change model" needs at least four periods of data, and at the same time the "three-period double moving average change model" requires at least six periods of data. For a Box Jenkins model, some feel at least six years of data are needed if weekly or monthly forecasts are to be prepared and the data contain seasonality. In a regression-based model, the minimum observations required depend, among other things, on the number of independent variables. The more independent variables you incorporate in a model, the more observations will be needed.

Ex-Post Forecasts

Above all, the data required depend on how many observations, on the average, give the best forecasts. Using the best model, one can prepare ex-post forecasts on the basis of, say, one year of data, two years of data, and three years of data. (Ex-post forecasts are forecasts of those periods for which actuals are known.) If, on the average, three years of data give the lowest error, you need three years of data; if two years of data give the lowest error, you need two years of data; and so on.

Source: Chaman L. Jain, "How Much Data Should You Use to Prepare Forecasts?" *The Journal of Business Forecasting,* Winter 1994–1995, p. 2.

Techniques Available

Economic Forecasts

At one time, only forecasts of economic variables were used in strategic management. The forecasts were primarily concerned with remote factors, such as general economic conditions, disposable personal income, the consumer price index, wage rates, and

FIGURE 5–3
Popular Approaches to Forecasting

Technique	Short Description	Cost	Popularity	Complexity	Association with Life Cycle Stage
Quantitative–Causal Models					
Econometric models	Simultaneous systems of multiple regression equations.	High	High	High	Steady state
Single and multiple regression	Variations in dependent variables are explained by variations in one or more independent variables.	High/medium	High	Medium	Steady state
Time series models	Linear, exponential, S-curve, or other types of projections.	Medium	High	Medium	Steady state
Trend extrapolation	Forecasts obtained by linear or exponential smoothing or averaging of past actual values.	Medium	High	Medium	Steady state
Qualitative or Judgmental Models					
Sales force estimate	A bottom-up approach aggregating salespersons' forecasts.	Low	High	Low	All stages
Juries of executive opinion	Forecasts jointly prepared by marketing, production, finance, and purchasing executives.	Low	High	Low	Product development
Customer surveys; market research	Learning about intentions of potential customers or plans of businesses.	Medium	Medium	Medium	Market testing and early introduction
Scenario development	Impacts of anticipated conditions imagined by forecasters.	Low	Medium	Low	All stages
Delphi method	Experts guided toward a consensus.	Low	Medium	Medium	Product development
Brainstorming	Idea generation in a noncritical group situation.	Low	Medium	Medium	Product development

productivity. Derived from government and private sources, these economic forecasts served as the framework for industry and company forecasts, which dealt with task-environment concerns, such as sales, market share, and other pertinent economic trends.

Econometric Models

With the advent of sophisticated computers, the government and some wealthy firms contracted with private consulting firms to develop "casual models," especially models involving econometrics. These econometric models utilize complex simultaneous regression equations to relate economic occurrences to areas of corporate activity. They are especially useful when information on casual relationships is available and large changes are anticipated. During the relatively stable decade of the 1970s, econometrics was one of the nation's fastest-growing industries. In the 1980s, however, the three biggest econometric firms—Data Resources (McGraw-Hill), Chase Econometric (Chase Manhattan Bank), and Wharton Econometric Forecasting Associates (Ziff-Davis Publishing)—fell on hard times. The explosion of oil prices, inflation, and the growing interdependence in the world economy created problems that fell beyond the inherent limits of econometric models. And despite enormous technological resources, such models still depend on the often undependable judgment of the model builders.

FIGURE 5–4
Interpretations in Trend Analysis

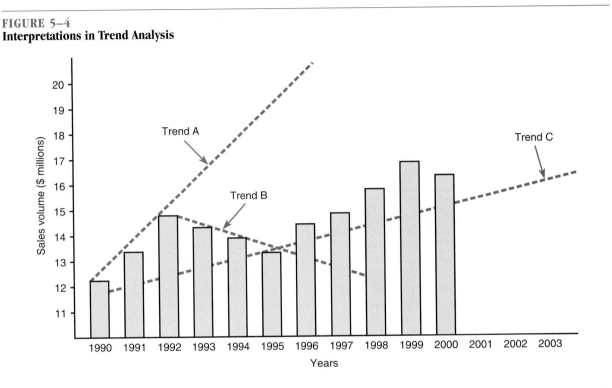

Two more widely used and less expensive forecasting techniques are *time series models* and *judgmental models.* Time series models attempt to identify patterns based on combinations of historical trends and seasonal and cyclical factors. This technique assumes that the past is a prologue to the future. Time series techniques, such as exponential smoothing and linear projections, are relatively simple, well known, inexpensive, and accurate.

Of the time series models, *trend analysis* models are the most frequently used. Such models assume that the future will be a continuation of the past, following some long-range trend. If sufficient historical data are available, such as annual sales, a trend analysis can be done quickly at a modest cost.

In the trend analysis depicted in Figure 5–4, concern should focus on long-term trends, such as Trend C, which is based on 11 years of fluctuating sales. Trend A, which is based on three excellent years, is much too optimistic. Similarly, Trend B, which is based on four bad years, is much too pessimistic.

The major limitation of trend analysis is the assumption that all of the relevant conditions will remain relatively constant. Sudden changes in these conditions falsify trend predictions.

Judgmental models are useful when historical data are unavailable or hard to use. *Sales force estimates* and *juries of executive opinion* are examples of such models. Sales force estimates consolidate salespeople's opinions of customer intentions regarding specific products. These estimates can be relevant if customers respond honestly and their intentions remain consistent. Juries of executive opinion average the estimates made by executives from marketing, production, finance, and purchasing. No elaborate math or statistics are required.

Customer surveys are conducted by means of personal interviews or telephone questionnaires. The questions must be well stated and easily understood. The respondents are a random sample of the relevant population. Customer surveys can provide valuable in-depth information. Although they are often difficult to construct and time-consuming to administer, many marketing research firms use them.

Global Strategy in Action 5–1 provides an interesting and fast developing use of sales force estimates. They are used to provide companies with recommendations for internationally marketable products—their own successful products currently sold in limited geographic areas.

Social Forecasts

If strategic forecasting relies only on economic indicators, social trends that can have a profound impact may be neglected. Some firms have recognized this and identify social trends and underlying attitudes as part of their environmental scanning. Recent social forecasting efforts have involved analysis of such areas as population, housing, Social Security and welfare, health and nutrition, education and training, income, and wealth and expenditures.

A variety of approaches are used in social forecasting, including time series analysis and the judgmental techniques described earlier. However, *scenario development* is probably the most popular approach. Scenarios, the imagined stories that integrate objective and subjective parts of other forecasts, are designed to help prepare strategic managers for alternative possibilities, thus enabling them to develop contingency plans. Because scenarios can be presented in easily understood forms, they often are used in social forecasting. They can be developed by the following process:

1. Prepare the background by assessing the overall social environment under investigation (such as social legislation).
2. Select critical indicators, and search for future events that may affect them (e.g., growing distrust of business).
3. Analyze the reasons for the past behavior of each indicator (e.g., perceived disregard for air and water quality).
4. Forecast each indicator in three scenarios—showing the least favorable environment, the likely environment, and the most favorable environment.
5. Write the scenarios from the viewpoint of someone at a given future time.
6. Condense each scenario to a few paragraphs.

Strategy in Action 5–2 presents the "most likely" scenario of the ecology in the 21st century as judged by a panel of experts. It shows how social, political, and technological concerns can be blended to produce a useful forecast.

Strategy in Action 5–3 presents a scenario that was developed in 1987 for Georgia Power Company. Its purpose was to determine how the future environment might influence the firm's load and energy growth to the year 1995. With the help of Battelle Columbus Division, a consulting firm, Georgia Power identified five broad areas of influence—the same areas you studied in Chapter 3 as the constituents of the remote external environment. From these areas, 15 key factors were isolated for investigation, of which 5 were judged to be critical to Georgia Power's planning. Several scenarios were developed based on forecasts of these five factors. The scenario presented in Strategy in Action 5–3 showed the greatest economic growth.

When a situation is dominated by a few highly influential factors, scenario developers often develop different forecasts based on the possible emergence of each factor as the dominant one. This approach is shown in Strategy in Action 5–4. It provides three scenarios for the advertising industry centered on the factors of globalization, polarization, and mega-shops.

BusinessWeek

IT WAS A HIT IN BUENOS AIRES—SO WHY NOT BOISE?

GLOBAL STRATEGY IN ACTION 5–1

In June of 1997, Häagen-Dazs began serving a new flavor called *dulce de leche* at its sole ice cream shop in Buenos Aires. Named after the caramelized milk that is one of the most popular flavors in Argentina, the locally developed line was an immediate hit. Within weeks, the super-sweet, butterscotch-like confection was the store's best-seller.

Just one year later, consumers from Boston to Los Angeles to Paris can find *dulce de leche* at the supermarket or in one of Häagen-Dazs's 700 retail stores. In U.S. stores that carry it, only vanilla sells better. In Miami, *dulce* sells twice as fast as any other flavor. In the U.S., it does $1 million a month in revenue. And in Europe, it will soon move up from a seasonal flavor to year-round status.

FERTILE FEEDBACK

The dessert is just the latest example of an emerging two-way trend among American marketers. No longer does the shrinking of the globe mean simply that U.S. companies pump out hamburgers, sneakers, and movies for the world to consume—or that Asian and European companies readily sell their goods in the U.S.

In globalization's latest twist, American companies from Levi Strauss & Co. to Nike Inc. are lifting products and ideas from their international operations and bringing them home. Although U.S. companies have long exported their products, a few have now begun using their international operations as incubators for the next big hit.

It's not just happenstance, either. Companies are reorganizing so that hot products from one region of the world can be more readily spotted and shipped elsewhere—either to the U.S. or other international markets. Reliance on the home office for product research, development, and ideas is shrinking. Within companies, says Jane Fraser, a consultant in McKinsey & Co.'s global practice, "the importance of the product is rising, and the importance of the country is beginning to decline."

Take Pillsbury Co., which owns Häagen-Dazs. After consolidating its international division last year, it now invites U.S. executives to training seminars to swap ideas. North American executives who had tried *dulce de leche* at a brand conference in January, 1997, realized it might fit with the company's recent move to target Latinos in the U.S. But the product did more than that. Today, U.S. sales of the flavor are growing by about 27% monthly—compared with 6% for another specialty flavor, coffee mocha chip.

Source: David Leonhardt in Chicago, "It Was a Hit in Buenos Aires—So Why Not Boise?" *Business Week:* September 7, 1998.

Political Forecasts

Some strategic planners want to give political forecasts the same serious consideration that is given to economic forecasts. They believe that business success can be profoundly affected by shifts in a broad range of political factors, such as the size of government budgets, tariffs, tax rates, defense spending, the growth of regulatory bodies, and the extent of business leaders' participation in government planning.

Political forecasts for foreign countries also are important. Political risks in those countries affect firms that are in any way dependent on international subsidiaries, on suppliers for customers, or on critical resources. Increasing worldwide interdependence

BusinessWeek

continued

BUYING NON-AMERICAN

An increasingly diverse U.S. customer base has companies searching for ways to connect with fast-growing ethnic groups. Rising levels of immigration also have brought salsa, soccer, and Thai food into the mainstream. At the same time, Americans of all backgrounds have become increasingly willing to choose more adventurous products. Altoids, a 200-year-old British product originally used to calm upset stomachs, now holds 17% of the $281 million U.S. breath-mint category, having edged aside tamer candies such as Certs. "The popularity of stronger, more intense flavors has soared," says Liz Smith, general manager of Callard & Bower-Suchard, a Kraft subsidiary that owns the Altoids mint.

Moreover, the vast increase in imported products in the U.S. over the last two decades has made consumers and marketers far more comfortable with the idea of products with international roots than they once were. With U.S. households increasingly buying Japanese electronics and German cars, the "Not Invented Here" impulse no longer applies. "Most Americans who buy a Mercedes or Toyota don't think they're buying a value system along with a product," says Richard Pelles, a history professor at the University of Bonn.

To be fair, the trend is in its early stages. A good number of giant marketers, such as Coca-Cola Co. and RJR Nabisco Inc., say they have never taken a product or ad campaign from abroad and brought it into the U.S.

But others are happy to take the plunge. Nike has found success with shoes that don't appear to jibe with U.S. tastes. A soccer boot, designed with and worn by Brazilian national team member Ronaldo, was a hit at stores, especially during this summer's playing of the World Cup. Two running shoes have also been imported to the U.S. A long-distance running shoe called the Air Rift, which fits like a mitten with the big toe separate to better simulate running barefoot, was designed with the help of Kenyan runners. And the Air Streak was introduced first in Japan and a year later in the U.S.

The reason for the moves? Nike based them in part on an internal consumer study, which shows a decline in nativistic consumer sentiment in the U.S., especially among young buyers.

Other companies are hoping for similar outcomes. Levi Strauss, famous for exporting the all-American look of blue jeans to the world, is hoping to bring an offshore trend to U.S. consumers. For three years, a dark version of Levi's denim has been the hot seller in Japan. This year, Levi's is launching an offshoot called "hard jeans" that will be darker and stiffer than typical denim. Levi's has told its U.S. managers that looking abroad for ideas is part of their job. "Three or four years ago, that would have been inconceivable in this company," says Robert Holloway, Levi Strauss's vice-president for business development. "People had a much narrower view."

makes it imperative for firms of all sizes to consider the international political implications of their strategies.

Because of the billions of U.S. dollars lost in the last two decades as a result of revolutions, nationalization, and other manifestations of political instability, multinational firms and consultants have developed a variety of approaches to international forecasting. Some of the better known are:

Haner's Business Environmental Risk Index, which monitors 15 economic and political variables in 42 countries.

Frost and Sullivan's World Political Risks Forecasts, which predict the likelihood of various catastrophes befalling an individual firm.

SCENARIO ON THE ECOLOGY IN THE 21ST CENTURY

STRATEGY IN ACTION 5–2

Imagine how the world will look from a technological standpoint in the year 2050. It seems likely that the combination of environmental constraints and consumer desires for functionality rather than ownership will have had profound impacts on the global economy, government policies, private corporations, and individuals. As a result of environmental constraints, for example, energy and resource conservation will have become increasingly critical. Energy- and resource-efficient corporations will have gained substantial competitive advantages. This trend in particular may favor Japanese companies, because as an island nation, the Japanese have already internalized a parsimonious attitude toward energy and resources. This attitude, which at least initially was quite independent of the environment, will serve them well in an environmentally constrained world. Americans, on the other hand, with their "cowboy economy" and propensity for resource depletion, may have a considerably rougher time.

Price structures, a serious impediment to industrial ecology during the 1990s, will undergo considerable evolution in the next few decades, as more and more externalities become captured either through market mechanisms or fees and taxes. The adjustment of the pricing structure will be sporadic and will make business planning quite difficult. Those corporations that fail to internalize environmental considerations into their product and process planning in the late twentieth or early twenty-first centuries will find their costs escalating wildly and unpredictably, and will have few options when changes have to be made rapidly.

A concomitant development will be the ascendancy of materials science in many corporations. The ability to predict environmental impacts of materials across their life cycles and to implement alternatives in response to regulatory bans and rapidly changing costs will prove to be an important competency for any extractive or manufacturing corporation. Much of the progress in achieving sustainable manufacturing practices will rely on new materials—superconductors, buckyball derivatives, and enzymes used in bioprocessing factories, for example—and those corporations that stay abreast of the "learning curve" on new materials will do well.

The crucial role of new materials will be reinforced by an explicit policy on the part of many governments to allocate the transfer of functionality to the consumer marketplace and to place the responsibility for the underlying product on manufacturing corporations. The trend, initiated by postconsumer product take-back legislation in Germany and Japan in the 1990s, will be extended to most product categories. Governments will increasingly realize that environmental impacts arise predominantly from the nature of the material stocks and flows underlying the economy

Source: *Industrial Ecology* by Graedel/Allenby, © 1995. Adapted by permission of Prentice Hall, Inc., Upper Saddle River, NJ.

Probe International's custom reports for specific firms, which examine broad social trends.

The developmental forecasts of Arthur D. Little (ADL), which examine a country's progress.

Of all the approaches in use, those of ADL may be the most ambitious and sophisticated. With computer assistance, ADL follows the progress of each country by looking at five criteria: social development, technological advancement, abundance of natural resources, level of domestic tranquility, and type of political system. When a country's development in any one of these areas gets too far ahead of its development in the other areas, tension builds and violence often follows. Using this system, ADL

continued

rather than from the quality of life the economy provides to consumers. They will react more and more by imposing on business the responsibility for materials, from extraction to rebirth to safe disposal.

On a broader front, as more and more operations of corporations become subject to public approval processes, either formally through regulatory mechanisms or informally through public activism, manufacturing will become a true partnership among the corporation, the community in which it exists, and the society in which it is embedded. The idea of a corporation as responsible to only its shareholders and perhaps to its employees or management is rapidly becoming obsolescent, although the details of balancing desirable competitive incentives against a broader social role are difficult and still evolving. Nonetheless, in the future corporations will not quickly put profit ahead of social responsibility; so deeply will environmental concerns redefine our society.

What of various industrial sectors? Electronics manufacturing and software development will boom as the creation of intelligent resource- and energy-conserving systems permeates the economy. Some power utilities will suffer, but many will prosper by increasing their energy networking capabilities and becoming turnkey energy-efficiency consultants, an extension of the demand management efforts that began in the early 1990s. The transportation sector will see enormous change, best characterized by saying that customers will be offered "transparent transportation" for goods and services, where conditions and timing are specified but modes and interconnections are chosen by the service vendor. "Transparent commuting" will operate much the same way, except that many people will remain where they are and commute electronically. An economy based on intellectual capital requires an infrastructure emphasizing electronic networks, not civil engineering.

A SUMMARY OF THE VISION

The future for purposes of the practitioner of industrial ecology is essentially captured in two propositions: that it is an increasingly environmentally constrained world, and that customers will soon be buying functionality, not material. Thus, the long-term vision of industrial ecology centers both on a technological development and on changes in the structure of societal demand. Industrial ecology recognizes that technology is the source of our environmental problems and that it may be the only feasible way to solve them. Technology alone cannot achieve the transformation we envision; it must work within the societal system to move closer to that goal.

---

forecast political turbulence in Iran eight years before the U.S. hostage crisis. ADL foresees that uneven development probably will produce similar turmoil in 20 other countries, such as Peru, Chile, Malaysia, and the Philippines. It believes the world is highly predictable if the right questions are asked. Unfortunately, too many executives fail to use the same logic in analyzing political affairs that they use in other strategic areas. Political analysis should be routinely incorporated into economic analyses. Ford, General Motors, PepsiCo, Singer, Du Pont, and United Technologies are among the many firms that follow ADL's advice.

Global Strategy in Action 5–2 provides a guide to political evaluation that is popular among executives who are responsible for international operations. Global Strategy in Action 5–3 presents an actual scenario that was developed to assess political and economic conditions in the Americas.

STRATEGY IN ACTION 5–3

GEORGIA POWER PLANNING SCENARIOS FOR 1995

HIGH ECONOMIC GROWTH SCENARIO

The average annual growth rate of the real U.S. gross national product (GNP) will exceed 3.2 percent between now and the year 2010. This growth rate is about the same as the growth rate of 3.4 percent experienced during the post–World War II era but is greater than the average growth rate for the 1980s. Economic growth in Georgia will exceed that of the nation as a whole by as much as one percentage point. This growth pattern is expected to result from a continuation of the Sunbelt phenomenon that drove Georgia's strong growth over the past two decades. With higher economic growth elsewhere, net migration to Georgia will slow down.

Higher productivity growth and lower real interest rates will be associated with higher U.S. economic growth. Higher productivity growth will occur as the baby boom generation matures and the work experience of its members increases. Interest rates will remain lower as long as inflationary pressures do not reemerge.

The average price of oil in 1985 dollars will remain under $18 per barrel as a result of the transformation of the OPEC-dominated world oil market into a commodity-based market. The surplus of natural gas will diminish, but not until the middle 1990s. Industrial demand for natural gas will dampen, as lower oil prices encourage substitution to oil. Coal prices will increase more slowly. Real electricity prices will decline if the free market energy policy pursued by the Reagan Administration continues. Emissions will remain essentially stable through 1995.

Real U.S. GNP will grow at an annual rate of less than 2.7 percent, a rate lower than the average growth rate experienced so far in the 1980s. This decline will result from a worsening trade imbalance and from large deficit spending that exerts an upward pressure on interest rates. Georgia's personal income growth will exceed that of the United States as a whole by over one percentage point. Higher levels of net migration into Georgia will occur as economic circumstances worsen elsewhere. This will accelerate growth in the state.

The annual increase in U.S. productivity will be less than 1.5 percent, an increase consistent with the slow growth of the 1970s. The low growth rate will result from a decline in demand for most goods and services as the population ages. Taxes will increase to support the aged population. Both higher taxes and higher interest rates will accelerate the shift from a manufacturing to a service economy.

By 1995, oil prices will average over $30 per barrel in 1985 dollars. The current world surplus will erode quickly in the early years as the current strong economic growth increases oil demand. This will cause a return to OPEC price controls. Deregulation will free natural gas prices to adjust rapidly to supply and demand imbalances. Exploration and development will be dampened by the initial lower prices and by inconsistent and unpredictable government energy policy. Real electricity prices will decline. Some acid rain legislation will be passed, but not enough to significantly discourage growth in the utility industry.

Source: D. L. Goldfarb and W. R. Huss, "Building Scenarios for an Electric Utility," *Long Range Planning,* June 1988, pp. 78–85.

Technological Forecasts

Such rapidly developed and revolutionary technological innovations as lasers, nuclear energy, satellites and other communication devices, desalination of water, electric cars, and miracle drugs have prompted many firms to invest in technological forecasts. Knowledge of probable technological development helps strategic managers prepare their firms to benefit from change. Except for econometrics, all of the previously described techniques can be used to make technological forecasts. However, uncertainty of information favors the use of scenarios and two additional forecasting approaches: brainstorming and the Delphi technique.

Brainstorming helps a group generate new ideas and forecasts. With this technique, analysis or criticisms of participants' contributions are postponed so creative thinking is not stifled or restricted. Because there are no interruptions, group members are encouraged to offer original ideas and to build on one another's innovative thoughts. The most promising ideas generated in this way are thoroughly evaluated at a later time.

The *Delphi method* is a systematic procedure for obtaining consensus among a group of experts. This method includes:

1. A detailed survey of opinions of experts, usually obtained through a mail questionnaire.
2. Anonymous evaluation of the responses by the experts involved.
3. One or more revisions of the experts' answers until convergence has been achieved.

Relatively inexpensive, the Delphi method can be successful in social and political forecasting.

A firm's use of a particular forecasting technique is often highly dependent on the industry in which it is involved. For product necessities such as electric power, food, and pharmaceuticals, corporations are often able to perform forecasts several months in advance. However, for newly introduced products or products with volatile demand, forecasting efforts become daily challenges in satisfying fluctuating demand patterns. A means to alleviate the pressures of dealing with such patterns can be the recognition of early warning signals. Proactive steps such as customer surveys or early tests of response can help to provide early warning signs. Figure 5–5 provides a comparison of where early warning systems have greater or less value in predicting demand.

At the end of this chapter, Appendix 5–B briefly describes the 20 most frequently used forecasting approaches.

INTEGRATE FORECAST RESULTS INTO THE STRATEGIC MANAGEMENT PROCESS

Once the forecasting techniques have been selected and the forecasts made, the results must be integrated into the strategic management process. For example, the economic forecast must be related to analyses of the industry, suppliers, competition, and key resources. Figure 5–6 presents a format for displaying interrelationships between forecast remote environment variables and the influential task environment variables. The resulting predictions become a part of the assumed environment in formulating strategy.

It is critical that strategic decision makers understand the assumptions on which environmental forecasts are based. The experience of Itel, a computer-leasing firm, illustrates the consequences of a failure to understand these assumptions. Itel had been able to lease 200 plug-in computers made by Advance Systems and by Hitachi largely because IBM could not deliver its newest AT systems. Consequently, Itel bullishly forecast that it would place 430 of its systems in the following year—despite the rumor that IBM would announce a new line of aggressively priced systems in the first quarter of that year. Even Itel's competitors felt that customers would hold off their purchasing decisions until IBM made the announcement. However, Itel signed long-term purchase contracts with its suppliers and increased its marketing staff by 80 percent.

SCENARIOS FOR THE ADVERTISING INDUSTRY

STRATEGY IN
ACTION
5–4

TOTAL GLOBALIZATION

The mega-shops dominate the world marketing scene in Europe, China, Japan, Korea, and beyond. The issue of agency account conflicts disappears. Advanced communication technology speeds up the homogenization of the world's cultures as global marketers expand. Attempts to create regional trading blocks fail, and global brand names flourish. Cars, electronic products, packaged foods, clothing, and many other products compete in a global marketplace with global competitors. Although media are fragmented locally, the information highway permits the transmission of targeted messages to increasingly smaller segments (i.e., mass customization).

Agencies provide a broad range of services in view of the external complexities facing clients. As agencies and advertising grow together, they become inextricably linked in terms of profits and information. The world marketing front becomes a battleground of Titans. The profits are enormous, since the barriers to entry are substantial. Fee and performance compensation structures are common, with long-term relationships being the norm. The mega-agencies thrive in part because of their more professional approach to business, with better-trained account executives and office managers. Many mega-agencies invest heavily in managerial training and development, via "in-house universities," which give them a strong edge.

POLARIZATION IS "HOT"

Globalization and localization flourish side by side, due to the emergence of strong regional trade-blocks (NAFTA, the European Community, Pacific Blocks, etc.). Negative reactions to the export of U.S. pop culture is on the rise (e.g., Disney's theme park in France). Mega-shops serve global marketers of consumer products, providing a broad range of services and developing close relationships. Global marketers consolidate accounts among a few key agencies. The issue of account conflicts among the high rollers exists in some accounts, in part because of a few well-reported leaks. Compensation structure varies depending on billings and client/agency relationships.

Localized, specialized, or "boutique" agencies also flourish as the mega-shops cannot maintain profitable relationships with specialized industries, small regional advertisers, or controversial

Source: Paul J. H. Schoemaker, "Scenario Planning: A Tool for Strategic Thinking," *Sloan Management Review,* Winter 1995, pp. 25–39.

Itel's forecasting mistake and its failure to examine its sales forecasts in relationship to the actions of competitors and suppliers were nearly disastrous. It slipped close to bankruptcy within less than a year.

Forecasting external events enables a firm to identify its probable requirements for future success, to formulate or reformulate its basic mission, and to design strategies for achieving its goals and objectives. If the forecast identifies any gaps or inconsistencies between the firm's desired position and its present position, strategic managers can respond with plans and actions. When Apple successfully introduced its new low-priced personal computers, sales climbed 85 percent for the quarter. However, because the firm failed to forecast that sales of the low-price computers would cannibalize the sales of its more expensive models, profits slipped, forcing Apple to lay off 10 percent of its work force, or 1,500 employees.

Dealing with the uncertainty of the future is a major function of strategic managers. The forecasting task requires systematic information gathering coupled with the utilization of a variety of forecasting approaches. A high level of insight also is needed

continued

products (e.g., condoms). Specialized support services such as marketing research firms continue to flourish. Some big, disillusioned clients turn increasingly toward nontraditional sources for creative ideas, notably film producers. The mega-agencies are unable to compete for new advertising, and attempts at strategic alliances with Hollywood studios fail due to culture and ego clashes. Also, the increasing fragmentation of media (with more than 500 cable channels, CD-ROMs, radio, print, etc.) favors more specialized players that understand selected niches better. In an attempt to boost their tax revenues, various governments institute percentage caps on the deductible ad expenses.

Mega-Shop Dinosaurs

The mega-shops reign for a short time, just beyond the turn of the century. They are eventually crippled by their sheer size, central ownership, and the bureaucracy that often accompanies such structures. They are slow to adapt to media changes (especially interactive), relying instead on personal relationships through account executives. As a consequence, their flexibility and creativity suffers. Advertising by mega-agency is increasingly seen as a commodity and bought on price. The lumbering mega-shops gradually lose business to the smaller but "hotter" agencies, especially as clients restructure into networked entities with high personnel turnover. Military conflicts around the world (especially in Eastern Europe and the Middle East) lead to isolationism and nationalism and frustrate any attempts at the creation of truly global markets.

In addition, advertisers in many countries remain highly sensitive to agency account conflicts. Privately held start-ups emerge with revolutionary creative and management styles. Specialized media agencies and cooperatives develop, pooling client resources to profit from media-buying leverage. Creative compensation structures emerge as advertisers demand that agencies be financially accountable and as agencies' competition heats up. On top of this, the Democrats (in their quest to fund social programs) limit the tax deductions associated with advertising. This further undermines firms' investments in brand equity, which together with a poor economy puts an emphasis on value and price discounts.

to integrate risks and opportunities in formulating strategy. However, intentional or unintentional delays or the inability to understand certain issues may prevent a firm from using the insights gained in assessing the impact of broad environmental trends. Sensitivity and openness to new and better approaches and opportunities, therefore, are essential.

Monitor the Critical Aspects of Managing Forecasts

Although almost all aspects of forecast management may be critical in specific situations, three aspects are critical over the lifetime of a firm.

The first is the identification of the environmental factors that deserve forecasting. Hundreds of factors may affect a firm, but often the most important of these factors are a few of immediate concern, such as sales forecasts and competitive trends. The time and resources needed to completely understand all the environmental factors that might be critical to the success of a strategy are seldom available. Therefore, executives must

GLOBAL STRATEGY IN ACTION 5–2

A GUIDE TO POLITICAL EVALUATION

The following is an abridged version of the popular Political Agenda Worksheet developed by Probe, a consulting firm that specializes in political analysis, which may serve as a guide for corporate executives initiating their own political evaluations.

EXTERNAL FACTORS AFFECTING SUBJECT COUNTRY

Prospects for foreign conflict.

Relations with border countries.

Regional instabilities.

Alliances with major and regional powers.

Sources of key raw materials.

Major foreign markets.

Policy toward United States.

U.S. policy toward country.

INTERNAL GROUPINGS (POINTS OF POWER)

Government in Power

Key agencies and officials.

Legislative entrenched bureaucracies.

Policies—economic, financial, social, labor, and so on.

Pending legislation.

Attitude toward private sector.

Power networks.

Political Parties (in and out of power)

Policies.

Leading and emerging personalities.

Source: Benjamin Weiner, "What Executives Should Know about Political Risk," *Management Review,* January 1992, p. 21.

depend on their collective experience and perception to determine which factors are worth the expense of forecasting.

The second aspect is the selection of reputable, cost-efficient forecasting sources outside the firm that can expand its forecasting database. Strategic managers should identify federal and state government agencies, trade and industry associations, and individuals or other groups that can provide data forecasts at reasonable costs.

The third aspect is the selection of forecasting tasks that are to be done in-house. Given the great credence that often is accorded to formally developed forecasts—despite the inherent uncertainty of the database—the selection of forecasting techniques is indeed critical. A firm beginning its forecasting efforts is well advised to start with less technical methods, such as sales force estimates and the jury of executive opinion, rather than highly sophisticated forecasting techniques, such as econometrics, and to

continued

Internal power struggles.

Sector and area strengths.

Future prospects for retaining or gaining power.

Other Important Groups

Unions and labor movements.

Military, special groups within military.

Families.

Business and financial communities.

Intelligentsia.

Students.

Religious groups.

Media.

Regional and local governments.

Social and environmental activists.

Cultural, linguistic, and ethnic groups.

Separatist movements.

Foreign communities.

Potential competitors and customers.

INTERNAL FACTORS

Power struggles among elites.

Ethnic confrontations.

Regional struggles.

Economic factors affecting stability (consumer inflation, price and wage controls, unemployment, supply shortages, taxation, and so on).

Anti-establishment movements.

add approaches requiring greater analytic sophistication as its experience and understanding increase. In this way, its managers can learn how to deal with the varied weaknesses and strengths of forecasting techniques.

SUMMARY

Environmental forecasting starts with the identification of critical factors external to the firm that might provide opportunities or pose threats in the future. Both quantitative and qualitative strategic forecasting techniques are used to project the long-range direction and impact of these factors in the remote and task environments. To select the forecasting techniques that are most appropriate for the firm, the strengths and weaknesses of the various techniques must be understood. To offset the potential biases or

THE AMERICAS

GLOBAL
STRATEGY IN
ACTION
5–3

In general, political and economic conditions are likely to be more stable in Central and South America in 1992 than they have been for several years. The debt crisis has receded as a prime concern; and while political violence may increase, most regimes are not likely to change during 1992. The biggest headlines will be devoted to the free-trade movements in the region, especially the North American Free Trade Area (NAFTA).

Some type of free-trade agreement between Mexico and the United States is likely in 1992, but its economic impact will not be nearly as important as its symbolic significance. Rather than stimulating new trade in Mexico, it will open up new opportunities for joint venture investments. The most important consequence of such an agreement may well be to sustain political support for President Salinas of Mexico. Other free-trade agreements among South American countries will also evolve during 1992, but they will have only limited impact on the local economies.

Since Brazil and Argentina together account for 50 percent of all economic activity in South America, these are the countries to watch closely. Brazil continues to make little headway against inflation or toward meaningful economic reform. Prospects for improvement are not good while President Collor battles a recalcitrant congress and the stubbornly independent state governments.

Argentina, on the other hand, has shown significant signs of economic improvement under a new minister of the economy and President Menem, who has regained much of his earlier popularity. As more privatization has occurred, the international financial community appears to have talked itself back into believing in Argentina. Nevertheless, prospects for comprehensive privatization remain limited, and labor is becoming increasingly opposed to Menem's policies. A new acceleration of inflation could destroy Menem's chances of implementing the nascent program of far-reaching economic reform now in process.

Source: *Planning Review* 20, no. 2 (March–April 1992), p. 27. Published with permission of The Planning Forum, P.O. Box 70, Oxford, OH 45056.

FIGURE 5–5
Where an Early Warning System Has Greater or Less Value in Business

Greater Value	Less Value
Long or lengthening supply lead times.	Easy resupply "off the shelf."
Lean inventories.	Ample inventories.
High fraction of new products; apparel, book publishing.	Well-established products such as aspirin and corn flakes.
Customers can easily go elsewhere if item is unavailable: department stores, airlines.	Unique items with limited competition: high-performance car accessories.
Perishable or rapid-obsolescence items: theater seats, cut flowers.	Products can be easily carried over for future sale: blue jeans, office supplies.
Short, intense selling season: Christmas decorations, skiwear.	Selling seasons that permit enough time to expand or contract supplies.
Suppliers to JIT or Quick Response customers, for example, to auto companies, Wal-Mart.	Suppliers of capital equipment and systems that are made to order: mainframe computers, aircraft.

Source: Paul V. Teplitz, "Do You Need an Early Warning System?" *The Journal of Forecasting*, 1995, p. 9.

FIGURE 5–6
Task and Remote Environment Impact Matrix

Remote Environments	Task Environments			
	Key Customer Trends	**Key Competitor Trends**	**Key Supplier Trends**	**Key Labor Market Trends**
Economic	*Example:* Trends in inflation and unemployment rates.		*Example:* Annual domestic oil demand and worldwide sulfur demand through the year 2020.	
Social	*Example:* Increasing numbers of single-parent homes.			*Example:* Rising education level of U.S. population.
Political	*Example:* Increasing numbers of punitive damage awards in product liability cases.		*Example:* Possibility of oil boycotts.	
Technological		*Example:* Increasing use of superchips and computer-based instrumentation for synthesizing genes.	*Example:* Use of cobalt 60 gamma irradiation to extend shelf life of perishables.	
Ecological		*Example:* Increased use of biodegradable fast-food packaging.		*Example:* Increasing availability of mature workers with experience in "smokestack" industries.

errors individual techniques involve, employment of more than one technique usually is advisable.

Critical aspects in forecast management include the identification of the environmental factors that deserve forecasting, the selection of forecasting sources outside the firm, and the selection of forecasting tasks that are to be done in-house.

QUESTIONS FOR DISCUSSION

1. Identify five changes in the remote environment that you believe will affect major U.S. industries over the next decade. What forecasting techniques could be used to assess the probable impact of these changes?

2. Construct a matrix with forecasting techniques on the horizontal axis and at least five qualities of forecasting techniques across the vertical axis. Indicate the relative strengths and weaknesses of each technique.

3. Develop three rules of thumb for guiding strategic managers in their use of forecasting.

4. Develop a typewritten two-page forecast of a variable that you believe will affect the prosperity of your business school over the next 10 years.

5. Using prominent business journals, find two examples of firms that either benefited or suffered from environmental forecasts.

6. Describe the background, skills, and abilities of the individual you would hire as the environmental forecaster for a firm with $500 million in annual sales. How would the qualifications of such an individual differ for a much smaller firm? For a much larger firm?

BIBLIOGRAPHY

Alerthal, Lester M., Jr. "Keeping the Lead in an Ever-Changing Global Landscape." *Planning Review* 23, no. 8 (September–October 1995), p. 13.

Alexander, Marcus; Andrew Campbell; and Michael Gorld. "A New Model for Reforming the Planning Review Process." *Planning Review* 23, no. 1 (January–February 1995), p. 12.

Allaire, Y., and M. E. Firsirotu. "Coping with Strategic Uncertainty." *Sloan Management Review,* Spring 1989, pp. 7–16.

Barndt, W. D., Jr. "Profiling Rival Decision Makers." *The Journal of Business Strategy,* January–February 1991, pp. 8–11.

Coplin, W. D., and M. K. O'Leary. "1991 World Political Risk Forecast." *Planning Review,* January–February 1991, pp. 16–23.

Czinkota, M. R. "International Information Needs for U.S. Competitiveness." *Business Horizons,* November–December 1991, pp. 86–91.

Fuld, L. "A Recipe for Business Intelligence Success." *The Journal of Business Strategy,* January–February 1991, pp. 12–17.

—————. "Achieving Total Quality through Intelligence." *Long Range Planning,* February 1992, pp. 109–15.

Fulmer, W., and R. Fulmer. "Strategic Group Technique: Involving Managers in Strategic Planning." *Long Range Planning,* April 1990, pp. 79–84.

Gelb, B. D.; M. J. Saxton; G. M. Zinkhan; and N. D. Albers. "Competitive Intelligence: Insights from Executives." *Business Horizons,* January–February 1991, pp. 43–47.

Gilad, B. "U.S. Intelligence System: Model for Corporate Chiefs?" *The Journal of Business Strategy,* May–June 1991, pp. 20–25.

Herring, J. P. "The Role of Intelligence in Formulating Strategy." *The Journal of Business Strategy,* September–October 1992, pp. 54–60.

Kahane, A. "Scenarios for Energy: Sustainable World vs. Global Mercantilism." *Long Range Planning,* August 1992, pp. 38–46.

Keiser, B. "Practical Competitor Intelligence." *Planning Review,* September 1987, pp. 14–19.

Lederer, A. L., and V. Sethi. "Guidelines for Strategic Information Planning." *The Journal of Business Strategy,* November–December 1991, pp. 38–43.

Pant, P. N., and W. H. Starbuck. "Innocents in the Forest: Forecasting and Research Methods." *Yearly Review of Management,* June 1990, pp. 433–60.

Pine, B. Joseph, II. "Peter Schwartz Offers Two Scenarios for the Future." *Planning Review* 23, no. 5 (September–October 1995), p. 30.

Premkumar, G., and W. R. King. "Assessing Strategic Information Systems Planning." *Long Range Planning,* October 1991, pp. 41–58.

Rousch, G. B. "A Program for Sharing Corporate Intelligence." *The Journal of Business Strategy,* January–February 1991, pp. 4–7.

Schoemaker, Paul J. H. "Scenario Planning: A Tool for Strategic Thinking." *Sloan Management Review* 36, no. 2 (Winter 1995), p. 25.

Schriefer, Audrey E. "Getting the Most Out of Scenarios: Advice from the Experts." *Planning Review* 23, no. 5 (September–October 1995), p. 33.

Simpson, Daniel. "The Planning Process and the Role of the Planner." *Planning Review* 23, no. 1 (January–February 1995), p. 20.

Stokke, P. R.; W. K. Ralston; T. A. Boyce; and I. H. Wilson. "Scenario Planning for Norwegian Oil and Gas." *Long Range Planning,* April 1990, pp. 17–26.

Thurow, Lester C. "Surviving in a Turbulent Environment." *Planning Review* 23, no. 5 (September–October 1995), p. 24.

Wilson, Ian; Oliver W. Markley; Joseph F. Coates; and Clement Bezold. "A Forum of Futurists." *Planning Review* 23, no. 6 (November–December 1995), p. 10.

Appendix 5–A

Sources for Environmental Forecasts

Remote and Industry Environments

A. Economic considerations:
1. *Predicasts* (most complete and up-to-date review of forecasts).
2. National Bureau of Economic Research.
3. *Handbook of Basic Economic Statistics.*
4. *Statistical Abstract of the United States* (also includes industrial, social, and political statistics).
5. Publications by Department of Commerce agencies:
   a. Office of Business Economics (e.g., *Survey of Business*).
   b. Bureau of Economic Analysis (e.g., *Business Conditions Digest*).
   c. Bureau of the Census (e.g., *Survey of Manufacturers* and various reports on population, housing, and industries).
   d. Business and Defense Services Administration (e.g., *United States Industrial Outlook*).
6. Securities and Exchange Commission (various quarterly reports on plant and equipment, financial reports, working capital of corporations).
7. The Conference Board.
8. *Survey of Buying Power.*
9. *Marketing Economic Guide.*
10. *Industrial Arts Index.*
11. U.S. and national chambers of commerce.
12. American Manufacturers Association.
13. *Federal Reserve Bulletin.*
14. *Economic Indicators,* annual report.
15. *Kiplinger Newsletter.*
16. International economic sources:
    a. *Worldcasts.*
    b. Master key index for business international publications.
    c. Department of Commerce.
       (1) Overseas business reports.
       (2) Industry and Trade Administration.
       (3) Bureau of the Census—*Guide to Foreign Trade Statistics.*
17. *Business Periodicals Index.*

Sources: Adapted with numerous additions from C. R. Goeldner and L. M. Kirks, "Business Facts: Where to Find Them," *MSU Business Topics,* Summer 1976, pp. 23–76, reprinted by permission of the publisher, Division of Research, Graduate School of Business Administration, MSU; F. E. deCarbonnel and R. G. Donance, "Information Source for Planning Decisions," *California Management Review,* Summer 1973, pp. 42–53; and A. B. Nun, R. C. Lenz, Jr., H. W. Landford, and M. J. Cleary, "Data Source for Trend Extrapolation in Technological Forecasting," *Long Range Planning,* February 1972, pp. 72–76.

B. Social considerations:
   1. Public opinion polls.
   2. Surveys such as *Social Indicators and Social Reporting,* the annals of the American Academy of Political and Social Sciences.
   3. Current controls: Social and behavioral sciences.
   4. Abstract services and indexes for articles in sociological, psychological, and political journals.
   5. Indexes for *The Wall Street Journal, New York Times,* and other newspapers.
   6. Bureau of the Census reports on population, housing, manufacturers, selected services, construction, retail trade, wholesale trade, and enterprise statistics.
   7. Various reports from such groups as the Brookings Institution and the Ford Foundation.
   8. World Bank Atlas (population growth and GNP data).
   9. World Bank–World Development Report.
C. Political considerations:
   1. *Public Affairs Information Services Bulletin.*
   2. CIS Index (Congressional Information Index).
   3. Business periodicals.
   4. Funk & Scott (regulations by product breakdown).
   5. Weekly compilation of presidential documents.
   6. *Monthly Catalog of Government Publications.*
   7. *Federal Register* (daily announcements of pending regulations).
   8. *Code of Federal Regulations* (final listing of regulations).
   9. Business International Master Key Index (regulations, tariffs).
   10. Various state publications.
   11. Various information services (Bureau of National Affairs, Commerce Clearing House, Prentice Hall).
D. Technological considerations:
   1. *Applied Science and Technology Index.*
   2. *Statistical Abstract of the United States.*
   3. Scientific and Technical Information Service.
   4. University reports, congressional reports.
   5. Department of Defense and military purchasing publishers.
   6. Trade journals and industrial reports.
   7. Industry contacts, professional meetings.
   8. Computer-assisted information searches.
   9. National Science Foundation annual report.
   10. *Research and Development Directory* patent records.
E. Industry considerations:
   1. *Concentration Ratios in Manufacturing* (Bureau of the Census).
   2. *Input-Output Survey* (productivity ratios).
   3. *Monthly Labor Review* (productivity ratios).
   4. *Quarterly Failure Report* (Dun & Bradstreet).
   5. *Federal Reserve Bulletin* (capacity utilization).
   6. *Report on Industrial Concentration and Product Diversification in the 1,000 Largest Manufacturing Companies* (Federal Trade Commission).
   7. Industry trade publications.
   8. Bureau of Economic Analysis, Department of Commerce (specialization ratios).

Industry and Operating Environments

A. Competition and supplier considerations:
1. Target Group Index.
2. U.S. Industrial Outlook.
3. Robert Morris annual statement studies.
4. Troy, Leo Almanac of Business & Industrial Financial Ratios.
5. Census of Enterprise Statistics.
6. Securities and Exchange Commission (10-K reports).
7. Annual reports of specific companies.
8. *Fortune 500 Directory, The Wall Street Journal, Barron's, Forbes, Dun's Review.*
9. Investment services and directories: Moody's, Dun & Bradstreet, Standard & Poor's, Starch Marketing, Funk & Scott Index.
10. Trade association surveys.
11. Industry surveys.
12. Market research surveys.
13. *Country Business Patterns.*
14. *Country and City Data Book.*
15. Industry contacts, professional meetings, salespeople.
16. *NFIB Quarterly Economic Report for Small Business.*

B. Customer profile:
1. *Statistical Abstract of the United States,* first source of statistics.
2. *Statistical Sources* by Paul Wasserman (a subject guide to data—both domestic and international).
3. *American Statistics Index* (Congressional Information Service Guide to statistical publications of U.S. government—monthly).
4. Office to the Department of Commerce:
   a. Bureau of the Census reports on population, housing, and industries.
   b. U.S. Census of Manufacturers (statistics by industry, area, and products).
   c. Survey of Current Business (analysis of business trends, especially February and July issues).
5. Market research studies (*A Basic Bibliography on Market Review,* compiled by Robert Ferber et al., American Marketing Association).
6. *Current Sources of Marketing Information: A Bibliography of Primary Marketing Data* by Gunther & Goldstein, AMA.
7. *Guide to Consumer Markets,* The Conference Board (provides statistical information with demographic, social, and economic data—annual).
8. *Survey of Buying Power.*
9. *Predicasts* (abstracts of publishing forecasts of all industries, detailed products, and end-use data).
10. *Predicasts Basebook* (historical data from 1960 to present, covering subjects ranging from population and GNP to specific products and services; series are coded by Standard Industrial Classifications).
11. *Market Guide* (individual market surveys of over 1,500 U.S. and Canadian cities; includes population, location, trade areas, banks, principal industries, colleges and universities, department and chain stores, newspapers, retail outlets, and sales).

12. *Country and City Data Book* (includes bank deposits, birth and death rates, business firms, education, employment, income of families, manufacturers, population, savings, and wholesale and retail trade).
13. *Yearbook of International Trade Statistics* (UN).
14. *Yearbook of National Accounts Statistics* (UN).
15. *Statistical Yearbook* (UN—covers population, national income, agricultural and industrial production, energy, external trade, and transport).
16. *Statistics of (Continents): Sources for Market Research* (includes separate books on Africa, America, Europe).

C. Key natural resources:
1. *Minerals Yearbook, Geological Survey* (Bureau of Mines, Department of the Interior).
2. *Agricultural Abstract* (Department of Agriculture).
3. Statistics of electric utilities and gas pipeline companies (Federal Power Commission).
4. Publications of various institutions: American Petroleum Institute, Atomic Energy Commission, Coal Mining Institute of America, American Steel Institute, and Brookings Institution.

Appendix 5–B

Strategic Planning Forecasting Tools and Techniques

1. **Dialectical Inquiry.**
   Development, evaluation, and synthesis of conflicting points of view by (1) having separate assigned groups use debate format to formulate and refine each point of view and (2) then bringing two groups together for presentation of debate between and synthesis of their points of view.
2. **Nominal Group Technique.**
   Development, evaluation, and synthesis of individual points of view through an interactive process in a group setting.
3. **Delphi Method.**
   Development, evaluation, and synthesis of individual points of view by systematically soliciting and collating judgments on a particular topic through a set of carefully designed sequential questionnaires interspersed with summarized information and feedback of opinions derived from earlier responses.
4. **Focus Groups.**
   Bringing together recognized experts and qualified individuals in an organized setting to develop, evaluate, and synthesize their individual points of view on a particular topic.
5. **Simulation Technique.**
   Computer-based technique for simulating future situations and then predicting the outcome of various courses of action against each of these situations.
6. **PIMS Analysis.**
   Application of the experiences of a diverse sample of successful and unsuccessful firms.
7. **Market Opportunity Analysis.**
   Identification of markets and market factors in the economy and the industry that will affect the demand for and marketing of a product or service.
8. **Benchmarking.**
   Comparative analysis of competitor programs and strategic positions for use as reference points in the formulation of organization objectives.
9. **Situational Analysis (SWOT or TOWS).**
   Systematic development and evaluation of past, present, and future data to identify internal strengths and weaknesses and external threats and opportunities.
10. **Critical Success Factors/Strategic Issues Analysis.**
    Identification and analysis of a limited number of areas in which high performance will ensure a successful competitive position.
11. **Product Life Cycle Analysis.**
    Analysis of market dynamics in which a product is viewed according to its position within distinct stages of its sales history.

Source: Excerpted with updates from J. Webster, W. Reif, and J. Bracker, "The Manager's Guide to Strategic Planning Tools and Techniques," *Planning Review,* November–December 1989, pp. 4–13, 48.

12. **Future Studies.**
Development of future situations and factors based on agreement of a group of "experts," often from a variety of functional areas within a firm.

13. **Multiple Scenarios.**
Smoothly unfolding narratives that describe an assumed future expressed through a sequence of time frames and snapshots.

14. **SPIRE** (Systematic Procedure for Identification of Relevant Environments).
A computer-assisted, matrix-generating tool for forecasting environmental changes that can have a dramatic impact on operations.

15. **Environmental Scanning, Forecasting, and Trend Analysis.**
Continuous process, usually computer based, of monitoring external factors, events, situations, and projections of forecasts of trends.

16. **Experience Curves.**
An organizing framework for dynamic analyses of cost and price for a product, a company, or an industry over an extended period.

17. **Portfolio Classification Analysis.**
Classification and visual display of the present and prospective positions of firms and products according to the attractiveness of the market and the ability of the firms and products to compete within that market.

18. **Metagame Analysis.**
Arriving at a strategic direction by thinking through a series of viewpoints on a contemplated strategy in terms of every competitor and every combination of competitive responses.

19. **Strategic Gap Analysis.**
Examination of the difference between the extrapolation of current performance levels (e.g., current sales) and the projection of desired performance objectives (e.g., a desired sales level).

20. **Sustainable Growth Model.**
Financial analysis of the sales growth rate that is required to meet market share objectives and the degree to which capacity must be expanded to achieve that growth rate.

CHAPTER 5 DISCUSSION CASE

BusinessWeek

DO YOU KNOW WHO YOUR MOST PROFITABLE CUSTOMERS ARE?

> The tremendous data processing power of computers and the development of user-friendly statistical packages has led to the demand for evermore detailed information bases on consumers. In turn, the growing underutilized data pools of information about consumer demographics, lifestyles, and spending patterns have led to an ability for businesses to develop detailed profiles on customers. Foremost among the analyses that is generated is an assessment whether doing business with a particular customer is likely to provide a profit for the company. This burgeoning form of forecasting is known as *data mining* and it is the topic of the Chapter 5 discussion case.

Like most companies, Federal Express Corp. has some customers that are losers: The cost of doing business with them is greater than the profits they return to the shipper. But FedEx has an edge that most companies lack—it knows who those customers are. That knowledge has kicked off a marketing revolution inside FedEx, where customers sometimes are rated as the good, the bad, and the ugly. "We want to keep the good, grow the bad, and the ugly we want nothing to do with," says Sharanjit Singh, managing director for marketing analysis at FedEx.

It's relatively easy for companies to recognize who is spending money with them. But surprisingly, identifying which customers are profitable for them requires a quantum leap in sophistication. Confounded by technical difficulties and the high cost of software and data storage, many businesses muddle along with only a rough approximation of which customers make them money. "Not too many people have actually done this yet because it's difficult to pull off," says Wayne Eckerson, a principal analyst at Data Warehouse Institute.

But those few that have begun are finding that determining each customer's profitability can pay big dividends. Savvy companies are conducting behind-the-scenes beauty contests to determine who they like and who they wish would go away. Companies such as U S West, Bank of America, and The Limited are creating vast information warehouses stocked with customer data that allow them to compare the complex mix of marketing and servicing costs that go into retaining each individual consumer, versus the revenues he or she is likely to bring in. "Some companies are building a profit-and-loss statement for each customer," says Mike Caccavale, president of Aperio Inc., a consulting firm that specializes in customer-relationship management.

Of course, companies have been using large databases to help refine their marketing efforts for years. But previous attempts focused on the average behavior of large demographic groups, while the newer efforts allow marketers to target individual customers with pinpoint accuracy. And the latest techniques go well beyond determining whether a marketing campaign encourages a consumer to buy—they focus on whether or not that consumer spends enough to make a campaign worthwhile.

Source: Paul C. Judge in Boston, "Do You Know Who Your Most Profitable Customers Are?" *Business Week:* September 14, 1998.

At FedEx, customers who spend a lot with little service and marketing investment get different treatment than, say, those who spend just as much but cost more to keep. The "good" can expect a phone call if their shipping volume falters, which can head off defections before they occur. As for the "bad"—those who spend but are expensive to the company—FedEx is turning them into profitable customers, in many cases, by charging higher shipping prices. And the "ugly"? Those customers who spend little and show few signs of spending more in the future? They can catch the TV ads. "We just don't market to them anymore," says Singh. "That automatically brings our costs down."

The power of such an approach lies in a company's ability to determine how much to spend on marketing campaigns—and where to direct those dollars. Twice a year, U S West sifts through its customer list looking for money-losers who have the potential to be more profitable in the future. The starting point is a database containing as many as 200 observations about each customer's calling patterns. By looking at demographic profiles, plus the mix of local versus long-distance calls, or whether a customer has voice mail, they can estimate a customer's potential telecom spending.

Next, U S West determines how much of the customer's likely telecom budget is already coming its way. Armed with that knowledge, "we can set a cutoff point for how much to spend marketing to this customer before it begins to deteriorate our profitability," says Dennis J. DeGregor, chief database marketing executive for U S West. Those savings fall straight to the bottom line.

Seems like the kind of information marketers would die for. But so far, only a handful have taken the plunge. For one thing, it's expensive. Fleet Bank, one of the few big companies to break out its costs, is spending $38 million just to get started. Also, details about which customers are profitable and which aren't is not always welcome news. "It means the things you did in the past were wrong," says Scott Nelson, an analyst at Gartner Group. "Big advertising campaigns, product introductions—all might be mistakes because you find out they didn't contribute profit."

WRONG REVENUES

That's what executives at Glasgow-based Standard Life Assurance, Europe's largest mutual life-insurance company, discovered earlier this year. They were stunned when the first cut of a profitability survey showed that the insurer was loading up fast on policyholders who held little or no potential for making money. Instead of bringing in the affluent customers Standard Life wanted, its direct-mail marketing campaign was encouraging elderly couples and stay-at-home mothers to sign up for costly home visits by sales agents. Revenues were up—but they were the wrong kind of revenues. "It was an exact mismatch," says Graham Wilson, Standard's database and statistics manager. "These are people who love to sit down and have a cup of tea with someone, but they typically buy only one policy, and margins are small."

Even motivated companies may find mining for profitable customers a tough task. The mechanics are demanding. To get a true picture of customer profitability, Bank of America calculates its profits every month on each of its more than 75 million accounts. Mortgages, for instance, have different costs than checking accounts, car loans, or home-equity credit accounts. And service costs vary by how customers bank—whether they use ATMs, tellers, or the Net.

By wading through all that data, however, BofA is able to zero in on the 10% of households that are most profitable. It assigns a financial adviser to track about 300 accounts at a time. Their job: to answer questions, coordinate the bank's efforts to sell more services, and—perhaps most important—watch for warning flags that these lucrative customers may be moving their business elsewhere.

If the bank's computer notes a change in the customer's normal pattern of transactions or a falling balance, for example, it alerts the account manager, who may post a flag to the tellers at the customer's branch warning that the account is in danger of moving.

The next time the customer walks into the bank, a teller asks if they have any concerns about the account and offers them a chat with the bank manager. The heavy intervention seems to be working. Since BofA launched the program 18 months ago, customer defections are down, and account balances in the top 10% have grown measurably. "When such a small percentage of customers generate such a large percentage of profits, this kind of program is critical," says Christopher Kelly, senior vice-president for database marketing at Bank of America. "We view it as a strategic weapon."

HANDHOLDING

Often, the strategy is used not to jettison low-spending customers or to reward the cream of the crop. Efforts are focused on those in the middle—customers who aren't yet profitable but whose demographics suggest that they could be. Consider Joseph Taylor, a 62-year-old minister in the United Church of Christ and a professor of pastoral theology at Howard University in Washington. When First Union Bank bought Signet Bank in 1997, Taylor's accounts moved, too. As First Union combed through Signet's records looking for customers with higher profit potential, up popped Taylor. Soon, a marketing push to profitability began.

First Union's buyout of Signet was the third time Taylor's bank had been acquired, and he was fed up. But he dropped his plans to switch when he received a phone call from a First Union marketer. "He talked as if he had known me, even though we had never met," Taylor says. Taylor maintained high balances in his bank accounts, frequently writing large checks to help church members in need. The marketer suggested that Taylor consolidate his checking and savings accounts in one interest-bearing account, providing income to Taylor while reducing the bank's servicing costs. First Union also persuaded Taylor to sign up for a home-equity loan, and he brought over the accounts from his ministry as well.

Customers who cost more to lure than they're worth aren't likely to see the same pampering. For those who enjoy browsing through catalogs without buying much, the days of receiving free reading material may be numbered. Mail-order retailers such as Victoria's Secret are winnowing their lists to focus on the most profitable recipients. "Some we expect to drop—those we don't get any return from at all," says Frank Giannantonio, chief information officer for Victoria's Secret.

"Free money" offers are already on the wane. MCI Communications, Sprint, and AT&T have largely dropped their once-omnipresent offers of cash for customers who switch their long-distance service. "They were offering $20, $30, $50 to all takers, without any understanding about whether they actually would want to retain those customers once they had won them," says Thomas Tague, chief operations officer for Tessera Enterprise Systems Inc., a data-warehouse builder. Now, focusing on profitability gives the phrase "valued customer" a whole new twist.

6

INTERNAL ANALYSIS

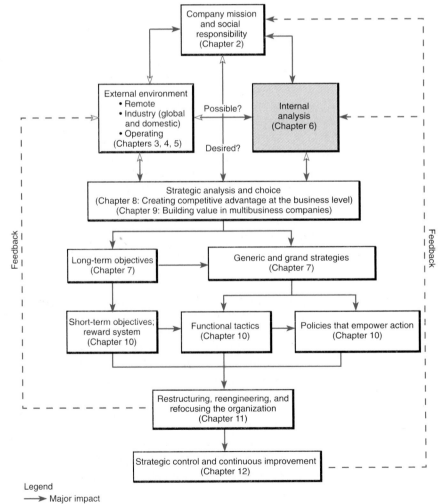

Company mission and social responsibility (Chapter 2)

External environment
• Remote
• Industry (global and domestic)
• Operating
(Chapters 3, 4, 5)

Possible?

Desired?

Internal analysis (Chapter 6)

Strategic analysis and choice
(Chapter 8: Creating competitive advantage at the business level)
(Chapter 9: Building value in multibusiness companies)

Long-term objectives (Chapter 7)

Generic and grand strategies (Chapter 7)

Short-term objectives; reward system (Chapter 10)

Functional tactics (Chapter 10)

Policies that empower action (Chapter 10)

Restructuring, reengineering, and refocusing the organization (Chapter 11)

Strategic control and continuous improvement (Chapter 12)

Feedback

Feedback

Legend
⟶ Major impact
⟶▷ Minor impact

Three ingredients are critical to the success of a strategy. First, the strategy must be *consistent* with conditions in the competitive environment. Specifically, it must take advantage of existing or projected opportunities and minimize the impact of major threats. Second, the strategy must place *realistic* requirements on the firm's resources. In other words, the firm's pursuit of market opportunities must be based not only on the existence of external opportunities but also on competitive advantages that arise from the firm's key resources. Finally, the strategy must be *carefully executed.* The focus of this chapter is on the second ingredient: *realistic analysis of the firm's resources.*

Managers often do this subjectively, based on intuition and "gut feel." Years of seasoned industry experience positions managers to make sound subjective judgments. But just as often, or more often, this may not be the case. In fast-changing environments, reliance on past experiences can cause management myopia or a tendency to accept the status quo and disregard signals that change is needed. And with managers new to strategic decision making, subjective decisions are particularly suspect. A lack of experience is easily replaced by emotion, narrow functional expertise, and the opinions of others creating the foundation on which newer managers build strategic recommendations. So it is that new managers' subjective assessments often come back to haunt them.

Strategy in Action 6–1 helps us understand this "subjective" tendency among both new as well as experienced managers. It looks at what happened a few years ago at Navistar when CEO John R. Horne admonished his management team to join him in buying their rapidly deteriorating (in price) stock as a sign to Wall Street that they had confidence in their company. Most managers declined, as their subjective sense of the company's situation and resources was quite negative. Some were reported to have even shorted the stock. The CEO acted virtually alone based on his view that several Navistar resources provided potential competitive advantages. Two years later, Navistar stock was up 400 percent. Subjective assessment had probably been holding the company back. It undoubtedly hit hard in the pocketbooks of several key managers that saw their own stock as an unwise investment.

Internal analysis has received increased attention in recent years as being a critical underpinning to effective strategic management. Indeed many managers and writers have adopted a new perspective on understanding firm success based on how well the firm uses its internal resources—the *resource-based view* (RBV) of the firm. This chapter will start with a look at the RBV to provide a useful vocabulary for identifying and examining internal *resources.* Next the chapter looks at ways managers achieve greater objectivity and rigor as they analyze their company's resources. Managers often start their internal analysis with questions like: "How well is the current strategy working? What is our current situation? Or what are our strengths and weaknesses?" Traditional *SWOT analysis* is then presented because it remains an approach that managers frequently use to answer these questions. More recently, insightful managers have begun to look at their business as a chain of activities that add value by creating the products or services they sell. Associated with this perspective is a powerful concept for introducing rigor and objectivity into internal analysis, the *value chain,* which this chapter will examine in great detail. Finally, objectivity and realism are enhanced when managers use meaningful standards for comparison regardless of the particular analytical framework they employ in internal analysis. We conclude this chapter by examining how managers do this using *past performance, stages of industry evolution, comparison with competitors* or other *"benchmarks," industry norms,* and traditional *financial analysis.*

BusinessWeek

NAVISTAR: AN OBJECTIVE INTERNAL ANALYSIS LETS IT GUN THE ENGINES FOR 2002

STRATEGY IN
ACTION
6–1

Early 1997 saw things looking bleak for Navistar International Corp. After decades of crippling labor problems and manufacturing snafus, the $6.4 billion Chicago truck and engine maker had suffered another steep earnings slide last year. Then, in a showdown with United Auto Workers members over costs, CEO John R. Horne had been forced to scrap the company's latest truck introduction. By midyear, disheartened investors let the stock drop to $9 a share, just 50¢ above its low.

That's when Horne called his 30 top executives into his office to make a personal plea. Looking for a show of faith in the company, he implored all of them to spend their own money to buy as many shares of Navistar stock as they could. Horne knew it was a lot to ask. Over the last 10 years, the company—once known as International Harvester—had tallied the worst total return to shareholders of all publicly traded U.S. companies. But he was convinced that if his managers bought, Wall Street would see that as a sign that Navistar's fortunes were turning.

Management's reply was a unanimous no. Many felt that Navistar's shares might drop as low as 6, and all 30 backed away. So Horne bit the bullet alone, buying as much as he could for cash and also turning his 401(k) account entirely into Navistar stock. "I couldn't force them because it was their money," he says. "I laugh at them some now."

All the way to the bank, he might add. By early 1998, Navistar's stock hit 27, a blazing 200% return to shareholders.

What Horne—a 31-year veteran who became president in 1991 and CEO in 1995—convinced himself about was the presence of key resources that were on the verge of becoming distinctive competencies, and key strengths, at Navistar.

TANGIBLE ASSET: CLEANEST BURNING DIESEL ENGINE

Navistar's diesel engine business was the first to be worked over. Horne immediately cut the number of engines in production to two, down from 70 in the mid-80s, for example. And by 1994, with Navistar's balance sheet improving, he introduced a new engine.

Navistar's offering, still the cleanest burning model on the market, quickly attracted major truck manufacturers such as Ford Motor Co. Ford puts the engine in vans and pickups and will soon offer it on its hot Expedition sport utility vehicle. Thanks largely to this model, Navistar's share of the diesel engine market rose from 25% in 1990 to 38% in 1998. That's one big reason operating results climbed from a $355 million loss in 1993 to a $266 million profit for the fiscal year ended October 1997.

TANGIBLE ASSET: EXCESS TRUCK AND ENGINE MANUFACTURING CAPACITY

Horne began a wide-ranging overhaul of Navistar's remaining truck and engine manufacturing lines. He started by drastically slicing the number of products Navistar made. Assembly was rationalized too. While Navistar plants used to build multiple trucks for several different markets, today each one specializes in one type of truck with fewer models.

Source: "Navistar: Gunning the Engines," *Business Week:* February 2, 1998, pp. 135–36.

RESOURCE-BASED VIEW OF THE FIRM

Coca-Cola versus Pepsi is a competitive situation virtually all of us recognize. Stock analysts look at the two and frequently conclude that Coke is the clear leader. They cite Coke's superiority in tangible assets (warehouses, bottling facilities, computerization,

continued

Tackling problems in Navistar's truck and tractor division proved far tougher. Two years ago, for example, Horne laid out a plan to introduce a new generation of trucks. By simplifying the design of components, Horne hoped to bring out a series of truck and trailer models with interchangeable designs and standardized parts, thus cutting costs while reducing errors on the assembly line. Horne's goal: to reduce the 19 heavy-duty and medium truck designs in his main Springfield (Illinois) plant to one or two.

ORGANIZATIONAL CAPABILITY: IMPROVED UNION RELATIONS

Before he got that far, Horne ran smack into the problem that has dogged Navistar for more than a decade: He needed significant concessions from the UAW, which represents almost 80% of Navistar's truck workers. Horne demanded a wage freeze until 2002 and the flexibility to consolidate production. He took a direct approach. "I showed them the books," he says. "They knew survival of the plants depended on the changes."

Union leaders may have known it, but U.S. union members weren't convinced. They rejected the contract outright. Convinced that he could never achieve his profitability goals without the changes, Horne cancelled the new trucks. He took a $35 million charge and made clear his next step would be to look abroad for lower labor costs. By August 1997, the workers folded their cards and approved the plan. Horne's tough stance has paid off. He quickly revived plans for the new truck. And since the new labor contract and other manufacturing changes went into effect last fall, productivity at U.S. plants has already risen 15%.

ORGANIZATIONAL CAPABILITY: NEW PRODUCT DEVELOPMENT PROCESS

Just as important, Horne got Navistar working on new models again for the first time in years. Having brought out few new products during Navistar's long slide, most of the company's models were aging. But to make sure the new products pay off, Horne also introduced tight financial discipline: Today, new projects only win the nod if they can earn a 17.5% return on equity and a 15% return on assets through a business cycle.

INTANGIBLE ASSET: A VISIONARY LEADER WITH STRONG LEADERSHIP SKILLS

"Horne has done a magnificent job," says David Pedowitz, director of research at New York's David J. Greene & Co. brokerage firm, the largest outside investor with a 5% stake. "For the first time since the breakup of International Harvester, they're in a position to be a world-class competitor."

In the meantime, Horne continues to spread his penny-pinching gospel. Indeed, though he's a big basketball fan, he won't buy courtside seats to see his favorite competitor, Chicago Bulls' Michael Jordan, hit the court. When Horne does make it to a home game, it's as a guest. He has other things to do with the fortune he's made in Navistar stock. Like reinvest.

cash, etc.) and intangible assets (reputation, brand name awareness, tight competitive culture, global business system, etc.). They also mention that Coke leads Pepsi in several capabilities to make use of these assets effectively—managing distribution globally, influencing retailer shelf space allocation, managing franchise bottler relations, marketing savvy, investing in bottling infrastructure, and speed of decision making to

FIGURE 6–1
Examples of Different Resources

Tangible Assets	Intangible Assets	Organizational Capabilities
Hampton Inn's reservation system	Nike's brand name	Dell Computer's customer service
Ford Motor Company's cash reserves	Dell Computer's reputation	Wal-Mart's purchasing and inbound logistics
3M's patents	Wendy's advertising with Dave Thomas	Sony's product-development processes
Georgia Pacific's land holdings	Jack Welch as GE's leader	Coke's global distribution coordination
Virgin Airlines' plane fleet	IBM's management team	3M's innovation process
Coca-Cola's Coke formula	Wal-Mart's culture	

take quick advantage of changing global conditions are just a few that are frequently mentioned. The combination of capabilities and assets, most analysts conclude, creates several competencies that give Coke several competitive advantages over Pepsi that are durable and not easily imitated.

The Coke-Pepsi situation provides a useful illustration for understanding several concepts central to the resource-based view (RBV) of the firm. The RBV's underlying premise is that firms differ in fundamental ways because each firm possesses a unique "bundle" of resources—tangible and intangible assets and organizational capabilities to make use of those assets. Each firm develops competencies from these resources and, when developed especially well, these become the source of the firm's competitive advantages. Coke's decision to buy out weak bottling franchisees, and regularly invest in or own newer bottling locations worldwide has given Coke a competitive advantage analysts estimate Pepsi will take at least 10 years or longer to match. Coke's strategy for the last 15 years was based in part on the identification of this resource and the development of it into a distinctive competence—a sustained competitive advantage. The RBV is a useful starting point for understanding internal analysis. Let's look at the basic concepts underlying the RBV.

Three Basic Resources: Tangible Assets, Intangible Assets, and Organizational Capabilities

In the 1990s, executives charting the strategy of their businesses were encouraged by the notion of a "core competence." Basically, a core competence was seen as a capability or skill running through a firm's businesses and that once identified, nurtured, and deployed throughout the firm, became the basis for lasting competitive advantage. Executives, enthusiastic about the notion that their job as strategists was to identify and leverage core competencies, encountered difficulty applying the concept because of the generality of its level of analysis. The RBV emerged as a way to make the core competency concept more focused and measurable—creating a more meaningful internal analysis. Central to the RBV's ability to do this is its notion of three basic types of resources that together create the building blocks for distinctive competencies. They are defined below and illustrated in Figure 6–1.

Tangible assets are the easiest to identify and are often found on a firm's balance sheet. They include production facilities, raw materials, financial resources, real estate, and computers. Tangible assets are the physical and financial means a company uses to provide value to its customers.

Intangible assets are things like brand names, company reputation, organizational morale, technical knowledge, patents and trademarks, and accumulated experience within an organization. While they are not assets that you can touch or see, they are very often critical in creating competitive advantage.

Organizational capabilities are not specific "inputs" like tangible or intangible assets; rather, they are the skills—the ability and ways of combining assets, people, and processes—that a company uses to transform inputs into outputs. Dell Computer built its first 10 years of unprecedented growth by creating an organization capable of the speedy and inexpensive manufacture and delivery of custom-built PCs. Gateway and Micron have attempted to copy Dell for most of that time but remain far behind Dell's diverse organizational capabilities. Now Dell is attempting to revolutionize its own "system" using the Internet to automate and customize service, creating a whole new level of organizational capability that combines assets, people, and processes throughout and beyond their organization. Concerning this organizational capability, Michael Dell recently said: "Anyone who tries to go direct now will find it very difficult—like trying to jump over the Grand Canyon." Finely developed capabilities, such as Dell's Internet-based customer-friendly system, can be a source of sustained competitive advantage. They enable a firm to take the same input factors as rivals (like Gateway and Micron) and convert them into products and services, either with greater efficiency in the process or greater quality in the output or both.

What Makes a Resource Valuable?

Once managers begin to identify their firm's resources, they face the challenge of determining which of those resources represent strengths or weaknesses—which resources generate core competencies that are sources of sustained competitive advantage. This has been a complex task for managers attempting to conduct a meaningful internal analysis. The RBV has addressed this by setting forth some key guidelines that help determine what constitutes a valuable asset, capability, or competence—that is, what makes a resource valuable.

1. Competitive superiority: Does the resource help fulfill a customer's need better than those of the firm's competitors? Two restaurants offer similar food, at similar prices, but one has a location much more convenient to downtown offices than the other. The tangible asset, location, helps fulfill daytime workers' lunch eating needs better than its competitor, resulting in greater profitability and sales volume for the conveniently located restaurant. Wal-Mart redefined discount retailing and outperformed the industry in profitability by 4.5 percent of sales—a 200 percent improvement. Four resources—store locations, brand recognition, employee loyalty, and sophisticated inbound logistics—allowed Wal-Mart to fulfill customer needs much better and more cost effectively than Kmart and other discount retailers, as shown in Figure 6–2. In both of these examples, *it is important to recognize that only resources that contributed to competitive superiority were valuable.* At the same time, other resources such as the restaurant's menu and specific products or parking space at Wal-Mart were essential to doing business but contributed little to competitive advantage because they did not distinguish how the firm fulfilled customer needs.

2. Resource scarcity: Is the resource in short supply? When it is, it is more valuable. When a firm possesses a resource and few if any others do, and it is central to fulfilling customers' needs, then it becomes a distinctive competence for the firm. The real way resource scarcity contributes value is when it can be sustained over time. To really answer this very basic question we must explore the following questions.

FIGURE 6–2
Wal-Mart's Resource-Based Competitive Advantage

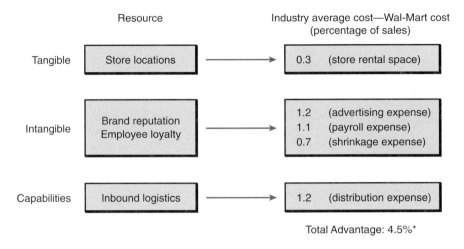

*Wal-Mart's cost advantage as a percent of sales. Each percentage point advantage is worth
$500 million in net income to Wal-Mart.

Source: Pankaj Ghemawat, "Wal-Mart Stores' Discount Operations," Harvard Business School case number
9-387-018.

3. Inimitability: Is the resource easily copied or acquired? A resource that competitors can readily copy can only generate temporary value. It cannot generate a long-term competitive advantage. When Wendy's first emerged, it was the only major hamburger chain with a drive-through window. This unique organizational capability was part of a "bundle" of resources that allowed Wendy's to provide unique value to its target customers, young adults seeking convenient food service. But once this resource, or organizational capability, proved valuable to fast-food customers, every fast-food chain copied the feature. Then Wendy's continued success was built on other resources that generated other distinctive competencies.

Inimitability doesn't last forever, as the Wendy's example illustrates. Competitors will match or better any resource as soon as they can. It should be obvious, then, that the firm's ability to forestall this eventuality is very important The RBV identifies four characteristics, called *isolating mechanisms,* that make resources difficult to imitate:

- **Physically unique resources** are virtually impossible to imitate. A one-of-a-kind real estate location, mineral rights, and patents are examples of resources that cannot be imitated. Disney's Mickey Mouse copyright or Winter Park, Colorado's Iron Horse resort possess physical uniqueness. While many strategists claim that resources are physically unique, this is seldom true. Rather, other characteristics are typically what make most resources difficult to imitate.
- **Path-dependent resources** are very difficult to imitate because of the difficult "path" another firm must follow to create the resource. These are resources that cannot be instantaneously acquired but rather must be created over time in a manner that is frequently very expensive and always difficult to accelerate. When Michael Dell said that "anyone who tries to go direct now will find it very difficult—like trying to jump over the Grand Canyon" (see page 195), he was asserting that Dell's system of selling customized PCs direct via the Internet and Dell's unmatched customer

service is in effect a path-dependent organizational capability. It would take any competitor years to develop the expertise, infrastructure, reputation, and capabilities necessary to compete effectively with Dell. Coca-Cola's brand name, Gerber Baby Food's reputation for quality, and Steinway's expertise in piano manufacture would take competitors many years and millions of dollars to match. Consumers' many years of experience drinking Coke or using Gerber or playing a Steinway would also need to be matched.

• **Causal ambiguity** is a third way resources can be very difficult to imitate. This refers to situations where it is difficult for competitors to understand exactly how a firm has created the advantage it enjoys. Competitors can't figure out exactly what the uniquely valuable resource is, or how resources are combined to create the competitive advantage. Causally ambiguous resources are often organizational capabilities that arise from subtle combinations of tangible and intangible assets and culture, processes, and organizational attributes the firm possesses. Southwest Airlines has regularly faced competition from major and regional airlines, with some like United and Continental eschewing their traditional approach and attempting to compete by using their own version of the Southwest approach—same planes, routes, gate procedures, number of attendants, and so on. They have yet to succeed. The most difficult thing to replicate is Southwest's "personality," or culture of fun, family, and frugal yet focused services and attitude. Just how that works is hard for United and Continental to figure out.

• **Economic deterrence** is a fourth source of inimitability. This usually involves large capital investments in capacity to provide products or services in a given market that are scale sensitive. It occurs when a competitor understands the resource that provides a competitive advantage and may even have the capacity to imitate, but chooses not to because of the limited market size that realistically would not support two players the size of the first mover.

While we may be inclined to think of a resource's inimitability as a yes-or-no situation, inimitability is more accurately measured on a continuum that reflects difficulty and time. Figure 6–3 illustrates such a continuum. Some resources may have multiple imitation deterrents. For example, 3M's reputation for innovativeness may involve path dependencies and causal ambiguity.

4. Appropriability: Who actually gets the profit created by a resource? Warren Buffet is known worldwide as one of the most successful investors of the last 25 years. One of his legendary investments was the Walt Disney Company, which he once said he liked "because the Mouse does not have an agent."[1] What he was really saying was that Disney owned the Mickey Mouse copyright, and all profits from that valuable resource went directly to Disney. Other competitors in the "entertainment" industry generated similar profits from their competing offerings, for example movies, but they often "captured" substantially less of those profits because of the amounts that had to be paid to well-known actors or directors or other entertainment contributors seen as the real creators of the movie's value.

Sports teams, investment services, and consulting businesses are other examples of companies that generate sizable profits based on resources (key people, skills, contacts, for example) that are not inextricably linked to the company and therefore do not allow the company to easily capture the profits. Superstar sports players can move from

---

[1] *The Harbus,* March 25, 1996, p. 12.

FIGURE 6–3
Resource Inimitability

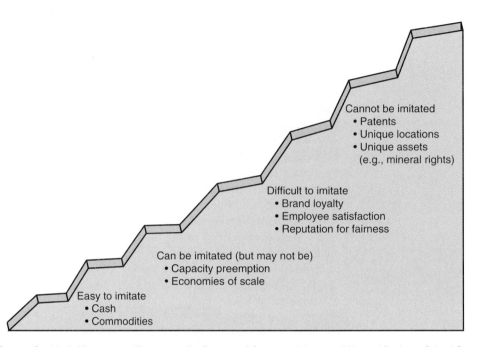

Cannot be imitated
• Patents
• Unique locations
• Unique assets
(e.g., mineral rights)

Difficult to imitate
• Brand loyalty
• Employee satisfaction
• Reputation for fairness

Can be imitated (but may not be)
• Capacity preemption
• Economies of scale

Easy to imitate
• Cash
• Commodities

Source: Cynthia A. Montgomery, "Resources: the Essence of Corporate Advantage," Harvard Business School Case N1-792-064.

one team to another, or command excessively high salaries, and this circumstance could arise in other personal services business situations. It could also occur when one firm joint ventures with another, sharing resources and capabilities and the profits that result. Sometimes restaurants or lodging facilities that are franchisees of a national organization are frustrated by the fees they pay the franchisor each month and decide to leave the organization and go "independent." They often find, to their dismay, that the business declines significantly. The value of the franchise name, reservation system, and brand recognition is critical in generating the profits of the business.

Bottom line, resources that one develops and controls—where ownership of the resource and its role in value creation is obvious—are more valuable than resources that can be easily bought, sold, or moved from one firm to another.

5. Durability: How rapidly will the resource depreciate? The slower a resource depreciates, the more valuable it is. Tangible assets, like commodities or capital, can have their depletion measured. Intangible resources, like brand names or organizational capabilities, present a much more difficult depreciation challenge. The Coca-Cola brand has continued to appreciate, whereas technical know-how in various computer technologies depreciates rapidly. In the increasingly hypercompetitive global economy of the 21st century, distinctive competencies and competitive advantages can fade quickly, making the notion of durability a critical test of the value of key resources and capabilities. Some believe that this reality makes well-articulated visions and associated cultures within organizations potentially the most important contributor to long-term survival.[2]

[2]James C. Collins and Jerry L. Porras, *Built to Last: Successful Habits of Visionary Companies* (New York: Harper Business, 1994).

6. Substitutability: Are other alternatives available? We discussed the threat of substitute products in Chapter 3 as part of the five forces model for examining industry profitability. The basic idea can be taken further and used to gauge the value of particular resources. DeLite's of America was a hot IPO in the last decade as a new fast-food restaurant chain focused exclusively on selling lite food—salads, lean sandwiches, and so on. The basic idea was to offer, in a fast-food format, food low in calories and saturated fat. Investors were very excited about this concept because of the high-calorie, high-fat content of the foods offered by virtually every existing chain. Unfortunately for these investors, several key fast-food players, like Wendy's and later McDonalds, Burger King, and Hardees, adapted their operations to offer salad bars or premade salads and other "lean" sandwich offerings without disrupting their more well known fare. With little change and adaptation of their existing facility and operational resources, these chains quickly created alternatives to DeLite's offerings and the initial excitement about those offerings faded. DeLite's was driven out of business by substitute resources and capabilities rather than substitute products.

Using the Resource-Based View in Internal Analysis

To use the RBV in internal analysis, a firm must first identify and evaluate its resources to find those that provide the basis for future competitive advantage. This process involves defining the various resources the firm possesses, and examining them based on the above discussion to gauge which resources truly have strategic value. Four final guidelines have proven helpful in this undertaking:

- Disaggregate resources—break them down into more specific competencies—rather than stay with broad categorizations. Saying that Domino's Pizza has better marketing skills than Pizza Hut conveys little information. But dividing that into subcategories such as advertising that, in turn, can be divided into national advertising, local promotions, and couponing allows for a more measurable assessment. Figure 6–4 provides a useful illustration of this at Whitbread's Restaurant.

- Utilize a functional perspective. Looking at different functional areas of the firm, disaggregating tangible and intangible assets as well as organizational capabilities that are present, can begin to uncover important value-building resources and activities that deserve further analysis. Figure 6–5 lists a variety of functional area resources and activities that deserve consideration.

- Look at organizational processes and combinations of resources and not only at isolated assets or capabilities. While disaggregation is critical, you must also take a creative, gestalt look at what competencies the firm possesses or has the potential to possess that might generate competitive advantage.

- Use the value chain approach to uncover organizational capabilities, activities, and processes that are valuable potential sources of competitive advantage. Value chain analysis is discussed starting on page 206.

Although the RBV enables a systematic assessment of internal resources, it is important to stress that a meaningful analysis of those resources best takes place in the context of the firm's competitive environment. Possessing valuable resources will not generate commensurate profits unless resources are applied in an effective product market strategy; they must be deployed in an optimum way and align related activities for the firm to pursue its chosen sources of competitive advantage. Traditional strategy formulation—externally positioning a firm to capitalize on its strengths and opportunities and to minimize its threats and weaknesses—remains essential to realizing the

FIGURE 6–4
Disaggregating Whitbread Restaurant's Customer Service Resource

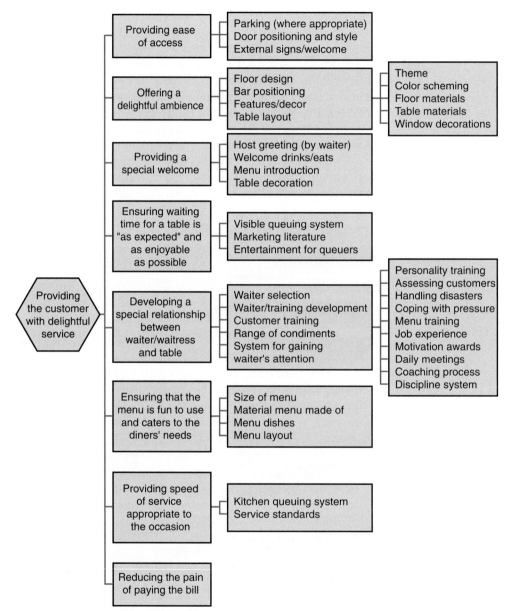

Source: Andrew Campbell and Kathleen Luchs, *Strategic Synergy* (London: Butterworth-Heineman, 1992).

competitive advantage envisioned from an RBV of the firm.[3] The next section examines this traditional approach, often called *SWOT analysis,* as a conceptual framework that may complement the RBV in conducting a sound internal analysis.

---

[3]David J. Collins and Cynthia A. Montgomery, *Corporate Strategy: Resources and Scope of the Firm* (Chicago: Irwin/McGraw-Hill, 1997), p. 30.

FIGURE 6–5
Key Resources across Functional Areas

Marketing

Firm's products-services: breadth of product line.
Concentration of sales in a few products or to a few customers.
Ability to gather needed information about markets.
Market share or submarket shares.
Product-service mix and expansion potential: life cycle of key products; profit-sales balance in product-service.
Channels of distribution: number, coverage, and control.
Effective sales organization: knowledge of customer needs.
Product-service image, reputation, and quality.
Imaginativeness, efficiency, and effectiveness of sales promotion and advertising.
Pricing strategy and pricing flexibility.
Procedures for digesting market feedback and developing new products, services, or markets.
After-sale service and follow-up.
Goodwill—brand loyalty.

Financial and Accounting

Ability to raise short-term capital.
Ability to raise long-term capital; debt-equity.
Corporate-level resources (multibusiness firm).
Cost of capital relative to that of industry and competitors.
Tax considerations.
Relations with owners, investors, and stockholders.
Leverage position; capacity to utilize alternative financial strategies, such as lease or sale and leaseback.
Cost of entry and barriers to entry.
Price-earnings ratio.
Working capital; flexibility of capital structure.
Effective cost control; ability to reduce cost.
Financial size.
Efficiency and effectiveness of accounting system for cost, budget, and profit planning.

Production, Operations, Technical

Raw materials cost and availability, supplier relationships.
Inventory control systems; inventory turnover.
Location of facilities; layout and utilization of facilities.
Economies of scale.
Technical efficiency of facilities and utilization of capacity.
Effectiveness of subcontracting use.
Degree of vertical integration; value added and profit margin.
Efficiency and cost-benefit of equipment.
Effectiveness of operation control procedures: design, scheduling, purchasing, quality control, and efficiency.
Costs and technological competencies relative to those of industry and competitors.
Research and development—technology—innovation.
Patents, trademarks, and similar legal protection.

Personnel

Management personnel.
Employees' skill and morale.
Labor relations costs compared to those of industry and competitors.
Efficiency and effectiveness of personnel policies.
Effectiveness of incentives used to motivate performance.
Ability to level peaks and valleys of employment.
Employee turnover and absenteeism.
Specialized skills.
Experience.

Quality Management

Relationship with suppliers, customers.
Internal practices to enhance quality of products and services.
Procedures for monitoring quality.

FIGURE 6–5
(concluded)

Information Systems

Timeliness and accuracy of information about sales, operations, cash, and suppliers.
Relevance of information for tactical decisions.
Information to manage quality issues: customer service.
Ability of people to use the information that is provided.

Organization and General Management

Organizational structure.
Firm's image and prestige.
Firm's record in achieving objectives.
Organization of communication system.
Overall organizational control system (effectiveness and utilization).
Organizational climate; organizational culture.
Use of systematic procedures and techniques in decision making.
Top-management skill, capabilities, and interest.
Strategic planning system.
Intraorganizational synergy (multibusiness firms).

SWOT ANALYSIS

SWOT is an acronym for the internal Strengths and Weaknesses of a firm and the environmental Opportunities and Threats facing that firm. SWOT analysis is a widely used technique through which managers create a quick overview of a company's strategic situation. It is based on the assumption that an effective strategy derives from a sound "fit" between a firm's internal resources (strengths and weaknesses) and its external situation (opportunities and threats). A good fit maximizes a firm's strengths and opportunities and minimizes its weaknesses and threats. Accurately applied, this simple assumption has powerful implications for the design of a successful strategy.

Environmental industry analysis (Chapters 3 through 5) provides the information needed to identify opportunities and threats in a firm's environment, the first fundamental focus in SWOT analysis.

Opportunities

An *opportunity* is a major favorable situation in a firm's environment. Key trends are one source of opportunities. Identification of a previously overlooked market segment, changes in competitive or regulatory circumstances, technological changes, and improved buyer or supplier relationships could represent opportunities for the firm.

Threats

A *threat* is a major unfavorable situation in a firm's environment. Threats are key impediments to the firm's current or desired position. The entrance of new competitors, slow market growth, increased bargaining power of key buyers or suppliers, technological changes, and new or revised regulations could represent threats to a firm's success.

Understanding the key opportunities and threats facing a firm helps its managers identify realistic options from which to choose an appropriate strategy and clarifies the most effective niche for the firm. The second fundamental focus in SWOT analysis is the identification of internal strengths and weaknesses.

Strengths

A *strength* is a resource advantage relative to competitors and the needs of the markets a firm serves or expects to serve. It is a *distinctive competence* when it gives the firm a comparative advantage in the marketplace. Strengths arise from the resources and competencies available to the firm.

Weaknesses

A *weakness* is a limitation or deficiency in one or more resources or competencies relative to competitors that impedes a firm's effective performance.

The sheer size and level of Microsoft's user base have proven to be a key strength on which it built its aggressive entry into Internet services. Limited financial capacity was a weakness recognized by Southwest Airlines, which charted a selective route expansion strategy to build the best profit record in a deregulated airline industry.

SWOT analysis can be used in many ways to aid strategic analysis. The most common way is to use it as a logical framework guiding systematic discussion of a firm's resources and the basic alternatives that emerge from this resource-based view. What one manager sees as an opportunity, another may see as a potential threat. Likewise, a strength to one manager may be a weakness to another. Different assessments may reflect underlying power considerations within the firm or differing factual perspectives. Systematic analysis of these issues facilitates objective internal analysis.

The diagram in Figure 6–6 illustrates how SWOT analysis builds on the results of an RBV of a firm to aid strategic analysis. Key external opportunities and threats are systematically compared with internal resources and competencies—that is, strengths and weaknesses—in a structured approach. The objective is identification of one of four distinct patterns in the match between a firm's internal resources and external situation. Cell 1 is the most favorable situation; the firm faces several environmental opportunities and has numerous strengths that encourage pursuit of those opportunities. This situation suggests growth-oriented strategies to exploit the favorable match. America OnLine's intensive market development strategy in the online services market is the result of a favorable match of its strong technical expertise, early entry, and reputation resources with an opportunity for impressive market growth as millions of people joined the information highway in the latter 1990s. Cell 4 is the least favorable situation, with the firm facing major environmental threats from a weak resource position. This situation clearly calls for strategies that reduce or redirect involvement in the products or markets examined by means of SWOT analysis. Citicorp's successful turnaround from the verge of insolvency due to massive defaults on many international loans is an example of such a strategy in the early 1990s.

In cell 2, a firm whose RBV has identified several key strengths faces an unfavorable environment. In this situation, strategies would seek to redeploy those strong resources and competencies to build long-term opportunities in more opportunistic product markets. Greyhound, possessing many strengths in intercity bus transportation, still faced an environment dominated by fundamental, long-term threats, such as airline competition and high costs. The result was product development into nonpassenger (freight) services, followed by diversification into other businesses (e.g., financial services).

FIGURE 6–6
SWOT Analysis Diagram

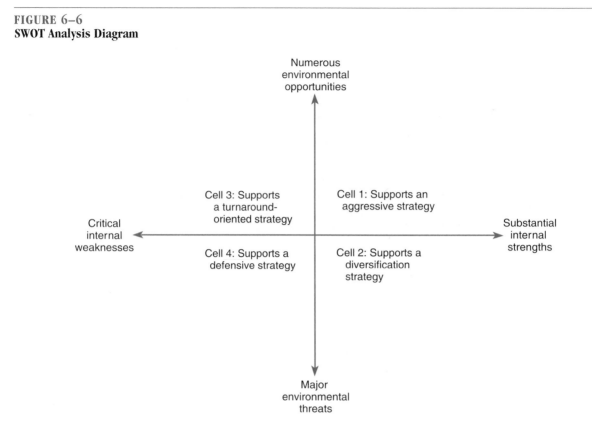

A firm in cell 3 faces impressive market opportunity but is constrained by weak internal resources. The focus of strategy for such a firm is eliminating the internal weaknesses so as to more effectively pursue the market opportunity. Disney's acquisition of ABC/Capital Cities was in part an attempt to overcome key weaknesses in Disney's control of distribution outlets for its varied, excellent programming so that it could more easily pursue global opportunities in the entertainment industry of the 21st century.

SWOT analysis has been a framework of choice among many managers for a long time because of its simplicity and its portrayal of the essence of sound strategy formulation—matching a firm's opportunities and threats with its strengths and weaknesses. Central to making SWOT analysis effective is accurate internal analysis—the identification of specific strengths and weaknesses around which sound strategy can be built. One of the historical deficiencies of SWOT analysis was the tendency to rely on a very general, categorical assessment of internal capabilities. The resource-based view came to exist in part as a remedy to this void in the strategic management field. It is an excellent way to identify internal strengths and weaknesses and use that information to enhance the quality of a SWOT analysis. The RBV perspective was presented earlier in this chapter. While the conceptual appeal of the RBV is compelling, many managers remain comfortable with a functional approach to isolate and evaluate internal strengths and weaknesses. The next section describes the functional approach so that you will be aware of how management teams that don't use the RBV identify internal strengths and weaknesses.

THE FUNCTIONAL APPROACH

Key internal factors are a firm's basic capabilities, limitations, and characteristics. Figure 6–5 (page 201) lists typical internal factors, some of which would be the focus of internal analysis in most firms. The list is broken along functional lines for one logical reason. Most firms organize their operations at some level along functional lines to get their products or services sold, produced, delivered, financed, and accounted. It stands to reason that close scrutiny of each of these functions serves as a compelling, strategically relevant focus for internal analysis.

Firms are not likely to evaluate all of the resources listed in Figure 6–5 as potential strengths or weaknesses. To develop or revise a strategy, managers would prefer to identify the few factors on which its success is most likely to depend. Equally important, a firm's reliance on particular internal factors will vary by industry, market segment, product life cycle, and the firm's current position. Managers are looking for what Chester Barnard calls the "strategic factors," those internal capabilities that are most critical for success in a particular competitive area. The strategic factors of firms in the oil industry, for example, will be quite different from those of firms in the construction industry or the hospitality industry. Strategic factors also can vary among firms within the same industry. In the mechanical writing industry, for example, the strategies of BIC and Cross, both successful firms, are based on different internal strengths: BIC's on its strength in mass production, extensive advertising, and mass distribution channels; Cross's on high quality, image, and selective distribution channels.

Strategists examine a firm's past performance to isolate key internal contributors to favorable (or unfavorable) results. What did we do well, or poorly, in marketing, operations, and financial management that had a major influence on our past results? Was our sales force effectively organized? Were we in the right channels of distribution? Did we have the financial resources needed to support our past strategy? The same examination can be applied to a firm's current situation, with particular emphasis on changes in the importance of key dimensions over time. For example, heavy advertising, mass production, and mass distribution were strategic internal factors in BIC's initial strategy for ballpoint pens and disposable lighters. With the product life cycle fast reaching maturity, BIC later determined that cost-conscious mass production was a strategic factor, whereas heavy advertising was not.

Analysis of past trends in a firm's sales, costs, and profitability is of major importance in identifying its strategic internal factors. And that identification should be based on a clear picture of the nature of the firm's sales. An anatomy of past sales trends broken down by product lines, channels of distribution, key customers or types of customers, geographic region, and sales approach should be developed in detail. A similar anatomy should be developed on costs and profitability. Detailed investigation of the firm's performance history helps isolate the internal factors that influence its sales, costs, and profitability or their interrelationships. For example, one firm may find that 83 percent of its sales result from 25 percent of its products, and another firm may find that 30 percent of its products (or services) contribute 78 percent of its profitability. On the basis of such results, a firm may determine that certain key internal factors (e.g., experience in particular distribution channels, pricing policies, warehouse location, technology) deserve major attention in the formulation of future strategy.

The identification of strategic internal factors requires an external focus. A strategist's efforts to isolate key internal factors are assisted by analysis of industry conditions and trends and by comparisons with competitors. BIC's identification of mass production and advertising as key internal factors was based as much on analysis of industry and competitive characteristics as on analysis of its own past performance. Changing conditions in an industry can lead to the need to reexamine a firm's internal strengths and weaknesses in light of newly emerging determinants of success in that industry.

It is important to see that a functional approach, regardless of situational differences, focuses managers on basic business functions leading to a more objective, relevant internal analysis that enhances strategic decision making. Whether looking at attributes of marketing, production, financing, information systems, or human resource management, the functional approach structures managers' thinking in a focused, potentially objective manner.

While SWOT analysis (supported by the functional approach or the RBV) offers a simple, logical approach to guide internal analysis, managers that endured the downsizing and reengineering 1990s found the need for an approach that focused them even more narrowly on how work actually took place within their companies as they sought to meet customer needs. What these managers were responding to was the reality that producing goods or services and handling customers often necessitated the simultaneous involvement of multiple functions to be effective. They needed a way to look at their business as a series of activities that took place to create value for a customer—and to use this view as the framework to guide internal analysis. The RBV, which we discussed earlier, is one important perspective. The value chain concept is another popular framework.

VALUE CHAIN ANALYSIS

The term *value chain* describes a way of looking at a business as a chain of activities that transform inputs into outputs that customers value. Customer value derives from three basic sources: activities that differentiate the product, activities that lower its cost, and activities that meet the customer's need quickly. *Value chain analysis* (VCA) attempts to understand how a business creates customer value by examining the contributions of different activities within the business to that value.

VCA takes a process point of view: It divides (sometimes called disaggregates) the business into sets of activities that occur *within the business,* starting with the inputs a firm receives and finishing with the firm's products (or services) and after-sales service to customers. VCA attempts to look at its costs across the series of activities the business performs to determine where low-cost advantages or cost disadvantages exist. It looks at the attributes of each of these different activities to determine in what ways each activity that occurs between purchasing inputs and after-sales service helps differentiate the company's products and services. Proponents of VCA believe VCA allows managers to better identify their firm's strengths and weaknesses by looking at the business as a process—a chain of activities—of what actually happens in the business rather than simply looking at it based on arbitrary organizational dividing lines or historical accounting protocol.

Figure 6–7 shows a typical value chain framework. It divides activities within the firm into two broad categories: primary activities and support activities. *Primary activities* (sometimes called *line* functions) are those involved in the physical creation of the product, marketing and transfer to the buyer, and after-sale support. *Support activities* (sometimes called *staff* or *overhead* functions) assist the firm as a whole by providing infrastructure or inputs that allow the primary activities to take place on an

FIGURE 6–7
The Value Chain

The Value Chain

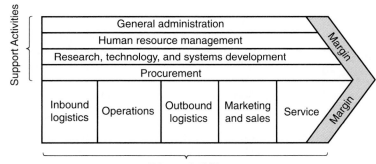

Primary Activities

Primary Activities

- **Inbound Logistics**—Activities, costs, and assets associated with obtaining fuel, energy, raw materials, parts components, merchandise, and consumable items from vendors; receiving, storing, and disseminating inputs from suppliers; inspection; and inventory management.

- **Operations**—Activities, costs, and assets associated with converting inputs into final product form (production, assembly, packaging, equipment maintenance, facilities, operations, quality assurance, environmental protection).

- **Outbound Logistics**—Activities, costs, and assets dealing with physically distributing the product to buyers (finished goods warehousing, order processing, order picking and packing, shipping, delivery vehicle operations).

- **Marketing and Sales**—Activities, costs, and assets related to sales force efforts, advertising and promotion, market research and planning, and dealer/distributor support.

- **Service**—Activities, costs, and assets associated with providing assistance to buyers, such as installation, spare parts delivery, maintenance and repair, technical assistance, buyer inquiries, and complaints.

Support Activities

- **General Administration**—Activities, costs, and assets relating to general management, accounting and finance, legal and regulatory affairs, safety and security, management information systems, and other "overhead" functions.

- **Human Resources Management**—Activities, costs, and assets associated with the recruitment, hiring, training, development, and compensation of all types of personnel; labor relations activities; development of knowledge-based skills.

- **Research, Technology, and Systems Development**—Activities, costs, and assets relating to product R&D, process R&D, process design improvement, equipment design, computer software development, telecommunications systems, computer-assisted design and engineering, new database capabilities, and development of computerized support systems.

- **Procurement**—Activities, costs, and assets associated with purchasing and providing raw materials, supplies, services, and outsourcing necessary to support the firm and its activities. Sometimes this activity is assigned as part of a firm's inbound logistic purchasing activities.

Source: Adapted from Michael E. Porter, *Competitive Advantage: Creating and Sustaining Superior Performance* (New York: The Free Press, 1985). Copyright © 1985 by Michael E. Porter.

ongoing basis. The value chain includes a *profit margin* since a markup above the cost of providing a firm's value-adding activities is normally part of the price paid by the buyer—creating value that exceeds cost so as to generate a return for the effort.

Judgment is required across individual firms and different industries because what may be seen as a support activity in one firm or industry may be a primary activity in

VALUE CHAIN ANALYSIS "MORPHS" FEDERAL EXPRESS INTO AN INFORMATION COMPANY

STRATEGY IN ACTION 6–2

Founder Fred Smith and executives running companies controlled by FedEx say they are planning a monumental shift in the FedEx mission. They are accelerating plans to focus on information systems that track and coordinate packages. They are seeking to "morph" themselves from being a transportation company into an information company.

FedEx already has one of the most heavily used websites on the Internet. Company management claims to have 1,500 in-house programmers writing more software code than almost any other non-software company. To complement package delivery, FedEx designs and operates high-tech warehouses and distribution systems for big manufacturers and retailers around the world. For almost two decades, FedEx has been investing massive amounts to develop software and create a giant digital network. FedEx has built corporate technology campuses around the world, and its electronic systems are directly linked via the Internet or otherwise to over 1 million customers worldwide. That system now allows FedEx to track packages on an hourly basis, but it also allows FedEx to predict future flow of goods and then rapidly refigure the information and logistical network to handle those flows.

"Moving an item from point A to point B is no longer a big deal," say James Barksdale, CEO of Netscape and early architect of FedEx's information strategies. "Having the information about that item, and where it is, and the best way to use it. . . . That is value. The companies that will be big winners will be the ones who can best maximize the value of these information systems." Where FedEx's value has long been built on giant airplanes and big trucks, founder Smith sees a time when it will be built on information, computers, and the allure of the FedEx brand name.

If it works, FedEx's value chain will shrink in areas involved with inbound and outbound operations—taking off and landing on the tarmac—and will expand in areas involved with zapping around the pristine and pilot-free world of cyberspace.

Source: "Do You Know Who Your Most Profitable Customers Are?" *Business Week:* September 14, 1998; "Online Original: FedEx: an Internet Stock?" *Business Week:* June 22, 1998; "Management: Will FedEx Shift from Moving Boxes to Bytes?" *The Wall Street Journal,* November 20, 1998.

another. Computer operations might typically be seen as infrastructure support, for example, but may be seen as a primary activity in airlines, newspapers, or banks. Strategy in Action 6–2 describes how Federal Express reconceptualized its company using a value chain analysis that ultimately saw its information support become its primary activity and source of customer value.

Conducting a Value Chain Analysis

Identify Activities

The initial step in value chain analysis is to divide a company's operations into specific activities or business processes, usually grouping them similarly to the primary and support activity categories shown in Figure 6–7. Within each category, a firm typically performs a number of discrete activities that may represent key strengths or weaknesses. Service activities, for example, may include such discrete activities as installation, repair, parts distribution, and upgrading—any of which could be a major source of competitive advantage or disadvantage. The manager's challenge at this point is to

FIGURE 6–8

The Difference between Traditional Cost Accounting and Activity-Based Cost Accounting

Traditional Cost Accounting in a Purchasing Department		Activity-Based Cost Accounting in the Same Purchasing Department for its "Procurement" Activities	
Wages and salaries	$350,000	Evaluate supplier capabilities	$135,750
Employee benefits	115,000	Process purchase orders	82,100
Supplies	6,500	Expedite supplier deliveries	23,500
Travel	2,400	Expedite internal processing	15,840
Depreciation	17,000	Check quality of items purchased	94,300
Other fixed charges	124,000	Check incoming deliveries against purchase orders	48,450
Miscellaneous operating expenses	25,250	Resolve problems	110,000
	$640,150	Internal administration	130,210
			$640,150

Source: Adapted from Terence P. Pare, "A New Tool for Managing Costs," *Fortune,* June 14, 1993, p. 124. © 1993, Time, Inc. All rights reserved.

be very detailed attempting to "disaggregate" what actually goes on into numerous distinct, analyzable activities rather than settling for a broad, general categorization.

Allocate Costs

The next step is to attempt to attach costs to each discrete activity. Each activity in the value chain incurs costs and ties up time and assets. Value chain analysis requires managers to assign costs and assets to each activity, thereby providing a very different way of viewing costs than traditional cost accounting methods would produce. Figure 6–8 helps illustrate this distinction. Both approaches in Figure 6–8 tell us that the purchasing department (procurement activities) cost $640,150. The traditional method lets us see that payroll expenses are 73 percent [(350 + 115)/640] of our costs with "other fixed charges" the second largest cost, 19 percent [124/640] of the total procurement costs. VCA proponents would argue that the benefit of this information is limited. Their argument might be the following:

> With this information we could compare our procurement costs to key competitors, budgets, or industry averages, and conclude that we are better, worse, or equal. We could then ascertain that our "people" costs and "other fixed charges" cost are advantages, disadvantages, or "in line" with competitors. Managers could then argue to cut people, add people, or debate fixed overhead charges. However, they would get lost in what is really a budgetary debate without ever examining what it is those people do in accomplishing the procurement function, what value that provides, and how cost effective each activity is.

VCA proponents hold that the activity-based VCA approach would provide a more meaningful analysis of the procurement function's costs and consequent value-added. The activity-based side of Figure 6–8 shows that approximately 21 percent of the procurement cost or value-added involves evaluating supplier capabilities. A rather sizeable cost, 20 percent, involves internal administration, with an additional 17 percent spent resolving problems and almost 15 percent spent on quality control efforts. VCA advocates see this information as being much more useful than traditional cost accounting information, especially when compared to the cost information of key competitors or other "benchmark" companies. VCA supporters might assert the following argument that the benefit of this activity-based information is substantial:

Rather than analyzing just "people" and "other charges," we are now looking at meaningful categorizations of the work that procurement actually does. We see, for example, that a key value-added activity (and cost) involves "evaluating supplier capabilities." The amount spent on "internal administration" and "resolving problems" seems high, and may indicate a weakness or area for improvement if the other activities' costs are in line and outcomes favorable. The bottom line is that this approach lets us look at what we actually "do" in the business—the specific activities—to create customer value, and that in turn allows more specific internal analysis than traditional, accounting-based cost categories.

Recognize the Difficulty in Activity-Based Cost Accounting It is important to note that existing financial management and accounting systems in many firms are not set up to easily provide activity-based cost breakdowns. Likewise, in virtually all firms, the information requirements to support activity-based cost accounting can create redundant work because of the financial reporting requirements that may force firms to retain the traditional approach for financial statement purposes. The time and energy to change to an activity-based approach can be formidable, and still typically involves arbitrary cost allocation decisions trying to allocate selected asset or people costs across multiple activities in which they are involved. Challenges dealing with a cost-based use of VCA have not deterred use of the framework to identify sources of differentiation. Indeed, conducting a VCA to analyze competitive advantages that differentiate the firm is compatible with the RBV's examination of intangible assets and capabilities as sources of distinctive competence.

Identify the Activities that Differentiate the Firm

Scrutinizing a firm's value chain may not only reveal cost advantages or disadvantages, it may also bring attention to several sources of differentiation advantage relative to competitors. Dell Computer considers its Internet-based after-sales service (activities) to be far superior to any competitor. Dell knows they have a cost advantage because of the time and expense replicating this activity would take. But they consider it an even more important source of value to the customer because of the importance customers place on this activity, which differentiates Dell from many similarly priced competitors. Likewise Federal Express, as we noted earlier, considers its information management skills to have become the core competence and essence of the company because of the value these skills allow FedEx to provide its customers and the importance they in turn place on such skills. Figure 6–9 suggests some factors for assessing primary and support activities' differentiation and contribution.

Examine the Value Chain

Once the value chain has been documented, managers need to identify the activities that are critical to buyer satisfaction and market success. It is those activities that deserve major scrutiny in an internal analysis. Three considerations are essential at this stage in the value chain analysis. First, the company's basic mission needs to influence managers' choice of the activities they examine in detail. If the company is focused on being a low-cost provider, then management attention to lower costs should be very visible; and missions built around commitment to differentiation should find managers spending more on activities that are differentiation cornerstones. Retailer Wal-Mart focuses intensely on costs related to inbound logistics, advertising, and loyalty to build its competitive advantage (see Figure 6–2) while Nordstrom builds its distinct position in retailing by emphasizing sales and support activities on which they spend twice the

FIGURE 6–9
Possible Factors for Assessing Sources of Differentiation in Primary and Support Activities

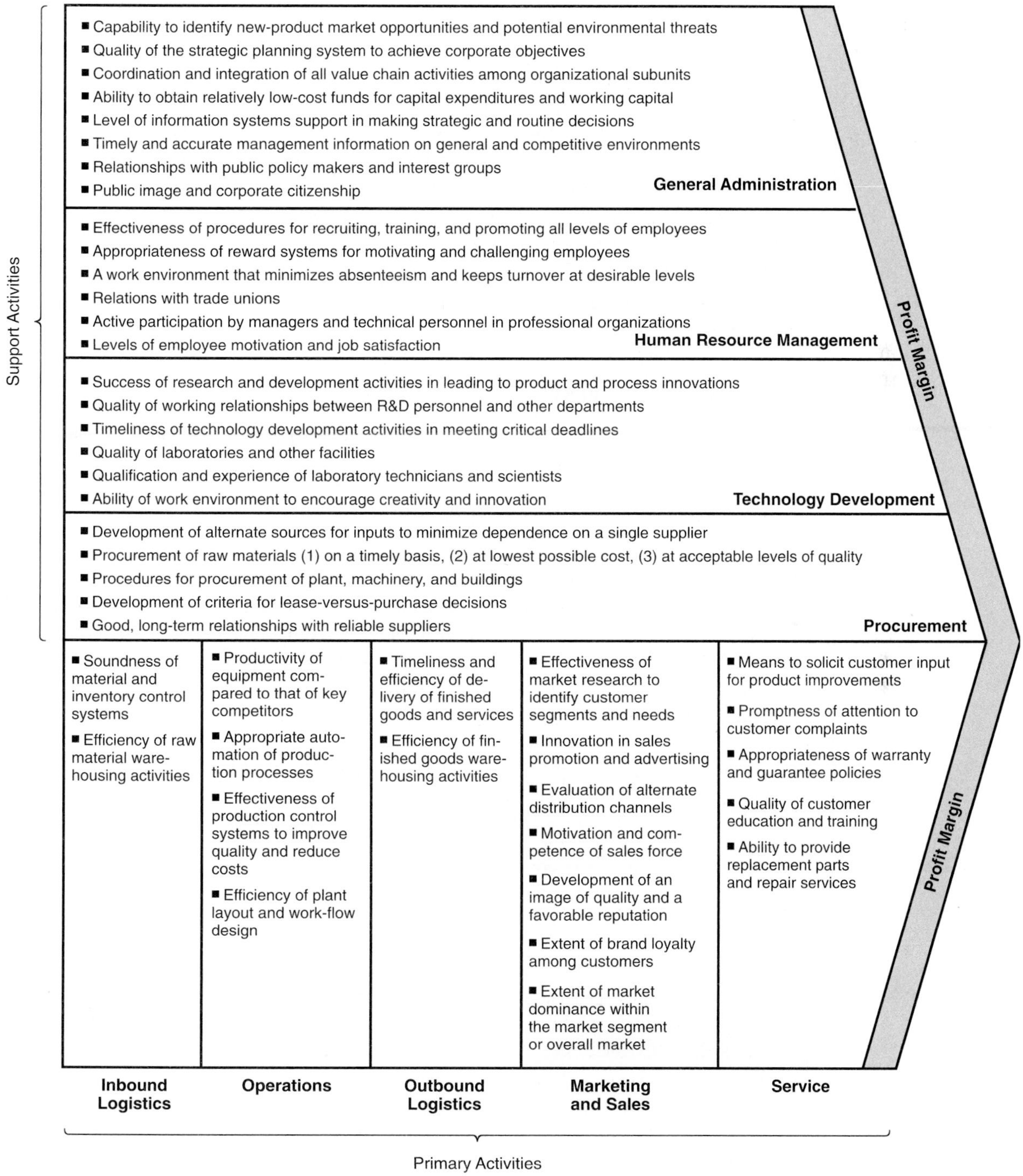

- Capability to identify new-product market opportunities and potential environmental threats
- Quality of the strategic planning system to achieve corporate objectives
- Coordination and integration of all value chain activities among organizational subunits
- Ability to obtain relatively low-cost funds for capital expenditures and working capital
- Level of information systems support in making strategic and routine decisions
- Timely and accurate management information on general and competitive environments
- Relationships with public policy makers and interest groups
- Public image and corporate citizenship

General Administration

- Effectiveness of procedures for recruiting, training, and promoting all levels of employees
- Appropriateness of reward systems for motivating and challenging employees
- A work environment that minimizes absenteeism and keeps turnover at desirable levels
- Relations with trade unions
- Active participation by managers and technical personnel in professional organizations
- Levels of employee motivation and job satisfaction

Human Resource Management

- Success of research and development activities in leading to product and process innovations
- Quality of working relationships between R&D personnel and other departments
- Timeliness of technology development activities in meeting critical deadlines
- Quality of laboratories and other facilities
- Qualification and experience of laboratory technicians and scientists
- Ability of work environment to encourage creativity and innovation

Technology Development

- Development of alternate sources for inputs to minimize dependence on a single supplier
- Procurement of raw materials (1) on a timely basis, (2) at lowest possible cost, (3) at acceptable levels of quality
- Procedures for procurement of plant, machinery, and buildings
- Development of criteria for lease-versus-purchase decisions
- Good, long-term relationships with reliable suppliers

Procurement

(Support Activities — left vertical label; Profit Margin — right diagonal label)

Inbound Logistics	Operations	Outbound Logistics	Marketing and Sales	Service
■ Soundness of material and inventory control systems ■ Efficiency of raw material warehousing activities	■ Productivity of equipment compared to that of key competitors ■ Appropriate automation of production processes ■ Effectiveness of production control systems to improve quality and reduce costs ■ Efficiency of plant layout and work-flow design	■ Timeliness and efficiency of delivery of finished goods and services ■ Efficiency of finished goods warehousing activities	■ Effectiveness of market research to identify customer segments and needs ■ Innovation in sales promotion and advertising ■ Evaluation of alternate distribution channels ■ Motivation and competence of sales force ■ Development of an image of quality and a favorable reputation ■ Extent of brand loyalty among customers ■ Extent of market dominance within the market segment or overall market	■ Means to solicit customer input for product improvements ■ Promptness of attention to customer complaints ■ Appropriateness of warranty and guarantee policies ■ Quality of customer education and training ■ Ability to provide replacement parts and repair services

Primary Activities

Source: Adapted from Alex Miller, *Strategic Management* (Burr Ridge, IL: Irwin/McGraw-Hill, 1998), pp. 127–28.

THE GAP'S SPECTACULAR RETAILING SUCCESS WAS BASED ON VALUE CHAIN ANALYSIS

STRATEGY IN ACTION 6–3

Melvin Jacobs, chairman of the New York–based Saks Fifth Avenue, observed: "The Gap is a huge success, while retailers around the world are struggling like crazy." Dean Witter analyst Donald Trott says The Gap is expected to reach 3,000 stores in time for its 30th birthday in 2000 after a one-store start in San Francisco. While The Gap has been a Wall Street darling for some time, president Mickey Drexler says, "We've been doing the same thing for seven or eight years. This company is no overnight success."

What Drexler and founder Donald Fisher did was apply a type of value chain look at specialty retail clothing to identify key value activities around which they could build a long-term competitive advantage. They identified four components of the value chain within which they saw the opportunity to create new, value-added approaches that could become sustained competitive advantages.

1. PRODUCT DEVELOPMENT

Drexler's concept for The Gap was and is: simple, quality, and comfort. Gap's designers are told to design clothes they themselves would wear, to guide their search for merchandise. At a meeting in San Francisco, about 30 merchandisers were showing their proposed fall collection for GapKids to Drexler and his staff. The woman in charge of jackets held up a hooded coat. After viewing it, Drexler's reaction: "I hate it." A loud cheer among the staff goes up—the New York designers were pushing the item, but The Gap staff found it ugly.

The Gap staff members feel their strong involvement in clothing design choices, rather than the usual reliance on New York or Dallas merchandisers, is a distinct advantage. The Gap designs its own clothes, chooses its own material, and monitors manufacturing so closely that it can keep quality high and costs low.

2. INBOUND LOGISTICS

The Gap has over 200 quality-control inspectors working inside factories in 40 countries to make sure specifications are met right from the start. Like Wal-Mart, The Gap has computerized, highly automated, carefully located distribution centers serving as hubs directly linked to store groupings.

Source: "The World According to GAP," *Business Week:* January 27, 1997, p. 72; "The Gap," *Business Week:* March 9, 1992, p. 58.

retail industry average. The Gap's use of value chain analysis to guide its spectacular retail success is described in Strategy in Action 6–3.

Second, the nature of value chains and the relative importance of the activities within them vary by industry. Lodging firms like Holiday Inn's major costs and concerns involve operational activities—it provides its service instantaneously at each location—and marketing activities, while having minimal concern for outbound logistics. Yet for a distributor, such as the food distributor PYA, inbound and outbound logistics are the most critical area. Major retailers like Wal-Mart have built value advantages focusing on purchasing and inbound logistics while the most successful personal computer companies have built via sales, outbound logistics, and service through the mail order process.

continued

For example, a $75 million automated distribution center recently opened outside Baltimore, allowing The Gap to supply New York City stores daily instead of three times a week. Few in specialty retailing can match this logistical capability.

3. OPERATIONS

Every Gap store is the same—a clean, well-lit place where harried consumers can shop easily and quickly. Every detail is fussed over, from cleaning the store's floors to rounding the counter corners at GapKids for safety's sake to the detailed instructions on where to display clothes and touching up white walls weekly and polishing wood floors every three days. Already in 800 of the U.S.'s 1,500 largest malls, it lowered operating costs long term by taking advantage of incidents of commercial property excess capacity, locking up sweet lease deals, moving into downtowns and urban neighborhoods, and opening new stores on the declining main streets of midsized cities. Each of these operational activities ensured higher quality and ease of management, and sustained lower costs.

4. HUMAN RESOURCE MANAGEMENT

In an industry that is low base pay and commission based, The Gap salespeople receive no commission. But compensation exceeds the industry average. The Gap's COO motivates salespeople with constant contests. The most multiple purchases to the register in one day wins a Gap-logo watch. The Thanksgiving weekend rush saw COO O'Donnell have Pizza Hut and Domino's deliver 15,000 pizzas and 72,000 Pepsis to store personnel on the job. And The Gap's training program is detailed and rigorous before you are free to "work the floor." Again, The Gap pursues policies that differentiate it from current industry practices in a way that adds incremental value—well trained, fairly compensated, highly motivated store personnel, resulting in lower turnover costs and a favorable image for service-leery retail shoppers.

Drexler and Fisher have driven The Gap's success in these and many other ways. But disaggregating specialty clothing retailing into distinct activities in order to better understand their costs and sources of differentiation has led them to design unique approaches (described above) in four strategically important activities that created sustained competitive advantages through lower costs, higher quality, and clear differentiation from all other clothing retailers.

Third, the relative importance of value activities can vary by a company's position in a broader value system that includes the value chains of its upstream suppliers and downstream customers or partners involved in providing products or services to end users. A producer of roofing shingles depends heavily on the downstream activities of wholesale distributors and building supply retailers to reach roofing contractors and do-it-yourselfers. Maytag manufactures its own appliances, sells them through independent distributors, and provides warranty service to the buyer. Sears outsources the manufacture of its appliances while it promotes its brand name—Kenmore—and handles all sales and service.

As these examples suggest, it is important that managers take into account their level of vertical integration when comparing their cost structure for activities on their value chain to those of key competitors. Comparing a fully integrated rival with a partially integrated one requires adjusting for the scope of activities performed to achieve meaningful comparison. It also suggests the need for examining costs associated with activities provided by upstream or downstream companies; these activities ultimately determine comparable, final costs to end users. Said another way, one company's comparative cost disadvantage (or advantage) may emanate more from activities undertaken by upstream or downstream "partners" than from activities under the direct control of that company—therefore suggesting less of a relative advantage or disadvantage within the company's direct value chain.

Compare to Competitors

The final basic consideration when applying value chain analysis is the need to have a meaningful comparison to use when evaluating a value activity as a strength or weakness. Value chain analysis is most effective when comparing the value chains or activities of key competitors. Whether using the value chain approach or an examination of functional areas, or both approaches, the strategist's next step in a systematic internal analysis is to compare the firm's status with meaningful standards to determine which of its value activities are strengths or weaknesses. Four sources of meaningful standards for evaluating internal factors and value activities are discussed in the next section.

INTERNAL ANALYSIS: MAKING MEANINGFUL COMPARISONS

Managers need objective standards to use when examining internal resources and value-building activities. Whether applying the RBV, SWOT analysis, or the value chain approach, strategists rely on four basic perspectives to evaluate where their firm stacks up on its internal capabilities. These four perspectives are discussed in this section.

Comparison with Past Performance

Strategists use the firm's historical experience as a basis for evaluating internal factors. Managers are most familiar with the internal capabilities and problems of their firm because they have been immersed in its financial, marketing, production, and R&D activities. Not surprisingly, a manager's assessment of whether a certain internal factor—such as production facilities, sales organization, financial capacity, control systems, or key personnel—is a strength or a weakness will be strongly influenced by his or her experience in connection with that factor. In the capital-intensive airline industry, for example, debt capacity is a strategic internal factor. Delta Airlines managers view Delta's debt-equity ratio of less than 1.5 brought on by its acquisition of PanAm's international operations as a real weakness limiting its flexibility to invest in facilities because it maintained a ratio less than 0.6 for over 20 years. American Airlines managers, on the other hand, view American's much higher 1.8 debt-equity ratio as a growing strength, because it is down 50 percent from its 3.5 level five years earlier.

Although historical experience can provide a relevant evaluation framework, strategists must avoid tunnel vision in making use of it. NEC, Japan's IBM, has dominated Japan's PC market with a 70 percent market share using a proprietary hardware system, much higher screen resolution, powerful distribution channels, and a large software library from third-party vendors. Far from worried, Hajime Ikeda, manager of NEC's planning division, said recently: "We don't hear complaints from our users."

But the 1990s has seen IBM and Macintosh filling shelves in Japan's famous consumer electronics district, Akihabara. Hiroki Kamata, president of a Japanese computer research firm, reports that Japan's PC market is worth over $25 billion in 2001, with Apple and IBM compatibles each having more market share than NEC because of better technology, software, and the restrictions created by NEC's proprietary technology. Clearly, using only historical experience as a basis for identifying strengths and weaknesses can prove dangerously inaccurate.

Stages of Industry Evolution

The requirements for success in industry segments change over time. Strategists can use these changing requirements, which are associated with different stages of industry evolution, as a framework for identifying and evaluating the firm's strengths and weaknesses.

Figure 6–10 depicts four stages of industry evolution and the typical changes in functional capabilities that are often associated with business success at each of these stages. The early development of a product market, for example, entails minimal growth in sales, major R&D emphasis, rapid technological change in the product, operating losses, and a need for sufficient resources or slack to support a temporarily unprofitable operation. Success at this introduction stage may be associated with technical skill, with being first in new markets, or with having a marketing advantage that creates widespread awareness. Radio Shack's initial success with its TRS–80 home computer was based in part on its ability to gain widespread exposure and acceptance in the ill-defined home computer market via the large number of existing Radio Shack outlets throughout the country.

The strengths necessary for success change in the growth stage. Rapid growth brings new competitors into the product market. At this stage, such factors as brand recognition, product differentiation, and the financial resources to support both heavy marketing expenses and the effect of price competition on cash flow can be key strengths. IBM entered the personal computer market in the growth stage and was able to rapidly become the market leader with a strategy based on its key strengths in brand awareness and possession of the financial resources needed to support consumer advertising. But IBM lost that lead in the next stage as speed in distribution and cost structures became the key success factors—strengths for Compaq and several mail order–oriented computer assemblers.

As the industry moves through a shakeout phase and into the maturity stage, industry growth continues, but at a decreasing rate. The number of industry segments expands, but technological change in product design slows considerably. As a result, competition usually becomes more intense, and promotional or pricing advantages and differentiation become key internal strengths. Technological change in process design becomes intense as the many competitors seek to provide the product in the most efficient manner. Where R&D was critical in the introduction stage, efficient production is now crucial to continued success in the broader industry segments. Ford's emphasis on quality control and modern, efficient production has helped it prosper in the maturing U.S. auto industry, while General Motors, which pays almost 50 percent more than Ford to produce a comparable car, continues to decline.

When the industry moves into the decline stage, strengths and weaknesses center on cost advantages, superior supplier or customer relationships, and financial control. Competitive advantage can exist at this stage, at least temporarily, if a firm serves gradually shrinking markets that competitors are choosing to leave.

FIGURE 6–10
Sources of Distinctive Competence at Different Stages of Industry Evolution

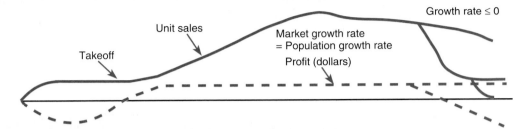

Functional Area	Introduction	Growth	Maturity	Decline
Marketing	Resources/skills to create widespread awareness and find acceptance from customers; advantageous access to distribution	Ability to establish brand recognition, find niche, reduce price, solidify strong distribution relations, and develop new channels	Skills in aggressively promoting products to new markets and holding existing markets; pricing flexibility; skills in differentiating products and holding customer loyalty	Cost-effective means of efficient access to selected channels and markets; strong customer loyalty or dependence; strong company image
Production operations	Ability to expand capacity effectively, limit number of designs, develop standards	Ability to add product variants, centralize production, or otherwise lower costs; ability to improve product quality; seasonal subcontracting capacity	Ability to improve product and reduce costs; ability to share or reduce capacity; advantageous supplier relationships; subcontracting	Ability to prune product line; cost advantage in production, location or distribution; simplified inventory control; subcontracting or long production runs
Finance	Resources to support high net cash overflow and initial losses; ability to use leverage effectively	Ability to finance rapid expansion, to have net cash outflows but increasing profits; resources to support product improvements	Ability to generate and redistribute increasing net cash inflows; effective cost control systems	Ability to reuse or liquidate unneeded equipment; advantage in cost of facilities; control system accuracy; streamlined management control
Personnel	Flexibility in staffing and training new management; existence of employees with key skills in new products or markets	Existence of an ability to add skilled personnel; motivated and loyal work force	Ability to cost effectively, reduce work force, increase efficiency	Capacity to reduce and reallocate personnel; cost advantage
Engineering and research and development	Ability to make engineering changes, have technical bugs in product and process resolved	Skill in quality and new feature development; ability to start developing successor product	Ability to reduce costs, develop variants, differentiate products	Ability to support other grown areas or to apply product to unique customer needs
Key functional area and strategy focus	Engineering: market penetration	Sales: consumer loyalty; market share	Production efficiency; successor products	Finance; maximum investment recovery

Figure 6–10 is a rather simple model of the stages of industry evolution. These stages can and do vary from the model. What should be borne in mind is that the relative importance of various determinants of success differs across the stages of industry evolution. Thus, the state of that evolution must be considered in internal analysis. Figure 6–10 suggests dimensions that are particularly deserving of in-depth consideration when a company profile is being developed.

Benchmarking—Comparison with Competitors

A major focus in determining a firm's resources and competencies is comparison with existing (and potential) competitors. Firms in the same industry often have different marketing skills, financial resources, operating facilities and locations, technical know-how, brand images, levels of integration, managerial talent, and so on. These different internal resources can become relative strengths (or weaknesses) depending on the strategy a firm chooses. In choosing a strategy, managers should compare the firm's key internal capabilities with those of its rivals, thereby isolating its key strengths and weaknesses.

In the home appliance industry, for example, Sears and General Electric are major rivals. Sears's principal strength is its retail network. For GE, distribution—through independent franchised dealers—has traditionally been a relative weakness. GE's possession of the financial resources needed to support modernized mass production has enabled it to maintain both cost and technological advantages over its rivals, particularly Sears. This major strength for GE is a relative weakness for Sears, which depends solely on subcontracting to produce its Kenmore appliances. On the other hand, maintenance and repair service are important in the appliance industry. Historically, Sears has had strength in this area because it maintains fully staffed service components and spreads the costs of components over numerous departments at each retail location. GE, on the other hand, has had to depend on regional service centers and on local contracting with independent service firms by its independent local dealers. Among the internal factors that Sears and GE must consider in developing a strategy are distribution networks, technological capabilities, operating costs, and service facilities. Managers in both organizations have built successful strategies yet those strategies are quite different. Benchmarking each other, they have identified ways to build on relative strengths while avoiding dependence on capabilities at which the other firm excels.

Benchmarking, comparing the way "our" company performs a specific activity with a competitor or other company doing the same thing, has become a central concern of managers in quality commitment companies worldwide. Particularly as the value chain framework has taken hold in structuring internal analysis, managers seek to systematically benchmark the costs and results of the smallest value activities against relevant competitors or other useful standards because it has proven to be an effective way to continuously improve that activity. The ultimate objective in benchmarking is to identify the "best practices" in performing an activity, to learn how lower costs, fewer defects, or other outcomes linked to excellence are achieved. Companies committed to benchmarking attempt to isolate and identify where their costs or outcomes are out of line with what the best practicers of a particular activity experience (competitors and noncompetitors) and then attempt to change their activities to achieve the new best practices standard.

Comparison with key competitors can prove useful in ascertaining whether their internal capabilities on these and other factors are strengths or weaknesses. Significant favorable differences (existing or expected) from competitors are potential cornerstones

BusinessWeek

SAS AIRLINES BENCHMARKS USING DELTA AIRLINES

GLOBAL
STRATEGY IN
ACTION
6–1

For many years, Scandinavian Airline System (SAS) was a premier European airline. Benefiting from International Airline Transportation Association (IATA), a protective European airline industry trade organization, SAS was profitable for 17 straight years. But changes in the global

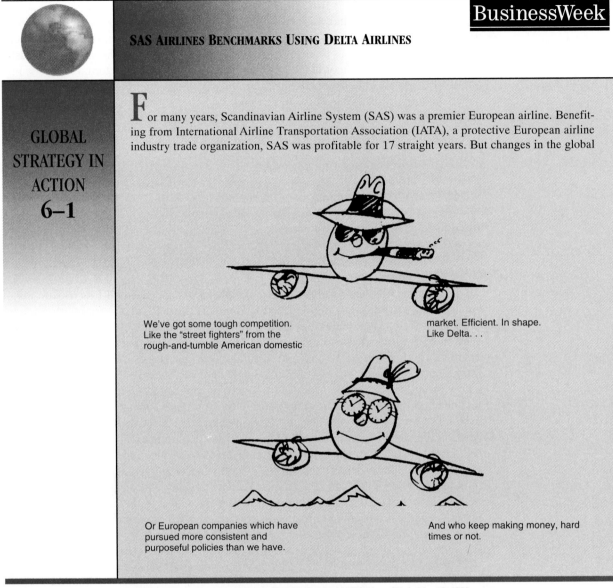

We've got some tough competition. Like the "street fighters" from the rough-and-tumble American domestic

market. Efficient. In shape. Like Delta. . .

Or European companies which have pursued more consistent and purposeful policies than we have.

And who keep making money, hard times or not.

Source: SAS documents and "Ready for TransEurope Air?" *Business Week:* May 10, 1993.

of a firm's strategy. Moreover, through comparison with major competitors, a firm may avoid strategic commitments that it cannot competitively support. Global Strategy in Action 6–1 shows how the Scandinavian Airline System (SAS) used competitor comparison to assess its strengths and weaknesses in the global airline industry.

Comparison with Success Factors in the Industry

Industry analysis (see Chapter 3) involves identifying the factors associated with successful participation in a given industry. As was true for the evaluation methods discussed above, the key determinants of success in an industry may be used to identify a firm's internal strengths and weaknesses. By scrutinizing industry competitors, as well as customer needs, vertical industry structure, channels of distribution, costs, barriers

continued

airline industry caused its earnings to plummet in the last few years. When SAS was on the verge of folding, its new CEO undertook an extensive competitor comparison as a basis for finding a strategy to turn it around. The CEO shared the following assessment in an employee pamphlet communicating the firm's new strategy and rationale behind it.

Look at the Differences:

	Swissair International	SAS International
Cabin Factor	63.60	59.30
Load Factor	59.20	47.60
Passenger revenue USD/RPK*	0.09	0.08
Cargo revenue USD/RFTK	0.37	0.31
Total revenue USD/RTK	0.79	0.73
Operating cost USD/ATK	0.45	0.42
Revenue-cost relationship (Over 100% profit)	103.50	99.70
Average flight leg/km	1051.00	967.00

Delta Has:

40% more revenue tonne kms per employee

120% more passengers per employee

14% more available tonne kms per pilot

40% more passenger kms per cabin attendant

35% more passenger kms per passenger sales employee

It is difficult to make similar comparisons in the technical and maintenance fields, but even in these areas Delta has a substantially higher productivity than SAS.

*USD = U.S. Dollars; RPK = Revenue passenger-kilometers; RFTK = Revenue freight tonne-kilometers; RTK = Revenue tonne-kilometers; ATK = Available tonne-kilometers. Exchange rate: one USD = 4.65 Swedish kronor.

to entry, availability of substitutes, and suppliers, a strategist seeks to determine whether a firm's current internal capabilities represent strengths or weaknesses in new competitive arenas. The discussion in Chapter 3 provides a useful framework—five industry forces—against which to examine a firm's potential strengths and weaknesses. General Cinema Corporation, the largest U.S. movie theater operator, determined that its internal skills in marketing, site analysis, creative financing, and management of geographically dispersed operations were key strengths relative to major success factors in the soft-drink bottling industry. This assessment proved accurate. Within 10 years after it entered the soft-drink bottling industry, General Cinema became the largest franchised bottler of soft drinks in the United States, handling Pepsi, 7UP, Dr Pepper, and Sunkist. Global Strategy in Action 6–2 describes how Avery Dennison used industry evolution benchmarking versus 3M to create a new, successful strategy.

BusinessWeek

AVERY DENNISON USES BENCHMARKING AND STAGE OF INDUSTRY EVALUATION TO TURN WEAKNESS INTO STRENGTH

GLOBAL STRATEGY IN ACTION 6–2

Avery Dennison has long made adhesives and what it calls "sticky papers" for business customers. Ten years ago, AD decided to take on 3M with its own version of 3M's highly successful Post-It notes and Scotch transparent tape.

How frequently did you buy Avery Notes and Avery Tape? You probably have never heard of them, right? That is because Avery was beat up in that market by 3M and AD exited the business after just a few years. Key strengths, distribution and brand name, that 3M used to build those products were major weaknesses at AD. Plus, in President Charles Miller's way of viewing it, 3M remained aggressive and true to an innovative culture to back its products while AD had grown rusty and "me too" rather than being the innovator it had traditionally been with pressure-sensitive papers. So faced with considerable weakness competing against a major threat, Miller refocused AD on getting innovative in areas of traditional technical strength.

Today, AD has 30 percent of its sales from products introduced in the past five years. It has half the market for adhesive paper stock and 40 percent of the market for coated paper films for package labels. Says Miller, "We believe in market evolution. The best way to control a market is to invent it. With innovative products, superstores aren't able to squeeze margins, as they can in commodity products." New products now pour out of AD labs to position AD strengths against early life cycle stage opportunities.

Source: "The Business Week 50," *Business Week:* March 30, 1998.

SUMMARY

This chapter looked at several ways managers achieve greater objectivity and rigor as they analyze their company's internal capabilities. Managers often start their internal analysis with questions like: "How well is the current strategy working? What is our current situation? Or what are our strengths and weaknesses?" The resource-based view provides a key, fundamental framework for analyzing firm success based on the firm's internal resources and competencies. *SWOT analysis,* a widely used approach to internal analysis, provides a logical way to apply the results of an RBV. Managers frequently use RBV and SWOT analysis to introduce realism and greater objectivity into their internal analysis. This chapter also described how insightful managers look at their business as a chain of activities that add value creating the products or services they sell—this is called *value chain analysis.* Managers who use value chain analysis to understand the value structure within their firm's activities and look at the value system, which also includes upstream suppliers and downstream partners and buyers, often gain very meaningful insights into their company's strategic resources, competencies, and options. Finally, this chapter covered four ways objectivity and realism are enhanced when managers use meaningful standards for comparison regardless of the particular analytical framework they employ in internal analysis. This chapter is followed by an appendix covering traditional financial analysis to serve as a refresher and reminder about this basic internal analysis tool.

When matched with management's environmental analyses and mission priorities, the process of internal analysis provides the critical foundation for strategy formulation.

Armed with an accurate, thorough, and timely internal analysis, managers are in a better position to formulate effective strategies. The next chapter describes basic strategy alternatives that any firm may consider.

QUESTIONS FOR DISCUSSION

1. Describe SWOT analysis as a way to guide internal analysis. How does this approach reflect the basic strategic management process?

2. What is the resource-based view of the firm? Give examples of three different types of resources.

3. What are three characteristics that make resources more, or less, valuable? Provide an example of each.

4. Apply SWOT analysis to yourself and your career aspirations. What are your major strengths and weaknesses? How might you use your knowledge of these strengths and weaknesses to develop your future career plans?

5. Why do you think value chain analysis has become a preferred approach to guide internal analysis? What are its strengths? Its weaknesses?

6. In what ways do the approaches to internal analysis at The Gap (see Strategy in Action 6–3) and Scandinavian Airline System (see Global Strategy in Action 6–1) appear to be similar and in what ways are they different?

BIBLIOGRAPHY

Barney, J. "Firm Resources and Sustained Competitive Advantage." *Journal of Management* 17 (1991), pp. 99–120.

Collins, David J., and Cynthia A. Montgomery. "Competing on Resources: Strategy in the 1990s." *Harvard Business Review* 73, no. 4 (July–August 1995), pp. 118–28.

Collins, James C., and Jerry L. Porras. *Built to Last: Successful Habits of Visionary Companies.* New York: Harper Business, 1994.

Conner, Kathleen R. "A Historical Comparison of Resource-Based Theory and Five Schools of Thought Within Industrial Organization Economics: Do We Have a New Theory of the Firm?" *Journal of Management* (March 1991), p. 121.

D'Aveni, Richard A. *Hypercompetition: The Dynamics of Strategic Maneuvering.* New York: Free Press, 1994, chaps. 1, 2, 3, and 4.

Davis, Stan, and Jim Botkin. "The Coming of Knowledge-Based Business." *Harvard Business Review* 72, no. 5 (September–October 1994), pp. 165–70.

Grant, R. M. "The Resource-Based Theory of Competitive Advantage: Implications for Strategy Formulation." *California Management Review* (Spring 1991), pp. 119–45.

Kaplan, Robert S. "Designing a Balanced Scorecard Matched to Business Strategy." *Planning Review* 22 (September–October 1994), pp. 15–19.

Kaplan, Robert S., and David P. Norton. "The Balanced Scorecard—Measures That Drive Performance." *Harvard Business Review* (January–February 1992), p. 166.

————. "Putting the Balanced Scorecard to Work." *Harvard Business Review* (September–October 1993), p. 205.

————. "Using the Balanced Scorecard as a Strategic Management System." *Harvard Business Review* 74 (January–February 1996), pp. 75–85.

Kiernan, Matthew J. "The New Strategic Architecture: Learning to Compete in the Twenty-First Century." *Academy of Management Executive* 7, no. 1 (1993), pp. 7–21.

Klein, Jeremy A.; Gordon M. Edge; and Tom Kass. "Skill-Based Competition." *Journal of General Management* 16 (Summer 1991), pp. 1–15.

McGrath, Michael E., and Richard W. Hoole. "Manufacturing's New Economies of Scale." *Harvard Business Review* (May–June 1992), pp. 94–102.

Peteraf. "The Cornerstone of Competitive Advantage: A Resource-Based View." *Strategic Management Journal* 14 (1993), pp. 179–91.

Prahalad, C. K., and Gary Hamel. "The Core Competence of the Corporation." *Harvard Business Review* 90, no. 3 (May–June 1990), pp. 79–93.

Prusak, Laurence. "The Knowledge Advantage." *Strategy and Leadership* 24, no. 2 (March–April 1966), pp. 6–8.

Rayport, Jeffrey F., and John J. Sviokla. "Exploiting the Virtual Value Chain." *Harvard Business Review* 73, no. 6 (November–December 1995), pp. 75–85.

Rumelt, Richard P. "How Much Does Industry Matter?" *Strategic Management Journal* 12 (March 1991), pp. 167–85.

Shank, John K., and Vijay Govindarajan. *Strategic Cost Management: The New Tool for Competitive Advantage.* New York: The Free Press, 1993.

Stalk, George; Philip Evans; and Lawrence E. Shulman. "Competing on Capabilities: The New Rules of Corporate Strategy." *Harvard Business Review* 70, no. 2 (March–April 1992), pp. 57–69.

Ulrich, Dave, and Dale Lake. "Organizational Capability: Creating Competitive Advantage." *Academy of Management Executive* 5 (February 1991), pp. 77–92.

Watson, Gregory H. *Strategic Benchmarking: How to Rate Your Company's Performance Against the World's Best.* New York: John Wiley & Sons, 1993.

Wernerfelt. "A Resource-Based View of the Firm." *Strategic Management Journal* 5 (1984), pp. 171–80.

APPENDIX

USING FINANCIAL ANALYSIS

One of the most important tools for assessing the strength of an organization within its industry is financial analysis. Managers, investors, and creditors all employ some form of this analysis as the beginning point for their financial decision making. Investors use financial analyses in making decisions about whether to buy or sell stock, and creditors use them in deciding whether or not to lend. They provide managers with a measurement of how the company is doing in comparison with its performance in past years and with the performance of competitors in the industry.

Although financial analysis is useful for decision making, some weaknesses should be noted. Any picture that it provides of the company is based on past data. Although trends may be noteworthy, this picture should not automatically be assumed to be applicable to the future. In addition, the analysis is only as good as the accounting procedures that have provided the information. When making comparisons between companies, one should keep in mind the variability of accounting procedures from firm to firm.

There are four basic groups of financial ratios: liquidity, leverage, activity, and profitability.

Depicted in Exhibit 6–1 are the specific ratios calculated for each of the basic groups. Liquidity and leverage ratios represent an assessment of the risk of the firm. Activity and profitability ratios are measures of the return generated by the assets of the firm. The interaction between certain groups of ratios is indicated by arrows.

Typically, two common financial statements are used in financial analyses: the balance sheet and the income statement. Exhibit 6–2 is a balance sheet and Exhibit 6–3 an income statement for the ABC Company. These statements will be used to illustrate the financial analyses.

LIQUIDITY RATIOS

Liquidity ratios are used as indicators of a firm's ability to meet its short-term obligations. These obligations include any current liabilities, including currently maturing long-term debt. Current assets move through a normal cash cycle of inventories—sales—accounts receivable—cash. The firm then uses cash to pay off or reduce its current liabilities. The best-known liquidity ratio is the current ratio: current assets divided by current liabilities. For the ABC Company, the current ratio is calculated as follows:

$$\frac{\text{Current assets}}{\text{Current liabilities}} = \frac{\$4,125,000}{\$2,512,500} = 1.64 \ (2002)$$

$$= \frac{\$3,618,000}{\$2,242,250} = 1.161 \ (2001)$$

Prepared by Elizabeth Gatewood, Indiana University. ©Elizabeth Gatewood, 2000. Reprinted by permission of Elizabeth Gatewood.

EXHIBIT 6–1
Financial Ratios

	Liquidity	Leverage	Activity	Profitability

Liquidity:
$$\frac{\text{Current assets}}{\text{Current liabilities}}$$

$$\frac{\text{Current assets–inventory}}{\text{Current liabilities}}$$

Leverage:
$$\frac{\text{Total debt}}{\text{Total assets}}$$

$$\frac{\text{Long-term debt}}{\text{Equity}}$$

Activity:
$$\frac{\text{Net sales}}{\text{Assets}}$$

$$\frac{\text{Net sales}}{\text{Fixed assets}}$$

$$\frac{\text{Net sales}}{\text{Inventory}}$$

$$\frac{\text{Net sales}}{\text{Accounts receivable}}$$

Profitability:
$$\frac{\text{Net income}}{\text{Sales}}$$

$$\frac{\text{Net income}}{\text{Total assets}}$$

$$\frac{\text{Net income}}{\text{Net worth}}$$

Return measures

Most analysts suggest a current ratio of 2 to 3. A large current ratio is not necessarily a good sign; it may mean that an organization is not making the most efficient use of its assets. The optimum current ratio will vary from industry to industry, with the more volatile industries requiring higher ratios.

EXHIBIT 6–2

ABC Company
Balance Sheet
As of December 31, 2001, and 2002

		2002		2001
Assets				
Current assets:				
Cash		$ 140,000		$ 115,000
Accounts receivable		1,760,000		1,440,000
Inventory		2,175,000		2,000,000
Prepaid expenses		50,000		63,000
Total current assets		4,125,000		3,618,000
Fixed assets:				
Long-term receivable		1,255,000		1,090,000
Property and plant	$2,037,000		$2,015,000	
Less: Accumulated depreciation	862,000		860,000	
Net property and plant		1,175,000		1,155,000
Other fixed assets		550,000		530,000
Total fixed assets		2,980,000		2,775,000
Total assets		$7,105,000		$6,393,000
Liabilities and Stockholders' Equity				
Current liabilities:				
Accounts payable		$1,325,000		$1,225,000
Bank loans payable		475,000		550,000
Accrued federal taxes		675,000		425,000
Current maturities (long-term debt)		17,500		26,000
Dividends payable		20,000		16,250
Total current liabilities		2,512,500		2,242,250
Long-term liabilities		1,350,000		1,425,000
Total liabilities		3,862,000		3,667,250
Stockholders' equity:				
Common stock (104,046 shares outstanding in 1995;				
101,204 shares outstanding in 1994)		44,500		43,300
Additional paid-in capital		568,000		372,450
Retained earnings		2,630,000		2,310,000
Total stockholders' equity		3,242,500		2,725,750
Total liabilities and stockholders' equity		$7,105,000		$6,393,000

Since slow-moving or obsolescent inventories could overstate a firm's ability to meet short-term demands, the quick ratio is sometimes preferred to assess a firm's liquidity. The quick ratio is current assets minus inventories, divided by current liabilities. The quick ratio for the ABC Company is calculated as follows:

$$\frac{\text{Current assets} - \text{Inventories}}{\text{Current liabilities}} = \frac{\$1,950,000}{\$2,512,500} = 0.78 \ (2002)$$

$$= \frac{\$1,618,000}{\$2,242,250} = 0.72 \ (2001)$$

EXHIBIT 6–3

ABC Company
Income Statement
For the Years Ending December 31, 2001, and 2002

		2002		2001
Net sales		$8,250,000		$8,000,000
Cost of goods sold	$5,100,000		$5,000,000	
Administrative expenses	1,750,000		1,680,000	
Other expenses	420,000		390,000	
Total		7,270,000		7,070,000
Earnings before interest and taxes		980,000		930,000
Less: Interest expense		210,000		210,000
Earnings before taxes		770,000		720,000
Less: Federal income taxes		360,000		325,000
Earnings after taxes (net income)		$ 410,000		$ 395,000
Common stock cash dividends		$ 90,000		$ 84,000
Addition to retained earnings		$ 320,000		$ 311,000
Earnings per common share		$ 3.940		$ 3.90
Dividends per common share		$ 0.865		$ 0.83

A quick ratio of approximately 1 would be typical for American industries. Although there is less variability in the quick ratio than in the current ratio, stable industries would be able to operate safely with a lower ratio.

LEVERAGE RATIOS

Leverage ratios identify the source of a firm's capital—owners or outside creditors. The term *leverage* refers to the fact that using capital with a fixed interest charge will "amplify" either profits or losses in relation to the equity of holders of common stock. The most commonly used ratio is total debt divided by total assets. Total debt includes current liabilities and long-term liabilities. This ratio is a measure of the percentage of total funds provided by debt. A total debt–total assets ratio higher than 0.5 is usually considered safe only for firms in stable industries.

$$\frac{\text{Total debt}}{\text{Total assets}} = \frac{\$3,862,500}{\$7,105,000} = 0.54 \ (2002)$$

$$= \frac{\$3,667,250}{\$6,393,000} = 0.57 \ (2001)$$

The ratio of long-term debt to equity is a measure of the extent to which sources of long-term financing are provided by creditors. It is computed by dividing long-term debt by the stockholders' equity.

$$\frac{\text{Long-term debt}}{\text{Equity}} = \frac{\$1,350,000}{\$3,242,500} = 0.42 \ (2002)$$

$$= \frac{\$1,425,000}{\$2,725,750} = 0.52 \ (2001)$$

ACTIVITY RATIOS

Activity ratios indicate how effectively a firm is using its resources. By comparing revenues with the resources used to generate them, it is possible to establish an efficiency of operation. The asset turnover ratio indicates how efficiently management is employing total assets. Asset turnover is calculated by dividing sales by total assets. For the ABC Company, asset turnover is calculated as follows:

$$\text{Asset turnover} = \frac{\text{Sales}}{\text{Total assets}} = \frac{\$8,250,000}{\$7,105,000} = 1.16 \ (2002)$$

$$= \frac{\$8,000,000}{\$6,393,000} = 1.25 \ (2001)$$

The ratio of sales to fixed assets is a measure of the turnover on plant and equipment. It is calculated by dividing sales by net fixed assets.

$$\text{Fixed asset turnover} = \frac{\text{Sales}}{\text{Net fixed assets}} = \frac{\$8,250,000}{\$2,980,000} = 2.77 \ (2002)$$

$$= \frac{\$8,000,000}{\$2,775,000} = 2.88 \ (2001)$$

Industry figures for asset turnover will vary with capital-intensive industries, and those requiring large inventories will have much smaller ratios.

Another activity ratio is inventory turnover, estimated by dividing sales by average inventory. The norm for U.S. industries is 9, but whether the ratio for a particular firm is higher or lower normally depends on the product sold. Small, inexpensive items usually turn over at a much higher rate than larger, expensive ones. Since inventories normally are carried at cost, it would be more accurate to use the cost of goods sold in place of sales in the numerator of this ratio. Established compilers of industry ratios, such as Dun & Bradstreet, however, use the ratio of sales to inventory.

$$\text{Inventory turnover} = \frac{\text{Sales}}{\text{Inventory}} = \frac{\$8,250,000}{\$2,175,000} = 3.79 \ (2002)$$

$$= \frac{\$8,000,000}{\$2,000,000} = 4 \ (2001)$$

The accounts receivable turnover is a measure of the average collection period on sales. If the average number of days varies widely from the industry norm, it may be an indication of poor management. A too-low ratio could indicate the loss of sales because of a too restrictive credit policy. If the ratio is too high, too much capital is being tied up in accounts receivable, and management may be increasing the chance of bad debts. Because of varying industry credit policies, a comparison for the firm over time or within an industry is the only useful analysis. Because information on credit sales for other firms generally is unavailable, total sales must be used. Since not all firms have the same percentage of credit sales, there is only approximate comparability among firms.

$$\frac{\text{Accounts receivable}}{\text{turnover}} = \frac{\text{Sales}}{\text{Accounts receivable}} = \frac{\$8,250,000}{\$1,760,000} = 4.69 \ (2002)$$

$$= \frac{\$8,000,000}{\$1,440,000} = 5.56 \ (2001)$$

$$\text{Average collection period} = \frac{360}{\text{Accounts receivable turnover}}$$

$$= \frac{360}{4.69} = 77 \text{ days (2002)}$$

$$= \frac{360}{5.56} = 65 \text{ days (2001)}$$

PROFITABILITY RATIOS

Profitability is the net result of a large number of policies and decisions chosen by an organization's management. Profitability ratios indicate how effectively the total firm is being managed. The profit margin for a firm is calculated by dividing net earnings by sales. This ratio is often called *return on sales* (ROS). There is wide variation among industries, but the average for U.S. firms is approximately 5 percent.

$$\frac{\text{Net earnings}}{\text{Sales}} = \frac{\$410,000}{\$8,250,000} = 0.0497 \text{ (2002)}$$

$$= \frac{\$395,000}{\$8,000,000} = 0.0494 \text{ (2001)}$$

A second useful ratio for evaluating profitability is the return on investment—or *ROI,* as it is frequently called—found by dividing net earnings by total assets. The ABC Company's ROI is calculated as follows:

$$\frac{\text{Net earnings}}{\text{Total assets}} = \frac{\$410,000}{\$7,105,000} = 0.0577 \text{ (2002)}$$

$$= \frac{\$395,000}{\$6,393,000} = 0.0618 \text{ (2001)}$$

The ratio of net earnings to net worth is a measure of the rate of return or profitability of the stockholders' investment. It is calculated by dividing net earnings by net worth, the common stock equity and retained earnings account. ABC Company's return on net worth, also called ROE, is calculated as follows:

$$\frac{\text{Net earnings}}{\text{Net worth}} = \frac{\$410,000}{\$3,242,500} = 0.1264 \text{ (2002)}$$

$$= \frac{\$395,000}{\$2,725,750} = 0.1449 \text{ (2001)}$$

It is often difficult to determine causes for lack of profitability. The Du Pont system of financial analysis provides management with clues to the lack of success of a firm. This financial tool brings together activity, profitability, and leverage measures and shows how these ratios interact to determine the overall profitability of the firm. A depiction of the system is set forth in Exhibit 6–4.

The right side of the exhibit develops the turnover ratio. This section breaks down total assets into current assets (cash, marketable securities, accounts receivable, and inventories) and fixed assets. Sales divided by these total assets gives the turnover on assets.

EXHIBIT 6–4
Du Pont's Financial Analysis

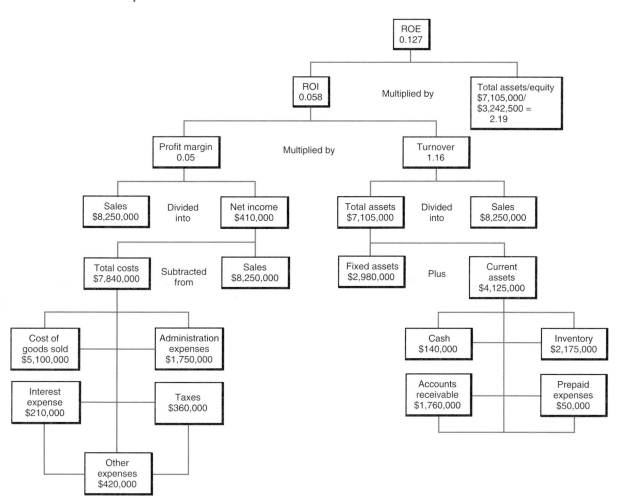

The left side of the exhibit develops the profit margin on sales. The individual expense items plus income taxes are subtracted from sales to produce net profits after taxes. Net profits divided by sales gives the profit margin on sales. When the asset turnover ratio on the right side of Exhibit 6–4 is multiplied by the profit margin on sales developed on the left side of the exhibit, the product is the return on assets (ROI) for the firm. This can be shown by the following formula:

$$\frac{\text{Sales}}{\text{Total assets}} \times \frac{\text{Net earnings}}{\text{Sales}} = \frac{\text{Net earnings}}{\text{Total assets}} = \text{ROI}$$

The last step in the Du Pont analysis is to multiply the rate of return on assets (ROI) by the equity multiplier, which is the ratio of assets to common equity, to obtain the rate of return on equity (ROE). This percentage rate of return, of course, could be calculated directly by dividing net income by common equity. However, the Du Pont analysis demonstrates how the return on assets and the use of debt interact to determine the return on equity.

The Du Pont system can be used to analyze and improve the performance of a firm. On the left, or profit, side of the exhibit, attempts to increase profits and sales could be investigated. The possibilities of raising prices to improve profits (or lowering prices to improve volume) or seeking new products or markets, for example, could be studied. Cost accountants and production engineers could investigate ways to reduce costs. On the right, or turnover, side, financial officers could analyze the effect of reducing investment in various assets as well as the effect of using alternative financial structures.

There are two basic approaches to using financial ratios. One approach is to evaluate the corporation's performance over several years. Financial ratios are computed for different years, and then an assessment is made about whether there has been an improvement or deterioration over time. Financial ratios also can be computed for projected, pro forma, statements and compared with present and past ratios.

The other approach is to evaluate a firm's financial condition and compare it with the financial conditions of similar firms or with industry averages in the same period. Such a comparison gives insight into the firm's relative financial condition and performance. Financial ratios for industries are provided by Robert Morris Associates, Dun & Bradstreet, and various trade association publications. (Associations and their addresses are listed in the *Encyclopedia of Associations* and in the *Directory of National Trade Associations*.) Information about individual firms is available through *Moody's Manual,* Standard & Poor's manuals and surveys, annual reports to stockholders, and the major brokerage houses.

To the extent possible, accounting data from different companies must be so standardized that companies can be compared or so a specific company can be compared with an industry average. It is important to read any footnotes of financial statements, since various accounting or management practices can have an effect on the financial picture of the company. For example, firms using sale-leaseback methods may have leverage pictures quite different from what is shown as debts or assets on the balance sheet.

ANALYSIS OF THE SOURCES AND USES OF FUNDS

The purpose of this analysis is to determine how the company is using its financial resources from year to year. By comparing balance sheets from one year to the next, one may determine how funds were obtained and how these funds were employed during the year.

To prepare a statement of the sources and uses of funds, it is necessary to (1) classify balance sheet changes that increase and decrease cash, (2) classify from the income statement those factors that increase or decrease cash, and (3) consolidate this information on a sources and uses of funds statement form.

Sources of funds that increase cash are:

1. A net decrease in any other asset than a depreciable fixed asset.
2. A gross decrease in a depreciable fixed asset.
3. A net increase in any liability.
4. Proceeds from the sale of stock.
5. The operation of the company (net income, and depreciation if the company is profitable).

Uses of funds include:

1. A net increase in any other asset than a depreciable fixed asset.
2. A gross increase in depreciable fixed assets.

3. A net decrease in any liability.
4. A retirement or purchase of stock.
5. Payment of cash dividends.

We compute gross changes to depreciable fixed assets by adding depreciation from the income statement for the period to net fixed assets at the end of the period and then subtracting from the total net fixed assets at the beginning of the period. The residual represents the change in depreciable fixed assets for the period.

For the ABC Company, the following change would be calculated:

Net property and plant (2002)	$1,175,000
Depreciation for 2002	+ 80,000
	$1,255,000
Net property and plant (2001)	−1,155,000
	$ 100,000

To avoid double counting, the change in retained earnings is not shown directly in the funds statement. When the funds statement is prepared, this account is replaced by the earnings after taxes, or net income, as a source of funds, and dividends paid during the year as a use of funds. The difference between net income and the change in the retained earnings account will equal the amount of dividends paid during the year. The accompanying sources and uses of funds statement was prepared for the ABC Company.

A funds analysis is useful for determining trends in working-capital positions and for demonstrating how the firm has acquired and employed its funds during some period.

ABC Company
Sources and Uses of Funds Statement
For 2002

Sources:	
Prepaid expenses	$ 13,000
Accounts payable	100,000
Accrued federal taxes	250,000
Dividends payable	3,750
Common stock	1,200
Additional paid-in capital	195,000
Earnings after taxes (net income)	410,000
Depreciation	80,000
Total sources	$1,053,500
Uses:	
Cash	$ 25,000
Accounts receivable	320,000
Inventory	175,000
Long-term receivables	165,000
Property and plant	100,000
Other fixed assets	20,000
Bank loans payable	75,000
Current maturities of long-term debt	8,500
Long-term liabilities	75,000
Dividends paid	90,000
Total uses	$1,053,500

EXHIBIT 6–5
A Summary of the Financial Position of a Firm

Ratios and Working Capital	1998	1999	2000	2001	2002	Trend	Industry Average	Interpre-tation
Liquidity: Current								
Quick								
Leverage: Debt-assets								
Debt-equity								
Activity: Asset turnover								
Fixed asset ratio								
Inventory turnover								
Accounts receivable turnover								
Average collection period								
Profitability: ROS								
ROI								
ROE								
Working-capital position								

CONCLUSION

It is recommended that you prepare a chart, such as that shown in Exhibit 6–5, so you can develop a useful portrayal of these financial analyses. The chart allows a display of the ratios over time. The "Trend" column could be used to indicate your evaluation of the ratios over time (e.g., "favorable," "neutral," or "unfavorable"). The "Industry Average" column could include recent industry averages on these ratios or those of key competitors. These would provide information to aid interpretation of the analyses. The "Interpretation" column could be used to describe your interpretation of the ratios for this firm. Overall, this chart gives a basic display of the ratios that provides a convenient format for examining the firm's financial condition.

Finally, Exhibit 6–6 is included to provide a quick reference summary of the calculations and meanings of the ratios discussed earlier.

EXHIBIT 6–6
A Summary of Key Financial Ratios

Ratio	Calculation	Meaning
Liquidity Ratios:		
Current ratio	$\dfrac{\text{Current assets}}{\text{Current liabilities}}$	The extent to which a firm can meet its short-term obligations.
Quick ratio	$\dfrac{\text{Current assets} - \text{Inventory}}{\text{Current liabilities}}$	The extent to which a firm can meet its short-term obligations without relying on the sale of inventories.
Leverage Ratios:		
Debt-to-total-assets ratio	$\dfrac{\text{Total debt}}{\text{Total assets}}$	The percentage of total funds that are provided by creditors.
Debt-to-equity ratio	$\dfrac{\text{Total debt}}{\text{Total stockholders' equity}}$	The percentage of total funds provided by creditors versus the percentage provided by owners.
Long-term-debt-to-equity ratio	$\dfrac{\text{Long-term debt}}{\text{Total stockholders' equity}}$	The balance between debt and equity in a firm's long-term capital structure.
Times-interest-earned ratio	$\dfrac{\text{Profits before interest and taxes}}{\text{Total interest charges}}$	The extent to which earnings can decline without the firm becoming unable to meet its annual interest costs.
Activity Ratios:		
Inventory turnover	$\dfrac{\text{Sales}}{\text{Inventory of finished goods}}$	Whether a firm holds excessive stocks of inventories and whether a firm is selling its inventories slowly compared to the industry average.
Fixed assets turnover	$\dfrac{\text{Sales}}{\text{Fixed assets}}$	Sales productivity and plant equipment utilization.
Total assets turnover	$\dfrac{\text{Sales}}{\text{Total assets}}$	Whether a firm is generating a sufficient volume of business for the size of its assets investment.
Accounts receivable turnover	$\dfrac{\text{Annual credit sales}}{\text{Accounts receivable}}$	In percentage terms, the average length of time it takes a firm to collect on credit sales.
Average collection period	$\dfrac{\text{Accounts receivable}}{\text{Total sales/365 days}}$	In days, the average length of time it takes a firm to collect on credit sales.
Profitability Ratios:		
Gross profit margin	$\dfrac{\text{Sales} - \text{Cost of goods sold}}{\text{Sales}}$	The total margin available to cover operating expenses and yield a profit.
Operating profit margin	$\dfrac{\text{Earnings before interest and taxes (EBIT)}}{\text{Sales}}$	Profitability without concern for taxes and interest.
Net profit margin	$\dfrac{\text{Net income}}{\text{Sales}}$	After-tax profits per dollar of sales.
Return on total assets (ROA)	$\dfrac{\text{Net income}}{\text{Total assets}}$	After-tax profits per dollar of assets; this ratio is also called *return on investment* (ROI).
Return on stockholders' equity (ROE)	$\dfrac{\text{Net income}}{\text{Total stockholders' equity}}$	After-tax profits per dollar of stockholders' investment in the firm.

EXHIBIT 6–6
(concluded)

Ratio	Calculation	Meaning
Earnings per share (EPS)	$$\frac{\text{Net income}}{\text{Number of shares of common stock outstanding}}$$	Earnings available to the owners of common stock.
Growth Ratio:		
Sales	Annual percentage growth in total sales	Firm's growth rate in sales.
Income	Annual percentage growth in profits	Firm's growth rate in profits.
Earnings per share	Annual percentage growth in EPS	Firm's growth rate in EPS.
Dividends per share	Annual percentage growth in dividends per share	Firm's growth rate in dividends per share.
Price-earnings ratio	$$\frac{\text{Market price per share}}{\text{Earnings per share}}$$	Faster-growing and less risky firms tend to have higher price-earnings ratios.

CHAPTER 6 DISCUSSION CASE

BusinessWeek

TOYOTA'S MIDLIFE CRISIS: CAN TOYOTA PRODUCE CARS THAT APPEAL TO YOUNG JAPANESE BUYERS?

Toyota has been a major power in the global automotive industry for some time. Key to that accomplishment has been the strength and dominance it has at home in Japan. That situation has rapidly changed for the worse as the following three graphs from 1999 illustrate. What to do? What was going on? Why was Toyota in this situation? Toyota managers, led by Hiroshi Okuda, conducted an extensive internal analysis to answer these questions and generate a strategic response that would turn the situation around. *Business Week* correspondents Emily Thornton, Kathleen Kerwin and Inka Resch talked with Okuda and others in Toyota and the industry to provide you with an interesting description of Toyota's internal analysis at the time.

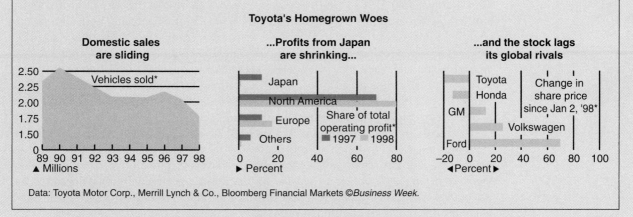

Toyota's Homegrown Woes

Domestic sales are sliding — Vehicles sold* — ▲ Millions

...Profits from Japan are shrinking... — Share of total operating profit* — ■ 1997 □ 1998 — ► Percent

...and the stock lags its global rivals — Change in share price since Jan 2, '98* — ◄Percent►

Data: Toyota Motor Corp., Merrill Lynch & Co., Bloomberg Financial Markets ©*Business Week.*

Toyota Motor Corp.'s commander in chief, Hiroshi Okuda, is beaming. Hundreds of French citizens are gathered to celebrate his latest conquest: a sprawling site for a $727 million factory near Valenciennes, in northeastern France. Okuda seals the deal by laying two stones for the plant, making $177,000 in donations to local causes, and planting several cherry trees—proof that Toyota wants to take root in Europe. Then he dons a short kimono and takes up a wooden mallet to open four barrels of hot sake as part of Japanese ritual. The spectacle leaves little doubt that Okuda is serious about extending Toyota's reach around the world.

But back at home, road warrior Toyota looks battered. Japan's No. 1 carmaker managed record pretax operating profits of $3.4 billion, on sales of $52 billion, for the first half of this year. Yet these figures obscure something important: Toyota is barely breaking even in its most critical market, Japan.

Some analysts believe the company has started to lose money in its domestic car business. Merrill Lynch & Co. reckons Toyota loses $423 on every car it sells at home. Only the sale of spare parts and accessories pushes domestic operations into the black. Toyota slices the data differently: It lumps export profits from Japanese plants together with domestic sales. But even its executives admit conditions in the home market are dreadful. Toyota's vehicle sales in Japan have tumbled 31% since 1990. Its market

Source: Emily Thornton, Kathleen Kerwin, and Inka Resch, "Toyota's Midlife Crisis," *Business Week.*

share has been below 40% since 1995, and the company must spend more than ever to lure customers into showrooms. Even if Toyota recovers a 40% share by year-end, it will sell less than 2 million vehicles in Japan for the first time in a decade. Japan's economy, it seems, has become Toyota's Achilles' heel.

To Toyota's North American rivals, none of this matters for now. All they see is the Toyota juggernaut in the U.S., which in November upped its share of the world's biggest market by more than a full percentage point, to 9.1%. Detroit executives are only dimly aware of Toyota's woes at home and probably figure the giant will recover its momentum when the recession ends. "Toyota is a tough, tough competitor," says Ronald L. Zarrella, head of General Motors North America.

SHORT ON ZIP

But the question still demands an answer: How long can any carmaker afford to give up profits in its core market? Japan accounts for just 38% of Toyota's worldwide car sales—down from 52% in 1990. Those sales generate little in the way of profit, while North America accounts for an estimated 80% of operating income, with Europe accounting for most of the rest. "Americans have been feeding us," concedes Kanji Kurioka, executive vice-president for domestic sales. Yet with the yen now strengthening against the dollar, every one-yen increase knocks an estimated $68 million off Toyota's net profit. Partly because of the currency situation, Toyota has just lowered its 1999 profit forecast. Says Fujio Cho, executive vice-president for corporate planning: "I tell people, 'You can't rely forever on a weaker yen.'"

The recession has certainly taken a bite out of Toyota's Japanese results, but the company must accept much of the blame for its troubles. It has failed to cater to younger buyers' desires for zippy compact minivans and sport-utility vehicles. Shrinking sales mean that Toyota must pay for factory and dealership workers it doesn't need. Toyota also worries investors by spending billions on investments such as housing and telecoms that could yield minimal returns.

Increasingly, Toyota's woes typify the problems plaguing Japan Inc. Until the mid-1990s, Toyota could depend on strong results at home to drive rapid expansion abroad: Some analysts believe Toyota earned as much as 90% of operating income from its domestic operations at its peak in 1990. The Japanese car market was predictable, with Toyota firmly on top. It faced weak rivals, was supported by dealers who felt little need to discount, and sold to consumers who meekly accepted high prices. Japanese officials helped by conducting such stiff vehicle inspections that most consumers were forced to buy a new car every three years. Toyota could keep its Toyota City plants operating at full tilt because of the steady growth of export markets and a booming local economy.

Now, the pattern is reversed, and overseas profits are propping up Japan. Excess capacity, picky consumers, surplus workers, price wars, and hemorrhaging affiliates have become the rule of the Japanese market. Honda Motor Co., which for years played a small role in Japan, is attacking Toyota's domestic market with a vengeance. Already, Toyota must worry about keeping its No. 3 ranking among the world's auto makers. DRI/McGraw-Hill automotive analyst Philip Rosengarten estimates that Toyota and Volkswagen will each sell 4.5 million vehicles this year. "Toyota has not changed, but the world has changed," says Shoichiro Toyoda, Toyota's chairman.

If these conditions persist, even Toyota's $25 billion cash hoard could start to dwindle, as the giant wages a war of attrition against rivals at home. Eventually, a low-profit domestic market could sap its ability to finance its global ambitions and fend off rivals. "In a sense, we are troubled," admits Okuda. "We set a target of selling 6 million vehicles [a year] by the early 21st century. However, because of the recession, it's necessary to extend that target."

Some Toyota executives even compare their problems in Japan with those GM faced more than a decade ago. "In a way, we have gotten too big, and it's tough to manage Toyota," says Chairman Toyoda. "Sometimes, we face difficulties deciding which direction to go. I used to think that [GM Chairman] Roger Smith had [that] trouble." Toyota is much healthier than GM—but Toyota executives know how foreign profits dulled GM management's sense of crisis at home. In the U.S. GM's market share has shrunk from 40.3% in 1985 to 29.4% this year.

SACRED GROUND

Recognizing that Toyota must fix its domestic sales to remain a leader, Okuda has embarked on an aggressive restructuring. "Toyota has a sense of crisis, and it is making efforts, but it takes time," says Takaki Nakanishi, an automotive analyst at Merrill Lynch. Yet watching competitors such as Nissan Motor Co. and Mitsubishi Corp. approach the brink has convinced Okuda that the longer he waits, the more painful the process will be.

So Toyota has started to tread on sacred territory. Some investors remain frustrated that it keeps workers on the payroll even as its factories run at 85% of capacity. But next year, Toyota will hire 9% fewer high school and university graduates. More important some of these new hires will be contract employees with no expectation of lifetime employment. If all goes as scheduled, such hires will make up one-third of the payroll by early in the next century. "We will be streamlining and gradually reducing our workforce," says Okuda.

Toyota also expects to shed $678 million in costs this year, largely by designing cars with fewer, simpler parts and sharing more parts between models. To shave an estimated 30% off development costs, Toyota is using the chassis from its European-designed Yaris for a new subcompact in Japan and for at least two other models.

Such efforts should lessen the blow of smaller sales volumes during Japan's deepening recession. Toyota's engineers used to develop cars on the assumption that the company would sell 10,000 units per month. Now, many must design cars to make profits at lower prices and monthly volumes as low as 2,500. So engineers on the $26,270 Progres luxury sedan shared parts with other vehicles and overhauled everything from the development process to the stamping equipment to squeeze enough costs out to compete with the low-end Mercedes C class.

Beyond that, Okuda is shaking up the chain of command. After he became president in 1995, the sales staff showed him a report that described how Toyota's well-built blandness turned off the younger customers. More alarming, Toyota was losing ground with its core customers—folks in their 40s and 50s. So Okuda ordered a task force of thirtysomething managers to make up a youth division and to think big—fast. "He said that if we couldn't think of anything in three months, then we probably wouldn't be able to come up with an idea," recalls Hideaki Homma, 35. The result was a new company to design and sell cars for young people. Dubbed the Virtual Venture Co. (VVC), its managers answer only to Okuda. The company is housed in the hip Tokyo district of Sangenjaya, safe from contagion from Toyota's stodgy headquarters.

"NOT FOR US"

Although VVC is keeping mum on details, it is scheduled to develop at least one cool car by 2000. But the longer VVC takes, the more opportunities Toyota misses to lure younger buyers. If Toyota wants to regain the volumes it had in 1990, it will have to go at full throttle. "Toyota is for old people; not for us," says Ken Nomura, 29, who cruises around Tokyo with his girlfriend in a Honda $19,200 CR-V sport-utility vehicle.

In the meantime, the VVC subsidiary is experimenting with unconventional sales strategies to jazz up Toyota's image. For a small fee, it is allowing the public to test-drive most of the cars in Toyota's lineup in a Kobe parking lot. It's building an $83 million amusement park on the edge of Tokyo that will open in April, complete with everything from displays of Toyota's visions for vehicles of the future to an area where people can design their own cars. VVC estimates that these efforts have boosted sales of some Toyota models by 10%, and recent consumer surveys show an improvement in Toyota's brand image, even though it still trails Honda.

A MODICUM OF FLOPS

Good stuff, but Toyota continues to struggle to regain its 40% market share. Many of Toyota's attempts to create entirely new markets aren't working. The Altezza and Progres luxury cars are hits. But the $18,600 Vista next-generation sedan and the $16,000 Nadia "monospace" sedan, which looks like a cross between a station wagon and a minivan, continue to fall far short of sales targets. Some dealers fear that just at the time Toyota is discovering what Japan's youth really want, youngsters aren't able or willing to afford it.

Even Toyota's revolutionary hybrid, the Prius—which runs both on gasoline and an electric battery to cut the emissions dramatically—may be an example of a superb technology with no real market. Okuda's launch of the Prius one year ago is still remembered with awe and bewilderment by everyone from Toyota's competitors to its suppliers to its stockholders. That's because the $16,500 Prius is being sold at a price that analysts estimate is only about half what it costs to build the car. Toyota makes 2,000 Prius cars a month. Yet starting in August this year, consumers have bought only 1,561 of them on average. "The Prius is being sold near [other Toyotas] that are discounted. And only cheap cars are selling now," says a disappointed Akihiro Wada, executive vice-president for research and development. Toyota now wants its dealership chains to specialize in different parts of its lineup.

Toyota has also started to pressure dealers. Its sprawling network of more than 300 dealerships—with 5,600 outlets—has long been regarded as the key to its might. No rival can match Toyota's reach. Yet sometimes, Toyota outlets are located one block from each other. They may even display some of the same models.

Now, Toyota wants to overhaul this crazy-quilt system, an act previously considered taboo. It has stopped supplying dealers with look-alike models, to eliminate unnecessary price competition. It has pulled the plug on monetary incentives for dealers. Instead, starting next year, if dealers cannot meet sales targets, they run the risk of losing their franchise. Toyota has also asked some dealers to rebuild and rename outlets to attract more young people. In the past year, for example, 66 dealers have established 1,074 "Netz" dealerships intended to attract women and youth with showrooms that are brighter and swankier than most Toyota outlets. On its own, Toyota has begun constructing a massive "auto mall" in the Japanese Alps that will sell every model in Toyota's lineup—in addition to prefabricated houses—from November, 2000.

Dealers are getting the message. Toyota's second-largest dealer, Tokyo Corolla, closed down a dozen of its outlets in the capital this year and has drawn up a blueprint for paring down its payroll by 300 employees in two years. Tokyo Corolla is also trying to build trust among customers, revamping one of its main outlets so that passersby can see through a window how workmen fix cars. "We dealers are trying things that we have never tried before," says Akira Nishimura, chairman of Tokyo Corolla.

Okuda figures that a lot more has to be done before Japan can once again be an engine of growth, even while shrugging off the naysayers. "Financial analysts are saying all sorts of things about our company," he says. "They don't know anything about the future, and they don't know the details of our operations. I don't care that much about what they're saying."

Yet he admits Toyota must go ahead at full speed. Says Okuda: "Recession is a time to overwhelm the enemy." And, he hopes, the best time to fix what ails Japan's preeminent company.

FORMULATING LONG-TERM OBJECTIVES AND GRAND STRATEGIES

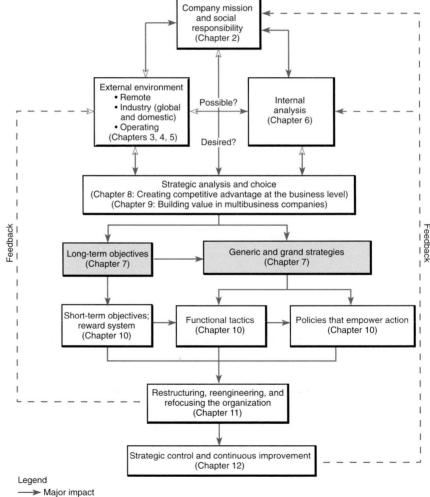

Legend

⟶ Major impact

⟶ Minor impact

The company mission was described in Chapter 2 as encompassing the broad aims of the firm. The most specific statement of aims presented in that chapter appeared as the goals of the firm. However, these goals, which commonly dealt with profitability, growth, and survival, were stated without specific targets or time frames. They were always to be pursued but could never be fully attained. They gave a general sense of direction but were not intended to provide specific benchmarks for evaluating the firm's progress in achieving its aims. Providing such benchmarks is the function of objectives.[1]

The first part of this chapter will focus on long-term objectives. These are statements of the results a firm seeks to achieve over a specified period, typically five years. The second part will focus on the formulation of grand strategies. These provide a comprehensive general approach in guiding major actions designed to accomplish the firm's long-term objectives.

The chapter has two major aims: (1) to discuss in detail the concept of long-term objectives, the topics they cover, and the qualities they should exhibit; and (2) to discuss the concept of grand strategies and to describe the 15 principal grand strategy options that are available to firms singly or in combination, including three newly popularized options that are being used to provide the basis for global competitiveness.

LONG-TERM OBJECTIVES

Strategic managers recognize that short-run profit maximization is rarely the best approach to achieving sustained corporate growth and profitability. An often repeated adage states that if impoverished people are given food, they will eat it and remain impoverished; however, if they are given seeds and tools and shown how to grow crops, they will be able to improve their condition permanently. A parallel choice confronts strategic decision makers:

1. Should they eat the seeds to improve the near-term profit picture and make large dividend payments through cost-saving measures such as laying off workers during periods of slack demand, selling off inventories, or cutting back on research and development?
2. Or should they sow the seeds in the effort to reap long-term rewards by reinvesting profits in growth opportunities, committing resources to employee training, or increasing advertising expenditures?

For most strategic managers, the solution is clear—distribute a small amount of profit now but sow most of it to increase the likelihood of a long-term supply. This is the most frequently used rationale in selecting objectives.

To achieve long-term prosperity, strategic planners commonly establish long-term objectives in seven areas:

Profitability The ability of any firm to operate in the long run depends on attaining an acceptable level of profits. Strategically managed firms characteristically have a profit objective, usually expressed in earnings per share or return on equity.

---

[1]Throughout this text, the terms *goals* and *objectives* are each used to convey a special meaning, with goals being the less specific and more encompassing concept. Most authors follow this usage; however, some use the two words interchangeably, while others reverse the usage.

GLOBAL STRATEGY IN ACTION 7–1

FROM STRATEGIC INTENT TO CORPORATE PURPOSE: THE REMAKING OF KOMATSU

When he succeeded his father as Komatsu's president in 1964, Ryoichi Kawai articulated an objective that the company would pursue for more than 20 years. Komatsu's strategic intent, Kawai announced, was to "catch up with and surpass Caterpillar."

The management approach Kawai adopted to pursue this goal became a well-studied and widely emulated model in the West. Each year, Kawai would define a clear and specific operating priority—for example, improving quality, reducing costs, or expanding exports—that used Caterpillar's performance as a standard and sited Caterpillar itself as the competitive target. Then each year's priority would be translated into detailed action plans through PDCA (plan, do, check, act), Komatsu's tightly controlled management system.

Kawai's strategy worked well, and by 1982, when he was choosing his successor, Komatsu had grown from a tiny local competitor with poor product quality to Caterpillar's most serious global challenger in the construction equipment market. But the market was about to change. By 1989, when Tetsuya Katada became the third president to follow Kawai, worldwide demand for construction equipment was down, competition was up, and Komatsu's profits were in steady decline.

As Katada saw the situation, Komatsu's management had become so obsessed with catching Caterpillar that it had stopped thinking about strategic choices. For instance, its product development efforts were biased toward Caterpillar's high-end bulldozers rather than toward smaller, lower-priced products like hydraulic excavators, for which market demand was growing. Katada worried that Komatsu's top management had stopped questioning the business the company was in. Further, he was concerned that the inflexible, top-down style that had become embedded at Komatsu had crushed "the spirit of enterprise" among middle and frontline managers.

Source: Reprinted by permission of *Harvard Business Review.* An excerpt from "Changing the Role of Top Management: Beyond Strategy to Purpose," by Christopher A. Bartlett and Sumantra Ghoshal, November–December 1994. Copyright © 1995 by the President and Fellows of Harvard University, all rights reserved.

Productivity Strategic managers constantly try to improve the productivity of their systems. Firms that can improve the input-output relationship normally increase profitability. Thus, firms almost always state an objective for productivity. Commonly used productivity objectives are the number of items produced or the number of services rendered per unit of input. However, productivity objectives sometimes are stated in terms of desired cost decreases. For example, objectives may be set for reducing defective items, for customer complaints leading to litigation, or for overtime. Achieving such objectives increases profitability if unit output is maintained.

Competitive Position One measure of corporate success is relative dominance in the marketplace. Larger firms commonly establish an objective in terms of competitive position, often using total sales or market share as measures of their competitive position. An objective with regard to competitive position may indicate a firm's long-term priorities. For example, Gulf Oil set a five-year objective of moving from third to second place as a producer of high-density polypropylene. Total sales were the measure.

Competitive positioning, however, may sometimes result in a firm subordinating its main objective. As was the case with Komatsu, management became so concerned

continued

Managers, Katada decided, "can no longer operate within the confines of a defined objective. They need to go out and see the needs and opportunities and operate in a creative and innovative way, always encouraging initiative from below." In other words, he told the company, "I want everyone to stop concentrating simply on catching up with Caterpillar."

At meetings and discussions, Katada challenged managers at several levels to find ways for the company to double its sales by the mid-1990s. What emerged from these and subsequent discussions was a new definition of the company. Rather than thinking of Komatsu as a construction equipment company trying to catch Caterpillar, management began to describe it as a ``total technology enterprise" with an opportunity to leverage its existing resources and expertise in electronics, robotics, and plastics.

Under a new banner of "Growth, Global, Groupwide" (the Three Gs), Katada encouraged management at all levels to find new growth opportunities through expanding geographically and leveraging competences. He appointed a Committee for the 1990s to determine how Komatsu could enrich its corporate philosophy, broaden its social contributions, and revitalize its human resources. His objective was to create an organization that could attract and stimulate the best people. "Compared with our old objective," Katada acknowledged, "the Three Gs slogan may seem abstract, but it was this abstract nature that stimulated people to ask what they could do and respond creatively."

More than a strategy, Komatsu now had a corporate purpose, to which its managers could commit and in which they had a voice. In the first three years after Katada articulated the Three Gs, Komatsu's sales, which had been declining since 1982, perked up. That surge was driven almost entirely by a 40 percent growth in Komatsu's nonconstruction equipment business.

with the company's performance relative to its competitor, Caterpillar, that the company found itself forgoing opportunities for growth, which led to the company's decline in profits. As Global Strategy in Action 7–1 demonstrates, the company's strategy was successfully restructured before any further damage was caused.

Employee Development Employees value growth and career opportunities. Providing such opportunities often increases productivity and decreases turnover. Therefore, strategic decision makers frequently include an employee development objective in their long-range plans. For example, PPG has declared an objective of developing highly skilled and flexible employees and, thus, providing steady employment for a reduced number of workers.

Employee Relations Whether or not they are bound by union contracts, firms actively seek good employee relations. In fact, proactive steps in anticipation of employee needs and expectations are a characteristic concern of strategic managers. Strategic managers believe that productivity is linked to employee loyalty and to perceived management interest in workers' welfare. They, therefore, set objectives to improve employee relations. Among the outgrowths of such objectives are safety programs, worker representation on management committees, and employee stock option plans.

Technological Leadership Firms must decide whether to lead or follow in the market-place. Either approach can be successful, but each requires a different strategic posture. Therefore, many firms state an objective with regard to technological leadership. For example, Caterpillar Tractor Company established its early reputation and dominant position in its industry by being in the forefront of technological innovation in the manufacture of large earthmovers. Because of an advanced technological design, Daihatsu Mira became the most popular car in Japan in 1991. The four-seat minicar held a 660cc engine that provided the customer with 30 percent more miles per gallon than any competitor, and it had a 25 percent smaller sales tax.

Public Responsibility Firms recognize their responsibilities to their customers and to society at large. In fact, many firms seek to exceed the demands made by government. They work not only to develop reputations for fairly priced products and services but also to establish themselves as responsible corporate citizens. For example, they may establish objectives for charitable and educational contributions, minority training, public or political activity, community welfare, or urban revitalization. In an attempt to exhibit their sense of public responsibility in the United States, Japanese companies, such as Toyota, Hitachi, and Matsushita, contributed more than $500 million to American educational projects, charities, and nonprofit organizations, a 67 percent increase over the previous year.

Qualities of Long-Term Objectives

What distinguishes a good objective from a bad one? What qualities of an objective improve its chances of being attained? Perhaps these questions are best answered in relation to seven criteria that should be used in preparing long-term objectives: acceptable, flexible, measurable over time, motivating, suitable, understandable, and achievable.

Acceptable Managers are most likely to pursue objectives that are consistent with their preferences. They may ignore or even obstruct the achievement of objectives that offend them (e.g., promoting a non-nutritional food product) or that they believe to be inappropriate or unfair (e.g., reducing spoilage to offset a disproportionate allocation of fixed overhead). In addition, long-term corporate objectives frequently are designed to be acceptable to groups external to the firm. An example is efforts to abate air pollution that are undertaken at the insistence of the Environmental Protection Agency.

Flexible Objectives should be adaptable to unforeseen or extraordinary changes in the firm's competitive or environmental forecasts. However, such flexibility usually is increased at the expense of specificity. Moreover, employee confidence may be tempered because adjustment of flexible objectives may affect their jobs. One way of providing flexibility while minimizing its negative effects is to allow for adjustments in the level, rather than in the nature, of objectives. For example, the personnel department objective of providing managerial development training for 15 supervisors per year over the next five-year period might be adjusted by changing the number of people to be trained. In contrast, changing the personnel department's objective of "assisting production supervisors in reducing job-related injuries by 10 percent per year" after three months had gone by would understandably create dissatisfaction.

Measurable Objectives must clearly and concretely state what will be achieved and when it will be achieved. Thus, objectives should be measurable over time. For example, the objective of "substantially improving our return on investment" would be better stated as "increasing the return on investment on our line of paper products by a minimum of 1 percent a year and a total of 5 percent over the next three years."

Motivating Studies have shown that people are most productive when objectives are set at a motivating level—one high enough to challenge but not so high as to frustrate or so low as to be easily attained. The problem is that individuals and groups differ in their perceptions of what is high enough. A broad objective that challenges one group frustrates another and minimally interests a third. One valuable recommendation is that objectives be tailored to specific groups. Developing such objectives requires time and effort, but objectives of this kind are more likely to motivate.

Suitable Objectives must be suited to the broad aims of the firm, which are expressed in its mission statement. Each objective should be a step toward the attainment of overall goals. In fact, objectives that do not coincide with the company mission can subvert the firm's aims. For example, if the mission is growth oriented, the objective of reducing the debt-to-equity ratio to 1.00 would probably be unsuitable and counterproductive.

Understandable Strategic managers at all levels must understand what is to be achieved. They also must understand the major criteria by which their performance will be evaluated. Thus, objectives must be so stated that they are as understandable to the recipient as they are to the giver. Consider the misunderstandings that might arise over the objective of "increasing the productivity of the credit card department by 20 percent within five years." What does this objective mean? Increase the number of outstanding cards? Increase the use of outstanding cards? Increase the employee workload? Make productivity gains each year? Or hope that the new computer-assisted system, which should improve productivity, is approved by year 5? As this simple example illustrates, objectives must be clear, meaningful, and unambiguous.

Achievable Finally, objectives must be possible to achieve. This is easier said than done. Turbulence in the remote and operating environments affects a firm's internal operations, creating uncertainty, and limiting the accuracy of the objectives set by strategic management. To illustrate, the wildly fluctuating prime interest rates in 1980 made objective setting extremely difficult for the years 1981 to 1985, particularly in such areas as sales projections for producers of consumer durable goods like General Motors and General Electric.

An especially fine example of long-term objectives is provided in CACI, Inc.'s strategic plan. Shown in Strategy in Action 7–1 are CACI's major financial objectives for the period. The firm's approach is wholly consistent with the list of desired qualities for long-term objectives. In particular, CACI's objectives are flexible, measurable over time, understandable, and suitable for a high-technology and professional services organization.

The Balanced Scorecard

The Balanced Scorecard is a set of measures that are directly linked to the company's strategy. Developed by Robert S. Kaplan and David P. Norton, it allows a company to link its own long-term strategy with tangible goals and actions. The scorecard allows managers to evaluate the company from four perspectives: financial performance, customer knowledge, internal business processes, and learning and growth.

CACI's Long-Term Objectives, 1990–1997

STRATEGY IN
ACTION
7–1

REVENUE

Increase revenue range to $167–$176M or better in FY 90 (FY 90 bookings at $170M).

FY 91: Revenue in the $193–$202M range; bookings at $195–$205M range.

Increase company revenue 15–20 percent per year steadily over next decade.

Consistently increase revenues to $500 M per annum by 1997 or earlier. Steady manageable and consistent profitable growth.

PROFITABILITY

Achieve 4 percent NAT or better as an annual corporate target for return on revenues, moving to 5 percent CAT by mid-90s.

Individual departments and divisions must target NAT percentage profits at 50–100 percent above company levels (i.e., 6–8 percent moving to 7.5–10 percent).

SHAREHOLDERS' VALUE

Increase stock price (market value) to $20 per share or better by 1997 (current share basis).

The Balanced Scorecard, as shown in Figure 7–1, contains a concise definition of the company's vision and strategy. Surrounding the vision and strategy are four additional boxes; each box contains the objectives, measures, targets, and initiatives for one of the four perspectives:

- The box at the top of Figure 7–1 represents the financial perspective, and answers the question, "To succeed financially, how should we appear to our shareholders?"
- The box to the right represents the internal business process perspective and addresses the question, "To satisfy our shareholders and customers, what business processes must we excel at?"
- The learning and growth box at the bottom of Figure 7–1 answers the question, "To achieve our vision, how will we sustain our ability to change and improve?"
- The box at the left reflects the customer perspective, and responds to the question, "To achieve our vision, how should we appear to our customers?"

All of the boxes are connected by arrows to illustrate that the objectives and measures of the four perspectives are linked by cause-and-effect relationships that lead to the successful implementation of the strategy. Achieving one perspective's targets should lead to desired improvements in the next perspective, and so on, until the company's performance increases overall.

A properly constructed scorecard is balanced between short- and long-term measures; financial and nonfinancial measures; and internal and external performance perspectives.

FIGURE 7–1
The Balanced Scorecard

The balanced scorecard provides a framework to translate a strategy into operational terms

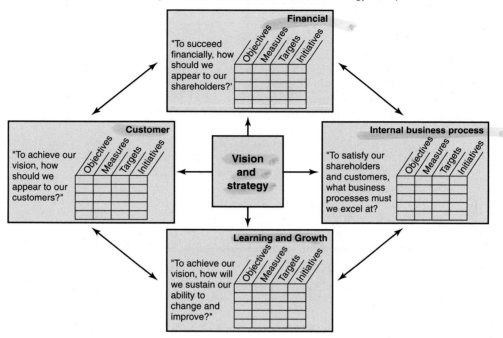

Source: Robert S. Kaplan and David P. Norton, "Using the Balanced Scorecard as a Strategic Management System," *Harvard Business Review,* January–February 1996, p. 76. Reprinted with permission.

The Balanced Scorecard is a management system that can be used as the central organizing framework for key managerial processes. Chemical Bank, Mobil Corporation's US Marketing and Refining Division, and CIGNA Property and Casualty Insurance have used the Balanced Scorecard approach to assist in individual and team goal setting, compensation, resource allocation, budgeting and planning, and strategic feedback and learning.

GENERIC STRATEGIES

Many planning experts believe that the general philosophy of doing business declared by the firm in the mission statement must be translated into a holistic statement of the firm's strategic orientation before it can be further defined in terms of a specific long-term strategy. In other words, a long-term or grand strategy must be based on a core idea about how the firm can best compete in the marketplace.

The popular term for this core idea is *generic strategy*. From a scheme developed by Michael Porter, many planners believe that any long-term strategy should derive from a firm's attempt to seek a competitive advantage based on one of three generic strategies:

1. Striving for overall low-cost leadership in the industry.
2. Striving to create and market unique products for varied customer groups through *differentiation*.

IT'S NOT EASY BEING CHEAP: AFTER EARLY STUMBLES, INTEL SHAPES UP ITS LOW-END GAME

GLOBAL STRATEGY IN ACTION 7–2

For a company whose credo is "only the paranoid survive," Intel Corp. was dangerously slow to respond to the low-cost personal-computer craze of the last 18 months. While customers opted for cheaper models, Intel focused mostly on the pricey high-end chips that made it one of the world's most profitable companies.

Now, Intel is fighting back. It will roll out a new Celeron chip, codenamed Mendocino, that could boost Intel's share of the sub-$1,000 PC market. And to ensure it doesn't miss the next big thing, Intel has taken a radical step toward grabbing a bigger role in the market for "embedded" processors, the ultracheap chips used in cellular phones, TV settop boxes, and handheld gizmos. To do that, the company has tossed aside its famous bias for homegrown technology by using an embedded chip it neither designed nor completely controls—the StrongARM, a variant of the ARM processor created by ARM Ltd. of Cambridge, England.

PROFIT PUNCTURE

Has Intel Chairman Andrew S. Grove gone bonkers? Not at all. He's just facing up to the new realities. Thanks to the low-price boom, Asian flu, and slowing PC growth, analysts expect Intel's sales to fall slightly this year, to $24.9 billion, along with a gut-wrenching 25% drop in profits, to $5.2 billion—Intel's first year-over-year decline in a decade.

Worse, it now seems the double whammy of soft PC sales and falling prices could be around for years. Sales of more profitable $1,000-plus PCs are expected to grow just 10% annually for the next five years, while bargain basement computers will surge an average 55%, says International Data Corp. That's why Intel is heading downstream, even though processors for cheap PCs earn margins of just 50% versus the fat 80% Intel gets on more powerful chips.

The Internet explosion, along with falling component prices, is expected to fuel sales of Web phones and other handheld devices from fewer than 5 million units this year to 43 million in 2001, says IDC. "Intel is going to need new opportunities," says analyst Scott Miller of Dataquest Inc., "and appliances could be one of them."

This new low-price plan won't be easy for Intel. In sub-$1,000 PCs, the chipmaker has 45% market share—far below its 99% lock on the $1,500-plus market.

The new Celeron won't rid Intel of its pesky low-end rivals. Analysts expect AMD to keep gaining share through the end of 1998 as it cranks up production of its K6 chips to 3.3 million

Source: Andy Reinhardt in Santa Clara, California, with Peter Burrows in New York, "It's Not Easy Being Cheap," *Business Week:* August 17, 1998.

3. Striving to have special appeal to one or more groups of consumer or industrial buyers, *focusing* on their cost or differentiation concerns.

Advocates of generic strategies believe that each of these options can produce above-average returns for a firm in an industry. However, they are successful for very different reasons.

Low-cost leaders depend on some fairly unique capabilities to achieve and sustain their low-cost position. Examples of such capabilities are: having secured suppliers of scarce raw materials, being in a dominant market share position, or having a high degree of capitalization. Low-cost producers usually excel at cost reductions and efficiencies. They maximize economies of scale, implement cost-cutting technologies, stress reductions in overhead and in administrative expenses, and use volume sales

continued

BusinessWeek

units this quarter. Dataquest chip analyst Nathan Brookwood expects Intel's sub-$1,000 PC share to grow just one percentage point per year through 2002.

Prospects in the emerging information-appliance sector are brighter, since Intel seems to have picked up a gem in StrongARM technology. StrongARM is considered by many the best version of ARM's hot-selling chip design. Sales of ARM-based chips by licensees such as NEC and Samsung have exploded to 15 million units in the first half of 1998, up from around 7 million units all last year, says Mark Edelstone of Morgan Stanley Dean Witter. ARM- based chips power RCA Thomson's DSS set-top box, and will likely be the standard in smart phones: In July, giants Nokia, L. M. Ericsson, and Motorola committed to use the chip.

StrongARM is a tiny fraction of total ARM sales. But with Intel's backing and a new version of Microsoft's Windows CE software for ARM due out this fall, it could become a frontrunner in handheld devices. With blazing speed and very low power consumption—and a price as low as $30, versus $86 for Intel's cheapest Celeron—it's well-suited for battery-operated devices.

But Intel has yet to prove it can cut it in the down-and-dirty appliance market. While PC makers line up to buy Intel's latest, most powerful processors, appliance makers require customized chips that aren't going to become obsolete every six months. They also don't care about the reams of PC software—Intel's biggest advantage in the PC segment. "In this market, Intel is like anybody else," says Lavi Lev, senior vice-president of engineering for em-bedded-chip rival MIPS Technologies Inc. And that's an unfamiliar place for the king of chips.

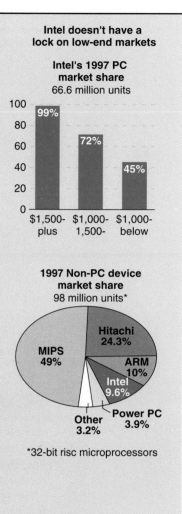

Intel doesn't have a lock on low-end markets

Intel's 1997 PC market share
66.6 million units

1997 Non-PC device market share
98 million units*

*32-bit risc microprocessors

techniques to propel themselves up the earning curve. The commonly accepted requirements for successful implementation of the low-cost and the other two generic strategies are overviewed in Figure 7–2.

A low-cost leader is able to use its cost advantage to charge lower prices or to enjoy higher profit margins. By so doing, the firm effectively can defend itself in price wars, attack competitors on price to gain market share, or, if already dominant in the industry, simply benefit from exceptional returns. As an extreme case, it has been argued that National Can Company, a corporation in an essentially stagnant industry, is able to generate attractive and improving profits by being the low-cost producer.

Intel Corporation is a company that has decided to pursue a low-cost strategy for a growing segment of the PC chip market, the sub-$1,000 computer models. The problems that it faces and the likelihood of its success are discussed in Global Strategy in Action 7–2.

FIGURE 7–2
Requirements for Generic Competitive Strategies

Generic Strategy	Commonly Required Skills and Resources	Common Organizational Requirements
Overall cost leadership	Sustained capital investment and access to capital.	Tight cost control.
	Process engineering skills.	Frequent, detailed control reports.
	Intense supervision of labor.	Structured organization and responsibilities.
	Products designed for ease in manufacture.	Incentives based on meeting strict quantitative targets.
	Low-cost distribution system.	
Differentiation	Strong marketing abilities.	Strong coordination among functions in R&D, product development, and marketing.
	Product engineering.	
	Creative flare.	Subjective measurement and incentives instead of quantitative measures.
	Strong capability in basic research.	
	Corporate reputation for quality or technological leadership.	Amenities to attract highly skilled labor scientists, or creative people.
	Long tradition in the industry or unique combination of skills drawn from other businesses.	
	Strong cooperation from channels.	
Focus	Combination of the above policies directed at the particular strategic target.	Combination of the above policies directed at the regular strategic target.

Source: Free Press COMPETITIVE STRATEGY: Techniques for Analyzing Industries and Competitors, pp. 40–41. Reprinted with permission of the Free Press, a division of Simon & Schuster, from Competitive Strategy: Techniques for Analyzing Industries and Competitors, by Michael E. Porter. Copyright © 1980 by Michael E. Porter.

Strategies dependent on differentiation are designed to appeal to customers with a special sensitivity for a particular product attribute. By stressing the attribute above other product qualities, the firm attempts to build customer loyalty. Often such loyalty translates into a firm's ability to charge a premium price for its product. Cross-brand pens, Brooks Brothers suits, Porsche automobiles, and Chivas Regal Scotch whiskey are all examples.

The product attribute also can be the marketing channels through which it is delivered, its image for excellence, the features it includes, and the service network that supports it. As a result of the importance of these attributes, competitors often face "perceptual" barriers to entry when customers of a successfully differentiated firm fail to see largely identical products as being interchangeable. For example, General Motors hopes that customers will accept "only genuine GM replacement parts."

A focus strategy, whether anchored in a low-cost base or a differentiation base, attempts to attend to the needs of a particular market segment. Likely segments are those that are ignored by marketing appeals to easily accessible markets, to the "typical" customer, or to customers with common applications for the product. A firm pursuing a focus strategy is willing to service isolated geographic areas; to satisfy the needs of customers with special financing, inventory, or servicing problems; or to tailor the product to the somewhat unique demands of the small-to-medium-sized customer. The focusing firms profit from their willingness to serve otherwise ignored or underappreciated customer segments. The classic example is cable television. An entire industry was born because of a willingness of cable firms to serve isolated rural locations that were ignored by traditional television services. Brick producers that typically service

FIGURE 7–3
Risks of the Generic Strategies

Risks of Cost Leadership	Risks of Differentiation	Risks of Focus
Cost of leadership is not sustained: • Competitors imitate. • Technology changes. • Other bases for cost leadership erode.	Differentiation is not sustained: • Competitors imitate. • Bases for differentiation become less important to buyers.	The focus strategy is imitated. The target segment becomes structurally unattractive: • Structure erodes. • Demand disappears.
Proximity in differentiation is lost.	Cost proximity is lost.	Broadly targeted competitors overwhelm the segment: • The segment's differences from other segments narrow. • The advantages of a broad line increase.
Cost focusers achieve even lower cost in segments.	Differentiation focusers achieve even greater differentiation in segments.	New focusers subsegment the industry.

Source: Free Press *Competitive Advantage: Creating and Sustaining Superior Performance,* p. 21. Adapted with the permission of the Free Press, a division of Simon & Schuster, from *Competitive Strategy: Creating and Sustaining Superior Performance,* by Michael E. Porter. Copyright © 1985 by Michael E. Porter.

a radius of less than 100 miles and commuter airlines that serve regional geographic areas are other examples of industries where a focus strategy frequently yields above-average industry profits.

While each of the generic strategies enables a firm to maximize certain competitive advantages, each one also exposes the firm to a number of competitive risks. For example, a low-cost leader fears a new low-cost technology that is being developed by a competitor; a differentiating firm fears imitators; and a focused firm fears invasion by a firm that largely targets customers. As Figure 7–3 suggests, each generic strategy presents the firm with a number of risks.

GRAND STRATEGIES

While the need for firms to develop generic strategies remains an unresolved debate, designers of planning systems agree about the critical role of grand strategies. *Grand strategies,* often called master or business strategies, provide basic direction for strategic actions. They are the basis of coordinated and sustained efforts directed toward achieving long-term business objectives.

The purpose of this section is twofold: (1) to list, describe, and discuss 14 grand strategies that strategic managers should consider and (2) to present approaches to the selection of an optimal grand strategy from the available alternatives.

Grand strategies indicate the time period over which long-range objectives are to be achieved. Thus, a grand strategy can be defined as a comprehensive general approach that guides a firm's major actions.

The 15 principal grand strategies are: concentrated growth, market development, product development, innovation, horizontal integration, vertical integration, concentric diversification, conglomerate diversification, turnaround, divestiture, liquidation, bankruptcy, joint ventures, strategic alliances, and consortia. Any one of these strategies could serve as the basis for achieving the major long-term objectives of a single firm. But a firm involved with multiple industries, businesses, product lines, or customer groups—as many firms are—usually combines several grand strategies. For clarity, however, each of the principal grand strategies is described independently in this section, with examples to indicate some of its relative strengths and weaknesses.

Concentrated Growth

Many of the firms that fell victim to merger mania were once mistakenly convinced that the best way to achieve their objectives was to pursue unrelated diversification in the search for financial opportunity and synergy.[2] By rejecting that "conventional wisdom," such firms as Martin-Marietta, Kentucky Fried Chicken, Compaq, Avon, Hyatt Legal Services, and Tenant have demonstrated the advantages of what is increasingly proving to be sound business strategy. A firm that has enjoyed special success through a strategic emphasis on increasing market share through concentration is Chemlawn. With headquarters in Columbus, Ohio, Chemlawn is the North American leader in professional lawn care. Like others in the lawn-care industry, Chemlawn is experiencing a steadily declining customer base. Market analysis shows that the decline is fueled by negative environmental publicity, perceptions of poor customer service, and concern about the price versus the value of the company's services, given the wide array of do-it-yourself alternatives. Chemlawn's approach to increasing market share hinges on addressing quality, price, and value issues; discontinuing products that the public or environmental authorities perceive as unsafe; and improving the quality of its work force.

These firms are just a few of the majority of American firms that pursue a concentrated growth strategy by focusing on a specific product and market combination. *Concentrated growth* is the strategy of the firm that directs its resources to the profitable growth of a single product, in a single market, with a single dominant technology. The main rationale for this approach, sometimes called a market penetration or concentration strategy, is that the firm thoroughly develops and exploits its expertise in a delimited competitive arena.

Rationale for Superior Performance

Concentrated growth strategies lead to enhanced performance. The ability to assess market needs, knowledge of buyer behavior, customer price sensitivity, and effectiveness of promotion are characteristics of a concentrated growth strategy. Such core capabilities are a more important determinant of competitive market success than are the environmental forces faced by the firm. The high success rates of new products also are tied to avoiding situations that require undeveloped skills, such as serving new customers and markets, acquiring new technology, building new channels, developing new promotional abilities, and facing new competition.

A major misconception about the concentrated growth strategy is that the firm practicing it will settle for little or no growth. This is certainly not true for a firm that correctly utilizes the strategy. A firm employing concentrated growth grows by building on its competences, and it achieves a competitive edge by concentrating in the product-market segment it knows best. A firm employing this strategy is aiming for the growth that results from increased productivity, better coverage of its actual product-market segment, and more efficient use of its technology. Strategy in Action 7–2

---

[2]Portions of this section were adapted from John A. Pearce II and J. Harvey, "Risks and Rewards of a Concentrated Growth Strategy," *Academy of Management Executive,* February 1990, pp. 62–69.

describes how Federated Department Stores has shifted from an acquisition strategy to one of concentrated growth to reinvigorate its store sales. This example is especially useful because Federated has been explicit in telling how its new strategy will be implemented.

Conditions That Favor Concentrated Growth

Specific conditions in the firm's environment are favorable to the concentrated growth strategy. The first is a condition in which the firm's industry is resistant to major technological advancements. This is usually the case in the late growth and maturity stages of the product life cycle and in product markets where product demand is stable and industry barriers, such as capitalization, are high. Machinery for the paper manufacturing industry, in which the basic technology has not changed for more than a century, is a good example.

An especially favorable condition is one in which the firm's targeted markets are not product saturated. Markets with competitive gaps leave the firm with alternatives for growth, other than taking market share away from competitors. The successful introduction of traveler services by Allstate and Amoco demonstrates that even an organization as entrenched and powerful as the AAA could not build a defensible presence in all segments of the automobile club market.

A third condition that favors concentrated growth exists when the firm's product markets are sufficiently distinctive to dissuade competitors in adjacent product markets from trying to invade the firm's segment. John Deere scrapped its plans for growth in the construction machinery business when mighty Caterpillar threatened to enter Deere's mainstay, the farm machinery business, in retaliation. Rather than risk a costly price war on its own turf, Deere scrapped these plans.

A fourth favorable condition exists when the firm's inputs are stable in price and quantity and are available in the amounts and at the times needed. Maryland-based Giant Foods is able to concentrate in the grocery business largely due to its stable long-term arrangements with suppliers of its private-label products. Most of these suppliers are makers of the national brands that compete against the Giant labels. With a high market share and aggressive retail distribution, Giant controls the access of these brands to the consumer. Consequently, its suppliers have considerable incentive to honor verbal agreements, called *bookings,* in which they commit themselves for a one-year period with regard to the price, quality, and timing of their shipments to Giant.

The pursuit of concentrated growth also is favored by a stable market—a market without the seasonal or cyclical swings that would encourage a firm to diversify. Night Owl Security, the District of Columbia market leader in home security services, commits its customers to initial four-year contracts. In a city where affluent consumers tend to be quite transient, the length of this relationship is remarkable. Night Owl's concentrated growth strategy has been reinforced by its success in getting subsequent owners of its customers' homes to extend and renew the security service contracts. In a similar way, Lands' End reinforced its growth strategy by asking customers for names and addresses of friends and relatives living overseas who would like to receive Lands' End catalogs.

A firm also can grow while concentrating, if it enjoys competitive advantages based on efficient production or distribution channels. These advantages enable the firm to formulate advantageous pricing policies. More efficient production methods and better handling of distribution also enable the firm to achieve greater economies of scale or, in conjunction with marketing, result in a product that is differentiated in the mind of the consumer. Graniteville Company, a large South Carolina textile manufacturer,

BusinessWeek

TIME TO STOP BUYING—AND START SELLING:
FEDERATED IS SPENDING BILLIONS SPRUCING UP ITS STORES

STRATEGY IN
ACTION
7–2

On Manhattan's Herald Square, Macy's 96-year-old flagship is getting a face-lift. A restaurant is under construction, new floors have been laid throughout the store, and brighter halogen lights seem to illuminate every pile of towels.

Even the merchandise is under repair. Next to the usual designer names, Macy's is increasingly hawking private brands created by its owner, Federated Department Stores Inc. From the rows of INC suits for young working women on the second floor to a bed covered with Charter Club striped damask sheets on the sixth, the company is pushing its own labels. "This is what the other stores won't do," says Federated President Terry J. Lundgren. "It takes a major commitment."

The Macy's makeover is part of a renewed push for top-line growth at Cincinnati-based Federated. Since emerging from a painful bankruptcy in 1992, the chain—which also owns Bloomingdale's and a flock of regional chains—has focused on two things: cutting costs to bolster profits and acquiring new stores to fuel growth. Spearheading the strategy was Allen Questrom, the smooth and stylish retailer whose remarkable ability to control spending and cut deals with vendors sparked the turnaround.

After Questrom retired unexpectedly in early 1997, his successor, James M. Zimmerman, found himself facing a new problem. Survival was by then assured, but the new CEO needed to find a way to boost internal growth. For years, the focus was on cutting costs and not on sprucing up stores or basic merchandising.

That's why Zimmerman, Questrom's soft-spoken protégé, is now zeroing in on boosting performance far closer to home. In addition to broadening brands such as Charter House from clothes into housewares and other areas, he is pouring $2.3 billion into capital investments over the next two years. "The most important growth now," says Zimmerman, 54, "is growth from the stores we have."

BUYING SPREE

The changes are coming none too soon. Sure, Federated's earnings have more than doubled, from $635 million in 1995 to $1.34 billion in 1997, on sales that have soared from $8.3 billion to $15.7 billion. But most of that growth has come from rapid-fire acquisitions: Federated swallowed Macy's, then bought Broadway Stores.

Questrom focused on improving each store's return on investment.

They sold underperforming stores and exited lower-margin merchandise such as consumer electronics. Financial controls were tightened, and extensive point-of-sale bar scanners were added to let Federated tally prices and keep close tabs on inventory. Questrom's strong relationship with vendors helped him win money-saving concessions such as having vendors put clothes on hangers before delivery. And as earnings recovered, Questrom paid down debt, shaving off $70 million in interest payments in 1997 alone. The result: Net margins blossomed from 1.9% in 1992 to 3.7% last year, sending the stock soaring. Up more than 300% since emerging from bankruptcy, it now trades around 52.

Still, Zimmerman and his execs have plenty of work ahead. Of particular concern is Federated's sales growth in stores open for more than a year. An anemic 2.7% last year, that growth is a full percentage point less than prime competitors.

Moreover, Zimmerman will have to boost those numbers at a tough time for the industry. Department stores continue to lose market share to discount stores and other venues. Among younger

Source: Peter Galuszka in Cincinnati, "Time to Stop Buying—and Start Selling," *Business Week:* September 7, 1998.

BusinessWeek

continued

consumers in particular, department stores are generally as out of style as last year's merchandise. Questrom points out that it will be hard for Federated to grow faster than the economy's 2% to 3% expansion without further acquisitions.

While not ruling out an acquisition, Zimmerman prefers an internal focus. To lure customers back, he plans to spend $1.6 billion renovating Federated's 400 U. S. stores, many of which had gotten somewhat dowdy during the cost-cutting years. A big chunk will go to spiffing up the chains' flagships in hopes of making them must-stop stores.

To attract younger shoppers, Lundgren has selected a team of execs to rethink Federated's format. The idea is to target younger buyers without alienating the baby boomers who are department stores' core shoppers. "We're going to stay with it until the whole store has changed," says Lundgren, who says an entirely redone test store should open sometime in 1999.

Another top priority: continuing to add to Federated's stock of private brands. With margins that average 2% higher than what Federated makes on outside brands, private labels have been Lundgren's biggest success so far. They are now 15% of Federated's wares, or $2.3 billion in sales last year, up from 5% three years ago. But Lundgren doesn't plan to go beyond 20% of sales.

That's because Federated, in boosting its own labels, is competing more and more with the national brands that are its main suppliers. And the risks of missing a fashion trend are greater when the store owns the merchandise.

Zimmerman is also investing heavily in such alternative ways of selling as the Net and mail-order. An expanded macys.com will move beyond showing goods to selling products online.

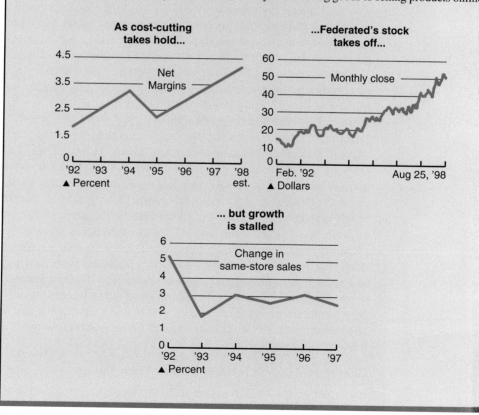

enjoyed decades of growth and profitability by adopting a "follower" tactic as part of its concentrated growth strategy. By producing fabrics only after market demand had been well established, and by featuring products that reflected its expertise in adopting manufacturing innovations and in maintaining highly efficient long production runs, Graniteville prospered through concentrated growth.

Finally, the success of market generalists creates conditions favorable to concentrated growth. When generalists succeed by using universal appeals, they avoid making special appeals to particular groups of customers. The net result is that many small pockets are left open in the markets dominated by generalists, and that specialists emerge and thrive in these pockets. For example, hardware store chains, such as Stanbaugh-Thompsons and Hechinger, focus primarily on routine household repair problems and offer solutions that can be easily sold on a self-service, do-it-yourself basis. This approach leaves gaps at both the "semiprofessional" and "neophyte" ends of the market—in terms of the purchaser's skill at household repairs and the extent to which available merchandise matches the requirements of individual homeowners.

Risk and Rewards of Concentrated Growth

Under stable conditions, concentrated growth poses lower risk than any other grand strategy; but, in a changing environment, a firm committed to concentrated growth faces high risks. The greatest risk is that concentrating in a single product market makes a firm particularly vulnerable to changes in that segment. Slowed growth in the segment would jeopardize the firm because its investment, competitive edge, and technology are deeply entrenched in a specific offering. It is difficult for the firm to attempt sudden changes if its product is threatened by near-term obsolescence, a faltering market, new substitutes, or changes in technology or customer needs. For example, the manufacturers of IBM clones faced such a problem when IBM adopted the OS/2 operating system for its personal computer line. That change made existing clones out of date.

The concentrating firm's entrenchment in a specific industry makes it particularly susceptible to changes in the economic environment of that industry. For example, Mack Truck, the second-largest truck maker in America, lost $20 million as a result of an 18-month slump in the truck industry.

Entrenchment in a specific product market tends to make a concentrating firm more adept than competitors at detecting new trends. However, any failure of such a firm to properly forecast major changes in its industry can result in extraordinary losses. Numerous makers of inexpensive digital watches were forced to declare bankruptcy because they failed to anticipate the competition posed by Swatch, Guess, and other trendy watches that emerged from the fashion industry.

A firm pursuing a concentrated growth strategy is vulnerable also to the high opportunity costs that result from remaining in a specific product market and ignoring other options that could employ the firm's resources more profitably. Overcommitment to a specific technology and product market can hinder a firm's ability to enter a new or growing product market that offers more attractive cost-benefit trade-offs. Had Apple Computers maintained its policy of making equipment that did not interface with IBM equipment, it would have missed out on what have proved to be its most profitable strategic options.

Concentrated Growth Is Often the Most Viable Option

Examples abound of firms that have enjoyed exceptional returns on the concentrated growth strategy. Such firms as McDonald's, Goodyear, and Apple Computers have used firsthand knowledge and deep involvement with specific product segments to become powerful competitors in their markets. The strategy is associated even more often with successful smaller firms that have steadily and doggedly improved their market position.

The limited additional resources necessary to implement concentrated growth, coupled with the limited risk involved, also make this strategy desirable for a firm with limited funds. For example, through a carefully devised concentrated growth strategy, medium-sized John Deere & Company was able to become a major force in the agricultural machinery business even when competing with such firms as Ford Motor Company. While other firms were trying to exit or diversify from the farm machinery business, Deere spent $2 billion in upgrading its machinery, boosting its efficiency, and engaging in a program to strengthen its dealership system. This concentrated growth strategy enabled it to become the leader in the farm machinery business despite the fact that Ford was more than 10 times its size.

The firm that chooses a concentrated growth strategy directs its resources to the profitable growth of a narrowly defined product and market, focusing on a dominant technology. Firms that remain within their chosen product market are able to extract the most from their technology and market knowledge and, thus, are able to minimize the risk associated with unrelated diversification. The success of a concentration strategy is founded on the firm's use of superior insights into its technology, product, and customer to obtain a sustainable competitive advantage. Superior performance on these aspects of corporate strategy has been shown to have a substantial positive effect on market success.

A grand strategy of concentrated growth allows for a considerable range of action. Broadly speaking, the firm can attempt to capture a larger market share by increasing the usage rates of present customers, by attracting competitors' customers, or by selling to nonusers. In turn, each of these options suggests more specific options, some of which are listed in the top section of Figure 7–4.

When strategic managers forecast that their current products and their markets will not provide the basis for achieving the company mission, they have two options that involve moderate costs and risk: market development and product development.

Market Development

Market development commonly ranks second only to concentration as the least costly and least risky of the 14 grand strategies. It consists of marketing present products, often with only cosmetic modifications, to customers in related market areas by adding channels of distribution or by changing the content of advertising or promotion. Several specific market development approaches are listed in Figure 7–4. Thus, as suggested by the figure, firms that open branch offices in new cities, states, or countries are practicing market development. Likewise, firms are practicing market development if they switch from advertising in trade publications to advertising in newspapers or if they add jobbers to supplement their mail-order sales efforts.

Market development allows firms to practice a form of concentrated growth by identifying new uses for existing products and new demographically, psychographically, or geographically defined markets. Frequently, changes in media selection, promotional appeals, and distribution are used to initiate this approach. Du Pont used market development when it found a new application for Kevlar, an organic material that police, security, and military personnel had used primarily for bulletproofing. Kevlar now is being used to refit and maintain wooden-hulled boats, since it is lighter and stronger than glass fibers and has 11 times the strength of steel.

FIGURE 7–4
Specific Options under the Grand Strategies of Concentration, Market Development, and Product Development

Concentration (increasing use of present products in present markets):

1. Increasing present customers' rate of use:
   a. Increasing the size of purchase.
   b. Increasing the rate of product obsolescence.
   c. Advertising other uses.
   d. Giving price incentives for increased use.
2. Attracting competitors' customers:
   a. Establishing sharper brand differentiation.
   b. Increasing promotional effort.
   c. Initiating price cuts.
3. Attracting nonusers to buy the product:
   a. Inducing trial use through sampling, price incentives, and so on.
   b. Pricing up or down.
   c. Advertising new uses.

Market development (selling present products in new markets):

1. Opening additional geographic markets:
   a. Regional expansion.
   b. National expansion.
   c. International expansion.
2. Attracting other market segments:
   a. Developing product versions to appeal to other segments.
   b. Entering other channels of distribution.
   c. Advertising in other media.

Product development (developing new products for present markets):

1. Developing new product features:
   a. Adapt (to other ideas, developments).
   b. Modify (change color, motion, sound, odor, form, shape).
   c. Magnify (stronger, longer, thicker, extra value).
   d. Minify (smaller, shorter, lighter).
   e. Substitute (other ingredients, process, power).
   f. Rearrange (other patterns, layout, sequence, components).
   g. Reverse (inside out).
   h. Combine (blend, alloy, assortment, ensemble; combine units, purposes, appeals, ideas).
2. Developing quality variations.
3. Developing additional models and sizes (product proliferation).

Source: Adapted from Philip Kotler, *Marketing Management Analysis, Planning, and Control,* 10th ed., 1999. Reprinted by permission of Prentice Hall, Inc., Englewood Cliffs, NJ.

The medical industry provides other examples of new markets for existing products. The National Institutes of Health's report of a study showing that the use of aspirin may lower the incidence of heart attacks was expected to boost sales in the $2.2 billion analgesic market. It was predicted that the expansion of this market would lower the market share of nonaspirin brands, such as industry leaders Tylenol and Advil. Product extensions currently planned include Bayer Calendar Pack, 28-day packaging to fit the once-a-day prescription for the prevention of a second heart attack.

Another example is Chesebrough-Ponds, a major producer of health and beauty aids, which decided several years ago to expand its market by repacking its Vaseline Petroleum Jelly in pocket-size squeeze tubes as Vaseline "Lip Therapy." The corporation decided to place a strategic emphasis on market development, because it knew from market studies that its petroleum-jelly customers already were using the product to prevent chapped lips. Company leaders reasoned that their market could be expanded significantly if the product were repackaged to fit conveniently in consumers' pockets and purses.

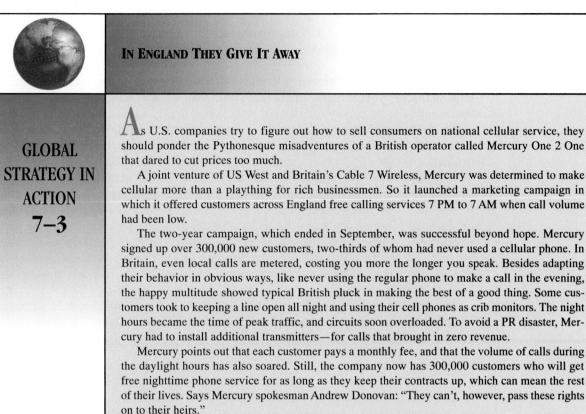

GLOBAL
STRATEGY IN
ACTION
7–3

IN ENGLAND THEY GIVE IT AWAY

As U.S. companies try to figure out how to sell consumers on national cellular service, they should ponder the Pythonesque misadventures of a British operator called Mercury One 2 One that dared to cut prices too much.

A joint venture of US West and Britain's Cable 7 Wireless, Mercury was determined to make cellular more than a plaything for rich businessmen. So it launched a marketing campaign in which it offered customers across England free calling services 7 PM to 7 AM when call volume had been low.

The two-year campaign, which ended in September, was successful beyond hope. Mercury signed up over 300,000 new customers, two-thirds of whom had never used a cellular phone. In Britain, even local calls are metered, costing you more the longer you speak. Besides adapting their behavior in obvious ways, like never using the regular phone to make a call in the evening, the happy multitude showed typical British pluck in making the best of a good thing. Some customers took to keeping a line open all night and using their cell phones as crib monitors. The night hours became the time of peak traffic, and circuits soon overloaded. To avoid a PR disaster, Mercury had to install additional transmitters—for calls that brought in zero revenue.

Mercury points out that each customer pays a monthly fee, and that the volume of calls during the daylight hours has also soared. Still, the company now has 300,000 customers who will get free nighttime phone service for as long as they keep their contracts up, which can mean the rest of their lives. Says Mercury spokesman Andrew Donovan: "They can't, however, pass these rights on to their heirs."

Source: "The Trouble with Cellular," November 13, 1995, p. 186. By Andrew Jupfer, FORTUNE, © 1995, Time, Inc. All rights reserved.

As shown in Global Strategy in Action 7–3, a British joint venture called Mercury One 2 One was able to successfully market its cellular service to a new target segment. The company changed the promotion of its existing product to appeal to more than the traditional wealthy businessman, offering free calling services during downtime hours. The company's strategy proved disastrously successful as the company has gained over 300,000 new customers.

Product Development

Product development involves the substantial modification of existing products or the creation of new but related products that can be marketed to current customers through established channels. The product development strategy often is adopted either to prolong the life cycle of current products or to take advantage of a favorite reputation or brand name. The idea is to attract satisfied customers to new products as a result of their positive experience with the firm's initial offering. The bottom section in Figure 7–4 lists some of the options available to firms undertaking product development. A revised edition of a college textbook, a new car style, and a second formula of shampoo for oily hair are examples of the product development strategy.

The product development strategy is based on the penetration of existing markets by incorporating product modifications into existing items or by developing new products with a clear connection to the existing product line. The telecommunications industry provides an example of product extension based on product modification. To increase its estimated 8–10 percent share of the $5–$6 billion corporate user market, MCI Communication Corporation extended its direct-dial service to 146 countries, the same as those serviced by AT&T, at lower average rates than those of AT&T. MCI's addition of 79 countries to its network underscores its belief in this market, which it expects to grow 15–20 percent annually. Another example of expansions linked to existing lines is Gerber's decision to engage in general merchandise marketing. Gerber's recent introduction included 52 items that ranged from feeding accessories to toys and children's wear. Likewise, Nabisco Brands seeks competitive advantage by placing its strategic emphasis on product development. With headquarters in Parsippany, New Jersey, the company is one of three operating units of RJR Nabisco. It is the leading producer of biscuits, confections, snacks, shredded cereals, and processed fruits and vegetables. To maintain its position as leader, Nabisco pursues a strategy of developing and introducing new products and expanding its existing product line. Spoon Size Shredded Wheat and Ritz Bits crackers are two examples of new products that are variations on existing products.

To attract more attention from car buyers is the affluent-male-over-35 segment, Chrysler developed the dramatically designed Plymouth Prowler. As discussed in Strategy in Action 7–3, this new product has been a stunning success.

Innovation

In many industries, it has become increasingly risky not to innovate. Both consumer and industrial markets have come to expect periodic changes and improvements in the products offered. As a result, some firms find it profitable to make *innovation* their grand strategy. They seek to reap the initially high profits associated with customer acceptance of a new or greatly improved product. Then, rather than face stiffening competition as the basis of profitability shifts from innovation to production or marketing competence, they search for other original or novel ideas. The underlying rationale of the grand strategy of innovation is to create a new product life cycle and thereby make similar existing products obsolete. Thus, this strategy differs from the product development strategy of extending an existing product's life cycle. For example, Intel, a leader in the semiconductor industry, pursues expansion through a strategic emphasis on innovation. With headquarters in California, the company is a designer and manufacturer of semiconductor components and related computers, of microcomputer systems, and of software. Its Pentium microprocessor gives a desktop computer the capability of a mainframe.

While most growth-oriented firms appreciate the need to be innovative occasionally, a few firms use it as their fundamental way of relating to their markets. An outstanding example is Polaroid, which heavily promotes each of its new cameras until competitors are able to match its technological innovation; by this time, Polaroid normally is prepared to introduce a dramatically new or improved product. For example, it introduced consumers in quick succession to the Swinger, the SX-70, the One Step, and the Sun Camera 660.

Few innovative ideas prove profitable because the research, development, and premarketing costs of converting a promising idea into a profitable product are extremely high. A study by the Booz Allen & Hamilton management research department provides some understanding of the risks. As shown in Figure 7–5, Booz Allen & Hamilton found that less than 2 percent of the innovative projects initially considered by 51 companies eventually reached the marketplace. Specifically, out of every 58 new

BusinessWeek

ON THE PROWL IN PLYMOUTH'S BAD BOY

STRATEGY IN ACTION 7–3

There's no such thing as a routine spin around the block in Chryslers new *Plymouth Prowler*. Minutes after pulling out of my driveway, I cruise by a neighborhood park in the low-slung, purple roadster modeled after 1930s-era hotrods. As if on cue, a sandlot baseball game freezes in mid-pitch. The preteen players stare in my direction, and then begin a rhythmic chant: *"Prowler . . . Prowler . . . Prowler!"*

Talk about an attention-getter. Outrageous by design, *Prowler* is the spiritual successor to the wildly popular Dodge Viper muscle car. The idea behind *Prowler* was to inject some excitement into Chrysler's tired *Plymouth* brand. On that score, the *Prowler* delivers big time.

BIT OF A BRUTE

With a $39,000 price tag, *Prowler* can't succeed on looks alone. Luxury carmakers Porsche, Mercedes-Benz, and BMW have all rolled out new two-seat roadsters since last year, and the rivalry in this sporty segment has never been tougher. With its unique wedge-shaped body, huge 20-inch rear tires, and sinister-looking headlamps and grille, *Prowler* won't get lost in the crowd of snubnosed European convertibles. Compared with the fine road manners and sophistication of vehicles such as the Porsche Boxster and Mercedes SLK, *Prowler* is a bit of a brute. Yet Chrysler revels in the car's image as the antithesis of the slick, luxury roadster. "It's thumbing your nose at conventional things," says Thomas Gale, executive vice-president of product development. "There's a bad-boy mentality about *Prowler.*"

Like any bad boy, *Prowler* does its share of misbehaving. Its ride is rough, and hitting a serious pothole can rattle your teeth. Other drawbacks include a trunk barely big enough to store a garment bag, and a windshield so narrow that the rear-view mirror nearly obstructs your vision.

But you flat-out don't care about those flaws because driving the *Prowler* is so much fun. So what if it comes in just one color—"*Prowler* Purple"—and is only equipped with a 3.5-liter, V-6 engine? Chrysler programmed the automatic transmission to shift hard and abruptly, providing a satisfying kick from first to second gears. Or the driver can use the clutchless AutoStick to shift. Aluminum body panels keep *Prowler's* weight down to a trim 2,862 pounds, so its 214-horsepower engine can hit a top speed of 120 miles per hour.

This is the perfect car for the exhibitionist in the family (who, based on the price and target market, is likely to be an affluent male over 35). Chrysler plans to build about 3,000 *Prowlers* a year and parcel them out only to their best dealers. The thinking is that part of the car's mystique will be its scarcity.

Source: Bill Vlasic, "On the Prowl in Plymouth's Bad Boy," *Business Week:* September 1, 1997.

product ideas, only 12 pass an initial screening test that finds them compatible with the firm's mission and long-term objectives, only 7 remain after an evaluation of their potential, and only 3 survive development attempts. Of the three survivors, two appear to have profit potential after test marketing and only one is commercially successful.

Horizontal Integration

When a firm's long-term strategy is based on growth through the acquisition of one or more similar firms operating at the same stage of the production-marketing chain, its grand strategy is called *horizontal integration.* Such acquisitions eliminate competitors and provide the acquiring firm with access to new markets. One example is

FIGURE 7–5
Decay of New Product Ideas (51 Companies)

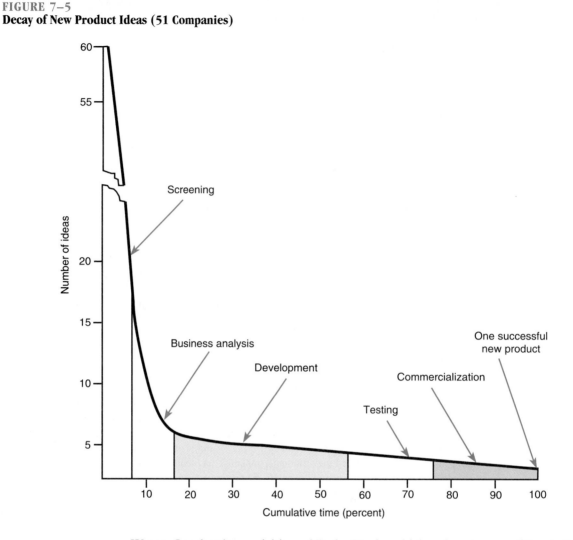

Warner-Lambert's acquisition of Parke Davis, which reduced competition in the ethical drugs field for Chilcott Laboratories, a firm that Warner-Lambert previously had acquired. Another example is the long-range acquisition pattern of White Consolidated Industries, which expanded in the refrigerator and freezer market through a grand strategy of horizontal integration, by acquiring Kelvinator Appliance, the Refrigerator Products Division of Bendix Westinghouse Automotive Air Brake, and Frigidaire Appliance from General Motors. Nike's acquisition in the dress shoes business and N. V. Homes's purchase of Ryan Homes have vividly exemplified the success that horizontal integration strategies can bring.

Vertical Integration

When a firm's grand strategy is to acquire firms that supply it with inputs (such as raw materials) or are customers for its outputs (such as warehousers for finished products), *vertical integration* is involved. To illustrate, if a shirt manufacturer acquires a textile producer—by purchasing its common stock, buying its assets, or exchanging ownership interests—the strategy is vertical integration. In this case, it is *backward* vertical integration, since the acquired firm operates at an earlier stage of the production-marketing process. If the shirt manufacturer had merged with a clothing store, it would have been *forward* vertical integration—the acquisition of a firm nearer to the ultimate consumer.

Amoco emerged as North America's leader in natural gas reserves and products as a result of its acquisition of Dome Petroleum. This backward integration by Amoco was made in support of its downstream businesses in refining and in gas stations, whose profits made the acquisition possible.

In contrast, Amazon.com is employing a forward vertical integration as its strategy for the year 2000. Strategy in Action 7–4 tells how the company will use vertical integration to redefine itself in the marketplace with an eventual plan to eliminate its well-known E-commerce book business.

Figure 7–6 depicts both horizontal and vertical integration. The principal attractions of a horizontal integration grand strategy are readily apparent. The acquiring firm is able to greatly expand its operations, thereby achieving greater market share, improving economies of scale, and increasing the efficiency of capital use. In addition, these benefits are achieved with only moderately increased risk, since the success of the expansion is principally dependent on proven abilities.

The reasons for choosing a vertical integration grand strategy are more varied and sometimes less obvious. The main reason for backward integration is the desire to increase the dependability of the supply or quality of the raw materials used as production inputs. That desire is particularly great when the number of suppliers is small and the number of competitors is large. In this situation, the vertically integrating firm can better control its costs and, thereby, improve the profit margin of the expanded production-marketing system. Forward integration is a preferred grand strategy if great advantages accrue to stable production. A firm can increase the predictability of demand for its output through forward integration; that is, through ownership of the next stage of its production-marketing chain.

Some increased risks are associated with both types of integration. For horizontally integrated firms, the risks stem from increased commitment to one type of business. For vertically integrated firms, the risks result from the firm's expansion into areas requiring strategic managers to broaden the base of their competences and to assume additional responsibilities.

Concentric Diversification

Grand strategies involving diversification represent distinctive departures from a firm's existing base of operations, typically the acquisition or internal generation (spin-off) of a separate business with synergistic possibilities counterbalancing the strengths and weaknesses of the two businesses. For example, Head Ski initially sought to diversify into summer sporting goods and clothing to offset the seasonality of its "snow" business. However, diversifications occasionally are undertaken as unrelated investments, because of their high profit potential and their otherwise minimal resource demands.

Regardless of the approach taken, the motivations of the acquiring firms are the same:

Increase the firm's stock value. In the past, mergers often have led to increases in the stock price or the price-earnings ratio.

Increase the growth rate of the firm.

BusinessWeek

A NEW CHAPTER FOR AMAZON.COM

STRATEGY IN ACTION 7–4

From the start, Jeffrey P. Bezos, founder and chief executive officer of Amazon.com Inc., wanted to do more than just run the biggest bookstore on earth—or in cyberspace. Now, it's becoming clearer how much more: On Aug. 4, Amazon.com purchased two Net startup companies for a total of $280 million that will help elevate his online store into an Internet commerce hub—like Yahoo! and other Web portals, but one aimed at shoppers, not merely fickle cybercruisers who want to hang out, browse, and chat. Says Bezos: "Our goal is to be an E-commerce destination."

How so? Software from Junglee Corp. in Sunnyvale, Calif., for which Amazon is paying $180 million, will help consumers who visit Amazon.com to comparison-shop for everything from personal computers to perfume. PlanetAll in Cambridge, Mass., another of the new Amazon ventures, offers a service that currently lets some 1.5 million people keep in touch with each other online by organizing their address books and coordinating their appointment calendars. With its already flourishing online bookshop, these recent acquisitions will give Amazon the potential to become "the Wal-Mart of online," according to Aberdeen Group analyst Mark P. Peabody.

The moves raise the stakes for Amazon's current rivals, such as Barnes & Noble Inc. and Borders Group Inc. And they put Amazon in more direct competition with such darlings of the Net as Yahoo!, Excite, and America Online. All aim to make E-commerce a central piece of their business models.

"UBER-PORTAL"

Bezos remains coy about specific plans for Amazon's expansion. Recently, however, he started selling CDs and will soon move into videos. Junglee's shopping search engine opens up the potential for Amazon to offer products from other sites, for which it could charge a commission or advertising fees.

Source: Robert D. Hof in San Mateo, California, "A New Chapter for Amazon.com," *Business Week:* August 17, 1998.

Make an investment that represents better use of funds than plowing them into internal growth.

Improve the stability of earnings and sales by acquiring firms whose earnings and sales complement the firm's peaks and valleys.

Balance or fill out the product line.

Diversify the product line when the life cycle of current products has peaked.

Acquire a needed resource quickly (e.g., high-quality technology or highly innovative management).

Achieve tax savings by purchasing a firm whose tax losses will offset current or future earnings.

Increase efficiency and profitability, especially if there is synergy between the acquiring firm and the acquired firm.[3]

---

[3]Godfrey Devlin and Mark Bleackley, "Strategic Alliances—Guidelines for Success," *Long Range Planning,* October 1988, pp. 18–23.

FIGURE 7–6
Vertical and Horizontal Integrations

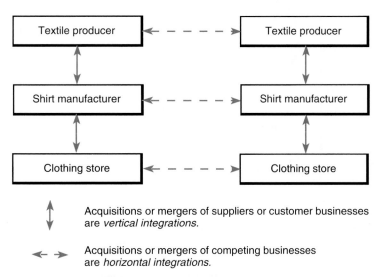

Acquisitions or mergers of suppliers or customer businesses are *vertical integrations.*

Acquisitions or mergers of competing businesses are *horizontal integrations.*

Concentric diversification involves the acquisition of businesses that are related to the acquiring firm in terms of technology, markets, or products. With this grand strategy, the selected new businesses possess a high degree of compatibility with the firm's current businesses. The ideal concentric diversification occurs when the combined company profits increase the strengths and opportunities and decrease the weaknesses and exposure to risk. Thus, the acquiring firm searches for new businesses whose products, markets, distribution channels, technologies, and resource requirements are similar to but not identical with its own, whose acquisition results in synergies but not complete interdependence.

A. T. Cross provides an excellent example of concentric diversification. As discussed in Strategy in Action 7–5, the maker of the universally recognized golden pen has created the CrossPad with partner IBM in a strategy designed to expand its sales potential.

Conglomerate Diversification

Occasionally a firm, particularly a very large one, plans to acquire a business because it represents the most promising investment opportunity available. This grand strategy is commonly known as *conglomerate diversification.* The principal concern, and often the sole concern, of the acquiring firm is the profit pattern of the venture. Unlike concentric diversification, conglomerate diversification gives little concern to creating product-market synergy with existing businesses. What such conglomerate diversifiers as ITT, Textron, American Brands, Litton, U.S. Industries, Fuqua, and I. C. Industries seek is financial synergy. For example, they may seek a balance in their portfolios between current businesses with cyclical sales and acquired businesses with countercyclical sales, between high-cash/low-opportunity and low-cash/high-opportunity businesses, or between debt-free and highly leveraged businesses.

The principal difference between the two types of diversification is that concentric diversification emphasizes some commonality in markets, products, or technology, whereas conglomerate diversification is based principally on profit considerations.

BusinessWeek

DON'T CROSS OFF CROSS

STRATEGY IN
ACTION
7–5

Since 1952, when A. T. Cross (ATX.A) introduced its gold-plated ballpoint pen now synonymous with the Cross name, the product had been a huge success—until 1995, when sales peaked. And after hitting a high of 41 in mid-1996, its stock has since slid downhill, closing at 10% on Apr. 7. Earnings have followed suit, falling from 80 cents in 1995 to 40 cents in 1996 and a loss of 26 cents in 1997. End of the line for Cross?

Value investor Mark Boyar thinks not. He says Cross is one of the best bargains around, so has accumulated a big stake. Two factors whet his appetite. Cross has launched new computing products, including CrossPad—with IBM as its partner. The CrossPad, designed by Cross and IBM, transforms how users store, organize, and share notes by writing in ink on a pad and unloading the handwriting directly to a PC.

And there is a buyout angle: With the family of Chairman Bradford Boss and CEO Russell Boss owning 100% of Cross Class B stock, which elects two-thirds of the board, a friendly buyout could be easy to achieve—if a serious suitor comes along. "There are no buyout rumors, and the family claims no interest in selling," notes Boyar. But the family might be enticed by a tax-free stock deal, he argues, with the likes of Fortune Brands, formerly called American Brands before it got out of the tobacco business. With its famous name in pens and new computing products, Cross could be a compelling *acquisition* for Fortune, a global consumer products company, says Boyar.

Given its "solid consumer franchise, a strong balance sheet, significant cash flow-generating abilities, and new computer products," says Boyar, Cross has an intrinsic value of 28 a share. A Fortune spokesman wouldn't go beyond saying the company continues to look for acquisitions, Cross CFO John Ruggieri says the company is investing heavily in new products to turn it around. Cross, he adds, is not for sale.

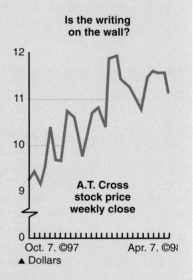

Is the writing on the wall?

A.T. Cross
stock price
weekly close

Oct. 7. ©97   Apr. 7. ©9{
▲ Dollars

Source: Gene G. Marcial, "Don't Cross Off Cross," *Business Week:* April 20, 1998.

Several of the grand strategies discussed above, including concentric and conglomerate diversification and horizontal and vertical integration, often involve the purchase or acquisition of one firm by another. It is important to know that the majority of such acquisitions fail to produce the desired results for the companies involved. Strategy in Action 7–6 provides seven guidelines that can improve a company's chances of a successful acquisition.

Turnaround

For any one of a large number of reasons, a firm can find itself with declining profits. Among these reasons are economic recessions, production inefficiencies, and innovative breakthroughs by competitors. In many cases, strategic managers believe that such a firm can survive and eventually recover if a concerted effort is made over a period of a few years to fortify its distinctive competences. This grand strategy is known as *turnaround.* It typically is begun through one of two forms of retrenchment, employed singly or in combination:

1. *Cost reduction.* Examples include decreasing the work force through employee attrition, leasing rather than purchasing equipment, extending the life of machinery, eliminating elaborate promotional activities, laying off employees, dropping items from a production line, and discontinuing low-margin customers.

2. *Asset reduction.* Examples include the sale of land, buildings, and equipment not essential to the basic activity of the firm and the elimination of "perks," such as the company airplane and executives' cars.

Interestingly, the turnaround most commonly associated with this approach is in management positions. In a study of 58 large firms, researchers Shendel, Patton, and Riggs found that turnaround almost always was associated with changes in top management.[4] Bringing in new managers was believed to introduce needed new perspectives on the firm's situation, to raise employee morale, and to facilitate drastic actions, such as deep budgetary cuts in established programs.

Strategic management research provides evidence that the firms that have used a *turnaround strategy* have successfully confronted decline. The research findings have been assimilated and used as the building blocks for a model of the turnaround process shown in Figure 7–7.

The model begins with a depiction of external and internal factors as causes of a firm's performance downturn. When these factors continue to detrimentally impact the firm, its financial health is threatened. Unchecked decline places the firm in a turnaround situation.

A *turnaround situation* represents absolute and relative-to-industry declining performance of a sufficient magnitude to warrant explicit turnaround actions. Turnaround situations may be the result of years of gradual slowdown or months of sharp decline. In either case, the recovery phase of the turnaround process is likely to be more successful in accomplishing turnaround when it is preceded by planned retrenchment that results in the achievement of near-term financial stabilization. For a declining firm, stabilizing operations and restoring profitability almost always entail strict cost reduction followed by a shrinking back to those segments of the business that have the best prospects of attractive profit margins. The need for retrenchment was shown during the 1990–92 recession when half of all U.S. companies reduced their work forces by an average of 11 percent (especially hard hit were real estate, transportation, and electronic company middle managers).

The immediacy of the resulting threat to company survival posed by the turnaround situation is known as *situation severity.* Severity is the governing factor in estimating the speed with which the retrenchment response will be formulated and activated. When severity is low, a firm has some financial cushion. Stability may be achieved through cost retrenchment alone. When turnaround situation severity is high, a firm must immediately stabilize the decline or bankruptcy is imminent. Cost reductions must be supplemented with more drastic asset reduction measures. Assets targeted for divestiture are those determined to be underproductive. In contrast, more productive resources are protected from cuts and represent critical elements of the future core business plan of the company (i.e., the intended recovery response).

---

[4]Other forms of joint ventures (such as leasing, contract manufacturing, and management contracting) offer valuable support strategies. They are not included in the categorization, however, because they seldom are employed as grand strategies.

SEVEN DEADLY SINS OF STRATEGY ACQUISITION

STRATEGY IN ACTION 7–6

1. *The wrong target.* This error becomes increasingly visible as time passes after the acquisition, when the acquiror may realize that anticipated synergies just don't exist, that the expanded market just isn't there, or that the acquiror's and target's technologies simply were not complementary.

The first step to avoid such a mistake is for the acquiror and its financial advisors to determine the strategic goals and identify the mission. The product of this strategic review will be specifically identified criteria for the target.

The second step required to identify the right target is to design and carry out an effective due diligence process to ascertain whether the target indeed has the identified set of qualities selected in the strategic review.

2. *The wrong price.* Even in a strategic acquisition, paying too much will lead to failure. For a patient strategic acquiror with long-term objectives, overpaying may be less of a problem than for a financial acquiror looking for a quick profit. Nevertheless, overpaying may divert needed acquiror resources and adversely affect the firm's borrowing capacity. In the extreme case, it can lead to continued operating losses and business failure.

The key to avoiding this problem lies in the acquiror's valuation model. The model will incorporate assumptions concerning industry trends and growth patterns developed in the strategic review.

3. *The wrong structure.* Both financial and strategic acquisitions benefit by the structure chosen. This may include the legal structure chosen for the entities, the geographic jurisdiction chosen for newly created entities, and the capitalization structure selected for the business after the acquisition. The wrong structure may lead to an inability to repatriate earnings (or an ability to do so only at a prohibitive tax cost), regulatory problems that delay or prevent realization of the anticipated benefits, and inefficient pricing of debt and equity securities or a bar to chosen exit strategies due to inflexibility in the chosen legal structure.

The two principal aspects of the acquisition process that can prevent this problem are a comprehensive regulatory compliance review and tax and legal analysis.

Source: Excerpted from D. A. Tanner, "Seven Deadly Sins of Strategic Acquisition," *Management Review,* June 1991, pp. 50–53. Reprinted by permission of publisher, from MANAGEMENT REVIEW, June 1991, © 1991. American Management Association, New York, All rights reserved.

Turnaround responses among successful firms typically include two stages of strategic activities: retrenchment and the recovery response. *Retrenchment* consists of cost-cutting and asset-reducing activities. The primary objective of the retrenchment phase is to stabilize the firm's financial condition. Situation severity has been associated with retrenchment responses among successful turnaround firms. Firms in danger of bankruptcy or failure (i.e., severe situations) attempt to halt decline through cost and asset reductions. Firms in less severe situations have achieved stability merely through cost retrenchment. However, in either case, for firms facing declining financial performance, the key to successful turnaround rests in the effective and efficient management of the retrenchment process.

continued

4. *The lost deal.* Lost deals often can be traced to poor communication. A successful strategic acquisition requires agreement upon the strategic vision, both with the acquiring company and between the acquiror and the continuing elements of the target. This should be established in the preliminary negotiations that lead to the letter of intent.

The letter must spell out not only the price to be paid but also many of the relational aspects that will make the strategic acquisition successful. Although an acquiror may justifiably focus on expenses, indemnification, and other logical concerns in the letter of intent, relationship and operational concerns are also important.

5. *Management difficulties.* Lack of attention to management issues may lead to a lost deal. These problems can range from a failure to provide management continuity or clear lines of authority after a merger to incentives that cause management to steer the company in the wrong direction.

The remedy for this problem must be extracted from the initial strategic review. The management compensation structure must be designed with legal and business advisors to help achieve those goals. The financial rewards to management must depend upon the financial and strategic success of the combined entity.

6. *The closing crisis.* Closing crises may stem from unavoidable changed conditions, but most often they result from poor communication. Negotiators sometimes believe that problems swept under the table maintain a deal's momentum and ultimately allow for its consummation. They are sometimes right—and often wrong. Charting a course through an acquisition requires carefully developed skills for every kind of professional—business, accounting, and legal.

7. *The operating transition crisis.* Even the best conceived and executed acquisition will prevent significant transition and postclosing operation issues. Strategic goals cannot be achieved by quick asset sales or other accelerated exit strategies. Management time and energy must be spent to assure that the benefits identified in the strategic review are achieved.

The principal constraints on smooth implementation are usually human: poor interaction of personnel between the two preexisting management structures and resistance to new systems. Problems also may arise from too much attention to the by now well-communicated strategic vision and too little attention to the nuts and bolts of continuing business operations.

The primary causes of the turnaround situation have been associated with the second phase of the turnaround process, the *recovery response.* For firms that declined primarily as a result of external problems, turnaround most often has been achieved through creative new entrepreneurial strategies. For firms that declined primarily as a result of internal problems, turnaround has been most frequently achieved through efficiency strategies. *Recovery* is achieved when economic measures indicate that the firm has regained its pre-downturn levels of performance.

Looking at Strategy in Action 7–7, it is evident that the need for a turnaround that was faced by Red Ant Entertainment was caused by internal factors. The relatively high severity level is a also clearly evident. Less certain is whether CEO Bruce Wasserstein is prepared to take the strategic actions needed to turn his fledgling music company around.

FIGURE 7–7
A Model of the Turnaround Process

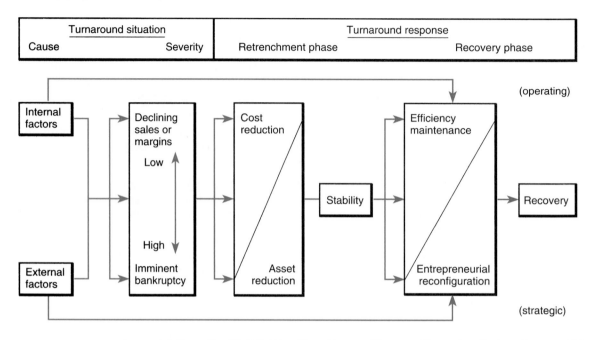

Source: J. A. Pearce II and D. K. Robbins, "Toward Improved Theory and Research on Business Turnaround," *Journal of Management,* 1993, 19 (3): 613–636.

Divestiture

A *divestiture strategy* involves the sale of a firm or a major component of a firm. For example, in March 1992, Goodyear Tire and Rubber announced its decision to sell its polyester business to Shell Chemical to cut its $2.6 billion debt. The sale was part of Goodyear's strategy to bring its debt below $2 billion within 18 months.

When retrenchment fails to accomplish the desired turnaround, as in the Goodyear situation, or when a nonintegrated business activity achieves an unusually high market value, strategic managers often decide to sell the firm. However, because the intent is to find a buyer willing to pay a premium above the value of a going concern's fixed assets, the term *marketing for sale* is often more appropriate. Prospective buyers must be convinced that, because of their skills and resources or because of the firm's synergy with their existing businesses, they will be able to profit from the acquisition.

The reasons for divestiture vary. They often arise because of partial mismatches between the acquired firm and the parent corporation. Some of the mismatched parts cannot be integrated into the corporation's mainstream activities and, thus, must be spun off. A second reason is corporate financial needs. Sometimes the cash flow or financial stability of the corporation as a whole can be greatly improved if businesses with high market value can be sacrificed. The result can be a balancing of equity with long-term risks or of long-term debt payments to optimize the cost of capital. A third, less frequent reason for divestiture is government antitrust action when a firm is believed to monopolize or unfairly dominate a particular market.

Although examples of the divestiture grand strategy are numerous, CBS, Inc., recently provided an outstanding example. In a two-year period, the once diverse entertainment and publishing giant sold its Records Division to Sony, its magazine publishing business to Diamandis Communications, its book publishing operations to Harcourt Brace Jovanovich, and its music publishing operations to SBK Entertainment World. Other firms that recently have pursued this type of grand strategy include Esmark, which divested Swift & Company, and White Motors, which divested White Farm.

Liquidation

When liquidation is the grand strategy, the firm typically is sold in parts, only occasionally as a whole—but for its tangible asset value and not as a going concern. In selecting liquidation, the owners and strategic managers of a firm are admitting failure and recognize that this action is likely to result in great hardships to themselves and their employees. For these reasons, liquidation usually is seen as the least attractive of the grand strategies. As a long-term strategy, however, it minimizes the losses of all the firm's stockholders. Faced with bankruptcy, the liquidating firm usually tries to develop a planned and orderly system that will result in the greatest possible return and cash conversion as the firm slowly relinquishes its market share.

Planned liquidation can be worthwhile. For example, Columbia Corporation, a $130 million diversified firm, liquidated its assets for more cash per share than the market value of its stock.

Bankruptcy

Business failures are playing an increasingly important role in the American economy. In an average week, more than 300 companies fail. More than 75 percent of these financially desperate firms file for a *liquidation bankruptcy*—they agree to a complete distribution of their assets to creditors, most of whom receive a small fraction of the amount they are owed. Liquidation is what the layperson views as bankruptcy: The business cannot pay its debts, so it must close its doors. Investors lose their money, employees lose their jobs, and managers lose their credibility. In owner-managed firms, company and personal bankruptcy commonly go hand-in-hand.[5]

The other 25 percent of these firms refuse to surrender until one final option is exhausted. Choosing a strategy to recapture its viability, such a company asks the courts for a *reorganization bankruptcy*. The firm attempts to persuade its creditors to temporarily freeze their claims while it undertakes to reorganize and rebuild the company's operations more profitably. The appeal of a reorganization bankruptcy is based on the company's ability to convince creditors that it can succeed in the marketplace by implementing a new strategic plan, and that when the plan produces profits, the firm will be able to repay its creditors, perhaps in full. In other words, the company offers its creditors a carefully designed alternative to forcing an immediate, but fractional repayment of its financial obligations. The option of reorganization bankruptcy offers maximum repayment of debt at some specified future time if a new strategic plan is successful.

Consider the case of Today's Man retail clothing stores. Led by the dynamic entrepreneur David Feld, who owns 52 percent of the corporation or about 5.5 million shares, Today's Man was enjoying explosive success in 1993, trading at $15 to $18 a

---

[5]The section was developed from an article by John A. Pearce II and Samuel A. DiLullo, "When a Strategic Plan Includes Bankruptcy," which appeared in the September–October 1998 issue of *Business Horizons,* pp. 67–73.

BusinessWeek

A SOUR NOTE FOR WASSERSTEIN

STRATEGY IN ACTION 7-7

Overall, it has been a great year for the 50-year-old Bruce Wasserstein. He published a definitive book on mergers called *Big Deal*. The firm he co-founded, Wasserstein Perella & Co., just celebrated its 10th anniversary. One of the most prominent M&A bankers in the 1980s, he is still sought out for advice on megamergers.

Although Wasserstein appears to have it all, there's still the embarrassing Red Ant matter. Red Ant Entertainment is a startup record label that over the past 18 months has cost Wasserstein some $32 million worth of grief and a hard lesson in the trendy and treacherous rock-music business.

Red Ant is part of Wasserstein's efforts to become a media mogul. In the past four years, his leveraged-buyout fund bought *The American Lawyer* from Time Warner Inc. and the *The National Law Journal* from Boston Ventures. He owns 35% of IMAX Corp., the Toronto-based 3-D large-screen movie-projection company.

Most financial investors avoid the industry, but Wasserstein thought music had better returns than film or TV. Six weeks after starting Red Ant, he got in bed with Alliance Entertainment Corp., a troubled record distributor, with the grand notion of becoming the next Sony or Polygram. But within a year, Alliance was bankrupt.

Unwilling to call it quits, Wasserstein bought Red Ant from bankruptcy court last summer and poured in $12 million more. Now, the hope is that Red Ant will hold its own like another of Wasserstein's music holdings, H.O.L.A., a fledgling Latin-music label run by Madonna's boyfriend, John "Jellybean" Benitez. But the jury is still out as to whether a firm of pinstriped investment bankers can strike it rich in the hip, fickle world of alternative urban music.

TIGHTER BUDGET

Alvin Teller, former head of MCA Music Entertainment Group and CBS Records, seemed like just the man to help. A Harvard B-school grad, he was considered one of the music-industry greats, having turned MCA's music unit into the most profitable part of MCA. But Teller was also a man used to having hundreds of millions of dollars at his fingertips, not to being a bootstrapping entrepreneur.

The decision to fund yet another music company was controversial among the Wasserstein partners. The firm had already invested in H.O.L.A., which is focused on Latino crossover artists,

Source: Debra Sparks and Leah Nathans Spiro in New York, "A Sour Note for Wasserstein," *Business Week:* August 17, 1998.

share. The company was entering a four-year expansion that would increase the number of retail outlets from 16 to 35. Feld had hired a professional management team, and the company greatly increased its promotional budget in support of its increased sales objectives.

Just two years later, Today's Man's creditors were concerned. Despite 1995 sales of $263 million, up 21 percent from 1994 up more than 50 percent from 1993, the company's principal lender, Alex. Brown & Sons, feared for its investment. The brokerage firm had extended Feld a personal loan of $7.5 million, collateralized by 5 million shares of Today's Man's stock. Feld then lent his company $5 million. When the value of the shares declined to $10 per share in the fall of 1995, Alex. Brown & Sons began to consider calling in the collateral on the loan. Soon after, the stock price dropped to $3 a share. In response, Today's Man's corporate bankers froze the company's credit line.

BusinessWeek

continued

and more in JB Music Publishing, which owns copyrights to such songs as Will Smith's hit *Gettin' Jiggy Wit It*. The firm then ponied up $20 million to back Teller and start Red Ant—the "ant" came from Teller's initials.

And Teller's goals went beyond startups. He wanted distribution to the masses, something he had at MCA. He was receptive when Alliance, then the country's largest record distributor, agreed to acquire Red Ant in August, 1996, six weeks after Red Ant was formed. That left Wasserstein with only 15% of Alliance—and only two out of the nine board seats. But Teller became CEO of the combined company.

The deal quickly transformed Red Ant from a fledgling label to a division of a large company, Alliance. Red Ant's mission was to create an independent music label concentrating on rock, urban, and hip-hop music, with artists such as The Sunz of Man, Crumb, naked, and ultrahorse.

Extravagant spending was rampant, with fingers pointing all around.

In hindsight, it's clear Red Ant would have been better off on its own. By 1996, the music industry was in a slump. Many independent record labels went bust, leaving Alliance holding the bag to refund record returns.

In late August, Alliance sank into Chapter 11. While Red Ant was left out of the bankruptcy proceedings, it was still owned by a bankrupt company. Red Ant, out of capital, shut down for three months.

"NIGHTMARE"

Undaunted, Wasserstein bought the label back from bankruptcy court by agreeing to pump in $12 million more, which got Red Ant through part of '98.

A year after the bankruptcy, the prospects for Red Ant, independent again, are still unclear. One record exec says the cloud of the Alliance bankruptcy still haunts Red Ant's acts. Many radio stations are gun-shy about giving them airtime, because they're not sure the promotional dollars will follow. Others in the music industry call the company Dead Ant.

Yet the company isn't dead. On July 21, the label released a new rap album by The Sunz of Man, which landed on Billboard's top 200 best-selling album charts that week. Plus, Red Ant has three acts in the R&B chart's top 10, including Voices of Theory and Tami Davis. But even if these artists don't provide the major hits Wasserstein has paid so dearly for, expect more media purchases. He's just starting to "get jiggy wit it."

On February 2, 1996, Today's Man filed for corporate bankruptcy in Wilmington, Delaware, while, simultaneously, David Feld filed for personal bankruptcy in Camden, Delaware. During his hearings, Feld argued successfully for the court to restrain Alex. Brown & Sons from selling its shares of Today's Man until a corporate restructuring under the reorganization bankruptcy laws could be considered by the court.

The Bankruptcy Situation

Imagine that your firm's financial reports have shown an unabated decline in revenue for seven quarters. Expenses have increased rapidly, and it is becoming difficult, and at times not possible, to pay bills as they become due. Suppliers are concerned about shipping goods without first receiving payment and some have refused to ship without advanced payment in cash. Customers are requiring assurances that future orders will be delivered and some are beginning to buy from competitors. Employees are listening seriously to rumors of financial problems and a higher than normal number have accepted other employment. What can be done? What strategy can be initiated to protect the company and resolve the financial problems in the short term?

The Harshest Resolution

If the judgment of the owners of a business is that its decline cannot be reversed, and the business cannot be sold as a going concern, then the alternative that is in the best interest of all may be a liquidation bankruptcy, also known as Chapter 7 of the Bankruptcy Code. The court appoints a trustee, who collects the property of the company, reduces it to cash, and distributes the proceeds proportionally to creditors on a pro rata basis as expeditiously as possible. Since all assets are sold to pay outstanding debt, a liquidation bankruptcy terminates a business. This type of filing is critically important to sole proprietors or partnerships. Their owners are personally liable for all business debts not covered by the sale of the business assets unless they can secure a Chapter 7 bankruptcy, which will allow them to cancel any debt in excess of exempt assets. Although they will be left with little personal property, the liquidated debtor is discharged from paying the remaining debt.

The shareholders of corporations are not liable for corporate debt and any debt existing after corporate assets are liquidated is absorbed by creditors. Corporate shareholders may simply terminate operations and walk away without liability to remaining creditors. However, filing a Chapter 7 proceeding will provide for an orderly and fair distribution of assets to creditors and thereby may reduce the negative impact of the business failure.

A Conditional Second Chance

A proactive alternative for the endangered company is reorganization bankruptcy. Chosen for the right reasons, and implemented in the right way, reorganization bankruptcy can provide a financially, strategically, and ethically sound basis on which to advance the interests of all of the firm's stakeholders.

A thorough and objective analysis of the company may support the idea of it continuing its operations if excessive debt can be reduced and new strategic initiatives can be undertaken. If the realistic possibility of long-term survival exists, a reorganization under Chapter 11 of the Bankruptcy Code can provide the opportunity. Reorganization allows a business debtor to restructure its debts and, with the agreement of creditors and approval of the court, to continue as a viable business. Creditors involved in Chapter 11 actions often receive less than the total debt due to them but far more than would be available from liquidation.

A Chapter 11 bankruptcy can provide time and protection to the debtor firm (which we will call the *Company*) to reorganize and use future earnings to pay creditors. The Company may restructure debts, close unprofitable divisions or stores, renegotiate labor contracts, reduce its work force, or propose other actions that could create a profitable business. If the plan is accepted by creditors, the Company will be given another chance to avoid liquidation and emerge from the bankruptcy proceedings rehabilitated.

For example, Today's Man filed a bankruptcy reorganization plan in June 1997 that promised to repay creditors in full, but without accrued interest. Under the plan, Feld would remain in control of the company and a $42.5 million loan would be secured from Foothill Capital in New York to reestablish the financial stability of the firm. This plan was proposed after the company took some important preliminary steps under the protection of the court, including the closing of 10 stores, the reduction of its work force by 400 employees, the reduction of its advertising budget, and the return of its original everyday low price marketing strategy.

The Company will usually file a reorganization plan during the first 120 days after the proceeding is started. Today's Man was given until July 1997 to present its creditor-approved plan to the bankruptcy court. If Feld's reorganization plan succeeded, the company's current creditors would be substantially repaid, but Today's Man would be taking on $42.5 million of new debt.

Seeking Protection of the Bankruptcy Court

If creditors file lawsuits or schedule judicial sales to enforce liens, the Company will need to seek the protection of the Bankruptcy Court. Filing a bankruptcy petition will invoke the protection of the court to provide sufficient time to work out a reorganization that was not achievable voluntarily. If reorganization is not possible, a Chapter 7 proceeding will allow for the fair and orderly dissolution of the business.

If a Chapter 11 proceeding is the required course of action, the Company must determine what the reorganized business will look like, if such a structure can be achieved, and how it will be accomplished while maintaining operations during the bankruptcy proceeding. Will sufficient cash be available to pay for the proceedings and reorganization? Will customers continue to do business with the Company or seek other more secure businesses with which to deal? Will key personnel stay on or look for more secure employment? Which operations should be discontinued or reduced?

Emerging from Bankruptcy

Bankruptcy is only the first step toward recovery for a firm. Many questions should be answered: How did the business get to the point at which the extreme action of bankruptcy was necessary? Were warning signs overlooked? Was the competitive environment understood? Did pride or fear prevent objective analysis? Did the business have the people and resources to succeed? Was the strategic plan well designed and implemented? Did financial problems result from unforeseen and unforeseeable problems or from bad management decisions?

Commitments to "try harder," "listen more carefully to the customer," and "be more efficient" are important but insufficient grounds to inspire stakeholder confidence. A recovery strategy must be developed to delineate how the company will compete more successfully in the future.

An assessment of the bankruptcy situation requires executives to consider the causes of the Company's decline and the severity of the problem it now faces. Investors must decide whether the management team that governed the company's operations during the downturn can return the firm to a position of success. Creditors must believe that the company's managers have learned how to prevent a recurrence of the observed and similar problems. Alternatively, they must have faith that the company's competencies can be sufficiently augmented by key substitutions to the management team, with strong support in decision making from a board of directors and consultants, to restore the firm's competitive strength.

The great severity of Today's Man's financial problems prompted the need to undertake bankruptcy, but the sales growth of the firm argued in favor of reorganization rather than liquidation. As a result of successful negotiations during its protection under Chapter 11, Today's Man was able to secure the $42.5 million financial package from Foothill Capital Corporation. Today's Man repaid bank group claimants from a cash distribution pool of $21.9 million taken from the Foothill investment, while other investor claims were kept pending. The financing was possible because of the success of some aggressive strategic reorganization moves by Today's Man. The new strategic initiatives included closing 10 retail stores and an outlet center, opening shoe departments in 9 stores, reducing budgets sharply, and succeeding with a turnaround plan. These initiatives enabled Today's Man to generate $7.6 million in EBITDA in fiscal 1996. Coincidentally, Feld also emerged from his personal bankruptcy protection.

CORPORATE COMBINATIONS

The 12 grand strategies discussed above, used singly and much more often in combinations, represent the traditional alternatives used by firms in the United States. Recently, three new grand types have gained in popularity; all fit under the broad category of corporate combinations. Although they do not fit the criterion by which executives retain a high degree of control over their operations, these grand strategies deserve special attention and consideration especially by companies that operate in global, dynamic, and technologically driven industries. These three newly popularized grand strategies are joint ventures, strategic alliances, and consortia.

Joint Ventures

Occasionally two or more capable firms lack a necessary component for success in a particular competitive environment. For example, no single petroleum firm controlled sufficient resources to construct the Alaskan pipeline. Nor was any single firm capable of processing and marketing all of the oil that would flow through the pipeline. The solution was a set of *joint ventures,* which are commercial companies (children) created and operated for the benefit of the co-owners (parents). These cooperative arrangements provided both the funds needed to build the pipeline and the processing and marketing capacities needed to profitably handle the oil flow.

The particular form of joint ventures discussed above is *joint ownership.* In recent years, it has become increasingly appealing for domestic firms to join foreign firms by means of this form. For example, Diamond-Star Motors is the result of a joint venture between a U.S. company, Chrysler Corporation, and Japan's Mitsubishi Motors corporation. Located in Normal, Illinois, Diamond-Star was launched because it offered Chrysler and Mitsubishi a chance to expand on their long-standing relationship in which subcompact cars (as well as Mitsubishi engines and other automotive parts) are imported to the United States and sold under the Dodge and Plymouth names.

The joint venture extends the supplier-consumer relationship and has strategic advantages for both partners. For Chrysler, it presents an opportunity to produce a high-quality car using expertise brought to the venture by Mitsubishi. It also gives Chrysler the chance to try new production techniques and to realize efficiencies by using the work force that was not included under Chrysler's collective bargaining agreement with the United Auto Workers. The agreement offers Mitsubishi the opportunity to produce cars for sale in the United States, without being subjected to the tariffs and restrictions placed on Japanese imports.

As a second example, Bethlehem Steel acquired an interest in a Brazilian mining venture to secure a raw material source. The stimulus for this joint ownership venture was grand strategy, but such is not always the case. Certain countries virtually mandate that foreign firms entering their markets do so on a joint ownership basis. India and Mexico are good examples. The rationale of these countries is that joint ventures minimize the threat of foreign domination and enhance the skills, employment, growth, and profits of local firms.

It should be noted that strategic managers understandably are wary of joint ventures. Admittedly, joint ventures present new opportunities with risks that can be shared. On the other hand, joint ventures often limit the discretion, control, and profit potential of partners, while demanding managerial attention and other resources that might be directed toward the firm's mainstream activities. Nevertheless, increasing globalization in many industries may require greater consideration of the joint venture approach, if historically national firms are to remain viable. Advantages and disadvantages of an international joint venture are highlighted in Global Strategy in Action 7–4.

Strategic Alliances

Strategic alliances are distinguished from joint ventures because the companies involved do not take an equity position in one another. In many instances, strategic alliances are partnerships that exist for a defined period during which partners contribute their skills and expertise to a cooperative project. For example, one partner provides manufacturing capabilities while a second partner provides marketing expertise. Many times, such alliances are undertaken because the partners want to learn from one another with the intention to be able to develop in-house capabilities to supplant the partner when the contractual arrangement between them reaches its termination date. Such relationships are tricky since in a sense the partners are attempting to "steal" each other's know-how. Global Strategy in Action 7–5 lists many important questions about their learning intentions that prospective partners should ask themselves before entering into a strategic alliance.

In other instances, strategic alliances are synonymous with licensing agreements. Licensing involves the transfer of some industrial property right from the U.S. licensor to a motivated licensee in a foreign country. Most tend to be patents, trademarks, or technical know-how that are granted to the licensee for a specified time in return for a royalty and for avoiding tariffs or import quotas. Bell South and U.S. West, with various marketing and service competitive advantages valuable to Europe, have extended a number of licenses to create personal computer networks in the United Kingdom (U.K.).

Another licensing strategy open to U.S. firms is to contract the manufacturing of its product line to a foreign company to exploit local comparative advantages in technology, materials, or labor. For example, MIPS Computer Systems has licensed Digital Equipment Corporation, Texas Instruments, Cypress Semiconductor, and Bipolar Integrated Technology in the United States, and Fujitsu, NEC, and Kubota in Japan to market computers based on its designs in the partner's country.

Service and franchise-based firms—including Anheuser-Busch, Avis, Coca-Cola, Hilton, Hyatt, Holiday Inns, Kentucky Fried Chicken, McDonald's, and Pepsi—have long engaged in licensing arrangements with foreign distributors as a way to enter new markets with standardized products that can benefit from marketing economies.

Outsourcing is a rudimentary approach to strategic alliances that enables firms to gain a competitive advantage. Significant changes within many segments of American business continue to encourage the use of outsourcing practices. Within the health care arena, an industry survey recorded 67 percent of hospitals using provider outsourcing

GLOBAL STRATEGY IN ACTION 7–4

The name White Nights Joint Enterprise plays off the Siberian summer and off the reason U.S. oil companies are here. And while the mission of the first working Russian–U.S. oil venture is simple, the details aren't.

"This is the first arrangement of its kind in all of the oil industry," says Gerald Walston, the Denver oil man who is White Nights' director.

The arrangement he refers to is incremental sharing, which entitles White Nights to all the oil recovered from three fields, above what the Russians had expected to get out, for 25 years.

Varyegan Oil and Gas, the state-owned company that controls the oil, is the Russian partner in White Nights. In exchange for turning its oil fields over to the joint venture, Varyegan gets all the oil up to its production estimates, plus half the oil that comes in addition to that. It also gets 10 percent in royalties.

The U.S. partners, Anglo-Suisse and Philbro Energy Production, split what's left, which is 40 percent of the extra production. They can make their money by shipping their oil out of the country to sell for hard currency.

The venture is pumping ahead of the Russians' estimated production. "Production in all of Russia was down 9.5 percent in 1991. Our fields were up about 40 percent," says Walston.

Anatoly Sivak, director general of Varyegan Oil and Gas, says, "This joint venture will serve as an example. It is the wave of the future."

The reason Sivak turned to the West for help was simple: "The question was how to stop the production decline. For that, we needed money and equipment and technology not available here." Completed wells were sitting idle for lack of parts.

Although the venture has succeeded in boosting production, "We've had some problems," Sivak says.

Anglo-Suisse was designated operator of the venture, and Russian oil people, who have been drilling here since the 1960s, couldn't understand why a U.S. company is running the show.

On top of that resentment were more obvious obstacles: different languages, clashing cultures, huge gaps in economic circumstances among the workers, different drilling techniques, and radically different organizational mindsets.

The Russians, with their five-year plans and strict instructions, "tended to organize and plan down to the last jot and tiddle," says Walston, a graying, unflappable gentleman who appears to keep the joint venture on an even keel via strings of Post-It notes splayed over the top of his desk. "The watchword for us is flexibility," he says.

Source: Excerpted from J. T. Buckley, ``Joint Venture Boosts Siberian Oil Flows," *USA Today,* March 12, 1992, section 5B. Copyright 1992, USA TODAY. Reprinted with permission.

for at least one department within their organization. Services such as information systems, reimbursement, and risk and physician practice management are outsourced by 51 percent of the hospitals that use outsourcing. Global Strategy in Action 7–6 describes how the newest form of global outsourcers, known as *supercontractors,* are revolutionizing manufacturing.

Another successful application of outsourcing is found in human resources. A survey of human resource executives revealed 85 percent have personal experience leading an outsourcing effort within their organization. In addition, it was found that two-thirds of pension departments have outsourced at least one human resource function.

KEY ISSUES IN STRATEGIC ALLIANCE LEARNING

GLOBAL
STRATEGY IN
ACTION
7–5

Objective	Major Questions
1. Assess and value partner knowledge.	• What were the strategic objectives in forming the alliance? • What are the core competencies of our alliance partner? • Which partner contributes key alliance inputs? • What specific knowledge does the partner have that could enhance our competitive strategy? Is that knowledge or some of the knowledge embodied in the alliance? • What are the core partner skills relevant for our product/markets? • Are we realistic about partner skills and capabilities relevant to our strategy and capabilities?
2. Determine knowledge accessibility.	• Have learning issues been discussed in the alliance negotiations? • How have key alliance responsibilities been allocated to the partners? Which partner controls key managerial responsibilities? • Do we have easy geographic access to the alliance operations? • Does the alliance agreement specify restrictions on our access to the alliance operations? • Has our partner taken explicit steps to restrict our access? If yes, can we eliminate these restrictions through negotiation or assignment of managers to the alliance?
3. Evaluate knowledge tacitness and ease of transfer.	• Is our learning objective focused on explicit operational knowledge? • Where in the alliance does the knowledge reside? • Is the knowledge strategic or operational? • Reality check: Do we understand what we are trying to learn and how we can use the knowledge?
4. Establish knowledge connections between the alliance and the partner.	• Do parent managers visit the alliance on a regular basis? • Has a systematic plan been established for managers to rotate between the alliance and the parent? • Are parent managers in regular contact with senior alliance managers? • Has the alliance been incorporated into parent strategic plans and do alliance managers participate in parent strategic planning discussions? • What is the level of trust between parent and alliance managers? • Do alliance financial issues dominate meetings between alliance and parent managers?
5. Draw on existing knowledge to facilitate learning.	• Have the partner firms worked together in the past? • In the learning process, have efforts been made to involve managers with prior experience in either/both alliance management and partner ties? • Are experiences with other alliances being used as the basis for managing the current alliance? • Are we realistic about our partner's learning objectives? • Are we open-minded about knowledge without immediate short-term applicability?
6. Ensure that partner and alliance managerial cultures are in alignment.	• Is the alliance viewed as a threat or an asset by parent managers? • In the parent, is there agreement on the strategic rationale for the alliance? • In the alliance, do managers understand the importance of the parent's learning objective?

Source: Andrew C. Inkpen. "Learning and Knowledge Acquisition Through International Strategic Alliances," *Academy of Management Executive* 12, no. 4 (1998), p. 78.

SOUPING UP THE SUPPLY CHAIN

GLOBAL
STRATEGY IN
ACTION
7–6

Today's supercontractors are turning manufacturers into models of efficiency.

Even in this "just-in-time" age, the production line that churns out Hewlett-Packard ink-jet printers in Newark, California, is impressive. In response to electronic orders from customers around the country, parts trucked in moments earlier are loaded onto a 110-foot assembly line. Finished printers fly off the other end—and soon are aboard another truck heading to a distributor. The operation is seamless and speedy. But then, what would you expect from one of America's premier high-tech corporations?

You might think the factory belongs to Hewlett-Packard Co. Instead it's owned by Solectron Corp., a contract manufacturer. What's more, even as Milpitas (California)-based Solectron pumps out HP's printers, its 24 production lines are simultaneously assembling everything from pagers to television decoding boxes for some of the biggest brand names in electronics.

Solectron is part of a new breed of U.S. supercontractors that promise to revolutionize manufacturing well into the next century. They command dozens of factories and supply networks around the world. Increasingly, they also manage their customers' entire product lines, offering an array of services from design to inventory management to delivery and after-sales service. Their unusually flexible operations are surprisingly profitable, producing returns on assets in the range of 20%.

"Outsourcing," a practice that has been around for decades, doesn't begin to describe the phenomenon. In place of traditional contracting relationships between client and supplier, arrangements with companies such as Solectron represent a sort of extended enterprise—a set of partnerships between product developers and specialists in components, distribution, retailing, and manufacturing.

The resulting organization can be so tight as to behave like a single, closely knit company— only better. Its strategies can slash time and costs out of the supply chain, the process between the invention of a new product and the time it reaches the consumer. Customers say they have achieved cost efficiencies of 15% to 25% already. And that, says James E. Morehouse, a logistics expert at A. T. Kearny Inc., is only 5% to 10% of U.S. industry's potential savings.

BUSTED BARRIERS

The effect on innovation could be huge. Spinning off manufacturing and other noncore functions allows industrial titans to focus new investment where it gets the most bang: on research and marketing. Because the strategy reduces the need for capital and in-house operations expertise, moreover, startups face far lower barriers in bringing new technologies to market.

In 1996, for example, Egyptian-born engineers Zaki and Shlomo Raqib came up with a modem, capable of advanced services such as teleconferencing, that could be deployed over any cable system without needing costly upgrades by cable operators. But while their Santa Clara (California) company, Terayon Communications Systems Corp., had $45 million in venture capital, it lacked manufacturing facilities. So it went to Solectron, and four months later Terayon's modems were being shipped to cable operators in the U.S. and abroad. In terms of manufacturing capability, boasts Zaki Raqib, "this puts us on a par with the Motorolas of the world."

Source: Pete Engardio in Milpitas, California, "Souping Up the Supply Chain," *Business Week:* August 31, 1998.

continued

BusinessWeek

COST BENEFIT

Far from eroding American industry, the new manufacturing paradigm is one of the surprise strengths of America's high-tech economy. Because independent contractors can better meet demands for quick delivery, the U.S. is actually becoming more competitive as a production base—even in mass-volume assembly work. As Asia's cheap wages are offset by higher shipping costs, "the cost difference between the U.S. is now virtually gone," says Michael E. Marks, chief executive at Flextronics International USA Inc., a major contract manufacturer.

Not everyone is abandoning their factories. Compaq Computer, Intel, National Semiconductor, and Merck are among the corporate giants that keep manufacturing in-house to protect their competitive edge. They fear losing control over intellectual property and quality, or that secrets will leak to competitors. They also worry about losing touch with clients and industry trends.

But in many industries, vertical integration is giving way to virtual integration. General Motors Corp.'s Aug. 3 decision to spin off its $31 billion Delphi Automotive Systems components unit is part of the auto industry's shift toward "modular" production, where prefabricated chunks with scores of parts are supplied by outsiders and bolted together at the last minute. Delphi, for example, makes full instrument panels for M-class sport-utility vehicles assembled at Mercedes Benz's modular plant in Vance, Alabama. Some experts believe the Big Three also will eventually sell off their engine and auto assembly plants.

The same trend is emerging in pharmaceuticals, where the cost of bringing a new drug to market—as high as $500 million—and the high risk of failure have long been barriers to entry. Covance Inc., one of the world's largest contract research organizations for drugmakers, has just opened a $55 million plant in North Carolina's Research Triangle Park that CEO Christopher A. Kuebler likens to a "sterile version of a microbrewery," capable of making up to five biological drug products simultaneously. Among its first customers is seven-year-old StressGen Biotechnologies Corp. of Victoria, British Columbia, which has hired Covance to make its new vaccine for treating cervical cancer.

The movement is much further along in electronics, where a $90 billion contract manufacturing sector is growing three times faster than overall electronics sales, according to Technology Forecasters Inc. of Alameda, California. Semiconductor startups can turn to a growing number of silicon-wafer foundries—highly flexible shops willing to produce small runs of a few thousand units at first and ramp up to mass production if demand takes off. That allows "fabless" Silicon Valley to design houses like Xilinx Inc., 3Dfx Interactive, and Broadcom Corp. to market innovative telecom, graphics, and video chips that power the myriad multimedia gadgets of the Digital Age. With billions of dollars in new capacity coming online, analysts expect the supply of new chips to explode.

As virtual integration evolves, futurists envision a time when product developers, manufacturers, and distributors will be so tightly linked through data networks that inventory will all but disappear. Companies will make goods based on the daily needs of retailers. Even automobiles will be assembled to a customer's specifications within days, just as Dell Computer Corp. and Cisco Systems do now with computers and networking equipment. A sunset industry no longer, manufacturing will help drive innovation.

FIGURE 7–8
The Top Five Strategic Reasons for Outsourcing

1. **Improve Business Focus.**
   For many companies, the single most compelling reason for outsourcing is that several "how" issues are siphoning off huge amounts of management's resources and attention.

2. **Access to World-Class Capabilities.**
   By the very nature of their specialization, outsourcing providers bring extensive worldwide, world-class resources to meeting the needs of their customers. According to Norris Overton, vice president of reengineering, AMTRAK, partnering with an organization with world-class capabilities, can offer access to new technology, tools, and techniques that the organization may not currently possess; better career opportunities for personnel who transition to the outsourcing provider; more structured methodologies, procedures, and documentation; and competitive advantage through expanded skills.

3. **Accelerated Reengineering Benefits.**
   Outsourcing is often a byproduct of another powerful management tool—business process reengineering. It allows an organization to immediately realize the anticipated benefits of reengineering by having an outside organization—one that is already reengineered to world-class standards—take over the process.

4. **Shared Risks.**
   There are tremendous risks associated with the investments an organization makes. When companies outsource they become more flexible, more dynamic, and better able to adapt to changing opportunities.

5. **Free Resources for Other Purposes.**
   Every organization has limits on the resources available to it. Outsourcing permits an organization to redirect its resources from noncore activities toward activities that have the greater return in serving the customer.

Source: Material prepared for a paid advertising section which appeared in the October 16, 1995, issue of *Fortune* © 1995, Time, Inc. All rights reserved.

Within customer service and sales departments, outsourcing increased productivity in such areas as product information, sales and order taking, sample fulfillment, and complaint handling. Figure 7–8 presents the top five strategic and tactical reasons for exploiting the benefits of outsourcing.

Consortia, Keiretsus, and Chaebols

Consortia are defined as large interlocking relationships between businesses of an industry. In Japan such consortia are known as *keiretsus,* in South Korea as *chaebols.*

In Europe, consortia projects are increasing in number and in success rates. Examples include the Junior Engineers' and Scientists' Summer Institute, which underwrites cooperative learning and research; the European Strategic Program for Research and Development in Information Technologies, which seeks to enhance European competitiveness in fields related to computer electronics and component manufacturing; and EUREKA, which is a joint program involving scientists and engineers from several European countries to coordinate joint research projects.

A Japanese *keiretsu* is an undertaking involving up to 50 different firms that are joined around a large trading company or bank and are coordinated through interlocking directories and stock exchanges. It is designed to use industry coordination to minimize risks of competition, in part through cost sharing and increased economies of scale. Examples include Sumitomo, Mitsubishi, Mitsui, and Sanwa. Global Strategy in Action 7–7 presents a new side to keiretsus, namely, that they are adding global partners, including several from the United States. Their cooperative nature is growing in evidence as is their market success.

A South Korean chaebol resembles a consortium or keiretsu except that they are typically financed through government banking groups and largely are run by professional managers trained by participating firms expressly for the job.

LIMITATIONS OF THE GRAND STRATEGIES

Throughout the chapter both the advantages and disadvantages of each of the 14 grand strategies have been explored. Before we delve into the complex issues of strategy implementation and control, it is important to take one final look at the most popularly recognized shortcomings of some of the strategy formulation–related ideas that we have explored. Figure 7–9 presents a description and expert assessment of the potential problems that each idea presents for its adopters.

SELECTION OF LONG-TERM OBJECTIVES AND GRAND STRATEGY SETS

At first glance, the strategic management model, which provides the framework for study throughout this book, seems to suggest that strategic choice decision making leads to the sequential selection of long-term objectives and grand strategies. In fact, however, strategic choice is the simultaneous selection of long-range objectives and grand strategies. When strategic planners study their opportunities, they try to determine which are most likely to result in achieving various long-range objectives. Almost simultaneously, they try to forecast whether an available grand strategy can take advantage of preferred opportunities so the tentative objectives can be met. In essence, then, three distinct but highly interdependent choices are being made at one time. Several triads, or sets, of possible decisions are usually considered.

A simplified example of this process is shown in Figure 7–10. In this example, the firm has determined that six strategic choice options are available. These options stem from three interactive opportunities (e.g., West Coast markets) that present little competition. Because each of these interactive opportunities can be approached through different grand strategies—for options 1 and 2, the grand strategies are horizontal integration and market development—each offers the potential for achieving long-range objectives to varying degrees. Thus, a firm rarely can make a strategic choice only on the basis of its preferred opportunities, long-range objectives, or grand strategy. Instead, these three elements must be considered simultaneously, because only in combination do they constitute a strategic choice.

In an actual decision situation, the strategic choice would be complicated by a wider variety of interactive opportunities, feasible company objectives, promising grand strategy options, and evaluative criteria. Nevertheless, Figure 7–10 does partially reflect the nature and complexity of the process by which long-term objectives and grand strategies are selected.

In the next chapter, the strategic choice process will be fully explained. However, knowledge of long-term objectives and grand strategies is essential to understanding that process.

BusinessWeek

KEIRETSU CONNECTIONS

GLOBAL STRATEGY IN ACTION 7–7

Amid rolling hills outside Nagoya, Toshiba Corp. recently took the wraps off a new $1 billion chipmaking facility that uses ultraviolet lithography to etch circuits less than one micron wide—a tiny fraction of the width of a human hair.

The Toshiba chip site owes much to a strategic alliance with IBM and Siemens of Germany. In fact, IBM's knowhow in chemical mechanical polishing, essential to smoothing the tiny surfaces of multilayered chips, played a critical role. "We had little expertise here," concedes Toshiba's Koichi Suzuki.

QUIET CHANGE

What's more, about 20 IBM engineers will show up shortly to transfer the technology back to an IBM-Toshiba facility in Manassas, Virginia. In addition to the semiconductor cooperation, IBM and Toshiba jointly make liquid-crystal display panels—even though they use the LCDs in their fiercely competitive lines of laptop computers. "It's no longer considered a loss of corporate manhood to let others help out," says IBM Asia Pacific President Robert C. Timpson.

For years, many U.S. tie-ups with Japanese companies tended to be defensive in nature, poorly managed, and far removed from core businesses. Now, the alliances are deepening, taking on increasingly important products, and expanding their geographic reach in terms of sales. U.S.-Japanese partnerships are, for example, popping up in Asia's emerging but tricky markets, reducing the risks each company faces.

This deepening web of relationships reflects a quiet change in thinking by Japanese and U.S. multinationals in an era when keeping pace with technological change and competing globally have stretched the resources of even the richest companies. "The scale and technology are so great that neither can do it alone," says Jordan D. Lewis, author of *The Connected Corporation*.

Source: Brian Bemner in Toyko, with Zachary Schiller in Cleveland, Tim Smart in Fairfield, William J. Holstein in New York, and bureau reports, "Keiretsu Connections," *Business Week:* July 22, 1996.

SEQUENCE OF OBJECTIVES AND STRATEGY SELECTION

The selection of long-range objectives and grand strategies involves simultaneous, rather than sequential, decisions. While it is true that objectives are needed to prevent the firm's direction and progress from being determined by random forces, it is equally true that objectives can be achieved only if strategies are implemented. In fact, long-term objectives and grand strategies are so interdependent that some business consultants do not distinguish between them. Long-term objectives and grand strategies are still combined under the heading of company strategy in most of the popular business literature and in the thinking of most practicing executives.

However, the distinction has merit. Objectives indicate what strategic managers want but provide few insights about how they will be achieved. Conversely, strategies indicate what types of actions will be taken but do not define what ends will be pursued or what criteria will serve as constraints in refining the strategic plan.

Does it matter whether strategic decisions are made to achieve objectives or to satisfy constraints? No, because constraints are themselves objectives. The constraint of

continued

Overall, instances of joint investment in research, products, and distribution by Japanese companies and foreign counterparts, mostly American, have jumped 26%, to 155, in the first quarter of 1996—on top of a 33% increase between 1993 and 1995—according to the Sakura Institute of Research.

ENVY

And while Uncle Sam and U.S. companies with grievances have attacked Japan's system of big industrial groups, called keiretsu, as exclusionary, other chieftains of Corporate America have quietly become *stakeholders* of sorts. The list includes companies as diverse as IBM, General Motors, TRW, Boeing, and Caterpillar.

Many American executives who have established these alliances say they appreciate the attributes of Japan's big industrial groups. U.S. managers have always envied the keiretsu edge in spreading risk over a cluster of companies when betting big on a new technology or blitzing emerging markets.

In one industry after another, U.S. and Japanese partners are breaking new ground in their level of cooperation. The impact is felt far beyond the U.S. and Japanese home markets. Take the 50-50 venture between Caterpillar Inc. and Mitsubishi Heavy Industries Ltd., part of Japan's $200 billion keiretsu of the same name. Early on, Cat wanted a way to sell its construction equipment in Japan and compete with rival Komatsu Ltd. on its home turf. Mitsubishi wanted to play catch-up with Komatsu, too, and expand its export markets.

Their alliance played a key role in taming Komatsu. But the partners have broader ambitions. Since Cat shifted all design work for its "300" series of excavators to the partnership back in 1987, the venture's two Japanese factories have emerged as Cat's primary source of production for sales to fast-growing Asia. The alliance's products reach the world market through Cat's network of 186 independent dealers in 197 countries.

increased inventory capacity is a desire (an objective), not a certainty. Likewise, the constraint of an increase in the sales force does not assure that the increase will be achieved, given such factors as other company priorities, labor market conditions, and the firm's profit performance.

SUMMARY

Before learning how strategic decisions are made, it is important to understand the two principal components of any strategic choice; namely, long-term objectives and the grand strategy. The purpose of this chapter was to convey that understanding.

Long-term objectives were defined as the results a firm seeks to achieve over a specified period, typically five years. Seven common long-term objectives were discussed: profitability, productivity, competitive position, employee development, employee relations, technological leadership, and public responsibility. These, or any other long-term objectives, should be acceptable, flexible, measurable over time, motivating, suitable, understandable, and achievable.

FIGURE 7–9
Shortcomings of Popular Strategy-Related Ideas

Strategy-Related Idea	Brief Description	Problems or Unrealistic Assumptions
Centralized corporate strategy	Strategy must be formulated at the top, where the whole picture of corporate goals and long-term visions is available.	Individual managers have little or no say in determining the strategy for their units/departments.
Competitive strategies	Analyze the competitive situation in your industry and learn to read competitive signals.	The challenge is to predict future competition, not analyze that of the past or present.
Conglomerates	Acquiring dissimilar businesses under a single corporation.	By definition the most conglomerates can achieve is average returns.
Core competences	Special skills or technologies that provide lasting competitive advantages to firms.	Core competences can change and be a disadvantage to firms that do not recognize the change.
Decentralization	Decision-making is placed in the hands of functional managers.	Without effective coordination, decision-making can become ineffective.
Diversification	To maintain high growth, companies must diversify into promising industries or new markets.	Difficulty in accurately forecasting promising industries/markets.
Experience curves	As production doubles, nondirect costs decrease by a constant percentage.	It might work for mass production, but bureaucracy can wipe out economies of scale.
Global rationalization	The marketplace is the world. Thus, production, marketing, finance, and R&D decisions must be made with such a view in mind.	How do you know future conditions? A change in exchange rates, for instance, can make all plans useless.
PIMS	An empirical database containing company-supplied information whose purpose is to discover the relationship between profitability and other factors.	Too many methodological problems and tautologies to make the result reliable and useful.
Portfolio matrix	Products or business units are classified as dogs, cows, question marks, and stars. The objective is to get rid of dogs and to promote stars, financing them with cash generated from cows.	It assumes futures stars can be identified, it ignores synergies, it can drop profitable products, it disregards competitive action and learning.
Restructuring	Getting rid of unprofitable businesses or those that do not fit the corporate identity.	The challenge is to know which businesses to get rid of.
Searching for excellence	Through empirical research, identify the factors common to excellent companies and use them to become excellent too.	Past excellence cannot be used to achieve excellence in the future.
Strategic alliances	Form alliances (if necessary even with your arch-rival(s)) to improve your competitive position.	Long-term effects can be detrimental, as they provide a false sense of security.

Source: Extracted from Spyros Makridakis, "Metastrategy: Learning and Avoiding Past Mistakes," *Long Range Planning* 30, no. 1 (1997), p. 130.

Grand strategies were defined as comprehensive approaches guiding the major actions designed to achieve long-term objectives. Fifteen grand strategy options were discussed: concentrated growth, market development, product development, innovation, horizontal integration, vertical integration, concentric diversification, conglomerate diversification, turnaround, divestiture, liquidation, bankruptcy, joint ventures, strategic alliances, and consortia.

FIGURE 7–10
A Profile of Strategic Choice Options

	Six Strategic Choice Options					
	1	**2**	**3**	**4**	**5**	**6**
Interactive opportunities	West Coast markets present little competition		Current markets sensitive to price competition		Current industry product lines offer too narrow a range of markets	
Appropriate long-range objectives (limited sample): Average 5-year ROI. Company sales by year 5. Risk of negative profits.	15% +50% .30	19% +40% .25	13% +20% .10	17% +0% .15	23% +35% .20	15% +25% .05
Grand strategies	Horizontal integration	Market development	Concentration	Selective retrenchment	Product development	Concentration

QUESTIONS FOR DISCUSSION

1. Identify firms in the business community nearest to your college or university that you believe are using each of the 15 grand strategies discussed in this chapter.

2. Identify firms in your business community that appear to rely principally on 1 of the 15 grand strategies. What kind of information did you use to classify the firms?

3. Write a long-term objective for your school of business that exhibits the seven qualities of long-term objectives described in this chapter.

4. Distinguish between the following pairs of grand strategies:

   a. Horizontal and vertical integration.

   b. Conglomerate and concentric diversification.

   c. Product development and innovation.

   d. Joint venture and strategic alliance.

5. Rank each of the 15 grand strategy options discussed in this chapter on the following three scales:

   High   Low
   Cost

   High   Low
   Risk of failure

   High   Low
   Potential for exceptional growth

6. Identify firms that use one of the eight specific options shown in Figure 7–4 under the grand strategies of concentration, market development, and product development.

BIBLIOGRAPHY

Anderson, E. "Two Firms, One Frontier: On Assessing Joint Venture Performance." *Sloan Management Review,* Winter 1990, pp. 19–30.

Badaracco, J. L. "Alliances Speed Knowledge Transfer." *Planning Review,* March–April 1991, pp. 10–17.

Beamish, Paul W., and Andrew C. Inkpen. "Keeping International Joint Ventures Stable and Profitable." *Long Range Planning* 28, no. 3 (June 1995), p. 26.

Bleeke, J., and D. Ernst. "The Way to Win in Cross-Border Alliances." *Harvard Business Review,* November–December 1991, pp. 127–35.

Brannen, M. Y. "Culture as the Critical Factor in Implementing Innovation." *Business Horizons,* November–December 1991, pp. 59–67.

Bronthers, Keith D.; Lane Eliot Bronthers; and Timothy J. Wilkinson. "Strategic Alliances: Choose Your Partners." *Long Range Planning* 28, no. 3 (June 1995), p. 68.

Ettlie, J. E. "What Makes a Manufacturing Firm Innovative?" *Academy of Management Executive,* November 1990, pp. 7–20.

Evan, W. M., and P. Olk. "R&D Consortia: A New U.S. Organizational Form." *Sloan Management Review,* Spring 1990, pp. 37–46.

Gopinath, C. "Turnaround: Recognizing Decline and Initiating Intervention." *Long Range Planning,* December 1991, pp. 96–101.

Grossi, G. "Promoting Innovation in a Big Business." *Long Range Planning,* February 1990, pp. 41–52.

Haspeslagh, P. C., and D. B. Jemison. "The Challenge of Renewal through Acquisitions." *Planning Review,* March–April 1991, pp. 27–33.

Houlden, Brian T. "How Corporate Planning Adopts and Survives." *Long Range Planning* 28, no. 4 (August 1995), p. 99.

Hughes, G. D. "Managing High-Tech Product Cycles." *Academy of Management Executive,* May 1990, pp. 44–55.

Kanter, R. M. "When Giants Learn Cooperative Strategies." *Planning Review,* January–February 1990, pp. 15–25.

Keller, R., and R. Chinta. "International Technology Transfer: Strategies for Success." *Academy of Management Executive,* May 1990, pp. 33–43.

Kukolis, Sal, and Mark Jungemann. "Strategic Planning for a Joint Venture." *Long Range Planning* 28, no. 3 (June 1995), p. 46.

Lengnick-Hall, C. A. "Innovation and Competitive Advantage: What We Know and What We Need to Learn." *Journal of Management,* June 1992, p. 399.

Leontiades, M. "The Case for Nonspecialized Diversification." *Planning Review,* January–February 1990, pp. 26–33.

Lewis, J. "Using Alliances to Build Market Power." *Planning Review,* September–October 1990, pp. 4–9.

Littler, Dole, and Fiona Leverick. "Joint Ventures for Product Development: Learning from Experience." *Long Range Planning* 28, no. 3 (June 1995), p. 58.

Lowry, James R. "A Partnering Approach to Mass Merchandising in Russia." *Business Horizons* 38, no. 4 (July–August 1995), p. 28.

Miller, D. "The Generic Strategy Trap." *The Journal of Business Strategy,* January–February 1992, pp. 37–41.

Newman, W. H. "Focused Joint Ventures in Transforming Economies." *Academy of Management Executive,* February 1992, pp. 67–75.

Paap, J. E. "A Venture Capitalist's Advice for Successful Strategic Alliances." *Planning Review,* September–October 1990, pp. 20–26.

Pearce, J. A., II, and J. W. Harvey. "Concentrated Growth Strategies." *Academy of Management Executive,* February 1990, pp. 61–68.

Pearce, J. A., II, and D. K. Robbins. "Toward Improved Theory and Research on Business Turnaround." *Journal of Management,* 1993.

————. "Entrepreneurial Recovery Strategies among Small Market Share Manufacturers." *Journal of Business Venturing,* 1994.

Peters, T. "Get Innovative or Get Dead." *California Management Review,* Winter 1991, pp. 9–23.

Reimann, B. C. "Corporate Strategies That Work." *Planning Review,* January–February 1992, pp. 41–46.

Robbins, D. K., and Pearce, J. A., II. "Entrepreneurial Retrenchment among Small Manufacturing Firms." *Journal of Business Venturing,* July 1993, pp. 301–18.

Sankar, Chetan S.; William R. Boulton; Nancy W. Davidson; Charles A. Snyder; and Richard W. Ussery. "Building a World-Class Alliance: The Universal Card—TSYS Case." *The Academy of Management Executive* 9, no. 2 (May 1995), p. 20.

Shanklin, William L. "Offensive Strategies for Defense Companies." *Business Horizons* 38, no. 4 (July–August 1995), p. 53.

Stiles, Jan. "Collaboration for Competitive Advantage: The Changing World of Alliances and Partnerships." *Long Range Planning* 28, no. 5 (October 1995), p. 109.

CHAPTER 7 DISCUSSION CASE

BusinessWeek

MOBILEMEDIA: ANATOMY OF A BANKRUPTCY

> Corporate bankruptcies are occurring in America in unprecedented numbers. The Chapter 7 discussion case discusses one of the most celebrated of these business failures, but the objective is not simply to document a bankruptcy. The real value in the story is seeing that danger lurks in every major strategic decision. Mobile-Media was a dominant player in a high-growth market whose success was undermined by cutthroat competition, impressive new competitor technologies, and problems of integrating corporate acquisitions. As you will read, flawed strategic management, ill-timed financing, slow board of director involvement, and flagging supplier confidence all converged to limit MobileMedia's flexibility, producing the eventual bankruptcy outcome.

In 1996, MobileMedia Corp., the country's second-largest paging company, was transmitting nothing but good news. A successful initial public offering had returned hefty paper profits to stockholders, new customers were signing on at a blistering pace, and two lightning-fast acquisitions costing more than $1 billion were winning praise. On Jan. 4, 1996, then-CEO Greg M. Rorke called MobileMedia's recent purchase of BellSouth subsidiary MobileComm "a milestone in the personal communications industry."

Millstone was more like it. In the end, integrating the two companies proved too much for MobileMedia to handle. On Jan. 30, 1997, the $567 million company filed for bankruptcy. While it is preparing to emerge from *Chapter 11,* MobileMedia still faces a Federal Communications Commission investigation into possible improprieties in the licensing process, as well as shareholder lawsuits and bitter creditors.

CUTTHROAT

In part, MobileMedia's decline mirrors that of the paging industry, which has lost some $4 billion in market capitalization since September, 1995, because of cutthroat competition and new technologies. But MobileMedia's woes go deeper. It suffered from poor management, a disastrous acquisitions strategy, and a disengaged board. "It's a tragedy," says one creditor. "It should not have happened."

But it did. And when MobileMedia crashed, nearly everyone connected with the Ridgefield Park, New Jersey, company got burned, including executives, lenders, shareholders, and analysts who talked up MobileMedia's stock as it fell from a high of 29¼ in September, 1995, to about 1 in March. Their enthusiasm, typical of bull-market excess, continued long after glaring evidence to the contrary should have sobered them up.

One of the biggest hits to reputation and pocketbook was taken by Hellman & Friedman, the highly regarded San Francisco–based investment firm that made its

Source: Jennifer Reingold in New York, "MobileMedia: Anatomy of a Bankruptcy," *Business Week:* March 17, 1997.

name taking Levi Strauss & Co. private in 1988. H&F poured $180 million into MobileMedia, owned a controlling interest in the stock, and dominated the board, which changed CEOs three times in three years but still failed to avert disaster. H&F, which sat on paper profits of $347 million in the months after MobileMedia's June, 1995, IPO, referred all questions to a MobileMedia spokesman. The three former CEOs either could not be reached or declined to answer most questions publicly.

In theory, the acquisition strategy made sense. From a fragmented, local industry, paging was quickly becoming a business of scale. Since 1982, the top 10 companies have moved from a 28% market share to an estimated 70% in 1996. Convinced they needed an executive with broader experience to make MobileMedia a dominant player, the board brought in Rorke in October, 1994, replacing CEO Charles J. Payer, Jr. With no telecommunications experience, Rorke, who had turned around Washington Post Co.'s Kaplan Educational Centers Ltd., was supposed to bring strategic thinking to his new job.

In August, 1995, Rorke completed his first acquisition, snapping up Dial Page Inc.'s paging operations for $189 million. That was just a warmup. A month later, the company announced it would buy BellSouth Corp.'s paging arm, MobileComm. The $930 million deal doubled MobileMedia's subscriber base to more than 4 million and made it No. 2 in the industry, behind Paging Network Inc. Although MobileComm's subscriber growth rates had slowed, investors were thrilled: On Sept. 15, MobileMedia stock hit its all-time high of 29¼.

There was no shortage of heavy hitters willing to help fund the deal. In November, the company raised $355 million through a secondary offering at 23¾ a share led by Lehman Brothers Inc. and issued $250 million in subordinated debt. The next month it opened a $750 million credit line with a Chase Manhattan–led group of banks, pushing debt to nearly five times cash flow at the company, which lost $44 million in 1995. Says Glenn W. Marschel, CEO of Paging Network: "They overpaid."

Even worse, merging the two companies proved tougher than anyone expected. A customer service center in Dallas, one of two sites where Rorke hoped to consolidate MobileComm's 26 centers, choked on its share of the company's 1.8 million new subscribers. Operators sat around waiting for calls that were never patched through, and customer service rapidly deteriorated. "You could page yourself and it would take seven to 10 minutes," says Kenneth A. Toudouze, a Dallas securities analyst and MobileMedia customer.

Former executives acknowledge they underestimated the problems. And, in the rush to meet Wall Street's growth expectations, MobileMedia kept adding new customers: 300,000 in the first half of 1996 alone. Meanwhile, customer turnover rose to 3.8% in the first quarter, from 3.6% in 1995's fourth quarter. Despite the growing difficulties, former executives said they had no signal the board was worried.

RED FLAG

The numbers should have told the story: MobileMedia's operating cash flow fell from $50.5 million in the fourth quarter of 1995 to $43.6 million in the first quarter of 1996. Nevertheless, MobileMedia's May 13 press release—reporting record first-quarter revenues—was titled "Acquisition integration running ahead of schedule."

So, it seems, were expenses. Just three weeks later, on June 6, MobileMedia announced a private stock offering to help pay skyrocketing integration costs that helped push MobileMedia's overhead expenses up 50% in the first quarter. Shares fell 19%, to about 14. On June 26, with cash flow stalled, MobileMedia was forced to ask bank lenders to loosen the covenants on its line of credit. Predictably, missed supplier payments followed, including some to its primary pager supplier, Motorola Inc.

That finally kicked the board into action. In late July, H&F general partners John L. Bunce Jr. and Mitchell R. Cohen flew to New Jersey and, insiders say, fired Rorke. MobileMedia says he resigned. "The reaction was to shoot [Rorke]," says a creditor. "That caused the company to go into a tailspin." Two other top execs soon followed. In the aftermath, the offering was halted, and H&F heavyweight F. Warren Hellman joined the board. Board member David A. Bayer, a frequent co-investor with H&F, became acting chairman and CEO.

Two weeks later, Bayer announced CEO No. 3: Michael K. Lorelli, then president of the Americas Div. at Tambrands Inc. and a former PepsiCo Inc. marketer. The choice of a marketing specialist surprised some, given the financial crisis. Still, analysts remained upbeat. In the last week of August, both Smith Barney Inc. and Lehman reaffirmed their buy recommendations. But it soon became obvious that Lorelli was a bad fit. "The agenda of the CEO's office changed very substantially since my first conversations with the board," he says. "Lorelli was a deer in the headlights," says a supplier. On Nov. 19, after less than three months on the job, Lorelli resigned, collecting an exit package of almost $1 million.

Before leaving, Lorelli dropped another bombshell. On Sept. 27, the company announced that it had discovered "certain errors" in its FCC licensing applications. In applying for approval to expand, the company had overstated the number of transmitters it had in place, a violation of FCC rules that could result in heavy fines. If nothing else, the errors show the degree of chaos at MobileMedia. Motorola stopped shipping equipment in November and MobileMedia filed for *Chapter 11* on Jan. 30.

The aftershocks have been felt far and wide. Although creditors have approved payments to Motorola and a few other key suppliers, others were not so lucky. Greg L. Reyes, CEO of Wireless Access Inc., a Santa Clara, California, developer of next-generation pagers, doesn't expect to see the $700,000 MobileMedia owes his company anytime soon, part of the reason Wireless postponed its own IPO. Unsecured creditors hold some $500 million worth of bonds now trading at less than a fifth of their original value. Shareholders have filed suit against MobileMedia and Lehman, alleging the brokerage was too upbeat about the paging industry. Lehman analyst John L. Bauer III left the brokerage in October and could not be reached for comment.

While MobileMedia still has more than 4 million subscribers, its challenges are formidable. Rivals have swooped in to capture market share. Forced to abandon plans to

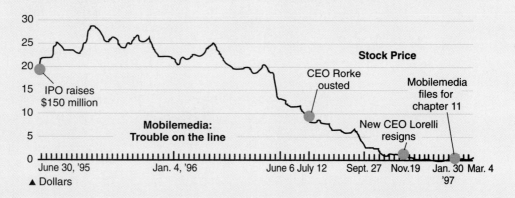

upgrade its technology, the company risks falling behind. Chief executive No. 4, Ronald R. Grawert, who was hired from GTE Corp. on Feb. 10, has a strong technology background, but that may not be enough. "There's been a gap in serious management," says one analyst. "It's a real mess."

In the end, the H&F-dominated board remains the only constant at MobileMedia. "It was said what they touch turns to gold," says a former executive. "I'm sure they're not proud of what's happened." In a statement, Bayer, who is still chairman, acknowledged mistakes. "In retrospect," he said, "the timeline for the integration of the two companies was too aggressive and there were differences between the companies that were not fully accounted for." Translation: We blew it.

8

STRATEGIC ANALYSIS AND CHOICE IN SINGLE- OR DOMINANT-PRODUCT BUSINESSES: BUILDING SUSTAINABLE COMPETITIVE ADVANTAGES

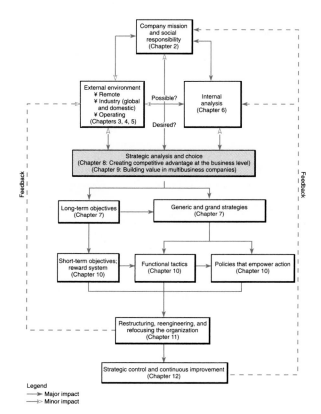

Strategic analysis and choice is the phase of the strategic management process when business managers examine and choose a business strategy that allows their business to sustain or create a sustainable competitive advantage. Their starting point is to evaluate and determine which value chain activities provide the basis for distinguishing the firm in the customer's mind from other reasonable alternatives. Businesses with a dominant product or service line must also choose among alternate grand strategies to guide the firm's activities, particularly when they are trying to decide about broadening the scope of the firm's activities beyond its core business.

This chapter examines strategic analysis and choice in single- or dominant-product/ service businesses by addressing two basic issues:

1. **What strategies are most effective at building sustainable competitive advantages for single business units?** What competitive strategy positions a business most effectively in its industry? For example, Scania, the most productive truck manufacturer in the world, joins its major rival Volvo as two anchors of Sweden's economy. Scania's return on sales of 9.9 percent far exceeds Mercedes (2.6 percent) and Volvo (2.5 percent), which it has achieved most of the last 60 years. Scania has built a sustainable competitive advantage with a strategy of focusing solely on heavy trucks, in a limited geographic area—Europe—and by providing customized trucks with standardized components (20,000 components per truck versus 25,000 for Volvo and 40,000 for Mercedes). Scania is a low-cost producer of a differentiated truck that can be custom-manufactured quickly and sold to a regionally focused market.

2. **Should dominant-product/service businesses diversify** to build value and competitive advantage? What grand strategies are most appropriate? For example, Compaq Computers and Coca-Cola managers have examined the question of diversification and apparently concluded that continued concentration on their core products and services and development of new markets for those same core products and services are best. IBM and Pepsi examined the same question and concluded that related diversification and vertical integration were best. Why?

EVALUATING AND CHOOSING BUSINESS STRATEGIES: SEEKING SUSTAINED COMPETITIVE ADVANTAGE

Business managers evaluate and choose strategies that they think will make their business successful. Businesses become successful because they possess some advantage relative to their competitors. The two most prominent sources of competitive advantage can be found in the business's cost structure and its ability to differentiate the business from competitors. Disney World in Orlando offers theme park patrons several unique, distinct features that differentiate it from other entertainment options. Wal-Mart offers retail customers the lowest prices on popular consumer items because they have created a low-cost structure resulting in a competitive advantage over most competitors.

Businesses that create competitive advantages from one or both of these sources usually experience above-average profitability within their industry. Businesses that lack a cost or differentiation advantage usually experience average or below-average profitability. Two recent studies found that businesses that do not have either form of competitive advantage perform the poorest among their peers while businesses that possess both forms of competitive advantage enjoy the highest levels of profitability within their industry.[1] The average return on investment for over 2,500 businesses across seven industries looked as follows:

Differentiation Advantage	Cost Advantage	Overall Average ROI across Seven Industries
High	High	35.0%
Low	High	26.0
High	Low	22.0
Low	Low	9.5

Initially, managers were advised to evaluate and choose strategies that emphasized one type of competitive advantage. Often referred to as *generic strategies,* firms were encouraged to become either a differentiation-oriented or low-cost-oriented company. In so doing, it was logical that organizational members would develop a clear understanding of company priorities and, as these studies suggest, likely experience profitability superior to competitors without either a differentiation or low-cost orientation.

The studies mentioned above, and the experience of many other businesses, indicate that the highest profitability levels are found in businesses that possess both types of competitive advantage at the same time. In other words, businesses that have one or more value chain activities that truly differentiate them from key competitors and also have value chain activities that let them operate at a lower cost will consistently outperform their rivals that don't. So the challenge for today's business managers is to evaluate and choose business strategies based on core competencies and value chain activities that sustain both types of competitive advantage simultaneously. Global Strategy in Action 8–1 shows Honda Motor Company attempting to do just this in the new millennium.

Evaluating Cost Leadership Opportunities

Business success built on cost leadership requires the business to be able to provide its product or service at a cost below what its competitors can achieve. And it must be a sustainable cost advantage. Through the skills and resources identified in Figure 8–1, a business must be able to accomplish one or more activities in its value chain activities—procuring materials, processing them into products, marketing the products, and distributing the products or support activities—in a more cost-effective manner than that of its competitors or it must be able to reconfigure its value chain so as to achieve a cost advantage. Figure 8–1 provides examples of ways this might be done.

Strategists examining their business's value chain for low-cost leadership advantages evaluate the sustainability of those advantages by *benchmarking* (refer to Chapter 6 for a discussion of this comparison technique) their business against key competitors and by considering the impact of any cost advantage on the five forces in

---

[1]R. B. Robinson and J. A. Pearce, "Planned Patterns of Strategic Behavior and Their Relationship to Business Unit Performance," *Strategic Management Journal* 9, no. 1 (1988), pp. 43–60; G. G. Dess and A. Miller, *Strategic Management* (New York: McGraw-Hill, 1993), pp. 110–11.

BusinessWeek

HONDA: EVALUATING LOW-COST AND DIFFERENTIATION OPPORTUNITIES

GLOBAL STRATEGY IN ACTION 8–1

For the last decade, Honda Motor Co. has been the carmaker that could do no wrong. By almost any measure—sales, profits, market share—Japan's No. 3 carmaker is one of the country's few winners. Honda closed in on the rear bumper of titan Toyota Motor Corp. and raced ahead of rivals such as Mitsubishi Motors Corp. In the U. S., it built such a successful franchise that customers now demand more Accords than the carmaker can pump out of its Marysville (Ohio) plant. And as a latecomer to Southeast Asia, it has escaped the region's free fall mostly unscathed. As a result, Honda posted record profits of $1.8 billion on revenues of $41 billion for the year ended last March.

That's the legacy left for Hiroyuki Yoshino, who took over as Honda's CEO this summer. Yoshino, 58, would like to maintain Honda's Midas touch through the millennium, but he couldn't be taking the helm at a worse time. Japan's economy is in recession, shrinking the market for cars there, and competition is increasing.

COST LEADERSHIP OPPORTUNITIES

To face these challenges Yoshino is trying to squeeze costs even more while counting on strong U.S. sales. And rather than build new factories, he's ramping up production at existing ones, despite being close to capacity. "First, we will try to increase production by strengthening our existing operations," says Yoshino.

Yet some analysts worry that there are few places left to squeeze. In the past, Honda has been able to reduce production costs by as much as 30%. But that leaves little to cut. More than 80% of Honda's cars are built from the same bases, and many share as much as 60% of the same parts. "They can only milk the existing platforms so much more," says Stephen Usher, automotive analyst at Jardine Fleming Securities.

That means in order to cut costs, Yoshino, who trained as an aeronautical engineer and oversaw research and development before becoming CEO, may need a technological breakthrough. Yoshino wants to implement flexible production methods that will enable the company to keep profitable small-car and small-volume operations. But no one is sure how this will be done.

Honda is now selling all the cars it can make in the U.S., where its $19,500 Accord is the top-selling car. It recently launched a new near-luxury Acura TL sedan and its largest vehicle—the 3.5-liter, V-6 engine Odyssey minivan, which sell in the $20,000 to $30,000 range. With those launches, Honda will be able to produce nearly 1 million vehicles in North America annually.

Source: "Honda: A Heckuva Time to Switch Drivers," *Business Week:* August 31, 1998, p. 42.

their business's competitive environment. Low-cost activities that are sustainable and that provide one or more of these advantages relative to key industry forces should become the basis for the business's competitive strategy.[2]

Low-Cost Advantages That Reduce the Likelihood of Pricing Pressure from Buyers When key competitors cannot match prices from the low-cost leader, customers pressuring the leader risk establishing a price level that drives alternate sources out of business.

---

[2]G. G. Dess and A. Miller, *Strategic Management* (New York: McGraw Hill, 1993), p. 116.

continued

Yoshino has the flexibility of cranking up overtime assembly, which could push production to 1.2 million by 2000.

DIFFERENTIATION OPPORTUNITIES

The new, larger minivan for the U.S., the size of a Dodge Caravan, is part of Honda's strategy of developing vehicles suited for the world's diverging car markets. In Europe, it's the opposite tack—a fleet of smaller cars as part of its "small is smart" strategy. Honda now plans to boost European capacity 40%, to 250,000 vehicles per year by 2000.

Skeptical analysts think Yoshino may have a hard time making money in Europe. Standard & Poor's DRI forecasts that Honda's market share will climb from 1.6% this year to 2.2% in 2002 after Honda makes inroads into Europe's market with a new 2.0-liter compact car later this year. But price competition in compact cars will be brutal. "With that volume, there is no way they can make money in Europe," says Koji Endo, automotive analyst at Schroders Japan Ltd.

First, though, Honda needs to prove it can keep the market share it won last year at home. "Honda gained share because it had good cars and its dealers cooperated," says Toshio Nakata, president of the Honda Clio Tokyo dealership. "Now we have to work even more closely together to make sure these new customers are satisfied and continue to drive Honda cars." Led by the $9,590 Capa, a hip, ultrasmall minivan, and the $12,330 Stepwagon sport-utility, Honda continues to gain ground with fashion-conscious young buyers. It racked up 7% more car sales in July, even though the market overall slid by 8.4%.

In a scramble to woo buyers in a recession, carmakers plan to launch 64 new cars this year in Japan, more than twice last year's number, estimates Jardine Fleming Securities. Toyota plans a new, aggressively styled compact car. It will also slash the car's production cost by 30%, compared with its previous compact models. Yoshino revised Honda's calendar-year sales target for Japan down to 764,000 cars from 810,000. Honda will not easily suffer defeat, however. The company aims to repeat last year's success by counterattacking with two new minicars, a classy SSM sports car, and a new subcompact sport-utility.

Despite the tough road ahead, Yoshino is making it clear he thinks Honda can make it as a nimble player. He says Honda will not pursue any megamergers like the Daimler-Chrysler tie-up, nor will it invest aggressively in more capacity worldwide. Instead, Yoshino plans to follow a contrarian strategy of going it alone at a time when the rest of the world's auto heavies are joining forces. And, make no mistake about it, he wants to take them head-on.

Truly Sustained Low-Cost Advantages May Push Rivals into Other Areas, Lessening Price Competition Intense, continued price competition may be ruinous for all rivals, as seen occasionally in the airline industry.

New Entrants Competing on Price Must Face an Entrenched Cost Leader without the Experience to Replicate Every Cost Advantage Delite entered the fast-food market with great fanfare in the 1980s as the first low-fat fast-food chain emphasizing salads and lean hamburgers. Wendy's simply expanded its inexpensive salad bar and, already serving fresh lean meat, quickly saw Delite disappear from NASDAQ. Delite could not begin to match Wendy's cost structure, built on inbound logistics and lower location costs, and still charge a price close to what Wendy's charged for lean, fresh fast food.

FIGURE 8-1
Evaluating a Business's Cost Leadership Opportunities

A. Skills and Resources That Foster Cost Leadership

Sustained capital investment and access to capital.
Process engineering skills.
Intense supervision of labor or core technical operations.
Products or services designed for ease of manufacture or delivery.
Low-cost distribution system.

B. Organizational Requirements to Support and Sustain Cost Leadership Activities

Tight cost control.
Frequent, detailed control reports.
Continuous improvement and benchmarking orientation.
Structured organization and responsibilities.
Incentives based on meeting strict, usually quantitative targets.

C. Examples of Ways Businesses Achieve Competitive Advantage via Cost Leadership

Technology Development	Process innovations that lower production costs.		Product redesign to reduce the number of components.		
Human Resource Management	Safety training for all employees reduces absenteeism, downtime, and accidents.				
General Administration	Reduced levels of management cuts corporate overhead.		Computerized, integrated information system reduces errors and administrative costs.		
Procurement	Favorable long-term contracts; captive suppliers or key customer for supplier.				
	Global, online suppliers provide automatic restocking of orders based on our sales.	Economy of scale in plant reduces equipment costs and depreciation.	Computerized routing lowers transportation expense.	Cooperative advertising with distributors creates local cost advantage in buying media space and time.	Subcontracted service technicians repair product correctly the first time or they bear all costs.
	Inbound logistics	Operations	Outbound logistics	Marketing and Sales	Service

Profit margin

Source: Adapted with permission of The Free Press, a Division of Simon and Schuster, from *Competitive Advantage: Creating and Sustaining Superior Performance,* by Michael E. Porter. Copyright © 1985 by Michael E. Porter.

Low-Cost Advantages Should Lessen the Attractiveness of Substitute Products A serious concern of any business is the threat of a substitute product in which buyers can meet their original need. Low-cost advantages allow the holder to resist this happening because it allows them to remain competitive even against desirable substitutes and it allows them to lessen concerns about price facing an inferior, lower priced substitute.

Higher Margins Allow Low-Cost Producers to Withstand Supplier Cost Increases and Often Gain Supplier Loyalty over Time Sudden, particularly uncontrollable increases in the costs suppliers face can be more easily absorbed by low-cost, higher margin producers. Severe droughts in California quadrupled the price of lettuce—a key restaurant demand. Some chains absorbed the cost; others had to confuse customers with a "lettuce tax."

Furthermore, chains that worked well with produce suppliers gained a loyal, cooperative "partner" for possible assistance in a future, competitive situation.

Once managers identify opportunities to create cost advantage–based strategies, they must consider whether key risks inherent in cost leadership are present in a way that may mediate sustained success. The key risks with which they must be concerned are discussed next.

Many Cost-Saving Activities Are Easily Duplicated Computerizing certain order entry functions among hazardous waste companies gave early adopters lower sales costs and better customer service for a brief time. Rivals quickly adapted, adding similar capabilities with similar impacts on their costs.

Exclusive Cost Leadership Can Become a Trap Firms that emphasize lowest price and can offer it via cost advantages where product differentiation is increasingly not considered must truly be convinced of the sustainability of those advantages. Particularly with commodity-type products, the low-cost leader seeking to sustain a margin superior to lesser rivals may encounter increasing customer pressure for lower prices with great damage to both leader and lesser players.

Obsessive Cost Cutting Can Shrink Other Competitive Advantages Involving Key Product Attributes Intense cost scrutiny can build margin, but it can reduce opportunities for or investment in innovation—processes and products. Similarly, such scrutiny can lead to the use of inferior raw materials, processes, or activities that were previously viewed by customers as a key attribute of the original products. Some mail-order computer companies that sought to maintain or enhance cost advantages found reductions in telephone service personnel and automation of that function backfiring with a drop in demand for their products even though their low prices were maintained.

Cost Differences Often Decline over Time As products age, competitors learn how to match cost advantages. Absolute volumes sold often decline. Market channels and suppliers mature. Buyers become more knowledgeable. All of these factors present opportunities to lessen the value or presence of earlier cost advantages. Said another way, cost advantages that are not sustainable over a period of time are risky.

Once business managers have evaluated the cost structure of their value chain, determined activities that provide competitive cost advantages, and considered their inherent risks, they start choosing the business's strategy. Those managers concerned with differentiation-based strategies, or those seeking optimum performance incorporating both sources of competitive advantage, move to evaluating their business's sources of differentiation.

Evaluating Differentiation Opportunities

Differentiation requires that the business have sustainable advantages that allow it to provide buyers with something uniquely valuable to them. A successful differentiation strategy allows the business to provide a product or service of perceived higher value to buyers at a "differentiation cost" below the "value premium" to the buyers. In other words, the buyer feels the additional cost to buy the product or service is well below what the product or service is worth compared to other available alternatives.

Differentiation usually arises from one or more activities in the value chain that create a unique value important to buyers. Perrier's control of a carbonated water spring in France, Stouffer's frozen food packaging and sauce technology, Apple's highly integrated chip designs in its Mac computers, American Greeting Card's automated inventory system for retailers, and Federal Express's customer service capabilities are all examples of sustainable advantages around which successful differentiation strategies have been built. A business can achieve differentiation by performing its existing value activities or reconfiguring in some unique way. And the sustainability of that differentiation will depend on two things—a continuation of its high perceived value to buyers and a lack of imitation by competitors.

Figure 8–2 suggests key skills that managers should ensure are present to support an emphasis on differentiation. Examples of value chain activities that provide a differentiation advantage are also provided.

Strategists examining their business's value chain for differentiation advantages evaluate the sustainability of those advantages by *benchmarking* (refer to Chapter 6 for a discussion of this comparison technique) their business against key competitors and by considering the impact of any differentiation advantage on the five forces in their business's competitive environment. Sustainable activities that provide one or more of the following opportunities relative to key industry forces should become the basis for differentiation aspects of the business's competitive strategy:

Rivalry Is Reduced When a Business Successfully Differentiates Itself BMW's new Z23 made in Greer, South Carolina, does not compete with Saturns made in central Tennessee. A Harvard education does not compete with a local technical school. Both situations involve the same basic needs, transportation or education. However, one rival has clearly differentiated itself from others in the minds of certain buyers. In so doing, they do not have to respond competitively to that competitor.

Buyers Are Less Sensitive to Prices for Effectively Differentiated Products The Highlands Inn in Carmel, California, and the Ventana Inn along the Big Sur charge a minimum of $400 per night for a room with a kitchen, fireplace, hot tub, and view. Other places are available along this beautiful stretch of California's spectacular coastline, but occupancy rates at these two locations remain over 90 percent. Why? You can't get a better view and a more relaxed, spectacular setting to spend a few days on the Pacific Coast. Similarly, buyers of differentiated products tolerate price increases low-cost–oriented buyers would not accept. The former become very loyal to certain brands.

Brand Loyalty Is Hard for New Entrants to Overcome Many new beers are brought to market in the United States, but Budweiser continues to gain market share. Why? Brand loyalty is hard to overcome! And Anheuser-Busch has been clever to extend its brand loyalty from its core brand into newer niches, like nonalcohol brews, that other potential entrants have pioneered.

Managers examining differentiation-based advantages must take potential risks into account as they commit their business to these advantages. Some of the more common ways risks arise are discussed next.

Imitation Narrows Perceived Differentiation, Rendering Differentiation Meaningless AMC pioneered the Jeep passenger version of a truck 40 years ago. Ford created the Explorer, or luxury utility vehicle, in 1990. It took luxury car features and put them inside a jeep. Ford's payoff was substantial. The Explorer has become Ford's most popular domestic vehicle. However, virtually every vehicle manufacturer offered a luxury utility in 1997, with customers beginning to be hard pressed to identify clear distinctions between lead models. Ford's Explorer managers were looking for a new business strategy for the next decade that relied on new sources of differentiation and placed greater emphasis on low-cost components in their value chain.

FIGURE 8-2
Evaluating a Business's Differentiation Opportunities

A. Skills and Resources That Foster Differentiation

Strong marketing abilities.
Product engineering.
Creative talent and flair.
Strong capabilities in basic research.
Corporate reputation for quality or technical leadership.
Long tradition in an industry or unique combination of skills drawn from other businesses.
Strong cooperation from channels.
Strong cooperation from suppliers of major components of the product or service.

B. Organizational Requirements to Support and Sustain Differentiation Activities

Strong coordination among functions in R&D, product development, and marketing.
Subjective measurement and incentives instead of quantitative measures.
Amenities to attract highly skilled labor, scientists, and creative people.
Tradition of closeness to key customers.
Some personnel skilled in sales and operations—technical and marketing.

C. Examples of Ways Businesses Achieve Competitive Advantage via Differentiation

Technology Development	Cutting-edge production technology and product features to maintain a distinct image and actual product.
Human Resource Management	Programs to ensure technical competence of sales staff and a marketing orientation of service personnel.
General Administration	Comprehensive, personalized database to build knowledge of groups of customers and individual buyers to be used in customizing how products are sold, serviced, and replaced.
Procurement	Quality control presence at key supplier facilities; work with suppliers' new product development activities

Inbound logistics	Operations	Outbound logistics	Marketing and Sales	Service
Purchase superior quality, well-known components, raising the quality and image of final products.	Careful inspection of products at each step in production to improve product performance and lower defect rate.	JIT coordination with buyers; use of own or captive transportation service to ensure timeliness.	Expensive, informative advertising and promotion to build brand image.	Allowing service personnel considerable discretion to credit customers for repairs.

Profit margin

Source: Adapted with permission of The Free Press, a division of Simon and Schuster, from *Competitive Advantage: Creating and Sustaining Superior Performance,* by Michael E. Porter. Copyright © 1985 by Michael E. Porter.

Technological Changes That Nullify Past Investments or Learning The Swiss controlled over 95 percent of the world's watch market into the 1970s. The bulk of the craftspeople, technology, and infrastructure resided in Switzerland. U.S.-based Texas Instruments decided to experiment with the use of its digital technology in watches. Swiss producers were not interested.

The Cost Difference between Low-Cost Competitors and the Differentiated Business Becomes Too Great for Differentiation to Hold Brand Loyalty Buyers may begin to choose to sacrifice some of the features, services, or image possessed by the differentiated business for large cost savings. The rising cost of a college education, particularly at several "premier" institutions, has caused many students to opt for lower-cost destinations that offer very similar courses without image, frills, and professors that seldom teach undergraduate students anyway.

Evaluating Speed as a Competitive Advantage

While most telecommunication companies have used the last decade to leap aboard the information superhighway, GTE continued its impressive turnaround focusing on its core business—providing local telephone services. Long lagging behind the Baby Bells in profitability and efficiency, GTE has emphasized improving its poor customer service throughout the decade. The service was so bad in Santa Monica, California, that officials once tried to remove GTE as the local phone company. Candidly saying "we were the pits," new CEO Chuck Lee largely did away with its old system of taking customer service requests by writing them down and passing them along for resolution. Now, using personal communication services and specially designed software, service reps can solve 70 percent of all problems on the initial call—triple the success rate at the beginning of the last decade. Repair workers meanwhile plan their schedules on laptops, cutting downtime and speeding responses. CEO Lee has spent $1.5 billion on reengineering that slashed 17,000 jobs, replaced people with technology, and prioritized *speed* as the defining feature of GTE's business practices.

Speed, or rapid response to customer requests or market and technological changes, has become a major source of competitive advantage for numerous firms in today's intensely competitive global economy. Speed is certainly a form of differentiation, but it is more than that. Speed involves the *availability of a rapid response* to a customer by providing current products quicker, accelerating new product development or improvement, quickly adjusting production processes, and making decisions quickly. While low cost and differentiation may provide important competitive advantages, managers in tomorrow's successful companies will base their strategies on creating speed-based competitive advantages. Figure 8–3 describes and illustrates key skills and organizational requirements that are associated with speed-based competitive advantage. Jack Welch, the CEO who transformed General Electric from a fading company into one of Wall Street's best performers over the last 15 years, had this to say about speed:

> Speed is really the driving force that everyone is after. Faster products, faster product cycles to market. Better response time to customers. . . . Satisfying customers, getting faster communications, moving with more agility, all these things are easier when one is small. And these are all characteristics one needs in a fast-moving global environment.[3]

Speed-based competitive advantages can be created around several activities:

Customer Responsiveness All consumers have encountered hassles, delays, and frustration dealing with various businesses from time to time. The same holds true when dealing business to business. Quick response with answers, information, and solutions to mistakes can become the basis for competitive advantage . . . one that builds customer loyalty quickly.

Product Development Cycles Japanese car makers have focused intensely on the time it takes to create a new model because several experienced disappointing sales growth in the mid-1990s in Europe and North America competing against new vehicles like

---

[3]"Jack Welch on the Art of Thinking Small," *Business Week*, Enterprise 1993 issue, p. 212.

FIGURE 8-3
Evaluating a Business's Rapid Response (Speed) Opportunities

A. Skills and Resources That Foster Speed

Process engineering skills.
Excellent inbound and outbound logistics.
Technical people in sales and customer service.
High levels of automation.
Corporate reputation for quality or technical leadership.
Flexible manufacturing capabilities.
Strong downstream partners.
Strong cooperation from suppliers of major components of the product or service.

B. Organizational Requirements to Support and Sustain Rapid Response Activities

Strong coordination among functions in R&D, product development, and marketing.
Major emphasis on customer satisfaction in incentive programs.
Strong delegation to operating personnel.
Tradition of closeness to key customers.
Some personnel skilled in sales and operations—technical and marketing.
Empowered customer service personnel.

C. Examples of Ways Businesses Achieve Competitive Advantage via Speed

Technology Development	Use of companywide technology sharing activities and autonomous product development teams to speed new product development.				
Human Resource Management	Develop self-managed work teams and decision making at the lowest levels to increase responsiveness.				
General Administration	Highly automated and integrated information processing system. Include major buyers in the "system" on a real-time basis.				
Procurement	Preapproved, online suppliers integrated into production.				
	Working very closely with suppliers to include their choice of warehouse location to minimize delivery time.	Standardize dies, components, and production equipment to allow quick changeover to new or special orders.	JIT delivery plus partnering with express mail services to ensure very rapid delivery.	Use of laptops linked directly to operations to speed the order process and shorten the sales cycle.	Locate service technicians at customer facilities that are geographically close.
	Inbound logistics	Operations	Outbound logistics	Marketing and Sales	Service

(Profit margin)

Source: Adapted with permission of The Free Press, a Division of Simon and Schuster, from *Competitive Advantage: Creating and Sustaining Superior Performance,* by Michael E. Porter. Copyright © 1985 by Michael E. Porter.

Ford's Explorer and Renault's Megane. By 1997, Honda, Toyota, and Nissan had lowered the cycle from 24 months to 11 months from conception to production. This capability is old hat to 3M Corporation, which is so successful at speedy product development that one-fourth of its sales and profits each year are from products that didn't exist five years earlier.

Product or Service Improvements Like development time, companies that can rapidly adapt their products or services and do so in a way that benefits their customers or creates new customers have a major competitive advantage over rivals that cannot do this.

Speed in Delivery or Distribution Firms that can get you what you need when you need it, even when that is tomorrow, realize that buyers have come to expect that level of responsiveness. Federal Express's success reflects the importance customers place on speed in inbound and outbound logistics.

Information Sharing and Technology Speed in sharing information that becomes the basis for decisions, actions, or other important activities taken by a customer, supplier, or partner has become a major source of competitive advantage for many businesses. Telecommunications, the Internet, and networks are but a part of a vast infrastructure that is being used by knowledgeable managers to rebuild or create value in their businesses via information sharing.

These rapid response capabilities create competitive advantages in several ways. They create a way to lessen rivalry because they have *availability* of something that a rival may not have. It can allow the business to charge buyers more, engender loyalty, or otherwise enhance the business's position relative to its buyers. Particularly where impressive customer response is involved, businesses can generate supplier cooperation and concessions since their business ultimately benefits from increased revenue. Finally, substitute products and new entrants find themselves trying to keep up with the rapid changes rather than introducing them. Global Strategy in Action 8–2 describes key steps Procter & Gamble has recently taken to make speed, rather than cost leadership, its new core competence.

While the notion of speed-based competitive advantage is exciting, it has risks managers must consider. First, speeding up activities that haven't been conducted in a fashion that prioritizes rapid response should only be done after considerable attention to training, reorganization, and/or reengineering. Second, some industries—stable, mature ones that have very minimal levels of change—may not offer much advantage to the firm that introduces some forms of rapid response. Customers in such settings may prefer the slower pace or the lower costs currently available or they may have long time frames in purchasing such that speed is not that important to them.

Evaluating Market Focus as a Way to Competitive Advantage

Small companies, at least the better ones, usually thrive because they serve narrow market niches. This is usually called *focus,* the extent to which a business concentrates on a narrowly defined market. Take the example of Soho Beverages, a business former Pepsi manager Tom Cox bought from Seagram after Seagram had acquired it and was unable to make it thrive. The tiny brand, once a healthy niche product in New York and a few other east coast locations, muddled within Seagrams because its sales force was unused to selling in delis. Cox was able to double sales in one year. He did this on a lean marketing budget that didn't include advertising or database marketing. He hired Korean- and Arabic-speaking college students and had his people walk into practically every deli in Manhattan in order to reacquaint owners with the brand, spot consumption trends, and take orders. He provided rapid stocking services to all Manhattan-area delis, regardless of size. The business has continued sales growth at over 50 percent per year. Why? Cox says "It is attributable to focusing on a niche market, delis; differentiating the product and its sales force; achieving low costs in promotion and delivery; and making rapid, immediate response to any deli owner request its normal practice."

Two things are important in this example. First, this business focused on a narrow niche market in which to build a strong competitive advantage. But focus alone was not enough to build competitive advantage. Rather, Cox created several value chain activities that achieved differentiation, low-cost, and rapid response competitive advantages within this niche market that would be hard for other firms, particularly mass market–oriented firms, to replicate.

Focus allows some businesses to compete on the basis of low cost, differentiation, and rapid response against much larger businesses with greater resources. Focus lets a business "learn" its target customers—their needs, special considerations they want accommodated—and establish personal relationships in ways that "differentiate" the smaller firm or make it more valuable to the target customer. Low costs can also be achieved filling niche needs in a buyer's operations that larger rivals either do not want to bother with or cannot do as cost effectively. Cost advantage often centers around the high level of customized service the focused, smaller business can provide. And perhaps the greatest competitive weapon that can arise is rapid response. With enhanced knowledge of its customers and intricacies of their operations, the small, focused company builds up organizational knowledge about timing sensitive ways to work with a customer. Often the needs of that narrow set of customers represent a large part of the small, focused business's revenues. Global Strategy in Action 8–3 illustrates how Sweden's Scania has become the global leader in heavy trucks via the focused application of low cost, differentiation, and speed.

The risk of focus is that you attract major competitors that have waited for your business to "prove" the market. Domino's proved that a huge market for pizza delivery existed and now faces serious challenges. Likewise, publicly traded focused companies become takeover targets for large firms seeking to fill out a product portfolio. And perhaps the greatest risk of all is slipping into the illusion that it is focus itself, and not some special form of low cost, differentiation, or rapid response, that is creating the business's success.

Managers evaluating opportunities to build competitive advantage should link strategies to value chain activities that exploit low cost, differentiation, and rapid response competitive advantages. When advantageous, they should consider ways to use focus to leverage these advantages. One way business managers can enhance their likelihood of identifying these opportunities is to consider several different "generic" industry environments from the perspective of the typical value chain activities most often linked to sustained competitive advantages in those unique industry situations. The next section discusses five key generic industry environments and the value chain activities most associated with success.

SELECTED INDUSTRY ENVIRONMENTS AND BUSINESS STRATEGY CHOICES

The analysis and choice of the ways a business will seek to build competitive advantage can be enhanced when managers take industry conditions into account. Chapters 3 and 5 discussed ways to examine industry conditions, so we do not repeat that here. Likewise, Chapter 6 showed how the market life cycle concept can be used to examine business strengths. What is important to recognize as managers evaluate opportunities to emphasize a narrow set of core competencies and potential competitive advantages is that different sets appear to be more useful in different, unique industry environments. We examine five "typical" industry settings and opportunities for generating competitive advantages that strategists should look for in their deliberations. Three of these five settings relate to industry life cycle. Managers use these as ways to

VODAFONE USES *SPEED AND FOCUS* TO BUILD A GLOBAL CELLULAR PHONE EMPIRE AHEAD OF GLOBAL TELECOMMUNICATION GIANTS LIKE AT&T, SPRINT, AND BRITISH TELECOMMUNICATION

BusinessWeek

GLOBAL STRATEGY IN ACTION 8–2

Vodaphone, a small British military electronics firm called Racal-Vodaphone, landed Britain's first cellular license in 1983. Five years later its IPO in 1988 raised the funds it needed to stave off a challenge by British Telecommunication's mobile operator, Cellnet.

Now a dominant player in the U.K., Vodaphone is quickly becoming a global leader in the cellular industry. It continues, at each step in its development, to use speed and focus as the centerpiece of its strategy to achieve global success. This Strategy in Action tells how Vodaphone is doing this.

SPEED

As a public-relations stunt, it would have been a tad heavy-handed. But there was Vodafone Group PLC chief executive Chris C. Gent, orchestrating the biggest merger in the history of the mobile phone industry—via cell phone from Australia. It started over New Year's weekend, when word got out that Bell Atlantic Corp. was offering $45 billion for AirTouch Communications Inc., the largest independent U.S. mobile company. Gent, watching cricket down under, didn't fuss with flights back to London. He simply pressed the call button and started talking. By Jan. 3, he had put together his own $55 billion stock and cash offer for AirTouch. If it goes through, as analysts now expect, Vodafone, Europe's leading mobile phone company, could become the first global giant of the wireless age. "Sizewise, nobody else would come anywhere near," says Jonathan Lewis, Dresdner Kleinwort Benson Inc. telecom analyst.

A Vodafone-AirTouch team would create a titan with annual sales of $10 billion. At current valuations, its capitalization of $105 billion would rank it third in Britain. More important, by consuming AirTouch, which is strong in Europe's booming south, Gent would enjoy supremacy in Europe's cellular-phone market, the world's biggest At the same time, he would acquire 8.5 million U.S. customers in California.

FOCUS

The result of the deal would be a wireless empire, one entirely focused on a mobile phone business projected to double, globally, to 550 million subscribers within two years, according to International Data Corp. This is a heady time for Gent. The 50-year-old marketing maven was dreaming of cellular as a global business way back when the unwieldy gadgets were more like police radios. Now the global business is taking shape—and he may wind up running it.

Vodafone's European roots give Gent a technical edge over American competitors, such as AT&T and Sprint Corp. That's because the cellular industry is preparing to launch the next generation of cell phones within two or three years—and the new system should open in Britain shortly after Japan, a year or two before reaching the U.S. This so-called third generation would

Source: Stephen Baker in Paris and Kerry Capell in London, "Vodafone Calling," *Business Week:* January 25, 1999.

evaluate their value chain activities and then select the ones around which it is most critical to build competitive advantage.[4]

---

[4]These industry characterizations draw heavily on the work of Michael E. Porter, *Competitive Advantage: Creating and Sustaining Superior Performance* (New York: Free Press, 1985).

continued

BusinessWeek

enable users to send E-mail, download stereo compact discs, and even video-conference on mobile phones. With cell-phone rates falling by 10% to 20% annually in most markets, the move to third generation is vital: It promises crucial new markets for handheld devices. But for Vodafone and other cell-phone operators, the switch to the third generation requires multibillion-dollar investments on costly licenses and infrastructure—"a fair old sum," Gent calls it. He is determined to spend it, even with only the sketchiest notion of return.

SPEED

Vodafone seemed to be losing ground to aggressive newcomers when Gent, who had been developing Vodafone's international portfolio, took over as CEO in early 1997. He immediately canned the old ad agency and set about building a network of 250 company stores in towns and villages throughout Britain. The idea: to build brand recognition and neighborhood service that would keep customers, especially business users, loyal to Vodafone. Gent's timing couldn't have been better. He had Vodafone ready just as Britain's market was taking off. In the last two years, the combination of lower prices and a booming economy have fueled cell-phone mania in Britain—a phenomenon that Gent and others expect to hit the U.S. soon. Last year alone, British subscriptions grew by 53%, to 13 million, or 22.4% of the population.

SPEED & FOCUS

The phenomenal growth is rooted in the ABCs of the phone business. The company bids high and early for cellular licenses, builds market share while holding down costs, and focuses on rich business customers. The formula runs like a cash-generating machine—which is what gave Gent the opportunity to follow Britain's Vodafone-sponsored cricket team to Australia. In fact, after making the bid for AirTouch, he stayed to watch a four-day match.

Already, Vodafone and AirTouch know each other well, although they hardly seem like a close match culturally. Vodafone, with its history as a military supplier, is known as a tightly run ship, while AirTouch says an executive at its Spanish affiliate, "is California loose, with no dress code." The two are partners in a Swedish joint venture and were mulling over a merger last summer, say analysts, but could not reach agreement on a price. Bell Atlantic, as it turns out, set the price for them. And for Chris Gent, the move to become leader of the wireless world was simply a matter of fishing a cell phone out of his pocket, and putting it to use.

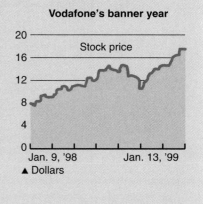

Vodafone's banner year

Stock price

20
16
12
8
4
0

Jan. 9, '98   Jan. 13, '99
▲ Dollars

Competitive Advantage in Emerging Industries

Emerging industries are newly formed or re-formed industries that typically are created by technological innovation, newly emerging customer needs, or other economic or sociological changes. Emerging industries of the last decade have been the Internet browser, fiber optics, solar heating, cellular telephone, and on-line services industries.

SWEDEN'S SCANIA COMBINES LOW COST, SPEED, DIFFERENTIATION, AND FOCUS TO CONSISTENTLY BEAT OTHER GLOBAL TRUCK MANUFACTURERS

GLOBAL STRATEGY IN ACTION 8–3

The preeminent consulting firm McKinsey and Company recently studied the global truck industry to understand which producers had the strongest competitive advantages and why they did. It quickly became a study of the Swedish firm, Scania, and its long time rival, Volvo. On an index that measured value added per hour worked, Scania scored 100 with Volvo close behind. The best Japanese, U.S., and German truck makers trailed by more than 25 points.

Leif Ostling, Scania's burly CEO, attributes the business's success to a determination to stick to its strategy of concentrating on heavy trucks, and rely on its own resources to deliver quality products commanding market leading prices. McKinsey's analysis broadens the explanation as it sought an answer to how Scania had arrived at its enviable position and what its prospects were for remaining a world leader. McKinsey concluded:

1. Benchmarking: Intense competition between Scania and Volvo in tiny Sweden prepared them both to compete better than other rivals in the global market because the truck industry is much less international than the car industry, leaving newer rivals less competitive even on their home turf. Scania and Volvo have been benchmarking each other for years.

2. Low cost: Scania uses a building principle of maximization of standardization of parts across many brands while also leading the industry in responding to the demand for customization of each vehicle that is sold. How? While every truck is a unique order, Scania uses less than 20,000 components to build their truck compared to 25,000 for Volvo and 40,000 for Mercedes. Fewer parts mean lower development costs, lower manufacturing costs, and lower distribution costs.

3. Speed: Scania produces all main components in house, which allows them to maximize integration of design, development, and production, thus saving time, allowing for greater customization, and fewer parts.

4. Differentiation: There is strong emphasis on customization of each vehicle: "We have to supply a specific truck to a customer's specific needs," said Kaj Holmelius, head of chassis development, pointing to a production line, "Each of these is for a specific order and almost every one will be different in some way when they come off the end of the line. At the same time we want to get as large volumes as possible for individual components."

5. Focus: Scania will not expand into lighter trucks because it would dilute the efficiencies it has wrung out of its modular system. It has no plans to enter the North American market because of very different truck specifications and lower margins. The intention is to grow chiefly in Central and Eastern Europe and in the Pacific region. "We will stick to what we know how to do in limited, margin favorable markets," said Ostling.

The bottom line is, Scania has built a variety of sustainable competitive advantages that promise to keep it on top the world heavy truck market for a long time.

Sources: By Stanley Reed, with Ariane Sains, in Stockholm, "The Young Wallenbergs," *Business Week* International Edition: October 20, 1997; "Scania Pulls Ahead of the Crowd," *Financial Times,* October 16, 1995.

From the standpoint of strategy formulation, the essential characteristic of an emerging industry is that there are no "rules of the game." The absence of rules presents both a risk and an opportunity—a wise strategy positions the firm to favorably shape the emerging industry's rules.

Business strategies must be shaped to accommodate the following characteristics of markets in emerging industries.

Technologies that are mostly proprietary to the pioneering firms and technological uncertainty about how product standardization will unfold.

Competitor uncertainty because of inadequate information about competitors, buyers, and the timing of demand.

High initial costs but steep cost declines as the experience curve takes effect.

Few entry barriers, which often spurs the formation of many new firms.

First-time buyers requiring initial inducement to purchase and customers confused by the availability of a number of nonstandard products.

Inability to obtain raw materials and components until suppliers gear up to meet the industry's needs.

Need for high-risk capital because of the industry's uncertainty prospects.

For success in this industry setting, business strategies require one or more of these features:

1. The ability to *shape the industry's structure* based on the timing of entry, reputation, success in related industries or technologies, and role in industry associations.
2. The ability to *rapidly improve product quality* and performance features.
3. *Advantageous relationships* with key suppliers and promising distribution channels.
4. The ability to *establish the firm's technology as the dominant one* before technological uncertainty decreases.
5. The early acquisition of *a core group of loyal customers* and then the expansion of that customer base through model changes, alternative pricing, and advertising.
6. The ability to *forecast future competitors* and the strategies they are likely to employ.

A firm that has had repeated successes with business in emerging industries is 3M Corporation. In each of the last 20 years, over 25 percent of 3M's annual sales have come from products that did not exist 5 years earlier. Start-up companies enhance their success by having experienced entrepreneurs at the helm, a knowledgeable management team and board of directors, and patient sources of venture capital. Amazon.com's dramatic debut on Wall Street symbolically ushering in the emerging E-commerce industry era for investors will certainly lead to questions about the lasting competitive advantage at Amazon.com. Strategy in Action 8–1 examines whether Amazon.com has the capacity to prevail in this emerging industry.

Competitive Advantage in the Transition to Industry Maturity

As an industry evolves, its rate of growth eventually declines. This "transition to maturity" is accompanied by several changes in its competitive environment:

Competition for market share becomes more intense as firms in the industry are forced to achieve sales growth at one another's expense.

Firms in the industry sell increasingly to experienced, repeat buyers that are now making choices among known alternatives.

Competition becomes more oriented to cost and service as knowledgeable buyers expect similar price and product features.

DOES AMAZON.COM HAVE A SUSTAINABLE COMPETITIVE ADVANTAGE IN THE EMERGING "E-COMMERCE" INDUSTRY?

BusinessWeek

STRATEGY IN ACTION 8–1

When giant retailer Wal-Mart Stores Inc. sued upstart Internet bookseller Amazon.com Inc. in late 1998, jaws dropped. Wal-Mart accused Amazon of raiding its executives to steal its computerized merchandising and distribution trade secrets. The amazing part: Wal-Mart said tiny, money-losing Amazon had caused it "economic damage" and continues to do so. Regardless of the outcome, this case may well signal a watershed in the history of the Internet: the moment when cyberspace retailers began to turn the tables on earthly ones. Indeed, Amazon is blazing a trail in the world of commerce where no merchant has gone before.

Can it shape the E-commerce industry structure? By pioneering—and possibly perfecting—the art of selling online, it is forcing the titans of retail to scramble onto the Net. More than that it's jolting them into rethinking whether their traditional advantages—physical size, mass-media branding, and even the sensory appeal of shopping in stores—will be enough to thrive in the New Economy. Says Duke University marketing professor Martha Rogers: "Amazon is an example of how an upstart can redefine its whole industry."

Can it rapidly improve product quality & features? Consider this: Amazon offers an easily searchable trove of 3.1 million titles—15 times more than any bookstore on the planet and without the costly overhead of multimillion-dollar buildings and scads of store clerks. That paves the way for each of its 1,600 employees to generate, on average, $375,000 in annual revenues—almost four times that of No. 1 bricks-and-mortar bookseller Barnes & Noble Inc.'s 27,000 employees. It has 24 inventory turns per year versus 3 for Barnes & Noble, and high cash flow versus low cash flow at B&N.

Can its technology become the dominant one? Amazon's cutting-edge technology gives it a leg up, too, by automatically analyzing past purchases to make recommendations customized to each buyer—a trick that confounds 20th century mass marketing. And with a single mouse click, an order can be placed on its Web site, making shopping a friendly, frictionless, even fun experience that can take less time than finding a parking space at the mall.

Does it have a core group of loyal customers that might buy other things? It has a two-year head start, unheard of in the software industry, on key software that handles millions of transactions and personalizes the customers' experience. It gathers instant information on customer preferences to help understand what else [books and other things] they might want to buy. "We want Amazon.com to be the right store for you as an individual," says founder Jeffrey Bezos. "If we have 4.5 million customers, we should have 4.5 million stores."

While these observations seem favorable, Merrill Lynch analyst Jonathan Cohen is not. "The company has been able to show it can sell lots of books for less without making money," he says, "and now it has shown it can sell lots of music without making money." Forrester Research CEO George Colony, pointing out entrenched rivals in every sector Amazon.com seeks to enter/redefine, declared that it would soon become known as "Amazon.toast." Nonetheless, 6 out of every 7 stock analysts in early 1999 believe Amazon.com is a sure winner. You get to see who was right! Look up Amazon.com and see if it met their predictions and leads the emerging E-commerce industry.

Source: "Amazon.com: The Wild World of E-commerce," *Business Week:* December 14, 1998, p. 106.

Industry capacity "tops out" as sales growth ceases to cover up poorly planned expansions.

New products and new applications are harder to come by.

International competition increases as cost pressures lead to overseas production advantages.

Profitability falls, often permanently, as a result of pressure to lower prices and the increased costs of holding or building market share.

These changes necessitate a fundamental strategic reassessment. Strategy elements of successful firms in maturing industries often include:

1. *Pruning the product line* by dropping unprofitable product models, sizes, and options from the firm's product mix.
2. *Emphasis on process innovation* that permits low-cost product design, manufacturing methods, and distribution synergy.
3. *Emphasis on cost reduction* through exerting pressure on suppliers for lower prices, switching to cheaper components, introducing operational efficiencies, and lowering administrative and sales overhead.
4. *Careful buyer selection* to focus on buyers that are less aggressive, more closely tied to the firm, and able to buy more from the firm.
5. *Horizontal integration* to acquire rival firms whose weaknesses can be used to gain a bargain price and are correctable by the acquiring firms.
6. *International expansion* to markets where attractive growth and limited competition still exist and the opportunity for lower-cost manufacturing can influence both domestic and international costs.

Business strategists in maturing industries must avoid several pitfalls. First, they must make a clear choice among the three generic strategies and avoid a middle-ground approach, which would confuse both knowledgeable buyers and the firm's personnel. Second, they must avoid sacrificing market share too quickly for short-term profit. Finally, they must avoid waiting too long to respond to price reductions, retaining unneeded excess capacity, engaging in sporadic or irrational efforts to boost sales, and placing their hopes on "new" products, rather than aggressively selling existing products.

Competitive Advantage in Mature and Declining Industries

Declining industries are those that make products or services for which demand is growing slower than demand in the economy as a whole or is actually declining. This slow growth or decline in demand is caused by technological substitution (such as the substitution of electronic calculators for slide rules), demographic shifts (such as the increase in the number of older people and the decrease in the number of children), and shifts in needs (such as the decreased need for red meat).

Firms in a declining industry should choose strategies that emphasize one or more of the following themes:

1. *Focus* on segments within the industry that offer a chance for higher growth or a higher return.
2. *Emphasize product innovation and quality improvement,* where this can be done cost effectively, to differentiate the firm from rivals and to spur growth.
3. *Emphasize production and distribution efficiency* by streamlining production, closing marginal productions facilities and costly distribution outlets, and adding effective new facilities and outlets.
4. *Gradually harvest the business*—generate cash by cutting down on maintenance, reducing models, and shrinking channels and make no new investment.

Strategists who incorporate one or more of these themes into the strategy of their business can anticipate relative success, particularly where the industry's decline is

BusinessWeek

PENN RACQUET SPORTS SEEKS CONCENTRIC DIVERSIFICATION AS THE ANSWER TO DECLINING SALES IN A DECLINING INDUSTRY—TENNIS BALLS

STRATEGY IN ACTION 8–2

Suppose your industry were in free fall. Yet you were the leader in that industry . . . the strongest! What would you do to find more customers? Would you go global in search of sales? Try the Internet? Refocus your business? How about switching species?

That's the drastic move made by Penn Racquet Sports, the nation's No. 1 maker of tennis balls. Penn recently began marketing its fuzzy orbs to some undeniably loyal customers: dogs. *R. P. Fetchem*'s is a traditional tennis ball that has been gussied up as a "natural felt fetch toy" for pooches. "Ten times more people own pets than play tennis," explains Penn President Gregg R. Weida. Tennis may be stalled, but pet-pampering is booming. Human beings will shell out $5.95 a box for doggie pasta and will pay $59.95 for a pet canopy bed. Most important to Penn, they buy toys: Last year, owners lavished $41.7 million on dog toys sold in pet stores. While $5 a can might make tennis players gasp, it's no barrier for dog lovers in search of the perfect treat. New York dog owner Joel Katz didn't balk at the Fetchem's price tag. "This guy will do anything for a ball," he said of his cocker spaniel, Max. "He loves them more than food."

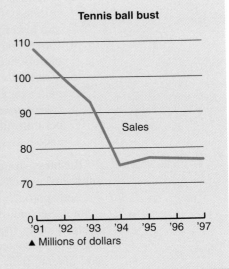

Tennis ball bust

Sales

▲ Millions of dollars

Source: "Now, Tennis Balls Are Chasing the Dogs," *Business Week:* July 13, 1998, p. 138.

slow and smooth and some profitable niches remain. Strategy in Action 8–2 describes how Penn Racquet Sports went from "humans to dogs" to reenergize the declining tennis ball market. At the same time, three pitfalls must be avoided: (1) being overly optimistic about the prospects for a revival of the industry, (2) getting trapped in a profitless war of attrition, and (3) harvesting from a weak position.

Competitive Advantage in Fragmented Industries

A fragmented industry is one in which no firm has a significant market share and can strongly influence industry outcomes. Fragmented industries are found in many areas of the economy and are common in such areas as professional services, retailing, distribution, wood and metal fabrication, and agricultural products. The funeral industry is an example of a highly fragmented industry. Business strategists in fragmented industries pursue low-cost, differentiation, or focus competitive advantages in one of five ways.

Tightly Managed Decentralization

Fragmented industries are characterized by a need for intense local coordination, a local management orientation, high personal service, and local autonomy. Recently, however, successful firms in such industries have introduced a high degree of professionalism into the operations of local managers.

"Formula" Facilities

This alternative, related to the previous one, introduces standardized, efficient, low-cost facilities at multiple locations. Thus, the firm gradually builds a low-cost advantage over localized competitors. Fast-food and motel chains have applied this approach with considerable success.

Increased Value Added

The products or services of some fragmented industries are difficult to differentiate. In this case, an effective strategy may be to add value by providing more service with the sale or by engaging in some product assembly that is of additional value to the customer.

Specialization

Focus strategies that creatively segment the market can enable firms to cope with fragmentation. Specialization can be pursued by:

1. *Product type.* The firm builds expertise focusing on a narrow range of products or services.
2. *Customer type.* The firm becomes intimately familiar with and serves the needs of a narrow customer segment.
3. *Type of order.* The firm handles only certain kinds of orders, such as small orders, custom orders, or quick turnaround orders.
4. *Geographic area.* The firm blankets or concentrates on a single area.

Although specialization in one or more of these ways can be the basis for a sound focus strategy in a fragmented industry, each of these types of specialization risks limiting the firm's potential sales volume.

Bare Bones/No Frills

Given the intense competition and low margins in fragmented industries, a "bare bones" posture—low overhead, minimum wage employees, tight cost control—may build a sustainable cost advantage in such industries.

Competitive Advantage in Global Industries

A global industry is one that comprises firms whose competitive positions in major geographic or national markets are fundamentally affected by their overall global competitive positions. To avoid strategic disadvantages, firms in global industries are virtually required to compete on a worldwide basis. Oil, steel, automobiles, apparel, motorcycles, televisions, and computers are examples of global industries.

Global industries have four unique strategy-shaping features:

Differences in prices and costs from country to country due to currency exchange fluctuations, differences in wage and inflation rates, and other economic factors.

Differences in buyer needs across different countries.

Differences in competitors and ways of competing from country to country.

Differences in trade rules and governmental regulations across different countries.

These unique features and the global competition of global industries require that two fundamental components be addressed in the business strategy: (1) the approach used to gain global market coverage and (2) the generic competitive strategy.

Three basic options can be used to pursue global market coverage:

1. *License* foreign firms to produce and distribute the firm's products.
2. *Maintain a domestic production base* and export products to foreign countries.
3. *Establish foreign-based plants and distribution* to compete directly in the markets of one or more foreign countries.

Along with the market coverage decision, strategists must scrutinize the condition of the global industry features identified earlier to choose among four generic global competitive strategies:

1. *Broad-line global competition*—directed at competing worldwide in the full product line of the industry, often with plants in many countries, to achieve differentiation or an overall low-cost position.
2. *Global focus* strategy—targeting a particular segment of the industry for competition on a worldwide basis.
3. *National focus* strategy—taking advantage of differences in national markets that give the firm an edge over global competitors on a nation-by-nation basis.
4. *Protected niche* strategy—seeking out countries in which governmental restraints exclude or inhibit global competitors or allow concessions, or both, that are advantageous to localized firms.

Competing in global industries is an increasing reality for many U.S. firms. Strategists must carefully match their skills and resources with global industry structure and conditions in selecting the most appropriate strategy option.

In conclusion, the analysis and choice of business strategy involves three basic considerations. First, strategists must recognize that their overall choice revolves around three sources of competitive advantage that require total, consistent commitment. Second, strategists must carefully weigh the skills, resources, organizational requirements, and risks associated with each source of competitive advantage. Finally, strategists must consider the unique influence that the generic industry environment most similar to the firm's situation will have on the set of value chain activities they choose to build competitive advantage.

DOMINANT PRODUCT/SERVICE BUSINESSES: EVALUATING AND CHOOSING TO DIVERSIFY TO BUILD VALUE

McDonald's has frequently looked at numerous opportunities to diversify into related businesses or to acquire key suppliers. Its decision has consistently been to focus on its core business using the grand strategies of concentration, market development, and product development. Rival Pepsi, on the other hand, has chosen to diversify into related businesses and vertical integration as the best grand strategies for it to build long-term value. Both firms experienced unprecedented success during the last 20 years.

Many dominant product businesses face this question as their core business proves successful: What grand strategies are best suited to continue to build value? Under what circumstances should they choose an expanded focus (diversification, vertical integration); steady continued focus (concentration, market or product development); or a narrowed focus (turnaround or divestiture)? This section examines two ways you can analyze a dominant product company's situation and choose among the 14 grand strategies identified in Chapter 7.

FIGURE 8–4
Grand Strategy Selection Matrix

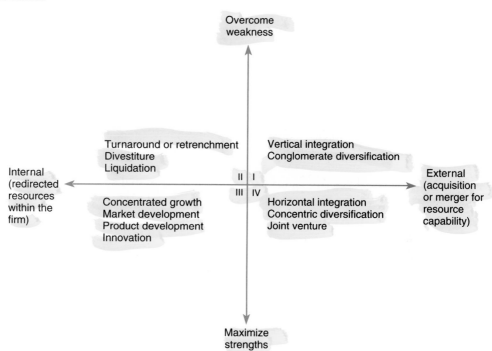

Grand Strategy Selection Matrix

One valuable guide to the selection of a promising grand strategy is the matrix shown in Figure 8–4. The basic idea underlying the matrix is that two variables are of central concern in the selection process: (1) the principal purpose of the grand strategy and (2) the choice of an internal or external emphasis for growth or profitability.

In the past, planners were advised to follow certain rules or prescriptions in their choice of strategies. Now, most experts agree that strategy selection is better guided by the conditions of the planning period and by the company strengths and weaknesses. It should be noted, however, that even the early approaches to strategy selection sought to match a concern over internal versus external growth with a desire to overcome weaknesses or maximize strengths.

The same considerations led to the development of the grand strategy selection matrix. A firm in quadrant I, with "all its eggs in one basket," often views itself as over-committed to a particular business with limited growth opportunities or high risks. One reasonable solution is *vertical integration,* which enables the firm to reduce risk by reducing uncertainty about inputs or access to customers. Another is *conglomerate diversification,* which provides a profitable investment alternative with diverting management attention from the original business. However, the external approaches to overcoming weaknesses usually result in the most costly grand strategies. Acquiring a second business demands large investments of time and sizable financial resources. Thus, strategic managers considering these approaches must guard against exchanging one set of weaknesses for another.

More conservative approaches to overcoming weaknesses are found in quadrant II. Firms often choose to redirect resources from one internal business activity to another.

This approach maintains the firm's commitment to its basic mission, rewards success, and enables further development of proven competitive advantages. The least disruptive of the quadrant II strategies is *retrenchment,* pruning the current activities of a business. If the weaknesses of the business arose from inefficiencies, retrenchment can actually serve as a *turnaround* strategy—that is, the business gains new strength from the streamlining of its operations and the elimination of waste. However, if those weaknesses are a major obstruction to success in the industry and the costs of overcoming them are unaffordable or are not justified by a cost-benefit analysis, then eliminating the business must be considered. *Divestiture* offers the best possibility for recouping the firm's investment, but even *liquidation* can be an attractive option if the alternatives are bankruptcy or an unwarranted drain on the firm's resources.

A common business adage states that a firm should build from strength. The premise of this adage is that growth and survival depend on an ability to capture a market share that is large enough for essential economies of scale. If a firm believes that this approach will be profitable and prefers an internal emphasis for maximizing strengths, four grand strategies hold considerable promise. As shown in quadrant III, the most common approach is *concentrated growth,* that is, market penetration. The firm that selects this strategy is strongly committed to its current products and markets. It strives to solidify its position by reinvesting resources to fortify its strengths.

Two alternative approaches are *market development* and *product development.* With these strategies, the firm attempts to broaden its operations. Market development is chosen if the firm's strategic managers feel that its existing products would be well received by new customer groups. Product development is chosen if they feel that the firm's existing customers would be interested in products related to its current lines. Product development also may be based on technological or other competitive advantages. The final alternative for quadrant III firms is *innovation.* When the firm's strengths are in creative product design or unique production technologies, sales can be stimulated by accelerating perceived obsolescence. This is the principle underlying the innovative grand strategy.

Maximizing a firm's strengths by aggressively expanding its base of operations usually requires an external emphasis. The preferred options in such cases are shown in quadrant IV. *Horizontal integration* is attractive because it makes possible a quick increase in output capability. Moreover, in horizontal integration, the skills of the managers of the original business often are critical in converting newly acquired facilities into profitable contributors to the parent firm; this expands a fundamental competitive advantage of the firm—its management.

Concentric diversification is a good second choice for similar reasons. Because the original and newly acquired businesses are related, the distinctive competencies of the diversifying firm are likely to facilitate a smooth, synergistic, and profitable expansion.

The final alternative for increasing resource capability through external emphasis is a *joint venture* or *strategic alliance.* This alternative allows a firm to extend its strengths into competitive arenas that it would be hesitant to enter alone. A partner's production, technological, financial, or marketing capabilities can reduce the firm's financial investment significantly and increase its probability of success.

Model of Grand Strategy Clusters

A second guide to selecting a promising grand strategy is shown in Figure 8–5. The figure is based on the idea that the situation of a business is defined in terms of the growth rate of the general market and the firm's competitive position in that market.

FIGURE 8–5
Model of Grand Strategy Clusters

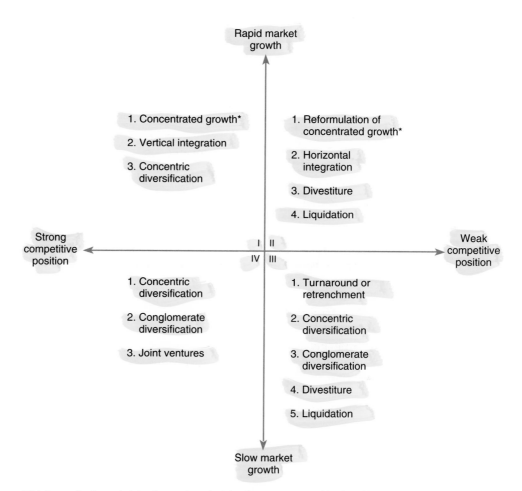

*This is usually via market development, product development, or a combination of both.

When these factors are considered simultaneously, a business can be broadly categorized in one of four quadrants: (I) strong competitive position in a rapidly growing market, (II) weak position in a rapidly growing market, (III) weak position in a slow-growth market, or (IV) strong position in a slow-growth market. Each of these quadrants suggests a set of promising possibilities for the selection of a grand strategy.

Firms in quadrant I are in an excellent strategic position. One obvious grand strategy for such firms is continued concentration on their current business as it is currently defined. Because consumers seem satisfied with the firm's current strategy, shifting notably from it would endanger the firm's established competitive advantages. McDonald's Corporation has followed this approach for 25 years. However, if the firm has resources that exceed the demands of a concentrated growth strategy, it should consider vertical integration. Either forward or backward integration helps a firm protect its profit margins and market share by ensuring better access to consumers or material inputs. Finally, to diminish the risks associated with a narrow product or service line, a quadrant I firm might be wise to consider concentric diversification; with this strategy, the firm continues to invest heavily in its basic area of proven ability.

Firms in quadrant II must seriously evaluate their present approach to the marketplace. If a firm has competed long enough to accurately assess the merits of its current grand strategy, it must determine (1) why that strategy is ineffectual and (2) whether it is capable of competing effectively. Depending on the answers to these questions, the firm should choose one of four grand strategy options: formulation or reformulation of a concentrated growth strategy, horizontal integration, divestiture, or liquidation.

In a rapidly growing market, even a small or relatively weak business often is able to find a profitable niche. Thus, formulation or reformulation of a concentrated growth strategy is usually the first option that should be considered. However, if the firm lacks either a critical competitive element or sufficient economies of scale to achieve competitive cost efficiencies, then a grand strategy that directs its efforts toward horizontal integration is often a desirable alternative. A final pair of options involve deciding to stop competing in the market or product area of the business. A multiproduct firm may conclude that it is most likely to achieve the goals of its mission if the business is dropped through divestiture. This grand strategy not only eliminates a drain on resources but also may provide funds to promote other business activities. As an option of last resort, a firm may decide to liquidate the business. This means that the business cannot be sold as a going concern and is at best worth only the value of its tangible assets. The decision to liquidate is an undeniable admission of failure by a firm's strategic management and, thus, often is delayed—to the further detriment of the firm.

Strategic managers tend to resist divestiture because it is likely to jeopardize their control of the firm and perhaps even their jobs. Thus, by the time the desirability of divestiture is acknowledged, businesses often deteriorate to the point of failing to attract potential buyers. The consequences of such delays are financially disastrous for firm owners because the value of a going concern is many times greater than the value of its assets.

Strategic managers who have a business in quadrant III and expect a continuation of slow market growth and a relatively weak competitive position will usually attempt to decrease their resource commitment to that business. Minimal withdrawal is accomplished through retrenchment; this strategy has the side benefits of making resources available for other investments and of motivating employees to increase their operating efficiency. An alternative approach is to divert resources for expansion through investment in other businesses. This approach typically involves either concentric or conglomerate diversification because the firm usually wants to enter more promising arenas of competition than integration or concentrated growth strategies would allow. The final options for quadrant III businesses are divestiture, if an optimistic buyer can be found, and liquidation.

Quadrant IV businesses (strong competitive position in a slow-growth market) have a basis of strength from which to diversify into more promising growth areas. These businesses have characteristically high cash flow levels and limited internal growth needs. Thus, they are in an excellent position for concentric diversification into ventures that utilize their proven acumen. Strategy in Action 8–2 (on p. 312) describes how the number-one tennis ball maker, Penn Racquet Sports, chose concentric diversification from humans to dogs as their best option. A second option is conglomerate diversification, which spreads investment risk and does not divert managerial attention from the present business. The final option is joint ventures, which are especially attractive to multinational firms. Through joint ventures, a domestic business can gain competitive advantages in promising new fields while exposing itself to limited risks.

Opportunities for Building Value as a Basis for Choosing Diversification or Integration

The grand strategy selection matrix or the model of grand strategy clusters are useful tools to help dominant product company managers evaluate and narrow their choices among alternative grand strategies. When considering grand strategies that would broaden the scope of their company's business activities through integration, diversification, or joint venture strategies, managers must examine whether opportunities to build value are present. Opportunities to build value via diversification, integration, or joint venture strategies are usually found in market-related, operating-related, and management activities. Such opportunities center around reducing costs, improving margins, or providing access to new revenue sources more cost effectively than traditional internal growth options via concentration, market development, or product development. Major opportunities for sharing and value building as well as ways to capitalize on core competencies are outlined in the next chapter, which covers strategic analysis and choice in diversified companies.

Dominant product company managers who choose diversification or integration eventually create another management challenge. That challenge is charting the future of a company that becomes a collection of several distinct businesses. These distinct businesses often encounter different competitive environments, challenges, and opportunities. The next chapter examines ways managers of such diversified companies attempt to evaluate and choose corporate strategy. Central to their challenge is the continued desire to build value, particularly shareholder value.

SUMMARY

This chapter examined how managers in businesses that have a single or dominant product or service evaluate and choose their company's strategy. Two critical areas deserve their attention: first, their business's value chain; second, the appropriateness of 12 different grand strategies based on matching environmental factors with internal capabilities.

Managers in single-product-line business units examine their business's value chain to identify existing or potential activities around which they can create sustainable competitive advantages. As managers scrutinize their value chain activities, they are looking for three sources of competitive advantage: low cost, differentiation, and rapid response capabilities. They also examine whether focusing on a narrow market niche provides a more effective, sustainable way to build or leverage these three sources of competitive advantage.

Managers in single or dominant product/service businesses face two interrelated issues. First, they must choose which grand strategies make best use of their competitive advantages. Second, they must ultimately decide whether to diversify their business activity. Twelve grand strategies were identified in this chapter along with three frameworks that aid managers in choosing which grand strategies should work best and when diversification or integration should be the best strategy for the business. The next chapter expands the coverage of diversification to look at how multibusiness companies evaluate continued diversification and how they construct corporate strategy.

QUESTIONS FOR DISCUSSION

1. What are three activities or capabilities a firm should possess to support a low-cost leadership strategy? Use Figure 8–1 to help you answer this question. Can you give an example of a company that has done this?

2. What are three activities or capabilities a firm should possess to support a differentiation-based strategy? Use Figure 8–2 to help you answer this question. Can you give an example of a company that has done this?

3. What are three ways a firm can incorporate the advantage of speed in its business? Use Figure 8–3 to help you answer this question. Can you give an example of a company that has done this?

4. Do you think is it better to concentrate on one source of competitive advantage (cost versus differentiation versus speed) or to nurture all three in a firm's operation? What did Caterpillar do in the *Business Week* Discussion Case?

5. How does market focus help a business create competitive advantage? What risks accompany such a posture? How did market focus come to play at Caterpillar?

6. Using Figures 8–4 and 8–5, describe situations or conditions under which horizontal integration and concentric diversification would be preferred strategic choices.

BIBLIOGRAPHY

Chen, Ming-Jer, and Donald C. Hambrick. "Speed, Stealth, and Selective Attack." *Academy of Management Journal* 38 (April 1995), pp. 453–82.

Covin, J. G., and D. P. Slevin. "New Venture Strategic Posture, Structure, and Performance: An Industry Life Cycle Analysis." *Journal of Business Venturing* 5 (1990), pp. 123–35.

Eisenhardt, K. M. "Speed and Strategic Choice: How Managers Accelerate Decision Making." *California Management Review* 32, no. 3 (1990), pp. 39–54.

Fierman, Jaclyn. "The Fine Art of Niche-Picking." *Fortune* (Autumn–Winter 1993), pp. 80–83.

Fulmer, William E., and Jack Goodwin. "Differentiation: Begin with the Consumer." *Business Horizons,* September–October 1988, p. 55.

Hamilton, W. F.; J. Vila; and M. D. Dibner. "Patterns of Strategic Choice in Emerging Firms." *California Management Review* 32, no. 3 (1990), pp. 73–86.

Jennings, Suzanne L. "Niches Within a Niche." *Forbes* (April 25, 1994), p. 122.

Kelly, K. "Suddenly, Big Airlines Are Saying: 'Small Is Beautiful.' " *Business Week,* January 1994, p. 37.

Kennedy, C. "Planning Global Strategies for 3M." *Long Range Planning,* February 1988, pp. 9–17.

Lado, A. A.; N. G. Boyd; and P. Wright. "A Competency-Based Model of Sustainable Competitive Advantage: Toward a Conceptual Integration." *Journal of Management* 18, no. 1 (1992), pp. 77–91.

Mitchell, W. "Dual Clocks: Entry Order Influence on Incumbent and Newcomer Market Share and Survival When Specialized Assets Retain Their Value." *Strategic Management Journal* 12 (February 1991), pp. 85–100.

Raynor, Michael E. "The Pitfalls of Niche Marketing." *Journal of Business Strategy* (March–April 1992), p. 29.

Ries, Al. "The Discipline of the Narrow Focus." *Journal of Business Strategy* 13 (November–December 1992).

Schofield, M., and D. Arnold. "Strategies for Mature Businesses." *Long Range Planning,* October 1988, pp. 69–76.

Schrage, Michael. "A Japanese Firm Rethinks Globalization: Interview with Yoshihisa Tabuchi." *Harvard Business Review,* July–August 1989, p. 70.

Sfiligh, E. "Ice Beers Give Stroh Another Excuse to Keep Coming Out With New Brews." *Beverage World,* January 31, 1994, p. 3.

Stalk, G. "Time—The Next Source of Competitive Advantage." *Harvard Business Review,* July–August 1988, pp. 41–53.

Stalk, G.; P. Evans; and L. E. Shulman. "Competing on Capabilities: The New Rules of Corporate Strategy." *Harvard Business Review* 70, no. 2 (1992), pp. 57–69.

Stuckey, John, and David White. "When and When *Not* to Vertically Integrate." *Sloan Management Review* (Spring 1993), pp. 71–83.

Sugiura, Hideo. "How Honda Localizes Its Global Strategy." *Sloan Management Review* 3 (Fall 1990), pp. 77–82.

Varadarajan, P. R. "Product Portfolio Analysis and Market Share Objectives: An Exposition of Certain Underlying Relationships." *Journal of the Academy of Marketing Science* 18, no. 1 (1990), pp. 17–29.

Varadarajan, P. R.; T. Clark; and W. M. Pride. "Controlling the Uncontrollable: Managing Your Market Environment." *Sloan Management Review* 33, no. 2 (1992), pp. 39–47.

Venkatesan, Ravi. "Strategic Outsourcing: To Make or Not to Make." *Harvard Business Review* 7, no. 6 (November–December 1992) , pp. 98–107.

Watts, L. R. "Degrees of Entrepreneurship and Small Firm Planning." *Journal of Business and Entrepreneurship* 2, no. 2 (1992), pp. 59–67.

Yip, George S. *Total Global Strategy.* Englewood Cliffs, N.J.: Prentice-Hall, 1992, chaps. 1, 2, 3, 5, and 7.

Zahra, Shaker; Sarah Nash; and Deborah J. Bickford. "Transforming Technological Pioneering into Competitive Advantage." *Academy of Management Executive* 9 (February 1995), pp. 17–31.

Zimmerman, Frederick M. *The Turnaround Experience: Real-World Lessons in Revitalizing Corporations.* New York: McGraw-Hill, 1991.

CHAPTER 8 DISCUSSION CASE

BusinessWeek

STRATEGIC ANALYSIS AND CHOICE IN THE 1990S AT CATERPILLAR, INC.

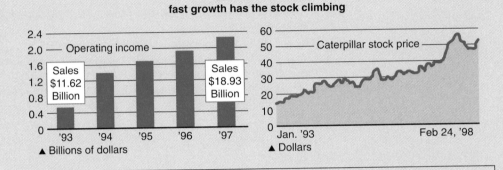

Cat in the 1990s: fast growth has the stock climbing

> Caterpillar, long the global standard in heavy-duty construction equipment was almost destroyed by the painful industry collapse in the 1980s and subsequent union difficulties. Global demand was dropping fast, and the weak yen allowed Cats biggest rival, Japan's Komatsu Ltd., to undercut prices by 40%. When Komatsu began to gain share, Cat's new CEO Donald Fites—and Cat—got the scare of their lives. And a lengthy, debilitating strike with the United Auto Workers in 1990–91 made matters even more difficult. Fites, who became CEO coming from Caterpillar's marketing organization, took an aggressive stance toward the UAW and sought to craft a strategy for the 1990s that would rebuild Caterpillar as the industry leader. *Business Week*'s De'Ann Weimer recently visited Caterpillar to report on the strategic analysis and choices Fites made during that time that led to the outstanding turnaround she summarized for you in the chart above. Her findings from mid-1998 illustrate how one company analyzed and chose to build a strategy around key cost, differentiation, and speed competitive advantages in existing markets and eventually new, growth markets.

STRATEGIC ANALYSIS: Core operations were too costly—old equipment; slow production processes; numerous dedicated production lines for individual truck and tractor models; product design activities for each model, again quite costly; Problematic union agreement.

STRATEGIC CHOICE: **Seek low-cost and speed enhancing leadership advantages** by integrating production activities across multiple models to gain economies of scale; speeding up production processes with newer technology; and reducing inventory costs with increased JIT accommodated with speedier production activities:

> *Fites began by overhauling manufacturing in Cat's core truck and tractor operations. He invested almost $2 billion to modernize his U.S. plants. New state-of-the-art machinery helped Cat **slash time** out of such mundane tasks as painting, for example,*

Source: Adapted from De'Ann Weimer, "A New Cat on the Hot Seat," *Business Week:* March 9, 1998, p. 56.

*and **vastly simplified production.** Today, Cat can build 20 different models from the same basic design. The changes—together with the increased use of temporary workers in its nonunion plants—have also greatly **improved Cat's flexibility.** The company can now **change production levels with a week's notice**—down from six months at the height of its 1980s crisis. Altogether, Cat's manufacturing time has fallen 75%—one key reason operating margins have exploded, from 5.2% in 1993, to 12.6% in 1997. **Faster production** has also allowed Fites to **slash inventories.** Gone are the long order backlogs and dealer inventories that weighed heavily on Cat's books; today, it **refuses orders more than three months in advance.***

STRATEGIC ANALYSIS: Caterpillar was getting hurt not only on price, but because many models had changed very little compared to key Japanese competitors. Newer competitors had begun to differentiate themselves based on providing product line extensions with varying product features.

STRATEGIC CHOICE: **Seek to differentiate Caterpillar's products** by introducing products that enhance construction efficiency while representing basic product line extensions or adaptations of Caterpillar's manufacturing and design capabilities.

*While aggressively redesigning its manufacturing system, **Cat broadened its products.** In the last two years, it has introduced 90 offerings—**some all-new, some well-targeted fine extensions** that enhance construction site efficiency and capabilities in very specific construction tasks. In 1997, for example, Cat introduced a telescopic handler—essentially a tractor with an arm on it that allows masons to work their way up the side of a building eliminating the need for scaffolding so expensive in traditional construction methods.*

STRATEGIC ANALYSIS: Caterpillar is a global business. It is affected significantly by currency fluctuations, by development opportunities outside the U.S. and cyclical downturns, and labor costs in the U.S. versus overseas markets.

STRATEGIC CHOICE: **Focus on selected national markets** where establishing **incountry plants** and distribution provide cost advantages while allowing potential synergy across global markets in selected product offerings.

Good timing helped with the turnaround, too. As the combination of reduced costs and the end of recession restored the company's financial health, Fites pushed into new markets. He focused on Asia, where infrastructure development created huge demand. Markets in Latin America, Central Europe, Russia, and other former Soviet states.

STRATEGIC ANALYSIS: The heavy construction industry is very cyclical. The global nature of the industry heightens the potential cyclical impact and adds currency risks from fluctuating currency values. Restrictive UAW contracts in the U.S. add to the cost impact of these risks when demand, and sales, decrease due to global cyclical pressures yet higher labor costs remain built into Cat's cost structure.

STRATEGIC CHOICE: **Concentric diversification** into related product-markets that leverage key strengths making engines **into less cyclical markets** than trucks and tractors; and into product-markets that leverage sales and distribution strengths. **Use acquisitions** to accelerate this effort. **Increase global presence of facilities over time** to decrease currency fluctuation impact and reliance on UAW labor.

Some 51% of Cat sales come from overseas—though Fites wants to hit 75% by 2008. To cut the risk of fluctuating currencies—and trim labor costs—Fites has also pushed much manufacturing abroad Today, roughly half of Cat's 74 plants are abroad, versus just 39% of its 38 plants a decade ago. In the wake of the UAW's rejection of the labor contract—which will prevent Cat from hiring new workers at lower wages or demanding more flexible scheduling in union plants—analysts say the percentage of foreign production could go even higher.

Fites has also bulked up in less-cyclical businesses like electric power generation. An offshoot of its long-standing engine business, the move into power gained steam in 1996 when Fites purchased a German maker of engines for generators. Driven by demand for power in developing countries—where governments often don't want to build big power plants—generation has helped boost engines to more than 25% of Cat sales. "They are trending toward smaller, easier-to-operate generators," says Siegfried R. Ramseyer, vice-president of Cat Asia. "This we can do very, very well." He says sales could triple in the next few years.

The company's largest acquisition to date—the $1.3 billion purchase of Britain's Perkins Engines, which closed in February—was directed at another target altogether: the fast-growing $3.6 billion market for compact construction machinery. These machines, typically operated by one person, are the industry's hottest segment. The star of the category: skid-steer loaders, which break up asphalt, move dirt, and do such a variety of useful things that sales are growing a red-hot 11% a year.

Cat is all but absent in the lucrative small-equipment market, but Fites wants a 20% share by 2003. He's counting on big gains from Perkins, which makes engines for skid-steers. Since engines account for 25% of the costs of a skid-steer, Cat figures that trimming those expenses will allow it to undercut rivals while maintaining margins. Elsewhere, Fites has tapped other new markets by focusing dealers on rental equipment. Initially unpopular with dealers, who must keep rental gear on their books as assets, the change drew lots of smaller customers. The added demand also helped keep prices strong. In 1997, for example, when few companies could do so, Cat raised prices.

What Was the Result of Caterpillar's Strategic Analysis and Choice?

The reborn company skyrocketed through the upturn with flying colors. Since 1993, when Cat completed its manufacturing overhaul amid soaring demand for construction equipment in the U.S. and developing nations, sales leaped from $11.6 billion to $18.9 billion, an average of 13% a year. Meanwhile, earnings have risen a stunning 45% annually, jumping from just $626 million to $2.3 billion in 1997. Investors have also won big: In five years, Cat's stock more than tripled.

The U.S. market, where Cat sells 49% of its goods, was expected to slow by 1999. And Asia, Cat's fastest-growing market suffered a headline-grabbing downturn. American dealers quickly started seeing barely used, heavily discounted Cat equipment begin to trickle into the U.S. from Asia, as customers dumped equipment to raise cash. The slowdown promised the biggest test yet of the "New Cat" the combative CEO has built.

The question in early 1999 was whether Fites can keep up the performance. Speaking to investors at a Boston conference, he promised sustained sales growth of 5% to 7% annually for the next decade. Now you can look up Caterpillar in *Business Week,* Standard & Poor's, and other business periodicals to see whether Fites's strategic choices achieved what he expected them to do.

9

STRATEGIC ANALYSIS AND CHOICE IN THE MULTIBUSINESS COMPANY: RATIONALIZING DIVERSIFICATION AND BUILDING SHAREHOLDER VALUE

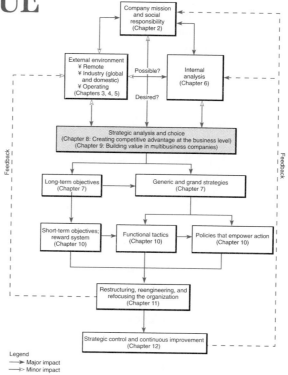

Strategic analysis and choice is more complicated for corporate-level managers because they must create a strategy to guide a company that contains numerous businesses. They must examine and choose which businesses to own and which ones to forgo or divest. They must consider business managers' plans to capture competitive advantage, and then decide how to allocate resources among businesses as part of this phase. This chapter will first examine diversified, multibusiness companies. Specifically, how should the diversified business build shareholder value? For example, MCI has decided to pursue an aggressive diversification program to expand its presence in a variety of different industries; AT&T has recently decided to split into three separate companies while divesting itself of other businesses. Why?

A final topic that is important to an understanding of strategic analysis and choice in business organization is the "nonbusiness," behavioral factors that often exert a major influence on strategic decisions. This is true in the single-product business as well as the multibusiness company. What behavioral considerations often influence how managers analyze strategic options and make strategic choices? For example, J. E. Schrempp became CEO of Germany's Daimler Benz in mid-1995 as planned, having taken over from his mentor, Edzard Reuter, with whom he had charted a steady 10-year diversification to build a $74 billion company. Three months later, Schrempp reversed the strategy to break up the company, focus on core businesses, and reconstruct a new management team. How could such a dramatic, sudden shift take place? Answering that question requires you to consider behavioral factors as well as strategic issues at Daimler Benz.

RATIONALIZING DIVERSIFICATION AND INTEGRATION

When a single- or dominant-business company is transformed into a collection of numerous businesses across several industries, strategic analysis becomes more complex. Managers must deal not only with each business's strategic situation, they must set forth a corporate strategy that rationalizes the collection of businesses they have amassed. Two key audiences are listening. First, managers within the organization want to understand their role and access to resources relative to other businesses within the company. Second, and of greatest importance, stockholders deserve to understand how this collection of businesses is expected to build shareholder value over the long term more effectively than simply investing in separate businesses. In a sense the question is: "Are there compelling reasons why corporate management is better able to invest shareholder value in a variety of other businesses versus allowing shareholders to make that decision themselves?"

Stockholder value in a diversified company is ultimately determined by how well its various businesses perform and/or how compelling potential synergies and opportunities appear to be. Business-level performance is enhanced by sustained competitive advantages. Wise diversification has at its core the search for ways to build value and sustained competitive advantage across multiple business units. We saw several ways opportunities for sharing and building value may be present across different businesses. The bottom line is that diversification that shares skills and core competencies across multiple businesses to strengthen value chains and build competitive advantage enhances shareholder value. And so it is that strategic analysis and choice for corporate managers overseeing multibusiness companies involves determining whether their portfolio of business units is capturing the synergies they intended, how to respond accordingly, and choosing among future diversification or divestiture options. Managers address the following four basic questions to do this.

Are Opportunities for Sharing Infrastructure and Capabilities Forthcoming?

Opportunities to build value via diversification, integration, or joint venture strategies are usually found in market-related, operating-related, and management activities. Each business's basic value chain activities or infrastructure become a source of potential synergy and competitive advantage for another business in the corporate portfolio. Morrison's Cafeteria, long a mainstay in U.S. food services markets, rapidly accelerated its diversification into other restaurant concepts like Ruby Tuesdays. Numerous opportunities for shared operating capabilities and management capabilities drove this decision and, upon repeated strategic analysis, has accelerated corporate managers to move Morrison's totally out of the cafeteria segment by 2000. Some of the more common opportunities to share value chain activities and build value are identified in Figure 9–1.

Strategic analysis is concerned with whether or not the potential competitive advantages expected to arise from each value opportunity have materialized. Where advantage has not materialized, corporate strategists must take care to scrutinize possible impediments to achieving the synergy or competitive advantage. We have identified in Figure 9–1 several impediments associated with each opportunity, which strategists are well advised to examine. Good strategists assure themselves that their organization has ways to avoid or minimize the impact of any impediments or they recommend against further integration or diversification and consider divestiture options.

Two elements are critical in meaningful shared opportunities. First, the shared opportunities must be a significant portion of the value chain of the businesses involved. Returning to Morrison's Cafeteria, its purchasing and inbound logistics infrastructure give Ruby Tuesday's operators an immediate cost-effective purchasing and inventory management capability that lowered its cost in a significant cost activity. Second, the businesses involved must truly have shared needs—need for the same activity—or there is no basis for synergy in the first place. Novell, the U.S.-based networking software giant, paid $900 million for WordPerfect in late 1994, envisioning numerous synergies serving offices globally not to mention 15 million WordPerfect users. By late 1995 Novell would sell WordPerfect for less than $300 million, because, as new CEO Bob Frankenberg said, "It is not because WordPerfect is not a business without a future, but for Novell it represented a distraction from our strategy." Corporate strategies have repeatedly rushed into diversification only to find perceived opportunities for sharing were nonexistent because the businesses did not really have shared needs. Strategy in Action 9–1 examines just this dilemma at several well-known U.S. companies that have botched their synergy searches.

Are We Capitalizing on Our Core Competencies?

Perhaps the most compelling reason companies should diversify can be found in situations where core competencies—key value-building skills—can be leveraged with other products or into markets that are not a part of where they were created. Where this works well, extraordinary value can be built. Managers undertaking diversification strategies should dedicate a significant portion of their strategic analysis to this question.

General Cinema was a company that grew from drive-in theaters to eventually dominate the multicinema, movie exhibition industry. Next, they entered soft-drink bottling and became the largest bottler of soft drinks (Pepsi) in North America. Their stock value rose 2,000 percent in 10 years. They found that core competencies in movie exhibition—managing many small, localized businesses; dealing with a few large

FIGURE 9-1
Value Building in Multibusiness Companies

Opportunities to Build Value or Sharing	Potential Competitive Advantage	Impediments to Achieving Enhanced Value
Market-Related Opportunities:		
Shared sales force activities or shared sales office, or both.	Lower selling costs. Better market coverage. Stronger technical advice to buyers. Enhanced convenience for buyers (can buy from single source). Improved access to buyers (have more products to sell).	• Buyers have different purchasing habits toward the products. • Different salespersons are more effective in representing the product. • Some products get more attention than others. • Buyers prefer to multiple-source rather than single-source their purchases.
Shared after-sale service and repair work.	Lower servicing costs. Better utilization of service personnel (less idle time). Faster servicing of customer calls.	• Different equipment or different labor skills, or both, are needed to handle repairs. • Buyers may do some in-house repairs.
Shared brand name.	Stronger brand image and company reputation. Increased buyer confidence in the brand.	• Company reputation is hurt if quality of one product is lower.
Shared advertising and promotional activities.	Lower costs. Greater clout in purchasing ads.	• Appropriate forms of messages are different. • Appropriate timing of promotions is different.
Common distribution channels.	Lower distribution costs. Enhanced bargaining power with distributors and retailers to gain shelf space, shelf positioning, stronger push and more dealer attention, and better profit margins.	• Dealers resist being dominated by a single supplier and turn to multiple sources and lines. • Heavy use of the shared channel erodes willingness of other channels to carry or push the firm's products.
Shared order processing.	Lower order processing costs. One-stop shopping for buyer enhances service and, thus, differentiation.	• Differences in ordering cycles disrupt order processing economies.

suppliers; applying central marketing skills locally; and acquiring or crafting a "franchise"—were virtually the same in soft-drink bottling. Disney and ABC see shared core competencies as central in the entertainment industry of the 21st century. AT&T and TCI see shared core competencies as central to telecommunications success. These and many more companies look to three basic considerations to evaluate whether they are capitalizing on core competencies.[1]

Is Each Core Competency Providing a Relevant Competitive Advantage to the Intended Businesses?

The core competency must assist the intended business in creating strength relative to key competition. This could occur at any step in the business's value chain. But it must represent a major source of value to be a basis for competitive advantage—and the

---

[1]C. K. Prahalad and G. Hamel, "The Core Competence of the Corporation," *Harvard Business Review,* May–June 1990, pp. 79–91; and M. Porter, "From Competitive Advantage to Corporate Strategy," *Harvard Business Review,* May–June 1987, pp. 43–59.

FIGURE 9-1
concluded

Opportunities to Build Value or Sharing	Potential Competitive Advantage	Impediments to Achieving Enhanced Value
Operating Opportunities:		
Joint procurement of purchased inputs.	Lower input costs. Improved input quality. Improved service from suppliers.	• Input needs are different in terms of quality or other specifications. • Inputs are needed at different plant locations, and centralized purchasing is not responsive to separate needs of each plant.
Shared manufacturing and assembly facilities.	Lower manufacturing/assembly costs. Better capacity utilization, because peak demand for one product correlates with valley demand for other. Bigger scale of operation improves access to better technology and results in better quality.	• Higher changeover costs in shifting from one product to another. • High-cost special tooling or equipment is required to accommodate quality differences or design differences.
Shared inbound or outbound shipping and materials handling.	Lower freight and handling costs. Better delivery reliability. More frequent deliveries, such that inventory costs are reduced.	• Input sources or plant locations, or both, are in different geographic areas. • Needs for frequency and reliability of inbound/outbound delivery differ among the business units.
Shared product and process technologies or technology development or both.	Lower product or process design costs, or both, because of shorter design times and transfers of knowledge from area to area. More innovative ability, owing to scale of effort and attraction of better R&D personnel.	• Technologies are the same, but the applications in different business units are different enough to prevent much sharing of real value.
Shared administrative support activities.	Lower administrative and operating overhead costs.	• Support activities are not a large proportion of cost, and sharing has little cost impact (and virtually no differentiation impact).
Management Opportunities:		
Shared management know-how, operating skills, and proprietary information.	Efficient transfer of a distinctive competence—can create cost savings or enhance differentiation. More effective management as concerns strategy formulation, strategy implementation, and understanding of key success factors.	• Actual transfer of know-how is costly or stretches the key skill personnel too thinly, or both. • Increased risks that proprietary information will leak out.

Source: Adapted with the permission of The Free Press, a Division of Simon and Schuster, from *Competitive Advantage: Creating and Sustaining Superior Performance,* by Michael E. Porter. Copyright © 1985 by Michael E. Porter.

core competence must be transferrable. Honda of Japan viewed itself as having a core competence in manufacturing small, internal combustion engines. It diversified into small garden tools, perceiving that traditional electric tools would be much more attractive if powered by a lightweight, mobile, gas combustion motor. Their core competency created a major competitive advantage in a market void of gas-driven hand tools. When Coca-Cola added bottled water to its portfolio of products, it expected its extraordinary core competencies in marketing and distribution to rapidly build value in this business. Ten years later, Coke sold its water assets concluding that the product did

BusinessWeek

STRATEGY IN ACTION 9–1

STORIES AND LESSONS IN THE SAD SEARCH FOR SYNERGY

AT&T shelled out $7 billion for NCR Corp. early in the 1990s and finally staked out the strategic beachhead in computers that it had failed, despite billions of dollars spent, to achieve on its own. When AT&T succeeded in taking over computer maker NCR, it figured it had won a major victory in its dream of linking computers and telecommunications. As things turned out, the dream proved to be wishful thinking. Four years and $4 billion in net NCR losses later, AT&T was ready to cut its losses and spin off NCR. AT&T had also invested an additional $3.2 billion into NCR by the time it was spun off to the public. And after its initial emotional IPO market reception in early 1997, NCR stock quickly nosedived as its longterm prospects became more obvious, and unattractive. Analysts and competitors say NCR's computer problems are a lingering result of neglect under AT&T. For starters, NCR's computer sales force was allowed to shrink too much. And though it boasted customers such as H&R Block Inc. and J.C. Penney Co., outsiders say NCR was far too dependent on sales to AT&T. Worse, the phone giant failed to invest enough in the business or expand NCR's computer product lines, especially its Unix-based servers. "What NCR found, because of the AT&T screwup, is that their critical mass in the Unix business is not that big," says Nick Earle, worldwide marketing manager for Hewlett-Packard Co.'s enterprise systems group, a strong NCR rival in both servers and data warehousing.

Although consolidation of health-care providers has made sense for some, it certainly didn't for Dallas-based Medical Care International Inc. and Critical Care America, based in Westborough, Massachusetts. If ever there was a marriage made in hell, this combination of the nation's largest surgery-center chain and largest independent operator of home intravenous services was it. The concept—to create a hospital without walls and enable Medical Care America to profit from the rising demand for low-cost outpatient services—certainly sounded good. But virtually everything that could go wrong in a merger went wrong in this one. Poor timing, faulty due diligence, culture clashes, and big egos doomed the deal from the start. The merger took place just as intensified competition began driving down prices for home infusion services. Critical Care's problems were masked by slow insurer payments and infrequent internal reporting, which made it difficult to spot trends. Less than three weeks after the merger, Chairman and CEO Donald E. Steen announced that third-quarter results would fall below expectations, triggering a free fall in Medical Care America's shares. Management responded by slashing Critical Care's staff, which, in turn, caused it to lose customers. Shareholder lawsuits followed. "The Critical Care merger was bad, really bad," says Steen. "It's something I'm trying to forget." Soon thereafter Medical Care America sold off Critical Care to Caremark International Inc. and six months later sold out to Columbia/HCA Healthcare Corp. for $850 million. "This has been a very good merger," Steen says,

Sources: "The Case Against Mergers," *Business Week:* October 30, 1995; "Is NCR Ready To Ring Up Some Cash?" *Business Week:* October 14, 1996; and "Still Waiting for the New NCR," *Business Week:* December 15, 1997.

not have enough margin to interest its franchised bottlers and that marketing was not a significant value-building activity among many small suppliers competing primarily on the cost of "producing" and shipping water.

Are Businesses in the Portfolio Related in Ways That Make the Company's Core Competence(s) Beneficial?

Related versus unrelated diversification is an important distinction to understand as you evaluate the diversification question. "Related" businesses are those that rely on

BusinessWeek

continued

largely because its broad geographic coverage and supply contracts have enabled it to lower prices.

Other attempts at expanding by acquiring closely related companies have also bombed. Take, for example, Kmart Corp.'s 1990s acquisitions strategy. Instead of focusing on its core discount business, it lost more ground to Wal-Mart Stores Inc. when it diverted its attention and capital to buying up fast-growing specialized retailers, sometimes paying top dollar. Before long, Kmart had become a $30 billion-sales retail conglomerate with seven specialty store chains and 2,300 Kmart stores. But overhead was higher than rival Wal-Mart and sales per square foot lower. "The Kmart stores were totally neglected," says Trish Reopelle, an analyst with the State of Wisconsin Investment Board. Mid-decade, Kmart was forced to begin selling its specialty stores and CEO Joseph Antonini was out of a job. Kmart has continued to try to avoid bankruptcy protection as it seeks to survive its mistake pursuit of synergy and diversification.

Few deals made more sense on paper yet so little sense culturally than the merger of Price Club and Costco Wholesale to create Price/Costco Inc., which became the second-largest operator of warehouse clubs after Wal-Mart's Sam's Club. "The economies of the two companies coming together to compete with Sam's Club were compelling," says Jeffrey Atkin, principal of the Seattle money-management firm of Kunath Karren Rinne & Atkin.

The deal had many problems, but the worst were cultural. The Price and Costco people just didn't seem to hit it off. Says analyst Michael J. Shea of Charter Investment Group: "The Price guys had much more of a real estate strip-mall mentality. The Costco guys were the type who started working at grocery stores bagging groceries when they were 10 years old and worked their way up the ladder." In one of the shortest corporate marriages ever, Price and Costco broke up after less than a year. Says analyst Mark Byl, of Laird Norton Trust Co.: "The best thing to happen to that marriage was the divorce."

All this indicates that many large-company CEOs are making multibillion-dollar decisions about the future of their companies, employees, and shareholders in part by the seat of their pants. When things go wrong, as the evidence demonstrates that they often do, these decisions create unnecessary tumult, losses, and heartache. While there clearly is a role for thoughtful and well-conceived mergers in American business, all too many don't meet that description. Moreover, in merging and acquiring mindlessly and flamboyantly, dealmakers may be eroding the nation's growth prospects and global competitiveness. Dollars that are wasted needlessly on mergers that don't work might better be spent on research and new-product development. And in view of the growing number of corporate divorces, it's clear that the best strategy for most would-be marriage partners is never to march to the altar at all.

the same or similar capabilities to be successful and attain competitive advantage in their respective product markets. The discussion case at the end of Chapter 8 described how Caterpillar pursued related diversification into the portable power generation business from its core truck and tractor focus. This related move was very successful in part because Caterpillar's expertise in diesel engine manufacturing, indeed its same engines, could be used to strategic advantage in small scale, portable power generation. Earlier, we described General Cinema's spectacular success in both movie exhibition and soft-drink bottling. Seemingly unrelated, they were actually very related businesses in terms of key core competencies that shaped success—managing a network of diverse business locations, localized competition, reliance on a few large suppliers, and centralized marketing advantages. Thus, the products of various businesses do not necessarily have to be similar to leverage core competencies. While their products may not be related, it is essential that some activities in their value chains require similar skills to create competitive advantage if the company is going to leverage its core competence(s) in a value-creating way.

Situations that involve "unrelated" diversification occur when no real overlapping capabilities or products exist other than financial resources. We refer to this as *conglomerate diversification* in Chapter 7. Recent research indicates that the most profitable firms are those that have diversified around a set of resources and capabilities that are specialized enough to confer a meaningful competitive advantage in an attractive industry, yet adaptable enough to be advantageously applied across several others. The least profitable are broadly diversified firms whose strategies are built around very general resources (e.g., money) that are applied in a wide variety of industries, but are seldom instrumental to competitive advantage in those settings.[2]

Are Our Combination of Competencies Unique or Difficult to Recreate?

Skills that corporate strategists expect to transfer from one business to another, or from corporate to various businesses, may be transferrable. They may also be easily replicated by competitors. When this is the case, no sustainable competitive advantage is created. Sometimes strategists look for a combination of competencies, a package of various interrelated skills, as another way to create a situation where seemingly easily replicated competencies become unique, sustainable competitive advantages. 3M Corporation has the enviable record of having 25 percent of its earnings always coming from products introduced within the last five years. 3M has been able to "bundle" the skills necessary to accelerate the introduction of new products so that it consistently extracts early life cycle value from adhesive-related products that hundreds of competitors with similar technical or marketing competencies cannot touch.

All too often companies envision a combination of competencies that make sense conceptually. This vision of synergy develops an energy of its own leading CEOs to relentlessly push the merger of the firms involved. But what makes sense conceptually and is seen as difficult for competitors to recreate often proves difficult if not impossible to create in the first place. Strategy in Action 9–2 discusses this dilemma, making a case against merger and diversification.

Does the Company's Business Portfolio Balance Financial Resources?

Multibusiness companies usually find that their various businesses generate and consume very different levels of cash. Some generate more cash than they can use to maintain or expand their business while others consume more than they generate. Corporate managers face the very important challenge of determining the best way to generate and use financial resources among the businesses within their company. Faced with this challenge, managers historically looked to balance cash generators and cash users so that, along with outside capital sources, they can efficiently manage the cash flows across their business portfolio.

Responding to this challenge during the diversification explosion of the 1970s, the Boston Consulting Group pioneered an approach called *portfolio techniques* that attempted to help managers "balance" the flow of cash resources among their various

---

[2]David J. Collis and Cynthia A. Montgomery, *Corporate Strategy* (Chicago: Irwin), 1997, p. 88.

BusinessWeek

THE CASE AGAINST MERGERS AND DIVERSIFICATION

STRATEGY IN ACTION 9–2

American companies are in the grip of full-blown merger mania. Each of the last ten years has topped the previous year's merger and acquisition activity. This historic surge of consolidations and combinations is occurring in the face of strong evidence that mergers and acquisitions, at least over the past 35 years or so, have hurt more than helped companies and shareholders. The conglomerate deals of the 1960s and 1970s that gave rise to such unwieldy companies as ITT Corp. and Litton Industries have since been thoroughly discredited, and most of these behemoths have been broken up. The debt-laden leveraged buyouts and bust-ups of the 1980s didn't fare any better, and many surely did a whole lot worse. That era ended not with a whimper but with a bang: In October, 1989, when bankers couldn't raise the money for the ill-conceived buyout of UAL Corp., the deal collapsed, dragging the stock market down with it.

But by the 1990s, chief executives and investment bankers figured that they had finally gotten it right. If UAL marked the end of the 1980s crazy season, then the July, 1991, announcement by Chemical Bank Corp. and Manufacturers Hanover Corp. that they would join in a $2.3 billion stock swap to create the nation's second-largest banking company and produce $650 million in annual expense savings by 1994, seemed to signal that the Age of Reason in mergers and acquisitions had begun. This was to be the era of strategic deals—friendly, intelligent, and relatively debt-free transactions done mostly as stock swaps, which were supposed to enrich shareholders by producing synergies in which two plus two would equal five or more. These synergies would take the form of economies of scale, improved channels of distribution, greater market clout, and ultimately higher profits for surviving companies. Although Harvard University's Michael Porter in a seminal *Harvard Business Review* article argued persuasively that most would-be deal synergies are never realized, the new strategic transactions, Wall Street promised, would be different.

It turns out they're not. Indeed, with investment bankers singing their new, improved siren song, many big company CEOs are demonstrating that they still are as vulnerable to the latest fad as the most naive individual investor. An exhaustive analysis by *Business Week* and Mercer Management Consulting Inc., a leading management consulting firm, of hundreds of deals in this decade indicates that their performance has fallen far short of their promise. Deals that were announced with much fanfare such as AT&T's acquisition of NCR and Matsushita's acquisition of MCA, have since unraveled. Acquisitions by big pharmaceutical manufacturers of drug wholesalers, as well as software and entertainment deals aren't producing the results the acquirers had hoped for. Some recent megadeals like Turner Broadcasting's takeover by Time Warner, itself a value-destroying combination, and Disney's acquisition of Capital Cities/ABC leave many media-industry observers scratching their heads over where the gains are going to come from. "For all these deals to work out, you have to believe that the American public is underentertained," says Wilbur L. Ross, senior managing director at Rothschild Inc.

These anecdotal findings are supported statistically. The *Business Week*/Mercer analysis indicates that companies performed better in the wake of '90s deals, most of which have been done ostensibly for business reasons, than they did after '80s transactions, a high proportion of which were financially driven. But the analysis also concluded that most of the '90s deals still haven't worked. Of 150 recent deals valued at $500 million or more, about half destroyed shareholder wealth, judged by stock performance in relation to Standard & Poor's industry indexes. Another third contributed only marginally to it. Further, says James Quella, director of Mercer

(continued)

Source: Phillip L. Zweig in New York, with Judy Perlman Kline in Pittsburgh, Stephanie Anderson Forest in Dallas, and Kevin Gudridge, "The Case Against Mergers," *Business Week:* October 30, 1995.

BusinessWeek

continued

STRATEGY IN
ACTION
9–2

Management Consulting, "many deals destroy a lot of value." Mergers and acquisitions, he declares, "are still a slippery slope." Key reasons mergers fail were:

Deal performance has been poor because melding two companies is enormously difficult and only a few companies are very good at it. One reason is that buyers often stack the odds against success by rushing headlong into mergers and acquisitions for the wrong reasons in search of synergies that don't exist. To make matters worse, they often pay outlandish premiums that can't be recovered even if everything goes right. And finally—and this is the real deal-killer—they fail to effectively integrate the two companies after the toasts have been exchanged. Good postmerger integration rarely makes a really bad deal work, but bad execution almost always wrecks one that might have had a shot. Says Kenneth W. Smith, a Mercer vice-president based in Toronto: "The deal is won or lost after it's done."

Most transactions fall below expectations, but an even greater percentage of companies lose in the M&A game. That's because **a few large, proficient acquirers,** such as General Electric Co. and Dover Corp. (BW—Jan. 23), tend to **do a lot of successful deals while a much larger number of less adept companies execute one or two unsuccessful mergers.** In the 5½ years ending July 31, 72% of companies that completed six or more deals valued over $5 million each yielded returns above the industry average, compared with 54% of companies that closed just one to five transactions.

Nonacquirers are more likely to outperform their respective industry indices than are **active acquirers.** Only about a fourth of the nation's 500 largest companies have not yet made a single acquisition larger than $5 million in this decade. But over 70% of companies that made no acquisitions larger than $5 million outperformed their respective Standard & Poor's industry indices. Only 50% of all acquirers did better than their industry indices. Many companies—notably Andrew Corp. and Coca Cola Co.—whose industry rivals are bent on growing through acquisition, have delivered superior returns by keeping investment bankers at bay and sticking to their knitting.

Many deals are poorly thought out, founded on dubious assumptions about the potential benefits by CEOs with questionable motivations. "There's tremendous allure to mergers and acquisitions," says Porter. "It's the big play, the dramatic gesture. With the stroke of a

businesses while also identifying their basic strategic purpose within the overall portfolio. Three of these techniques are reviewed here. Once reviewed, we will identify some of the problems with the portfolio approach that you should keep in mind when considering its use.

The BCG Growth-Share Matrix

Managers using the BCG matrix plotted each of the company's businesses according to market growth rate and relative competitive position. *Market growth rate* is the projected rate of sales growth for the market being served by a particular business. Usually measured as the percentage increase in a market's sales or unit volume over the two most recent years, this rate serves as an indicator of the relative attractiveness of the markets served by each business in the firm's portfolio of businesses. *Relative competitive position* usually is expressed as the market share of a business divided by the market share of its largest competitor. Thus, relative competitive position provides a basis for

BusinessWeek

continued

pen you can add billions to size, get a front-page story, and create excitement in the markets." Numerous companies have blundered lately when they tried to engineer a major redefinition of their businesses through merger and acquisition—often in response to sea changes in regulation, technology, and even geopolitics. If the spate of copycat deals in computers, telecommunications, media, and technology are any indication, these companies seem to fear they will be left behind forever if they don't do something and do it fast. "Nobody wants to be marooned," says David A. Nadler, chairman of Delta Consulting Group.

Optimism is bolstered by a variety of rationales. One is that vertical integration—linking manufacturing with distribution—will yield vast synergies. On that theory, Merck, Eli Lilly, and SmithKline paid handsomely for drug wholesalers, but the prospects for those deals are looking bleaker and bleaker. Such linkages are behind the Hollywood deals, such as Disney's acquisition of Capital Cities/ABC. "I hate to use the 's' word," says Disney Chairman Michael Eisner, "but that's synergy at work." Others are skeptical. Says Tele-Communications Inc. CEO John C. Malone: "It's an industry that's as certain as betting on a race horse."

Many experts say that the deal-breaker is usually **bad postmerger planning and integration.** If a deal is to stand any chance of success, companies must move quickly and decisively to appoint the new management team, cut costs, reassure customers, and resolve cultural conflicts.

To be sure, some strategic transactions have worked well. The Chemical-Manny Hanny merger; Primerica's acquisition of Travelers Corp.; Toymaker Mattel Corp.'s acquisition of Fisher-Price; and Campbell Soup–Pace Foods have worked. But the kinds of mergers and acquisitions with a better-than-even shot at success are limited indeed. Small and midsize deals—notably leveraged "buildups" in such fragmented industries as funeral homes and health clubs—frequently work. The best acquisitions, says Harvard's Porter, involve "gap-filling," including those in which one company buys another to strengthen its product line or expand its territory. "Globalizing" acquisitions, such as those that enable companies to expand their core business into other countries, may make sense, though culture and language problems undermine many of these deals. Mergers of direct competitors aimed at dominating a market, such as marriages of big banks with overlapping branches, often have worked out.

comparing the relative strengths of the businesses in the firm's portfolio in terms of their positions in their respective markets. Figure 9–2 illustrates the growth-share matrix.

The *stars* are businesses in rapidly growing markets with large market shares. These businesses represent the best long-run opportunities (growth and profitability) in the firm's portfolio. They require substantial investment to maintain (and expand) their dominant position in a growing market. This investment requirement is often in excess of the funds that they can generate internally. Therefore, these businesses are often short-term, priority consumers of corporate resources.

Cash cows are businesses with a high market share in low-growth markets or industries. Because of their strong positions and their minimal reinvestment requirements, these businesses often generate cash in excess of their needs. Therefore, they are selectively "milked" as a source of corporate resources for deployment elsewhere (to stars and question marks). Cash cows are yesterday's stars and the current foundation of corporate portfolios. They provide the cash needed to pay corporate overhead and

FIGURE 9–2
The BCG Growth-Share Matrix

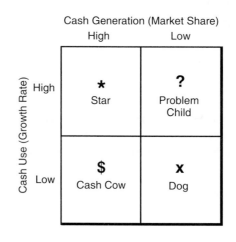

Source: The growth-share matrix was originally developed by the Boston Consulting Group.

dividends and provide debt capacity. They are managed to maintain their strong market share while generating excess resources for corporatewide use.

Low market share and low market growth businesses are the *dogs* in the firm's portfolio. Facing mature markets with intense competition and low profit margins, they are managed for short-term cash flow (through ruthless cost cutting, for example) to supplement corporate-level resource needs. According to the original BCG prescription, they are divested or liquidated once this short-term harvesting has been maximized.

Question marks are businesses whose high growth rate gives them considerable appeal but whose low market share makes their profit potential uncertain. Question marks are cash guzzlers because their rapid growth results in high cash needs, while their small market share results in low cash generation. At the corporate level, the concern is to identify the question marks that would increase their market share and move into the star group if extra corporate resources were devoted to them. Where this long-run shift from question mark to star is unlikely, the BCG matrix suggests divesting the question mark and repositioning its resources more effectively in the remainder of the corporate portfolio.

The Industry Attractiveness–Business Strength Matrix

Corporate strategists found the growth-share matrix's singular axes limiting in their ability to reflect the complexity of a business's situation. Therefore, some companies adopted a matrix with a much broader focus. This matrix, developed by McKinsey & Company at General Electric, is called the Industry Attractiveness–Business Strength Matrix. This matrix uses multiple factors to assess industry attractiveness and business

FIGURE 9-3
Factors Considered in Constructing an Industry Attractiveness–Business Strength Matrix

Industry Attractiveness	Business Strength
Nature of Competitive Rivalry	**Cost Position**
Number of competitors	Economies of scale
Size of competitors	Manufacturing costs
Strength of competitors' corporate parents	Overhead
Price wars	Scrap/waste/rework
Competition on multiple dimensions	Experience effects
	Labor rates
Bargaining Power of Suppliers/Customers	Proprietary processes
Relative size of typical players	**Level of Differentiation**
Numbers of each	Promotion effectiveness
Importance of purchases from or sales to	Product quality
Ability to vertically integrate	Company image
	Patented products
Threat of Substitute Products/New Entrants	Brand awareness
Technological maturity/stability	**Response Time**
Diversity of the market	
Barriers to entry	Manufacturing flexibility
Flexibility of distribution system	Time needed to introduce new products
	Delivery times
Economic Factors	Organizational flexibility
Sales volatility	**Financial Strength**
Cyclicality of demand	
Market growth	Solvency
Capital intensity	Liquidity
	Break-even point
Financial Norms	Cash flows
Average profitability	Profitability
Typical leverage	Growth in revenues
Credit practices	**Human Assets**
Sociopolitical Considerations	Turnover
Government regulation	Skill level
Community support	Relative wage/salary
Ethical standards	Morale
	Managerial commitment
	Unionization
	Public Approval
	Goodwill
	Reputation
	Image

strength rather than the single measures (market share and market growth, respectively) employed in the BCG matrix. It also has nine cells as opposed to four—replacing the high/low axes with high/medium/low axes to make finer distinctions among business portfolio positions.

The company's businesses are rated on multiple strategic factors within each axis, such as the factors described in Figure 9–3.[3] The position of a business is then calculated by "subjectively" quantifying its rating along the two dimensions of the matrix. Depending on the location of a business within the matrix as shown in Figure 9–4, one of the following strategic approaches is suggested: (1) invest to grow, (2) invest selectively and manage for earnings, or (3) harvest or divest for resources. The resource allocation decisions remain quite similar to those of the BCG approach.

---

[3]A. Miller, *Strategic Management* (New York: McGraw-Hill, 1998), p. 263.

FIGURE 9–4
The Industry Attractiveness–Business Strength Matrix

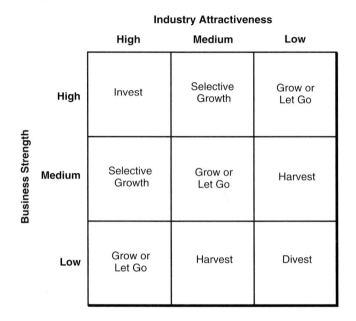

Industry Attractiveness

	High	Medium	Low
High	Invest	Selective Growth	Grow or Let Go
Medium	Selective Growth	Grow or Let Go	Harvest
Low	Grow or Let Go	Harvest	Divest

Business Strength

Description of Dimensions

Industry Attractiveness: Subjective assessment based on broadest possible range of external opportunities and threats beyond the strict control of management

Business Strength: Subjective assessment of how strong a competitive advantage is created by a broad range of the firm's internal strengths and weaknesses.

Source: McKinsey & Company and General Electric.

Although the strategic recommendations generated by the Industry Attractiveness–Business Strength Matrix are similar to those generated by the BCG matrix, the Industry Attractiveness–Business Strength Matrix improves on the BCG matrix in three fundamental ways. First, the terminology associated with the Industry Attractiveness–Business Strength Matrix is preferable because it is less offensive and more understandable. Second, the multiple measures associated with each dimension of the business strength matrix tap many factors relevant to business strength and market attractiveness besides market share and market growth. And this, in turn, makes for broader assessment during the planning process, bringing to light considerations of importance in both strategy formulation and strategy implementation.

The Life Cycle–Competitive Strength Matrix

One criticism of the first two portfolio methods was their static quality—their portrayal of businesses as they exist at one point in time, rather than as they evolve over time. A third portfolio approach was introduced that attempted to overcome these deficiencies and better identify "developing winners" or potential "losers."[4] This approach uses the multiple-factor approach to assess competitive strength as one dimension and stage of the market life cycle as the other dimension.

The life cycle dimension allows users to consider multiple strategic issues associated with each life cycle stage (refer to the discussion in Chapter 6), thereby enriching the discussion of strategic options. It also gives a "moving indication" of both issues—those strategy needs to address currently and those that could arise next. Figure 9–5 on page 340 provides an illustration of this matrix. It includes basic strategic investment parameters recommended for different positions in the matrix. While this approach seems valuable, its recommendations are virtually identical to the previous two portfolio matrices.

Limitations of Portfolio Approaches

Portfolio approaches made several contributions to strategic analysis by corporate managers convinced of their ability to transfer the competitive advantage of professional management across a broad array of businesses. They helped convey large amounts of information about diverse business units and corporate plans in a greatly simplified format. They illuminated similarities and differences between business units and helped convey the logic behind corporate strategies for each business with a common vocabulary. They simplified priorities for sharing corporate resources across diverse business units that generated and used those resources. They provided a simple prescription that gave corporate managers a sense of what they should accomplish—a balanced portfolio of businesses—and a way to control and allocate resources among them. While these approaches offered meaningful contributions, they had several critical limitations and shortcomings:

- A key problem with the portfolio matrix was that it did not address how value was being created across business units—the only relationship between them was cash. Because of this, its valued simplicity encouraged a tendency to trivialize strategic thinking among users that did not take proper time for thorough underlying analysis.
- Truly accurate measurement for matrix classification was not as easy as the matrices portrayed. Identifying individual businesses, or distinct markets, was not often as precise as underlying assumptions required.
- The underlying assumption about the relationship between market share and profitability—the experience curve effect—varied across different industries and market segments. Some have no such link. Some find that firms with low market share can generate superior profitability with differentiation advantages.
- The limited strategic options, intended to describe the flow of resources in a company, came to be seen more as basic strategic missions. Doing this creates a false sense of what strategies were when none really existed. This becomes more acute when attempting to use the matrices to conceive strategies for average businesses in average growth markets.
- The portfolio approach portrayed the notion that firms needed to be self-sufficient in capital. This ignored capital raised in capital markets.
- The portfolio approach typically failed to compare the competitive advantage a business received from being owned by a particular company with the costs of owning

[4]Attributed to Arthur D. Little, a consulting firm, and to Charles W. Hofer in "Conceptual Constructs for Formulating Corporate and Business Strategies" (Boston: Harvard Case Services, #9-378-754, 1977).

FIGURE 9–5
The Market Life Cycle–Competitive Strength Matrix

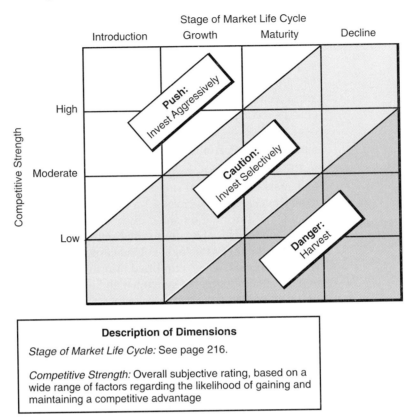

it. The 1980s saw many companies build enormous corporate infrastructures that created only small gains at the business level. The deconstruction in the 1990s of some "model" portfolio companies reflects this important omission.

Constructing business portfolio matrices must be undertaken with these limitations in mind. Perhaps it is best to say that they provide one form of input to corporate managers seeking to balance financial resources. They should be used merely to provide a basis for further discussion of corporate strategy and the allocation of corporate resources, and to provide a picture of the "balance" of resource generators and users to test underlying assumptions about these issues in more involved corporate planning efforts to leverage core competencies to build sustained competitive advantages. For while the portfolio approaches have serious limitations, the challenge for corporate managers overseeing the allocation of resources among a variety of business units is still to maintain a balanced use of the company's financial resources.

Does Our Business Portfolio Achieve Appropriate Levels of Risk and Growth?

Diversification has traditionally been recommended as a way to manage, or diversify, risk. Said another way, "not having all your eggs in one basket" allows corporate managers to potentially reduce risk to company stockholders. Balancing cyclical revenue streams to reduce earnings volatility is one way diversification may reduce risk. So

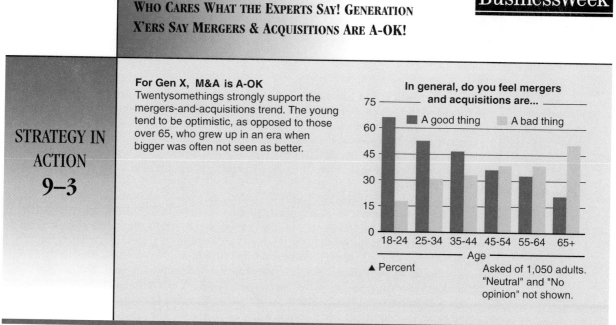

STRATEGY IN ACTION 9–3

WHO CARES WHAT THE EXPERTS SAY! GENERATION X'ERS SAY MERGERS & ACQUISITIONS ARE A-OK!

BusinessWeek

For Gen X, M&A is A-OK
Twentysomethings strongly support the mergers-and-acquisitions trend. The young tend to be optimistic, as opposed to those over 65, who grew up in an era when bigger was often not seen as better.

In general, do you feel mergers and acquisitions are...
■ A good thing ■ A bad thing

Age: 18-24, 25-34, 35-44, 45-54, 55-64, 65+

▲ Percent

Asked of 1,050 adults. "Neutral" and "No opinion" not shown.

Source: "Up Front" section, *Business Week:* August 10, 1998, p. 6.

managers need to ask this question as a part of their strategic analysis and subsequent choice. Likewise, revenue growth can be enhanced by diversification. Many companies in the hazardous waste industry maintained the steady growth investors had come to expect by continuously making acquisitions of other businesses to gain immediate sales growth. Indeed, Strategy in Action 9–3 reports that Generation X managers are much more comfortable with "M&A" diversification growth than their elderly counterparts.

Both risk and growth are assumptions or priorities corporate managers should carefully examine as they undertake strategic analysis and choice. Is growth always desirable? Can risks truly be managed most effectively by corporate management? Many companies have pursued growth to gain market share without accompanying attention to profitability. Similarly, companies have built diverse business portfolios in part to manage overall risk. In both instances, the outcome is often a later time when subsequent management must "look in the bag" of businesses and aggressively divest and downsize the company until true value-adding activities and synergies linked to sustained competitive advantages are uncovered. Strategy in Action 9–4 shows Finland's Nokia outdistancing Motorola and Ericsson due to the advantage Nokia's focus provides over the others' portfolio problems.

BEHAVIORAL CONSIDERATIONS AFFECTING STRATEGIC CHOICE

After alternative strategies have been analyzed, managers choose one of those strategies. If the analysis identified a clearly superior strategy or if the current strategy will clearly meet future company objectives, then the decision is relatively simple. Such clarity is the exception, however, and strategic decision makers often are confronted with several viable alternatives rather than the luxury of a clear-cut choice.

BusinessWeek

NOKIA'S SECRET FOR SUCCESS

**STRATEGY IN
ACTION
9–4**

Focused growth in new geographic cell phone markets and related products, rather than product and technology diversification, is Finland's Nokia's impressive secret.

Six years ago, as an untested CEO, Jorma Ollila bet Nokia, the 133-year-old Finnish conglomerate, on cellular phones, challenging rivals Motorola Inc. and L. M. Ericsson. In the struggle that ensued, Ollila's Finns outdid themselves. Fast and focused, with a canny eye for design, Nokia wrested market share from entrenched competitors and emerged as the most profitable player in the industry.

All told, Nokia is providing troubled Motorola Inc., the leader in old-fashioned analog phones, with a humiliating tutorial on digital communications. Motorola CEO Christopher B. Galvin glumly concedes that "the analog business is trending down." Ollila, for his part, predicts that Nokia will be "No. 1 in the world in the number of phones sold, in growth, and return on capital employed." Rapid growth should about double the worldwide number of cellular subscribers, now equally divided among Europe, Asia, and the Americas, to 550 million by 2001. This benefits the big three—Motorola, Ericsson, and, of course, Nokia—which rule three-quarters of the cellular market with nearly equal shares. Motorola, though, is struggling to escape from dying analog, where prices are collapsing. And Ericsson, while fully in stride with Nokia in digital sets, is far larger and more diverse and is burdened with less profitable old-line businesses.

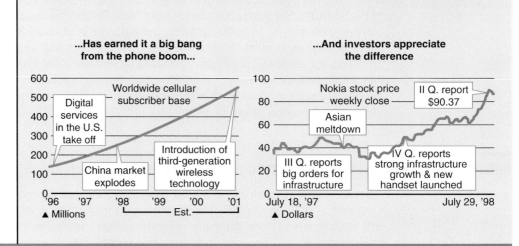

**Nokia is battling
two Goliaths...**

	Motorola	Ericsson	**Nokia**
1997 Sales	$29.8	$21.17	**$9.64**
% Increase	+6.5%	+35%	**+34%**
Operating profits*	$1.95	$2.37	**$1.58**
% Increase	Flat	75%	**+98%**

*Billions of dollars

**...But its laserlike focus
on cell phones...**

Cell phones and infrastructure as percent of sales**

Motorola Ericsson Nokia

** Includes infrastructure

**...Has earned it a big bang
from the phone boom...**

Worldwide cellular subscriber base

Digital services in the U.S. take off

China market explodes

Introduction of third-generation wireless technology

'96 '97 '98 '99 '00 '01
▲ Millions   —— Est. ——

**...And investors appreciate
the difference**

Nokia stock price weekly close

II Q. report $90.37

Asian meltdown

III Q. reports big orders for infrastructure

IV Q. reports strong infrastructure growth & new handset launched

July 18, '97   July 29, '98
▲ Dollars

Source: "Can CEO Ollila Keep the Cellular Superstar Flying High?" *Business Week:* August 10, 1998, p. 55.

Under these circumstances, several factors influence the strategic choice. Some of the more important are:

1. Role of the current strategy.
2. Degree of the firm's external dependence.
3. Attitudes toward risk.
4. Managerial priorities different from stockholder interests.
5. Internal political considerations.
6. Competitive reaction.

Role of the Current Strategy

Current strategists are often the architects of past strategies. If they have invested substantial time, resources, and interest in those strategies, they logically would be more comfortable with a choice that closely parallels or involves only incremental alterations to the current strategy.

Such familiarity with and commitment to past strategy permeates the entire firm. Thus, lower-level managers reinforce the top managers' inclination toward continuity with past strategy during the choice process. Research in several companies found lower-level managers suggested strategic choices that were consistent with current strategy and likely to be accepted while withholding suggestions with less probability of approval. Research by Henry Mintzberg suggests that past strategy strongly influences current strategic choice. The older and more successful a strategy has been, the harder it is to replace. Similarly, once a strategy has been initiated, it is very difficult to change because organizational momentum keeps it going. Even as a strategy begins to fail due to changing conditions, strategists often increase their commitment to it. Thus, firms may replace top executives when performance has been inadequate for an extended period because replacing these executives lessens the influence of unsuccessful past strategy on future strategic choice.

Degree of the Firm's External Dependence

If a firm is highly dependent on one or more environmental elements, its strategic alternatives and its ultimate strategic choice must accommodate that dependence. The greater a firm's external dependence, the lower its range and flexibility in strategic choice.

Bama Pies is a great family business success story. It makes excellent pies—apple turnovers. For many years, Bama Pies sold most of its pie output to one customer—McDonald's. With its massive retail coverage and its access to alternative suppliers. McDonald's was a major external dependence for Bama Pies. Bama Pies' strategic alternatives and ultimate choice of strategy were limited and strongly influenced by McDonald's demands.

Numerous small software companies and even many larger computer, software, and Internet-related businesses have considerable external dependence on Microsoft's operating system for their main products and services. Decisions to pursue options that put that relationship at risk are weighed with much hesitation because of the impact a negative Microsoft reaction could have on their company's survival. Or consider Amazon.com, the Internet bookseller and 1999 Wall Street darling company. As that year began, arch rival Barnes and Noble acquired the leading book distributor Ingram Book Group, which supplied 60 percent of Amazon.com's books. Barnes & Noble promises "no favoritism," but Amazon's high external dependence on Ingram will no doubt be reevaluated and other sources considered even at a higher cost.

While external dependence can restrict options, it isn't necessarily a strategic threat. The last decade has seen firms' efforts to enhance quality and cost include decisions to "sole-source" certain supplies or services, even ones central to the firm's strategic capabilities. This increases "external dependence," but it is seen as a way to "strategically partner" that allows both firms to share information, and improve and integrate product and process design and development, to mention a few benefits that may accrue to both partners. More on this in Chapter 11.

Attitudes toward Risk

Attitudes toward risk exert considerable influence on strategic choice. Where attitudes favor risk, the range of the strategic choices expands and high-risk strategies are acceptable and desirable. Where management is risk averse, the range of strategic choices is limited and risky alternatives are eliminated before strategic choices are made. Past strategy exerts far more influence on the strategic choices of risk-averse managers. Strategy in Action 9–4 shows how the highly focused, risk-tolerant Nokia has flown past risk-averse Motorola in cell phones.

Industry volatility influences the propensity of managers toward risk. Top managers in highly volatile industries absorb and operate with greater amounts of risk than do their counterparts in stable industries. Therefore, top managers in volatile industries consider a broader, more diverse range of strategies in the strategic choice process.

Industry evolution is another determinant of managerial propensity toward risk. A firm in the early stages of the product-market cycle must operate with considerably greater risk and uncertainty than a firm in the later stages of that cycle.

In making a strategic choice, risk-oriented managers lean toward opportunistic strategies with higher payoffs. They are drawn to offensive strategies based on innovation, company strengths, and operating potential. Risk-averse managers lean toward safe, conservative strategies with reasonable, highly probable returns. They are drawn to defensive strategies that minimize a firm's weaknesses, external threats, and the uncertainty associated with innovation-based strategies.

Managerial Priorities Different from Stockholder Interests

Corporate managers are hired, theoretically, to act as agents of shareholders and to make decisions that are in shareholders' best interests. An increasing area of research known as *agency theory* suggests that managers frequently place their own interests above those of their shareholders.[5] This appears to be particularly true when the strategic decisions involve diversification. While stockholder value may be maximized by selling a company, for example, managers in the acquired company may lose their jobs—a potential conflict of interests. In these circumstances, several of the benefits sought through diversification give rise to potential manager-stockholder conflicts. The idea of "sharing core competencies" may encounter resistance from managers suspicious about diluting their valued capability. "Shared infrastructure" usually means fewer managers are needed. "Balancing financial resources" realistically means resources controlled by one management group become shared or diluted to support other businesses.

---

[5]K. M. Eisenhardt, "Agency Theory: An Assessment and Review," *Academy of Management Review* 14 (1989), pp. 57–74; B. M. Oviatt, "Agency and Transaction Cost Perspectives on the Manager-Shareholder Relationship: Incentives for Congruent Interests," *Academy of Management Review* 13 (1988), pp. 214–25.

FIGURE 9-6
Political Activities in Phases of Strategic Decision Making

Phases of Strategic Decision Making	Focus of Political Action	Examples of Political Activity
Identification and diagnosis of strategic issues.	Control of: Issues to be discussed. Cause-and-effect relationships to be examined.	Control agenda. Interpretation of past events and future trends.
Narrowing the alternative strategies for serious consideration.	Control of alternatives.	Mobilization: Coalition formation. Resource commitment for information search.
Examining and choosing the strategy.	Control of choice.	Selective advocacy of criteria. Search and representation of information to justify choice.
Initiating implementation of the strategy.	Interaction between winners and losers.	Winners attempt to "sell" or co-opt losers. Losers attempt to thwart decisions and trigger fresh strategic issues.
Designing procedures for the evaluation of results.	Representing oneself as successful.	Selective advocacy of criteria.

Source: Adapted from Liam Fahey and V. K. Naroyanan, "The Politics of Strategic Decision Making," in *The Strategic Management Handbook,* ed. Kenneth J. Albert (New York: McGraw-Hill, 1983), pp. 20–21.

Similarly, some managers may seek diversification to accelerate sales growth, although continued focus in a narrow market area ensures increased competitive advantage to sustain long-term shareholder value. "Growth" achieved by combining two companies increases the basis on which some managers are compensated, regardless of whether the combination is truly advantageous to stockholders. The bottom line is, particularly where diversification decisions are being made, managerial self-interests can result in strategic choices that benefit managers to the detriment of stockholders. In these situations, strategic decision making can take on a political context like that described in the next section and Figure 9–6.

Internal Political Considerations

Power/political factors influence strategic choice. The use of power to further individual or group interest is common in organizational life. A major source of power in most firms is the chief executive officer (CEO). In smaller firms, the CEO is consistently the dominant force in strategic choice. Regardless of firm size, when the CEO begins to favor a particular choice, it is often selected unanimously.

Coalitions are power sources that influence strategic choice. In large firms, subunits and individuals (particularly key managers) have reason to support some alternatives and oppose others. Mutual interest draws certain groups together in coalitions to enhance their position on major strategic issues. These coalitions, particularly the more powerful ones (often called *dominant coalitions*), exert considerable influence on the strategic choice process. Numerous studies confirm the frequent use of power and coalitions in strategic decision making.

Figure 9–6 shows that the *content* of strategic decisions and the *processes* of arriving at such decisions are politically charged. Each phase in the process of strategic choice presents an opportunity for political action intended to influence the outcome. The challenge for strategists lies in recognizing and managing this political influence. For example, selecting the criteria used to compare alternative strategies or collecting and appraising information regarding those criteria may be particularly susceptible to political influence. This possibility must be recognized and, where necessary, "managed" to avoid dysfunctional political bias. Relying on different sources to collect and appraise information might serve this purpose.

Organizational politics must be viewed as an inevitable dimension of organizational decision making that strategic management must accommodate. Some authors argue that politics is a key ingredient in the "glue" that holds an organization together. Formal and informal negotiating and bargaining between individuals, subunits, and coalitions are indispensable mechanisms for organizational coordination. Accommodating these mechanisms in the choice of strategy will result in greater commitment and more realistic strategy. The costs of doing so, however, are likely to be increased time spent on decision making and incremental (as opposed to drastic) change.

Competitive Reaction

In weighing strategic choices, top management frequently incorporates perceptions of likely competitor reactions to those choices. For example, if it chooses an aggressive strategy directly challenging a key competitor, that competitor can be expected to mount an aggressive counterstrategy. In weighing strategic choices, top management must consider the probable impact of such reactions on the success of the chosen strategy.

The beer industry provides a good illustration. In the early 1970s, Anheuser-Busch dominated the industry, and Miller Brewing Company, recently acquired by Philip Morris, was a weak and declining competitor. Miller's management decided to adopt an expensive advertising-oriented strategy that challenged the big three (Anheuser-Busch, Pabst, and Schlitz) head-on because it assumed that their reaction would be delayed due to Miller's current declining status in the industry. This assumption proved correct, and Miller was able to reverse its trend in market share before Anheuser-Busch countered with an equally intense advertising strategy.

Miller's management took another approach in its next major strategic decision. In the mid-1970s, it introduced (and heavily advertised) a low-calorie beer—Miller Lite. Other industry members had introduced such products without much success. Miller chose a strategy that did not directly challenge its key competitors and was not expected to elicit immediate counterattacks from them. This choice proved highly successful, because Miller was able to establish a dominant share of the low-calorie beer market before those competitors decided to react. In this case, as in the preceding case, expectations regarding the reactions of competitors were a key determinant in the strategic choice made by Miller's management.

SUMMARY

This chapter examined how managers evaluate and choose their company's strategy in multibusiness settings. They look to rationalize their efforts to diversify and their current or anticipated collection of businesses. Doing this means identifying opportunities to share skills and core competencies across businesses or from corporate capabilities to business operational needs. Such opportunities usually arise in marketing, operations, management, or a combination of these activities when a capability in one area contributes to a competitive advantage in another.

Diversified, multibusiness companies face yet another, more complicated process of strategy analysis and choice. This chapter looked at the evolution of this challenge from portfolio approaches to value-based ways to decide which set of businesses maximizes opportunities to build shareholder value.

Critical, often overlooked in the process of strategic analysis and choice, are behavioral considerations that may well determine a company's choice of strategy as much or more so than solely rational analysis. Commitment to the current strategy, external dependence, managerial self-interests, political considerations, and competitive considerations combine to exercise a major influence on how managers eventually evaluate and choose strategies.

QUESTIONS FOR DISCUSSION

1. How does strategic analysis at the corporate level differ from strategic analysis at the business unit level? How are they related?

2. When would multi-industry companies find the portfolio approach to strategic analysis and choice useful?

3. What are three types of opportunities for sharing that form a sound basis for diversification or vertical integration? Give an example of each from companies you have read about.

4. What role might power and politics play in strategic analysis within a multibusiness company? Strategic choice within that same company? Would you expect these issues to be more prominent in a diversified company or in a single–product line company? Why or why not?

5. Several behavioral considerations discussed in this chapter appear to influence strategic analysis and choice within many companies as they seek to chart future direction. From your reading of current business publications, select and explain an example of a company where one of these behavioral considerations influenced strategic analysis and choice.

BIBLIOGRAPHY

Badaracco, Joseph L., Jr. "Alliances Speed Knowledge Transfer." *Planning Review* (March–April 1991), pp. 10–16.

Bettis, Richard A., and William K. Hall. "The Business Portfolio Approach—Where It Falls Down in Practice." *Long Range Planning* 16, no. 2 (April 1983), pp. 95–104.

Bulkeley, William M. "Conglomerates Make a Comeback—with a '90s Twist," *The Wall Street Journal* (March 1, 1994), p. 1.

Buzzell, R. D. "Is Vertical Integration Profitable?" *Harvard Business Review* 61 (January–February 1994), pp. 92–102.

Calori, Roland, CESMA. "How Successful Companies Manage Diverse Businesses." *Long Range Planning* 21, no. 3 (1988), pp. 80–89.

Chatterjee, Sayan. "Sources of Value in Takeovers: Synergy or Restructuring—Implications for Target and Bidder Firms." *Strategic Management Journal* 13 (1992), pp. 267–86.

Davis, R., and L. G. Thomas. "Direct Estimation of Synergy: A New Approach to the Diversity-Performance Debate." *Management Science* 39 (1993), pp. 1334–46.

Ewaldz, D. B. "How Integrated Should Your Company Be?" *Journal of Business Strategy* (July–August 1991), pp. 52–55.

Fisher, Anne B. "How to Make a Merger Work." *Fortune* (January 24, 1994), pp. 66–70.

Fry, J. N., and P. J. Killing. "Vision-Check." *Business Quarterly* [Canada] 54, no. 2 (1989), pp. 64–69.

Ginter, P. M.; W. J. Duncan; L. E. Swayne; and A. G. Shelfer. "When Merger Means Death: Organizational Euthanasia and Strategic Choice." *Organizational Dynamics* 20, no. 3 (1992), pp. 21–33.

Goold, Michael, and Kathleen Luchs. "Why Diversify? Four Decades of Management Thinking." *Academy of Management Executive* 7, no. 3 (1993), p. 7.

Haspeslagh, Phillippe C., and David B. Jamison. *Managing Acquisitions: Creating Value through Corporate Renewal.* New York: Free Press, 1991.

Hoskisson, Robert E. "Multidivisional Structure and Performance: The Contingency of Diversification Strategy." *Academy of Management Journal,* December 1987, p. 621.

Lei, David, and John W. Slocum Jr. "Global Strategy, Competence-Building and Strategic Alliances." *California Management Review* (Fall 1992), pp. 81–97.

Lorange, P., and J. Roos. "Why Some Strategic Alliances Succeed and Others Fail." *Journal of Business Strategy* (January–February 1991), pp. 25–30.

Lubatkin, M., and S. Chatterjee. "Extending Modern Portfolio Theory into the Domain of Corporate Diversification: Does It Apply?" *Academy of Management Journal* 37 (1994), pp. 109–36.

Lubatkin, Michael. "Value-Creating Mergers: Fact or Folklore?" *Academy of Management Executive* 2 (November 1988), pp. 295–302.

Mahoney, Joseph T. "The Choice of Organizational Form: Vertical Financial Ownership Versus Other Methods of Vertical Integration." *Strategic Management Journal* 13 (1992), pp. 559–84.

Naugle, David G., and Garret A. Davies. "Strategic-Skill Pools and Competitive Advantage." *Business Horizons* 30, no. 6 (November–December 1987), pp. 35–42.

Nord, Walter R. "Do Mergers Make Acquired Executives Feel Inferior? You Bet!" *Academy of Management Executive* 8, no. 2 (1994), pp. 81–82.

Porter, Michael E. *Competitive Advantage.* New York: Free Press, 1984, chaps. 9–11.

—————. "From Competitive Advantage to Corporate Strategy." *Harvard Business Review* 65, no. 3 (May–June 1987), pp. 43–59.

Rappaport, Alfred. "CFOs and Strategists: Forging a Common Framework." *Harvard Business Review* (May–June 1992), pp. 84–91.

Stuckey, John, and David White. "When and When *Not* to Vertically Integrate." *McKinsey Quarterly* (Summer 1993), pp. 3–27.

Tichy, Noel M., and Stratford Sherman. *Control Your Destiny or Someone Else Will.* New York: Doubleday, 1993.

Tully, Shawn. "The Real Key to Creating Wealth." *Fortune* (September 20, 1993), p. 38.

Walsh, James P., and John W. Ellwood. "Mergers, Acquisitions, and the Pruning of Managerial Deadwood." *Strategic Management Journal* 12 (1991), pp. 201–17.

Zweig, L. "Who Says the Conglomerate is Dead?" *Business Week,* January 23, 1995, p. 92.

CHAPTER 9 DISCUSSION CASE

BusinessWeek

DAIMLER'S DIVERSIFICATION DANCE

Chapter 9 has helped you look at companies' decisions to become more diversified, to become multibusiness companies, or to narrow their scope to fewer businesses.

Daimler Benz is an interesting company for you to examine in the *Business Week* Discussion Case because it has had such a varied diversification experience in the decade just ended. You might say that this last decade has been Daimler Benz's *decade-long dance with the diversification devil.*

So *Business Week* reporters John Templeton, Bill Vlasic, Kathleen Kerwin, David Woodruff, Thane Peterson, Leah Nathans, and Jeff Garten take you through *Daimler's Diversification Dance* to illustrate some of the concepts about strategic analysis and choice involving multibusiness companies. They examine it in three phases, or dance steps, ending with the Daimler-Chrysler waltz, which they examine in the greatest detail.

Daimler Benz has "danced" an incredible and varied dance with diversification in the 1990s. You could say there were three segments, steps, or eras to the dance:

- *Obsession* with Diversification—Be all we can possibly be—in the decade's first half
- *Revulsion* with Diversification—Be only what we have to be—in the mid-decade
- *Simple related* Diversification—Be the global car company we have to be—decade's end

OBSESSION WITH DIVERSIFICATION—BE ALL WE CAN POSSIBLY BE—IN THE DECADE'S FIRST HALF

Daimler Benz spent billions of dollars on acquisitions in the early 1990s to try to transform itself from an auto maker into a high-tech conglomerate excelling at everything from telecommunications to jet planes. In perhaps the most critical step toward that goal, CEO Edzard Reuter laid out an additional $1.9 billion—and even billions more later—in a bid to succeed in an industry where his European rivals have failed and become a global heavyweight in microelectronics.

Reuter thought he didn't have much choice. Whether in aerospace or autos, Daimler needs to become a leader in microelectronics if it hopes to stay competitive with the U.S. and Japan. Daimler's new venture would steer clear of standard memory chips, which have led to huge losses. Instead, it will make specialized chips that are custom-designed to control everything from automobile engines to computerized production lines. Daimler executives worried that if they don't make their own chips they

Source: *Business Week:* November 16, 1998; July 20, 1998; September 21, 1995; July 4, 1994; and June 22, 1992.

will be increasingly dependent on Japanese and American technology for their next generation of products. It would mean sharing sensitive product knowhow with outsiders who design the chips. That's a risk the Germans didn't want to take. One way or another, microelectronics influences two-thirds of Germany's gross national product, said Frank Dieter Maier, head of the new Daimler chip unit. Daimler wasn't alone. Other German industrial giants, such as Siemens and Robert Bosch, also ramped up production of application-specific chips, called ASICs, and other logic products. In fact, the Germans moved toward Japanese-style integration, where systems manufacturers and electronics companies often share space under the same keiretsu roof. Without a competitive chip operation, "Daimler's engineers will lose touch with fast-paced semiconductor developments that have a huge impact on their automotive electronics," said Tomihiro Matsumura, the senior executive vice-president who heads chip operations at NEC Corp.

Despite Daimler's deep pockets, Reuter's bet was a risky one. Competition in the multibillion dollar ASIC business gets hotter every day as well-heeled memory-chip makers from South Korea to Tokyo to the Silicon Valley seek to step up production of custom chips. That means learning the hard way. Early in its efforts, when Daimler sold bipolar chips to Mitsubishi Electric, Mitsubishi rejected them, saying they weren't good enough. Daimler engineers redoubled their efforts, revamping test procedures from start to finish on the production line. Said a hopeful Maier: "It's a learning experience. It will pay off."

By the mid-1990s Edzard Reuter was ready to retire at 66 years old having returned Daimler to profitability ($750 million on $74 billion in sales versus a $1.3 billion loss the previous year). He was still passing out copies of his glossy document called The New Age in which Reuter boasted that he had transformed Daimler from a luxury car maker into an "integrated technology group" involved in aerospace, microelectronics, and many kinds of transportation. His heir apparent Jurgen E. Schrempp, had been the leading CEO candidate ever since Reuter appointed him CEO of Deutsche Aerospace (DASA). His mission there was to weld a grab bag of outfits making engines, rockets, planes, and helicopters into a coherent company. That job was a small-scale version of what Reuter has been trying to do with all of Daimler—pool the technical knowhow of its autos to avionics units into an integrated high-technology concern, a sort of Teutonic General Electric Co. The effort included pouring $6.25 billion into acquisitions over five years. Reuter left saying the strategy was working. There was little evidence it would pay off soon.

REVULSION WITH DIVERSIFICATION—BE ONLY WHAT WE HAVE TO BE—IN THE MID-DECADE

It could have been the smoothest of handovers. When Jurgen E. Schrempp became chief executive of Germany's Daimler Benz, he was expected to inherit a $74 billion industrial empire restored to financial health. His predecessor and mentor, Edzard Reuter, boasted of a return to profitability and promised another boost the next year. But less than three months later, the empire was in disarray. Hit by the soaring German mark, management disputes, and losses from Reuter's own diversification strategy, Daimler was faced another dangerous slide in profits. Brokers have stamped "sell" recommendations on the stock. In a fight to restore the company's credibility, Schrempp, 50, reversed Reuter's forecast and warned of "severe losses" in his first full year.

It turned out that Schrempp, while learning under diversification champion Reuter, had been spending his final year of grooming to become CEO preparing a very different, anti-diversification strategy for Daimler. All that year, Schrempp prepared his strategy, and once in power, he executed it with exacting swiftness. The goal: to reverse his former mentor's grand scheme of building an integrated technology company. First, he streamlined head-office hierarchy, cutting staff by more than 75%. "You have to sweep the stairs from the top down," he says. Then he examined each business unit, grilling frightened managers nearly to tears and set a 12% return-on-capital target for each unit. When the dust had settled, Daimler was down to 23 units from 35 and carried 63,000 fewer people on the payroll within six months after Schrempp became CEO.

That year observers described his longterm strategy as:

- Make a decisive break with failed diversification strategy
- Focus on core automotive and truck businesses, which provide most of the group's profits
- Close the money-losing Daimler Benz Industrie unit with sell-offs and transfers of profitable operations to other divisions
- Slim down DASA Daimler Benz Aerospace, reducing its workforce of 40,000 by up to 50%, and step up sourcing of parts from dollar and other weak-currency areas
- Speed up globalization of manufacturing by locating big-ticket plant investments outside Germany

By 1997, focus had started to pay off and the "swagger" was back at Mercedes. Take the U.S. market for example. It has been a remarkable turnaround for the German company, whose U.S. sales hit rock bottom in 1991 in the face of a successful onslaught by Japanese luxury brands. But they have since left rivals behind in the slow lane. Bolstered by a stable of new products and aggressive marketing campaigns, Mercedes (and BMW) again rank as the hottest luxury brands in the U.S. They ended 1997 in a dead heat for preeminence among luxury import brands, with BMW's sales of 122,500 vehicles edging out Mercedes' 122,417. And in a luxury-car market that grew just 6% from 1991 to 1997, BMW sales soared 130%, while Mercedes rose 83%. That has allowed the German brands to leapfrog past their top two Japanese rivals, Lexus and Acura. If BMW and Mercedes keep accelerating, they could roar past the faltering U.S. market leaders, General Motors' Cadillac Div. and Ford's Lincoln unit, within the next five years.

Competitors now hold Mercedes and BMW up as the standard to beat. "They have clearly reframed the luxury market," says John F. Smith, general manager of GM's Cadillac Div. "I think they've been much more responsive to a variety of consumer tastes." That's just the opposite of the reputations BMW and Mercedes carried at their low point in 1991. Back then, the pair admittedly lost touch with consumers. They paid the price: Sales bottomed out at 53,343 vehicles for BMW and 58,869 for Mercedes—down 45% and 41%, respectively, from their high five years earlier. "The key issue then was to survive," says Michael Jackson, president of Mercedes-Benz of North America.

The bottomline was a resounding rejection of the prior diversification strategy choosing instead to focus on stablizing the business around core competencies and capabilities relative to automotive and key transportation products, and to globalize its operations where cost benefits were derived.

SIMPLE RELATED DIVERSIFICATION—BE THE GLOBAL CAR COMPANY WE HAVE TO BE—DECADE'S END

CEO Schrempp led an aggressive effort to refocus and simplify Daimler Benz. It worked. But as he looked toward the 21st century's global automotive industry, he had some concerns. Daimler Benz had a limited, upper scale product line with an industry becoming truly global with overcapacity and increasing full product line competitors. Globally, in 1998 there was plant capacity to build at least 15 million more vehicles each year than could realistically be sold. And overcapacity was expected to balloon to 18.2 million vehicles by 2002. So while he was dismantling Daimler Benz and refocusing it around the automotive industry, Schrempp was thinking about eventually seeking a partner for Daimler that would diversify its product line and geographic presence in the global automotive industry. He had decided that a carmaker can't compete without a full range of products, and he couldn't stretch the Mercedes brand any further downmarket.

But first he had to get Daimler in shape for a merger. Mercedes-Benz was a separate operating company with its own board, run by Helmut Werner, who was a hero in Germany for reviving the Mercedes lineup. Schrempp wanted to give Daimler direct operating control of Mercedes. "We had steps and steps, and layers and layers," Schrempp explains, moving Marlboros around the table to illustrate. "It took months to make a decision." In 1995 and early 1996, talks between Chrysler CEO Eaton and Mercedes CEO Werner about a joint venture for all their international businesses outside Europe and North America had bogged down because of this structure. That failure helped spur Schrempp's reorganization. Although Werner fought to keep Mercedes independent, Schrempp prevailed with the supervisory board. By early 1997, Mercedes was folded into Daimler, Werner was out, and Schrempp was running a car business. A year later the lean, chainsmoking 54-year-old chief executive of Daimler Benz approached Chrysler CEO Robert J. Eaton in his office in Auburn Hills, Michigan with a scheme to merge their two companies. In a steak house with Daimler colleagues after the 17-minute chat, Schrempp worried that he may have been too bold. His fears were unfounded. America's scrappy No. 3 car company and Germany's most revered brand name quickly decided to combine to become the world's fifth-largest carmaker when shares in DaimlerChrysler first traded in November, 1998.

Schrempp and Eaton are entering into an unprecedented business experiment. The auto industry has long been among the world's most international. But the DaimlerChrysler merger ushers in a new phase of global competitiveness when the very biggest players in the world's main regions unite as industrial powerhouses of tremendous scope. Schrempp will be judged both on his ability to run this ungainly giant and on whether he can emerge as Europe's most forceful business leader.

The megadeal unites two of the world's most profitable auto companies—with combined 1997 net earnings of $4.6 billion. And if ever a merger had the potential for that elusive quality—synergy—this could be the one. Mercedes-Benz passenger cars are synonymous with luxury and sterling engineering. Chrysler is renowned for its low-cost production of trucks, minivans, and sport-utility vehicles. Chrysler is almost wholly domestic, and Mercedes is increasing global sales—albeit within the confines of the luxury-car market. By spreading Chrysler's production expertise to Daimler operations and merging both product-development forces, the new company could cut costs by up to $3 billion annually—including $1.1 billion in purchasing costs, analysts say. And fundamental synergies are as follows:

Product Synergies: There is almost no product overlap. Mercedes-Benz luxury cars compete in a market beyond Chrysler's mainstream offerings. Chrysler brings strength in minivans, profitable pickups, and sport-utility vehicles. Mercedes has hot-sellers like the E-class sedan and SLK roadster. The only overlapping model: Mercedes M-class, which goes against Jeep Grand Cherokee.

Geographic Synergies: Each company is strong where the other is weak. Chrysler derives 93% of its sales from North America. Mercedes-Benz depends on Europe for 63% of its business. Each company is looking to strengthen its position in its partner's home market and conquer emerging markets together.

One of the biggest opportunities is for the paired company to plunge into new markets that neither could assay alone. Neither has much of a presence in Latin America or Asia, although Daimler does sell heavy trucks there. Chrysler's inexpensive small cars will give Daimler a vehicle to drive into emerging markets. "With our [upscale] product portfolio, we will never be a mass marketer," says a source close to Daimler. "There are some markets where [Mercedes] will never be able to have an impact."

Operational Synergies: Chrysler's slowly improving quality could take a quantum leap forward with help from Daimler engineers. And Daimler's diesel engines, for example, could help Chrysler in its efforts to sell subcompacts and minivans in Europe and elsewhere. Chrysler, for its part, has the industry's best supplier relations, while Daimler still relies on strong-arm techniques to get lower prices from its suppliers. Together, they can save on warehousing and logistics for cars and spare parts in both Europe and the U.S. They also can jointly make internal components like air-conditioning systems and door latches and pool their resources in developing basic technology.

COMBINING DIVERGENT CORPORATE CULTURES: THE KEY CHALLENGE

Most rivals were too stunned to react when the merger was first announced. Both Ford and GM declined to comment in the U.S. as did BMW in Germany. On the other hand, many industry watchers immediately questioned whether the enormously divergent cultures of Auburn Hills and Stuttgart won't get in the way of all that synergy. "I can't imagine two more different cultures," says Furman Selz auto analyst Maryann N. Keller. Chrysler's brushes with bankruptcy forged a culture dedicated to speedy product development, lean operations, and flashy design. Daimler remains a buttoned-down, engineering-driven bureaucracy known for conservatively styled products. "The reaction here is shock, excitement, enthusiasm, and concern," said one Chrysler exec.

Indeed, most observers feel that DaimlerChrysler's success hinges on melding two starkly different corporate cultures. Daimler's methodical decision making could squelch Chrysler's famed creativity. Mercedes' reputation for luxury and quality could be tarnished by Chrysler's downmarket image. If they can't create a climate of learning from each other, warns Ulrich Steger, a management professor at IMD, the Lausanne business school, "they could be heading for unbelievable catastrophe."

If that happens, it won't be the first time. Big cross-border mergers have a poor track record. In most cases, the hoped-for savings are not realized, the weaker partner is stripped of its best assets, and margins plunge. For instance, BMW's merger with Rover floundered because BMW lacked a clear strategy, and the companies' models cannibalized each other. BMW has asked the British government for aid. Another deal involving a high-profile takeover by an admired foreign company of prized American assets: Sony Corp.'s acquisition of both CBS Records Inc. and Columbia Pictures saw Sony start off mistakenly thinking that it could oversee its freewheeling American companies from afar and with a light touch. It failed to put its own strong management structure in the U.S. It neglected to build links between Sony's American subsidiaries on the two coasts. It lost control of expenses, and by 1994, Sony was forced to take a $2.7 billion write-off.

Sony and Daimler are in different businesses, of course, and no one blueprint applies to all big international mergers. But the most successful global companies, such as Nestlé, ABB Asea Brown Boveri, and General Electric, have put their unambiguous imprint on all their operations by imposing one strong corporate culture with central management for the most critical functions. Someone must articulate overall philosophy and values and establish companywide investment priorities. Someone must set financial and operational performance requirements, compensation policies, and development paths for senior executives. Unless Daimler takes charge of these kinds of tasks immediately, don't be surprised if the deal comes unwound.

To avoid a similar fate, Schrempp and Eaton analyzed 50 large-scale mergers from many industries before launching their own. They found that 70% had stumbled, most for lack of clear targets and speed. "What you don't do in the first 12 to 24 months will be very difficult to do later," Schrempp said.

That's especially true for two industrial icons from business cultures that couldn't be more different. Chrysler is the very symbol of American adaptability and resilience. Having survived a near-death experience that required a 1979 government bailout, it scrambled under legendary CEO Lee A. Iacocca, and then Eaton, to become one of the world's leanest and nimblest car companies.

Daimler Benz, meanwhile, has long represented the epitome of German industrial might, its Mercedes cars the purest examples of German quality and engineering. But despite Schrempp's shakeup at the top, its middle ranks exemplify the hierarchical, procedure-driven German management style that could smother an agile company like Chrysler.

He was certainly the dominant player in forging the merger. "I wasn't going to sit passively and be the object of someone else's decision," Schrempp told 1,000 of Munich's glitterati as he introduced the new Mercedes S-Class sedan last month. Schrempp had talked to Ford Motor Co. in 1997, but the U.S. company's family-ownership structure would have complicated a merger. Sources close to Daimler say that Schrempp also approached Honda Motor Co., but found the cultural differences too great.

Investors immediately applauded—pushing Chrysler shares up $7\frac{3}{8}$ to $48\frac{13}{16}$ on May 6. "Chrysler has the trucks, vans, and SUVs, and Daimler has the luxury cars," says Seth M. Glickenhaus of Glickenhaus & Co., an investment firm that holds 8 million Chrysler shares. "There are enormous synergies in product." Amid the initial euphoria, *Business Week*'s Jeffrey E. Garten offered perhaps the most objective summary of the cultural challenge to make the Daimler-Chrysler merger work: The new company will face massive challenges. Daimler Chrysler will still be only the fifth-largest car company, behind General Motors, Ford, Toyota, and Volkswagen. Its product line, ranging from an $11,000 Dodge to a $130,000 Mercedes, could foster a confused image and culture. The German corporate governance system in which labor and banks hold board seats in order to take a longer-term view could collide with the obsession of American shareholders with immediate returns. Compensation philosophies could be irreconcilable: Just compare Chrysler Chairman and CEO Robert J. Eaton's 1997 pay package of $16 million with that of Daimler chief Jurgen E. Schrempp's $1.9 million.

And politically explosive decisions are sure to arise about how to apportion layoffs between America and Germany when downsizing occurs because of the overcapacity in the global auto industry.

One final likely outcome from this merger, well before anyone knows if Daimler-Chrysler is a success—its very existence could reshape the industry. Look for automakers to scramble for partners to ensure survival as one of the 21st century 20. How that plays out is anybody's guess. "The odd man out here seems to be the Japanese," says Phillippi of Lehman Brothers. "Nissan and Honda in particular have only two legs to stand on: North America and Japan." That won't be enough in this race.

III

STRATEGY IMPLEMENTATION

The last section of this book examines what is often called the *action phase* of the strategic management process: implementation of the chosen strategy. Up to this point, three phases of that process have been covered—strategy formulation, analysis of alternative strategies, and strategic choice. Although important, these phases alone cannot ensure success. To ensure success, the strategy must be translated into carefully implemented action. This means that:

1. The strategy must be translated into guidelines for the daily activities of the firm's members.
2. The strategy and the firm must become one—that is, the strategy must be reflected in the way the firm organizes its activities and in the firm's values, beliefs, and tone.
3. In implementing the strategy, the firm's managers must direct and control actions and outcomes and adjust to change.

Chapter 10 explains how organizational action is successfully initiated in four interrelated steps:

1. Creation of clear *short-term objectives* and *action plans.*
2. Development of specific *functional tactics* that create competitive advantage.
3. Empowerment of operating personnel through *policies* to guide decisions.
4. Implementation of effective *reward system.*

Short-term objectives and action plans guide implementation by converting long-term objectives into short-term actions and targets. Functional tactics translate the business strategy into activities that build advantage. Policies empower operating personnel by defining guidelines for making decisions. Reward systems encourage effective results.

Today's competitive environment often necessitates restructuring and reengineering the organization to sustain competitive advantage. Chapter 11 examines how restructuring and reengineering are pursued in three organizational elements that provide fundamental, long-term means for institutionalizing the firm's strategy:

1. The firm's *structure.*
2. The *leadership* provided by the firm's CEO and key managers.
3. The fit between the strategy and the firm's *culture.*

Since the firm's strategy is implemented in a changing environment, successful implementation requires that execution be controlled and continuously improved. The control and improvement process must include at least these dimensions:

1. *Strategic controls* that "steer" execution of the strategy.
2. *Operations control systems* that monitor performance, evaluate deviations, and initiate corrective action.
3. *Continuous improvement* through total quality initiatives.

Chapter 12 examines the dimensions of the control and improvement process. It explains the essence of change as an ever-present force driving the need for strategic control. The chapter concludes with a look at the global "quality imperative," which is redefining the essence of control into the 21st century.

Implementation is "where the action is." It is the arena that most students enter at the start of their business careers. It is the strategic phase in which staying close to the customer, achieving competitive advantage, and pursuing excellence become realities. The chapters in this part will help you understand how this is done.

10

IMPLEMENTING STRATEGY THROUGH SHORT-TERM OBJECTIVES, FUNCTIONAL TACTICS, REWARD SYSTEM, AND EMPLOYEE EMPOWERMENT

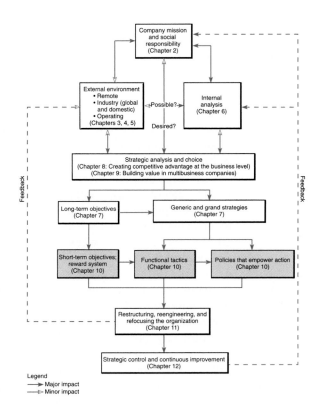

Once corporate and business strategies have been agreed upon and long-term objectives set, the strategic management process moves into a critical new phase—translating strategic thought into organizational action. In the words of two well-worn phrases, they move from "planning their work" to "working their plan" as they shift their focus from strategy formulation to strategy implementation. Managers successfully make this shift when they do four things well:

1. Identify short-term objectives.
2. Initiate specific functional tactics.
3. Communicate policies that empower people in the organization.
4. Design effective rewards.

Short-term objectives translate long-range aspirations into this year's targets for action. If well developed, these objectives provide clarity, a powerful motivator and facilitator of effective strategy implementation.

Functional tactics translate business strategy into daily activities people need to execute. Functional managers participate in the development of these tactics, and their participation, in turn, helps clarify what their units are expected to do in implementing the business's strategy.

Policies are empowerment tools that simplify decision making by empowering operating managers and their subordinates. Policies can empower the "doers" in an organization by reducing the time required to decide and act.

A powerful part of getting things done in any organization can be found in the way its reward system rewards desired action and results. Rewards that align manager and employee priorities with organizational objectives and shareholder value provide very effective direction in strategy implementation.

SHORT-TERM OBJECTIVES

Chapter 7 described business strategies, grand strategies, and long-term objectives that are critically important in crafting a successful future. To make them become a reality, however, the people in an organization that actually "do the work" of the business need guidance in exactly what needs to be done today and tomorrow to make those long-term strategies become reality. Short-term objectives help do this. They provide much more specific guidance for what is to be done, a clear delineation of impending actions needed, which helps translate vision into action.

Short-term objectives help implement strategy in at least three ways. First, short-term objectives "operationalize" long-term objectives. If we commit to a 20 percent gain in revenue over five years, what is our specific target or objective in revenue during the current year, month, or week to indicate we are making appropriate progress? Second, discussion about and agreement on short-term objectives help raise issues and potential conflicts within an organization that usually require coordination to avoid otherwise dysfunctional consequences. Figure 10–1 illustrates how objectives within marketing, manufacturing, and accounting units within the same firm can be very different even when created to pursue the same firm objective (e.g., increased sales, lower costs). The third way short-term objectives assist strategy implementation is to identify measurable outcomes of action plans or functional activities, which can be used to make feedback, correction, and evaluation more relevant and acceptable.

Short-term objectives are usually accompanied by action plans, which enhance these objectives in three ways. First, action plans usually identify functional tactics and

FIGURE 10–1
Potential Conflicting Objectives and Priorities

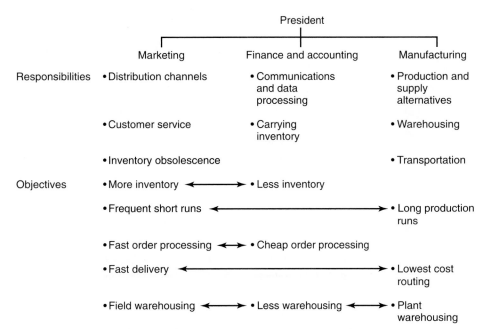

Source: John F. Stolle, "How to Manage Physical Distribution," *Harvard Business Review,* July–August 1967, p. 95. Used by permission.

activities that will be undertaken in the next week, month, or quarter as part of the business's effort to build competitive advantage. The important point here is *specificity*—what exactly is to be done. We will examine functional tactics in a subsequent section of this chapter. The second element of an action plan is a clear *time frame for completion*—when the effort will begin and when its results will be accomplished. A third element action plans contain is identification of *who is responsible* for each action in the plan. This accountability is very important to ensure action plans are acted upon. Strategy in Action 10–1 provides excerpts from the short-term objectives and action plans of a small oil distribution company in the northeastern United States that was part of its 2000–2002 strategic plan.

Because of the particular importance of short-term objectives in strategy implementation, the next section addresses how to develop meaningful short-term objectives.

Qualities of Effective Short-Term Objectives

Measurable

Short-term objectives are more consistent when they clearly state *what* is to be accomplished, *when* it will be accomplished, and *how* its accomplishment will be *measured.* Such objectives can be used to monitor both the effectiveness of each activity and the collective progress across several interrelated activities. Figure 10–2 illustrates several effective and ineffective short-term objectives. Measurable objectives make misunderstanding less likely among interdependent managers who must implement action plans. It is far easier to quantify the objectives of *line* units (e.g., production) than of certain *staff* areas (e.g., personnel). Difficulties in quantifying objectives often

FROM OBSCURITY TO BEING A LEADER IN FUEL DISTRIBUTION ALONG VIRGINIA'S COAST

STRATEGY IN ACTION 10–1

EnergyCo is an exciting, closely-held fuel distribution company located in coastal Virginia. Its management team has undertaken regular strategic analysis and planning to guide its growth aspirations. Its most recent planning efforts generated a comprehensive strategic plan to exploit several attractive opportunities. A key part of their ongoing strategic planning effort is the identification of action plans and annual objectives to make their wide-ranging planning discussions and efforts become concrete actions for which each member of the management team accepts some responsibility. They also insist on reducing the action plans into a few pages with minimal wording so that they can easily be reviewed, updated, and discussed at each weekly management meeting. Included below is an excerpt from their most recent action plan.

Objective	Assumption	2000	2002
Sales: Commercial fuels	12.5% annual growth	$ 16.9 mm	$ 21.0 mm
Sales: Oil futures hedging	Approximately 5% annual growth	$ 6.5 mm	$ 7.0 mm
Sales: Retail/C stores	Approximately 5% annual growth	$ 4.3 mm	$ 5.0 mm
Sales: Branding	4 sites per year 2001–02	$ 4.0 mm	$ 12.0 mm
Sales: Home heat	1 or 2 acquisitions 2001–02	$ 1.5 mm	$ 3.0 mm
Sales: Fleet pump	Aggressive growth 2001–02	$ 750 k	$ 2.5 mm
Sales: Lubricants	12.5% + growth	$ 2.3 mm	$ 2.6 mm
Sales: Marine	Approximately 5% annual growth	$ 3.7 mm	$ 4.0 mm
Sales: Heating & cooling	Flat with 2002 acquisition?	$ 530 k	$ 800 k
Sales: Trucking	Approximately 5% annual growth	$ 2.7 mm	$ 3.0 mm
Total sales		$ 43.9 mm	$ 60.9 mm
Operating income		$ 1.2 mm	$ 1.7 mm
Return on equity		40%	37%
Debt to equity		3.5/1	3/1

Strategic Assignment	Who's Responsible	Due
Present outline of timing/format for sharing the results of EnergyCo planning retreat and the 2000 Vision with Eees (see 3/1/00 too).	Sam	Xmas Party
Get info on employee leasing from Laser Tech to Sarah	Richard	12/20/00

can be overcome by initially focusing on *measurable activity* and then identifying *measurable outcomes.*

Priorities

Although all annual objectives are important, some deserve priority because of a timing consideration or their particular impact on a strategy's success. If such priorities are not established, conflicting assumptions about the relative importance of annual

continued

Strategic Assignment	Who's Responsible	Due
Sales—Operations Coordination and Integration—Report on initial ideas to increase the level of coordination and to pursue group meetings; after work meetings; coordination and interaction with admin personnel to. . . . Report on initial thoughts & get input	Leigh Jack Kate	Report initial ideas by 1/3/01
Real good assessment & recommendations on HVAC situation	Jack and Ginger	2/3/01
Create drawings and explanation of the adjacent property deal/use	Jack, Sarah, & Sam	3/3/01
Sales—Operations (Administration) Coordination Procedure Plan (the plan that results from the above ideas discussed, refined, etc.)	Leigh and Jack	4/30/01
Assess, do P&L, & implement hiring of Harbor Lube sales rep	Sam & Sarah	5/30/01
Computerization Task Force—assemble team, set agenda, and plan to proceed to examine, get a handle on, get input/involvement of EnergyCo employees doing the real work, and implement a comprehensive, integrated computer automation of the daily management of all of EnergyCo's sales, operations, administrative activities . . . & consideration of hiring someone to help early on	Sarah Kate Leigh Jack	6/30/01
Analysis, evaluation & develop a plan to deal with out of town product acquisition & $0.015 premium on low rack	Sarah & Jack	7/15/01
Retail Joint Venture: Evaluate EnergyCo direct ownership; franchise operations; owner equity lease financing to EnergyCo; and the potential for real estate syndication	Sam Sarah Kate	8/15/01
Partner buyout life insurance and evaluate risk of shared ownership	Leigh & Jack	9/15/01
EnergyCo Proformas on D/E ratios with capital proposed; set up EnergyCo's financial report to reflect investment by revenue stream/division and calculate ROI & SPI for each, etc.	Sarah	10/1/01
Implement series of meetings with employees to explain EnergyCo 2000 strategic plan and to answer questions; get their feedback, etc. One of the key issues to develop and discuss with EnergyCo employees is the new, greater emphasis and commitment to the retail and branding sides of the business.	Sam with management team	11/1/01
Finish Commission Program for Sales organization	Sarah and Leigh	12/30/01

objectives may inhibit progress toward strategic effectiveness. Facing the most rapid, dramatic decline in profitability of any major computer manufacturer as it confronted relentless lower pricing by Dell Computer and AST, Compaq Computer formulated a retrenchment strategy with several important annual objectives in pricing, product design, distribution, and financial condition. But its highest priority was to dramatically lower overhead and production costs so as to satisfy the difficult challenge of dramatically lowering prices while also restoring profitability.

FIGURE 10–2
Creating Measurable Objectives

Examples of Deficient Objectives	Examples of Objectives with Measurable Criteria for Performance
To improve morale in the division (plant, department, etc.)	To reduce turnover (absenteeism, number of rejects, etc.) among sales managers by 10 percent by January 1, 2001.
	Assumption: Morale is related to measurable outcomes (i.e., high and low morale are associated with different results).
To improve support of the sales effort	To reduce the time lapse between order data and delivery by 8 percent (two days) by June 1, 2001.
	To reduce the cost of goods produced by 6 percent to support a product price decrease of 2 percent by December 1, 2001.
	To increase the rate of before- or on-schedule delivery by 5 percent by June 1, 2001.
To improve the firm's image	To conduct a public opinion poll using random samples in the five largest U.S. metropolitan markets to determine average scores on 10 dimensions of corporate responsibility by May 15, 2001. To increase our score on those dimensions by an average of 7.5 percent by May 1, 2002.

Priorities are established in various ways. A simple *ranking* may be based on discussion and negotiation during the planning process. However, this does not necessarily communicate the real difference in the importance of objectives, so such terms as *primary, top,* and *secondary* may be used to indicate priority. Some firms assign *weights* (e.g., 0 to 100 percent) to establish and communicate the relative priority of objectives. Whatever the method, recognizing priorities is an important dimension in the implementation value of short-term objectives.

Linked to Long-Term Objectives

Short-term objectives can add breadth and specificity in identifying *what* must be accomplished to achieve long-term objectives. For example, Wal-Mart's top management recently set out "to obtain 45 percent market share in five years" as a long-term objective. Achieving that objective can be greatly enhanced if a series of specific short-term objectives identify what must be accomplished each year in order to do so. If Wal-Mart's market share is now 25 percent, then one likely annual objective might be "to have each regional office achieve a minimum 4 percent increase in market share in the next year." "Open two regional distribution centers in the Southwest in 2002" might be an annual objective that Wal-Mart's marketing and distribution managers consider essential if the firm is to achieve a 45 percent market share in five years. "Conclude arrangements for a $1 billion line of credit at 0.25 percent above prime in 2001" might be an annual objective of Wal-Mart's financial managers to support the operation of new distribution centers and the purchase of increased inventory in reaching the firm's long-term objective.

The link between short-term and long-term objectives should resemble cascades through the firm from basic long-term objectives to specific short-term objectives in key operation areas. The cascading effect has the added advantage of providing a clear reference for communication and negotiation, which may be necessary to integrate and coordinate objectives and activities at the operating level.

The qualities of good objectives discussed in Chapter 7—acceptable, flexible, suitable, motivating, understandable, and achievable—also apply to short-term objectives.

They will not be discussed again here, but the reader should review the discussion in Chapter 7 to appreciate these qualities, common to all good objectives.

The Value-Added Benefits of Short-Term Objectives and Action Plans

One benefit of short-term objectives and action plans is that they give operating personnel a better understanding of their role in the firm's mission. "Achieve $2.5 million in 2002 sales in the Chicago territory," "Develop an OSHA-approved safety program for handling acids at all Georgia Pacific plants in 2002," and "Reduce Ryder Truck's average age of accounts receivable to 31 days by the end of 2002" are examples of how short-term objectives clarify the role of particular personnel in their firm's broader mission. Such *clarity of purpose* can be a major force in helping use a firm's "people assets" more effectively, which may add tangible value.

A second benefit of short-term objectives and action plans comes from the process of developing them. If the managers responsible for this accomplishment have participated in their development, short-term objectives and action plans provide valid bases for addressing and accommodating conflicting concerns that might interfere with strategic effectiveness (see Figure 10–1). Meetings to set short-term objectives and action plans become the forum for raising and resolving conflicts between strategic intentions and operating realities.

A third benefit of short-term objectives and action plans is that they provide *a basis for strategic control*. The control of strategy will be examined in detail in Chapter 12. However, it is important to recognize here that short-term objectives and action plans provide a clear, measurable basis for developing budgets, schedules, trigger points, and other mechanisms for controlling the implementation of strategy.

A fourth benefit is often a *motivational payoff*. Short-term objectives and action plans that clarify personal and group roles in a firm's strategies and are also measurable, realistic, and challenging can be powerful motivators of managerial performance—particularly when these objectives are linked to the firm's reward structure.

Strategy in Action 10–1 excerpts selected short-term objectives and action plans from the strategic plan of EnergyCo Fuel Company. Bought out of bankruptcy 10 years ago, founder Sam Rutledge has led an outstanding management team that has made EnergyCo a major player in eastern Virginia. Short-term objectives and action plans with the attributes we have discussed were key management tools for implementing their turnaround strategy successfully.

FUNCTIONAL TACTICS THAT IMPLEMENT BUSINESS STRATEGIES

Functional tactics are the key, routine activities that must be undertaken in each functional area—marketing, finance, production/operations, R&D, and human resource management—to provide the business's products and services. In a sense, functional tactics translate thought (grand strategy) into action designed to accomplish specific short-term objectives. Every value chain activity in a company executes functional tactics that support the business's strategy and help accomplish strategic objectives.

Figure 10–3 illustrates the difference between functional tactics and corporate and business strategy. It also shows that functional tactics are essential to implement business strategy. The corporate strategy defined General Cinema Corporation's general posture in the broad economy. The business strategy outlined the competitive posture of its operations in the movie theater industry. To increase the likelihood that these

FIGURE 10–3
Functional Tactics at General Cinema Corporation

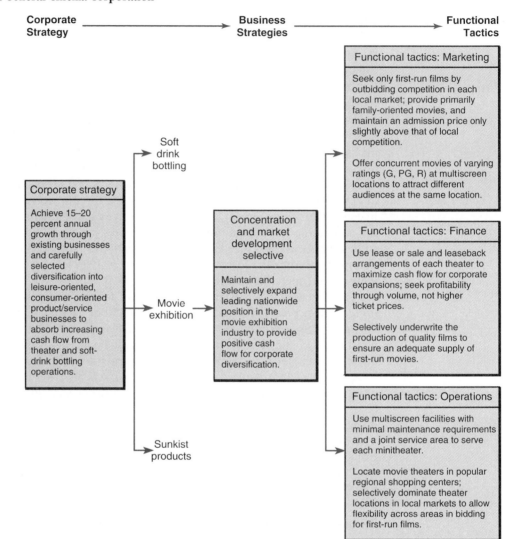

strategies would be successful, specific functional tactics were needed for the firm's operating components. These functional tactics clarified the business strategy, giving specific, short-term guidance to operating managers in the areas of marketing, operations, and finance.

Differences between Business Strategies and Functional Tactics

Functional tactics are different from business or corporate strategies in three fundamental ways:

1. Time horizon.
2. Specificity.
3. Participants who develop them.

Time Horizon

Functional tactics identify activities to be undertaken "now" or in the immediate future. Business strategies focus on the firm's posture three to five years out. Delta Air lines is committed to a concentration/market development business strategy that seeks competitive advantage via differentiation in its level of service and focus on the business traveler. Its pricing tactics are often to price above industry averages, but it often lowers fares on selected routes to thwart low-cost competition. Its business strategy is focused 10 years out; its pricing tactics change weekly.

The shorter time horizon of functional tactics is critical to the successful implementation of a business strategy for two reasons. First, it focuses the attention of functional managers on what needs to be done *now* to make the business strategy work. Second, it allows functional managers like those at Delta to adjust to changing current conditions.

Specificity

Functional tactics are more specific than business strategies. Business strategies provide general direction. Functional tactics identify the specific activities that are to be undertaken in each functional area and thus allow operating managers to work out *how* their unit is expected to pursue short-term objectives. General Cinema's business strategy gave its movie theater division broad direction on how to pursue a concentration and selective market development strategy. Two functional tactics in the marketing area gave managers specific direction on what types of movies (first-run, primarily family-oriented, G, PG, R) should be shown and what pricing strategy (competitive in the local area) should be followed.

Specificity in functional tactics contributes to successful implementation by:

- Helping ensure that functional managers know what needs to be done and can focus on accomplishing results.
- Clarifying for top management how functional managers intend to accomplish the business strategy, which increases top management's confidence in and sense of control over the business strategy.
- Facilitating coordination among operating units *within* the firm by clarifying areas of interdependence and potential conflict.

Strategy in Action 10–2 illustrates the nature and value of specificity in functional tactics versus business strategy in an upscale pizza restaurant chain.

Participants

Different people participate in strategy development at the functional and business levels. Business strategy is the responsibility of the general manager of a business unit. That manager typically delegates the development of functional tactics to subordinates charged with running the operating areas of the business. The manager of a business unit must establish long-term objectives and a strategy that corporate management feels contributes to corporate-level goals. Similarly, key operating managers must establish short-term objectives and operating strategies that contribute to business-level goals. Just as business strategies and objectives are approved through negotiation between corporate managers and business managers, so, too, are short-term objectives and functional tactics approved through negotiation between business managers and operating managers.

THE NATURE AND VALUE OF SPECIFICITY IN FUNCTIONAL TACTICS VERSUS BUSINESS STRATEGY

STRATEGY IN ACTION 10–2

A restaurant business was encountering problems. Although its management had agreed unanimously that it was committed to a business strategy to differentiate itself from other competitors based on concept and customer service rather than price, it continued to encounter inconsistencies across different store locations in how well it did this. Consultants indicated that the customer experience varied greatly from store to store. The conclusion was that while the management understood the "business strategy," and the employees did too in general terms, the implementation was inadequate because of a lack of specificity in the functional tactics—what everyone should do every day in the restaurant—to make the vision a reality in terms of the customers' dining experience. The following breakdown of part of their business strategy into specific functional tactics just in the area of customer service helps illustrate the value specificity in functional tactics brings to strategy implementation.

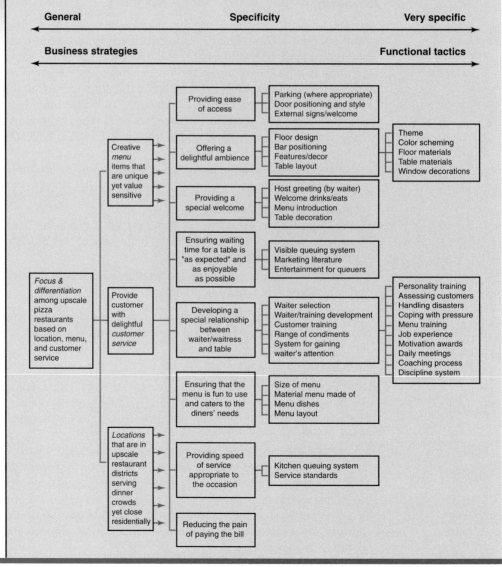

Source: Adapted from "How to Have Your Pizza and Eat It, Too," *Business Week,* November 16, 1998; and A. Campbell and K. Luchs, *Strategic Synergy* (London: Butterworth-Heineman, 1992).

FIGURE 10–4
Key Functional Tactics in POM

Functional Tactic	Typical Questions That the Functional Tactic Should Answer
Facilities and equipment	How centralized should the facilities be? (One big facility or several small facilities?)
	How integrated should the separate processes be?
	To what extent should further mechanization or automation be pursued?
	Should size and capacity be oriented toward peak or normal operating levels?
Sourcing	How many sources are needed?
	How should suppliers be selected, and how should relationships with suppliers be managed over time?
	What level of forward buying (hedging) is appropriate?
Operations planning and control	Should work be scheduled to order or to stock?
	What level of inventory is appropriate?
	How should inventory be used (FIFO/LIFO), controlled, and replenished?
	What are the key foci for control efforts (quality, labor cost, downtime, product use, other)?
	Should maintenance efforts be oriented to prevention or to breakdown?
	What emphasis should be placed on job specialization? Plant safety? The use of standards?

Involving operating managers in the development of functional tactics improves their understanding of what must be done to achieve long-term objectives and, thus, contributes to successful implementation. It also helps ensure that functional tactics reflect the reality of the day-to-day operating situation. And perhaps most important, it can increase the commitment of operating managers to the strategies developed.

The next several sections will highlight key tactics around which managers can build competitive advantage and add value in each of the various functional areas.

Functional Tactics in Production/Operations

Basic Issues

Production/operations management (POM) is the core function of any organization. That function converts inputs (raw materials, supplies, machines, and people) into value-enhanced output. The POM function is most easily associated with manufacturing firms, but it also applies to all other types of businesses (service and retail firms, for example). POM tactics must guide decisions regarding (1) the basic nature of the firm's POM system, seeking an optimum balance between investment input and production/operations output and (2) location, facilities design, and process planning on a short-term basis. Figure 10–4 highlights key decision areas in which the POM tactics should provide guidance to functional personnel.

POM facility and equipment tactics involve decisions regarding plant location, size, equipment replacement, and facilities utilization that should be consistent with grand strategy and other operating strategies. In the mobile home industry, for example, the facilities and equipment tactic of Winnebago was to locate one large centralized, highly integrated production center (in Iowa) near its raw materials. On the other extreme, Fleetwood, Inc., a California-based competitor, located dispersed, decentralized

BusinessWeek

WHAT DOES THE TRULY RESPONSIVE FACTORY OF
THE 21ST CENTURY GLOBAL ECONOMY LOOK LIKE?

STRATEGY IN
ACTION
10–3

Manufacturers worldwide are scrambling to create the factories of the future today. Flexible manufacturing systems are an important component. But that's not all. Total quality control, concurrent engineering, process reengineering, computerization, and computer-aided logistical support are just some of today's insisted-upon characteristics. Convened by *Business Week* to probe the vision of the responsive factory more clearly, operations managers around the globe agreed on five key characteristics.

Characteristics of the Truly Responsive Factory

Concurrent everything	Enterprisewide computer integration, with electronic links to customers and suppliers, means that transactions occur mostly between computers, which will automatically route information to all the proper departments or operations.
Fast development cycles	A real-time database will unite the distributed-processing computers used by design, engineering, production, logistics, marketing, and customer service—whether the work is done in-house or outsourced. All parties will have instant access to the latest information, eliminating the rework now caused by delays in shuffling paper.
Flexible production	Flexibility will be built into all levels of manufacturing, from the controls on each machine to the computers that coordinate work cells and factorywide systems. Products can thus be turned out in greater variety and customized easily, with no cost penalty for small production runs.
Quick response	Dynamic factory-scheduling systems will put production "on call" and thus pare inventories to the bone. Production will begin only after a customer places an order.
Commitment to lifelong quality	Ongoing quality programs will lead to continuous improvement of both processes and products. A primary focus will be to make products easier to recycle or dispose of in environmentally sound ways.

Source: Reprinted from October 22, 1993, issue of *Business Week* by special permission. Copyright © 1993 by The McGraw-Hill Companies.

production facilities near markets and emphasized maximum equipment life and less-integrated, labor-intensive production processes. Both firms are leaders in the mobile home industry, but have taken very different tactical approaches.

The interplay between computers and rapid technological advancement has made flexible manufacturing systems (FMS) a major consideration for today's POM tacticians. FMS allows managers to automatically and rapidly shift production systems to retool for different products or other steps in a manufacturing process. Changes that previously took hours or days can be done in minutes. The result is decreased labor cost, greater efficiency, and increased quality associated with computer-based precision. Strategy in Action 10–3 summarizes the "responsive factory" of tomorrow based on a global study by *Business Week*.

Sourcing has become an increasingly important component in the POM area. Many companies now accord sourcing a separate status like any other functional area. Sourcing tactics provide guidelines about questions such as: Are the cost advantages of using only a few suppliers outweighed by the risk of overdependence? What criteria (e.g., payment requirements) should be used in selecting vendors? Which vendors can provide "just-in-time" inventory and how can the business provide it to our customers? How can operations be supported by the volume and delivery requirements of purchases?

POM planning and control tactics involve approaches to the management of ongoing production operations and are intended to match production/operations resources with longer range, overall demand. These tactical decisions usually determine whether production/operations will be demand oriented, inventory oriented, or outsourcing oriented to seek a balance between the two extremes. Tactics in this component also address how issues like maintenance, safety, and work organization are handled. Quality control procedures are yet another focus of tactical priorities in this area.

Just-in-time (JIT) delivery, outsourcing, and statistical process control (SPC) have become prominent aspects of the way today's POM managers create tactics that build greater value and quality in their POM system. JIT delivery was initially a way to coordinate with suppliers to reduce inventory carrying costs of items needed to make products. It also became a quality control tactic because smaller inventories made quality checking easier on smaller, frequent deliveries. It has become an important aspect of supplier-customer relationships in today's best businesses.

Outsourcing, or the use of a source other than internal capacity to accomplish some task or process, has become a major operational tactic in today's downsizing-oriented firms. Outsourcing is based on the notion that strategies should be built around core competencies that add the most value in the value chain, and functions or activities that add little value or that cannot be done cost effectively should be done outside the firm—outsourced. When done well, the firm gains a supplier that provides superior quality at lower cost than it could provide itself. JIT and outsourcing have increased the strategic importance of the purchasing function. Outsourcing must include intense quality control by the buyer. ValuJet's tragic 1996 crash in the Everglades was caused by poor quality control over its outsourced maintenance providers.

The Internet and "E-commerce" have begun to revolutionize functional tactics in operations and marketing. How we sell, where we make things, how we logistically coordinate what we do, all of these basic business functions and questions have new perspectives and ways of being addressed because of the technological impact of the globally emerging ways we link together electronically, quickly, and accurately. Amazon.com became perhaps the breakthrough lightning rod of this E-commerce revolution with its spectacular stock run-up in early 1999. Strategy in Action 10–4 illustrates how Amazon.com, and many more companies to follow, will usher in a new strategic era blending and changing the way companies manage functions like POM and marketing.

Functional Tactics in Marketing

The role of the marketing function is to achieve the firm's objectives by bringing about the profitable sale of the business's products/services in target markets. Marketing tactics should guide sales and marketing managers in determining who will sell what, where, to whom, in what quantity, and how. Marketing tactics at a minimum should address four fundamental areas: products, price, place, and promotion. Figure 10–5 highlights typical questions marketing tactics should address.

In addition to the basic issues raised in Figure 10–5, marketing tactics today must guide managers addressing the impact of the *communication revolution* and the *increased diversity* among market niches worldwide. The Internet and the accelerating

BusinessWeek

THE E-COMMERCE REVOLUTION: AMAZON.COM

STRATEGY IN ACTION 10–4

Amazon is blazing a trail in the world of commerce where no merchant has gone before. By pioneering—and darn near perfecting—the art of selling online, it is forcing the titans of retail to scramble onto the Net. More than that, it's jolting them into rethinking whether their traditional advantages—physical size, mass-media branding, and even the sensory appeal of shopping in stores—will be enough to thrive in the new economy. Says Duke University marketing professor Martha Rogers: "Amazon is an example of how an upstart can redefine its whole industry." Amazon offers an easily searchable trove of 3.1 million titles—15 times more than any bookstore on the planet and without the costly overhead of multimillion-dollar buildings and scads of store clerks. That paves the way for each of its 1,600 employees to generate, on average, $375,000 in annual revenues—more than triple that of No. 1 bricks-and-mortar bookseller Barnes & Noble Inc.'s 27,000 employees at over 1,000 retail outlets worldwide.

Amazon's cutting-edge technology gives it a leg up by automatically analyzing past purchases to make recommendations customized to each buyer—a trick that confounds 20th century mass marketing. And with a single mouse click, an order can be placed on its Web site, making shopping a friendly, frictionless, even fun experience that can take less time than finding a parking space at the mall. It has an almost unheard-of two-year head start on key software that handles millions of transactions and personalizes the customers' experience. Besides spurring more purchases, there's another huge bonus for Amazon: It can gather instant feedback on customer preferences to divine what else they might want to buy. Such valuable information has proven forbiddingly effective in capturing new markets online. While it may appear as though the company is careening willy-nilly into new terrain, Amazon is in fact targeting areas its customers have already requested. "We want Amazon.com to be the right store for you as an individual," says Founder Bezos. "If we have 4.5 million customers, we should have 4.5 million stores."

Not since superstores and mail-order catalogers came along in the 1980s have merchants faced such a wrenching shift to a new way of doing business. It's a lot like what Wal-Mart did in the past decade: It used computers to transform the entire process of getting products to customers, all the way from the warehouse to Wal-Mart's welcome mats. Now Bezos is using Net technologies to shatter the perennial retail trade-off—he can offer a rich selection and personalized service, while still reaching millions of customers.

But technology is just one way Amazon is trying to rewrite the rules of retail. Bookstore and other retail chains largely depend on opening new stores to boost revenues—a huge cost that Amazon completely avoids. In the reverse of traditional retailers, Amazon has relatively high

Source: "Amazon.com: The Wild World of E-Commerce," *Business Week,* December 14, 1998.

blend of computers and telecommunications has facilitated instantaneous access to several places around the world. A producer of plastic kayaks in Easley, South Carolina, receives orders from somewhere in the world about every 30 minutes over the Internet without any traditional distribution structure or global advertising. It fills the order within five days without any transportation capability. Speed linked to the ability to communicate instantaneously is causing marketing tacticians to radically rethink what they need to do to remain competitive and maximize value. Strategy in Action 10–4 tells a similar story about Amazon.com.

Diversity has accelerated because of communication technology, logistical capability worldwide, and advancements in flexible manufacturing systems. The diversity that

BusinessWeek

continued

initial costs for things such as computer systems and editorial staff—which partly explain its red ink today. But unlike retailers, who must continually invest in new stores to hike revenues, Amazon can boost sales by simply getting more people to come to its single online store. Says Chief Financial Officer Joy Covey: "I don't think we could have grown a physical store base four times in one year." For now, Amazon has to spend millions on marketing to bring in new customers— about 24 cents per dollar of revenue last quarter, compared with 4 cents for traditional retailers. But it's little understood just how much leverage Amazon's low capital costs provide to support that spending. Here's how it works: Physical bookstores must stock up to 160 days' worth of inventory to provide the kind of in-store selection people want. Yet they must pay distributors and publishers 45 to 90 days after they buy the books—so on average, they carry the costs of those books for up to four months. Amazon, by contrast, carries only 15 days' worth of inventory and is paid immediately by credit card. So it gets about a month's use of interest-free money. That float—amounting to well over $25 million so far this year—actually provides a large chunk of the cash Amazon needs to cover its operating expenses. In its latest quarter, Amazon used a mere $600,000 in operating cash while jacking up its customer base by 37%, or 1.4 million customers. Even though Amazon is still a long way from making a profit, its basic economics suggest the upstart will someday look more like a fat-cat software company than a scrambling-for-profits retailer. Once Amazon gets enough customers and sales to pay off its initial marketing and technology investments—and as that technology pays off in falling labor costs—additional revenue drops to the bottom line. "Amazon's changing the business model of retailing," says Ann Winblad, a principal at Hummer Winblad Venture Partners.

Amazon	versus	Barnes & Noble
1 website	Number of stores	1,011
3.1 million	Titles per superstore	175,000
2%	Book returns	30%
306%	Sales growth	10%
$375,000	Sales per employee (annual)	$100,000
24	Inventory turnovers per year	3
Low	Long-term capital requirements	High
High	Cash flow	Low

has resulted is a virtual explosion of market niches, adaptations of products to serve hundreds of distinct and diverse customer segments that would previously have been served with more mass-market, generic products or services. Where firms used to rely on volume associated with mass markets to lower costs, they now encounter smaller niche players carving out subsegments they can serve more timely *and* more cost effectively. These new, smaller players lack the bureaucracy and committee approach that burdens the larger firms. They make decisions, outsource, incorporate product modifications, and make other agile adjustments to niche market needs before their larger competitors get through the first phase of committee-based decision making. Jack Welch, the CEO of General Electric, commented on this recently with the editors of *Business Week:*

FIGURE 10–5
Key Functional Tactics in Marketing

Functional Tactic	Typical Questions That the Functional Tactic Should Answer
Product (or service)	Which products do we emphasize? Which products/services contribute most to profitability? What product/service image do we seek to project? What consumer needs does the product/service seek to meet? What changes should be influencing our customer orientation?
Price	Are we competing primarily on price? Can we offer discounts or other pricing modifications? Are our pricing policies standard nationally, or is there regional control? What price segments are we targeting (high, medium, low, and so on)? What is the gross profit margin? Do we emphasize cost/demand or competition-oriented pricing?
Place	What level of market coverage is necessary? Are there priority geographic areas? What are the key channels of distribution? What are the channel objectives, structure, and management? Should the marketing managers change their degree of reliance on distributors, sales reps, and direct selling? What sales organization do we want? Is the sales force organized around territory, market, or product?
Promotion	What are the key promotion priorities and approaches? Which advertising/communication priorities and approaches are linked to different products, markets, and territories? Which media would be most consistent with the total marketing strategy?

Size is no longer the trump card it once was in today's brutally competitive world marketplace—a marketplace that is unimpressed with logos and sales numbers but demands, instead, value and performance. At GE we're trying to get that small-company soul—and small-company speed—inside our big-company body. Faster products, faster product cycles to market. Better response time. New niches. Satisfying customers, getting faster communications, moving with more agility, all these are easier when one is small. All these are essential to succeed in the diverse, fast-moving global environment.

Functional Tactics in Accounting and Finance

While most functional tactics guide implementation in the immediate future, the time frame for functional tactics in the area of finance varies, because these tactics direct the use of financial resources in support of the business strategy, long-term goals, and annual objectives. Financial tactics with longer time perspectives guide financial managers in long-term capital investment, debt financing, dividend allocation, and leveraging. Financial tactics designed to manage working capital and short-term assets have a more immediate focus. Figure 10–6 highlights some key questions that financial tactics must answer.

Accounting managers have seen their need to contribute value increasingly scrutinized. Traditional expectations centered around financial accounting; reporting requirements from bank and SEC entities and tax law compliance remain areas in which actions are dictated by outside governance. Managerial accounting, where managers are responsible for keeping records of costs and the use of funds within their company, has taken on increased strategic significance in the last decade. This change has involved two tactical areas: (1) how to account for costs of creating and providing their

FIGURE 10–6
Key Functional Tactics in Finance and Accounting

Functional Tactic	Typical Questions That the Functional Tactics Should Answer
Capital acquisition	What is an acceptable cost of capital?
	What is the desired proportion of short- and long-term debt? Preferred and common equity?
	What balance is desired between internal and external funding?
	What risk and ownership restrictions are appropriate?
	What level and forms of leasing should be used?
Capital allocation	What are the priorities for capital allocation projects?
	On what basis should the final selection of projects be made?
	What level of capital allocation can be made by operating managers without higher approval?
Dividend and working capital management	What portion of earnings should be paid out as dividends?
	How important is dividend stability?
	Are things other than cash appropriate as dividends?
	What are the cash flow requirements? The minimum and maximum cash balances?
	How liberal/conservative should the credit policies be?
	What limits, payment terms, and collection procedures are necessary?
	What payment timing and procedure should be followed?

business's products and services, and (2) valuing the business, particularly among publicly traded companies.

Managerial cost accounting has traditionally provided information for managers using cost categories like those shown on the left side below. However, value chain advocates have been increasingly successful getting managers to seek activity-based cost accounting information like that shown on the right side below. In so doing, accounting is becoming a more critical, relevant source of information that truly benefits strategic management.

Traditional Cost Accounting in a Purchasing Department		Activity-Based Cost Accounting in the Same Purchasing Department	
Wages and salaries	$350,000	Evaluate supplier capabilities	$135,750
Employee benefits	115,000	Process purchase orders	82,100
Supplies	6,500	Expedite supplier deliveries	23,500
Travel	2,400	Expedite internal processing	15,840
Depreciation	17,000	Check quality of items purchased	94,300
Other fixed charges	124,000	Check incoming deliveries against purchase orders	48,450
Miscellaneous operating expenses	25,250	Resolve problems	110,000
		Internal administration	130,210
	$640,150		$640,150

Source: Adapted from information in Terence P. Paré, "A New Tool for Managing Costs," *Fortune,* June 14, 1993, pp. 124–29. *Fortune,* © 1993, Time, Inc. All rights reserved.

FIGURE 10–7
Key Functional Tactics in R&D

R&D Decision Area	Typical Questions That the Functional Tactics Should Answer
Basic research versus product and process development	To what extent should innovation and breakthrough research be emphasized? In relation to the emphasis on product development, refinement, and modification?
	What critical operating processes need R&D attention?
	What new projects are necessary to support growth?
Time horizon	Is the emphasis short term or long term?
	Which orientation best supports the business strategy? The marketing and production strategy?
Organizational fit	Should R&D be done in-house or contracted out?
	Should R&D be centralized or decentralized?
	What should be the relationship between the R&D units and product managers? Marketing managers? Production managers?
Basic R&D posture	Should the firm maintain an offensive posture, seeking to lead innovation in its industry?
	Should the firm adopt a defensive posture, responding to the innovations of its competitors?

Functional Tactics in Research and Development

With the increasing rate of technological change in most competitive industries, research and development (R&D) has assumed a key strategic role in many firms. In the technology-intensive computer and pharmaceutical industries, for example, firms typically spend between 4 and 6 percent of their sales dollars on R&D. In other industries, such as the hotel/motel and construction industries, R&D spending is less than 1 percent of sales. Thus, functional R&D tactics may be more critical instruments of the business strategy in some industries than in others.

Figure 10–7 illustrates the types of questions addressed by R&D tactics. First, R&D tactics should clarify whether basic research or product development research will be emphasized. Several major oil companies now have solar energy subsidiaries in which basic research is emphasized, while the smaller oil companies emphasize product development research.

The choice of emphasis between basic research and product development also involves the time horizon for R&D efforts. Should these efforts be focused on the near term or the long term? The solar energy subsidiaries of the major oil companies have long-term perspectives, while the smaller oil companies focus on creating products now in order to establish a competitive niche in the growing solar industry.

R&D tactics also involve organization of the R&D function. For example, should R&D work be conducted solely within the firm, or should portions of that work be contracted out? A closely related issue is whether R&D should be centralized or decentralized. What emphasis should be placed on process R&D versus product R&D?

Decisions on all of the above questions are influenced by the firm's R&D posture, which can be offensive or defensive, or both. If that posture is offensive, as is true for small high-technology firms, the firm will emphasize technological innovation and new product development as the basis for its future success. This orientation entails high risks (and high payoffs) and demands considerable technological skill, forecasting expertise, and the ability to quickly transform innovations into commercial products.

FIGURE 10–8
Key Functional Tactics in HRM

Functional Tactic	Typical Questions That HRM Tactics Should Answer
Recruitment, selection, and orientation	What key human resources are needed to support the chosen strategy?
	How do we recruit these human resources?
	How sophisticated should our selection process be?
	How should we introduce new employees to the organization?
Career development and training	What are our future human resource needs?
	How can we prepare our people to meet these needs?
	How can we help our people develop?
Compensation	What levels of pay are appropriate for the tasks we require?
	How can we motivate and retain good people?
	How should we interpret our payment, incentive, benefit, and seniority policies?
Evaluation, discipline, and control	How often should we evaluate our people? Formally or informally?
	What disciplinary steps should we take to deal with poor performance or inappropriate behavior?
	In what ways should we "control" individual and group performance?
Labor relations and equal opportunity requirements	How can we maximize labor-management cooperation?
	How do our personnel practices affect women/minorities?
	Should we have hiring policies?

A defensive R&D posture emphasizes product modification and the ability to copy or acquire new technology. Converse Shoes is a good example of a firm with such an R&D posture. Faced with the massive R&D budgets of Nike and Reebok, Converse placed R&D emphasis on bolstering the product life cycle of its prime products (particularly canvas shoes).

Large companies with some degree of technological leadership often use a combination of offensive and defensive R&D strategy. GE in the electrical industry, IBM in the computer industry, and Du Pont in the chemical industry all have a defensive R&D posture for currently available products *and* an offensive R&D posture in basic, long-term research.

Functional Tactics in Human Resource Management (HRM)

The strategic importance of HRM tactics received widespread endorsement in the 1990s. HRM tactics aid long-term success in the development of managerial talent and competent employees; the creation of systems to manage compensation or regulatory concerns; and guiding the effective utilization of human resources to achieve both the firm's short-term objectives and employees' satisfaction and development. HRM tactics are helpful in the areas shown in Figure 10–8. The recruitment, selection, and orientation should establish the basic parameters for bringing new people into a firm and adapting them to "the way things are done" in the firm. The career development and training component should guide the action that personnel takes to meet the future human resources needs of the overall business strategy. Merrill Lynch, a major brokerage firm whose long-term corporate strategy is to become a diversified financial service institution, has moved into such areas as investment banking, consumer credit, and venture capital. In support of its long-term objectives, it has incorporated extensive early-career training and ongoing career development programs to meet its expanding need for personnel with multiple competencies. Larger organizations need HRM tactics that guide decisions regarding labor relations; EEOC requirements; and employee compensation, discipline, and control.

Current trends in HRM parallel the reorientation of managerial accounting by looking at their cost structure anew. HRM's "paradigm shift" involves looking at people expense as an investment in human capital. This involves looking at the business's value chain and the "value" of human resource components along the various links in that chain. One of the results of this shift in perspective has been the downsizing and outsourcing phenomena of the last quarter century. While this has been traumatic for millions of employees in companies worldwide, its underlying basis involves an effort to examine the use of "human capital" to create value in ways that maximize the human contribution. This scrutiny continues to challenge the HRM area to include outsourcing all HRM as described in Strategy in Action 10–5 on page 379. The emerging implications for human resource management tactics may be a value-oriented perspective on the role of human resources in a business's value chain as suggested below.

Traditional HRM Ideas	Emerging HRM Ideas
Emphasis solely on physical skills	Emphasis on total contribution to the firm
Expectation of predictable, repetitious behavior	Expectation of innovative and creative behavior
Comfort with stability and conformity	Tolerance of ambiguity and change
Avoidance of responsibility and decision making	Accepting responsibility for making decisions
Training covering only specific tasks	Open-ended commitment; broad continuous development
Emphasis placed on outcomes and results	Emphasis placed on processes and means
High concern for quantity and throughput	High concern for total customer value
Concern for individual efficiency	Concern for overall effectiveness
Functional and subfunctional specialization	Cross-functional integration
Labor force seen as unnecessary expense	Labor force seen as critical investment
Work force is management's adversary	Management and work force are partners

Source: A. Miller, *Strategic Management,* p. 400. © 1998 by McGraw-Hill, Inc. Reproduced with the permission of The McGraw-Hill Companies.

To summarize, functional tactics reflect how each major activity of a firm contributes to the implementation of the business strategy. The specificity of functional tactics and the involvement of operating managers in their development help ensure understanding of and commitment to the chosen strategy. A related step in implementation is the development of policies that empower operating managers and their subordinates to make decisions and to act autonomously.

BusinessWeek

WHAT'S NEXT FOR HRM? AN EXPERT SAYS IT'S TIME FOR HRM DEPARTMENTS TO PUT UP OR SHUT UP!

STRATEGY IN ACTION 10–5

European and U.S. companies are accelerating outsourcing to include their whole HRM function. Tom Stewart (74774.3555@compuserve.com), editor of *Fortune,* made these observations recently:

> Nestling warm and sleepy in your company is a department whose employees spend 80 percent of their time on routine administrative tasks. Nearly every function of this department can be performed more expertly for less by others. It is your human resources department. Consider what HR does and whether it should do it.

Start with payroll. Outside providers now cut an estimated 25 percent of all paychecks issued in the United States. The reason, says payroll services leader ADP's CFO: "As companies move off mainframes, they are taking a look at what applications are strategic to them. When they decide that payroll and HR functions are not strategic, they outsource them."

The same is happening with benefits administration. A 1995 survey of 314 large U.S. companies found 87 percent outsource record keeping and 59 percent administration service. The Corporate Leadership Council, which conducts research for 500 member companies, concluded that there is significant potential and value in outsourcing four HR functions: benefit design and administration; information systems and record keeping; employee services such as retirement counseling, outplacement, and relocation; and health and safety. None, the Council noted, have much potential to produce competitive advantage for a company that does them especially well in-house.

But why stop there? Take recruiting. The rule of thumb among managers is to involve HR as little as possible in the recruiting process. While HR professionals are themselves looking for work, two-thirds of the time they find it by networking or using (outside) search firms. Another candidate is designing and running compensation and reward systems—ironically, especially when state-of-the-art reward mechanisms are of paramount importance to competing. Many managers have decided that it is much better to buy the state of the art from outside, customize it, and instill responsibility for running it as far down in the organization as possible. And as for training: Will every reader who has taken a training course sponsored by their HR department and found it very valuable raise his hand? There's lot of evidence that training is a good thing . . . if it's just-in-time, close-to-the-work training—training that should be lodged in the line function, not off the shelf.

Says Vikesh Mahendroo, Executive VP of HR consultants W. M. Mercer, "HR is often out of sync with the needs of the business." He thinks reengineering HR can fix that. But how far should they go? Steel giant Nucor, with 6,000 employees, runs HR with a headquarters staff of three people—a secretary and two HR professionals, one HR agent at each plant reporting to the plant manager, and a set of company HR principles. Says Corporate Leadership Council executive director Matt Olsen: "This is a make-or-break moment for the HR function."

HR people say that they are the trustee of the asset that matters above all others, proactive custodians of our core competence, holders of the keys to competitive advantage in the new economy. Just so much rhetoric say others. There may be a reason that more and more new HR executives come to the post with backgrounds in line management or consulting rather than from HR's own ranks. Says Mahendroo, "There are two messages here. One is that human capital management is important enough that it is an acceptable career path for an up-and-comer. The second is that many people doing the work now can't cut it in the HR of the future."

Source: "A Tidal Wave of Temps," *Business Week:* November 24, 1997; and "Taking on the Last Bureaucracy," January 15, 1996, pp. 105–7. By Tom Stewart, *FORTUNE,* © 1996, Time, Inc. All rights reserved.

EMPOWERING OPERATING PERSONNEL: THE ROLE OF POLICIES

Specific functional tactics provide guidance and initiate action implementing a business's strategy, but more is needed. Supervisors and personnel in the field have been charged in today's competitive environment with being responsible for customer value—for being the "front line" of the company's effort to truly meet customers' needs. Meeting customer needs, becoming obsessed with quality service, was the buzzword that started organizational revolutions in the 1980s. Efforts to do so often failed because employees that were the real contact point between the business and its customers were not *empowered* to make decisions or act to fulfill customer needs. One solution has been to empower operating personnel by pushing down decision making to their level. General Electric allows appliance repair personnel to decide about warranty credits on the spot, a decision that used to take several days and multiple organizational levels. Delta Air Lines allows customer service personnel and their supervisors wide range in resolving customer ticket pricing decisions. Federal Express couriers make decisions and handle package routing information that involves five management levels in the U.S. Postal Service.

Empowerment is being created in many ways. Training, self-managed work groups, eliminating whole levels of management in organizations, and aggressive use of automation are some of the ways and ramifications of this fundamental change in the way business organizations function. At the heart of the effort is the need to ensure that decision making is consistent with the mission, strategy, and tactics of the business while at the same time allowing considerable latitude to operating personnel. One way operating managers do this is through the use of policies.

Policies are directives designed to guide the thinking, decisions, and actions of managers and their subordinates in implementing a firm's strategy. Previously referred to as *standard operating procedures,* policies increase managerial effectiveness by standardizing many routine decisions and clarifying the discretion managers and subordinates can exercise in implementing functional tactics. Logically, policies should be derived from functional tactics (and, in some instances, from corporate or business strategies) with the key purpose of aiding strategy execution.[1] Strategy in Action 10–6, on page 382, illustrates selected policies of several well-known firms.

Creating Policies That Empower

Policies communicate guidelines to decisions. They are designed to control decisions while defining allowable discretion within which operational personnel can execute business activities. They do this in several ways:

1. *Policies establish indirect control over independent action* by clearly stating how things are to be done *now.* By defining discretion, policies in effect control decisions

[1]The term *policy* has various definitions in management literature. Some authors and practitioners equate policy with strategy. Others do this inadvertently by using *policy* as a synonym for company mission, purpose, or culture. Still other authors and practitioners differentiate policy in terms of "levels" associated respectively with purpose, mission, and strategy. "Our policy is to make a positive contribution to the communities and societies we live in" and "our policy is not to diversify out of the hamburger business" are two examples of the breadth of what some call policies. This book defines *policy* much more narrowly as specific guides to managerial action and decisions in the implementation of strategy. This definition permits a sharper distinction between the formulation and implementation of functional strategies. And, of even greater importance, it focuses the tangible value of the policy concept where it can be most useful—as a key administrative tool to enhance effective implementation and execution of strategy.

yet empower employees to conduct activities without direct intervention by top management.

2. *Policies promote uniform handling of similar activities.* This facilitates the coordination of work tasks and helps reduce friction arising from favoritism, discrimination, and the disparate handling of common functions—something that often hampers operating personnel.

3. *Policies ensure quicker decisions* by standardizing answers to previously answered questions that otherwise would recur and be pushed up the management hierarchy again and again—something that required unnecessary levels of management between senior decision makers and field personnel.

4. *Policies institutionalize basic aspects of organization behavior.* This minimizes conflicting practices and establishes consistent patterns of action in attempts to make the strategy work—again, freeing operating personnel to act.

5. *Policies reduce uncertainty in repetitive and day-to-day decision making,* thereby providing a necessary foundation for coordinated, efficient efforts and freeing operating personnel to act.

6. *Policies counteract resistance to or rejection of chosen strategies by organization members.* When major strategic change is undertaken, unambiguous operating policies clarify what is expected and facilitate acceptance, particularly when operating managers participate in policy development.

7. *Policies offer predetermined answers to routine problems.* This greatly expedites dealing with both ordinary and extraordinary problems—with the former, by referring to these answers; with the latter, by giving operating personnel more time to cope with them.

8. *Policies afford managers a mechanism for avoiding hasty and ill-conceived decisions in changing operations.* Prevailing policy can always be used as a reason for not yielding to emotion-based, expedient, or temporarily valid arguments for altering procedures and practices.

Policies may be written and formal or unwritten and informal. Informal, unwritten policies are usually associated with a strategic need for competitive secrecy. Some policies of this kind, such as promotion from within, are widely known (or expected) by employees and implicitly sanctioned by management. Managers and employees often like the latitude granted by unwritten and informal policies. However, such policies may detract from the long-term success of a strategy. Formal, written policies have at least seven advantages:

1. They require managers to think through the policy's meaning, content, and intended use.
2. They reduce misunderstanding.
3. They make equitable and consistent treatment of problems more likely.
4. They ensure unalterable transmission of policies.
5. They communicate the authorization or sanction of policies more clearly.
6. They supply a convenient and authoritative reference.
7. They systematically enhance indirect control and organizationwide coordination of the key purposes of policies.

The strategic significance of policies can vary. At one extreme are such policies as travel reimbursement procedures, which are really work rules and may not be linked to the implementation of a strategy. At the other extreme are organizationwide policies that are virtually functional strategies, such as Wendy's requirement that every location invest 1 percent of its gross revenue in local advertising.

SELECTED POLICIES THAT AID STRATEGY IMPLEMENTATION

3M Corporation has a *personnel policy,* called the *15 percent rule,* that allows virtually any employee to spend up to 15 percent of the workweek on anything that he or she wants to, as long as it's product related.

(This policy supports 3M's corporate strategy of being a highly innovative manufacturer, with each division required to have a quarter of its annual sales come from products introduced within the past five years.)

Wendy's has a *purchasing policy* that gives local store managers the authority to buy fresh meat and produce locally, rather than from regionally designated or company-owned sources.

(This policy supports Wendy's functional strategy of having fresh, unfrozen hamburgers daily.)

General Cinema has a *financial policy* that requires annual capital investment in movie theaters not to exceed annual depreciation.

(By seeing that capital investment is no greater than depreciation, this policy supports General Cinema's financial strategy of maximizing cash flow—in this case, all profit—to its growth areas. The policy also reinforces General Cinema's financial strategy of leasing as much as possible.)

IBM had a *marketing policy* of not giving free IBM personal computers (PCs) to any person or organization.

(This policy attempted to support IBM's image strategy by maintaining its image as a professional, high-value, service business as it sought to dominate the PC market.)

Crown, Cork, and Seal Company has an *R&D policy* of not investing any financial or people resources in basic research.

(This policy supports Crown, Cork, and Seal's functional strategy, which emphasizes customer services, not technical leadership.)

Bank of America has an *operating policy* that requires annual renewal of the financial statement of all personal borrowers.

(This policy supports Bank of America's financial strategy, which seeks to maintain a loan-to-loss ratio below the industry norm.)

Policies can be externally imposed or internally derived. Policies regarding equal employment practices are often developed in compliance with external (government) requirements, and policies regarding leasing or depreciation may be strongly influenced by current tax regulations.

Regardless of the origin, formality, and nature of policies, the key point to bear in mind is that they can play an important role in strategy implementation. Communicating specific policies will help overcome resistance to strategic change, empower people to act, and foster commitment to successful strategy implementation.

Policies empower people to act. Compensation, at least theoretically, rewards their action. The last decade has seen many firms realize that the link between compensation, particularly executive management compensation, and value-building strategic outcomes within their firms was uncertain. The recognition of this uncertainty has brought about increased recognition of the need to link management compensation with the successful implementation of strategies that build long-term shareholder value. The next section examines this development and major types of executive bonus compensation plans.

EXECUTIVE BONUS COMPENSATION PLANS[2]

Major Plan Types

The goal of an executive bonus compensation plan is to motivate executives to achieve maximization of shareholder wealth—the underlying goal of most firms. Since shareholders are both owners and investors of the firm, they desire a reasonable return on their investment. Because they are absentee landlords, shareholders want the decision-making logic of their firm's executives to be concurrent with their own primary motivation.

However, agency theory instructs us that the goal of shareholder wealth maximization is not the only goal that executives may pursue. Alternatively, executives may choose actions that increase their personal compensation, power, and control. Therefore, an executive compensation plan that contains a bonus component can be used to orient management's decision making toward the owners' goals. The success of bonus compensation as an incentive hinges on a proper match between an executive bonus plan and the firm's strategic objectives. As one author has written: "Companies can succeed by clarifying their business vision or strategy and aligning company pay programs with its strategic direction."[3]

Stock Options

A common measure of shareholder wealth creation is appreciation of company stock price. Therefore, a popular form of bonus compensation is stock options. Stock options currently represent 55 percent of a chief executive officer's average pay package.[4] Stock options provide the executive with the right to purchase company stock at a fixed price in the future. The precise amount of compensation is based on the difference, or "spread," between the option's initial price and its selling, or exercised, price. As a result, the executive receives a bonus only if the firm's share price appreciates. If the share price drops below the option price, the options become worthless. Strategy in Action 10–7 summarizes the Microsoft stock option story.

The largest single option sale of all time occurred on December 3, 1997. Disney Chief Executive Officer Michael D. Eisner exercised more than 7 million options on Disney stock that he had been given in 1989 as part of his bonus plan. Eisner sold his shares for more than $400 million.

Although stock options only compensate an executive when wealth is created for shareholders, some critics question whether options truly gauge executive performance. Those doubting the accuracy of options as performance measures question why an executive should profit by merely riding a bull market where virtually every blue-chip firm's stock appreciates. In essence, they argue that the stock market may lack a correlation with firm operational performance, thus the movement of a company's stock price may be mostly outside the influence of most executives.[5] The case involving Michael King of King World Productions is noteworthy.

---

[2]We wish to thank Roy Hossler for his assistance on this section.

[3]James E. Nelson, "Linking Compensation to Business Strategy," *The Journal of Business Strategy* 19, no. 2 (1998), pp. 25–27.

[4]Gary McWilliams, Richard A. Melcher, and Jennifer Reingold, "Executive Pay," *Business Week,* April 20, 1998, pp. 64–70.

[5]William Franklin, "Making the Fat Cats Earn Their Cream," *Accountancy,* July 1998, pp. 38–39.

BusinessWeek

**MICROSOFT STOCK OPTIONS AND BILL GATES'S
BOOKING WEALTH**

**STRATEGY IN
ACTION
10–7**

Microsoft has issued 807 million stock options to employees since 1990—worth $80 billion if they were exercised today.

Analysts estimate several thousand of Microsoft's 28,000 employees are stock-option millionaires. Even relatively low-level managers can tuck away a small fortune.

The option plan has made some veteran executives fabulously wealthy, including Michel Lacombe, president, Microsoft Europe, $152 million; Paul Maritz, group vice-president, $176 million; Nathan Myrhvold, chief technology officer, $179 million; Jeffrey Raikes, group vice-president, $237 million.

But the biggest winner is Bill Gates, whose 20.8% stake in Microsoft was worth a staggering $50 billion in 1998.

Source: Table: "The Microsoft Money Machine," *Business Week,* October 26, 1998.

Chief Executive Officer Michael King was granted options on December 20, 1995, at the then-market price of $39.50. In about two years the stock rose about 40 percent to $55^{13}⁄₁₆. Over the same period, the Standard & Poor's 500 stock index gained 61 percent. Although King World shareholders realized wealth creation over this period, the level was mediocre compared to what an average blue-chip stock achieved. While King's wealth increased $24 million, other shareholders would have profited more by investing in a security that mirrored the stock market.

Although the indexing of stock option plans is rare in bull markets, indexing these plans in bear markets is not uncommon. During a bear market, stock prices will decline due to outside factors such as investor uncertainly resulting from volatile international markets. In this market environment, some firms will re-price their executives' options at the lower current market value. In truth, the credibility of options may be strengthened at any time by indexing firm stock performance against a peer group of stocks, or against a popular market barometer. "Indexing some of the Chief Executive Officer's options to general stock market measures, such as the Standard & Poor's 500 index, will neither reward them for bull markets, nor penalize them for bear markets; such indexing can help mitigate the effect of overall market moves on executives' pay."[6]

Research suggests that stock option plans lack the benefits of plans that include true stock ownership. Stock option plans provide unlimited upside potential for executives, but limited downside risk since executives incur only opportunity costs. Because of the tremendous advantages to the executive of stock price appreciation, there is an incentive for the executive to take undue risk. Thus, supporters of stock ownership plans argue that direct ownership instills a much stronger behavioral commitment, even when the stock price falls, since it binds executives to their firms more than do options.[7]

---

[6]Nicholas Carr, "Compensation: Refining CEO Stock Options," *Harvard Business Review* 76, no. 5 (September–October 1998), pp. 15–18.

[7]Jeffrey Pfeffer, "Seven Practices of Successful Organizations," *California Management Review,* Winter 1998.

Additionally, "Executive stock options may be an efficient means to induce management to undertake more risky projects."[8]

By providing stock option plans with a so-called "reload" feature, firms may reap the previously mentioned benefits of direct executive stock ownership. A *reload* is a bonus of stock options given to executives when options are exercised.[9] In other words, when the executive converts her options into shares, thereby making a very sizable personal investment in the stock of the company, she receives a second bonus grant of stock options to continue to incentivize her to perform. The reload feature allows executives to realize present-day profits, while being rewarded with new options with the potential for future share price appreciation. Because the executive can take advantage of the reload feature only when she is willing to invest her own money into the company, the reload feature achieves the firm's goal of more tightly linking shareholders' and executives' wealth.

Restricted Stock

A restricted stock plan is designed to provide benefits of direct executive stock ownership. In a typical restricted stock plan, an executive is given a specific number of company stock shares. The executive is prohibited from selling the shares for a specified time period. Should the executive leave the firm voluntarily before the restricted period ends, the shares are forfeited. Therefore, restricted stock plans are a form of deferred compensation that promotes longer executive tenure than other types of plans.

In addition to being contingent on a vesting period, restricted stock plans may also require the achievement of predetermined performance goals. Price-vesting restricted stock plans tie vesting to the firm's stock price in comparison to an index, or to reaching a predetermined goal or annual growth rate. If the executive falls short on some of the restrictions, a certain amount of shares are forfeited. The design of these plans motivates the executive to increase shareholder wealth while promoting a long-term commitment to stay with the firm.

If the restricted stock plan lacks performance goal provisions, the executive needs only to remain employed with the firm over the vesting period to cash in on the stock. Performance provisions make sure executives are not compensated without achieving some level of shareholder wealth creation. Like stock options, restricted stock plans offer no downside risk to executives, since the shares were initially gifted to the executive. Shareholders, on the other hand, do suffer a loss in personal wealth resulting from a share price drop.

Investment bank Lehman Brothers has a restricted stock plan in place for hundreds of managing directors and senior vice presidents. The plan vests with time and does not include stock price performance provisions. It is a two-tiered plan consisting of a principal stock grant and a discounted share plan. For managing directors, the discount is 30 percent. For senior vice presidents, the discount is 25 percent. The principal stock grant is a block of shares given to the executive. The discounted share plan allows executives to purchase shares with their own money at a discount to current market prices.

Managing directors at Lehman are able to cash in on one-half the principal portion of their stock grant three years after the grant is awarded. The rest of the principal and

---

[8]Richard A. DeFusco, Robert R. Johnson, and Thomas S. Zorn, "The Effect of Executive Stock Option Plans on Stockholders and Bondholders," *Journal of Finance* 45, no. 2 (1990), pp. 617–35.

[9]Jennifer Reingold and Leah Nathans Spiro, "Nice Option If You Can Get It," *Business Week,* May 4, 1998, pp. 111–14.

any shares bought at a discount must vest for five years. Senior vice presidents receive the entire principal after two years and any discounted shares after five years. Provisions also exist for resignation. If managing directors leave Lehman for a competitor within three years of the award, all stock compensation is forfeited. For senior vice presidents, the period is two years, and the penalties for jumping to a noncompetitor of Lehman's are not as severe.

Golden Handcuffs

The rationale behind plans that defer compensation forms the basis for another type of executive compensation called *golden handcuffs.* Golden handcuffs refer to either a restricted stock plan, where the stock compensation is deferred until vesting time provisions are met, or to bonus income deferred in a series of annual installments. This type of plan may also involve compensating an executive a significant amount upon retirement or at some predetermined age. In most cases, compensation is forfeited if the executive voluntarily resigns or is discharged before certain time restrictions.

Many boards consider their executives' skills and talents to be their firm's most valuable assets. These "assets" create and sustain the professional relationships that generate revenue and control expenses for the firm. Research suggests that the departure of key executives is unsettling for companies and often disrupts long-range plans when new key executives adopt a different management strategy.[10] Thus, the golden handcuffs approach to executive compensation is more congruent with long-term strategies than short-term performance plans, which offer little staying-power incentive.

Firms may turn to golden handcuffs if they believe stability of management is critical to sustain growth. Jupiter Asset Management tied 10 fund managers to the firm with golden handcuffs in 1995. The compensation scheme calls for a cash payment in addition to base salaries if the managers remain at the firm for five years. From 1995 to 1996, the firm's pretax profits more than doubled, and their assets under management increased 85 percent. The firm's chairman has also signed a new incentive deal that will keep him at Jupiter for four years.

Deferred compensation is worrisome to some executives. In cases where the compensation is payable when the executives are retired and no longer in control, as when the firm is acquired by another firm or a new management hierarchy is installed, the golden handcuff plans are considerably less attractive to executives.

Golden handcuffs may promote risk averseness in executive decision making due to the huge downside risk borne by executives. This risk averseness could lead to mediocre performance results from executives' decisions. When executives lose deferred compensation if the firm discharges them voluntarily or involuntarily, the executive is less likely to make bold and aggressive decisions. Rather, the executive will choose safe, conservative decisions to reduce the downside risk of bold decision making.

Golden Parachutes

Golden parachutes are a form of bonus compensation that is designed to retain talented executives. A *golden parachute* is an executive perquisite that calls for a substantial cash payment if the executive quits, is fired, or simply retires. In addition, the golden parachute may also contain covenants that allow the executive to cash in on noninvested stock compensation.

---

[10]William E. Hall, Brian J. Lake, Charles T. Morse, and Charles T. Morse, Jr., "More Than Golden Handcuffs," *Journal of Accountancy* 184, no. 5 (1997), pp. 37–42.

The popularity of golden parachutes grew during the 1980s, when abundant hostile takeovers would often oust the acquired firm's top executives. In these cases, the golden parachutes encouraged executives to take an objective look at takeover offers. The executives could decide which move was in the best interests of the shareholders, having been personally protected in the event of a merger. The "parachute" helps soften the fall of the ousted executive. It is "golden" because the size of the cash payment often varies from several to tens of millions of dollars.

AMP Incorporated, the world's largest producer of electronic connectors, has golden parachutes for several executives. On August 4, 1998, Allied Signal proclaimed itself an unsolicited suitor for AMP. The action focused attention on the AMP parachutes for its three top executives.

Robert Ripp became AMP's chief executive officer in August 1998. If Allied Signal ousted him, he stood to receive a cash payment of three times the amount of his salary as well as his highest annual bonus from the previous three years. His current salary in 1998 was $600,000 and his 1997 bonus was almost $200,000. The cash payment to Ripp would therefore exceed $2 million. Parachutes would also open for William Hudson, the former chief executive officer, and James Marley, the former chairman. Hudson and Marley were slated to officially retire on June 1, 1999, and August 1, 2000, respectively. Since they remain on the payroll, they stand to receive their parachutes if they are ousted before their respective retirement dates. Hudson and Marley's parachutes are both valued at more than $1 million.

In addition to cash payments, these three executives' parachutes also protect existing blocks of restricted stock grants and nonvested stock options. The restricted stock grants were scheduled to become available within three years. Should the takeover come to fruition, the executives would receive the total value of the restricted stock even if it was not yet vested. The stock options would also become available immediately. Some of the restricted stock was performance restricted. Under normal conditions this stock would not be available without the firm reaching certain performance levels. However, the golden parachutes allow the executives to receive double the value of the performance-restricted stock.

Golden parachutes are designed in part to anticipate hostile takeovers like this. In AMP's case, Ripp's position is to lead the firm's board of directors in deciding if Allied Signal's offer is in the long-term interests of shareholders. Since Ripp is compensated heavily whether AMP is taken over or not, the golden parachute has helped remove the temptation that Ripp could have of not acting in the best interests of shareholders.

By design, golden parachutes benefit top executives whether or not there is evidence that value is created for shareholders. In fact, research has suggested that since high-performing firms are rarely taken over, golden parachutes often compensate top executives for abysmal performance.[11] For example, in 1998, AMP went through a troubled period that included plant closings and layoffs, which depressed its stock price.

Cash

Executive bonus compensation plans that focus on accounting measures of performance are designed to offset the limitations of market-based measures of performance. This type of plan is most usually associated with the payment of periodic (quarterly or

---

[11]Graef S. Crystal, *In Search of Excess* (New York: W. W. Norton & Company, 1991).

annual) cash bonuses. Market factors beyond the control of management, such as pending legislation, can keep a firm's share price repressed even though a top executive is exceeding the performance expectations of the board. In this situation, a highly performing executive loses bonus compensation due to the undervalued stock. However, accounting measures of performance correct for this problem by tying executive bonuses to improvements in internally measured performance.

Traditional accounting measures, such as net income, earnings per share, return on equity and return on assets, are used because they are easily understood, are familiar to senior management, and are already tracked by firm data systems.[12]

Sears, Roebuck and Company bases annual bonus payments on such performance criteria, given an executive's business unit and level with the firm. The measures used by Sears include return on equity, revenue growth, net sales growth, and profit growth.

Critics argue that due to inherent flaws in accounting systems, basing compensation on these figures may not result in an accurate gauge of managerial performance. Return on equity estimates, for example, are skewed by inflation distortions and arbitrary cost allocations.[13] Accounting measures are also subject to manipulation by firm personnel to artificially inflate key performance figures. Firm performance schemes, critics believe, need to be based on a financial measure that has a true link to shareholder value creation.[14] This issue led to the creation of the Balanced Scorecard, which emphasizes not only financial measures, but also such measures as new product development, market share, and safety.

Matching Bonus Plans and Corporate Goals

Figure 10–9 provides a summary of the five types of executive bonus compensation plans. The figure includes a brief description, a rationale for implementation, and the identification of possible shortcomings for each of the compensation plans. Not only do compensation plans differ in the method through which compensation is rewarded to the executive, but they also provide the executive with different incentives.

Figure 10–10 matches a company's strategic goal with the most likely compensation plan. On the vertical axis are common strategic goals. The horizontal axis lists the main compensation types that serve as incentives for executives to reach the firm's goals. A rationale is provided to explain the logic behind the connection between the firm's goal and the suggested method of executive compensation.

Researchers emphasize that fundamental to these relationships is the importance of incorporating the level of strategic risk of the firm into the design of the executive's compensation plan. Incorporating an appropriate level of executive risk can create a desired behavioral change commensurate with the risk level of strategies shareholders and their firms want.[15] To help motivate an executive to pursue goals of a certain

[12]Francine C. McKenzie and Matthew D. Shilling, "Avoiding Performance Measurement Traps: Ensuring Effective Incentive Design and Implementation," *Compensation and Benefits Review,* July–August 1998, pp. 57–65.

[13]Fred K. Foulkes, *Executive Compensation: A Strategic Guide for the 1990s* (Boston: Harvard Business School, 1985).

[14]William Franklin, "Making the Fat Cats Earn Their Cream," *Accountancy,* July 1998, pp. 38–39.

[15]Ira T. Kay, *Value at the Top* (New York: HarperCollins, 1992).

FIGURE 10–9
Types of Executive Bonus Compensation

Bonus Type	Description	Rationale	Shortcomings
Stock option grants	Right to purchase stock in the future at a price set now. Compensation is determined by "spread" between option price and exercise price.	Provides incentive for executive to create wealth for shareholders as measured by increase in firm's share price.	Movement in share price does not explain all dimensions of managerial performance.
Restricted stock plan	Shares given to executive who is prohibited from selling them for a specific time period. May also include performance restrictions.	Promotes longer executive tenure than other forms of compensation.	No downside risk to executive, who always profits unlike other shareholders.
Golden handcuffs	Bonus income deferred in a series of annual installments. Deferred amounts not yet paid are forfeited with executive resignation.	Offers an incentive for executive to remain with the firm.	May promote risk-averse decision making due to downside risk borne by executive.
Golden parachute	Executives have right to collect the bonus if they lose position due to takeover, firing, retirement, or resignation.	Offers an incentive for executive to remain with the firm.	Compensation is achieved whether or not wealth is created for shareholders. Rewards either success or failure.
Cash based on internal business performance using financial measures	Bonus compensation based on accounting performance measures such as return on equity.	Offsets the limitations of focusing on market-based measures of performance.	Weak correlation between earnings measures and shareholder wealth creation. Annual earnings do not capture future impact of current decisions.

risk-return level, the compensation plan can quantify that risk-return level and reward the executive accordingly.

The links we show between bonus compensation plans and strategic goals were derived from the results of prior research. The basic principle underlying Figure 10–10 is that different types of bonus compensation plans are intended to accomplish different purposes; one element may serve to attract and retain executives, another may serve as an incentive to encourage behavior that accomplishes firm goals.[16] Although every strategy option has probably been linked to each compensation plan at some time, experience shows that there may be scenarios where a plan type best fits a strategy option. Figure 10–10 attempts to display the "best matches."

Once the firm has identified strategic goals that will best serve shareholders' interests, an executive bonus compensation plan can be structured in such a way as to provide the executive with an incentive to work toward achieving these goals.

---

[16]James E. Nelson, "Linking Compensation to Business Strategy," *The Journal of Business Strategy* 19, no. 2 (1998), pp. 25–27.

FIGURE 10–10
Compensation Plan Selection Matrix

Strategic Goal	Type of Bonus Compensation					Rationale
	Cash	Golden Handcuffs	Golden Parachutes	Restricted Stock Plans	Stock Options	
Achieve corporate turnaround					X	Executive profits only if turnaround is successful in returning wealth to shareholders.
Create and support growth opportunities					X	Risk associated with growth strategies warrants the use of this high-reward incentive.
Defend against unfriendly takeover			X			Parachute helps remove temptation for executive to evaluate takeover based on personal benefits.
Evaluate suitors objectively			X			Parachute compensates executive if job is lost due to a merger favorable to the firm.
Globalize operations					X	Risk of expanding overseas requires a plan that compensates only for achieved success.
Grow share price incrementally	X					Accounting measures can identify periodic performance benchmarks.
Improve operational efficiency	X					Accounting measures represent observable and agreed-upon measures of performance.
Increase assets under management				X		Executive profits proportionally as asset growth leads to long-term growth in share price.
Reduce executive turnover		X				Handcuffs provide executive tenure incentive.
Restructure organization					X	Risk associated with major change in firm's assets warrant the use of this high-reward incentive.
Streamline operations				X		Rewards long-term focus on efficiency and cost control.

SUMMARY

The first concern in the implementation of business strategy is to translate that strategy into action throughout the organization. This chapter discussed four important tools for accomplishing this.

Short-term objectives are derived from long-term objectives, which are then translated into current actions and targets. They differ from long-term objectives in time frame, specificity, and measurement. To be effective in strategy implementation, they must be integrated and coordinated. They also must be consistent, measurable, and prioritized.

Functional tactics are derived from the business strategy. They identify the specific, immediate actions that must be taken in key functional areas to implement the business strategy.

Employee empowerment through policies provides another means for guiding behavior, decisions, and actions at the firm's operating levels in a manner consistent with its business and functional strategies. Policies empower operating personnel to make decisions and take action quickly.

Compensation rewards action and results. Once the firm has identified strategic objectives that will best serve stockholder interests, there are five bonus compensation plans that can be structured to provide the executive with an incentive to work toward achieving those goals.

Objectives, functional tactics, policies, and compensation represent only the start of the strategy implementation. The strategy must be institutionalized—it must permeate the firm. The next chapter examines this phase of strategy implementation.

QUESTIONS FOR DISCUSSION

1. How does the concept "translate thought into action" bear on the relationship between business strategy and operating strategy? Between long-term and short-term objectives?

2. How do functional tactics differ from corporate and business strategies?

3. What key concerns must functional tactics address in marketing? Finance? POM? Personnel?

4. How do policies aid strategy implementation? Illustrate your answer.

5. Use Figures 10–9 and 10–10 to explain five executive bonus compensation plans.

6. Illustrate a policy, an objective, and a functional tactic in your personal career strategy.

7. Why are short-term objectives needed when long-term objectives are already available?

BIBLIOGRAPHY

Carr, Nicholas G. "Compensation: Refining CEO Stock Options." *Harvard Business Review* 76, no. 5 (September–October 1998), pp. 15–18.

Coy, P. "The New Realism in Office Systems." *Business Week,* June 15, 1992, p. 128.

Crystal, Graefs. *In Search of Excess.* New York: W. W. Norton & Company, 1991.

DeFusco, Richard A.; Robert R. Johnson; and Thomas S. Zorn. "The Effect of Executive Stock Option Plans on Stockholders and Bondholders." *Journal of Finance* 45, no. 2 (June 1990), pp. 617–35.

Foulkes, Fred. K. *Executive Compensation: A Strategic Guide for the 1990's.* Boston: Harvard Business School, 1985.

Franklin, William. "Making the Fat Cats Earn Their Cream." *Accountancy* (July 1998), pp. 38–39.

Fulmer, William E. "Human Resource Management: The Right Hand of Strategy Implementation." *Human Resource Planning* 13, no. 1 (1990), pp. 1–11.

Garavan, Thomas N. "Strategic Human Resource Development." *International Journal of Manpower* 12, no. 6 (1991), pp. 21–34.

Giles, William D. "Making Strategy Work." *Long Range Planning* 24, no. 5 (1991), pp. 75–91.

Hall, William E.; Brian J. Lake; Charles T. Morse; and Charles T. Morse, Jr. "More Than Golden Handcuffs." *Journal of Accountancy* 184, no. 5 (1997), pp. 37–42.

Kay, Ira T. *Value at the Top.* New York: HarperCollins, 1992.

Lado, A. A., and M. C. Wilson. "Human Resource Systems and Sustained Competitive Advantage: A Competency Based Perspective." *Academy of Management Review* 19 (1994), pp. 699–727.

Marucheck, Ann; Ronald Pamnesi; and Carl Anderson. "An Exploratory Study of the Manufacturing Strategy Process in Practice." *Journal of Operations Management* 9, no. 1, pp. 101–23.

McKenzie, Francine C., and Matthew D. Shilling. "Avoiding Performance Measurement Traps: Ensuring Effective Incentive Design and Implementation." *Compensation and Benefits Review* (July–August 1998), pp. 57–65.

McWilliams, Gary; Richard A. Melcher; and Jennifer Reingold. "Executive Pay." *Business Week* (April 20, 1998), pp. 64–70.

Nelson, James E. "Linking Compensation to Business Strategy." *The Journal of Business Strategy* 19, no. 2 (1998), pp. 25–27.

Ohmae, K. "Getting Back to Strategy." *Harvard Business Review,* September–October 1988, pp. 149–56.

Parnell, J. A. "Functional Background and Business Strategy: The Impact of Executive Strategy Fit on Performance." *Journal of Business Strategies* 11, no. 1 (1994), pp. 49–62.

Perkins, A. G. "Manufacturing: Maximizing Service, Minimizing Inventory." *Harvard Business Review* 72, no. 2, pp. 13–14.

Pfeffer, Jeffrey. "Seven Practices of Successful Organizations." *California Management Review* (Winter 1998).

Prahalad, C. K., and Gary Hamel. "The Core Competence of the Corporation." *Harvard Business Review* 68 (May–June 1990), pp. 79–93.

Quinn, James Brian. *Intelligent Enterprise* (New York: Free Press, 1992), chaps. 2 and 3.

Randolph, W. A., and B. Z. Posner. "What Every Manager Needs to Know about Project Management." *Sloan Management Review,* Summer 1988, pp. 64–74.

Reingold, Jennifer, and Leah Nathans Spiro. 1998. "Nice Option If You Can Get It." *Business Week* (May 4, 1998), pp. 111–14.

Roth, Kendall; David M. Schweiger; and Allen J. Morrison. "Global Strategy Implementation at the Business Unit Level: Operational Capabilities and Administrative Mechanisms." *Journal of International Business Studies* 22, no. 3 (1991), pp. 369–402.

Stalk, George; Philip Evans; and Lawrence E. Shulman. "Competing on Capabilities: The New Rules of Corporate Strategy." *Harvard Business Review* 70, no. 2 (March–April 1992), pp. 57–69.

Wright, Norman B. "The Driving Force: An Action-Oriented Solution to Strategy Implementation." *Canadian Business Quarterly* 54, no. 1 (1989), pp. 51–54, 66.

Yip, George S. *Total Global Strategy: Managing for Worldwide Competitive Advantage* (Englewood Cliffs, NJ: Prentice Hall, 1992), chap. 8.

CHAPTER 10 DISCUSSION CASE   BusinessWeek

AMAZING AMAZON.COM

Who would believe that you could start a company in your garage and three years later have it worth over $17 billion as a public company with only about $500 million in annual sales and a sizable loss? Jeff Bezos did just that at Amazon.com!

A few stock analysts think Amazon.com is way overvalued; that investors are "nuts" to pay an amount equal to five times Barnes & Noble for this company. You can examine that valuation today as you read this discussion case and see whether they, or the "nutty" investors, were wisest.

Regardless, the value of the Amazon.com story for you is to see why those E-commerce- and Internet-savvy people, many somewhat ahead of the curve in the Internet world of online purchasing, liked the company. And what you will see is that they liked Amazon.com because of the functional tactics and activities—how Amazon.com conducted its business each day.

Those functional activities allowed Amazon.com's strategy to be the first true E-commerce company to become a reality such that these "nutty" investors invested because they could get on the Net and experience those tactics working every day! Amazon.com is a company that *Business Week* journalists Robert Hof, Ellen Neuborne, and Heather Green found to have pioneered and perfected the simple idea of selling online to anyone anywhere in mass before any other business did.

Amazon offers an easily searchable trove of 3.1 million titles—15 times more than any bookstore on the planet and without the costly overhead of multimillion-dollar buildings and scads of store clerks. That paves the way for each of its 1,600 employees to generate, on average, $375,000 in annual revenues—more than triple that of No. 1 bricks-and-mortar bookseller Barnes & Noble Inc.'s 27,000 employees.

Amazon's cutting-edge technology gives it a leg up, too, by automatically analyzing past purchases to make recommendations customized to each buyer—a trick that confounds 20th century mass marketing. And with a single mouse click, an order can be placed on its Web site, making shopping a friendly, frictionless, even fun experience that can take less time than finding a parking space at the mall.

Amazon is extending its warm and fuzzy formula far beyond the bibliophile set. 1999 saw the online merchant debuted a video store, as well as an expanded gift shop—a clear sign that founder Jeff Bezos aimed to make Amazon the Net's premier shopping destination. Buyers who visit the Web site can now find everything from Pictionary games and Holiday Barbies to Sony Walkmen and watches. And Amazon isn't apt to stop there. Not surprisingly, Bezos, who abruptly left a cushy job as a Wall Street hedge-fund manager in 1994 to race across the country and launch Amazon in his Seattle garage, keeps his plans close to the vest. But experts say he's eyeing everything

Source: Robert Hof, Ellen Neuborne, and Heather Green, "Amazon.com: The Wild World of E-Commerce," *Business Week:* December 14, 1998.

from software and apparel to flowers and travel packages—markets that could pit the upstart against more heavyweights, such as Microsoft Corp. and Nordstrom Inc., as early as next year.

Can Bezos, a 34-year-old computer whiz with no previous experience in retail, pull it off? Don't bet against him: In Amazon's first full quarter selling music CDs, it drew $14.4 million in sales, quickly edging out two-year-old cyberleader CDnow Inc. Says analyst Lauren Cooks Levitan of BancBoston Robertson Stephens: "When you think of Web shopping, you think of Amazon first." But as Bezos moves into new markets, he will run smack into traditional retailers that are starting to wield their brands online. A new study by Boston Consulting Group found that 59% of consumer E-commerce revenues—including retail sites and online financial and travel services—are generated by companies such as Eddie Bauer and 1-800-FLOWERS that also sell through traditional channels. Says Carol Sanger, a vice-president at Macy's parent Federated Department Stores Inc.: "We think the brand of Macy's is far more meaningful to the consumer who is looking for traditional department-store goods than any Internet brand name."

As if all the rivals aren't scary enough, Amazon faces an even more fundamental uncertainty: Retailing is a business with razor-thin margins, prompting some analysts to question whether the company will ever be profitable. The theory: Its ambitious growth plans will keep it on the fast track for entering new markets, propelling costs ever upward—and earnings out of reach. Analysts estimate that Amazon will spend nearly $200 million on marketing next year, up 50% over a year ago. "The company has been able to show it can sell lots of books for less without making money, and now it has shown it can sell lots of music for less without making money," says Merrill Lynch & Co. analyst Jonathan Cohen, one of only two analysts with a sell rating on the stock.

For every Cohen, though, there are seven analysts who think Amazon ultimately will fulfill investors' seemingly outsized expectations. For one thing, it has an almost unheard-of two-year head start on key software that handles millions of transactions and personalizes the customers' experience. Amazon, for instance, was the first commerce site to use so-called collaborative-filtering technology, which analyzes a customer's purchases and suggests other books that people with similar purchase histories bought: the ultimate in targeted marketing.

Besides spurring more purchases, there's another huge bonus for Amazon: It can gather instant feedback on customer preferences to divine what else they might want to buy. Such valuable information has proven forbiddingly effective in capturing new markets online. While it may appear as though the company is careening willy-nilly into new terrain, Amazon is in fact targeting areas its customers have already requested. "We want Amazon.com to be the right store for you as an individual," says Bezos. "If we have 4.5 million customers, we should have 4.5 million stores."

Not since superstores and mail-order catalogers came along in the 1980s have merchants faced such a wrenching shift to a new way of doing business. It's a lot like what Wal-Mart did in the past decade: It used computers to transform the entire process of getting products to customers, all the way from the warehouse to Wal-Mart's welcome mats. Now Bezos is using Net technologies to shatter the perennial retail trade-off—he can offer a rich selection and personalized service, while still reaching millions of customers.

But technology is just one way Amazon is trying to rewrite the rules of retail. Bookstore and other retail chains largely depend on opening new stores to boost revenues—a huge cost that Amazon completely avoids. In the reverse of traditional retailers, Amazon has relatively high initial costs for things such as computer systems and editorial staff—which partly explain its red ink today. But unlike retailers, who must continually invest in new stores to hike revenues, Amazon can boost sales by simply getting more people to come to its single online store. Says Chief Financial Officer Joy Covey: "I don't think we could have grown a physical store base four times in one year."

Of course, for now, Amazon has to spend millions on marketing to bring in new customers—about 24 cents per dollar of revenue last quarter, compared with 4 cents for traditional retailers. But it's little understood just how much leverage Amazon's low capital costs provide to support that spending. Here's how it works: Physical bookstores must stock up to 160 days' worth of inventory to provide the kind of in-store selection people want. Yet they must pay distributors and publishers 45 to 90 days after they buy the books—so on average, they carry the costs of those books for up to four months. Amazon, by contrast, carries only 15 days' worth of inventory and is paid immediately by credit card. So it gets about a month's use of interest-free money.

That float—amounting to well over $25 million so far this year—actually provides a large chunk of the cash Amazon needs to cover its operating expenses. In its latest quarter, Amazon used a mere $600,000 in operating cash while jacking up its customer base by 37%, or 1.4 million customers.

Even though Amazon is still a long way from making a profit, its basic economics suggest the upstart will someday look more like a fat-cat software company than a scrambling-for-profits retailer. Once Amazon gets enough customers and sales to pay off its initial marketing and technology investments—and as that technology pays off in falling labor costs—additional revenue drops to the bottom line. "Amazon's changing the business model of retailing," says Ann Winblad, a principal at Hummer Winblad Venture Partners.

It's no accident that Bezos named Amazon after the river that carries the greatest volume of water. "He wants Amazon to be a $10 billion [in revenues] company," says early investor and board member Tom A. Alberg. To look at Amazon's crowded, grubby Seattle headquarters, you'd never suspect such grand ambitions: It's an unmarked building across from Wigland, the Holy Ghost Revivals mission, and the Seattle–King County needle-exchange program. Unlike most of his Silicon Valley colleagues, Bezos is so cheap that the desks are made of doors and four-by-fours, while computer monitors sit on stacks of phone books. Of course, there's one big bonus: Everyone gets stock options, which have made dozens of Amazonians millionaires. But the usual Valley perks such as free neck massages? Yeah, right.

And it's only natural that in a company where everything is being created from whole cloth, the people don't exactly fit either the Silicon Valley or the Microsoft mold. Dogs, sometimes including Bezos' golden retriever, Kamala (named after a minor Star Trek character), and green-haired twentysomethings with multiple piercings run loose, often around the clock. Says Acting Customer Service Director Jane Slade: "We tell the temp agencies, 'Send us your freaks.' "

Bezos' executive staff is nearly as eclectic. It's a motley, though whip-smart, band of executives ranging from Microsoft refugees to liberal-arts majors and rock musicians. Ryan Sawyer, for instance, the vice-president for strategic growth, was a Rhodes scholar who studied poetry at Oxford. "They don't care what has been done in the past," says Anne Martin, a principal at BT Alex. Brown Inc., who was on Amazon's IPO road show.

And that includes Bezos. What he understood before most people was that the ability of the Web to connect almost anyone with almost any product meant that he could do things that couldn't be done in the physical world—such as sell 3 million books in a single store. Starting the company in his suburban Bellevue (Washington) garage, Bezos interviewed suppliers and prospective employees at, ironically, a nearby cafe inside a Barnes & Noble superstore. Launching Amazon.com quietly in July, 1995, Bezos quickly set out to make the customer's experience as appealing as sipping a latte in a bookstore cafe.

Besides the huge selection and simple Web pages that load fast, he created a sense of online community. He invited people to post their own reviews of books; some 800,000 are now up. He brought in authors for chats and more: John Updike started a short story, and 400,000 people sent in contributions to finish it.

Most important, Bezos made it irresistibly easy to buy a book. After the first purchase, a customer's shipping and credit-card information are stored securely, so the next time, all it takes is a single click to send the books winging their way to a mailbox. And to assure people that their purchase went through, Amazon sent E-mail confirmations of orders—which were often upgraded to priority shipping for free.

Rivals have since copied those tactics, but Amazon continues to give customers the red-carpet treatment. This month, it introduced GiftClick, which lets customers choose a gift and simply type in the recipient's E-mail address—Amazon takes care of the rest. The result: Some 64% of orders are from repeat customers, and that's rising steadily. For many, Amazon's a lifeline to literature. Marcia Ellis, an American attorney working in Hong Kong, used to drag home a suitcase full of books when she visited the U.S. Now, she orders two books a month online. "Most of the people we know here get books from Amazon," she says.

Bezos also was one of the first merchants to leverage the Web's power in unique ways to spread the Amazon brand. Early on, he offered other Web sites the chance to sell books related to their visitors' interests through a link to Amazon. Their inducement: a cut of up to 15% of sales. Now, he has 140,000 sites in the so-called Associates Program.

That's what has kept even the online arm of Barnes & Noble at bay. Certainly the No. 1 bookseller, which built its first store 125 years ago, is a savvy merchant, but it proved vulnerable when it came to the ways of the Web. For one thing, it was late in arriving, and its store-trained executives took longer to learn the new rules of E-commerce than Amazon's Net-centric staff. "In the early days, there's a big advantage in not having that baggage," says William McKiernan, chairman of E-commerce services provider CyberSource Corp.

Even after Barnes & Noble went online, it was slower to take advantage of the Net's ability to customize its site to each shopper. That allowed Amazon to use its appealing customer experience as a branding tool far more powerful than conventional advertising. And Barnes & Noble? Despite its well-known name and huge online marketing campaign, only 37% of Internet users recognized the brand without prompting, versus 50% that knew Amazon, according to Intelliquest Information Group.

The result: 18 months after Barnes & Noble went online, Amazon.com's $153.6 million in third-quarter sales, up 306% from a year ago, still overwhelm the book giant's online sales by 11 times. And Barnes & Noble's online customer base rose 29%, to 930,000—still less than a quarter of Amazon's.

Still, the bottom line is that Amazon needs to get customers to buy more. Indeed, with the bruising price wars that are sure to come, getting each customer to spend a tad extra may be critical for survival. It's just that the next step—the first beyond entertainment media—is a doozy. For one thing, it's unclear that the Amazon brand will extend into, say, toys or consumer electronics. "I get the combination of books and music and videos," says Robert Kagle, a venture capitalist who invests in Internet startups for Benchmark Capital. "Beyond that, I don't know how far their brand goes."

Even if the brand does travel well, it's almost guaranteed that other products won't be as profitable. Take CDs: They have lower margins than books. Same for videos. Toys have the disadvantage of not having as established a distribution network as books and music. So Amazon may have to stock more on its own, increasing its inventory costs and skimming off some of that nice float.

Already, established competitors are forcing it to do just that. Reel. com says 96% of the 20,000 titles it stocks are on the backlist. Those videos constitute most of its sales—and by far the most profitable portion. "If Amazon wants to ship them in a reasonable time, they'll have to stock them," says Reel.com CEO Julie Wainwright. And some products, such as cars, real estate, or office products, are simply too cumbersome or expensive to ship. Or they may require too much aftersale support—which makes software a dicey product for Amazon to sell.

That's why Bezos will likely branch out beyond retail. In August, he spent $270 million for two companies that steer Amazon even more firmly toward becoming a shopping service rather than just a retailer. One of them, Junglee, has technology that makes it easy to scour the Web for products and compare prices or other features. "We don't even necessarily have to be selling all those things," says Bezos. "We just help people find things that are being sold elsewhere on the Web." Amazon might take a cut of revenues from other retailers if its customers buy their products. Says marketing prof Rogers, who is a partner in consultancy Peppers & Rogers: "Their next mission is to be a service agent."

TENUOUS ADVANTAGE

It's a tricky mission. Why? It will be tough to guarantee that the entire customer experience will measure up to Amazon's standard. Any glitches could quickly damage the company's carefully crafted brand name. "In three or four years, they'll be known for 'big,'" says CDnow CEO Jason Olim. "Well, whoop-di-do."

In the end, Amazon's success or failure will ride on maintaining a delightful experience for all of those new customers. Indeed, satisfied Amazon customers may well be helping more than most people realize: Analysts say one key to the sky-high stock price, which underwrites so much of its coming opportunity, is that investors can get a personal feel for Amazon's prospects by trying it out—something that's tough to do with most technology companies. Says Halsey Minor, CEO of online network CNET Inc.: "His [Bezos'] greatest advantage is a lot of people who buy his stock buy his books.

11

IMPLEMENTING STRATEGY THROUGH RESTRUCTURING AND REENGINEERING THE COMPANY'S STRUCTURE, LEADERSHIP, AND CULTURE

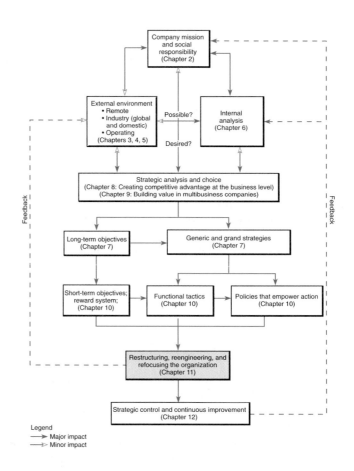

Until this point in the strategic management process, managers have maintained a decidedly market-oriented focus as they formulate strategies and begin implementation through action plans detailing the tactics and actions that will be taken in each functional activity. Now the process takes a decidedly operations focus—getting the work of the business done efficiently and effectively so as to make the strategy work. What is the best way to organize ourselves to accomplish the mission? Where should leadership come from? What values should guide our activities each day? What should this organization and its people be like? These are some of the fundamental issues managers face as they turn to the heart of strategy implementation.

While the focus is internal, the firm must still consider external factors as well. The intense competition in today's global marketplace has led most companies to consider their structure, or how the activities within their business are conducted, with an unprecedented attentiveness to what that marketplace—customers, competitors, suppliers, distribution partners—suggests or needs from the "internal" structure, business processes, leadership, and culture of their company. *Downsizing, restructuring, reengineering, outsourcing,* and *empowerment* are all emblazoned in our minds as a result of the extraordinary speed with which companies worldwide have incorporated them as part of their adjustment to the rigors of competing as a part of the global economic village of the 21st century. You no doubt recognize and have been touched in several ways by the ramification of these concepts over the last five years. This contemporary vocabulary reflects managers' attempts to rationalize their organizational structure, leadership, and culture to ensure a basic level of cost competitiveness, capacity for responsive quality, and the need to shape each one of them to accommodate the requirements of their strategies.

These topics received considerable attention from executives, authors, and researchers during the last decade as they sought to understand the reasons behind the superior performance of the world's "best companies." One of the early and widely accepted frameworks that identify the key factors that best explain superior performance was the McKinsey 7-S Framework, provided in Figure 11–1. This framework provides a useful visualization of the key components managers must consider in making sure a strategy permeates the day-to-day life of the firm.

Once the strategy has been designed, the McKinsey Framework suggests that managers focus on six components to ensure effective execution: structure, systems, shared values (culture), skills, style, and staff. This chapter organizes these six components into three basic "levers" through which managers can implement strategy. The first lever is structure—the basic way the firm's different activities are organized. Second is leadership, encompassing the need to establish an effective style as well as the necessary staff and skills to execute the strategy. The third lever is culture—the shared values that create the norms of individual behavior and the tone of the organization.

STRUCTURING AN EFFECTIVE ORGANIZATION

Successful strategy implementation depends in large part on a firm's "primary organizational structure." *Primary organizational structure* refers to the way work is "organized" within an organization or business entity. Various activities that reflect the work of the enterprise are divided in ways that are intended to help get work done efficiently and effectively. Dividing activities in this way is part organizing and is sometimes called *differentiation.* But separate activities must be coordinated and "integrated" back together in some fashion so that the business as a whole functions effectively. The result of these efforts to differentiate and integrate work activities is a firm's primary

FIGURE 11–1
McKinsey 7-S Framework

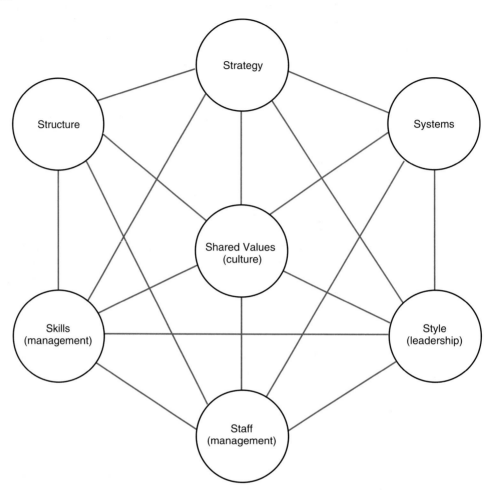

organizational structure. Managers quickly learn that designing the "right" structure can enhance the chances a strategy will succeed, while designing a structure without regard to the needs of their strategy, or more often simply staying with a long-standing organizational structure, can cause that strategy to fail regardless of other well-intended efforts.

Strategy in Action 11–1 tells the recent and unfolding story of Procter & Gamble's aggressive reorganization to make itself more competitive and responsive in an increasingly global retailing environment. While its strategy of product development has led to over 100 years of impressive successes, large international retail customers like Wal-Mart have become increasingly frustrated with the difficulties they encountered dealing with P&G's geographic-based structure. While Wal-Mart CEO David Glass describes his company's goal as "global sourcing," which includes worldwide relationships on pricing and distribution, P&G's geography-based structure had country managers who ruled as "colonial governors, setting pricing and handling products as they saw fit." So while P&G's strategy sought to build its consumer product excellence into a solid international image for its products, P&G's primary organizational structure was systematically hindering the implementation and subsequent success of that strategy. P&G's subsequent shift, from a long-standing geographical driven structure to global business units organized by seven product categories, reflects a two-year effort on the part of its top-management team to design a primary organizational structure that was better "organized" to build sales of various products on a global scale and speed new product development.

Primary Organizational Structures and Their Strategy-Related Pros and Cons

Matching the structure to the strategy is a fundamental task of company strategists. To understand how that task is handled, we first must review the five basic primary structures. We will then turn to guidelines for matching structure to strategy.

The five basic primary structures are: (1) functional, (2) geographic, (3) divisional, or strategic business unit, (4) matrix, and (5) product team. Each structure has advantages and disadvantages that strategists must consider when choosing an organization form.

Functional Organizational Structure

Functional structures predominate in firms with a single or narrow product focus. Such firms require well-defined skills and areas of specialization to build competitive advantages in providing their products or services. Dividing tasks into functional specialties enables the personnel of these firms to concentrate on only one aspect of the necessary work. This allows use of the latest technical skills and develops a high level of efficiency.

Product, customer, or technology considerations determine the identity of the parts in a functional structure. A hotel business might be organized around housekeeping (maids), the front desk, maintenance, restaurant operations, reservations and sales, accounting, and personnel. An equipment manufacturer might be organized around production, engineering/quality control, purchasing, marketing, personnel, and finance/accounting. Two examples of functional organizations are illustrated in Figure 11–2.

The strategic challenge presented by the functional structure is effective coordination of the functional units. The narrow technical expertise achieved through specialization can lead to limited perspectives and to differences in the priorities of the functional units. Specialists may see the firm's strategic issues primarily as "marketing" problems or "production" problems. The potential conflict among functional units makes the coordinating role of the chief executive critical. Integrating devices (such as project teams or planning committees) are frequently used in functionally organized firms to enhance coordination and to facilitate understanding across functional areas.

Geographic Organizational Structure

Firms often grow by expanding the sale of their products or services to new geographic areas. In these areas, they frequently encounter differences that necessitate different approaches in producing, providing, or selling their products or services. Structuring by geographic areas is usually required to accommodate these differences. Thus, Holiday Inns is organized by regions of the world because of differences among nations in the laws, customs, and economies affecting the lodging industry. And even within its U.S. organization, Holiday Inns is organized geographically because of regional differences in traveling requirements, lodging regulations, and customer mix.

The key strategic advantage of geographic organizational structures is responsiveness to local market conditions. Figure 11–3 illustrates a typical geographic organizational structure and itemizes the strategic advantages and disadvantages of such structures.

BusinessWeek

P&G's REVOLUTION: A NEW ORGANIZATIONAL STRUCTURE FOR GLOBAL SPEED AND FOCUS

STRATEGY IN ACTION

11–1

THE PRESSURE

Big international retailers such as Wal-Mart Stores and Carrefour are pushing suppliers such as P&G for standardized worldwide pricing, marketing, and distribution.

THE PLAN

P&G is undergoing a major shift in its organization, moving away from a country-by-country setup to a handful of powerful departments that will supervise categories such as hair care, diapers, and soap on a global scale

THE RISKS

Procter's plan will take two years to implement and depends heavily on increasing market share and sales volume in international markets, many of which are reeling from economic instability.

P&G, a company notorious for secrecy, has set itself on a remarkably outward-looking self-improvement plan. Breaking from decades of tradition, it has sought external advice. It is undergoing a structural shift prompted at least in part by outsiders—namely, its big chain-store customers. And it is already rolling out an aggressive global marketing blitz, from working the fairgrounds to marshaling the Internet.

Chief Executive John E. Pepper will step down about two years early to make way for President and Chief Operating Officer Durk I. Jager, who will drive the changes. It's a shift away from internal themes of recent years in which Procter focused heavily on such tasks as cost-cutting and shedding underperforming brands.

In preparation for the task, Pepper and other top execs have been traversing the country, visiting the CEOs of a dozen major companies, including Kellogg Co. and 3M, in search of advice. Pepper went to Jack Welch at General Electric Co. to learn how the company streamlined global marketing. He persuaded Hewlett-Packard Co. CEO Lewis E. Platt to share enough secrets about new-product development to make a 30-minute instructional video for P&G staffers. The message from all was clear, says Pepper: "What thousands of people have been telling us is that we need to be simpler and move faster."

The result of this unprecedented road trip is Organization 2005, a shuffling of the P&G hierarchy and a new product-development process designed to speed innovative offerings to the global market. The old bureaucracy, based on geography, will be reshaped into seven global business units organized by category, such as baby care, beauty care, and fabric-and-home care. The global business units will develop and sell products on a worldwide basis, erasing the old system

Source: "P&G's Hottest New Product: P&G," *Business Week:* October 5, 1998, pp. 92–93.

Divisional or Strategic Business Unit Structure

When a firm diversifies its product/service lines, utilizes unrelated market channels, or begins to serve heterogeneous customer groups, a functional structure rapidly becomes inadequate. If a functional structure is retained under these circumstances, production managers may have to oversee the production of numerous and varied products or services, marketing managers may have to create sales programs for vastly different products or sell through vastly different distribution channels, and top management may be confronted with excessive coordination demands. A new organizational structure is

continued

that let Procter's country managers rule as colonial governors, setting prices and handling products as they saw fit.

P&G didn't come to this global focus entirely on its own. Its biggest chain-store customers, such as Wal-Mart Stores Inc. and French-owned Carrefour, have been agitating for just such a program to mirror their own global expansion. It has been Topic A at retail conventions for months, says Robin Lanier, senior vice-president for industry affairs at the International Mass Retail Assn. While P&G craves an international image for its products, retailers want something more tangible: a global price. As it stands, prices are negotiable on a country or regional basis. What an international retailer pays for Crest in the U.S. could be considerably less than what it costs the chain in Europe or Latin America. A consistent global price gives big chains more power to plan efficiently and save money. Wal-Mart Chief Executive David D. Glass describes his company's goal as "global sourcing," which includes worldwide relationships on pricing and distribution. Moving P&G products from regional to global management is pointing somewhat in that direction," Glass says.

In addition to marketing and pricing, global business units will supervise new-product development. P&G will move away from its long-used "sequential" method, which tested products first in midsize U.S. cities and then gradually rolled them out to the world.

This new global vision has already had an accidental test run. Last year, P&G introduced an extension of its Pantene shampoo line. The ad campaign for the product was almost entirely visual, with images of beautiful women and their lustrous hair, and had a very limited script. That meant the campaign was easily translated and shipped to P&G markets around the world without the usual months of testing and tinkering. The result: P&G was able to introduce the brand extension in 14 countries in six months, versus the two years it took to get the original shampoo into stores abroad. "It's a success story that gets quite a bit of talk internally," says Chris T. Allen, a marketing professor at the University of Cincinnati, who spent his sabbatical year working in the P&G new-products department. "I see the reorganization as an attempt to do more Pantenes on a regular basis."

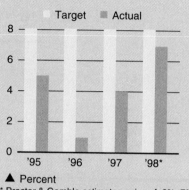

Missing the mark

Procter & Gamble's net sales growth hasn't been strong enough to propel it to its goal of $70 billion by 2006

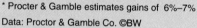

▲ Percent
* Procter & Gamble estimates gains of 6%–7%
Data: Proctor & Gamble Co. ©BW

often necessary to meet the increased coordination and decision-making requirements that result from increased diversity and size, and the divisional or strategic business unit (SBU) organizational structure is the form often chosen.

For many years, Ford and General Motors have used divisional/SBU structures organized by product groups. Manufacturers often organize sales into divisions based on differences in distribution channels.

A divisional/SBU structure allows corporate management to delegate authority for the strategic management of distinct business entities—the division/SBU. This expedites decision making in response to varied competitive environments and enables

FIGURE 11–2
Functional Organization Structures

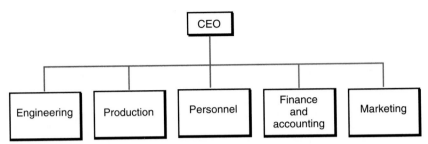

A process-oriented functional structure (an electronics distributor):

Strategic Advantages	Strategic Disadvantages
1. Achieves efficiency through specialization.	1. Promotes narrow specialization and functional rivalry or conflict.
2. Develops functional expertise.	2. Creates difficulties in functional coordination and interfunctional decision making.
3. Differentiates and delegates day-to-day operating decisions.	3. Limits development of general managers.
4. Retains centralized control of strategic decisions.	4. Has a strong potential for interfunctional conflict—priority placed on functional areas, not the entire business.
5. Tightly links structure to strategy by designating key activities as separate units.	

corporate management to concentrate on corporate-level strategic decisions. The division/SBU usually is given profit responsibility, which facilitates accurate assessment of profit and loss.

Figure 11–4 illustrates a divisional/SBU organizational structure and specifies the strategic advantages and disadvantages of such structures. Strategy in Action 11–1 describes how a global geographic structure's disadvantages necessitated a recent change to a division/SBU structure at Procter & Gamble.

Matrix Organizational Structure

In large companies, increased diversity leads to numerous product and project efforts of major strategic significance. The result is a need for an organizational form that provides skills and resources where and when they are most vital. For example, a product development project needs a market research specialist for two months and a financial analyst one day per week. A customer site application needs a software engineer for one month and a customer service trainer one day per month for six weeks. Each of

FIGURE 11–3
A Geographic Organizational Structure

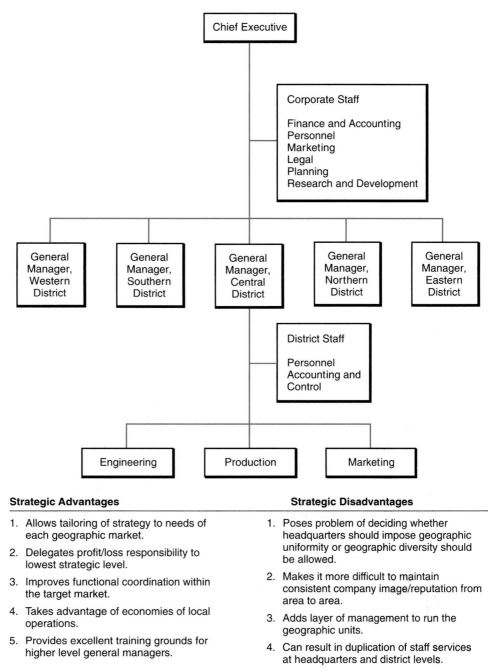

Strategic Advantages	Strategic Disadvantages
1. Allows tailoring of strategy to needs of each geographic market.	1. Poses problem of deciding whether headquarters should impose geographic uniformity or geographic diversity should be allowed.
2. Delegates profit/loss responsibility to lowest strategic level.	
3. Improves functional coordination within the target market.	2. Makes it more difficult to maintain consistent company image/reputation from area to area.
4. Takes advantage of economies of local operations.	3. Adds layer of management to run the geographic units.
5. Provides excellent training grounds for higher level general managers.	4. Can result in duplication of staff services at headquarters and district levels.

these situations is an example of a matrix organization that has been used to temporarily put people and resources where they are most needed. Among the firms that now use some form of matrix organization are Citicorp, Matsushita, DaimlerChrysler, Microsoft, Dow Chemical, and Texas Instruments.

FIGURE 11–4
Divisional or Strategic Business Unit Structure

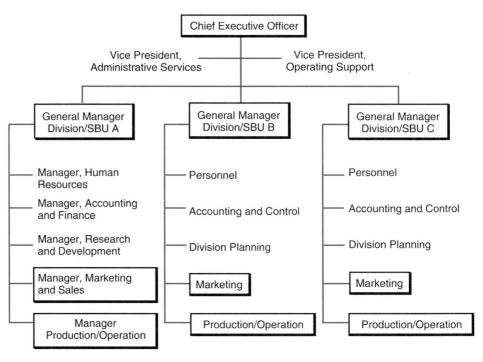

Strategic Advantages

1. Forces coordination and necessary authority down to the appropriate level for rapid response.
2. Places strategy development and implementation in closer proximity to the unique environments of the divisions/SBUs.
3. Frees chief executive officer for broader strategic decision making.
4. Sharply focuses accountability for performance.
5. Retains functional specialization within each division/SBU.
6. Provides good training grounds for strategic managers.
7. Increases focus on products, markets, and quick response to change.

Strategic Disadvantages

1. Fosters potentially dysfunctional competition for corporate-level resources.
2. Presents the problem of determining how much authority should be given to division/SBU managers.
3. Creates a potential for policy inconsistencies among divisions/SBUs.
4. Presents the problem of distributing corporate overhead costs in a way that's acceptable to division managers with profit responsibility.
5. Increases costs incurred through duplication of functions.
6. Creates difficulty maintaining overall corporate image.

The matrix organization provides dual channels of authority, performance responsibility, evaluation, and control, as shown in Figure 11–5. Essentially, subordinates are assigned both to a basic functional area and to a project or product manager. The matrix form is intended to make the best use of talented people within a firm by combining the advantages of functional specialization and product-project specialization.

The matrix structure also increases the number of middle managers who exercise general management responsibilities (through the project manager role) and, thus,

FIGURE 11–5
Matrix Organizational Structure

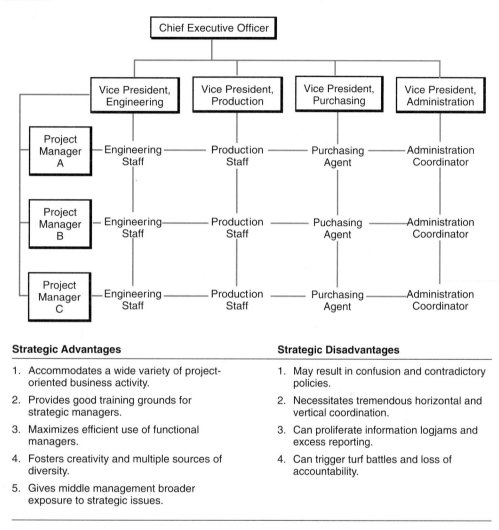

Strategic Advantages	Strategic Disadvantages
1. Accommodates a wide variety of project-oriented business activity.	1. May result in confusion and contradictory policies.
2. Provides good training grounds for strategic managers.	2. Necessitates tremendous horizontal and vertical coordination.
3. Maximizes efficient use of functional managers.	3. Can proliferate information logjams and excess reporting.
4. Fosters creativity and multiple sources of diversity.	4. Can trigger turf battles and loss of accountability.
5. Gives middle management broader exposure to strategic issues.	

broaden their exposure to organizationwide strategic concerns. In this way, the matrix structure overcomes a key deficiency of functional organizations while retaining the advantages of functional specialization.

Although the matrix structure is easy to design, it is difficult to implement. Dual chains of command challenge fundamental organizational orientations. Negotiating shared responsibilities, the use of resources, and priorities can create misunderstanding or confusion among subordinates. These problems are heightened in an international context with the complications introduced by distance, language, time, and culture.

To avoid the deficiencies that might arise from a permanent matrix structure, some firms are accomplishing particular strategic tasks, by means of a "temporary" or "flexible" *overlay structure.* This approach, used recently by such firms as NEC, Matsushita, Phillips, and Unilever, is meant to take *temporary* advantage of a matrix-type team while preserving an underlying divisional structure. Thus, the basic idea of the

FIGURE 11–6
Product-Team Structure

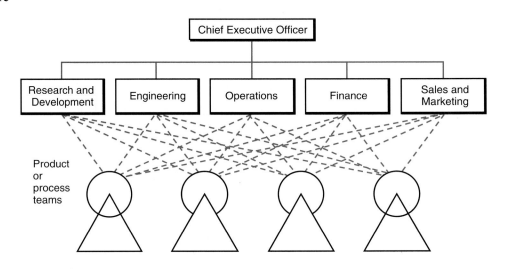

matrix structure—*to simplify and amplify the focus of resources on a narrow but strategically important product, project, or market*—appears to be an important structural alternative for large, diverse organizations.

Product-Team Structure

Cross-functional collaboration has become an increasing concern for companies facing rapid change and global competitors in the 21st century. The product-team structure has emerged as a way many firms are restructuring to meet this challenge. Drawing on the ideas underlying the matrix structure and the division/SBU structure, this new approach seeks to allocate people across all functions onto teams that manage a particular product or process. Figure 11–6 illustrates how the product-team structure might look.

The product-team structure assigns functional managers and specialists (e.g., engineering, marketing, financial, R&D, operations) to a new product, project, or process team that is empowered to make major decisions about their product. The team is usually created at the inception of the new product idea, and they stay with it indefinitely if it becomes a viable business. Instead of being assigned on a temporary basis, as in the matrix structure, team members are assigned permanently to that team in most cases. This results in much lower coordination costs and, since every function is represented, usually reduces the number of management levels above the team level needed to approve team decisions.

It appears that product teams formed at the beginning of product-development processes generate cross-functional understanding that irons out early product or process design problems. They also reduce costs associated with design, manufacturing, and marketing, while typically speeding up innovation and customer responsiveness because authority rests with the team allowing decisions to be made more quickly. That ability to make speedier, cost-saving decisions has the added advantage of eliminating the need for one or more management layers above the team level, which would traditionally have been in place to review and control these types of decisions. While seemingly obvious, it has only recently become apparent that those additional management layers were also making these decisions with less firsthand understanding of the issues involved than the cross-functional team members brought to the product or process in the first place. Strategy in Action 11–2 gives examples of a product-team approach at several well-known companies and some of the advantages that appear to have accrued.

Guidelines to Match Structure to Strategy

Which organizational structure is the best? Considerable research has addressed this issue, and the consensus is that *it depends on the strategy of the firm.* Since the structural design ties together key activities and resources of the firm, it must be closely aligned with the demands of the firm's strategy. What follows are some guidelines that emerge from this line of research and the restructuring revolution that has altered the corporate landscape at the dawn of the 21st century.

Restructure to Emphasize and Support Strategically Critical Activities

Restructuring has been the buzzword of global enterprise for the last 10 years. Its contemporary meaning is multifaceted. At the heart of the restructuring trend is the notion that some activities within a business's value chain are more critical to the success of the business's strategy than others. Wal-Mart's organizational structure is designed to ensure that its impressive logistics and purchasing competitive advantages operate flawlessly. Coordinating daily logistical and purchasing efficiencies among separate stores lets Wal-Mart lead the industry in profitability yet sell retail for less than many competitors buy the same merchandise at wholesale. Motorola's organizational structure is designed to protect and nurture its legendary R&D and new product development capabilities—spending over twice the industry average in R&D alone each year. Motorola's R&D emphasis continually spawns proprietary technologies that support its technology-based competitive advantage. Coca-Cola emphasizes the importance of distribution activities, advertising, and retail support to its bottlers in its organizational structure. All three of these companies emphasize very different parts of the value chain process, but they are extraordinarily successful in part because they have designed their organizational structures to emphasize and support strategically critical activities. Strategy in Action 11–3 provides some guidelines that should influence how an organization is structured depending on which among five different sources of competitive advantage are emphasized in its strategy.

Two critical considerations arise when restructuring the organization to emphasize and support strategically critical activities. First, managers need to make the strategically critical activities the central building blocks for designing organization structure. Those activities should be identified and separated as much as possible into self-contained parts of the organization. Then the remaining structure must be designed so as to ensure timely integration with other parts of the organization.

While this is easily proposed, managers need to recognize that strategically relevant activities may still reside in different parts of the organization, particularly in functionally organized structures. Support activities like finance, engineering, or information processing are usually self-contained units, often outside the unit around which core competencies are built. This often results in an emphasis on departments obsessed with performing their own tasks more than emphasizing the key results (customer satisfaction, differentiation, low costs, speed) the business as a whole seeks. So the second consideration is to design the organizational structure so that it helps coordinate and integrate these support activities to (1) maximize their support of strategy-critical primary activities in the firm's value chain and (2) does so in a way to minimize the costs for support activities and the time spent on internal coordination. Managerial

BusinessWeek

INCREASED USE OF CROSS-FUNCTIONAL PRODUCT
TEAMS IN 21ST CENTURY WINNERS

STRATEGY IN
ACTION
11–2

Building teams is a new organization art form for Corporate America. Getting people to work together successfully has become a critical managerial skill. Those companies that learn the secrets of creating cross-functional teams are winning the battle for global market share and profits. Those that don't are losing out.

Take General Motors. Both Ford and Chrysler are picking up market share in the U.S. because each in its own way has discovered how to build product-development teams that generate successful new models. Their method: Bring together people from engineering, design, purchasing, manufacturing, and marketing, and make them responsible as a group for the new car. Then destroy all bureaucracy above them, except for service support. GM has yet to do this. Its team members remain tied to their old structures—the engineers to engineering, purchasing agents to the purchasing department. Decisions aren't made for the good of the new product but to satisfy atavistic requirements of ancient bureaucracies.

Consider Modicon Inc., a North Andover (Massachusetts) maker of automation-control equipment with annual revenues of $300 million. Instead of viewing product development as a task of the engineering function, President Paul White defined it more broadly as a process that would involve a team of 15 managers from engineering, manufacturing, marketing, sales, and finance. By working together, Modicon's team avoided costly delays from disagreements and misunderstandings. "In the past," says White, "an engineering team would have worked on this alone with some dialogue from marketing. Manufacturing wouldn't get involved until the design was brought into the factory. Now, all the business issues are right on the table from the beginning." The change allowed Modicon to bring six software products to market in one-third the time it would normally take. The company still has a management structure organized by function. But many of the company's 900 employees are involved in up to 30 teams that span several functions and departments. Predicts White: "In five years, we'll still have some formal functional structure, but people will probably feel free enough to spend the majority of their time outside their functions."

Eastman Chemical Co., the $3.5 billion unit of Eastman Kodak Co. recently spun off as a stand-alone company, replaced several of its senior vice-presidents in charge of the key functions with "self-directed work teams." Instead of having a head of manufacturing, for example, the company uses a team consisting of all its plant managers. "It was the most dramatic change in the company's 70-year history," maintains Ernest W. Deavenport Jr., president of Eastman Chemical. "It makes people take off their organizational hats and put on their team hats. It gives people a much broader perspective and forces decision-making down at least another level." In creating the new organization, the 500 senior managers agreed that the primary role of the functions was to support Eastman's business in chemicals, plastics, fibers, and polymers. "A function does not and should not have a mission of its own," insists Deavenport. Common sense? Of course. But over the years, the functional departments had grown strong and powerful, as they have in many organizations, often at the expense of the overall company as they fought to protect and build turf. Now, virtually all of the company's managers work on at least one cross-functional team, and most work on two or more on a daily basis. For example, Tom O. Nethery, a group vice-president, runs an industrial-business group. But he also serves on three other teams that deal with such diverse issues as human resources, cellulose technology, and product-support services.

Source: John A. Byrne, "The Horizontal Corporation," *Business Week:* December 20, 1993; and "What GM Needs To Do," *Business Week:* November 1, 1993.

GUIDELINES FOR DESIGNING A STRUCTURE TO ACCOMMODATE FIVE DIFFERENT STRATEGIC PRIORITIES

STRATEGY IN ACTION 11–3

One of the key things business managers should keep in mind when restructuring their organizations is to devise the new structure so that it emphasizes strategically critical activities within the business's value chain. This means that the structure should allow those activities to have considerable autonomy over issues that influence their operating excellence and timeliness; they should be in a position to easily coordinate with other parts of the business—to get decisions made fast.

Below are five different types of critical activities that may be at the heart of a business's effort to build and sustain competitive advantage. Beside each one are typical conditions that will affect and shape the nature of the organization's structure:

Potential Strategic Priority and Critical Activities	Concomitant Conditions That May Affect or Place Demands on the Organizational Structure and Operating Activities to Build Competitive Advantage
1. Compete as low-cost provider of goods or services.	Broadens market. Requires longer production runs and fewer product changes. Requires special-purpose equipment and facilities.
2. Compete as high-quality provider.	Often possible to obtain more profit per unit, and perhaps more total profit from a smaller volume of sales. Requires more quality-assurance effort and higher operating cost. Requires more precise equipment, which is more expensive. Requires highly skilled workers, necessitating higher wages and greater training efforts.
3. Stress customer service.	Requires broader development of servicepeople and service parts and equipment. Requires rapid response to customer needs or changes in customer tastes, rapid and accurate information system, careful coordination. Requires a higher inventory investment.
4. Provide rapid and frequent introduction of new products.	Requires versatile equipment and people. Has higher research and development costs. Has high retraining costs and high tooling and changeover costs. Provides lower volumes for each product and fewer opportunities for improvements due to the learning curve.
5. Seek vertical integration.	Enables firm to control more of the process. May not have economies of scale at some stages of process. May require high capital investment as well as technology and skills beyond those currently available within the firm.

efforts to do this in the 1990s have placed reengineering, downsizing, and outsourcing as prominent tools for strategists restructuring their organizations.

Reengineer Strategic Business Processes

Business process reengineering (BPR), popularized by consultants Michael Hammer and James Champy,[1] is one of the more popular methods by which organizations

---

[1] Michael Hammer and James Champy, *Reengineering the Corporation* (New York: HarperBusiness, 1993).

worldwide are undergoing restructuring efforts to remain competitive in the 21st century. BPR is intended to reorganize a company so that it can best create value for the customer by eliminating barriers that create distance between employees and customers. It involves fundamental rethinking and radical redesign of a business process. It is characterized as radical because it strives to structure organizational efforts and activities around results and value creation by focusing on the processes that are undertaken to meet customer needs, not specific tasks and functional areas such as marketing and sales.

Business reengineering reduces fragmentation by crossing traditional departmental lines and reducing overhead to compress formerly separate steps and tasks that are strategically intertwined in the process of meeting customer needs. This "process orientation," rather than a traditional functional orientation, becomes the perspective around which various activities and tasks are then grouped to create the building blocks of the organization's structure. This is usually accomplished by assembling a multifunctional, multilevel team that begins by identifying customer needs and how the customer wants to deal with the firm. Customer focus must permeate all phases. Companies that have successfully reengineered their operations around strategically critical business processes have pursued the following steps:[2]

- Develop a flow chart of the total business process, including its interfaces with other value chain activities.
- Try to simplify the process first, eliminating tasks and steps where possible and analyzing how to streamline the performance of what remains.
- Determine which parts of the process can be automated (usually those that are repetitive, time-consuming, and require little thought or decision); consider introducing advanced technologies that can be upgraded to achieve next-generation capability and provide a basis for further productivity gains down the road.
- Evaluate each activity in the process to determine whether it is strategy-critical or not. Strategy-critical activities are candidates for benchmarking to achieve best-in-industry or best-in-world performance status.
- Weigh the pros and cons of outsourcing activities that are noncritical or that contribute little to organizational capabilities and core competencies.
- Design a structure for performing the activities that remain; reorganize the personnel and groups who perform these activities into the new structure.

When asked recently about his new networking-oriented direction for IBM, IBM CEO Gerstner responded: "It's called *reengineering*. It's called *getting competitive*. It's called *reducing cycle time and cost, flattening organizations, increasing customer responsiveness*. All of these require a collaboration with the customer and with suppliers and with vendors."

Downsize, Outsource, and Self-Manage

Reengineering and a value orientation have led managers to scrutinize even further the way their organizational structures are crucial to strategy implementation. That scrutiny has led to downsizing, outsourcing, and self-management as three important themes influencing the organizational structures into the 21st century. *Downsizing* is eliminating the number of employees, particularly middle management, in a company.

---

[2]Judy Wade, "How to Make Reengineering Really Work," *Harvard Business Review* 71, no. 6 (November–December 1993), pp. 119–31.

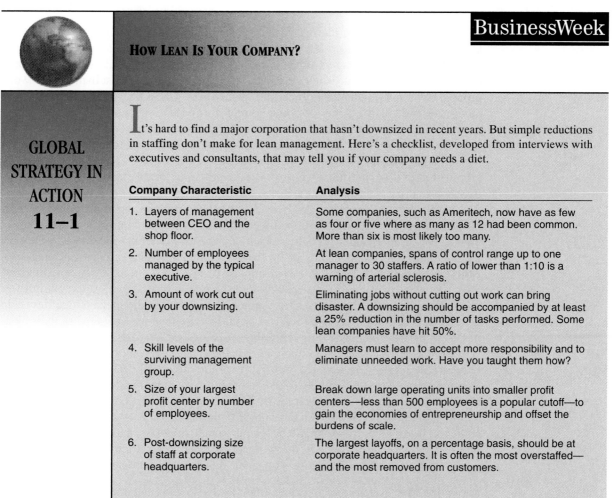

BusinessWeek

HOW LEAN IS YOUR COMPANY?

GLOBAL
STRATEGY IN
ACTION
11–1

It's hard to find a major corporation that hasn't downsized in recent years. But simple reductions in staffing don't make for lean management. Here's a checklist, developed from interviews with executives and consultants, that may tell you if your company needs a diet.

Company Characteristic	Analysis
1. Layers of management between CEO and the shop floor.	Some companies, such as Ameritech, now have as few as four or five where as many as 12 had been common. More than six is most likely too many.
2. Number of employees managed by the typical executive.	At lean companies, spans of control range up to one manager to 30 staffers. A ratio of lower than 1:10 is a warning of arterial sclerosis.
3. Amount of work cut out by your downsizing.	Eliminating jobs without cutting out work can bring disaster. A downsizing should be accompanied by at least a 25% reduction in the number of tasks performed. Some lean companies have hit 50%.
4. Skill levels of the surviving management group.	Managers must learn to accept more responsibility and to eliminate unneeded work. Have you taught them how?
5. Size of your largest profit center by number of employees.	Break down large operating units into smaller profit centers—less than 500 employees is a popular cutoff—to gain the economies of entrepreneurship and offset the burdens of scale.
6. Post-downsizing size of staff at corporate headquarters.	The largest layoffs, on a percentage basis, should be at corporate headquarters. It is often the most overstaffed—and the most removed from customers.

Source: Reprinted from October 22, 1993 issue of *Business Week* by special permission, copyright © 1993 by The McGraw-Hill Companies.

The arrival of a global marketplace, information technology, and intense competition caused many companies to reevaluate middle management activities to determine just what value was really being added to the company's products and services. The result of this scrutiny, along with continuous improvements in information processing technology, has been widespread downsizing in the number of management personnel in thousands of companies worldwide. These companies often eliminate whole levels of management. General Electric went from 400,000 to 280,000 employees in this decade while its sales have almost tripled and its profit risen fivefold. AT&T has experienced similar numbers of job reductions. The results of a survey of companies worldwide that have been actively downsizing (which attempts to extract guidelines for downsizing) is shown in Global Strategy in Action 11–1.

One of the outcomes of downsizing was increased *self-management* at operating levels of the company. Cutbacks in the number of management people left those that remained with more work to do. The result was that they had to give up a good measure of control to workers, and they had to rely on those workers to help out. Spans of control, traditionally thought to maximize under 10 people, have become much larger due to information technology, running "lean and mean," and delegation to lower levels. Ameritech, one of the Baby Bells, has seen its spans of control rise to as much as 30 to 1 in some divisions because most of the people that did staff work—financial analysts, assistant managers, and so on—have disappeared. This delegation, also known as empowerment, is accomplished through concepts like self-managed work groups, reengineering, and automation. It is also seen through efforts to create distinct businesses within a business—conceiving a business as a confederation of many "small" businesses, rather than one large, interconnected business. Whatever the terminology, the idea is to push decision making down in the organization by allowing major management decisions to be made at operating levels. The result is often the elimination of up to half the levels of management previously existing in an organizational structure.

Another driving force behind downsizing has been outsourcing. *Outsourcing* is simply obtaining work previously done by employees inside the companies from sources outside the company. Managers have found that as they attempt to restructure their organizations, particularly if they do so from a business process orientation, numerous activities can often be found in their company that are not "strategically critical activities." This has particularly been the case of numerous staff activities and administrative control processes previously the domain of various middle management levels in an organization. But it can also refer to primary activities that are steps in their business's value chain—purchasing, shipping, making certain parts, and so on. Further scrutiny has led managers to conclude that these activities not only add little or no value to the product or services, but that they are either unnecessary or they can be done much more cost effectively (and competently) by other businesses specializing in these activities. If this is so, then the business can enhance its competitive advantage by outsourcing the activities it can't outright eliminate. Many organizations have outsourced information processing, various personnel activities, and production of parts that can be done better outside the company. Outsourcing, then, can be a source of competitive advantage and result in a leaner, flatter organizational structure.

Recognize That Strategy and Structure Often Evolve in a Predictable Pattern

Predating some of the recent guidelines reviewed above, still-relevant research suggests businesses frequently grow in a rather predictable pattern that has ramifications for which structure would be most effective. Alfred Chandler first observed a common sequence of evolution in strategy and structure among American firms.[3] The sequence reflected their increasing scope. Most firms began as simple functional units operating at a single site (e.g., a plant, a warehouse, or a sales office) and within a single industry. The initial growth strategy of such firms was *volume expansion,* which created a need for an administrative office to manage the increased volume. The next growth strategy was *geographic expansion,* which required multiple field units, still performing the same function but in different locations. Administrative problems with regard to standardization, specialization, and interunit coordination then gave rise to the need for geographic units and for a central administrative unit to oversee them. *Vertical integration* was usually the next growth strategy. Firms remained within the same industry but performed additional functions. Problems associated with the flow of information and materials among the various functions led to the functional organization, in which staff personnel developed forecasts and schedules that facilitated overall coordination.

---

[3]Alfred D. Chandler, *Strategy and Structure* (Cambridge, MA: MIT Press, 1962).

The final growth strategy was *product diversification*. Firms entered other industries in which they could use their existing resources. Problems in managing diverse product divisions and evaluating their capital investment proposals led to the multidivisional structure in which similar activities were grouped. Separate divisions handled independent products and were responsible for short-run operating decisions. General managers (i.e., group managers) at a central office were responsible for long-term strategic decisions. These managers had to relate divisional decisions and performance to strategic direction and to balance divisional autonomy against central control.

Larry Wrigley and Richard Rumelt built on Chandler's work by examining how a firm's degree of diversification from its core business affected its choice of structure. They identified four growth strategies: (1) *single-product businesses;* (2) *single dominant businesses,* with one business accounting for 70–95 percent of sales; (3) *related diversified businesses* based on a common distribution channel or technology, with more than 30 percent of sales outside the primary business; and (4) *unrelated diversified businesses,* with more than 30 percent of sales outside the primary business.[4] They found that greater diversity led to greater divisionalization: single-product businesses used a functional structure; related and unrelated businesses used a divisionalized structure; and single dominant businesses used a functional structure in the dominant business and a divisional structure in the remaining businesses.

More-recent research has extended our understanding of the strategy-structure fit.[5] This research continues to suggest that, in smaller firms with a single product or product line, the functional structure significantly outperforms the multidivisional structure. In larger firms, however, the roles of corporate- and lower-level staffs significantly affect performance. The greater the diversity among a firm's businesses, the more desirable it is to have strong, decentralized staffs within the businesses (or divisions); with less diversity, firms with strong staffs at higher organizational levels are more effective. In other words, the greater the diversity among the businesses in multibusiness firms, the greater is the necessary degree of decentralization and self-containment. This need has only been heightened by the rapid globalization among many countries. On the other hand, where the diversity among a firm's businesses is low and the interdependence of these businesses is high, more integration at the corporate level is needed.

Four significant conclusions can be drawn from this research:[6]

1. *A single-product firm or single dominant business firm should employ a functional structure.* This structure allows for strong task focus through an emphasis on specialization and efficiency, while providing opportunity for adequate controls through centralized review and decision making.

2. *A firm in several lines of business that are somehow related should employ a multidivisional structure.* Closely related divisions should be combined into groups within this structure. When synergies (i.e., shared or linked activities) are possible within such a group, the appropriate location for staff influence and decision making is at the group

[4]Larry Wrigley, *Divisional Autonomy and Diversification,* doctoral dissertation, Harvard Business School, 1970; Richard Rumelt, "Diversification Strategy and Performance," *Strategic Management Journal* 3 (January–February 1982), pp. 359–69; Richard Rumelt, *Strategy, Structure and Economic Performance* (Boston: HBS Press, 1986). Rumelt used a similar, but more detailed classification scheme.

[5]D. A. Nathanson and J. S. Cassano, "Organization, Diversity, and Performance," *Wharton's Magazine* 6 (1982), pp. 19–26; and Christopher A. Bartlett and Sumantra Ghoshal, "Matrix Management: Not a Structure, a Frame of Mind," *Harvard Business Review* 68, no. 4 (1990), pp. 138–45.

[6]V. R. Galbraith and R. K. Kazanjian, *Strategy Implementation: Structure, Systems & Processes* (St. Paul, MN: West Publishing, 1986).

level, with a lesser role for corporate-level staff. The greater the degree of diversity across the firm's businesses, the greater should be the extent to which the power of staff and decision-making authority is lodged within the divisions.

3. *A firm in several unrelated lines of business should be organized into strategic business units.* Although the strategic business unit structure resembles the multidivisional structure, there are significant differences between the two. With a strategic business unit structure, finance, accounting, planning, legal, and related activities should be centralized at the corporate office. Since there are no synergies across the firm's businesses, the corporate office serves largely as a capital allocation and control mechanism. Otherwise, its major decisions involve acquisitions and divestitures. All operational and business-level strategic plans are delegated to the strategic business units.

4. *Early achievement of a strategy-structure fit can be a competitive advantage.* A competitive advantage is obtained by the first firm among competitors to achieve appropriate strategy-structure fit. That advantage will disappear as the firm's competitors also attain such a fit. Moreover, if the firm alters its strategy, its structure must obviously change as well. Otherwise, a loss of fit will lead to a competitive disadvantage for the firm.

ORGANIZATIONAL LEADERSHIP

The introduction to this chapter showed the McKinsey 7-S framework as a way to understand the implementation challenge. Figure 11–1 shows that framework identifies management and leadership as two separate elements. Management is identified with skills and leadership with style. This distinction is important. John Kotter, a widely recognized leadership expert, helps explain this distinction:[7]

> Management is about coping with complexity. Its practices and procedures are largely a response to one of the most significant developments of the 20th century: the emergence of large organizations. Without good management, complex enterprises tend to become chaotic in ways that threaten their very existence. Good management brings a degree of order and consistency to key dimensions like the quality and profitability of products.
>
> Leadership, by contrast, is about coping with change. Part of the reason it has become so important in recent years is that the business world has become more competitive and more volatile. . . . The net result is that doing what was done yesterday, or doing it 5 percent better, is no longer a formula for success. Major changes are more and more necessary to survive and compete effectively in this new environment. More change always demands more leadership.

Organizational leadership, then, involves two considerations. One is strategic leadership, usually coming from the CEO. The other is management skill to cope with complexity.

Strategic Leadership: Embracing Change

The blending of telecommunications, computers, the Internet, and one global marketplace have increased the pace of change exponentially during the last 10 years. All business organizations are affected. Change has become an integral part of what leaders and managers deal with daily.

---

[7]John P. Kotter, "What Leaders Really Do," *Harvard Business Review* 68, no. 3 (May–June 1990), p. 104.

The leadership challenge is to galvanize commitment among people within an organization as well as stakeholders outside the organization to embrace change and implement strategies intended to position the organization to do so. Leaders galvanize commitment to embrace change through three, interrelated activities: clarifying strategic intent, building an organization, and shaping organizational culture.

Clarifying Strategic Intent

Leaders help stakeholders embrace change by setting forth a clear vision of where the business's strategy needs to take the organization. Traditionally, the concept of vision has been a description or picture of what the company could be that accommodates the needs of all its stakeholders. The intensely competitive, rapidly changing global marketplace has refined this to be targeting a very narrowly defined strategic intent—*an articulation of a simple criterion or characterization of what the company must become to establish and sustain global leadership.* Lou Gerstner is a good example of a leader in the middle of trying to shape strategic intent. "One of the great things about this industry is that every decade or so, you get a chance to redefine the playing field," said Gerstner. "We're in that phase of redefinition right now, and winners or losers are going to emerge from it. We've got to become *the leader in 'network-centric computing.'*" It's an opportunity brought about by telecommunications-based change that will change IBM more than semiconductors did in the 1980s. Says Gerstner, "I sensed there were too many people inside IBM who wanted to fight the war we lost," referring to PCs and PC software, so now he is aggressively trying to shape network-centric computing as the strategic intent for IBM in the next century.

Clarifying strategic intent can come in many different forms. Coca-Cola's legendary former CEO and Chairman Roberto Goizueta said "the company lead is a global business system for which we raise capital to make concentrate and sell it at an operating profit. Then we pay the cost of that capital. Shareholders pocket the difference." Coke averaged 27% annual return on stockholder equity for 18 years under his leadership. Travelers Insurance lost $200 million in 1992. Sanford Weill assumed leadership, focusing on a short-term turnaround. Recalling that time, he said, "We sent letters to all suppliers saying: Dear Supplier, either we rebid your business or you lower your costs 15%." Within two years, nonpersonnel costs were cut 49% in addition to 15,000 jobs. Travelers made $700 million in 1996. Mr. Weill was effective in setting forth strategic intent for Travelers' turnaround. While Coke and Travelers are very different situations, their leaders were both very effective in shaping and clarifying strategic intent in a way that helped stakeholders understand what needed to be done.

Building an Organization

The previous section examined alternative structures to use in designing the organization necessary to implement strategy. Leaders spend considerable time shaping and refining their organizational structure and making it function effectively to accomplish strategic intent. Since leaders are attempting to embrace change, they are often rebuilding or remaking their organization to align it with the ever-changing environment and needs of the strategy. And since embracing change often involves overcoming resistance to change, leaders find themselves addressing problems like the following as they attempt to build or rebuild their organization:

- Ensuring a common understanding about organizational priorities.
- Clarifying responsibilities among managers and organizational units.
- Empowering newer managers and pushing authority lower in the organization.

- Uncovering and remedying problems in coordination and communication across the organization.
- Gaining the personal commitment to a shared vision from managers throughout the organization.
- Keeping closely connected with "what's going on in the organization and with its customers."

Leaders do this in many ways. Larry Bossidy, the CEO who had quadrupled Allied Signal's stock price in the last four years, spends 50 percent of his time each year flying to Allied Signal's various operations around the world meeting with managers and discussing decisions, results, and progress. Bill Gates at Microsoft spends two hours each day reading and sending E-mail to any of Microsoft's 16,000 employees that want to contact him. All managers adapt structures, create teams, implement systems, and otherwise generate ways to coordinate, integrate and share information about what their organization is doing and might do. Others create customer advisory groups, supplier partnerships, R&D joint ventures and other adjustments to build an adaptable, learning organization that embraces the leader's vision and strategic intent and the change driving the future opportunities facing the business. These, in addition to the fundamental structural guidelines described in the previous section for restructuring to support strategically critical activities, are the issues leaders constantly address as they attempt to build a supportive organization.

Shaping Organization Culture

Leaders know well that the values and beliefs shared throughout their organization will shape how the work of the organization is done. And when attempting to embrace accelerated change, reshaping their organization's culture is an activity that occupies considerable time for most leaders. Listen to these observations by and about MCI and its CEO Bert Roberts about competing in the rapidly changing telecommunications industry prior to its merger with WorldCom:[8]

> Says Roberts: "We run like mad and then we change directions." Indeed, the ever-changing wireless initiative (reselling wireless services rather than creating its own capacity) illustrates a trait that sets apart MCI from its competitors—a willingness to try new things, and if they don't work, to try something else. "Over at AT&T, people are afraid to make mistakes," says Jeff Kagan, president of Kagan Telecom in Atlanta, Ga. "At MCI, people are afraid not to make mistakes."

It appears that MCI CEO Bert Roberts wanted an organizational culture that was risk taking and somewhat free wheeling in order to take advantage of change in the telecommunications industry. He did this by example, by expectations felt by his managers, and in the way decision making is approached within MCI.

Leaders use reward systems, symbols, and structure among other means to shape the organization's culture. Travelers' turnaround was accomplished in part by changing its "hidebound" culture through a change in its agent reward system. Employees previously on salary with occasional bonuses were given rewards that involved substantial cash bonuses and stock options. Observed a customer and risk management director at drugmaker Becton Dickinson, "They're hungrier now. They want to make deals. They're different than the old, hidebound Travelers' culture."

---

[8]Alison Sprout, "MCI: Can It Become the Communications Company of the Next Century?" *Fortune,* October 2, 1995, p. 110.

As leaders clarify strategic intent, build an organization, and shape their organization's culture, they look to one key element to help—their management team throughout their organization. As Allied Signal's visible CEO Larry Bossidy candidly observed when asked about how after 38 years at General Electric and now at Allied Signal with seemingly drab businesses he could expect exciting growth: "There's no such thing as a mature market. What we need is mature executives who can find ways to grow." Leaders look to managers they need to execute strategy as another source of leadership to accept risk and cope with the complexity that change brings about. So assignment of key managers becomes a leadership tool.

Assignment of Key Managers

A major concern of top management in implementing a strategy, particularly if it involves a major change, is that the right managers be in the right positions to facilitate execution of the new strategy. Of all the means for ensuring successful implementation, this is the one that CEOs mention first. Confidence in the individuals occupying pivotal managerial positions is directly correlated with top-management expectations that a strategy can be executed successfully.

This confidence is based on the answers to two fundamental questions:

1. Which persons hold the leadership positions that are especially critical to execution of the strategy?
2. Do these persons have the characteristics needed to ensure effective implementation of the strategy?

Although it is impossible to specify the characteristics that are most important in this context, they probably include (1) ability and education, (2) previous track record and experience, and (3) personality and temperament. An individual's suitability on these counts, combined with top managers' gut feelings about the individual, provides the basis for top management's confidence in the individual.

One practical consideration in making key managerial assignments when implementing strategy is whether to utilize current (or promotable) executives or bring in new personnel. This is obviously a difficult, sensitive, and strategic issue. Figure 11–7 highlights the key advantages and disadvantages of these alternatives.

The other consideration that has become prominent in an environment of restructuring, downsizing, and self-management is managers' ability to delegate and to handle larger spans of control. As companies adapt employee empowerment and self-managed work group practices, managers that remain face greater workloads and different management challenges. The result is the need for skills consistent with this new environment—delegation, coaching, electronic savvy, and a results orientation.

Strategy in Action 11–4 (page 422) describes the remarkable leadership achievements of Finlander Jorma Ollila in successfully betting the 133-year-old Finnish conglomerate Nokia on cellular phones.

ORGANIZATIONAL CULTURE

Organizational culture is the set of important assumptions (often unstated) that members of an organization share in common. Every organization has its own culture. An organization's culture is similar to an individual's personality—an intangible yet

FIGURE 11–7
**Using Existing Executives versus Bringing in Outsiders for
Managerial Assignments to Implement a New Strategy**

	Advantages	Disadvantages
Using existing executives to implement a new strategy	Existing executives already know key people, practices, and conditions. Personal qualities of existing executives are better known and understood by associates. Existing executives have established relationships with peers, subordinates, suppliers, buyers, and the like. Use of existing executives symbolizes organizational commitment to individual careers.	Existing executives are less adaptable to major strategic changes because of their knowledge, attitudes, and values. Past commitments of existing executives hamper the hard decisions required in executing a new strategy. Existing executives have less ability to become inspired and credibly convey the need for change.
Bringing in outsiders to implement a new strategy	Outsiders may already believe in and have "lived" the new strategy. Outsiders are unencumbered by internal commitments to people. Outsiders come to the new assignment with heightened commitment and enthusiasm. Bringing in outsiders can send powerful signals throughout the organization that change is expected.	Bringing in outsiders often is costly in terms of both compensation and "learning-to-work-together" time. Candidates suitable in all respects (i.e., exact experience) may not be available, leading to compromise choices. Uncertainty exists in selecting the right outsiders to bring in. "Morale costs" are incurred when an outsider takes a job that several insiders want. The "what to do with poor ol' Fred" problem arises when outsiders are brought in.

ever-present theme that provides meaning, direction, and the basis for action. In much the same way as personality influences the behavior of an individual, the shared assumptions (beliefs and values) among a firm's members influence opinions and actions within that firm.

A member of an organization can simply be aware of the organization's beliefs and values without sharing them in a personally significant way. Those beliefs and values have more personal meaning if the member views them as a guide to appropriate behavior in the organization and, therefore, complies with them. The member becomes fundamentally committed to the beliefs and values when he or she internalizes them; that is, comes to hold them as personal beliefs and values. In this case, the corresponding behavior is *intrinsically rewarding* for the member—the member derives personal satisfaction from his or her actions in the organization because those actions are congruent with corresponding personal beliefs and values. *Assumptions become shared assumptions through internalization among an organization's individual members.* And those shared, internalized beliefs and values shape the content and account for the strength of an organization's culture.

Leaders typically attempt to manage and create distinct cultures through a variety of ways. Some of the most common ways are as follows:

Emphasize Key Themes or Dominant Values Businesses build strategies around distinct competitive advantages they possess or seek. Quality, differentiation, cost advantages, and speed are four key sources of competitive advantage. So insightful leaders nurture key themes or dominant values within their organization that reinforce competitive advantages they seek to maintain or build. Key themes or dominant values may center around wording in an advertisement. They are often found in internal company communications. They are most often found as a new vocabulary used by company personnel to explain "who we are." At Xerox, the key themes include respect for the individual and services to the customer. At Procter & Gamble (P&G), the overarching value is product quality; McDonald's uncompromising emphasis on QSCV—quality, service, cleanliness, and value—through meticulous attention to detail is legendary; Delta Airlines is driven by the "family feeling" theme, which builds a team spirit and nurtures each employee's cooperative attitude toward others, cheerful outlook toward life, and pride in a job well done. Du Pont's safety orientation—a report of every accident must be on the chairman's desk within 24 hours—has resulted in a safety record that was 17 times better than the chemical industry average and 68 times better than the all-manufacturing average.

Encourage Dissemination of Stories and Legends about Core Values Companies with strong cultures are enthusiastic collectors and tellers of stories, anecdotes, and legends in support of basic beliefs. Frito-Lay's zealous emphasis on customer service is reflected in frequent stories about potato chip route salespeople who have slogged through sleet, mud, hail, snow, and rain to uphold the 99.5 percent service level to customers in which the entire company takes great pride. Milliken (a textile leader) holds "sharing" rallies once every quarter at which teams from all over the company swap success stories and ideas. Typically, more than 100 teams make five-minute presentations over a two-day period. Every rally is designed around a major theme, such as quality, cost reduction, or customer service. No criticisms are allowed, and awards are given to reinforce this institutionalized approach to storytelling. L. L. Bean tells customer service stories; 3M tells innovation stories; P&G, Johnson & Johnson, IBM, and Maytag tell quality stories. These stories are very important in developing an organizational culture, because organization members identify strongly with them and come to share the beliefs and values they support.

Institutionalize Practices That Systematically Reinforce Desired Beliefs and Values Companies with strong cultures are clear on what their beliefs and values need to be and take the process of shaping those beliefs and values very seriously. Most important, the values these companies espouse undergird the strategies they employ. For example, McDonald's has a yearly contest to determine the best hamburger cooker in its chain. First, there is a competition to determine the best hamburger cooker in each store; next, the store winners compete in regional championships; finally, the regional winners compete in the "All-American" contest. The winners, who are widely publicized throughout the company, get trophies and All-American patches to wear on their McDonald's uniforms.

Adapt Some Very Common Themes in Their Own Unique Ways The most typical beliefs that shape organizational culture include (1) a belief in being the best (or, as at GE, "better than the best"); (2) a belief in superior quality and service; (3) a belief in the importance of people as individuals and a faith in their ability to make a strong contribution; (4) a belief in the importance of the details of execution, the nuts and bolts of doing the job well; (5) a belief that customers should reign supreme; (6) a belief in inspiring people to do their best, whatever their ability; (7) a belief in the importance of informal communication; and (8) a belief that growth and profits are essential to a company's well-being. Every company implements these beliefs differently (to fit its particular situation), and every company's values are the handiwork of one or two legendary

LEADERSHIP AND CULTURE SHAPE
SUCCESS AT FINLAND'S NOKIA

STRATEGY IN
ACTION
11–4

Behind his gentlemanly demeanor, Jorma Ollila, CEO of Nokia Corp., is a man of extremes. As his wife, Liisa Annikki, tells it, her husband fires up the Finnish sauna a good 15 degrees warmer than she likes it, all the way to 212F—hot enough to boil a pot of tea. It was late March, ice was still floating on Lake Pukala north of Helsinki, and the kids challenged their father to dive in. Emerging from the sauna, Ollila paused, then plunged naked into the icy lake.

Ollila, a 47-year-old former banker, lives by the plunge. He believes people get comfy and complacent and that it takes a dive into the unknown, or a push, to tap into their strongest instincts—those that guide survival. Six years ago, as an untested CEO, he bet the 133-year-old Finnish conglomerate on cellular phones, challenging rivals Motorola Inc. and L. M. Ericsson. In the struggle that ensued, Ollila's Finns outdid themselves. Fast and focused, with a canny eye for design, Nokia wrested market share from entrenched competitors and emerged as the most profitable player in the industry.

The company's startling climb has provided the Continent with something it was sorely lacking: a new high-tech superstar. What's more, that triumph is in a crucial technology—mobile communications. That's the next frontier for the Internet, and one of the few areas where Europe is racing ahead of the U.S.

Smack in the middle of Nokia's success stands Ollila, whose name is accented on the "O." He's a self-avowed nontechie who hasn't even put plumbing in his lakeside cabin. But it's Ollila who is improvising a brand-new style of high-tech management. Refuting the common "slip-and-you-die" thinking, Ollila sticks with slip and you grow.

In a sense, this model is a variation on the man's freezing plunge at the lake. Ollila views disasters as education, and he fires almost no one. While others rush to the world's high-tech hot spots, Ollila created one of his own in an underpopulated stretch between Russia and the Arctic Circle. From there, he nurtures a network of suppliers around the globe. And just when Nokia seems to be performing in top gear, as it is now, Ollila risks disarray by switching the jobs of all his top managers.

Trouble is, Nokia isn't the only one searching for a digital El Dorado in the form of convergence. While Ollila's sharp and nimble Finns ambushed Ericsson and Motorola in the telephone market, they're now converging right into a Silicon Valley traffic jam. To sell pocket-size Net devices, Ollila must maneuver his way among the brightest stars of America's high-tech economy, where everyone from Microsoft Corp. to 3Com Corp. wants to own a piece of the same business.

And few of them are convinced that this next revolution is going to be conducted through mobile telephones. Who's to say, after all, that mobile Web surfers won't use palmtop computers equipped with telephone chips? And there's always the chance the public will shrug at the entire selection of these tiny devices. "You have to think hard," says Richard Howard, director of the wireless research lab at Lucent Technologies Inc.'s Bell Labs. "Do you really need full-motion video in a car phone?"

So despite his laid-back manner, Ollila has no time to catch his breath. He must prepare Nokia for a metamorphosis. Like a snake growing out of its skin, the company has to emerge sleek and

Source: "Nokia," *Business Week:* August 10, 1998.

figures in leadership positions. Accordingly, every company has a distinct culture that it believes no other company can copy successfully. And in companies with strong cultures, managers and workers either accept the norms of the culture or opt out from the culture and leave the company.

BusinessWeek

continued

strong in the next generation, when simple handsets are stocking stuffers and mobile phones molt into powerful new be-alls. Ollila's tried-and-true motivator is the plunge. In the past, there have been plenty of crises around which to rally the team. Ollila recalls them with great fondness.

So how does Ollila conjure up a sense of fear and urgency? For starters, on July 1, he reached into Nokia's sparkling glass-and-steel headquarters on the shore of the Baltic, took the inner circle of four fortysomething Finns who run the company's main divisions, and switched all their jobs. His infrastructure executive, Matti Alahuhta, was rotated from his customer-schmoozing position into the marketing vortex of handsets. Asia-Pacific chief Sari Baldauf was told to head up infrastructure, as well as development on Third Generation. Handset chief Pekka Ala-Pietila, who oversaw the spectacular development of the 6100s, became vice-chairman, charged with exploring new ventures. Later this year, Ollila will bring back his chief executive for U.S. operations, Olli-Pekka Kallasvuo, to be chief financial officer. In short, except for Ollila, every top person at the company is getting ready for a brand-new job—all in the name of "removing people from their comfort areas," as Ollila puts it.

Despite the upheaval, Ollila is determined to preserve a corporate culture in Helsinki dominated by Finns. He jokes about this, explaining that the best brains in Silicon Valley, London, or Hong Kong recoil from moving to icy Helsinki, where it's dark all winter. The trick is to give his new recruits autonomy and let them pursue their careers in Nokia's big markets, where taxes are far lower and the lakes thaw by Easter. But Ollila also believes that Nokia draws strength from its understated collegiality, which he associates with the Finnish character. "We don't snap our suspenders," he says in his fluent British English.

The culture Ollila struggles to preserve goes back a ways. Founded in 1865 in a mill town 100 miles north of Helsinki, Nokia has made just about everything at one time or another. Many Finns still associate the name with the rubber snow boots they wore as children. A hundred years later, Nokia had grown into a regional conglomerate.

While Nokia, Ericsson, and Motorola are all preparing to battle one another with Internet phones and intelligent base stations, they've been forced to join forces on the Third Generation. Their worst nightmare: All the new features arrive on schedule—on palmtop computers instead of cell phones. To avoid that scenario, in June the three companies formed a London joint venture with British computer maker Psion PLC. The deal establishes a common software platform—Psion's operating system—for the coming generation of mobile Net devices.

In linking up with tiny Psion, Ollila and his competitors jilted none other than William H. Gates III. Earlier in the year, the Microsoft chairman toured Europe, plugging Microsoft's Windows CE software for Third Generation machines. He lost out. His software, phonemakers complained, was wrenched from the PC and not created for next-generation machines. Gates's loss, though, means that cellular phones could eventually be battling a slew of Microsoft-powered handheld devices in the same mobile market.

Ollila claims not to be worried. "The market will be big enough for all of us," he says. But don't misread the man. He's plenty competitive: He can recite the exact ages of his two sons when they finally beat him in tennis. When it comes time to plunge, Ollila is extreme—a man of fire and ice, leading Nokia into cyberspace.

The stronger a company's culture and the more that culture is directed toward customers and markets, the less the company uses policy manuals, organization charts, and detailed rules and procedures to enforce discipline and norms. The reason is that the guiding values inherent in the culture convey in crystal-clear fashion what everybody is supposed to do in most situations. Poorly performing companies often have strong cultures. However, their cultures are dysfunctional, being focused on internal politics or operating by the numbers as opposed to emphasizing customers and the people who make and sell the product.

Managing Organizational Culture in a Global Organization[9]

The reality of today's global organizations is that organizational culture must recognize cultural diversity. *Social norms* create differences across national boundaries that influence how people interact, read personal cues, and otherwise interrelate socially. *Values* and *attitudes* about similar circumstances also vary from country to country. Where individualism is central to a North American's value structure, the needs of the group dominate the value structure of their Japanese counterparts. *Religion* is yet another source of cultural differences. Holidays, practices, and belief structures differ in very fundamental ways that must be taken into account as one attempts to shape organizational culture in a global setting. Finally, *education,* or ways people are accustomed to learning, differ across national borders. Formal classroom learning in the United States may teach things that are only learned via apprenticeship in other cultures. Since the process of shaping an organizational culture often involves considerable "education," leaders should be sensitive to global differences in approaches to education to make sure their cultural education efforts are effective. The discussion case on General Electric at the end of this chapter provides some relevant examples of how GE has successfully managed organizational culture in a global organization.

Managing the Strategy-Culture Relationship

Managers find it difficult to think through the relationship between a firm's culture and the critical factors on which strategy depends. They quickly recognize, however, that key components of the firm—structure, staff, systems, people, style—influence the ways in which key managerial tasks are executed and how critical management relationships are formed. And implementation of a new strategy is largely concerned with adjustments in these components to accommodate the perceived needs of the strategy. Consequently, managing the strategy-culture relationship requires sensitivity to the interaction between the changes necessary to implement the new strategy and the compatibility or "fit" between those changes and the firm's culture. Figure 11–8 provides a simple framework for managing the strategy-culture relationship by identifying four basic situations a firm might face.

Link to Mission

A firm in cell 1 is faced with a situation in which implementing a new strategy requires several changes in structure, systems, managerial assignments, operating procedures,

---

[9]Differing backgrounds, often referred to as *cultural diversity,* is something that most managers will certainly see more of, both because of the growing cultural diversity domestically and the obvious diversification of cultural backgrounds that result from global acquisitions and mergers. For example, Harold Epps, manager of DEC's computer keyboard plant in Boston, manages 350 employees representing 44 countries of origin and 19 languages. Useful reading on cultural diversity can be found in David Jamieson and Julie O'Mara, *Managing Workforce 2000: Gaining the Diversity Advantage* (San Francisco: Jossey-Bass, 1991), and R. R. Thomas, *Beyond Race and Gender: Unleashing the Power of Your Total Workforce by Managing Diversity* (New York: AMACOM Books, 1991). To get an informative appreciation of the global scene, see Rosabeth Moss Kanter, "Transcending Business Boundaries: 12,000 World Managers View Change," *Harvard Business Review* 69, no. 3 (1991), pp. 151–64.

FIGURE 11–8
Managing the Strategy-Culture Relationship

	High	Low
Many	Link changes to basic mission and fundamental organizational norms. 1	Reformulate strategy or prepare carefully for long-term, difficult cultural change. 4
Few	2 Synergistic—focus on reinforcing culture.	3 Manage around the culture.

Changes in key organizational factors that are necessary to implement the new strategy

Potential compatibility of changes with existing culture

or other fundamental aspects of the firm. However, most of the changes are potentially compatible with the existing organizational culture. Firms in this situation usually have a tradition of effective performance and are either seeking to take advantage of a major opportunity or are attempting to redirect major product-market operations consistent with proven core capabilities. Such firms are in a very promising position: they can pursue a strategy requiring major changes but still benefit from the power of cultural reinforcement.

Four basic considerations should be emphasized by firms seeking to manage a strategy-culture relationship in this context. First, *key changes should be visibly linked to the basic company mission.* Since the company mission provides a broad official foundation for the organizational culture, top executives should use all available internal and external forums to reinforce the message that the changes are inextricably linked to it. Second, *emphasis should be placed on the use of existing personnel* where possible to fill positions created to implement the new strategy. Existing personnel embody the shared values and norms that help ensure cultural compatibility as major changes are implemented. Third, *care should be taken if adjustments in the reward system are needed.* These adjustments should be consistent with the current reward system. If, for example, a new product-market thrust requires significant changes in the way sales are made, and, therefore, in incentive compensation, common themes (e.g., incentive oriented) should be emphasized. In this way, current and future reward approaches are related and the changes in the reward system are justified (encourage development of less familiar markets). Fourth, *key attention should be paid to the changes that are least compatible with the current culture,* so current norms are not disrupted. For example, a firm may choose to subcontract an important step in a production process because that step would be incompatible with the current culture.

IBM's strategy in entering the Internet-based market is an illustration. Serving this radically different market required numerous organizational changes. To maintain maximum compatibility with its existing culture while doing so, IBM went to considerable public and internal effort to link its new Internet focus with its long-standing mission. Numerous messages relating the network-centric computing to IBM's tradition of top-quality service appeared on television and in magazines, and every IBM manager was encouraged to go online. Where feasible, IBM personnel were used to fill the new positions created to implement the strategy. But because the software require-ments were not compatible with IBM's current operations, virtually all of its initial ef-forts were linked to newly acquired Lotus Notes.

Maximize Synergy

A firm in cell 2 needs only a few organizational changes to implement its new strategy, and those changes are potentially quite compatible with its current culture. A firm in this situation should emphasize two broad themes: (1) *take advantage of the situation to reinforce and solidify the current culture* and (2) *use this time of relative stability to remove organizational roadblocks to the desired culture.* Holiday Inns' move into casino gambling required a few major organizational changes. Holiday Inns saw casi-nos as resort locations requiring lodging, dining, and gambling/entertainment services. It only had to incorporate gambling/entertainment expertise into its management team, which was already capable of managing the lodging and dining requirements of casino (or any other) resort locations. It successfully inculcated this single major change by selling the change internally as completely compatible with its mission of providing high-quality accommodations for business and leisure travelers. The resignation of Roy Clymer, its CEO, removed an organizational roadblock, legitimizing a culture that placed its highest priority on quality service to the middle-to-upper-income business traveler, rather than a culture that placed its highest priority on family-oriented service. The latter priority was fast disappearing from Holiday Inns' culture, with the encour-agement of most of the firm's top management, but its disappearance had not yet been fully sanctioned because of Clymer's personal beliefs. His voluntary departure helped solidify the new values that top management wanted.

Manage around the Culture

A firm in cell 3 must make a few major organizational changes to implement its new strategy, but these changes are potentially inconsistent with the firm's current organi-zational culture. The critical question for a firm in this situation is whether it can make the changes with a reasonable chance of success.

A firm can manage around the culture in various ways: create a separate firm or di-vision; use task forces, teams, or program coordinators; subcontract; bring in an out-sider; or sell out. These are a few of the available options, but the key idea is to create a method of achieving the change desired that avoids confronting the incompatible cul-tural norms. As cultural resistance diminishes, the change may be absorbed into the firm.

In the Southeast, Rich's was a highly successful, quality-oriented department store chain that served higher income customers in several southeastern locations. With Wal-Mart and Kmart experiencing rapid growth in the sale of mid- to low-priced mer-chandise, Rich's decided to serve this market as well. Finding such merchandise in-consistent with the successful values and norms of its traditional business, it created a separate business called *Richway* to tap this growth area in retailing. Through a new store network, it was able to *manage around its culture.* Both Rich's and Richway ex-perienced solid regional success, though their cultures are radically different in some respects.

Reformulate the Strategy or Culture

A firm in cell 4 faces the most difficult challenge in managing the strategy-culture re-lationship. To implement its new strategy, such a firm must make organizational changes that are incompatible with its current, usually entrenched, values and norms.

A firm in this situation faces the complex, expensive, and often long-term challenge of changing its culture; it is a challenge that borders on impossible. Strategy in Action 11–4 describes the exciting success at Finland's Nokia where CEO Jorma Ollila transformed a 125-year-old company into a world technology leader.

When a strategy requires massive organizational change and engenders cultural resistance, a firm should determine whether reformulation of the strategy is appropriate. Are all of the organizational changes really necessary? Is there any real expectation that the changes will be acceptable and successful? If these answers are yes, then massive changes in management personnel are often necessary. AT&T offered early retirement to over 20,000 managers as part of a massive recreation of its culture to go along with major strategic changes in recent years. If the answer to these questions is no, the firm might reformulate its strategic plan so as to make it more consistent with established organizational norms and practices.

Merrill Lynch faced the challenge of strategy-culture incompatibility in the last decade. Seeking to remain number one in the newly deregulated financial services industry, it chose to pursue a product development strategy in its brokerage business. Under this strategy, Merrill Lynch would sell a broader range of investment products to a more diverse customer base and would integrate other financial services, such as real estate sales, into the Merrill Lynch organization. The new strategy could succeed only if Merrill Lynch's traditionally service-oriented brokerage network became sales and marketing oriented. Initial efforts to implement the strategy generated substantial resistance from Merrill Lynch's highly successful brokerage network. The strategy was fundamentally inconsistent with long-standing cultural norms at Merrill Lynch that emphasized personalized service and very close broker-client relationships. Merrill Lynch ultimately divested its real estate operation, reintroduced specialists that supported broker/retailers, and refocused its brokers more narrowly on basic client investment needs.

STRUCTURE, LEADERSHIP, AND CULTURE IN THE 21ST CENTURY[10]

The once unthinkable decline of many of the world's largest corporations has become all too common as we enter the 21st century global economy. Strategic blunders and oversights by management have pulled down such powerful and mighty giants as AT&T, Eastman Kodak, and General Motors. Hesitancy to change, clinging to an outdated organizational structure, antiquated leadership and change-resistant cultures have found many well-known companies suddenly losing sales and slipping into a survival crisis.

Yet there is a less visible but even more critical danger: the inability to adapt to the speed and turbulence of technological change. After massive high-tech investments, management is only beginning to make the organizational changes needed to transform information technology into the potent competitive weapon that it will need to be in the 21st century.

Few companies have grasped the far-reaching importance of the new technology for management better than Cisco Systems, Inc. Cisco has become the global leader in networking for the Internet, with annual revenues over $10 billion. It's also a Wall Street

[10]This section is adapted and provided by *Business Week*'s senior writer, John A. Byrne, from his work on "The Corporation of the Future," *Business Week*, August 31, 1998; and *Business Week*'s "Special Report—The 21st Century Economy—How It Will Work."

darling, with a market cap exceeding $100 billion. Cisco could well provide one of the best road maps to a new model of management. Partly because it makes the tools to build the powerful networks that link businesses to their customers and suppliers, Cisco itself has been at the forefront of using technology to transform management practices.

Truly *Customer-Focused* Leadership and Culture   It's not only Cisco's innovative use of technology that wins favorable reviews. It's also the company's mind-set and culture, its willingness to team up with outsiders to acquire and retain intellectual assets, its near-religious focus on the customer, and its progressive human resource policies. "Cisco is the quintessential outside-in company" says James F. Moore, chairman of consultants GeoPartners Research, Inc. "They have mastered how to source talent, products, and momentum from outside their own walls. That's a powerful advantage."

This corporate adolescent—founded in 1984 by a group of computer scientists from Stanford University—is headed by a leader, John T. Chambers, who cut his teeth at successful companies that stumbled. At both IBM and Wang Laboratories, Inc., the soft-spoken West Virginian got a firsthand glimpse of how arrogance and reluctance to change caused a severe pain and dislocation. Those experiences—including a traumatic time when he survived five layoffs in 15 months at Wang, before resigning in 1990—colored his view of what a healthy organization should be. "It taught me how a company should be built in the first place and how to do things dramatically different the next time," says Chambers, 48, who joined Cisco in 1991 and became CEO in 1995. "Laying off people was the toughest thing I ever did. I'll move heaven and earth to avoid doing that again."

To hear Chambers tell it, his people and his organization are "in the sweet spot"—where technology and the future meet to transform not only business but all of life. His vision is simple: "We can change the way people live and work, play and learn." It is an idealistic phrase that falls out of his mouth repeatedly and unabashedly. It is also an inspiring and motivating declaration for each of Cisco's 13,000-plus employees. Chambers aims to be the Jack Welch of the new millennium. Like General Electric Co.'s Chairman Welch, he has decided he wants to be no. 1 or no. 2 in every market, a condition that already exists in 14 of the 15 markets in which Cisco competes.

Fluid, Network-Based Organizational Structures   Cisco managers believe that the new rules of competition demand organizations built on change, not stability; organized around networks, not a rigid hierarchy; based on interdependencies of partners, not self-sufficiency; and constructed on technological advantage, not old-fashioned bricks and mortar. The network structure has vast implications for managing in the next century. GM's Saturn Division and Dell Computer Corporation have shown how the network can eliminate inventory, by connecting with partners that deliver goods only when they are needed. In the new model that Chambers is creating at Cisco, however, the network is pervasive, central to nearly everything.

The company's network structure is designed to seamlessly link Cisco to its customers, prospects, business partners, suppliers, and employees. Last year, Cisco sold more than $5 billion worth of goods—more than half its total—over the Internet, nearly three times the Internet sales booked by pioneer Dell. So successful has Cisco been in selling complex, expensive equipment over the Net that Cisco alone accounted for one-third of all electronic commerce in 1999.

Seven out of 10 customer requests for technical support are filled electronically—at satisfaction rates that eclipse those involving human interaction. Using the network for tech support allows Cisco to save more money than its nearest competitor spends on research and development. "It has saved me 1,000 engineers," gushes Chambers. "I take those 1,000 engineers, and instead of putting them into support, I put them into building new products. That gives you a gigantic competitive advantage."

The network also is the glue for the internal workings of the company. It swiftly connects Cisco with its web of partners, making the constellation of suppliers, contract manufacturers, and assemblers look like one company—Cisco—to the outside world. Via the company's intranet, outside contractors directly monitor orders from Cisco customers and ship the assembled hardware to buyers later in the day—often without Cisco even touching the box. By outsourcing production of 70 percent of its products, Cisco has quadrupled output without building new plants and has cut the time it takes to get a new product to market by two-thirds, to just six months.

A Network-Based "Personal Touch" Culture The network also is Cisco's primary tool for recruiting talent, with half of all applications for jobs coming over the Net. When an employee wants information about a company event or health benefits, or needs to track an expense report, the network is the place to go at Cisco. The upshot: More than 1.7 million pages of information are accessible by employees who use the Cisco network thousands of times every day. "We are," says Chambers, "the best example of how the Internet is going to change everything."

Technology aids and abets this business model, but it does not completely displace human interaction. "The network works better when you've already had a personal touch," insists Chambers. That's why he does quarterly meetings with employees at a nearby convention center, why all employees in the month of their birth are invited to one of his 1½-hour "birthday breakfasts," and why he works harder than most to encourage open and direct communication with all of Cisco's leaders.

A Propensity to Partner Chambers also believes in partnering with other businesses. Plenty of companies forge new links with others, but Cisco has a track record of making them work. "Partnerships are key to the new world strategies of the 21st century," says Donald J. Listwin, a Cisco senior vice president. "Partners collapse time because they allow you to take on more things and bring them together quicker."

A good example is Cisco's partnership with Microsoft Corp., which last year resulted in a new technology to make networks more intelligent. The software lets networks know immediately a user's identity and location, and respond differently to each one. The partnership allows both companies to expand this market together more rapidly. "From initial discussion to technology, it took 18 months to get the product out," says Listwin. "It would have taken us four years to get to where we are [without such a partnership], and it's not clear we had the competence to get there alone."

And Partner with Key Customers Another theme—often heard but seldom exercised by corporate leaders—is the central importance of the customer. Nothing causes Chambers more restless nights than worry over how to serve customers better. That's why he spends as much as 55 percent of his time with customers and why he receives every night, 365 nights a year, voice mail updates on as many as 15 key clients.

In this new model, strategic direction is not formed by an insular group of top executives, but by the company's leading customers. It's an outside-in approach, as opposed to inside out. The customer is the strategy. "There is nothing more arrogant than telling a customer: 'Here is what you need to know,'" says Chambers. "Most of the time, you are not going to be right." Rather, Cisco's leading-edge customers are seen as partners in forming the company strategy. For example, after Boeing Co. and Ford Motor Co. informed Chambers that their future network needs were unlikely to be satisfied by Cisco, Chambers went out to make his first acquisition to solve the problem. That deal, to acquire local-area-network switchmaker Crescendo Communications in 1993, put the company into a sector of the industry that now accounts for $2.8 billion in annual revenue.

Acquire Talent, Not Sales Growth Even such tactical moves as acquisitions and mergers are seen differently by a new-world company. Rather than acquire merely to speed growth or swell market share, Cisco routinely employs acquisitions to capture intellectual assets and next-generation products. "Most people forget that in a high-tech acquisition, you really are acquiring only people," says Chambers. "That's why so many of them fail. At what we pay, at $500,000 to $2 million an employee, we are not acquiring current market share. We are acquiring futures."

While most companies immediately cut costs and people from newly acquired outfits, Cisco adheres to what it calls the "Mario rule"—named after Senior Vice President Mario Mazzola, who had been CEO of Crescendo when it was bought by Cisco. Before any employee in a newly acquired company can be terminated, both Chambers and the former CEO must give their consent. "It tells new employees that Cisco wants them, that Cisco cares about them, and that we're not just another big company," says Daniel Scheinman, vice president for legal and government affairs. "It buys the trust of the people . . . and their passion is worth a lot more than any of the downside legal protection."

In talent-hungry Silicon Valley, Cisco measures the success of every acquisition first by employee retention, then by new product development, and finally return on investment. The company has been phenomenally successful at holding on to the intellectual assets it buys: Overall turnover among acquired employees is just 6 percent a year, two percentage points lower than Cisco's overall employee churn. The company works hard to embrace employees acquired in deals, often giving top talent key jobs in the new organization. Three of Cisco's main businesses are led by former CEOs of acquired companies.

Every acquisition, moreover, must meet Cisco guidelines. For years, Chambers watched IBM and other high-tech outfits acquire and then slowly smother any number of entrepreneurial companies. What he learned was that you never buy a company whose values and culture are much different from your own. Nor do you buy a company that is too far away from your central base of operations. The latter makes a cultural fit less likely and severely limits the speed a company needs to compete in the new economy.

Chambers also believes that each deal must boast both short-term and long-term wins for customers, shareholders, and employees. "If there are no results in three to six months, people begin to question the acquisition," says Charles H. Giancarlo, vice president for global alliances. "If you have good short-term wins, it's a virtuous cycle."

Demand Excellence, and Share Success Through it all, the emphasis is on doing it faster, cheaper, and better—an integral part of success in the new economy. At Cisco, wages are less important than ownership. Some 40 percent of the stock options at the company are held by "individual contributors" who on average boast more than $200,000 in option gains. Egalitarianism is critical to successful teamwork and to morale. "You never ask your team to do something you wouldn't do yourself," says Chambers, who flies coach and has no reserved parking space at headquarters.

STRATEGY IN ACTION 11–5

A NEW MANAGEMENT PRIMER FOR THE 21ST CENTURY ECONOMY: SIX KEY ORGANIZATIONAL CHARACTERISTICS

BusinessWeek

1. NETWORK, NETWORK, NETWORK
   Technology allows links with customers, suppliers, business partners, and employees. So take advantage of the speed and productivity it affords.

2. FOCUS ON THE CUSTOMER
   Let your core customers determine your strategy. They know more about what they need than your top executives do.

3. BUY SMART
   Pursue acquisitions not to speed growth or increase market share per se, but to capture intellectual assets and next-generation products.

4. TEAM UP FOR SUCCESS
   Create alliances with partners based on trust and the potential for achieving mutual short- and long-term wins.

5. SHARE THE WEALTH
   Use broad-based stock option plans to reward and retain key employees.

6. THAT PERSONAL TOUCH
   Technology goes only so far. Face-time counts. Corporate leaders must spend lots of time coaching, mentoring, and communicating with employees in person.

Source: John A. Byrne, from his work on "The Corporation of the Future," *Business Week:* August 31, 1998; and *Business Week*'s "Special Report—The 21st Century Economy—How It Will Work."

Cisco provides a compelling example of what structure, leadership, and culture in the leading 21st century companies may look like. Change, technology, speed, egalitarianism, customer partners, and value appear to be elements their leaders will embrace and their structures and cultures reflect. Strategy in Action 11–5 shows some additional characteristics of 21st century winning companies based on the conclusions of their Special Report examining the 21st century economy.

SUMMARY

This chapter examined the idea that a key aspect of implementing a strategy is the *institutionalization* of the strategy so it permeates daily decisions and actions in a manner consistent with long-term strategic success. The "recipe" that binds strategy and organization involves three key ingredients: *organizational structure, leadership,* and *culture.*

Five fundamental organizational structures were examined, and the advantages and disadvantages of each were identified. Institutionalizing a strategy requires a good strategy-structure fit. This chapter dealt with how this requirement often is overlooked until performance becomes inadequate and then indicated the conditions under which the various structures would be appropriate.

Organizational leadership is essential to effective strategy implementation. The CEO plays a critical role in this regard. Assignment of key managers, particularly within the top-management team, is an important aspect of organizational leadership. Deciding whether to promote insiders or hire outsiders is often a central leadership issue in strategy implementation. This chapter showed how this decision could be made in a manner that would best institutionalize the new strategy.

Organizational culture has been recognized as a pervasive influence on organizational life. Organizational culture, which is the shared beliefs and values of an organization's members, may be a major help or hindrance to strategy implementation. This chapter discussed an approach to managing the strategy-culture fit. It identified four fundamentally different strategy-culture situations and provided recommendations for managing the strategy-culture fit in each of these situations.

The chapter concluded with an examination of structure, leadership, and culture for 21st century companies. Networked organizations, with intense customer focus, and alliances are keys to success. Talent-focused acquisitions, success sharing, and leaders as coaches round out the future success scenario.

QUESTIONS FOR DISCUSSION

1. What key structural considerations must be incorporated into strategy implementation? Why does structural change often lag a change in strategy?

2. Which organizational structure is most appropriate for successful strategy implementation? Explain how state of development affects your answer.

3. Why is leadership an important element in strategy implementation? Find an example in a major business periodical of the CEO's key role in strategy implementation.

4. Under what conditions would it be more appropriate to fill a key management position with someone from outside the firm when a qualified insider is available?

5. What is organizational culture? Why is it important? Explain two different situations a firm might face in managing the strategy-culture relationship.

6. Compare the company Cisco to one you are familiar with in terms of structure, leadership, and culture.

BIBLIOGRAPHY

"If You Want to Lead, First Learn to Speak." *Success* 39 (April 1992), pp. 42–43.

"The Outing of Outsourcing." *Economist,* November 25, 1995, p. 36.

Amason, A. C. "Distinguishing the Effects of Functional and Dysfunctional Conflict on Strategic Decision Making: Resolving a Paradox for Top Management Teams." *Academy of Management Journal* 1 (1996), pp. 123–148.

Argyris, Chris. "Teaching Smart People How to Learn." *Harvard Business Review* (May–June 1991), p. 191.

Bailey, G., and J. Szerdy. "Is There Life after Downsizing?" *Journal of Business Strategy,* January 1988, pp. 8–11.

Barney, J. B. "Organizational Culture: Can It Be a Source of Sustained Competitive Advantage?" *Academy of Management Review,* July 1986, p. 656.

Bartlett, Christopher A., and Sumantra Ghoshal. "Matrix Management: Not a Structure, a Frame of Mind." *Harvard Business Review* (July–August 1990), p. 168.

Bethel, J. E., and J. Liebeskind. "The Effects of Ownership Structure on Corporate Restructuring." *Strategic Management Journal* 14 (1993), pp. 15–31.

Bettinger, Cass. "Use Corporate Culture to Trigger High Performance." *Journal of Business Strategy* 10, no. 2 (March–April 1989), pp. 38–42.

Block, Barbara. "Creating a Culture All Employees Can Accept." *Management Review,* July 1989, p. 41.

Boje, David M. "The Storytelling Organization: A Study of Story Performance in an Office-Supply Firm." *Administrative Science Quarterly* 36 (March 1991), pp. 106–26.

Botterill, M. "Changing Corporate Culture." *Management Services* (UK) 34, no. 6 (1990), pp. 14–18.

Bower, Joseph Lyon, and Martha Wagner Weinberg. "Statecraft, Strategy, and Corporate Leadership." *California Management Review,* Winter 1988, p. 107.

Bowman, E. H., and H. Singh. "Corporate Restructuring: Reconfiguring the Firm." *Strategic Management Journal* 14 (1993), pp. 5–14.

Bruton, G. D.; J. K. Keels; and C. L. Shook. "Downsizing the Firm: Answering the Strategic Questions." *Academy of Management Executive,* May 1996, pp. 38–45.

Bryne, John A. "The Horizontal Corporation." *Business Week* (December 20, 1993), pp. 76–81.

Fincham, Robin. "Perspectives on Power: Processual, Institutional, and 'Internal' Forms of Organizational Power." *Journal of Management Studies* 29 (November 1992), pp. 741–59.

Ghoshal, Sumantra, and Nitin Nohria. "Horses for Courses: Organizational Forms for Multinational Corporations." *Sloan Management Review* 34 (Winter 1993), pp. 23–35.

Gomez-Mejia, L.R. "Structure and Process of Diversification, Compensation Strategy, and Performance." *Strategic Management Journal* 13 (1992), pp. 381–97.

Gordon, George D., and Nancy DiTomaso. "Predicting Corporate Performance from Organizational Culture." *Journal of Management Studies* 29 (November 1992), pp. 783–98.

Hamel, G., and C. K. Prahalad. *Competing for the Future* (Cambridge, Mass.: Harvard Business School Press, 1994).

Harrison, J. Richard, and Glenn R. Carroll. "Keeping the Faith: A Model of Cultural Transmission in Formal Organizations." *Administrative Science Quarterly* 36 (December 1991), pp. 552–82.

Henkoff, Ronald. "CEOs Still Don't Walk the Talk." *Fortune* (April 18, 1994), pp. 14–15.

Herman, Stanley M. *A Force of Ones: Reclaiming Individual Power in a Time of Teams, Work Groups, and Other Crowds* San Francisco: Jossey-Bass, 1994.

Hoskisson, R. E. "Multidivisional Structure and Performance: The Contingency of Diversification Strategy." *Academy of Management Journal* 30 (1987), pp. 625–44.

Huey, John. "The New Post-Heroic Leadership." *Fortune* (February 21, 1994), pp. 42–56.

Kanter, Rosabeth Moss. "The New Managerial Work." *Harvard Business Review* (November–December 1989), pp. 85–92.

Keys, Bernard, and Thomas Case. "How to Become an Influential Manager." *Academy of Management Executive,* 4 (November 1990), pp. 38–51.

Krackhardt, David, and Jeffrey R. Hanson. "Informal Networks: The Company Behind the Chart." *Harvard Business Review* (July–August 1993), pp. 104–11.

Larson, E. W., and D. H. Gobeli. "Matrix Management: Contradictions and Insights." *California Management Review* 29 (1987), pp. 126–38.

Manz, Charles C., and Henry P. Sims, Jr. "Superleadership: Beyond the Myth of Heroic Leadership." *Organizational Dynamics* 19 (Spring 1991), pp. 18–35.

Markides, C. C., and P. J. Williamson. "Related Diversification, Core Competencies, and Corporate Performance." *Strategic Management Journal,* Special Issue, 15 (1994), pp. 149–65.

Maruca, Regina Fazio. "The Right Way to Go Global." *Harvard Business Review* (March–April 1994), pp. 134–45.

McDonald, Paul, and Jeffrey Gandz. "Getting Value from Shared Values." *Organizational Dynamics* 20 (Winter 1992), pp. 64–77.

Miles, Raymond E., and Charles C. Snow. "Causes of Failure in Network Organizations." *California Management Review* 34 (Summer 1992), pp. 53–72.

Nadler, David A., and Michael L. Tushman. "Beyond the Charismatic Leader: Leadership and Organizational Change." *California Management Review* 32 (Winter 1990), pp. 77–97.

Pfeffer, Jeffrey. "Understanding Power in Organizations." *California Management Review* 34 (Winter 1992), pp. 29–50.

Senge, Peter M. "The Leader's New Work: Building Learning Organizations." *Sloan Management Review* 32 (Fall 1990), pp. 7–23.

Snow, Charles C.; Raymond E. Miles; and Henry J. Coleman, Jr. "Managing 21st Century Network Organizations." *Organizational Dynamics* 20 (Winter 1992), pp. 5–20.

Soloman, C. "Amoco to Cut More Jobs and Radically Alter Its Structure." *The Wall Street Journal,* July 22, 1995, p. B4.

Uttal, B. "The Corporate Culture Vultures." *Fortune* 66 (October 17, 1983), pp. 68–72.

Zaleznik, Abraham. "The Leadership Gap." *Academy of Management Executive* 4 (1990), pp. 7–22.

CHAPTER 11 DISCUSSION CASE

BusinessWeek

LEADERSHIP, CULTURE, AND STRUCTURE: THE SECRETS OF THE MOST SUCCESSFUL BUSINESS MANAGER OF THE 20TH CENTURY— JACK WELCH AT GE

> If leadership is an art, then surely GE's Jack Welch has proved himself a master painter. Few have personified corporate leadership more dramatically. Fewer still have so consistently delivered on the results of that leadership. For 17 years, while big companies and their chieftains tumbled like dominoes in an unforgiving global economy, Welch has led GE to one revenue and earnings record after another.

"The two greatest corporate leaders of this century are Alfred Sloan of General Motors and Jack Welch of GE," says Noel Tichy, a longtime GE observer and University of Michigan management professor. "And Welch would be the greater of the two because he set a new, contemporary paradigm for the corporation that is the model for the 21st century."

It is a model that has delivered extraordinary growth, increasing the market value of GE from just $12 billion in 1981 to over $400 billion today. "This guy's legacy will be to create more shareholder value on the face of the planet than ever—forever," says Nicholas P. Heymann, a onetime GE auditor who follows the company for Prudential Securities.

Much has been said and written about how Welch has transformed what was an old-line American industrial giant into a keenly competitive global growth engine, how he has astutely moved the once-establishment maker of things into services. Welch has reshaped the company through more than 600 acquisitions and a forceful push abroad into newly emerging markets.

Less well understood, however, is how Jack Welch is able to wield so much influence and power over the most far-flung, complex organization in all of American business. Many managers struggle daily to lead and motivate mere handfuls of people. Many CEOs wrestle to squeeze just average performance from companies a fraction of GE's size. How does Welch, who sits atop a business empire with $304 billion in assets, $89.3 billion in sales, and 276,000 employees scattered in more than 100 countries around the globe, do it?

Senior *Business Week* reporter John Byrne recently spent a great deal of time with Jack Welch and within GE to try and answer this question for you. His close-up look at how Jack Welch runs GE reveals the importance of leadership, culture, and structure in strategy implementation and it gives you some exciting examples to take with you and apply in your management career. Enjoy.

Whisked by chopper from New York City, Jack Welch arrives early at the General Electric Co. training center at Croton-on-Hudson. He scoots down to The Pit—the well of a bright multitiered lecture hall—peels off his blue suit jacket, and drapes it over one of the swivel seats.

Source: John A. Byrne, "How Jack Welch Runs GE," *Business Week:* June 8, 1998.

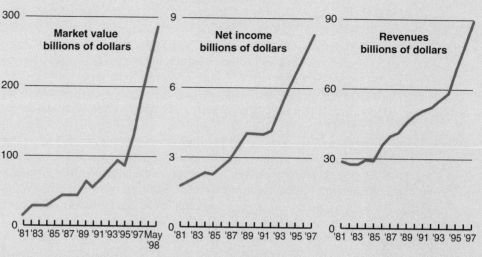

GE under Jack Welch

Data: Company reports ©BW

This is face-to-face with Jack, not so much as the celebrated chairman and chief executive of GE, the company he has made the most valuable in the world, but rather as Professor Welch, coach and teacher to 71 high-potential managers attending a three-week development course.

The class sits transfixed as Welch's laser-blue eyes scan the auditorium. He hardly appears professorial. With his squat, muscular, five-foot, eight-inch frame, pasty complexion, and Boston accent, the 62-year-old balding man looks and sounds more like the guy behind the wheel of a bus on Beacon Hill. And he isn't there to deliver a monologue to a polite group.

For nearly four hours, he listens, lectures, cajoles, and questions. The managers push right back, too. They grouse that despite the rhetoric about managing for the long term at GE, they are under too much pressure to produce short-term results. They say that for all the Welch talk about "sharing best practices" and "boundaryless behavior," they are missing many opportunities to learn and sell services across the vast network of GE companies. Some worry that the company's gargantuan Six Sigma program, the largest quality initiative ever mounted in Corporate America, is allowing bureaucracy to creep back into GE.

Pacing the floor with a bottle of water in hand, Welch passionately attacks each question.

"You can't grow long-term if you can't eat short-term," he states flatly. "Anybody can manage short. Anybody can manage long. Balancing those two things is what management is."

"I think someone is smoking pot here," he quips about the complaint over the lack of synergy among GE units. "We've got enormous sharing going on."

In this classroom, where Welch has appeared more than 250 times in the past 17 years to engage some 15,000 GE managers and executives, something extraordinary happens. The legendary chairman of GE, the take-no-prisoners tough guy who gets results at any cost, becomes human. His slight stutter, a handicap that has bedeviled him since childhood, makes him oddly vulnerable. The students see all of Jack here: the management theorist, strategic thinker, business teacher, and corporate icon who made it to the top despite his working-class background. No one leaves the room untouched.

Of course, GE's success is hardly Welch's alone. The company boasts what most headhunters believe to be the most talent-rich management bench in the world. Gary C. Wendt has led GE Capital Corp. to extraordinary heights, where it contributes nearly 40% of the company's total earnings. Robert C. Wright has managed an astounding turnaround at NBC, leading it to a fifth straight year of double-digit earnings gains in 1997 and a No. 1 position in prime-time ratings. Nor does Welch's magic work everywhere in GE. The huge appliance operation, for instance, saw operating earnings fall 39% last year, to $458 million, largely due to restructuring charges. Nonetheless, Welch has led and managed GE to nearly unprecedented prosperity.

How does Jack Welch wield so much influence and power over the most far-flung, complex organization in all of American business. Many managers struggle daily to lead and motivate mere handfuls of people. Many CEOs wrestle to squeeze just average performance from companies a fraction of GE's size. How does Welch, who sits atop a business empire with $304 billion in assets, $89.3 billion in sales, and 276,000 employees scattered in more than 100 countries around the globe, do it?

He does it through sheer force of personality, coupled with an unbridled passion for winning the game of business and a keen attention to details many chieftains would simply overlook. He does it because he encourages near-brutal candor in the meetings he holds to guide the company through each work year. And he does it because, above all else, he's a fierce believer in the power of his people.

Welch's profound grasp on General Electric stems from knowing the company and those who work for it like no other. First off, there are the thousands of "students" he has encountered in his classes at the Croton-on-Hudson campus, which everyone at GE just calls Crotonville. Then there's the way he spends his time: More than half is devoted to "people" issues. But most important, he has created something unique at a big company: informality.

Welch likes to call General Electric the "grocery store." The metaphor, however quirky for such a colossus, allows Welch to mentally roll up his sleeves, slip into an apron, and get behind the counter. There, he can get to know every employee and serve every customer. "What's important at the grocery store is just as important in engines or medical systems," says Welch. "If the customer isn't satisfied, if the stuff is getting stale, if the shelf isn't right, or if the offerings aren't right, it's the same thing. You manage it like a small organization. You don't get hung up on zeros."

You don't get hung up on formalities, either. If the hierarchy that Welch inherited, with its nine layers of management hasn't been completely nuked, it has been severely damaged. Everyone, from secretaries to chauffeurs to factory workers, calls him Jack. Everyone can expect—at one time or another—to see him scurry down an aisle to pick through the merchandise on a bottom shelf or to reach into his pocket and surprise with an unexpected bonus. "The story about GE that hasn't been told is the value of an informal place," says Welch. "I think it's a big thought. I don't think people have ever figured out that being informal is a big deal."

Making the company "informal" means violating the chain of command, communicating across layers, paying people as if they worked not for a big company but for a demanding entrepreneur where nearly everyone knows the boss. It has as much to do with Welch's charisma as it has to do with the less visible rhythms of the company—its meetings and review sessions—and how he uses them to great advantage.

When he became CEO, he inherited a series of obligatory corporate events that he has since transformed into meaningful levers of leadership. These get-togethers—from the meeting in early January with GE's top 500 executives in Boca Raton, Florida, to the monthly sessions in Croton-on-Hudson—allow him to set and abruptly change the corporation's agenda, to challenge and test the strategies and the people that populate each of GE's dozen divisions, and to make his formidable presence and opinions known to all.

Welch also understands better than most the value of surprise. Every week, there are unexpected visits to plants and offices, hurriedly scheduled luncheons with managers several layers below him, and countless handwritten notes to GE people that suddenly churn off their fax machines, revealing his bold yet neat handwriting. All of it is meant to lead, guide, and influence the behavior of a complex organization.

"We're pebbles in an ocean, but he knows about us," says Brian Nailor, a fortysomething marketing manager of industrial products who was at the Croton-on-Hudson session. "He's able to get people to give more of themselves because of who he is. He lives the American dream. He wasn't born with a silver spoon in his mouth. He got himself out of the pile. He didn't just show up."

Jack Welch received a standard $1,000 raise after his first year at GE, and he was disgusted at the lack of rationale behind it—the bureaucracy, his lethargic boss, and the civil-service style approach. So he accepted another job offer. But Reuben Gutoff, then a young executive a layer up from Welch, had other ideas. He had been mightily impressed by the young upstart and was shocked to hear of his impending departure. Desperate to keep him, Gutoff coaxed Welch and his wife, Carolyn, out to dinner that night. For four straight hours at the Yellow Aster in Pittsfield, he made his pitch: Gutoff swore he would prevent Welch from being entangled in GE red tape and vowed to create for him a small-company environment with big-company resources. These were themes that would later dominate Welch's own thinking as CEO. "Trust me," Gutoff remembers pleading. "As long as I am here, you are going to get a shot to operate with the best of the big company and the worst part of it pushed aside."

"Well, you are on trial," retorted Welch.

"I'm glad to be on trial," Gutoff said. "To try to keep you here is important."

Gutoff's story is cute, but it contains within it hints of Welch's future management style. Indeed, the decades have failed to diminish for Welch the potency of combining big-company might with small-company nimbleness. If Gutoff, who remained Welch's boss until 1973, could do that for Welch—and he did—then Welch could do that for others, many others. And so for much of his professional life, as he climbed the corporate totem, Welch has been preoccupied with harnessing the brute strength of bigness while ridding GE of big-company paralysis.

MORE THAN SHOW AND TELL

Welch kicks off each year with a confab for the top 500 executives at Boca Raton, Florida. Amid the ocean breezes and palms, it is Welch's opportunity to set the year's agenda and toast the company's newest heroes. An invitation by Welch to pitch in front of GE's most accomplished executives is like winning an Olympic medal in GE's intense locker-room culture. This past January, 29 managers gained the privilege, most of whom spoke glowingly about their quality improvement projects.

With Welch in the front row of the auditorium furiously scribbling notes on a yellow pad, the managers recounted how they used new ideas to squeeze still more profit out of the lean machine that is GE. One after another explained how quality efforts cut costs and mistakes, enhanced productivity, led to greater market share, and eliminated the need for investment in new plant and equipment.

It's more than a bragging fest. The show-and-tell routine allows managers in plastics to exchange lessons with their counterparts in GE Capital. It's a place, like Croton-on-Hudson, where "best practices" get transferred among GE's differing businesses. In between sessions, managers who make bulbs or locomotives swap ideas with those who finance cars and service credit-card accounts.

Welch seldom disappears early. One night, for example, he was up until 3, shooting the breeze with 20 executives—half of them fast-rising women. But the main event is Welch's wrap-up comments when he steps out onto the stage under a spotlight and a pair of video cameras. Even though GE had just ended a record year, with earnings up 13%, to more than $8.2 billion. Welch wants more. Most CEOs would give a feel-good, congratulatory chat. But Welch dispenses with the kudos and warns the group that it will face one of the toughest years in a decade. It's no time to be complacent, he says, not with the Asian economic crisis, not with deflation in the air.

"The one unacceptable comment from a GE leader in '98 was 'Prices are lower than we thought, and we couldn't get costs out fast enough to make our commitments.' Unacceptable," he shouts, like a preacher. "Unacceptable behavior, because prices will be lower than you're planning, so you better start taking action this week."

Then, after asking every GE business to resubmit annual budgets by the end of the month to account for deflation, the ideas tumble out of him for how they can combat it. "Don't add costs," he advises. "Increase inventory turns. Consolidate acquisitions. Use intellectual capital to replace plant and equipment investment. Raise approvals for price decisions. Make it harder to give away prices."

Welch then throws out yet another challenge. "The market is rewarding you like Super Bowl winners or Olympic gold medalists," he says. "I know I have such athletes reporting to me. Can you put your team against my team? Are you proud of everyone who reports to you? If you aren't, you can't win. You can't win the game."

When the executives return to work on Friday morning, a videotape of Welch's talk is already on their desks along with a guide for how to use it with their own teams. Within one week, more than 750 videos in eight different languages, including Mandarin and Hungarian, are dispatched to GE locations around the world. Welch's words will be absorbed and reinforced by as many as 150,000 employees by month's end.

What happens in Boca, in the management development courses at Crotonville, or in the quarterly CEC sessions promptly spills down into the organization's guts, where people at every layer digest it. William Woodburn, a 47-year-old former McKinsey & Co. consultant who heads GE's industrial diamonds business in Worthington, Ohio, was one of this year's heroes at Boca. Since taking over the business four years ago, Woodburn had increased the operation's return on investment fourfold and halved the cost structure.

On Monday, after returning from Boca, Woodburn gathers his 15 direct reports and uses Welch's video as the centerpiece for a discussion of what he learned in Florida. They then do the same with their staffs. On Wednesday, Woodburn uses the video again with 100 staffers in the plant. A week later, he goes through the process yet again with the region's "orphans"—GE staffers in the area who aren't in a major facility. "They see the tape. They hear the message. It gets people pumped up," he says.

Most great leaders, of course, are masters at communicating their desires. In his early years as chief executive, Welch discovered that you can't will things to happen, nor can you simply communicate with a few hundred people at the top and expect change to occur. So he doggedly repeats the key messages over and over again, reinforcing them at every opportunity.

Welch is uncommonly conscious of the signals and symbolism of leadership. Rarely does he miss a chance to make his presence felt. His handwritten notes sent to everyone from direct reports to hourly workers possess enormous impact, too, because they are intimate and spontaneous. Moments after Welch lifts his black felt-tip pen from the chairman's stationery, they are sent via fax direct to the employee. Two days later, the original arrives in the mail.

They are written to inspire and motivate as often as to stir and demand action. Two years ago, for example, Woodburn turned down a promotion from Welch that would have required a transfer because he didn't want to move his teenage daughter out of school. Woodburn does not report directly to Welch but to Gary L. Rogers, CEO of GE Plastics. Yet Welch spoke to Woodburn about the decision on the telephone and within a day dashed off a personal note to him.

"Bill," wrote Welch, "we like you for a lot of reasons—one of them is that you are a very special person. You proved it again this morning. Good for you and your lucky family. Make Diamonds a great business and keep your priorities straight." To Woodburn, the note was an important gesture. "It showed me he cared about me not as a manager but as a person," he says. "That means a lot."

As if in lockstep, each business chieftain then emulates the behavior of his boss, and their reports, in turn, do the same. After Welch's Boca meeting in January, for instance, Lloyd G. Trotter, CEO of GE's electrical-distribution and -control business, had his own 2½ day leadership conference in Orlando with his top 250 people. And in February, after Welch gave him his bonus and reiterated the targets for the remainder of the year, Trotter then followed through in similar fashion with the 97 people in his organization who received cash bonuses. Other GE businesses follow the same format. As Thomas E. Dunham, who runs services in GE Medical Systems, puts it, "Welch preaches it from the top, and people see it at the bottom." The result: Welch's leadership style is continually reinforced up and down the organization.

Above all, however, Welch skillfully uses rewards to drive behavior. Those rewards are not inconsequential at GE, in part because of Welch's determination not to hand out the kind of standard $1,000 raise that he got back in 1961. To this day, Welch demands that the rewards a leader disburses to people be highly differentiated—especially because GE is in so many different businesses. "I can't stand nondifferential stuff," he says. "We live in differentiation. You can't run these 12 businesses as if they were one institution."

Although GE set an overall 4% salary increase as a target last year, base salaries can rise by as much as 25% in a year without a promotion. Cash bonuses can increase as much as 150% in a year, to between 20% and 70% of base pay. Stock options, once reserved for the most senior officers at GE, have been broadly expanded under Welch. Now, some 27,000 employees get them, nearly a third of GE's professional employees. More than 1,200 employees, including over 800 below the level of senior management, have received options that are now worth over $1 million. Yet, unlike many companies that hand out options as automatic annual grants, Welch doesn't want GE's program to be perceived as a "dental plan." So everyone who receives option grants doesn't necessarily get them every year. In fact, Welch insists that at least 25% of the employees receiving options should be getting them for the first time, and no more than 50% of the executives should get more than three grants in a row.

USE SURPRISE

Welch's reach is long, frequent, and idiosyncratic. "It's part of living with Jack," a former General Electric executive says. "If you're doing well, you probably have more freedom than most CEOs of publicly traded companies. But the leash gets pulled very tightly when a unit is underperforming."

When Welch intervenes, he is rarely indecisive. "Welch will say yes. Welch will say no. But he never says maybe. A lot of CEOs do, and decisions lay there like three-legged horses that no one wants to shoot," says George Stalk Jr., a partner with Boston Consulting Group Inc. who has worked with GE. Late last year, for instance, GE Capital argued in favor of buying AT&T Universal Card, the credit-card operation of AT&T. Within 24 hours of the presentation, Welch vetoed the idea and sent a note to the GE Capital manager who had spent hundreds of hours studying it. Welch wanted her to know that despite his decision, he had been impressed with the quality of her analysis and her presentation.

FIND AND KEEP THE BEST PEOPLE

While analysts on Wall Street or GE's own investors view Welch's likely legacy as creating the world's most valuable company in stock market terms, Welch himself sees things quite differently. The man who spends more than 50% of his time on people issues considers his greatest achievement the care and feeding of talent. "This place runs by its great people," says Welch. "The biggest accomplishment I've had is to find great people. An army of them. They are all better than most CEOs. They are big hitters, and they seem to thrive here."

Welch knows by sight the names and responsibilities of at least the top 1,000 people at GE. "He knows their names. He knows what they do. That's an incredible reinforcement to the individual that he or she counts," says Dunham of GE's Medical Systems business.

His premium on people knows no bounds Three years ago, GE's transportation business, struggling to attract topnotch talent at its headquarters in Erie, Pennsylvania, began recruiting junior military officers. So successful were they that other GE units did the same. When GE had 80, Welch asked all of them to come to Fairfield, where he spent an entire day with them. Impressed with the quality and track record of the recruits, he insisted that the company hire 200 junior military officers annually. In less than three years, GE now has 711 of them on the payroll and many have already gained significant promotions.

That message has been consistently hammered home by Welch since he became CEO in 1981. Nowhere does Welch put greater focus on people and performance than in the company's annual Session C reviews that begin in April and last through May. With three of his senior executives, Welch travels into the field to each of his 12 businesses to review the progress of the company's top 3,000 executives and keeps closest tabs on the upper 500.

Typically Session C reviews begin at 8 A.M. and end at 10 P.M., with the CEO of the business and his senior human-resources executive. These are intensive reviews that force those running the units to identify their future leaders, make bets on early-career "stretch" assignments, develop succession plans for all key jobs, and decide which high-potential executives should be sent to Croton-on-Hudson for leadership training.

How can Welch possibly weigh in with intelligent comments about so many diverse managers and executives? Largely, it's because he has met so many of them. In an average year, Welch directly meets and interacts with several thousand GE employees. At the session, moreover, he sits behind a briefing book that contains every employee's assessment of their strengths and weaknesses, developmental needs, and short- and long-term goals, together with their supervisor's analysis. Photos of the employees being tracked and reviewed accompany the package.

In every potential leader, Welch is looking for what he now calls "E to the fourth power." That's his term for people who have enormous personal energy, the ability to motivate and energize others, "edge"—the GE code word for being instinctively competitive—and the skill to execute on those attributes. He's also pressuring leaders to ditch their C players. "He doesn't suffer fools gladly, and he doesn't have a high tolerance for mediocrity, that's for sure," says director Gertrude G. Michelson.

Welch's frequent teaching assignments at Croton-on-Hudson are clearly one of the favorite parts of his job. He typically appears at these three-week courses toward the end, after an array of other GE executives have psyched the group up to ask Welch tough questions. His appearance is unscripted, without notes. If there aren't a dozen hands up wanting to take a swat at Welch at any time, the CEO would consider the group a dull bunch, a group of turkeys.

Nearly four hours after this session at Croton-on-Hudson began, when the class disbands at 5 P.M., Welch doesn't just head for the chopper on the nearby pad. Instead, as he always does, he invites the class to have a drink with him at the White House, the spacious rec center on campus. There, at the bar, with a Buckler nonalcoholic beer bottle in hand, Welch is just one of the guys. "I was expecting this halo above him, this deity," says Robert Callahan, who has been with GE Plastics for six years. "It was like talking to your grandfather. You feel comfortable around him. You don't expect him to be so down-to-earth."

END GAME

Back in his office at 30 Rockefeller Plaza, Welch can't contain his excitement. "Ro!" he shrieks through a sliding door to his secretary, Rosanne Badowski. "Bring it in! You know what it is. Bring it in!" he shouts. "This is the most exciting thing that has ever happened to me."

A few moments pass and the sliding door disappears into a wall with a whoosh. His secretary gives Welch a scorecard from his latest golf game. He hides the results with his hand and jumps into the story. "I'm playing golf, O.K.?" he says. "And the players are Jack, Matt Lauer, Bob Wright, Greg Norman, and Wayne Huizenga at Wayne's course. Greg plays terrific. He shoots a 70, two under par."

Welch's hand slowly slides down the scorecard to reveal Norman's name and score. "Bob has a 96. Wayne has a 92. Matt has a 78. And Jack has a 69 and beats Greg Norman!" declares Welch, finally revealing his total score. "Isn't that the greatest thing? Is that a turn-on? That's everything! The rest of it is all nonsense. This is the real stuff. If you are going to shoot a 69, what better moment?"

Indeed. The Irish-Catholic kid who learned to play golf as a 12-year-old caddy beat a champion. "If I had my preference," Welch says, "I would have loved to have been a great professional golfer. Oh. God! But if you've got to pick a job in business, this is the best job God ever created. Every day is a whole new event. You're not dealing with products as much here as you're dealing with people. It's a kick."

In 2001, Welch will lose that kick when he steps down as chairman and CEO of General Electric after nearly 20 years at the top, as he reaches the mandatory retirement age of 65. No one, not even Welch, knows who his successor will be. Nonetheless, Welch's leadership style has become so embedded in the organization that even his retirement is unlikely to erode his impact.

12 STRATEGIC CONTROL AND CONTINUOUS IMPROVEMENT

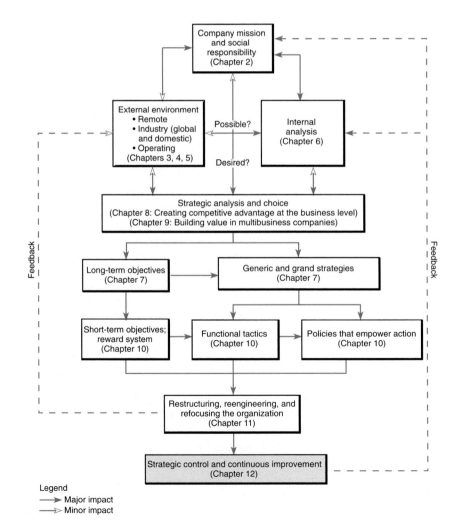

Company mission and social responsibility (Chapter 2)

External environment
• Remote
• Industry (global and domestic)
• Operating
(Chapters 3, 4, 5)

Possible?

Internal analysis (Chapter 6)

Desired?

Strategic analysis and choice
(Chapter 8: Creating competitive advantage at the business level)
(Chapter 9: Building value in multibusiness companies)

Long-term objectives (Chapter 7)

Generic and grand strategies (Chapter 7)

Short-term objectives; reward system (Chapter 10)

Functional tactics (Chapter 10)

Policies that empower action (Chapter 10)

Restructuring, reengineering, and refocusing the organization (Chapter 11)

Strategic control and continuous improvement (Chapter 12)

Feedback

Feedback

Legend
——→ Major impact
——▷ Minor impact

Strategies are forward looking, designed to be accomplished several years into the future, and based on management assumptions about numerous events that have not yet occurred. How should managers control a strategy? The traditional approach to control compares actual results against a standard. After work is done, the manager evaluates it and then uses that evaluation as input to control further work. Although this approach has its place, it is inappropriate as a means for controlling a strategy. The full execution of a strategy often takes five or more years, during which time many changes occur that have major ramifications for the strategy's ultimate success. Consequently, the traditional approaches to control must be replaced by an approach that recognizes the unique control needs of long-term strategies.

Strategic control is concerned with tracking a strategy as it is being implemented, detecting problems or changes in its underlying premises, and making necessary adjustments. In contrast to postaction control, strategic control is concerned with guiding action in behalf of the strategy as that action is taking place and when the end result is still several years off. Managers responsible for the success of a strategy typically are concerned with two sets of questions:

1. Are we moving in the proper direction? Are key things falling into place? Are our assumptions about major trends and changes correct? Are we doing the critical things that need to be done? Should we adjust or abort the strategy?
2. How are we performing? Are objectives and schedules being met? Are costs, revenues, and cash flows matching projections? Do we need to make operational changes?

The rapid, accelerating change of the global marketplace of the last 10 years has made *continuous improvement* another aspect of strategic control in many business organizations. Synonymous with the total quality movement, continuous improvement provides a way for organizations to provide strategic control that allows an organization to respond more proactively and timely to rapid developments in hundreds of areas that influence a business's success. This chapter discusses traditional strategic controls and then explains ways that the *continuous improvement quality imperative* can be a vehicle for strategic control.

ESTABLISHING STRATEGIC CONTROLS

The control of strategy can be characterized as a form of "steering control." Ordinarily, a good deal of time elapses between the initial implementation of a strategy and achievement of its intended results. During that time, investments are made and numerous projects and actions are undertaken to implement the strategy. Also, during that time, changes are taking place in both the environmental situation and the firm's internal situation. Strategic controls are necessary to steer the firm through these events. They must provide the basis for adapting the firm's strategic actions and directions in response to these developments and changes.

Prudential Insurance Company provides a useful example of the proactive, steering nature of strategic control. Several years ago, Prudential adopted a long-term market development strategy in which it sought to attain the top position in the life insurance industry by differentiating its level of service from those of its competitors. It decided to achieve a differential service advantage by establishing regional home offices. Exercising strategic control, its managers used the experience of the first regional offices to reproject the overall expenses and income associated with this strategy. The

FIGURE 12–1
Four Types of Strategic Control

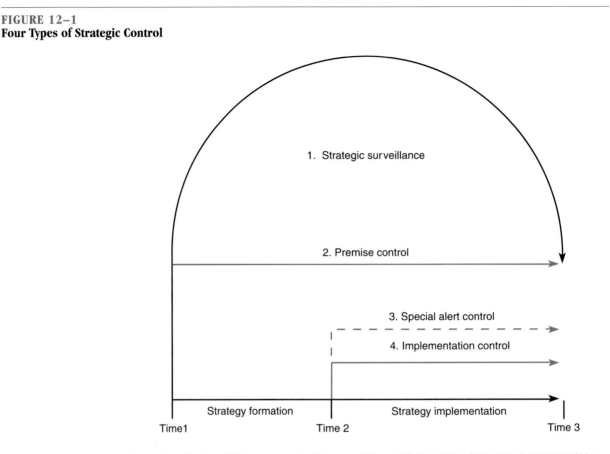

Source: Adapted from G. Schreyogg and H. Steinmann, "Strategic Control: A New Perspective," *Academy of Management Review* 12, no. 1 (1987), p. 96.

predicted expenses were so high that the original schedule for establishing other regional offices had to be modified. And on the basis of other early feedback, the restructuring of the services performed at Prudential's corporate headquarters was sharply revised. Thus, the steering control (or strategic control) exercised by Prudential managers significantly altered the firm's strategy. In this case, the major objectives of the strategy remained in place; in other cases, strategic control has led to changes in the major strategic objectives.

The four basic types of strategic control are:

1. Premise control.
2. Implementation control.
3. Strategic surveillance.
4. Special alert control.

The nature of these four types is summarized in Figure 12–1.

Premise Control

Every strategy is based on certain planning premises—assumptions or predictions. *Premise control is designed to check systematically and continuously whether the premises on which the strategy is based are still valid.* If a vital premise is no longer valid, the strategy may have to be changed. The sooner an invalid premise can be recognized and rejected, the better are the chances that an acceptable shift in the strategy can be devised.

Which Premises Should Be Monitored?

Planning premises are primarily concerned with environmental and industry factors. These are described next.

Environmental Factors Although a firm has little or no control over environmental factors, these factors exercise considerable influence over the success of its strategy, and strategies usually are based on key premises about them. Inflation, technology, interest rates, regulation, and demographic/social changes are examples of such factors.

EPA regulations and federal laws concerning the handling, use, and disposal of toxic chemicals have a major effect on the strategy of Velsicol Chemical Company, a market leader in pesticide chemicals sold to farmers and exterminators. So Velsicol's management makes and constantly updates premises about future regulatory actions.

Industry Factors The performance of the firms in a given industry is affected by industry factors. These differ among industries, and a firm should be aware of the factors that influence success in its particular industry. Competitors, suppliers, product substitutes, and barriers to entry are a few of the industry factors about which strategic assumptions are made.

Rubbermaid has long been held up as a model of predictable growth, creative management, and rapid innovation in the plastic housewares and toy industry. Its premise going into the 21st century was that large retail chains would continue to prefer its products over competitors' because of this core competence. This premise included continued receptivity to regular price increases when necessitated by raw materials costs. Late 1998 found retailers, most notably Wal-Mart, balking at Rubbermaid's attempt to raise prices to offset the doubling of resin costs. Furthermore, traditionally overlooked competitors have begun to make inroads with computerized stocking services. Rubbermaid is moving aggressively to adjust its strategy because of the response of Wal-Mart and other key retailers.

Strategies are often based on numerous premises, some major and some minor, about environmental and industry variables. Tracking all of these premises is unnecessarily expensive and time consuming. Managers must select premises whose change (1) is likely and (2) would have a major impact on the firm and its strategy.

How Are Premise Controls Enacted?

A strategy's key premises should be identified and recorded during the planning process. Responsibility for monitoring those premises should be assigned to the persons or departments that are qualified sources of information. To illustrate, members of the sales force might be assigned to monitor the expected price policy of major competitors and the finance department might be assigned to monitor interest rate trends. The required amount of monitoring effort varies for different premises; to avoid information overload, emphasis should be placed on the monitoring of key premises. These premises should be updated (and new predictions should be made) on the basis of updated information. Finally, key areas within the firm, or key aspects of the strategy that would be significantly affected by changes in certain premises, should be preidentified so adjustments necessitated by revisions in those premises can be determined and initiated. For example, senior marketing executives should be alerted to changes in

BusinessWeek

PREMISE CONTROL AT JAPAN'S MAZDA MOTOR CORPORATION

STRATEGY IN ACTION 12–1

Mazda Motor Corp. lost face back in May 1996. After five years of increasing losses, the management team was convinced something drastic needed to be done. Two premises that formed the underpinnings of its long-range automotive strategy were finally being challenged: (1) Strength comes from remaining an independently operated Japanese company, and (2) competitive advantage is built based on Mazda's engineering expertise. After heated board debate that spread over one year, the hemorrhaging, Hiroshima-based company turned to a "gaijin" for help: Ford Motor Co. took control by boosting its stake in Mazda Motor Corp. from 25% to 33.4%.

Just the thought of foreign control sent shock waves through Japan's No. 5 carmaker. Outside the company, commentators referred to the deal as the second atomic bomb dropped on Hiroshima. Customers deserted Mazda's showrooms.

In a turnabout, the alliance with Ford is now seen as crucial to Mazda's pulling out of its skid. While the slowdown in Japan and Southeast Asia has Japan's auto heavies—Toyota, Nissan, Honda, and Mitsubishi—throttling back production, Mazda is more than holding its own. Its sales in Japan are off only 5.8% so far this year, versus 14.9% for the industry. Facing increasingly harsh competition, Mazda employees from the executive offices to its showrooms are accepting the U.S. auto giant as a necessary ticket to the millennium. "Ford's involvement was essential for Mazda's recovery," admits Kei Kado, managing director of product development.

With guidance from Ford, Mazda has trimmed costs while wheeling out a string of popular new models, including the $11,900 Familia compact station wagon in Japan. At the same time, it's gaining enough ground in North America and Europe to reach breakeven after losing $93 million in those markets last year. Overall, after five years in the red, the company expects to net $215 million on sales of $15.3 billion in the fiscal year ending next March.

"LIKE A GOD"

Mazda has pulled the plug on unprofitable lines, such as 660cc minicars. It now slaps its nameplates on minicars produced by Suzuki Motor Corp. Ford executives have reined in Mazda's freewheeling engineers, forcing them to share auto "platforms" and source more components overseas. A company that used to roll out a dizzying array of expensive sporty sedans now produces cars that people want at affordable prices. "We were engineering-driven," says Kado. "Now we treat the customer like a god."

By following Ford's advice to use customer clinics, Mazda took the lead in one of the few growing segments of Japan's hammered auto market: car-based compact sport utilities. Its $8,800 Demio compact SUV is a hit because it gives young families what they asked for—a roomy interior.

Source: Emily Thornton. "Mazda Learns to Like Those Intruders," *Business Week:* September 14, 1998.

competitors' pricing policies so these executives can determine whether revised pricing, product repositioning, or other strategy adjustments are necessary. Strategy in Action 12–1 reports the result of premise control–driven strategic changes at Japan's Mazda Motor Corporation.

Implementation Control

Strategy implementation takes place as series of steps, programs, investments, and moves that occur over an extended time. Special programs are undertaken. Functional areas initiate strategy-related activities. Key people are added or reassigned. Resources are mobilized. In other words, managers implement strategy by converting broad plans into the concrete, incremental actions and results of specific units and individuals.

Implementation control is the type of strategic control that must be exercised as those events unfold. *Implementation control is designed to assess whether the overall strategy should be changed in light of the results associated with the incremental actions that implement the overall strategy.* Prudential's updating of cost and revenue projections based on early experiences with regional home offices is an example of implementation control. The two basic types of implementation control are (1) monitoring strategic thrusts and (2) milestone reviews.

Monitoring Strategic Thrusts

As a means of implementing broad strategies, narrow strategic projects often are undertaken—projects that represent part of what needs to be done if the overall strategy is to be accomplished. These strategic thrusts provide managers with information that helps them determine whether the overall strategy is progressing as planned or needs to be adjusted.

Although the utility of strategic thrusts seems readily apparent, it is not always easy to use them for control purposes. It may be difficult to interpret early experience or to evaluate the overall strategy in light of such experience. One approach is to agree early in the planning process on which thrusts or which phases of thrusts are critical factors in the success of the strategy. Managers responsible for these implementation controls will single them out from other activities and observe them frequently. Another approach is to use stop/go assessments that are linked to a series of meaningful thresholds (time, costs, research and development, success, and so forth) associated with particular thrusts. A program of regional development via company-owned inns in the Rocky Mountain area was a monitoring thrust that Days Inn used to test its strategy of becoming a nationwide motel chain. Problems in meeting time targets and unexpectedly large capital needs led Days Inn's executives to abandon the overall strategy and eventually sell the firm.

The speed of change in the "Internet sector" compresses the time in which strategic thrusts are monitored and milestones reviewed. Strategy in Action 12–2 examines this fast-paced setting as it faced Netscape co-founder Mark Andreessen.

Milestone Reviews

Managers often attempt to identify significant milestones that will be reached during strategy implementation. These milestones may be critical events, major resource allocations, or simply the passage of a certain amount of time. The milestone reviews that then take place usually involve a full-scale reassessment of the strategy and of the advisability of continuing or refocusing the firm's direction.

A useful example of implementation control based on milestone review is offered by Boeing's product-development strategy of entering the supersonic transport (SST) airplane market. Boeing had invested millions of dollars and years of scarce engineering talent during the first phase of its SST venture, and competition from the British/French Concorde effort was intense. Since the next phase represented a billion-dollar decision, Boeing's management established the initiation of the phase as a milestone. The milestone reviews greatly increased the estimates of production costs; predicted relatively few passengers and rising fuel costs, thus raising the estimated operating costs; and noted that the Concorde, unlike Boeing, had the benefit of massive government subsidies. These factors led Boeing's management to scrap its SST

BusinessWeek

IMPLEMENTATION CONTROL IN THE LIGHTNING FAST INTERNET ARENA: NETSCAPE'S STORY

STRATEGY IN ACTION 12–2

It was like a slow-motion train wreck. Marc Andreessen, 26-year-old co-founder of Netscape Communications Corp., was basking in last December's post-holiday glow when troubling reports began trickling in from Netscape's sales force. Instead of the big numbers he had hoped for, each report was more discouraging than the last. Corporate customers just weren't buying Netscape software fast enough.

By late January, the full extent of the damage was clear. Because of a huge fourth-quarter revenue shortfall, the company that had nearly turned the computing world upside down would report an $88 million loss and fire 400 of its 3,200 employees. The news was so bad that analysts began to question the Mountain View (California) company's ability to survive.

What had happened to Marc Andreessen's charmed life? It was only four years ago that this big, apple cheeked programming whiz kid left college in the Midwest and arrived in California seeking fame and fortune. With their Web browser, Andreessen and his Netscape cohorts launched the Internet gold rush. And, thanks to the company's initial public offering, his net worth soared to $171 million. At just 24, he appeared—barefoot and wearing a crown—on the cover of Time. Hyped as the next Bill Gates, he became a model for every brainy kid who dreamed of striking it rich on the Net. "He's the icon for his 20s generation—just as Gates is for his generation," says Eric Schmidt, CEO of Novell Inc.

But Andreessen had a problem Netscape was only beginning to detect. Gates has already chosen the next Bill Gates, and it's . . . Bill Gates. Not content just to be king of the PC realm, Gates set out two years ago to rule the Internet, too. Indeed, his move to give away much of Microsoft Corp.'s Internet software is working so well that it threatens to level Netscape. Nor has a convincing counterattack been mounted by Netscape. "I give them an A for putting together a solid technology strategy," says Dan Lynch, an investor in Net startups. "But unfortunately you need an A+. I don't think they appreciated the lengths to which Microsoft would go to crush them."

Soon, Andreessen was in the fight of his young life. No longer the hot new programming wunderkind, he has been forced to grow up fast. During his brief tenure in Silicon Valley, he has learned just how quickly fortunes can change in his cut-throat industry. Now, he needs to prove himself all over again—and the company's fate rests in part on his ability to remake himself as a more mature, market-savvy manager.

Two years ago, it looked as if Netscape's path would always lead upward. So it would be understandable if Andreessen were emotionally devastated. He says he's not. He swears he never believed the hype that surrounded Netscape. "What happened to me happened so quickly and was so far out of proportion to anything that would be considered reasonable that I treat it as an external phenomenon," he says in his rapid-fire delivery. He was happy to be a high-profile evangelist for the Internet—as long as it helped boost Netscape's fortunes.

FASTER TREADMILL

But Andreessen couldn't have guessed his glory days would be so brief. Indeed, he has had to grow up in Internet Time, a term first used to describe how quickly Netscape delivered new products (originally every six months, a breakneck pace). Bill Gates got to run Microsoft for more than

Source: "The Education of Marc Andreessen," *Business Week:* April 13, 1998; and "Power Play: AOL-Netscape-Sun," *Business Week:* December 7, 1998.

continued

a dozen years before IBM set its sights on him. For Netscape and Andreessen, the trip from phenom to potential has-been was over in a blink of an eye.

It's one thing to learn to dress well and show up on time and quite another to help save a troubled company. Some observers question whether Andreessen has the management skills needed for the job. After all, before his promotion last summer, he had never managed more than a handful of people. "In the Internet market, things are changing so fast," says the CEO of another Internet software company. "Marc's youth and inexperience are hard to overcome."

SHOWTIME

Others say it's time for the sometimes-cocky Andreessen to deliver the goods. "The challenge for Netscape is to live up to the story they've been telling everyone—that they were going to be the next Microsoft, they were going to put us out of business and become the next platform for the industry," says Nathan P. Myhrvold, CTO at Microsoft.

Netscape was losing its technology lead over Microsoft, particularly in browsers. And the company's two top engineers were in transition—one, Hahn, was going on sabbatical, and the other, Rick Schell, had asked for a less intense job. So Barksdale created a single engineering group and put Andreessen in charge of it—backing him up with a cadre of seasoned engineering managers.

Is Barksdale's strategy a stroke of genius or an act of desperation? He insists no one at Netscape has better technical know-how than Andreessen. And he is convinced that, with guidance, Andreessen will succeed as a manager. "Marc was frustrated with the problems in engineering, so I said if he's so frustrated, why not let him do it," says Barksdale.

Will the latest strategy be enough to stave off Microsoft and save Netscape? It's a long shot, according to analysts and industry players. Despite Netscape's risky giveaway of its source code, most predict it will lose browser market share even more quickly once Microsoft comes out with Windows 98. And in servers, Microsoft keeps upping the ante by adding new features to basic servers it gives away with its Windows NT operating system.

To stay in the race, Netscape will have to bolster its own server technology while holding prices low enough to keep corporate customers in its fold. Mary McCaffrey of BT Alex. Brown Inc. says she expects more bad financial news for the next couple of quarters. Longer term, there's a ray of hope. "If they knuckle down and get focused on the strengths of their product line, they've got a shot at turning this around," she says.

OUTCOME 1999

AOL announced in early 1999 its acquisition of Netscape as part of a blockbuster deal with Sun Microsystems which stunned the internet world. While the deal may worry rivals, it helps assuage Netscape customers, who have grown wary of the company's ability to deliver on its promises of producing key software. "It's reassuring to us," says Charlotte Decker, a marketing manager with Visteon Automotive Systems, a $17 billion auto-components division of Ford Motor Co. based in Dearborn, Michigan.

strategy in spite of high sunk costs, pride, and patriotism. Only an objective, full-scale strategy reassessment could have led to such a decision.

In this example, a milestone review occurred at a major resource allocation decision point. Milestone reviews may also occur concurrently when a major step in a strategy's implementation is being taken or when a key uncertainty is resolved. Managers even may set an arbitrary period, say two years, as a milestone review point. Whatever the basis for selecting that point, the critical purpose of a milestone review is to thoroughly scrutinize the firm's strategy so as to control the strategy's future.

Strategic Surveillance

By their nature, premise control and implementation control are focused controls; strategic surveillance, however, is unfocused. *Strategic surveillance is designed to monitor a broad range of events inside and outside the firm that are likely to affect the course of its strategy.*[1] The basic idea behind strategic surveillance is that important yet unanticipated information may be uncovered by a general monitoring of multiple information sources.

Strategic surveillance must be kept as unfocused as possible. It should be a loose "environmental scanning" activity. Trade magazines, *The Wall Street Journal,* trade conferences, conversations, and intended and unintended observations are all subjects of strategic surveillance. Despite its looseness, strategic surveillance provides an ongoing, broad-based vigilance in all daily operations that may uncover information relevant to the firm's strategy. Citicorp benefited significantly from a Peruvian manager's strategic surveillance of political speeches by Peru's former president, as discussed in Strategy in Action 12–3.

Special Alert Control

Another type of strategic control, really a subset of the other three, is special alert control. *A special alert control is the thorough, and often rapid, reconsideration of the firm's strategy because of a sudden, unexpected event.* A political coup in the Middle East, an outside firm's sudden acquisition of a leading competitor, an unexpected product difficulty, such as the poisoned Tylenol capsules—events of these kinds can drastically alter the firm's strategy.

Such an event should trigger an immediate and intense reassessment of the firm's strategy and its current strategic situation. In many firms, crisis teams handle the firm's initial response to unforeseen events that may have an immediate effect on its strategy. Increasingly, firms have developed contingency plans along with crisis teams to respond to circumstances such as those illustrated in Strategy in Action 12–3.

Figure 12–2 summarizes the major characteristics of the four types of strategic control. Unlike operational controls, which are concerned with the control of action, strategic controls are designed to continuously and proactively question the basic direction and appropriateness of a strategy. Each type of strategic control shares a common purpose: to assess whether the strategic direction should be altered in light of unfolding events. Many of us have heard the axiom, "The only thing that is constant is change itself." Organizations face the constancy of change from endless sources within and without the organization, all occurring at an ever accelerating pace. There is very little

[1]G. Schreyogg and H. Steinmann, "Strategic Control: A New Perspective," *Academy of Management Review* 12, no. 1 (1987), p. 101.

BusinessWeek

EXAMPLES OF STRATEGIC CONTROL

STRATEGY IN ACTION 12–3

IMPLEMENTATION CONTROL AT DAYS INN

When Days Inn pioneered the budget segment of the lodging industry, its strategy placed primary emphasis on company-owned facilities and it insisted on maintaining a roughly 3-to-1 company-owned/franchise ratio. This ratio ensured the parent company's total control over standards, rates, and so forth.

As other firms moved into the budget segment, Days Inn saw the need to expand rapidly throughout the United States and, therefore, reversed its conservative franchise posture. This reversal would rapidly accelerate its ability to open new locations. Longtime executives, concerned about potential loss of control over local standards, instituted *implementation controls* requiring both franchise evaluation and annual milestone reviews. Two years into the program, Days Inn executives were convinced that a high franchise-to-company ratio was manageable, and so they accelerated the growth of franchising by doubling the franchise sales department.

STRATEGIC SURVEILLANCE AT CITICORP

Citicorp has been pursuing an aggressive product development strategy intended to achieve an annual earnings growth of 15 percent while it becomes an institution capable of supplying clients with any kind of financial service anywhere in the world. A major obstacle to the achievement of this earnings growth is Citicorp's exposure to default because of its extensive earlier loans to troubled Third World countries. Citicorp is sensitive to the wide variety of predictions about impending Third World defaults.

Citicorp's long-range plan assumes an annual 10 percent default on its Third World loans over any five-year period. Yet it maintains active *strategic surveillance control* by having each of its international branches monitor daily announcements from key governments and from inside contacts for signs of changes in a host country's financial environment. When that surveillance detects a potential problem, management attempts to adjust Citicorp's posture. For example, when Peru's former president, Alan Garcia, stated that his country would not pay interest on its debt as scheduled, Citicorp raised its annual default charge to 20 percent of its $100 million Peruvian exposure.

SPECIAL ALERT CONTROL AT UNITED AIRLINES

The sudden impact of an airline crash can be devastating to a major airline. United Airlines has made elaborate preparations to deal with this contingency. Its executive vice president, James M. Guyette, heads a crisis team that is permanently prepared to respond. Members of the team carry beepers and are always on call. If United's Chicago headquarters receives word that a plane has crashed, for example, they can be in a "war room" within an hour to direct the response. Beds are set up nearby so team members can catch a few winks; while they sleep, alternates take their places.

Members of the team have been carefully screened through simulated crisis drills. "The point is to weed out those who don't hold up well under stress," says Guyette. Although the team was established to handle flight disasters, it has since assumed an expanded role. The crisis team was activated when American Airlines launched a fare war. And according to Guyette, "We're brainstorming about how we would be affected by everything from a competitor who had a serious problem to a crisis involving a hijacking or taking a United employee hostage."

Source: Adapted from conversations with selected Days Inn executives; "Is the Worst over for Citi?" *Forbes,* May 11, 1992; and "How Companies Prepare for the Worst," *Business Week,* December 23, 1985, p. 74.

FIGURE 12-2
Characteristics of the Four Types of Strategic Control

Basic Characteristics	Types of Strategic Control			
	Premise Control	Implementation Control	Strategic Surveillance	Special Alert Control
Objects of control	Planning premises and projections	Key strategic thrusts and milestones	Potential threats and opportunities related to the strategy	Occurrence of recognizable but unlikely events
Degree of focusing	High	High	Low	High
Data acquisition:				
Formalization	Medium	High	Low	High
Centralization	Low	Medium	Low	High
Use with:				
Environmental factors	Yes	Seldom	Yes	Yes
Industry factors	Yes	Seldom	Yes	Yes
Strategy-specific factors	No	Yes	Seldom	Yes
Company-specific factors	No	Yes	Seldom	Seldom

Source: Adapted from G. Schreyogg and H. Steinmann, "Strategic Control: A New Perspective," *Academy of Management Review* 12, no. 1 (1987), pp. 91–103.

that organizations can do to directly control the many sources of change. Yet, with performance and long-term survival at stake, better organizations adopt and regularly refine strategic controls as a way to deal with pervasive change.

IBM's CEO Lou Gerstner's explanation of the rationale behind some of the fundamental changes at IBM toward the end of the 20th century illustrates the pervasive, dramatic character of change and the essence of strategic control as a means to deal with it:

> One of the great things about this [computer] industry is that every decade or so, you get a chance to redefine the playing field. We're in that phase of redefinition right now, and winners or losers are going to emerge from it . . . Network centric computing . . . Providing time on computers rather than selling the hardware . . . The Internet . . . There's no question that the speed with which the Internet has emerged has caught all industries related to this technology by surprise . . . But there is no question that the PC-based model is now not the future.

Both operational and strategic controls are needed to guide the strategic management process. The next section examines the key types of operational control systems that are used to aid the strategic management process.

OPERATIONAL CONTROL SYSTEMS

Operational control systems guide, monitor, and evaluate progress in meeting short-term objectives. While strategic controls attempt to steer the company over an extended period (usually five years of more), operational controls provide postaction evaluation and control over short periods—usually from one month to one year. To be effective, operational control systems must take four steps common to all postaction controls:

1. Set standards of performance.
2. Measure actual performance.

3. Identify deviations from standards set.
4. Initiate corrective action.

Three types of operational control system are *budgets, schedules,* and *key success factors.* The nature and use of these three types of systems are described in the next sections.

Budgets

The budgetary process was the forerunner of strategic planning. A budget is a resource allocation plan that helps managers coordinate operations and facilitates managerial control of performance. Budgets themselves do not control anything. They simply set standards against which action can be measured. They also provide a basis for negotiating short-term resource requirements to implement strategy at the operating level. Most firms employ at least three budgets as a part of their planning and control activities. These types of budgets are the following:

1. *Profit and loss (P&L) budgets* are perhaps the most common. These budgets serve as the basis to monitor sales on a monthly or more frequent basis, as well as to monitor expense categories on a comparable time frame against what has actually occurred. Sales and expense numbers often are subdivided by department, location, product lines, and other relevant subunits to more closely project and monitor organizational activities.

2. *Capital budgets* usually are developed to show the timing of specific expenditures for plant, equipment, machinery, inventories, and other capital items needed during the budget period.

3. *Cash flow budgets* forecast receipt and disbursement of cash during the budget period. They tie together P&L expectations, capital expenditures, collection of receivables, expense payments, and borrowing needs to show just where the life blood of any business—cash—will come from and go to each month.

The budgeting system serves as an important and early indicator about the effectiveness of a firm's strategy by serving as a frame of reference against which to examine month-to-month results in the execution of that strategy.

Scheduling

Timing is often a key factor in the success of a strategy. Scheduling considerations in allocating time-constrained resources and sequencing interdependent activities often determine the success of strategy implementation. Scheduling offers a mechanism with which to plan for, monitor, and control these dependencies.[2] For example, a firm committed to a vertical integration strategy must carefully absorb expended operations into its existing core. Such absorption, given either forward or backward integration, will require numerous changes in the operational practices of the firm's organizational units. A good illustration is Coors Brewery's decision to integrate backward by producing its own beer cans. A comprehensive two-year schedule of actions and targets for incorporating the manufacture of beer cans and bottles into the product chain contributed

---

[2]A useful primer on scheduling considerations in strategic project planning is provided by Steven Wheelwright and Kim Clark in "Creating Project Plans to Focus Project Development," *Harvard Business Review* 70, no. 2 (1992), pp. 70–82; and Steven Wheelwright and Kim Clark, *Revolutionizing Product Development: Quantum Leaps in Speed, Efficiency, and Quality* (New York: The Free Press, 1992).

FIGURE 12-3
Key Success Factors at IBM's Lotus Notes Division

Key Success Factor	Measurable Performance Indicator
1. Product quality	a. Performance data versus specification. b. Percentage of product returns. c. Number of customer complaints.
2. Customer service	a. Delivery cycle in days. b. Percentage of orders shipped complete. c. Field service delays.
3. Employee morale	a. Trends in employee attitude survey. b. Absenteeism versus plan. c. Employee turnover trends.
4. Competition	a. Number of firms competing directly. b. Number of new products introduced. c. Percentage of bids awarded versus the standard.

to the success of this strategy. Purchasing, production scheduling, machinery, and production systems were but a few of the critical operating areas that Coors's scheduling efforts were meant to accommodate and coordinate.

Key Success Factors

Another useful way to effect operational control is to focus on "key success factors." These factors identify the performance areas that are of greatest importance in implementing the company's strategies and, therefore, must receive continuous management attention. Each key success factor must have measurable performance indicators. Lotus Notes' management, for example, having identified product quality, customer service, employee morale, and competition as the key determinants of success in the firm's strategy of rapidly expanding its software offerings, then specified three indicators to monitor and control each of these key success factors, as shown in Figure 12–3.

Key success factors succinctly communicate the critical elements for which operational managers are responsible. These factors require the successful performance of several key individuals and, thus, can be a foundation for teamwork among managers in meeting the firm's strategic objectives.

Budgeting, scheduling, and monitoring key success factors are important means of controlling strategy implementation at the operational level. Common to all of these operational control systems is the need to establish measurable standards and to monitor performance against those standards. The next section examines how to accomplish this.

USING OPERATIONAL CONTROL SYSTEMS: MONITORING PERFORMANCE AND EVALUATING DEVIATIONS

Operational control systems require performance standards. *Control* is the process of obtaining timely information on deviations from these standards, determining the causes of the deviations, and taking corrective action.

Figure 12–4 illustrates a simplified report that links the current status of key performance indicators to a firm's strategy. These indicators represent progress after two

FIGURE 12-4
Monitoring and Evaluating Performance Deviations

Key Success Factors	Objective, Assumption, or Budget	Forecast Performance at This Time	Current Performance	Current Deviation	Analysis
Cost control:					
Ratio of indirect overhead cost to direct field and labor costs	10%	15%	12%	+3 (ahead)	Are we moving too fast, or is there more unnecessary overhead than was originally thought?
Gross profit	39%	40%	40%	0%	
Customer service:					
Installation cycle in days	2.5 days	3.2 days	2.7 days	+0.5 (ahead)	Can this progress be maintained?
Ratio of service to sales personnel	3.2	2.7	2.1	−0.6 (behind)	Why are we behind here? How can we maintain the installation-cycle progress?
Product quality:					
Percentage of products returned	1.0%	2.0%	2.1%	−0.1% (behind)	Why are we behind here? What are the ramifications for other operations?
Product performance versus specification	100%	92%	80%	−12% (behind)	
Marketing:					
Monthly sales per employee	$12,500	$11,500	$12,100	+$600 (ahead)	Good progress. Is it creating any problems to support?
Expansion of product line	6	3	5	+2 products (ahead)	Are the products ready? Are the perfect standards met?
Employee morale in service area:					
Absenteeism rate	2.5%	3.0%	3.0%	(on target)	
Turnover rate	5%	10%	15%	−8% (behind)	Looks like a problem! Why are we so far behind?
Competition:					
New product introductions (average number)	6	3	6	−3 (behind)	Did we underestimate timing? What are the implications for our basic assumptions?

years of a five-year strategy intended to differentiate the firm as a customer-service-oriented provider of high-quality products. Management's concern is to compare *progress to date* with *expected progress*. The *current deviation* is of particular interest, because it provides a basis for examining *suggested actions* (usually suggested by subordinate managers) and for finalizing decisions on changes or adjustments in the firm's operations.

From Figure 12–4, it appears that the firm is maintaining control of its cost structure. Indeed, it is ahead of schedule on reducing overhead. The firm is well ahead of its delivery cycle target, while slightly below its target service-to-sales personnel ratio. Its product returns look OK, although product performance versus specification is below standard. Sales per employee and expansion of the product line are ahead of schedule. The absenteeism rate in the service area is on target, but the turnover rate is higher than that targeted. Competitors appear to be introducing products more rapidly than expected.

After deviations and their causes have been identified, the implications of the deviations for the ultimate success of the strategy must be considered. For example, the rapid product-line expansion indicated in Figure 12–4 may have been a response to the increased rate of competitors' product expansion. At the same time, product performance is still low; and, while the installation cycle is slightly above standard (improving customer service), the ratio of service to sales personnel is below the targeted ratio. Contributing to this substandard ratio (and perhaps reflecting a lack of organizational commitment to customer service) is the exceptionally high turnover in customer service personnel. The rapid reduction in indirect overhead costs might mean that administration integration of customer service and product development requirements has been cut back too quickly.

This information presents operations managers with several options. They may attribute the deviations primarily to internal discrepancies. In that case, they can scale priorities up or down. For example, they might place more emphasis on retaining customer service personnel and less emphasis on overhead reduction and new product development. On the other hand, they might decide to continue as planned in the face of increasing competition and to accept or gradually improve the customer service situation. Another possibility is reformulating the strategy or a component of the strategy in the face of rapidly increasing competition. For example, the firm might decide to emphasize more standardized or lower-priced products to overcome customer service problems and take advantage of an apparently ambitious sales force.

This is but one of many possible interpretations of Figure 12–4. The important point here is the critical need to monitor progress against standards and to give serious in-depth attention to both the causes of observed deviations and the most appropriate responses to them. After the deviations have been evaluated, slight adjustments may be made to keep progress, expenditure, or other factors in line with the strategy's programmed needs. In the unusual event of extreme deviations—generally because of unforeseen changes—management is alerted to the possible need for revising the budget, reconsidering certain functional plans related to budgeted expenditures, or examining the units concerned and the effectiveness of their managers.

An acceptable level of deviation should be allowed; otherwise, the control process will become an administrative overload. Standards should not be regarded as absolute, because the estimates used to formulate them typically are based on historical data, which, by definition, are after the fact. Absolute standards (keep equipment busy 100 percent of the time or meet 100 percent of quota) make no provision for variability. Standards are also often derived from averages, which, by definition, ignore variability. These difficulties suggest the need to define acceptable *ranges* of deviation in budgetary figures or key indicators of strategic success. This approach helps in avoiding administrative difficulties, in recognizing measurement variability, in delegating more realistic authority for short-term decisions to operating managers, and in improving motivation.

Some firms use trigger points for the clarification of standards, particularly in monitoring key success factors. A *trigger point* is a level of deviation of a key indicator or figure (such as a competitor's actions or a critical cost category) that management identifies in the planning process as representing either a major threat or an unusual opportunity. When that point is reached, management immediately is altered (triggered) to consider necessary adjustments in the firm's strategy. Some firms take this idea a step forward and develop one or more *contingency plans* that are to be implemented when predetermined trigger points are reached. These contingency plans redirect priorities and actions so rapidly that valuable reaction time is not wasted on administrative assessment of the extreme deviation.

Correcting deviations in performance brings the entire management task into focus. Managers can correct such deviations by changing measures or plans. They also can eliminate poor performance by changing how things are done, by hiring or retraining workers, by changing job assignments, and so on. Correcting deviations, therefore, can involve all of the functions, tasks, and responsibilities of operations managers. Managers in other cultures, most notably Japan, have for some time achieved operational control by seeking their unit's continuous improvement. Companies worldwide have adapted this point of view that operational control is best achieved through a pervasive commitment to quality, often called *total quality management* (TQM), which is seen as essential to strategic success into the 21st century.

THE QUALITY IMPERATIVE: CONTINUOUS IMPROVEMENT TO BUILD CUSTOMER VALUE

The initials TQM have become the most popular abbreviation in business management literature since MBO (management by objectives).[3] TQM Stands for *total quality management,* an umbrella term for the quality programs that have been implemented in many businesses worldwide in the last two decades. TQM was first implemented in several large U.S. manufacturers in the face of the overwhelming success of Japanese and German competitors. Japanese manufacturers embraced the quality messages of Americans W. Edwards Deming and J. M. Juran following World War II, and by the 1970s Japanese products had acquired unquestioned reputations for superior high quality.

Growing numbers of U.S. manufacturers have attempted to change this imbalance with their own quality programs, and the practice has spread to large retail and service companies as well. Increasingly, smaller companies that supply big TQM companies have adopted quality programs, often because big companies have required small suppliers to adopt quality programs of their own. Strategy in Action 12–4 describes the quality program in one such company, Dallas-based Marlow Industries, a recent winner of the Malcolm Baldrige National Quality Award.

TQM is viewed as virtually a new organizational culture and way of thinking. It is built around an intense focus on customer satisfaction; on accurate measurement of every critical variable in a business's operation; on continuous improvement of products, services, and processes; and on work relationships based on trust and teamwork. One useful explanation of the quality imperative suggests 10 essential elements of implementing total quality management, as follows:[4]

1. **Define *quality* and *customer value*.** Rather than be left to individual interpretation, company personnel should have a clear definition of what *quality* means in the job, department, and throughout the company. It should be developed from your customer's perspective and communicated as a written policy.

---

[3]This section draws on total quality management ideas found in the following: G. Stalk, P. Evans, and L. E. Shulman, "Competing on Capabilities: The New Rules of Corporate Strategy," *Harvard Business Review,* March–April 1992, pp. 57–69; M. Barrier, "Small Firms Put Quality First," *Nation's Business,* May 1992, pp. 22–31; Ernst & Young, *Total Quality,* SCORE Retrieval File no. A49003, 1991; and Mary Walton, *The Deming Management Method* (New York: Perigee Books, 1986).

[4]Ideas about these 10 elements are based in part on excellent work by the firm Ernst and Young, in *Total Quality,* SCORE Retrieval File no. A49003, 1991.

STRATEGY IN ACTION 12–4

BusinessWeek

DO OR DIE: MARLOW INDUSTRIES ADOPTS TOTAL QUALITY MANAGEMENT

Congress created the Baldridge Award in 1987 to recognize U.S. firms with outstanding records of quality improvement and quality management. Marlow Industries, the Dallas-based firm that was a small-business winner of the Malcolm Baldridge National Quality Award, is one of those companies that adopted TQM under pressure from its customers.

There's a simple reason for such customer pressure: When an appliance maker is trying to produce defect-free products, it cannot tolerate defects in the parts provided by its small suppliers.

Marlow, with 160 employees, is the smallest business yet to win the award. Only three small firms have ever won, out of 125 that have applied. Marlow makes thermoelectric coolers—small solid-state devices used to spot cooling in critical applications for telecommunications, aerospace, and the military. Most of Marlow's products are custom made for customers who impose their own quality requirements on their suppliers. Marlow had to come up with comprehensive quality systems that would meet all of those requirements.

That might sound like an intimidating task for so small a company, but Marlow successfully introduced profound changes in the way it operates. For example, about two years ago Marlow broke up its quality-assurance department, assigning product inspectors to "minifactories"—self-contained units, made up of approximately 15 people each. Today, according to Chris Witzke, Marlow's COO, the inspectors "look after the quality systems, set training standards, do audits—but they're not in the product-inspection business."

In other words, Marlow switched from product inspection to process control—from catching and correcting defects at the end of the process to monitoring the process itself, so defects do not occur. It was not easy to adopt TQM at Marlow. Raymond Marlow, founder and president of Marlow, said "You've got to have patience, because it takes a couple of years" before employees can work together smoothly in problem-solving teams. While the transition is taking place, Marlow says, top management must display "consistency of purpose. You have to keep the quality thing moving."

Measurement was critical at Marlow. "If you measure something," said Chris Witzke, "it improves." Simply posting measurements—putting up a chart showing how well departments are

Source: "Quality," *Business Week:* November 30, 1992, and "Small Firms Put Quality First," *Nation's Business,* May 1992, pp. 22–31.

Thinking in terms of customer value broadens the definition of *quality* to include efficiency and responsiveness. Said another way, quality to your customer often means that the product performs well; that it is priced competitively (efficiency); and that you provide it quickly and adapt it when needed (responsiveness). Customer value is found in the combination of all three—quality, price, and speed.

2. **Develop a customer orientation.** Customer value is what the customer says it is. Don't rely on secondary information—talk to your customers directly. Also recognize your "internal" customers. Usually less than 20 percent of company employees come into contact with external customers, while the other 80 percent serve internal customers—other units with real performance expectations.

The value chain provides an important way to think about customer orientation, particularly to recognize *internal* as well as external (ultimate) customers. Operating personnel are *internal* customers of the accounting department for useful information and

continued

doing at turning in their time cards on schedule, for instance—can sometimes solve a problem. But deciding what to measure is not always easy. Marlow devoted a full year to developing statistical process controls. "We really dedicated ourselves to understanding our processes and finding the key variables," Witzke said. "All this stuff used to be black art. Now it's science." Marlow at one time measured 52 variables in a plating process—but had constant problems anyway. Now it measures only 14 variables (including seven new ones), and the problems have disappeared. Measurements sometimes can reveal things about a business that no one would have suspected if the measurements hadn't been made. When Marlow began subjecting employee turnover to Pareto analysis, it discovered that a 90-day probationary period was contributing to turnover by encouraging supervisors to make marginal hires. Once the supervisors understood the cost of that turnover, they tightened their hiring practices. At Marlow, decisions on what should be measured usually have followed surveys of "internal customers" so what was important could be measured.

As any TQM company would be expected to do, Marlow measures its suppliers' performances—and it also tells them how they're doing. "It's amazing how quick a reaction you can get just from sending out a letter saying, 'Hey, your supplier index has dropped to 1.1,'" said Marlow's Witzke. One of Marlow's minifactories, responding to just such a review, came up with a "service guarantee" for its internal customers. Posted prominently in a hall at the plant, the guarantee promises replacement of any unsatisfactory part within 24 hours. After that guarantee went up, Witzke said, "it wasn't long before they started popping up in other places. That's the ideal situation—where management doesn't have to spend all of its time making things happen."

Marlow does a lot of in-house training, in both work skills and quality techniques—the average employee spent almost 50 hours in training last year—and the training helps managers as well as employees. Said Witzke: "By the time you've taught a course three or four times, you begin to believe it."

When a quality program is working, Witzke says—when customers are happy, products are defect-free, deliveries are on time—"all of a sudden you've got 30 percent more staff than you thought you had," because employees are spending less time correcting problems.

also the purchasing department for quality, timely supplies. When they are "served" with quality, efficiency, and responsiveness, value is added to their efforts, and is passed on to their internal customers and, eventually, external (ultimate) customers.

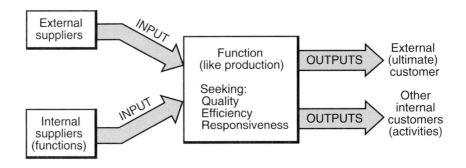

3. **Focus on the company's business processes.** Break down every minute step in the process of providing the company's product or service and look at ways to improve it, rather than focusing simply on the finished product or service. Each process contributes value in some way, which can be improved or adapted to help other processes (internal customers) improve. Examples of ways customer value is enhanced across business processes in several functions are:

	Quality	Efficiency	Responsiveness
Marketing	Provides accurate assessment of customer's product preferences to R&D	Targets advertising campaign at customers, using cost-effective medium	Quickly uncovers and reacts to changing market trends
Operations	Consistently produces goods matching engineering design	Minimizes scrap and rework through high-production yield	Quickly adapts to latest demands with production flexibility
Research and development	Designs products that combine customer demand and production capabilities	Uses computers to test feasibility of idea before going to more expensive full-scale prototype	Carries out parallel product/process designs to speed up overall innovation
Accounting	Provides the information that managers in other functions need to make decisions	Simplifies and computerizes to decrease the cost of gathering information	Provides information in "real time" (as the events described are still happening)
Purchasing	Selects vendors for their ability to join in an effective "partnership"	Given the required vendor quality, negotiates prices to provide good value	Schedules inbound deliveries efficiently, avoiding both extensive inventories and stock-outs
Personnel	Trains work force to perform required tasks	Minimizes employee turnover reducing hiring and training expenses	In response to strong growth in sales, finds large numbers of employees and quickly teaches needed skills

4. **Develop customer and supplier partnerships.** Organizations have a destructive tendency to view suppliers and even customers adversarily. It is better to understand the horizontal flow of a business—outside suppliers to internal suppliers/customers (a company's various departments) to external customers. This view suggests suppliers are partners in meeting customer needs, and customers are partners by providing input so the company and suppliers can meet and exceed those expectations.

Ford Motor Company's Dearborn, Michigan, plant is linked electronically with supplier Allied Signal's Kansas City, Missouri, plant. A Ford computer recently sent the design for a car's connecting rod to an Allied Signal factory computer, which transformed the design into instructions that it fed to a machine tool on the shop floor. The result: quality, efficiency, and responsiveness.

5. **Take a preventive approach.** Many organizations reward "fire fighters," not "fire preventers," and identify errors after the work is done. Management, instead, should be rewarded for being prevention oriented and seeking to eliminate nonvalue-added work.

Strategy in Action 12–4 describes how Marlow Industries discovered that a traditional 90-day probationary period for new hires was increasing employee turnover, encouraging marginal hires, and lowering all three sources of customer value.

6. **Adopt an error-free attitude.** Instill an attitude that "good enough" is not good enough anymore. "Error free" should become each individual's performance standard,

with managers taking every opportunity to demonstrate and communicate the importance of this imperative.

Strategy in Action 12–4 describes how Marlow Industries reoriented its complete organization from a "get the job done no matter what" attitude to a "no job is done until it's done right" way of thinking.

7. **Get the facts first.** Continuous improvement–oriented companies make decisions based on facts, not on opinions. Accurate measurement, often using readily available statistical techniques, of every critical variable in a business's operation—and using those measurements to trace problems to their roots and eliminate their causes—is a better way.

8. **Encourage every manager and employee to participate.** Employee participation, empowerment, participative decision making, and extensive training in quality techniques, in statistical techniques, and in measurement tools are the ingredients continuous improvement companies employ to support and instill a commitment to customer value.

9. **Create an atmosphere of total involvement.** Quality management cannot be the job of a few managers or of one department. Maximum customer value cannot be achieved unless all areas of the organization apply quality concepts simultaneously.

10. **Strive for continuous improvement.** Stephen Yearout, director of Ernst & Young's Quality Management Center, recently observed that, "Historically, meeting your customers' expectations would distinguish you from your competitors. The 21st century will require you to anticipate customer expectations and deliver quality service faster than the competition." Quality, efficiency, and responsiveness are not one-time programs of competitive response, for they create a new standard to measure up to. Organizations quickly find that continually improving quality, efficiency, and responsiveness in their processes, products, and services is not just good business; it's a necessity for long-term survival.

Continuous improvement and strategic control are two sides of the same "coin"—attention to factors that, in themselves, or because of change impacting them, influence the long-term success and survival of an organization. So it is not surprising, in the face of increasing global competition, that continuous improvement has evolved as a prominent factor that strategic-thinking managers are instilling in the way their organizations do business in the 21st century.

SUMMARY

Three fundamental perspectives—strategic control, operational control, and total quality/continuous improvement—provide the basis for designing strategy control systems. Strategic controls are intended to steer the company toward its long-term strategic goals. Premise controls, implementation controls, strategic surveillance, and special alert controls are types of strategic control. All four types are designed to meet top management's needs to track the strategy as it is being implemented, to detect underlying problems, and to make necessary adjustments. These strategic controls are linked to the environmental assumptions and the key operating requirements necessary for successful strategy implementation. Ever-present forces of change fuel the need for and focus of strategic control.

Operational control systems identify the performance standards associated with allocation and use of the firm's financial, physical, and human resources in pursuit of its strategy. Budgets, schedules, and key success factors are the primary means of operational control.

Operational control systems require systematic evaluation of performance against predetermined standards or targets. A critical concern here is identification and evaluation of performance deviations, with careful attention paid to determining the underlying reasons for and strategic implications of observed deviations before management reacts. Some firms use trigger points and contingency plans in this process.

The "quality imperative" of the last 20 years has redefined global competitiveness to include reshaping the way many businesses approach strategic and operational control. What has emerged is a commitment to continuous improvement in which personnel across all levels in an organization define customer value, identify ways every process within the business influences customer value, and seek continuously to enhance the quality, efficiency, and responsiveness with which the processes, products, and services are created and supplied. This includes attending to internal as well as external customers.

QUESTIONS FOR DISCUSSION

1. Distinguish strategic control from operating control. Give an example of each.
2. Select a business whose strategy is familiar to you. Identify what you think are the key premises of the strategy. Then select the key indicators that you would use to monitor each of these premises.
3. Explain the differences between implementation controls, strategic surveillance, and special alert controls. Give an example of each.
4. Why are budgets, schedules, and key success factors essential to operations control and evaluation?
5. What are key considerations in monitoring deviations from performance standards?
6. What are five key elements of quality management? How are quality imperative and continuous improvement related to strategic and operational control?
7. How might customer value be linked to quality, efficiency, and responsiveness?
8. Is it realistic that a commitment to continuous improvement could actually replace operational controls? Strategic controls?

BIBLIOGRAPHY

Asch, D. "Strategic Control: A Problem Looking for a Solution." *Long Range Planning* 25, no. 2 (1992), pp. 97–104.

Bart, C. K., "Budgeting Gamesmanship." *Academy of Management Executive* 2 (1988), pp. 285–94.

Baysinger, B., and R. E Hoskisson. "The Composition of Boards of Directors and Strategic Control: Effects on Corporate Strategy." *Academy of Management Review* 15, no. 1 (1990), pp. 72–87.

Boeker, Warren. "Strategic Change: The Effects of Founding and History." *Academy of Management Journal,* September 1989, p. 489.

Bungay, S., and M. Goold. "Creating a Strategic Control System." *Long Range Planning* 24, no. 3 (1991), pp. 32–39.

Bureau of Business Practice, *Profiles of Malcolm Baldrige Award Winners* (Boston: Allyn & Bacon, 1992).

Cowen, S. S., and J. K. Middaugh. "Designing an Effective Financial Planning and Control System." *Long Range Planning,* December 1988, pp. 83–92.

Duchessi, P., and J. Hobbs. "Implementing a Manufacturing Planning and Control System." *California Management Review,* Spring 1989, pp. 75–90.

Eccles, Robert G. "The Performance Measurement Manifesto." *Harvard Business Review* (January–February 1991), pp. 131–37.

Finkin, E. F. "Expense Control in Sales and Marketing." *Journal of Business Strategy,* May 1988, pp. 52–55.

Goold, M. "Strategic Control in the Decentralized Firm." *Sloan Management Review* 32, no. 2 (1991), pp. 69–81.

Goold, M., and J. J. Quinn. "The Paradox of Strategic Control." *Strategic Management Journal* 11, no. 1 (1990), pp. 43–57.

Grant, Robert M.; Rami Shani; and R. Krishnan. "TQM's Challenge to Management Theory and Practice." *Sloan Management Review,* Winter 1994, pp. 25–35.

Gundy, T., and D. King. "Using Strategic Planning to Drive Strategic Change." *Long Range Planning* 25, no. 1 (1992), pp. 100–09.

Gupta, A. K., and V. Govindarajan. "Knowledge Flows and the Structure of Control within Multinational Corporations." *Academy of Management Review* 16, no. 4 (1991), pp. 768–92.

Hamel, Gary, and C. K. Prahalad. *Competing for the Future.* Boston: Harvard Business School Press, 1994.

Harrison, E. F. "Strategic Control at the CEO Level." *Long Range Planning* 24, no. 6 (1991), pp. 78–87.

Herzberg, Frederick. "One More Time: How Do You Motivate Employees?" *Harvard Business Review* 65, no. 4 (September–October 1987), pp. 109–20.

Hiam, Alexander. "Exposing Four Myths of Strategic Planning." *Journal of Business Strategy* 11 (September–October 1990), pp. 23–28.

Hill, C. W. L. "Corporate Control Type, Strategy, Size and Financial Performance." *Journal of Management Studies,* September 1988, pp. 403–18.

Johnson, G. N. "Managing Strategic Change: Strategy, Culture and Action." *Long Range Planning* 25, no. 1 (1992), pp. 28–36.

Johnson, H. Thomas. *Relevance Regained.* New York: Free Press, 1992.

Kaplan, R. S., and D. P. Norton. "The Balanced Scorecard—Measures that Drive Performance." *Harvard Business Review* (January–February 1992), pp. 71–79.

Kaplan, R. S., and D. P. Norton. "Using the Balanced Scorecard as a Strategic Management System." *Harvard Business Review* (January–February 1996), pp. 75–85.

Kaplan, R. S., and D. P. Norton. "Putting the Balanced Scorecard to Work." *Harvard Business Review* (September–October 1993), pp. 134–47.

Kellinghusen, G., and K. Wiebbenhorst. "Strategic Control for Improved Performance." *Long Range Planning* 25, no. 3 (1992), pp. 30–37.

Kelly, D., and T. L. Amburgey. "Organizational Inertia and Momentum: A Dynamic Model of Strategic Change." *Academy of Management Journal* 34, no. 3 (1991), pp. 591–612.

Kerr, Steven. "On the Folly of Rewarding A While Hoping for B." *Academy of Management Executive* (February 1995), pp. 7–14.

Kiernan, Matthew J. "The New Strategic Architecture: Learning to Compete in the Twenty-First Century." *Academy of Management Executive* 7, no. 1 (February 1993), pp. 7–21.

King, E. M.; W. Norvell; and D. Deines. "Budgeting: A Strategic Managerial Tool." *Journal of Business Strategy,* Fall 1988, pp. 69–75.

Klein, Howard J. "An Integrated Control Theory Model of Work Motivation." *Academy of Management Review,* April 1989, p. 50.

Kohn, Alfie. "Why Incentive Plans Cannot Work." *Harvard Business Review* 71, no. 5 (September–October 1993), pp. 54–63.

McCrory, Francis V., and Peter G. Gerstberger. "The New Math of Performance Measurement." *Journal of Business Strategy* (March–April 1992), pp. 33–43.

Meyer, Christopher. "How the Right Measures Help Teams Excel." *Harvard Business Review* (May–June 1994), pp. 95–103.

Murphy, T. "Pay for Performance—An Instrument of Strategy." *Long Range Planning,* August 1989, pp. 40–45.

Norburn, D., and S. Birley. "The Top Management Team and Corporate Performance." *Strategic Management Journal,* May 1988, pp. 225–38.

Odiorne, George S. "Measuring the Unmeasurable: Setting Standards for Management Performance." *Business Horizons,* July–August 1987, p. 69.

Olian, Judy D., and Sara L. Rynes. "Making Total Quality Work: Aligning Organizational Processes, Performance Measures, and Stakeholders." *Human Resource Management* 30, no. 3 (Fall 1991), pp. 303–33.

Quinn, James Brian. *Intelligent Enterprise.* New York: Free Press, 1992, chap. 4.

Reichheld, F. F., and W. E. Sasser. "Zero Defects: Quality Comes to Services." *Harvard Business Review* 68, no. 3 (1990), pp. 94–111.

Rodgers, R., and J. E. Hunter. "Impact of Management by Objectives on Organizational Productivity." *Journal of Applied Psychology* 76 (1991), pp. 322–26.

Rogers, T. J. "No Excuses Management." *Harvard Business Review* 68, no. 4 (1990), pp. 105–13.

Ross, Joel, and David Georgoff. "A Survey of Productivity and Quality Issues in Manufacturing: The State of the Industry." *Industrial Management* 33, no. 1 (1991), pp. 3–5, 22–25.

Schmidt, Jeffrey A. "Is It Time to Replace Traditional Budgeting?" *Journal of Accountancy* 174 (October 1992), pp. 103–07.

Shetty, Y. K. "Aiming High: Competitive Benchmarking for Superior Performance." *Long Range Planning* 26, no. 1 (February 1993), pp. 39–44.

Simmons, R. "How New Top Managers Use Control Systems as Levers of Strategic Renewal." *Strategic Management Journal* 15 (1994), pp. 169–89.

Taguchi, G., and D. Clausing. "Robust Quality." *Harvard Business Review* 68, no. 1 (1990), pp. 65–75.

Tosi, Jr., H. L.., and L. R. Gomez-Mejia. "CEO Compensation and Firm Performance." *Academy of Management Journal* 37 (1994), pp. 1002–16.

Wiley, Carolyn. "Incentive Plan Pushes Production." *Personnel Journal* (August 1993), pp. 86–91.

Zahra, S. "Increasing the Board's Involvement in Strategy." *Long Range Planning* 23, no. 6 (1990), pp. 10–16.

Zent, Charles H. "Using Shareholder Value to Design Business Unit Manager Incentive Plans." *Planning Review,* March–April 1988, p. 40.

CHAPTER 12 DISCUSSION CASE

BusinessWeek

STRATEGIC CONTROL AND QUALITY MANAGEMENT AT GENERAL ELECTRIC

Jack Welch achieves strategic control through a seasonal ritual he repeats each year at GE:

EARLY JANUARY
Sets agenda for the year with top 500 executives at a session in Boca Raton, Florida.

MARCH
Tracks progress and swaps ideas with top 30 executives at quarterly Corporate Executive Council in Croton-on-Hudson.

APRIL/MAY
Goes into the field to each of GE's 12 businesses for full-day Session C meetings to personally review the performance and developmental plans for GE's top 3,000 managers. Also sends out a survey to thousands of employees to find out what they're thinking.

JUNE
Quarterly CEC meeting at Croton-on-Hudson.

JUNE/JULY
Spends full day with leadership of each of GE's businesses to review their three-year strategic plans at headquarters in Fairfield.

SEPTEMBER
Quarterly CEC meeting at Croton-on-Hudson.

OCTOBER
Convenes top 140 executives in Croton-on-Hudson at corporate officers' meeting to set the stage for the upcoming Boca meeting.

OCTOBER/NOVEMBER
Invests full day with leadership of each of GE's businesses to review budgets and follow up on human-resource reviews earlier in year.

DECEMBER
Quarterly CEC meeting at Croton-on-Hudson.

The discussion case in Chapter 11 told about GE's outstanding leader, Jack Welch. It also described ways he leads and manages on a daily basis. His hands on approach, even for such a large organization, undertaken through a repetitive routine which is emulated by all of his direct reports, and they to their direct reports, achieves excellent strategic control and operational control. That repetitive routine is described above.

In recent years, Jack Welch and GE have adopted an unparalleled commitment to a "Six Sigma" quality program as a virtual strategy to lower cost, increase productivity, and keep the organization focused on ways to make itself better for the 21st century. Let's return to John Byrne's excellent analysis of GE to see some of the quality efforts Jack Welch has implemented.

Source: John Bryne, "How Jack Welch Runs GE," *Business Week:* June 8, 1998.

Just look at the Corporate Executive Council (CEC) sessions, where GE's top 30 officers gather before the close of each financial quarter. The antithesis of the staid, staged off-site meeting, these sessions earn descriptions from executives like "food fights" and "free-for-alls." They are where Welch collects unfiltered information, challenges and tests his top players, and makes sure that the organization's triumphs and failures are openly shared. "I may be kidding myself," says Welch, "but going to a CEC meeting for me is like going to a fraternity party and hanging around friends. When I tell my wife I can hardly wait to go, she says, 'Well, why wouldn't you? You hired them all!' If you like business, sitting in that room with all these different businesses, all coming up with new ideas, is just a knockout."

If Welch's intellect and fervor make a strong impression, it is his near spiritual belief in the promise of the individual that made his early mentor and other observers that have followed really sit up and take notice. Welch believes that efficiencies in business are infinite, a faith grounded in the belief that there are no bounds to human creativity. "The idea flow from the human spirit is absolutely unlimited," Welch declares. "All you have to do is tap into that well. I don't like to use the word efficiency. It's creativity. It's a belief that every person counts."

It is not surprising, then, that Welch chose to embrace—as the ultimate expression of those beliefs—the largest corporate quality initiative ever undertaken. GE's Six Sigma program, Welch is convinced, can add up to $5 billion to GE's net earnings through the year 2000.

For years, Welch had been skeptical of the quality programs that were the rage in the 1980s. He felt that they were too heavy on slogans and too light on results. That was before he heard former GE Vice Chairman Lawrence A. Bossidy, a longtime friend, wax on about the benefits he was reaping from a quality initiative he had launched at AlliedSignal Inc., where he has been CEO since 1991. Bossidy had borrowed the Six Sigma program from Motorola Inc. and reported that the company was lowering costs, increasing productivity, and realizing more profits out of operations.

Welch invited Bossidy to share his story with GE's top management at the June, 1995, CEC meeting. As it turned out, that was the only one Welch ever missed—he was home recovering from open-heart surgery. However, Bossidy's presentation won such rave reviews that when Welch returned to work in August, he agreed to pursue it.

A Six Sigma quality level generates fewer than 3.4 defects per million operations in a manufacturing or service process. GE is running at a Sigma level of three to four. The gap between that and the Six Sigma level is costing the company between $8 billion and $12 billion a year in inefficiencies and lost productivity.

Still, it was no small decision to launch a quality initiative because it called for massive investment in training tens of thousands of employees in a disciplined methodology heavily laden with statistics. To make the ideas take hold throughout General Electric would require the training of so-called master black belts, black belts, and green belts to impose the quality techniques on the organization.

Welch launched the effort in late 1995 with 200 projects and intensive training programs, moved to 3,000 projects and more training in 1996, and undertook 6,000 projects and still more training in 1997. So far, the initiative has been a stunning success, delivering far more benefits than first envisioned by Welch. Last year, Six Sigma delivered $320 million in productivity gains and profits, more than double Welch's original goal of $150 million. This year, he expects GE to get about $750 million in net benefits. "Six Sigma has spread like wildfire across the company, and it is transforming everything we do," boasts Welch.

SHOW AND TELL

The success of the program was evident this January at Boca Raton, where Welch kicks off each year with a confab for the top 500 executives. Amid the ocean breezes and palms, it is Welch's opportunity to set the year's agenda and toast the company's newest heroes. An invitation by Welch to pitch in front of GE's most accomplished executives is like winning an Olympic medal in GE's intense locker-room culture. This past January, 29 managers gained the privilege, most of whom spoke glowingly about their Six Sigma projects.

With Welch in the front row of the auditorium furiously scribbling notes on a yellow pad, the managers recounted how they used new ideas to squeeze still more profit out of the lean machine that is GE. One after another explained how quality efforts cut costs and mistakes, enhanced productivity, led to greater market share, and eliminated the need for investment in new plant and equipment.

It's more than a bragging fest. The show-and-tell routine allows managers in plastics to exchange lessons with their counterparts in GE Capital. It's a place, like Croton-on-Hudson, where "best practices" get transferred among GE's differing businesses. In between sessions, managers who make bulbs or locomotives swap ideas with those who finance cars and service credit-card accounts.

Welch seldom disappears early. One night, for example, he was up until 3, shooting the breeze with 20 executives—half of them fast-rising women. But the main event is Welch's wrap-up comments when he steps out onto the stage under a spotlight and a pair of video cameras. Even though GE had just ended a record year, with earnings up 13%, to more than $8.2 billion, Welch wants more. Most CEOs would give a feel-good, congratulatory chat. But Welch dispenses with the kudos and warns the group that it will face one of the toughest years in a decade. It's no time to be complacent, he says, not with the Asian economic crisis, not with deflation in the air.

"The one unacceptable comment from a GE leader in '98 will be 'Prices are lower than we thought, and we couldn't get costs out fast enough to make our commitments.' Unacceptable," he shouts, like a preacher. "Unacceptable behavior, because prices will be lower than you're planning, so you better start taking action this week."

Then, after asking every GE business to resubmit annual budgets by the end of the month to account for deflation, the ideas tumble out of him for how they can combat it. "Don't add costs," he advises. "Increase inventory turns. Consolidate acquisitions. Use intellectual capital to replace plant and equipment investment. Raise approvals for price decisions. Make it harder to give away prices."

Welch then throws out yet another challenge. "The market is rewarding you like Super Bowl winners or Olympic gold medalists," he says. "I know I have such athletes reporting to me. Can you put your team against my team? Are you proud of everyone who reports to you? If you aren't, you can't win. You can't win the game."

When the executives return to work on Friday morning, a videotape of Welch's talk is already on their desks along with a guide for how to use it with their own teams. Within one week, more than 750 videos in eight different languages, including Mandarin and Hungarian, are dispatched to GE locations around the world. Welch's words will be absorbed and reinforced by as many as 150,000 employees by month's end.

ROSES AND CHAMPAGNE

What happens in Boca, in the management development courses at Crotonville, or in the quarterly CEC sessions promptly spills down into the organization's guts, where people at every layer digest it. William Woodburn, a 47-year-old former McKinsey & Co. consultant who heads GE's industrial diamonds business in Worthington, Ohio, was one of this year's heroes at Boca. Since taking over the business four years ago, Woodburn had increased the operation's return on investment fourfold and halved the cost structure.

Employing Six Sigma ideas, he and his team have squeezed so much efficiency out of their existing facilities that they believe they have eliminated the need for all investment in plant and equipment for a decade. Some 300 other managers from GE have visited the plant to learn directly how Woodburn has done it so they, too, can transfer the ideas to their own operations.

Like so many GE managers raised in Welch's intense hothouse, Woodburn's tough talk is pure Welch. To get the improvements, he has had to "take out" over a third of the workforce, including more than half the salaried staff. "We've been open and fair," he insists. "That doesn't mean being easy. You perform, or you're gone. There's tension in the rubber band."

On Monday, after returning from Boca, Woodburn gathers his 15 direct reports and uses Welch's video as the centerpiece for a discussion of what he learned in Florida. They then do the same with their staffs. On Wednesday, Woodburn uses the video again with 100 staffers in the plant. A week later, he goes through the process yet again with the region's "orphans"—GE staffers in the area who aren't in a major facility. "They see the tape. They hear the message. It gets people pumped up," he says.

Most great leaders, of course, are masters at communicating their desires. In his early years as chief executive, Welch discovered that you can't will things to happen, nor can you simply communicate with a few hundred people at the top and expect change to occur. So he doggedly repeats the key messages over and over again, reinforcing them at every opportunity.

And the commitment to quality through the Six Sigma program, Jack Welch believes, is destined to focus and guide the strategic management of GE through brutally competitive global markets to unprecedented levels of success in the new millennium.

GUIDE TO STRATEGIC MANAGEMENT CASE ANALYSIS

THE CASE METHOD

Case analysis is a proven educational method that is especially effective in a strategic management course. The case method complements and enhances the text material and your professor's lectures by focusing attention on what a firm has done or should do in an actual business situation. Use of the case method in a strategic management course offers you an opportunity to develop and refine analytical skills. It also can provide exciting experience by allowing you to assume the role of the key decision maker for the organizations you will study.

When assuming the role of the general manager of the organization being studied, you will need to consider all aspects of the business. In addition to drawing on your knowledge of marketing, finance, management, production, and economics, you will be applying the strategic management concepts taught in this course.

The cases in this book are accounts of real business situations involving a variety of firms in a variety of industries. To make these opportunities as realistic as possible, the cases include a variety of quantitative and qualitative information in both the presentation of the situation and the exhibits. As the key decision maker, you will need to determine which information is important, given the circumstances described in the case. Keep in mind that the results of analyzing one firm will not necessarily be appropriate for another since every firm is faced with a different set of circumstances.

PREPARING FOR CASE DISCUSSION

The case method requires an approach to class preparation that differs from the typical lecture course. In the typical lecture course, you can still benefit from each class session even if you did not prepare, by listening carefully to the professor's lecture. This approach will not work in a course using the case method. For a case course, proper preparation is essential.

Suggestions for Effective Preparation

1. *Allow adequate time in preparing a case.* Many of the cases in this text involve complex issues that are often not apparent without careful reading and purposeful reflection on the information in the cases.

2. *Read each case twice.* Because many of these cases involve complex decision making, you should read each case at least twice. Your first reading should give you an overview of the firm's unique circumstances and the issues confronting the firm. Your second reading allows you to concentrate on what you feel are the most critical issues and to understand what information in the case is most important. Make limited notes identifying key points during your first reading. During your second reading, you can add details to your original notes and revise them as necessary.

3. *Focus on the key strategic issue in each case.* Each time you read a case you should concentrate on identifying the key issue. In some cases, the key issue will be identified by the case writer in the introduction. In other cases, you might not grasp the key strategic issue until you have read the case several times. (Remember that not every piece of information in a case is equally important.)

4. *Do not overlook exhibits.* The exhibits in these cases should be considered an integral part of the information for the case. They are not just "window dressing." In fact, for many cases you will need to analyze financial statements, evaluate organizational charts, and understand the firm's products, all of which are presented in the form of exhibits.

5. *Adopt the appropriate time frame.* It is critical that you assume the appropriate time frame for each case you read. If the case ends in 1999, that year should become the present for you as you work on that case. Making a decision for a case that ends in 1999 by using data you could not have had until 2000 defeats the purpose of the case method. For the same reason, although it is recommended that you do outside reading on each firm and industry, you should not read material written after the case ended unless your professor instructs you to do so.

6. *Draw on all of your knowledge of business.* As the key decision maker for the organization being studied, you will need to consider all aspects of the business and industry. Do not confine yourself to strategic management concepts presented in this course. You will need to determine if the key strategic issue revolves around a theory you have learned in a functional area, such as marketing, production, finance, or economics, or in the strategic management course.

USING THE INTERNET IN CASE RESEARCH

The proliferation of information available on the Internet has direct implications for business research. The Internet has become a viable source of company and industry data to assist those involved in case study analysis. Principal sources of useful data include company websites, U.S. government web sites, search engines, investment research sites, and online data services. This section will describe the principal Internet sources of case study data and offer means of retrieving that data.

Company Websites

Virtually every public and private firm has a website that any Internet user can visit. Accessing a firm's web site is easy. Many firms advertise their web address through both TV and print advertisements. To access a site when the address is known, enter the address into the address line on any Internet service provider's homepage. When the address is not known, use of a search engine will be necessary. The use of a search engine will be described later. Often, but not always, a firm's web address is identical to its name, or is at least an abbreviated form of its name.

Company web sites contain data that are helpful in case study analysis. A firm's website may contain descriptions of company products and services, recent company accomplishments and press releases, financial and stock performance highlights, and an overview of a firm's history and strategic objectives. A company's web site may also contain links to relevant industry web sites that contain industry statistics as well as current and future industry trends. The breadth of data available on a particular firm's web site will vary but in general larger, global corporations tend to have more complete and sophisticated web sites than smaller, regional firms.

U.S. Government Web Sites

The U.S. government allows the public to access virtually all of the information that it collects. Most of this information is available online to Internet users. The government collects a great range of data types, from firm-specific data the government mandates all publicly traded firms to supply, to highly regarded economic indicators. The usefulness of many U.S. government web sites depends on the fit between the case you are studying and the data located on the web site. For example, a study of an accounting firm may be supplemented with data supplied by the Internal Revenue Service web site, but not the Environmental Protection Agency website. A sampling of prominent government web sites and their addresses is shown below.

> Environmental Protection Agency: www.epa.gov
> General Printing Office: www.gpo.gov
> Internal Revenue Service: www.irs.ustreas.gov
> Libraries of Congress: www.loc.gov
> National Aeronautics and Space Administration: www.hq.nasa.gov
> SEC's Edgar Database: www. sec.gov/edgarhp.htm
> Small Business Administration: www.sba.gov
> STAT-USA: www.stat-usa.gov
> U.S. Department of Commerce: www.doc.gov
> U.S. Department of Treasury: www.ustreas.gov

One of the most useful sites for company case study analysis is the Securities and Exchange Commission's EDGAR database listed above. The EDGAR database contains the documents that the government mandates all publicly traded firms to file including 10-Ks and 8-Ks. A form 10-K is the annual report that provides a comprehensive overview of a firm's financials in addition to discussions regarding industry and product background. Form 8-K reports the occurrence of any material events or corporate changes that may be of importance to investors. Examples of reported occurrences include key management personnel changes, corporate restructures, and new debt or equity issuance. This site is very user friendly and requires the researcher to provide only the company name in order to produce a listing of all available reports.

Search Engines

Search engines allow a researcher to locate information on a company or industry without prior knowledge of a specific Internet address. Generally, to execute a search the search engine requires the entering of a keyword, for example, a company name. However, each search engine differs slightly in its search capabilities. For example, to narrow a search on one search engine may be accomplished differently than narrowing a search on another.

The information retrieved by search engines typically includes articles and other information that contain the entered keyword or words. Because the search engine has retrieved data that contain keywords does not necessarily mean that the information is useful. Internet data are unfiltered, meaning they may not be checked for accuracy before the data are posted online. However, data copyrighted or published by a reputable source may greatly increase the chance that the data are indeed accurate. A list of popular Internet search engines is shown below:

Alta Vista: www.altavista.digital.com

Deja News: www.dejanews.com

DogPile: www.dogpile.com

Excite: www.excite.com

HotBot: www.hotbot.com

InfoSeek: www.infoseek.com

Lycos: www.lycos.com

Magellan Internet Guide: www.mckinley.com

Metacrawler: www.metacrawler.com

Starting Point: www.stpt.com

WebCrawler: www.webcrawler.com

Yahoo!: www.yahoo.com

Although Yahoo! appears in the above list, it is not a true search engine. Yahoo! actually catalogs web sites for users. When keywords are entered into Yahoo!'s search mechanism, Yahoo! will return Internet addresses that contain the keywords. Therefore, Yahoo! is regarded as a very efficient means of locating a firm's web site without prior knowledge of its exact web address.

Investment Research Sites

Investment research sites provide company stock performance data including key financial ratios, competitor identification, industry data, and links to research reports and SEC filings. These sites provide support for the financial analysis portion of a case study, but only for publicly traded businesses. Most investment research sites also contain macro market data that may not be company specific, but may still affect many investors of equities.

Investment research sites usually contain a search mechanism if a desired stock's ticker symbol is not known. In this case, the company name is entered to enable the site to find the corresponding equity. Since these sites are geared toward traders who want recent stock prices and data, searching for data relevant to a case may require more elaborate investigations at multiple sites. The list below includes many popular investment research sites:

American Stock Exchange: www.amex.com

DBC Online: www.dbc.com

Hoover's Online: www.hoovers.com

InvestorGuide: www.investorguide.com

Wall Street Research Net: www.wsrn.com

Market Guide: www.marketguide.com

Money Search: www.moneysearch.com

NASDAQ: www.nasdaq.com

New York Stock Exchange: www.nyse.com/public/home.html

PC Financial Network: www.dljdirect.com

Quote.Com: www.quote.com

Stock Smart: www.stocksmart.com

Wright Investors' Service on the World Wide Web: www.wisi.com

Zacks Investment Research: www.zacks.com/docs/Bob/hotlinks.htm

One site that conveniently contains firm, industry, and competitor data is Hoover's Online. Hoover's also provides financials, stock charts, current and archived news stories, and links to research reports and SEC filings. Some of these data, most notably the lengthy research reports produced by analysts, are fee-based and must be ordered.

Online Data Sources

Online data sources provide wide access to a huge volume of business reference material. Information retrieved from these sites typically includes descriptive profiles, stock price performance, SEC filings, and newspaper, magazine, and journal articles related to a particular company, industry, or product. Online data services are popular with educational and financial institutions. While some services are free to all users, to utilize the entire array of these sites' services, a fee-based subscription is usually necessary.

Accessing these sites requires only the source's address, or the use of a search engine to find the address. The source's homepage will clearly indicate the nature of the information available and describe how to search for and access the data. Most sites have help screens to assist in locating the desired information.

One of the most useful online sources for business research is the Lexis-Nexis Universe. This source provides a wide array of news, business, legal, and reference information. The information is categorized into dozens of topics including general news, company and industry news, company financials that include SEC filings, government and political news, accounting auditing and tax data, and legal research. One particularly impressive service is a search mechanism that allows a user to locate a particular article when the specific citation is known. A list of several notable online data sources is shown below:

ABI/Inform (Proquest Direct): www.umi.com/proquest/
Bloomberg Financial News Services: www.bloomberg.com
Dow Jones News Retrieval: http://bis.dowjones.com
EconLit: www.econlit.org
Lexis-Nexis Universe: www.lexis-nexis.com

PARTICIPATING IN CLASS

Because the strategic management course uses the case method, the success and value of the course depend on class discussion. The success and value of the class discussion, in turn, rely on the roles both you and your professor perform. Following are aspects of your role and your professor's, which, if kept in mind, will enhance the value and excitement of this course.

Students as Active Learners

The case method requires your active participation. This means your role is no longer one of sitting and listening.

1. *Attend class regularly.* Not only is your grade likely to depend on your involvement in class discussions, but the benefit you derive from this course is directly related to your involvement in and understanding of the discussions.

2. *Be prepared for class.* The need for adequate preparation already has been discussed. You will benefit more from the discussions, will understand and participate in

the exchange of ideas, and will avoid the embarrassment of being called on when not prepared. By all means, bring your book to class. Not only is there a good chance you will need to refer to a specific exhibit or passage from the case, you may need to refresh your memory of the case (particularly if you made notes in the margins while reading).

3. *Participate in the discussion.* Attending class and being prepared are not enough; you need to express your views in class. You can participate in a number of ways: by addressing a question asked by your professor, by disagreeing with your professor or your classmates (by all means, be tactful), by building on an idea expressed by a classmate, or by simply asking a relevant question.

4. *Participate wisely.* Although you do not want to be one of those students who never raises his or her hand, you also should be sensitive to the fact that others in your class will want to express themselves. You have probably already had experience with a student who attempts to dominate each class discussion. A student who invariably tries to dominate the class discussion breeds resentment.

5. *Keep a broad perspective.* By definition, the strategic management course deals with the issues facing general managers or business owners. As already mentioned, you need to consider all aspects of the business, not just one particular functional area.

6. *Pay attention to the topic being discussed.* Focus your attention on the topic being discussed. When a new topic is introduced, do not attempt to immediately introduce another topic for discussion. Do not feel you have to have something to say on every topic covered.

Your Professor as Discussion Leader

Your professor is a discussion leader. As such, he or she will attempt to stimulate the class as a whole to share insights, observations, and thoughts about the case. Your professor will not necessarily respond to every comment you or your classmates make. Part of the value of the case method is to get you and your classmates to assume this role as the course progresses.

The professor in a strategic management case course performs several roles:

1. *Maintaining focus.* Because multiple complex issues need to be explored, your professor may want to maintain the focus of the class discussion on one issue at a time. He or she may ask you to hold your comment on another issue until a previous issue is exhausted. Do not interpret this response to mean your point is unimportant; your professor is simply indicating there will be a more appropriate time to pursue that particular comment.

2. *Getting students involved.* Do not be surprised if your professor asks for input from volunteers and nonvolunteers alike. The value of the class discussion increases as more people share their comments.

3. *Facilitating comprehension of strategic management concepts.* Some professors prefer to lecture on strategic management concepts on a "need-to-know" basis. In this scenario, a lecture on a particular topic will be followed by an assignment to work on a case that deals with that particular topic. Other professors will have the class work through a case or two before lecturing on a topic to give the class a feel for the value of the topic being covered and for the type of information needed to work on cases. Still other professors prefer to cover all of the theory in the beginning of the course, thereby allowing uninterrupted case discussion in the remaining weeks of the term. All three of these approaches are valued.

4. *Playing devil's advocate.* At times your professor may appear to be contradicting many of the comments or observations being made. At other times your professor may adopt a position that does not immediately make sense, given the circumstances of the case. At other times your professor may seem to be equivocating. These are all examples of how your professor might be playing devil's advocate. Sometimes the professor's goal is to expose alternative viewpoints. Sometimes he or she may be testing your resolve on a particular point. Be prepared to support your position with evidence from the case.

ASSIGNMENTS

Written Assignments

Written analyses are a critical part of most strategic management courses. Each professor has a preferred format for these written analyses, but a number of general guidelines will prove helpful to you in your written assignments.

1. *Analyze.* Avoid merely repeating the facts presented in the case. Analyze the issues involved in the case and build logically toward your recommendations.

2. *Use headings or labels.* Using headings or labels throughout your written analysis will help your reader follow your analysis and recommendations. For example, when you are analyzing the weaknesses of the firm in the case, include the heading Weaknesses. Note the headings in the cases that follow.

3. *Discuss alternatives.* Follow the proper strategic management sequence by (1) identifying alternatives, (2) evaluating each alternative, and (3) recommending the alternative you think is best.

4. *Use topic sentences.* You can help your reader more easily evaluate your analysis by putting the topic sentence first in each paragraph and following with statements directly supporting the topic sentence.

5. *Be specific in your recommendations.* Develop specific recommendations logically and be sure your recommendations are well defended by your analysis. Avoid using generalizations, clichés, and ambiguous statements. Remember that any number of answers are possible, and so your professor is most concerned about how your reasoning led to your recommendations and how well you develop and support your ideas.

6. *Do not overlook implementation.* Many good analyses receive poor evaluations because they do not include a discussion of implementation. Your analysis will be much stronger when you discuss how your recommendation can be implemented. Include some of the specific actions needed to achieve the objectives you are proposing.

7. *Specifically state your assumptions.* Cases, like all real business situations, involve incomplete information. Therefore, it is important that you clearly state any assumptions you make in your analysis. Do not assume your professor will be able to fill in the missing points.

Oral Presentations

Your professor is likely to ask you and your classmates to make oral presentations on a particular case. Oral presentations usually are done by groups of students. In these groups, each member will typically be responsible for one aspect of the overall case. Keep the following suggestions in mind when you are faced with an oral presentation:

1. *Use your own words.* Avoid memorizing a presentation. The best approach is to prepare an outline of the key points you want to cover. Do not be afraid to have the outline in front of you during your presentation, but do not just read the outline.

2. *Rehearse your presentation.* Do not assume you can simply read the outline you have prepared or that the right words will come to you when you are in front of the class making your presentation. Take the time to practice your speech, and be sure to rehearse the entire presentation with your group.

3. *Use visual aids.* The adage "a picture is worth a thousand words" contains quite a bit of truth. The people in your audience will more quickly and thoroughly understand your key points—and will retain them longer—if you use visual aids. Think of ways you and your team members can use the blackboard in the classroom; a graph, chart, or exhibit on a large posterboard; or, if you will have a number of these visual aids, a flip chart.

4. *Be prepared to handle questions.* You probably will be asked questions by your classmates. If questions are asked during your presentation, try to address those that require clarification. Tactfully postpone more elaborate questions until you have completed the formal phase of your presentation. During your rehearsal, try to anticipate the types of questions that you might be asked.

Working as a Team Member

Many professors assign students to groups or teams for analyzing cases. This adds more realism to the course, since most strategic decisions in business are addressed by a group of key managers. If you are a member of a group assigned to analyze a case, keep in mind that your performance is tied to the performance of the other group members, and vice versa. The following are some suggestions to help you be an effective team member:

1. *Be sure the division of labor is equitable.* It is not always easy to decide how the workload can be divided equitably, since it is not always obvious how much work needs to be done. Try breaking down the case into the distinct parts that need to be analyzed to determine if having a different person assume responsibility for each part is equitable. All team members should read and analyze the entire case, but different team members can be assigned primary responsibility for each major aspect of the analysis. Each team member with primary responsibility for a major aspect of the analysis also will be the logical choice to write that portion of the written analysis or to present it orally in class.

2. *Communicate with other team members.* This is particularly important if you encounter problems with your portion of the analysis. Since, by definition, the team members are dependent on each other, it is critical that you communicate openly and honestly with each other. It, therefore, is essential that your team members discuss problems, such as some members not doing their fair share of work or members insisting that their point of view dominate the team's report.

3. *Work as a team.* Since a group's output should reflect a combined effort, the whole group should be involved in each part of the analysis, even if different individuals assume primary responsibility for different parts of the analysis. Avoid having the marketing major do the marketing portion of the analysis, the production major handle the production issues, and so forth. This will both hamper the group's aggregate analysis and do all of the team members a disservice by not giving each member exposure to decision making involving the other functional areas. The strategic management course provides an opportunity to look at all aspects of the

business situation, to develop the ability to see the big picture, and to integrate the various functional areas.

4. *Plan and structure team meetings.* When working with a group on case analysis, it is impossible to achieve the team's goals and objectives without meeting outside of class. As soon as the team is formed, establish mutually convenient times for regular meetings, and be sure to keep this time available each week. Be punctual in going to the meetings, and manage the meetings so they end at a predetermined time. Plan several shorter meetings, as opposed to one longer session right before the case is due. (This, by the way, is another way realism is introduced in the strategic management course. Planning and managing your time is essential in business, and working with others to achieve a common set of goals is a critical part of life in the business world.)

SUMMARY

The strategic management course is your opportunity to assume the role of a key decision maker in a business organization. The case method is an excellent way to add excitement and realism to the course. To get the most out of the course and the case method, you need to be an active participant in the entire process.

The case method offers you the opportunity to develop your analytical skills and to understand the interrelationships of the various functional areas of business; it also enables you to develop valuable skills in time management, group problem solving, creativity, organization of thoughts and ideas, and human interaction.

A

BUSINESS WEEK CASES

THE CORPORATION OF THE FUTURE

1   The once unthinkable decline of many of the world's largest corporations has become all too common in recent years. Strategic blunders and oversights by management have pulled down such powerful and mighty giants as AT&T, Eastman Kodak, and General Motors.

2   Yet there is a less visible but even more critical danger: the inability to adapt to the speed and turbulence of technological change. After massive high-tech investments, management is only beginning to make the organizational changes needed to transform information technology into the potent competitive weapon that it will need to be in the 21st century.

3   Few companies have grasped the far-reaching importance of the new technology for management better than Cisco Systems Inc. The San Jose (Calif.) company has become the global leader in networking for the Internet, with annual revenues of more than $8 billion. It's also a Wall Street darling, with a market cap approaching $100 billion.

4   Cisco could well provide one of the best road maps to a new model of management. Partly because it makes the tools to build the powerful networks that link businesses to their customers and suppliers, Cisco itself has been at the forefront of using technology to transform management practices.

NEAR-RELIGIOUS

5   But it's not only the company's innovative use of technology that wins favorable reviews. It's also the company's mind-set and culture, its willingness to team up with outsiders to acquire and retain intellectual assets, its near-religious focus on the customer, and its progressive human resource policies. "Cisco is the quintessential outside-in company" says James F. Moore, chairman of consultants GeoPartners Research Inc. "They have mastered how to source talent, products, and momentum from outside their own walls. That's a powerful advantage."

Source: John A. Byrne in San Jose, California, "The Corporation of the Future," *Business Week:* August 31, 1998.

6 This corporate adolescent—founded in 1984 by a group of computer scientists from Stanford University—is headed by a leader, John T. Chambers, who cut his teeth at successful companies that stumbled. At both IBM and Wang Laboratories Inc., the soft-spoken West Virginian got a firsthand glimpse of how arrogance and reluctance to change caused severe pain and dislocation.

7 Those experiences, including a traumatic time when he survived five layoffs in 15 months at Wang—before resigning in 1990—colored his view of what a healthy organization should be. "It taught me how a company should be built in the first place and how to do things dramatically different the next time," says Chambers, 48, who joined Cisco in 1991 and became CEO in 1995. "Laying off people was the toughest thing I ever did. I'll move heaven and earth to avoid doing that again."

8 To hear Chambers tell it, his people and his organization are "in the sweet spot"—where technology and the future meet to transform not only business but all of life. His vision is simple: "We can change the way people live and work, play and learn." It is an idealistic phrase that falls out of his mouth repeatedly and unabashedly. It is also an inspiring and motivating declaration for each of Cisco's 13,000-plus employees.

9 Chambers aims to be the Jack Welch of the new millennium. Like General Electric Co.'s Chairman Welch, he has decided he wants to be No. 1 or No. 2 in every market, a condition that already exists in 14 of the 15 markets in which Cisco competes. Beyond that strategic goal, Chambers believes that the new rules of competition demand organizations built on change, not stability; organized around networks, not a rigid hierarchy; based on interdependencies of partners, not self-sufficiency; and constructed on technological advantage, not old-fashioned bricks and mortar.

10 The network structure has vast implications for managing in the next century. GM's Saturn Div. and Dell Computer Corp. have shown how the network can eliminate inventory, by connecting with partners that deliver goods only when they are needed. In the new model that Chambers is creating at Cisco, however, the network is pervasive, central to nearly everything.

11 It seamlessly links Cisco to its customers, prospects, business partners, suppliers, and employees. This year, Cisco will sell more than $5 billion worth of goods—more than half its total—over the Internet, nearly three times the Internet sales booked by pioneer Dell. So successful has Cisco been in selling complex, expensive equipment over the Net that last year Cisco alone accounted for one-third of all electronic commerce.

12 Seven out of 10 customer requests for technical support are filled electronically—at satisfaction rates that eclipse those involving human interaction. Using the network for tech support allows Cisco to save more money than its nearest competitor spends on research and development. "It has saved me 1,000 engineers," gushes Chambers. "I take those 1,000 engineers, and instead of putting them into support, I put them into building new products. That gives you a gigantic competitive advantage."

13 The network also is the glue for the internal workings of the company. It swiftly connects Cisco with its web of partners, making the constellation of suppliers, contract manufacturers, and assemblers look like one company—Cisco—to the outside world. Via the company's intranet, outside contractors directly monitor orders from Cisco customers and ship the assembled hardware to buyers later in the day—often without Cisco even touching the box. By outsourcing production of 70% of its products, Cisco has quadrupled output without building new plants and has cut the time it takes to get a new product to market by two-thirds, to just six months.

"PERSONAL TOUCH"

14 The network also is Cisco's primary tool for recruiting talent, with half of all applications for jobs coming over the Net. When an employee wants information about a company event or health benefits, or needs to track an expense report, the network is the place to go at Cisco. The upshot: More than 1.7 million pages of information are accessible by employees who use the Cisco network thousands of times every day. "We are," says Chambers, "the best example of how the Internet is going to change everything."

15   Technology aids and abets this business model, but it does not completely displace human interaction. "The network works better when you've already had a personal touch," insists Chambers. That's why he does quarterly meetings with employees at a nearby convention center, why all employees in the month of their birth are invited to one of his 1 1/2-hour "birthday breakfasts," and why he works harder than most to encourage open and direct communication with all of Cisco's leaders.

16   Chambers also believes in partnering with other businesses. Plenty of companies forge links with others, but Cisco has a track record of making them work. "Partnerships are key to the new world strategies of the 21st century," says Donald J. Listwin, a Cisco senior vice-president. "Partners collapse time because they allow you to take on more things and bring them together quicker."

17   A good example is Cisco's partnership with Microsoft Corp., which last year resulted in a new technology to make networks more intelligent. The software lets networks know immediately a user's identity and location and to respond differently to each one. The partnership allows both companies to expand this market together more rapidly. "From initial discussion to technology, it took 18 months to get the product out," says Listwin. "It would have taken us four years to get to where we are [without such a partnership], and it's not clear we had the competence to get there alone."

18   Another theme—often heard but seldom exercised by corporate leaders—is the central importance of the customer. Nothing causes Chambers more restless nights than worry over how to serve customers better. That's why he spends as much as 55% of his time with customers and why he receives every night, 365 nights a year, voice mail updates on as many as 15 key clients.

"ARROGANT"

19   In this new model, strategic direction is not formed by an insular group of top executives, but by the company's leading customers. It's an outside-in approach, as opposed to an inside-out. The customer is the strategy. "There is nothing more arrogant than telling a customer: 'Here is what you need to know,'" says Chambers. "Most of the time, you are not going to be right." Rather, Cisco's leading-edge customers are seen as partners in forming the company strategy. Example: After Boeing Co. and Ford Motor Co. informed Chambers that their future network needs were unlikely to be satisfied by Cisco, Chambers went out to make his first acquisition to solve the problem. That deal, to acquire local-area-network switchmaker Crescendo Communications in 1993, put the company into a sector of the industry that now accounts for $2.8 billion in annual revenue.

20   Even such tactical moves as acquisitions and mergers are seen differently by a new-world company. Rather than acquire merely to speed growth or swell market share, Cisco routinely employs acquisitions to capture intellectual assets and next-generation products. "Most people forget that in a high-tech acquisition, you really are acquiring only people," says Chambers. "That's why so many of them fail. At what we pay, at $500,000 to $2 million an employee, we are not acquiring current market share. We are acquiring futures."

21   While most companies immediately cut costs and people from newly acquired outfits, Cisco adheres to what it calls the "Mario rule"—named after Senior Vice-President Mario Mazzola, who had been CEO of Crescendo when it was bought by Cisco. Before any employee in a newly acquired company can be terminated, both Chambers and the former CEO must give their consent. "It tells new employees that Cisco wants them, that Cisco cares about them, and that we're not just another big company," says Daniel Scheinman, vice-president for legal and government affairs. "It buys the trust of the people . . . and their passion is worth a lot more than any of the downside legal protection."

22   In talent-hungry Silicon Valley, Cisco measures the success of every acquisition first by employee retention, then by new product development, and finally return on investment. The company has been phenomenally successful at holding on to the intellectual assets it buys: Overall turnover among acquired employees is just 6% a year, two percentage points lower than Cisco's overall employee churn. The company works hard to embrace employees acquired in deals, often giving top talent key jobs in the new organization. Three of Cisco's main businesses are led by former CEOs of acquired companies.

GOOD FIT

23 Every acquisition, moreover, must meet Cisco guidelines. For years, Chambers watched IBM and other high-tech outfits acquire and then slowly smother any number of entrepreneurial companies. What he learned was that you never buy a company whose values and culture are much different from your own. Nor do you buy a company that is too far away from your central base of operations. The latter makes a cultural fit less likely and severely limits the speed a company needs to compete in the new economy.

24 Chambers also believes that each deal must boast both short-term and long-term wins for customers, shareholders, and employees. "If there are no results in three to six months, people begin to question the acquisition," says Charles H. Giancarlo, vice-president for global alliances. "If you have good short-term wins, it's a virtuous cycle."

25 Through it all, the emphasis is on doing it faster, cheaper, and better—an integral part of success in the new economy. At Cisco, wages are less important than ownership. Some 40% of the stock options at the company are held by "individual contributors" who on average boast more than $150,000 in option gains. Egalitarianism is critical to successful teamwork and to morale. "You never ask your team to do something you wouldn't do yourself," says Chambers, who flies coach and has no reserved parking space at headquarters.

26 There are other leaders, of course, besides Chambers, who hope to create an organization that may very well revolutionize the fundamental business models of major global companies. But he's surely in the "sweet spot," helping to write the new rules for managing.

TABLE 1
A New Management Primer

Some key lessons from Cisco Systems and other progressive companies:

Network, Network, Network

Technology allows links with customers, suppliers, business partners, and employees. So take advantage of the speed and productivity it affords.

Focus on the Customer

Let your core customers determine your strategy. They know more about what they need than your top executives do.

Buy Smart

Pursue acquisitions not to speed growth or increase market share per se, but to capture intellectual assets and next-generation products.

Team Up for Success

Create alliances with partners based on trust and the potential for achieving mutual short- and long-term wins.

Share the Wealth

Use broad-based stock option plans to reward and retain key employees.

That Personal Touch

Technology goes only so far. Face-time counts. Corporate leaders must spend lots of time coaching, mentoring, and communicating with employees in person.

CASE 2   BusinessWeek

GENERATION Y

1   At malls across America, a new generation is voting with its feet.

2   At Towson Town Center, a mall outside of Baltimore, Laura Schaefer, a clerk at the Wavedancer surf-and-skateboard shop, is handling post-Christmas returns. Coming back: clothes that fit snugly and shoes unsuitable for skateboarding. Schaefer, 19, understands. "They say 'My mom and dad got me these'," she says.

3   At the Steve Madden store in Roosevelt Mall on Long Island, N.Y., parents, clad in loafers and Nikes, are sitting quietly amid the pulsating music while their teenage daughters slip their feet into massive Steve Madden platform shoes. Many of the baby boomer-age parents accompanying these teens look confused. And why not? Things are different in this crowd.

4   Asked what brands are cool, these teens rattle off a list their parents blank on. Mudd. Paris Blues. In Vitro. Cement. What's over? Now, the names are familiar: Levi's. Converse. Nike. "They just went out of style," shrugs Lori Silverman, 13, of Oyster Bay, N.Y.

5   Ouch. Some of the biggest brands on the market are meeting with a shrug of indifference from Lori and her cohorts. A host of labels that have prospered by predicting—and shaping—popular tastes since the baby boomers were young simply aren't kindling the same excitement with today's kids. Already, the list includes some major names: PepsiCo Inc. has struggled to build loyalty among teens. Nike Inc.'s sneaker sales are tumbling as the brand sinks in teen popularity polls. Levi Strauss & Co., no longer the hippest jeanmaker on the shelf, is battling market share erosion. Meanwhile, newcomers in entertainment, sports equipment, and fashion have become hot names.

6   What's the problem? These kids aren't baby boomers. They're part of a generation that rivals the baby boom in size—and will soon rival it in buying clout. These are the sons and daughters of boomers.

7   Born during a baby bulge that demographers locate between 1979 and 1994, they are as young as five and as old as 20, with the largest slice still a decade away from adolescence. And at 60 million strong, more than three times the size of Generation X, they're the biggest thing to hit the American scene since the 72 million baby boomers. Still too young to have forged a name for themselves, they go by a host of taglines: Generation Y, Echo Boomers, or Millennium Generation.

8   Marketers haven't been dealt an opportunity like this since the baby boom hit. Yet for a lot of entrenched brands, Gen Y poses mammoth risks. Boomer brands flopped in their attempts to reach Generation X, but with a mere 17 million in its ranks, that miss was tolerable. The boomer brands won't get off so lightly with Gen Y. This is the first generation to come along that's big enough to hurt a boomer brand simply by giving it the cold shoulder—and big enough to launch rival brands with enough heft to threaten the status quo. As the leading edge of this huge new group elbows its way into the marketplace, its members are making it clear that companies hoping to win their hearts and wallets will have to learn to think like they do—and not like the boomers who preceded them.

9   Indeed, though the echo boom rivals its parent's generation in size, in almost every other way, it is very different. This generation is more racially diverse: One in three is not Caucasian. One in four lives in a single-parent household. Three in four have working mothers. While boomers are still mastering Microsoft Windows 98, their kids are tapping away at computers in nursery school.

10   With the oldest Gen Yers barely out of high school, it's no surprise that the brands that have felt their disdain so far have been concentrated in fashion, entertainment, and toys. But there's a lot more going on here than fickle teens jumping on the latest trend. While some of Gen Y's choices have been

Source: Ellen Neuborne in New York, with Kathleen Kerwin in Detroit and bureau reports, "Generation Y," *Business Week:* February 15, 1999; Ellen Neuborne, "We Are Going to Own This Generation," *Business Week:* February 15, 1999; and Amey Stone in New York, "Can Gen Yers Down Enough Mountain Dew to Lift Pepsi's Stock?" *Business Week:* February 15, 1999.

driven by faddishness and rebellion, marketing experts say those explanations are too simplistic. "Most marketers perceive them as kids. When you do that, you fail to take in what they are telling you about the consumers they're becoming," says J. Walker Smith, a managing partner at Yankelovich Partners Inc. who specializes in generational marketing. "This is not about teenage marketing. It's about the coming of age of a generation."

11   Smith and others believe that behind the shift in Gen Y labels lies a shift in values on the part of Gen Y consumers. Having grown up in an even more media-saturated, brand-conscious world than their parents, they respond to ads differently, and they prefer to encounter those ads in different places. The marketers that capture Gen Y's attention do so by bringing their messages to the places these kids congregate, whether it's the Internet, a snowboarding tournament, or cable TV. The ads may be funny or disarmingly direct. What they don't do is suggest that the advertiser knows Gen Y better than these savvy consumers know themselves.

12   Soon a lot of other companies are going to have to learn the nuances of Gen Y marketing. In just a few years, today's teens will be out of college and shopping for their first cars, their first homes, and their first mutual funds. The distinctive buying habits they display today will likely follow them as they enter the high-spending years of young adulthood. Companies unable to click with Gen Y will lose out on a vast new market—and could find the doors thrown open to new competitors. "Think of them as this quiet little group about to change everything," says Edward Winter of The U30 Group, a Knoxville (Tenn.) consulting firm.

13   Nike has found out the hard way that Gen Y is different. Although still hugely popular among teens, the brand has lost its grip on the market in recent years, according to Teenage Research Unlimited, a Northbrook (Ill.) market researcher. Nike's slick national ad campaigns, with their emphasis on image and celebrity, helped build the brand among boomers, but they have backfired with Gen Y. "It doesn't matter to me that Michael Jordan has endorsed Nikes," says Ben Dukes, 13, of LaGrange Park, Ill.

14   Missteps such as Nike's disastrous attempt to sponsor Olympic snowboarders two years ago and allegations of inhumane overseas labor practices added to Gen Y's scorn. As Nike is discovering, success with this generation requires a new kind of advertising as well as a new kind of product. The huge image-building campaigns that led to boomer crazes in everything from designer vodka to sport-utility vehicles are less effective with Gen Y. "The old-style advertising that works very well with boomers, ads that push a slogan and an image and a feeling, the younger consumer is not going to go for," says James R. Palczynski, retail analyst for Ladenburg Thalmann & Co. and author of YouthQuake, a study of youth consumer trends.

15   Instead, Gen Yers respond to humor, irony, and the (apparently) unvarnished truth. Sprite has scored with ads that parody celebrity endorsers and carry the tagline "Image is nothing. Obey your thirst." J.C. Penney & Co.'s hugely successful Arizona Jeans brand has a new campaign showing teens mocking ads that attempt to speak their language. The tagline? "Just show me the jeans."

NET EFFECT

16   Which isn't to say echo boomers aren't brand-conscious. Bombarded by ad messages since birth, how could they not be? But marketing experts say they form a less homogeneous market than their parents did. One factor is their racial and ethnic diversity. Another is the fracturing of media, with network TV having given way to a spectrum of cable channels and magazine goliaths such as Sports Illustrated and Seventeen now joined by dozens of niche competitors. Most important, though, is the rise of the Internet, which has sped up the fashion life cycle by letting kids everywhere find out about even the most obscure trends as they emerge. It is the Gen Y medium of choice, just as network TV was for boomers. "Television drives homogeneity," says Mary Slayton, global director for consumer insights for Nike. "The Internet drives diversity."

17   Nowhere is that Net-driven diversity more clear than in the music business. On the Web, fans of even the smallest groups can meet one another and exchange information, reviews, even sound clips. Vicki Starr, a partner in Girlie Action, a New York-based music promoter, last year booked No Doubt, a band with a teen following, into a small Manhattan venue. She says that on opening night the house

was packed with teenage girls dressed just like the lead singer. "How do they know this? How do they keep up with what she's wearing? It's not from network television," says Starr. "It's online."

18   The Internet's power to reach young consumers has not been lost on marketers. These days, a well-designed Web site is crucial for any company hoping to reach under-18 consumers. "I find out about things I want to buy from my friends or from information on the Internet," says Michael Elia-son, 17, of Cherry Hill, N.J. Even popular teen TV shows, such as Warner Bros. Television Network's "Buffy the Vampire Slayer" and "Dawson's Creek," have their own Web sites.

19   Other companies are keeping in touch by E-mail. American Airlines Inc. recently launched a college version of its popular NetSaver program, which offers discounted fares to subscribers by E-mail. "They all have E-mail addresses," says John R. Samuel, director of interactive marketing for American. "If a company can't communicate via E-mail," he says, "the attitude is 'What's wrong with you?'"

20   This torrent of high-speed information has made Gen Y fashions more varied and faster-changing. Young consumers have shown that they'll switch their loyalty in an instant to marketers that can get ahead of the style curve. No brand has done a better job of that than Tommy Hilfiger. When Hilfiger's distinctive logo-laden shirts and jackets starting showing up on urban rappers in the early '90s, the company started sending researchers into music clubs to see how this influential group wore the styles. It bolstered its traditional mass-media ads with unusual promotions, from giving free clothing to stars on VH1 and MTV to a recent deal with Miramax Film Corp., in which teen film actors will appear in Hilfiger ads. Knowing its customers' passion for computer games, it sponsored a Nintendo competition and installed Nintendo terminals in its stores. Gen Y consumers have rewarded that attentiveness by making Hilfiger jeans their No. 1 brand in a recent American Express Co. survey.

21   Compare that record with Levi's, one of the world's most recognized brands and an icon of boomer youth. It got a harsh wake-up call in 1997, when its market share slid, and research revealed that the brand was losing popularity among teens. With its core boomer customers hitting middle age, both Levi's advertising and its decades-old five-pocket jeans were growing stale. "We all got older, and as a consequence, we lost touch with teenagers," says David Spangler, director of market research for the Levi's brand. Now, Levi's is fighting back with new ads, new styles, a revamped Web site, and ongoing teen panels to keep tabs on emerging trends. "We never put much muscle into this sort of thing before, but now, we are dead serious about it," says Spangler. "This is a generation that must be reckoned with. They are going to overtake the country."

22   Marketers who don't bother to learn the interests and obsessions of Gen Y are apt to run up against a brick wall of distrust and cynicism. Years of intense marketing efforts aimed directly their way have taught this group to assume the worst about companies trying to coax them into buying something. Ads meant to look youthful and fun may come off as merely opportunistic to a Gen Y consumer. That's what happened to PepsiCo in its attempts to earn Gen Y loyalty with its Generation Next campaign, says William Strauss, co-author of the 1991 book *Generations: The History of America's Future.* The TV ads, in which kids showed off branded trinkets, from jackets to gym bags, fell flat. "They were annoying," says Philip Powell, 14, of Houston. "It was just one long 'Please, please, buy me.'"

23   Ironically, Pepsi already has one of the biggest teen soda hits with Mountain Dew, but the drink's success has little to do with advertising. Instead, kids found out about Dew from their most trusted endorsers—each other. "[Kids] believe—true or not—that they're the ones who figured out and spread the word that the drink has tons of caffeine," says Marian Salzman, head of the brand futures group at Young & Rubicam Inc. "The caffeine thing was not in any of Mountain Dew's television ads. This drink is hot by word of mouth."

24   Along with cynicism, Gen Y is marked by a distinctly practical world view, say marketing experts. Raised in dual-income and single-parent families, they've already been given considerable financial responsibility. Surveys show they are deeply involved in family purchases, be they groceries or a new car. One in nine high school students has a credit card co-signed by a parent, and many will take on extensive debt to finance college. Most expect to have careers and are already thinking about home ownership, according to a 1998 survey of college freshman for Northwestern Mutual Life Insurance Co. "This is a very pragmatic group. At 18 years old, they have five-year plans. They are already looking at how they will be balancing their work/family commitments," says Deanna Tillisch, who directed the survey.

GRASSROOTS

25   That means marketers who want to reach worldly wise Gen Yers need to craft products and pitches that are more realistic. To rejuvenate its Gen X hit "House of Style," for example, MTV switched the emphasis on the weekly fashion show from celebrity lifestyles to practical information, with segments on decorating your bedroom and buying a prom dress. "We adapted the show to be more of what they wanted to see," said Todd Cunningham, director of brand research for MTV.

26   To break through Gen Y's distrust, marketers are also trying to make their campaigns more subtle and more local. A growing number, including Universal Studios, Coca-Cola, and McDonald's, use "street teams." Made up of young people, the teams hang out in clubs, parks, and malls talking to teens about everything from fashion to finance, trying to pinpoint trends as they emerge. Other marketers are trying to build grassroots support for their brands. Following the lead of underground rock bands, mass marketers have taken to "wild postings," that is, tacking up ad posters on street corners and construction sites. Others sponsor community events or hand out coupons and T-shirts at concerts and ball games. Golden Books Publishing Co. distributed sample chapters from a new teen book series at movie theaters. The idea is to let kids stumble onto the brand in unexpected places.

27   Last year, when Lee Apparel introduced Pipes, a line of oversize, multipocketed pants aimed at 10- to 14-year-old boys, it spent its marketing dollars on the Internet, outdoor posters, and skateboard magazines. "As a brand, you need to go where they are, not just pick a fashion statement, put it on TV, and wait for them to come to you," says Terry Lay, president of the Lee brand. Even Coke, a master of slick advertising, looks for more personal ways to reach Gen Y. Last summer, it courted teens with discount cards good for movies and fast food. To build credibility, it mailed them directly to high school sports stars and other leaders first before handing out more at stores.

28   Of course, plenty of marketers continue to reach for this group with national TV campaigns. The ones that work are funny, unpretentious, and often confusing to older consumers. Consider Volkswagen of America Inc. Although VW doesn't market directly to teens, both its Golf and Passat models show up on surveys as Gen Y faves. Part of the credit goes to the carmaker's quirky TV commercials, which are about as far from the traditional image-building ads Detroit churns out as possible. "We're a little edgier, a little more risk-tolerant, and not so mainstream," says VW marketing director Liz Vanzura. While other marketers fled the airwaves when Ellen DeGeneres came out of the closet on her show last spring, VW used the groundbreaking episode to introduce a new commercial showing two guys in a car who pick up a discarded chair. The ad, funny and oblique, became a favorite among young adults and teens.

29   With the oldest Gen Yers turning 20 this year, a lot of other companies will soon find themselves grappling with this new generation. Toyota Motor Corp., noting that 4 million new drivers will come of age each year until 2010, unveiled the Echo at this year's Detroit auto show. With low emissions and a price well below the Corolla, the new subcompact is aimed squarely at boomers' kids who are buying their first cars. General Motors Corp. is putting together a task force to figure out how to appeal to Gen Y. The auto maker brings teens and children as young as sixth-graders into car clinics, where researchers probe their opinions of current models and prototypes of future cars. Michael C. DiGiovanni, GM's head of market research and forecasting, says Gen Y kids have an entirely different aesthetic from their parents. Their sense of how a product should look and feel has been shaped by the hours they spend at the keyboard. "One of the trends that will manifest itself is computers," says DiGiovanni. "The design of products will be influenced by the way a computer screen looks."

30   Meanwhile, computers and other high-tech products are starting to look less industrial and more sleek in an effort to attract younger buyers. By using bright colors and cool designs, Motorola Inc. helped transform the pager from a lowly tool for on-call workers to a must-have gizmo for teens. Apple Computer Inc. appeals directly to the same group with products such as its rounded, space-age-looking iMac computer. "For this generation, the computer is like a hot rod," says Allen Olivo, Apple's senior director for worldwide marketing, who says kids are constantly comparing features and styling with their friends' systems.

31   Apple's stylish iMac may or may not become the computer of choice for this new generation. But Apple and other marketers that attempt to chart the Gen Y psyche now could have an advantage as this generation moves into adulthood. After all, some of the biggest brands on the market today got their start by bonding with boomers early and following them from youth into middle age. Will the

TABLE 1
Cool Stuff

According to Boomers . . .

- Lexus LS400

  What to drive when you have your own parking spot. It says you've arrived without the ostentation of a Beemer.

- Major League Baseball

  Mark McGwire and the New York Yankees have made the game hot again.

- Gap

  Those chinos and jeans still look cool. Really.

- "ER"

  A worthy successor to Marcus Welby, MD.

- Superbowl Ads

  Usually they're more entertaining than the game.

- Harrison Ford

  Tough and fiftysomething. Plus, his action figure is a hot collectible.

- Estee Lauder

  For the way we ought to look.

- L. L. Bean

  A favorite for decades, but does anyone actually go duck-hunting in those boots?

- Palm Pilot

  A Rolodex for your pocket, with a high-tech edge.

- Nick at Nite

  All our favorite reruns in one convenient place.

- Political Activism

  Make yourself heard.

- The Beatles

  Rock 'n' roll as the signal artistic achievement of a generation.

- Coke

  Water + sugar + caffeine. Besides, it's the real thing.

- David Letterman

  Late-night TV, slightly mellowed with age. Still among the Top Ten reasons to stay awake.

- Nikes

  From Michael to Tiger, no shortage of sports celebs saying Just Do it.

According to Generation Y . . .

- Jeep Wrangler

  Who cares about gas mileage? It looks great in the high school parking lot.

- Skateboard Triple Crown

  Stars compete for glory instead of multiyear contracts.

- Delia's

  Definitely not your mother's dress catalog.

- "Dawson's Creek"

  High school drama with sizzle.

- Lilith Fair Sponsorship

  Supporting the sound of new voices.

- Leonardo Dicaprio

  Dashing, sensitive, and irresistible to 12-year-olds.

TABLE 1
concluded

- Hard Candy

  For the way we really look.
- The North Face

  Does anyone actually go mountain climbing in that stuff?
- Motorola Flex Pagers

  Stay in touch anytime, anyplace.
- WB Network

  Creating new favorites and a new look for prime time television.
- Volunteerism

  Make yourself useful.
- Spice Girls

  Rock 'n' roll packaged and marketed to children.
- Mountain Dew

  Water + sugar + more caffeine. Besides, it's an extreme thing.
- Jenny McCarthy

  Think Carol Burnett with a bad attitude.
- Vans

  No sports celebs allowed. And they're the coolest shoes on skateboards.

labels that grew up with baby boomers reinvent themselves for Generation Y? Or will the big brands of the new millennium bear names most of us have not yet heard of?

"WE ARE GOING TO OWN THIS GENERATION"

32 The morning after the Delia's catalog arrives, the halls of Paxton High School in Jacksonville, Fla., are buzzing. That's when all the girls bring in their copies from home and compare notes. "Everyone loves Delia's," says Emily Garfinkle, 15. "It's the big excitement."

33 If you've never heard of Delia's, chances are you don't know a girl between 12 and 17. The five-year-old direct mailer has become one of the hottest names in Gen Y retailing by selling downtown fashion to girls everywhere. Already, the New York cataloger, which racked up sales of $98 million over the past three quarters, has a database of 4 million names, and its fastest growth may still lie ahead: Gen Y's teen population won't peak for five or six years.

Tight Focus

34 A lot of thriving Gen Y companies fell into the market by accident. Not Delia's. Founders Stephen Kahn, a 33-year-old ex-Wall Streeter, and Christopher Edgar, his ex-roommate at Yale University, re- alized that few retailers had taken the trouble to learn this market. So they carefully honed the Delia's concept: cutting-edge styles and mail-order distribution with a Gen Y twist.

35 Delia's trendy apparel is definitely not designed with mom and dad in mind. "I think the clothes are too revealing," says Emily's mother, Judy. "I tell her I'll buy her anything she wants at the Gap." But Emily dismisses the Gap as "too preppy," preferring Delia's long, straight skirts and tops with bra-exposing spaghetti straps. Delia's order form even includes tips on how to order pants so they conform to the parentally despised fashion of drooping well below the hips, with hems dragging. In

EXHIBIT A

The second booming

The number of new babies surged
with the baby boom, and then again
as boomers had their own kids

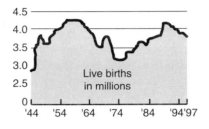

keeping with Gen Y preferences, the catalog illustrates these fashions with models who look like regular teenagers, not superglam androgynes.

36   Delia's youthful image isn't just a facade. Most of the company's 1,500 employees are well under 30. And its phone reps—mostly high school and college students—do more than take orders: They offer tips and fashion advice. "Delia's speaks the language of its consumers," says Wendy Liebmann, president of consultant WSL Marketing.

37   Instead of mass-market advertising, Delia's gets the word out in the ways Gen Y prefers: with local campaigns such as catalog drops in schools and with hot Web sites. In 1997, the company bought gURL.com, a popular fashion, chat, and game site for girls. It also launched its own Web site, with news and entertainment stories, catalog-request forms, E-mail, and online shopping. That effort helped buy some buzz for Delia's stock, which has gyrated between $4 and $32 a share over the past year. In December, buoyed by news of an online shopping venture, the stock shot up more than 50%, to a recent 15.

38   So far, the company has sold mostly clothing, but it has recently branched out into home furnishings, such as bean bag chairs and throw rugs. "Girls like to do their rooms," says Kahn, who defines his business by its customers rather than by a product category. He foresees a day when Delia's will get these girls their first credit card, first car loan, and first mortgage. "We'll follow them and broaden our offerings," says Kahn.

39   Next up: boys. The company recently bought TSI Soccer Corp., a sportswear catalog and launched Droog, a catalog for boys. "We are going to own this generation," Kahn says. Or at least a sizable portion of its members' wallets.

CAN GEN YERS DOWN ENOUGH MOUNTAIN DEW TO LIFT PEPSI'S STOCK?

40   As a leading maker of soda and snacks, PepsiCo (PEP) seems poised to benefit from the approaching wave of 60 million teenagers who'll roll through the economy in the next decade or so. Already, Generation Y clamors for the company's caffeine-charged Mountain Dew soft drink.

41   Indeed, strong Mountain Dew sales for the second straight year were one of the bright spots in the company's Feb. 1 earnings release. However, that was one of the few bright spots.

42   PepsiCo reported fourth-quarter net profits of $361 million, or earnings per share of 24 cents—a 20% decline from 29 cents for the fourth quarter a year ago. Net sales climbed to $7.2 billion in the quarter, up from $6.3 billion in the fourth quarter of 1997. The combination of higher advertising and marketing expenses, primarily to launch low-cal Pepsi One and the Wow! line of Olean-based chips, ate into profits—as did a weak global environment. In the conference call with analysts that followed its earnings announcement, PepsiCo warned that first-quarter 1999 results could be hurt by economic woes in Brazil.

43   After a volatile 1998, in which the stock traded as high as 45 in April and as low as 28 in August, PepsiCo shares have ended up in the same high-30s trading range where they were 18 months ago: The stock closed Feb. 4 at 38 1/16, down 3/4.

"A New Era"?

44   The lackluster earnings and stock performance are trying the patience of investors who expected Chairman Roger Enrico's strategy for overhauling the company to improve bottom-line results by now. Enrico has focused Pepsi on its core beverage and Frito-Lay snack business: In 1997, it spun off its restaurant division into Tricon Global Restaurants (YUM), and it will soon spin off its bottling business. PepsiCo acquired Tropicana juices from Seagram Co. for $3.3 billion in cash last July and also made several investments in snack products in international markets, including Europe and Australia. "The year 1998 was a transitional one," summed up Merrill Lynch analyst Emanuel Goldman in a Feb. 4 report that raised the question in its title: "A New Era for Pepsi?" He continues to rate the stock a buy.

45   "We're trying to be patient with the stock," says Jay Sekelsky, lead equity manager for Mosaic Funds, who concedes that he expected to see better performance by now. He bought the stock about a year ago, and it has climbed only about 10%, while the S&P 500 has gained nearly 30% over the same period. "We thought results from the fourth quarter of 1998 would be a launch pad," he says. "Now we think it will be more like the second half of 1999, where we'll really see the acceleration in growth. That's what we're betting on."

46   Some Wall Street analysts still rate PepsiCo among their favorite stocks, because they believe that the turning point is nigh. "We're at an inflection point where after two years of going through a strategic overhaul of its business, the company will emerge in 1999 as a much stronger organization," says Skip Carpenter, an analyst with Donaldson, Lufkin & Jenrette.

Forget Cola Wars

47   PepsiCo did have positive news in 1998, even if the earnings weren't sparkling. The company repurchased nearly 60 million shares, and it could use proceeds from the spin-off of its bottling operations to buy back more, analysts say. Soft-drink sales volume grew 10% in North America in the fourth quarter, thanks to sales of Pepsi One, Mountain Dew, and the bottled water Aquafina. Its 1998 soft-drink volume gain of 6% was the company's largest in four years, points out Goldman. Pepsi-Cola also gained market share against rival Coca-Cola. Coke now claims 37.1% of the soft-drink market vs. Pepsi's 31.7%, meaning that Coke's lead of 5.8 percentage points a year ago has narrowed to a 5.4-point spread.

48   As much as investors love to compare Coke and Pepsi, the cola wars aren't that important to the overall investment scenario, says Carpenter. Although Pepsi's sales of beverages and snacks were roughly equal last year, Frito-Lay generates nearly 70% of the company's operating profits. "Global snack food is what will ultimately carry, drive, and continue growth for the company for the long term," he adds. Frito-Lay already dominates the market in salty snacks, with a 55% share, according to Merrill Lynch. But even Carpenter concedes that unless PepsiCo's new products and new focus translate soon into strong earnings growth, he may have to temper his positive outlook.

CASE 3

BusinessWeek

ZAP! HOW THE YEAR 2000 BUG WILL HURT THE ECONOMY

1 No one can accuse Genzyme Corp., the biotech giant based in Cambridge, Mass., of being a technological laggard. Its scientists work at the forefront of biological research, while computer-controlled production equipment churns out hundreds of different advanced compounds.

2 So imagine the reaction of Robert Cowie, Genzyme's chief information officer, when he realized in 1996 that nearly every major system at Genzyme would be unable to cope with dates in the next century—the so-called Year 2000, or Y2K, computer bug. If left unfixed, the production equipment, the research and development computers used to analyze DNA, and the computers handling order-taking and billing would all fail on or before Jan. 1, 2000. Thanks to an early start, Cowie expects to have all his systems repaired well ahead of the deadline. Other businesses won't be so fortunate, he believes. "People will have to be complete by the end of this year, or it will be too late," says Cowie. "But there are still many companies that haven't done anything yet."

3 If Cowie is right about the overall lack of preparedness for Year 2000—and there's growing evidence that he is—a lot of businesses are in for a nasty shock. Up to now, skeptics have been able to pooh-pooh Year 2000 as a relatively easy-to-fix bug, an example of overheated hype by consultants looking for a quick buck. But there's growing alarm in Washington and elsewhere. The Securities & Exchange Commission has recently been strongly urging companies to start reporting the effect of Year 2000 on their earnings. "Many people think it is vastly exaggerated," says Percy Barnevik, chairman of Swiss-Swedish industrial giant ABB Asea Brown Boveri Ltd., one of the world's largest companies. "But it is a really big challenge."

ARMIES OF PROGRAMMERS

4 Indeed, the Y2K bug is shaping up to have a profoundly negative impact on the U.S. economy—starting almost immediately. According to a new analysis prepared for BUSINESS WEEK by Standard & Poor's DRI, the growth rate in 1999 will be 0.3 percentage points lower as companies divert resources to fix the problem. Then Y2K could cut half a percentage point off growth in 2000 and early 2001. That would be the same size as the expected economic damage from the turmoil in East Asia.

5 All told, the Year 2000 bug could cost the U.S. about $119 billion in lost economic output between now and 2001. "The Year 2000 bug will certainly hurt the economy," says DRI chief economist David A. Wyss, "and it could be a real killer if more of the problems are not fixed."

6 It's not only the growth rate that will be affected. Starting in 1999, inflation will be higher than it otherwise would have been and productivity growth will be lower. The reason: Instead of creating or installing new productivity-enhancing programs, every company that uses computers is diverting money and skilled workers into patching old programs.

7 Think of it as a town threatened by a rising river. Every able-bodied person—no matter what their job—is put to work stacking sandbags, while economic activity in the rest of the town slows down. In the case of the Y2K bug, experienced programmers and computer-science PhDs are doing what is essentially unproductive labor.

8 And the amount of skilled labor needed is enormous. Finding, fixing, and testing all Y2K-affected software would require over 700,000 person-years, calculates Capers Jones, head of Software Productivity Research, a firm that tracks programmer productivity. "People are spending huge sums of

Source: Michael J. Mandel, with Peter Coy in New York, Paul C. Judge in Boston and bureau reports, "Zap! How the Year 2000 Bug Will Hurt the Economy," *Business Week:* March 2, 1998.

money fixing problems that are 35 or 40 years old, just to stay in business," says John Bace, research director at Gartner Group Inc.

9   Indeed, the demand for Year 2000 fixes helps explain why management consulting and accounting firms have added a stunning 200,000 new workers over the past two years. Moreover, with programmers' wages soaring because of the overpowering need to fix the problem, Year 2000 has the potential to push up inflation.

10   Then, at the beginning of 2000, the economy is almost certain to be hit by some computer failures, since it's becoming clear that many companies have gotten a late start attacking their Y2K problems. The BUSINESS WEEK/DRI estimate assumes that 85% of software programs will be fixed or replaced, which may be optimistic: A December, 1997, survey by Howard Rubin, a computer-science professor at Hunter College in New York, indicated that two out of three large companies did not yet have detailed plans in place to address Year 2000. Small companies and government agencies are even further behind.

11   Year 2000 is going to pose a serious policy dilemma for the Federal Reserve, which has been trying to steer a tricky course. Over the next couple of years, Fed Chairman Alan Greenspan is going to be under increasing pressure to raise interest rates as labor shortages for information-technology workers send wages skyrocketing. The problem: A rate hike in 1999 would run the risk of worsening the post-2000 slowdown.

12   Some analysts even worry that Y2K could send the economy into a recession. Edward E. Yardeni, chief economist at investment bank Deutsche Morgan Grenfell Inc., sees a 40% chance of a sharp downturn. One way that could happen is if there's a major failure in the government's computer systems. Each week, the federal government sends out $32 billion in Social Security and payroll checks and payments for such mundane items as rent. Even a short delay could be a major shock to the economy.

13   Unfortunately, when the Office of Management & Budget issues the next official report on the government's Y2K readiness on Mar. 15, the news is not likely to be good. On Feb. 6, the Defense Dept.'s Inspector General issued a report saying that the military has no assurance that it is purchasing Year 2000-compliant products, "which may seriously hamper the ability of DOD to perform its administrative and warfighting mission requirements." The Internal Revenue Service is struggling to meet the deadline, as is the Health Care Financing Administration (HCFA), which handles the enormous flow of Medicare and Medicaid funds. In the worst case, the tax system and the Medicare payment system will experience severe disruptions in 2000, halting the delivery of refund and reimbursement checks. "What is going to happen is the government is going to say, 'It's O.K., trust us,'" says Richard M. Kovacevich, CEO of Minneapolis-based Norwest Corp. "It could get scary."

NOT LOSING SLEEP

14   To be sure, there are some, especially in Silicon Valley, who aren't concerned. "Frankly, I don't lose any sleep on worrying about being Year 2000-ready," says Eric Benhamou, CEO of 3Com Corp., the large network-equipment maker. Adds Tony Hampel, group manager for Year 2000 Marketing at Sun Microsystems Inc.: "Year 2000 is an annoyance, a speed bump. We're overassessing the end-of-the-world aspect of the Year 2000 problem."

15   Perhaps. But other knowledgeable people are more worried about the widespread economic impact of the Y2K bug, including the Federal Reserve. "The failure to get it right will affect the integrity of the payment system, financial markets, and the performance of the domestic and the global economies," said William McDonough, president of the Federal Reserve Bank of New York, in a recent speech.

16   How can a single computer bug turn out to be so potentially hazardous to the economy? In theory, any single instance of the 2000 bug is relatively easy to repair. But the sheer number and complexity of computer programs that use dates turn the process of fixing the programs—also known as "remediation"—into a herculean task.

17   Consider a household analogy. If you have to change one lightbulb or one electric switch in your house, there's no problem. But if you have to replace the lightbulbs and electric switches in

everything you own, including your refrigerator, your car dashboard, and your furnace, it becomes a very time-consuming and expensive process.

18   Indeed, what makes Year 2000 particularly vexing is that it affects both stand-alone computers and the embedded processors built into all sorts of modern equipment, from automated factory equipment to power plants to cars to cellular telephones. Last fall, Phillips Petroleum Co. engineers ran Year 2000 tests on an oil-and-gas production platform in the North Sea. The result: In a simulation, an essential safety system for detecting harmful gases such as hydrogen sulfide got confused and shut down. In real life, that would have rendered the platform unusable. Similar problems can occur in almost any sort of modern manufacturing that involves sensors and "smart" machinery. "There will be facilities where they go in and turn on the machines and they won't go on," says Dean Kothmann, head of the technology division at engineering firm Black & Veatch, the world's largest provider of power plants.

19   In particular, electric utilities are only now becoming aware that programmable controllers—which have replaced mechanical relays in virtually all electricity-generating plants and control rooms—may behave badly or even freeze up when 2000 arrives. Many utilities are just getting a handle on the problem. "It's probably six months too soon for anyone to try to guess the complete extent of the problem," says Charlie Siebenthal, manager of the Year 2000 program at the Electric Power Research Institute, the industry group that serves as an information clearinghouse. "We don't know if electricity flow will be affected," he said.

20   Nuclear power plants, of course, pose an especially worrisome problem. While their basic safety systems should continue to work, other important systems could malfunction because of the 2000 bug. In one Year 2000 test, notes Jared S. Wermiel, who is leading the millennium bug effort at the Nuclear Regulatory Commission, the security computer at a nuclear power plant failed by opening vital areas that are normally locked. For that reason, the NRC is in the process of issuing a letter requesting confirmation from utilities that their plants will operate safely come Jan. 1, 2000. Given the complexity and the need to test, "it wouldn't surprise me if certain plants find that they are not Year 2000-ready and have to shut down," says Wermeil.

21   By contrast, the securities industry, big banks, and the Federal Reserve have been taking Year 2000 seriously for years. Chase Manhattan Corp. is spending $250 million on the problem, while Wells Fargo & Co. will ultimately deploy 400 people to fix Y2K. Later this year and next year, Wall Street firms will run an industrywide test simulating the rollover to Jan. 1, 2000.

22   But smaller banks are lagging way behind. According to an extensive new survey from accounting firm Grant Thornton, community banks are only spending an average of $7,000 each on the bug. "They are not taking it seriously enough," says Diane Casey, national director of Thornton's financial-services practice. Only 44% have tested their vaults and other time-sensitive security systems for Year 2000, raising the possibility that they will either be locked out or that doors and vaults will spring open on New Year's Day, 2000.

PREOCCUPIED IN ASIA

23   These smaller banks, which typically outsource check processing and other computer-dependent operations to outside service providers, are assuming that those companies will handle the problem. But bank-service providers themselves are faced with the tough prospect of fixing their own systems. If outside vendors don't get the problem corrected, "banks are then in a real bind," says Mark L. O'Dell, director of the bank-technology division at the Office of the Comptroller of the Currency.

24   Another danger to the U.S. financial system comes from abroad. European and Asian banks are far behind their U.S. counterparts. In Europe, banks are focusing on the enormous task of converting their financial programs to handle the euro, rather than fixing Y2K. "Western Europe will not achieve Year 2000 compliance for even 65% of the applications that need Year 2000 repair," says software expert Jones.

25   And the situation in Asia may be even worse, since banks in those countries are more preoccupied with surviving the current economic threat than worrying about Year 2000. "Y2K could trigger a whole new round of country debt negotiations," warned Philip Kozloff, a member of Citibank's

EXHIBIT A

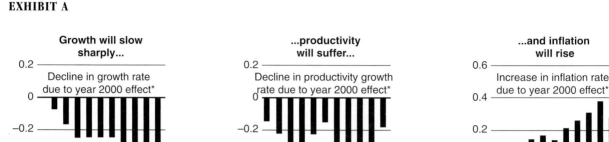

* All changes measured over previous four quarters

Credit Policy Committee, speaking at a Securities Industry Assn. conference in January. Adds Yardeni: "If foreign banks fail to comply, that could have a serious impact on world trade."

26   Closer to home, state and local governments are lagging even further behind the federal government. In Massachusetts, for example, according to a report released on Feb. 3, more than 40% of state agencies had not yet even begun an effort to become Year 2000-compliant. "It is likely that certain systems will not attain Year 2000 compliance in time and that alternative processing methods will be needed," wrote State Auditor A. Joseph DeNucci, whose office prepared the report.

27   Massachusetts isn't alone. Only about one-third of states are in decent shape, estimates Larry Olson, chief information officer of Pennsylvania, which got an early start on fixing Year 2000 problems. "Everybody else will have significant problems." What's more, the problems reach down to local levels, including school systems, which must run payroll systems, track student records, and operate other date-sensitive systems. The fixes could be quite expensive: The Columbus (Ohio) school system, with 65,000 students, may have to pay $8 million to fix its most significant applications.

"NO SILVER-BULLET SOLUTION"

28   Is there any chance of avoiding major economic upheaval from Y2K? Yes, but it will take a huge effort. Smaller companies and organizations still have time to fix their typically less complicated computers and software. And utilities and manufacturers with embedded chip problems can fix them—if they start right now. "It's not something they can study for a year," says Kothmann.

29   But a large company or organization that has not yet started dealing with Year 2000 is in big trouble. While software tools do exist for identifying trouble spots and speeding fixes, they only solve part of the problem. "There is no silver-bullet solution," says Jean- Charles Andre, director of Year 2000 Services for IBM Global Services.

30   In particular, no software tool can eliminate the need for testing Year 2000 fixes once they are made—and testing a complicated software program is so time-consuming that it may prove to be one of the biggest barriers to finishing on time. A large company that has not started making fixes will have great difficulty completing tests before the deadline, according to Jones. The same is true for governments: "If you're not well on your way now, you just don't have time to do everything," says Olson.

31   Companies and other organizations may also have trouble finding the trained workers they need to fix their Year 2000 woes. A just-released study from the Information Technology Association of America shows that the U.S. already has 350,000 job vacancies for computer scientists and programmers that are not getting filled. "The big issue for corporations is going to be around resources,"

TABLE 1
Where the Bug Will Bite

ELECTRIC POWER

Many electric utilities realized only last year that their generating plants were susceptible to Y2K problems. Scattered power outages are likely, and some nuclear power plants may be shut down temporarily.

GOVERNMENT

Major problems exist at the Internal Revenue Service and many other agencies. Most state and local governments are way behind fixing date-sensitive programs needed for tax collection, payrolls, and welfare payments.

BANKING AND FINANCIAL SERVICES

Most large banks, the Federal Reserve, and the exchanges should be well prepared. But foreign banks and small U.S. banks are lagging. The result: Disruptions in the financial system.

MANUFACTURING

Most large companies are on top of the problem, but they are vulnerable to problems at smaller suppliers. Industries such as pharmaceuticals and petroleum refining depend on timing-sensitive computer programs.

TOTAL LOSS OF OUTPUT

1998–2001

says Cowie. "If you need to change your systems, and you have to get programmers in to do that, it will be very hard."

32   To be sure, farsighted companies have up to now solved their Y2K problems by simply installing new software and hardware. But such major productivity-enhancing projects take even longer than fixing old software. "Until now, many people have been ripping things out, installing new software," says William T. Ruckle, managing director of Ernst & Young's Year 2000 business. "It's getting too late to do that." Adds ABBs Barnevik: "Some of the biggest problems will come when people have planned to substitute new systems for old ones. If there are problems, it will be too late to rebuild the old system."

33   What happens next, aside from everyone working very hard to fix the problem? Some organizations that have their Year 2000 bug under control are getting ready to turn it into a competitive advantage. "Solving this problem gives us a marketing tool that we plan on using," says Pennsylvania Governor Tom Ridge.

34   Most managers, though, are going to have to start thinking about contingency plans and workarounds. "There's no question that things will fail," says Judith List, who runs the Year 2000 effort for Bellcore, which develops communications software. "What Bellcore recommends is that you focus on the mission-critical systems first."

35   Year 2000 is a unique and unprecedented economic event. Previous jolts to the economy, like the gulf war and the oil price shocks of the 1970s, were surprises. But Year 2000 is the first economic disaster to arrive on a schedule. The great danger is that the U.S. economy will not be ready to welcome the millennium.

CASE 4

BusinessWeek

WHAT EVERY CEO NEEDS TO KNOW ABOUT ELECTRONIC BUSINESS: A SURVIVAL GUIDE

From: Paul Revere, director of business development
To: J. R. Biggenslow, chief executive officer
Organization: Mid-America Paper Corp.

Date: Mar. 29, 1999
Subject: E-business—NOW!
Priority: URGENT

Jack,

1. You don't know me very well, so I will warn you up front: This memo may come as a shock. After all, I joined Mid-America Paper just a few months ago, and I'm way down on the org chart. But it's my job to scout out new market opportunities—and I've found the only one that matters. This is a call to arms-straight, no chaser, no PowerPoint slides.

2. We have to get off our butts and get wired. Not just E-mail. Not just Web browsers or a Web site. I mean the big kahuna: electronic commerce. Our future depends on nothing less than transforming our company into a full-fledged E-business. Now.
    Or else we're roadkill.

3. Oh, I know you're thinking: Who is this clown? Sales are up 10% in the latest quarter, to $1.2 billion for 1998, and profits have rebounded since the pulp shortage of 1996. And yes, I know we already have a Web site. But—not to put too fine a point on it—it stinks. Yes, it's got reams of information and pretty pictures of our products—well, actually, they're pretty ugly on the screen. And although it took me five mouse clicks, I finally found an 800 number to order a catalog.

4. So what's missing? The money, Jack—THE MONEY! You can't buy anything on the whole damned site. There aren't even links to the Web sites of Office Depot and Staples, our biggest customers. For Pete's sake, even the Netherlands' association of wooden-shoe makers just opened a global electronic-commerce site (www.woodenshoes.nl). Jack, E-commerce is where it's at. And with the exception of some creaky old Electronic Data Interchange links with pulp suppliers, it's where we're not.

5. Now, I won't deny that our industry is unique. We sell paper office supplies and corrugated boxes to corporations and retail stores—not books and CDs to Web surfers. And we sure can't ship them three tons of colored stock in a FedEx package. But lots of traditional companies have discovered there are all kinds of ways to do business on the Net.

6. Check out these numbers: E-commerce between businesses is five times as much as consumer E-commerce, or about $43 billion last year. And by 2003, Forrester Research Inc. figures it will balloon to $1.3 trillion. That's 10 times consumer E-commerce, constituting 9% of all U.S. business trade—and more than the gross domestic product of either Britain or Italy. Around 2006 or so, it might reach up to 40% of all U.S. business. Wow!

7. Problem is, our rivals are a lot closer to grabbing that business than we are—because most of them are already selling online. And as you know from our slumping stock price, our investors see this all too well. With every price drop, we have fewer resources to invest in online ventures. The premium for Net savviness is huge: Amazon.com had $610 million in sales last year—about half of ours. Amazon's market value, however, is almost $20 billion—more than 20 times ours. What's wrong with this picture, Jack?

8. I'll tell you: It's not just a few crazy day traders having fun with their new E*Trade accounts. The Internet is nothing less than a revolution in commerce. Think railroads. Automobiles. Computers. Each of them kicked off an explosion of new markets and new businesses. Today, these businesses

account for most of the largest companies in the world—after giving a lot of companies that didn't get it an up-close-and personal reading of Chapters 7 and 11.

9   Don't you hate it? These Yahooligans and Amazonians sport earrings, tap away on Palm computers, and sip lattes while pushing their net worths higher than most undeveloped nations' gross domestic product. These are captains of industry? Get used to it. It won't matter if nine out of 10 of them disappear into the depths of cyberspace. Just one of them can steal our customers while we're twiddling our thumbs.

10   And that could happen faster than you can say "dot com." On the Net, more than anywhere in the physical world, the first mover grabs the lion's share. Moreover, the Net is quickly breaking down industry boundaries, creating new competitors that spread like flu viruses. Media companies once dismissed Yahoo! as a silly search engine. Intuit wasn't on banks' radar screens until it had already morphed from a software to an online financial-services company.

11   Yes, the Net has changed the rules. For good. If we're to thrive, or even survive, we must live, eat, and breathe the Net. Starting yesterday. How? Forgive my audacity, but I've come up with a survival guide, a list of our top 10 must-do action items. I'm also attaching a magazine article on each point.

1. REENGINEERING YOUR COMPANY

12   Get ready for another round of reengineering. Brace yourself—this one's on steroids. The Internet lets us communicate instantly with every supplier, partner, and customer—and, in many cases, lets them communicate with each other. This supply chain we've built up so carefully? Boom! Eventually, it will explode into a supply web: Trucking companies will tap directly into our ordering system for earlier visibility on shipping schedules. Retailers and corporations will monitor our inventory database instead of placing orders through sales. Uh-oh, what's that mean for all those shipping dock workers and all our salespeople? Big, big changes ahead, Jack.

13   Ultimately, the Net promises to change our whole manufacturing process. Dell Computer, for instance, lets customers configure their own PC online and track assembly and shipping status. The result: happy customers. Even with a recent slowdown, sales for the build-to-order pioneer, are still growing 38% a year, more than double the industry's 15% average. And lest you think this is just a silicon sensation, get this: Ford Motor and Weyerhaeuser are at the head of the pack.

2. THROW OUT THE OLD BUSINESS MODEL

14   Ask yourself a very basic question: Just who are we in the Internet Age? As we face more global competition online and have to cut our prices, we need to reexamine our business model. Maybe we should take a cue from MicroAge Inc., the PC distributor. Realizing the Net would make it easier for resellers to bypass distributors, it started transforming itself in 1995 into a service company, helping corporations with installation and training. Get this—now it even offers data on rival distributors' inventory in case MicroAge's fulfillment arm is out of stock on something—a way to earn customers' loyalty. Nothing's too strange to consider: The online superstore Buy.com, for instance, undersells rivals, sometimes at or below cost, hoping to make profits off advertising. It hit $125 million in sales its first full year in 1998—more than any company in history.

3. THE BUYER ALWAYS WINS

15   Understand that the buyer runs the show on the Net. Up to now, buyers faced big obstacles to getting the best prices and service—limited time and data to compare vendors' products and the cost of dealing with far-flung suppliers. No more. The anytime-anywhere Net knocks down those barriers. It's spawning middlemen galore to give buyers more information. One of these guys will give you nightmares. PaperExchange.com is acting like a NASDAQ for paper products—and you know what that

means: lower prices and a tougher time building our brand. We can't just ignore them, either—market researcher Keenan Vision Inc. figures these exchanges will handle 29% of all Internet commerce by 2002. We'd better be there.

4. HOLD YOUR CUSTOMER'S HAND

16   Roll out the red carpet—or whatever the cyber-quivalent is. Have you bought a book at Amazon.com? Try it—they've reinvented customer service. Don't be surprised if our rivals start copying Amazon's methods. The first couple of times I ordered, they automatically upgraded me to free priority shipping—nice touch. And they use some nifty software from Net Perceptions that analyzes my purchases and suggests other books I'll probably like. They're often dead-on. That kind of software would help us sell more to our customers at little extra cost and treat them as individuals. There's also a raft of new programs from startups such as Kana Communications that automate E-mail service and promotions. Bottom line: We wouldn't have to hire a bunch of people to support the online site.

5. GO AHEAD, FARM OUT THOSE JOBS

17   Cancel that vacation—we've got to move fast! None of our usual round of studies and meetings. And we have no time to do everything ourselves—nor any need to. The instant communications power of the Net shatters the physical-world need to do product development, manufacturing, distribution, marketing, and customer management all in-house. Now, there are lots of specialists that can do everything from hosting our Web site to running our warehouses. Look at personal-computer maker Monorail. Using intimate communications links, it has been able to outsource manufacturing and assembly, financing, and shipping to other companies. The result: The company can offer among the lowest-priced PCs—and increase sales with almost no constraints.

6. NO WEB SITE IS AN ISLAND

18   We should not treat cyberspace as a separate universe. Look at Charles Schwab. By leveraging its brand name online and using its offices as a place to introduce clients to Web access, it has managed to stay far ahead of upstarts like E*Trade Group. Likewise, Day-Timers recently launched a free Web calendar to compete with a raft of online upstarts while also promoting its traditional paper and software schedulers. As we go online, our brand name and purchasing power can work to our advantage.

7. CREATE AN ONLINE SENSE OF COMMUNITY

19   Think global. People all over the world are congregating into virtual communities on the Web, and we want to be part of that. My wife just joined a site called FortuneCity.com—which was founded in London. She can chat online about our little girl's teething problems with other moms around the world. Maybe that's not our customers' thing, but as these communities embrace E-biz, we need to help our retailers plug into them—perhaps by offering them bundles of services such as chat and free E-mail.

8. FOLLOW THE MONEY

20   Now that the Silicon Valley venture capitalists are scouring the country for new industries to wire up, we need to keep our eyes on what startups are getting funded in the online world. This upstart,

PaperExchange.com, came out of nowhere. Had we subscribed to one of the services that track venture-capital investments, we would have seen that coming long ago.

9. A WEB OF NERDS? DON'T BELIEVE IT

21   We need to persuade everyone at Mid-America Paper that the Web is not Nerdville anymore. It's becoming part of everyday life. By 2003, International Data estimates 510 million people will be online worldwide. (By the way, why on earth do only half our employees have browser access? No wonder we're behind. Some 159 million people worldwide are now online!)

10. LOG ON, BOSS

22   Get wired—or we'll get whacked. And Jack, I'm talking to you. Sorry if this seems harsh, but you've got to get closer to the Net than reading the E-mail your secretary prints out. You're not alone—only 25% of CEOs in a recent PricewaterhouseCoopers survey regularly log on to the Net. But you've got to get your fingers on that keyboard every day. Surf the Web. Talk to the nerds in the systems department. You'll see what I mean. This is something you can't delegate.

23   Jack, I know this must feel like a slap in the face. Please understand I would never suggest such radical change unless the costs of not changing were so high. Maybe you'll decide I'm an uppity jerk and reengineer me to the parking lot. But if we don't get E-bized, we'll soon be pulp—and I'll be out of a job anyway.

SURVIVAL GUIDE 1: FROM REENGINEERING TO E-ENGINEERING[1]

24   Men and women who have spiced up their sex lives with Viagra can thank the Web for its quick arrival on the market. Here's why: Pfizer Inc. now dashes off electronic versions of its drug applications to Washington for Food & Drug Administration approval. In the old days, it had to truck tons of paper to regulators and thumb through copies of all those pages manually whenever the feds had a question. By managing documents on the Web, Pfizer sliced the old one-year approval timetable nearly in half and sped Viagra into the world's boudoirs.

25   Post-Viagra, Pfizer's drugs will move through the pipeline even faster. The company's wired researchers now use the Web to mine libraries of technical data and collaborate on new drug development. "We've reengineered our business—digitally," says Vice-President for Research James Milson.

26   Reengineering. It was all the rage in the mid-'90s. But the vast and speedy Internet is ushering in an even bigger wave of business transformation. Call it E-engineering. Companies realize it's not enough to put up simple Web sites for customers, employees, and partners. To take full advantage of the Net, they've got to reinvent the way they do business—changing how they distribute goods, collaborate inside the company, and deal with suppliers.

27   This isn't just about saving time and money. The Web gets creative juices flowing, too. Employees who formerly spent their days faxing and phoning basic information to customers and suppliers are freed by the Net's magic to do more valuable work.

New Believers

28   Technology companies like Intel, Dell, and Cisco Systems were among the first to seize on the Net to overhaul their operations. At Intel Corp., for example, Web-based automation has liberated 200

---

[1]From Steve Hamm and Marcia Stepanek, "From Reengineering to E-Engineering," *Business Week e.biz:* March 22, 1999.

salesclerks from tediously entering orders. Now, they concentrate instead on analyzing sales trends and pampering customers. Cisco Systems Inc., for its part, handles 75% of sales online. And 45% of its online orders for networking gear never touch employees' hands. They go directly from customers to the company's software system and on to manufacturing partners. That helped Cisco hike productivity by 20% over the past two years. But what grabs attention is sales: The troika is doing a booming $70 million in online business each day.

29   With numbers like that, it's no wonder the tech jocks are being joined by a second wave of believers, ranging from Rust Belt manufacturing giants like Ford Motor Co. to foreign companies like Mexican cement seller Cemex. Even Corporate America's walking wounded are joining in. Just last month, troubled silicone supplier Dow Corning Corp. appointed an E-commerce czar. "Every businessperson I call on today is filled with greed or fear when it comes to the Internet," says James L. Barksdale, CEO of Netscape Communications Corp. "They're asking, `How do I do it to them before they do it to me?' "

30   Doing it is no simple matter. Reengineering projects can be hugely complicated, with technology, business, and organizational upheavals all rocking the corporate foundations at once. There are harrowing risks. Casualties will include some companies that were too bold—but even more that were too timid.

31   Ford plans to be neither. It's taking on the E-engineering challenge holistically. One executive, Bernard Mathaisel, is both chief information officer and leader of its reengineering efforts. His plan is to fundamentally retool the way Ford operates with the help of the Web, cementing lifelong relationships with customers and slashing costs. "We're bringing new practices into every aspect of the company," says Mathaisel.

32   Already, E-business has begun to spread through the organization from front to back. Rather than relying on dealers to handle all customer contacts, Ford has put up a Web site that lets tire-kickers pick and price cars—then refers them to dealers. Ford then routes the customer feedback from the Web site to its marketers and designers to help them plan new products.

33   In the design process, the Web brings 4,500 Ford engineers from labs in the U.S., Germany, and England together in cyberspace to collaborate on projects. The idea is to break down the barriers between regional operations so basic auto components are designed once and used everywhere. When design plans conflict, the software automatically sends out E-mail alerts. Next, Ford's going to roll out a system for ordering parts from suppliers. When all of these pieces are in place, the company hopes to transform the way it produces cars—building them to order rather than to forecasts.

34   Other companies need to get wired to defend themselves. In the PC industry, the threat comes from Dell Computer Corp., which has deftly translated its hugely successful direct sales model to the Internet. Other PC companies have to match Dell's efficiencies—or die. Enter Ingram Micro Inc., the PC industry's largest distributor, which has teamed up with Solectron Corp., a giant contract manufacturer of high-tech gear.

Team Effort

35   In April, they plan to launch a brand-new way to build custom-made PCs inexpensively for companies like Hewlett-Packard Co. and Compaq Computer Corp. Instead of the PC companies handling orders and manufacturing, Ingram and Solectron will do it for them using a Web-based system that will hasten communications and slash assembly times. The PC companies are still in the driver's seat. They continue to build the value of their brands, designing and marketing their products and handling quality assurance. But now it's a team effort. "Customers are doing business with a virtual company," says Ingram President Jeffrey R. Rodek.

36   Figuring out what you do best is a crucial piece of Web reengineering. Few companies have pursued that philosophy as aggressively as Provident American Corp. in Norristown, Pa. In December, it took a radical step. It sold off nearly all of its life-insurance business and reinvented itself as HealthAxis.com, an online service that sells insurance products from other companies. CEO Michael Ashker decided the company was best at selling simple, high-volume insurance policies to consumers and taking a commission—rather than managing risk and independent agents.

The Internet Supply Chain

These days, most PCs for business customers are made by PC companies based on sales forecasts and shipped through distributors. The PC company, distributors, and the resellers who deal with customers all keep inventories and often have to reconfigure computers to a customer's specifications. Ingram Micro, a distributor and assembler, and Solectron, a contract manufacturer, have come up with a system that will build computers to order and cut costs substantially. The amount of time a PC sits in inventory is expected to be reduced from months to hours.

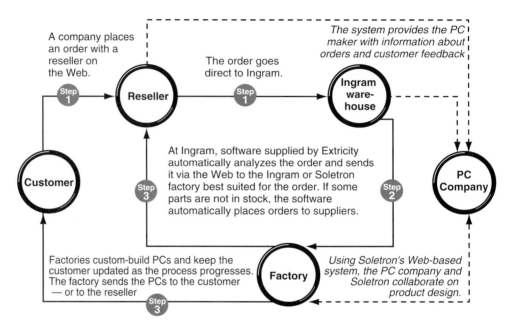

Source: Solectron Corp., Ingram Micro Inc., and Extricity Inc.

37   There are some real shockers in this process. Like: Not all your customers are equal, or worthy. Weyerhaeuser Co. Inc., the forest-products company uses the Web to help it mine information from its suppliers, price products, and measure demand. More down-to-the-minute knowledge paid off: The plant boosted production by 60% to 800,000 doors last year. Weyerhaeuser can also offer more accurate bids to builders. In some cases, it can charge $40 less for certain doors—and still make a profit. That spells entré into some new markets. What's more, it now knows which customers bring in the big revenues and which don't. It can shed the ones that eat up too much time and order little.

38   That's painful for some customers. But E-engineering, badly executed, is even tougher on organizations. Just ask the engineers at NASA's Ames Research Center in Moffett Field, Calif. They spent $100 million building a Web-based collaborative engineering system to help accelerate development of the space station. Turned out they didn't have the technology plumbing in place to handle the job and lost some valuable data. Among the missing information: the plans for the Saturn V rocket.

39   Technology isn't always the hangup. In some cases, it's a stodgy corporate culture. "For many older executives, converting to E-business is like changing their religion," says John Thorp, vice-president of DMR Consulting Group Inc. And sometimes resistance comes from a pencil pusher down in purchasing. At Canadian Imperial Bank of Commerce in Toronto, purchasing agents missed the point of a new Web-based system for ordering supplies. They tried squeezing suppliers for price cuts when in fact the point was for everyone to buy from an electronic catalog—to land volume discounts. The bank set them straight with tailored incentive bonuses.

40   Perhaps the greatest danger is that business units will act independently, and the results will be piecemeal. The last thing you want is "tack-on" technology. To work, this effort must be coordinated at a high level—and changes should be fundamental, says analyst Bobby Cameron of Forrester Research Inc.

Change Fatigue

41   Citigroup gets it. As an executive vice-president in charge of advanced technologies, Edward D. Horowitz defines his job this way: to get the company's top 200 executives marching to the same drumbeat when it comes to the Internet. Horowitz's first salvo was to send them all copies of Clayton M. Christensen's best-selling book *The Innovator's Dilemma: When New Technologies Cause Great Firms to Fail,* about managing the dislocating effects of technology. Then he gave them a homework assignment: start banking online. At the time, only a handful were doing it. "The message was you've got to use the product you're selling," says Horowitz.

42   That's a lot to ask of busy executives who are scrambling to complete the $80 billion merger of Citicorp and Travelers Group. But these days, change is relentless. Many corporate executives are just now finishing up major retooling of their financial and manufacturing processes. Plus, there's the Y2K problem. After a while, change fatigue sets in. "Companies are exhausted," says Michael Hammer, author of the 1993 book *Reengineering the Corporation: A Manifesto for Business Revolution.* His advice: "Suck it up. You have to face it again." In the era of E-engineering, risking burnout is better than getting fried.

SURVIVAL GUIDE 2: THROW OUT YOUR OLD BUSINESS MODEL[2]

43   In February, a cool Web startup called AllApartments changed its name. While it was at it, the company rehauled its business model. What started out two years ago as a simple online listing of apartment rentals available in the U.S. suddenly was something far more provocative. The new business, called SpringStreet, still sells ads on its site, where it lists some 7 million apartments. But now the startup wants to make money in completely new, weird, and unexpected ways.

44   These days, the San Francisco-based company throws in quotes and deals on furniture, moving-truck rentals, and loan possibilities—all for free and often at a discount. SpringStreet makes money by collecting transaction and commission fees from about 35 partners, including Visa and Ryder Moving Services. Every time a consumer requests a car insurance quote or applies for a loan, SpringStreet gets a fee that starts at $4. "We want to provide people with free services and save them money," says Sophia Kabler, SpringStreet's vice-president for marketing. "The good part is, we make money off of all that." And how. SpringStreet expects the new fees to account for nearly 50% of revenues this year.

45   Like SpringStreet, online businesses old and new are re-creating themselves, jolting their rivals, and sending their investors scurrying for their calculators. Let's face it, a lot of the ideas will be duds. But amid the dozens of wacky proposals, propositions, business makeovers, and other E-business madness, ideas are taking shape that will define commerce for decades to come.

Radical

46   Today there are a bewildering number of signposts, each pointing to a different business model or revenue opportunity: ads, subscriptions, transaction fees, direct sales to consumers or businesses, and commissions for matching buyers to sellers. To make the most of any of these, you must pinpoint your core strength, then turn on the creative juices to come up with new revenue streams. Take San Francisco-based Web-design shop Organic Online Inc. Increasingly, it is paid in stock and transaction fees from the E-commerce sites it helps set up, including electronics merchant E/Town. This year, Organic expects 25% to 35% of its revenue to come from such deals. That way, Organic sticks to its knitting while cashing in on its clients' success.

47   The Net provides just such opportunities for companies to rejigger their business models. Last fall, CNET Inc. began to use its four-year-old tech news and reviews sites to make money in a slew

---

[2]From Heather Green, with Linda Himelstein, "Throw Out Your Old Business Model," *Business Week e.biz:* March 22, 1999.

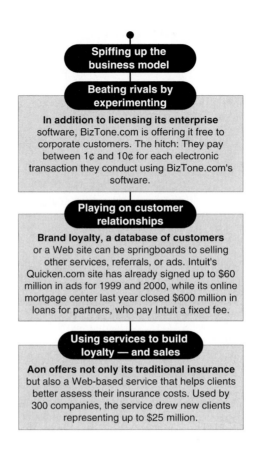

Spiffing up the business model

Beating rivals by experimenting

In addition to licensing its enterprise software, BizTone.com is offering it free to corporate customers. The hitch: They pay between 1¢ and 10¢ for each electronic transaction they conduct using BizTone.com's software.

Playing on customer relationships

Brand loyalty, a database of customers or a Web site can be springboards to selling other services, referrals, or ads. Intuit's Quicken.com site has already signed up to $60 million in ads for 1999 and 2000, while its online mortgage center last year closed $600 million in loans for partners, who pay Intuit a fixed fee.

Using services to build loyalty — and sales

Aon offers not only its traditional insurance but also a Web-based service that helps clients better assess their insurance costs. Used by 300 companies, the service drew new clients representing up to $25 million.

of ways besides ad revenue. Its Computers.com service, for one, provides information on 120,000 products from 86 merchants, charging those vendors a flat fee for each customer it sends them. CNET says it generates 90,000 leads a day, with 8% to 10% of those turning into purchases. CNET drummed up $80 million in purchases for its vendor partners last quarter. Last month it snapped up AuctionGate, an auction site for computer products that lets CNET make money by charging a listing fee.

48   BizTone.com is testing a far more radical approach. While the three-year-old Malaysian company sells its enterprise software the traditional way, through licenses and installment fees, in January it began offering an alternative. Now, corporate customers can pay from 1 cent to 10 cents per electronic transaction a company conducts using BizTone.com's software. "In the new world, no one will have to pay to license the software itself, just to transact," says Miko Matsumura, BizTone.com's vice-president for strategy. He predicts fees from "software as services" will one day account for most of the company's revenues.

49   Figuring out a company's chief strength may be the most wrenching part of dreaming up such novel approaches. Established players, such as Intuit Inc., have gone through high-level soul searching. "We had to think long and hard about what we did best as a company," says Intuit CEO Bill Harris. That led Intuit in the past two years to add alternatives to straight-out licenses of shrink-wrapped software—such as subscription, usage, ad, and transaction fees. Although Intuit doesn't break down revenues, it says the Quicken.com site already has signed up $60 million in ads for this year and next, while the online mortgage center on its Web site last year closed $600 million in loans for partners. Those include First Union Corp. and Chase Manhattan Corp., which pay Intuit fixed fees.

50   By offering new services, companies not only expand sales but also instill customer loyalty. That's what Aon Corp., a Chicago insurance-services company that raked in $6.5 billion in sales last year, is doing. In addition to its traditional business, Aon offers a Web-based service that pulls together a database—of, say, the latest changes in government regulations—that's matched with

information on each of its client's operations. The clients can then access the database to better analyze and manage insurance costs.

51   Some 300 companies use the service, which starts at $10,000 a year, and the number of clients is expected to double by yearend. AonLine has helped bring in new clients representing up to $25 million in business, and it gives the parent company a better understanding of its existing clients. "This is a service that enhances our new business," says Mia Shernoff, AonLine's managing director. "But over time it will be an important part of our revenue."

At a Loss

52   To be sure, some of the new schemes are far from proven. Three-year-old Buy.com, for instance, sells products from computers to books at impossibly low prices to attract an audience. The company raked in $125 million in revenues in its first year of operations in 1998, and it expects to do as much as $100 million in sales this quarter. Still, it remains unprofitable and is betting it can earn most of its net on ads.

53   Crazy or insanely smart? Only time will tell. But one thing is certain, these wild and varying approaches will rewrite the old business rules. Says John Hummer, co-founding partner of Hummer Winblad Venture Partners in San Francisco: "Whether Buy.com is successful is beside the point. They don't have to be successful to have a huge impact on all of business." So toss out that dusty old business plan, think weird, and try the unexpected.

SURVIVAL GUIDE 3: "THE BUYER ALWAYS WINS"[3]

54   Hoping to save a few bucks, United Technologies Corp. decided to try something new last year. Once, it would have spent months haggling individually with dozens of vendors to supply printed circuit boards for various subsidiaries worldwide. Instead, UTC put the contract out on FreeMarkets On-Line Inc., a Web marketplace for industrial goods. Bids from 39 suppliers poured in—and the winners managed to slash a cool $10 million off the initial $24 million estimate. Says Ed Williams, vice-president for supply management at UTC subsidiary Carrier Corp.: "The technology drives to the lowest price in a hurry."

55   E-business deals like that are fast driving home a startling shift in the commercial balance of power: To a greater extent than ever before, the customer is king. In the physical world, buyers face all kinds of obstacles to getting the best deal—far-flung suppliers, limited time to do research, middlemen who keep a tight lid on information. "It's a pain to drive three different places to save a dollar," says Jeffrey P. Bezos, chief executive of online megastore Amazon.com Inc.

No Distance

56   On the Web, shopping's a snap. Buyers can quickly compare information about products and vendors almost anywhere. Suppliers are only a click apart and an E-mail message away, giving buyers unprecedented influence to demand lower prices, better service—even a direct say in product design. Dell Computer Corp., for instance, lets buyers configure their own personal computers and track them through manufacturing and shipping—all online. Says FreeMarkets CEO Glen Meakem: "If you're surviving on schmoozy sales relationships, you're not going to make it in this world."

57   It's a world where the virtual distance between the producers and their ultimate customers has collapsed, sometimes to near zero. All of a sudden, relationships among producers, wholesalers, distributors, and retailers, once virtually sacrosanct, are up for grabs—and along with them, their customers.

[3]From Robert D. Hof, "'The Buyer Always Wins,'" *Business Week e.biz:* March 22, 1999.

58   That's prompting a goodly number of producers to reach customers more directly by making an end run around the traditional channels. Although they won't talk about it publicly, says Gartner Group analyst Beth Enslow, auto makers, consumer-electronics companies, and almost all other large manufacturers are looking for ways to shorten their selling chains—even if by doing so they risk alienating partners. Says Enslow: "If they don't, somebody else in their industry will."

59   Or already is: Dell is growing more than twice as fast as other PC makers, thanks largely to its $14 million a day in Web sales. Any company whose main edge was privileged pricing, product, and other information—travel agents, car dealers, stockbrokers, industrial-parts distributors—risks being cut out of transactions.

60   In many cases, buyers are starting to skip past the old industrial distributor and the neighborhood insurance salesman. Web efficiencies are freeing up money to fund a whole new class of Web-savvy middlemen—from consumer sites such as Amazon.com and Autoweb.com to a trucking spot market called National Transportation Exchange and a seafood exchange called GoFish. They're providing a more direct conduit between producers and the ultimate buyers. And a much cheaper one. Chemdex Inc., an online site where scientists can buy biochemical supplies, takes a 10% cut of transactions from vendors—less than a quarter of most distributors' take—and passes the savings on to buyers.

Infomediary

61   Naturally, not all distributors and merchants are ecstatic about this development. Sellers in some industries worry that listing their products in an online market could bring unbearable pressure, prompting them to erect filters on their sites to repel automated shopping comparison software—or else forcing them to refuse to take part in online markets. GoFish, for instance, netted new buyers for

some seafood companies, but other merchants have been more reticent—perhaps with good reason. Neal Workman, who started GoFish last year as an outgrowth of his credit reports company, Seafax Inc. in Portland, Me., concedes that GoFish may well bring seafood prices down. "The buyer always wins," he shrugs.

62   Unlike many existing middlemen, a growing number of these upstarts claim allegiance to the buyer, instead of to the producers whose wares they offer. That is bound to amplify the power that the Net already gives buyers, says McKinsey & Co. principal John Hagel III, co-author of a new book called *Net Worth* on these new middlemen, whom he calls information intermediaries, or "infomediaries." He estimates that consumer infomediaries can save an average client household the tidy sum of $1,110 a year by searching for the best deals on its behalf. Says Hagel: "The reduction of transaction costs will give more power to the buyer."

63   These dynamics are playing out in business trade as well. IMX Exchange, for example, provides an online marketplace for mortgage brokers to find loans. Instead of having to comb through dozens of daily faxes of lender rate sheets, brokers place requested loans on the exchange, and lenders bid on them. San Jose (Calif.) real estate broker Cecelia Babkirk says IMX saves her up to a half-point on loans and another half-point for the home buyers she serves—adding $60,000 to her annual revenues.

64   These upstart middlemen may be poised to play a commanding role in their industries. Infomediaries aimed at trade between businesses alone will grow from $290 million in revenues last year to about $20 billion by 2002—a quarter of all business trade, predicts Charles H. Finnie, an analyst with investment bank Volpe Brown Whelan & Co. Says Finnie: "Infomediaries have the potential to fundamentally reorder the economy."

65   Over the long haul, these infomediaries will be able to pool enormous buying power over the Net to extract even more from vendors. Early results from individual buyers point to potentially huge savings. General Electric Co., for instance, has reduced prices by 20% on more than $1 billion in purchases of operating materials by pooling various divisions' orders online—something too cumbersome in the physical world—to demand volume discounts.

66   *Caveat emptor* may be the byword of traditional commerce, but E-business has added a new twist: *Caveat venditor.* Let the vendor beware.

SURVIVAL GUIDE 4: YOU'LL WANNA HOLD THEIR HANDS[4]

67   The big myth about E-commerce is that it's about as close to self-service as you can get. At last—or so the theory goes—companies no longer have to sweat customer hand-holding, staff huge call centers, and suffer the dings and slings of customer gripes. But oh, how wrong that is.

        Four years into E-commerce, and the shrewdest Web operators are finding that the velvet-glove-treatment may be more crucial in cyberspace than it has ever been on Main Street.

68   Gone are the days of the geographically captive customer, when merchants had the advantage of being the only store within driving distance. On the Web, the next shop is seconds away. What's more, it's open 24 hours. If cybershoppers can't get products or answers instantly—which happens all too often—they are off in a heartbeat. "Better service is no longer just a nice thing to do. It's mandatory," says Amir Aghdaei, Hewlett-Packard Co.'s call-center manager.

69   From Chase Manhattan Bank to Thomas Cook Travel Group Ltd., companies are waking up to the need for so-called E-service. It takes many forms: schmoozing shoppers over the Web through E-mail and Web chats, or sophisticated software that tracks buyers' habits and supplies instant help. There's even software that will respond automatically to the avalanche of E-mail Web sites are getting. The beauty of it? Done right, E-service can dish up more than just digital warm-and-fuzzies. It can improve the bottom line.

---

[4]From Marcia Stepanek, with Larry Armstrong, "You'll Wanna Hold Their Hands," *Business Week e.biz:* March 22, 1999.

When E-Mail Is E-Normous

Ideally, E. Cameron King would like his service reps to answer all E-mails personally. "For selling mortgages, that's the right thing to do," says King, executive vice-president at Countrywide Home Loans Inc. in Calabasas, Calif. But when interest rates started falling last September, E-mail overwhelmed Countrywide, swelling to more than 2,000 a day, triple the normal rate. Says King: "They all ask the same thing—'What's your 30-year fixed rate?'"

Now there's software to help. Such companies as Mustang Software, eGain Communications, and Kana Communications have sprung up with programs that record, acknowledge, route, queue, and generate reports on E-mail. Others, such as Aptex Software Inc., supply artificial-intelligence tools to understand questions without human intervention, and even get the tone of E-mail—whether angry, sarcastic, or humorous. Those can then generate a response, either sent automatically or as a suggested answer for the service representative.

Many Web businesses don't realize how essential automated help can be until they're barraged by incoming E-mail. And the problem is getting worse. A Jupiter Communications survey earlier this year found that 44% of retail Web sites either didn't respond or didn't even offer an E-mail address. That is up from 28% last fall.

Countrywide chose a system from Brightware Inc. in Novato, Calif. Now, 70% of that E-mail receives an automatic response that asks whether it's a new loan or a refinance, and whether it's a conventional or jumbo loan. "We can prequalify consumers," says King, who estimates that reps now spend only 5% of their precious time on E-mail instead of 35%. Most Web sites need to figure out some way to respond, or run the risk of losing customers.

Red Carpet

70   Whether a company rolls out the red carpet or tries to scrimp with linoleum could be one of the biggest factors in deciding tomorrow's E-business winners and losers. Amazon.com CEO Jeff Bezos says over the Internet, word of mouth has a far wider reach. In the offline world, he says, 30% of a company's resources are spent providing a good customer experience and 70% goes to marketing. But online, he says, 70% should be devoted to creating a great customer experience and 30% should be spent "shouting" about it.

71   That's the idea at furniture.com, a startup in Worcester, Mass., whose state-of-the-art digital aid provides a glimmer of the future. Visitors to its Web site type in style preferences, and within seconds a live company rep is at their service, ready to talk via Web chat or Netphone about the personalized showroom that has just been created and sent to their computer. From there, buyers can haggle over colors, fabrics, prices, and dimensions.

72   The service doesn't stop there. After the sale, customers are "adopted" by the reps, who E-mail or phone from time to time to vet complaints or offer a new fabric-coordinated accessory. The result: While shoppers who use the personalized showroom take 20% longer, the orders are, on average, 50% larger. CEO Andrew Brooks says furniture.com can afford to spend more on service because doing business over the Web is cheaper. "The fundamental earth-shaking event that's being shaped by E-business is a radical shift in bargaining power from sellers to buyers," says Brooks. "What does that mean? Service is everything."

73   Sometimes that means combining all the different complaint boxes at a company—call centers, faxes, and E-mails—into one Web site. "Many companies haven't yet equipped their service staff to handle both E-mail and phone traffic," says analyst Jeff Snyder of market researcher International Data Corp. Or they have separate staffs handling each, without much integration or communication between the two.

74   Companies such as Thomas Cook, the travel and financial-services firm, are avoiding that trap, using software to coordinate all queries. Sprint Corp. is taking another tack: With each request for help, its software automatically dips into a database to find similar questions, then automatically provides an answer. Sprint is using each exchange to build its problem-solving and marketing database. This helps Sprint handle a glut of new service traffic and E-mail without adding to service costs.

75   E-service savings can be huge. A Forrester Research Inc. study of financial institutions says Web service costs companies just 4 cents per customer on average for a simple Web page query, vs. $1.44 per live phone call. Shifting service to the Net, says Forrester, could let companies handle up to one-third more service queries at 43% of the cost.

76   The ultimate money-saver, though, is automating service so thoroughly that few reps are needed at all. The idea: let the Web do for customer service what automated tellers did for dispensing cash. One example: Using software from Motive Communications Inc. in Austin, Tex., companies including Netscape and Dell can take a digital "snapshot" of a customer's troubled computer system, pinpoint the problem, and send repairs over the Web—all without human intervention.

77   And E-service sells. HP is using homegrown tracking software to create a database of corporate customers who call or E-mail for service. That way, HP can chart their concerns and, when they E-mail or call again, identify them by specialty before automatically routing them to agents with the right knowhow. The payoff so far: an estimated $180 million in incremental sales. With those kinds of results, E-service can pay for itself.

Survival Guide 5: Go Ahead, Farm Out Those Jobs[5]

78   Speed kills—if you don't have it. Whether it's product development, marketing, or customer service, there's no need—or time—for companies to try to do everything in-house. "E-commerce is putting a supercharger on the pace of business," says Jeff McKeever, chairman of MicroAge Inc., an electronics distributor that is using the Net to move faster.

79   In the computer industry, you used to be able to tell the technology pioneers by the arrows in their backs. Those who took a more measured pace, pushing widely used products such as IBM-compatible personal computers, were the ones reaping the rewards. But the Net has turned that notion on its head. Now, the E-business innovators such as Amazon.com, Yahoo!, and eBay are cashing in on lofty stock valuations and heavy traffic flowing to their Web sites. "We were first to market, and it was a huge advantage," says Stuart Wolff, CEO of RealSelect Inc., which attracts 6 million people a day to its REALTOR.com Web site, where 1.2 million homes from around the world are posted for sale. "People who don't understand the importance of speed are making a huge mistake."

Lighter Load

80   Think Internet time. Hire help—there's plenty. For every wannabe.com, there are scores of companies eager to run entire online businesses or take some of the load off by handling just one cyber operation—say, E-mail—for a fee. Instead of spending six months to build a portal site for your employees or customers, software from San Francisco-based startup Epicentric, for example, can do it in a few days. Or tiny Be Free Inc. in Marlborough, Mass., helps you set up virtual sales booths on more than 100,000 sites. Need to turn on more computer power—fast, and only when you need it? Interpath Communications Inc. can host your Web site at its computer center where it can handle peak loads.

81   Moving fast can also mean spending less. Take RadNet Corp., a $3\frac{1}{2}$-year-old company that makes radiology data in hospitals available to nearly 600 physicians. About 18 months ago, the company decided to make its services available over the Net, instead of just through private networks. Management wanted it done this year. But an internal technology group estimated that it couldn't complete the job before 2001 because of all the staff it needed to develop new software and systems. That wouldn't do. RadNet hired Interpath Communications to develop and host the Web site—for one-third of what the company figures it would have cost in-house. Says Al Majkowski, RadNet's founder and chief technology officer: "We can't be burdened by having to build a large IT [Information Technology] organization."

82   It's not just about getting into cyberspace quickly. Once on the Web, companies have to keep moving fast. Consider distribution. "Anybody can build a Web site and take orders," says David Crampton, president of PC Flowers & Gifts Inc., a Web site that takes about 110,000 orders a year. "The biggest challenge we face is the shipping, the fulfillment end of our business."

[5]From Ira Sager, with Peter Elstrom, "Go Ahead, Farm Out Those Jobs," *Business Week e.biz:* March 22, 1999.

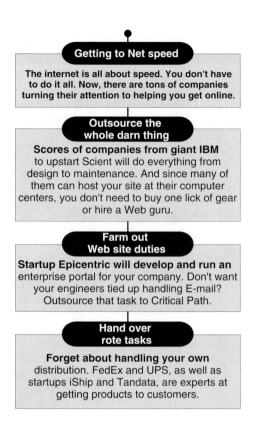

Getting to Net speed

The internet is all about speed. You don't have to do it all. Now, there are tons of companies turning their attention to helping you get online.

Outsource the whole darn thing

Scores of companies from giant IBM to upstart Scient will do everything from design to maintenance. And since many of them can host your site at their computer centers, you don't need to buy one lick of gear or hire a Web guru.

Farm out Web site duties

Startup Epicentric will develop and run an enterprise portal for your company. Don't want your engineers tied up handling E-mail? Outsource that task to Critical Path.

Hand over rote tasks

Forget about handling your own distribution. FedEx and UPS, as well as startups iShip and Tandata, are experts at getting products to customers.

83   Fortunately, there's help. Companies are ditching company-owned trucks and outsourcing to United Parcel Service, Federal Express Corp., and the like. UPS and FedEx both consult with E-business players to help establish shipping procedures. And they've opened up their databases so these customers can track their packages from the Web. The day before Christmas, 1 million people checked on their UPS packages over the Net. Now, imagine how many people will be checking next Christmas. Will you be quick enough?

SURVIVAL GUIDE 6: NO WEB SITE IS AN ISLAND[6]

84   Even though he's CEO of a wedding-planning Web site called the Knot, David Liu isn't pledging any till-death-do-us-part fidelity to the Internet. Rather, he's finding out that a fling on terra firma can bring him added exposure—and more cybershoppers. On Jan. 6, Liu and co-founder Carley Roney published The Knot's Complete Guide to Weddings in the real world, the first of what are expected to be three paperback books based on advice and discussions culled from the site. With its books perched on store shelves, the Knot's Web traffic surged to 900,000 visitors in January, up from 400,000 a month earlier. Even for a Net company, "the best way to [build a brand] is through the power of the printed word and TV," says Liu.

85   He's not the only one who thinks so. As electronic commerce evolves, it's becoming clear that earthly and cyberspace companies can benefit by operating on both sides of the digital divide. Slapping together a Web site to sell stuff isn't enough. Companies need to leverage both virtual and real-world businesses off one another to get the full wallop of the Web.

---

[6]From Catherine Yang, "No Web Site Is an Island," *Business Week e.biz:* March 22, 1999.

Interactive Kiosks

86   Already, some companies are blurring the boundaries of the two worlds. In certain Levi Strauss & Co. stores, you can plug your measurements into a Web kiosk and have custom-made jeans delivered to your home in about two weeks. On Walt Disney Co.'s cable-TV Disney Channel, buglike creatures called Zoogs encourage kids to log onto Disney's Web site to send fan mail to their favorite stars. And even if you never fire up a Web browser, you'll see more of the Knot: It plans to produce a 13-part Public Broadcasting System series and launch a wedding magazine in June.

87   There are certain to be miscues. When America Online Inc. and ABC produced a Christmas special based on AOL's online character Ozzie the Elf in 1997, it yielded disappointing ratings. All the same, Net companies know they need to reach into the real world—even if it's something as simple as Amazon.com advertising on TV or on Wells Fargo Co.'s automated teller machines. "To get inside the brains of the three-quarters of the population that's not online, you'd better build your brand in traditional channels," says analyst Melissa Bane of Yankee Group Research Inc.

88   This is where physical stores—once scoffed at as ball-and-chain relics by some "pure" Net companies—are proving invaluable. Gap Inc. has installed interactive kiosks, called Web Lounges, in some of its stores so that customers can get gift ideas or match up outfits without going into a dressing room. Discount broker Charles Schwab & Co. is installing about 500 PCs in 300 branches so investors can try its online-trading site. "The branches are a comfortable place for investors to get started on the Web," says Daniel Leemon, the company's chief strategy officer.

89   Outdoor equipment retailer REI is one of the trailblazers in bringing the Web to the real world. Last June, the company outfitted stores with kiosks so that customers could get product information and place orders online. Now, REI is upgrading all its cash registers so that cashiers can order merchandise from its Web site when they don't have it in stock at the store. Result: REI's online traffic is up about 10% since June, and the site is expected to be more profitable than any of its 55 shops by yearend.

90   Web companies are finding innovative ways to market in the real world, too. BabyCenter.com, a Web site that sells products to new parents, has cut a deal so that 320 SmithKline Beecham salespeople will distribute educational pamphlets with BabyCenter's Web address to 17,000 obstetricians' offices. "Only a small portion of expectant parents use Web sites, " says Mark Selcow, BabyCenter's president.

91   As E-business takes off, cyberspace and the real world are becoming tightly intertwined. For most companies, it pays to plant a flag in both.

SURVIVAL GUIDE 7: BUILDING GLOBAL COMMUNITIES[7]

92   Executives at Warner Brothers Online were fed up. For years, they had looked on as fans of Bugs Bunny, Batman, the Tazmanian Devil, and other characters banded together and hoisted brand images and sound clips onto personal home pages in cybercommunities such as GeoCities and Tripod. What really grated was the way the site operators were selling ad space on those pages. "They were underwriting the cost of copyright infringement," fumes Warner Online President Jim Moloshok.

93   Warner wasn't about to sue its own fans. Instead, in January, Moloshok formed a joint venture with FortuneCity, a fast-growing online community based in London. Together, they created a site called ACMEcity as a beacon for fans around the world. The site has built home pages for 150,000 registered members in two months—luring many of them away from GeoCities and Tripod with giveaways.

94   Companies like Warner are finding much to love about online communities. Once the frontier towns of the Net, these sites have blossomed into digital metropolises. Their combined membership probably exceeds 25 million, if you count some 16 million subscribers to America Online Inc. Few of the sites are profitable as businesses. But companies are racing to partner with online

[7]From Neil Gross, "Building Global Communities," *Business Week e.biz:* March 22, 1999.

communities—or build their own—in hopes of solving two of the toughest challenges on the Net: Reaching customers all over the planet and understanding who they are.

95   Like the Internet itself, online communities are often global from Day One. As Net-based communications obliterate national boundaries, these sites draw together like-minded individuals who would never converge in the real world. A unit of AOL called ICQ, for example, provides instant messaging to hip young members scattered from Fresno to Finland, and provides space for their home pages. Jupiter Communications figures 45% of new home pages at community sites are now going up outside the U.S.

96   Just as important to businesses, communities thrive on experimentation. First, they popularized online chat and "buddies" networks. Today, these neighborhoods are incubators for trends in E-business. "We've built massive Web sites with millions of relationships to consumers," says Bo Peabody, President and CEO of Tripod, a trendy community owned by Internet portal Lycos. "Now, we're finding ways to make those relationships profitable."

97   The road to community business is already strewn with advertising. In both GeoCities and Tripod, banner ads blink and scroll across most prominent Web pages. But like neighborhoods in the real world, online communities have unique sensibilities. So site owners and marketers are struggling to invent what Peabody calls "commerce plus compassion."

Info in Exchange

98   To see how it works, consider the reasons cybernauts flock to communities. Mostly, it's the desire to know your neighbors and interact with them. Many sites encourage this by offering free or discounted real estate—meaning storage space for personal home pages on a computer server. Many sites build the home page for new members—asking for nothing in return except personal information on a registration form that includes name and address, marital status, and hobbies.

99   Site owners can use this information to fine-tune the online experience by making advertising, contests, and rewards programs more relevant. At sites for music and film buffs, the banner ads flog online music stores and DVDs. These vendors usually can't access the sites' registration lists. But site owners will give them enough general data for them to target ad pitches.

100   Even without registration details, marketers on community sites are swimming in info. They can visit neighborhood chat rooms and bulletin boards or browse photo galleries and music rooms on personal home pages. With smart software tools, vendors can parse these snippets for tips on consumer trends. Sometimes, site owners do it for them. Exploiting such tools, Tripod has managed to sort over 85% of its Web pages into categories.

101   When it comes to raising money, however, most sites are looking beyond banner ads. Tripod's owner, Lycos, is now merging with USA Network to create a sprawling conglomerate that includes an online auction site called First Auction, TicketMaster Online-CitySearch, and a separate community called Angelfire. As these properties become integrated, Tripod and Lycos will be able to aggregate member purchasing power to win discounts on consumer products and services. First Auction will help homesteaders conduct personal auctions from their home pages. "These online properties will link up to form massive electronic buying and selling chains," predicts Tripod's Peabody.

102   Companies like Warner that run their own sites acquire a precious commodity: knowledge. In return for low-cost giveaways and perks—character images, film previews, and online chat with actors from TV shows such as Friends and Babylon 5—Warner gets personal info galore from the registration forms.

103   With that comes responsibilities for site owners. Fresh in everyone's memory is the scandal that engulfed GeoCities last summer, when the Federal Trade Commission accused the site owners of selling members' personal information to outside marketers. GeoCities denied the charge but agreed to bolster privacy enforcement.

104   Even without abuse of privacy, however, advertising can rub homesteaders the wrong way. Stick a Coca-Cola ad in a chat room, and participants will quickly start flaming Coke, notes Jupiter analyst Patrick Keane. So when Japan's Fujitsu Ltd. introduced advertisements on its 3-D site called Worlds-Away, it tastefully disguised them as objects. Click on a flower pot, and it takes you to PC Flowers. World manager Timothy J. Lavalli, a Ph.D. anthropologist, is now building incentives into

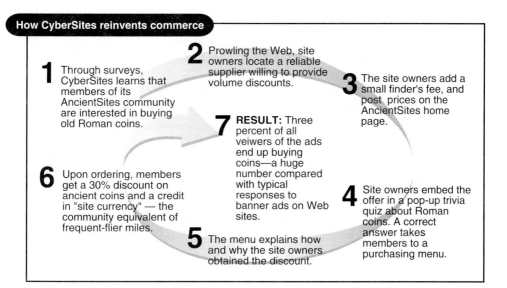

How CyberSites reinvents commerce

1 Through surveys, CyberSites learns that members of its AncientSites community are interested in buying old Roman coins.

2 Prowling the Web, site owners locate a reliable supplier willing to provide volume discounts.

3 The site owners add a small finder's fee, and post prices on the AncientSites home page.

4 Site owners embed the offer in a pop-up trivia quiz about Roman coins. A correct answer takes members to a purchasing menu.

5 The menu explains how and why the site owners obtained the discount.

6 Upon ordering, members get a 30% discount on ancient coins and a credit in "site currency" — the community equivalent of frequent-flier miles.

7 RESULT: Three percent of all veiwers of the ads end up buying coins—a huge number compared with typical responses to banner ads on Web sites.

the fiber of the virtual world. For example, members who spend $50 or more in on-site E-commerce might find their $9.95 monthly fee waved, he says. Advertisers also pay more when they see that members are willing to spend money.

105   A newer community called CyberSites goes even further: It tactfully surveys members before exposing them to ads, negotiates group discounts on products that are sold on-site, and allows each member to edit his or her online profile to accommodate shifting tastes. Step by step, companies and customers are learning to be neighbors. In a community, they can also be partners.

Survival Guide 8: Follow the Money[8]

106   So you're not a stockbroker, an auto dealer, or some other poor sap trying to fight off a dozen E-commerce startups. No need to worry, right? Wrong. Like objects in a rearview mirror, Internet rivals are closer than they appear. And there's only one sure way to know how soon they'll be riding your bumper.

107   Keep your eye on the money. Since 1995, venture capitalists have poured nearly $3.8 billion into some 530 electronic-commerce companies, according to VentureOne Corp., a San Francisco researcher. Checking out who's getting that dough is a little-known way of discovering what businesses might be next on the Internet hit list. Although many of these ventures are still fledglings, their backers say they're poised to infiltrate a wide swath of industries, from postal services to human-resource management.

108   It has happened before. In the past four years, venture capitalists have funneled $263 million into online news services and Web sites related to cars and travel. Already, a quarter of new-car buyers consult the Web before making their purchases, and nearly 4% of all airline tickets are bought over the Net. Now, venture capitalists are turning their attention—with a vengeance—to other markets. "Everybody is potentially vulnerable," says Jean Yaremchuk, vice-president for research and technology at VentureOne. "It's just a matter of timing."

109   Batteries included. If you're in financial services, the time is now. More than $300 million has gone into 34 companies focused on everything from mortgages to insurance in 1998, up from $81 million in 22 companies a year earlier. One newcomer even hopes to shake up the staid credit-card

[8]From Linda Himelstein, "Follow the Money," *Business Week e.biz:* March 22, 1999.

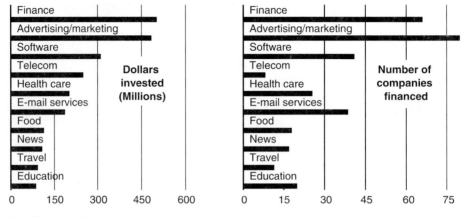

Where the dough went (1995–98)

How venture capitalists are investing in E-commerce

Data: Ventureone Corp.

industry: San Francisco's NextCard's Web site lets its customers apply for Visa cards, get online statements, and design their own cards with images of Elvis, Mom, or whomever.

110   There are plenty of other industries on the Web radar screen. Internet advertising and marketing outfits attracted $245 million in 1998 as 34 upstarts were launched. Palo Alto (Calif.)-based AdKnowledge Inc., which helps companies decide how and where to advertise on the Web, landed $14 million in February. Health-care upstarts, including online pharmacies and medical information sites, also are popular. In 1998, they took in $96 million, up 57% from the previous year. Even niche categories, such as battery retailing, now boast multiple venture- backed startups. Duracell, are you ready?

111   What makes these businesses so enticing is that they promise to eliminate inefficiencies in their markets. Businesses with multiple distribution channels, a slew of middlemen, or massive product selections are ripe for invasion. Art.com Inc. in Lake Forest, Ill., for example, sells more than 100,000 prints over the Net. The average brick-and-mortar shop carries 1,000. "When you look at the efficiencies that the Web creates, they're too powerful to ignore," says Robert C. Kagle, a partner at Benchmark Capital, an Art.com investor.

112   Even established companies are backing the small fry. Intel Corp. has invested in 50 E-commerce startups to fuel demand for personal computers that use Intel chips. And venture-capital firm Kleiner Perkins Caufield & Byers has built a grid of virtually every sector of the U.S. economy—from wine to steel—to pinpoint areas in need of Web treatment. "It's an exploding universe of opportunities," says Kleiner Perkins partner L. John Doerr. Traditional businesses intent on outracing Web upstarts had better step on the gas pedal, while keeping their eye on the latest venture investments.

SURVIVAL GUIDE 9: A WEB THAT LOOKS LIKE THE WORLD[9]

113   Doral Main, a 51-year-old mother of two and office manager of a low-income property company in Oakland, Calif., saves precious time by shopping the Internet for greeting cards and getaways. Her Net-newbie father, Charles F. Bumcrot, 73, goes online to buy supplies for his wood-carving hobby. Even niece Katrina, 11, finds excitement on the Web, picking gifts she wants from the Disney.com site. "It's addictive," Main says of the Net.

[9]From Roger O. Crockett, "A Web That Looks Like the World," *Business Week e.biz:* March 22, 1999.

114   The Web isn't mostly a hangout for techno-nerds anymore. On the cusp of a new century, it is being embraced by every age and ethnic group. Indeed, Internet demographics are quickly coming to match America's diversity. Combined BUSINESS WEEK and Harris polls conducted in January and February reveal that 46% of those who use the Internet are women, compared with 37% three years ago. And the number of cybersurfers over 50 has doubled, to 20%.

115   Indeed, research shows just how rapidly the Web is losing its male-geek status. Women account for more than half of new Internet users, according to a recent Pew Research Center study. By yearend, predicts Forrester Research Inc., 32% of black households in the U.S., 43% of Hispanic, and 67% of Asian-American households will be online. These proportions compare with 39% of white households expected to be online by yearend. Cybersurfing is becoming a global pastime, too: The number of Europeans hopscotching across Web sites is expected to jump from 4% of the population to 13% by 2001, says Forrester, while the number of Chinese Netizens will more than quadruple, to 9.4 million, by 2002, according to researcher International Data Corp.

A Simple Plan

116   For E-businesses and traditional merchants, that means adapting to the Web's mass-market following. What was cool to the propeller-head may be a turnoff to the cyber-granny. And there's no time to waste. According to the recent BUSINESS WEEK/Harris poll, the number of people who have made purchases online jumped to 31% of online users, from 19% in 1997. What's more, the new Net shoppers pack a mighty economic punch. Consider this: Some 80% of all household purchases are made or influenced by women, according to WomanTrend, a Washington consulting firm. This year, about 28% of those buying online are expected to be women, up from 21% last year, according to Forrester Research.

117   As the type of users snared by the Web broadens, Net operators are beginning to think outside the box. Savvy online merchants realize they have to expand their product mix to reflect the interests of different groups. And to capture new users with less technological knowhow, they're focusing on making sites more appealing and easier to use. For example, many women dislike black backgrounds, says Fran Maier, senior vice-president for marketing at Women.com Networks, a site devoted to women's issues.

118   Minding female tastes pays off. Although nearly twice as many men buy goods online, studies show women are boosting online commerce in areas such as travel, gifts, clothing, toys, flowers, and cards. Web women, for example, have helped iVillage grow from a tiny parenting site on America Online Inc. in 1996 to one of the Internet's bigger success stories. The New York startup has seen its number of users boom 52% from 2.1 million in April, 1998, to 3.2 million in January, according to Web ratings service Media Metrix Inc. And an initial public offering is in the works.

119   And move over, kids—seniors are elbowing their way online. Those aged 55 to 64 make up some 22% of online households today—and will reach 40% by 2003, according to Forrester Research. With substantial incomes—their median household incomes hover above $60,000, dwarfing younger users, Forrester says—older Netizens make an attractive target for Web businesses, ranging from florists to automotive retailers. Still, seniors are less familiar with techie lingo and gadgets, and they admit that they approach Internet shopping with some trepidation. "It's because there's an erosion of a feeling of security," says Rosina Lassalle, 66. Lassalle, a Castro Valley (Calif.) homemaker, had some of her fears about online credit-card theft calmed when she bought a satellite dish last fall without any problems.

Getting Personal

120   Web-site operators interested in luring seniors are toning down the technology. The American Association of Retired Persons' site doesn't require lengthy downloads or complicated plug-ins, and it's light on graphics. "Our major mantra is keeping it simple," says Mark D. Carpenter, AARP's online-communications developer. The site, an information source for some 33,000 members, features a popular section on computers and technology. In fact, high-tech education has driven more than 500,000 users a month to SeniorNet, a site for the over-50 crowd.

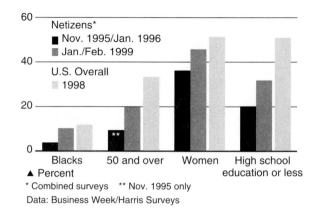

A wider net

Net demographics are moving to match U.S. diversity

Netizens*
■ Nov. 1995/Jan. 1996
■ Jan./Feb. 1999

U.S. Overall
□ 1998

▲ Percent
* Combined surveys   ** Nov. 1995 only
Data: Business Week/Harris Surveys

121   Simplicity counts, but success online really means just what it meant in the pre-Web days: matching the right goods to the right group. It's no secret why Bluemountain.com shot to the top of Media Metrix' list of popular Web sites, with 12.5 million visitors in December. The site's mix of electronic greeting cards attracts women, seniors, and minorities. Some 57% of Bluemountain's users are female, says Executive Director Jared Schutz. And while he doesn't keep data by ethnic group, he says cards that focus on ethnic and specialty subjects, such as Buddhism and Kwanzaa, are among the most popular on the site. Bluemountain also has Spanish- and French-language sections and will soon add German and Italian. "For many of these people, we are one of the few sites that caters to them," Schutz says.

122   That's because narrowly targeted sites have a better read on what their audience wants. Women.com's online store includes everything from deals on roses to baby carriages. The site also builds a database of about 500,000 customers and zaps them E-mail notices when there's a sale on an item they are listed as liking. The approach has helped Women.com generate millions in sales from the store since it was launched last July. Rather than the price of products, "Personalization makes women feel more comfortable making purchases," says Women.com's Maier.

123   Online businesses also are waking up to the economic clout of different ethnic groups. For example, black Americans' total buying power increased 7% in 1997, to $392 billion, according to a study of the latest Census Bureau data released in February by Target Market News Inc. in Chicago. Blacks spent $60 million—a sixfold increase—on Internet access and $3.3 billion on electronic gear. "The black dollar spends just like the white dollar," says B. Keith Fulton, director of technology programs and policy at the National Urban League. Catering to African Americans helped NetNoir generate thousands of dollars a month from its Web mall. In less than a year, the mall has grown from 20 vendors to about 100, which sell everything from books and cards to clothing. As the Web morphs into tomorrow's marketplace, its shoppers will come in every culture, gender, and age group.

SURVIVAL GUIDE 10: LOG ON, BOSS[10]

124   Dennis M. Kubit, chief executive of Trans-General Group, a Pittsburgh insurance outfit, used to be like most executives in his stodgy industry. He rarely surfed the Internet, and his company's Web site was little more than a shingle emblazoned with the corporate name and a list of services. But last

─────

[10]From Linda Himelstein, with Gary Silverman, "Log On, Boss," *Business Week e.biz:* March 22, 1999.

year, customers and brokers began asking about the insurer's Internet strategy. Banks, for instance, wanted to sell Trans-General's products over the Web. So, six months ago, Kubit decided he had to get wired—and fast. Now he spends one to two hours a day online, checking out rivals' Web sites and surfing for industry news. "We felt we were behind and we needed to catch up," he says.

125   Kubit isn't the only one. Even as electronic commerce is poised to bring sweeping changes to virtually every industry, fewer than one-third of CEOs in the U.S. consider themselves Web-literate, according to a PricewaterhouseCoopers survey of more than 800 CEOs that was released in January. Only one in four surf the Web regularly, and 69% describe their Internet sophistication as fair or poor.

126   Here's the problem with such Luddite behavior: The vast majority of these same chief executives say that electronic business will be central to their future. Will top execs be able to learn how to navigate the cyberworld without getting their fingers dirty on a computer keyboard? Don't count on it. CEOs who don't get down to some serious, hands-on Net prowling may soon find themselves with little else to do. Says Thornton A. May, vice-president for research and education at Cambridge Technology Partners Inc.: "We're living in a brand new economy and some of these guys are still in the Middle Ages bleeding patients."

One-on-One

127   Mindful of the threats posed by Web-centric rivals, companies are scrambling to bring their most senior executives into the Information Age. At Visa International, at least 30 high-ranking officials have been treated to "Web tours" to learn everything from checking stock quotations to buying golf clubs. Visa also has offered these tours to senior executives in the banking and retail sectors. Visa is so serious about the Web that it has made online commerce one of the company's top five strategic initiatives and has cut a series of deals to promote Visa on the Net with the likes of Web pioneer Yahoo! Inc. and eToys. "You need high-level support to get an entire organization to embrace E-commerce," explains Joseph A. Vause, vice-president for electronic-commerce, who has been dubbed Visa International's resident "dot com."

128   At Trans-General, Kubit might be considered the house "dot com" these days. Since the fall, he has hired a chief information officer, Charles Klein, and gotten himself some one-on-one training to learn how the Web might be used to lower costs, provide better customer service, and conduct research on competitors. Starting this March, Kubit began requiring top lieutenants to spend an hour a week in "nerd training" to make them cybersmart. "People wonder if I'm really embracing the Internet or just sitting there not walking the walk," observes Kubit.

129   Beyond mastering the Web's ABC's, Kubit is overseeing the launch of an extensive corporate intranet, while weaving technology into all his strategic thinking. For instance, the company's market researchers routinely use the Net to check out other insurers' products and prices before Trans-General's sales force pitches new business. The company's tech staff regularly meets with senior executives and quarterly with the company's board of directors. Trans-General has even established a high-tech advisory board to ensure that the company stays on the right track—and doesn't cede any territory to startups that are creeping into the insurance industry.

No, Thanks

130   To be sure, many chief executives don't believe they need to be the one combing the Web. George L. Engelke Jr., the 60-year-old chairman, president, and CEO of Astoria Financial Corp., a $20 billion thrift in Lake Success, N.Y., has no computer in his office and doesn't plan on getting one. Engelke says his job has nothing to do with the nuts and bolts of opening accounts or processing mortgages. Even voicemail, he says, is overrated, since it's far less customer-friendly than a real person. For tasks that require technical assistance, Engelke says his computer-savvy aides or a calculator he picked up for free 15 years ago are more than adequate. "As an executive, your biggest role is being a devil's advocate," says Engelke, who keeps an old Mercury 2300 adding machine in his office. "Devil's advocacy isn't on a PC. It doesn't have that key."

131   Although honchos such as Engelke are still in the majority, most experts and Net-smart CEOs say they won't be for long—not if they hope to survive in the coming decade. "How can you lead your

You know you don't "Get it" when...

...the CIO position constantly need refilling.

...executives rely on staff to handle E-mail.

...technology issues are rarely discussed by the board of directors.

...senior managers are not accountable for high-tech projects and budgets.

company into this new era if you're not conversant and comfortable in this new technology and able to envision its opportunities?" asks David S. Pottruck, co-CEO of Charles Schwab & Co.

132   Pottruck knows firsthand how important Net experience is to corporate leadership. In early 1998, the company decided to move its Internet business from a separate operation into the core of Schwab's financial-services strategy. Initially, the move was painful—the company's stock and revenues started to sink as it cut trading fees. But the gambit worked. Today, 54% of Schwab's trades are done online—a key reason it's one of the fastest-growing companies in the country. If senior management had not personally understood the Web and its potential impact on the brokerage industry, Pottruck says, Schwab could have been left in the dust.

133   Levi Strauss & Co. doesn't want to be left behind. It's going through an entire reorganization. In February, the giant jeans maker started assigning a technology manager to business-unit executives to help them grapple with techie issues that arise. "There's a fundamental technology level of literacy that people have to have to operate today," says Thomas M. Kasten, vice president of information technology for Levi Strauss Americas.

134   That's what Henry's Marketplace, a 14-store grocery chain based in La Mesa, Calif., is finding out. Top execs there admit that they are still struggling with basic technology issues, let alone sophisticated uses of the Internet. In the past, some of the top brass didn't even check E-mail routinely—and missed out on critical notices such as the agendas for board meetings.

High Price

135   But Stanley A. Boney, the chairman and CEO at Henry's, has had enough of that. He learned that more than a third of his customers are regularly surfing the Web. With a little help, Boney says, he has begun to understand how to use the Internet to lower inventories of specialty items, serve up information to his customers, and expand Henry's beyond Southern California. The transition, however, has been difficult. "We weren't brought up in the computer generation, so we weren't computer literate," Boney explains. "Even though the Internet isn't that much of a threat to us at this point, we know it's coming and we've got to prepare."

136   There's still time for Boney and other CEOs to get Net-wise—but not a lot of time. Those top execs who continue to relegate Web responsibility to their information systems staff, or to hide behind their calculators and secretaries, will pay a high price. "You either get on to technology and into E-commerce, or you probably get out of business or have a shrinking business," says San Diego consultant Gerald W. Faust. That may be bitter medicine. But better to take it before it's too late.

CASE 5

BusinessWeek

PORTAL COMBAT COMES TO THE NET

1   Microsoft Corp.'s 10 Web sites are among the biggest draws on the Internet, visited by a third of all U.S. Web surfers. Yet it's just not enough. So the software giant is whipping up a super Web site that will showcase all its online properties, from travel to car-buying to news, and include services such as free E-mail and a search engine to explore the rest of the Web. The new site, which could be ready as early as this summer, will be called "Microsoft Start"—a telling name, since the software maker is hoping all these goodies will persuade cybernauts to make it their first stop on the Net.

2   It's home sweet home page. And Microsoft isn't the only business trying to create the best one. Yahoo!, CNET's Snap! Online, Excite, Netscape, and half a dozen others are making bids to become the launchpad to the rest of the Net. They are jamming their Web sites chock-full of free services—chat, customized news pages, entertainment listings, even personal finance advice—hoping Netizens will visit them first to get most of the stuff they need.

3   The theory: If a Web site becomes a major gateway to the Net, or "portal," it will boast traffic from a big chunk of the 55 million Web surfers. That could draw advertising dollars, online shoppers, and lucrative sponsorship deals, transforming money-losing sites into cash machines. The prize is huge: Advertising on the Net is expected to hit $7.7 billion by 2002, up from $940 million in 1997, and E-commerce could balloon to $37.5 billion, up from $2.6 billion last year, according to market researcher Jupiter Communications Co. "It's hard to find any of the major sites that aren't seeking to be the start site," says Laura Jennings, vice-president at Microsoft Network, the No. 2 online service.

4   The idea of portals marks the latest twist in the Web's evolution. A year ago, search-engine sites such as Yahoo! and Lycos feared they would become commodities. So they began touting themselves as newfangled "networks" that—much as in the TV world—would act as channels funneling programs, information, and news to subscribers. Now, they and other ambitious Web-site operators are taking it further, attempting to become one-stop, full-service sites.

5   And none is more successful at it today than America Online Inc. AOL is the No. 1 doorway to the Net, with its 11 million subscribers accounting for a hefty 39% of Web traffic, according to Media Metrix-The PC Meter Co. AOL's oodles of content, shopping, chat, and E-mail have drawn hordes to the proprietary online service. Now AOL is beefing up its Web site, AOL.com, to ward off the portal wannabes. Its site offers features once only available on the online service, such as instant messaging—a real-time E-mail exchange much like chat—and NetMail, which lets AOL users check E-mail from the Web without having to use the AOL service.

PILING ON

6   So far, it's paying off. AOL's revenue from advertising, goods, and services sold electronically rose to $108.8 million in the December quarter, up 87% from a year ago. But AOL is facing stiffer competition. CNET Inc., for example, is muscling in by licensing Snap!—a collection of Web content created by others—to such biggies as Toshiba, GTE, and Compaq Computer. "Our bet," says Halsey M. Minor, chief executive at CNET, "is that everybody combined will be able to generate more customers than AOL."

7   But first, CNET and the others must outdo the online giant—a task that's triggering an all-out features war. Excite Inc., Yahoo! Inc., and others are piling on services that are being matched almost

Source: Heather Green in New York and Linda Himelstein in San Francisco, with Paul C. Judge in Boston, "Portal Combat Comes to the Net," *Business Week*: March 2, 1998; and Ronal Grover in North Hollywood, California, "The Wonderful World of Disney.com," *Business Week*: March 2, 1998.

instantly by rivals. Last October, for example, Excite paid $35 million in stock for Netbot Inc., which developed an online shopping technology that helps find products across a welter of Web merchants. But before Excite could launch the shopping service on Nov. 26, Yahoo! trumped it by unveiling a similar comparison-shopping feature through a licensing deal with Junglee Corp. of Sunnyvale, Calif.

8   The latest must-add feature: online communities. These let Web surfers homestead by setting up their own pages around common interests. "Neighbors" chat online and exchange information on topics ranging from Southern living to Broadway. Yahoo! kicked that off in January by taking a $5 million minority stake in GeoCities, a privately owned Santa Monica (Calif.) online community that was ranked the seventh most popular site, according to RelevantKnowledge Inc. Lycos Inc. followed by acquiring Tripod Inc. on Feb. 3 for $58 million in stock. The Web community for twentysomethings boasts 1 million members. Now, AOL says it's considering a similar service. "This space is very unforgiving because your competition is one click away," says Jeff Mallett, vice-president of business operations at Yahoo!

9   It's also getting more expensive by the day. Take Yahoo!, which licensed a search service two years ago and developed features in-house before buying additional ones in the past year—at a total cost of $205.5 million. To recreate that same service from the ground up today would cost between $500 million and $1 billion, analysts say. "The separation between the haves and the have-nots will begin in earnest in 1998," says analyst Mary G. Meeker of Morgan Stanley, Dean Witter, Discover & Co.

BULKING UP

10   So, too, will the pace of acquisitions, as the "haves" bulk up with extra features and make a grab for subscribers, figuring they don't have much time left to get established. One likely buyout candidate, say analysts, is Mirabilis Ltd., an Israeli startup that has developed real-time chat now used by 4 million people. Also attractive: WhoWhere? Inc., a Mountain View (Calif.) company that provides free E-mail and was the 15th most popular site in January. Experts also bet iVillage Inc. will be snapped up soon. The New York-based company, which owns the popular Parentsoup site, is one of the top Net communities, with 2 million monthly users, offering information targeted at women on finance, parenting, and work. Co-founder Candice Carpenter says iVillage has been approached by media companies, though she won't name them. "We've had inquiries, and it's speeding up," she says. "This is in the air."

11   So who will be standing when the portal combat is over? Experts say there will be four major doorways to the Net, maybe six—including AOL, Yahoo!, and Microsoft, which are sitting pretty with the most traffic and the deepest pockets. Experts say Excite and media companies such as Time Warner or Disney—which is starting to put its gateway pieces together—will duke it out for the other spots.

12   The smaller players, such as Lycos, which had 18 million daily page views in the latest quarter, and Infoseek, with 12.5 million, need to partner up, says analyst Alan M. Braverman of Credit Suisse First Boston. That's because their numbers—and ability to attract advertisers—are dwarfed by the 65 million page views and the breadth of the services Yahoo! is putting together. Infoseek executives decline comment about a partnership, saying they are in a quiet period after a secondary stock offering. Lycos, which turned profitable in the October quarter, says partners have indicated interest in the startup. But, says CEO Robert J. Davis, "we're completely committed to growing as an independent company."

13   The way the competition is shaping up, even small fry can leverage the success of the biggies to draw a crowd.

14   No one loves brand names more than Michael D. Eisner. Whether it's the Beauty and the Beast Broadway show that kids drag their parents to or the new ESPN store that lures sports nuts to a shopping mall in Glendale, Calif., the Disney chairman has long preached that the best way to draw a crowd is to give them something they'll recognize in a crowd. It should be the same on the Internet.

15   Certainly, that's the mantra at Walt Disney Co.'s online unit, Buena Vista Internet Services. As Web usage, advertising, and E-commerce catch on, so too has Disney's interest in carving out a piece of the Internet pie. Indeed, the company has been in talks to buy the remaining two-thirds it doesn't already

TABLE 1
Bigger, Better, Faster

Company	Features	% of Users' Visits	
		Home	Work
AOL.com	Offers a link to the Internet for AOL's 11 million subscribers, with loads of content, E-mail, news, and chat	46%	41%
Yahoo! sites	A top Web brand that's setting the pace for new features—such as free E-mail, chat, local listings, customized Web pages	42	51
Microsoft sites	Building a supersite called Microsoft Start that will tie together all its properties in travel, personal finance, games, news, and car buying	33	40
Excite network	Signing exclusive deals with companies such as Intuit to offer financial services and investment information	24	30
Walt Disney sites	Using its stable of properties—Mickey Mouse, ESPN sports, ABC entertainment and news—to draw a wide audience, including kids and sports buffs	14	12
CNET network	Tops in technology news and software sites, it's now branching out by licensing its Snap! service, a collection of content with search and chat	11	13

Data: Media Metrix—THE PC METER CO.

own of Web-site owner and designer Starwave Corp., say insiders. Starwave, which operates the popular ESPN SportsZone and Mr. Showbiz sites, would give Disney a key property that would help tie together a collection of two dozen sites aimed at doing what Disney does best—entertainment.

Pushing Pooh Grams

16   No major media company is more aggressively pushing to cash in on the Web than Disney, whose on-line expenditures were an estimated $150 million in the last year alone. As many as 25% of Netizens visit at least one of the Disney sites each month, whether to send "Pooh grams" or to "own" one of the 100,000 or so football, basketball, or baseball teams that compete in ESPN SportsZone's fantasy leagues.

17   Disney has the combination of technical savvy, brand name, and deep pockets it takes to compete. Working out of a six-floor office building in North Hollywood, many of its 300 artists, writers, and programmers create as much new Web content as any company in the industry. To get the technical expertise it lacked, Disney plunked down an estimated $80 million last April for one-third of Starwave, which was launched by Microsoft Corp. co-founder Paul Allen. "They're aggressive, and they have a lot of resources," says Scott Webb, senior vice-president of Viacom Inc.'s Nickelodeon Media Works.

18   Disney is pulling all its strings to make a profit on its money-losing Net operations. It generates healthy distribution fees from America Online Inc., which features its ABCnews.com site. Its sites take in an estimated $25 million a year in ad revenues. And www.Disney.com sells some $8 million in trinkets. The company also boasts an estimated 70,000 members at $5.95 a month to its 10-month old Disney's Daily Blast service for kids.

19   Can Disney's Web sites keep the rivals at bay? The kiddie sites have heavy competition from the likes of AOL, Warner Brothers and Nickelodeon. Disney's ABCnews.com is No. 4 in news. And even ESPN, which handily leads all sports sites, faces mounting competition from CNN/SI and CBS's

SportsLine. Still, among the media industry's best marketers, Disney has an arsenal of promotional tools that includes its theme parks, movies, TV shows, and even its Mighty Ducks hockey team. For instance, the company slipped promotions for the Daily Blast into 8 million copies of George of the Jungle videocassettes, and will soon pitch the service at the Innoventions booth at Epcot Center.

20   Down the road, the company sees its place in the world of convergence, with ESPN offering on-line sports statistics for the cable channel or www.Disney.com offering a quick way to buy products that a kid might see in a movie on ABC's Wonderful World of Disney. "The companies that will win on the Internet are those who have the ability to create content, and no one does that better than we do," says Jake Winebaum, Buena Vista's president. But in the hotly competitive Web world, Disney may need some Tinkerbell dust, too.

CASE 6

BusinessWeek

INTERNET ANXIETY

1   For years, Toys 'R' Us has struggled against giant discounters like Wal-Mart and Target. But this past holiday season brought into focus an even more formidable threat: a tiny online retailer called eToys. The Net startup's $30 million in sales last year equaled that of maybe two—out of 1,486—Toys 'R' Us stores. But when it came to ringing up the online register at Christmas, eToys left toysrus.com in the dust. Even worse, eToys scored a market cap of $7.8 billion on its first trading day, in May, dwarfing Toys 'R' Us's $5.6 billion.

2   With visions of an Amazon.com-type rival emerging in his own backyard, Toys 'R' Us CEO Robert C. Nakasone went into overdrive. But rather than attempting to refine his online operation in-house, he has set it up as a separate unit. Nakasone formed a partnership with Silicon Valley venture capitalists Benchmark Capital, funded it with $80 million from his own coffers, and moved the budding online business from Toys' New Jersey headquarters to Northern California. "Over time, we could have gotten it right," says Nakasone. "But we don't have the time."

3   Nakasone is not the only executive with an urgent desire to rush onto the Net. In industry after industry, Corporate America is suddenly feeling the uncomfortable gnaw of Internet Anxiety—a stomach-churning mixture of envy, resentment, and increasingly, just plain fear. "It was easy for people up front to dismiss online business as the flavor of the day," says Frank J. Drazka, managing director and head of technology investment banking at PaineWebber Inc. "But in the last year there have been a lot of board meetings in which management was asked, 'How do we compete against the newbies on the block?'" Driving those meetings, says Drazka: "The threat of extinction."

4   The phenomenon started, of course, with those incredible, indefensible, often downright insane valuations investors began bestowing on their "dot.com" favorites around the fall of last year. After all, with the Goldman Sachs Internet Index (GIN) climbing a phenomenal 453% between last September and its early April high, who wouldn't get a little green watching from the sidelines?

5   But what began as simply the lust for a red-hot stock has turned into something far deeper recently—something even the 34% nosedive of Net stocks over the past two months has done little to dispel. More galling than Internet stock prices is the way Net companies are allowed to operate. In the Net's through-the-looking-glass world, earnings hardly seem to matter, investors have been happy to hand over buckets of money to speed development, and the lucky devils running Net businesses are getting filthy rich besides. Meanwhile, even at their current levels, Net stocks have proved to be powerful currency that gives Internet companies a huge advantage when it comes to making acquisitions or hiring the best talent.

WAMPUM

6   At a fundamental level, there's a clash of business models under way, and the new model springing up among Net companies bears little resemblance to the old rules by which most managers have learned to play the game. To the dumbstruck executives at conventional companies—who have spent their careers forced into slavish obeisance to Wall Street's incessant demands for a penny or two more in earnings per share—it's all a bit much.

7   A prime example? Look no further than the adventures of Margaret C. Whitman, who went from being a senior manager at Hasbro Inc. to a billionaire Internet exec in just 14 months after joining

Source: Nanette Byrnes in New York and Paul C. Judge in Boston, "Internet Anxiety," *Business Week*: June 28, 1999.

online swap meet eBay Inc. With a net worth on paper of $1.1 billion, Whitman now boasts personal wealth almost twice the size of the $503 million family stockholdings of her former boss, Hasbro Chairman Alan G. Hassenfeld. It took the Hassenfelds 75 years to build a business with a $5.7 billion market cap. After nine months as a public company, eBay is worth more than three times that. "That drives Alan crazy," says Gary Jacobson, a onetime top-ranked toy analyst who—surprise!—spent several months recently trying to launch his own Net startup. "A lot of people are seeing things like this and saying, 'I want my shot.'"

8   Hassenfeld declined to speak to BUSINESS WEEK, saying through a spokesperson that he doesn't recall commenting on Whitman's wealth. But listen to the comments of other blue-chip CEOs and a certain note of surprise comes through. No slouch himself when it comes to pumping up his stock price, General Electric Chairman John F. Welch jokingly derides lofty Net stocks as "wampum," while IBM Chairman Louis V. Gerstner Jr. scoffs at the new Net companies as "fireflies before the storm"—they shine now, but will eventually dim out.

9   Mock the phenomenon as they may, however, these two are far too smart not to recognize that something more important than soaring stock prices is going on. Simply put, there's a revolution under way, and mastering the Net has moved front and center on Corporate America's agenda. The Internet model, with fewer hard assets, a direct pipeline to customers, and freedom from the hierarchical management structure of most of Corporate America, offers a new level of speed and operational efficiency for those who master it—and huge dislocations for those who don't. "I don't think there's been anything more important or more widespread in all my years at GE," says Welch. "Where does the Internet rank in priority? It's No. 1, 2, 3, and 4." By yearend, every one of GE's 200 odd businesses will be able to do E-commerce transactions. Eventually, billing, quality monitoring, and other things now done on paper will move onto the Net.

10   Certainly, established companies can bring considerable strengths of their own to the online battle. Strong brands, customer-service expertise, and management depth will help. And with their positive cash flow and borrowing power, they could find that the financing advantage swings in their favor if the market for Net stocks continues to weaken.

11   But for the time being, it's the Net business model that's ascendant—and throughout Corporate America, executives are suddenly waking to the realization that those who don't move fast to get in on the game risk having their lunch eaten by tiny rivals who may have barely existed just a few years ago. In industry after industry, fledgling Net companies have transformed the way business is done and snatched market share from their much bigger, established rivals. Retailing and financial services got whacked first. Now media, entertainment, telecommunications, and health-care companies are feeling the heat.

DAY OF RECKONING

12   Old-line industries such as autos, oil, and utilities could be next, warns market researcher Forrester Research Inc., which believes that brokers in these industries—either independent or owned by the established players—will set up more efficient online sites for reaching customers. "Americans perfected a business model that became the most important in the world," says Lawrence A. Bossidy, CEO of industrial-products giant AlliedSignal Inc. "But it's obsolete now because it requires too much working capital. The Internet allows you to be far more virtual with customers and suppliers. If I don't embrace the Net, I can't reduce those investments."

13   Or you could be cut out altogether—disintermediated, in Internet parlance. That's what spooked John Steffens, vice-chairman at broker Merrill Lynch & Co. He held out for months, arguing that Merrill's superior service and market savvy would allow the world's largest brokerage firm to trump nascent online rivals. But then the unthinkable happened: Merrill began to lose business to Charles Schwab and E*Trade. In an abrupt about-face, Merrill announced on June 1 that it would rush to build an online brokerage service in six months. With the titan of broker-generated sales conceding the online threat, any company that relies on a traditional sales force will now have to do some soul-searching.

14   Elsewhere, too, the past few months have seen a dizzying series of announcements and deals as other mainstream corporate giants have raced to solidify their Web strategy. Faced with the potentially catastrophic threat of digitized music available over the Web, BMG and Universal have created online CD seller getmusic.com. In the media and entertainment world, it seems, nearly everyone from Walt Disney to NBC to TCI is scrambling to create separate Web stocks in a mad rush to get some Internet currency. Even before Merrill's announcement, other brokerages had been hustling to prepare for the Internet. Donaldson, Lufkin & Jenrette Inc., for example, floated a tracking stock tied to its online efforts.

15   Those who don't attempt to navigate the Internet may be taking the biggest risk of all. Almost overnight, the Net has become a huge part of the economy. A recent study by the Center for Research on Electronic Commerce at the University of Texas, commissioned by Cisco Systems Inc., found that the Internet economy grew at an astonishing annual 174.5% rate from 1995 through 1998. At $300 billion today, that rivals sectors like telecommunications and autos.

YOUNG AND HUNGRY

16   Anyone who doubts the vibrancy of this new world need only follow the money. Net-based IPOs and deals are restructuring the corporate landscape. Through June 10, 66 Internet companies went public, up from 40 in all of 1998, according to Securities Data Corp. So far this year, they've raised $5.5 billion—fully 25% of the $21.9 billion raised by U.S. public offerings, compared with 6% of the total raised by all IPOs last year. And though the IPO parade could slow if the Internet stocks don't regain their footing, it is worth remembering that Net-stock valuations remain stratospheric compared with the blue chips. The GIN's average p-e is a breathtaking 674, dwarfing the 34 averaged by the companies in the S&P 500 index. Moreover, armed with their high-priced stocks, Internet highfliers continue to be aggressive acquirers. In the first five months of 1999, Internet outfits have snatched up companies worth $48 billion, according to Securities Data, up from $28 billion in all of 1998.

17   Until now, many of those deals have involved Net companies buying up other Net companies in a dash to capture market share. But the disparity of valuations between pumped-up Net stocks and their real-world brethren has allowed Net businesses to begin buying up rivals with real-world assets—making the Net companies a threat to more established players. Take Yellow Page ad agency TMP Worldwide Inc., which garnered a Net-like stock valuation by relentlessly promoting its online job-search site, monster.com. That helped its stock rise from $15.50 to a high of $93. Though the stock has since dropped to $56, TMP has used that currency to consolidate a foray into the headhunting business by snapping up LAI Worldwide Inc. From out of nowhere, it's suddenly breathing down the neck of established rivals such as Heidrick & Struggles Inc. and Korn/Ferry International Inc.

18   Stories like that have awakened many executives at old-line companies to the need to develop a little Net currency of their own. ''If we have a currency, we can be consolidators instead of the consolidatee,'' says Fredric G. Reynolds, chief financial officer at CBS Corp.

19   The issue of Internet currency is also closely linked to one of the most intractable problems lurking beneath Internet Anxiety: Will brick-and-mortar companies still be able to attract good people? The ability to hire and keep top-notch employees, of course, goes to the heart of any company's ability to prosper and grow. But without the lure of high-flying stocks and big options gains, traditional companies are hardly playing on a level field.

20   Just ask Disney's Michael D. Eisner. The Internet ambitions of the entertainment giant he runs have been hampered by a revolving door in the online unit. Executives arrive, earn their stripes online, and get snatched away to run their own show with a startup that can offer a big equity stake. The latest to leave: Internet honcho Jake Winebaum, who gave up one of the best perches in media to run his own Net outfit in partnership with Sky Dayton, a 27-year-old entrepreneur. Dayton, with whom Winebaum often went snowboarding, founded ISP giant Earthlink Network Inc. "There's real-world wealth and Internet wealth," says Winebaum, who made a fortune selling a group of magazines to Disney. "I'd like to see what Internet wealth feels like."

Jumping on the Bandwagon
Traditional companies in all kinds of industries are furiously mapping out Net strategies.

- **Universal Music**

What It's Doing Getting ready for the time, probably later this year, when their music is available over the Net. Working out piracy guards and supporting online CD seller getmusic.com.

Goal Compete with smaller labels already selling online and ensure that Universal isn't cut out as the middleman between artist and audience.

- **Merrill Lynch**

What It's Doing Recognizing that not all customers will remain true to traditional brokers and brokerage services, it's setting up online trading.

Goal Stem the tide of customers moving to online leaders such as Charles Schwab and E*Trade. Lure E-traders' assets with a supermarket of services from financial-planning advice to Visa cards.

- **NBC**

What It's Doing Merging several of its Web sites—but not its interest in MSNBC—with Xoom.com to create publicly traded NBC Interactive.

Goal Gain Internet currency to acquire Net-content companies and build a bigger presence online.

- **QVC**

What It's Doing Expanding iQVC so television shoppers can turn to the Web for greater selection and variety.

Goal Support the TV shopping business with Web-based sales and use the mass reach of television to steer customers online.

- **ALLIEDSIGNAL**

What It's Doing Pushing top executives to include the Internet in their business plans for 1999.

Goal Dramatically reduce the amount of working capital AlliedSignal uses to manufacture and distribute its products by establishing virtual networks with customers and suppliers that can cut inventory and time to market.

- **AMERICAN AIRLINE'S SABRE INC.**

What It's Doing Considering a tracking stock for its Travelocity travel reservations Web site.

Goal Cash in on the multi-billion dollar values accorded the stocks of much smaller Net-based rivals without risking Travelocity's key role linking SABRE's reservations system with airlines and travel agents.

JUMPING SHIP

21   Disney isn't the only company watching as online upstarts seduce some of their most talented executives. As the Web matures, Net companies are finding they need new skills, from logistics and distribution to marketing. Recruiting isn't a hard sell when the Net seems to mint a fresh set of millionaires with each IPO. "Comments like 'someone's brother went over to work for Excite as an assistant marketer and is now worth $10 million to $20 million' and so on—that noise is already seeping in, and we are nervous about it," says Alan Kaye, head of human resources at toymaker Mattel Inc.

22   Still, money is not the only reason talent is moving to the Net. Some top execs have looked around at the speed with which the Net is transforming the economy and have decided that a move online is a simple matter of survival. Neil S. Braun left a job at the pinnacle of broadcasting as president of the NBC Television Network to take his chance on the Internet. With $100 million in backing from Net investor CMGI Inc., Braun is launching iCast to develop video and audio services for the Web. "The Internet will be the growth medium for the rest of my career," says Braun, 46. "Not to be part of it would be an incredible missed opportunity."

23   If poaching can't be stopped, some have stepped up the efforts to fight back. Federal Express Corp., whose expertise at computerized logistics has made it a prime hunting ground for hungry E-biz startups, is hoping a more balanced work environment will help it to keep its remaining high-

tech workers. Unlike the work-around-the-clock ethos Silicon Valley demands, FedEx offers flexible schedules, telecommuting, and on-site degree programs through a local university—all at a leafy campus 18 miles from its Memphis headquarters.

24   As tough as it is to attract and hold on to talent, traditional companies face an even bigger challenge when it comes to deploying capital in an online initiative. Net-based rivals have created a new model for doing business that rewards them for plowing every cent into development—even if it means losses. Real-world companies, however, are still expected to show earnings growth quarter after quarter.

25   For those tied to the earnings-driven way of doing business, there are anguishing choices to be made about how much to invest in a still-emerging medium with huge up-front costs and profits that remain only theoretical. "In getting from A to C, B is hell," says Avram C. Miller, who guided Intel Corp.'s Internet investments as vice-president of business development before forming his own consultancy. "B is where your revenues decline and your profits go down. But there may be no way for large companies to get to where they need to be in the future without going through this valley of death."

26   It's not just about shrinking earnings—it's also about having the stomach to take money away from other businesses within the company that are actually generating cash. Take the case of Charles Schwab, which has been one of the most successful in its migration to the Net. An early challenge managers of the fledgling unit faced back in 1995 was fighting the expanding international unit and others for corporate-investment dollars. "We had hard decisions to make," says Dawn G. Lepore, Schwab's chief information officer.

27   Even Wal-Mart Stores Inc., which brought retailing into the computer age, is groping to find its way in the new environment. "No one seems to understand that there is not a general consensus as to what's going to happen on the Internet," says CEO David D. Glass. He says the best estimates he has found for total retail sales transacted over the Internet next year range from $10 billion all the way up to $100 billion. That makes it all but impossible for him to figure how much Wal-Mart, with sales of $138 billion, should invest.

TOUGH SLOG

28   Making matters worse, the Internet is not a world that tolerates caution or deliberation. In a medium where brand-name recognition is everything, losing the "first-mover advantage" can be a handicap. That's the big lesson Corporate America learned when Barnes & Noble Inc. got blindsided by Amazon.com Inc. Despite huge capital expenditures and massive advertising since then, Barnes & Noble remains barely more than one-tenth Amazon's size online.

29   It's hardly surprising that Barnes & Noble wasn't first to the party. Selling direct on the Net, after all, required it to cannibalize its own core franchise. That's a problem a lot of other conventional companies will face as they contemplate an online push. By cutting out the middleman, the Net makes it possible to reach buyers faster and cheaper. But for many, taking advantage of those efficiencies will mean going into direct competition with themselves or their distributors.

30   Any company that tries to minimize cannibalization risks losing the customer altogether to more aggressive outsiders—as Merrill Lynch learned to its chagrin. Similar issues torpedoed former Compaq Computer CEO Eckhard Pfeiffer. He was ousted on Apr. 17 in part because he was unwilling to cut out his distributors and sell computers direct online. Compaq's sales stalled any way when customers went to rivals' online sites. E-commerce players like CompUSA Inc. and Staples Inc. figure the only course is to forge ahead and not fret about cannibalization. "Right now, someone else is trying to get that customer, and that's Dell and Gateway," says Stephen B. Polley, CEO of CompUSA Direct. "We have to be just as aggressive."

31   Another thorny issue that established companies face is the question of how to structure their online unit. Should it be kept in-house or spun off? The answer has profound implications for everything from a company's ability to offer its best employees options to how deeply it can integrate the Net into its core business.

SPLITSVILLE

32   Given the potential Net IPO's still have for big runups, it's no surprise that investors—as well as employees who work for online units—are increasingly pressuring managers to cash in by floating a separate stock. But if few would quarrel with the joys of stuffing the corporate coffers, it's often far from clear that spinning off an online unit is the best choice strategically. That's one reason, for example, why Microsoft Corp. hasn't spun off its MSN portal. A separately traded MSN with its array of E-commerce and online content sites might gain a big market cap in its own right to help it compete against Yahoo! and AOL. But it would leave Microsoft on the outside looking in as software becomes more tightly integrated with online content.

33   Those issues are behind a debate that is now raging inside SABRE Inc., the big computer-reservations system majority owned by AMR Corp., parent of American Airlines Inc. Travelocity, the popular online travel site, is just a small part of SABRE, which has a current market value of $8 billion. Yet Priceline.com Inc., a far smaller, money-losing rival to Travelocity, has a market cap of $13 billion. That has some investors pushing for a separate tracking stock for Travelocity. With estimates of its value ranging up to $10 billion, says SABRE CEO Michael J. Durham, "you start forgetting how to spell 'synergies.'"

34   So how can real-world companies pick their way through the competing demands of investors, employees, and their own business imperatives? Catalog retailer Fingerhut Cos. may offer a model. Already famed for its database expertise, Fingerhut began buying up promising Web ventures such as PCFlowers and MountainZone in 1998. But rather than take full control and an earnings hit as these embryonic businesses struggle toward profitability, Fingerhut buys stakes of less than 20%. Keeping below that threshold lets Fingerhut avoid having to recognize losses at those ventures. To make sure it doesn't miss out on the upside, Fingerhut holds options to raise its share if the companies start showing a profit. The minority positions also allow Fingerhut to attract and reward E-workers with stakes in their own ventures. "It's a very good structure for a company like ours, which is earnings-driven," says President Will Lansing.

35   Lansing isn't the only one in search of a solution. And as older companies adjust to the new technology—and learn to exploit it—they should be able to counterpunch with some formidable strengths of their own. Says GE's Welch: "There are advantages for existing companies: They have the business processes, they have the fulfillment capabilities, they have the brand recognition, and they often have the technology."

36   Some have already begun to exploit those advantages. QVC's Internet shopping subsidiary, iQVC, racked up a respectable $50 million in sales last year by piggybacking on QVC's existing order-fulfillment and customer-service operations. That lets QVC sell a lot more items than it can showcase each hour on TV. Says Jeffrey F. Rayport, an associate professor at Harvard Business School who praises QVC as a case study in hybrid business models: "They stood back and said, 'What is it we can do uniquely for our customers offline and online?' and then built around that."

37   Still, the anxiety unleashed in the past year is likely just a taste of what's ahead. The two competing business models have only begun to clash, and the new rules have yet to gel. "No one can tell you today what the impact of any move on the chessboard will be," says PaineWebber's Drazka. The only certainty: The earlier you get in on the game, the greater your chances of winning.

BusinessWeek

CASE 7

COMPAQ'S POWER PLAY

1   Since taking over the world's largest maker of personal computers six years ago, Compaq Chief Executive Eckhard Pfeiffer has regularly sent shock waves through the PC business. Back in 1992, the Houston-based PC maker slashed prices by up to 32%, sending competitors scrambling to lower costs and match Compaq Computer Corp. Last year the German-born executive set the consumer-PC business on its ear with a line of home computers priced below $1,000, again forcing rivals to react swiftly or lose out on one of the fastest-growing segments of the PC business.

2   Get ready for another shakeup—only this one will reach far beyond the PC crowd and into every corner of the $700 billion computer world. On Jan. 26, Pfeiffer and Digital Equipment Corp. Chief Executive Robert B. Palmer concluded four days of intense negotiations by shaking hands on a record-breaking $8.7 billion acquisition. When completed in June, the deal will be the largest in the annals of the computer industry—topping AT&T's $7.4 billion purchase of NCR Corp. and IBM's $3.5 billion buyout of Lotus Development. It will create a new computer colossus with some $37.5 billion in revenues, second only to giant IBM in computer sales.

NEW LANDSCAPE

3   The import of this mega-merger, though, goes far beyond computer rankings. By acquiring Digital, Compaq is catapulted from the upstart, wild-and-woolly PC generation into the high-tech big leagues of companies that supply the world's most complex and critical information systems. Compaq's product offerings will now span the computing landscape, from $649 handheld computers to superpowerful $2 million fail-safe computer servers. More important, the company will command Digital's vaunted service and consulting staff of 22,000 people, who know their way around the computing back offices of the world's largest corporations—customers Compaq has been striving to reach, with modest success, for the past three years.

4   Compaq's timing couldn't be better. The merger comes just as corporations are grappling with wrenching change in their computing options and the way they do business. The move away from mainframe-style computing to cheaper, powerful servers tied to banks of PCs is accelerating as companies buy new equipment to ward off potential software problems posed by the year 2000. At the same time, the race is on to figure out how to link a mish-mash of corporate networks to the Internet for speedy access to customers and suppliers. Compaq will now be able to offer solutions on all fronts—low-cost, powerful computing systems, along with a cadre of consultants to install and maintain the high-tech gear.

5   Suddenly, the 16-year-old company has the key pieces to reshuffle the tech deck. Compaq is expected to bring its low-cost, take-no-prisoners PC economics into the high-end computing markets that IBM, Hewlett-Packard, and Sun Microsystems have long dominated. Compaq's lean operations, for instance, require it to spend just 15 cents for every $1 in sales, far below Hewlett-Packard and IBM, which spend 24 cents and 27 cents, respectively, for every $1 they add to the top line. "This is an example of a New Economy company growing up to replace a company that dominated in an earlier era," says John T. Chambers, chief executive of Cisco Systems Inc., the No. 1 supplier of networking gear.

Source: Gary McWilliams in Houston, with Ira Sager in New York, Paul C. Judge in Boston, and Peter Burrows in San Mateo, California, "Compaq's Power Play," *Business Week:* February 9, 1998; and Robert D. Hof in San Mateo, California, "Now What's in the Forecast for Sun?" *Business Week:* February 9, 1998.

6   Even PC highfliers Dell Computer Corp. and Gateway 2000 Inc., long accustomed to running no-frills operations, can't assume it's business as usual. Now, their biggest competitor just upped the ante by adding a service and support team that will give business customers the velvet-glove treatment. This deal, says Pfeiffer, will "force others to rethink their positions."

7   Indeed, Compaq's sheer muscle and broad new reach may put it on a par with the industry's two agenda-setters: Microsoft Corp. and Intel Corp. Today, Microsoft calls the shots with its Windows software, which runs on 87% of desktop machines, while Intel's microprocessors claim 89% of the world's $21 billion computer processor market—a duopoly dubbed Wintel.

8   Now, Compaq, already the biggest seller of Windows software and Intel chips in its PCs, could be the flag bearer that pushes Wintel technologies upstream in servers for heavy-duty computing jobs—everything from inventory management to complex financial databases. A crucial ingredient: Digital has one of the largest trained sales and support staffs for hawking Microsoft's powerful Windows NT, which is Microsoft's linchpin for moving into the lucrative $30 billion corporate-software market. In the past, customers gravitated to Compaq's aggressively priced products but often would use a service company like Digital because of its superior systems-integration skills, says Microsoft Chairman William H. Gates III. "This gives them the best of both worlds," he says.

9   Or three worlds. The Microsoft-Intel-Compaq troika could be a hugely powerful combination that gives NT the oomph it needs to edge out the huge numbers of mainframes and Unix servers that corporations now rely on to run their businesses. Already, NT has captured 40% of the server market, with unit sales up a huge 80% from last year.

10   In essence, the three companies may well wind up acting like a virtual corporation lined up against IBM, Sun, Silicon Graphics, and the like. While Microsoft spends a hefty 17% of sales on research and development and Intel spends 9.4%, Compaq invests a measly 3.3%. Even after the merger, analysts expect Compaq will be able to keep its R&D costs to just 4.6%, thanks to Digital's decade of downsizing. That makes it possible for the Houston computer maker to undercut competitors across its product line, from bargain-basement PCs to powerful servers. Says Pfeiffer: "We want to do it all, and we want to do it now."

11   But first Compaq must digest Digital, which promises to be one of the biggest challenges Pfeiffer has faced to date. For years, Compaq has prospered through its single-minded focus on selling Wintel machines. Now it vows to turn itself into a one-stop shop, selling Wintel, as well as Digital's proprietary VMS computers and Unix machines—both used for big computing tasks. That means Compaq will likely face a massive sales reorganization as it melds its PC sales group with Unix sales reps. That's no small thing. Just this November, HP finished merging its Unix and PC sales staffs into one integrated force—a two-year effort that changed the jobs of 5,000 people. "It was big for us, and it will be orders of magnitude greater for them," says William V. Russell, HP's server chief.

12   Then there's the task of folding Digital's 54,300 employees into Compaq's considerably smaller 33,000-strong workforce. Worse, this must be done by companies based some 2,000 miles apart. To be sure, Compaq is credited with the smooth $3 billion acquisition of Tandem Computers Inc. last June. But Tandem, a Silicon Valley maker of high-end computers, had just 7,000 employees, and they weren't as demoralized as Digital's workers, who have weathered years of layoffs, losses, and flip-flop strategies. "Compaq could really get locked up in an execution nightmare," says Silicon Graphics Chief Executive Rick Belluzzo, who until recently ran HP's computer business.

13   And, face it, big tech mergers have a lousy track record, chiefly because it's so tough fusing differing product lines and corporate cultures. "Compaq will have to spend the next two years integrating and reinventing," says Edward J. Zander, Chief Operating Officer of Sun Microsystems Inc. "We'll spend it innovating."

14   Rivals dismiss the deal as only the final chapter in Digital's long decline. "We don't see DEC in the marketplace very much at all," says HP's Russell. "We don't even track our win rate against them anymore." Dell Computer Corp. CEO Michael S. Dell, whose company now uses Digital for customer service, says the merger is more likely to balloon Compaq's operating costs than its sales. "Companies with higher cost structures do very poorly," he says.

15   Still, it's hard to bet against Pfeiffer. Under the 56-year-old CEO, Compaq's run has been phenomenal. Revenues are up 500% since 1992 and show no sign of slowing—they're expected to climb 26% this year, to $31 billion, even without Digital. Last year, Compaq sold 10.1 million PCs worldwide, up a stunning 43%—more than double the industry growth rate. "If you look at the over-all market, there were 11 million more PCs sold than in 1996, and Compaq picked up 30% of that," says analyst Ashok Kumar, of Loewenbaum & Co. Among rivals, none matches Compaq's sizzling pace—certainly not IBM, whose sales rose an anemic 3% last year. Not even Sun, whose revenues shot up 21% last year.

NEW RESPECT

16   In almost every business it has entered, Compaq has driven rivals to distraction. Three years after it charged into the home-PC business, Compaq's sales are running neck-and-neck with Packard Bell NEC Inc., the market leader. Packard Bell held a 31% share of retail PC sales to Compaq's 29% during October, according to researchers Audits & Surveys Worldwide. Even in segments with well-entrenched suppliers, such as engineering workstations, Compaq has marched in unimpeded. Just a year after shipping its first PC-based workstations, it held a market-leading 16% share, leapfrogging Hewlett-Packard, Intergraph, and IBM. Meanwhile, Compaq has held the lead in PC servers since 1993.

17   Now, Compaq will cast an even bigger shadow. Analysts say Sun will have to speed up investments in customer services, a notoriously weak area for the $8.6 billion computer maker. "We typically viewed Compaq as a supplier in the middle tier, not for our big transaction systems," says Monsanto Corp. Chief Information Officer Patrick Fortune. "Now, within one company, we can have that whole line."

18   The deal also is bad news for HP. Given Digital's problems and HP's ascent in the PC business in recent years, HP has carved out a position as the only soup-to-nuts supplier to challenge IBM for the biggest corporate customers. Should Compaq resuscitate Digital's computer business, HP would face a competitor with a product lineup not unlike its own—but with a history for slashing costs and forcing margins down industrywide. "This puts a strong new player into the mix," admits HP CEO Lewis E. Platt. "We'll be watching with interest and won't let any time pass before we respond."

19   IBM, the company Compaq must now surpass to become No. 1, may be forced to revisit lagging PC operations. Until now, IBM has fended off efforts to match the sector's cutthroat pricing by linking PC sales with services. "This may be a wake-up call for IBM," says a consultant close to both companies. Further evidence of IBM's declining share of home-PC sales came on Jan. 28, when retailer Tandy Corp. announced it would no longer sell IBM PCs, opting for an exclusive 3-year Compaq deal. With IBM's sales dragging behind the PC industry's worldwide 15% growth rate, it could be forced to match Compaq's ultrathin hardware margins. That will likely require IBM to take additional steps to lower its manufacturing and distribution costs, they say. IBM declines comment.

20   Even Dell, the master of cheap PC assembly and delivery to corporations, can't blithely ignore the bulked-up Compaq. Dell will no doubt remain the lowest-cost PC maker—its overhead amounts to just 11.6% of sales vs. Compaq's 15%. But the move to networked computing and the rush to tap into the Net are prompting more companies to seek advice—not just machines. IBM's service business, for example, has ballooned from $2 billion to $19 billion in the past seven years. This trend could force Dell to invest heavily in a service and support team, raising its overhead costs. "Dell will have to fight fire with fire," says analyst John B. Jones Jr. of Salomon Smith Barney, "or change the game."

21   Changing the game is Pfeiffer's specialty. By tackling Digital, the computer world's longest-running tough-luck story, he is again flaunting conventional wisdom. He's betting that PC economics, where huge volumes make up for slim margins, can make Digital a winner. "What we realized before anyone, is the unlimited potential of the PC," says Pfeiffer.

22   That became clear to him in 1991 when he took over a bloated Compaq, slashed the workforce by 12%, and depth-charged prices on Compaq's PCs. The result: Compaq reset the competitive landscape, forcing PC rivals to whack costs and squeeze efficiencies out of manufacturing. Those that couldn't make the grade, such as AST Research Inc. and Apple Computer Inc., lost market share and were sidelined.

TABLE 1
Compaq and Digital

Armed with Digital Equipment's products—not to mention its vaunted service and support staff—Compaq will bring its own low-cost, take-no-prisoners PC economics into high-end corporate markets that have long been dominated by Hewlett-Packard and IBM.

The Might of Compaq and Digital Will Boost Some . . .

Intel Revenues

. . . And Threaten Others

IBM Revenues

MARGIN MAGIC

23   Four years later, Pfeiffer disproved the notion that home PCs were money-losers. He further tackled costs and brought consumer marketing and retail skills to the computer maker. Last year, Pfeiffer drove the concept to new heights. By using low-cost chips, outsourcing assembly, and tightening sales policies, Compaq released a $799 PC with the same 11% gross margin as its most expensive home computer.

24   To get these tough jobs done, Pfeiffer has shown he's willing to do just about anything—even go up against Intel and Microsoft. Take the recent sales explosion in sub-$1,000 PCs, a segment Compaq jump-started late last year. At the time, Intel didn't offer a low-cost processor that would make it possible to sell a no-frills machine and still make money. Pfeiffer didn't wait for Intel to come around. He cut a deal with Cyrix Corp. and, more recently, Advanced Micro Devices Inc. to use their Intel-clone chips.

25   Absorbing Digital will put such skills to the test. Digital, after all, is no plum. The company recently swung earnings into the black with a $75 million profit for the quarter ended Dec. 27. But its $13 billion in revenues are the lowest since 1990. And Digital has suffered $5.9 billion in cumulative losses since 1991. Addressing the company's low morale and leisurely release of new products will be Pfeiffer's first priority. There are signs Digital's culture may be waking up to what's ahead. At a meeting last week, a Digital manager asked the correct pronunciation of Pfeiffer's first name. "Aggressive," came the response from a co-worker.

26   Pfeiffer has a plan, as well as a reputation. "We believe we can apply a lot of the management abilities we've shaped very successfully in the last two years—be it asset management or combining some functions," he says. "There's lots of leverage there." Pfeiffer, however, won't reveal any restructuring plans until the merger officially closes in June. But analysts say he will likely pare Digital back to two pieces: a systems and software unit and a services business.

27   That means Compaq may jettison Digital's remaining software and peripheral product lines. Analysts also are betting he will fold Digital's lackluster notebook and PC operations and sell off some businesses, such as Digital's storage unit, to recoup a part of its purchase price. The result: Digital's workforce could shrink to about 45,000, from 54,000 currently, say experts.

28   Analysts agree the acquisition can deliver significant new revenues. "You have to ask how much of Digital's growth has been limited by its financial uncertainties," says technology analyst William C. Conroy of the Houston-based brokerage Sanders Morris Mundy Inc. "There may be some nice pickups" from customers' faith in Compaq, he says. Indeed, Compaq Chief Financial Officer Earl L. Mason says Digital will contribute to earnings within a year.

29   Achieving that goal will require a sizable hike in revenues from Digital's business. Compaq expects Digital's $5.8 billion service group to play a big role in that. "There is a very big multiplier effect," says a source close to the merger talks. "That's where IBM is using frontline services to drag big-iron sales along." Compaq's willingness to pay a nearly $2.5 billion premium to the company's Jan. 23 market cap reflects the conviction that Compaq's management can rapidly expand sales to Digital's 20,000 customers.

EXHIBIT A

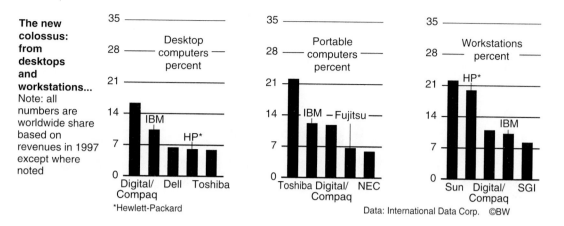

The new colossus: from desktops and workstations...
Note: all numbers are worldwide share based on revenues in 1997 except where noted

*Hewlett-Packard

Data: International Data Corp.   ©BW

30   What made the deal happen now? Talks between the two companies had been on and off over the past three years. In mid-1995, when the two first began negotiating, Digital's stock was depressed to $42 and its market cap less than half its $13.8 billion in sales. At the time, the Digital board was unwilling to consider a sale, believing its shares were undervalued and Compaq would likely gut the company, according to a source close to the talks. Then last December, when discussions resumed, Palmer was joined in the negotiations by outside Digital director Frank P. Doyle, a retired General Electric Co. executive.

31   Doyle, who had played a key role in brokering the October sale of Digital's chipmaking operations to Intel, swayed the board in favor of a sale this time. "He helped the Digital board wrestle with the economic consequences of a stand-alone strategy," says a source close to the talks.

ROSE'S RAIDS

32   There also was a new team evaluating the deal for Compaq. Pfeiffer assigned CFO Mason and Enterprise Computing Group Senior Vice-President John T. Rose, who oversees Compaq's corporate-computing efforts. They have the background for the task—both are former Digital executives. They spent weeks evaluating Digital's products, customers, and finances. Rose's ties have helped land former Digital executives at Compaq, including vice-president for enterprise marketing Robert Fernander and vice-president of Compaq's networking division, William R. Johnson.

33   A gregarious manager who began his computer industry career at IBM and later ran Digital's PC business for seven years, Rose will be on the hot seat to make the deal work. "He's been the champion. This [acquisition] affects his ability to compete in the marketplace. More than anybody else, he's the guy Eckhard and the board are looking to say why this is the right target," says a Compaq insider.

34   Pfeiffer is looking to another former Digital manager to get the business contributing to profits by the end of the year. Under CFO Mason, who joined the company in 1996, Compaq has become a cash machine intensely focused on boosting return on invested capital. Since the start of 1996, Compaq has trimmed inventories by 27% even as it added nearly $10 billion in revenues. Compaq now turns over inventories 14 times a year, up from nine times at the end of September. The payoff from that ultrafast turnover: Compaq generated $6 billion in cash since the start of 1996.

35   Not bad returns for what is largely a low-margin PC business. Now, consider the potential impact of that operating style on big-ticket packages of servers, networks, software, and services. That's the landscape Pfeiffer now sketches for a dramatically bigger Compaq—and the world of computers.

EXHIBIT B

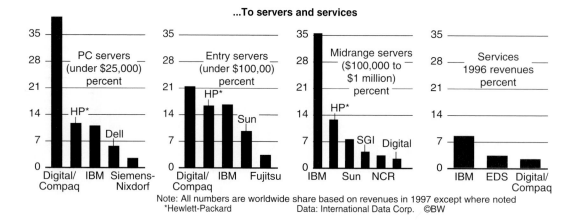

...To servers and services

Note: All numbers are worldwide share based on revenues in 1997 except where noted
*Hewlett-Packard   Data: International Data Corp.   ©BW

NOW WHAT'S IN THE FORECAST FOR SUN?

36   Scott G. McNealy, chief executive of Sun Microsystems Inc., loves to compare the computer business to the auto industry: If you're not one of the top two or three, he says, you're nowhere. Now, Compaq Computer Corp.'s planned purchase of Digital Equipment Corp. suddenly vaults the PC maker into the top trio of computer makers, along with IBM and Hewlett-Packard Co. What does McNealy—whose father was once vice-chairman of also-ran American Motors Corp.—have to say now?

37   Nothing. McNealy declined to comment, though his chief operating officer, Edward J. Zander, says that as far as Sun is concerned, it's merely a chance to raid Digital's customers and employees: "This is IBM's and HP's problem more than ours," he says. But some analysts and customers say that Sun, which only recently joined computerdom's top-tier suppliers, had better pay closer attention. If Compaq manages to swallow Digital without too much indigestion, they say, McNealy could be the odd man out.

Stunted Growth?

38   Why? Unlike its chief rivals, Sun still makes computers based solely on its own Unix operating software and its own microprocessor chips. It's the only major computer maker without machines based on Intel Corp.'s Pentium chips, and it's the only one still shunning Microsoft Corp.'s Windows NT operating software. Contends Bruce L. Claflin, Digital's senior vice-president for worldwide sales and marketing: "[McNealy] has painted himself into a corner."

39   Sun can't afford that. According to market researcher International Data Corp., 1997 sales of all Unix servers grew 9%, to $24.7 billion. But NT server sales shot up 66%, to $6.1 billion. And early next year, the newest version of Windows NT will present an even more direct challenge. Although NT still won't match powerful Unix systems, it will make NT more competitive with Sun's bread-and-butter midrange servers.

40   That's not Sun's only challenge. Buyers often rank Sun behind IBM, HP, and DEC in service. With Digital, Compaq gains a large service organization and more Windows NT support personnel than any of its rivals.

41   Not surprisingly, Sun dismisses any immediate impact from the merger. "DEC has tried more strategies than Heinz has flavors, and none of them has worked," says Zander. "We haven't had DEC on our radar screen in a long time."

42   Zander isn't just whistling past the high-tech boneyard. The PC wolves haven't yet gotten much past Sun's door. In its second quarter, ended on Dec. 28, Sun reported better-than-expected earnings thanks to strong server sales. Indeed, several observers think Sun could actually clean up for the next

year or so, thanks to Digital customers wary of what may happen. "In the short term, it might add some power to Sun," says Stuart Davie, information technology vice-president for Pfizer Inc.'s orthopedic subsidiary, Howmedica, which uses Sun and Compaq NT servers.

43   And Sun's not sitting idle. It's going on the offensive against PC makers on several fronts. On Jan. 19, it introduced a $2,995 workstation aimed squarely at staving off Compaq's PC business. And servers introduced last fall included easier-to-use software designed to combat NT servers.

44   Still, Sun could find itself more isolated than ever. That's one reason the Silicon Valley highflier is spending $30 million this year to take its message to the general public—most recently with its first-ever Super Bowl advertisements. One ad, poking fun at PCs' notorious unreliability, shows bank robbers who explain they need all that money to pay for PC support. To stay ahead of Compaq, McNealy will need big bucks, too.

CASE 8   BusinessWeek

FOR LUCENT, HUNTING SEASON IS ABOUT TO BEGIN

1   Even in the red-hot telecom-equipment market, Lucent Technologies Inc. has been a star. Still, CEO Richard A. McGinn hasn't hesitated to point out Lucent's weaknesses, conceding that it needs to offer better gear for data networking and participate more aggressively in overseas markets. The simple solution would be to buy companies that fill those strategic holes.

2   Until now, however, McGinn has been limited in his ability to do that. Despite Lucent's soaring stock, up sixfold to $80 a share since its public offering in 1996, the company hasn't been as free as rivals such as Cisco Systems Inc. to use its shares as acquisition currency. The reason: Accounting rules bar spin-offs such as Lucent—formerly a unit of AT&T—from using an accounting method called "pooling of interests" for deals until they have been independent for two years. Pooling lets companies avoid taking charges against earnings to write down "goodwill"—the price above book value they pay. Lucent's second birthday is Oct. 1.

PLUGGING HOLES

3   So what will Lucent buy itself as a gift? The company won't comment. But investors and analysts are buzzing about possible targets, including networking-equipment maker Ascend Communications, France's Alcatel, and Finland's Nokia. With a market capitalization of more than $100 billion, Lucent could pull off deals that would set records in an industry already marked by merger mania. Targets could include Ascend, with a market capitalization of $9 billion, or even Nokia, valued at $48 billion. "Everybody's sort of holding their breath to see what Lucent will do," says William Schaff, chief investment officer at San Francisco-based Bay Isle Financial Corp., a Lucent shareholder.

4   Lucent is actively looking at networking and international deals, according to two investment bankers who have talked to company executives. William O'Shea, the head of Lucent's data-networking group, is spearheading the networking initiative. Ben J.M. Verwaayen, Lucent's co-chief operating officer, is trolling for global deals. Lucent has used Goldman, Sachs & Co. or Morgan Stanley Dean Witter for big deals in the past but does not have an exclusive investment bank this time, the bankers say.

5   Lucent's most immediate need is for data networking. The market for data gear is growing 25% a year, says BancBoston Robertson Stephens, about double the traditional telecom-equipment market. And Lucent is weak in two fast-growing areas: asynchronous transfer mode (ATM) and Internet protocol (IP) routing technology.

6   That's where Ascend comes in. The Alameda (Calif.) company is the market leader in ATM and has some IP routing expertise. "That's not rocket science," says Mark Dicioccio, a managing director and head of Lehman Brothers Inc.'s telecom-equipment practice. "Ascend is pretty much the last one standing." Ascend says it plans to remain independent but would listen to an overture. If Ascend balks, Lucent could target other networking companies such as Newbridge Networks, the No. 2 ATM player.

7   Overseas, where Lucent generated only about $6 billion of its $26.4 billion in 1997 revenue, bankers say the strongest candidate would be Finland's Nokia Corp. Nokia would give Lucent expertise in Europe's most popular wireless technology and would provide valuable customer relationships in some 45 countries. Nokia declined comment.

Source: Peter Elstrom in New York, "For Lucent, Hunting Season Is about to Begin," *Business Week:* September 21, 1998.

TABLE 1
Lucent's Most-Wanted List

Ascend Communications

The $1.2 billion company would give Lucent additional expertise in the fast-growing market for data networks. The firm would probably cost more than $10 billion, and Wall Street deems it Lucent's most likely target.

Nokia

The $9.8 billion Finnish telephone-equipment maker has been a rising star, thanks partly to its wireless technology. It would give Lucent a needed boost in Europe and a presence in a total of 45 countries.

Siemens' Telecom Unit

The German conglomerate, which makes everything from locomotives to medical equipment, has a strong $16 billion telecom-equipment business.

Alcatel

The $30 billion French giant offers international reach, with operations in 130 countries. It has bulked up its digital capabilities, notably with its $4.4 billion acquisition of DSC Communications in June.

Data: *Business Week*.

8   Several other companies would also help in foreign markets. France's Alcatel has operations in 130 countries and growing data expertise. But the company, which declined comment, may resist a takeover, and Lucent is unlikely to attempt a hostile deal. Siemens' telecom unit would also give Lucent greater international reach. But a spokesman for Siemens says it would not sell the telecom business on its own.

9   How soon will Lucent make its move? It can't have substantial negotiations before Oct. 1 without running afoul of accounting guidelines. But McGinn has a head start—the shopping list he has been carrying around for two years.

CASE 9

LUCENT'S ASCENT

1   Whether it's bushels of rabbits' feet or just good management, Lucent Technologies Inc. has led a charmed life. Since it was spun off from AT&T in 1996, it has been on a dizzying three-year streak, acting more like a Silicon Valley startup than a 123-year-old maker of phone equipment. Since Lucent went public, its shares soared from 13 1/2 to a high of 120 on Jan. 8. Meanwhile, the Standard & Poor's 500-stock index hasn't even doubled. Last year alone, Lucent nearly tripled shareholders' money, compared with a 29% return for the S&P 500. Says Mark Herskovitz, co-manager of the Dreyfus Technology Growth Fund, one of Lucent's largest shareholders: "The stock has been just a monster."

2   Until lately, that is. On Jan. 21, Lucent Chairman and CEO Richard A. McGinn reported that revenues for the first fiscal quarter had fallen well short of what Wall Street had forecast—even though profits were better than expected. Instead of $10 billion in sales, Lucent chalked up $9.2 billion. The news fueled worries that phone companies have begun to buy less gear from Lucent and others. Lucent's stock took a drubbing that day, down 7%, to 106.94, although it came back to close at 110 on Jan. 26.

3   And McGinn? Despite the revenue shortfall, he's feeling luckier than ever. He dismisses the notion that overall spending on telecom gear is slowing. Oh sure, big guys such as MCI WorldCom, Bell Atlantic, and BellSouth are paring back their capital expenditures. But purchases by telecom upstarts that are building whizzy Internet-like networks will make up the difference, he says. And thanks to Lucent's Jan. 13 deal to buy Ascend Communications Inc. for $20 billion, McGinn thinks his company now has the cutting-edge technologies to land those new contracts. "We intend to lead the networking revolution," he says. "With Ascend, we will become the clear leader."

AMBITIOUS

4   Indeed, Ascend is crucial to McGinn's plan of transforming Lucent from the musty old maker of plain-vanilla phone gear into a colossus supplying the communications gear for the Internet era. He's so certain that Lucent is on the fast track that he vows the company's revenues, not counting Ascend, will hit $36 billion this year, up from $30.1 billion in 1998—an ambitious 20% increase.

5   To put that in perspective, consider this: No other $30 billion company is growing 20% or more a year, according to S&P. To be sure, Silicon Valley archrival Cisco Systems Inc., the leading maker of this new digital networking gear, has been growing at a 35% clip—but Cisco is less than one-third Lucent's size. For McGinn to deliver on his pledge, Lucent must win $6 billion in new business this year, while Cisco needs to add just half that to keep up its torrid pace.

6   Can McGinn do it? Despite his assurances, slowing demand for communications gear may trip him up. Several analysts insist that spending on telecom gear will drop from 15% growth in 1998 to just 5% this year. "Even Lucent's management can't really know [what spending will be]," says Jeffrey Heil, director of equity investments for the Regents of the University of California, a top Lucent shareholder. In the longer term, though, the Lucent-Ascend combo is a powerful one that could make the equipment supplier a leader in next-generation networks.

7   There's little doubt that the feisty 52-year-old McGinn revels in such challenges. His idea of relaxation is going head-to-head with friends in their own version of "Ironman" races—competing in

Source: Peter Elstrom in Murray Hill, New Jersey, with Andy Reinhardt in San Mateo, California, "Lucent's Ascent," *Business Week*, February 8, 1999.

swimming, billiards, golf, and basketball, all in one day. Once, rather than lose a fish he had hooked, he swam around a pier to untangle his line.

8   At Lucent, he's just as relentless. Since stepping up to the CEO post 15 months ago, McGinn has turned around what was widely considered a fading technology power by persuading employees to set aside their internal differences and focus on beating the pants off rivals such as Cisco and Canada's Northern Telecom Ltd. He pushes his staff to set sky-high goals for themselves—and then do whatever is necessary to accomplish them. The result: Lucent's sales are climbing twice as fast as before it became independent.

9   But this year, McGinn may find his Ironman ways are put to the test. The telecom industry is entering a time of wrenching change, as old phone systems give way to digital gear that will be the underpinning of tomorrow's global communications. The rise of the Internet is at the heart of this profound change. Its explosive traffic, combined with the oodles of data that corporations are zapping between offices, demands speedy networks that can chop up information into bite-size digital pieces that wing their way fast.

"IN OUR FAVOR"

10   What's more, this new equipment is so efficient that it may eventually carry both data and voice traffic. Most phone companies already are testing the gear for voice service—and a handful are offering it commercially. That has made data-networking equipment a $45 billion market today—just 10% of the total communications-equipment market—but it's growing twice as fast as sales of standard equipment. So far, that has been a boon to Cisco, which dominates the U.S. market with a 55% share, vs. Lucent's piddling 2%, according to BancBoston Robertson Stephens analyst Paul Johnson. "I think the odds of Cisco leading the market are in our favor," says John T. Chambers, Cisco's CEO.

11   Not anymore, argues McGinn. With Ascend, McGinn believes Lucent has bought its way into the new digital future. Under CEO Mory Ejabat, the Alameda, Calif., company has developed products that are good enough to compete with Cisco's. When you combine Ascend's technology with Lucent's strong relationships with phone companies and its reputation for reliability, McGinn thinks he has the industry's odds-on front-runner. Others agree. "Of all the companies out there, Lucent is the one that's closest to the Holy Grail of offering customers a complete solution," says Mukesh Chatter, founder and CEO of Nexabit Networks Inc., a Marlborough (Mass.) startup.

12   The data market is so crucial to Lucent and its rivals that it reduces normally civil execs to snarling rivals. At a retreat for its top 60 executives last year outside Tucson, Lucent put up "Wanted" posters with the faces of Cisco's Chambers, Nortel CEO John A. Roth, and other executives from equipment makers. Chambers was not amused: "McGinn made it personal," he says. "It sent a bad message to his employees."

SHORT END?

13   McGinn and Nortel's Roth are just as quick to sling barbs. McGinn ridicules Roth for saying that Nortel was buying Bay Networks Inc. to help sell new digital equipment to phone companies—and then backpedaling to say that Bay would instead sell to corporations, its traditional customer base. "At least, you should get your message consistent," he snaps. As for Roth, he criticizes McGinn's purchase of Ascend as buying the wrong digital technology at a sky-high price. "Twenty billion later, Lucent still needs to go shopping," he says.

14   Indeed, technologically, McGinn may yet find himself on the short end of the stick. What Lucent is buying in Ascend is the top maker of phone switches that use a technology called asynchronous transfer mode (ATM). This is the first generation of the technology that most phone companies are using to carry both voice and data traffic. But over time, carriers are itching to move beyond ATM to a technology called Internet protocol (IP). Just like it sounds, this is what's used on the Net. Most phone companies don't think IP is reliable enough for voice calls now—but it's getting better every

EXHIBIT A

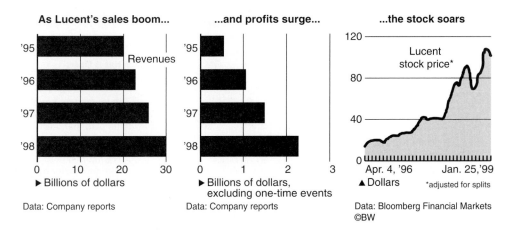

As Lucent's sales boom...

'95 ▮ Revenues
'96 ▮
'97 ▮
'98 ▮

0   10   20   30
▶ Billions of dollars

Data: Company reports

...and profits surge...

'95 ▮
'96 ▮
'97 ▮
'98 ▮

0   1   2   3
▶ Billions of dollars,
   excluding one-time events

Data: Company reports

...the stock soars

120
         Lucent
         stock price*
80
40
0
Apr. 4, '96   Jan. 25,'99
▲ Dollars   *adjusted for splits

Data: Bloomberg Financial Markets
©BW

day. The problem for Lucent: Cisco holds 67% of the IP market, while Lucent is a tiny blip on the radar screen. "Even after Ascend, they still have a lot of work to do," says BancBoston's Johnson.

15   Navigating such digital divides may prove to be as tough for McGinn as what he went through overhauling Lucent. For decades, the business that is now Lucent had been the sleepy maker of phone equipment for AT&T. It included the vaunted Bell Laboratories and its Nobel prize-winning technology. But a history of supplying the country's phone monopoly made Lucent the opposite of scrappy successes like Cisco. Lucent's engineers emphasized bulletproof reliability instead of rapid innovation. They often took years to develop products and tended to work on what they—not their customers—wanted. This was, after all, the company that became known for a variation on Henry Ford's old saw: "You can have any color phone you want, as long as it's black."

16   Times have changed. A galvanizing moment came in 1995, when McGinn sat down with his top 15 execs at Bernards Inn in Bernardsville, N.J. He told them Lucent's spin-off was "the chance of a lifetime" to create the kind of company they had always wanted. When it had been buried inside AT&T, the only expectation was that the unit should increase its profits 10% a year.

AIMING HIGH

17   The executives studied how the best big companies of that time—Motorola Inc. and Hewlett-Packard Co.—had achieved preeminence. With McGinn guiding them, the execs concluded they would have to meet an audacious goal: increasing revenues twice as fast as they had in the past. "You could just see the change in energy," says Henry B. Schacht, the former Cummins Engine Co. chief who was brought in to head Lucent during the spin-off so that McGinn could learn the ropes of running a public company. "Rich gets people to have expectations of themselves that are greater than what they would have on their own," adds Schacht.

18   And not just in the executive suite. McGinn also has been instrumental in revitalizing Bell Labs. Just before Lucent's spin-off, according to Schacht, McGinn told a group of 300 scientists: "You are our future." He also linked their research budget directly to Lucent's fortunes. It would start out at 1% of sales—and for every 10% increase in Lucent's revenues, the research budget would rise 10%. And he set up an internal venture-capital fund so that scientists could get money to start their own businesses—eight have been funded. "We went from less than one patent a day to three patents a day within the first calendar year," says Schacht.

19   The approach is paying off. In 1997, tiny Ciena Corp. clobbered Lucent with a new optical networking product that greatly increased the capacity of long-distance networks. Bell Labs' engineers scrambled to come up with a competing product—and delivered it to customers last September, in

TABLE 1
Lucent Buys into the Future

In the past two years, Lucent has gone on a buying spree, snatching up 14 companies with key market positions or technologies. Here's a sampling:

Company and Acquisition Date	Price	What It Does
Voice Systems		
Octel Communications July '97	$1.8 billion	The leading maker of voice-mail systems teams up with the top rival to its own market.
Data Networking		
Yurie Systems April '98	$1.06 billion	A startup maker of data switches aimed at smaller networks, but it hasn't made big inroads yet.
Livingston Enterprises October '97	$610 million	A rival to Ascend and 3Com in Net access gear. Hasn't gained much market share to date.
Prominet December '97	$164 million	One of a dozen pioneers in fast switches for corporate networks.
Ascend Communications January '99	$19.7 billion	The No. 1 seller of Net access gear and high-octane data switches for the Internet.
Software		
Kenan Systems January '99	$1.48 billion	A provider of advanced billing and customer care software.

just 12 months. "We didn't even have a market position a year ago," says Daniel C. Stanzione, co-chief operating officer and president of Bell Labs. And McGinn's recent spate of purchases sends a signal, too: If Bell Labs doesn't come up with vital technology, Lucent will go out and buy it.

20   At first blush, it seems odd that McGinn is the one shaking up Lucent, given that he worked at AT&T for 27 years. But he was always something of an outsider. Instead of working in AT&T's core phone business, he labored in international operations, ran its computer unit, and moved to the equipment-making division in 1991.

21   He was known for his outspoken views in the hushed suites where radical views were largely unwelcome. McGinn, for example, objected strongly to AT&T's disastrous 1991 acquisition of NCR Corp., and he pushed for years for the Lucent spin-off. "He was always part of the outside renegade culture at AT&T," says David A. Nadler, a friend of McGinn and chairman of the telecom industry's Delta Consulting Group Inc.

22   McGinn's business sense surfaced at an early age. When the New Jersey native arrived at Iowa's Grinnell College in 1964, he set up a late-night snack service operating from his dorm room so students and professors could buy sandwiches after the stores had closed. McGinn jokes that he "had a positive cash flow" by the end of his first year.

PLAIN FOLKS

23   McGinn still seems more entrepreneurial than wing-tip corporate. He's "Rich" to everyone at Lucent, and he fetches his own lunch from the cafeteria. He favors black mock-turtlenecks over collars and ties. "Ties restrict blood flow to the brain," he says. And he says his idols are Dell Computer Corp.'s Michael S. Dell and Nelson Mandela. Indeed, McGinn pushed for Lucent to give $5 million to improve graduation rates at the predominantly African American Malcolm X Shabazz High School in Newark, N.J. McGinn also has little tolerance for those who think technology developments begin

TABLE 2
Duking It Out in the New World of Data Networks

Lucent Technologies

Revenues: $30.1 billion

Profits: $970 million

Market cap: $134 billion

The Murray Hill (N.J.)-based company grew up as the telephone equipment maker for Ma Bell during its days as the country's telephone monopoly, making it the No. 1 seller of standard phone gear. But Lucent is still just a bit player in the hot market for converged voice-and-data networks. That could change, though, with its $20 billion purchase of Ascend, which has cutting-edge technology rivaling Cisco.

Northern Telecom (Nortel)

Revenues: $15.4 billion

Profits: $829 million

Market cap: $36.2 billion

The Canadian player is No. 2 to Lucent in sales of regular phone gear in North America. Nortel has a bigger international presence than Lucent and a stronger position selling data equipment to corporations—thanks to last year's $9 billion acquisition of Cisco rival Bay Networks. The merger has had a rocky start: Nortel warned of soft demand for its equipment last year and laid off 10,000 workers in early January.

Cisco Systems

Revenues: $8.5 billion

Profits: $1.35 billion

Market cap: $162 billion

The Silicon Valley powerhouse is the No. 1 seller of corporate data switches and routers—specialized computers that direct traffic around the Internet and corporate networks. Now Cisco is marketing aggressively to telephone companies that want to build whizzy new networks that can handle data and voice. It has won key orders from startup phone companies such as Qwest Communications, but has had a harder time selling to the Baby Bells, which worry about reliability.

and end in Silicon Valley. At a recent speech in the Valley, he thanked the organizers "for getting me a visa" so he could visit.

24   What drives McGinn more than anything is his need to win. Ben J.M. Verwaayen, co-chief operating officer, recalls how McGinn reacted the first time he told the CEO that Lucent had lost what was a very small piece of business. "He turned gray," Verwaayen says. "It was like somebody had hit him in the stomach." Verwaayen tried to reassure McGinn. "You win some, you lose some," he told his boss. But McGinn would not be consoled. "I don't want anyone here to be a good loser," he snapped. "We are winners."

25   McGinn won't settle for anything less. He has told analysts that he expects to grow 2% to 5% faster than the industry average. How will Lucent reach that mark? By luring business away from rivals while expanding overseas and focusing on the fastest-growing markets. Besides data networking, that means Lucent must sell loads more wireless equipment, optical-networking gear, services, and software. "We're not exactly limited by opportunity," McGinn says, pointing out that Lucent may be the No. 1 equipment maker but still has less than 10% of the $400 billion worldwide market.

26   If McGinn's tactics of the past few years are any indication, he may yet outfox his rivals. For one thing, Lucent executives don't just listen to customers, they pepper them with questions—and then deliver the goods they need. Last year, that helped Lucent elbow its way further into the wireless market. There, it won a contract from PrimeCo Personal Communications, a top U.S. wireless company, after its equipment from Motorola had quality problems. "They spend a lot of time thinking about how to make life easier for us," says Lowell McAdam, PrimeCo's CEO. Overall, Lucent claims

30% of the U.S. wireless market, up from 25% three years ago, estimates Salomon Smith Barney analyst Alex Cena.

27   With the Ascend acquisition, McGinn is betting that he can make the same kind of progress in the data-networking market. Clearly, Ascend's tried-and-true ATM technology will help Lucent win over big phone companies nervous about the less proven IP technology promoted by Cisco and Nortel. But Ascend may not be the answer for the new telecom cowboys cropping up since deregulation. For example, when ICG Communications in Englewood, Colo., decided to offer voice service on an IP network, it asked Lucent to demonstrate its equipment. "It didn't meet the mark," says Robert Flood, ICG's chief technical officer. Instead, Cisco got the contract, estimated at $5 million. Analysts say Lucent will eventually acquire an IP company, such as Juniper Networks or Nexabit Networks.

28   While McGinn vows to improve Lucent's technology, he has more immediate concerns. He managed to calm jitters over Lucent's first-quarter shortfall by making hefty promises for the second quarter and fiscal year ending Sept. 30. A good chunk of Lucent's market cap is riding on whether he can meet his goal. "He has called the corner pocket," says Johnson. "Just winning the game isn't enough. He has to win the way he said." With Ascend in hand, McGinn is betting he has the winning shot lined up.

CASE 10   BusinessWeek

IBM: BACK TO DOUBLE-DIGIT GROWTH?

1   Listening to Louis V. Gerstner Jr. talk about IBM, you could hardly tell revenue growth is in the low single digits. But on May 13, there was the CEO, reciting for Wall Street a unit-by-unit rundown of IBM's businesses that amounted to a bullish analysis of the computer giant. Gerstner even made a bold prediction: It is "possible" IBM will return to double-digit revenue growth in the next few years.

2   Investors ate it up. The next day, IBM shares shot up four points, to nearly 126. And why not? For five years, Gerstner has been masterminding one of the most remarkable revivals in corporate history: double-digit earnings growth, a laser focus on costs, and one of the industry's most aggressive beads on electronic commerce. For the first time in years, pockets of the company are excelling. In '97, Gerstner turned up the heat on high-tech services, a $19.3 billion business that grew 22%. Chip and disk-drive operations racked up sales at a 20% clip. And software acquisitions, such as Lotus Development Corp. and Tivoli Systems Inc., are paying off big time.

3   Sounds like nirvana. The trouble is whether Gerstner can rev up a huge chunk of IBM's business that is nowhere near the fast lane. Despite the upbeat performance Gerstner gave analysts, IBM is losing ground in personal computers, servers, storage systems, and its bread-and-butter—mainframes. Consider the math: Big Blue ended 1997 with nearly 64%—a staggering $50 billion—of its business flat to down. It was the same in the first quarter, a red flag that major segments of IBM's computer business are either losing market share or just not keeping up with fast-growing rivals.

4   Gerstner aims to make up a lot of the difference with hyper-growth in just one key area: high-tech services. Although IBM execs have cautioned analysts for more than a year that the company's services business can't grow at a 20%-plus rate forever, Gerstner now says he's unwilling to accept that. Why? The services sector is going global—a trend, Gerstner says, that should fuel IBM's business strongly enough to carry the company even if its other businesses stay at '97 growth rates. In '96, IBM snagged 27 computer-service deals, each worth more than $100 million, 21 of them in the U.S. Last year, 14 of 24 big contracts were outside the U.S. And so far this year, five out of seven deals are global. "I have never seen a better growth business than [information-technology] services," says Gerstner.

OTHERS' INNARDS

5   Still, services alone may not be enough to lift IBM into double digits. That's why Gerstner also has staked out expanding businesses such as collaborative software, PC servers, and disk drives. Longer term, though, he's betting on new terrain. Gerstner wants to reenergize revenues by making Big Blue the premier supplier of electronic-commerce software and services and the maker of raw technology to build Net-ready information appliances—the innards of everything from Internet phones to handheld computers to TV set-top boxes.

6   While Gerstner thinks IBM can reach double-digit growth in a few years, some analysts figure it may take longer. Gerstner is making his prediction based on an 8.5% 1997 growth rate adjusted for the negative impact of currency. But some analysts don't see it that way. Based on nonadjusted growth rates and a 20% growth in the services business, it'll be 2002 before IBM hits an overall growth rate of 10%, figures analyst Steven Milunovich of Merrill Lynch & Co. The only way IBM can reach that sooner is if the company's software and hardware businesses kick in. While software

Source: Ira Sager in New York, with Gary McWilliams in Houston, Andy Reinhardt in San Mateo, California, and bureau reports, "IBM: Back to Double-Digit Growth?" *Business Week:* June 1, 1998.

EXHIBIT A

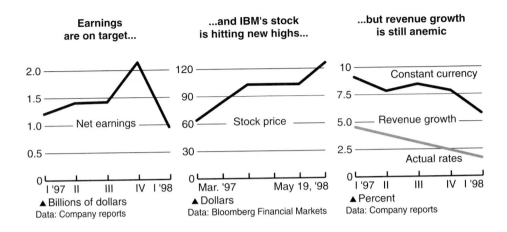

Earnings are on target...

2.0
1.5
1.0 ——— Net earnings ———
0.5
0
I '97   II   III   IV   I '98
▲ Billions of dollars
Data: Company reports

...and IBM's stock is hitting new highs...

120
90
60 ——— Stock price ———
30
0
Mar. '97   May 19, '98
▲ Dollars
Data: Bloomberg Financial Markets

...but revenue growth is still anemic

10 ——— Constant currency
7.5
5.0 ——— Revenue growth ———
2.5 ——— Actual rates
0
I '97   II   III   IV   I '98
▲ Percent
Data: Company reports

has been inching back into the growth column—it posted a 2% gain in the first quarter—hardware has been a bummer. IBM's computer sales were down 8% in the first quarter, to $7.1 billion, from $7.8 billion a year ago.

7   Gerstner knows he must do better. In the high-tech world, single-digit revenue growth doesn't cut it. Overall, IBM's revenue rose a piddling 3.4% last year and a scant 1.8% during the first quarter of this year. Worse, at the same time, major rivals—Compaq Computer, Sun Microsystems, Cisco Systems, Hewlett-Packard, and Microsoft—were growing 4 to 17 times faster. "Every year, IBM grows slower than the industry," says International Data Corp. analyst Frank Gens. "There is a possibility that five years down the road, IBM may not be the largest information-technology supplier." Says Soundview Financial Group analyst Gary Helmig: "1998 is the turning point here."

8   Indeed, Big Blue is looking smaller by the day. Microsoft Corp. is now the world's largest software provider, having edged past IBM with $13.1 billion in software sales during 1997, vs. $12.8 billion for IBM. In the $6.6 billion database-software market, Oracle Corp. slipped past IBM last year to become tops in that field—Oracle's database revenue jumped 20%, to $1.82 billion, while IBM's grew 8%, to $1.8 billion, according to market researcher Dataquest Inc.

9   What's more, IBM, once the undisputed king of hardware, is about to lose that title, too. When Compaq Computer Corp. completes its $9 billion merger with Digital Equipment Corp., their combined hardware operations will be $34 billion by yearend. IBM's computer sales are expected to be $26 billion, essentially flat from '97. Says Compaq Senior Vice-President John T. Rose: "If you're not quick enough, the competition will get by you."

10   Gerstner wants to get quicker. On Feb. 2, in his annual employee pep talk, he told IBM's 270,000 workers via a televised speech: "We've got to gain market share," he snapped. "This is the year we've got to make it happen." Then, poking a finger at his troops, Gerstner declared: "None of us at IBM is here, certainly not me, because we want to work on a perpetual turnaround. We're finished with the turnaround."

11   Tough talk aside, Gerstner insists IBM's growth over the past few years has not been shabby. The way he sees it, Big Blue didn't grow a measly 3.4% last year but a respectable 8.5%. How so? IBM calculates the different currency values against the dollar in the 160 countries it does business in to come up with a figure it calls "constant currency." Gerstner argues that since IBM conducts 55% of its business overseas, the only way to get a true measure of how the company is doing is to factor in currency fluctuations around the globe. If you do, he says, IBM is on target: high single-digit revenue growth and double-digit earnings. "You have to look at [growth] from the perspective of constant currency or it really isn't very meaningful," he says.

12   But even using that logic, IBM's growth doesn't measure up to that of rivals. Hewlett-Packard Co., for example, conducts 56% of its business outside the U.S., yet its revenue still grew 12% last

EXHIBIT B

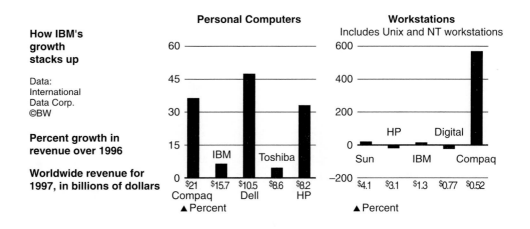

How IBM's growth stacks up

Data: International Data Corp. ©BW

Percent growth in revenue over 1996

Worldwide revenue for 1997, in billions of dollars

year, without adjusting for constant currency. And in the first quarter, HP's revenue shot up 16%—even with falling PC prices, a problem IBM and Compaq share. "If I'm looking at the growth rate of the company, I'm not going to use constant currency," says analyst Bret Rekas of BancAmerica Robertson Stephens. Even at the 8.5% constant-currency rate IBM executives are using, Rekas isn't impressed. "I'm supposed to get excited about that?" he asks.

13   Gerstner, however, is excited about IBM's opportunities for growth in an increasingly digital world. He says Big Blue has two skills it can capitalize on: services and microchip knowhow. Gerstner is betting that the Internet will set off demand for IBM chip technology as well as services to manage new generations of low-cost digital gear. "The network world is the ultimate manifestation of what this technology is going to do," says Gerstner. "It's going to connect everybody and everything." But don't expect IBM to build toasters with tiny computers inside or even handheld computers. It views its role strictly as a components supplier to other companies.

14   Odds are that Big Blue, already a big technology supplier, will eke a good business out of this IBM Inside strategy. But it's too early to tell whether it will boost growth substantially. The company already supplies superfast slivers of silicon for Silicon Graphics Inc.'s Cray Research Inc. supercomputers. Networking giants Cisco Systems Inc. and 3Com Corp. use IBM microchips in their communications gear. And phonemaker Qualcomm has adopted IBM chips to make digital phones. In disk drives, rivals—including Compaq, Dell Computer, and EMC—are lining up to buy IBM products. And thanks to leading-edge technology in the components that go into its drives, IBM's gross profit margin is 40%, nearly twice that of competitors'. Concedes Jack Egan, vice-president for rival storage maker EMC: "Periodically, IBM does a great job of getting technology out of its labs and into products."

15   There's more to come. Companies such as National Semiconductor, Harris, and Northern Telecom are paying just for the right to have early access to IBM's state-of-the-art work with silicon geranium. With this technology, IBM can make tiny parts using little power.

TRUMP CARD?

16   That, says Big Blue, will be a boon to communications companies, such as cell-phone makers, especially as they start building next-generation devices that have Net access built in. Hughes Electronics Corp. is planning to use IBM chips in communications satellites it will launch next year. Says Michael Attardo, general manager for IBM's Microelectronics Div.: "My objective is to be the premier [chip] supplier in the networked world."

EXHIBIT C

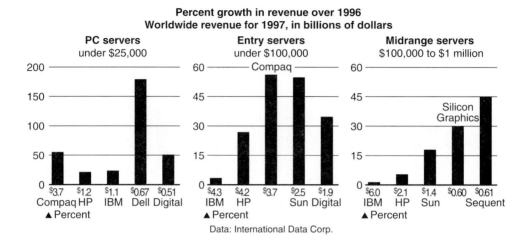

Percent growth in revenue over 1996
Worldwide revenue for 1997, in billions of dollars

Data: International Data Corp.

17   By then, Gerstner hopes to be the top supplier of E-commerce tools and services, ranging from Web servers to 3D software for online video to data-mining over the Net. Gerstner is focused heavily on Internet security, Web-management software, even whizzy software in its labs that will translate foreign-language Web pages into English. IBM also beat most companies to market with network computers and is getting ready to launch a line of powerful servers that let companies pull the latest programs right off the Net.

18   With the help of a $100 million ad blitz, the company is gaining mind share—and business. Gerstner says that research shows IBM is considered by other companies to be a leader in E-commerce. In a coup, retail giant Wal-Mart Stores Inc. dumped Microsoft products in favor of IBM mainframe systems to run its online operations. The Microsoft technology just couldn't handle the load. IBM, says Wal-Mart Chief Information Officer Randy Mott, has improved the power of its large systems to handle massive online volumes. "It's a different company than it was two to three years ago," he says.

NET SHIFT

19   But E-commerce is not translating into higher product sales for IBM yet. And E-commerce is not as big a catalyst as Gerstner expected two years ago, when he predicted that the Net would set off demand for IBM's big mainframe computers and huge storage systems.

20   Gerstner is working on that. The company is pumping resources into making PC servers as reliable as mainframes. IBM also is rewriting huge chunks of its mainframe software for Microsoft's Windows NT software, a top seller for servers and workstations.

21   But IBM must still fight its tendency to move slowly. In the past, the company has hesitated to jump into areas of the industry that have fueled spectacular growth for rivals. Fearful of damaging what's left of its mainframe business, which produces 70% gross profit margins, IBM only recently started to aggressively push corporate systems using NT or low-cost PC servers.

22   Then there's SAP, the software of choice for most major corporations to run all facets of business, from manufacturing to finance to human resources. It has been one of the hottest areas in the industry, now, it's part of IBM's growth plan. But Big Blue was painfully slow to get onboard—turning off customers and missing out on a booming business. Eli Lilly Co. decided against an IBM mainframe because it wanted to run SAP software. Now, the company is using a Sun Microsystems computer.

EXHIBIT D

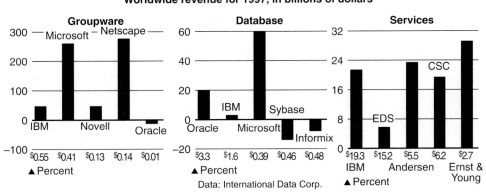

Percent growth in revenue over 1996
Worldwide revenue for 1997, in billions of dollars

Data: International Data Corp.

23 New blood might help. On May 19, IBM's top salesman, Ned C. Lautenbach, retired from the computer maker to look for a CEO job elsewhere. Lautenbach, a quiet, cerebral executive, will be replaced by William A. Etherington, an energetic salesman who has been running IBM's sales operations in Europe, the Middle East, and Africa.

24 In hardware, Gerstner has promised analysts that IBM will get its act together. The company is working through an inventory glut of PCs and PC servers. New mainframes and midrange computers should help. But revenue is going to be under pressure from falling prices, and most analysts expect growth in this segment to be flat this year.

25 Still, Gerstner is a believer—as are investors. He recently took advantage of IBM'S high stock price and, for the first time since joining the company, sold 3% of his IBM stock for a neat $14 million profit. If Gerstner wants to profit handsomely on his remaining shares, he will need to hit his growth target.

CASE 11

HOW MEDTRONIC SETS THE PACE

1   By the time Maurice Long put in an appearance before a Food & Drug Administration panel last year, he could joke about the wires running from his brain to a pacemaker-like device implanted in his chest. The contraption had ended the debilitating tremors that cut short his career as a financial-services executive and reduced his life to that of a hermit on his Hutchinson (Kan.) farm. Now, Long could keep his hands still. He could even play golf.

2   Just by sitting still, Long, 73, provided powerful testimony for the FDA panel. Last August, it approved Activa, a device made by Medtronic Inc., for widespread use in controlling tremors. Then, in April, Medtronic won European clearance to market the device to treat the shaking and other symptoms of Parkinson's disease. Today, the Minneapolis company is hoping that more testimonials will sway U.S. regulators and eventually open a worldwide market of 300,000 Parkinson's patients.

3   Stories like Long's are stirring. But for Medtronic, the stakes in the success of this new product are also dramatic. Best known as the leading supplier of heart pacemakers, Medtronic badly needs to crank out new applications of that maturing technology if it's going to extend an enviable record for earnings growth—a compounded annual rate of 25% over the past five years.

"EXCITING"

4   Over the past two years, those gains have slowed sharply as Medtronic's pacemaker share has been eaten away by hard-charging rival Guidant Corp. William W. George, who joined Medtronic as chief operating officer in 1989 and became chief executive officer two years later, is counting on a host of state-of-the-art pacemaker products—along with Activa and other devices from its fast-growing, $400 million neurology unit—to help push sales to $6 billion in five years. Medtronic's revenues in the fiscal year ended Apr. 30 rose 7%, to $2.6 billion; net income was up 12%, to $594 million.

5   Anticipation of those breakthroughs have helped push Medtronic shares up 24% since January, to about 57. "What's exciting about this stock is its product innovation," says Jane R. Davenport, vice-president at Montag & Caldwell Inc., which holds a $750 million position.

6   A close look at Activa's development shows how Medtronic has institutionalized the process of innovation. Since its founding in 1949, the company has nurtured and invested in ideas from a world-wide network of doctors. But as pacemaking competition heated up in the early 1990s, Medtronic intensified a search for new ways to use its core implantation and stimulation technologies. "We looked at diseases with no treatment or for which drugs didn't work," says George. But he also directed an overhaul of product-development efforts, tightening their focus and forcing shorter delivery times.

7   Now, proposals are judged on their medical value but also against tough financial measures, including affordability. That's crucial in today's managed-care environment, says Medtronic President Arthur D. Collins Jr. "The onus is on the provider of the product to demonstrate it is not only good but cost-effective," he says. "There is a belief that technology is just adding cost to the system."

8   Medtronic's selection process can be brutal, but it offers avenues of appeal. For staffers who can't get over the initial hurdles, there's the Quest program, which frees up employee time to work on out-of-the-box ideas. Once approved, three-quarters of Quest ideas fail. However, the program can also salvage ideas such as Reveal, a heart-monitoring device that hit the market earlier this year after nearly being short-circuited several times.

Source: Richard A. Melcher in Minneapolis, "How Medtronic Sets the Pace," *Business Week:* June 29, 1998.

9   Winning projects emerge through a mixture of perseverance, serendipity, and back-channel support. And in Activa's case, the product would never have survived without the passion of an outsider.

10   Since the 1970s, neurosurgeons had been experimenting with electrical stimulation of the spinal chord to alleviate pain. But only drug therapy or brain surgery were being used to treat the tremors that accompany diseases such as Parkinson's. In 1985, French neurosurgeon Alim-Louis Benabid was experimenting with electrical stimulation of a Parkinson's patient's brain to help determine which tissues he should cut away. He was stunned by what he saw. "As I increased the frequency, the tremor stopped," he says. "I saw the patient's shaking hand stop."

11   What Benabid had done was show that tremors could be manipulated through different electric frequency levels. In early 1987, working on his own at the University of Grenoble in France with what was essentially a jerry-built Medtronic pacemaker, Benabid performed his first implant of what eventually became the Activa. The device was placed just under the skin in the patient's chest, with wires running to the thalmic region of the brain. The results seemed promising—and came as evidence was growing that conventional drug therapy had diminishing benefits.

TRICKY ISSUES

12   But Benabid recalls that Medtronic's interest in funding his research was lukewarm at best. The market seemed minuscule—maybe 60,000 people worldwide. Among the doubters was John A. Meslow, the president of Medtronic's neurology unit. "Remember, it took seven hours of surgery, and who knew whether physicians would get operating time or any payers to pay," says Meslow, who later became a key supporter. "Could Benabid's results even be duplicated?" The ethical issues were tricky, too: To some, rooting around the brain and leaving wires there conjured up Frankenstein-like images.

13   When it came time to whittle 42 neurology prospects down to six that would get company backing, Benabid's tremor-control device didn't make the cut. Benabid was frustrated, but he continued to lobby. As more doctors picked up the procedure, operating time was cut in half and costs were greatly reduced. And the increased interest showed Medtronic that it may have underestimated the number of patients who might benefit.

14   Scott R. Ward, then head of the neurology group reviewing new ventures, pushed to have the device presented to the executive committee even though it hadn't made the initial cut. After viewing dramatic videos that showed patients entering surgery with uncontrollable shaking and emerging without a sign of tremors, the committee cleared a place on its funding list.

15   The new device had now crossed enough thresholds that it was given a team of seven Medtronic employees to guide it through product launch. Headed by Noreen Thompson, director of neurostimulation movement disorders, the team was charged with training doctors, educating patients, and arguing for insurance companies' approval. It was a tough sell. Activa, like all of Medtronic's neurology products, addresses a quality-of-life issue. And insurers won't pay up as readily as for lifesaving pacemakers.

16   To build momentum, Thompson focused on the "thought leaders" among European and Canadian doctors—top-flight surgeons who were willing to perform the surgery, publish the results in professional journals, and otherwise spread the word. As FDA consideration neared, Thompson compiled a list of 200 neurosurgeons capable of implanting the device. Marketing, sales, and reimbursement experts began to visit them and conduct workshops. At every stop, they showed the breathtaking videos.

17   In early '97, the product was far enough along that Thompson's team began planning for the actual launch. Some officials suggested a gold-plated $16,000 price tag. "It took about three minutes to convince them it wasn't going to work," laughs Barbara Veath, the company's reimbursement specialist. However, Medtronic wanted a strong margin to begin to recoup its multimillion-dollar investment. In the end, the device was priced at about $10,000. The procedure cost hospitals another $10,000 or so for surgery time, room costs, and other expenses. Of the total, Medicare or private insurance typically picks up about $15,000; the rest is absorbed by hospitals or patients.

18   But the FDA had yet to give its nod. Investigators wanted to know how patients would fare years after they had received the implants. Medtronic pointed to Benabin's early patients in France who were doing fine after seven or eight years. But the patient videos, which had been so successful at

TABLE 1
Innovation Machine

Medtronic has cranked out a stream of new electrical stimulators and implant devices based on its old heart pacemaker technology.

Product	Condition	Approval Status	World Market by 2002
Activa	Tremors, Parkinson's symptoms	Europe, all symptoms; U.S., more limited	$150 million to $200 million
Gem DR	Fast and slow heart rate	Europe; pending in U.S.	$225 million to $300 million
Insync	Congestive heart failure	Europe, expected 1998; U.S., expected 2000	$125 million to $175 million
Synchromed	Lou Gehrig's disease, Parkinson's symptoms	Clinical trials	$50 million to $100 million

Data: Medtronic, Cowen & Co.

winning internal Medtronic support and doctors' interest, failed to wow the FDA. Among those who were unimpressed was Dr. Daniel A. Spyker, a senior FDA official with medical device responsibility. "In God we trust," says Dr. Spyker, "but everybody else has to bring data."

NAIL-BITER

19   In August, 1996, four months after Medtronic submitted its application for approval, a long list of questions came back from the FDA. The team that had prepared the application scurried to rework and reanalyze reams of data. In March, 1997, as the final panel hearing took place in Washington, Thompson gathered with about 20 colleagues at Medtronic headquarters to listen via audio hookup. By this point, the team had spent more than two years shepherding the device. "We were chewing our nails, cheering, cursing," Thompson recalls.

20   The outcome, announced preliminarily after the hearing, was a partial win. Activa was approved for tremor applications—but only for implanting in one side of the brain at a time. Before it could gain approval for both sides and for implanting deeper in the brain to control other Parkinson's symptoms, further clinical studies would be necessary.

21   There was no time for celebration or disappointment. Medtronic officials now faced tedious, word-by-word negotiating with the FDA on labels and manuals for doctors and patients—a five-month-long process. Then came the actual rollout. In a fashion typical of the understated culture of the Upper Midwest, the neuro team didn't celebrate until the company's annual holiday party. Patients like those in the videos were invited to give live testimonials. There wasn't a dry eye in the house, says Paul Citron, vice-president for science and technology.

22   Medtronic hopes to get U.S. approval of Activa for Parkinson's symptoms in 12 to 36 months and is searching for a wide range of new applications. Tops on Medtronic's hit list: Alzheimer's, epilepsy, Lou Gehrig's disease, and dystonia, a debilitating contraction of the muscles that affects young children. Some see a future where Medtronic's devices will have sensors in the brain that detect the onset of seizures and also trigger the delivery of drugs to disrupt them.

23   Medtronic CEO George craves the growth these innovations promise but recognizes the price it may exact. "Size and creativity are inversely related," he says. "We can't achieve our growth objectives unless we stay nimble and break ourselves into teams. Everyone—sales, manufacturing, engineers, me—we all need to be out among doctors and in the operating rooms, staying in touch. It's a lot easier when you're small." Maintaining that edge will be critical if Medtronic is to satisfy patients such as Maurice Long—as well as its investors.

CASE 12

REMAKING SCHWAB

1   Quick. Which stock performed best in the bull market of the 1990s: Microsoft, Intel, or Charles Schwab? If you picked either of the dynamic duo of high tech, you guessed wrong. Schwab left both in the dust. A dollar invested in Microsoft at the start of 1991 grew to a little more than $15 by the end of 1997; Intel, a little less. But during the same period, a dollar put into the discount brokerage firm blossomed into $39.

2   The rising tide of a bull market lifts all securities firms, but no firm rode the bull like Schwab. Customer accounts more than tripled, customer assets swelled tenfold, revenues jumped by a factor of six, and best of all, net income rose nearly fourteenfold.

3   But 1998 is unfolding as a different story. Competition from both deep-discount Internet brokers and full-service investment firms is keener than ever. Commission rates are collapsing while expenses are surging.

4   True, judged by what's coming through the doors, the Schwab juggernaut has lost none of its momentum. In the first quarter, 358,000 new accounts were opened, bringing the total to 5 million, and customer assets climbed $55 billion—$21 billion of which is new money—and now is over $400 billion. But here's the bottom line: Revenue growth slowed to 13% and profit gains to just 2%. The stock, now at 35, is down more than 20% from its all-time high of 44, and it's the only major brokerage stock with negative returns this year.

5   Over the past two years, daily trades have jumped 60% to 85,400, but commissions income is up only 23%. Now, commissions make up 49% of revenues, vs. 53% in 1995. "We can't build a business on trading anymore because that service is a commodity," says Susanne D. Lyons, president of Schwab's Specialized Investor Services unit.

NO PROTOTYPE

6   Is the Schwab era about to end? In one sense, yes. The old Schwab that catered to the investors who knew exactly what they wanted is disappearing. What is emerging is Schwab II, shaped by the explosive growth of Internet trading and the mounting demand from investors for help and advice on where to put their money.

7   The Schwab team is striving to build a brokerage firm for which there is no prototype. "Schwab has got to become more of a full-service brokerage firm," says David S. Pottruck, 49, president, co-CEO, and heir apparent to Chairman and co-CEO Charles R. Schwab, now 60. "But we're not going to become another Merrill Lynch or Dean Witter." Schwab doesn't plan to spoon-feed investments to its customers. But with a strategy built around the Internet, the company aims to teach investors to feed themselves. "Our mission," says Schwab, "is to coach people on investing."

8   Schwab's full-service competitors point out that investors already suffer from too much information and too little time—and that's what will keep people coming to the full-service firms. "You need help in sorting out the information and figuring out what it means for you," says Jay Mandelbaum, senior vice-president at Salomon Smith Barney. And John L. Steffens, vice-chairman of Merrill Lynch & Co., argues that while the bull market has made it easy for investors to fend for themselves, many will seek Merrill's advice when times get tougher. Not that business is bad now. Both firms have been signing up customers at the rate of more than 30,000 a week.

Source: Jeffrey M. Laderman in San Francisco, "Remaking Schwab," *Business Week:* May 25, 1998.

TABLE 1
Schwab's New Direction

Advice

Written and online tools to help investors set up asset allocation plans and choose stocks and mutual funds. Customers can also sit down with representatives at branches for more personal help.

Internet

Encourage clients to make use of schwab.com, the company's Web site, for advice, research, and account servicing as well as transactions. Offer seminars to familiarize investors with online resources.

Service

Offer personalized services to customers depending on how frequently they trade or by the amount of assets held at the company. Assign higher-end clients to teams of service representatives.

Referrals

Customers who want investment advisers can get referrals to Schwab-screened money managers. Those with more complex needs like estate planning can also get leads on outside experts.

Data: *Business Week.*

9   Schwab is banking that more attention and service will keep customers from bolting. That's what often happens as investors age, grow wealthier, and have larger and more complex portfolios. The average age of a Schwab customer is 47, vs. 57 for the full-service firms, and the challenge will be to keep older ones in the fold. Last year, 35,000 accounts left Schwab for full-service, or what Pottruck calls "full-cost" firms. True, 60,000 came in from those firms, but it burns the competitive Pottruck to lose even one. That's why Schwab developed AdvisorSource, a network of 425 independent money managers. This way, clients who want advisers can get them, but the assets remain at Schwab.

10   For the take-charge types, Schwab offers enhanced services. Those who make at least four trades a month and maintain $50,000 in their account qualify for the Schwab 500 Active Trader service. Two monthly trades and $25,000 get customers into Schwab Select service. There's no trading requirement for Priority service, just $500,000 in assets. Those with $1 million get the Priority Gold treatment.

11   With these services, clients don't get personal brokers, but each is assigned to a small team in one of several national call centers with which he or she can plot a strategy for a large trade, discuss the merits of an investment idea, exercise stock options, or get a referral to an estate-planning attorney. "Your team is your concierge," says Lyons.

12   Increased help and advice is the strategy that Schwab is using to build customer assets. And at Schwab, the key to profitability is gathering those assets, not trading them frequently. Schwab's customer representatives are salaried, not commissioned, and incentive bonuses to branch staff are paid based on asset growth and the quality of the customer service provided.

13   The bigger the asset base, the less dependence the firm will have on commissions where competition is cutthroat. From the asset base, the firm can make money from margin lending, customer cash balances, and mutual-fund servicing fees.

14   Schwab insists his firm can remake itself without getting swept up in the merger mania engulfing the brokerage business. "I have no interest in participating in these megamergers," says Schwab. "What for? We don't need anybody else's capital, and we don't need anybody else's technology, and we already have a national brand name." He sold Schwab to BankAmerica Corp. in the early 1980s, only to buy it back and take it public in 1987. He does not rule out making an acquisition "if it would enhance customer service."

15   Schwab says the firm can benefit from the merger wave without becoming part of it. "Those mergers are about cost-cutting and balance sheets and capital," he says. "They're not about serving the customers." The founder's opinion counts plenty. He owns 20.2% of the stock, worth $1.9 billion. An employee stock option plan has an additional 8.6%. Other employee holdings bring total inside ownership to around 40%.

16   Schwab II is a far cry from the novel idea Chuck Schwab had when he started the firm in the depths of the 1970s bear market. Investors were angry with their brokers, who were not only handing

EXHIBIT A

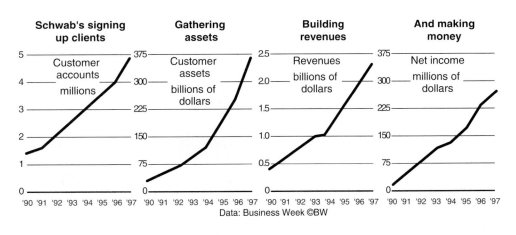

Schwab's signing up clients — Customer accounts millions
Gathering assets — Customer assets billions of dollars
Building revenues — Revenues billions of dollars
And making money — Net income millions of dollars

Data: Business Week ©BW

out bad advice but also were charging like bandits. Schwab positioned the firm as the un-broker. His goal was to give top-notch service but not push products or make recommendations on which stocks to buy. That worked well during the 1980s as the bull market took off. Even 10 years ago, says Pottruck, nearly all of Schwab's new customers had had at least two years of investing experience.

"WARM CALLS"

17   But in the 1990s, customers arrived at Schwab's doors who didn't know a stock from a bond, let alone a mutual fund. Rather than turn them away, Schwab slowly moved into the advice business, plying newcomers with asset-allocation planners and investment tool kits, and offering them a select list of outside mutual funds that could be purchased through the no-fee OneSource program.

18   Schwab has even crossed some lines into what was once taboo. It now has proprietary products that carry the Schwab name, like a series of asset-allocation and index mutual funds. But here, too, Schwab differentiates its product from the house-brand funds at full-service firms: Schwab funds have lower management fees and levy no loads or sales charges. And, unlike most other brokerage funds, the Schwab equity funds are either index portfolios or funds that invest in other managers' funds.

19   Another change in the Schwab culture: Customers never had to tell a Schwab broker "don't call me, I'll call you." Now the firm makes "warm calls." If you ask for an account application, but don't fill it out, you'll get a phone call to ask if you have questions or need assistance. Schwab is also testing software that will identify accounts where activity seems to have stopped, or cash has built up. "That could be a sign the investor is confused," says Pottruck. In the future, such customers might get a call to ask if he or she wants help.

20   Then there's the red-hot call. Frequent trader Joe Parascandolo of Holmdel, N.J., recalls that on a day the stock market was taking a dive, one of his Schwab 500 team reps insisted his wife rouse him from his sickbed. "I had several hundred index options and they collapsed from $15 to $2 that day," says Parascandolo, who owns a printing business. "Because of that call, I got out at $12, and I saved $75,000 to $100,000." He thinks Schwab's team service beats the one-on-one approach at Merrill Lynch, where he has a small account. "It' s like having eight pair of eyes working for me," he says.

21   The mass of Schwab clients, though, will have to use their own eyes. For stockpickers, the Analyst Center on the Schwab Web site rivals what many stockbrokers have on their desks: company and industry research reports from Standard & Poor's Corp.; earnings forecasts by First Call Corp.; data on corporate insiders' trading from Vickers Inc.; price and volume charts by BigCharts; interviews with executives and industry experts from Briefing.com; and news stories from Dow Jones & Co. Schwab now delivers Web users some reports for free that might cost a few dollars if ordered by mail or phone.

EXHIBIT B

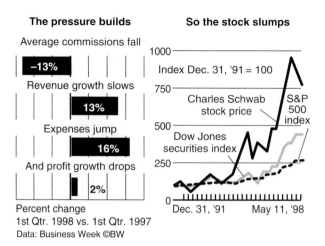

The pressure builds

Average commissions fall

So the stock slumps

Percent change
1st Qtr. 1998 vs. 1st Qtr. 1997
Data: Business Week ©BW

IPO ACCESS

22   Customers in the Schwab 500 and Priority services have access to their own Web pages, including a powerful sorting tool called Stock Screener, which allows users to hunt down stocks according to a myriad of different criteria such as stock-price performance, earnings expectations, market capitalization, or sectors and industries. Other perks include access to initial public offerings and online interviews with top executives like Intel Corp.'s Andrew S. Grove and Dell Computer Corp.'s Michael S. Dell.

23   All this data is generated elsewhere, and Schwab collects and delivers it. One thing you don't get from Schwab is an official opinion on a particular company. That's the stock-in-trade of full-service brokerage firms, and verboten at Schwab.

24   Schwab is beefing up its advisory services for mutual-fund investors, who hold about $131 billion in funds at the firm. Late last year, Schwab hired Mark W. Riepe from investment consultant Ibbotson Associates to head up the Charles Schwab Center for Investment Research. The in-house think tank tackles such questions as what are the rules to follow in deciding whether to sell a fund and what happens to performance after funds close to new investors.

25   Riepe is also studying such questions as what's the impact on a fund of getting tapped for the Schwab Mutual Fund Select List. Making the quarterly list can lead to huge inflows that swamp a fund and undercut the reason for which it was selected. "Is it the dollar value of the assets that go in, or the amount of assets relative to size of the fund?" asks Riepe. "We're still trying to nail that one."

26   The Select List runs about 90 funds, a mix of domestic and international equity, asset allocation, and bond funds. Most, but not all, are in the no-fee OneSource program. The current list includes offerings from rival Fidelity Investments and even has several Vanguard index funds that compete head-on with Schwab products. Other information available to investors includes a one-page Mutual Fund Report Card on about 7,000 funds, highlighting performance, risk, ratings, and expenses. And this month, Schwab will introduce a customized one-page Mutual Fund Performance Snapshot that compares all the funds held by an investor with market indexes and other funds in the same peer group.

27   In reshaping the company, the branches—now 274—have been revamped in look and in mission. Gone are the teller-like counters for transactions, replaced with desks and private conference areas for meeting customers. Call the local branch, and you are switched through to one of five national call centers where much branch-like business can be handled by an automated line or rep—a trade, a request for a prospectus, or a question about an account. Customers can also ask to talk to an individual at the branch, but most queries never go that far.

28   That frees up time for branch reps to discuss with investors such topics as financial planning, mutual-fund selection, or the pros and cons of variable annuities. Over the last several years, reps have

EXHIBIT C

How Schwab makes its money

First quarter, 1998

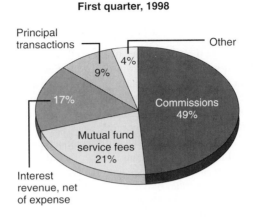

Principal transactions 9%

Other 4%

Commissions 49%

17%

Mutual fund service fees 21%

Interest revenue, net of expense

been replaced or retrained as the job has been upgraded from order-taking to help and advice. Reps are also encouraged to develop a specific field of expertise, like retirement planning, fixed-income investing, or insurance, which Schwab also sells.

29   Stocks, bonds, or funds, Schwab's strategy relies on moving as many of its customers as it can onto the Internet. The more they go online for routine business—checking balances, requesting quotes, or making trades—the less the staffing needs at service centers and branches. On that score, Schwab starts with a solid base: 70% of customers own PCs, and 50% have Net access. About 29% of total accounts are online, and 300,000 of the 500,000 new customers who joined since January are also online.

PRIVATE CLASS

30   To speed the move to the Web, Schwab is putting Net-linked PCs in branches and offering training sessions. One branch manager even gave an in-home session to a customer who wasn't able to make the classes. The company has also increased Web-trading capacity. Arthur V. Shaw, senior vice-president of electronic brokerage, says the Web system has already experienced several days when online trading exceeded that on Oct. 27, 1997, the day of the stock market's minicrash. It's a relevant comparison: Online customers of Schwab and others complained about inability to gain access to Web sites or execute trades that day.

31   Clients remain free to contact Schwab by other means. One criticism of its earlier Web service, e.Schwab, was that all contact had to be online, and phone calls or branch visits cost extra. That service has since been folded into Web trading.

32   The more customers migrate to the Web, the less pressure the company will face on broker-age rates. Schwab's new charge for Internet trading—$29.95 for trades up to 1,000 shares and an additional 3 cents a share after that—is expensive by Net standards. In fact, it's six times higher than the cheapest online discounters. "Others charge less, but I don't trade daily or even weekly," says Schwab customer James Willis, an automotive engineer from Frankenmuth, Mich. "The breadth of the information and the ability to talk to someone is worth a few dollars more."

33   Indeed, for millions of Schwab clients, $29.95 is still far less than the standard commission rates. Right now, purchasing 200 shares of $40 stock would cost $103 in commissions in a branch or through telephone reps, and $93 if ordered through TeleBroker or using StreetSmart, a pre-Web online system.

34   Pottruck says that the company has bitten the bullet on commission rates—and shouldn't need to go any lower. If anything, the rate cut spurred usage. Web trades now account for about half of all Schwab trades, vs. 37% last year. Schwab is by far the largest online broker, with 1.5 million accounts and 30% of the daily trading and 67% of all online assets.

FALLING BEHIND

35   But even if rates hold steady, the Web is a place where standing pat means falling behind. In the first quarter, Schwab ranked 7th out of 52 sites by Gomez Advisors Inc., which rates Internet brokerage sites. But in second-quarter rankings, Schwab dropped to 20th out of 69. "New entries and site redesigns have raised the bar," says Alexander Stein of Gomez Advisors. What's more, the fuller-service discounters like Quick & Reilly and Fidelity Brokerage Services now earn higher ratings than Schwab for their Internet brokerage sites.

36   Schwab's Web service earns its highest ratings on "customer confidence." But it does not fare as well in "ease-of-use," and that's critical if the company is going to get more people to use it. Web-meister Shaw takes issue with the criticism, since schwab.com is by far the Net's most active brokerage site. "Part of our Web experience is, if you have a problem, you can get service and support right away," says Shaw. "But we're always trying to improve the ease of use." Shaw is planning to redesign the opening pages with "clearer customer pathing" to the services they want.

37   Can Schwab succeed in planting a new sort of firm in a business that's polarizing between deep-discount and full-service? Daniel O. Leemon, Schwab's chief strategy officer, argues that demographics and technology will help make it happen. Of some 30 million U.S. households which have brokerage accounts, says Leemon, about 12 million are "delegators"—those who want to offload the investment chores to others—and 3 million are largely self-directed. But in the middle are 15 million households, what Leemon calls the "validators," these are people who know what they want, but at times need some information or advice to confirm it.

38   Validators usually turn to full-service firms to get that support. But Leemon thinks Schwab can win over some of the validators' business with the right mix of information, advice, and technology, and says extensive customer research bears this out. "Where we're going," he says, "is the direction in which our customers are leading us."

39   Certainly, Schwab has ample resources with which to pursue its new strategy: a strong foothold on the Net, a young customer base, a branch network, and high brand-name recognition. It also plans to boost its ad budget by more than 20%, to over $100 million this year, and recently hired a new agency to promote retail brokerage. And it spends about 13% of revenues on technology. But the competition's getting keener, too, and not just from the big Wall Street firms. Privately held Fidelity Brokerage Services competes for the same customers as Schwab. And a few rivals recently hooked up with deeper-pocketed parents: Quick & Reilly with Fleet Financial, and Jack White & Co. with the Waterhouse Investors Services division of the Toronto Dominion Bank.

40   Chuck Schwab believes he can harness the power of the Net to create a firm that delivers the kind of advice and services investors want. Considering his record as an innovator and judge of what investors really need, it would be foolish to bet against him.

CASE 13

BusinessWeek

No Slacking in Silicon Valley

1   Jeff Thermond could have happily stayed at 3Com Corp. for the rest of his career. After $8^{1}/_{2}$ years helping build the computer networking company into a giant, he was a top manager with a fortune in stock options. But last summer, Thermond felt the Silicon Valley itch—and jumped ship to become chief executive of Epigram Inc. The Sunnyvale (Calif.) startup is about to unveil technology he hopes will become essential in every home—a way to link together PCs, consumer electronics, and appliances for the smart house. "We can create a market that didn't exist before," effuses Thermond. "We're going for a home run."

2   Take a look at an amazing phenomenon. After one of the most astounding outpourings of ideas and products in history, Silicon Valley's legendary innovation machine is still in overdrive. If anything, the Valley's stature as the world's high-tech capital is growing. Last year, 3,575 new businesses were launched, and venture capitalists poured a record $3.7 billion into startups—60% more than the year before, according to PriceWaterhouseCoopers. And 1998 is shaping up as another banner year: Venture capitalists dumped $1.87 billion into Valley companies in the first quarter, up slightly from the same period a year ago, says researcher VentureOne Corp. in San Francisco. "Silicon Valley is the single most important center for innovation," says Mitchell L. Moss, a professor at New York University. "Money follows ideas, and money flows to money."

MAGIC MIX

3   Signs are strong that the region will continue to churn out new ideas and new companies for some time. The reason? The Valley still possesses the combination of ingredients that nurtured Intel, Apple Computer, and Cisco Systems. The key is the sheer density of more than 7,000 tech companies crammed into a 50-mile corridor. That gives startups access to a deep talent pool of smart, experienced engineers, programmers, and managers, as well as the infrastructure—from legal to technical to marketing—that can transform an entrepreneur's idea into a company overnight. Add to that the unmatched availability of venture-capital and funding from larger corporations, and a climate that rewards risk-taking and tolerates failures, and you have the recipe for a technological hothouse.

4   True, Silicon Valley runs the risk of tripping over its own success. Explosive growth has left the region with a shortage of engineers, a lack of affordable housing, and sky-high business costs that make it ever more expensive to start a company there.

5   Despite these problems, the Valley is moving into the 21st century at top speed. In the past, innovation focused on producing more powerful hardware and whizzy packaged software. Now, the hot investment fields are ones that aim to reshape entire industries: electronic commerce, digital consumer electronics, and communications. "The game now is structural changes in the economy itself," says John Seely Brown, director of the Xerox Palo Alto Research Center.

6   And Silicon Valley is playing the new game well. Take E-commerce, where the pace has accelerated to warp speed. Hundreds of startups such as E-Loan and Autoweb.com are devising ways to cut out middlemen and speed product cycles by connecting buyers and sellers directly over the Internet.

Source: Andy Reinhardt in San Mateo, California, "No Slacking in Silicon Valley," *Business Week:* August 31, 1998.

E-MAILROOM

7 Not all of these will succeed—but the sheer number of startups is an essential part of the Silicon Valley creative process. In E-commerce, where no one yet knows the best ways of doing things, the advantage of Silicon Valley is that it gives bright ideas a chance to prove themselves.

8 Nothing shows this better than Palo Alto's Kana Communications Inc., launched in 1996 by Mark Gainey, then 28 years old. Gainey had the idea of making software that categorizes and sorts E-mail. Potential buyers: companies that took the plunge into the Net but couldn't cope with the avalanche of customer E-mail generated by their new Web sites. Kana's software would enable companies to eliminate expensive brick-and-mortar call centers one day and, by having instant E-feedback from customers, quickly modify or customize products.

9 Gainey, who previously worked at venture-capital firm TA Associates, was able to raise more than $5 million to get started. Today, the startup has customers such as Netscape Communications, online auctioneer eBay, and cable company Cox Communications. "The global 2000 are waking up to the leverage they can get from electronic business," says Gainey. "And we're providing the plumbing."

10 But good ideas and cash alone are not enough to keep innovation going. Where Silicon Valley also shines is in the availability of talent that's seasoned and willing to take risks. At Epigram, for example, the five-person management team came to the startup with a total of 110 years of experience at such high-tech companies as 3Com, Sun, Rockwell, BBN Communications, and Cisco. Backers are betting that such hands will help the company get a big chunk of the home networking market, expected to reach $1 billion in sales by 2002, according to Forrester Research. Venture capitalists have funneled $13 million into the company, which will ship its technology early next year.

11 Startups such as Epigram have to find their way in a business dominated by giants. Indeed, one danger to Silicon Valley's innovative vigor is the growth of megacompanies such as Microsoft, Intel, and Cisco. In other industries, the emergence of such behemoths has typically signaled the maturing of the industry and the slowdown of innovation.

12 That has not turned out to be true in Silicon Valley—at least not yet. Instead, the giants have been a further source of funds backing innovation. They have been pouring money into the Valley for several years, investing in or snapping up more than 200 companies. Intel alone has taken equity stakes in 125 fledgling companies, while Microsoft has poured money into more than 50 deals.

WIDER BETS

13 Association with the giants gives startups access to huge resources and marketing clout. For big companies, spreading R&D money beyond their walls is a way of stimulating innovation—and upping their chances of not missing the next thing. Intel, for example, has invested in companies doing everything from improving chip design and manufacturing to building Internet communities. "It's our equivalent of a Bell Labs," says Michelangelo A. Volpi, manager of Cisco's investment portfolio. "Instead of betting on one technology, we can place our bets on 10."

14 More and more, corporate investors are taking the next step and actually buying up startups with promising technology. "We don't invest in companies with the idea of selling," says C. Richard Kramlich, managing partner of venture capitalist New Enterprise Associates in Menlo Park, Calif. "But we've had 10 companies acquired this past year."

15 Motorola Inc., for example, recently paid an estimated $400 million for Starfish Software Inc. of Scotts Valley, Calif., which was started in 1994 by Philippe Kahn, founder of former software giant Borland International Inc. For Motorola, it was an opportunity to acquire Starfish's TrueSync technology, which reconciles data between handheld computers, PCs, and mobile phones. For Kahn, who together with his wife owned 75% of Starfish, it meant both vindication and riches. "It's almost embarrassing," says the 46-year-old Kahn. "It's more money than we'll need for the rest of our lives."

16 Often, such a purchase can give a new technology a jump-start. Take WebTV Networks Inc., a Mountain View (Calif.) company that was developing a digital set-top box for viewing the Web via TV. In August, 1997, Microsoft Corp. bought the company for $425 million and quickly brought in research and development funds—in addition to Microsoft's considerable marketing might. Sales of

TABLE 1
The Valley Is Still Hot . . . But There Are Some Warning Flags

The Valley Is Still Hot . . .

- Venture capitalists poured a record $3.7 billion into Silicon Valley startups in 1997—up 60% from 1996.

- More than 53,000 jobs were created in 1997. Wages grew at nearly twice the national average.

- 34 companies went public, raising $1.1 billion and earning a market valuation of $7.4 billion.

. . . But There Are Some Warning Flags

- While some startups still aim to create new industries, many others are digging for smaller niches in the "Wintel" mainstream.

- Only 15 Valley companies issued IPOs in the first half of 1998. That's against 34 for all of 1997—and 74 in all of 1996.

- Success has a price. Freeway delays have doubled since 1994, and housing costs are the nation's highest.

Data: PriceWaterhouseCoopers, California Employment Development Dept., Ventureone Corp., Broadview, *Business Week.*

the WebTV box jumped from 50,000 at the time of purchase to 400,000 today. "They got a great exit and a better shot at realizing their dream under Microsoft's umbrella," says Andy Duncan, CEO of E-commerce startup EC Co.

17   But it's not just the big outfits that are funding new firms: The Valley's abundance of wealthy entrepreneurs continues to be an essential ingredient to the innovation cycle. Even after an entrepreneur is flush with cash, few stray far before returning to the high-tech hunt—to start another company or invest in other hopefuls. "They get the new house, the new wife, the boat, and they don't really like to play golf. So what then?" asks Hans C. Severens, a former investment banker who now backs tech startups. "They have business in their blood. They have money in their pockets. It's about reinvesting."

BAND OF ANGELS

18   That part of the equation could become more critical in the years ahead. The sheer abundance of startup capital is beginning to have one ironic consequence: Venture funds are bulging to the point where many investors no longer want to be bothered with small-fry opportunities. The average size of deals has climbed 27%, to $5.3 million, in the past two years, according to PriceWaterhouseCoopers.

19   In typical fashion, the Valley is plugging the hole. To seed deals too small for venture capitalists, private investors are jumping into the fray, including one group of 120 industry execs led by Severens, known as the Band of Angels. Since it was formed in January, 1995, the Band has helped launch 62 startups, pouring an average of $1.1 million a month into the market. This reinvestment is helping the Valley refuel itself—and is apt to continue doing that as even more wealth is spun off. One enterprise that benefited from such funding was EC Co. Duncan started with some of his own money, then brought in a half-dozen angels. Funding from four corporations, including Intel, followed. Only then did venture capitalists add their contributions.

20   Could anything slow the rate of innovation in Silicon Valley? As dynamic as it is, the Valley isn't immune to larger economic forces. The Asian economic crisis is making a dent: Layoffs have already occurred at Intel, Sun Microsystems, and Applied Materials. Last year also saw a sharp drop in the number of initial public offerings for local companies: There were just 34 IPOs, vs. a record 74 in 1996, according to VentureOne. Just 15 went public in the first half of 1998. Part of the slowdown reflects a return to more tempered conditions after the Internet stock frenzy of 1996.

21   Another drag is the Valley's physical limits. It's bursting at the seams: Commercial real estate vacancies hit a 10-year low in 1997, and traffic delays on the region's clogged freeways have doubled

---

Voices: Michael Moritz

Title

Partner, Sequoia Capital. 43.

Contributions

The venture capitalist has scored big on electronic commerce, notably with Yahoo! Inc., the hot Internet search engine company. Sequoia's $2 million investment is now worth $1.3 billion. His latest play: online retailer eToys Inc.

In His Words

"If anybody's between you and your customers, you had better be shaking in your boots. Figure out how to profit from the Net, or it will drain the juice out of your marrow."

---

since 1994. The cost of housing, too, is the highest in the country, making it harder to recruit top talent. That's prompting some companies to expand elsewhere in California or into other states.

RESILIENCE

22   But the nerve center of the tech world is still firmly planted in the Valley. Even when companies set up shop elsewhere, says Becky Morgan, chief executive of the public/private partnership Joint Venture: Silicon Valley Network, "research and development incubators will still be here." SAP, L.M. Ericsson, and AT&T, for example, have all established R&D centers in the Valley in recent years. Even Microsoft, long rooted in Seattle, plans to build a 32-acre campus in Mountain View.

23   It's that constant supply of fresh talent that will continue to keep Silicon Valley on the cutting edge. Despite periodic downturns, the region has shown a remarkable ability to catch the latest technical wave. Is it home networking, automating customer service, or connecting buyers and sellers over the Net? Or maybe it's as simple as transforming the lowly TV into a tech-savvy device. That's what 48-year-old Mike Ramsay, a former marketer at Silicon Graphics Inc., thinks. In Sunnyvale, he launched TiVo Inc. to create a smart set-top box that recommends shows to viewers based on their preferences and records programs for later viewing as easily as clicking a remote. "We're dealing with a whole new category," Ramsay says. "We're on the edge."

24   It's the Valley's siren song. Every day, seasoned managers and fresh-scrubbed MBAs alike throw caution to the wind and try their luck at building the next Yahoo! Inc. or Sun Microsystems Inc. As long as they do, the land of startup dreams, breakthrough technologies, and fast fortunes will keep its innovative verve.

CASE 14

BusinessWeek

THE CENDANT MESS GETS MESSIER

1 When franchising giant HFS Inc. and discount-shopping-club operator CUC International Inc. merged late last year, the new company, dubbed Cendant Corp., was supposed to become a marketing powerhouse selling millions of customers everything from travel services to mortgages. But that wasn't the only behemoth the deal spawned. When the company's board gathered in April—shortly after a bombshell disclosure that accounting irregularities had been discovered in CUC's books—the meeting had to be held at the law firm of Battle Fowler. The reason? Cendant's Manhattan offices didn't have a conference room that would hold 28 board members and their advisers.

2 That logistical headache speaks volumes about the struggle for control of Cendant. The company's unwieldy board is effectively paralyzed, split between directors who support Walter A. Forbes, the Cendant chairman who founded CUC, and those who back Henry R. Silverman, the Cendant chief executive and HFS founder. Some investors say Silverman wants Forbes out. In the wake of the April bombshell, the CUC and HFS directors hired separate lawyers—and things have since gone from bad to worse. On July 14, the company disclosed that the accounting woes went far deeper than expected. And on July 22, Ernst & Young LLP, CUC's former auditor, said in a statement that "from information provided by Cendant to the media, it appears that efforts may have been taken to deceive the auditors." With the stock now trading around 17—down from 41 in April—investors have become increasingly vocal about hastening Forbes's exit.

3 Resolution may come quickly. As *Business Week* went to press, sources familiar with discussions said talks had been held recently between representatives for Forbes and representatives of the company about terms of his possible departure. Reached by phone, Forbes issued a terse "no comment." A spokesman for Forbes says he has no plans to leave.

4 Certainly, the heat has been turned up on the CUC founder. Silverman has been telling big shareholders who want Forbes removed to write or call board members. Says Director John D. Snodgrass: "I do receive faxes from large shareholders that request the board to take action." Even if the talks fall through, pressure is building for the board to act before a report ordered by the Cendant audit committee is completed in August.

5 Looking at the makeup of the Cendant board, it's easy to see why the management issue hasn't been resolved quickly. It's twice as big as the boards of most large public companies, says Thomas J. Neff, U.S. chairman of headhunter SpencerStuart. That alone impedes decisive action. And more than half of the directors could be described as insiders, ex-insiders, or business associates of Cendant, of its two predecessors, or of Forbes.

6 Seven of the directors are Cendant executives; an eighth resigned his executive post just before the accounting disclosures but remains as a director. Six other directors—including two on the four-member audit committee that is overseeing the accounting probe—have current or recent business dealings with Cendant, directly or through other companies in which they're involved. And the head of that committee, Frederick D. Green, has partnered with Forbes in developing golf courses in such spots as Nantucket, Mass.

Source: Amy Barrett in Philadelphia and Jennifer Reingold in New York, "The Cendant Mess Gets Messier," *Business Week:* August 3, 1998.

TABLE 1
No Way to Run a Board

Why Cendant's board is under fire:

• Overcrowding

With 28 directors, Cendant has about twice the average for a large publicly held company, split between the CUC and HFS sides.

• Few Outsiders

Many are executives or former execs of the merged company, leaving few strong outsiders to advocate an independent position.

• Business Links

Some directors appear to have had conflicts of interest, including contracts to do work for Cendant, and private ventures with Cendant or Walter Forbes.

JOB SWAP?

7   None of that sits well with big investors, some of whom have already dumped blocks of shares. And governance experts say the board's makeup raises questions about its directors' independence. "Those are warning signs . . . that you have CEOs [meaning Silverman and Forbes] who have appointed people with conflicts," says Sarah A.B. Teslik, executive director of the Council of Institutional Investors. "That can make oversight difficult."

8   Both executives deny problems with the board. "I think that is off-base," says Forbes. "The former CUC directors now on the board are decent people trying to do a good job in a difficult period." Adds Silverman: "If the board listens to the facts in a dispassionate way, I would expect them to do the right thing."

9   For now though, board action does not appear imminent. One director from the CUC side says he doesn't think the board should meet until the auditors' report comes out. He's paying little attention to Cendant's statements about revenue restatement. "I've known Walter for . . . years and never caught him lying," he says. But Snodgrass, from the HFS side, says: "If all that has been written is true, I think he should go." Other directors didn't return calls or would not comment on the record.

10   Under terms of the merger, Forbes and Silverman were to swap jobs in January, 2000. Many investors say it is inevitable that Forbes will exit. But if he does not go voluntarily, an 80% vote of the board is required to remove him. To avoid paying Forbes a severance package worth at least $50 million, Cendant must terminate him "for cause," according to the company's proxy. Included in that definition: "serious, willful misconduct" such as fraud.

11   That doesn't mean shareholders are sitting on their hands. Hans Utsch, president of the Kaufmann Fund and a large Cendant investor, plans to write a letter urging the board to remove Forbes. And at last count, 68 shareholder lawsuits had been filed against the company. A spokesman for Cendant says the company does not comment on pending litigation.

12   Silverman, meanwhile, is facing pressures of his own from investors to boost the stock. According to sources familiar with the position of veteran Wall Street investor Leon G. Cooperman, he wants the Cendant CEO to sell off some noncore operations, including CUC's software businesses. That would raise money that could be used toward completing the planned $3.1 billion acquisition of credit insurer American Bankers Insurance Group Inc. using all cash instead of the cash-and-stock deal now planned, which some investors worry will be dilutive. And another big shareholder has been pressing Silverman to explore a complete spin-off of CUC, effectively undoing that merger. Silverman says it is "premature" to talk about restructuring the American Bankers deal and that a CUC spin-off would be impractical. "You can't unscramble the eggs," he says.

EXHIBIT A

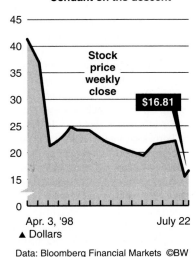

Cendant on the descent

Stock price weekly close

$16.81

Apr. 3, '98   July 22

▲ Dollars

Data: Bloomberg Financial Markets ©BW

13   Certainly, no investor could have imagined the scope of the problem. When Cendant announced on Apr. 15 that it had uncovered accounting irregularities, most analysts and investors figured the company had, if anything, overstated the problem to protect management's credibility. But it was worse than expected. Auditors from Arthur Andersen & Co., which had been hired to comb through CUC's numbers, uncovered what was described as a "widespread and systemic" practice of overstating or fabricating results. Net income before charges for 1997 would have to be reduced by $200 million to $250 million, the company announced, twice the original estimate. Earnings for 1996 and 1995 would also have to be revised based in part on the discovery of fictitious CUC revenues.

14   It also turned out that a big chunk of a CUC charge taken at the time of the merger, about $200 million after taxes, would have to be reversed. That occurred on Henry Silverman's watch. "I was in shock when I read that," says David P. Brady, a senior portfolio manager at Stein Roe & Farnham Inc., a large Cendant shareholder. Silverman says that portion of the yearend charge was handled by CUC execs and auditors.

15   Barring a quick resolution of the management crisis, the ball will be in the hands of the Cendant board, which includes several directors who go back years with Forbes or Silverman. Three directors who were on the board at CUC—Bartlett Burnap, T. Barnes Donnelley, and Stanley M. Rumbough Jr.—were among its early investors, and have made substantial money in the past under Forbes's leadership.

16   Directors from the HFS side of the aisle also have connections. Several current Cendant directors bought limited partnership interests through a private placement in a new HFS hotel chain called Wingate. Included: Silverman, Snodgrass, who was the HFS president until last December, Cendant execs-and-board-members James E. Buckman and Stephen P. Holmes, and Cendant director and now president of America Online Robert W. Pittman. Cendant bought out those interests earlier this year. Silverman says the five directors did not vote on that decision, and that it was made by disinterested directors. In addition, Snodgrass served as a consultant this year for Cendant after it purchased Jackson Hewitt Inc., a tax-preparation company. Snodgrass says neither deal posed a conflict.

MAGIC MOMENT

17   No one has suggested these deals were improperly handled. Still, says governance expert Charles M. Elson, "If you are making a profit aside from other shareholders, that certainly raises a question about independence from management."

18   Some directors are also taking heat for selling shares soon before the April disclosure. According to CDA Investnet, which tracks insider sales, Silverman sold 1.7 million shares in February at about $36, while Forbes sold 300,000 shares in March. Directors Rumbough, Burnap, and Martin L. Edelman sold in March, and Snodgrass sold over 1 million shares in March and April, ending the week before problems were announced. Says Robert M. Gabele, president of CDA Investnet: "These were among the most timely sales we've ever seen at the company."

19   Silverman says that his sale was part of a pattern of selling shares each quarter, while a spokesman for Forbes says he sells a small amount of shares every year. Snodgrass says he was diversifying his holdings. All three deny any knowledge of the accounting problems at the time of the sales. The other directors wouldn't comment on their sales.

20   Once the boardroom battle is resolved, investors may see a rebound in Cendant stock. But a number of analysts warn that failure to resolve that issue quickly could result in deterioration of Cendant's underlying businesses. Merrill Lynch & Co. analyst Mark R. Miller reduced his Cendant rating last week to neutral, citing concerns that the battle could distract management. Miller also noted the risk of management defections now that Cendant's stock options are less attractive. Indeed, if the Cendant board doesn't take control of the situation, the bad news may be just beginning.

CASE 15   BusinessWeek

AETNA'S BRAVE OLD WORLD

1   Two years ago, Aetna Inc. seemed to be on the verge of transforming the health-care landscape. It bought U.S. Healthcare Inc. for an eyepopping $8.2 billion. Executives talked of creating the first national, fully integrated managed-health-care insurer. With the industry rapidly consolidating, Aetna would be among the handful of behemoths able to dictate terms to customers and health-care providers alike.

2   The rhetoric was quite different on Mar. 15, when Aetna agreed to buy New York Life Insurance Co.'s health-insurance business for $1.05 billion. "We've redefined what we are," says Chairman Richard L. Huber, an international banker who joined Aetna in 1995. While Aetna is still acquiring, the insurer has abandoned ambitious plans to expand aggressively into managed care. "We're an insurance company," he says.

3   NYLCare, which will add only 2.5 million members to Aetna's 13.7 million, lost $30 million last year on $3.2 billion in revenues. Last year, Aetna netted $901 million in revenues of $18.5 billion.

"A CRAPSHOOT"

4   Why the strategy shift? Melding U.S. Healthcare, a brash health-maintenance-organization operator, proved far more difficult and costly than anyone thought, and the process is not finished yet. Computer system snafus, exacerbated by overzealous staffing cuts, have alienated customers and fouled up pricing strategies. Originally, Aetna promised the merger would cut $300 million from costs by the end of 1997, but less than half that has been realized. Says J. Randall MacDonald, senior vice-president for human resources at GTE Corp., an Aetna customer: "One plus one doesn't equal three, and I'm not even sure it equals two."

5   Meanwhile, the managed-care merger wave Aetna hoped to lead hasn't happened: The balance of power is shifting away from insurers toward employers, doctors, and hospitals. Indeed, while Aetna has been struggling to rationalize two strikingly disparate organizations, doctors and employers have rebelled against its attempts to apply U.S. Healthcare's aggressive pricing and controls to Aetna's sclerotic existing business.

6   Back in 1996, the U.S. Healthcare deal looked like a winner. But it soon became apparent that Aetna had bought at the height of a market that quickly plummeted. Consolidation of claims-processing centers and 4,950 layoffs helped reduce Aetna's overhead expenses to 19.2% of revenues last year, from 22.3% in 1996. But cuts were too deep and too fast, as Huber now concedes. Corporate customers complained about problems matching employee files with data. Doctors and hospitals got testy about payment delays. Even now, getting paid properly is "a crapshoot," says the office manager for one Connecticut doctor.

HIRING AGAIN

7   With a huge lag in claims processing, executives didn't realize until the third quarter that medical costs were running as much as 2% higher than forecast. By then, Aetna was negotiating with 40% of its 1998 corporate contracts. Many of the resulting premiums were based on outdated cost information, so Aetna stands to see little profit on a big chunk of its business this year.

Source: Susan Jackson in Hartford, "Aetna's Brave Old World," *Business Week:* March 30, 1998.

8   To repair the damage, Aetna has hired 550 new full- and part-time operations employees and has slowed the closing of service centers. While it has put the vast majority of its HMO members on one computer system, Aetna still plans to merge the traditional insurance operations into the system as well, a feat that has yet to be performed anywhere in the industry.

9   In dealing with NYLCare, Huber is taking a tight, cost-effective approach to the deal and promising much less than Aetna did with U.S. Healthcare. That seems appropriate. The only NYLCare plans that make money are the biggest ones—in Dallas, Houston, and the Washington (D.C.) area. And those won't be integrated with Aetna's computer systems for more than two years.

10   Huber admits that Aetna's marriage to U.S. Healthcare has been messy. "It was a painful way to learn," he admits, but says he'll apply the lessons in the NYLCare merger—even if he has to sacrifice the grand vision that inspired Aetna's original expansion binge.

A TALK WITH AETNA'S BOSS

11   Richard L. Huber, a former banker who joined Aetna in 1995 and was named CEO and president in July, 1997, became chairman earlier this month. Huber has had to deal with the merging of two very different entities: Aetna and U.S. Healthcare, a tightly run health maintenance organization company that Aetna bought in July, 1996, for $8.2 billion. The purchase did make Aetna—which is also in the retirement services and life-insurance businesses—one of the largest players in health-care coverage. But making the combination work has proved much harder than expected, especially in a competitive health-care landscape. Then, on Mar. 15, Aetna bought NYLCare, the health-care unit of New York Life Insurance Co., for $1.05 billion. Business Week's Susan Jackson spoke with Huber about these challenges in a series of interviews in January and March, 1998. Here are some excerpts from those talks:

12   Q: Earlier this winter, your investors were pressuring you to sell off some assets and not do any-more health-care deals until U.S. Healthcare had been fully absorbed. Yet at the same time, you were negotiating with NY Life.

13   A: They approached us. They came to the conclusion that they want to concentrate on individual life insurance because to be competitive in health-care, they would have had to invest to get critical mass. [As for the timing,] you can't always pick when a great opportunity will present itself. In an ideal world, this would have happened three or so months from now, but it was a very attractive opportunity.

14   Q: NYLCare lost $30 million last year. Why is that so attractive?

15   A: They suffered some of the same problems that [all health-care organizations] did, with higher-than-perceived medical costs, some of which related to [a] prior year. And they have three large plans which are quite profitable and several small ones which lose money because they are expansions or startups which don't have critical mass. The smaller ones we will integrate pretty rapidly and put quickly into the black. The three large plans will run for 24–30 months as they are. We don't want to have a sizable systems integration at the same time we're dealing with the Year 2000.

16   Q: Part of the deal is that you will pay them $300 million if certain enrollment and earnings targets are met. Is that going to happen?

17   A: I hope we pay it all, because that will mean they're making very good money and our market cap will go up to several times the amount we've paid.

18   Q: The deal is much more cautious than the deal to buy U.S. Healthcare.

19   A: We have different objectives, and it's a different time. Right now, the market for HMOs is certainly nowhere near as hot as it was years ago. You pay the best possible price at the time. Everything we do is aimed at increasing our margins.

20   Q: There has been speculation that NY Life was interested in buying some of your life-insurance properties. Can you comment?

21   A: This transaction is totally stand-alone. If they or somebody else came along, we wouldn't refuse to talk to them. But there's a significant difference in the way our life-insurance businesses are structured [so it's an unlikely match].

TABLE 1
Back to Basics

November, 1995	Having gotten out of the reinsurance business, Aetna sells its underperforming property-casualty division. Chairman Ronald E. Compton says the company will focus on managed health care and financial services.
April, 1996	Aetna agrees to buy U.S. Healthcare for $8.2 billion.
July, 1997	Doctors complain about claims payment backlogs. Big employers chafe at tough, U.S. Healthcare-style sales tactics.
December, 1997	Richard L. Huber is named CEO of Aetna. He concedes consolidation snafus.
March, 1998	Huber is named chairman. Aetna agrees to buy NYLCare for $1.05 billion. Deal is far more conservative than U.S. Healthcare, and so is the consolidation timetable. Huber talks about Aetna reverting to being an insurer, rather than a managed-care company.

22 Q: Are you going to keep the NYLCare management?

23 A: That's one of the attractions. They have good sales and marketing, good growth in membership, and their systems are solid. We're not looking for a senior management team who's going to take over. We've got a great team now, but we're thin. The managers from NYLCare will fit in with our business model and strengthen our bench.

24 Q: Are you an insurer or a health-care company?

25 A: We're an insurance company—we do not practice medicine. We're a financial intermediary that bears insurance risk. It's the same [in life or property/casualty as] in health care: The public doesn't feel comfortable shouldering the risk of a catastrophic illness, so [people] buy insurance.

26 Q: What lessons have you learned from the U.S. Healthcare deal?

27 A: I have driven people hard. I knew there would be pain. There has been more than I expected, but the payoff will be dramatic. You'll see it in the Jan. 1, 1999 enrollment.

28 Q: Your goals now sound different from what they were when you bought U.S. Healthcare.

29 A: We've redefined what we are: We're an employee benefits company. Virtually all our products and services are distributed through plan sponsors, and through them, we sell [health and retirement services products] to employees and retirees. Our objective is to manage best what matters most to our end customers: their physical health and financial well-being. We've gotten a very clear vision of what we are and where we're going, which we didn't have three years ago.

CASE 16   **BusinessWeek**

FIXING FIDELITY

1   During the four-day, 1,000-point stock market debacle that started on Aug. 26, the atmosphere at Fidelity Investments in Boston was less hectic than on the floors of the stock exchanges. With many fund managers on vacation, trading fell to half its normal volume of 5% to 7% of all Wall Street trades. Telephone calls from shareholders increased. All told, customers moved some $2.5 billion from Fidelity's equity funds into money-market funds. That's nothing to sneeze at, but it's a pittance compared with the $487 billion in equity-fund assets managed by the nation's No. 1 fund company. Dividend Growth Fund manager Charles Mangum, who interrupted his beach vacation to go bargain-hunting for beaten-down financial stocks, says: "Hey, markets go down, too." He adds: "It's a good excuse to upgrade your portfolio."

2   Fidelity has been doing a lot of upgrading beyond Mangum's fund. Even with August's gruesome rout, Fidelity funds are holding up well against their peers. For the year through Sept. 1, Fidelity's U.S. diversified equity funds ranked No. 2 in performance among the nation's 10 largest fund companies, according to a Morningstar Inc. analysis conducted for *Business Week*.

3   Of course, nearly all funds are getting hit. Fidelity's average returns of −1.9% for 1998, and 0.6% for the past 12 months aren't anything to brag about. But this year's performance is only half a percentage point behind the leader, American Funds Group, and is nine percentage points ahead of Franklin, the laggard (see Table 2).

4   Indeed, Fidelity is mounting a comeback after its crisis in 1995 and 1996. In the midst of a strong bull market, many of its biggest funds turned in poor performances as a result of unchecked asset growth and wild bets that went bad. Many top fund managers bolted, and the company faced heavy criticism from customers and investment pros. The giant's returns so dismayed investors that in the fourth quarter of 1996, when its rivals were taking in billions, it suffered net outflows of $158 million. The flagship Fidelity Magellan Fund still has not recovered. Since April, 1996, investors have pulled more than $11 billion out of the roughly $70 billion fund even though performance has improved.

"OUT OF CONTROL"

5   Behind Fidelity's attempt at renewal is a complete overhaul of the mutual-fund operation and an even broader restructuring of the entire Fidelity empire. Those changes include a brand-new national TV and print advertising campaign featuring former Magellan manager Peter Lynch and comic Lily Tomlin. In a sharp break from past campaigns, this one doesn't push particular products but rather encourages people to seek advice at Fidelity. Later this fall, Fidelity will roll out new brokerage services aimed at making up ground lost to the growing number of financial industry giants targeting Fidelity's turf.

6   Orchestrating Fidelity's makeover is James C. Curvey, an unlikely character to lead Fidelity back to health. Until early last year, Curvey, 63, was president of Fidelity's venture-capital company, watching over a car service, a newspaper chain, and other pet investments of Chairman Edward C. "Ned" Johnson III. Though he had no role in overseeing mutual funds, he was a member of the parent company's nine-man operating committee.

7   But Curvey says he couldn't stand watching a disaster unfold. So on Mar. 24, 1997, he called a meeting of the operating committee, leaving Johnson out of the loop. Curvey went around the room,

Source: Geoffrey Smith in Boston, "Fixing Fidelity," *Business Week:* September 14, 1998; and Geoffrey Smith in Boston, " 'The Executioner' Takes Charge," *Business Week:* September 14, 1998.

TABLE 1
Curvey Shakes Up Fidelity

- Revives mutual-fund performance by installing new management
- Streamlines Fidelity's top management, consolidating 12 jobs into five
- Changes compensation to reward teamwork
- Forces executives to identify and train successors

---

criticizing his peers and telling them what he thought they were doing wrong. His primary target was J. Gary Burkhead, president of Fidelity's mutual-fund unit. Curvey also went after former marketing chief Paul J. Hondros, an abrasive former Philadelphia cop who was leading a marketing campaign that was not stopping the bloodletting. After two hours with the committee, Curvey went to the chairman. "Things are out of control," he recalls telling Johnson. His first recommendation: Replace Burkhead immediately. "We've got to get him out of there," Curvey recalls saying. "He's burned to a crisp."

8   Curvey's tirade was a turning point for Fidelity. Johnson agreed with Curvey. Within weeks, Burkhead was bumped upstairs to vice-chairman overseeing institutional strategy. The following week—on May 1, 1997—Johnson named Curvey chief operating officer, giving him sweeping power over operations. Hondros resigned a few months later. Sixteen months later, on Sept. 3, 1998, Johnson gave Curvey the added title of president, solidifying his authority as Johnson's right-hand man. Says Johnson: "I knew Curvey was right, and I knew he could fix it."

9   Curvey is radically shaking up Fidelity's corporate culture, trying to repair divisive, behind-the-scenes management problems that contributed to the 1995–96 crisis. He has totally realigned Fidelity's senior ranks and restructured virtually all of its operations aimed at selling products to individual investors, brokers, registered investment advisers, and banks.

10   Central to Curvey's approach has been to sharply rein in the decentralized, entrepreneurial culture that served Fidelity so well when it was small. Power, once spread among 12 senior managers reporting to Johnson, has been consolidated among five managers. All the top players now have 20% of their bonuses tied to their success in cooperating with one another.

11   This seemingly innocuous new compensation system is a dramatic step for Fidelity. In the old Fidelity, conflicting goals and competition among top executives led to numerous problems, including redundant technology development and marketing efforts and turf battles over customers. "Suspicion and mistrust among different units" was one factor behind the slow development of a Windows-based software program for retail brokerage customers called Fox On-Line Xpress, says Mark A. Peterson, president of Fidelity's computer operations. The three-year delay in developing Fox, followed by a shorter delay in launching stock trading on the Internet, allowed competitors, such as Charles Schwab & Co. to surge ahead in electronic brokerage. Curvey "has forced us to really rethink the way we did things here," says Abigail P. Johnson, daughter of Ned Johnson and a senior vice-president.

12   Curvey's insistence on ousting Burkhead as head of mutual funds has proved to be his most prescient move so far—and the one with the most impact on the company's 12 million fund shareholders. Burkhead's replacement is Fidelity's longtime general counsel, Robert C. Pozen, a government affairs specialist who declined an offer to become President Clinton's lead Far East trade negotiator when he signed on to his new job.

13   Since taking over in April, 1997, Pozen has restored order among Fidelity's force of 326 fund managers and analysts. No high-ranking equity managers have left Fidelity since. A key tool for doing this: money. Fidelity managers were hardly underpaid before, but in 1997 and 1998, Fidelity granted millions of dollars in stock of the privately held company to key fund managers, all deferred as an incentive to stay.

14   Size had become a handicap. Many Fidelity funds had grown so large they could no longer nimbly maneuver through the market as they had in the past. The size problem, many worried, made them less likely to ever again produce the spectacular returns they achieved when they were smaller. In 1993, for example, 19 out of 20 Fidelity growth funds beat the Standard & Poor's 500-stock index, many by a margin of more than 2 to 1.

CLIENTS DEFECT

15   That incredible performance led investors to pour money into Fidelity at unprecedented rates. Faced with billions of dollars in new cash, many fund managers in 1994 began sidestepping Fidelity's traditional approach of investing in a diversified array of hundreds of fast-growing small and midsize companies in favor of making big bets on whole sectors of the economy, such as technology stocks or government bonds. Some funds strayed wildly from the objectives described in their prospectuses. The Blue Chip Growth fund, for example, invested heavily in unknown small-cap stocks.

16   Even worse, performance was hurting Fidelity's reputation with companies that offer mutual funds in their 401(k) plans. It began losing new business to such rivals as Putnam Investments, which at the time had better returns.

17   Pozen's predecessor, Burkhead, put an end to the wild sector bets and ordered managers to stay within the investment objectives outlined in the prospectus. But Pozen directly responded to the most serious complaint from the outside: the unchecked growth of the funds. Soon after taking charge, he closed Fidelity's four biggest funds to new retail investors: Magellan, Contrafund, Low-Priced Stock, and Growth & Income.

18   A number of smaller fixes are also helping. Pozen cut the workload of some managers and appointed apprentice managers for some smaller funds. Fidelity's 248 analysts have been divided between small-cap and large-cap stocks and seven specific industry sectors. Analysts now cover only 35 companies instead of 68 and spend two years specializing in an area instead of one.

HONING DATA

19   Other changes, as well, are helping the funds gain against rivals. One is a new stock-picking approach that is changing the way Fidelity invests. Under the old system, devised by Lynch, Fidelity focused on buying companies with strong earnings growth that were likely to beat Wall Street earnings estimates, and it traded aggressively in and out of these mostly small- and mid-cap stocks.

20   Now, Fidelity is less concerned with beating the Street's earnings estimates and is focusing more on companies with consistent earnings growth. "We came to grips with the idea that even if the price is rich, if the earnings are good, you can still have good appreciation," Pozen says.

21   This has led many Fidelity funds into large stocks, such as Coca-Cola and Microsoft, that have high price-earnings multiples. Now, says Dividend Growth Fund manager Mangum, "I'm much more willing to take multiple risk than earnings risk," in part because the fast-growing, smaller companies Fidelity used to favor tend to get pummeled by investors if they have even slight earnings problems.

22   Another reason for the movement into large-cap stocks is a new, broad set of quantitative data designed to identify investments that drag down the fund's performance. Quarterly financial reports pick apart fund holdings and strategy. The data includes comparisons of each fund's industry sector weightings with those of competing non-Fidelity funds and analyses of what would happen if the fund doubled its bets on its 20 largest holdings.

23   The most valuable information, Pozen says, identifies holdings that are underweighted relative to a fund's benchmark. If a fund whose bogey is the Standard & Poor's 500-stock index has 1% of its money in Intel Corp., it's a negative bet, since Intel constitutes 1.6% of the index. The fund will suffer against its benchmark if Intel does well.

24   The system prods managers into paying more attention to their smaller holdings, which often get short shrift in a large portfolio. The idea is that if a manager likes the stock, he or she should consider increasing the position. Conversely, those positions that are underweighted because the manager has cooled on the company may be targets for sale. Fund manager Mangum says this analysis has helped him run his $7 billion fund by eliminating smaller positions, which take time to monitor but have little impact on returns. "If I can't own at least 1% of a company, why bother?" he says. So he has used the quarterly reports to help him trim his portfolio down to 123 stocks, from 250. Many of his top holdings are now also heavily overweighted compared with the weighting they get in the S&P 500, Mangum says.

TABLE 2
Fidelity's Looking Better Against the Competition

How it stacks up against its rivals, short- and long-term:

Fund Group	Cumulative Average Total Return Year to Date*
American	−1.4%
Fidelity	−1.9
Amer. Century	−5.1
Vanguard	−5.3
Putnam	−5.5
AIM	−6.8
IDS	−6.8
Merrill Lynch	−7.4
T. Rowe Price	−8.5
Franklin	−10.9

Fund Group	Cumulative Average Total Return 1-Year*
American	3.4%
Fidelity	0.6
Putnam	−2.3
T. Rowe Price	−3.6
Vanguard	−3.7
IDS	−4.7
AIM	−5.3
Amer. Century	−5.6
Merrill Lynch	−7.5
Franklin	−8.7

25   Fidelity has another analytical tool that can help improve performance. Funds that trade aggressively have high trading costs, which can hurt returns. So, Fidelity now produces a separate report monthly showing how much a fund might save if it reduced its trading. Not all managers use it—Mangum, for one, says smart stock-picking should more than overcome the increased cost of trading. But many Fidelity funds are trading noticeably less than before. Magellan, for example, turned over its portfolio about once every ten months in 1995, but now it's nearly once every three years.

26   The jury is still out on whether Fidelity's revamped stock-picking machine will bring back its halcyon days when many funds routinely beat the market. The new analytical tools may not help the behemoth funds very much if the market starts to favor small- and mid-cap stocks.

27   Some Fidelity watchers, including several former Fidelity fund managers, argue that some larger funds now look more like index funds. Eric Kobren, publisher of Fidelity Insight, calculates that some large funds, such as Growth & Income, have a 98% correlation with the S&P 500 over the past three years. One former manager says: "All these guys are getting paid to do is tweak indexes." Says another: "It's a form of indexing . . . a certain amount of S&P stocks need to be in the fund."

NEW CANDOR

28   Abigail Johnson, who oversees the Fidelity growth funds, dismisses that claim. "That's not supportable if you look at the data." Fewer than half of Magellan's holdings were in the S&P 500 earlier this summer. Pozen notes that most funds are invested in a wide variety of holdings beyond the S&P 500. For example, as of June 30, only 118 of Contrafund's 336 stocks were S&P 500 issues.

TABLE 2
concluded

Fund Group	Cumulative Average Total Return 3-Year*
American	55.2%
Vanguard	55.0
T. Rowe Price	50.3
Fidelity	48.1
Putnam	47.5
IDS	44.3
Franklin	41.9
Amer. Century	41.1
Merrill Lynch	38.2
AIM	36.3

Fund Group	Cumulative Average Total Return 5-Year*
Vanguard	112.7%
Fidelity	105.4
T. Rowe Price	103.0
Putnam	102.4
American	98.3
Franklin	95.2
AIM	91.4
Amer. Century	82.9
IDS	80.1
Merrill Lynch	77.3

Average returns are for 10 largest fund companies (excluding money-market funds); returns exclude index funds.

*Appreciation plus reinvestment of dividends and capital gains before taxes for time returns exclude index funds periods ending Sept. 1, 1998, preliminary results.

Data: Morningstar Inc.

29   Some of Fidelity's harshest critics from a few years ago now think it is making the right moves. David O'Leary, president of Alpha Equity Research Inc. in New Hampshire, had been a vocal critic of Fidelity's forays into sector bets and bonds in 1995 and 1996. But now he says: "Fidelity is back to doing what it does best: stock-picking." Russel Kinnel, editor of Morningstar Mutual Funds, says: "Fidelity is coming to grips with the problems of running enormous funds."

30   Fidelity's turnaround is a work in progress. Company officials have said little publicly about the changes until now, believing they were not complete. But Curvey says the company should acknowledge its past mistakes and move on: "We're almost a public trust here . . . and we have an obligation to tell people what the hell is going on."

31   Curvey's candor is refreshing for Fidelity. The privately held company in the past has been loathe to discuss its affairs with outsiders unless boasting about its successes. And Curvey's leadership comes none too soon. The crisis that prompted his secret meeting with the operating committee led to a sales slump from which Fidelity has yet to fully recover. In 1995, Fidelity collected nearly one-third of new money flowing into mutual funds. But through the first half of 1998, Fidelity's market share stood at just 7.3% (see Exhibit A).

32   Of course, there's more to this company than mutual funds. One long-held goal left unchanged by Curvey is to diversify the business and make the company's fortunes less dependent on mutual funds. Fidelity now sells dozens of products—both financial and nonfinancial—developed by more than 40 separate companies. The offerings range from stock trading to bond underwriting to insurance and back-office support for brokers, independent investment advisers, and corporate-benefits departments.

EXHIBIT A

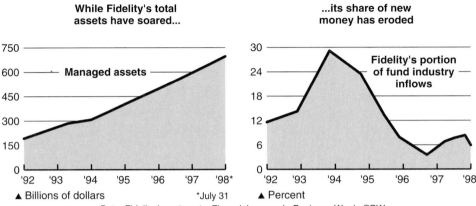

While Fidelity's total
assets have soared...

...its share of new
money has eroded

Data: Fidelity Investments, Financial research, Business Week ©BW

33   Johnson built these businesses by exploiting the advantages of being privately held. He incubated each one from scratch—sometimes doubling up efforts to create competition. Many he funded for years, even if they lost money. Several Fidelity sources say its retail brokerage unit hasn't made a dime in years. Fidelity declines to comment. Many of these units were run by high-ranking execs with their own budgets and total autonomy—and responsibility—to organize and market their products as they wished.

34   Curvey says this system broke down as Fidelity's growth soared. Before he become COO, Fidelity had 17 internal newspapers and five nearly identical software programs under development for five different parts of the company. Hundreds of millions of dollars in marketing and promotions were being spent on duplicate or competing projects.

35   Fidelity has been acclaimed for its technological expertise, but that has come at an enormous price. In one oft-cited case by former employees, Fidelity spent hundreds of millions of dollars over seven years developing competing data processing systems to handle customer accounts. Finally last year, one project, called Vantage 20/20, was scrapped despite an investment some former employees estimate at $500 million. Curvey won't confirm that figure, but he says not all of the money spent on Vantage was wasted, since parts of the project have been adopted in other company systems.

36   Curvey has started cleaning up the mess. He's consolidated Fidelity's computer operations under one executive, Mark A. Peterson, who has built a new computer center in New Hampshire to handle online transactions, which now amount to 60% of brokerage trades. Curvey also named Burkhead to oversee all brokerage and marketing operations, consolidating 11 units. Curvey has also assigned each operating committee member cross-company projects to force them to work together. And he bases part of their bonuses on how well they develop successors. "None of what I'm doing is rocket science, but we've never had any of this before," says Curvey.

37   Johnson has wisely decided not to try to rebuild his company alone. At 68, he is preparing for retirement, though he refuses even to hint at when that might come. He ran Fidelity without a second-in-command for 12 years, but he now is trying to build a management team capable of running Fidelity when he steps down. Although Curvey has been the mover behind Fidelity's shakeup, he will not necessarily succeed Johnson. Johnson says he will decide on his successor when he retires, based on "who's available at the time and what skills the company needs."

FAR ENOUGH?

38   His first choice is Abigail, 36. A former fund manager, she joined the executive ranks last year to help oversee funds and broaden her experience dealing with other parts of the company, including the

marketing, public relations, and legal departments. She owns 24.5% of Fidelity's voting stock, potentially worth $4 billion to $5 billion if Fidelity went public, according to industry estimates. Her father owns 12%, and other Johnson family members own an additional 13%.

39   Abigail is the beneficiary of a trust that grants her ownership of Fidelity "for her lifetime" and could keep ownership in the family for another generation as well, her father says. Two years ago, he gave 51% of the company's voting stock to 50 top employees, as a way to reduce estate taxes. Since then, many employees have hoped that Fidelity will go public, producing windfall profits. Fidelity may be worth $20 billion in an initial public offering, some estimate.

40   The trust allows Abigail to sell Fidelity or take it public. But Johnson says he does not want that to happen. "I'm not really going to reach out of the grave and curse her if she does that," Johnson quips. But, he adds, "there wouldn't be any strong financial incentive at all" for her to do so. "If there were good business reasons, maybe it would happen," Johnson adds. Abigail says she wants Fidelity to remain private.

41   Abigail has her choice of jobs, her father says. She can oversee strategy, head operations, or remain in a lesser role, he says. Abby says she will decide that when the time comes. Her father, she adds, is in excellent health and will "probably never" retire. He has worked out regularly with a personal trainer in his Boston home for the past 10 years, and occasionally challenges his aides to a game of tennis.

42   Whether Curvey and his changes go far enough to solve Fidelity's problems is still to be seen. The changes in the mutual-fund unit are untested, particularly in a bear market. The new marketing strategy, which emphasizes advice, is a sharp break from the past practice of promoting funds. And new brokerage products that Fidelity will roll out in coming months, including a voice-recognition trading system and a program to offer customers investment advice, are coming on the heels of similar products offered by competitors.

43   Fidelity is far from being the money machine it was in the early 1990s. But Curvey has stopped the bloodletting and has Fidelity back on the warpath.

"THE EXECUTIONER" TAKES CHARGE

44   James C. Curvey seems like an odd choice for president of Fidelity Investments. He joined Fidelity in 1982 as head of human resources and five years later moved on to run Fidelity Capital, a hodgepodge of businesses unrelated to Fidelity's core mutual-fund operations. But Curvey's ascent is no surprise to insiders at the company. He and Fidelity Chairman Edward C. "Ned" Johnson III hit it off from the start, and Johnson has long used him as a sounding board. A former top Fidelity executive says the two became so close that "Curvey is one of the few execs who will tell Ned he's full of it and not have Ned cut his throat."

45   It is no accident that Johnson calls Curvey "the Executioner," although for reasons other than his willingness to fire people. For starters, he has made millions for the parent company. Since taking over Fidelity Capital in 1987, revenues have grown from $10 million to over $270 million last year. Curvey also oversaw Fidelity's most profitable investment ever outside mutual funds—a 55% stake in British telecommunications company Colt Telecom Group PLC. Fidelity built the company from scratch in 1992, took it public in 1996, and its stake is now worth $3 billion.

RURAL BACKGROUND

46   Johnson makes no secret of his admiration for Curvey's ability to execute his business strategies. According to Fred K. Foulkes, a Boston University business professor and longtime Fidelity consultant, Curvey is well-organized and big on setting goals and making sure that they are achieved. "His eyes will roll if you talk about flaky HR [human resources] stuff, like organizational development programs," Foulkes adds.

47   Many current and former executives who have worked with Curvey describe him as someone adept at getting groups of senior managers to cooperate. "He has the ability to keep lots of very strong

EXHIBIT B

Resume of James C. Curvey

Born
June 9, 1935

Hometown
Mahanoy City, Pa.

Family
Married, two children

Pastimes
Golf, tennis

Employment
Fidelity Investments:

　1998 President

　1997 COO

　1987–97 President, Fidelity Capital

　1983–86 Sr. V.P. administration

　1982–83 V.P. human resources

　1976–82 Chase Manhattan Bank, V.P. human resources

　1956–76 U.S. government, various human resources jobs

Education
BS Accounting, Villanova University, 1957

MA Personnel Management, George Washington University, 1962

---

egos working together, " says Metropolitan Life Insurance Co. Chairman Robert H. Benmosche, who worked with Curvey at Chase Manhattan Bank in the early 1980s.

48　　　Despite Curvey's blunt style, the executive has made few enemies at Fidelity. Indeed, many considered him their first stop before approaching Johnson with a new idea or difficult problem.

49　　　Curvey's background could not have been more different than his Boston blueblood boss's. He grew up in rural Pennsylvania, the son of a co-owner of a coal mine who died in a car crash when Curvey was 12. He struggled in school, and his early career took him from accounting to the Army to law school. Around Fidelity, rumor has it that Curvey worked for the CIA. Not true, he says. Although he did get an offer from the Secret Service to guard President Dwight D. Eisenhower, Curvey turned down the job because it required too much travel, he says.

50　　　After Curvey received his BA from Villanova University, his home-town congressman landed him a job in the U.S. Treasury Dept. answering mail. From there, he jumped to a succession of human resources positions within the department and worked his way up to head of human resources at Housing & Urban Development. In 1976, Curvey moved to the private sector by nailing down the No. 2 human resources job at Chase Manhattan.

51　　　Is Curvey CEO material? "The answer is yes," says Benmosche. Still, the odds are against him. Only a handful of executives with human resources backgrounds have ever made it to chief executive, says Foulkes. Curvey won't say when he plans to retire, but he may pack it in before Johnson, who is five years his senior. The current chairman has no plans to go anywhere, and he seems determined to stay on long enough to let his daughter Abigail, a rising executive at Fidelity, grow into his job. No matter who ends up succeeding Johnson, Curvey will remain the key man at Fidelity at least for a few more years.

CASE 17

BusinessWeek

LOUD NOISES AT BOMBARDIER

1. For Laurent Beaudoin, the 59-year-old chief executive of Montreal-based Bombardier Inc., 1997 was a bumpy ride. First, Bombardier's Sea-Doo, a sit-down water bike that had blasted past stand-up models like Kawasaki Heavy Industries Ltd.'s Jet Ski to sales growth of more than 30% a year, began to sputter. By August, a growing chorus of complaints about waterway congestion, noise, and safety had forced Bombardier to cut production, and unhappy investors were selling stock. Some $1 billion in market value disappeared in a few weeks.

2. The next month, stockholders were rocked again when a political flap cost the company's mass transit division a lucrative Mexican subway car contract. These troubles, combined with Bombardier's long struggle to turn around its money-losing Learjet Div., ended the company's hot growth streak. After a five-year ride in which operating profits raced ahead by an average 39% a year, the maker of trains, planes, and snowmobiles had been stopped cold. Net earnings for the fiscal year ending this month are expected to be flat at $285 million, on a paltry 5% sales gain, to $5.9 billion. And at around 19, Bombardier stock remains roughly 20% below its mid-1997 high.

3. None of that means Beaudoin is swearing off risky innovations such as the Sea-Doo. Instead, he's diving in deeper. To rev Bombardier back up, he's counting on a bevy of new products—everything from the Global Express, a top-of-the-line corporate jet, to a new series of New York City subway cars.

4. That has convinced some investors that Bombardier's setback is nothing but a short-lived squall. Indeed, analyst Peter A. Rozenberg of Toronto's TD Securities Inc. forecasts net income will rise 33% for the coming fiscal year, to $377.8 million, as sales grow 24%, to $7.3 billion. Adds John G. Ambrose, a portfolio manager with Toronto's Nigel Stephens, one of Bombardier's largest shareholders: "The stock market is focusing on the disappointing results in personal watercraft, but seems to be ignoring other aspects of the company which have much better growth potential."

5. Certainly, Beaudoin appears to have good reason to be unruffled: He has faced much worse. In 1973, eight years after he took charge at age 27, the company's Ski-Doo snowmobiles came under attack as unsafe, polluting gas-guzzlers. As the energy crisis ground on, Ski-Doo sales—then more than 90% of Bombardier's $127 million in annual revenues—began to melt away.

"A HUGE LEAP"

6. Beaudoin determined to diversify. Over the next two decades, he engineered a series of ambitious purchases that have built Bombardier into a premier worldwide manufacturer of transportation equipment. The shift has brought balance to Bombardier's product line—and kudos for its CEO. Beaudoin has "done a remarkable job moving from snowmobiles to Global Expresses," says Joe Leonard, president of the aerospace marketing unit of Bombardier partner Allied Signal Inc. "That is a huge leap."

7. Much of the company's growth has come from new products, long its forte. Snowmobiles were primitive and cumbersome devices until inventor J. Armand Bombardier figured out in the late 1950s how to mass-produce a user-friendly model. Today, Bombardier's annual snowmobile sales top $400 million. Beaudoin, the son-in-law who took the helm a year after the inventor died, has continued to innovate. "We're selling technology, and we're selling new products," he says. "That's what makes us a success."

Source: Joseph Weber in Montreal, with Wendy Zellner in Dallas and Geri Smith in Mexico City, "Loud Noises at Bombardier," *Business Week:* January 26, 1998.

8   But will Bombardier be able to keep it up? This year's offerings start with the Learjet 45, a midsize plane priced like a light jet but capable of nonstop transcontinental flights. The $8 million plane boasts 135 orders outstanding. Hitting the tarmac in 2000 will be a plane with even greater potential: the 70-seat Canadair Regional Jet Series 700. Already, it has won over such customers as American Eagle, the commuter division of American Airlines Inc., which has 25 on order. "Bombardier did a very good job of listening to us about the customer features," says Peter A. Pappas, American Eagle's senior vice-president for planning, who praises the plane's large windows and ease of servicing. The plane has taken off so fast that Aero International (Regional), a European consortium, last month opted not to build a competitor. Analysts estimate that sales for 70-seaters may reach $20 billion over 15 years, and for now, Bombardier has the market to itself.

9   These planes join strong Bombardier names like the Challenger 604, a long-range widebody jet designed to ferry up to 11 passengers on routes stretching over 4,000 miles. Microsoft Corp. Chairman William H. Gates III recently paid $21 million for one. Analyst Rozenberg of TD Securities expects pretax profits at the $3 billion aerospace division to soar 41% in 1998, to $328 million.

10   Still, Bombardier's planemakers can't just cruise—they're in the midst of a furious dogfight with rival Gulfstream Aircraft Inc. in the market for ultralong-range corporate jets. Gulfstream's top-of-the-line jets have long been the ultimate executive perk, and in Bombardier they face their most serious head-to-head competition yet. With its entrant, the Global Express, Bombardier wants to carve out a larger share of that market. The company says the plane, which will be able to ferry 16 or so people from New York to Tokyo nonstop, should reach customers later this year. Gulfstream is already delivering its newest planes and has sold more than 70, claiming a superior cabin pressure system that will make long rides more comfortable. But the Global Express is expected to fly faster and longer and has won customers like Las Vegas architect Anthony A. Marnell, designer of the Mirage casino hotel. "They've really gone out and designed a 21st century airplane," says Marnell, who's flying an old-model Gulfstream but has ordered a Global Express.

11   While Bombardier appears to be holding its own in the battle so far, serious concerns remain about whether the ultralong-range market will ever pay off for either player. Richard T. Santulli, chairman of Executive Jet Inc., the largest buyer of corporate jets, believes demand for this latest iteration may be running out. That would be bad news for Bombardier, which says it has more than 73 on order but must sell at least 100 to break even on its investment of about $280 million. Bombardier says it expects strong demand.

BIG-TICKET WINS

12   Concerns about other business lines—particularly Bombardier's $1.2 billion transportation unit—have begun to lift. Countering the stalled Mexican effort and erratic and declining sales in Europe are recent big-ticket wins in the U.S. Bombardier is building 680 highly automated New York City subway cars for nearly $1 billion and Amtrak's first high-speed trains, set to hit the Boston-Washington route by 1999, for $419 million. And Bombardier's Mexican prospects may also be on the rise again. On Jan. 12, Mexican officials told a visiting Canadian trade delegation that bidding for the subway cars will re-open in two to three months.

13   Elsewhere, Beaudoin is introducing entirely new products, such as his electric "Neighborhood Vehicle," or NV. After brainstorming sessions on the kind of vehicles people will drive in the future, Bombardier executives began researching this souped-up golf cart. Aimed at gated or retirement communities, it features a windshield and seatbelts and whizzes along at up to 25 mph. Says Police Chief James V. Murray, whose force is using one to patrol Peachtree City, Ga.: "It's a spectacular little machine." Introduced last year, analysts say sales of the $8,000 carts could hit $33 million this year. Also in the works: an unmanned hovering aircraft to detect buried land mines, as well as a sporty all-terrain recreational vehicle to be introduced this spring that will compete with popular models now sold by Honda Motor Co. and Yamaha Corp.

TABLE 1
Planes, Trains, and Snowmobiles

Bombardier figures a host of new products will fuel growth in 1998

Aerospace:

Learjet 45: The midsize business jet is in hot demand. With 135 orders outstanding, factories will be humming at least through 2000.

Global Express: Bombardier's top-of-the-line executive jet is late and faces a tough rival in the Gulfstream V, but they say they've presold more than 73.

Transportation:

Subway cars: Deliveries start in 1999 on a nearly $1 billion contract for New York City featuring cars with automatic announcements and electronic information signs.

American Flyer: New high-speed trains will carry Amtrak passengers from Boston to Washington at 150 miles per hour starting in 1999.

Consumer Products:

Ski-Doo: New models of Bombardier's workhorse snowmobile—which claims 30% of the North American market and half of Europe's—should ensure continued dominance.

Neighborhood Vehicle: A souped-up, two-passenger golf cart featuring an electric motor capable of 25 mph could forge a $33 million market by yearend.

Data: TD Securities, Bombardier.

14   Of course, new projects such as those bring high risk and high costs. Witness the slow takeoff of Bombardier's de Havilland Dash 8 Series 400 turboprop, a regional plane that will carry as many as 78 passengers and cost Bombardier some $319 million to develop. So far, U.S. demand has been weak. But for now, the success stories seem to outweigh the risks: Bombardier's backlog of orders is up to $10.3 billion, from less than $7 billion a year ago. That's the kind of bump Beaudoin, a snowmobiler for 40 years, can enjoy.

CASE 18   BusinessWeek

AT&T-TCI: TELECOM UNBOUND

---

1   We've all seen it before—two powerful executives, presiding over a hastily convened news conference to announce their new world-shaping combination. They stand, gripping and grinning for the cameras, zipping off sound bites for the evening news, and predicting that their megamerger will be the combination of resources, talents, and technology that finally brings the future into the present.

2   Indeed, as John Malone stood on stage with AT&T CEO C. Michael Armstrong on June 24 to announce their $48 billion deal, it was impossible not to recall how five years ago, he stood with Bell Atlantic CEO Ray Smith to announce a similar groundbreaking deal. That botched merger attempt led many to question the whole concept of "digital convergence"—the notion that telecommunications, television, and computers would all come together in a single, digitized system of electronic communications.

3   Well, a lot has changed since then. The technology to transport high-speed digital signals—for voice calls, video, or virtually any form of communication you can name—is vastly more powerful and less costly. The Internet and the Web have created a standard "platform" for managing all this digital traffic, and the Telecommunications Act of 1996 has reduced—but not eliminated—anachronistic barriers between communications markets.

4   And in an ironic twist, AT&T, the company that has perhaps missed the most opportunities in the new world of digital communications, has come up with the deal that, if it works, will take advantage of all these trends—and could be the catalyst for other deals and business plans that break the bottleneck and finally deliver on the promise of digital convergence. "This is the deal that's going to get competition going," says former FCC Commissioner Reed Hundt. "This is exactly what regulators envisioned—consumers having choice."

5   What will that choice be? For starters, the new AT&T is now in position to be the first nationwide communications company—since the breakup of the old Bell system—that solves the "last mile" problem. Now, the only way to bridge that final gap to the user's home is via a local phone company. Because of the last mile bottleneck, there has been virtually no competition in local residential phone service, innovation is almost nonexistent, and connections to the Internet have been painfully slow. Once TCI's cable network and set-top boxes are upgraded to handle a two-way flow—no easy feat, mind you—AT&T can use the cable company's coaxial connections to transmit local and long-distance voice calls, Internet traffic, and the usual cable fare.

6   And then? Let your imagination run wild. Video voicemail will be a cinch. If a guest comes to stay for the weekend, you'll be able to order him a second phone line—and probably even give him the same number he has at home. Electronic commerce is likely to flourish as consumers can more easily cruise the Internet and as television melds with the Net. As TCI Chairman and CEO John Malone puts it, you'll be able to order Viagra online while you're watching your favorite show. "Just point and click," he says. "Do it on the fly."

7   What puts this vision within reach now is a host of new technologies that are smoothing digital connections. Most important, the technology for providing telephone service over the cable network is now developed enough to offer an economically feasible—and potentially much better—alternative to the existing copper wire. While the costs of cable telephony have been prohibitive in the past, they've now dropped to the point where Armstrong expects to spend as much as $400 to $500 per home. Other cable companies have also shown that it works. MediaOne Group is offering cable telephony in Atlanta and Los Angeles—and says it has captured a 10% market share in the slices of those markets it has entered.

Source: Peter Elstrom with Catherine Arnst in New York, Roger Crockett in Chicago, and bureau reports, "AT&T-TCI: Telecom Unbound," *Business Week:* July 6, 1998.

TABLE 1
Building a Better Bundle . . .

AT&T provides:
- 70 million long-distance customers
- 4 million wireless customers
- 1.1 million dial-up Internet access customers
- 15 million business customers
- Local access networks in 250 cities through Teleport
- Strong brand awareness
- 128,000 employees
- 1997 revenues—$51.32 billion

TCI provides:
- 10.5 million cable subscribers out of 33 million homes passed
- 10 million subscribers through affiliates out of 16 million homes passed
- @Home Network, an Internet access and content provider
- Access cable and sports networks through Liberty Media Group
- 31,500 employees
- 1997 revenues—$7.57 billion

8   Cable isn't the only way to bridge the final mile, either. While TCI and its affiliates can reach 33 million homes in the U.S., AT&T plans to continue to experiment with wireless technology that it will deploy outside of the TCI region. That technology will be tested in several thousand homes next year and, if the tests are successful, it will be rolled out commercially in 2000. "We need to own our own facilities," says Armstrong. "We need to control our service, and we need to control our costs."

9   However AT&T—and rivals that follow—approach these new networks, it won't be cheap. The costs of upgrading TCI's entire infrastructure so that it can provide telephony and high-speed Internet access are enormous—about $15 billion for TCI and its affiliates, by Armstrong's reckoning. And some analysts think those numbers are low. They forecast that the costs could hit $20 billion or more.

10   Think of it this way: AT&T has bought the dirt road that leads to American homes. Now it must grade it and pave it to carry all the new traffic. "What's wrong about this deal is that TCI is not in the local phone business," says Mark R. Bruneau, president of Renaissance Worldwide Inc. "So it is a big gamble." On the other hand, AT&T is one of the few companies that can fund such an undertaking: It has $8 billion in annual cash flow and little debt.

11   Cost isn't the only issue, however. Although the technology for pushing voice traffic over cable works with small numbers of customers, some experts think it will be problematic if used widely. "That technology is just not at hand," says Michael Noll, a business professor at the University of Southern California.

12   Another risk to the deal? Under current telecom law, if AT&T pays to upgrade TCI's network for telephone service, AT&T will have to let competitors also use the infrastructure at a wholesale discount. That prospect convinced Sprint Corp. CEO William T. Esrey to walk away from a similar deal with a group of cable companies including TCI. "If we provided telephony service over cable, we recognized that they would have to make it available to competitors."

13   That may not be such a big issue for AT&T, however. By using the cable network to provide high-speed connections to the home that are 20 to 30 times faster than what the Baby Bells and GTE now provide, AT&T expects to produce a massive pipeline that can carry all sorts of traffic at relatively low cost. "We could have a universal pipe in the home that handles all flavors of what will then be digital, including video, voice, and data," says Van Baker, director of consumer research at market researcher Dataquest.

TABLE 2
. . . And Making It Work

How the combined company will be structured:

AT&T Consumer Services (separate tracking stock)

- All-consumer long-distance, wireless, cable, and Internet businesses

- 1999 projected revenues—$33 billion

AT&T Business Services and Wholesale Networking (wholly owned)

- All telecom and outsourcing services provided to business, including Teleport, and network access sold to other phone companies

- 1999 projected revenues—$29 billion

Liberty Media (separate tracking stock)

- Stakes in several cable networks including Discovery Channel and Black Entertainment Television

14   That opens up a potential bonanza of services beyond telephony. Web sites will be able to incorporate video. You'll be able to jump from a commercial to the advertiser's Web address. And video telephony will become much simpler and more affordable. "Your grandkids are going to laugh at us for using these little black things to talk on without looking at each other."

15   That poses the most profound challenge the local phone companies have ever encountered. So far, the Baby Bells have rolled out broadband services for consumers slowly—if at all. Few want to market a low cost alternative that could cannibalize their high-margin sales to businesses. But with AT&T planning to roll out high-speed services, the Bells will have to get serious about providing high-speed access of their own or face a revolt from customers. "If the AT&T-TCI deal goes through, that will create more competition, which in turn will accelerate the buildout of high-bandwidth connections to the home," says Lawrence E. Ellison, CEO of Oracle Corp.

16   AT&T isn't the only company using new technologies to muscle in on the local phone companies' markets. Earlier this summer, Sprint announced plans for a number of "integrated services," including local service, over high-speed connections. And cable companies trying to sell telecom services think AT&T's entry into cable telephony will help them. "By virtue of AT&T battling, that helps any cable operator, even those that aren't affiliated with AT&T," says Dallas Clement, treasurer for Cox Communications.

17   Local phone companies will have to scramble to find ways to provide similar services to their customers. So far, U S West is the only Bell that has announced aggressive plans to roll out high-speed Net connections.

18   The Bells certainly have the opportunity to provide high-speed connections—and the additional services that they make possible. The Bells have started to deploy digital subscriber lines (DSL), which provide speeds as fast as 1.5 megabits per second over copper wire. Although there are now several different flavors of DSL, which has contributed to a delay in wholesale rollout, many experts think the phone companies are further along than the cable companies.

19   Time to market, rather than technology, is likely to separate the winners from the losers. The first to offer high-speed connections is likely to be able to skim off the cream of consumers, who most value use of the Internet. Since there are economies of scale to be had from rolling out high-speed connections, the company that gets a headstart will have a significant advantage. Asks Christopher Mines, telecom analyst with Forrester Research, "Can AT&T-TCI be the first one there? They take a giant step with this deal."

20   It's a step that some observers say AT&T almost had to take. "Frankly, it allows AT&T to diversify out of the consumer long-distance business before it completely collapses," says Craig Moffett, vice-president and telecom specialist at Boston Consulting Group. In fact, as part of the June 24 announcement, AT&T disclosed its plan to separate the consumer business into a new unit with TCI's cable service called AT&T Consumer Services. The $33 billion group, with AT&T President John D.

Zeglis as its CEO and TCI's Leo J. Hindery as president, will have its own stock. Its mission will be to sell all sorts of consumer services—cable, wireless, local and long-distance, and Internet services. What remains of AT&T will be the long-distance network and the corporate business.

21   Armstrong describes the new consumer company as the high-growth—and high-risk—portion of the AT&T portfolio. Indeed, there are plenty of doubters who wonder why AT&T, which has failed so often in its attempts to conquer cyberspace, will now prevail. Such concerns helped knock AT&T's stock down 8%, to $60, on the day of the announcement.

22   Still, AT&T's deal with TCI likely marks a turning point in the evolution of communications. It's the beginning of the breakdown of the Baby Bells' monopoly over the last mile. "This looks like the break in the dam," says Kevin Costello, a partner in global communications and entertainment at Arthur Andersen. A flood of new communications services is on the way.

CASE 19

BusinessWeek

STEVE JOBS, MOVIE MOGUL

1   The euphoria in the air is as thick as the fog in nearby San Francisco. One by one, employees of Pixar Animation Studios jump onto a makeshift stage on the company's outdoor patio to compete in the annual Halloween costume contest. A Roller Derby team cavorts to a 1970s' disco beat as Pixar's 400-plus employees hoot and holler. A decrepit John Glenn look-alike in a space suit canes his way onstage, waves weakly, and shuffles off. And, natch, Francis the Ladybug, a character from Pixar's upcoming movie *A Bug's Life,* waddles up for a moment in the spotlight. Nice try, but first prize—free airplane tickets to Europe or Hawaii—goes to A. J. Riebli. At 295 pounds, with a shaved head and clad only in diapers, he flops around in a perfect imitation of the infant star of Pixar's 1988 Academy Award-winning short film, *Tin Toy.*

2   So how did Pixar's real larger-than-life character, Chairman and Chief Executive Steven P. Jobs, dress? Silicon Valley's numero uno visionary was attired in jeans, a plaid shirt, and New Balance running shoes because, well, he just didn't have time to get all gussied up. No problem, he's wearing what really matters anyway—a grin that stretches from ear to ear.

3   He has reason to be gleeful. After years of Pixar chasing its dream of making full-length movies using computers, the company is preparing to release what's expected to become its second box-office hit. Pixar's first feature film, 1995's *Toy Story,* became the third-highest grossing animated film of all time, with $350 million in worldwide box-office revenues. On Nov. 25, Pixar will debut *A Bug's Life,* the story of a courageous ant named Flik who fights back against extortionist grasshoppers. The movie is not expected to reach the extraordinary box-office highs of *Toy Story*—analysts peg *A Bug's Life* at $250 million worldwide—but it could be a gold mine for Pixar.

4   Thanks to a cushy deal that Jobs cut with Walt Disney Co. last year, Pixar will get an equal share of the profits, after Disney's 12.5% distribution fee, and the full backing of Disney's unbeatable marketing and distribution clout. That has drawn merchandising deals like bees to honey: Everyone from Mattel Inc. to McDonald's Corp. is churning out *A Bug's Life* paraphernalia—toothbrushes, candy bars, even bed sheets. There will be caterpillar Beanie Babies modeled after the movie's Heimlich, $30 voice-activated Fliks, and no less than 65 million Happy Meal toys. The bottom line: After spending $45 million on its half of the production costs, Pixar could reap as much as $200 million in merchandising royalties, video sales, and box-office receipts, vs. $53.8 million so far from *Toy Story.*

5   Wall Street is clearly starstruck. Pixar's stock has soared to 48 from 23 a year ago based on the high expectations for *A Bug's Life* and two other movies in the works. Indeed, Pixar's revenues are projected to rocket from $11.5 million this year to $193 million in 2001, with profits soaring from $3.9 million to $87 million, according to Merrill Lynch & Co. analyst Jessica Reif Cohen. That has earned Jobs membership in the billionaires' club, with his 73% stake worth $1.4 billion.

INDENTURED SERVANTS

6   But Jobs is after much more than money. What he's planning is nothing less than building Pixar into a movie studio for the 21st century—one that will rival Disney for the hearts and minds of families around the world. In a sense, the influence he's seeking is as pervasive as what he sought when he founded Apple Computer Inc.: He wants Pixar to tell the stories that children grow up with—the Snow Whites, Mary Poppinses, and Lion Kings for future generations. "I think Pixar has the opportunity to be the next Disney—not replace Disney—but be the next Disney," he says.

7   That's quintessential Jobs—sweeping, bold, and, as always, audacious. While Disney has built its reputation over 70 years with gobs of talent and billions of dollars, Pixar has made all of two feature

Source: Peter Burrows in Point Richmond, California, and Ronald Grover in Los Angeles, "Steve Jobs, Movie Mogul," *Business Week:* November 23, 1998.

films so far—counting *A Bug's Life.* Credit Jobs for cutting a sweet deal with Disney in which Pixar has a shot at rich profits. Still, it's Disney that controls the future use of all the Pixar characters and films that they develop together. And it is Disney that possesses the marketing might to transform Flik from a mere image on the big screen into a household name.

8   So how will Jobs achieve his dream? Not surprisingly, he's tapping into his Silicon Valley roots and using computers to forge a unique style of moviemaking. In *A Bug's Life,* Pixar has developed computer animation that allows more lifelike backgrounds, texture, and movement than ever before—from the stars of the show right down to a simple leaf. Since real leaves are translucent, Pixar's engineers developed special software algorithms that both reflect and absorb light, creating luminous scenes among jungles of clover. As for the characters in *A Bug's Life,* they have up to 3,900 potential movements, vs. 700 in *Toy Story*'s characters.

9   What's more, films using computer animation are very lucrative. They cost 30% to 40% less to make than traditional animated films because only one-third as many staffers are needed. And the process yields digitally stored characters and backdrops that can be recast inexpensively into sequels.

10   Of course, films that touch our hearts require far more than great technology. They depend upon the creative spark. To get that, Jobs has fostered a campuslike environment at Pixar similar to the freewheeling, charged atmosphere in the early days of his beloved Apple, where he has returned as acting CEO. Instead of just computer experts, the company hires an eclectic mix, including landscape artists, puppeteers, even a Danish rock star. And no one is more essential to stoking the creative fires than John Lasseter, Pixar's Academy Award-winning vice-president of creative. The 41-year-old Lasseter, known for his Hawaiian shirts and irrepressible playfulness, was director of *Toy Story* and *A Bug's Life.* "He is to animation what Steven Spielberg is to live-action films," gushes Disney Studios Chairman Joe Roth.

SETTING THE PACE

11   With Pixar's unique combination of technology and creativity, Jobs could become Silicon Valley's first movie mogul. Should *A Bug's Life* approach the box-office success of *Toy Story,* Pixar will have made the two most popular animated films since Disney's 1994 megahit *The Lion King.* "In Hollywood, there are very few brands—really just two—Disney and Spielberg," says Jobs. "We want to be one, too." To do that, Pixar must churn out hits at an aggressive pace—Jobs aims to make roughly one movie a year. "They will emerge as a leading digital animation studio—a filmmaker that parents and children will appreciate and trust," says analyst Paul W. Noglows of Hambrecht & Quist, which does investment banking for the company.

12   But many in Hollywood think Jobs is living in Fantasyland. The industry's cognoscenti consider the computer exec another movie-industry wannabe, and Pixar, they say, acts as little more than a well-paid subcontractor to Disney. Indeed, some say Pixar's fate rests almost entirely in the hands of Disney—its partner but also a potential competitor. The Hollywood powerhouse holds script approval on Pixar films and is doing some of the heavy lifting on the creative end. All the casting, music production, and some of the screenwriting for *A Bug's Life* was handled by Disney. Sure, Pixar will be able to reap royalty checks, but that's far from operating as an independent studio. "There is no such thing as a great deal with Disney," says David Geffen, co-founder of Pixar rival DreamWorks SKG. "They control the property, and they are just giving [Pixar] some of the profits."

13   Already, Disney is hard at work ginning up its own technical wizardry—100 of its employees are quietly honing their computer-animation skills at a former Lockheed Martin Corp. airplane plant near Burbank Airport. Their task: to produce Disney's first completely computer-animated film by 2000, called *Dinosaurs,* which will mix photorealistic, computer-generated tyrannosaurs and brontosaurs with real-life backgrounds. Disney also has invested in Tippett Studio, a Berkeley (Calif.) special-effects house that is developing a computer-animated space adventure for adults, code-named Expedition. And Disney bought the rights to a claymation script about animals escaping from a zoo from writers Mark Gibson and Phil Halprin.

14   These ventures could cause a rift in the seven-year-old Pixar-Disney marriage. Should Disney develop other sources of top-notch computer-animation fare, Pixar may find it tough to land another

TABLE 1
A Bug Farm's Life

Twenty years of buzz in the evolution of a toon shop:

1984

Disney animator John Lasseter joins filmmaker George Lucas' computer special-effects group, which later becomes Pixar.

1986

Steve Jobs purchases Pixar from Lucas for $10 million, and Lasseter creates a short computer-animated film called *Luxo Jr.,* which draws rave reviews at a technical trade show.

1988

Lasseter's *Tin Toy* wins an Academy Award for Best Short Animated Film.

1991

After giving Lasseter the go-ahead to make *Toy Story,* Disney signs Pixar to a three-film deal that gives Pixar roughly 10% of movie profits.

1995

Jobs decides to de-emphasize computer-animated software and to focus Pixar on making movies. He seeks counsel from superagent Michael Ovitz, Universal chief Edgar Bronfman, and investment banker Herb Allen. *Toy Story* is released in November, and Pixar goes public, raising $140 million—nudging out Netscape Communications as the biggest IPO of the year. Lasseter later wins an Academy Award for *Toy Story.*

1996

As *Toy Story* mania fades, so does Pixar's stock, dropping from 29 to 13 during the year. In March, Jobs and Eisner agree on a framework for a new agreement.

1997

Disney and Pixar announce a five-film deal that gives Pixar roughly 50% of the profits on its films. Jobs scraps a CD-ROM game division to focus only on movies.

1998

Pixar wins an Academy Award for *Geri's Game,* a short film with advances in animating human skin. On Nov. 25, after months of heavy marketing, *A Bug's Life* will debut.

1999

Pixar plans to release *Toy Story II.*

2000

Pixar plans to release a film code-named Hidden City—and take a year off from its flick-a-year pace in 2001.

2004

John Lasseter's contract, a key reason Disney signed the 1997 agreement, will end.

lucrative deal with the Hollywood giant after the current five-film deal expires—especially if Pixar produces any mediocre movies. That could leave the upstart with a smaller slice of profits, less guaranteed financial support from Disney—or no deal at all.

15   As dire as that sounds, Pixar executives aren't fretting. They say they will have options beyond Disney—especially if they continue making blockbusters. Under the five-film deal, Jobs can start talks with other studios after completion of a third movie, probably in 2002. With a few hits to its name, Pixar could either go it alone or turn to players like Paramount Pictures Corp. that are eager to get into the kid-flick market. There is a precedent. Jobs, for example, points to filmmaker George Lucas, who has remained independent and still gotten strong distribution from studios by making supernova hits like *Star Wars.* "If we're as successful as we hope we'll be, we should have that kind of clout," says Pixar CFO Lawrence Levy.

16   Besides, Jobs says he's not planning on leaving the Magic Kingdom anytime soon. "I hope we're doing business with them for another 20 years," he says. He may get his wish—and more. Analysts say that if Pixar stays at the top of its game, Disney may try to snap it up. "If they paid $19 billion for

TABLE 2
Pixar's All-Star Team

Lawrence Levy, Executive VP, CFO

He joined in 1995 from graphics company Electronics For Imaging—in time to help pull off Pixar's blockbuster, $140 million IPO. He's the company's voice of reason on Wall Street.

Edwin Catmull, Executive VP, CTO

A cartoonist who couldn't draw, he has developed many core concepts for computer animation. He runs the technical team that's essential to Pixar's success and remains the keeper of its free-spirited culture.

Steve Jobs, Chairman, CEO

His Apple Computer is on the rebound, and Pixar is headed for high times. He landed the critical partnership with mighty Disney that could help him achieve his vision of building his own Digital Age Disney.

John Lasseter, Creative VP

Pixar could be called Lasseter Studios—such is his reputation in Hollywood. Disney tried to hire him away from Pixar three times before agreeing to a long-term contract to get access to his services at Pixar.

Sarah McArthur, VP of Production

The executive producer of Disney's animation unit before joining Pixar in 1997, she helped make *The Lion King* a hit. Now, she will bring big-studio processes to Pixar so it can make one film a year.

ABC, they can probably afford us," quips Jobs. But he points out he doesn't have to sell unless it's an exceptional offer because he owns almost three-quarters of the stock. For Disney's part, execs say they have no plans to make a bid for Pixar.

17   If there's tension about what the future may hold, there's no evidence of it today. Lasseter's moviemaking is in line with Disney's penchant for heartwarming fare. And the companies developed a considerable amount of trust during the development of *Toy Story*—when Disney taught Pixar how to handle production and budgeting and Pixar proved its artistic mettle. Lasseter, for example, had to convince Disney that *Toy Story* could succeed without being a musical like Disney's other animated hits. And while Disney closely monitors Pixar's spending and progress via weekly videoconferences and visits every two weeks or so, the relationship seems more collaborative than contractual. "We act like partners are supposed to act," says Peter Schneider, president of Walt Disney Feature Animation. "We look every day at what they are doing, we demand, we push, we talk, and the end result is a better product. Who gets the credit really is never the issue for us, although I know sometimes it is for Steve."

18   Pixar will need all the help it can get. An increasing number of studios are cranking out children's films to try to get a piece of what's long been considered the most lucrative part of Hollywood. Witness the crowded schedule this fall. On Nov. 20, Paramount will release a movie based on the popular "Rugrats" TV show. Universal Studio Inc.'s live-action *Babe: Pig in the City* debuts Nov. 25, and *The Prince of Egypt*, the story of Moses as told by DreamWorks, will open on Dec. 18.

INFESTATION?

19   Worse, Pixar's days as the only computerized show in town are over. Industrial Light & Magic is working on a Frankenstein remake. Fox will do Planet Ice, a computerized futuristic look at space travel that's also pegged for 2000. And then there's archrival DreamWorks, the talented and well-funded partnership of Geffen, Steven Spielberg, and Jeffrey Katzenberg that brought *Antz* to the screen on Oct. 2.

20   How the DreamWorks film was released sparked something of a Bugs War between the two rival studios. DreamWorks was concerned *A Bug's Life* would overshadow its own *The Prince of Egypt*, originally scheduled for movie theaters about the same time. So it tried a maneuver Jobs flatly labels

EXHIBIT A

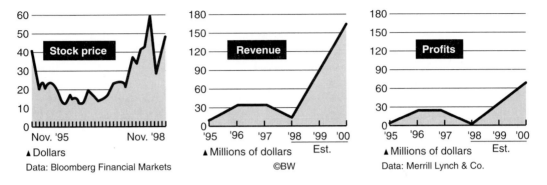

Thriller
After a rocky start, Pixar's stock has recovered, thanks to prospects of higher revenues and profits.

▲ Dollars
Data: Bloomberg Financial Markets

▲ Millions of dollars   Est.
©BW

▲ Millions of dollars   Est.
Data: Merrill Lynch & Co.

"extortion." According to Jobs, Katzenberg told Pixar to delay the release of *A Bug's Life* or Dream-Works would make its similarly insect-filled *Antz*. When Jobs said he couldn't control Disney's schedule, Katzenberg suggested that Pixar not deliver the film on time, says Jobs. "I said to him, 'Don't even go there.' " Katzenberg declined to comment. *Antz* beat *A Bug's Life* into theaters and already holds the record for a non-Disney film, with nearly $75 million in revenues.

21   How will Jobs and Pixar stay ahead of DreamWorks and the rest of the pack? So far, the company's powerful mix of technology and talent is probably two years ahead of competitors. Employees have published more than 50 papers on computer graphics, earned 18 patents, and won 14 Academy Awards since 1986. "We're not jumping on the bandwagon, we're making it," says Pixar's founder and Chief Technologist Edwin E. Catmull. Jules Engel, head of the experimental animation department at the Disney-supported California Institute of the Arts, the nation's top animation training ground, agrees. "They're the best when it comes to producing computer-animated films," he says.

22   Pixar has earned such kudos not just because of its technology but also because of its heartwarming storytelling. When it's time to start a project, Lasseter isolates his eight or so writers and directs them to forget about the constraints of technology. While many studios try to rush from script to production, Lasseter takes up to two years just to get the story right. "It's not simply the technology that makes Pixar," says Dick Cook, president of Walt Disney studios. Once the story is done, artists create storyboards and copy them onto videotapes called reels—a standard industry practice. "A sequence has to play great in reels, and then it'll be gangbusters," says Lasseter. "That's our No. 1 rule."

MOUSE POWER

23   Once a story is approved by Lasseter and Disney, Pixar's creative staffers go to work. Landscape artists paint lush backgrounds, sculptors create 3-D models of characters, and animators set about giving the characters life. But that doesn't mean the creative process is done. Everything can change right up to the last minute—taking full advantage of the fact that, unlike live-action films or even traditional hand-drawn animated films, the director can change sets, characters, or story lines with a few clicks of a mouse.

24   In *A Bug's Life,* the story was totally revamped after more than a year of work had been completed. Originally, it was about a troupe of circus bugs run by P. T. Flea that tries to rescue a colony of ants from marauding grasshoppers. But because of a flaw in the story—why would the circus bugs risk their lives to save stranger ants?—co-director Andrew Stanton recast the story to be about Flik, the heroic ant who recruits Flea's troupe to fight the grasshoppers. "You have to rework and rework it," says Lasseter. Indeed, one scene was rewritten 30 times.

TABLE 3
Just How Big Will *A Bug's Life* Be?

Two different scenarios for how the film will fare:

	Ho-Hum	Megahit
Worldwide box office receipts	$186*	$438*
Disney's and Pixar's cut of the receipts	94	219
Revenues from video sales	330	577.5
Revenues from merchandise royalties	50	187.5
Revenues from broadcast rights	10	50
Production costs	90	90
Disney's marketing costs and distribution fee	292.9	449.4
Total profits to Disney and Pixar	110.8	584.4
Pixar's profits	55.4	252.2

*In millions.
Data: Merrill Lynch.

25   Only after the basic story is set does Lasseter begin to think about what he'll need from Pixar's technologists. And it's always more than the engineers expect. Lasseter, for example, demanded that the crowds of ants in the movie not be a single mass of look-alike faces. To solve the problem, engineer William T. Reeves developed software that randomly applied physical and emotional characteristics to each ant. In another instance, writers brought a model of a butterfly named Gypsy to researchers, asking them to write code so that when she rubs her antennas, you can see the hairs press down and pop back up.

26   That attention to detail keeps Pixar on the cutting edge. It has turned out ever more lifelike short films, including 1998's Oscar-winning *Geri's Game*, which used a technology called subdivision surfaces. This makes realistic simulation of human skin and clothing possible. "They're absolute geniuses," gushes Jules Roman, co-founder and CEO of rival Tippett Studio. "They're the people who created computer animation really."

27   To achieve such feats, Pixar tends to the care and feeding of its creative stable. Each new hire spends 10 weeks at Pixar University, an in-house training program that includes courses in live improvisation, drawing, and cinematography. The school's dean is Randall E. Nelson, a former juggler known to perform his act using chain saws so students in animation classes have something compelling to draw.

28   Pixar is different from big studios in another way: There's an undercurrent of nearby Silicon Valley. Other than Lasseter, no one has long-term, Hollywood-style contracts. Everyone instead gets stock options. "We're blessed to be 600 miles apart from Hollywood," says Lasseter.

29   If Pixar has arrived, it certainly wasn't an easy trip. The roots of the company stretch back to 1975 and a vocational school in Old Westbury, N.Y., called the New York Institute of Technology. It was there that Catmull, a straitlaced Mormon from Salt Lake City who loved animation but couldn't draw, teamed up with the people who would later form the core of Pixar. "It was artists and technologists from the very start," says Alvy Ray Smith, who worked with Catmull and is now at Microsoft Corp. "It was like a fairy tale."

EARLY LOSSES

30   But there was no happy ending. In 1979, Catmull and his team grew disillusioned with New York Tech and went to work at Lucas' Industrial Light and Magic in San Rafael, Calif. Catmull decided to leave there after seven years when it became apparent Lucas only wanted computer animation for special effects, not feature-length films.

TABLE 4
How Flik Comes to Life

From pen strokes to pixels to projectors: How a little critter evolved from concept to screen:

Flik Is Born

Once the team of story writers hatches the idea for a movie, artists create hundreds of detailed drawings of the characters, such as the star of *A Bug's Life*.

. . . In Wireframe

Experts create wireframe models of the characters on computers and give them control points—computerized marionette strings—that allow animators to move an arm or eyebrow.

. . . In Polygons

Solid surfaces are added to give animators a sense of what the characters look like. This is what animators manipulate on their screens to make the characters act their parts.

. . . Rendered

After the animators are through, a program called a shader gives each character its color and texture in different lighting. He's ready for show time.

31   That's when Jobs appeared on the scene. Less than a year after being ousted from Apple in 1985, Jobs bought what then became known as Pixar from Lucas for just $10 million—one-third of Lucas' asking price. Still, it was hardly a bargain. As losses mounted over the next five years, Jobs invested an additional $50 million—more than 25% of his total wealth at the time. "There were times that we all despaired, but fortunately not all at the same time," says Jobs.

32   Still, Catmull's team of technologists was making major breakthroughs, and in 1991, Disney gave Pixar a three-film contract that included *Toy Story*. As the film neared completion in early 1995, Jobs decided to take a bold step. Since it was clear Pixar couldn't prosper selling its technology to others, it was time to recast the company as a moviemaker. A novice in Hollywood, he and CFO Levy visited moguls, including Universal parent Seagram CEO Edgar M. Bronfman, then superagent Michael Ovitz, investment banker Herbert A. Allen, and Disney CFO Robert Moore.

33   Pixar's luck began to change—fast. Rather than the nice little film Disney expected, *Toy Story* became the sensation of 1995. Within days, Pixar went public. When the shares, priced at $22, shot past $33, Jobs called his best friend, Oracle CEO Lawrence J. Ellison, to tell him he had company in the billionaires' club.

34   With Pixar's sudden success, Jobs returned to strike a new deal with Disney. In March, 1996, at a lunch with Walt Disney Co. chief Michael D. Eisner, Jobs made his demands: an equal share of the profits, equal billing on merchandise and on-screen credits, and guarantees that Disney would market Pixar films as they did its own. Disney, particularly worried about losing Lasseter, agreed. "[Jobs] had the brains, energy, and chutzpah to protect Pixar's interests. He enabled us to negotiate as equals," says former Pixar marketing executive Pamela J. Kerwin, who is now COO of GeoVector Corp., a maker of handheld computing devices.

35   Pixar's future now rests on how its partnership with Disney plays out. As long as Jobs and his team provide the types of films Eisner wants on schedule, Pixar will prosper. With Disney's help, Pixar could find that *A Bug's Life* is just the first of many rich paydays ahead. "They're in the most profitable part of the film business and are partnered with the most powerful company in that industry," says Merrill Lynch's Cohen. "They're in a very good position."

BACK DOOR

36   Indeed, with Disney as a partner, Pixar almost can't lose money so long as it keeps the movies coming. Morgan Stanley Dean Witter analyst Richard Bilotti figures Pixar breaks even so long as its films do $70 million at the box office—and no Disney film has failed to bring in that much since *Oliver and Company* in 1988.

37   And Pixar's upside is tremendous. In a business where the best moviemakers are lucky to get a 15% share of box-office receipts from stingy studios, Pixar will get 50% of total profits. That's defined as what's left of the ticket sales, video sales, and merchandising royalties after production costs and Disney's reimbursement for marketing and distribution fees.

38   Still, something as nebulous as "artistic differences" could get in the way. Disney has a back door that could leave Pixar on its own—and vulnerable. It's simple: If Disney doesn't get a Pixar pitch it likes within a contractually prescribed time, it can abandon the partnership. "The risk is the creative risk—that they become wedded to something we're not crazy about," says Disney's Roth, who adds he doubts the two studios will have such differences.

39   Still, the fiery, opinionated Jobs typically doesn't go for very long without creating controversy. He did elicit warnings from Disney execs for going public with his beefs that DreamWorks' *Antz* was a rip-off from Pixar. "We talked about it," says Roth. "We knew we had a great film. We didn't have to [have Jobs] go around talking about anyone else's film."

40   Investors had better hope that's as rough as relations with Disney ever get. For now, Disney and Jobs say they have a good thing going, and Jobs is clearly enjoying his second career as a movie mogul. Maybe the Pixar-Disney drama will have a happy ending, after all.

CASE 20

BusinessWeek

ROMANCING THE RUGRATS CROWD

1   When it comes to reeling in young TV watchers, it has been hard to beat Viacom Inc. Need to reach grade schoolers with your ads? Try the Nickelodeon cable channel, which has a near-strangle-hold on the 2- to 11-year-old viewer. High school and college age? Go to MTV. Gen-X through boomers? VH1.

2   Trouble is, these days Viacom has plenty of company chasing those markets. Sports channel ESPN has been airing everything from spelling bees to snowboarding competitions. Time Warner Inc. is lacing teen hits "Dawson's Creek" and "Felicity" on its WB Television Network with full-length songs by acts like Hootie & the Blowfish and Savage Garden. At the lucrative children's end of the market, a crop of competitors, including Ted Turner's Cartoon Network and a revitalized Disney Channel, has been luring viewers away from Nick, Viacom's most-watched channel. "It's always a great thing to be the first in a market," says Anne M. Sweeney, president of Disney/ABC Cable Networks and a former Nickelodeon executive. "What is more difficult is staying there."

3   To do just that, Viacom has been mounting an aggressive counter-offensive. Since 1994, when the alarm bells were sounded during a strategic review, Viacom has spent more than $500 million—serious money in the rerun world of cable TV—to fight off its suddenly robust competition. And the music channels are staging a comeback. The average number of people watching MTV was up 15% in the 12 months ending in September, reversing two straight years of decline. And the much smaller VH1 saw its audience grow by more than twice that rate. Things aren't nearly as cheery at Nick, however. After almost doubling its viewing audience between 1993 and 1997, viewership is slipping, as more kids click away to the Cartoon Network, Fox Family Channel, or broadcast networks' kiddie fare.

CASH OUTFLOW

4   In this crowded cable world, Wall Street is looking anxiously at the amounts Viacom needs to spend on new programming for its channels to stand out. In mid-September, two prominent analysts, citing added spending on cable and Viacom's Blockbuster Entertainment unit, cut their earnings estimate for the company. NationsBanc Montgomery Securities Inc. analyst John Tinker expects cash flow from the cable-channel unit to grow by 17% for the year, down from a 20% rise last year, and to slow to 13% growth next year.

5   Reversing that trend is critical to Viacom. MTV Networks this year will contribute 13% of the company's anticipated $14.3 billion in revenue but 30% of its operating cash flow of $2.5 billion. Moreover, notes Tinker, the cable unit and its 41% profit margins will represent even more of the company's fortunes as it completes the $4.6 billion sale of its educational publishing unit to Pearson PLC and the planned spin-off of Blockbuster to the public. "They keep asking me to spend money," Viacom Chairman Sumner M. Redstone says of his MTV Networks programmers. "I hate doing it, but look at the results they're getting."

6   Central to that spending strategy is more original programming, particularly in the children's field. Nickelodeon spent $350 million to build a 72,000-square-foot animation studio in Burbank, Calif., doubled the channel's animation staff, and will churn out up to 10 new shows this year to back up Nick hits such as "Blue's Clues" and "Rugrats." In October, Nickelodeon also launched a $22 million

Source: Ronald Grover in Los Angeles, with Richard Siklos in New York, "Romancing the Rugrats Crowd," *Business Week:* November 2, 1998.

EXHIBIT A

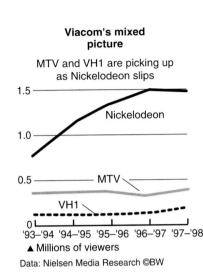

Viacom's mixed picture

MTV and VH1 are picking up as Nickelodeon slips

Data: Nielsen Media Research ©BW

ad blitz, including an estimated $10 million, one-month run of network spots on big draws like "ER" and "The Today Show."

RATES CUT

7   The channel is also tapping studio expertise at Viacom's Paramount Pictures unit to bring *The Rugrats Movie* to theaters on Nov. 20. "Nickelodeon is clearly feeling the pressure, but they're reacting appropriately," says Jon Mandel, co-managing director at MediaCom, the media-buying arm of Grey Advertising Inc. One tactic: In an effort to stop defections among its advertisers, media buyers say Nickelodeon has offered to trim pre-arranged 1999 rate hikes in exchange for extending contracts with advertisers. Meanwhile, the programming overhaul seems to be working. Boosted by new shows such as "The Wild Thornberrys," ratings of Nickelodeon's 8 p.m. to 9 p.m. "Nickel-O-Zone" block is up 11% since September. "Even with all the competition out there, we're still getting more than 57% of the ad market," says Tom Freston, chairman of MTV Networks.

8   Viacom knows well the power of programming. Moribund VH1 was overhauled in 1995 by adding such new fare as documentary-style profiles of rock stars called "Behind the Music" and "Pop-Up Video," which features irreverent captions in cartoonish balloons superimposed on music videos. A ratings revival at MTV began last year, after Viacom execs realized the channel had strayed too far from its music roots with a schedule heavy on game shows and dramas. The key to MTV's turnaround was the hiring last year of Brian Gradden, a 35-year-old former Fox programming exec who helped discover the irreverent cartoon "South Park" for Comedy Central (jointly owned by Viacom and Time Warner). Gradden has refocused the channel on music with new shows like "Artist Cut," where an artist describes the making of a song or video.

9   And the channels continue to go beyond straight video as they look for ways to attract viewers. For the first time, both MTV and VH1 intend to fashion their own made-for-television movies, including biographical features on former Beatles John Lennon and Paul McCartney and Latina singer Gloria Estefan. As long as such new fare can keep viewers tuning in at home, Viacom can also seek growth abroad—MTV is already in 85 countries and Nickelodeon in more than 100. "These are brands our company intends to nurture," says Redstone. That means spending more money, of course. Because in the TV business, staying young doesn't come cheap or easy.

CASE 21

BusinessWeek

THE GAMES SONY PLAYS

1   A recent episode of the hit U.S. comedy show "Friends" tells it all. One of the characters offers to bear a baby for a childless couple. "I'm going to be giving someone the greatest gift you can possibly give," she says. Replies Chandler, the show's resident wiseacre: "You're going to carry their child and give them a Sony PlayStation?"

2   The Sony PlayStation. It seems that just a few nanoseconds ago, we lived in a world where video games meant Nintendo and Sega. Now, PlayStation's sales, profits, and—most important—its buzz are so strong that the 32-bit game machine has become a fixture in the popular imagination. Its quirky menagerie of sports, action, and cartoon characters has romped across four continents and made Sony Corp. the Master of the Game Universe—for now.

BANNER YEAR

3   Sony Computer Entertainment, the company's four-year-old game division, has sold more than 33 million units of PlayStation worldwide, along with 236 million game CDs. In the fiscal year that ended March 31, the PlayStation business accounted for $5.5 billion, or 10%, of Sony's worldwide revenue, but it chipped in $886 million, or 22.5%, of its operating income. Thanks to PlayStation and a weak yen, Sony notched up a banner year, with record operating income of $3.9 billion on record sales of $51 billion. "We've never had a business like this," exclaims Chairman and Chief Executive Norio Ohga.

4   That's impressive, especially because Sony stumbled into the game business almost by accident. Now, PlayStation is a moneymaker for the company, one of the few Japanese multinationals to shrug off the country's dire recession. More important, PlayStation has proven a point that Sony managers have long felt intuitively: that digital, interactive entertainment offers the only plausible future. In recent years, the company has produced a string of turn-of-the-screw product innovations from Mini-Disc players to flatter television screens. Yet the margins on "boxes" get lower and lower. And none of these developments has unleashed either the profits or excitement of PlayStation.

5   Thus PlayStation has provided a glimpse of what the new Sony could be capable of—a company with great hardware that spawns even more exciting and much more profitable software. Sony wants to apply the lessons of PlayStation to its marketing and distribution of music, film, TV, and games on the Internet. And it wants to achieve something unheard of in the PC world—make it all as easy and crashproof as the PlayStation. Masayuki Nozoe, executive vice-president at Sony Pictures Entertainment, is one of the architects of this strategy. As Sony nurtures these new businesses, he says, "It will be a 3- to 5-year period of adjustment and then a 10-year cycle of real changeover."

6   Looking ahead, the company sees fresh profit streams in music and video downloaded from Sony Web sites straight to Sony home-entertainment systems. Movies from its Hollywood studios could morph into PlayStation and Internet games. As the innovations multiply, the PlayStation hardware itself could evolve. Imagine, muses Trip Hawkins, CEO of game-software maker 3DO Co., that you are shopping for the latest game console that doubles as a digital VCR: "What brand would a customer rather play movies on? Sony, Nintendo, or Sega?"

7   Yet the pitfalls in Sony's path outnumber the ones that beset its hyperenergetic game mascot, Crash Bandicoot. Challenge No. 1: catch up with America's high-tech leaders, from Microsoft Corp. to

Source: Irene Kunii in Tokyo and Steven V. Brull in Los Angeles, with Peter Burrows in San Mateo, California, and Edward C. Baig in Atlanta, "The Games Sony Plays," *Business Week* (international edition): June 15, 1998.

Amazon.com Inc., which are running circles around Sony in cyberspace. Challenge No. 2 (and this is the big one): stay ahead in the hideously fickle game business, so that PlayStation can bankroll all this development. Initially, Nintendo gave Sony plenty of competition, with its more sophisticated N64 console. Now, Nintendo of America Chairman Howard Lincoln admits, the N64 has lost some U.S. market share. But he says a very strong summer software lineup could even the score. "We're not selling cat food. This is the video game business, and market shares move very dramatically," he says.

8   Quick action is essential. With Japan stuck in recession and the Asian crisis deepening, Sony managers estimate that profits will probably decline some 10% this year. Some analysts are more bullish. Still, Sony's stock on the New York exchange has drifted from 96 in February to a recent 83. Even though PlayStation could continue to win converts in the West, the Japanese market is nearly saturated. "Sony is at the peak of its cycle now and has nowhere to go but down," says Kimihide Takano, senior analyst at Tokyo's Dresdner Kleinwort Benson. Long term, the Internet could also bring new upheavals. "The digital explosion is creating drastic change and forcing Sony to transform itself," says Sony President Nobuyuki Idei.

9   The wizards of Silicon Valley wonder if Sony can hack it. After a noisy entry into the PC market with the much admired VAIO line, Sony priced the machine out of most people's reach last year—just when Compaq and others were launching sub-$1,000 PCs. Valley mavens—and some recently departed Sony execs—wonder why Sony hasn't merged PlayStation with its slow-selling PC products, to give them a little lift. And they note that Sony's experimental digital communicators and DVD machines have not sold any better than its rivals'.

10   Nonetheless, with the PlayStation, serendipity has favored Sony mightily. The origins of the game are perfectly in sync with the helter-skelter nature of digital invention. A decade ago, Ken Kutaragi, a Sony computer engineer with a passion for video games, proposed a console that would combine the graphic capabilities of a workstation with Sony's CD-ROM drive. When Nintendo Co. jumped on board, Ohga gave Kutaragi the go-ahead to set up a joint development team. But several years later, in 1992, Nintendo abruptly pulled out, leaving Kutaragi in the lurch.

11   Bad move, Nintendo. When Ohga confronted Nintendo President Hiroshi Yamauchi, the latter denied any knowledge of a binding agreement. "Ohga was so furious, he told me to proceed with my project," says Kutaragi, now head of R&D for the PlayStation. Today, Nintendo says it preferred to stick with its ROM cartridge approach, which has less memory but more speed. Whatever transpired, Sony enticed most of Japan's game developers to its platform—along with top U.S. developers such as Electronic Arts—by offering some 4,000 game development tools and a bigger share of the profits than Nintendo.

12   All told, Sony has swamped the $8 billion Japanese game-software market with nearly 1,300 titles, prompting an outraged Nintendo President Yamauchi to warn last year that Sony could kill off the industry with all of "its garbage." Nintendo was right: Its carefully chosen N64 titles sell well. But in Japan, the paucity of game titles turned off fans—many of whom turned to the PlayStation.

SPORTS SPLASH

13   From the day it was launched, the PlayStation has projected an aura of hipness. For one thing, Sony largely ignored Nintendo's subteen following and zoned in on older customers, offering racier, more complex games. They enlisted athletes such as Terrell Davis, running back for the Denver Broncos football team, and Charles "Bo" Outlaw of the Orlando Magic basketball team to help promote world-beating sports titles.

14   Now the challenge is to move beyond PlayStation's hip franchise into even more lucrative and far-reaching businesses. In the world as Idei sees it, Sony will supply "content" to homes via digital satellite, cable, and the Internet. Compaq Computer, Hewlett-Packard, and IBM also believe that PCs and entertainment devices will merge. But Sony is the one that dominates the living room. And it understands that movies and games are a bigger draw than word processors or electronic checkbooks. As Nick Donatiello, president of U.S. market researcher Odyssey Ventures, puts it: "Entertainment is an 800-pound gorilla, and productivity tools [such as spreadsheets] are just Chihuahuas."

EXHIBIT A

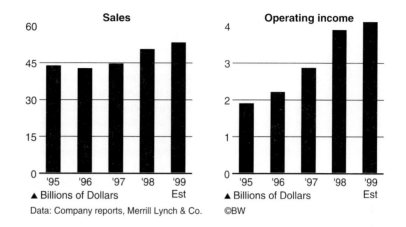

Sony's record performance

Sales

60
45
30
15
0
'95 '96 '97 '98 '99
                    Est
▲ Billions of Dollars

Operating income

4
3
2
1
0
'95 '96 '97 '98 '99
                    Est
▲ Billions of Dollars

Data: Company reports, Merrill Lynch & Co.   ©BW

15   The computer and TV, or a hybrid, would anchor this multimedia world, and Sony is now squarely in the game. Although its VAIO PC has flopped in the U.S., Sony can barely keep up with demand in Japan for its two notebook versions. The VAIO comes with an interface that makes it compatible with all of Sony's digital products. Eventually, it may have some unique, PlayStation-derived game feature.

16   In the meantime, the company is rolling out some exotic digital toys. In May, it took the wraps off a $30 handheld game code-named "PDA," for personal digital assistant. It plugs into the PlayStation and shares bits of software such as digital pets. Players can nurture their critters on the PDA alone, swap them with friends over an infrared link, and input their digital pets back into the PlayStation game. The PDA could grow, critterlike, into an information and communications device. Ditto, the welter of cool ideas in Sony's Computer Science Lab in Tokyo. Ever see a data wand? You point it at an interactive poster, a TV, or a printer and capture the information, which you can transport to a computer. Sony engineers also dig robots and like to match their creations in RoboCup events. There's a creative entertainment twist: Animated commentators whose words and facial expressions track developments in the race.

TITANIC TRACKS

17   In the U.S., Sony's networked future is in sharper relief. Today, Sony's Web site promotes music with snippets of songs sent in streaming formats. But as bandwidth becomes more plentiful, Sony plans to harness the power of the Web with a plethora of new services marketed directly to consumers—by-passing the middleman and pocketing higher margins for itself. Indeed, the Web looms so large that even though Sony is among the best-known brands in the world, Idei wants to create a new name for its online ventures that will resonate as clearly as, say, MTV.

18   Sonymusic.com is already among the most popular music sites, thanks to hits such as the *Titanic* soundtrack and Celine Dion's *Let's Talk about Love*. The site is linked to all of Sony's labels, including Columbia, Epic, and Sony Classical, and attracts up to 1 million visits per week, says Fred Ehrlich, senior vice-president and general manager for new technology and business development at Sony Music Entertainment Inc. in New York. The attractions are many. At subsidiary site bobdylan.com, fans can watch a six-minute streaming video of Dylan's recent hit "Not Dark Yet" and search for lyrics from his records on Columbia stretching back to the '60s. Fans can also buy CDs and concert tickets online, read liner notes, and listen to previously unreleased material.

19   Another tactic is to connect multimedia content on the Web directly to music CDs. When played on a CD-ROM in a PC linked to the Web, so-called ConnecteD CDs let listeners click on a menu and

search CDs for lyrics or guitar licks or view fresh material such as musical scores and photographs of the artists—tasks that would boggle your boom box.

20   High-quality motion pictures still can't be distributed digitally to consumers. But Sony is rapidly earning a reputation in digital media, from film and special effects to the production of films in DVD and high-definition formats. Last year, Sony Picture's Imageworks digital studio did computer graphics for the films *Contact, Godzilla,* and *Starship Troopers,* and the latter received an Academy Award nomination for special effects.

21   Other Sony entertainment properties are already online, including such lucrative TV game shows, as "Jeopardy" and "Wheel of Fortune." Online games like these will eventually complement and even supplant its PlayStation business as game consoles add connectivity to the Web. Says Paul Matteucci, chief executive of Mpath Interactive, which runs a hot game and chat area on the Web: "Sony has a lead position in one segment—console games—and is taking a revolutionary strategy in another." International Data Corp. in Framingham, Mass., says online games could be worth $1 billion a year by 2000. Sony claims its game site already has 1.25 million users, half of them women.

22   But in the here-today, gone-tomorrow video-game industry, there's no guarantee Sony can keep PlayStation humming. Late last month, on the eve of the "E3" game industry event in Atlanta, Sega sneak-previewed its 128-bit Dreamcast console, which debuts in Japan this November. Later, Sega will spend $100 million on the U.S. launch.

23   Many game developers think Dreamcast has a chance only if either Sony or Nintendo fumbles. No chance, says Kutaragi. "We are working on plans for a next-generation machine, but I can't say more." Sony Computer Entertainment President Tokunaka, however, says a DVD game machine is a possibility. Tokunaka has been making the rounds of the top game-development companies, according to an executive at a major Osaka game-software maker. "He came around two months ago, asking us to support their new platform. A month later, the Sega president came around," he recalls. The word is that once PlayStation sales peak, Sony will be ready with something new. That, of course, is how Sony plays the game.

CASE 22

BusinessWeek

WHAT DOES NO. 1 DELL DO FOR AN ENCORE?

1   Dell Computer Corp. defies gravity. Whether you measure its growth in sales, profits, market share, or stock price, the company is simply weightless. Last year, sales climbed from $7.7 billion to $12.3 billion. Profits rose from $518 million to $944 million. And then there's Dell stock, which has split six times in the past six years and continues to soar, up 120% this year, to $53. To top it off, Dell is now the largest merchant on the Internet, selling $6 million worth of gear daily. And all of this after three previous years of similar pyrotechnics. That's why Dell ranks No. 1 on the Business Week Info Tech 100 list of top performers.

2   So what does the company do for an encore? Ask CEO Michael S. Dell, and he'll tell you with his typical straight face: more of the same. Well, sure, that's what you'd expect him to say. Except Dell—whose direct-manufacturing model shook up the industry by redefining customer service as the speedy delivery of custom-built PCs—now wants to get even more up close and personal with buyers. "Our industry has generally neglected the customer. I want to take the customer experience to a whole new level," Dell says.

3   That's not just marketing mumbo jumbo. For Dell, it's a new battle cry. The 33-year-old CEO sees customer service as the "next battleground for market share." And nowhere will that be more true, say analysts, than in the consumer and home-office PC markets, which Dell is just beginning to target. "The consumer and home-office markets are going to be where the growth is, and that's where I want us to go next to keep growing," Dell declares.

4   The message isn't lost on the troops at Dell's suburban Austin, Tex., headquarters. Pinned to a wall amid a sea of cluttered cubicles is a photograph of Dell. Someone has drawn a hat on him, the kind worn by Uncle Sam. A slogan scrawled below reads: "Michael wants YOU to OWN your relationship with the customer." Just in case there's any doubt, Dell has tied bonuses and profit-sharing to service improvements of at least 15% this year. Success will be measured by shipping deadlines, fixing machines on the first try, and getting repair people to customers within 24 hours.

5   Dell's new customer-service plan: Use the Internet to automate and customize service, in much the same way that Dell streamlined and customized PC production. The do-it-the-customer's-way mantra has created for Dell the tightest—and most envied—relationship with buyers in the PC business. By using communications links over speedy private networks and the vast Internet, Dell plans not only to provide personalized Web pages for non-corporate customers but also to answer knotty service questions with the lightning speed that only the Net can deliver. "All our customers have individual files with us online," says Scott Eckert, director of Dell Online. "Why not expand those files for a new kind of direct-service model, one that will enable conversations with customers about service, industry trends, and new products—or even, say, weather and news someday?"

6   Weather and news from your PC company? It couldn't hurt. Research results from PC users show consumers are not yet satisfied with the industry's track record on service. In the November issue of San Francisco-based *PC World* magazine, a reader survey found that Dell and Micron Electronics Inc. were the only two manufacturers (out of 17) that ranked "good" for "reasonably reliable systems and serviceable support." None of the companies, though, earned an "outstanding" rating on its work, home, or notebook PCs.

7   Dell scored high mostly for having a very low rate of out-of-box quality problems. But its ranking was dragged down by complaints of long waits on the phone and a relatively high percentage of unresolved problems. "Creating a new direct-service model is extremely important," says Dell strategist Kevin Rollins. "The first company to crack this—or who can do quality and service demon-

Source: Marcia Stepanek in Round Rock, Texas, "What Does No. 1 Do for an Encore?" *Business Week:* November 2, 1998.

EXHIBIT A

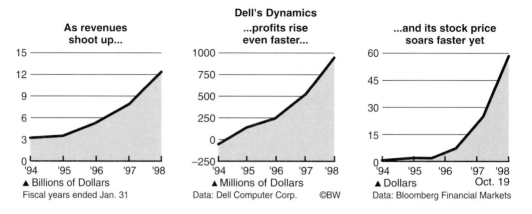

Dell's Dynamics

As revenues shoot up...

...profits rise even faster...

...and its stock price soars faster yet

▲ Billions of Dollars
Fiscal years ended Jan. 31

▲ Millions of Dollars
Data: Dell Computer Corp.   ©BW

▲ Dollars   Oct. 19
Data: Bloomberg Financial Markets

strably better—will have a new, sustainable advantage over everyone else." Today, only a third of Dell's customer-service force is dedicated to handling queries online.

8   So far, Dell has been better than most rivals at customer hand-holding, online and off. Last fall, Dell delivered eight customized PowerEdge servers to NASDAQ in New York in 36 hours so the exchange could handle higher trading volume during the first whiffs of the Asian crisis. "We didn't have to pay extra," says John Delta, director of NASDAQ's interactive services. "Originally, Dell got in with us on price, but that's not the issue now. Their customer support and service is what's driving our relationship."

9   That's what Dell wants to keep hearing, from a whole new crowd of less tech-savvy buyers—the small-business owners and the work-at-home crowd. "The Net allows us to take personalizaton to the next level," says Dell. Starting this fall, the company will expand its online forums with Dell executives, called "Breakfast with Dell," beyond big corporate buyers to small businesses. The live chats will cover topics ranging from the Year 2000 problem to trends in the server market. Further down the road, there will be a way for customers to ask hundreds of service questions, all of which, says Dell's senior Web manager Manish Mehta, will be answered automatically from Dell's online knowledge bank with the help of artificial-intelligence software.

"CUDDLY TOUCHES"

10   And coming in the next few months: more warm and fuzzy Web-service features, including "My Dell" Web pages—customized pages for small-business and home-office consumers. Such additions will enable these users to trade service tips, answer queries, and get weather, business information, and technical support papers over the Web. Also in the works is the "virtual account executive." Interested in a notebook but can't fly to Austin for a demonstration? "That's fine," says Rollins. "Go to our Web site, and get a full-motion video of someone explaining it."

11   To Dell, the benefits of dispensing more service over the Net are twofold: "It can be a great relief valve for disgruntled customers," says Mehta—and a relief for shareholders, too. Doug Chandler, a customer-service analyst at International Data Corp., estimates that phone calls to give service and support can cost PC companies $25 apiece. Dell's online service operation, he says, saves a bundle—thousands of calls per week and potentially millions of dollars. If that's extended to include a greater percentage of Dell's customers, it could save millions more.

12   Can Dell pull it off? The direct-service approach works well with corporate buyers—the bulk of Dell's business. Consumers and small businesses, though, expect far more hand-holding, and are more inclined to hunt for bargains. They're also often enamored of the marketing ploys and gee-whiz gizmos that make corporate-account managers cringe. "For all its success, Dell has had little experience with these cuddly touches," says Kevin Knox, senior analyst at Gartner Group.

13   And even if Dell persuades the masses it's tip-top in customer service, there are other challenges facing the company. At a Sept. 25 meeting for analysts, there were questions about price. While Dell's machines are still cheaper than comparable ones from Compaq and IBM, Dell hasn't been lowering prices as fast. "Normally, Dell had a $100 to $200 price advantage because of its direct model, but that advantage is nearly gone," says James Poyner, a PC analyst at CIBC Oppenheimer. "Isn't price supposed to be Dell's advantage?"

14   Not necessarily. Now that customer service is the new battleground, price may not be the main event. Says Dell: "IBM and Compaq are assuming that price is the problem. The problem is that the dealer channel they're using has fundamentally failed customers."

15   And what about continuing efforts by rivals to mimic Dell's direct model? Copycats such as Gateway and Micron still don't have the heft and market clout of Dell. As for rivals such as Compaq who use middlemen, Dell wins on cost. "Anyone who tries to go direct now will find it very difficult—like trying to jump over the Grand Canyon," says Dell. And now, with his efforts to get even more personal with customers over the Web, Dell's hoping that gap just got a lot wider.

CASE 23

UNILEVER FINALLY KNOWS WHERE IT'S GOING: EAST

1   The Billa supermarket in a drab residential neighborhood in Prague is hardly bustling on this weekday afternoon. But that doesn't faze Unilever's local chief, Nick Stenning, and its national sales manager, Richard Krejci, as they check out the store's well-stocked shelves. Krejci zeroes in on a competitor's poorly displayed toothpaste. It won't get much bang for the crown, he comments. Then, Stenning heaps scorn on a bar of Magnat ice cream—a local entrepreneur's knock-off of Unilever's 75 cents Magnum. "We'll have to have a word with him," he says.

2   Welcome to the new Unilever. Staking its future on emerging markets, the $46.2 billion company is dispatching expatriate marketing pros such as Stenning and hiring talented locals such as Krejci to go after the former Soviet bloc's 420 million consumers. Gone is the sluggish, directionless company that hawked everything from specialty chemicals to Caterpillar tractors alongside its soaps, margarines, and skin creams. After a blizzard of disposals, it is a leaner, nimbler company with a clear growth strategy (see Table 1). Last year alone, it invested $750 million in developing markets from Latin America to India.

3   Unilever has also reorganized management, set clear investment guidelines, and shaken up research and development. It is boosting profits by cutting costs and steering savings into higher-margin products such as ice cream. Before, managers could get almost "anything they wanted" financed by the company, says Co-Chairman Morris Tabaksblat. "We said 'No!' You have to have priorities. Certain things have to come first," he adds. With a war chest of $9.6 billion, Unilever is ready to make acquisitions. Indeed, says Finance Director Hans Eggerstedt, the company has the firepower to spend up to $20 billion on them.

4   Unilever's remake has been forged by Tabaksblat, 60, chairman of Unilever N.V., and by Niall FitzGerald, 52, chairman of Unilever PLC. Although Tabaksblat, a lawyer and marketing whiz, had been pushing hard to revamp the company since he took the job in 1994, the pace picked up after FitzGerald, an Irish financial specialist, joined him two years ago. FitzGerald orchestrated a raft of sell-offs—from the Caterpillar franchise to the Nordsee fast-food chain.

5   But the biggest move was last year's sale of Unilever's big specialty-chemical business to Imperial Chemical Industries PLC for $8 billion. It was a good business, but it didn't fit Unilever's consumer-products focus. "Specialty chemicals would have required massive investment going forward, and that would have meant consumer businesses would have been starved," says John Campbell, an analyst at London's Rabo Bank International.

SOAP CENTER

6   The shakeup has certainly pleased the markets. Once considered a doggy stock, the company's American depositary receipts (ADRs) have roughly doubled in price since early 1997, to $45. For the first quarter of 1998, operating profits jumped 41% to $1.16 billion, after rising a modest 7.3% to $4.6 billion last year. Operating profits in North America jumped by 17% last year, though sales fell by 1%. And Europe, where Unilever still makes 46% of its sales, saw a 17% profit rise despite slow volume growth.

7   But the company's heart is clearly in building new businesses in developing markets, such as the Czech Republic. Since it bought a former state-owned oils factory outside Prague in 1992, Unilever has invested $42 million to turn it into a center to make soaps, margarine, and Chesebrough Pond's skin creams for the region.

Source: Stanley Reed in Prague, "Unilever Finally Knows Where It's Going: East," *Business Week:* June 22, 1998.

TABLE 1
Unilever Cleans House

Sell-Offs

Sold noncore businesses, including its huge specialty-chemicals division

Key Products

Investing heavily to develop ice cream, tea, margarine, skin care, personal-wash products, fabric-wash products, and so-called prestige products, such as Calvin Klein fragrances

Target Markets

Pushing for fast growth in Central and Eastern Europe, China, Southeast Asia, southern Latin America, and India

Structure

Revamped operations in Europe and North America while naming 12 regional and product-line bosses to sharpen geographical focus

---

Data: *Business Week.*

8   More important, the company has harnessed the full power of its marketing savvy to soften up Czech consumers. A campaign on the dangers of cholesterol is turning Czechs from butter gluttons into margarine fans. Unilever has also brought in its Organics shampoo, developed in Asia, to seize top market share from Procter & Gamble Co.'s Pantene. Last year, Czech revenues increased about 20%, to $158 million, pushing up profits 31%, to $5.1 million.

9   Unilever is trying to repeat that performance from Budapest to Vladivostok. It has invested in detergent, ice-cream, fish-finger, and margarine factories in Poland. It also has a wide range of businesses in Hungary. It is scrambling to set up an ice-cream business in Russia in time for this summer. Meanwhile, it is shipping as many as 750 truckloads of margarine—15,000 tons of the stuff—to Russia every month. Sales in Central and Eastern Europe rose a stunning 42% last year, to $1 billion. And though the company isn't yet making money on the margarine shipments, Unilever considers Russia a potential gold mine. "All the way to the Urals, [people] are basically Western European," declares Jean Martin, Unilever's boss for Central and Eastern Europe. "They eat a lot of bread and spread something on it."

10   Now, the big question is where Unilever will apply its hefty war chest. Tabaksblat and FitzGerald say they want to speed up growth in emerging markets. Another possibility is to buy an additional hot product line to go with their Calvin Klein fragrances or Helene Curtis cosmetics. Last year, the company spent $930 million on Kibon, Brazil's leading ice-cream business, and added other cold-treat companies across Latin America. But prices, except in Asia, are high, and Unilever doesn't want to pay through the nose. "We sold in a seller's market," says Tabaksblat. "We have to take our time to see if anything comes forward."

11   Unilever bosses say that if they can't find satisfactory ways to spend the money, they will consider giving it back to shareholders in a couple of years. Already, laws in both the Netherlands and Britain are changing to make share buy-backs easier. "They have a collection of targets," says David Lang, an analyst at Henderson Crosthwaite Institutional Brokers Ltd. in London. "The question is whether a sufficient number will come up at attractive prices."

12   Unilever has other problems. It needs to fix its money-losing Elizabeth Arden cosmetics line. It has fallen way behind Procter & Gamble in its core European detergent business. And the company can also expect sterner challenges from P&G in emerging markets. As gains from cost-cutting run out, Unilever may have to consider more radical downsizing. Moreover, longtime observers wonder whether Unilever's two leaders bring a fresh enough perspective to a fast-changing world. Both FitzGerald and Tabaksblat have been with the company more than 30 years.

13   They are defying the conventional wisdom that two people can't run a company. "Any chief executive's role can be very lonely," says FitzGerald. "You are the person who has to take those final decisions, which are not always popular. To have two sharing that role enriches both the decision-taking and the decisions." They seem to enjoy hammering out the company's strategy together, spending as many as 10 days a month working together in the company's Rotterdam and London headquarters. The major test of their co-leadership will be making their big bet on emerging markets pay off.

CASE 24

BusinessWeek

JURGEN SCHREMPP: THE AUTO BARON

1   One August day four years ago, while climbing the 3,905-meter Ortler mountain in the Italian Alps, Jurgen Schrempp descended a sheer wall and got stuck. Groping about, he couldn't find a hand- or toehold. He was roped to mountaineering legend Reinhold Messner, the first person to climb Mt. Everest without oxygen. What would happen, Schrempp shouted up, if I fell? I'd catch you, replied Messner, and lower you down. Marvels Messner: "So he jumped."

2   Courageous or crazy, it was vintage Schrempp. The lean, chainsmoking 54-year-old chief executive of Daimler Benz took a similar leap of faith last January when he approached Chrysler CEO Robert J. Eaton in his office in Auburn Hills, Mich., with a scheme to merge their two companies. In a steak house with Daimler colleagues after the 17-minute chat, Schrempp worried that he may have been too bold. His fears were unfounded. America's scrappy No. 3 car company and Germany's most revered brand name will combine to become the world's fifth-largest carmaker when shares in DaimlerChrysler begin trading on Nov. 16.

3   The new giant is off to a good start. More than 97% of Daimler shareholders switched into DaimlerChrysler shares by Oct. 23, beating the 90% needed to avoid $33 billion in goodwill charges over 40 years. "Isn't this a glorious day!" declared Schrempp three days later, nearly skipping in excitement as he prepared to announce the news at Daimler's Stuttgart headquarters.

4   Schrempp and Eaton are entering into an unprecedented business experiment. The auto industry has long been among the world's most international. But the DaimlerChrysler merger ushers in a new phase of global competitiveness, when the very biggest players in the world's main regions unite as industrial powerhouses of tremendous scope. Schrempp will be judged both on his ability to run this ungainly giant and on whether he can emerge as Europe's most forceful business leader.

5   He was certainly the dominant player in forging the merger. "I wasn't going to sit passively and be the object of someone else's decision," Schrempp told 1,000 of Munich's glitterati as he introduced the new Mercedes S-Class sedan last month. Schrempp had talked to Ford Motor Co. in 1997, but the U.S. company's family-ownership structure would have complicated a merger. Sources close to Daimler say that Schrempp also approached Honda Motor Co., but found the cultural differences too great.

6   The timing of the DaimlerChrysler merger puts enormous pressure on the two companies. Schrempp and Eaton are trying to pull off their deal amid a global economic crisis that is expected to hit the world auto industry next year. Schrempp sees 1999 industrywide unit sales slipping by 4% in the U.S., by 2% to 3% in Western Europe, and stagnating in Germany.

7   As a global company, DaimlerChrysler will get a new kind of chief executive. Schrempp, who will take over on his own by 2001—and perhaps sooner—comes across as a macho, take-charge guy. But he is also a subtle man in many ways. He listens carefully to others before taking action. His close friends include artists, photographers, and mountain climbers, as well as other powerful executives.

8   Long tours of duty outside Germany have given him a business perspective broader than many of his countrymen's. As in mountain climbing, his clear thinking is balanced by instinct. "Many people think emotions are not needed in business," he says. "I think emotions, what I call the stomach and the heart, are the decisive factor at the end of the day."

9   The deal's acid test will come in the interplay of Schrempp's personality with those of Eaton and other Chrysler executives. "We, from day one, have been extremely direct with each other and open," Eaton says. If this merger is going to work, human factors will be of paramount importance.

Source: Karen Lowry Miller in Stuttgart, with Joann Muller in Auburn Hills, Michigan, "Jurgen Schrempp: The Auto Baron," *Business Week* (international edition): November 16, 1998.

LOGIC

10   There's plenty of logic behind the marriage. Chrysler's minivans and sport-utility vehicles—staples in suburban driveways across the U.S.—stretch Daimler into North America's vast middle market. Daimler can boost Chrysler's 1% market share in Europe, while also upgrading the Detroit carmaker's quality and technology with Mercedes' gold-plated engineering. Together, the auto makers believe they can conquer emerging markets in Asia by jointly developing a low-cost car.

11   Eaton and Schrempp are trying at every turn to demonstrate trust and cooperation. Last month Schrempp arrived for a meeting of 35 executives at a Stuttgart restaurant, after Eaton had spoken. "Whatever Bob said, I'll automatically sign on to right now," he said.

12   The first priority for both co-chairmen is to meet their pledge to cut $1.4 billion in costs in 1999. They will search for ways to save money in everything from shared overhead in finance and personnel to getting a better deal on steel. "First, we have to prove something to the world," says Schrempp, pounding his fist on the table over breakfast in his Stuttgart office. "We have to put that $1.4 billion on the table."

13   Preserving distinct brand identities while cutting costs will be tricky. The two companies will avoid a platform strategy that would muddy the Mercedes and Chrysler images, since customers might balk at paying up to $93,000 for an S-Class sedan with a Chrysler drive train. But there is room for common design and engineering in less visible areas, such as sound systems. And some production can be shared. For example, Chrysler's Jeep plant in Graz, Austria, will build the Mercedes sport-utility vehicle, the M-Class.

14   In the core markets of Europe and North America, Chrysler and Mercedes will maintain separate showrooms, even if they are owned by the same dealer. But combining logistics, service, warehousing, and technical training will dramatically boost sales volume, analysts figure. In markets where the companies have a weak presence, such as Asia, they are considering mixing the brands, perhaps selling Mercedes' heavy trucks and Chrysler's light trucks together, for example, to cut costs.

15   The company's big challenge will be reacting speedily to new trends with just the right models. While the U.S. will see a continued blurring of lines between cars and trucks, Europe has room to catch up in minivans and leisure vehicles. Schrempp expects to see several versions of sports cars. Inspired by Volkswagen's popular new Beetle, he has also asked his designers to think about a car with a retro look.

16   Yet at its most fundamental level, DaimlerChrysler's success hinges on melding two starkly different corporate cultures. Daimler's methodical decisionmaking could squelch Chrysler's famed creativity. Mercedes' reputation for luxury and quality could be tarnished by Chrysler's downmarket image. If they can't create a climate of learning from each other, warns Ulrich Steger, a management professor at IMD, the Lausanne business school, "they could be heading for unbelievable catastrophe."

17   If that happens, it won't be the first time. Big cross-border mergers have a poor track record. In most cases, the hoped-for savings are not realized, the weaker partner is stripped of its best assets, and margins plunge. For instance, BMW's merger with Rover is foundering because BMW lacked a clear strategy, and the companies' models cannibalized each other. BMW has asked the British government for aid.

18   To avoid a similar fate, Schrempp and Eaton analyzed 50 large-scale mergers from many industries before launching their own. They found that 70% had stumbled, most for lack of clear targets and speed. "What you don't do in the first 12 to 24 months will be very difficult to do later," Schrempp says.

19   That's especially true for two industrial icons from business cultures that couldn't be more different. Chrysler is the very symbol of American adaptability and resilience. Having survived a near-death experience that required a 1979 government bailout, it scrambled under legendary CEO Lee A. Iacocca, and then Eaton, to become one of the world's leanest and nimblest car companies.

20   Daimler Benz, meanwhile, has long represented the epitome of German industrial might, its Mercedes cars the purest examples of German quality and engineering. But despite Schrempp's shakeup at the top, its middle ranks exemplify the hierarchical, procedure-driven German management style that could smother an agile company like Chrysler.

TABLE 1
The Merger at a Glance

Employees
421,000

Performance
Operating earnings are forecast to hit $7.06 billion on revenues of $155.3 billion in 1999

1997 Combined Unit Sales
4 million cars and trucks

Global Reach
Manufacturing facilities in 34 countries, sales in more than 200 countries

Hot Models
Mercedes: S-Class luxury sedan, SLK 190 roadster. Chrysler: Dodge Durango, Plymouth Prowler

Data: Salomon Smith Barney, Company reports.

21   So over the next two years, he and Eaton will forge an identity for the new auto maker, creating a global company with its own product lineup and personality. For example, labor relations will break new ground. Based in Stuttgart, the company will retain the German two-tier board system, but a member of the United Auto Workers will join German union and Daimler works-council members on the supervisory board, which oversees management.

22   Schrempp and Eaton will also spend the next two years taking inventory. They'll look at the strength of each model and brand and decide which market segments to target. Schrempp sees potential in Europe for Chrysler's 300M, a luxury performance sedan. More pickups and heavy trucks will be directed to South America. Mercedes must decide whether to sell the little A-Class hatchback in the U.S. and what to do with Smart, the tiny city car built with the Swiss maker of Swatch that debuted to mixed reviews in October.

23   Together, the co-CEOs will assign a budget, select the appropriate technologies, and set a specific quality standard for each model. Once that process is completed in 2001, Eaton, now 58, will retire. There is much speculation in Detroit that he might leave earlier, and Eaton recently told senior Chrysler executives: "At any point that I feel redundant, I will go."

24   As far as products are concerned, DaimlerChrysler will start life in good health. Mercedes has a sexy new lineup, having launched 10 new models in the past three years, including the sleek SLK roadster. Daimler has little overlap with Chrysler, which brings strength in minivans, sport-utility vehicles, and pickups. Financially, too, the new company is strong. Daimler and Chrysler are among the world's most profitable carmakers. Salomon Smith Barney analyst John K. Lawson figures next year the combined company will have operating earnings of $7.06 billion on revenues of $155.3 billion. And with a cash stash of $19.4 billion, it could weather even a deep recession.

25   This auto juggernaut will loom large in Germany Inc. It will be the country's biggest industrial company by far, its shares amounting to a huge 13% of the DAX stock index. As DaimlerChrysler moves toward U.S.-style, profit-motivated management and compensation, the changes will reverberate throughout Germany's egalitarian business culture.

26   Schrempp, too, may come to represent a formidable presence on Germany's business landscape. If he decides to slash jobs, for example, or revamp costly German labor agreements, he may find himself going head to head with Gerhard Schroder, Germany's left-leaning new Chancellor. That could set a potent precedent for other German executives longing to break from the country's often strangling business regulations.

27   If there's a European executive whose style resembles that of a no-nonsense American CEO, though, it's Schrempp. He rattled Corporate Germany by nakedly pursuing profits when he took over Daimler Benz in 1995. That year the company posted a $3.45 billion operating loss, the worst in German postwar history. Schrempp restructured the industrial giant and axed businesses that couldn't

meet tough new standards, turning a profit again in 1996. In three years he has metamorphosed from one of German business's most vilified men to one of its most imitated.

28   Now, at DaimlerChrysler, some 98 integration teams are ready to hammer out details on topics from software to production. An 18-member management board is charting strategy. Where one company is clearly more advanced, decisions are easy: For instance, Daimler will handle fuel-cell and diesel technology, and Chrysler will keep its electric-vehicle project.

29   Other decisions are tougher. Chrysler invented the minivan, but Daimler is far along in developing its own. So the two are hotly debating whether to ditch Daimler's version or offer a separate luxury model. One senior Chrysler manager observing the process says that the way this decision is handled—rather than the outcome—will determine whether he chooses to stay with the company.

30   Another test will involve jobs. The new board is analyzing the next two management layers to decide between Daimler and Chrysler employees for each slot. "I suspect we'll lose some people," Eaton says. So far, though, decisions have been even-handed. On Nov. 3, the companies announced that Chrysler executives will run procurement and legal affairs, while Daimler execs will head finance and information technology.

NO REDUNDANCIES

31   Schrempp is playing his cards close to his Italian-cut vest, but industry experts who know him predict that by 2001 he will abandon the unwieldy new management board. Schrempp admits he can visualize a time when "you also have somebody in charge globally for production." He won't say more. But one likely option would be a lean corporate center for human resources, finance, and planning. Individual board members would be responsible for trucks, Chrysler cars, and Mercedes cars, as well as for purchasing, research and development, and production—with no redundancies. Sales and marketing units could be one level below the board.

32   Such a shakeup would not surprise employees from the Daimler side. Schrempp's focus on goals has earned him a reputation as cold-hearted. It started in 1989, when Daimler Benz Chairman Edzard Reuter put the young truck executive in charge of forming a new aerospace unit, now called Dasa. First, Schrempp pulled together four aerospace companies that Daimler controlled, and managed them as a holding company. Buffeted by defense cuts and a rising dollar, he needed more drastic steps. So he cut out the management and controlled each unit directly.

33   Then, in June, 1994, Reuter appointed Schrempp heir apparent to take over Daimler Benz in May, 1995. All that year, Schrempp prepared his strategy, and once in power, he executed it with exacting swiftness. The goal: to reverse his former mentor's grand scheme of building an integrated technology company. First, he streamlined head-office hierarchy, cutting staff by more than 75%. "You have to sweep the stairs from the top down," he says. Then he examined each business unit, grilling frightened managers nearly to tears and setting a 12% return-on-capital target for each unit. When the dust had settled, Daimler was down to 23 units from 35 and carried 63,000 fewer people on the payroll.

34   Meanwhile, Schrempp weathered two public humiliations. First, in July, 1995, word leaked out that Schrempp and two aides, one of them carrying a bottle of wine, were stopped by Italian police on the Spanish Steps of Rome for trying to walk through a blocked-off area late at night. After getting into an argument when the police demanded their passports, they were detained overnight. The German press had a field day. And as head of Dasa, he had bought Fokker, a loss-generating Dutch aircraft builder, in 1993. But in January, 1996, he cut Fokker loose, candidly admitting he had made a $1.4 billion mistake. But Schrempp's success at turning Daimler around outweighed the negative press on both incidents.

35   He did make one severe miscalculation. In 1996, the German government decided to cut sick pay to 80% of wages from 100%, and Mercedes was the first company to implement the policy. Works-council chief Karl Feuerstein immediately instructed workers across Germany to stage illegal work stoppages. Schrempp stood fast for three weeks. But when he realized he couldn't win, he called Feuerstein at home and gave in.

36   All along, Schrempp was thinking about seeking a partner for Daimler. By 1996, he had decided that a carmaker can't compete without a full range of products, and he couldn't stretch the Mercedes

TABLE 2
Targets and Action Plans

1999

- $1.4 billion in cost savings
- Schrempp and Eaton will consider joint procurement, combined overhead, and shared technology, such as for diesel engines.

1999–2000

- Complete integration
- Management will assess the market position of every model and brand, then assign appropriate technology, cost, and quality standards.

After 2001

- Realign top management
- Schrempp will become sole CEO. Leaner management could include a global R&D or manufacturing function, with sales and marketing one level below.

Data: *Business Week*.

brand any further downmarket. But first he had to get Daimler in shape for a merger. Mercedes-Benz was a separate operating company with its own board, run by Helmut Werner, who was a hero in Germany for reviving the Mercedes lineup. Schrempp wanted to give Daimler direct operating control of Mercedes. "We had steps and steps, and layers and layers," Schrempp explains, moving Marlboros around the table to illustrate. "It took months to make a decision."

37   In 1995 and early 1996, talks between Eaton and Werner about a joint venture for all their international businesses outside Europe and North America had bogged down because of this structure. That failure helped spur Schrempp's reorganization. Although Werner fought to keep Mercedes independent, Schrempp prevailed with the supervisory board. By January, 1997, Mercedes was folded into Daimler, Werner was out, and Schrempp was running a car business.

SKI BUM

38   Schrempp wasn't always so ambitious. He was raised in Freiburg, a university town in southwest Germany. But he had too much fun skiing and dancing to finish his high-school-level studies. His father, a clerk at the university, persuaded him to learn a trade, so Schrempp joined Daimler as a 15-year-old apprentice mechanic. "I learned to do the most with as little effort as possible—I still do," he says, grinning.

39   He met his wife, Renate, when he was 18 and she 19, and for 25 cents they would listen to records in the jazz cellars of Freiburg. Schrempp then borrowed $25 from his dad to buy a trumpet and taught himself to play jazz without reading music. The trumpet, which Schrempp still plays for fun, sits in his office. Eventually, Schrempp earned an engineering degree. He reentered Daimler in 1967.

40   But despite being a 31-year Daimler veteran, he escaped the stifling Stuttgart culture early on. After a decade mostly in sales, he lived in South Africa from 1974 to 1982. Responsible for customer service, he hosted lively parties that helped sell fleets of trucks. He left for a two-year stint in Cleveland, where he got rid of troubled truck unit Euclid. Then he returned to South Africa for two more years as vice-president and then president, lecturing against apartheid to the elite even as he sold them their cars. Indeed, Nelson Mandela has made him an honorary consul to South Africa. Schrempp still has a house in Capetown and owns a game reserve with two friends near Kruger National Park.

41   Returning to Stuttgart in 1987 as No. 2 in the truck division was a bit of a shock. "He displayed contempt for tribal wars and the small German mind-set," says an adviser who first met him then. So Schrempp has cultivated a circle of friends unrelated to Daimler's world. His modern, art-filled home

near the woods outside Stuttgart is warm and welcoming. Schrempp dispenses drinks and cigars from behind the bar to pals including famed photographers and painters.

42   He turned to this circle for help during the crisis over his new A-Class model last October. When a Swedish auto journalist tipped over the new hatchback in a test maneuver, Schrempp took personal charge of containing the potential public-relations disaster after three weeks of bad press. One Sunday evening he invited eight friends to his home, and over Italian sausages, bread, and wine he listened to their advice. By the time he met with public-relations specialists the next day, he had decided to stop shipping the car for two months until the problem was fixed. Mercedes installed an electronic stabilizing system that cost $182 million in 1997 and 1998 but has rescued the A-Class's reputation. Unit sales are expected to hit 200,000 next year.

43   Schrempp is a man of seemingly boundless stamina. He can socialize into the wee hours and still get up early to work out in his home gym. He is also a passionate mountain climber. "It's the only time in my life I do what others tell me to," he says. Indeed, he is accustomed to getting his way. Last August, the new management board gathered at a resort in West Virginia. One night after dinner, Schrempp asked Eaton if DaimlerChrysler's stock certificate could include a photo of Karl Benz, in addition to Gottlieb Daimler and Walter Chrysler as planned. Eaton said that wouldn't be fair. But Schrempp was getting heat from his home region, where Benz was founded. He cajoled Eaton for at least an hour, finally offering to donate his replica of the first Benz three-wheeler to the Chrysler museum. Eaton relented. "No one knows what a stock certificate looks like anyway," says Eaton.

44   There will be many more such sessions over the coming months as Daimler and Chrysler nail down the details of their merger. And if an economic downturn slams auto sales, there could be some tight moments. Chrysler execs, like Schrempp's climbing partners, may find that's when Schrempp is at his best. Last July, in the Italian Alps, a fierce storm forced Schrempp's climbing group to ditch all metal and take cover. As lightning ricocheted across the rocks, Schrempp remained serene. "He has no fear," says climbing partner Hubert Burda, a Munich publisher. Given the challenges this huge merger will face, Schrempp may be exactly what is called for: a tough man in a storm.

CASE 25

BusinessWeek

THE SHUTDOWN GM NEEDS?

1   How dramatically will General Motors Corp. change as a result of its latest showdown with the United Auto Workers? By late June—four weeks after workers struck two Flint (Mich.) plants and slowly brought GM's North American production to a halt—the auto maker was dropping tantalizing clues. Might the company use the shutdown to make fundamental changes—reducing plant capacity to match its reduced market share, killing off poor-selling models and, perhaps, getting rid of entire marketing divisions?

2   For investors eager to see such reforms, there are encouraging signs. A June 30 GM filing with the Securities & Exchange Commission stated that the company is "carefully reviewing future spending for products and facilities." That followed a series of internal memos leaked by GM that hinted at similar plans. And on July 1, Ronald L. Zarrella, GM's vice-president for sales and marketing, told reporters: "We may well take this situation as an opportunity to move up some future plans in terms of eliminating overlap in our portfolio."

WORRIED WALL STREET

3   Even if the auto maker isn't definitively signaling a major overhaul, many analysts and academics think it should. On Wall Street, where analysts are increasingly worried by the strike that has already cost GM $1.2 billion in net income, there's hope that this time the carmaker will go further than the long-expected cutbacks of a few more parts plants and a couple of car models. They would applaud a broad restructuring that would finally get GM in fighting trim. That would mean cuts in management and hourly ranks, and revamping products, marketing, and manufacturing. Furman Selz analyst Maryann N. Keller is eager for such a clean-sweep approach. "I would love it if they were making those decisions," she says.

4   Clearly, GM's decade-long "death by a thousand cuts" strategy of gradual downsizing isn't working. The company has not come close to its overall productivity goals. Its manufacturing inefficiency puts it at a $411-per-vehicle disadvantage to Ford Motor Corp., estimates Stephen J. Girsky, a Morgan Stanley Dean Witter analyst. And GM's declining market share in recent years has only made the need for lower costs more acute. At the same time, the never-ending cuts exact a high toll on labor relations. "Does GM honestly think there's going to be less pain in doing these things one at a time?" Keller asks. "It just makes the UAW madder."

5   True, getting all the bad news out at once might cause more labor friction in the near term. Analysts say GM needs to shrink hourly rolls by 40,000 to 50,000 workers out of 220,000 to match competitors' efficiency—hardly welcome news to the union and its members. But such moves are inevitable, and GM hopes to make many cuts through attrition over the next few years.

6   In some cases, workers whose plants are sold could be better off in the long run working for new owners, as former GM workers at Detroit Diesel and American Axle have discovered. Meanwhile, greater investment in new equipment for the remaining factories could improve productivity and preserve jobs.

7   A one-fell-swoop strategy could actually result in better labor relations in the long haul. Says Trevor Bain, a University of Alabama management professor: "Whatever it is, they need to enunciate it clearly and let the union in on the secret, too." Workers would stop waiting for the other shoe to drop—and looking for real or imagined actions against them by management—if they believed the

Source:Kathleen Kerwin in Detroit, "The Shutdown GM Needs?" *Business Week:* July 13, 1998.

EXHIBIT A

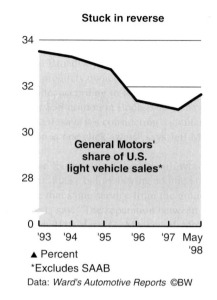

Stuck in reverse

General Motors'
share of U.S.
light vehicle sales*

▲ Percent
*Excludes SAAB

Data: *Ward's Automotive Reports* ©BW

cuts were over and the rebuilding was beginning. It worked at Ford and Chrysler Corp., both of which downsized radically in the early 1980s and went on to rebuild solid labor relations once the bloodletting was over. Says Merrill Lynch & Co. analyst Nicholas Lobaccaro: "Once you get right-sized and you don't need to lay people off any more, labor relations can improve dramatically."

8   And nobody should be surprised by more GM plant closings. The company is widely believed to be planning to close or sell both Flint plants that struck in June, as well as the Dayton brake plant that struck in 1996, and voted on June 30 to authorize another strike. "This strike may highlight a bunch of parts operations that have been living on borrowed time for quite a while and are finally going to be shuttered," says Lehman Brothers analyst Joseph S. Phillippi. Adds David E. Cole, director of the University of Michigan's Office for the Study of Automotive Transportation: "They'll probably clean the plate here. This is a crisis."

9   The auto maker is also expected to spin off all of its Delphi Automotive Systems parts maker, which had $26 billion in revenues in 1997. GM has said only that it is planning a partial spin-off. The sooner that happens, the better, analysts say. Likewise, GM is expected eventually to announce it will close at least one assembly plant—the Ste. Therese (Que.) factory that builds Chevrolet Camaros and Pontiac Firebirds that analysts say will be dropped. Wall Street would like to see the same discipline applied to salaried ranks. Analyst Girsky notes that GM's senior management ranks have ballooned 47% since its 1992 reorganization; rival Ford has reduced its top ranks by 37% in that time. GM would have to shrink its top management by 20% to 25% to match Ford's levels, he says. Labor experts say GM would gain credibility with its union workers if top management's bonuses were linked to the same efficiency standards being used to decide workers' fates.

"GRADE-B MOVIE"

10   The most painful reductions could come by streamlining GM's marketing system. It has more than twice as many brands and 70% more U.S. dealerships than Ford, Girsky points out—even though GM's unit sales are only 19% greater. Analysts and investors say GM should stop trying to resuscitate dying divisions, and instead spend more on promising newcomers like Saturn Corp. "This is like watching a grade-B movie—you know exactly how it ends," says Keller. "Either Buick or

TABLE 1
Whatever Happens in the Strike, Outsiders Say GM Should . . .

. . . BOOST productivity by investing in new equipment, improving manufacturing, and eliminating up to 50,000 workers.

. . . SELL or close inefficient parts plants. Accelerate the spin-off of the Delphi Automotive Systems operation.

. . . ELIMINATE excess capacity by shutting assembly plants. A top candidate: Ste. Therese, Que., which makes slow-selling Chevy Camaro and Pontiac Firebird.

. . . SLASH unprofitable cars from portfolio and add high-margin trucks or car-truck hybrids. Invest more resources in rising brands such as Saturn.

. . . KILL OFF or merge at least one marketing division—Buick or Oldsmobile—to cut engineering and marketing costs and speed consolidation of dealer network.

. . . SHRINK inflated management ranks and tie senior management bonuses more closely to the same productivity standards being used to slash hourly ranks.

Oldsmobile is going to have to disappear." Analysts also would like GM to add more high-profit trucks and new car-truck hybrids like Honda's CR-V and Lexus' RX300. Zarrella acknowledges that "we have more cars than we need, and not enough trucks." The strike may result "in getting out of those cars faster," he says.

11   GM's biggest problem is that it is chasing moving targets. When it comes to factory efficiency, "the competition is getting better faster than they are—and GM was already behind," says Phillippi. The company's U.S. market share has tumbled faster than it can close plants, and in June stood near 31%, down from 36% a decade ago. Even a rash of plant closings in the early '90s barely kept up with the declining demand. GM still has about 50% more assembly plants than Ford, which owns 24% of the market.

12   So how can GM level with the union about its capacity needs when management doesn't know how far market share will fall? Its executives will have to take a hard look at where sales are heading. For decades, they have declared that market share is about to rebound, only to be proven wrong. Early this year, market share tumbled below 29% for the second time in a year. A spring auto buying boom, fueled by a GM-led rebate push, helped the auto giant's share rebound temporarily. But Zarrella predicts that market share will be "well under 25%" in July and drop further if the strike continues. And some analysts believe the decline will continue longer term. Says Lobaccaro: "If you're doing long-term planning for GM, I think you have to look at 29% market share."

13   That's tough medicine for GM, its union, and its investors. But delaying the inevitable won't make it any less bitter—and will likely prolong the pain.

CASE 26

BusinessWeek

NISSAN IS BACK IN THE MUD

1 First we break even, then we make a profit. That was the simple plan of Yoshikazu Hanawa, president of Nissan Motor Co. In 1997, Japan's No. 2 carmaker posted a loss of $122 million on worldwide sales of $57 billion—and many investors hoped the worst was over. He had ambitious plans to cut administrative staff, build more models on fewer chassis, and streamline research and development. Good news seemed in sight.

2 Not so fast. Instead of reaching breakeven, Nissan now risks a 1998 loss much larger than last year's figure. Japan's stock market slide, marketing setbacks, and recessions in Japan and Asia are all combining to thwart Hanawa and deal him another setback. He says he's satisfied with Nissan's progress. But Nissan's problems may be so deep-rooted and Japan's financial crisis so severe that a healthy rebound may elude the company.

3 Nissan is now in its sixth year of trying to turn itself around. Problems started in the mid-1980s. In Japan, Nissan's engineers simply lost touch with what consumers wanted, rolling out dowdy sedans that didn't sell. In the all-important U.S. market, Nissan repatriated profits while Toyota and Honda reinvested them.

DEBT DILEMMA

4 Hanawa, who has been president since 1996, has done a lot. To raise cash, he has sold shares in subsidiaries unrelated to Nissan's core business of making cars and has even sold off Nissan's crown jewel—a swank 16-story headquarters in the chic Ginza district of Tokyo—for $125 million. To cut costs, he has slashed inventories by 100,000 vehicles in North America.

5 But that won't be enough. The company is saddled with $22 billion in debt and is running out of banks to borrow from. Meanwhile, Nissan's sales are dropping. On Nov. 10, the parent company is expected to announce a $289 million net loss for the first half of the fiscal year ending next March. According to some analysts, Nissan's losses could reach $626 million for the full year.

6 Ironically, the same cross-shareholdings that once propped up Nissan are starting to choke it. If not for the stock market crash, Nissan would have turned a profit in the first half. But the tumbling Nikkei blindsided Nissan with $661 million in securities-valuation losses from its holdings, including stakes in struggling Fuji Bank Ltd. and Industrial Bank of Japan Ltd. "If share prices continue to go down, it's a huge problem for Japan, not just Nissan," says Hanawa.

7 Yet the root of Nissan's problems remains unchanged: marketing. Nissan's failure to meet consumer preferences in the U.S. is a case in point. Last year, the U.S. operation lost $787 million, which pulled the parent company into the red. Nissan's U.S. sales are down 18% for the first nine months of this year, to 475,000 vehicles, while Toyota's are up 7% and Honda's have risen 8%. While Toyota and Honda are offering little by way of rebates, Nissan is giving back $2,000 on all models.

8 Nissan's greatest lost opportunity may be at home, however. To do it, the company has new models on the way. In October, Nissan launched its $13,565 Sunny sedan, outfitted with a safer frame; buyers can also choose one of several fuel-efficient engine options. The company plans to use the same chassis to roll out 10 other new models of cars and minivans worldwide.

Source: Emily Thornton in Tokyo, with Kathleen Kerwin in Detroit and bureau reports International Business, "Nissan Is Back in the Mud," *Business Week:* November 2, 1998.

TABLE 1
Auto Maker Besieged

Big Losses

Nissan may report a loss this year of $626 million, thanks to big losses in its stock portfolio. That's five times last year's loss.

Fire Sale

To raise badly needed cash, Nissan is selling its stake in an ad agency, its Ginza headquarters, and its Australian finance firm.

Big Debt

Total debt is still $22 billion. Top priority is to cut it.

Data: *Business Week,* Company reports.

IMAGE WOES

9   Nissan is not in immediate danger of collapse, of course. But still, Hanawa may have to make some painful decisions. Nissan closed one of its plants in 1995 and may have to close more. It's now operating below the critical threshold of 70% capacity. "Unless they shut down a plant, no matter how much debt they reduce, they can't make money," says Koji Endo, auto analyst at Schroders Japan Ltd.

10   For now, the company suffers from an image problem so severe that Japanese newspapers have run satirical poems from readers poking fun at the once-treasured carmaker. Investors are losing faith, too. Since Hanawa unveiled his latest restructuring plan, Nissan's share price has tumbled to $2.71 from $4. Hanawa's goals seem to grow more elusive every year.

CASE 27   BusinessWeek

GERMAN CARMAKERS IN THE FAST LANE

1   The U.S. luxury-vehicle market has pretty well stalled these days. Sales are expected to grow a scant 4% over the next two years. But around the New Jersey offices where both Mercedes-Benz and BMW have their American headquarters, optimism reigns. Flush with success from record sales in 1997, the German auto makers are loading up for a product blitz. Mercedes has a flashy new convertible, a souped-up version of its M-class sport-utility, a revamped line of large sedans, and maybe a luxury minivan on the way. BMW is gearing up for the launch of a new version of its popular 3-series sedans this fall, and has a hybrid sport-ute debuting in 1999. "We're going to keep pushing, no matter what," says Victor H. Doolan, president of BMW of North America Inc.

2   The swagger is back at BMW and Mercedes. It has been a remarkable dual turnaround for the German companies, whose U.S. sales hit rock bottom in 1991 in the face of a successful onslaught by Japanese luxury brands. But they have since left rivals behind in the slow lane. Bolstered by a stable of new products and aggressive marketing campaigns, BMW and Mercedes again rank as the hottest luxury brands in the U.S.

3   Indeed, both BMW and Mercedes have plenty of room to boast. They ended 1997 in a dead heat for preeminence among luxury import brands, with BMW's sales of 122,500 vehicles edging out Mercedes' 122,417. And in a luxury-car market that grew just 6% from 1991 to 1997, BMW sales soared 130%, while Mercedes rose 83%. That has allowed the German brands to leapfrog past their top two Japanese rivals, Lexus and Acura.

BACKLASH

4   What's more, if BMW and Mercedes keep accelerating, they could roar past the faltering U.S. market leaders, General Motors' Cadillac Div. and Ford's Lincoln unit, within the next five years. "Cadillac and Lincoln are definitely on the defensive," says Susan Jacobs, an independent auto analyst in Rutherford, N.J. Lincoln's car sales slipped 1% last year, to 139,540. Even with an all-new entry-level car, the Catera, Cadillac's sales rose just 7%, to 182,624. Lincoln is bringing out a small luxury car this fall, and Cadillac is banking on a redesigned DeVille in 1999. But few expect those additions to be strong enough to slow the Germans' momentum.

5   Competitors now hold Mercedes and BMW up as the standard to beat. "They have clearly re-framed the luxury market," says John F. Smith, general manager of GM's Cadillac Div. "I think they've been much more responsive to a variety of consumer tastes." That's just the opposite of the reputations BMW and Mercedes carried at their low point in 1991. Back then, the pair admittedly lost touch with consumers. They paid the price: Sales bottomed out at 53,343 vehicles for BMW and 58,869 for Mercedes—down 45% and 41%, respectively, from their high five years earlier. "The key issue then was to survive," says Michael Jackson, president of Mercedes-Benz of North America.

6   BMW suffered, in part, from a backlash against its yuppie image of the 1980s, when "Beemers" were the car of choice for nouveau-riche stockbrokers and investment bankers. They were known for performance, style, and such expensive maintenance that the brand's nickname was Break My Wallet. "The quality was always good, but maintenance was a huge issue," says Steve Thomas, a BMW dealer in Camarillo, Calif. "You'd spend $40,000 for the car, and a couple of thousand dollars a year to keep it on the road." Mercedes, on the other hand, was known as safe, reliable, exceptionally well-engineered—and dull.

Source: Bill Vlasic in Detroit, "German Carmakers in the Fast Lane," *Business Week*: April 13, 1998.

7   In other words, both companies were ripe for the picking. That's exactly what the Japanese auto makers set out to do, starting with Honda's Acura brand in 1986 and followed by Toyota with Lexus and Nissan with Infiniti in 1989. The Japanese luxury models had fresh styling, topped the quality charts, and were priced significantly lower than the competing BMW and Mercedes cars.

8   The way consumers flocked to the upstarts humbled the Germans. "We thought we couldn't be touched by them, that we were superior," says British-born Doolan, who joined BMW 20 years ago and has headed its U.S. sales operations since 1993. "There was a degree of complacency, maybe even arrogance." The attack came as the dollar was falling against the German mark, pushing up prices of BMW and Mercedes models. When Toyota introduced its LS 400 for $35,000 in 1989, the cheapest BMW 7-series sedan cost $55,000, and a Mercedes 300SE sold for $56,000. "Certainly, the Japanese did their homework, and we were vulnerable," says Jackson, a former Mercedes dealer who became president last year. "We had to change."

9   Their problems were all too apparent: bloated prices, antiquated dealer networks, and, most important, a lack of hot new cars. Both slashed prices across the board on existing products and held down costs on new models by opening their first assembly plants in the U.S. They pressured dealers to catch up to Lexus' standards for sales and service. BMW started a program that covered routine maintenance for a three-year period, for example.

10   The toughest challenge was to energize the tired lineups. Mercedes brought out two new C-class midsize sedans in 1994 and followed up with redesigned E-class full-size sedans and wagons two years later. Both new models were sportier, without a matching price hike. Mercedes ventured further into new territory last year with the SLK two-seat roadster and the CLK luxury coupe.

11   An even bigger gamble came with the introduction last year of Mercedes' first-ever sport-utility vehicle, the M-class, built at the company's new factory outside Tuscaloosa, Ala. It has been a runaway hit, with 21,000 vehicles sold in the first six months. Sometime later this year, Mercedes execs will decide whether to stretch their brand even further, to cover a uniquely American product—a luxury minivan.

12   BMW has matched Mercedes product for product. It radically redesigned the 3-series sedans in 1991 and made them more affordable to younger buyers. Currently, it offers seven versions of 3-series models, ranging in base price from $21,960 to $42,070. Another update set for this fall has already received rave reviews from the automotive press. BMW also rolled the first Z3 roadsters out of its new Spartanburg (S.C.) factory in 1996. And next year, BMW will introduce a "sports-activity-vehicle," described as a hybrid of an SUV and a performance sedan.

CACHET

13   Even as the Germans improved, they got a big break from an unexpected corner: Toyota and the other Japanese carmakers seemed to forget what had put them on the map in the first place. Lexus, for example, hit the market initially with less-expensive cars that mimicked Mercedes styling. But as Mercedes and BMW got nimble and held down prices, Lexus and other Japanese brands hiked prices to boost profits and promptly lost their edge. They have since tightened their belts by freezing and, in some cases, cutting prices.

14   But those moves have come too late to prevent BMW and Mercedes from recapturing the hearts of many luxury buyers with their new lineups. Don Busse, an engineer from Port Hueneme, Calif., recently traded in an Acura CL for a BMW Z3. "The Z3 is more sporty, more fun," says Busse. "BMW also has more cachet than a Japanese brand, or a Lincoln or Cadillac."

15   That's a message the German pair is also trying to hammer home in their advertising. In a new Mercedes ad campaign featuring its SUVs, for example, actors dressed as executives and engineers sing and dance to a 1950s-era rock beat. "I love my Benz now," croons an Elvis-like exec. The one-word tag line? "Fun." So far, the message seems to be resonating with Mercedes buyers. "It's the most reliable car on the road, but its image is hipper than before," says Kim Adams, a TV newswoman from Marlton, N.J., and owner of a C-class sedan.

16   Of course, the German competitors are not doing everything in lockstep. As their rivalry has intensified, executives of both Mercedes and BMW have begun to snipe at the other's

accomplishments. Before a speech in Detroit in January, Jurgen E. Schrempp, chairman of Mercedes' parent Daimler Benz, suggested that BMW may have manipulated its 1997 U.S. sales figures to beat Mercedes' numbers. "They reported their sales after us, right?" Schrempp said with a smile. "The point is, if we say our sales were 122,780, they would say they had 122,781." Retorts Doolan: "If it's a sales race, let's make it a level playing field. If we include [BMW-owned] Land Rover trucks, we beat them 144,000 to 122,000."

17   And even as the Germans enjoy their resurgence, rivals are hardly giving up. GM's Cadillac unit is entering the luxury sport-utility fray with the Escalade, due out this fall. Lincoln will court baby boomers—and potential C-class and 3-series buyers—with its own midsize luxury cars, the LS6 and LS8. The so-called Baby Lincolns come out this fall, with expected price tags around $30,000.

18   So far, the Japanese brands have yet to mount an effective response. Lexus is bringing out a car-like SUV called the RX300, aimed directly at the M-class. In a market that's largely product driven, however, more will be needed. "The Japanese counterpunch hasn't occurred yet," says John Casesa, an auto analyst with Schroder & Co. in New York.

19   With the market expected to slow, however, virtually all the luxury brands are holding the line on price hikes. That means competition is likely to get a lot tougher. But the German duo is expected to continue to grab new buyers. "BMW and Mercedes are riding the wave right now," says Lincoln Merrihew, an analyst with J.D. Power & Associates in Agoura Hills, Calif.

20   Mercedes and BMW executives vow that complacency will never creep into their companies again. Still, the surge in sales will level off, says Dieter Zetsche, a managing director of Daimler Benz. "You will not see continued 30% growth rates," he says. Helmut Panke, a BMW managing director, agrees. "When you get to the top of Mt. Everest, you have to take a deep breath," he says. For two companies that have been to the brink, it's remarkable enough that they're on the top, looking down.

CASE 28   **BusinessWeek**

REVIVING GM

1   As flashbulbs popped and music blared, General Motors President G. Richard Wagoner Jr. was beaming. Unveiling a crop of snazzy new concept cars at the Detroit auto show earlier this month, Wagoner's pride was palpable. "I pushed pretty hard for these," he said, momentarily shedding his customary aw-shucks modesty as he showed off three sleek hybrids that combine elements of cars, minivans, and sport-utility vehicles (SUVs). After years of churning out mostly unremarkable cars, GM finally had something to wow the audience. Wagoner couldn't have been happier.

2   That's not the only reason the athletic, 6-foot, 4-inch Wagoner is pleased. After a roller-coaster year in which GM was pummeled by a 54-day strike and a continuation of its seemingly endless market-share slide, the past few months have brought good news for Detroit's biggest carmaker. Six years of cutting costs and reshaping the way the lumbering giant designs and builds cars—much of it spearheaded by Wagoner, first as GM's chief financial officer and since 1994, as head of its core North American Operations (NAO)—seem to be paying off. GM has high hopes for its new Chevrolet Silverado and GMC Sierra full-size pickup trucks introduced last fall. And its once-sluggish manufacturing operations have succeeded in revving up production to take advantage of the hot market for high-margin light trucks. Flat-out production has sent GM's fourth-quarter earnings from operations up a stunning 55%, to $2.19 billion, as profits in its North American auto operations more than doubled, to $1.7 billion. And next year should be even better. Analysts now expect GM's operating profits to increase 62%, to $6 billion.

GIDDY

3   Behind the scenes, too, GM watchers see cause for optimism. After years of preparation, the company is pushing ahead with plans this spring to spin off its auto-components group, Delphi Automotive Systems. And even GM's most intractable problem, labor relations, shows signs of mending.

4   The combination has suddenly turned GM investors giddy. After driving the company's shares down from 76 to 47 over the course of last summer's strike, Wall Street has sent the stock up a stunning 89%, to a record high of 89, since October. In January alone, shares have risen almost 25%. "The market is telling us that this company is turning the corner," says Morgan Stanley Dean Witter auto analyst Stephen J. Girsky. And GM is likely to create more investor buzz on January 29 when analysts get a sneak peak at future models. Says Seth M. Glickenhaus of Glickenhaus & Co., a GM stockholder: "Finally, these people are coming out of their Rip Van Winkle sleep."

5   Investors are now counting on the 45-year-old Wagoner to keep up the momentum. Promoted last fall to president of GM's $130 billion global auto operations—which account for three-quarters of total revenues—Wagoner has played a pivotal role in getting GM back into fighting trim. His slow-but-steady overhaul of the North American unit won him the post—and has made him the leading candidate to succeed John F. Smith Jr., GM's 60-year old chairman and CEO. Smith, who has leaned heavily on Wagoner for years, credits him with doing a "superb" job. "We had to change virtually everything," Smith says. "Some things hadn't been touched since the beginning of time." The results are plain. After an $86 million loss in 1997, GM's North America auto business posted a $1.6 billion profit in 1998 and could soar to $3 billion in 1999. The improving outlook has won Wagoner kudos

Source: Kathleen Kerwin, with Joann Muller in Detroit, "Reviving GM," *Business Week:* February 1, 1999; Joann Muller in Detroit, "Delphi Pushes a Peace Program," *Business Week:* February 1, 1999; and Amey Stone in New York, "Is GM's Stock Heading for a Stall?" *Business Week* (online original): February 1, 1999.

from the board as well. Says director John G. Smale: "GM under Wagoner has made more money in North America than it had in decades before him."

"NO PLAN B"

6   Still, the year ahead will be Wagoner's acid test. The core of Wagoner's strategy for transforming GM has been a thorough renovation of its sagging product lineup. In the past two years, Wagoner has overseen the launch of 20 models—27% of GM's total 75 offerings—the Silverado and Sierra pickups, as well as a host of minivans and midsize cars. And later this year, GM will introduce four new SUVs, which could give another big jolt to profits. Wagoner and Smith had expected the new models to recharge GM's results throughout last year, but the strike cost it much momentum. In 1999, there are no excuses. "This is where the rubber hits the road," says Roy S. Roberts, GM's North American marketing chief. "There is no Plan B."

7   So how are they doing? Early indications seem promising: Sales of GM's redesigned minivans, such as the Chevy Venture and the Pontiac Montana, have more than doubled since 1995, the last year before redesigned models arrived. Sales for the seven new midsize models are up a more modest 5% since 1997, but even in this hugely competitive arena, GM has its stars: The Buick Century family sedan gained 38% for the year, while the Chevy Malibu rose 36%.

8   That's good—but is it good enough? For all his success, Wagoner still faces huge challenges. Overseas, Brazilian and Asian units are wracked by economic woes, even as GM's European operation—long one of the company's most profitable units—struggles to regain its footing. His biggest job, though, will be halting GM's decades-long market-share slide in the U.S. In the four years Wagoner headed the NAO's $94 billion business, GM's share of the U.S. market slipped down a further four percentage points, to 29.2%. The precipitous fall reflects myriad problems that can be boiled down to this: Many people today are turned off by GM cars. "At the end of the day, what really counts is the hardware," says Joseph S. Phillippi, an analyst at Lehman Brothers Inc. "GM is still, in most respects, one generation behind all its competitors."

9   Despite recent efforts to rejuvenate GM's brands and the progress with a smattering of new models, names like Oldsmobile and Buick seem tired. Even worse, GM remains years behind rivals in shifting production to the popular pickup and SUV models. And as car buyers defected in droves, GM has been left with a huge infrastructure of poorly located, aging dealerships and underutilized, outdated factories. Certainly, GM has made huge strides. But unless it generates excitement over new models and coaxes buyers back into its showrooms, GM faces many more years of cutbacks.

MORE DRAMATIC?

10   For all the problems Wagoner has solved, however, he still needs to do more to boost GM's profitability, which continues to lag the competition's. Net profit margins for the first half of 1998—before the strike wiped out earnings—fell back to 2.7%, right where they were when Wagoner took over the NAO in 1994. Meantime, Ford's margins for the period were 6.2% and growing, while Chrysler hit 6.7%. With GM's fourth-quarter margins roaring back to 5.7%, the outlook is brightening as GM snaps back from the effects of the strike. But, as production levels off later this year, it won't be easy to sustain those levels.

11   GM's critics say the profit lag points to the need for an even more dramatic remake of GM's product lineup. They argue that Wagoner needs to push harder for exciting new cars that will grab consumers. Volkswagen can point to its cute new Beetle, Ford has its lucrative Expedition SUVs, and Chrysler its pulse-pounding Dodge Viper. But even GM's brand-new Silverado, for which Wagoner has high expectations, is boxy and conservative compared with the competition. Says Merrill Lynch & Co. analyst Nicholas Lobaccaro: "The only way to truly fix this company is through a product renaissance."

12   With Smith focusing on strategy and trade issues, that job now falls squarely on Wagoner. But little in his background, or his makeup, suggests he's likely to push for more radical change. A

consensus-builder who methodically works his way through complex problems, Wagoner is the latest in a long line of GM insiders to get a shot at fixing GM. The quintessential company man, he has worked for GM since he graduated from Harvard business school in 1977, joining the auto company as an analyst in its New York treasurer's office.

13   During those 22 years, he has earned a reputation as a demanding boss, one who combines self-deprecating humor with a competitive streak honed during years of cutthroat basketball games. But he is also a conciliatory team player able to bring warring GM factions together. In a stint as CFO of GM Europe a decade ago, for instance, Wagoner was able to get GM's notoriously turf-conscious Swiss, German, and British units working smoothly together. "He does what's best for the company, not what's best for him personally," says Robert J. Eaton, now DaimlerChrysler co-chairman and the former head of GM Europe. "He's a very apolitical guy."

14   He has also come far from his roots in finance. As he moved quickly through a series of fast-track jobs in the U.S., Canada, and Latin America early in his career, co-workers remember that he gamely learned the ins and outs of every aspect of the business. DaimlerChrysler Senior Vice-President Gary L. Henson, who worked at GM's Vauxhall Motors Ltd. in Britain in the 1980s, recalls being teamed with the young finance whiz at a manufacturing workshop. Their task was to boost efficiency in the "cut-and-sew" area where seat covers were stitched together. He was amazed to see Wagoner plunge into the nitty-gritty of the shop floor. Marvels Henson: "He was up half the night, rearranging sewing machines."

15   It wasn't until 1991, however, that Wagoner got a chance to prove his mettle on the operations side. Taking over as head of Brazilian operations, he found them in chaos when he arrived in Sao Paulo. Wagoner showed that he had matured into far more than a number-cruncher. He was among the first in the auto industry to realize that Brazilians were no longer willing to accept decades-old models from Europe and the U.S. Employing the lean manufacturing techniques he had learned in Europe, he quickly built less expensive Brazilian versions of new Opel-designed cars and U.S.-engineered pickup trucks. "Rick got the whole product lineup modernized, well ahead of the competition," says Mark T. Hogan, the GM manager who ran things after Wagoner. "He read the tea leaves early on."

16   Wagoner's successes didn't go unnoticed back in Detroit, where—on the heels of 1991's $8 billion domestic auto loss—a boardroom coup had put Smith in charge. Just 16 months after he arrived in Sao Paulo, Smith named the then 39-year-old Wagoner CFO of the entire corporation. "He did a great job in Europe" and "really charged up that operation" in Brazil, says Smith. "He showed great leadership skills."

17   Wagoner became a member of the powerful inner circle that Smith brought in to perform triage on GM's battered domestic operations. With losses running $16 million a day, it was GM's darkest hour. As CFO, Wagoner made important contributions early on. One of his biggest: engineering a $6 billion contribution of EDS-backed stock to trim the company's gaping $24 billion pension deficit. He also restored the auto maker's credibility on Wall Street by replacing fancy accounting practices with a more conservative approach.

CONCILIATORY

18   Wagoner's talent as a peacemaker also helped GM weather its crisis. When GM purchasing czar Jose Ignacio "Inaki" Lopez de Arriortua bolted for Volkswagen in 1993, for instance, Smith charged Wagoner with making Lopez' $4 billion in price cuts stick. The challenge: Lopez had left behind a trail of enraged suppliers, who were upset by his tearing up of contracts and other high-handed tactics. Wagoner took a conciliatory approach—but gave back few of Lopez' price cuts. Instead, he sought cooperation and listened to suppliers. "People felt more like participating voluntarily," recalls Kenneth L. Way, chairman of seatmaker Lear Corp. Smith was so impressed by Wagoner's handling of both finance and purchasing that he chose Wagoner to succeed him in running GM's North American auto unit in 1994.

19   Ever since, Wagoner has been working doggedly to reinvent the way GM designs, builds, and sells its cars. A crucial step has been revamping GM's problem-ridden manufacturing techniques,

especially the all-critical changeover process from an old model to a new one. Once an industry laughingstock because of the months it took for model changeovers, GM's recent launches, notably last year's kickoff of the Grand Am sedan and the Silverado pickup truck, have been far smoother.

20   Drawing on his international experience, Wagoner has also worked to get more leverage out of GM's global expertise. He ordered his Michigan engineers to begin cooperating with their international counterparts to share platforms, engines, transmissions, and other key components. The move will allow GM to make Saturn, Chevy, and Pontiac models from the same chassis it uses to build Opels in Europe. And the number of platforms GM uses globally should drop from 22 today to 14 by 2005, holding out the promise of billions of dollars a year in savings.

21   At the same time, Wagoner recast GM's archaic product-development system along lines favored by Toyota Motor Corp. and other carmakers. Doing away with a mishmash of chief engineers and marketers who used to jostle for control at each stage, Wagoner shifted responsibility for each truck and car platform to a single executive. Today, these managers oversee a model's development from the early stages of design until it rolls off the assembly line. They also have profit-and-loss responsibility for their vehicles—another first at GM.

22   Given the strong results the shift has produced, it's easy to see why Smale counts it as one of Wagoner's biggest accomplishments. The head of the full-size pickup program, for instance, has mobilized his team to design the pickup with 25% fewer parts. That, in turn, has enabled factory workers to assemble Silverados 10% faster than previous models.

TOUGH DEMANDS

23   Indeed, as many of Wagoner's core organizational, engineering, and manufacturing reforms come together in the new generation of vehicles, nowhere is progress clearer than in GM's improving outlook in the highly profitable truck market. GM recently announced it would crank out 977,000 of its brand-new Chevy Silverado and GMC Sierra pickups this year, a 34% leap from the 727,000 built in 1998. Even compared with 1997, a year with far less labor strife, truck production will jump a healthy 11%. Better still, Wagoner expects premium features for which consumers are willing to pay more to add a full 2% to net profits on the new trucks. All told, Wasserstein Perella & Co. analyst Scott Merlis estimates GM's aftertax pickup-truck profits could soar by $1 billion in 1999.

24   There's more where that came from. GM will launch four new sport-utilities into the red-hot market for full-size SUVs late this year: the Chevy and GMC Suburbans, the Chevy Tahoe, and the GMC Yukon. With all based on the Silverado chassis, analysts figure the $6 billion in revenues from these SUVs will haul in similar profit increases.

25   Having focused much of his early energy on GM's core manufacturing and design difficulties, Wagoner has more recently turned to another perennial GM problem—spiraling warranty costs. And in the process, the usually gregarious manager has also proved he can be tough when he needs to be. Eighteen months ago, with warranty costs totaling a hefty 5% of net sales, Wagoner summoned senior North American managers to the company's design dome. Reduce warranty costs to 2% by 2001, to save $1 billion, or look for another job, he ordered. So far, GM has hit its interim targets, says Hogan, who now runs North American small-car operations: "He absolutely demanded it."

26   Wagoner is also learning how to deal with the thorny labor issues that have beset him and Smith for years. Long a hard-liner, Wagoner's efforts to increase productivity and assign more work to outside suppliers helped provoke 13 strikes, at a cost of more than $4 billion, over the past three years. As recently as last Memorial Day, Wagoner fueled the fire by ordering dies removed from a Flint factory that was about to start making critical truck parts.

27   It was a huge and costly mistake. Infuriated workers immediately brought all of GM to a screeching halt in a strike that would ultimately shave $2 billion off of '98 profits for little gain. "Just add that to the list of the other million things where we probably made the wrong call," Wagoner concedes now.

28   Since then, however, Wagoner has softened his approach. He recently consulted with top United Auto Workers leaders before naming new labor head Gary Cowger, whose years on the factory floor had earned the union's respect. "They were looking for someone who could work well with the

union," says UAW President Stephen P. Yokich. And Wagoner now participates far more frequently in meetings and phone calls with union leaders. "We're opening up the dialogue a lot more," he says.

29   That sort of cooperation is having an impact. Company and union officials are close to resolving union objections to GM's plans to replace older factories with newer plants that use just half as many workers. As part of the deal, the two sides are hashing out details of GM's proposal to assign work to outside suppliers, who would build entire sections of cars. To gain union support, GM is offering to back UAW efforts to unionize supplier plants. Even so, by unloading fixed costs such as factories and parts inventories to suppliers, Wagoner figures he can cut overall costs well below current levels.

30   Wagoner is also counting on closer union ties to smooth the way for GM's spin-off of Delphi, its $28.5 billion parts unit. GM plans a $1.5 billion initial public offering in early February and expects to divest the remainder of Delphi to its stockholders later this year. Keeping the peace will be key: Wagoner needs the Delphi spin-off to give another big boost to the efforts to reduce costs. Until now, he has been hampered by GM's obligation to buy Delphi parts, even when outside suppliers were cheaper or could handle more of the assembly task.

31   It all sounds promising. But will it be enough? Many experts believe Wagoner has just taken the initial steps in the uphill climb to revive GM. And his accomplishments may simply not be enough, according to some large investors. "The feeling is that these guys are not in a hurry," says Timothy M. Ghriskey, manager of the Dreyfus Fund, a big GM shareholder. "GM has a lot of catching up to do."

32   Here's why: Compared with the other big auto companies, GM still lags in almost every category. The biggest problem remains weak profit margins, even though GM's average profits per vehicle skyrocketed in the fourth quarter. Burnham Securities analyst David B. Healy estimates that GM made roughly $1,300 on each vehicle, corrected for the post-strike buildup and unusually low rebates. Though well above the roughly $874 GM made in 1998's first quarter, it's still much less than the estimated $1,872 Ford pulled in or the $2,266 Chrysler made. The new truck and SUV models, moreover, may not be enough to compensate for the less than stellar performance of GM's extensive car lineup. Overall mid-size car sales dropped 15% last year from 1995, the year before GM began revamping them. And GM's share of that segment slid from 35% to 29%, according to Ward's Automotive Report. "What have they put out, other than the Corvette, that created any buzz?" asks Wesley R. Brown, an analyst at Nextrend Inc., a Thousand Oaks (Calif.) auto consulting firm. "There's no emotion or passion surrounding any of their vehicles."

33   Many critics are urging Wagoner to scrap poorly performing models. GM has too many models—and too many facilities to produce them—for all of them to thrive. Indeed, the snazziest new models may simply be cannibalizing GM, rather than snatching share from rivals. Strong selling cars, like the Chevy Malibu or Buick Century, steal sales from older models. Sales of the bread-and-butter Chevy Lumina, for instance, plunged 22% last year, as many Chevy customers switched to the Malibu. And some new models have fizzled, pulling in far fewer sales than the older models they have replaced. Sales of the redesigned Olds Cutlass, at 53,000 last year, are down 59% from the 1995 sales of the Ciera, the car that it replaced.

34   Wagoner has made some moves in the right direction. To help clear the way for new models, he pulled the plug in 1994 on GM's three large, rear-wheel-drive cars—the Chevy Caprice, Buick Roadmaster, and Cadillac Fleetwood. It wasn't an easy move. "These are agonizing decisions," he says. But, in truth, he will need to make many more such painful choices in the near future or risk tying up resources in building poor performers that could be better employed building trucks and SUVs.

35   In the meantime, GM's much-ballyhooed brand-management efforts to tackle the problem of overlapping, look-alike models have not yet panned out. Wagoner has been relying heavily on Ronald L. Zarrella, hired four years ago from Bausch & Lomb Inc. as marketing chief, to introduce packaged-goods-style brand management for cars. GM is building 10 midsize models from just three platforms, for example, with each model tweaked to appeal to different consumers. The Century, for instance, is a traditional bench-seat Buick with a floaty ride, while the Buick Regal, based on the same chassis, has zippier handling and bucket seats. The Pontiac Grand Prix has muscle and sporty styling, while the sleeker Olds Intrigue that rolls off the same assembly line aims directly at import-driving baby boomers.

36   The problem facing Zarrella, who succeeded Wagoner as head of the NAO in October, is that consumers aren't really buying into the branding strategy. Sales of the redesigned Grand Prix were down

7% in 1998 while Regal, Century, and Intrigue sales haven't surpassed pre-brand-management levels. Even stand-out cars that should sell well don't because of the negative baggage of some GM brands. The appealing Intrigue offers an object lesson. "If that car carried the Toyota name, instead of Oldsmobile, it would be the hands-down best-seller in the category," says ING Barings Furman Selz analyst Maryann Keller. But GM sold only a disappointing 91,000 Intrigues last year. Says auto consultant John Wolkonowicz: "They're proving they can't sell Oldsmobiles, no matter how wonderful they make them."

37   Indeed, no amount of brand management can overcome a fundamental truth: Many of GM's brands still appeal primarily to older buyers. Even GM's most aggressive attempts to lure well-heeled baby boomers have backfired badly. Cadillac's $35,000 Catera, for instance, which was supposed to set a hipper, younger tone for GM's flagship division, needs $1,000 rebates to move a paltry 25,000 cars a year. And the average age of a Catera buyer remains 53.

"OLD MAN"

38   Even in those segments where GM is making strong progress, Wagoner needs to do more—and soon. Despite recent big gains in truck and SUV production, such vehicles still accounted for only 47% of GM's sales in 1998, compared with 71% at Chrysler and 61% at Ford. "The truck trend went much faster than our people ever expected," concedes Wagoner. Playing catch-up won't be easy. Japanese carmakers have solid hits with models such as Toyota's RAV4, Honda Motor Co.'s CR-V, and Subaru's Forester. And while crossovers from Ford and Chrysler will arrive next year, GM's versions—such as the models Wagoner introduced at the auto show—are at least two years away.

39   For all GM's continuing problems, Wagoner appears supremely self-assured—and some insiders find him even a bit complacent. Says one senior GM manager: "Rick is an old young man at GM." He rejects suggestions that he needs to do more to spark sales, because he sees evidence that they are already on the upswing. While he admits GM's lineup could use more flair, Wagoner is confident the organization now has "the passion, intensity, and thoughtfulness" to deliver that.

40   That hardly sounds like the radical steps many in the auto industry prescribe for GM. The consensus is that Wagoner needs to move quickly to kill more car models, close or merge marketing divisions, and rescue standouts like Saturn by giving it more models to sell. "They've got to bite the bullet," says Wolkonowicz. "What's wrong with letting Buick die?" Wagoner doesn't see it that way, though he won't make any promises about keeping divisions or models that don't earn their way. "Nobody's future is guaranteed," he says.

41   Wagoner and his team have declared that 1999 will be the year that the auto maker reverses its 20-year decline in market share. For that to happen, many of the models he's banking on—including a much-anticipated Saturn compact sedan and a reinvented Chevy Impala—will have to do well.

42   Wagoner remains confident that he can pull it off. "You kind of get a gut feeling that you're on the right track," he says. If he succeeds over the next couple of years, Wagoner will likely have earned himself the CEO job. If he doesn't, the GM board will be under increasing pressure to look outside the company for its next leader. Although Smale says no such move was contemplated when Wagoner was named president, the stakes get higher from here on out. With GM's biggest problems—shrinking market share and underperforming profits—still looming large, Rick Wagoner's toughest job still lies ahead.

DELPHI PUSHES A PEACE PROGRAM

43   When executives from GM's Delphi Automotive Systems unit hit the road on Jan. 25 to drum up investors for next month's initial public offering, they'll have help from some surprising allies. Union leaders, including some who forced the shutdown of General Motors Corp.'s auto unit just two years ago, are rallying to the cause of spinning off the parts giant. "I should go out and promote my team," says Harold W. "Nick" Nichols, chief negotiator for 14,500 Delphi workers represented by the International Union of Electronic, Electrical, Salaried, Machine, & Furniture Workers (IUE).

TABLE 1
Wagoner Is Driving GM Forward . . . But He Still Faces Major Challenges

- Restored domestic auto profits from a $982 million loss in 1993 to a $1.6 billion gain in '98 and an estimated $3 billion in '99.
- Whittled seven vehicle groups down to one car unit and one truck unit.
- Trimmed its product portfolio from 89 models in 1994 to 75 by dropping such slow sellers as the Chevy Caprice, Buick Roadmaster, Cadillac Fleetwood, and Buick Skylark. Merged GMC division with Pontiac.
- Streamlined product development by appointing one manager to head each vehicle program, replacing a mishmash of chief engineers, manufacturing bosses, and marketing managers.
- Cut manufacturing time by 10%, to an average of 30 hours per vehicle, and reduced the U.S. hourly workforce 14%, to 229,000 employees—all since '94. Closed two plants, with two more to shut down in '99.
- Needs to reach a new pact with the UAW while spinning off its unionized Delphi parts unit and replacing factories with new ones requiring fewer workers.
- Must develop breakthrough car and truck models to halt GM's 20-year slide in U.S. market share. Just 29.2% last year, it was 49% in '67.
- Needs to increase GM's sales of trucks, minivans, and SUVs from 47% of total vehicles sales to improve the company's lagging profits per vehicle.
- Must improve marketing efforts to lure younger consumers and more aggressively kill off dated, poorly performing models.

Data: General Motors Corp., Harbour & Associates, *Business Week.*

44   That's a remarkable shift, but Nichols and other union leaders figure that if they can help make Delphi a winner, they'll have more leverage at the bargaining table in the future. Even the more militant United Auto Workers (UAW), with its 46,000 Delphi members, isn't likely to throw a wrench into the spin-off plans. Although top leaders oppose the spin-off, some plant-level union leaders realize that cooperation may be the only way to save their jobs. Says Gary Hill, president of Local 696 at GM's Dayton brake factory, long a trouble spot for GM labor relations: "There's too much riding on the line for 'He said, she said.' "

45   Now, Chief Executive J. T. Battenberg III is keeping his fingers crossed that labor peace lasts. "We are trying to build a future together," he says. Small wonder. With some on Wall Street fearful that a renewed strike threat could scare away investors, bad news on the labor front could depress Delphi's stock. In the first phase of the spin-off, GM hopes to raise more than $1.5 billion by selling 17.7% of Delphi for 15 to 18 a share. The rest will be divested by late 1999.

More Disclosure

46   To ensure he has plenty of maneuvering room, Battenberg wants to negotiate a national labor agreement separate from the one GM will negotiate with its unions later this summer. Delphi's unions will likely fight that plan, but Battenberg hopes to win them over by disclosing more financial information to them than GM typically would. What they'll see isn't pretty: Delphi reported earnings before restructuring charges of just $370 million last year, on sales down 9%, to $28.5 billion.

47   Battenberg figures that as they pore over the numbers together, labor leaders will help him push through cost-cutting programs and more flexible work rules. Ultimately, though, he will also need wage cuts that the union now opposes. If all goes according to plan, Battenberg will be able to boost efficiency and make Delphi more competitive with nonunion suppliers.

48   Merely getting out from under the GM structure should go a long way. For starters, Delphi will be better positioned to win business from rival auto makers. Delphi now gets about 65% of revenues from GM's North American unit and another 16% from GM abroad. Battenberg wants to get North America down to 50%.

EXHIBIT A
Resume of Rick Wagoner

Born
1953

Education
Duke University, BA economics, 1975. Harvard, MBA, 1977.

First GM Job
Financial analyst at the New York office.

Current Job
President of GM.

What His Job Is Like
"Juggling while running on a treadmill."

Claim to Fame
Fixed GM's ailing Brazilian operations in the early '90s. Later, as CFO of GM, he overhauled the company's balance sheet. He also played a pivotal role in streamlining operations, helping to halt multibillion-dollar losses.

Office Decor
Duke jersey of Detroit Pistons star—and now Chevy pitchman—Grant Hill. A Duke banner signed by GM factory workers. A size XXL pair of boxer shorts emblazoned with GM slogan "Plan to Win."

First Car
A silver 1973 Camaro purchased with money from summer jobs.

What He Drives Now
1999 Chevy Suburban jumbo SUV.

Favorite Motivational Tool
Awarding Twinkies, which he dispenses for any job well done. "If you tasted one today and then tasted it next year, it would taste exactly the same."

Family
Married, and has three sons, ages 15, 13, and 8.

Favorite Hangout
Sidelines of middle-school football games, where he coaches his eldest son's team.

49   Still, Delphi has a rough road ahead. It will be hard pressed to compete against nonunion shops, whose workers earn about one-third the pay and benefits of Delphi's unionized employees. With a GM supply contract that guarantees Delphi the right to match the lowest bid on any GM contract until 2002, Delphi will have a couple of years before it truly has to fly on its own. But after that, GM will be free to take its business elsewhere. "Delphi has been in the GM cocoon so long, the risk is that they'll find the real world pretty cold out there," says Burnham Securities analyst David B. Healy. True enough, but it hasn't been too hot within GM lately, either.

IS GM'S HOT STOCK HEADING FOR A STALL?

50   General Motors Corp. (GM) has produced several positive earnings surprises recently, and its latest quarter was particularly upbeat. Thanks to surging North American vehicle sales and successful cost-cutting efforts, on Jan. 19 the company announced fourth-quarter earnings that far exceeded analysts' estimates.

51   The consensus guess was for GM to earn $2.65 a share on earnings from continuing operations. But excluding special items, it reported a record $3.25 a share, as fourth-quarter earnings from operations rose 55%, to $2.19 billion. Revenues in the quarter rose to $46.4 billion, up from $42.9 billion in last year. Clearly, management at the No. 1 carmaker is doing a lot right .

EXHIBIT B

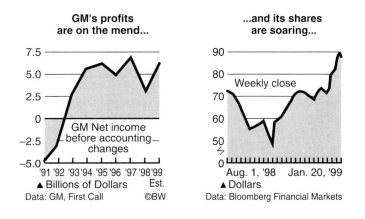

GM's profits
are on the mend...

GM Net income
before accounting
changes

▲ Billions of Dollars   Est.
Data: GM, First Call   ©BW

...and its shares
are soaring...

Weekly close

Aug. 1, '98   Jan. 20, '99
▲ Dollars
Data: Bloomberg Financial Markets

52   In the two days since GM surprised everyone, analysts have been busy ratcheting up their 1999 earnings estimates for the company. The consensus prediction for '99 climbed from $8.23 on Jan. 19 to $8.47 on Jan. 21, according to First Call Corp., which tracks such things. But while analysts might love the earnings report, they haven't raised their overall ratings on the stock. First Call says the average recommendation has remained at 2.1 (on a scale where 1 is a strong buy and 5 is a sell) since mid-December. This is GM's highest average rating since opinion on it hit a low of 2.6 in August, when the company was in the midst of a punishing strike.

53   This paradox—analysts raising earnings estimates, but not recommendations—shows that Wall Street still has reservations about the prospects for GM and the auto industry as a whole. "I'm constantly thinking about whether to raise my recommendation," says Efraim Levy, an analyst with Standard & Poor's equity research group, who maintained his neutral rating on the stock while hiking his 1999 full-year earnings estimate from $7.50 to an eye-opening $9.40 a share.

Cyclical Slide?

54   Although the strong fourth-quarter numbers markedly improved his outlook for GM and the auto industry, "I have to be careful here," Levy says. The auto industry is notoriously cyclical, and competitive pressures are increasing, he says. Plus, GM's stock has already moved up nearly 25% this year alone to close on Jan. 21 at 89 15/16, nearly double its 52-week low of 47 last October. "It's a cyclical company, so when things start tailing off, the stock will react violently to the downside," he says. However, based on the strong fourth-quarter revenues, he doesn't expect sales to start slowing as soon as he once did.

55   Some analysts think GM won't be able to maintain such strong earnings results into 1999. The fourth quarter benefited from a ramp up in production to rebuild inventory after the third quarter's strike, points out Merrill Lynch analyst Nicholas Lobaccaro, who had the highest fourth-quarter earnings estimate on the Street. Yet his 1999 estimate remains well below the $8.47 consensus (although he raised it from $7 to $7.50 on Jan. 21). He predicts that GM will post strong earnings for the first quarter (again, due to inventory building). But after that, slower inventory building, lower sales for the industry, and a need for higher incentives to build market share will crimp earnings in the last nine months of the year, Lobaccaro thinks. And thanks to Brazil's recent currency devaluation, Latin America could spell problems for GM's international operations, he believes.

56   Still, Wall Street has been warning for years that auto industry sales would slow—and they haven't yet. The industry sold 15.6 million units in 1998, when many analysts believed sales would top out at 15 million. Auto stocks were also dented in late summer and early fall because of fears of a global slowdown that never fully materialized. Value portfolio managers, who saw bargains in the group, have made money by ignoring Wall Street's concerns.

EXHIBIT C

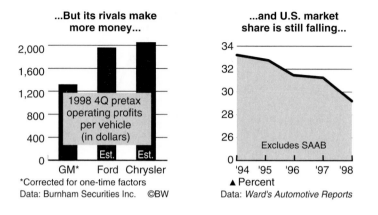

...But its rivals make more money...

1998 4Q pretax operating profits per vehicle (in dollars)

GM*   Ford   Chrysler

*Corrected for one-time factors
Data: Burnham Securities Inc.   ©BW

...and U.S. market share is still falling...

Excludes SAAB

'94   '95   '96   '97   '98
▲ Percent
Data: *Ward's Automotive Reports*

Stronger Now

57 "The economy is still flashing a green light for auto sales," says David Sowerby, a portfolio manager with Loomis, Sayles & Co. in Detroit who started buying GM last July and added to the position as recently as a month ago. Costs of financing are low, consumer confidence is strong, personal incomes are growing, and gas prices are low, he notes. Furthermore, when the economy does finally slow, Sowerby thinks the auto industry will hold up better than it has in the past, because inflation and interest rates are so low. In a normal recession, car sales drop 25% to 30%, he says. But next time, he thinks sales will drop only 10%.

58 Although GM's stock has risen dramatically, Sowerby thinks it has room to climb. It's still trading at a lower forward p-e—11—than Ford and DaimlerChrysler. Plus, GM has more room than the other two to improve earnings by cutting costs and spicing up its product lineup, he says. "Wall Street still needs to warm up perhaps a little bit more to the auto industry and to Detroit," he adds. "And that means there is still more potential for the stock to move higher. Hopefully this is just the start of good things to come."

CASE 29   BusinessWeek

NAVISTAR: GUNNING THE ENGINES

1   Early last year, things were looking bleak for Navistar International Corp. After decades of crippling labor problems and manufacturing snafus, the $6.4 billion Chicago truck and engine maker had suffered another steep earnings slide in fiscal 1996. Then, in a showdown with United Auto Workers members over costs, CEO John R. Horne had been forced to scrap the company's latest truck introduction. By April, disheartened investors let the stock drop to $9 a share, just 50 cents above its low.

2   That's when Horne called his 30 top executives into his office to make a personal plea. Looking for a show of faith in the company, he implored all of them to spend their own money to buy as many shares of Navistar stock as they could. Horne knew it was a lot to ask. Between 1986 to 1996, the company—once known as International Harvester—had tallied the worst total return to shareholders of all publicly traded U.S. companies. But he was convinced that if his managers bought, Wall Street would see that as a sign that Navistar's fortunes were turning.

3   Management's reply was a unanimous no. Many felt that Navistar's shares might drop as low as 6, and all 30 backed away. So Horne bit the bullet alone, buying as much as he could for cash and also turning his 401(k) account entirely into Navistar stock. "I couldn't force them because it was their money," he says. "I laugh at them some now."

4   All the way to the bank, he might add. By the end of 1997, Navistar's stock hit 25, a blazing 172% return to shareholders. In part, the turnaround came thanks to a strong economy and a fortuitously timed boom market for trucks. But Horne, 59, is also reaping the rewards of his fight with the UAW over labor costs and a four-year-long restructuring that is finally taking hold. Indeed, although analysts expect the overall market for heavy-duty tractors and midsize trucks—Navistar's bread and butter—to cool by fall, many believe the revived company could end up stealing share from rivals.

DOG DAYS

5   "Horne has done a magnificent job," says David Pedowitz, director of research at New York's David J. Greene & Co. brokerage firm, the largest outside investor with a 5% stake. "For the first time since the breakup of International Harvester, they're in a position to be a world-class competitor."

6   Certainly, Horne—a 31-year company veteran who stepped up as president in 1991 and as CEO in 1995—has brought Navistar a long way from its dog days in the late 1980s. A UAW strike against International Harvester in 1979, along with the recession, nearly bankrupted the company, which spent most of the decade shrinking just to survive.

7   But under Horne, Navistar began a wide-ranging overhaul of its remaining truck and engine manufacturing lines. He started by drastically slicing the number of products Navistar made. Assembly was rationalized too. While Navistar plants used to build multiple trucks for several different markets, today each one specializes in one type of truck with fewer models.

8   Just as important, Horne got Navistar working on new models again for the first time in years. Having brought out few new products during Navistar's long slide, most of the company's models were aging. But to make sure the new products pay off, Horne also introduced tight financial discipline: Today, new projects only win the nod if they can earn a 17.5% return on equity and a 15% return on assets through a business cycle.

Source: De'Ann Weimer in Chicago, "Navistar: Gunning the Engines," *Business Week:* February 2, 1998.

EXHIBIT A

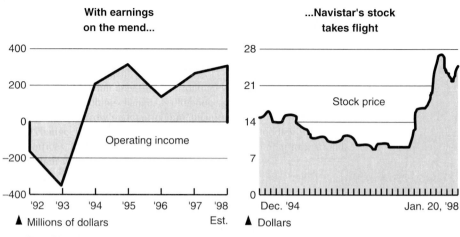

With earnings
on the mend...

...Navistar's stock
takes flight

Data: Bloomberg Financial Markets, Schroder & Co. ©BW

EASY PART

9   Navistar's diesel engine business was the first to be worked over. Horne immediately cut the number of engines in production to two, down from 70 in the mid-'80s, for example. And by 1994, with Navistar's balance sheet improving, he introduced a new engine.

10   Navistar's offering, still the cleanest burning model on the market, quickly attracted major truck manufacturers such as Ford Motor Co. Ford puts the engine in vans and pickups and will soon offer it on its hot Expedition sport utility vehicle. Thanks largely to this model, Navistar's share of the diesel engine market rose from 25% in 1990 to 38% today. That's one big reason operating results climbed from a $355 million loss in 1993 to a $266 million profit for the fiscal year ended last October.

11   Still, that was just the easy part. Tackling problems in Navistar's truck and tractor division proved far tougher. Two years ago, for example, Horne laid out a plan to introduce a new generation of trucks. By simplifying the design of components, Horne hoped to bring out a series of truck and trailer models with interchangeable designs and standardized parts, thus cutting costs while reducing errors on the assembly line. Horne's goal: to reduce the 19 heavy-duty and medium truck designs in his main Springfield (Ill.) plant to one or two.

12   But before he got that far, Horne ran smack into the problem that has dogged Navistar for more than a decade: He needed significant concessions from the UAW, which represents almost 80% of Navistar's truck workers. Horne demanded a wage freeze until 2002 and the flexibility to consolidate production. He took a direct approach. "I showed them the books," he says. "They knew survival of the plants depended on the changes."

13   Union leaders may have known it, but U.S. union members weren't convinced. They rejected the contract outright in August 1996. Convinced that he could never achieve his profitability goals without the changes, Horne cancelled the new trucks. He took a $35 million charge and made clear his next step would be to look abroad for lower labor costs. By August 1997, the workers folded their cards and approved the plan. Horne's tough stance has paid off. He quickly revived plans for the new truck. And since the new labor contract and other manufacturing changes went into effect last fall, productivity at U.S. plants has already risen 15%.

14   Even as it enjoys its status as most improved player, however, Navistar has plenty of battles ahead. The company's long decline has strengthened its competition, particularly Freightliner Corp. of Portland, Ore., which is owned by Germany's Daimler Benz and is now No. 1 in the heavy-truck market, a position Navistar held in 1990. Meanwhile, No. 2 PACCAR Inc. of Bellevue, Wash., has gained share by giving truckers what they want: bigger cabs, longer hoods, and lots of chrome.

15   Navistar is fighting back with two new heavy-duty truck lines produced in Canada, where the union contract was ratified a year ago. Navistar dealer Jerome J. Wahoff of Center City International Truck Inc. in Columbus, Ohio, says Navistar's new cab models such as the Sky-Rise Pro Sleeper will help the company gain market share in the first half of this year. Even rivals at Freightliner concede Navistar is becoming a "tougher competitor."

MEXICAN WAY

16   Still, no truck makers can count on the market's remaining as strong this year as last. Partly because of the strike against United Parcel Service and disrupted rail service in the wake of Union Pacific's troubled merger with Southern Pacific, sales of tractor-trailer rigs jumped an unexpected 10% in 1997.

17   With those gains unlikely to continue, Horne is looking elsewhere for growth. He has spent $167 million on a new Mexican plant that produces trucks for still strong markets such as Brazil and Mexico, for example. It also lets Navistar, which has a contract with Ford through 2013, stay close to that company's Latin American markets. Navistar already enjoyed explosive growth in the Mexican truck market, where it expanded sharply in 1996 and has built a 11.5% market share.

18   Horne has some time to keep inching ahead. Until 2002, Navistar's profits should be sheltered by the $2 billion in tax-loss carryforwards it accumulated in the 1980s. In the meantime, Horne continues to spread his penny-pinching gospel. Indeed, though he's a big basketball fan, he won't buy courtside seats to see his favorite competitor, Chicago Bulls' Michael Jordan, hit the court. When Horne does make it to a home game, it's as a guest. He has other things to do with the fortune he's made in Navistar stock. Like reinvest.

CASE 30

BusinessWeek

P&G's Hottest New Product: P&G

1   At Washington State's Clark County Fair last month, coffee lovers got a front-row seat at a corporate revolution in the making. The local sales force for Procter & Gamble Co. was out in force at the Pancake Feed, distributing samples of P&G's Millstone Coffee. To the amazement of the Fred Meyer supermarket employees running the pancake breakfast, the Procter reps worked the crowd, chatting with customers, even taking turns in the full-size coffee-maker costume with the cup-and-saucer hat. "You don't generally see them out there doing that kind of grassroots work with customers," says Jeanne Lawson, a Fred Meyer buyer. Procter is better known for serving up advertising dollars and display-design tips, she says. "I'd never seen anything like it."

2   But then, P&G has never needed ordinary customers quite so badly. Battered by disappointing revenue growth and demanding retail customers, Procter & Gamble is a company in a bind. Two years ago, its executives boldly declared that the consumer-products giant would double its net sales by 2006, to $70 billion. P&G has consistently missed its growth targets ever since. Olestra, the company's high-profile fat substitute, more than a decade in development, is showing weak sales. And global economic turmoil is crimping overseas operations. Shares have dropped from $94 apiece in July to $70. The behemoth so used to leading the pack is looking lost.

3   So P&G, a company notorious for secrecy, has set itself on a remarkably outward-looking self-improvement plan. Breaking from decades of tradition, it has sought external advice. It is undergoing a structural shift prompted at least in part by outsiders—namely, its big chain-store customers. And it is already rolling out an aggressive global marketing blitz, from working the fairgrounds to marshaling the Internet.

4   Chief Executive John E. Pepper will step down about two years early to make way for President and Chief Operating Officer Durk I. Jager, who will drive the changes. It's a shift away from internal themes of recent years in which Procter focused heavily on such tasks as cost-cutting and shedding underperforming brands. But even as the giant revs its engines to push for faster sales growth, critics wonder if it can overcome both economic turmoil around the world and what will surely be cultural turmoil within its own ranks. "This is a very big deal, for Procter and for all the companies that watch Procter's moves," says Watts Wacker, chairman of consulting firm FirstMatter in Westport, Conn. "But great plans often come with great obstacles."

SIMPLIFY, SIMPLIFY

5   In preparation for the task, Pepper and other top execs have been traversing the country, visiting the CEOs of a dozen major companies, including Kellogg Co. and 3M, in search of advice. Pepper went to Jack Welch at General Electric Co. to learn how the company streamlined global marketing. He persuaded Hewlett-Packard Co. CEO Lewis E. Platt to share enough secrets about new-product development to make a 30-minute instructional video for P&G staffers. The message from all was clear, says Pepper: "What thousands of people have been telling us is that we need to be simpler and move faster."

6   The result of this unprecedented road trip is Organization 2005, a shuffling of the P&G hierarchy and a new product-development process designed to speed innovative offerings to the global market. The old bureaucracy, based on geography, will be reshaped into seven global business units organized by category, such as baby care, beauty care, and fabric-and-home care. The global business units will

Source: Peter Galuszka in Cincinnati and Ellen Neuborne in New York, with Wendy Zellner in Dallas, "P&G's Hottest New Product: P&G," *Business Week:* October 5, 1998.

TABLE 1
Procter & Gamble's Gamble

The Pressure

Big international retailers such as Wal-Mart Stores and Carrefour are pushing suppliers such as P&G for standardized worldwide pricing, marketing, and distribution.

The Plan

Procter is undergoing a major shift in its organization, moving away from its country-by-country setup to a handful of powerful departments that will supervise categories such as hair care, diapers, and soap on a global scale.

The Risks

Procter's plan will take two years to implement and depends heavily on increasing market share and sales volume in international markets, many of which are reeling from economic instability.

develop and sell products on a worldwide basis, erasing the old system that let Procter's country managers rule as colonial governors, setting prices and handling products as they saw fit.

SWIFT ROLLOUT

7   This new global vision has already had an accidental test run. Last year, P&G introduced an extension of its Pantene shampoo line. The ad campaign for the product was almost entirely visual, with images of beautiful women and their lustrous hair, and had a very limited script. That meant the campaign was easily translated and shipped to P&G markets around the world without the usual months of testing and tinkering. The result: P&G was able to introduce the brand extension in 14 countries in six months, vs. the two years it took to get the original shampoo into stores abroad. "It's a success story that gets quite a bit of talk internally," says Chris T. Allen, a marketing professor at the University of Cincinnati, who spent his sabbatical year working in the P&G new-products department. "I see the reorganization as an attempt to do more Pantenes on a regular basis."

8   P&G didn't come to this global focus entirely on its own. Its biggest chain-store customers, such as Wal-Mart Stores Inc. and French-owned Carrefour, have been agitating for just such a program to mirror their own global expansion. It has been Topic A at retail conventions for months, says Robin Lanier, senior vice-president for industry affairs at the International Mass Retail Assn. While P&G craves an international image for its products, retailers want something more tangible: a global price. As it stands, prices are negotiable on a country or regional basis. What an international retailer pays for Crest in the U.S. could be considerably less than what it costs the chain in Europe or Latin America. A consistent global price gives big chains more power to plan efficiently and save money. Wal-Mart Chief Executive David D. Glass describes his company's goal as "global sourcing," which includes worldwide relationships on pricing and distribution. Moving P&G products from regional to global management is "pointing somewhat in that direction," Glass says.

9   In addition to marketing and pricing, global business units will supervise new-product development. P&G will move away from its long-used "sequential" method, which tested products first in midsize U.S. cities and then gradually rolled them out to the world. An example: Swiffer, a new disposable mop designed by P&G, is being tested simultaneously in Cedar Rapids, Iowa; Pittsfield, Mass.; and Sens, France, in hopes of sculpting a globally popular product right out of the box.

10   Jager concedes that it won't be a quick fix. The new regime won't start until January and won't really be functioning for about 18 to 24 months. He expects to see some top-line growth improvement within 12 to 16 months, with obviously better results two years out. Many observers doubt that will be fast enough to make the 2006 deadline. "[The plan] seems to work on paper, but it requires an accelerated sales growth in the final four years," says Constance M. Maneaty, an analyst at Bear, Stearns & Co. "We haven't seen that kind of sales growth from them in a while."

11   Even if P&G could implement its strategy more quickly, it would still run into the ugly realities of global economic markets. For its extra $35 billion in revenues through 2006, Procter is counting

EXHIBIT A

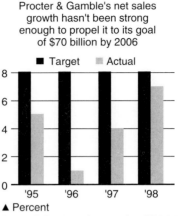

Missing the mark

Procter & Gamble's net sales growth hasn't been strong enough to propel it to its goal of $70 billion by 2006

■ Target   Actual

▲ Percent

*Procter & Gamble estimates gains of 6%–7%
Data: Procter & Gamble Co.   ©BW

on about $8 billion from emerging markets in Eastern Europe, China, and Latn America, says Clayton C. Daley Jr., P&G's treasurer, who becomes chief financial officer in October. Yet Asian emerging markets are likely to remain mired in deep economic slumps for at least two more years. Recent turmoil in Russia, which was a bright prospect for Procter just a year ago, has gotten so bad that the company has temporarily halted shipments there. "Growing in underdeveloped geographies is clearly questionable," says Jay Freedman, an analyst at Lincoln Capital, a big institutional holder of Procter & Gamble stock. "Whatever they thought the purchasing power of those new customers was going to be is less now."

"A LOT OF EX-CHIEFS"

12   Procter has additional obstacles closer to home. How, for example, will tradition-bound P&G managers react to the new hierarchy? "You're going from 144 chiefs to 8. That's a lot of ex-chiefs," says consultant Wacker. And everyone will be affected by the change in tone that is sure to come from the corner office. Gentlemanly Pepper, 60, will be succeeded by Jager, a Dutch-born P&G lifer with a reputation for aggressive moves and abrasiveness. In the 1980s, he turned around Procter's failing Japanese business with such a fury that his Japanese managers called him "Crazy Man Durk" behind his back.

13   Crazy or no, Jager is sticking to the 2006 target date. He's wasting no time stepping into his new role as champion of the global focus: Already, even before taking on the official title of CEO, he has started preaching the new structure to P&G managers. After all, the clock is ticking.

CASE 31   BusinessWeek

LEW PLATT'S FIX-IT PLAN FOR HEWLETT-PACKARD

1   For years, CEO Lewis E. Platt has used his annual management-review meeting to warn Hewlett-Packard Co.'s executives not to get sloppy. After all, the company was growing at more than 20% a year, making it the fastest-growing $30 billion company in the U.S. It would be easy for giddy executives to become less watchful. Sure enough, by last January's meeting, the company had missed Wall Street's expectations for five straight quarters. So to kick off the weekend meeting at a Monterey (Calif.) hotel, Platt tried a different tactic. The normally amiable CEO blasted his top 200-plus managers for shoddy execution, lax cost controls, and overreliance on slow-growth markets.

2   Then, a steely Platt told them to write down "two things you'll do differently on Monday morning." Since all the managers had laptops, Platt got their plans immediately. And he didn't like what he saw. Disappointed, he laid into them the next day. "You guys just don't get it, do you?" Platt scolded. "I expect more coherent plans from you moving forward," recalls an attendee.

FALLING SHORT

3   Now, Platt is facing similar expectations from investors. Since mid-1996, after years of blowing away the most bullish estimates, HP's sales have settled below the 20% growth clip analysts had come to expect. For the 1997 fiscal year, the company recorded a 12% revenue growth rate, down from 22% the year before. Worse, earnings have zigzagged wildly as the company has struggled with factors ranging from the Asian flu to erratic execution to falling prices for personal computers and printers.

4   The latest example: Although sales growth is back up—rising 16%, to $12 billion—HP shocked analysts with an 18% jump in operating expenses and a 12% dip in earnings in the quarter that ended on Apr. 30. That sent the stock spiraling downward 26%, where it is stuck at around 60. Concedes Platt: "The competition has closed the gap. Our execution just isn't what it used to be."

5   Wait a nanosecond. Not HP. This is the company that has been synonymous with progressive, top-notch management. HP is not only the inventor but also a top practitioner of many of the business philosophies and tactics that have led to Silicon Valley's global dominance of high tech—pushing the envelope by giving employees the freedom to innovate and take risks.

6   But in the past year, the Palo Alto (Calif.) giant has suffered a rash of embarrassing gaffes. In the summer of 1997, HP ran short on supplies of its flagship LaserJet printer for several months. Then it suffered two painful delays in the delivery of high-end computer servers. While HP prospered for decades on cushy 50%-plus gross profit margins, it now gets more than 60% of its revenue from lower-margin commodity products such as PCs and printers. That has dragged corporate gross margins down from 47.2% in 1990 to 34% in 1997—but operating costs have risen the past two quarters. "The conventional wisdom, that HP is a superbly managed company, is taking a bit of a body blow," says analyst Daniel R. Kunstler of J.P. Morgan Securities.

7   To be sure, HP remains a powerhouse by almost any measure. Despite falling short of Wall Street's expectations, the most recent quarterly sales growth topped the rate for IBM, Sun Microsystems, and Compaq Computer. As for earnings, which totaled $685 million in the quarter, HP has an insurance policy that rivals envy: a $4 billion annual annuity in lucrative paper, ink, and toner-cartridge sales from its printer business, where it enjoys 50%-plus U.S. market share. And HP remains a top player in most of its markets, including PCs, where it has vaulted from the 27th place in 1992 to No. 4 today.

Source: Peter Burrows in Palo Alto, California, "Lew Platt's Fix-It Plan for Hewlett-Packard," *Business Week:* July 13, 1998.

8   Still, the company hasn't come up with any blockbuster innovations of late, long an HP hallmark. The company has done some pioneering work in such areas as digital photography and printing off the Internet, but it has failed to transform these efforts into vibrant businesses. Instead, current and former executives say that HP has become so focused on protecting its existing businesses that it has taken its eye off the critical job of creating tomorrow's new markets.

"MAINTENANCE MODE"

9   Without breakthrough products—which typically command premium prices because competition is limited—the company is forced to compete largely on price. "I look at HP as being in maintenance mode," says former No. 2 Richard E. Belluzzo, who left in January to run Silicon Graphics Corp. "HP has got tremendous potential, people, technology, and a great brand, but there's something missing [that would] move the company to the next level."

10   Indeed, Belluzzo had been pressing hard for drastic change during his final months at HP. Former and current managers say this put him at loggerheads with Platt, who wanted to move more slowly. Belluzzo, for example, pushed to slash pricey overseas sales offices and divert investment from slower growth, old-line HP businesses to invest in high-growth areas such as PCs, say current and former executives. Platt complained to board members late last fall that Belluzzo's superaggressive efforts had become overly disruptive, they say. Platt won't discuss Belluzzo. "I'm not going down that rathole. It has nothing to do with the issues we face as a company."

11   Today, Platt is clearly focused on HP's future with a two-part fix-it plan firmly in motion. First, he needs to get HP's house in order by cutting costs and sharpening execution. Longer term, though, the 57-year-old CEO wants to ensure growth by extending current businesses and creating brand new ones. To do this, he is building on the belief of founders Bill Hewlett and David Packard that smart people will do great things if given the independence and authority to make their own decisions—fast. So Platt is easing back on corporate control of HP's business units. He is giving managers more freedom to define their own goals and policies.

COSTLY DISCOUNTS

12   But with freedom comes accountability. Through new pay policies, Platt hopes to tie each manager's salary to the performance of his or her unit. Platt was a guinea pig for this last year, when the board linked some 40% of his compensation to HP's performance. Now, Platt has asked the board to do the same for HP's top 40 executives.

13   The company's PC chief, Duane E. Zitzner, already is adopting the same philosophy. Starting this quarter, Zitzner will award stock options to his managers based on revenue growth, as well as shareholder value. That way, employees won't be tempted to offer unreasonable price breaks to make quota—a mistake that cost HP dearly last quarter, when it offered discounts of up to 50% to keep business from rivals such as Compaq. "We chased deals we shouldn't have chased," says Zitzner. "You get so into the battle that you can lose perspective."

14   Platt also is hacking away at the company's spiraling costs. He put out a call for a 5% cut in operating expenses—a pledge he made at a May analysts' meeting where he proclaimed: "I'm mad as hell, and I'm not going to take it anymore." Now, the newly empowered division heads are responding quickly. The personal-computer division, which shocked people by losing an estimated $50 million on a 70% increase in unit sales, is out banging on suppliers for price breaks. "We saw much more of a tough-guy attitude from HP within a week of the earnings announcement," says a top U.S. supplier of HP's PC unit. "They were saying: 'It's a new era, and you better cut our prices or we'll go somewhere else.'"

15   And then there's R&D, where the company spent $3 billion last year. In the past, each HP unit kicked in a portion of sales to fund the company's vaunted HP Labs. That's fine for high-margin businesses that need top-notch technology, but it's a financial ball and chain for the PC business, which must compete with the likes of Dell Computer. The new lab tab? HP businesses now pay the labs 8%

TABLE 1
The Diary of a Stumbling High-Tech Leader

November, 1995

With sales of printers and PCs booming, CEO Lew Platt tells Wall Street HP will increase investment to sustain its 20%-plus growth.

July, 1996

Third-quarter year-over-year sales growth dips below 20% for the first time in years, and earnings plunge by 26%—thanks mostly to a $150 million write-off in disk drives and margin pressure in PCs and printers.

Spring, 1997

While belt-tightening keeps earnings up, sales growth falls to a dismal 5% in the second quarter. Sales remain soft through the summer because of delays in the company's high-end servers and medical devices. Platt calls for cost-cutting, yet HP adds 2,600 new employees during its third quarter.

Fall, 1997

HP, the laser-printer king, botches a product transition, leaving the company with almost no inventory for months.

January, 1998

At a meeting of general managers just days after the departure of No. 2 Rick Belluzzo, Platt unveils a unit to seed new business opportunities, and demands better execution and cost controls.

May, 1998

The Asian crisis, PC price wars, and rising expenses cause HP to warn of yet another disappointing quarter. The stock drops 14% in one day, to 69. Platt cancels all new hiring, and cuts discretionary spending.

of their R&D budget, a figure tailored to the development needs of each division. "This is an example of Lew letting us run our own businesses," says Webb McKinney, who heads the consumer PC unit.

16   In the long run, though, Platt's No. 1 worry is growth. In late 1997, Chief Financial Officer Robert P. Wayman did a study of companies generating $40 billion-plus in annual sales and found that they grow, on average, less than a piddling 5%—not nearly enough to support HP's shrinking margins. That lit a fire under Platt, who is now trying to spark new innovation.

SKEPTICISM

17   One method: He has created a special unit to incubate promising new technology ideas. The first project is a whizzy new computer-display technology that Platt says could generate "billions" in sales. Unit chiefs must also show where they're spending their money. The goal: a higher mix of investment in new or fast-growing markets. "It's not enough anymore to just make your numbers," says Richard H. Lampman, who runs HP's efforts in computer research and development. "You have to show you're contributing to the future."

18   Will Platt's plan work? Some people are skeptical. His recent changes, they say, may not be enough to help HP address its biggest long-term challenge: developing new markets. After all, PCs and laser printers are a fixture in Corporate America, and penetration of home PCs is approaching 45%. Critics say that to meet its goal of continued 15%-plus growth, HP needs to plow fresh ground. Says former HP PC chief Robert Frankenberg, who now runs Encanto Networks Inc., a maker of networking gear: "HP needs to be less protective of its current kingdoms and go attack some undefended hills."

19   More than ever, that approach depends on Platt. After three months, the 32-year HP veteran decided in early May not to replace Belluzzo, who ran the printer and PC businesses that account for 83% of total revenue. Now, rather than just focusing on corporatewide functions, Platt is overseeing the major businesses himself. He heads an executive committee, which includes the chiefs of HP's six key business units. "We all love Rick [Belluzzo], but each of our businesses is big enough to deserve a closer relationship with Lew," says Antonio M. Perez, who runs the $8 billion ink-jet printer business.

TABLE 2
Platt's Fix-It Plan

Tighten Up Operations

With PC prices and Asian sales falling, he has called for 5% cuts in operating expenses.

Take the Day-to-Day Reins

Since the January departure of No. 2 Rick Belluzzo—who oversaw units accounting for 83% of total revenues—Platt has created an eight-person executive committee to stay in closer touch with all parts of the business.

Unshackle the Business Units

Platt is pushing HP's decentralization even further. Rather than companywide measures, managers are encouraged to devise financial models, compensation plans, and tactics for their own markets. He's also lighting a fire under HP's collegial culture with new pay-for-performance policies.

Hunt Out New Growth

A new unit will serve as an incubator for good ideas—many of which now get lost in HP Labs or dropped by overstretched product groups. Also, managers are now evaluated not just for financial performance but also by how much of their spending is allocated to emerging opportunities.

20   HP must do more. Under his six-year CEO tenure, HP has had plenty of good ideas, but little to show for them. Consider networked printers. Few analysts argue with HP's claim that networked printers will one day replace pricey copiers. The theory: Why should companies incur the high cost of copying and distributing documents that may not even be read when they could be stored on high-speed printers and printed out as needed? Boeing Co., for example, is moving to store its huge service manuals online so that technicians can print just the parts they need. Yet HP has made little headway pushing its "distribute-and-print" vision, say analysts.

21   Meanwhile, HP still hasn't made much of a dent on the Internet, a mark of shame for Silicon Valley's granddaddy. Having purchased VeriFone Inc., the leading manufacturer of credit-card readers and authorization software, HP hopes to become a top electronic-commerce player by outfitting PCs with VeriFone's credit-card readers. This would allow cybershoppers a secure way to buy products or download E-cash from home. So far, there's a small pilot program with Citicorp in Manhattan, but little other progress.

22   There's also been little movement in Internet imaging. Analysts drool over the potential sales of printers, inks, and computers if HP could accelerate development of technologies to let consumers and corporations print documents such as coupons, articles, and annual reports right off the Web. Many technical hurdles exist, but "as the overwhelming market leader, you look to HP to solve them," says Deutsche Bank Securities analyst Michael K. Kwatinetz.

23   The big digital photography initiation is off to a slow start, too. While HP's $400 PhotoSmart printer was the first machine capable of matching a snapshot in image quality, HP has failed to follow up with an all-out marketing blitz that could persuade consumers to give up their trusty old cameras. The result: HP has sold fewer than 25,000 PhotoSmart units since it hit the shelves a year ago, says analyst Marco Boer with market researcher IT Strategies. Later this year, however, the company is expected to roll out new products that let shutterbugs wirelessly zap their digital shots from HP cameras to special HP printers—a departure from most other schemes, which require a PC to do this.

24   Platt says give it time. He insists that HP launched its digital photography business knowing camera makers had yet to come up with digital gear offering the required image quality at a price most consumers could afford. "We could be accused of developing some of these markets too early," he says.

25   Besides, argues Platt, HP is turning up the innovation engine now. CFO Wayman says that with overall sales exceeding internal projections by 5% to 7% in recent years, unit chiefs were simply too busy keeping up with demand to focus on new opportunities. "When you're running as fast as we've been, you tend to pay less attention to cultivating seeds," he says.

26   That's about to change. In March, Platt O.K.'d a plan to hatch a series of internal "software startups" to attack promising cyberniches. Rather than get lost in HP's sprawling software organization,

TABLE 3
HP's Squeeze on Margins

1992

Total revenues: $16.4 billion

Overall gross margin: 44.2%

Business	Share of Revenues	Gross Margins
Laser printers	15.9%	43%
Services	14.0	NA
Test & measurement equipment	13.4	NA
Unix computers	11.0	47
Printer supplies	6.7	28
Ink-jet printers	5.7	40
PCs	5.7	31
Other	27.6	

1998

Total revenues: $48.8 billion

Overall gross margin: 32.7%

Business	Share of Revenues	Gross Margins
Laser printers	12.5%	39%
Services	12.1	NA
Test & measurement equipment	9.4	49
Unix computers	11.1	46
Printer supplies	13.3	33
Ink-jet printers	19.5	20
PCs	19.1	19
Other	3.0	

Data: Goldman, Sachs & Co.

these units are set off on their own. Staffers are measured and compensated for attaining the same milestones that venture capitalists demand of typical startups, such as delivering code on time or attaining a key customer. On June 29, HP unveiled the first of these: HP OpenPix ImageIgniter, which makes software to let cybershoppers easily view and manipulate high-resolution images. Says Platt: "If we see good ideas, we'll fund them."

SPOTTY RECORD

27 Now, Platt must prove he will move to turn these nascent efforts into big businesses capable of sustaining HP's growth goals. There are plenty of skeptics. "Under Lew's leadership, there's been an aversion to risk," says a former HP executive. "I can't point to one big new business that has been created since he's been in place." Argues Platt: "For those who say we're not attacking new kingdoms, look at PCs."

28   There are signs that HP may not have the stomach for the new fast-growth, low-margin businesses that dominate high-tech these days. Since its latest quarterly disappointment, the company has backed

away from a 1997 pledge to become the PC market share leader by 2001. "We're not going to chase market share at all costs," says PC chief Zitzner.

29   Instead, some board members are quietly wondering if PC sales are worth fighting for at all, admits Wayman. "This certainly raises questions about how good [the PC] business is," he says. Platt disagrees. The scrappy PC market is just the training ground HP needs to prove that big companies run as fast as little ones. "We envision a model where most of the computer business looks like the PC business," Platt says. "You can't duck that. It's the future." Platt has to move boldly to make that future as bright as HP's past.

CASE 32

BusinessWeek

HOW MOTOROLA LOST ITS WAY

1   For years, Motorola Inc. had supplied virtually all the wireless phones to Ameritech Corp. But when it came time to switch to the new digital technology, something went haywire: Motorola wasn't ready. So in the summer of 1997, Ameritech rolled out its digital service using phones from rival Qualcomm Inc., a San Diego upstart. "I could not stop my strategy or my business plan and was forced to go with vendors that were ready," says Marc Barnett, Ameritech Cellular's director of product marketing.

2   An isolated case? If only. Instead, one of the world's most admired companies, known for cutting-edge technology and gold-plated quality, is coming up stunningly short these days. The former trailblazer in two-way radios, cell phones, pagers, and computer chips has missed a digital beat and now finds itself scrambling to catch up. Even then, its products don't always pass muster. In 1994, Motorola claimed 60% of the U.S. market in wireless phones, according to Herschel Shosteck Associates. Today, it has 34%.

3   The company's wireless-equipment business hasn't fared any better. In the U.S., Motorola has lost crucial ground to Lucent Technologies Inc. and Northern Telecom Ltd.—in part because it has sold faulty products. On top of the problems Motorola has created for itself, a downturn in the semiconductor and paging industries and turmoil in Asia haven't helped.

4   Now, the go-go growth company of a few years ago is barely inching along. Revenue growth, which soared an average 27% a year between 1993 and 1995, has slowed to 5% in the past two years, to $29.8 billion in 1997. Profits have tumbled, too: down 33% since 1995, to $1.2 billion in 1997, with a 25% plunge expected this year. As for shareholder return, it has averaged less than 1% annually in the past three years, vs. an average 54% in the previous three years. Says Steven Goldman, a professor at Lehigh University who has done consulting work for Motorola: "It's hard to imagine that six or seven years ago Motorola was one of the most admired companies in the world. Now, you talk about Nokia and Ericsson and how they're eating Motorola's lunch."

5   Even worse for Motorola in the long haul, its hard-earned reputation for quality is being questioned. The same company that won the Malcolm Baldrige Quality Award in 1988 and once insisted that every executive presentation begin with an example of how to improve quality, now finds itself fielding customer complaints. These came to a head in March, when Motorola lost a $500 million contract with wireless carrier PrimeCo Personal Communications. The carrier's beef: Motorola's equipment would sometimes shut down, leaving customers unable to make calls.

6   Motorola admits to having problems in recent years but insists the future is bright. CEO Christopher B. Galvin declined to comment for this article, but Motorola executives who report to him say he has set a hurdle of 15% to 20% revenue growth and, despite the company's problems, expects to achieve that within the next year or two. Galvin is betting that the industries the company is in will grow 15% a year, and expansion into new markets will be frosting on the cake. "We're not very happy with the last few years of business results," says Merle L. Gilmore, an executive vice-president. "Just as we have renewed businesses regularly in our history . . . we expect to be able to renew our business again."

7   One promising new market: satellite communications. Motorola's flagbearer there, Iridium, will blast the last two pieces of a 66-satellite constellation into the sky on April 30 and begin offering new voice and paging services for business travelers in September. Iridium, 17.7% owned by Motorola, could generate revenues of $2.6 billion by 2000, says Chase Securities Inc. "If you throw our product in your briefcase, you know you can make a call from anywhere on the planet, and people can get

Source: Roger O. Crockett in Chicago, with Peter Elstrom in New York, "How Motorola Lost Its Way," *Business Week:* May 4, 1998.

to you," boasts Iridium chief Edward F. Staiano. Motorola has $6.3 billion in Iridium contracts and it's developing satellite expertise that should help win future business.

8   To be sure, Motorola remains a force to be reckoned with. Even with its market-share losses and customer complaints, it's still the world's largest maker of mobile phones and a top supplier of wireless equipment. It's a leading maker of digital phones overseas. And it remains the most sought-after brand name in mobile phones. Almost every carrier that criticizes the company for its late products says it does so because it wants them so badly. "We need them back in the game," says Dennis F. Strigl, CEO of Bell Atlantic Mobile.

9   But time is crucial. Galvin, 48, the grandson of Motorola's founder, is working furiously to stem market-share losses and return the company to its roots as a creator of top-notch products. Since taking over 16 months ago, he has replaced the heads of the wireless-phone and -equipment businesses and has installed top lieutenants in key posts throughout the company.

10   Galvin also has railed against a culture that he thinks, at times, has been too smug, too engineering driven, and too focused on internal rivalries. To foster cooperation among divisions, he's starting to pay top execs based on companywide performance—not just their own division's results. At the same time, Galvin has insisted that sales reps better serve customers. Already Motorola is working closely with AT&T Wireless Services to develop an innovative digital phone. "They're bending over backward for us," says an AT&T executive. "That's never happened before."

"WARRING TRIBES"

11   The most dramatic change is expected later this spring, when Galvin will restructure the company for the second time in his short tenure. His aim: to consolidate operations into three major groups, including a communications division that will pull together mobile phones, wireless equipment, two-way radios, pagers, and cable modems. This will encourage the communications teams to coordinate business plans, share ideas, and cut down on development costs.

12   This also could go a long way toward curbing Motorola's culture of "warring tribes." In recent years, division heads had almost total control of their operations, which meant they could compete or simply refuse to cooperate with other divisions. That culture worked well at times, especially when the cellular operations cannibalized Motorola's own two-way radio business and became a much bigger business. But recently, internal fiefdoms left Motorola's divisions badly out of step. The semiconductor group wouldn't make chips other divisions wanted to use. And the wireless-equipment group sold customers digital gear two years ago—while the wireless-phone unit is just now coming out with digital phones for those systems.

13   Hopes are high that these efforts will put the company back on track. To head the new communications division, Galvin has tapped Gilmore, a long-time confidant who had been running the company's operations in Europe, Africa, and the Middle East. "The most important objective," says Gilmore, "is that the organization will be able to serve the customer better."

14   But will it? Motorola has a good shot at recovering if Galvin is willing to make bold moves. Top of the list: He needs to decide whether to sell the company's struggling wireless-equipment business or buy a telecom-switch maker to bolster it. More important, he must take the starch out of Motorola's culture so its executives get back to listening to customers—instead of dictating to them.

JARRING PICTURE

15   So how did the once mighty Motorola lose its way? How could a company once dubbed the "American Samurai" for blazing a trail overseas, find itself being beaten to the punch by European giants and outfoxed by U.S. startups? Interviews with current and former Motorola executives, customers, rivals, and analysts paint a jarring picture of the company's fall from grace.

16   Motorola's tale is a cautionary one. It's a lesson in how a company reaches the pinnacle of its industry—and becomes blinded by its own success. It was hubris, say insiders, that kept executives from recognizing better technologies, changing markets, and customers' needs. What followed were management missteps, ill-timed strategies, and spotty execution.

EXHIBIT A

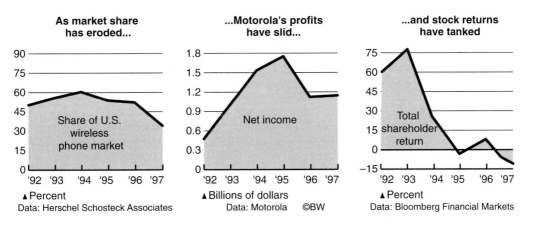

As market share has eroded...

Share of U.S. wireless phone market

▲ Percent
Data: Herschel Schosteck Associates

...Motorola's profits have slid...

Net income

▲ Billions of dollars
Data: Motorola ©BW

...and stock returns have tanked

Total shareholder return

▲ Percent
Data: Bloomberg Financial Markets

17   It began in the heady days of 1995. At the helm of the company sat Gary L. Tooker, a personable if not charismatic executive who had started working in Motorola's semiconductor operation 33 years earlier. He had replaced the much praised George M. C. Fisher, who had left to head Eastman Kodak Co. in 1993. At the time, Robert L. Galvin, the son of the founder and the company's chief for 27 years, polled the board to find out if they would name his son, Chris, then a senior executive vice-president, as CEO.

18   Board members balked. They thought the younger Galvin, then 43, was too green. He had started out at Motorola in 1973 selling two-way radios and had headed several key businesses, including the paging division. But some executives still considered him a lightweight, in part because he did not have an engineering degree like most of the other top brass. Still, it was a matter of when Galvin would become CEO, not if. "Inside, people knew it was a monarchy," says one former senior executive.

19   Tooker, by contrast, was an engineer who had helped Motorola prosper largely by giving division heads free rein to run their own show. The company owned the wireless-phone business: Its share of the U.S. market had increased to 60% in 1994—Nokia Corp. and L.M. Ericsson were barely a blip on the wireless scene. In January, 1995, Motorola announced results for 1994 that brought Wall Street to its feet: Revenues were up 31%, to $22.2 billion, and profits soared 53%, to $1.6 billion.

20   But this also was the year that U.S. wireless carriers began waking up to digital technology. The digital era promised new services like Caller I.D., paging, and short messaging. The carriers were hooked.

21   Not so Motorola. In one telling meeting in February, 1995, top execs from Ameritech met with Motorola's brass at the cellular industry's big trade show in New Orleans. "I need [digital] handsets . . . in a year," Barnett recalls saying. Motorola's cellular-phone chief, Robert N. Weisshappel, wasn't there, but his second-in-command did her best to reassure Barnett. "We want to meet your goals," said Suzette Steiger, according to Barnett. "Let me take it under review." AT&T, Bell Atlantic, and others were delivering the same message.

22   But inside Motorola, it was falling on deaf ears. Weisshappel, a bespectacled former engineer, had spent 24 years at Motorola and deserved much of the credit for making its cellular-phone business dominant. Known for his explosive temper, his greatest skill was in designing ever smaller stylish phones.

23   In 1995, he believed that what most consumers wanted was a better analog phone, not a digital phone that would have to be big and bulky because the technology was so new. "Forty-three million analog customers can't be wrong," he told a small gathering of execs at the cellular group's headquarters in suburban Chicago, according to one former employee. "It was hard to get him to stop talking about [analog]," recalls one executive. "The rank and file were scared to death."

24   But Weisshappel had what he thought was an ace up his sleeve. In January, 1996, Motorola introduced the ultrasleek StarTAC phone. The phone had taken two years and millions of dollars to develop—and it was a design marvel, smaller than a cigarette pack. "Motorola has taken what was never thought possible and made it a reality," Weisshappel crowed at the time.

25   Sure, the StarTAC wasn't digital, but Weisshappel thought he could use his design breakthrough to hold back the tide of technology. In the summer of 1996, he and his top execs introduced the so-called Signature program. The idea was simple: Motorola would distribute the StarTAC only to carriers that had bought a high percentage, typically 75%, of their mobile phones from Motorola—and agreed to promote the phones' features in stand-alone displays. The goal was to boost margins with higher-priced products such as the $1,500 StarTAC and, at the same time, protect Motorola's market share.

26   The Signature program turned into a fiasco. In one meeting in Bell Atlantic Mobile's executive conference room at its Bedminster (N.J.) headquarters, Weisshappel and his team laid out the requirements for the carrier's executives with what Bell Atlantic Corp. says was a "you-must" attitude. The carrier's Strigl quickly became furious. "Do you mean to tell me that [if we don't agree to the program] you don't want to sell the StarTAC in Manhattan?" he recalls telling Weisshappel. Weisshappel declined comment on the incident. Bell Atlantic wasn't the only company to take exception. GTE Corp. and BellSouth Corp. refused to participate in the program, and sales to both carriers dropped.

27   The company's digital delays weren't caused only by Weisshappel's preoccupation with StarTAC. Motorola tried buying semiconductors from rival Qualcomm to get into the digital game faster. But Weisshappel felt Qualcomm's prices were excessive, and he stopped buying in 1995 to develop the chips internally. As it turned out, the development took two years, cost millions of dollars, and lost the company precious time.

TENSE MEETING

28   Meanwhile, customers were launching digital service—without Motorola phones. In February, 1997, two years after he had first asked for digital phones, Ameritech's Barnett met again with Steiger. "We're placing orders now," he told her. "Do you have phones?" She didn't. Ameritech reluctantly turned to Qualcomm.

29   By early 1997, newly minted CEO Chris Galvin had had enough. Rivals Nokia and Qualcomm were putting a painful dent in Motorola's market share. In a tense meeting at Motorola's headquarters, Galvin demanded to know why the mobile-phone group hadn't released key digital phones. Weisshappel had heard all this before and was tired of the badgering. "I guess I'll just buy Qualcomm," he joked, according to one person at the meeting. Weisshappel left the company the following August.

30   By that time, Motorola had long ago made the decision to make digital phones. But it wasn't that simple. There were three competing digital standards to choose from in the U.S. Code Division Multiple Access (CDMA) technology offers six times the capacity of analog systems—and is now the most popular, with 50% of the U.S. market. Time Division Multiple Access (TDMA), which has three times the capacity, accounts for one-quarter of today's market. And Global Standard for Mobile Communications (GSM), the third standard with two to three times the capacity, claims 25% of the U.S. market and is the technology of choice in Europe.

31   Motorola developed its GSM phones first and has become a big supplier overseas, as well as in that segment of the U.S. market. But it has been slow to develop phones for the other two U.S. standards. "We underestimated the engineering effort to bring these products to market," says James P. Caile, corporate vice-president for marketing in Motorola's mobile-phone group. "It's an embarrassment to us."

32   By all accounts, Motorola's wireless-equipment group should be red-faced, too. In 1995, executives had been aggressively developing digital products, but they put all their chips on just one standard in the U.S.—CDMA. As it turned out, that eliminated Motorola from 50% of the U.S. market. The irony, say former executives, is the company had been developing TDMA equipment but abandoned it to focus on CDMA. "We were way ahead of everybody," laments one engineer who worked at the company during that period. Motorola says it dropped TDMA because it didn't think it had strong enough relationships with TDMA carriers to land deals.

33   Still, Motorola did have some big CDMA wins. In September, 1995, Primeco tapped the company to help build its national network. And Motorola would go on to nab $5 billion in equipment contracts in 1997.

TABLE 1
Motorola's History

It hit the pinnacle of success only to follow it with management missteps and ill-timed strategies.

September 25, 1928

Paul Galvin and his brother Joseph Galvin found Galvin Manufacturing in Chicago.

1948

Designs the first portable FM two-way radio, a backpack walkie-talkie that's the predecessor of today's cellular phones. The company goes public.

1955

Introduces its first pagers—a business Motorola comes to dominate with 85% market share.

1974

Unveils its first microprocessor, the 6800. By 1997, Motorola's computer chip business grows to $8 billion in sales—21% of the company's revenues.

1983

After 20 years and $200 million in development, the company's first cellular telephone network begins commercial operation.

1988

The company's nine-year push to emphasize quality products culminates when it receives the Malcolm Baldrige National Quality Award from Congress.

1988

George Fisher succeeds Robert Galvin as chief executive officer, the first non-Galvin to head the company.

1990

Motorola discontinues development of wireless infrastructure based on a standard called TDMA in favor of an alternative, CDMA, which is supposed to have higher capacity to carry phone calls. Today, the lack of TDMA equipment means Motorola can't supply 25% of the digital U.S. wireless infrastructure market.

1990

GTE, Southwestern Bell, BellSouth, and Metro One drop Motorola because of poor switching capabilities in its wireless equipment.

1993

Gary Tooker takes over as CEO after Fisher leaves for Eastman Kodak.

1993

Motorola raises $800 million for the Iridium satellite system, which promises to supply communications to every part of the world.

1993

Motorola and Northern Telecom discontinue their joint venture for wireless equipment. Lack of a strong switch partner hurts Motorola's ability to deliver end-to-end wireless networks.

1994

Top execs decide against buying General Instrument, a leader in cable TV set-top boxes. Tooker and others think Motorola's expertise is in wireless communications—not cable infrastructure. The decision keeps Motorola from wrapping its cable modem expertise into GI's set-top boxes.

1995

Execs decide not to buy CDMA chip from Qualcomm because of what it considers exorbitant costs. Developing CDMA chip internally slows introduction of Motorola phones.

Summer 1996

Discontinues production of its Marco and Envoy handheld computers, which are design marvels but commercial flops.

1996

Introduces the StarTAC, Motorola's smallest cellular phone. Motorola's decision to limit distribution to carriers that buy most of their phones from the company infuriates customers.

TABLE 1
concluded

January 1, 1997

Christopher Galvin, grandson of the founder, becomes CEO.

August 1997

Apple Computer interim CEO Steve Jobs pulls the plug on licensing the Macintosh to cloners. Motorola, which developed the PowerPC chip used in the Mac and had launched a Mac-clone business, has to fold its clone operation.

March 1998

Because its network shut down for up to two hours, wireless carrier PrimeCo replaces Motorola with Lucent Technologies as the supplier of wireless infrastructure for a $500 million contract.

April 7, 1998

First-quarter earnings plummet to half those of a year ago, and Motorola warns that profits will remain below forecasts for several quarters. The stock plunges 11%.

May 1998

Galvin plans to announce a restructuring into three major groups: communications, semiconductors, and components. The goal is to better coordinate the R&D and marketing in the divisions making consumer products such as cellular phones and pagers.

34   While Motorola was scrapping for contracts, it had to protect what has been the Achilles' heel of its wireless-equipment business: its lack of a telecom switch. A switch, a type of computer, is particularly important in digital networks, which need much more intelligence than the old analog systems. It's the switch that makes the snazzy new services possible. Motorola has established itself as the king of base stations, which send and receive sound over radio frequencies to mobile phones, but it doesn't make switches. Traditional telephone-company suppliers, such as Lucent and Northern Telecom, make both pieces so they can offer customers no-fuss integrated networks.

35   By 1995, the company had been trying for more than a decade to get a strong switch partner. In 1984, it signed an agreement with DSC Communications Corp. in Plano, Tex., for the two companies to market their equipment together. But in 1990, Motorola got dumped for poor switching capabilities by four key customers—GTE, Southwestern Bell, BellSouth, and Metro One Communications. In 1992, Motorola instead formed an alliance with Canada's Northern Telecom—but the partnership fell apart two years later when the competitors couldn't put aside their differences. The company again turned to DSC and at times Siemens and Alcatel Alsthom.

36   But problems continued. In early 1996, Bell Atlantic was getting more concerned about cellular fraud and asked its two equipment providers, Lucent and Motorola, to come up with solutions. Lucent provided a product within three months. In part because of switching problems, it took Motorola more than a year—and Bell Atlantic is still not satisfied. Strigl replaced Motorola with Lucent as his equipment provider in Connecticut. "We were very concerned that we were getting such fast response from Lucent and we were getting promises but no action from Motorola," he says. "I couldn't take them at their word anymore."

37   It got worse. In late 1996, PrimeCo started getting complaints from customers because Motorola's system would occasionally stop working—the lapses lasted between 30 minutes and two hours. PrimeCo traced the problem back to Motorola and, after Motorola tried in vain for several months to repair it, PrimeCo decided to bring in Lucent.

PRICE WARS

38   AirTouch Communications Inc., which owns half of PrimeCo, also has been experiencing a high number of dropped calls in its Los Angeles market, where it uses Motorola equipment. An AirTouch spokesperson declined to comment on whether Motorola would remain an equipment supplier. The

TABLE 2
How Motorola Missed the Mark

Customer	Problem
PrimeCo Personal Communications	Equipment problems in 1997–98 result in its network shutting down for up to two hours. PrimeCo drops Motorola's equipment in favor of Lucent's gear.
Bell Atlantic	In early 1996, the carrier asked both Lucent and Motorola for equipment to help prevent fraud. Lucent provided the technology within three months. Motorola took a year—and Bell Atlantic still isn't completely satisfied with its product.
Ameritech	In 1995, the Baby Bell told Motorola, which supplied most of its wireless phones, that it wanted to move to digital equipment. When Ameritech launched its digital network in spring 1997, Motorola still didn't have products ready. Ameritech turned to other suppliers, including Qualcomm and Sony.
U.S. Cellular	The carrier is forced to test four batches of Motorola's digital wireless phones over a six-month span before they finally work. Meanwhile, similar phones— all used in its Tulsa (Okla.) market—have been supplied by rival Nokia for two years. U.S. Cellular still can't get digital phones from Motorola for its Knoxville (Tenn.) and Yakima (Wash.) markets.

stumble in digital has taken its toll: Motorola's share of the U.S. digital equipment market was 13% last year, vs. Lucent's 38% share, says the Yankee Group.

39   Not all of Motorola's problems are of its own making. Despite a huge share of the pager and paging-equipment markets, price wars have left paging companies without the money to buy products. Revenues in the Motorola group that includes paging dropped 4% in 1997, to $3.8 billion. The problems at Apple Computer have devastated Motorola's computer-chip business, so it is pushing harder on specialized chips for airbags and other products.

40   The Asia turmoil also has contributed to Motorola's woes. In 1995, Motorola was beginning to reap substantial benefits from its two-decade push overseas, particularly in Asia. The company dominated the Asian market for two-way radios and pagers. It was running neck-and-neck with Ericsson for leadership of the mobile phone market and, after battering its way into Japan's protected telecom market, it held close to a quarter of the mobile-phone market.

41   But trouble lay ahead. The 200 engineers at Motorola's headquarters who were focused on the Japanese market were wedded to analog products—despite protests from Motorola's executives in Japan. "Motorola could be revered today if only it had embraced digital," says a former Motorola executive who was in Japan at the time. Motorola was late with digital phones and, in the past three years, has seen its market share slide to 3%. The recent economic downturn in the region also has hurt demand.

42   Questions about the company's future remain. Can it catch up in digital phones? Will it sell off its wireless equipment business? Can Galvin fix its culture, a task of no small magnitude?

43   Despite its problems, a sense of optimism is creeping through the company's headquarters. Galvin is telling executives that Motorola must strive for "renewal"—completely new businesses in which the company can recreate itself. After all, Motorola got its name because founder Paul V. Galvin developed a market in car radios, and then the company abandoned it as cellular service was taking off.

44   Now we'll see if Chris Galvin can truly follow in his grandfather's footsteps.

CASE 33

BusinessWeek

HOW AL DUNLAP SELF-DESTRUCTED

1   On June 9, Sunbeam Chairman and CEO Albert J. Dunlap stormed out of a board meeting in Rockefeller Center, leaving a conference room filled with puzzled and incredulous directors. Most of them thought the once celebrated champion of downsizing, under mounting pressure, was becoming unglued. One director, say three participants, openly expressed concerns about Dunlap's emotional state.

2   Demanding their support, Dunlap, 60, had just told his board that billionaire financier Ronald O. Perelman and others were engaged in a conspiracy to drive the small-appliance maker's already slumping stock down further so they could buy Sunbeam Corp. on the cheap. He suggested that if Michael Price, an influential mutual-fund manager who had recruited Dunlap nearly two years earlier, really backed him, he would buy out Perelman's $280 million stake.

3   Why Perelman, one of Sunbeam's largest investors, who owns 14% of the company, would do anything to diminish his investment, he could not explain. "We can't fight a battle on two fronts," said Dunlap, according to several directors. "Either we get the support we should have or [chief financial officer] Russ and I are prepared to go. . . . Just pay us."

NEAR TEARS

4   "Al, we don't know what you're talking about," retorted Director William T. Rutter, a banker patched into the meeting by phone from Florida, according to several participants. "We're supportive of both of you."

5   So were all the other four outside directors. Again and again they assured Dunlap and his close ally, Russell A. Kersh, of their support. Kersh, say several directors, seemed near tears. "I don't know what Al thought or what was going through his head," says Peter A. Langerman, Price's board representative. "But I didn't hear anything from Perelman, and Price was still behind him."

6   In four days, however, the directors voted to fire the man who has made a phenomenal business career out of firing others. Rarely does anyone express joy at another's misfortune, but Dunlap's ouster elicited unrestrained glee from many quarters. Former employees who had been victims of his legendary chainsaw nearly danced in the streets of Coshatta, La., where Dunlap shuttered a plant. Says David M. Friedson, CEO of Windmere-Durable Holdings Inc., a competitor of Sunbeam: "He is the logical extreme of an executive who has no values, no honor, no loyalty, and no ethics. And yet he was held up as a corporate god in our culture. It greatly bothered me." Other chief executives, many of whom considered him an extremist, agreed that Dunlap's demise was a welcome relief.

7   Even members of his own family—long estranged from the man—seemed ebullient. Upon hearing the news of his father's sacking on CNBC at 6:20 a.m. in Seattle, Troy Dunlap chortled. "I laughed like hell, " says Dunlap's 35-year-old son and only child. "I'm glad he fell on his ass. I told him Sunbeam would be his Dunkirk." Dunlap's sister, Denise, his only sibling, heard the news from a friend in New Jersey. Her only thought: "He got exactly what he deserved."

8   Sunbeam's stock, meanwhile, has plummeted from a high of 52 in early March to a low of 8 13/16 on June 22, below the level it traded when Sunbeam announced Dunlap's hiring in mid-1996. One analyst, Nicholas P. Heymann of Prudential Securities Inc., said the stock was trading "more on vindictive emotions than rational analysis."

Source: John A. Byrne in New York, "How Al Dunlap Self-Destructed," *Business Week:* July 6, 1998.

9   How could a single businessman arouse such emotions? In little more than four years, Al Dunlap made more than $100 million, ran two well-known public corporations, wrote a best-selling, vainglorious autobiography, and axed some 18,000 employees. Dunlap, of course, was hardly the only chieftain to order hefty workforce cuts or to say that the only stakeholders in a public corporation are its investors. But by eagerly seeking publicity to expound his simple philosophy, he emerged as the poster boy for "shareholder wealth." Since his departure from Sunbeam, Dunlap has been uncharacteristically silent. Along with his attorney, Christopher J. Sues, and CFO Kersh, he has not responded to repeated requests to be interviewed for this story.

10   To investors who made millions by following him, Dunlap was, if not a god, certainly a savior. He parachuted into poorly performing companies and made tough decisions that quickly brought shareholders sizable profits. "We're all seduced by the possibility of big wins," says PaineWebber Inc. analyst Andrew Shore, who follows Sunbeam. After meeting Dunlap in mid-1996, Shore immediately put out a buy on the stock. "I didn't necessarily like him or trust him," he recalls, "but I thought my clients could make money on him. I knew they just had to get out at the right time."

11   But if Chainsaw Al's rise to prominence was a '90s version of Barbarians at the Gate, his sudden demise may signal the beginnings of a more tempered era. With much of Corporate America considerably leaner and labor markets tight, taking a two-by-four to a problem is no longer perceived as a viable solution. "The need to do major downsizing is over. The opportunities to pick that kind of low-hanging fruit aren't as prevalent, and the second picking often requires different skills and methods than a Dunlap is known for," says Edward E. Lawler, a management professor at the University of Southern California. "Clearly, his era has come and is going."

DEMOLITION EXPERT

12   It was a supremely confident and triumphant Dunlap who arrived at the troubled appliance maker in July, 1996. Six months earlier, he had successfully completed the sale of Scott Paper Co. Wall Street lustily cheered his arrival at the $1.2 billion maker of electric blankets and outdoor grills. Sunbeam's stock surged nearly 50%, to 18 5/8, the day after his July 18 appointment. Less than four months later, Dunlap lived up to his reputation as a corporate demolition expert. He announced the shutdown or sale of two-thirds of Sunbeam's 18 plants and the elimination of half its 12,000 employees.

13   Predictably, Wall Street applauded Dunlap's actions, reporters wrote favorably of his exploits, and the stock zoomed up. It traveled so far in that direction, in fact, that it foiled Dunlap's initial strategy to sell the company. Although he hired investment banker Morgan Stanley Dean Witter & Co. to seek a buyer last October, no one would pay that large a premium (the stock had risen by 284% since July, 1996, to over 48). That forced Dunlap to consider another alternative: to scour the market for companies to buy. In early March, Dunlap bought not one but three companies in one fell swoop: Coleman, the camping-gear maker, from Perelman in a stock-and-cash deal; First Alert smoke alarms, and Signature Brands, the maker of Mr. Coffee.

14   Dunlap's most devoted fans, of course, resided on Wall Street. But Shore of PaineWebber wasn't one of them. Trained by the legendary Perrin Long, who made him come to work by 7 a.m. and labor over weekends, Shore, 37, had been following the household products and cosmetics industries for a decade when Dunlap arrived at Sunbeam.

15   When the stock spiked when Dunlap was appointed, Shore thought the reaction irrational and said so. His candor hardly pleased Dunlap, who would claim that Shore was biased against him because PaineWebber didn't get Sunbeam's investment banking business. (Shore denies that charge.) Still, the analyst jumped on the bandwagon himself, knowing Chainsaw Al could make his clients money. With each new earnings report, however, he carefully dissected Sunbeam's ever-improving results.

16   It didn't take long for alarm bells to sound. After the company reported its results in the second quarter of 1997, Shore says he began "getting pangs in my stomach." The numbers showed that Dunlap was building what Shore considered abnormally high inventory levels and accounts receivable. His trade contacts confirmed his suspicions that Sunbeam was giving lucrative terms to dealers to ship products aggressively.

"Bill and Hold"

17   "I said to myself: 'Let's play the game a little longer,' " remembers Shore. "No one [had] soured on him yet. Very few picked it up, only the smart shorts at the hedge funds. I thought it would take several more quarters to play out." Shore alerted his clients to the warning signs but continued to recommend the stock because he thought investors would keep bidding it up.

18   He was right. Sunbeam's shares kept climbing, even though the company's third-quarter results created even greater cause for concern. Shore noted in one of his reports that there were massive increases in sales of electric blankets, usually a fourth-quarter phenomenon. Then, in the fourth quarter of 1997, he was alarmed by enormous increases in sales of grills, at a time when virtually no one buys those products. Still, Shore says, "I didn't think the story was over just yet. The market hadn't caught it."

19   Although unknown at the time, Dunlap was aggressively trying to push out more and more product. As the company later acknowledged, he began to engage in so-called "bill and hold" deals with retailers in which Sunbeam products were purchased at large discounts and then held at third-party warehouses for delivery later. By booking these sales before the goods were delivered, Dunlap helped boost Sunbeam's revenues by 18% in 1997 alone. In effect, he was shifting sales from future quarters to current ones. The approach was not illegal, but the extraordinary volume made it unusual. Dunlap defended the practice, saying that it was an effort to extend the selling season and better meet surges in demand. Sunbeam's auditors, Arthur Andersen & Co., later insisted it met accounting standards.

20   On Mar. 19, Sunbeam acknowledged that first-quarter results would be below analysts' estimates. Two weeks later, on Apr. 2, Shore heard more disturbing news: Donald R. Uzzi, Sunbeam's well-regarded executive vice-president for worldwide consumer products, had been fired by Dunlap. Not able to reach Uzzi or Dunlap for confirmation, Shore sought out investor-relations chief Richard Goudis, only to discover that he had quit. Finally, the analyst thought, it was time to advise his clients to get out of the stock. He frantically downgraded the stock on Apr. 3 at 9:00 a.m., and it quickly fell by 4 points. Some two hours later, Sunbeam disclosed that it would post a first-quarter loss. By day's end, the stock fell 25%, to 34⅜, and shareholders soon filed lawsuits charging deception, an accusation that Sunbeam dismisses as "meritless."

21   Undaunted, Dunlap swiftly hatched a plan for a comeback. On May 11, before 200 major investors and Wall Street analysts—including Shore—he promised that the company would rebound from its dismal first-quarter loss of $44.6 million. Dunlap conceded that he had taken his "eye off the ball" to focus on the trio of acquisitions he made in March and had allowed underlings to offer "stupid, low-margin deals" on outdoor cooking grills. But he insisted that it would "never happen again," and that Sunbeam would post earnings of 5 cents to 10 cents a share in the second quarter and $1 a share for the full year.

22   Not everyone felt reassured, least of all Shore, who had several contentious exchanges with Dunlap at the meeting. Afterward, as Shore was heading out the door, Dunlap made a beeline for him. "I saw this wild man coming forward," recalls Shore. "He grabbed me by my left shoulder, put his hand over his mouth and near my left ear and said: 'You son of a bitch. If you want to come after me, I'll come after you twice as hard.' " One Sunbeam adviser corroborates Shore's account.

23   Dunlap's performance at that meeting—including his announcement of another 5,100 layoffs at Sunbeam and the newly acquired companies—didn't prevent the stock from dropping further. Nor did Dunlap's speech stop news reports about what Shore had discovered nearly nine months earlier: that Sunbeam was engaged in highly aggressive sales tactics and accounting practices that inflated revenues and profits. The most scathing analysis, in Barron's, alleged that Dunlap employed $120 million of "artificial profit boosters" last year when the company reported $109.4 million in net income.

24   Dunlap was so concerned about the effects of the story that he called an impromptu board meeting for June 9 to rebut the charges. He arrived for the session at 4 p.m. Besides the five outside board members, there was a bevy of external advisers, including lawyers, public relations consultants, and the company's accountant from Arthur Andersen. Dunlap, recalls one participant, "seemed strangely subdued and quiet."

EXHIBIT A

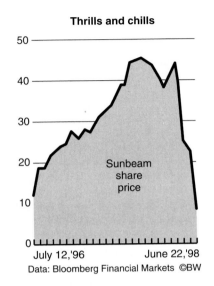

Thrills and chills

Sunbeam share price

July 12,'96   June 22,'98

Data: Bloomberg Financial Markets ©BW

25   Kersh and Controller Robert J. Gluck led the board through the charges, denying virtually all of them. The Arthur Andersen partner assured the board that the company's 1997 numbers were in compliance with accounting standards and firmly stood by the firm's audit of Sunbeam's books. The directors discussed a range of alternatives to deal with the story, from the filing of a libel suit to issuing a detailed letter of corrections to its shareholders.

26   The discussion was drifting when it was decided simply to draft a point-by-point rebuttal for the company's bankers and directors. Suddenly, Director Charles M. Elson, a Stetson University law professor and friend of Dunlap's, asked how the company's second quarter was shaping up. The following exchange then occurred, according to four of those who were present.

27   "Sales are a little soft," said Kersh.

28   "Well, do you think you're going to make the numbers?" asked Elson.

29   "It's going to be tough," replied Kersh.

30   "This is a transition year," Dunlap responded. "You've got to stop worrying about specific numbers. We're trying to prepare for 1999."

31   Dunlap then said he wanted to discuss something privately with the board. All the outside advisers departed, leaving only Dunlap, Kersh, and the five directors. Over the next 20 minutes, Dunlap told the board that either he needed the right level of support or he was prepared to go.

32   "If you really want me and Russ to go, then let's settle up the contract and we'll go," Dunlap said, according to several board members. "I have a document in my briefcase that we can go over and get it done."

33   The board was stunned. Dunlap told them he believed that Perelman was orchestrating a torrent of bad media coverage so he could buy the company at a bargain. Some of the directors said later that they thought Dunlap was becoming emotionally distraught. They did not believe that Perelman, who declined comment, would undermine himself that way. His ownership stake enabled him to affect change more directly.

SUSPICIONS

34   Shortly after the exchange, Dunlap and Kersh got up and marched out of the room. After allowing the pair enough time to reach the elevator bank, Howard G. Kristol broke the silence. Of all of them, he had known Dunlap the longest. For more than 20 years, Kristol had been his personal attorney. He had drafted Dunlap's employment pacts at Scott Paper and Sunbeam.

TABLE 1
Chainsaw Al's Waterloo

July 19, 1996	Dunlap is named chairman and CEO of Sunbeam. The stock jumps nearly 50%, from 12 1/2 to 18 5/8.
Nov. 13, 1996	Dunlap announces plans to ax half of Sunbeam's 12,000 employees and close or sell two-thirds of its 18 manufacturing plants.
Oct. 23, 1997	Dunlap hires Morgan Stanley to explore "strategic alternatives," including acquisitions or Sunbeam's sale.
Jan. 28, 1998	Dunlap declares a turnaround, reporting record sales and earnings for 1997.
Mar. 2, 1998	Dunlap announces a trio of acquisitions: camping-gear maker Coleman, smoke-alarm producer First Alert, and Mr. Coffee maker Signature Brands.
Mar. 4, 1998	Sunbeam stock closes at a record high of $52 a share.
Apr. 3, 1998	Stock falls 25%, to 34 3/8, after PaineWebber analyst Andrew Shore issues downgrade and company shocks Wall Street by posting a first-quarter loss.
May 11, 1998	Dunlap tells investors he took his eye "off the ball," says that it will "never happen again."
June 9, 1998	Dunlap demands board support or, he says, he and Vice-Chairman and CFO Russell Kersh will resign.
June 13, 1998	Outside directors fire Dunlap.
June 14, 1998	Board agrees to hire Jerry Levin, a longtime aide to financier Ronald Perelman, as new chief executive.

Data: *Business Week.*

35 "That is complete bullshit," Kristol blurted out, according to several directors. "Just bullshit."

36 Everyone in the room agreed. No one had uttered any doubt about Dunlap's ability to lead the company. No one thought he had cooked the books. So why would he bring up the possibility of resigning?

37 "I don't know about you, but what I'm clearly hearing is that Al and Russ want out," Kristol recalls saying. The others concurred. The timing could not have been worse. Although the company was in crisis, Dunlap was about to go to London to give a speech and promote his book, while Kersh was going off on vacation in Ohio. They were concerned that Dunlap lacked the resolve to continue in the job, was unaware of the deteriorating results, or worst of all, was being less than candid. "We all sat there feeling like we were going to throw up," says Elson. "It was horrible."

38 Dunlap's strange behavior led director Faith Whittlesey to openly suggest that perhaps the CEO was suffering from emotional distress, say three directors. She was not the first to wonder if he had lost perspective in the wake of the barrage of hostile media coverage. Some of his closest associates thought he had become oddly subdued and introspective—quite a departure from the volatile and voluble man they knew.

39 Before leaving the conference room, the directors exchanged personal phone numbers so they could stay in close touch. Several, particularly Langerman, agreed to dig more deeply into the company and question other Sunbeam executives over the next few days. When the session finally broke up around 8 p.m., Elson was so distraught that he spent the next three hours wandering the streets of Manhattan.

40 Over the following two days, Langerman did considerable homework. Unbeknownst to Dunlap, he called several Sunbeam insiders, including three top operating executives, Lee Griffith, Frank J. Feraco, and Franz Schmid. But the most important break came when he spoke with Sunbeam's Executive Vice-President David C. Fannin.

41 Fannin, 52, didn't fit the Dunlap mold. Unlike his tempestuous, self-promoting boss, Fannin is unassuming and mild-mannered. The Kentucky-born lawyer had worked at a blue-chip law firm in Louisville for nearly 20 years when a client recruited him to Sunbeam in 1993 as interim general counsel. Of Sunbeam's top dozen senior executives, he would be the only survivor, someone who viewed himself as a moderating influence on his mercurial boss.

IN CRISIS

42　　Dunlap not only brought Fannin into his inner circle, he handsomely rewarded the lawyer for his loyalty and commitment. In February, for example, Dunlap handed him a new three-year contract that raised his base salary by 90%, to $595,000, along with a huge stock option grant on 750,000 shares, now underwater. What Dunlap failed to notice, however, was that Fannin had become demoralized by what he saw at Sunbeam. It was hard to really like Dunlap, with his hair-trigger temper. Many times Fannin considered quitting. "But it was like being in an abusive relationship," he says. "You just didn't know how to get out of it."

43　　Fannin, however, had now reached the breaking point. Although Kersh told the board the second quarter would be soft, a week earlier Fannin had been at a Sunbeam meeting at which considerable concern was raised that the results would be far below Dunlap's May 11th forecast. At that session, the numbers coming in showed that revenues were falling by as much as $60 million in the quarter. In last year's second quarter, Sunbeam's sales were $287.6 million.

44　　When Langerman called Fannin on Wednesday morning at his office, Fannin was ready to reveal what he knew. "I was totally disillusioned," he said. "I felt this was not something I wanted to be involved in any further." Later that night, while at home, he told Langerman that the numbers were much worse than soft, and that the company was in crisis.

45　　Meanwhile, Fannin did some interviewing of his own from Wednesday to Friday of that week. He met with Gluck, the controller, a finance analyst who had been a pre-Dunlap holdover, and asked pointed questions about the quality of the 1997 earnings. "I didn't like the answers I got," recalls Fannin. "He said: 'Look, as much as possible, we tried to do things in accordance with GAAP, (generally accepted accounting principles), but everything has been pushed to the limit.' There was no smoking gun, but taken as a whole, this was not a sustainable situation." Gluck did not respond to requests to be interviewed.

46　　Langerman called his fellow directors and asked them to come to an emergency meeting in Kristol's Rockefeller Center offices on Saturday morning. Fannin agreed to come to report on what he had found. "Had he not come forward," says Elson, "it would have been extraordinarily difficult for us to act. He was the quiet hero. He really put his neck out."

47　　On Saturday morning, June 13, Sunbeam's outside directors solemnly gathered around the same rectangular conference room table where only four days earlier they had had their odd meeting with Dunlap and Kersh. A box of Krispy Kreme doughnuts served as breakfast. Four of the directors were there, along with Fannin and a pair of lawyers from Skadden Arps, Slate, Meagher & Flom. Director Rutter was on the telephone from Captiva Island, Fla., where he was on vacation with his family.

48　　The directors all agreed Dunlap had to go. With the exception of Langerman, the directors were Dunlap's friends. But they also felt betrayed by him, misled about the company's financial condition, its second-quarter earnings, and its yearly numbers as well, they later said. "We lost our confidence in him and the ability to sustain things was questionable," says Rutter.

49　　By noon, Skadden Arps lawyer Blaine V. "Finn" Fogg carefully scripted the words that Langerman would say to Dunlap when they placed the conference call. "All the outside directors have considered the options you presented to us last Tuesday and have decided that your departure from the company is necessary," Langerman read aloud.

50　　Elson then made the motion to dump Dunlap, but he couldn't bring himself to read it. "It felt too cruel," he recalls. "We had gone back a long way, and I just couldn't do it."

51　　So after Elson put forth the motion, it was quickly seconded by Kristol and dryly read by Fannin. The outside directors passed it unanimously.

NO EXPLANATION

52　　"I think I'm entitled to an explanation," Dunlap said finally, according to several participants in the meeting.

53　　He wouldn't get one. Instead, Langerman told him to contact the board's lawyer. Kristol adjourned the meeting shortly after. Three days later, during a telephone session, Kersh was fired as well.

54   The day after Dunlap was axed, the board met again in Skadden Arps' offices. It named as the new chief executive Jerry W. Levin, a longtime aide to Perelman and former CEO of Coleman, which now comprises about 40% of Sunbeam's revenues. Langerman, who agreed to serve as nonexecutive chairman, had called Perelman on Saturday afternoon to ask for help. Levin was on his way to see a movie that evening when Perelman asked if he would be interested in taking over.

55   Now, Levin has to sort out the mess. Not only is Sunbeam expected to report another loss in the second quarter and possibly for the year, but the company is also under an informal probe by the Securities & Exchange Commission. It is also expected to be in technical default on a $1.7 billion bank loan by June 30. Already, Levin is expected to win a reprieve from the banks, but it will take some time to turn Sunbeam around.

56   Dunlap still has followers who predict a comeback, though headhunters say it's unlikely he'll ever get another chance to run a major company. In the end, Al Dunlap, the kid from Hoboken, N.J., the son of a union steward, fell on his own weapon, the sword of shareholder value. "Dunlap got thrown out not because the board said his way was the wrong way to run a company," notes Peter D. Cappelli, chairman of the Wharton School's management department. "He was fired because he couldn't make his own numbers."

CASE 34

BusinessWeek

GILLETTE'S EDGE

1   Amid airtight security, workers at the Gillette Co.'s World Shaving Headquarters in South Boston are putting the finishing touches on the long-awaited successor to Sensor, the world's most successful razor. The stakes are high: To maintain Gillette's double-digit growth, the new razor must top Sensor, sold as "the best a man can get." Developing a new razor might seem like child's play for Gillette, which has dominated shaving for decades. But it has been a tortured, six-year marathon, involving thousands of shaving tests and design modifications.

2   But even as Gillette's marketers gear up for their biggest product launch ever—the new razor is expected to hit stores this spring along with a multimillion dollar global marketing blitz—a team of PhD scientists is using the latest high-tech equipment to burrow even deeper into the mysteries of shaving. There's high-speed video that can capture the act of a blade cutting a single whisker and even a microscope capable of examining a blade at atomic level. The mission is to create the next shaving breakthrough. Expected debut: 2006.

3   In coming months, the launch will get all the attention. But it's in labs like these that the more significant Gillette story is unfolding. They are at the heart of one of the consumer world's great innovation machines—a machine dedicated not just to churning out new products but to inventing entirely new ways of making them.

4   Now, Chief Executive Alfred M. Zeien wants to throw this machine into overdrive across Gillette's entire family of consumer products—from its Oral-B toothbrushes and Braun appliances to recently acquired Duracell batteries. He predicts that 50% of Gillette's sales will soon come from products introduced within the past five years, up from 41% in 1996 and twice the level of innovation at the average consumer-products company. But his ultimate aim is even more audacious. "If I can't make the next five years better than the last five," when Gillette net earnings grew at a sterling 17% annual clip, vows Zeien, "I wouldn't think I was doing a good job."

5   It's an especially tall order for a mass marketer like Gillette. Indeed, a recent Mercer Management Consulting study of 50 top consumer packaged-goods companies—including Coca-Cola, Procter & Gamble, and Johnson & Johnson—found that only 17 managed to achieve above-industry-average growth in both sales and profits from 1985 to 1990. More tellingly, just 7 of these 17 maintained this excellence during the following five years. True, Gillette—along with J&J and P&G—was among the stellar seven. But the study's sobering suggestion is that most of these seven are doomed to fall over the coming five years, if only because of the sheer difficulty of continually finding new products and markets that can excel.

OUT OF STEAM?

6   The odds seem even steeper in this era of low inflation, which makes it all but impossible to pass along cost increases. The supposed global cornucopia also has become more elusive, given the strong dollar and Asian flu. No wonder investors are edgy. It was bad enough that Gillette's sales grew just 3% in the first nine months of 1997—a far cry from the 9% pace of the past five years. But after Gillette advised analysts to modestly downgrade their 1997 estimates—from 17% to a 15% earnings increase—Gillette's stock plunged 24% below its July peak of $106. Investors worried that Gillette's steady growth machine was finally running out of steam—making it far harder to justify the sky-high

Source: William C. Symonds in Boston, with Carol Matlack in Moscow, "Gillette's Edge," *Business Week:* January 19, 1998; and William C. Symonds in Boston, "The Next CEO's Key Asset: A Worn Passport," *Business Week:* January 19, 1998.

price/earnings ratio of 41 times expected 1997 profits that its stock was then commanding. "Gillette took the 'p' out of predictable," says Morgan Stanley & Co. analyst Brenda Lee Landry, "and made people worry about the long term."

7   In part, that's because slow sales in Germany and Japan at its Braun division raised questions about Gillette's dependence on foreign markets to keep up its growth. Yet Gillette's problems in 1997 may prove less of a harbinger than first feared. Earnings were also hurt because it was a transition year in which the company absorbed Duracell even as it slowed shipments of its old razor products in anticipation of the launch this year. "People overreacted" to last summer's earnings revision, argues Landry. With many major investors still bullish, the stock has since recovered almost fully, to $100. "Their prospects are spectacular," says Jay Freedman of institutional shareholder Lincoln Capital.

8   Zeien's strategy is built on Gillette's three great strengths. He's planning the most ambitious roll-out of products in company history, with the razor just the beginning. It will be followed by a radically new toothbrush from Oral-B and a line of female-friendly razors designed to more than double that $250 million business. In time, he also hopes for battery breakthroughs that will leave the Energizer bunny in the dust.

9   Second, to ensure that earnings continue to outstrip revenue growth, Zeien plans to continue cutting manufacturing costs a full 4% annually, giving Gillette a huge edge in an era of low inflation. Third, Zeien is counting on Gillette's global strengths to produce growth overseas. True, those gains may be temporarily slowed by turmoil in Asia and the strong dollar. But longer term, few companies are better positioned. Some 1.2 billion people around the world now use at least one Gillette product daily, up from 800 million in 1990. With many of them now buying the cheapest products Gillette sells, Zeien figures over time the company can induce them to trade up.

10   Gillette's future hinges on a process its execs call "Gillettifying" a business. The model is Sensor, introduced at a time when even some Gillette executives feared blades were about to become a commodity, dominated by cheap disposables. Sensor reversed that trend by proving consumers could be induced to pay a premium for a high-tech shaving system delivering superior performance. Since 1990, Sensor and Sensor Excel have grabbed a leading 27% share of the U.S. market. The lessons: spend whatever it takes to gain technology supremacy in a category, and then produce innovative products that will capture consumers, even at premium prices.

11   To fulfill this promise, Gillette must overcome major challenges. Since King C. Gillette invented the safety razor early in the 20th century, the simple act of shaving has powered Gillette. But after the acquisition of Duracell International Inc., only 29% of sales and 52% of operating profits come from blades, the lowest levels ever. Now, at least half of Gillette's growth must come from other businesses—like batteries, toothbrushes, and toiletries—in which it faces far fiercer competition and has been far less successful in generating profits.

12   At the same time, Gillette faces a major transition. Zeien, 67, is nearing the end of the third one-year extension of his employment contract. Zeien refuses to be pinned down on when he'll step aside, saying only that it's "up to the board." But he is carefully grooming his No. 2, President Michael C. Hawley, 59, for the top job. When Zeien retires, Gillette will suddenly be in the hands of a man who, while highly regarded internally, is largely unknown outside.

13   And Zeien's leadership has been a crucial element of Gillette's success. By 1985, profits were flat, and sales had increased hardly at all since 1980. "There seemed to be little sense of urgency . . . to stretch, set tough goals, and make strong moves to reassure restless shareholders," writes Gorden McKibben in a new history of Gillette to be published by Harvard Business School Press on January 25. Highly vulnerable, Gillette faced a takeover bid from Ronald O. Perelman in 1986, and then a 1988 proxy fight.

14   Those narrowly won battles were a "wake-up call," says Zeien, who took over in early 1991 determined to shake things up. He insisted that Gillette must be the world leader, or have a plan to become leader, in all of its core businesses. He further decreed that at least 50 cents of every dollar in operating profit be plowed back into three growth drivers: research and development, capital spending, and advertising.

15   The results? Gillette is now the world leader in 13 product categories, accounting for 81% of its 1996 sales—up from just 50% in 1991. Although driven in part by acquisitions, sales have more than

doubled since 1991, to 1996's $9.7 billion, while net earnings soared 189%, to $1.2 billion. All told, it has posted 29 quarters of double-digit earnings gains. This has pushed Gillette's market value to $56 billion, 14 times what raider Perelman offered in 1986.

ENGLISH BORN

16   The new razor will be the first major test of whether Gillette can keep it up. To increase sales in the mature shaving market, Gillette must persuade men to pay a huge premium for the new razor—probably 15% to 25% over the current $5.25 U.S. retail price for a five-pack of Sensor Excels.

17   To meet such product-development challenges, Gillette religiously devotes 2.2% of its annual sales, or over $200 million, to R&D, roughly twice the average for consumer products. The company then uses a highly disciplined process to perfect its ideas. The original concept for Sensor, for instance, emerged all the way back in 1979. Gillette then developed seven different versions under the code name Flag. The winner incorporated many ideas from the six losers and 22 patentable innovations on top of the original idea. In similar fashion, Gillette set up three competing teams to produce what would be its breakthrough clear-gel deodorant, a product that has propelled that business to 21.5% of the U.S. market, its highest level in two decades. And the prototype for the new razor—which emerged from the company's lab in Reading, Britain in the early '90s—had to compete against two or three other contenders. Along the way, the razor was subjected to more than 15,000 shave tests.

18   To be sure, innovation is a goal of all major consumer-products companies. But the difference Gillette's approach can make is perhaps best illustrated by Oral-B, which Gillette acquired in 1984. At the time, "there wasn't a single person in R&D, and a new toothbrush hadn't been introduced since 1957," says Jacques Legarde, the executive vice-president who oversees Oral-B. Today, Gillette has a team of 150 researching manual plaque removal, "more than any other company in the world," he brags.

19   It has already produced a stream of new products—from a floss made with a proprietary fiber, to its top-of-the-line Advantage toothbrush, which retails for $3.49, compared with 99 cents for the brush Oral-B sold in 1984. This has pushed sales at Oral-B to $548 million, up from $110 million in 1984.

20   But Oral-B is just half the story. In 1989, Legarde ordered researchers at Braun, the German consumer-appliance giant Gillette acquired in 1967, to marry their expertise with Oral-B's bristles to create an electric toothbrush. The result—the Braun Oral-B Plaque Remover—is now the world leader, with over $400 million in annual sales. And with that market still tiny, Legarde figures Gillette can double its overall oral-care business to $2 billion in five years by marketing to aging baby boomers.

"TWO DWARFS"

21   Because only the best ideas make it through Gillette's innovation process, "they're one of the few consumer-products companies that really pick their shots," says Suzanne Hogan, a senior partner at marketing consultants Lippincott & Margulies Inc. Rather than "come out with a new razor every year," she adds, "they wait until they have something meaningful, and then go to the market with a bang."

22   But unlike Sensor in 1990, this time Gillette's new razor won't have the field to itself. Warner-Lambert Co.'s Schick—a distant second—soon will launch its largest ad campaign in history to promote its new Schick Protector shaving system. The bright-red Protector has blades wrapped with microfine wires to prevent nicks and cuts. Even so, "you're looking at Godzilla vs. the two dwarfs," Schick and Bic Corp., says Jack Trout, a Greenwich (Conn.) marketing consultant. Even Dick Jordan, Schick's vice-president of global business management, concedes Gillette "is a formidable competitor."

23   Yet Gillette is more than a new-products pipeline; it's equally expert at figuring out ways to make them more cheaply. To meet its annual 4% cost-cutting goal, engineers never stop searching for ways to run machinery faster and more efficiently. Such incremental gains have helped cut the cost of

making Sensor by 30% since 1993, while slashing the costs of Oral-B's Advantage a huge 60%. Meanwhile, materials costs have been trimmed 10% to 15% by intensifying competition between suppliers.

24   But the truly big manufacturing gains come when Gillette introduces products. Few companies "marry product and process innovation" to the same degree as Gillette, says Harvard Business School Professor Rosabeth Moss Kanter. After Zeien was told the new razor would be too expensive to produce with the setup Gillette has used to make cartridges since they were introduced in 1971, for example, he ordered the engineers to invent a new one. It was a staggering undertaking, requiring Gillette to "bring on 196 different pieces of equipment, each one essentially designed by us," says Executive Vice-President Robert G. King. The new system will spit out cartridges twice as fast as that used to make Sensor, enabling Gillette to roll out the razor in just over two years, half the time it took for Sensor.

25   Zeien hasn't managed to Gillettify everything. The biggest failure: an inability to gain a dominant edge in its nearly $1 billion writing-instrument business. Gillette achieved world leadership in pens by buying Parker for $458 million in 1993, creating a stable that included the low-priced Paper Mate and top-end Waterman pens. But it has yet to come up with a home-run product. "It's a much more challenging area" than shaving, admits Dr. John C. Terry, director of Gillette's Boston R&D lab. Some critics believe it's time to exit the business, but Zeien insists new products will save the day.

26   Braun also continues to weigh down Gillette's performance. Despite some successes, it is still burdened by slow-moving products such as electric razors, a big factor in last summer's earnings downgrade. To fix this, Braun is looking increasingly to faster-growing products, such as the electric toothbrush and personal-diagnostic equipment.

27   Perhaps the most pressing challenge is Duracell, acquired for over $7 billion in stock in late 1996. Duracell is already the world's leading producer of alkaline batteries, with nearly 50% of the U.S. market. Now, Gillette is determined "to escalate growth above and beyond that," says Edward F. DeGraan, the executive vice-president who took charge in early 1997. It's tripling spending on alkaline battery R&D. The aim, says DeGraan, is to build batteries so superior that the Duracell name will gain the same potency as the "Intel inside" logo.

28   But that's a huge challenge in what's essentially a commodity market, and most outsiders are skeptical. "I don't foresee any breakthroughs," says Martin Hersch, a battery expert at consultants Freedonia Group. Even if he's right, Gillette can do a lot to power Duracell simply by distributing its products more globally. Duracell—which in 1996 got only 20% of its sales from beyond North America and Europe—"didn't have the international organization" to exploit this opening, says Zeien. But Gillette does. That's why one of Gillette's first moves was to fold Duracell's distributors into its global juggernaut.

29   To be sure, Gillette is hardly immune to global turmoil. "Our growth [in Asia] might be less than what it has been for the next one to two years," concedes Jurgen Wedel, the executive vice-president heading Gillette's International Group. But he argues that Gillette will be far less affected than most. Asia still accounts for less than 10% of Gillette's sales. And Gillette has had success managing through troubled times.

30   Consider the former Soviet Union, one of the world's most challenging markets. When Gillette first opened its St. Petersburg office in 1992, it was all but unknown to Russian consumers and managed sales of just $150,000 a month. Gillette soon caught consumers' attention with colorful ads on billboards and buses. They then took their "best a man can get" campaign to televised sports. Today, the Gillette name is recognized by some 80% of Russia's city-dwellers, and Gillette has a leading 50% share of the Russian blade market. Gillette is expanding its marketing focus to promote batteries, toiletries, and toothbrushes. As it does, Wedel predicts Russian sales should explode to $500 million within five years, up from $200 million now.

31   As it pushes into brave new markets, Hawley readily admits Gillette "will hit some bumps along the way." But most observers are convinced that it still has a long ways to roll. Wall Street analysts expect Gillette earnings to grow at an 18% clip over the next five years, "slightly more than double the rate for the S&P 500," says Charles Hill, director of research at First Call Corp. And most are recommending the stock.

32   Of course, there are no guarantees. If Gillette's management becomes overconfident and complacent, it will begin to slip up and miss opportunities, just as it did in the early '80s. But say this for Al Zeien: He has laid a solid foundation for continued excellence. Now it's up to Hawley and his successors to execute.

TABLE 1
Gillette Has Big Plans for the Next Five Years . . . But Also Faces a Host of Challenges

Gillette Has Big Plans for the Next Five Years . . .

- Continued double-digit annual growth, matching the heady 17% rate of the past five years.
- Expansion of global markets in Asia, Russia, and Latin America.
- Increased emphasis on new products will include rolling out a new premium razor and inventions in oral care and batteries.

. . . But Also Faces a Host of Challenges

- CEO Al Zeien may retire soon. His contract expires in February, capping three one-year extensions. Heir apparent Michael Hawley is largely unknown outside Gillette.
- Lines such as Braun and the pen business continue to lag as researchers struggle to invent a "home-run" product like Sensor.
- Global currency jitters threaten international growth strategy.

THE NEXT CEO'S KEY ASSET: A WORN PASSPORT

33   In 1979, long before China was chic, Gillette Co.'s Michael C. Hawley flew into Shanghai. Hawley, then the Sydney-based head of Asia-Pacific operations, was on a mission to make Gillette one of the first Western companies to crack the Chinese market.

34   But his search for a joint venture to make razor blades was increasingly looking like Mission: Impossible. "We were flying blind," recalls Hawley. China didn't even have a law for joint ventures as yet. Worse, while Shanghai, home to China's largest razor-blade manufacturer was the natural site, the city was still under the sway of the Gang of Four.

35   Many American executives would have given up. But Hawley, an international veteran who had already broken ground in tough terrain from Teheran to Bogota, persevered. Eventually, he struck a deal in the northern city of Shenyang. It took over two dozen trips and nearly four years before the Shenyang Daily Use Metals Products Co., as Gillette's joint venture was called, began production. It was just a sliver of the market. But the payoff came in 1992 when Gillette beat the competition to buy 70% of the Shanghai operation, now the largest blade plant in Asia. As a result, Gillette controls over 80% of China's $51 million razor-blade market.

36   That achievement speaks volumes about why Hawley is being groomed as Gillette's next CEO. Foreign markets offer far more growth than the mature U.S., and Gillette is building an internationally seasoned management team to seize the opportunities.

TASKMASTER

37   While many American CEOs have done a brief stint abroad, Hawley, 59, built his career overseas. Although he joined Gillette in 1961 as an assistant to the controller in the Boston headquarters, by 1966 he was running Gillette's small import-export operation in Hong Kong. Promotions followed over the next two decades, taking him to five continents with a wife and three children in tow. Today, "he's the most skilled international manager in the company," says Chief Executive Alfred M. Zeien.

38   Hawley still spends much of his time traveling and garnering information—for example, on how Duracell batteries are moving in the open-air markets that ring Russian cities. Hawley isn't shy about shouting out overseas managers' errors: "Your name is right there, right across that really crappy display."

39   His years abroad have made Hawley opposed to any hint of a nationalistic approach to management. "I don't think you can be a global company and say you have to have Americans running it," he says. Two of Gillette's four executive vice-presidents, the traditional stepping-stone to the top, are Europeans. In some countries, Gillette management is beginning to rival the U.N. Its business in the

EXHIBIT A

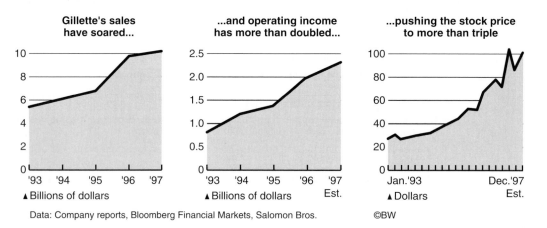

Gillette's sales have soared...
...and operating income has more than doubled...
...pushing the stock price to more than triple

Data: Company reports, Bloomberg Financial Markets, Salomon Bros.   ©BW

former Soviet Union, for instance, is headed by Albert Richard, a Frenchman backed up by an Egyptian controller, an English sales director, and officers from Pakistan and Ireland.

40   But with Al Zeien still firmly at the helm, even insiders are uncertain how Hawley will evolve as CEO. "He will have a different style" than Zeien, predicts Jacques Legarde, an executive vice-president who has worked with both men for years. "But I don't think we can see what his full style is until he is there." Zeien is known as a business theorist whose greatest contribution has been conceptualizing and then communicating Gillette's mission. The burly Hawley is more comfortable tackling nuts-and-bolts challenges. "He's a man who knows how to get things done," says Zeien. Gillette's board is betting that he is just the choice to see that the blueprint developed by Zeien is executed.

CASE 35

BusinessWeek

GILLETTE TAKES A SHAVE AND A BIG HAIRCUT

1   Through the long bull market, Wall Street had a love affair with Gillette. And why not? The company steadily produced double-digit earnings increases, and often came within a penny or two of analyst forecasts.

2   No more. In a hastily arranged Sept. 29 conference call, CEO Alfred M. Zeien stunned Wall Street by conceding that Gillette's operating earnings in the third quarter would reach just 30 cents a share, 20% below 1997's level and 25% below the Street's consensus expectation. Gillette will also ax 4,700 jobs, close 14 factories, and close or consolidate some 30 offices worldwide. The resulting $535 million restructuring charge—the largest ever at Gillette—will cut third-quarter results to no better than breakeven. The Gillette bulls are now in retreat: Its shares have dropped to 38, from 62 in July.

3   Even worse, Gillette's longer-term outlook is suddenly anything but certain. Zeien bravely suggests that Gillette "should be rolling again" in 1999, and he is not jettisoning his global ambitions. Still, even Zeien concedes that the emerging-markets crisis is "different than anything we've faced in the last 20 to 30 years," and "we don't know how long this is going to last." And since Gillette depends on markets outside the U.S. and Western Europe for 34% of sales, "no one really knows how Gillette will do," says Jay Freedman, an analyst at Lincoln Capital. "And if China and Brazil and Mexico go, it will be worse than the market thinks."

STIFF ARM

4   Gillette has compounded its problems by the way it managed the situation. For weeks, it stiff-armed inquiries from worried investors, even as the crisis spread from Asia to Russia and Brazil. Behind the scenes, Zeien was scrambling to contain the damage, in part by booking a gain on the sale of Gillette's Jafra Cosmetics unit, which even he says he tried to time for the third quarter. But in the end, his efforts may have done more harm than good. "I used to think I understood what was going on at Gillette," fumes one analyst. "But now I don't know what to believe."

5   Zeien created more confusion by refusing to be specific about closings. Soon, staffers from the governor of Massachusetts' office were calling to check out a Boston radio report that the company would eliminate jobs at its "World Shaving Headquarters" in South Boston—despite the fact that Gillette just invested $400 million in the plant.

6   Although Gillette's immediate problems stem from its overseas ambitions, it is not lowering its sights. The restructuring is aimed at completing the makeover of Gillette into a truly global company. Each of six business units—from shaving to Oral B toothbrushes—will have worldwide responsibility for its own product development and manufacturing. Gillette will also consolidate several sales units. Zeien says this should save $200 million.

7   But there is no global retreat. Even as he shuts factories, Zeien says he plans "huge capital expenditures to increase capacity in most product lines." At the same time, Gillette is gaining market share in some countries: Zeien says it now has 72% of the blade market in Russia and over 90% in Poland. Gillette is also shopping for acquisitions. Zeien notes that one troubled Korean battery maker already voiced a desire to be bought by Gillette. Even so, Gillette will face huge challenges in selling higher-priced products in these depressed markets.

Source: William C. Symonds in Boston, "Gillette Takes a Shave and a Big Haircut," *Business Week:* October 12, 1998.

EXHIBIT A

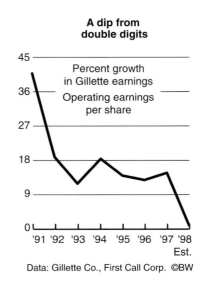

**A dip from
double digits**

Percent growth
in Gillette earnings

Operating earnings
per share

Data: Gillette Co., First Call Corp. ©BW

8   Gillette's woes have been compounded by the launch of its biggest bet for the future: the Mach3 razor. Even as overseas revenue falls off, Gillette is accounting for some of the $1 billion in startup costs in the early stages of the rollout, which began in late June.

BIG MACH

9   Zeien is certain Mach3 is well on its way to stellar sales. He says it already has 17.6% of the U.S. wet-shaving market. By 2002, he predicts, Mach3 will be a $2.5 billion business, adding $500 million a year to profits.

10   But that assumes a steady buildup from here. "Mach3 is still in the novelty stage," worries Jack Trout, a Greenwich, Conn., marketing consultant. Over time, "I'm not sure it is so dramatically better than Sensor" that U.S. consumers will pay a premium for it. And in the emerging markets, where Mach3 will debut in 1999, "they won't be selling a lot of expensive blades," Trout adds.

11   There's little doubt that Gillette will again enjoy vigorous growth—at some point. But for the first time in a decade, there's uncertainty about when and how fast Gillette will return to its glory days.

CASE 36

BusinessWeek

SMOKE ALARMS AT RJR

1 Steven F. Goldstone has been a busy guy. As head of RJR Nabisco Holdings Corp., he has spent the past year jetting from city to city as the tobacco industry's point man in a dramatic effort to reshape the most vilified business in America. Penitent, he admitted before Congress that his product is addictive. Then, defiant, he led a successful drive to kill federal legislation once it became clear the industry would have to pay billions of dollars more than it had agreed to in settlement talks with state attorneys general. Throughout, Goldstone has been front and center engaging in what he describes as a "public-policy debate on the issues that affect our industries and our customers."

2 Only problem is, while CEO Goldstone works tirelessly to extricate Big Tobacco from its legal quagmire, his company is being eaten alive on the operating front. At home, industry giant Philip Morris Cos. is kicking No. 2 RJR's cigarette butts with its Marlboro brand, outmarketing and out-spending its smaller rival to steal almost a full percentage point of U.S. market share so far this year. Things are even worse abroad. Although foreign markets are widely considered the tobacco makers' most fertile grounds for growth, RJR has let the opportunity slip away amid management missteps and economic malaise. It now plans to unload its hobbled international tobacco unit. To top things off, RJR's usually reliable profit machine, the Nabisco food division, is losing out to more nimble competitors as its cookie and cracker line grows stale as a week-old Oreo.

3 RJR's numbers show more smoke than fire. While Philip Morris posted third-quarter operating gains up 10%, RJR's operating profits slumped 14%. For the full year, analysts expect RJR's earnings to drop 11%, to $3.1 billion, on slightly lower sales of $16.9 billion. That's after operating earnings rose a paltry 3% last year.

4 The bottom line: Whatever comes of lawsuit-settlement discussions between tobacco companies and the states, RJR is in deep trouble. And the poor operating performance it has turned in lately has convinced many investors that part of the problem is Goldstone himself. While few doubt his smarts as a legal strategist, Wall Street has little regard for his management prowess. Critics complain he is too far removed from the fray. "This company has been very badly run," says Stephen Smith, executive vice-president of Brandywine Asset Management Inc., owner of 1 million RJR shares. "They need someone who can really turn it around."

LOOKING TO SPLIT?

5 But then, many investors admit that isn't the reason they're sticking around. They view Goldstone as a sort of Mikhail Gorbachev, presiding over the last days of a decrepit empire. They're counting on the lift that could come if the industry settles and Goldstone can then follow through with plans to split RJR in three. Says Arthur Cecil of T. Rowe Price Associates Inc., which owns 4 million RJR shares: "We're really, really banking on a reversal of fortune."

6 Goldstone, who admits his operational knowhow is limited, lets the division chiefs alone while he grapples with legal and financial matters. "I'm not going to follow their every footstep," says Goldstone, who after his elevation to CEO in December, 1995, replaced all three division heads. Industry insiders and analysts generally praise the credentials of that team—Andrew Schindler, president of R.J. Reynolds, Reynolds International President Pierre de Labouchere, and Nabisco President James M. Kilts. But they question their ability to rejuvenate RJR when the goal of the boss is to break up

Source: Larry Light in New York, with Irene Kunii in Tokyo, Carol Matlack in Moscow, and bureau reports, "Smoke Alarms at RJR," *Business Week:* November 16, 1998; and Carol Matlack in Moscow, "A Long Hard Slog on the Russian Front," *Business Week:* November 16, 1998.

the company. In fact, if he succeeds, Goldstone cheerfully admits he doesn't want to stay with any of the divisions. "My job here will be over," he says.

7   That's because a settlement would free Goldstone, finally, to spin off Nabisco. The long-anticipated move should boost share prices— indeed, reports in October that a settlement might be imminent following the elections hiked RJR's stock 19% in five days, to near 30. A spin-off would also help pay down further the mountainous debt RJR took on in its leveraged buyout 10 years ago. Even without a settlement, Goldstone has settled on what amounts to a strategic retreat, giving ground across all fronts. If there is no agreement, he insists RJR will wind up in bankruptcy court.

LBO HANGOVER

8   How did it come to this? Goldstone and other RJR executives blame the costs and distractions of two epic battles: the 1988 leveraged buyout of RJR by Kohlberg Kravis Roberts & Co., and the courtroom fight waged by states and individuals seeking redress for tobacco-related injuries. The LBO boosted RJR's debt load to $29 billion. KKR decamped in 1995. The debt has since been whittled down to $9.5 billion, but the upshot is that this year, through Sept. 30, RJR shelled out $664 million in interest payments. Add to that the charges that all tobacco companies already are paying states—$457 million so far this year for RJR. Philip Morris paid about the same in interest and twice as much to states but is three times RJR's size. "You can't operate on a shoestring against a competitor as powerful as Philip Morris," Goldstone says.

9   History alone, though, can't explain why RJR continues to lose ground. In the U.S., the company has been slow to defend its cigarette brands, which include Winston, Camel, and Salem. Philip Morris started the decade with 42% of the U.S. market, vs. 30% for RJR. Since then, Philip Morris has gained 8 points, while RJR lost 6%. Brown & Williamson, the U.S. subsidiary of Britain's well-heeled BAT Industries PLC, has also grabbed 6 share points this decade in the U.S. market. Sure, Philip Morris spent $212 million for U.S. cigarette ads in 1997, while RJR shelled out $126 million—a hair above its 1990 level. But the '90s are full of stories of smaller companies that outmaneuvered giants with a tighter brand focus. That hasn't been in evidence at RJR.

SALEM'S LOT

10   The situation is grimmest for RJR's lesser-ranked brands, which have suffered from a lack of marketing support. Salem, the company's No. 3-selling premium cigarette, hasn't had a new ad campaign since 1995. Salem's sales fell 5% in the first half of this year, part of a long-term slide that has cut market share in half since the LBO. The best that can be said is that RJR arrested the years-long decline of its flagship Winston brand with the "No Bull" ad campaign kicked off in August, 1997. These clever ads repositioned the brand as an unpretentious smoke for regular guys, free of sugar and licorice additives. Camel, meanwhile, has held its own, despite the retirement of its Joe Camel spokesfigure in 1997.

11   The marketing contrast between Philip Morris and RJR is seen at the Melton Food Mart in Louisville, where more than a quarter of the shop's 18,000 square feet is devoted to cigarette sales. Philip Morris has locked up the place by paying special bounties for favored treatment, an indulgence Reynolds can't as easily afford. Owner Joseph Melton III says Philip Morris' "contract money" is enough to pay his rent for the cigarette sales area. He also receives "flex funds" based on rising sales. Says Melton of his patron: "They've got the bucks." And, in return, the shelf space: Two-thirds of Melton's tobacco department is piled high with Philip Morris products. Though Winston and Camel occasionally put up displays, they remain for only a few days.

FOREIGN WOES

12   As bad as things are for RJR at home, they're worse overseas. R.J. Reynolds International, which provides one-third of RJR's cigarette revenues, saw tobacco sales fall 19% in the third quarter, while

EXHIBIT A

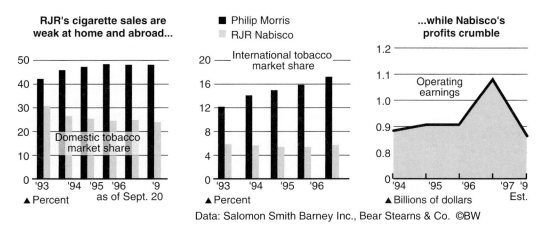

RJR's cigarette sales are weak at home and abroad...

■ Philip Morris
□ RJR Nabisco

...while Nabisco's profits crumble

Domestic tobacco market share

▲ Percent   as of Sept. 20

International tobacco market share

▲ Percent

Operating earnings

▲ Billions of dollars   Est.

Data: Salomon Smith Barney Inc., Bear Stearns & Co. ©BW

operating profits dropped by half. That followed a 5% sales slide in 1997. Says Reynolds International President de Labouchere: "1998 will be another year of disappointment." This summer, as it sought to cut costs, RJR shuttered three of its 28 foreign plants—in Hong Kong, Germany, and Hungary—partly because antiquated cigarette-making machines regularly mangled the product.

13   It wasn't supposed to turn out this way. Faced with stagnant U.S. and European markets, RJR began a big emerging-markets push in the late 1980s. Along with many of its rivals, RJR sought out countries where smoking rates were on the rise. But while Philip Morris and BAT have since surged ahead overseas, RJR spread its marketing too thin and moved too slowly as new opportunities arose. Those mistakes, compounded by economic recessions in Asia and Russia, have left RJR hustling for small pieces of many markets. Moreover, its expansion was haphazard, with much duplication of effort. There were 10 different Winston marketing campaigns around the globe, for instance, a mistake the company finally corrected this year by centralizing foreign operations in its international headquarters in Geneva.

14   Still, no structural revamping could make up for the fact that RJR has lacked the capital to gain significant market share in its far-flung outposts. "Their economies of scale are horrible in countries where they have just a percentage point or two," says Martin Feldman, a Salomon Smith Barney analyst. As a result, RJR belatedly plans to pull back from many nations where it has insignificant standing, particularly in Asia. Goldstone's fondest wish for Reynolds International is to see the suffering unit married off to a strong competitor, says a highly placed RJR executive.

15   The spin-off that RJR shareholders have been waiting forever to see, of course, is that of Nabisco. Goldstone says he can't do that until RJR's legal situation is resolved—otherwise, tobacco plaintiffs could get a court injunction to stop such a deal. In the meantime, though, the cookie and cracker empire continues to crumble. The first serious signs of weakness came last year, when revenue fell 1.7%, to $8.7 billion. This year, analysts expect operating profits to fall 20%, to $866 million, as sales drop another 4%. Nabisco shares—20% of the stock is publicly traded—have fallen to around 38, down 24% from a 52-week high of $50^1/8$ in April. No wonder Nabisco CEO Kilts likens his task to a trauma-team leader's: "We have to stop the bleeding."

16   But Nabisco executives have been pledging to turn things around for more than three years. Kilts took over in January from H. John Greeniaus, vowing to shed noncore operations and focus on snack foods. For the 12 months ended Sept. 30, market share for cookies in supermarkets slumped almost two full points, to 34%, and crackers slipped a half-point, to 47%. Kilts has yet to fill the void created by slowing demand for the Snackwells line of fat-free snacks. As consumers return to full-fat eats that taste better, Snackwells' sales have fallen steadily for three years and now stand at half of their 1995 peak. The best Nabisco can do is bring out a number of new Snackwells flavors. Says Andrew Carrano, vice-president for marketing at the Great Atlantic & Pacific Tea Co. supermarket chain: "Without any really new items, they're not going anywhere."

ELFIN RIVAL

17   Keebler Foods Co., with about half Nabisco's share in both categories, has gained the ground that Nabisco lost. For one thing, Keebler concentrated on some of the more consistent consumers around: children. And while Keebler only has a third of Nabisco's ad budget, its elves have new products to pitch. Keebler has offered up an ever-increasing and artful array of snacks, such as Heads and Tails animal-shaped cheese crackers. "We haven't seen that much from our competitors," chortled Keebler's retailing honcho, David B. Vermylen, in an analysts' conference call recently.

18   Now Kilts is in the midst of a massive restructuring that includes laying off 6% of his workforce and selling off brands like College Inn broths. That is supposed to let Nabisco scrape together enough savings to boost advertising. But he's haunted by a mess created in the last housecleaning, when Greeniaus trimmed the sales force by 1,000 people, most of them senior reps. Greeniaus figured less-experienced merchandisers could take up the slack. Wrong move: Stores started to complain of bad service. Shelves were disorganized or not stocked. "When you can't even get orders filled, you get very unhappy," says A&P's Carrano.

19   Of course, if Goldstone and other tobacco execs do patch together a sweeping settlement with the states, the stock market will be inclined to forgive a multitude of sins. Certainly some investors accepted long ago that Goldstone's legal abilities far exceed any hands-on management skills. Says Stephen A. Yacktman, vice-president of Yacktman Asset Management Co., which bailed out of RJR two years ago: "He's their lawyer, that's all. The game is over." But there's no telling when, or if, that settlement will arrive. And for RJR investors, there is a growing possibility that the end result will be three basket cases instead of one.

A LONG HARD SLOG ON THE RUSSIAN FRONT

20   Don't blame the Marlboro man for RJR's latest debacle. On its ride into Russia, R.J. Reynolds Tobacco Co. has shown an uncanny knack for shooting itself in the foot.

21   Only last winter, the company was savoring the success of Peter I, a locally produced cigarette that in just two years had become one of Russia's top-sellers. But then RJR sparked a dispute with local tobacco distributors that crippled sales. Peter I sales fell 20% in the second quarter, just as RJR was finishing a $120 million factory expansion in St. Petersburg. Making things worse, on August 17, Russia devalued the ruble, sending the economy tumbling. By September, weak sales forced the factory to shut for several days. RJR now says Russia was largely to blame for its poor overall third-quarter results.

22   The saga of RJR in Russia illustrates how the company has squandered opportunities in foreign markets once thought promising. True, all cigarette makers are struggling in crisis-stricken emerging markets, as consumers switch from premium imports to cheaper smokes. But for RJR, the stakes are especially high. Russia is one of its biggest overseas markets, accounting for 11% of foreign earnings, vs. only 3.7% for Philip Morris Cos. And RJR's position in Russia mirrors its vulnerability worldwide: Its leading brand, Peter I, is a lower-priced smoke with thin margins and weak consumer loyalty.

23   RJR had high hopes when it entered Russia in 1992. Russians, who smoke nearly 250 billion cigarettes a year, were eager to switch from harsh Soviet-style cigarettes and were entranced by Western advertising. Philip Morris was making inroads with images of the American West in Marlboro ads. But while RJR soon matched Philip Morris' ad spending, its Winston and Camel brands made little headway against its archrival's best-sellers, Marlboro and the mid-priced L&M. Industry-watchers say RJR scattered its ads over too many brands. "They diluted their marketing," says a Moscow ad exec familiar with the effort. RJR executives say ad spending early on was tiny, as it and rivals concentrated on distribution.

Rise and Fall

24   With Peter I, RJR's luck began to turn. Launched in 1995 to capitalize on Russian patriotism, its striking black package was embossed with the 18th century seal of Czar Peter the Great. But there was nothing imperial about its price: about 58 cents a pack, half the cost of Marlboro. Sales took off, and Peter I joined Russia's top brands. RJR cranked up production last year to 37 billion cigarettes.

25   From there, it went downhill. Last spring, RJR got into a spat with nine big Moscow-based distributors, who allege that it jacked up the prices they paid while maintaining lower prices for smaller regional distributors. The distributors perceived the move as an attempt to squeeze them out of certain markets and retaliated by refusing to carry RJR products. "We had to draw the line," says Mikhail Bukov of Yunakt, a member of the group. RJR, which will not comment publicly on the dispute, eventually made peace, and Peter I sales rebounded to pre-boycott levels. But the billions of cigarettes piling up in warehouses could not have come at a worse time. After devaluation, RJR had to discount heavily to pare inventory.

26   Even so, RJR has built a solid Russian beachhead with Peter I. But, says a Moscow-based executive at a rival tobacco company, "they made a mistake in believing that they could suddenly command brand loyalty." While Peter I has picked up smokers who traded down from costlier brands, it has also lost some who fled to even cheaper brands. Philip Morris admits that Marlboro sales have also softened but says its lower-priced brands are doing better than before. So instead of the sensational growth it expected, RJR will have to settle down for years of hard work—and no more fumbles—in Russia.

CASE 37   BusinessWeek

BOEING: FLY, DAMN IT, FLY

1   Since Alan R. Mulally was named president of Boeing Co.'s commercial airplane unit on Sept. 1, he has conferred with his top 14 managers every Thursday morning for four hours. The meetings move from one Puget Sound plant to another, but the agenda remains the same: fixing Boeing. These managers aren't jawboning about airy vision statements. They're poring over production numbers and cost reports, trying to drive operating margins for Boeing's largest business from near zero back up to 8% or more. Mulally recites the same mantra at each meeting: "The data will set us free."

2   That focus on numbers is a novel and long overdue change in Boeing's hidebound culture. Underlying its well-publicized travails—staggering production snafus and cost overruns that led to big losses despite a record boom in orders—are much deeper problems. In an era when price and efficiency are king, the company is saddled with bureaucracy, redundant processes, and antiquated information technology. "Boeing has not changed very much since World War II," says Bill Whitlow, investment manager for Safeco Northwest Fund, holder of $2.7 million in Boeing stock. Adds Paul H. Nisbet, president of aerospace analyst JSA Research Inc.: "Boeing needs a thorough scrubbing of its operations from top to bottom."

3   Now, after a management shakeup at its August board meeting, the scrubbing has begun in earnest. The reorganization came in the wake of $4.45 billion in writedowns over the past 18 months and net profits of only $308 million—or less than 1.2%—on first-half 1998 revenues of $26.3 billion. Boeing was split into three units—commercial, defense, and space—and the former head of commercial aircraft was forced out. New executives are now in charge of the units, including two who aren't Boeing lifers. That's almost unprecedented, and reflects how far Chief Executive Philip M. Condit, 57, and Chief Operating Officer Harry C. Stonecipher, 62, are willing to go.

4   They don't have much choice: Their own jobs are on the line if they can't end Boeing's seemingly endless litany of troubles. One Boeing director says privately that the pair still has board support. But Peter L. Aseritis, an analyst with Credit Suisse First Boston Corp., figures the board will give Condit a nine-month grace period before "taking him by the scruff of the neck and throwing him out the door."

5   Those nine months will go by fast. Condit and team say they are on the verge of fixing the bottlenecks that have slowed airplane deliveries and hammered profits. Facing enormous pressure to deliver airplanes on time, Boeing execs say they have to focus first on getting products out the door. "We have to get productivity back to the levels we've had before, and then redesign the process to take more cost out," Condit says. But beyond that, the plan Condit has spelled out is a course of incrementalism. And so far, it's lacking in details. The broad outlines: complete stalled plans to modernize the computer systems used to produce planes, trim tens of thousands of jobs, and remake relationships with Boeing's enormous supply chain.

6   Will it be enough? As long as Boeing continues to beat profit estimates, as it did for the third quarter, Wall Street seems to be regaining patience. Boeing's turmoil battered its stock by 50%, from 60 1/2 in July 1997 to 30 3/8 last August. But since the reorganization, it has recovered 16%, to around 35. "They've bought themselves some time," says investor Robert Finch, whose Aeltus Investment Management in Hartford, Conn., holds $4.6 million in Boeing shares. The reorganization, he says, shows the company is "paying attention to the bottom line."

7   Certainly the changes come none too soon. A redesign actually has been under way for five years, but it was seriously sidetracked by Boeing's production push. The process began in the early 1990s,

Source: Andy Reinhardt in San Mateo and Seanna Browder in Seattle, with bureau reports, "Boeing: Fly, Damn It, Fly," *Business Week:* November 9, 1998; and Andy Reinhardt in San Mateo, with Seanna Browder in Seattle, "A Space Venture That's Sputtering," *Business Week:* November 9, 1998.

during the trough of the last business cycle, when Boeing unveiled an ambitious plan to streamline aircraft assembly. But when business took off in 1995, Boeing focused on grabbing as many orders as it could. Management had been shocked the year before when its arch-rival, the European government-subsidized Airbus Industrie consortium, outsold it for the first time. To protect share, Boeing launched an all-out war, with discounts as high as 25%, analysts say.

8   Boeing won the battle, but ended up with a bulging order book of lowballed planes. Scaling up production to build all those planes sent costs soaring. That's why analysts expect the commercial airplane group, which lost $1.8 billion after charges in 1997, to end this year some $61 million in the red. "I'm convinced it was one of the most dysfunctional maneuvers in the history of American business," says Richard Aboulafia, director of aviation consulting for Teal Group Corp.

HOMELESS PLANES

9   Boeing is still digging out. Its anemic net margins, which are expected to be 1.7% this year, will creep up to 3.4% in 1999, analysts predict. Even customers are feeling the cost-cutting push; Boeing, for example, now makes them pay for nonstandard features on planes. In early October, both United Airlines Inc. and United Parcel Service Inc. complained to Boeing that it was balking at making minor fixes to planes they had ordered. After a heated meeting on Oct. 8, however, United went away satisfied. "I am very, very positive about the steps they are taking," says Andrew P. Studdert, a senior vice-president for United parent UAL Corp.

10   Customers and investors are pinning their hopes especially on Stonecipher. The hard-nosed former CEO of McDonnell Douglas Corp., who arrived in 1997 with Boeing's $16.3 billion acquisition, has already instilled a more by-the-numbers approach. He pressed Boeing, for the first time, to provide earnings guidance to Wall Street. And he supported Mulally's plan to push profit and loss responsibility down to individual plants, another first.

11   Still, any fixes could be swamped by worldwide economic problems. As America's largest exporter, Boeing is especially vulnerable to turmoil in Asia, where it sells a third of its commercial planes. Even as it gets production back on track, 34 finished aircraft are parked in the Arizona desert, unclaimed by strapped airlines such as Garuda Indonesia and Philippine Airlines. Condit himself now admits that earlier estimates of Asia's impact on orders may have been too low.

12   Those undelivered planes weigh heavily on the balance sheet, and Boeing can't turn off its production spigot quickly. Indeed, the company is still planning to raise output to a record 51 planes a month in the first quarter of 1999 because it has to meet longstanding delivery commitments. Yet it told analysts on Oct. 22 that up to 15% of its output for the next five quarters, or more than 120 planes, may go homeless, pending new financing deals or resales to other airlines.

13   Longer term, Condit must take a cold look at demand for aircraft. He still holds to forecasts that the global market will demand new planes at an average annual rate of 8% of the world's fleet for the next 20 years—5% growth and 3% replacement. But analysts and customers say that may be high. "Boeing is like a huge freight train that takes a couple of miles to slow down," says John Plueger, co-chief operating officer of International Lease Finance. "They have to talk to their customers now about deferrals." On October 20, Malaysian Airlines became the latest Asian carrier to back out, delaying 12 planes worth $2 billion.

14   Boeing's challenges aren't borne solely by the commercial-airplane unit, which accounts for 64% of revenues. In the defense arena, executives must figure out how to hike revenues while military budgets shrink. Indeed, some production lines could shut down in two years if new orders don't appear from the U.S. or abroad. And in the fast-developing space and communications business, a run of bad luck and heavy research spending are holding margins to less than 4%.

15   The new management team has a healthy dose of non-Boeing blood. The commercial airplane group, based near Seattle, is now under Mulally, 52, who previously headed Boeing's Information, Space & Defense Systems group. That group is now split in two: Michael M. Sears, 51, a veteran McDonnell Douglas exec, runs the defense operation out of McDonnell's old St. Louis home. And James F. Albaugh, 48, who came to Boeing when it bought Rockwell International Corp.'s space business in 1996 for $3.1 billion, heads space and communications in Southern California.

TABLE 1
Back to the Hangar

Boeing execs say they have production woes under control, but more steps are needed to assure long-term health

Fix Production for Good

Boeing has unkinked the snarls that plagued its Seattle factories for the past year. But computer systems that were supposed to streamline purchasing and production still aren't in place, and costs remain above historic levels. Fixing those problems is Job No. 1 for new management.

Make Up with Suppliers

During its ramp-up, Boeing stretched suppliers with extravagant demands for parts and raw materials—and then lured away many of their workers. Now, it is trying to treat those companies more like partners, including them on decisions and signing long-term contracts.

Push Back Deliveries

Given the state of the world economy, Boeing needs to take a reality check on its goal of making 620 jets next year. If Boeing can persuade customers to delay deliveries, it will gain some breathing room and hold on to the orders until 2001, when annual deliveries drop to 476.

Deal with Unneeded Assets

By 2001, all commercial McDonnell Douglas lines will have been shut down in Long Beach, Calif. The 100-seat 717 won't generate enough volume to carry the facility. Boeing needs to pare away or redeploy excess personnel and facilities like Long Beach that it acquired through mergers.

16   All three need to boost profit margins, but Mulally faces the toughest job. So far, though, his plans are short on specifics. Clearly, first priority is to finish cleaning up Boeing's production woes. Once parts are all arriving on time and workers are better trained, he'll focus on cutting costs. "We have another year to go before we get back to efficiency levels we had before we traumatized the whole system," he concedes.

17   Aside from tweaking the production flow, the only ways he can lower costs now are automation and layoffs. Both are already under way. Boeing has said it aims to cut total payroll, now at 235,000, to as low as 210,000 by the end of 1999. For a change, much of the pain could fall to white-collar workers, not to the factory staff Boeing needs to get planes out the door. Pink slips have already gone out to 1,100 employees. But analyst Nicholas P. Heymann of Prudential Securities Inc. thinks Boeing might have to cut as many as 70,000 people.

18   The automation problem is even more nagging. Boeing is one of the world's largest users of information technology, but it hosts a bewildering array of 400 systems. Data are so diffused that Boeing can't centralize procurement of the millions of parts used across its product line: An identical part may be manufactured in-house for one airplane and outsourced for another. Boeing is putting in place a new $1 billion system that ties together all its old computers, but it has ballooned in complexity and now won't be fully operational until after 2000.

PROCUREMENT OVERHAUL

19   With good systems in place, Mulally should eventually be able to better track inventory and forecast demand for parts. Even so, Boeing is years behind Airbus in electronically managing its supplier relations, a crucial step that saves costs on both sides. And software alone won't make partners of suppliers, many of whom felt burned by Boeing's extravagant demands for parts and raw materials during the production surge. For that, Boeing is overhauling procurement, forging long-term deals like the 10-year, $4.3 billion contract it announced Aug. 31 to buy aluminum from just five firms instead of the previous 50. Top suppliers invited to a two-day Boeing schmoozefest in early October say they were impressed by the company's new focus.

20   Still, Boeing has to prove it can keep that focus, even as boom times come to an end. But the economic crisis could have a silver lining: Order deferrals from carriers could help Boeing smooth the

EXHIBIT A

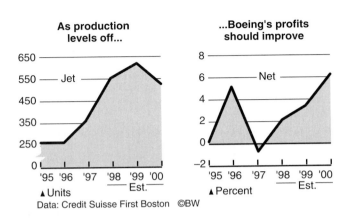

As production levels off...

As production
levels off...

650
550 — Jet
450
350
250
0
'95 '96 '97 '98 '99 '00
▲ Units
—— Est.——

...Boeing's profits
should improve

8
6 — Net
4
2
0
-2
'95 '96 '97 '98 '99 '00
▲ Percent
—— Est.——

Data: Credit Suisse First Boston ©BW

peaks and valleys of the cycle. "Just about the time we need another good kick, [Asian carriers] are going to be ready to go again," says Condit. "That'll help us carry on long-term." Assuming that by the time orders pick up again, Boeing has learned how to build planes for a profit.

A SPACE VENTURE THAT'S SPUTTERING

21   It wasn't supposed to work out this way. When Boeing Co. bought McDonnell Douglas Corp. and Rockwell International Corp.'s space and defense unit in 1996, the Seattle-based company's goal was to meld an assortment of products and services—rockets, satellite vehicles, launch operations, and electronics—into an entity that would dominate commercial and government space programs. Boeing wanted to grab hold of an industry set to blast off—and one able to balance the ebbs and flows of commercial aviation.

22   Oops. The strategy was valid, and the company is indeed No. 1 in space. But the past year has been nearly as trying for Boeing's $5.5 billion space operation as it was for the $26.9 billion commercial-airplane unit. At fault are geopolitics, unproven technology, and a remarkable run of bad luck. James F. Albaugh, the new president of Boeing's Space & Communications group, insists he will hit 1998 revenue and profit targets. "But it could have been better," Albaugh concedes.

23   What went wrong? Just about everything imaginable. Boeing's prized new Delta III rocket blew up on its maiden flight on Aug. 26, taking with it a $225 million PanAmSat Corp. satellite. Overconfidence lured Boeing into taking the risky step of carrying a live payload on the maiden voyage. The quirky Sea Launch program, which aims to loft rockets from a platform in the Pacific Ocean, is a year behind schedule because of difficulties coordinating with Ukrainian, Norwegian, and Russian partners. Boeing was outbid by Lockheed Martin Corp. on a $4 billion contract to manage NASA's ground operations. And the International Space Station, for which Boeing is the prime contractor, has been delayed by economic turmoil in Russia, where the main control module is being built.

"ENVIRONMENT OF EXTREMES"

24   As troubling as these setbacks are, analysts say that they're unsurprising. "Space is an environment of extremes," notes Brett Lambert of Washington-based researcher DFI International. Boeing certainly isn't alone: A Lockheed rocket blew up just weeks before the Delta III explosion, for instance. And the news isn't all bad. On October 16, Boeing bested Lockheed to win a $1.38 billion Air Force contract to launch a new generation of rockets.

25   Indeed, Boeing remains bullish on space despite all of its snafus. From about $40 billion this year, the industry could hit $150 billion in a decade, thanks to the global communications-satellite boom. Boeing has its hands in many of the key programs, as both an investor and a contractor, including the ambitious Teledesic Corp. "Internet-in-the-sky" venture backed by Craig O. McCaw and William H. Gates III.

26   Boeing's biggest challenge in space will be to drive down costs as relentlessly as it must in its jet airplane operations. "This is going to be a classic commercial business," says CEO Philip M. Condit—a far cry from the cushy government work of the past. Albaugh thinks that the space group can earn margins of 10% within five years. But with margins now less than 4%, Boeing has a ways to go before space takes its profits into orbit.

CASE 38

BusinessWeek

THEN CAME BRANSON

1   On a sultry September afternoon, a weary Richard Branson climbs aboard a Virgin Atlantic 747. Branson, founder and chairman of London-based Virgin Group, has just watched the jumbo jet unload 30 metric tons of relief equipment on hurricane-swept Antigua. He has also just come through a four-day publicity blitz that included celebrity cricket in Barbados and a catamaran cruise in St. Lucia to promote his airline's new Caribbean service. When the aftermath of Hurricane Georges forced him to cancel the Antigua leg of the V.I.P. junket, he quickly organized the relief effort, spotting a chance to engender local goodwill—and publicity. But ever the showman, Branson can't resist a final flourish. In the cool, darkened cabin of the nearly empty jet, he shakes a journalist's hand on a promise: to meet again on Virgin's inaugural flight into outer space.

2   Starship Virgin? Branson's dreams for his brand seem boundless. Since his counterculture days in the early '70s, when he lived on a houseboat in London, Europe's best-known entrepreneur has built an empire of some 200 companies with combined yearly revenues of an estimated $4 billion. His group spans three continents and includes planes, trains, financial services, music stores, cinemas, and cola. Restless and driven, Branson, who is worth an estimated $1.7 billion, according to London's Sunday Times, is a celebrity in Britain who rubs shoulders with royalty and pop stars. He's also an energetic self-promoter. It's no coincidence that *Losing My Virginity,* Branson's new autobiography, hits U.S. bookstores this month, just as he's expanding his airline, building new megastores, and rolling out his cola in the U.S. "I want Virgin to be as well-known around the world as Coca-Cola," he says.

3   With ambitions like these, some people wonder whether Branson, 48, is in outer space already. The flamboyant and media-savvy entrepreneur, who once promoted a new venture by donning a wedding gown for photographers, has helped make Virgin a recognized name with strong associations. But with that name now attached to dozens of unrelated ventures, marketing experts warn that Branson risks diluting his brand. "Overstretching ends up in only one way: snapping," says Jeremy Bullmore, an ad industry veteran and outside director for ad giant WPP Group PLC. "I can't think of a company that has put its brand on so many products."

4   Then there's the question of Branson and his ability to manage this chaotic empire. Few of Virgin's businesses make big profits, and two of the biggest cash generators, Virgin Atlantic Airways and an 18-month-old British railroad venture, are problematic. Analysts think the cyclical airline industry may be poised for a down cycle. Virgin Rail turns a profit with the help of government subsidies that will phase out by 2010. At a time when other companies are preparing for a global downturn, Branson is crisscrossing the U.S. on a book tour and gearing up for another attempt at circling the globe in a hot-air balloon in December.

TRUE LOVE

5   Branson knows firsthand the dangers of stretching his business too far. Virgin made its name as a record label in the '70s, signing punkers the Sex Pistols. But during the recession of the early 1990s, Branson was forced by his bankers to sell the record business to raise cash for his struggling startup, Virgin Air. Branson still mourns the loss of the music business. "I had to sell a company I loved," he says. Branson insists he'll never put himself at the mercy of bank lenders again.

Source: Julia Flynn in Antigua, with Wendy Zellner in Dallas, Larry Light in New York, and Joseph Weber in Toronto, "Then Came Branson," *Business Week* (international edition): October 26, 1998.

EXHIBIT A
Resumé of Richard Branson

Born
1950, son of an English barrister and his former airline hostess wife.

Education
Beaten at Scaitcliffe Preparatory School for poor grades. Skipped college and moved to London in the late 1960s to work on *Student,* a magazine he co-founded.

First Hit
Mike Oldfield's *Tubular Bells* album, released in 1973 by Branson's Virgin Records.

Family
Marriage to American Kristen Tomassi ends after wife-swapping episode. Marries Joan Templeman in 1989 after living together for a dozen years and having two children with her, Holly and Sam.

Personal Wealth
Estimated at $1.7 billion.

Data: *Losing My Virginity, Virgin King, Business Week.*

6   Instead, he has embarked on a strategy he calls "branded venture capital" that has allowed him to launch a hodgepodge of businesses with minimal investment. Essentially, Branson manages the business and puts up the Virgin name, usually in exchange for a controlling interest, while his wealthy partners put up most of the cash. In financial services, he has teamed up with insurer Australian Mutual Provident and Royal Bank of Scotland PLC to sell retirement and other investment products in Britain. In trains, he has hitched to Stagecoach Holdings PLC, which operates double-decker buses in London. And until recently, his cola venture was backed by Cott Corp., the Canadian private-label soda maker. "Not only does he come to us with great ideas, but he's willing to put in some of his own money to back them," says Randl L. Shure, managing director of BT Capital Partners Europe, an early partner in the rail venture and a current investor in Virgin Entertainment. When Stagecoach bought out its stake, BT nearly tripled its investment in less than two years.

7   The strategy has helped Branson expand his brand around the world. But teaming up with an equity partner carries its own risks, mainly that of having to buy out partners that are ready to move on. In the past several years, Branson has bought back stakes from Cott, Blockbuster Entertainment, and British retailer W.H. Smith, at a total cost of $270 million. And history shows the Virgin name is no guarantee of success. Notable nonstarters include ventures in vodka, computers, and a magazine.

8   Branson's toothy grin and corny publicity stunts have led some to dub him the P.T. Barnum of British business. But behind the scenes, he has assembled an executive team with solid Establishment credentials. A year ago, Branson brought in Gordon McCallum, a former McKinsey & Co. consultant, as group strategy director to impose some discipline on how the Virgin brand is used. Stephen Murphy, the group's finance chief, is ex-Mars, Unilever, and Quaker Oats. And behind his playful image, Branson himself is a tough competitor and negotiator.

SMALL STUFF

9   While most brand stewards use extreme caution before extending a valued name to a new product, Branson takes a different tack. He says Virgin is irreverent, eager to take on the Establishment, and dedicated to service. He believes that the occasional failure doesn't hurt, as long as Virgin is perceived to be fighting the good fight. Indeed, the one thread that runs through the tangle of Branson's business interests is his preference for entering industries where customers have few choices. "We like to use the brand to take on some very large companies that we believe exert too much power," he says.

10   Yet for a people's champion, Branson has created a complex and opaque empire. Most of his companies are private and domiciled in tax havens such as the Channel Islands. Because he's constantly shifting companies around and forging and discarding business partnerships, it's hard to gauge

TABLE 1
Branson's Bugaboos

Cola Competitors

Virgin Cola has made little headway against global giants Coca-Cola and Pepsi.

Train Trials

Service on newly acquired British train lines is shoddy. Dubbed "a national disgrace" by officials.

Airline Grounded

U.S. laws have blocked Branson's quest to fly the domestic skies.

Dangerous Hobbies

Branson already crashed a hot-air balloon in Algeria in 1997 while attempting to circle the globe. He plans another try in December.

Virgin's performance. Branson says he has built up a $420 million cash pile and that his companies produce a quarter-billion more in cash flow each year with scant debt. One reason its disparate ventures haven't hopelessly confused the Virgin image—or drained its finances—is that Branson doesn't mind starting small. Virgin's new bridal and fashion ventures, for example, are too tiny to matter much to the empire's financial well-being. And Branson says he's considering new ventures such as credit cards, phones, and health clubs.

11   No wonder it's a standing joke among Branson's top aides that they're paid to curb some of their boss's wilder schemes. "Richard comes up with ideas, and we say: 'Down, Richard,' " jokes Virgin Atlantic CEO Steve Ridgway. Yet Virgin Atlantic was once widely predicted to follow Freddy Laker's as another doomed transatlantic startup carrier. Instead, in its 15-year history, it has shaken up the industry and stolen share from giant British Airways. Instead of trying to compete just on price, Virgin has offered better creature comforts—seat-back videos, an upgraded business class, on-board manicures and massages, and curbside check-in. Virgin Atlantic earned $129 million on sales of $1.4 billion for the year that ended on Apr. 30, and it threw off nearly $340 million in cash, making it one of the healthiest airlines in the world, says Michael K. Lowry, publisher of industry newsletter AirWatch Report. Now, Branson is lobbying the U.S. Congress to change the law prohibiting foreign carriers from owning more than 25% of a U.S. airline. Airline experts say he has little chance of success, and some believe Branson's real purpose is to prevent approval for the planned alliance between British Air and American Airlines.

12   Even more quixotic is Branson's push to launch Virgin Cola in Europe and the U.S. The effort puts him squarely in competition with Coca-Cola Co. and PepsiCo—"cola duopolists," in Branson's words. Although he rode a vintage World War II tank through New York's Times Square last May to launch his soda, the brand's market share remains negligible. "It would be easier to make a snowman in July in Florida than to take on Coke and Pepsi," says Beverage Digest publisher John Sicher. For starters, Branson has been without a bottling-and-distribution network since buying out Cott last year after the Canadian bottler balked at Virgin's aggressive expansion plans. Although Virgin Cola's quirky TV ads are still running, Virgin's investment to date is minimal and Branson has little riding on the venture except his prestige.

NEW TIMES

13   Almost as unlikely as cola is a foray into financial services. Nonetheless, Virgin Direct has made a surprisingly credible assault on Britain's financial-services sector. During the early '90s, virtually every big player in Britain's fledgling private pensions industry was tainted by allegations of high-pressure sales tactics and fraud. Financial services may seem at odds with Virgin's irreverent image, but Branson says that once again it gives the brand a chance to take on established players in the name of giving the customer a better deal. Still, this is a long-term proposition at best. The

TABLE 2
Virgin Key Businesses

Company	1998		Change
Virgin Travel Group Ltd.* (includes Virgin Atlantic and Virgin Holidays)	Revenues	$1.6 billion	+20%
	Pretax profits	$151 million	+38%
Virgin Entertainment† (includes Megastore and Virgin Cinema)	Revenues	$1.3 billion	+10%
	Pretax profits	$81 million	+23%
Virgin Rail‡ (includes Cross Country and West Coast)	Revenues	$671 million	+2%
	Pretax profits	$22.9 million	NA

*For the year ended Apr. 30, 1998.
†For the year ended Jan. 31, 1998.
‡For 11-month period ending Feb. 28, 1998.

Data: Companies House, Virgin Group Ltd.

three-year-old venture has lost more than $33 million since it was launched, and CEO Rowan Gormley doesn't predict a profit until 2000 at the earliest.

14   Virgin Entertainment, which includes 148 book, music, and video megastores worldwide and a British cinema business, is a more obvious fit with the Virgin image. But though it makes money, it, too, has struggled. Last year, it closed six stores in Europe, and Branson has had to buy out two partners. Blockbuster wanted out after it was acquired by Viacom in 1994. W.H. Smith put its stake up for sale last fall, when it decided to focus on its bookselling business. Simon Burke, 40, who became head of Entertainment 11 years ago, downplays any problems caused by the buybacks. "Times are different now, and we have very strong cash flow," he says. "We are well able to finance our own expansion." He says the business will earn about $100 million this year on sales of $1.4 billion. Virgin plans to add close to 20 stores next year, including nine in the U.S.

15   Of all Branson's far-flung enterprises, perhaps the one posing the greatest risk to the Virgin name is the 19-month-old rail business. Virgin acquired two capital-starved rail lines as part of British Rail's privatization amid promises that Branson would do what the government couldn't: make the trains run on time. But he underestimated how difficult it would be to improve service given the decrepit track and unionized workforce. As a result, Virgin has been plagued by embarrassing missteps and bad publicity. In late September, while Branson was island-hopping across the Caribbean, Virgin trains carrying Cabinet ministers and other V.I.P.s to the Labor Party's annual meeting were delayed, prompting Deputy Prime Minister John Prescott to call the privatized rail system "a national disgrace" and to lash out that "when it comes to railways, I'm no Virgin."

16   Branson admits the company screwed up but insists that by spending more than $3 billion on high-speed trains over the next four years, service will improve. Meanwhile, the frequent delays hurt. "The experience is damaging Richard and Virgin's reputation overall," says Virgin Entertainment's Burke. "But if we do get it right, it will restore Richard's heroic status because he would have taken something that was hopeless and made it better."

17   It's crucial to the Virgin brand that Branson continue to be seen as a hero. And despite the rail problems, he still is, in Britain. For the second year in a row, Branson was named the country's best business leader in a survey of senior managers by KPMG Management Consultants, and his name is regularly floated as a possible Mayor of London.

18   Of course, that enormous personal appeal poses a difficult question. What are the prospects for Virgin if something should happen to Richard Branson? At the least, such a loss would leave Virgin without its ring-master. Branson, of course, emphasizes the positive: "When artists die, their products sell for twice or three times as much. Hopefully, the same thing will happen to Virgin products if I go." As P.T. Barnum might have said: "On with the show."

CASE 39   BusinessWeek

BASKETBALL'S DAVID STERN: THIS TIME, IT'S PERSONAL

---

1   If every aspiring athlete wants to "be like Mike," every budding sports-business executive wants to be like Dave. Named commissioner of the National Basketball Assn. in 1984, the year Michael Jordan entered the league, David J. Stern transformed the NBA from a dissolute, money-losing franchise into one of the premier brands in global entertainment. Now Stern, 56, must save it from an altogether more pernicious force: greed.

2   On June 30, NBA team owners locked out the players for the third time since 1995 after several months of fruitless negotiations over a new labor contract. During the lockout, teams can neither pay, re-sign, or trade players, nor operate basketball facilities. The immediate effect is limited, since most players have been paid for last season and training camps don't open until September. Unlike the other professional sports leagues, the NBA has never lost a game to lockout or strike. But with both sides talking tougher than ever before, that is one NBA record that might soon fall.

"THE BENCHMARK"

3   There were a number of new "player conduct" rules on the table, but the central issue could not be more elementally financial: Owners and players both want to maximize their share of league revenues, which hit a record $1.74 billion for the 1997–98 season. NBC and Turner Sports Inc. recently renewed their four-year contracts for U.S. rights to broadcast NBA games by agreeing to boost their payments to the league by 140%, to $2.65 billion. Buoyed by this fat new TV pact, league revenues are projected to hit $2 billion next season. "I just find it appalling that with all the money the NBA has to spread around that it's come to this," says Robert Williams, president of Burns Sports Celebrity Service Inc., a Chicago-based firm that pairs star athletes and advertisers.

4   But as any CEO worth his stock options can tell you, a business cannot live by revenues alone. Despite steady revenue growth, the league's operating profit peaked at $195 million in 1992–93 and has been sliding ever since. Last season, the NBA operated at a deficit for the first time since the bad old days of the early 1980s, losing $44 million.

5   The NBA's intramural conflict is attracting intense interest throughout the pro sports world, and for good reason. "David Stern and the NBA are still the benchmark of what a commissioner and a league can do right," says Allen Furst, managing director of D&F Group Inc., a sports-marketing firm in Washington. "If Stern can't handle this situation, it has got to worry all the leagues."

6   Although the NBA commissioner serves at the pleasure of team owners, Stern is a famously energetic and strong-willed sort who styles himself as basketball's "CEO." This is an expression of principle no less than ego, for Stern has always insisted that the league be run as a business in its own right. What could be more American? In practice, though, Stern often has bumped heads with owners who don't mind subsidizing money-losing teams to serve a larger corporate agenda or, worse, who look on basketball as a rich man's hobby and want to win at any cost.

7   It's no wonder that the players have come to think of team owners as men who plead poverty before fishing a $100 million contract out of mysteriously deep pockets. Last year, Kevin Garnett, a 21-year-old phenom, signed a $126 million, seven-year contract with the Minnesota Timberwolves, one of the league's least profitable teams. Stern took Glen Taylor, the Timberwolves' billionaire owner, to task privately but was powerless to block the deal. "David will always say to us, `You've hired me to be the boss, and I'll do it,'" says Taylor, who counts himself a Stern admirer. "But it's a different kind of CEO job, because in other instances, CEOs are the real boss."

Source: Anthony Bianco in New York, "Basketball's David Stern: This Time, It's Personal," *Business Week:* July 13, 1998.

EXHIBIT A

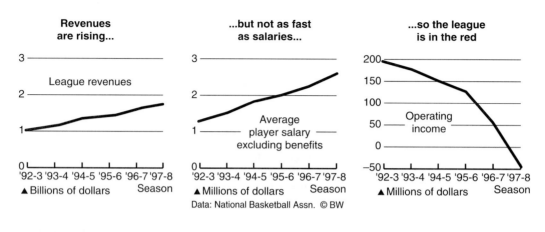

| Revenues are rising... | ...but not as fast as salaries... | ...so the league is in the red |

Data: National Basketball Assn. © BW

JUST SAY NO?

8   Stern now wants to force financial discipline on team owners by amending the league's labor contract to limit player salaries to a fixed percentage of total NBA revenues. He has suggested 48% in talks with the union but says that the number is negotiable. By the commissioner's analysis, the $1 billion in salary the players were paid last season amounted to 57.2% of total league revenues and would have risen to a ruinous 61% next year under the labor contract that the owners voided by imposing a lockout. "We simply cannot go on like this," Stern says.

9   If the owners feel threatened by player salary demands, "all they've got to do is say no," counters Jeffrey Kessler, a New York lawyer who represents the players association. Union officials also scoff at the league's claims of widespread financial distress, arguing that only a few franchises are actually losing money and that the league's real problem is not runaway player salaries but inefficient local management.

10   Stern, a lawyer by training, is known as a master labor negotiator who has done his fair share of posturing over the years. But never before has he publicly argued that the league has become so economically dysfunctional that many teams would be better off financially in the upcoming season if not a single game was played. The lockout frees teams of the obligation to pay their players— far and away management's largest operating cost. Meanwhile, the new TV contract is the first ever requiring broadcasters to make full payment even if there are no games to televise. In effect, Stern secured a strike fund of $475 million (the amount due in the contract's first year), courtesy of NBC and Turner.

11   On June 30, hours before the lockout went into effect, Stern imposed a league hiring freeze—the first of his tenure as commissioner. At the same time, he told the NBA's 800 employees to brace for "drastic reductions" in discretionary spending, including capital investment in a range of new ventures that Stern sees as crucial to the league's long-term revenue growth prospects.

12   Stern, the son of a New York deli owner, joined the NBA in 1978 and was the league's second-ranking executive when it hit bottom in 1980–81. The advent of free agency in 1976 had sent salaries spiraling upward even as attendance had dwindled to a pathetic 58% of capacity. It was Stern who saved the day by persuading the players to accept a league proposal to cap their salaries. A landmark contract signed in 1983 set a limit on the salaries teams could pay but guaranteed players that they would receive no less than 53% of revenues from the sale of tickets and domestic broadcast rights.

13   This management-labor pact undergirded enormous expansion. Attendance soared, handsome arenas were built, and a whole new infrastructure of regional, national, and international broadcasting was assembled. Stern set up NBA Properties Inc. to license the league logo to manufacturers of jerseys, caps, and some 70 other items. The commissioner also founded NBA Entertainment, which began as little more than a game-tape library and evolved into a mini-empire of proprietary multimedia products, including television programming, videos, books, and a Web site (NBA.com).

14   But by the time the league and the players union sat down to negotiate a new contract in 1995, their partnership was coming undone. To the players' annoyance, the league had been slow to cut them in on its growing merchandise and new-media businesses. Meanwhile, the salary cap system was leaking like a colander as owners and player agents exploited loopholes. Chief among them was the "Larry Bird exception." Named after the retired Boston Celtics great, it allowed teams to exceed the cap by any amount to re-sign a current employee. (Last year, the salary cap was set at $26.9 million, and 23 of the 29 teams exceeded it.)

15   Stern opened the contract bargaining with a proposal to turn the league's "soft" cap into a hard one by eliminating all loopholes other than the Bird exception. What's more, owners who made use of the Bird exception would have to pay a prohibitive "luxury tax." To Stern's delight, the union's executive director, an ex-league official named Simon Gourdine, accepted these terms and shook hands on a six-year deal. However, the players refused to ratify the agreement and even attempted to decertify their union.

16   In the end, it was Stern who blinked, recommending that the owners accept a new contract that preserved multiple loopholes and scuttled the luxury tax. However, he did wangle one important concession out of the union. If, after three years, the league's player payroll exceeded 51.8% of revenues, management could void the remainder of the contract. The owners exercised this option in March on a 27–2 vote, overriding the complaints of the union, which now is headed by Billy Hunter, a former federal prosecutor who is no stranger to hardball negotiating.

17   Even before push came to shove at the NBA bargaining table, America's love affair with pro basketball was cooling. The rising incidence of violence, notably the Latrell Sprewell coach-choking episode, has taken much of the sheen off the league's high-gloss image. And after many years of robust growth in gate receipts, average NBA attendance has leveled off in the past three years at slightly more than 17,000 a game.

18   The sports trading card business—once the NBA's single largest source of licensing fees—has all but imploded, and sales of all league-licensed apparel is stagnant at best. Makers of the glutted market in basketball shoes are paring back endorsement deals with NBA players. "The days of signing every single player on a team are over," says John Frascotti, vice-president for global marketing at Reebok International Ltd., which has slashed its roster of NBA endorsement contracts to 40 from 70 over the last year. On June 30, it even parted ways with Los Angeles Laker center Shaquille O'Neal, arguably the league's second-biggest star.

19   Like many longtime business partners of the NBA, Frascotti fears that the impending breakup of the Chicago Bulls—and the possible retirement of Jordan—will hurt the league across the board. "Core basketball fans will stay with the game," he says, "but those on the fringes, who turned on the TV to watch a dynasty, will lose interest."

20   Executives of NBC and Turner Sports disagree, of course, and still profess optimism that next season will come off without a hitch. While reluctant to directly criticize the players, their sympathies clearly lie with Stern. "It's easy to take shots at the leader," says Harvey W. Schiller, president of Turner Sports, dismissing union criticism of the commissioner.

BACKUP HELP

21   Stern concedes that the NBC and Turner contracts are likely to be the league's only major source of revenue growth in the next few years. In the long run, though, Stern sees "enormous potential" in three newly emergent revenue sources: the sale of foreign TV rights, NBA.com, and the Women's National Basketball Assn., the league's new distaff offshoot. Over the past two years alone, Stern has invested $35 million in these ventures, tapping into the league's share of income from merchandise and media sales.

22   Stern does not want to be the first NBA commissioner to lose a game to a labor disruption. It would sully his own image as well as that of the game. On the other hand, he is, above all, a business builder, whose battle with the union has become personal in the sense that he sees his life's work threatened: "Either we work with the players to restore the financial model on which the league's growth and success was based or NBA basketball becomes, I'm afraid, a bad investment." That is a startling statement coming from the biggest booster pro basketball has ever had.

CASE 40

BusinessWeek

FIRE AND ICE AT THE NHL

1   Gary B. Bettman, commissioner of the National Hockey League, has learned to skate a narrow, treacherous line. One moment, he is passionately promoting a sports enterprise that is thriving in such unlikely places as Nashville and Phoenix and that has seen the price of expansion franchises rise 60% in five years. The next moment, he is dousing financial fires from Pittsburgh to Vancouver, watching one NHL team declare bankruptcy, monitoring a half-dozen Canadian clubs mired in a currency-exchange crisis, and listening to team executives whine about a dangerous spiral in player salaries. The latest bad news: TV ratings for the NHL All-Star Game on January 24 were down 19% from last year.

2   Hired away from the National Basketball Assn. and from the shadow of his mentor, NBA Commissioner David J. Stern, Bettman's mission was to take the NHL out of the Ice Age. And certainly he has done that. He has also put millions into the pockets of owners and players alike. But Bettman, 46, has failed to contain costs. Despite all his marketing energy, the NHL remains a weak sibling to the other big-time sports leagues. With its fundamental flaws of low youth participation, few U.S.-born players, and relatively small TV audiences and revenues, can Bettman, or anyone, ever take the NHL to a higher level?

3   When Bettman arrived in February, 1993, the NHL had a public-relations staff of one, a tiny cable-TV contract, and, most assuredly, no vision. Its marketing was a shade better than second-graders hawking lemonade. Almost single-handedly, the new commish had to upgrade its TV deals, get the NHL into the Olympics, and introduce pro hockey to such new frontiers as Miami and Raleigh, N.C.

4   Now, Bettman, like Stern a lawyer by training, finds his hyperactive 5-foot, 6-inch body being checked into the boards by the harsh—"insane," as one former NHL owner says—realities of pro sports economics and the peculiarities of the NHL. In stark contrast to Stern's hard-nosed victory last month in containing basketball player costs, Bettman's tenure has seen average salaries rise 250%.

5   In part, Bettman and his owners boxed themselves in. They had their chance during contract talks in 1995 to press for a salary cap or some form of internal taxation from the National Hockey League Players Assn. (NHLPA). But the players held firm, and the owners rejected the union's modest proposals to tax teams that overpay players. The resulting agreement, twice amended, now runs until the 2004 season with no escape hatch.

6   NHLPA executive Bob Goodenow maintains that the agreement is working, well-managed teams are flourishing, and the league is healthy. Bettman is less sanguine, volunteering that player salaries have risen faster than league revenues in the past two years. "There are franchises spending more than they should. That's something we've got to continue to watch," he says.

7   In December, the Boston Bruins' veteran president, Harry Sinden, revealed that league-wide, the NHL is paying 72% of its revenues to its players. Bettman won't confirm that and cautions that such figures can be misleading. Still, on its face, Sinden's NHL calculation is 15% higher than NBA owners thought was enough to lock out its players and 17% more than NBA players will capture at the end of their just-signed six-year agreement.

8   For the truncated NBA season, the salary cap per team is $30 million. Fourteen of the NHL's 27 teams have payrolls higher than that this season. And under their national TV contracts, an NHL team gets $16 million less than an NBA franchise receives. The NHL relies more heavily on arena revenues, and ticket prices are now the highest in the major leagues, with an average this season of $42.79, according to Team Marketing Report, an industry newsletter.

Source: Jay Weiner in St. Paul and Mark Hyman in New York, "Fire and Ice at the NHL," *Business Week:* February 15, 1999.

BIG TEARS

9   "I think we have reached a crossroads where we need to address some things fairly quickly," says Pierre Gauthier, president of the Mighty Ducks of Anaheim. Gauthier claims his team, owned by Walt Disney Co., will run a $7 million to $9 million operating loss this season, even though it plays to 92% capacity in the Arrowhead Pond, its six-year-old arena, and even though its payroll, at $30.4 million, is only the 14th highest. "If we're starting to lose money, I suspect there's probably a lot of teams that are losing money," he says.

10   Of course, there is no major-league general manager who doesn't cry big tears on cue. And looking only at payrolls gives a distorted view, says Goodenow. "At the end of the day, franchise value . . . is the best indicator of the health of the league," he says. Under Bettman, franchise values have soared. As recently as 1993, new NHL franchises cost $50 million. In the latest round of expansion, which began this season in Nashville and will eventually mean new teams in Atlanta, St. Paul, and Columbus, Ohio, the price to join the NHL club has jumped to $80 million.

11   In 1995, the lowly Winnipeg Jets were sold for $67 million and at Bettman's urging, moved to Phoenix. Today, the Phoenix Coyotes have an estimated value of $87 million and are dickering to build a new arena in Scottsdale. That could push their value into the league's upper tier. According to some published estimates, 19 NHL franchises are worth at least $100 million.

12   Still, some NHL owners are looking doom in the face. Last October, the debt-strapped Pittsburgh Penguins, with $37.5 million in operating losses over the past two seasons, filed for Chapter 11. And last December, the partnership that owns the St. Louis Blues and privately built the $135 million, four-year-old Kiel Center, sent out a cash call to its investors seeking a $17.7 million infusion to cover operating losses. The Blues are now for sale.

SLOWPOKE

13   Meanwhile, the NHL's six remaining Canadian-based franchises are getting whacked by an unfavorable currency exchange rate that has teams taking in Canadian dollars—worth 65 cents U.S.—while paying out U.S. dollars to its players. The problem is so serious that Bettman engineered a modest revenue-sharing program that will give $3.5 million each to franchises in Calgary, Ottawa, and Edmonton. "Anything that would diminish our role as Canada's national pastime would be a severe negative to this league," says Bettman.

14   Add it all up, and there's an overarching question: Has Bettman moved too fast or too slow? More teams mean more of a national presence, added TV exposure, and greater brand recognition for the NHL and its increasing number of corporate sponsors. But it also has meant more jobs for players and thus, a seller's market when it comes to star free agents. TV ratings still bring up the rear, as do NHL rights fees, when compared with the other major leagues.

15   The pressure is to move faster. "This can't be the sport of the future forever," says Brian Lawton, a former union activist and now president of the hockey division of Advantage International, the agency that represents the NHL's best-paid player, Sergei Federov. "Gary looks at things and says, 'We've made enormous progress,' and he's right," says Richard Burke, owner of the Phoenix Coyotes. "But I look at the same thing and say, 'Gary, we need to go faster.' "

16   Bettman bristles at the notion that the league is behind schedule. "It's a slow build. You do it a step at a time," he says. "You won't see the impact of what we're doing—nobody will—for another 5 to 10 years."

17   In fact, Bettman's record suggests that he is anything but a slowpoke. In his first six years, league revenues have mushroomed. Corporate sponsorships are up from $25 million to $250 million, thanks to ties with national brands such as Nike, mbna, and Wendy's International. NHL licensed goods are hot, too, the greatest coup of all. When Bettman took over, the league had only a tiny cable-TV contract that gave each team less than $1 million a year. Compare that with the five-year, $600 million deal that the league signed with ABC Inc. and ESPN Inc. last August. Still small by National Football League and NBA standards, it was such an astonishingly large package for the NHL that Bettman felt obliged to say, with a wink that he hadn't negotiated "with a mask and a gun."

TABLE 1
Bumps, Body Checks . . . And Reasons for Optimism

Bumps, Body Checks . . .

- The bankruptcy of the Pittsburgh Penguins is but one sign that the rich team–poor team problem besetting other leagues may actually be worst in the NHL.

- When he became commissioner six years ago, Gary Bettman was essentially starting from scratch. But has he taken the league too far, too fast?

- NHL player salaries have risen 250% since Bettman took over. The owners had a chance to install a salary cap in 1995 but didn't. And their contract has no escape until 2004.

- Wayne Gretzky, the Great One, could hang up his skates after this season. For hockey, that would be a blow not quite comparable to Michael Jordan's retirement from the NBA, but the league would lose its most marketable player.

. . . And Reasons for Optimism

- NHL-licensed goods are hot in the face of a declining market for major-league merchandise. They accounted for $1.2 billion in revenue last year. And corporate sponsorships now bring in $250 million a year.

- The valuations of NHL franchises, while nowhere near those of the NFL or Major League Baseball, are rising swiftly. The Phoenix Coyotes, sold for $67 million in 1995, now command $87 million.

- Last August, the NHL signed a five-year, $600 million television deal with ABC and ESPN. That's far from the NFL's eight-year, $17.6 billion contract, but it's up from a tiny cable deal when Bettman took over.

- With no rules against corporate ownership, NHL teams have been bought or started by Disney (the Ducks), Comcast (the Flyers), Ascent Entertainment (the Avalanche), and Time Warner (the Thrashers). That strengthens hockey's underpinnings.

18   The NHL is also attracting a new breed of owners—media companies. Comcast Corp. bought the Philadelphia Flyers, Ascent Entertainment Group controls the Colorado Avalanche, and Time Warner's Turner Sports grabbed the expansion Atlanta Thrashers. Dallas broadcast mogul Thomas O. Hicks, chairman of Chancellor Media Corp. and owner of the Texas Rangers baseball team, owns the Dallas Stars.

19   Thus has the NHL laid the foundation for that immutable principle of sports ownership: The more money owners have, the more freely and irrationally they spend it. Average player compensation, despite a labor deal that the commissioner says restricts player movement, is up from $467,000 the year before Bettman took over to $1.17 million last season, union records show. Federov, whom most American sports fans might identify as a cosmonaut or victim of a Boris Yeltsin purge, will be paid $14 million by the Detroit Red Wings this season. That's the top salary allowed a 10-year NBA veteran this year. Just five years ago, the Wings' entire payroll was about $15 million.

20   While the NHL is playing with the big boys when it comes to costs, pro hockey still remains a virtual cult sport. Bettman points to the rapid growth of the game in nontraditional locales, but the absolute numbers are miniscule. So it's no wonder that hockey's ratings remain relatively flat. Still, that hasn't discouraged ABC and ESPN. Steven M. Bornstein, president and CEO of ESPN and ABC Sports, says sluggish ratings are not a concern because the NHL delivers "quality of audience." The league scores well with 18- to-34-year-old males that sponsors pay handsomely to reach.

21   Still, the NHL faces the bane of the major leagues: the rich market–poor market divide. Already, Detroit ($48.3 million) is paying players $35 million more than the expansion Nashville Predators ($13.6 million) pay theirs. For now, some lesser-paid teams are still high in the standings. But unless the owners with the new arenas, bigger markets, and deep pockets begin to share revenues with their poorer brethren, the NHL could be headed for a baseball-like quagmire: some teams with competitive hope, others without.

22   So the Bettman-driven economic growth of the past six years has created a hazy future. "I think the NHL was at a point where it had to move away from its roots to expose itself to all sorts of possibilities," says Bob Gainey, a Montreal Canadiens Hall of Fame defenseman who is now vice-president of the Dallas Stars. But, he cautions, sometimes you have to be careful what you wish for.

CASE 41

BusinessWeek

THE NOSTALGIA BOOM

1   To viewers watching the ad for the new Volkswagen Beetle, it is like squinting into the past. A vague image begins as a small circle set against a stark white background. As the picture sharpens, the circle becomes a flower—with seven daffodil-yellow New Beetles as its petals. The cute-as-a-Bug cars drive away, and a zippy black Beetle careens into view and skids to a stop. The tag line: "Less flower. More power."

2   Welcome back to the '60s—except this time, the revolution will be televised by Madison Avenue. Volkswagen's Flower Power commercial is only the first in a barrage of ads about to hit the airwaves as the German auto maker launches a new and improved version of the venerable Beetle to America after a 20-year absence. Volkswagen's strategy is simple: It plans to sell its back-to-the-future car by wrapping it in the symbols of the not-too-distant past.

3   Volkswagen is not the only marketer mining the warm associations of boomer youth and the Age of Aquarius to sell consumer goods. These days, nostalgia marketing is everywhere, from almost forgotten brands such as Burma Shave to jingles that borrow from classic rock. Pepsi uses the Rolling Stones' "Brown Sugar," while James Brown's "I Feel Good" helps sell Senokot Laxatives. Hollywood is awash with remakes of movies and TV shows plucked from an earlier era. Even retired slogans and mascots are being resurrected. Maxwell House has dusted off "Good to the last drop," while Charlie the Tuna is swimming his way through Starkist tuna ads once again.

4   Consumers can't seem to get enough of these airbrushed memories. Middle-aged boomers obsessed with their youth and movin' down the highway toward retirement clamor for retro roadsters such as the Porsche Boxster. Walt Disney Co. developed an entire town, Celebration, Fla., on the notion that Americans are pining for the look and feel of 1940s neighborhoods. Baseball fans step back in time by piling into Cleveland's Jacobs Field and Oriole Park at Camden Yards—new ballparks designed to look like they've been around since the turn of the century. Meanwhile, kids have reclaimed mom and dad's bell bottoms and platform shoes and brought back Diane Von Furstenberg's wrap dress.

5   No one, though, has as much riding on the nostalgia wave as Volkswagen. Its U.S. market share having withered to less than 1%, VW is wagering $560 million that its spunky little car can revive its fortunes. It's a very calculated bet. The new, postmodern Beetle has been reinvented with a message that slyly assuages end-of-the-millennium angst with a harkening back to the Summer of Love. The new version, which is about to hit the showrooms, comes with all the modern features car buyers demand, such as four air bags and power outlets for cell phones. But that's not why VW expects folks to buy it. With a familiar bubble shape that still makes people smile as it skitters by, the new Beetle offers a pull that is purely emotional. "If you sold your soul in the '80s," tweaks one ad, "here's your chance to buy it back."

STRESS RELIEF?

6   Why the intense yearning to turn back the clock? The faster we hurdle toward the millennium, it seems, the more we're reaching desperately backwards toward the halcyon days of mid-century, days of postwar prosperity and quaint notions of revolution that nowadays seem astonishing in their innocence and idealism. In their place have come growing anxiety about aging and a fear of hanging on in today's increasingly stressful society.

Source: Keith Naughton and Bill Vlasic in Detroit, with bureau reports, "The Nostalgia Boom," *Business Week:* March 23, 1998.

7   Americans are overwhelmed, social experts say, by the breathtaking onrush of the Information Age, with its high-speed modems, cell phones, and pagers. While we hail the benefits of the wired '90s, at the same time we are buffeted by the rapid pace of change. "We are creating a new culture, and we don't know what's going to happen," explains futurist Watts Wacker, co-author of *The 500-Year Delta.* "So we need some warm fuzzies from our past."

8   Just take a stroll through the supermarket. Shelves are now brimming with packaged goods that look as if they're from another era. After Coca-Cola Co. recreated a plastic version of its famous contour bottle in 1994, sales grew by double digits in some markets, says Frank P. Bifulco, vice-president for marketing of Coca-Cola USA. Necco wafers are enjoying a comeback—sales are up 25% in the past two years—thanks in part to a packaging redesign that harkens back to its roots. "There has been a flurry of clients coming to us and saying, 'We want that handcrafted look,'" says Jack Vogler, partner at SBG Enterprise, a San Francisco packaging-design house that recently restored the old packaging of the Sun-Maid raisin girl and Cracker Jack's Sailor Jack and Bingo.

9   Even old ads are being recycled to woo wistful customers. Sales of Maxwell House have perked up since it began including archival footage of percolating coffee pots in its ads. It's a startling departure from the modern image Maxwell House projected in the early 1990s as hip upstarts such as Starbucks Corp. became all the rage. "Consumers are not in a real experimental time now," says Richard S. Helstein, vice-president for advertising at Kraft Foods Inc. "They are looking for brands they can depend on—brands they grew up with."

10   Successes such as these have advertisers jumping on the bandwagon—even when they don't have archives to pillage. In February, Ford Motor Co. began airing a commercial commemorating how Henry Ford put America on wheels. The spot includes what appears to be grainy, historic footage of a Model T puttering down a long-ago Main Street. But the sepia-toned scene was actually shot last year on a Hollywood back lot and was given a vintage look by using a 1920s hand-cranked camera, old emulsion film, and special editing.

11   Why recreate history? Ford is hoping that consumers will equate longevity with quality. "People really respond to it. They say, 'This is a company that has lasted through a couple of world wars,'" says Bruce Rooke, executive creative director at Ford's agency, J. Walter Thompson Co.

12   Indeed, social experts say much of the appeal of nostalgia stems from a longing for a return to simpler times. Despite a robust economy, Americans remain an anxiety-ridden bunch. Not all the riches of a long bull market can make up for the rigors of overbooked working parents forced to reduce family life to an exercise in time management. Divorce rates remain high, job security is down, and saving enough to send the kids to college or for retirement can seem overwhelming. Is it any wonder that a new survey from Roper Starch Worldwide shows that 55% of Americans believe the "good old days" were better than today? That's an about-face from attitudes of a generation ago, when 54% of those surveyed in 1974 told Roper they believed there was no time better than the present.

GOLDEN MEMORIES

13   Naturally, baby boomers, ever powerful in their numbers, are driving this return to roots. The Roper survey identifies the most longed-for age as the 1950s, 1960s, and 1970s. "The '50s and '60s were a time of very high expectations for baby boomers," says J. Walker Smith, a partner with the Yankelovich Partners consumer-research firm. "But life didn't turn out to be the 1964 World's Fair."

14   In fact, life went on, and aging is yet another force at the root of nostalgia marketing. The oldest of the boomers are in their 50s and are resisting the aging process with the vigor they once reserved for protesting the war. While they snap up vitamins, diet pills, and other tonics touted to stop the clock, marketers are counting on the appeal of nostalgic products to salve the wounds of growing old. If nothing else, familiar products and jingles give boomers the chance to act and feel young. "Boomers are saying, 'Maybe my parents were old at 50, but I'm not,'" says Rick Adler, president of Senior Network Inc., a marketing consultant firm.

15   That's certainly a big reason why Dennis J. Berger, 52, waited six months to take delivery of his white $65,000 Porsche Boxster, a retro roadster styled like the 1950s vintage Porsche favored by movie stars like James Dean. "It opened up a memory of when I was a teenager in New Jersey," says

Berger, vice-president of Allied Plastics Co. in Jacksonville, Fla. "This car reminds me of the '50s, when there wasn't a care in the world."

16   Yet the nostalgia phenomenon is not simply about America reliving a Golden Age. It is also about reinterpreting it. We may look back through rose-colored glasses, but few want to live in the past for the sake of authenticity. The new retro ethos has a thoroughly modern cast. Log Cabin syrup brought back an old-timey label but sports a convenient squeeze-top bottle. When Coke redid its famous hourglass bottle, it made it in today's popular big-gulp sizes. And movie remakes come complete with the latest in special effects. "Americans want that Victorian house with the wraparound porch, but it had better be wired for all the latest technology," says Carolyn E. Setlow, senior vice-president at Roper.

17   Such reinterpretations are particularly popular among younger, Generation-X consumers. While they've adopted many products and fashions from the 1960s and 1970s as their own, they often up-date them with an ironic twist. And it has little to do with longing for an era they never experienced. "I see it more as rediscovering than retro," says 20-year-old Matthew Levy of New York City. "I don't want to be my father. I want to rediscover things he forgot about when he was out climbing the corporate ladder." Case in point: cigars. Both he and his dad smoke them. But Levy says his generation has reinvented the product to suit its lifestyle. "Where my dad smoked cigars, they didn't allow women. No one my age would go for that."

18   The vintage-style stadiums that have risen across the country embody this marriage of past and present. Camden Yards and Jacobs Field look like ballparks from a bygone era. Coming to New York might be a recreation of the old Brooklyn Dodgers' home turf, Ebbets Field. But this time, it would house the New York Mets. On the inside, these faux-historic stadiums are ringed with the luxury suites that make corporate customers comfortable and owners rich. Even regular fans are rewarded with wider seats and broad concourses dotted with more concession stands and restrooms than real old ballparks ever had. "People will go to see a place once because it's historic," says HOK Sport Senior Vice-President Joseph E. Spear, the architect of Camden Yards and Jacobs Field. "But they don't come back unless they have a good time."

POWER SUNROOF

19   The Beetle comeback is also based on a combination of romance and reason—wrapping up modern conveniences in an old-style package. Built into the dashboard is a bud vase perfect for a daisy plucked straight from the 1960s. But right next to it is a high-tech multi-speaker stereo—and options like power windows, cruise control, and a power sunroof make it a very different car than the rattly old Bug. So, too, does the sticker price: While a new Bug cost just $1,800 in 1968—$8,300 in today's dollars—a typically equipped new Beetle will run about $16,500.

20   But if the Beetle, like us, has grown up, Volkswagen is hoping it will still spark the same emotions as its younger self. With its simple design and no-frills engineering, the original Beetle was the antithesis of Detroit's gas-guzzlers. As boomers by the tens of thousands bought their first cars, it blossomed into an unlikely icon. By 1968, its peak year, VW sold 423,000 Beetles in the U.S. Cheap to own, easy to fix, and giddy fun to drive, the Beetle personified an era of rebellion against conventions. Says John Wright, a pop-culture expert at the Henry Ford Museum in Dearborn, Mich.: "When people look at Volkswagen, it looks like youth."

21   But youth fades, and by the late 1970s, the Bug had faded, too. VW was never the same after it dropped the Beetle from production for the U.S. in 1978. By 1993, says Jens Neumann, a member of Volkswagen's board of managers, with less than 1% of U.S. auto sales, "we were just about to drop out of this market."

MYSTERY MARKET

22   Instead, VW Chairman Ferdinand Piech decided to make an almost quixotic bid to recapture its former glory. In 1993, he ordered up a prototype of a new Beetle in what was essentially a last-ditch

**TABLE 1
Rock On!**

In the battle to win the hearts and minds of aging boomers, more and more marketers are turning to old rock and pop hits.

Brand	Artist	Song
Toyota	Sly and the Family Stone	"Everyday People"
AT&T	Elton John	"Rocket Man"
Senokot Laxative	James Brown	"I Feel Good"
Pepsi	The Rolling Stones	"Brown Sugar"
Microsoft	The Rolling Stones	"Start Me Up"
Ford	The Who	"I Can't Explain"
Intel	Bee Gees	"Stayin' Alive"
Levi's	The Partridge Family	"I Think I Love You"
Burger King	Squeeze	"Tempted"

effort to jump-start sales. The concept car was launched at the 1994 auto show in Detroit—and promptly stole the show as car shoppers and reporters mobbed the VW display. Crowds packed in several people deep just to get a look at the yellow Bug. The wildly enthusiastic reaction from the public astounded even VW execs. "We were, to say the least, overwhelmed," says Piech.

23   Still, VW is walking softly into the market. It plans to build just 100,000 Beetles a year at its plant in Puebla, Mexico, with half of those targeted for the U.S. and Canada. Company execs refuse to be pinned down on the Beetle's target market, saying only that it is designed for "optimists." Yet it's clearly aiming wide. While many of its ads sport jokes targeted at the previous Beetle generation, others are aimed squarely at Gen-X.

24   Early signs are that VW could have a cross-generational hit on its hands. Dealers across the country have been inundated with inquiries on the new Bug, and many now have long waiting lists. Jeff La Plant, sales manager for Volkswagen of Santa Monica, says he has already gotten orders from 100 customers. "It's like you have a rock star here and everybody wants an autograph," La Plant says. "I've never seen a car that had such a wide range of interest, from 16-year-olds to 65-year-olds."

25   Greg Stern, a 47-year-old film producer in Santa Monica, is No.1 on La Plant's list. Describing the car as—what else—"way cool," he's in line for a silver or white model. "In 1967, my Dad got me a VW. I loved it. I'm sure the new one will take me back," says Stern. "I'm getting the New Beetle as a surprise for my daughter, but I'm sure I'm going to be stealing it from her all the time."

26   Like Volkswagen, others have discovered that a history of warm memories is an exploitable asset these days. The Nickelodeon cable channel's Nick at Nite proved such a hit recycling sitcoms that it spawned TV Land and a host of other imitators. That's true even if the product itself has been gone for decades. Burma Shave is banking almost entirely on its nostalgic appeal as it returns to store shelves after a 30-year absence. The shaving cream's legendary rhyming roadside signs, last seen in 1964, will return this summer. And they may even begin showing up in the supermarkets and Wal-Marts where Burma Shave is now sold, says brand manager Steve Cochran. "Those signs evoke a lot of nostalgia about driving along the highway on vacation," he says.

27   At least Burma Shave's history is real. As nostalgia becomes ever more important as a marketing tool, companies are increasingly willing to fake it. Four years ago, Gap Inc. launched the Old Navy casual clothing chain with a series of old-timey black-and-white ads and store decor that recalled the '50s. "We used nostalgia in the very beginning to give credibility to the brand, so that it didn't feel like it was coming from nowhere," explains Richard Crisman, Old Navy's senior vice-president for marketing. Since then, Old Navy has modernized its marketing with new campaigns emphasizing value and fashion. But many of the original decor touches remain—all 300 stores sport a '50s Chevy pickup truck, for example, and the New York flagship store features a '50s-style diner.

DRAMA FLOP

28 For Old Navy, the tactic paid off. But not all efforts to manufacture nostalgia have been so successful. Executives at fast-food chain Kentucky Fried Chicken Corp. learned that you can go too far. Three years ago, they decided the brand needed some advertising help from founder Colonel Harlan Sanders. KFC's research showed that consumers still trusted the colonel. The problem: Sanders died in 1980, and KFC could not find old film clips of him that would work in a modern commercial. "Nothing was sound-bitey enough," explained Peter J. Foulds, KFC's advertising vice-president.

29 So KFC dressed up an actor in the colonel's starched white suit and broadcast black-and-white TV commercials that pretended to show the founder spouting his special brand of homespun wisdom. But the attempt to recreate history didn't wash, and KFC was roundly criticized for defaming the dead. After less than a year, the ads were pulled. Still, KFC hasn't given up on using the colonel altogether. Instead, the company decided the best—and safest—way to evoke his memory was to enlarge his image on buckets of chicken.

30 Celebrities who are dead, however, are hotter than ever in commercials. Ironically, one factor behind the wave of dead celebs who have come back to endorse products is sophisticated technology. Computer-generated imagery has made it appear that Fred Astaire had a new dancing partner—Dirt Devil vacuum cleaners. Lucille Ball sells diamond rings for Service Merchandise Co. And Ed Sullivan is back from the beyond to unveil one more phenom to the world: the Mercedes-Benz sportutility. "Who is Mr. Introduction-to-America more than Ed Sullivan?" says Mike Jackson, president of Mercedes-Benz of North America.

31 If only reviving a dying brand were as easy. A&W Restaurants Inc., once famous for carhops on roller skates, is attempting to reverse more than two decades of decline by overhauling its restaurants in a 1950s rock 'n' roll image. A&W Chairman Sidney Feltenstein, a former Burger King Corp. marketing executive, hopes the retro appeal will help them stand out in a crowded segment. Feltenstein says McDonald's Corp. and Burger King can fight over the kids; he's aiming for adults. So far, the makeover appears to be working: At one redone A&W in Dearborn, Mich., middle-age diners dominate the lunchtime crowd. "It reminds you of your youth," says salesman Kirk Pettit, 38, as Beach Boys music wafts from an old Wurlitzer jukebox. Overall, sales at the remodeled stores are up 20% over 1996.

32 So is nostalgia just the latest hype from Madison Avenue? Or is it the zeitgeist of a culture? While it clearly hits a chord, some worry that overkill can't be far off. "The grainy black-and-white commercials are the shaky camera of the late '90s," scoffs Martin Horn, Chicago-based research director at DDB Needham Worldwide Inc. "We in the ad business slide into derivative behavior." Also dubious is John K. Grace, executive director of Interbrand, a New York-based brand consultancy, who believes American culture in the late '90s lacks distinction, so young and old alike are clinging to the sights and sounds of the past until something better comes along. He compares it to the quiet 1950s, which led to the tumultuous 1960s: "There are no cultural hooks for youth to grab on to today, so they find comfort in what was. But nostalgia can't be sustained."

33 But others say advertisers are only reflecting Americans' deeper longings to take control of their lives by reconnecting with their idealized past. "If you want to understand values, study our advertising," says Seymour Leventman, a sociology professor at Boston College. He believes the nostalgia craze will only grow as trend-setting baby boomers age.

34 That's why the New Beetle just might be a tonic for the times. It is our romantic past, reinvented for our hectic here-and-now. "The Beetle is not just empty nostalgia," says Gerald Celente, publisher of *Trends Journal*. "It is a practical car that is also tied closely to the emotions of a generation."

35 To unleash that emotion, VW's staid German executives flew to Atlanta to stage a love-in to introduce the Love Bug last month to 300 journalists from around the world. Young women in tie-dyed T-shirts handed out daisies and peace medallions in a psychedelic rock hall. VW's Piech marveled at his little car's enduring appeal. "It is different, and it makes you feel different," he said. "It's like a magnet." Different, yet deeply familiar—a car for the times.

CASE 42

BusinessWeek

THE ATLANTIC CENTURY?

1   The global economy wasn't supposed to look like this. After the Berlin Wall crumbled and governments throughout the world cast their lots with capitalism, it seemed logical to envision a single, seamless system. Money, goods, and eventually people would move from market to market, unimpeded by ideology or protectionist barriers. Western wealth, seeking high returns in developing nations, would flow south and east, enriching recipient industries and consumers until a rising tide of growth lifted everyone into better living standards.

2   Instead, the new century will begin with an eerily familiar alignment. Once again, North America and Europe are the global anchors of prosperity and stability, while the rest of the world struggles in economic limbo. Far from counting on hot emerging markets to drive global growth, companies and investors are focused on the Atlantic zone. "The big growth engines are the U.S. and Europe," says Michael C. Hawley, president of Boston-based Gillette Co., which is spending $750 million to launch its pricey Mach III razor in the two regions.

3   Just three years ago, such optimism would have seemed misplaced. After all, the U.S. had been chugging through a six-year expansion. Surely, it had to run out of steam, most economists agreed. Even if growth continued, it could hardly be better than tepid, since the affluent American market seemed saturated with goods and services. And Europe? Pundits wrote it off as an also-ran in the race for global competitiveness, a continent hopelessly tangled in obsolete regulations and stubbornly refusing to change.

4   True, 1999 could bring a slowdown. But both regions have surprised us. The U.S., shattering traditional economic assumptions, may have created a new model for growth. Successive technology breakthroughs fuel productivity gains that have been running 2% a year since 1995—nearly twice the level of the previous two decades. Continued low-inflation, low-unemployment growth is defying the classic business cycle. Meanwhile, demographics have changed the face of finance. The baby boom generation saves for retirement by socking billions of dollars into stocks every month automatically—perhaps one reason for the market's long-term buoyancy. And boomers' insatiable appetite for investment advice has led to an explosion of lucrative financial services from banks, information companies, and the Internet.

5   Across the sea, Europe is going through many of the same changes. "The New Economy effect is still very much in the future," says University of Maastricht Professor Luc L. Soete. "But in many parts of Europe, it is starting to take form." Proof is in the Continent's two-tier economy: Manufacturers are in recession, while software and telecom companies are pumping out jobs.

6   Indeed, Europe increasingly mirrors its transatlantic trading partner. At $6.5 trillion, the euro zone's economy approaches the U.S.'s $8 trillion. The two continents' share of world trade is almost the same, about 18%, and they both export some 11% of GDP. Thanks to the euro, even their stock markets could soon be comparable. Barring any profit shocks, Europe's 9,100 listed companies should gradually grow in value close to that of America's 9,900.

7   Europe's new single currency will bring the continents even closer. By consolidating 11 different markets, the euro will create a source of capital far bigger than the sum of its parts, because it will be more liquid. Already, this market is taking shape along U.S. lines. That's partly because, like Americans, Europeans face an income crunch at retirement unless they begin shifting their savings into stocks and corporate bonds. The euro zone's fast-growing capital markets represent a fresh source of funds for U.S. and European companies alike. And as countries around the world stock up on euros

Source: Joan Warner, with Pete Engardio in New York and Thane Peterson in Frankfurt, "The Atlantic Century?" *Business Week:* February 8, 1999.

EXHIBIT A

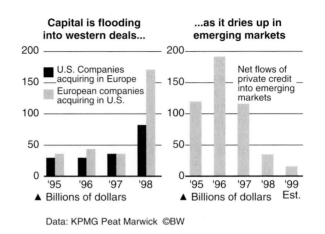

Capital is flooding into western deals... ...as it dries up in emerging markets

- U.S. Companies acquiring in Europe
- European companies acquiring in U.S.

Net flows of private credit into emerging markets

▲ Billions of dollars   ▲ Billions of dollars   Est.

Data: KPMG Peat Marwick ©BW

to cover trade with the euro zone, the currency could eventually share global reserve-currency status with the dollar.

8   On a less lofty but equally important level, transatlantic business values have more in common than ever. Executives share a focus on shareholder returns and an openness to ideas invented half a world away. Gradually, deregulation and more supply-side economics could solve Europe's remaining nagging unemployment problem. As the Continent gains in competitiveness and as its capital markets evolve, "you will have two virtually identical blocs," says Jan Svejnar, economics professor and head of the William Davidson Institute, a think tank in Ann Arbor, Mich. "Technologically, neither will be ahead, and institutionally they will be similar."

9   The upshot is that for now, U.S. and European companies no longer need look to the developing world for growth. For example, thanks to deregulation on both continents, a phone company formerly dependent on a single business repertoire can now branch out into cable and Internet services. And its once-regional customer base is the size of the entire transatlantic zone. "When we talk about globalization, we used to talk about emerging markets," says McKinsey & Co. global strategy expert Lowell L. Bryan. "But the most important integration now is occurring between Europe and America."

10   Already, gigantic mergers, from DaimlerChrysler to Deutsche Bank-Bankers Trust, signal that the biggest companies on both sides of the Atlantic want to exploit the two continents' growing similarities. Since size and market reach are more important than ever—especially in Europe whose national boundaries are gradually being razed—many more transatlantic deals are likely to follow. Mergers and acquisitions between the two continents totaled $256.5 billion in 1998, up from $69.4 billion in 1995.

LONG-TERM FOCUS

11   U.S. and European management styles are gradually converging, too. Multilingual executives believe in performance-based compensation and look for talent without regard to nationality. And the euro zone's monetary guardian, the new European Central Bank, seems committed to emulating the U.S. Federal Reserve, making steady, low-inflation growth its principal target. For the foreseeable future, investors on both sides of the Atlantic are likely to shun short-term high returns in emerging countries in favor of lower but less volatile rewards from each other's capital markets.

12   While North America and Europe increasingly look like twin pillars of global growth, the former stars of the world economy are in a tailspin. In Asia, the forces of economic integration are crumbling. The recession and financial debacle in Japan has deprived the region of its main growth engine. Self-obsessed China is turning more protectionist. Grand initiatives of the early 1990s to dismantle

TABLE 1
What's Driving the New Atlantic Economy

Deregulation

Opening of telecom, banking, and airlines is creating a continental market in Europe that parallels the U.S. Costs are falling as competition increases.

Technology

Companies in both Europe and the U.S. are rapidly absorbing technology, increasing productivity, and becoming more responsive to change. Technology is helping to turn once-mature economies into zones of growth.

Financial Markets

The euro has revolutionized European finance. It is reshaping capital markets along U.S. lines and will create a huge new pool of funding for both European and U.S. companies. The euro will likely take a bigger place alongside the dollar as a reserve currency.

Common Business Values

A generation of business-school trained, U.S.-style managers is taking over Europe's companies. On both sides of the Atlantic, companies are emphasizing shareholder value, focusing on profits, and paying for performance.

Merger Wave

A new breed of mega-corporation is emerging as transatlantic giants link up. These enormous companies can transfer technology, management skills, and money effortlessly between the world's two biggest and richest markets.

Data: *Business Week.*

regional barriers to trade, financial services, and telecommunications have fallen into disarray. In many industries, companies still must approach the region country by country, each with its own rules, currency regimes, and bureaucracies. That makes it tough to achieve critical mass.

13   Thanks to the Asian meltdown of 1997, Russia's devaluation and default last year, and a potential Latin American crisis in 1999, confidence in emerging markets has dissolved. At least in the midterm, these countries will pay dearly for every penny of Western capital as they try to repair their shattered economies. Private credit to emerging markets dwindled to $39 billion last year, from $196 billion in 1996.

14   The new divide between the economic haves and have-nots could be self-perpetuating. For example, the U.S. has benefited from the flood of cheap imports, which allowed the Federal Reserve to keep interest rates low. But developing nations get much less for the commodities they produce, be they oil, steel, or computer memory chips. And because their currencies have plunged in value, countries such as Indonesia, Thailand, and Brazil have much less buying power for machinery, raw materials, and fuel. Without such supplies, they can't get exports growing again.

15   Yet despite the reversal of the developing nations' fortunes, many opinion leaders reject the idea that the U.S. and Europe should be regarded as role models. "The emerging markets accepted unilateral imposition of dogmatic formulas because they feared a negative reaction from the market," says Eisuke Sakakibara, Japan's powerful vice-minister of finance for international affairs. But now, he says, the era of Western "market fundamentalism" is fading as a global ideology: "Global capitalism has turned inherently unstable."

16   Deprived of the hot Western money that fed their growth in the early 1990s, many developing markets are back to square one. But the tough times have brought valuable lessons. Perhaps the most fundamental is that capitalism isn't born fully formed. Throwing capital at an economy not yet equipped to handle cyclical downturns, inflation, and currency swings is unlikely to yield long-term gains.

17   Some government leaders, executives, and investors are calling for institutional and regulatory reforms in emerging markets. It could be years before these structural changes take root. But if nothing else, the cut-off of easy money from the West could ensure that Asia, Russia, and Latin America don't make the same mistakes again. Nor are they likely simply to turn back into cheap-export machines.

More probable is a gradual transition—no doubt with plenty of government intervention along the way—to a practice of capitalism that meshes with the trans-atlantic model but holds less built-in financial risk.

18   In fact, the new world order could introduce a set of global risks quite different from the emerging nations' boom-busts. Harmonious as the U.S. and European economies may be, a downturn in world growth could send the two continents into serious rivalry. Even now, Brussels and Washington are battling over banana and meat imports, with the U.S. threatening sanctions. Competitive devaluations between the dollar and the euro are not out of the question, and trade barriers and currency wars could be even more tempting. Says the Davidson Institute's Svejnar: "Since NAFTA and the euro zone are large blocs, it's easier for them to be self-sufficient."

UNITY GAP

19   Finally, it remains to be seen whether the U.S. can gracefully cede the geopolitical hegemony it has enjoyed for most of this century. America has traditionally shouldered much of the burden when a global crisis erupts, from wars to financial default. As the euro zone matures into a single, massive economy, its leaders could be called on more frequently to pull their weight in times of trouble. "But as long as Europe lacks political unity," says Andre Levy-Lang, chairman of French investment bank Paribas, "it's unlikely to assume a caretaker role, because countries still have conflicting interests."

20   The greatest danger to the transatlantic alliance, in fact, is an economic shock that somehow hits one bloc harder than the other. But as long as the two remain oases of growth in a turbulent world, they are likely to be more allies than rivals. Europeans and Americans may never define capitalism in exactly the same way. But for now, their definitions are close enough to ensure a fertile economic partnership for years to come.

B

TRADITIONAL CASES

CASE 43

McDONALD'S: HAS IT LOST THE GOLDEN TOUCH?

---

1   The McDonald brothers' first restaurant, founded in 1937 in a parking lot just east of Pasadena, Calif., didn't serve hamburgers. It had no playground and no Happy Meals. The most popular item on the menu was the hot dog, and most people ate it sitting on an outdoor stool or in their cherished new autos while being served by teenage carhops.

2   That model was a smashing success—for about a decade. Then America's tastes began to change, and the Golden Arches changed with them. As cars lost some of their romance, indoor restaurants took over. When adults became bored with the menu in the 1960s, a new sandwich called the Big Mac wooed them back. As consumers grew weary of beef, McDonald's introduced bite-size chunks of chicken in the early '80s and within four years was the nation's second-largest poultry seller.

3   The changes were vital, but never radical. McDonald's gave us what we wanted before we even knew we wanted it, whether it was movie tie-ins or Egg McMuffins. Along the way, it built one of the world's best-known corporate icons and its most ubiquitous store. The philosophy was neatly summarized by Ray Kroc's brash vow: whatever people ate, McDonald's would be the ones to sell it.

4   But now, two years shy of Kroc's benchmark for the far-off future, that goal seems less assured than ever. Forget for a moment all the recent talk about Burger King Corp. and Wendy's International Inc. stealing customers from McDonald's. With a 42% share of the U.S. fast-food burger market, McDonald's still easily outpaces its rivals. Nonetheless, the problems under the famous Golden Arches are far more serious than a failed Arch Deluxe here or a french-fry war there. Quite simply, McDonald's has lost some of its relevance to American culture—a culture that it, as much as any modern corporation, helped to shape. Not even a still booming international division, responsible for half of sales and 60% of profits, can mask the troubles.

©1998, The McGraw-Hill Companies, created and adapted by Richard Robinson, University of South Carolina, from David Leonhardt, "McDonald's," *Business Week:* March 9, 1998; and David Leonhardt, "Getting off Their McButts," *Business Week:* February 22, 1999.

EXHIBIT A

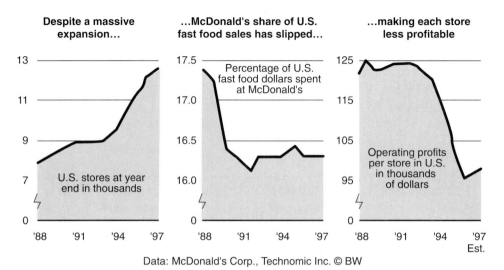

Despite a massive expansion...	...McDonald's share of U.S. fast food sales has slipped...	...making each store less profitable
U.S. stores at year end in thousands	Percentage of U.S. fast food dollars spent at McDonald's	Operating profits per store in U.S. in thousands of dollars

Data: McDonald's Corp., Technomic Inc. © BW

5   The company that once seemed a half-step ahead of pop culture today is unable to construct even an appealing new lunch sandwich. Its last successful new product was the Chicken McNugget, which launched in 1983. In the '90s, the company has careened from tests with pizza and veggie burgers to confusing discount promotions such as last year's Campaign 55. Earnings in 1997 inched up 4%, to $1.6 billion, on sales of $11.4 billion, up 7%. That's well below projections McDonald's itself made just a few years ago.

6   For a company that enjoyed sizzling growth for five decades based on its ability to read and shape popular trends, the breadth of its problems is astonishing. Since 1987, McDonald's share of fast-food sales in the U.S. has slipped almost two percentage points, to 16.2%. The drop has come even as the company has increased its number of restaurants by 50%, far outpacing the industry's expansion rate. The result: Domestic sales have climbed only 18% since 1989, while operating profits haven't even kept pace with inflation. They've risen just 2% a year in that period. That trend has slashed U.S. per-store profits by 20% since 1989—or a huge 40% after inflation. Meanwhile, nearly every other top consumer brand, from Disney to Marlboro, has prospered.

BRAND EQUITY—YES, . . . BUT?

7   McDonald's has chalked up that dismal record despite the fact that it owns one of the best known brands on the globe. The company has been unable to harness the strength of its brand to grow beyond its basic formula of burgers and fries. During a period when Americans have abandoned their kitchens in droves for food cooked elsewhere, the Golden Arches—easily the world's largest provider of prepared food—has failed to profit. It's as if hundreds of thousands of people started drinking soda for breakfast and Coca-Cola Co. wasn't benefiting. "McDonald's has totally failed to adapt its original concept," says Simon C. Williams, chairman of the Sterling Group, a New York-based brand consultancy that works with food companies.

8   Now, McDonald's is embarking on an effort at reform. Last year, Chief Executive Michael R. Quinlan shuffled his U.S. management team. He says the decentralized structure will rekindle the company's entrepreneurial flair. A new cooking system set for 2000 should make it easier to customize sandwiches, improve quality, and expand the menu. Fundamentally, however, tomorrow's McDonald's won't be much different. "Do we have to change?" asks Quinlan. "No, we don't have to change. We have the most successful brand in the world."

9   McDonald's, though, is doing some tinkering. The new head of the domestic division—Jack M. Greenberg, a pleasant 54-year-old lawyer who has been with the company 16 years—has brought in

a handful of new managers, including executives from Burger King, Boston Market, and General Electric Co. "We are not afraid to do things differently," Greenberg says. In a first for the burger giant, McDonald's in February bought a stake in another restaurant, a 14-outlet chain in Denver called Chipotle Mexican Grill.

10   But execs emphasized that the heart of the company's menu will remain the same—and that it believes it can squeeze new profits from the U.S. burger business, even though McDonald's already dominates the crowded segment. "We will extend our line, rather than going in more radical, different directions," says Quinlan, 53, who started in the company mailroom at age 19. "I'm a fan of menu tweaking."

11   Compare the McDonald's strategy with that at other companies that have prospered despite wrenching changes in their industries. When GE realized that manufacturing had become less profitable, it moved into financing. When Walt Disney Co. found it hard to lure more people to its theme parks, it built hotels and captured more dollars from the tourists already there. And Coca-Cola spun off its bottling business and focused instead on becoming a marketing powerhouse. The difference is profound: If McDonald's had added shareholder value at the same rate as Coca-Cola over the past ten years, its shares today would be worth $170 each. Instead, they bring less than $55.

"Family" Culture That Looks Inward, Not Outward

12   By contrast, McDonald's core recipe has changed little since the early '80s. "McDonald's needs to move the question from 'How can we sell more hamburgers?' to 'What does our brand allow us to consider selling to our customers?' " says Adrian J. Slywotzky, a partner at Corporate Decisions Inc., a consulting firm in Cambridge, Mass.

13   Such sweeping vision will not come easily. McDonald's is one of the nation's most insular large companies, with a management team more typical of a private company than a global powerhouse. The average top executive started working at the company when Richard Nixon was President. The 15-member board of directors has sat out the corporate-governance revolution and is more than two-thirds filled with current and former executives, vendors, and service providers [see p. 43-5].

14   As the company's performance has deteriorated, top execs have tended to blame others. They have publicly blasted dissident franchisees, whom they dismiss as a small faction. Negative news accounts are chalked up to misperceptions by reporters. And one persistently critical Wall Street analyst—Damon Brundage, now at J.P. Morgan & Co.—was barred from the company's latest biennial briefing.

15   And while some companies, such as IBM and AT&T, have brought in outside leaders—albeit reluctantly—to help guide management as the business changed, McDonald's has largely clung to the "McFamily" philosophy of the 1950s and 1960s, which rewards managers who start young and stay for life. Headhunters, noting that virtually no alumni from the McDonald's Oak Brook (Ill.) headquarters can be found running other companies, say it isn't where they look for talent. "They are no longer the beacon of great success they used to be," says a Chicago-area recruiter.

16   Wall Street seems to share that sentiment. Over the past two years, while the Standard & Poor's 500-stock index grew by 63%, McDonald's shareholders could have made more money in an insured savings account. Had you invested $100 in the company two years ago, you'd be holding $103 today. Of the world's 10 most powerful brands, as ranked by Interbrand, a New York consultant, only beleaguered Eastman Kodak Co. has had a worse run over that period (see table below). Shareholders of Gillette Co., meanwhile, have more than doubled their money.

Brand	2-Year Total Return
Coca-Cola	71%
Eastman Kodak	−8
Gillette	101
McDonald's	3
Sony	49
Walt Disney	78
S&P 500	63

HOLDING THE PAST SACRED VS. EMBRACING CHANGE?

17   Even some investors who still believe in the brand are concerned. Davis Selected Advisers, with $500 million in McDonald's stock, has been a shareholder since 1994 on the strength of the company's international operations, but the big investor believes there needs to be changes in management and in the business. "It means not holding the past sacred," says Chris Davis, a portfolio manager. "There needs to be a sense of urgency."

18   Even McDonald's formidable international business faces some serious challenges. On the plus side, operating earnings have more than doubled in the past five years, and some emerging markets will soon see economies of scale. Says James R. Cantalupo, who runs the division: "We're nowhere near any kind of penetration that I think is possible."

19   But the easy markets have been tapped. Now, McDonald's is expanding beyond the bustling Londons and Moscows. As it does, margins are dropping—from 20.5% in '94 to 19.1% last year in overseas company-owned outlets. In each of the past two years, McDonald's has badly missed its projection of 18% to 20% international earnings growth, falling short of 10% per year after accounting for currency fluctuations. In the fourth quarter, key markets such as Germany and Japan underperformed, largely because of local economic climates and a strong dollar. Overall, says analyst Dean T. Haskell of EVEREN Securities Inc., "the international story is not quite as good as McDonald's would have you believe."

20   And the Arches' domestic woes raise a troubling question for the overseas operations: If McDonald's cannot respond to changing market forces at home, how will it adapt over time as its most important overseas markets mature? "It's hugely problematic," Slywotzky says. "If the same set of conditions duplicate themselves abroad, then you have a dead end waiting to happen."

21   Of course, the strength of the McDonald's brand gives it opportunities to avoid that dead end. Thanks to the movie tie-in trinkets that it gives away, for example, McDonald's is hugely popular with kids. Imagine, says Slywotzky, if it used low-margin burgers to sell a line of high-margin toys—instead of vice-versa. McDonald's says that's not its core business. But the point, says Slywotzky, is that it needs to worry less about market share and more about new profit vehicles.

22   First, though, McDonald's needs to address an even more fundamental problem: the quality of its food. While the burger giant focused on building more stores, consumers have decided they want better food and more variety. Consumers who eat fast food at least once a month say that both Wendy's and Burger King offer better-tasting fare, according to a recent BUSINESS WEEK/Harris Poll. And in a soon-to-be-released survey for Restaurants & Institutions magazine in which 2,800 consumers graded chains based on the taste of their food, McDonald's ranked 87th out of 91—just behind Hooters. "We clearly think we have to do some things with our menu," says Greenberg, who believes the new cooking system will be a turning point.

23   The fact is, convenience is no longer enough. In the Harris Poll, more than 90% of consumers listed both taste and quality as "very important" factors in their choice of a restaurant, while location and speed were selected by barely half. Why? With an abundance of choices, consumers no longer choose McDonald's just because there's one around the corner. And with new entrants offering ethnic fare, vegetarian menus, and fully stocked salad bars, fast food no longer has to mean fried food.

MCDONALD'S CAN ONLY COUNT ON YOUNG KIDS

24   Take Stephen J. Char, a 31-year-old government scientist in Denver. He has cut his trips to McDonald's in half over the past few years. "A cheeseburger and fries will kill me for the day," he says. He's found tastier options near his office for about the same price: a taco restaurant, a German deli, and even Haji Babba's—a food counter at a Texaco station that serves stuffed grape leaves.

25   Even some regulars say it's not the food that keeps them coming back. Julie Lake is the Austin (Tex.) mother of 3-year-old Chloe and 5-year-old Evan. "After preschool, when they are whiny and hungry, we go there," she says, adding that she rarely eats the food herself. That's bad news for McDonald's, which has had little luck creating dishes that appeal to grown-ups. Last year's Arch Deluxe, though still on the menu, is hardly a blockbuster. As their kids move beyond the Ronald McDonald years, baby boomers like Lake will need a new reason to visit the Arches.

Change Comes Slow to McDonald's Board

Coca-Cola Co.'s largest customer is McDonald's Corp. Sonnenschein, Nath & Rosenthal has been the hamburger chain's lead law firm for decades. DDB Needham Worldwide Inc. and Leo Burnett Co. are two of its longtime ad agencies. And Dean Foods Co. supplies the Arches with pickles.

What else do these firms have in common? Each has an executive, retired executive, or director on the McDonald's board. In fact, by current standards of corporate governance, only 4 of McDonald's 15 directors can be called independent—meaning they don't work for the company, do outside business with it, or have a McDonald's exec sitting on their own board.

That's not all: Cross-directorships, in which directors serve on each other's boards, are common, too. Gordon C. Gray, for example, chairman of a Canadian mining company and an independent director, also sits on the board of a subsidiary of Stone Container Corp., a McDonald's packaging supplier whose CEO, Roger W. Stone, is a fellow McDonald's director.

Thanks to pressure from shareholders and regulators, Corporate America over the past decade has raised the quality of its boards and increased its directors' accountability. But that trend has passed McDonald's by. "They are not even close to keeping up with corporate-governance standards that most other companies their size meet," says Anne Hansen, deputy director of the Council of Institutional Investors in Washington. Adds Warren Bennis, a University of Southern California professor who studies leadership: "For a company that size, it's stunning." The National Association of Corporate Directors recommends "a substantial majority" of a company's directors be independent. And many shareholder groups discourage cross-directorships; governance experts say they can lead directors to look out for each others' interests, rather than those of shareholders.

McDonald's denies that the many relationships between its board members and the company are a problem. "We have always had a board that was fairly heavily peopled by inside directors. I am not troubled by that at all," says CEO and Chairman Michael R. Quinlan. He argues that insiders bring detailed knowledge of McDonald's to the board. And director Robert N. Thurston, a former Quaker Oats Co. executive, calls it an active board that "can stick our noses anywhere we want to." To suggest that directors are hampered by company ties "discounts the independence and the pride and the intelligence and the fortitude of the people on the board," he adds.

The proper question, though, may not be whether the directors have integrity—there is no evidence they don't—but whether, as a group, they bring the type of broad experience and objectivity that a company facing a watershed requires. Despite the hamburger chain's lackluster performance in the past few years, its board has done little to agitate for change, say people who follow the company. "This board is so stale, it's hard to imagine it asking the right questions," Bennis says. Or, as one major shareholder puts it: "If McDonald's is one of your largest customers, I don't think you're going to challenge the CEO too much."

Compare the McDonald's board with those at another globally branded company. Nine of Coca-Cola's 13 directors are independent. The board includes former Senator Sam Nunn, former baseball Commissioner Peter V. Ueberroth, former Delta Air Lines CEO Ronald W. Allen, and superinvestor Warren Buffett.

In fact, inspect almost any company with a brand similar in strength to McDonald's, and you will find more outside directors, a shorter average term, a younger board, and greater diversity of experience. Inspect McDonald's, on the other hand, and you will find a disproportionate number of directors who rely on the company for one kind of paycheck or another.

1998 McDonald's Board of Directors

HALL ADAMS JR., 64, former CEO of Leo Burnett & Co., a McDonald's ad agency (1993)

GORDON C. GRAY, 70, a Canadian mining executive; sits on another board with Stone (1982)

DONALD R. KEOUGH, 71, former president of Coca-Cola Co., a major McDonald's supplier (1993)

ENRIQUE HERNANDEZ JR., 42, CEO of California-based provider of security guards (1996)

DONALD G. LUBIN, 64, partner at McDonald's Chicago law firm, Sonnenschein, Nath & Rosenthal (1967)

TERRY L. SAVAGE, 53, Chicago-based television and print journalist (1990)

ANDREW J. McKENNA, 68, CEO of Schwarz Paper Co., a McDonald's supplier. Director of Aon Corp. (with former McDonald's CEO Fred Turner) and Dean Foods, another McDonald's supplier (1991)

ROGER W. STONE, 63, CEO of Stone Container Corp., a McDonald's supplier that also owns stake in supplier of take-out bags. Jack Greenberg, president of McDonald's USA, sits on Stone board (1989)

B. BLAIR VEDDER JR., 73, former COO of agency that became McDonald's lead ad agency (1988)

ROBERT N. THURSTON, 65, Former Quaker Oats executive (1974)

TABLE 1

Question: Which fast-food burger chain do you think serves the best-tasting food?

Wendy's: 36%

Burger King: 32%

McDonald's: 21%

Other: 8%

Don't know: 2%

Question: Which fast-food burger chain do you think serves the best-tasting burgers?

Burger King: 42%

Wendy's: 32%

McDonald's: 17%

Other: 7%

Don't know: 2%

The BW/Harris Poll also asked consumers what factors are most important to them when deciding whether to eat at a fast-food restaurant, another kind of restaurant, or at home. The results are intriguing. They indicate that simple convenience is by itself no longer enough to attract diners. The huge restaurant buildup of the last decade—led by the decline of stay-at-home parents and funded by an IPO boom on Wall Street—has left consumers with dozens of choices, often just a few minutes from their home or office. To a much lesser degree than before, people choose a restaurant simply because they happen to pass it. Taste and quality are paramount. Chains such as Starbucks and startups like the new "wrap" restaurants have benefitted from the trend.

Question: Thinking about the factors that are most important to you in choosing to eat at a fast-food hamburger restaurant rather than eating meals at home or at some other restaurant, how important to you is each of the following?

	Very	Somewhat	Not Very	n/a
The taste of the food	91%	8	1	
The quality of the food	93%	6	1	
The location	42%	39	18	
The speed and convenience	52%	39	9	
Low price	45%	4	13	
That your kids like the food	58%	12	5	24
That your kids like the atmosphere and giveaways	29%	27	21	23

(Note: Results cover only those who say they eat fast food at least once a month.)

26   All the while, McDonald's has concentrated on adding restaurants, angering store owners and cutting into margins. It began a major U.S. expansion in the early '90s, even as business was slowing. "They built a whole bunch of new stores in the wrong places," says Dick Adams, who heads up a group of concerned franchisees.

27   That single-minded focus left a huge opportunity for new competitors eager to take advantage of changing eating habits. In the same nine years that McDonald's U.S. profits have stagnated, Starbucks Corp. has become a $1 billion company. Supermarket sales of prepared food have doubled, and the "casual dining" segment has emerged. In fact, Americans now spend more on prepared meals sold at delis, supermarkets, and casual dining restaurants such as Applebee's International Inc. than they do at burger chains, according to Technomic Inc., a market-research firm based in Chicago.

28   Even among burger chains, McDonald's is no longer the shrewdest innovator. Burger King has nibbled at McDonald's market share with better-tasting burgers. Wendy's has used its new stuffed pitas and spicy chicken sandwich to drive it toward 21 months of sales gains in existing outlets. Carl's Jr., a 708-restaurant chain based in Anaheim, Calif., has opened a Mexican eatery called Green Burrito within 120 of its stores. That has helped boost the typically slow dinner business and led to a $250,000 revenue jump in some stores.

TABLE 2

In 1991, *Business Week* chronicled the millions McDonald's was pouring into experiments. Today, most of those items are off the menu.

Carrot Sticks

Still available as an optional item in some U.S. restaurants.

Fried Chicken

This was no McNuggets. Though available in much of Asia, it's off the menu in the U.S., along with the corn on the cob that came with it.

Pasta

McDonald's tried the old favorites, spaghetti and lasagna, with garlic bread. Neither is available anymore in the U.S.

Fajitas

The McDonald's version of this popular Mexican dish never took off, though it's still available in a few U.S. restaurants.

Pizza

The company devoted an entire annual franchisee meeting to talking up this fast-food favorite. Pizza survives in Canada, but it is no longer offered in the U.S.

McLean Deluxe

This low-fat sandwich debuted in 1991 to woo health-conscious customers. It was erased from the menu in 1996.

29   It's not that McDonald's hasn't made a stab at new products. The past decade has seen an array of test products, such as pasta, fried chicken, and fajitas. But customers have been unimpressed, and McDonald's invariably has returned to its core menu. It pulled the plug in 1995 on one of its most interesting ideas, a one-store test of a Boston Market-like chain called Hearth Express, saying it wanted to focus on building more hamburger restaurants. "The brand expectation, at least until now, hasn't been as broad [as it could be], and that's been an issue for us in the U.S.," Greenberg says. "When you try to sell something that doesn't necessarily fit people's expectations for the Golden Arches, you have a very difficult time." Analysts, however, say that too often the new products just didn't taste good.

30   The company's recent stake in Chipotle could be a sign that McDonald's is considering new ways to leverage its brand. Chipotle's fresh, inexpensive burrito wraps are precisely the type of food that has drawn consumers away from the Arches in recent years. Executives have said that they would like to eventually expand and franchise Chipotle, though they caution that the investment, estimated to be less than $15 million, is far too small to have any impact soon.

REENGINEERING, REORGANIZATION, OR WHITEWASH?

31   More significant than the Chipotle venture is McDonald's management reorganization of last summer. Quinlan nudged Edward H. Rensi, who formerly was head of the domestic division, into early retirement and replaced him with Greenberg, who franchisees say is easier to talk to. Five new regional division chiefs, whose territories divvy up the country, now report to Greenberg. The idea: create smaller companies within the larger McDonald's that will recapture its earlier entrepreneurial zeal.

32   But even the shuffling shows signs of McDonald's discomfort with change. Of the five new division heads, none has set up shop outside the Chicago area, and only one has immediate plans to do so. The majority of franchisees still report to the same person. The reorganization, charges EVEREN analyst Haskell, "is an effort to whitewash the public by trying to convince Wall Street things have changed when they really haven't." Says one investor who manages more than $30 million in McDonald's stock: "The changes were an improvement, but I don't think it's a dramatic improvement."

33   One of the most troubling signs of McDonald's unwillingness to grapple with underlying problems is its reaction to outside critics. Greenberg has dismissed the Consortium, a San Diego-based group of franchisees unhappy with the company's direction, as "eight people and a guy with a fax machine."

34   Adams, a former McDonald's owner who runs the Consortium, claims membership of 300 but refuses to release a list, saying franchisees fear reprisals. But other evidence indicates that unhappiness is more widespread than Greenberg's comment suggests. In a 1997 internal survey, only 28% of franchisees said they thought McDonald's was on the right track. The controversial push to put up more stores remains a flashpoint for many. Says one former operator who claims new stores helped to put him out of business: "Ray Kroc once told me, 'If you work hard, you get treated fairly.' But these guys don't care about the operators."

35   The media also get blamed for McDonald's bad news. During a guest lecture at Northwestern University's Medill School of Journalism last year, chief McDonald's spokesman Charles Ebeling lashed out at reporters. Ebeling dismissed as "bullshit" a story in *The Wall Street Journal* that prophetically detailed the problems with Campaign 55, a complicated discount promotion. Then he called *Crain's Chicago Business,* a respected weekly that had run critical stories on the company, "a scandal sheet" with a "corrupt" editor. Ebeling says the remarks, reported in *Rolling Stone* magazine, were taken out of context.

How [Not?] to Communicate With the Business Press, and Sustain Brand Identity

36   Indeed, after eight years in which real domestic operating profits have actually fallen, the head of marketing for McDonald's USA says the biggest problem with the brand is the media' s view of it. "If there were one thing I would want to change about McDonald's," says Senior Vice-President Brad A. Ball, "it would be to correct the misconceptions and perceptions that have become so pervasive in the last few years."

37   Wall Street analysts struggling to evaluate the company's prospects say they, too, have largely been frozen out. They say McDonald's is the only big company they follow in which top executives, including Quinlan, refuse to meet with them. "It's absolutely baffling," says Howard Penney of Morgan Stanley, Dean Witter, Discover & Co., one of four analysts McDonald's identifies as knowing the most about the corporation. "Here we are trying to educate people about what we think about the company, and the top management guy won't speak to us." Quinlan says he's in touch with Wall Street.

38   Through it all, he and other executives maintain that the company remains strong. Quinlan has cut his projections for future growth but still predicts a doubling or near-doubling of earnings per share over the next five years—which analysts call feasible, if optimistic. "In the U.S., we've made some mistakes," Quinlan acknowledges, but he says: "Our greatest days lie ahead."

39   So what's the problem? Simply put, it's hard to dismiss a lagging stock price, the end of growth in domestic profits, missed international projections, and a decade's worth of failed initiatives. This much is clear: The world's most successful restaurant company is far from achieving its potential— and may be sowing the seeds for further disappointment down the road.

40   It doesn't have to be that way. Imagine the possibilities: The company uses its powerful brand to figure out a way to grow in its own backyard. The new kitchen production system allows executives to think more broadly about high-quality menu additions. Domestic earnings no longer drag down international growth but add to it. And overseas markets, upon saturation, have a model for future growth.

41   Of course, doing all that requires thinking about the business in fundamentally new ways and refusing to be tied to the past. It wouldn't be the first time for McDonald's. After all, consider where the Golden Arches would be now if its first owners had insisted on keeping hot dogs as the centerpiece of the menu.

Initial Turnaround—Substance or Window Dressing?

42   One year ago, McDonald's Corp. was serving a menu that consumers ranked among the worst-tasting of any restaurant chain. The Golden Arches had not launched a successful new product since Chicken McNuggets in 1983. And the company's stock was performing worse than cash sitting in a

EXHIBIT B

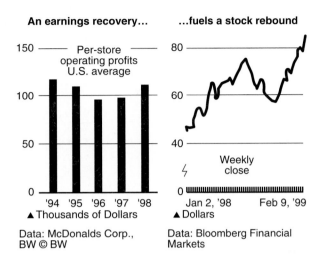

An earnings recovery...

150 — Per-store operating profits U.S. average

100

50

0

'94 '95 '96 '97 '98
▲ Thousands of Dollars

Data: McDonalds Corp., BW © BW

...fuels a stock rebound

80

60

40

Weekly close

0

Jan 2, '98   Feb 9, '99
▲ Dollars

Data: Bloomberg Financial Markets

bureau drawer. Today, the food still trails the competition's, and there is still no new blockbuster on the menu—but McDonald's shares have risen 67% in the past 12 months, to $80 each, about triple the growth rate of the Standard & Poor's 500-stock index.

43   What do investors see? It may not be obvious at your local Mickey D's, but a behind-the-scenes transformation is under way. New Chief Executive Jack M. Greenberg is leading an overhaul of the long-insular restaurant company that has made both franchisees and investors more optimistic than they have been in years. In a break with tradition, Greenberg has turned to outsiders to fill key posts. He is cutting 23% of headquarters staff, the first layoff in company history. And franchisees and corporate managers stationed in the field now make more of the decisions about when to discount and what food to test.

44   The result: McDonald's has found modest success with new products, including a bagel breakfast sandwich and the McFlurry sundae, and with regional discounts. Those were big reasons why average store sales climbed last year and overall company revenues rose 9%, to $12.4 billion. "We're doing better," Greenberg said late last year, "and sales are the best test of all." Operating profits, excluding charges for the layoffs and investments in new kitchens, climbed 10%, to $3.1 billion. "This was a company coming to a crisis," says Chris Davis, a portfolio manager at Davis Selected Advisers, which owns more than 9 million shares. "Greenberg's done a fantastic job bringing a new sense of urgency and getting rid of their corporate arrogance."

45   Still, much of the lift came from a one-time drop in advertising costs and last spring's wildly successful Teenie Beanie Babies promotion. McDonald's is looking for another home run with its upcoming promotion featuring miniature Furby dolls. But the success will be hard to maintain long-term without better food, says Everen Securities analyst Dean T. Haskell. Indeed, consumers ranked McDonald's food 87th out of 91 chains in a poll last year by *Restaurants and Institutions*— and its score will be slightly lower in a new poll out later this month. Says Alan D. Feldman, a former Pizza Hut Inc. exec who was named president of McDonald's USA last year: "We've got to improve our menu."

Big Retrofit

46   Enter "Made for You," a $500 million upgrade of virtually every U.S. McDonald's kitchen. Instead of keeping food in taste-killing warming bins, the system uses computers to project customer traffic and an assembly line to keep lettuce cold and burgers hot—while making custom orders as simple as they are at Burger King Corp. McDonald's says the retrofit will be almost complete by the end of 1999.

1997 Performance at a Glance

With more than 23,000 restaurants in over 100 countries, our global market potential is enormous. On any day, even as the market leader, McDonald's serves less than one percent of the world's population. Our outstanding brand recognition, experienced management, high-quality food, site development expertise, advanced operational systems, and unique global infrastructure position us to capitalize on global opportunities. We plan to expand our leadership position through convenience, superior value and excellent operations. Our efforts to increase market share, profitability, and customer satisfaction have produced high returns to shareholders—a compound annual total return of 17 percent over the past 10 years.

Compound annual growth rates
For the 10-year period ended December 31, 1997

Systemwide sales	8.9%
U.S.	4.9
Outside the U.S.	16.0
Total revenues	8.9
Operating income	9.2
U.S.	3.0
Outside the U.S.	19.4
Net income	11.6
Net income per common share	12.6
Net income per common share—diluted	12.4
Cash provided by operations	8.8
Total assets	10.1
Total shareholders' equity	11.7
Total return to investors on common stock	16.8

Market price per common share
In dollars, by quarter

	1997			1996		
	High	Low	Close	High	Low	Close
1st	$49^3/_8$	$42^1/_2$	$47^1/_4$	$54^1/_4$	$42^1/_2$	48
2nd	$54^7/_8$	$46^3/_4$	$48^5/_{16}$	$50^3/_8$	$45^3/_8$	$46^3/_4$
3rd	$54^3/_4$	$45^3/_4$	$47^5/_8$	49	41	$47^3/_8$
4th	$49^5/_8$	$42^1/_8$	$47^3/_4$	$49^3/_8$	$43^3/_4$	$45^3/_8$

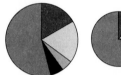

1997: 23,132   1992: 13,093

	1997	1992
United States	**12,380**	**8,959**
Europe	**3,886**	**1,534**
Andorra	2	1
Austria	103	35
Belarus	5	0
Belgium	60	16
Bulgaria	9	0
Croatia	8	0
Czech Republic	43	3
Denmark	78	21
England	746	429
Estonia	5	0
Finland	85	14
France	629	239
Germany	850	438
Greece	38	2
Hungary	62	10
Iceland	2	0
Ireland	38	16
Isle of Man	1	0
Italy	173	16
Jersey	1	0
Latvia	5	0
Liechtenstein	1	0
Lithuania	5	0
Luxembourg	4	2
Macedonia	1	0
Malta	6	0
Monaco	1	1
Netherlands	176	83
Northern Ireland	11	4
Norway	42	10
Poland	95	3
Portugal	45	4
Reunion Island	1	0
Romania	28	0
Russia	26	1
Scotland	47	24
Slovakia	5	0
Slovenia	9	0
Spain	150	50
Sweden	151	59
Switzerland	90	32
Ukraine	7	0
Wales	31	15
Yugoslavia	11	6
Asia/Pacific	**4,456**	**1,653**
Australia	642	338
Brunei	1	1
China	184	3
Fiji	2	0
Guam	6	4
Hong Kong	140	62
India	9	0
Indonesia	103	5
Japan	2,437	956
Macau	10	3
Malaysia	110	31
New Caledonia	1	0
New Zealand	137	61
Philippines	157	47
Saipan	2	0
Singapore	105	44
South Korea	114	15
Tahiti	1	0
Taiwan	233	67
Thailand	61	16
Western Samoa	1	0

Latin America

	1,091	274
Argentina	131	18
Aruba	2	1
Bahamas	3	4
Bermuda (U.S. Navy Base)	0	1
Bolivia	3	0
Brazil	480	107
Chile	27	3
Colombia	18	0
Costa Rica	19	8
Cuba (U.S. Navy Base)	1	1
Curacao	4	3
Dominican Rep.	4	0
Ecuador	2	0
El Salvador	0	3
Guadeloupe	4	1
Guatemala	23	6
Honduras	5	0
Jamaica	7	0
Martinique	5	1
Mexico	131	56
Panama	20	10
Paraguay	6	0
Peru	5	0
Puerto Rico	109	40
St. Maarten	1	0
Suriname	1	0
Trinidad	3	0
Uruguay	18	2
Venezuela	53	6
Virgin Islands	6	3

Other

	1,319	673
Bahrain	5	0
Canada	1,050	658
Cyprus	3	0
Egypt	20	0
Israel	53	0
Jordan	2	0
Kuwait	16	0
Morocco	6	1
Oman	2	0
Qatar	3	0
Saudi Arabia	27	0
South Africa	35	0
Turkey	84	14
United Arab Em.	13	0

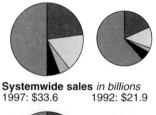

Systemwide sales *in billions*
1997: $33.6   1992: $21.9

Operating income *in billions*
1997: $2.8   1992: $1.9

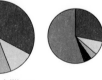

Assets *in billions*
1997: $18.2   1992: $11.7

- ● U.S.
- ● Europe
- ○ Asia/Pacific
- ◐ Latin America
- ● Other

1997 Performance at a Glance
concluded

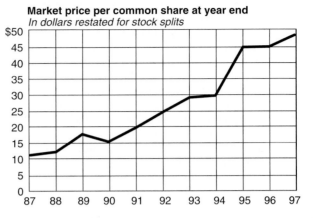

Market price per common share at year end
In dollars restated for stock splits

11-year summary	1997	1996	1995	1994	1993	1992	1991	1990	1989	1988	1987
(Dollars in millions, except per common share data and average restaurant sales)											
Systemwide sales	**$33,638**	31,812	29,914	25,987	23,587	21,885	19,928	18,759	17,333	16,064	14,330
Systemwide sales by type											
Operated by franchisees	**$20,863**	19,969	19,123	17,146	15,756	14,474	12,959	12,017	11,219	10,424	9,452
Operated by the Company	**$ 8,136**	7,571	6,863	5,793	5,157	5,103	4,908	5,019	4,601	4,196	3,667
Operated by affiliates	**$ 4,639**	4,272	3,928	3,048	2,674	2,308	2,061	1,723	1,513	1,444	1,211
Average sales by Systemwide restaurants *(in thousands)*	**$ 1,592**	1,708	1,844	1,800	1,768	1,733	1,658	1,649	1,621	1,596	1,502
Total revenues	**$11,409**	10,687	9,795	8,321	7,408	7,133	6,695	6,640	6,066	5,521	4,853
Revenues from franchised and affiliated restaurants	**$ 3,272**	3,116	2,931	2,528	2,251	2,031	1,787	1,621	1,465	1,325	1,186
Operating income	**$ 2,808**	2,633	2,601	2,241	1,984	1,862	1,679	1,596	1,438	1,288	1,160
Income before provision for income taxes	**$ 2,407**	2,251	2,169	1,887	1,676	1,448	1,299	1,246	1,157	1,046	959
Net income	**$ 1,643**	1,573	1,427	1,224	1,083	959	860	802	727	646	549[1]
Cash provided by operations	**$ 2,442**	2,461	2,296	1,926	1,680	1,426	1,423	1,301	1,246	1,177	1,051
Capital expenditures	**$ 2,111**	2,375	2,064	1,539	1,317	1,087	1,129	1,571	1,555	1,321	1,027
Treasury stock purchases	**$ 765**	605	321	500	628	92	117	157	497	136	143
Financial position at year end											
Net property and equipment	**$14,961**	14,352	12,811	11,328	10,081	9,597	9,559	9,047	7,758	6,800	5,820
Total assets	**$18,242**	17,386	15,415	13,592	12,035	11,681	11,349	10,668	9,175	8,159	6,982
Total debt	**$ 6,463**	5,523	4,836	4,351	3,713	3,857	4,615	4,792	4,036	3,269	2,784
Total shareholders' equity	**$ 8,852**	8,718	7,861	6,885	6,274	5,892	4,835	4,182	3,550	3,413	2,917
Per common share											
Net income[2]	**$ 2.35**	2.21	1.97	1.68	1.45	1.30	1.17	1.10	.97	.86	.72[1]
Net income—diluted[2]	**$ 2.29**	2.16	1.93	1.63	1.42	1.27	1.14	1.07	.96	.85	.71[1]
Dividends declared	**$ .32**	.29	.26	.23	.21	.20	.18	.17	.15	.14	.12
Market price at year end	**$ 47³/₄**	45³/₈	45¹/₈	29¹/₄	28¹/₂	24³/₈	19	14¹/₂	17¹/₄	12	11
Systemwide restaurants at year end	**23,132**	21,022	18,380	15,950	14,163	13,093	12,418	11,803	11,162	10,513	9,911
Systemwide restaurants by type											
Operated by franchisees	**14,265**	13,428	12,217	10,965	9,933	9,237	8,735	8,131	7,573	7,110	6,760
Operated by the Company	**5,000**	4,357	3,816	3,238	2,746	2,551	2,547	2,643	2,691	2,600	2,399
Operated by affiliates	**3,867**	3,237	2,347	1,747	1,484	1,305	1,136	1,029	898	803	752
Number of countries at year end	**109**	101	89	79	70	65	59	53	51	50	47

[1]Before the cumulative prior years' benefit from the change in accounting for income taxes.
[2]Net income per common share data is presented in conformity with SFAS 128.

47   Early response to the new system is promising. Frank Schley, a 42-year-old software company president, is impressed with the change at a McDonald's in Columbus, Ga., where he dines with his son, 8, of the same name. The restaurant is one of the 25% of U.S. McDonald's with Made for You already installed. "In the past, it was obviously an imposition to make a special order," Schley says. Adds little Frank: "I used to get some cold meals."

48   The improved performance is in stark contrast with recent years. McDonald's spent much of the '90s building hundreds of new U.S. restaurants, only to see its share of the fast-food pie shrink. Franchisees were unhappy, and domestic operating income wasn't even keeping pace with inflation. The situation came to a head last April, when Michael R. Quinlan abruptly announced his resignation as CEO. The board promoted Greenberg, who had come from Arthur Young & Co. in 1982 and risen to chief financial officer and then vice-chairman.

49   Greenberg has moved McDonald's away from big-bang initiatives—such as pizza, the Arch Deluxe, and the confusing "Campaign 55" discount—that flopped. Instead, he has focused on getting little things right. "They're being more conservative and more thoughtful," says Irwin S. Kruger, who owns six stores in Manhattan. McDonald's, with 24,800 restaurants worldwide, has closed almost 200 poorly performing U.S. units. It kept net U.S. expansion to less than 1% last year, compared with 9% a year from 1993 to 1996.

50   With new executives lured from companies ranging from Taco Bell Corp. to General Electric Co., the company is also starting to break from a past in which managers with a decade at McDonald's were considered new. Franchisees say there's also a new respect for consumer research. The company is using the data to help figure out when to discount. Starting in Florida and then on the West Coast, for example, store owners have responded to vigorous competition by selling burgers for less than the price of a candy bar on selected days. Says Tom Thompson, president of CKE Restaurants Inc. in Anaheim, Calif., which owns the Hardee's and Carl's Jr. chains: The "29 cents and 39 cents burgers have been wonderful for them."

GLOBAL SUCCESS

51   The chain is also experimenting with regional products. One, the bagel sandwich, will be available in about half of U.S. stores by midsummer. Containing meat, egg, and cheese, the bagel is an attempt to improve the Arches' appeal with adults. At almost $3 each, it's costlier than other breakfast options—but it has the potential to "change the whole mix," Greenberg says.

52   Investors like what they see so far: lower costs, higher earnings, and a buoyant new management team. They also are pleased with a powerhouse international division that is benefiting from the strong European economy while holding its own in Asia.

ACQUISITIONS TO "LEARN" HOW TO SELL TO ADULTS AND TO DIVERSIFY FRANCHISEE OPPORTUNITIES

53   You can find Steve Ells, a graduate of the Culinary Institute of America, zipping around Denver in a black BMW 540i. He likes to talk about cilantro, and he describes standard fast food as a warm piece of meat stuck inside a once-frozen bun. But when he names names, he's careful to talk only about Burger King Corp. and Wendy's International Inc.

54   That's the first clue that Ells, 33, doesn't specialize in haute cuisine. In fact, he is the founder and CEO of the only restaurant company in which McDonald's Corp. has ever invested. Named Chipotle Mexican Grill, it is a tiny but rapidly growing chain, which charges $5 apiece for enormous meat-, rice-, and bean-filled burritos that are made to order in not much more than a minute. The food is spicy and fresh, every restaurant is designed differently, and there is no kids' menu. "This is not the typical fast-food experience," says Ells. "This is something grown-up."

55   That is exactly what McDonald's executives like about the place. For the past decade, they have awkwardly tried to boost the Golden Arches' appeal to adults—from the failed test of a Boston

Market-like store to the disastrous Arch Deluxe ad campaign that depicted grimacing children. Early last year, McDonald's decided to look elsewhere for help and settled on taking a minority stake in Chipotle.

56   The investment is a tacit admission that in today's crowded restaurant field, even the biggest player may not be able to appeal to everybody. McDonald's says that within a year, it will likely determine whether to offer Chipotle franchises to existing McDonald's store owners. In the meantime, McDonald's hopes to glean some insights about how to appeal to adults in its own stores, says Pat J. Flynn, a McDonald's USA executive vice-president for strategic planning.

CROWDED FIELD

57   Chipotle runs 18 restaurants: 2 in Kansas City and 16 in the Denver area, where Ells launched the chain in 1993. Today, the outlets, with lines snaking out the door at lunch, bring in yearly sales of just above $1 million each—about 20% less than an average McDonald's. By yearend, Chipotle could be in a half-dozen more cities.

58   It will face some tough competition. The restaurant industry has overbuilt in recent years, and a number of other "fresh Mex" chains, such as La Salsa, are expanding, too. But compared with the Arches' massive global operation, the bet on Chipotle is a small one. And both McDonald's and Ells are hoping it turns out better than their last linkup, when the teenage Ells quit his job serving Big Macs after less than two months. "There was nothing fun about it," he says. Must have been the lack of cilantro.

CASE 44

KENTUCKY FRIED CHICKEN AND THE GLOBAL FAST-FOOD INDUSTRY

1   Kentucky Fried Chicken Corporation (KFC) was the world's largest chicken restaurant chain and third largest fast-food chain. KFC held over 55 percent of the U.S. market in terms of sales and operated over 10,200 restaurants worldwide in 1998. It opened 376 new restaurants in 1997 (more than one restaurant a day) and operated in 79 countries. One of the first fast-food chains to go international during the late 1960s, KFC has developed one of the world's most recognizable brands.

2   Japan, Australia, and the United Kingdom accounted for the greatest share of KFC's international expansion during the 1970s and 1980s. During the 1990s, KFC turned its attention to other international markets that offered significant opportunities for growth. China, with a population of over one billion, and Europe, with a population roughly equal to the United States, offered such opportunities. Latin America also offered a unique opportunity because of the size of its markets, its common language and culture, and its geographical proximity to the United States. Mexico was of particular interest because of the North American Free Trade Agreement (NAFTA), a free trade zone between Canada, the United States, and Mexico that went into effect in 1994.

3   Prior to 1990, KFC expanded into Latin America primarily through company-owned restaurants in Mexico and Puerto Rico. Company-owned restaurants gave KFC greater control over its operations than franchised or licensed restaurants. By 1995, KFC had also established company-owned restaurants in Venezuela and Brazil. In addition, it had established franchised units in numerous Caribbean countries. During the early 1990s, KFC shifted to a two-tiered strategy in Latin America. First, it established 29 franchised restaurants in Mexico following enactment of Mexico's new franchise law in 1990. This allowed KFC to expand outside of its company restaurant base in Mexico City, Guadalajara, and Monterrey. KFC was one of many U.S. fast-food, retail, and hotel chains to begin franchising in Mexico following the new franchise law. Second, KFC began an aggressive franchise building program in South America. By 1998, it was operating franchised restaurants in 32 Latin American countries. Much of this growth was in Brazil, Chile, Colombia, Ecuador, and Peru.

COMPANY HISTORY

4   Fast-food franchising was still in its infancy in 1952 when Harland Sanders began his travels across the United States to speak with prospective franchisees about his "Colonel Sanders Recipe Kentucky Fried Chicken." By 1960, "Colonel" Sanders had granted KFC franchises to over 200 take-home retail outlets and restaurants across the United States. He had also succeeded in establishing a number of franchises in Canada. By 1963, the number of KFC franchises had risen to over 300 and revenues had reached $500 million.

5   By 1964, at the age of 74, the Colonel had tired of running the day-to-day operations of his business and was eager to concentrate on public relations issues. Therefore, he sought out potential buyers, eventually deciding to sell the business to two Louisville businessmen—Jack Massey and John Young Brown Jr.—for $2 million. The Colonel stayed on as a public relations man and goodwill ambassador for the company.

6   During the next five years, Massey and Brown concentrated on growing KFC's franchise system across the United States. In 1966, they took KFC public and the company was listed on the New York Stock Exchange. By the late 1960s, a strong foothold had been established in the United States, and

This case was prepared by Professor Jeffrey A. Krug of the University of Illinois at Urbana-Champaign. The case was prepared for classroom purposes only and is not designed to show effective or ineffective handling of administrative situations.

Massey and Brown turned their attention to international markets. In 1969, a joint venture was signed with Mitsuoishi Shoji Kaisha, Ltd. in Japan, and the rights to operate 14 existing KFC franchises in England were acquired. Subsidiaries were also established in Hong Kong, South Africa, Australia, New Zealand, and Mexico. By 1971, KFC had 2,450 franchises and 600 company-owned restaurants worldwide, and was operating in 48 countries.

Heublein, Inc.

7   In 1971, KFC entered negotiations with Heublein, Inc. to discuss a possible merger. The decision to seek a merger candidate was partially driven by Brown's desire to pursue other interests, including a political career (Brown was elected Governor of Kentucky in 1977). Several months later, Heublein acquired KFC. Heublein was in the business of producing vodka, mixed cocktails, dry gin, cordials, beer, and other alcoholic beverages. However, Heublein had little experience in the restaurant business. Conflicts quickly erupted between Colonel Sanders, who continued to act in a public relations capacity, and Heublein management. Colonel Sanders became increasingly distraught over quality control issues and restaurant cleanliness. By 1977, new restaurant openings had slowed to about twenty per year. Few restaurants were being remodeled and service quality had declined.

8   In 1977, Heublein sent in a new management team to redirect KFC's strategy. A "back-to-the-basics" strategy was immediately implemented. New unit construction was discontinued until existing restaurants could be upgraded and operating problems eliminated. Restaurants were refurbished, an emphasis was placed on cleanliness and service, marginal products were eliminated, and product consistency was reestablished. By 1982, KFC had succeeded in establishing a successful strategic focus and was again aggressively building new units.

R.J. Reynolds Industries, Inc.

9   In 1982, R.J. Reynolds Industries, Inc. (RJR) merged Heublein into a wholly owned subsidiary. The merger with Heublein represented part of RJR's overall corporate strategy of diversifying into unrelated businesses, including energy, transportation, food, and restaurants. RJR's objective was to reduce its dependence on the tobacco industry, which had driven RJR sales since its founding in North Carolina in 1875. Sales of cigarettes and tobacco products, while profitable, were declining because of reduced consumption in the United States. This was mainly the result of an increased awareness among Americans about the negative health consequences of smoking.

10   RJR had no more experience in the restaurant business than did Heublein. However, it decided to take a hands-off approach to managing KFC. Whereas Heublein had installed its own top management at KFC headquarters, RJR left KFC management largely intact, believing that existing KFC managers were better qualified to operate KFC's businesses than were its own managers. In doing so, RJR avoided many of the operating problems that plagued Heublein. This strategy paid off for RJR as KFC continued to expand aggressively and profitably under RJR ownership. In 1985, RJR acquired Nabisco Corporation for $4.9 billion. Nabisco sold a variety of well-known cookies, crackers, cereals, confectioneries, snacks, and other grocery products. The merger with Nabisco represented a decision by RJR to concentrate its diversification efforts on the consumer foods industry. It subsequently divested many of its nonconsumer food businesses. RJR sold KFC to PepsiCo, Inc. one year later.

PEPSICO, INC.

Corporate Strategy

11   PepsiCo, Inc. was formed in 1965 with the merger of the Pepsi-Cola Co. and Frito-Lay Inc. The merger of these companies created one of the largest consumer products companies in the United States. Pepsi-Cola's traditional business was the sale of soft drink concentrates to licensed independent and company-owned bottlers that manufactured, sold, and distributed Pepsi-Cola soft drinks. Pepsi-Cola's best known trademarks were Pepsi-Cola, Diet Pepsi, Mountain Dew, and Slice.

Frito-Lay manufactured and sold a variety of snack foods, including Fritos Corn Chips, Lay's Potato Chips, Ruffles Potato Chips, Doritos, Tostitos Tortilla Chips, and Chee-tos Cheese Flavored Snacks. PepsiCo quickly embarked on an aggressive acquisition program similar to that pursued by RJR during the 1980s, buying a number of companies in areas unrelated to its major businesses. Acquisitions included North American Van Lines, Wilson Sporting Goods, and Lee Way Motor Freight. However, success in operating these businesses failed to live up to expectations, mainly because the management skills required to operate these businesses lay outside of PepsiCo's area of expertise.

12   Poor performance in these businesses led then-chairman and chief executive officer Don Kendall to restructure PepsiCo's operations in 1984. First, businesses that did not support PepsiCo's consumer product orientation, such as North American Van Lines, Wilson Sporting Goods, and Lee Way Motor Freight were divested. Second, PepsiCo's foreign bottling operations were sold to local businesspeople who better understood the culture and business environment in their respective countries. Third, Kendall reorganized PepsiCo along three lines: soft drinks, snack foods, and restaurants.

Restaurant Business and Acquisition of Kentucky Fried Chicken

13   PepsiCo first entered the restaurant business in 1977 when it acquired Pizza Hut's 3,200-unit restaurant system. Taco Bell was merged into a division of PepsiCo in 1978. The restaurant business complemented PepsiCo's consumer product orientation. The marketing of fast food followed many of the same patterns as the marketing of soft drinks and snack foods. Therefore, PepsiCo believed that its management skills could easily be transferred among its three business segments. This was compatible with PepsiCo's practice of frequently moving managers among its business units as a way of developing future top executives. PepsiCo's restaurant chains also provided an additional outlet for the sale of Pepsi soft drinks. Pepsi-Cola soft drinks and fast-food products could also be marketed together in the same television and radio segments, thereby providing higher returns for each advertising dollar. To complete its diversification into the restaurant segment, PepsiCo acquired Kentucky Fried Chicken Corporation from RJR-Nabisco for $841 million in 1986. The acquisition of KFC gave PepsiCo the leading market share in chicken (KFC), pizza (Pizza Hut), and Mexican food (Taco Bell), three of the four largest and fastest-growing segments within the U.S. fast-food industry.

Management

14   Following the acquisition by PepsiCo, KFC's relationship with its parent company underwent dramatic changes. RJR had operated KFC as a semi-autonomous unit, satisfied that KFC management understood the fast-food business better than they. In contrast, PepsiCo acquired KFC in order to complement its already strong presence in the fast-food market. Rather than allowing KFC to operate autonomously, PepsiCo undertook sweeping changes. These changes included negotiating a new franchise contract to give PepsiCo more control over its franchisees, reducing staff in order to cut costs, and replacing KFC managers with its own. In 1987, a rumor spread through KFC's headquarters in Louisville that the new personnel manager, who had just relocated from PepsiCo's headquarters in New York, was overheard saying that "There will be no more home grown tomatoes in this organization."

15   Such statements by PepsiCo personnel, uncertainties created by several restructurings that led to layoffs throughout the KFC organization, the replacement of KFC personnel with PepsiCo managers, and conflicts between KFC and PepsiCo's corporate cultures created a morale problem within KFC. KFC's culture was built largely on Colonel Sanders' laid-back approach to management. Employees enjoyed relatively good employment stability and security. Over the years, a strong loyalty had been created among KFC employees and franchisees, mainly because of the efforts of Colonel Sanders to provide for his employees' benefits, pension, and other nonincome needs. In addition, the Southern environment of Louisville resulted in a friendly, relaxed atmosphere at KFC's corporate offices. This corporate culture was left essentially unchanged during the Heublein and RJR years.

16   In stark contrast to KFC, PepsiCo's culture was characterized by a strong emphasis on performance. Top performers expected to move up through the ranks quickly. PepsiCo used its KFC, Pizza Hut, Taco Bell, Frito Lay, and Pepsi-Cola divisions as training grounds for its top managers, rotating

its best managers through the five divisions on average every two years. This practice created immense pressure on managers to continuously demonstrate their managerial prowess within short periods, in order to maximize their potential for promotion. This practice also left many KFC managers with the feeling that they had few career opportunities with the new company. One PepsiCo manager commented that "You may have performed well last year, but if you don't perform well this year, you're gone, and there are 100 ambitious guys with Ivy League MBAs at PepsiCo who would love to take your position." An unwanted effect of this performance driven culture was that employee loyalty was often lost and turnover tended to be higher than in other companies.

17   Kyle Craig, president of KFC's U.S. operations, was asked about KFC's relationship with its corporate parent. He commented:

> The KFC culture is an interesting one because I think it was dominated by a lot of KFC folks, many of whom have been around since the days of the Colonel. Many of those people were very intimidated by the PepsiCo culture which is a very high performance, high accountability, highly driven culture. People were concerned about whether they would succeed in the new culture. Like many companies, we have had a couple of downsizings which further made people nervous. Today, there are fewer old KFC people around and I think to some degree people have seen that the PepsiCo culture can drive some pretty positive results. I also think the PepsiCo people who have worked with KFC have modified their cultural values somewhat and they can see that there were a lot of benefits in the old KFC culture.
>
> PepsiCo pushes their companies to perform strongly, but whenever there is a slip in performance, it increases the culture gap between PepsiCo and KFC. I have been involved in two downsizings over which I have been the chief architect. They have been probably the two most gut-wrenching experiences of my career. Because you know you're dealing with peoples' lives and their families, these changes can be emotional if you care about the people in your organization. However, I do fundamentally believe that your first obligation is to the entire organization.

18   A second problem for PepsiCo was its poor relationship with KFC franchisees. A month after becoming president and chief executive officer in 1989, John Cranor addressed KFC's franchisees in Louisville, in order to explain the details of the new franchise contract. This was the first contract change in thirteen years. It gave PepsiCo greater power to take over weak franchises, relocate restaurants, and make changes in existing restaurants. In addition, restaurants would no longer be protected from competition from new KFC units and it gave PepsiCo the right to raise royalty fees on existing restaurants as contracts came up for renewal. After Cranor finished his address, there was an uproar among the attending franchisees, who jumped to their feet to protest the changes. The franchisees had long been accustomed to relatively little interference from management in their day-to-day operations (a tradition begun by Colonel Sanders). This type of interference, of course, was a strong part of PepsiCo's philosophy of demanding change. KFC's franchise association later sued PepsiCo over the new contract. The contract remained unresolved until 1996, when the most objectionable parts of the contract were removed by KFC's new president and CEO, David Novak. A new contract was ratified by KFC's franchisees in 1997.

PepsiCo's divestiture of KFC, Pizza Hut, and Taco Bell

19   PepsiCo's strategy of diversifying into three distinct but related markets—soft drinks, snack foods, and fast-food restaurants—created one of the world's largest consumer products companies and a portfolio of some of the world's most recognizable brands. Between 1990 and 1996, PepsiCo grew at an annual rate of over 10 percent, surpassing $31 billion in sales in 1996. However, PepsiCo's sale growth masked troubles in its fast-food businesses. Operating margins (profit as a percent of sales) at Pepsi-Cola and Frito Lay averaged 12 and 17 percent between 1990 and 1996, respectively. During the same period, margins at KFC, Pizza Hut, and Taco Bell fell from an average of over 8 percent in 1990 to a little more than 4 percent in 1996. Declining margins in the fast-food chains reflected increasing maturity in the U.S. fast-food industry, more intense competition among U.S. fast-food competitors, and the aging of KFC and Pizza Hut's restaurant base. As a result, PepsiCo's restaurant chains absorbed nearly one-half of PepsiCo's annual capital spending during the 1990s. However, they generated less than one-third of PepsiCo's cash flows. Therefore, cash was diverted from

TABLE 1
Tricon Global Restaurants, Inc.—Organizational Chart (1998)

PepsiCo's soft drink and snack food businesses to its restaurant businesses. This reduced PepsiCo's return on assets, made it more difficult to compete effectively with Coca-Cola, and hurt its stock price. In 1997, PepsiCo spun off its restaurant businesses into a new company called Tricon Global Restaurants, Inc. (see Table 1). The new company was based in KFC's headquarters in Louisville, Kentucky. PepsiCo's objective was to reposition itself as a packaged goods company, to strengthen its balance sheet, and to create more consistent earning growth. PepsiCo received a one-time distribution from Tricon of $4.7 billion, $3.7 billion of which was used to pay off short-term debt. The balance was earmarked for stock repurchases.

FAST-FOOD INDUSTRY

20 According to the National Restaurant Association (NRA), food-service sales topped $320 billion for the approximately 500,000 restaurants and other food outlets making up the U.S. restaurant industry in 1997. The NRA estimated that sales in the fast-food segment of the food service industry grew 5.2 percent to $104 billion, up from $98 billion in 1996. This marked the fourth consecutive year that fast-food sales either matched or exceeded sales in full-service restaurants, which grew 4.1 percent to $104 billion in 1997. The growth in fast-food sales reflected the long, gradual change in the restaurant industry from an industry once dominated by independently operated sit-down restaurants to an industry fast becoming dominated by fast-food restaurant chains. The U.S. restaurant industry as a whole grew by approximately 4.2 percent in 1997.

Major Fast-Food Segments

21 Six major business segments made up the fast-food segment of the food service industry. Sales data for the leading restaurant chains in each segment are shown in Table 2. Most striking is the dominance of McDonald's, which had sales of over $16 billion in 1996. This represented 16.6 percent of U.S. fast-food sales, or nearly 22 percent of sales among the nation's top 30 fast-food chains. Sales at McDonald's restaurants averaged $1.3 million per year, compared to about $820,000 for the average U.S. fast-food restaurant. Tricon Global Restaurants (KFC, Pizza Hut, and Taco Bell) had U.S. Sales of $13.4 billion in 1996. This represented 13.6 percent of U.S. fast-food sales and 17.9 percent of the top 30 fast-food chains.

TABLE 2
Leading U.S. Fast-Food Chains (Ranked by 1996 Sales, $000s)

Sandwich Chains	Sales	Share	Family Restaurants	Sales	Share
McDonald's	16,370	35.0%	Denny's	1,850	21.2%
Burger King	7,300	15.6%	Shoney's	1,220	14.0%
Taco Bell	4,575	9.8%	Big Boy	945	10.8%
Wendy's	4,360	9.3%	Int'l House of Pancakes	797	9.1%
Hardee's	3,055	6.5%	Cracker Barrel	734	8.4%
Subway	2,700	5.8%	Perkins	678	7.8%
Arby's	1,867	4.0%	Friendly's	597	6.8%
Dairy Queen	1,225	2.6%	Bob Evans	575	6.6%
Jack in the Box	1,207	2.6%	Waffle House	525	6.0%
Sonic Drive-In	985	2.1%	Coco's	278	3.2%
Carl's Jr.	648	1.4%	Steak 'n Shake	275	3.2%
Other Chains	2,454	5.2%	Village Inn	246	2.8%
Total	46,745	100.0%	Total	8,719	100.0%
Dinner Houses			**Pizza Chains**		
Red Lobster	1,810	15.7%	Pizza Hut	4,927	46.4%
Applebee's	1,523	13.2%	Domino's Pizza	2,300	21.7%
Olive Garden	1,280	11.1%	Little Caesars	1,425	13.4%
Chili's	1,242	10.7%	Papa John's	619	5.8%
Outback Steakhouse	1,017	8.8%	Sbarros	400	3.8%
T.G.I. Friday's	935	8.1%	Round Table Pizza	385	3.6%
Ruby Tuesday	545	4.7%	Chuck E. Cheese's	293	2.8%
Lone Star Steakhouse	460	4.0%	Godfather's Pizza	266	2.5%
Bennigan's	458	4.0%	Total	10,614	100.0%
Romano's Macaroni Grill	344	3.0%			
Other Dinner Houses	1,942	16.8%			
Total	11,557	100.0%			
Grilled Buffet Chains			**Chicken Chains**		
Golden Corral	711	22.8%	KFC	3,900	57.1%
Ponderosa	680	21.8%	Boston Market	1,167	17.1%
Ryan's	604	19.4%	Popeye's Chicken	666	9.7%
Sizzler	540	17.3%	Chick-fil-A	570	8.3%
Western Sizzlin'	332	10.3%	Church's Chicken	529	7.7%
Quincy's	259	8.3%	Total	6,832	100.0%
Total	3,116	100.0%			

Source: *Nation's Restaurant News.*

22   Sandwich chains made up the largest segment of the fast-food market. McDonald's controlled 35 percent of the sandwich segment, while Burger King ran a distant second with a 15.6 percent market share. Competition had become particularly intense within the sandwich segment as the U.S. fast-food market became more saturated. In order to increase sales, chains turned to new products to win customers away from other sandwich chains, introduced products traditionally offered by non-sandwich chains (such as pizzas, fried chicken, and tacos), streamlined their menus, and upgraded

product quality. Burger King recently introduced its "Big King," a direct clone of the Big Mac. Mc-Donald's quickly retaliated by introducing its "Big 'n Tasty," a direct clone of the Whopper. Wendy's introduced chicken pita sandwiches and Taco Bell introduced sandwiches called "wraps," breads stuffed with various fillings. Hardee's successfully introduced fried chicken in most of its restaurants. In addition to new products, chains lowered pricing, improved customer service, co-branded with other fast-food chains, and established restaurants in nontraditional locations (e.g., McDonald's installed restaurants in Wal-Mart stores across the country) to beef up sales.

23   The second largest fast-food segment was dinner houses, dominated by Red Lobster, Applebee's, Olive Garden, and Chili's. Between 1988 and 1996, dinner houses increased their share of the fast-food market from eight to over 13 percent. This increase came mainly at the expense of grilled buffet chains, such as Ponderosa, Sizzler, and Western Sizzlin'. The market share of steak houses fell from six percent in 1988 to under four percent in 1996. The rise of dinner houses during the 1990s was partially the result of an aging and wealthier population that increasingly demanded higher quality food in more upscale settings. However, rapid construction of new restaurants, especially among relative newcomers, such as Romano's Macaroni Grill, Lone Star Steakhouse, and Outback Steakhouse, resulted in overcapacity within the dinner house segment. This reduced per restaurant sales and further intensified competition. Eight of the sixteen largest dinner houses posted growth rates in excess of 10 percent in 1996. Romano's Macaroni Grill, Lone Star Steakhouse, Chili's, Outback Steakhouse, Applebee's, Red Robin, Fuddruckers, and Ruby Tuesday grew at rates of 82, 41, 32, 27, 23, 14, 11, and 10 percent, respectively.

24   The third largest fast-food segment was pizza, long dominated by Pizza Hut. While Pizza Hut controlled over 46 percent of the pizza segment in 1996, its market share has slowly eroded because of intense competition and its aging restaurant base. Domino's Pizza and Papa John's Pizza have been particularly successful. Little Caesars is the only pizza chain to remain predominately a take-out chain, though it recently began home delivery. However, its policy of charging customers $1 per delivery damaged its perception among consumers as a high value pizza chain. Home delivery, successfully introduced by Domino's and Pizza Hut, was a driving force for success among the market leaders during the 1970s and 1980s. However, the success of home delivery drove competitors to look for new methods of increasing their customer bases. Pizza chains diversified into non-pizza items (e.g., chicken wings at Domino's, Italian cheese bread at Little Caesars, and stuffed crust pizza at Pizza Hut), developed nontraditional units (e.g., airport kiosks and college campuses), offered special promotions, and offered new pizza variations with an emphasis on high quality ingredients (e.g., "Roma Herb" and "Garlic Crunch" pizza at Domino's and "Buffalo Chicken Pizza" at Round Table Pizza).

Chicken Segment

25   KFC continued to dominate the chicken segment, with 1997 sales of $4 billion (see Table 3). Its nearest competitor, Boston Market, was second with sales of $1.2 billion. KFC operated 5,120 restaurants in the United States in 1998, eight fewer restaurants than in 1993. Rather than building new restaurants in the already saturated U.S. market, KFC focused on building restaurants abroad. In the United States, KFC focused on closing unprofitable restaurants, upgrading existing restaurants with new exterior signage, and improving product quality. The strategy paid off. While overall U.S. sales during the last ten years remained flat, annual sales per unit increased steadily in eight of the last nine years.

26   Despite KFC's continued dominance within the chicken segment, it has lost market share to Boston Market, a new restaurant chain emphasizing roasted rather than fried chicken. Boston Market has successfully created the image of an upscale deli offering healthy, "home-style" alternatives to fried chicken and other "fast foods." It has broadened its menu beyond rotisserie chicken to include ham, turkey, meatloaf, chicken pot pie, and deli sandwiches. In order to minimize its image as a "fast-food" restaurant, it has refused to put drive-thrus in its restaurants and has established most of its units in outside shopping malls rather than in freestanding units at intersections so characteristic of other fast-food restaurants.

27   In 1993, KFC introduced its own rotisserie chicken, called "Rotisserie Gold," to combat Boston Market. However, it quickly learned that its customer base was considerably different from that of Boston Market's. KFC's customers liked KFC chicken despite the fact that it was fried. In addition,

TABLE 3
Top U.S. Chicken Chains

Sales ($ M)	1992	1993	1994	1995	1996	1997	Growth Rate (%)
KFC	3,400	3,400	3,500	3,700	3,900	4,000	3.3
Boston Market	43	147	371	754	1,100	1,197	94.5
Popeye's	545	569	614	660	677	727	5.9
Chick-fil-A	356	396	451	502	570	671	11.9
Church's	414	440	465	501	526	574	6.8
Total	4,758	4,952	5,401	6,118	6,772	7,170	8.5
U.S. Restaurants							
KFC	5,089	5,128	5,149	5,142	5,108	5,120	0.1
Boston Market	83	217	534	829	1,087	1,166	69.6
Popeye's	769	769	853	889	894	949	4.3
Chick-fil-A	487	545	534	825	717	762	9.0
Church's	944	932	937	953	989	1,070	2.5
Total	7,372	7,591	8,007	8,638	8,795	9,067	4.2
Sales per Unit ($ 000s)							
KFC	668	663	680	720	764	781	3.2
Boston Market	518	677	695	910	1,012	1,027	14.7
Popeye's	709	740	720	743	757	767	1.6
Chick-fil-A	731	727	845	608	795	881	3.8
Church's	439	472	496	526	531	537	4.1
Total	645	782	782	782	782	782	3.9

Source: Tricon Global Restaurants, Inc., 1997 Annual Report; Boston Chicken, Inc., 1997 Annual Report; Chick-fil-A, corporate headquarters, Atlanta; AFC Enterprises, Inc., 1997 Annual Report.

customers did not respond well to the concept of buying whole chickens for take-out. They preferred instead to buy chicken by the piece. KFC withdrew its rotisserie chicken in 1996 and introduced a new line of roasted chicken called "Tender Roast," which could be sold by the piece and mixed with its Original Recipe and Extra Crispy Chicken.

28   Other major competitors within the chicken segment included Popeye's Famous Fried Chicken and Church's Chicken (both subsidiaries of AFC Enterprises in Atlanta), Chick-fil-A, Bojangle's, El Pollo Loco, Grandy's, Kenny Rogers Roasters, Mrs. Winner's, and Pudgie's. Both Church's and Popeye's had similar strategies—to compete head-on with other "fried chicken" chains. Unlike KFC, neither chain offered rotisserie chicken and non-fried chicken products were limited. Chick-fil-A focused exclusively on pressure-cooked and char-grilled skinless chicken breast sandwiches, which it served to customers in sit-down restaurants located predominately in shopping malls. As many malls added food courts, often consisting of up to fifteen fast-food units competing side-by-side, shopping malls became less enthusiastic about allocating separate store space to food chains. Therefore, in order to complement its existing restaurant base in shopping malls, Chick-fil-A began to open smaller units in shopping mall food courts, hospitals, and colleges. It also opened freestanding units in selected locations.

Demographic Trends

29   A number of demographic and societal trends contributed to increased demand for food prepared away from home. Because of the high divorce rate in the United States and the fact that people married later in life, single-person households represented about 25 percent of all U.S. households, up from 17 percent in 1970. This increased the number of individuals choosing to eat out rather than

TABLE 4
The World's 30 Largest Fast-Food Chains (Year-end 1993, ranked by number of countries)

	Franchise	Location	Units	Countries
1	Pizza Hut	Dallas, Texas	10,433	80
2	McDonald's	Oakbrook, Illinois	23,132	70
3	KFC	Louisville, Kentucky	9,033	68
4	Burger King	Miami, Florida	7,121	50
5	Baskin Robbins	Glendale, California	3,557	49
6	Wendy's	Dublin, Ohio	4,168	38
7	Domino's Pizza	Ann Arbor, Michigan	5,238	36
8	TCBY	Little Rock, Arkansas	7,474	22
9	Dairy Queen	Minneapolis, Minnesota	5,471	21
10	Dunkin' Donuts	Randolph, Massachusetts	3,691	21
11	Taco Bell	Irvine, California	4,921	20
12	Arby's	Fort Lauderdale, Florida	2,670	18
13	Subway Sandwiches	Milford, Connecticut	8,477	15
14	Sizzler International	Los Angeles, California	681	14
15	Hardee's	Rocky Mount, North Carolina	4,060	12
16	Little Caesar's	Detroit, Michigan	4,600	12
17	Popeye's Chicken	Atlanta, Georgia	813	12
18	Denny's	Spartanburg, South Carolina	1,515	10
19	A&W Restaurants	Livonia, Michigan	707	9
20	T.G.I. Friday's	Minneapolis, Minnesota	273	8
21	Orange Julius	Minneapolis, Minnesota	480	7
22	Church's Fried Chicken	Atlanta, Georgia	1,079	6
23	Long John Silver's	Lexington, Kentucky	1,464	5
24	Carl's Jr.	Anaheim, California	649	4
25	Loterria	Tokyo, Japan	795	4
26	Mos Burger	Tokyo, Japan	1,263	4
27	Skylark	Tokyo, Japan	1,000	4
28	Jack in the Box	San Diego, California	1,172	3
29	Quick Restaurants	Berchem, Belgium	876	3
30	Taco Time	Eugene, Oregon	300	3

Source: *Hotels,* May 1994; 1994 PepsiCo, Inc. Annual Report.

Boston Market, which established its first restaurant in 1992, increased its market share from zero to 16.7 percent over the same period. On the surface, it appeared as though Boston Market's market share gain was achieved by taking customers away from KFC. However, KFC's sales growth has remained fairly stable and constant over the last ten years. Boston Market's success was largely a function of its appeal to consumers who did not regularly patronize KFC or other chicken chains that sold fried chicken. By appealing to a market niche that was previously unsatisfied, Boston Market was able to expand the existing consumer base within the chicken segment of the fast-food industry.

Refranchising Strategy

39 The relatively low growth rate in sales in KFC's domestic restaurants during the 1992–1997 period was largely the result of KFC's decision in 1993 to begin selling company-owned restaurants to

TABLE 5
Top U.S. Chicken Chains—Market Share (%)

	KFC	Boston Market	Popeye's	Chick-fil-A	Church's	Total
1988	72.1	0.0	12.0	5.8	10.1	100.0
1989	70.8	0.0	12.0	6.2	11.0	100.0
1990	71.3	0.0	12.3	6.6	9.8	100.0
1991	72.7	0.0	11.4	7.0	8.9	100.0
1992	71.5	0.9	11.4	7.5	8.7	100.0
1993	68.7	3.0	11.4	8.0	8.9	100.0
1994	64.8	6.9	11.3	8.4	8.6	100.0
1995	60.5	12.3	10.8	8.2	8.2	100.0
1996	57.6	16.2	10.0	8.4	7.8	100.0
1997	55.8	16.7	10.1	9.4	8.0	100.0
Change	−16.3	16.7	−1.9	3.6	−2.1	0.0

Source: *Nation's Restaurant News.*

franchisees. When Colonel Sanders began to expand the Kentucky Fried Chicken system in the late 1950s, he established KFC as a system of independent franchisees. This was done in order to minimize his involvement in the operations of individual restaurants and to concentrate on the things he enjoyed the most—cooking, product development, and public relations. This resulted in a fiercely loyal and independent group of franchises. PepsiCo's strategy when it acquired KFC in 1986 was to integrate KFC's operations into the PepsiCo system, in order to take advantage of operational, financial, and marketing synergies. However, such a strategy demanded that PepsiCo become more involved in decisions over franchise operations, menu offerings, restaurant management, finance, and marketing. This was met by resistance by KFC franchises, who fiercely opposed increased control by the corporate parent. One method for PepsiCo to deal with this conflict was to expand through company-owned restaurants rather than through franchising. PepsiCo also used its strong cash flows to buy back unprofitable franchised restaurants, which could then be converted into company-owned restaurants. In 1986, company-owned restaurants made up 26 percent of KFC's U.S. restaurant base. By 1993, they made up about 40 percent (see Table 6).

40   While company-owned restaurants were relatively easier to control compared to franchises, they also required higher levels of investment. This meant that high levels of cash were diverted from PepsiCo's soft drink and snack food businesses into its restaurant businesses. However, the fast-food industry delivered lowered returns than the soft drink and snack foods industries. Consequently, increased investment in KFC, Pizza Hut, and Taco Bell had a negative effect on PepsiCo's consolidated return on assets. By 1993, investors became concerned that PepsiCo's return on assets did not match returns delivered by Coca-Cola. In order to shore up its return on assets, PepsiCo decided to reduce the number of company-owned restaurants by selling them back to franchisees. This strategy lowered overall company sales, but also lowered the amount of cash tied up in fixed assets, provided PepsiCo with one-time cash flow benefits from initial fees charged to franchisees, and generated an annual stream of franchise royalties. Tricon Global continued this strategy after the spin-off in 1997.

Marketing Strategy

41   During the 1980s, consumers began to demand healthier foods, greater variety, and better service in a variety of nontraditional locations such as grocery stores, restaurants, airports, and outdoor events. This forced fast-food chains to expand menu offerings and to investigate nontraditional distribution channels and restaurant designs. Families also demanded greater value in the food they bought away from home. This increased pressure on fast-food chains to reduce prices and to lower operating costs in order to maintain profit margins.

TABLE 6
KFC Restaurant Count (U.S.A.)

	Company-Owned	% Total	Franchised/Licensed	% Total	Total
1986	1,246	26.4	3,474	73.6	4,720
1987	1,250	26.0	3,564	74.0	4,814
1988	1,262	25.8	3,637	74.2	4,899
1989	1,364	27.5	3,597	72.5	4,961
1990	1,389	27.7	3,617	72.3	5,006
1991	1,836	36.6	3,186	63.4	5,022
1992	1,960	38.8	3,095	61.2	5,055
1993	2,014	39.5	3,080	60.5	5,094
1994	2,005	39.2	3,110	60.8	5,115
1995	2,026	39.4	3,111	60.6	5,137
1996	1,932	37.8	3,176	62.2	5,108
1997	1,850	36.1	3,270	63.9	5,120
1986–1993 Compounded Annual Growth Rate	7.1%		−1.7%		1.1%
1993–1997 Compounded Annual Growth Rate	−2.1%		1.5%		0.1%

Source: Tricon Global Restaurants, Inc., 1997 Annual Report; PepsiCo, Inc., Annual Report, 1994, 1995, 1996, 1997.

42   Many of KFC's problems during the late 1980s surrounded its limited menu and inability to quickly bring new products to market. The popularity of its Original Recipe Chicken allowed KFC to expand without significant competition from other chicken competitors through the 1980s. As a result, new product introductions were never an important element of KFC's overall strategy. One of the most serious setbacks suffered by KFC came in 1989 as KFC prepared to add a chicken sandwich to its menu. While KFC was still experimenting with its chicken sandwich, McDonald's test-marketed its McChicken sandwich in the Louisville market. Shortly thereafter, it rolled out the McChicken sandwich nationally. By beating KFC to the market, McDonald's was able to develop strong consumer awareness for its sandwich. This significantly increased KFC's cost of developing awareness for its own sandwich, which KFC introduced several months later. KFC eventually withdrew its sandwich because of low sales.

43   In 1991, KFC changed its logo in the United States from Kentucky Fried Chicken to KFC, in order to reduce its image as a fried chicken chain. It continued to use the Kentucky Fried Chicken name internationally. It then responded to consumer demands for greater variety by introducing several products that would serve as alternatives to its Original Recipe Chicken. These included Oriental Wings, Popcorn Chicken, and Honey BBQ Chicken. It also introduced a dessert menu that included a variety of pies and cookies. In 1993, it rolled out Rotisserie Chicken and began to promote its lunch and dinner buffet. The buffet, which included 30 items, was introduced into almost 1,600 KFC restaurants in 27 states by year-end. In 1998, KFC sold three types of chicken—Original Recipe and Extra Crispy (fried chicken) and Tender Roast (roasted chicken).

44   One of KFC's most aggressive strategies was the introduction of its "Neighborhood Program." By mid-1993, almost 500 company-owned restaurants in New York, Chicago, Philadelphia, Washington, D.C., St. Louis, Los Angeles, Houston, and Dallas had been outfitted with special menu offerings to appeal exclusively to the Black community. Menus were beefed up with side dishes such as greens, macaroni and cheese, peach cobbler, sweet-potato pie, and red beans and rice. In addition, restaurant

employees wore African-inspired uniforms. The introduction of the Neighborhood Program increased sales by 5 to 30 percent in restaurants appealing directly to the Black community. KFC followed by testing Hispanic-oriented restaurants in the Miami area, offering side dishes such as fried plantains, flan, and tres leches.

45   One of KFC's most significant problems in the U.S. market was that overcapacity made expansion of freestanding restaurants difficult. Fewer sites were available for new construction and those sites, because of their increased cost, were driving profit margins down. Therefore, KFC initiated a new, three-pronged distribution strategy. First, it focused on building smaller restaurants in nontraditional outlets such as airports, shopping malls, universities, and hospitals. Second, it experimented with home delivery. Home delivery was introduced in the Nashville and Albuquerque markets in 1994. By 1998, home delivery was offered in 365 U.S. restaurants. Other nontraditional distribution outlets being tested included units offering drive-thru and carryout service only, snack shops in cafeterias, scaled-down outlets for supermarkets, and mobile units that could be transported to outdoor concerts and fairs.

46   A third focus of KFC's distribution strategy was restaurant co-branding, primarily with its sister chain, Taco Bell. By 1997, 349 KFC restaurants had added Taco Bell to their menus and displayed both the KFC and Taco Bell logos outside their restaurants. Co-branding gave KFC the opportunity to expand its business dayparts. While about two-thirds KFC's business was dinner, Taco Bell's primary business occurred at lunch. By combining the two concepts in the same unit, sales at individual restaurants could be increased significantly. KFC believed that there were opportunities to sell the Taco Bell concept in over 3,900 of its U.S. restaurants.

Operating Efficiencies

47   As pressure continued to build on fast-food chains to limit price increases, restaurant chains searched for ways to reduce overhead and other operating costs, in order to improve profit margins. In 1989, KFC reorganized its U.S. operations in order to eliminate overhead costs and to increase efficiency. Included in this reorganization was a revision of KFC's crew training programs and operating standards. A renewed emphasis was placed on improving customer service, cleaner restaurants, faster and friendlier service, and continued high-quality products. In 1992, KFC reorganized its middle management ranks, eliminating 250 of the 1,500 management positions at KFC's corporate headquarters. More responsibility was assigned to restaurant franchisees and marketing managers and pay was more closely aligned with customer service and restaurant performance. In 1997, Tricon Global signed a five-year agreement with PepsiCo Food Systems (which was later sold by PepsiCo to AmeriServe Food Distributors) to distribute food and supplies to Tricon's 29,712 KFC, Pizza Hut, and Taco Bell units. This provided KFC with significant opportunities to benefit from economies of scale in distribution.

INTERNATIONAL OPERATIONS

48   Much of the early success of the top ten fast-food chains was the result of aggressive building strategies. Chains were able to discourage competition by building in low population areas that could only support a single fast-food chain. McDonald's was particularly successful as it was able to quickly expand into small towns across the United States, thereby preempting other fast-food chains. It was equally important to beat a competitor into more largely populated areas where location was of prime importance. KFC's early entry into international markets placed it in a strong position to benefit from international expansion as the U.S. market became saturated. In 1997, 50 percent of KFC's restaurants were located outside of the United States. While 364 new restaurants were opened outside of the United States in 1997, only 12 new restaurants were added to the U.S. system. Most of KFC's international expansion was through franchises, though some restaurants were licensed to operators or jointly operated with a local partner. Expansion through franchising was an important strategy for penetrating international markets, because franchises were owned and operated by local entrepreneurs with a deeper understanding of local language, culture, and customs, as well as local law, financial markets, and marketing characteristics. Franchising was particularly important for expansion into smaller countries such as the Dominican Republic, Grenada, Bermuda, and Suriname, which could only support a single restaurant. Costs were prohibitively high for KFC to operate company-owned restaurants in these smaller markets. Of the 5,117 KFC restaurants located outside of the United States in 1997, 68 percent were franchised, while 22 percent were company-owned, and 10 percent were licensed restaurants or joint ventures.

49   In larger markets such as Japan, China, and Mexico, there was a stronger emphasis on building company-owned restaurants. By coordinating purchasing, recruiting and training, financing, and advertising fixed costs could be spread over a large number of restaurants and lower prices on products and services could be negotiated. KFC was also better able to control product and service quality. In order to take advantage of economies of scale, Tricon Global Restaurants managed all of the international units of its KFC, Pizza Hut, and Taco Bell chains through its Tricon International division located in Dallas, Texas. This enabled Tricon Global Restaurants to leverage its strong advertising expertise, international experience, and restaurant management experience across all its KFC, Pizza Hut, and Taco Bell restaurants.

Latin American Strategy

50   KFC's primary market presence in Latin America during the 1980s was in Mexico, Puerto Rico, and the Caribbean. KFC established subsidiaries in Mexico and Puerto Rico, from which it coordinated the construction and operation of company-owned restaurants. A third subsidiary in Venezuela was closed because of the high fixed costs associated with running the small subsidiary. Franchises were used to penetrate other countries in the Caribbean whose market size prevented KFC from profitably operating company restaurants. KFC relied exclusively on the operation of company-owned restaurants in Mexico through 1989. While franchising was popular in the United States, it was virtually unknown in Mexico until 1990, mainly because of the absence of a law protecting patents, information, and technology transferred to the Mexican franchise. In addition, royalties were limited. As a result, most fast-food chains opted to invest in Mexico using company-owned units.

51   In 1990, Mexico enacted a new law that provided for the protection of technology transferred into Mexico. Under the new legislation, the franchiser and franchisee were free to set their own terms. Royalties were also allowed under the new law. Royalties were taxed at a 15 percent rate on technology assistance and know-how and 35 percent for other royalty categories. The advent of the new franchise law resulted in an explosion of franchises in fast food, services, hotels, and retail outlets. In 1992, franchises had an estimated $750 million in sale in over 1,200 outlets throughout Mexico. Prior to passage of Mexico's franchise law, KFC limited its Mexican operations primarily to Mexico City, Guadalajara, and Monterrey. This enabled KFC to better coordinate operations and minimize costs of distribution to individual restaurants. The new franchise law gave KFC and other fast-food chains the opportunity to expand their restaurant bases more quickly into more rural regions of Mexico, where responsibility for management could be handled by local franchisees.

52   After 1990, KFC altered its Latin American strategy in a number of ways. First, it opened 29 franchises in Mexico to complement its company-owned restaurant base. It then expanded its company-owned restaurants into the Virgin Islands and reestablished a subsidiary in Venezuela. Third, it expanded its franchise operations into South America. In 1990, a franchise was opened in Chile and in 1993, a franchise was opened in Brazil. Franchises were subsequently established in Colombia, Ecuador, Panama, and Peru, among other South American countries. A fourth subsidiary was established in Brazil, in order to develop company-owned restaurants. Brazil was Latin America's largest economy and McDonald's primary Latin American investment location. By June 1998, KFC operated 438 restaurants in 32 Latin American countries. By comparison, McDonald's operated 1,091 restaurants in 28 countries in Latin America.

53   Table 7 shows the Latin American operations of KFC and McDonald's. KFC's early entry into Latin America during the 1970s gave it a leadership position in Mexico and the Caribbean. It had also gained an edge in Ecuador and Peru, countries where McDonald's had not yet developed a strong presence. McDonald's focused its Latin American investment in Brazil, Argentina, and Uruguay, countries where KFC had little or no presence. McDonald's was also strong in Venezuela. Both KFC and McDonald's were strong in Chile, Colombia, Panama, and Puerto Rico.

TABLE 7
Latin America Restaurant Count—KFC and McDonald's

(as of December 31, 1997)

	KFC Company Restaurants	KFC Franchised Restaurants	KFC Total Restaurants	McDonald's
Argentina	—	—	—	131
Bahamas	—	10	10	3
Barbados	—	7	7	—
Brazil	6	2	8	480
Chile	—	29	29	27
Colombia	—	19	19	18
Costa Rica	—	5	5	19
Ecuador	—	18	18	2
Jamaica	—	17	17	7
Mexico	128	29	157	131
Panama	—	21	21	20
Peru	—	17	17	5
Puerto Rico & Virgin Islands	67	—	67	115
Trinidad & Tobago	—	27	27	3
Uruguay	—	—	—	18
Venezuela	6	—	6	53
Other	—	30	30	59
Total	207	231	438	1,091

Source: Tricon Global Restaurants, Inc.; McDonald's, 1997 Annual Report.

Economic Environment and the Mexican Market

54   Mexico was KFC's strongest market in Latin America. While McDonald's had aggressively established restaurants in Mexico since 1990, KFC retained the leading market share. Because of its close proximity to the United States, Mexico was an attractive location for U.S. trade and investment. Mexico's population of 98 million people was approximately one-third as large as the United States and represented a large market for U.S. companies. In comparison, Canada's population of 30.3 million people was only one-third as large as Mexico's. Mexico's close proximity to the United States meant that transportation costs between the United States and Mexico were significantly lower than to Europe or Asia. This increased the competitiveness of U.S. goods in comparison with European and Asian goods, which had to be transported to Mexico across the Atlantic or Pacific Ocean at substantial cost. The United States was, in fact, Mexico's largest trading partner. Over 75 percent of Mexico's imports came from the United States, while 84 percent of its exports were to the U.S.A. (see Table 8). Many U.S. firms invested in Mexico in order to take advantage of lower wage rates. By producing goods in Mexico, U.S. goods could be shipped back into the United States for sale or shipped to third markets at lower cost.

55   While the U.S. market was critically important to Mexico, Mexico still represented a small percentage of overall U.S. trade and investment. Since the early 1900s, the portion of U.S. exports to Latin America had declined. Instead, U.S. exports to Canada and Asia, where economic growth outpaced growth in Mexico, increased more quickly. Canada was the largest importer of U.S. goods. Japan was the largest exporter of goods to the United States, with Canada a close second. U.S. investment in Mexico was also small, mainly because of past government restrictions on foreign investment. Most U.S. foreign investment was in Europe, Canada, and Asia.

TABLE 8
Mexico's Major Trading Partners—% Total Exports and Imports

	1992		1994		1996	
	Exports	Imports	Exports	Imports	Exports	Imports
U.S.A.	81.1	71.3	85.3	71.8	84.0	75.6
Japan	1.7	4.9	1.6	4.8	1.4	4.4
Germany	1.1	4.0	0.6	3.9	0.7	3.5
Canada	2.2	1.7	2.4	2.0	1.2	1.9
Italy	0.3	1.6	0.1	1.3	1.2	1.1
Brazil	0.9	1.8	0.6	1.5	0.9	0.8
Spain	2.7	1.4	1.4	1.7	1.0	0.7
Other	10.0	13.3	8.0	13.0	9.6	12.0
% Total	100.0	100.0	100.0	100.0	100.0	100.0
Value ($M)	46,196	62,129	60,882	79,346	95,991	89,464

Source: International Monetary Fund, *Direction of Trade Statistics Yearbook,* 1997.

56   The lack of U.S. investment in and trade with Mexico during this century was mainly the result of Mexico's long history of restricting trade and foreign direct investment. The Institutional Revolutionary Party (PRI), which came to power in Mexico during the 1930s, had historically pursued protectionist economic policies, in order to shield Mexico's economy from foreign competition. Many industries were government-owned or -controlled and many Mexican companies focused on producing goods for the domestic market without much attention to building export markets. High tariffs and other trade barriers restricted imports into Mexico and foreign ownership of assets in Mexico was largely prohibited or heavily restricted.

57   Additionally, a dictatorial and entrenched government bureaucracy, corrupt labor unions, and a long tradition of anti-Americanism among many government officials and intellectuals reduced the motivation of U.S. firms for investing in Mexico. The nationalization of Mexico's banks in 1982 led to higher real interest rates and lower investor confidence. Afterward, the Mexican government battled high inflation, high interest rates, labor unrest, and lost consumer purchasing power. Investor confidence in Mexico, however, improved after 1988, when Carlos Salinas de Gortari was elected president. Following his election, Salinas embarked on an ambitious restructuring of the Mexican economy. He initiated policies to strengthen the free market components of the economy, lowered top marginal tax rates to 36 percent (down from 60 percent in 1986), and eliminated many restrictions on foreign investment. Foreign firms can now buy up to 100 percent of the equity in many Mexican firms. Foreign ownership of Mexican firms was previously limited to 49 percent.

Privatization

58   The privatization of government-owned companies came to symbolize the restructuring of Mexico's economy. In 1990, legislation was passed to privatize all government-run banks. By the end of 1992, over 800 of some 1,200 government-owned companies had been sold, including Mexicana and AeroMexico, the two largest airline companies in Mexico, and Mexico's 18 major banks. However, more than 350 companies remained under government ownership. These represented a significant portion of the assets owned by the state at the start of 1988. Therefore, the sale of government-owned companies, in terms of asset value, was moderate. A large percentage of the remaining government-owned assets were controlled by government-run companies in certain strategic industries such as steel, electricity, and petroleum. These industries had long been protected by government ownership. As a result, additional privatization of government-owned enterprises until 1993 was limited. However, in 1993, President Salinas opened up the electricity sector to independent power producers and

Petroleos Mexicanos (Pemex), the state-run petrochemical monopoly, initiated a program to sell off many of its nonstrategic assets to private and foreign buyers.

North American Free Trade Agreement (NAFTA)

59   Prior to 1989, Mexico levied high tariffs on most imported goods. In addition, many other goods were subjected to quotas, licensing requirements, and other nontariff trade barriers. In 1986, Mexico joined the General Agreement on Tariffs and Trade (GATT), a world trade organization designed to eliminate barriers to trade among member nations. As a member of GATT, Mexico was obligated to apply its system of tariffs to all member nations equally. As a result of its membership in GATT, Mexico dropped tariff rates on a variety of imported goods. In addition, import license requirements were dropped for all but 300 imported items. During President Salinas' administration, tariffs were reduced from an average of 100 percent on most items to an average of 11 percent.

60   On January 1, 1994, the North American Free Trade Agreement (NAFTA) went into effect. The passage of NAFTA, which included Canada, the United States, and Mexico, created a trading bloc with a larger population and gross domestic product than the European Union. (See Table 9 for economic data on Canada, the United States, and Mexico.) All tariffs on goods traded among the three countries were scheduled to be phased out. NAFTA was expected to be particularly beneficial for Mexican exporters, because reduced tariffs made their goods more competitive in the United States compared to goods exported to the United States from other countries. In 1995, one year after NAFTA went into effect, Mexico posted its first balance of trade surplus in six years. Part of this surplus was attributed to reduced tariffs resulting from the NAFTA agreement. However, the peso crisis of 1995, which lowered the value of the peso against the dollar, increased the price of goods imported into Mexico and lowered the price of Mexican products exported to the United States. Therefore, it was still too early to assess the full effects of the NAFTA agreement.

Foreign Exchange and the Mexican Peso Crisis of 1995

61   Between 1982 and 1991, a two-tiered exchange rate system was in force in Mexico. The system consisted of a controlled rate and a free market rate. A controlled rate was used for imports, foreign debt payments, and conversion of export proceeds. An estimated 70 percent of all foreign transactions were covered by the controlled rate. A free market rate was used for other transactions. In 1989, President Salinas instituted a policy of allowing the peso to depreciate against the dollar by one peso per day. The result was a grossly overvalued peso. This lowered the price of imports and led to an increase in imports of over 23 percent in 1989. At the same time, Mexican exports became less competitive on world markets.

62   In 1992, the controlled rate was abolished and replaced with an official free rate. In order to limit the range of fluctuations in the value of the peso, the government fixed the rate at which it would buy or sell pesos. A floor (the maximum price at which pesos could be purchased) was established at Ps 3,056.20 and remained fixed. A ceiling (the maximum price at which the peso could be sold) was established as Ps 3,056.40 and allowed to move upward by Ps 0.20 per day. This was later revised to Ps 0.40 per day. In 1993, a new currency, called the new peso, was issued with three fewer zeros. The new currency was designed to simplify transactions and to reduce the cost of printing currency.

63   When Ernesto Zedillo became Mexico's president in December 1994, one of his objectives was to continue the stability of prices, wages, and exchange rates achieved by ex-president Carlos Salinas de Gortari during his five-year tenure as president. However, Salinas had achieved stability largely on the basis of price, wage, and foreign exchange controls. While giving the appearance of stability, an overvalued peso continued to encourage imports, which exacerbated Mexico's balance of trade deficit. Mexico's government continued to use foreign reserves to finance its balance of trade deficits. According to the Banco de Mexico, foreign currency reserves fell from $24 billion in January 1994 to $5.5 billion in January 1995. Anticipating a devaluation of the peso, investors began to move capital into U.S. dollar investments. In order to relieve pressure on the peso, Zedillo announced on December 19, 1994, that the peso would be allowed to depreciate by an additional 15 percent per year against the dollar compared to the maximum allowable depreciation of 4 percent per year established during the Salinas administration. Within two days, continued pressure on the peso forced Zedillo to

TABLE 9
Selected Economic Data for Canada, the United States, and Mexico

Annual Change (%)	1993	1994	1995	1996	1997
GDP Growth					
Canada	3.3	4.8	5.5	4.1	—
United States	4.9	5.8	4.8	5.1	5.9
Mexico	21.4	13.3	29.4	38.2	—
Real GDP Growth					
Canada	2.2	4.1	2.3	1.2	—
United States	2.2	3.5	2.0	2.8	3.8
Mexico	2.0	4.5	−6.2	5.1	—
Inflation					
Canada	1.9	0.2	2.2	1.5	1.6
United States	3.0	2.5	2.8	2.9	2.4
Mexico	9.7	6.9	35.0	34.4	20.6
Depreciation Against $U.S.					
Canada (C$)	4.2	6.0	−2.7	0.3	4.3
Mexico (NP)	−0.3	71.4	43.5	2.7	3.6

Source: International Monetary Fund, *International Financial Statistics,* 1998.

allow the peso to float freely against the dollar. By mid-January 1995, the peso had lost 35 percent of its value against the dollar and the Mexican stock market plunged 20 percent. By November 1995, the peso had depreciated from 3.1 pesos per dollar to 7.3 pesos per dollar.

64   The continued devaluation of the peso resulted in higher import prices, higher inflation, destabilization within the stock market, and higher interest rates. Mexico struggled to pay its dollar-based debts. In order to thwart a possible default by Mexico, the U.S. government, International Monetary Fund, and World Bank pledged $24.9 billion in emergency loans. Zedillo then announced an emergency economic package called the "pacto" that included reduced government spending, increased sales of government-run businesses, and a freeze on wage increases.

Labor Problems

65   One of KFC's primary concerns in Mexico was the stability of labor markets. Labor was relatively plentiful and wages were low. However, much of the work force was relatively unskilled. KFC benefited from lower labor costs, but labor unrest, low job retention, high absenteeism, and poor punctuality were significant problems. Absenteeism and punctuality were partially cultural. However, problems with worker retention and labor unrest were also the result of workers' frustration over the loss of their purchasing power due to inflation and government controls on wage increases. Absenteeism remained high at approximately 8 to 14 percent of the labor force, though it was declining because of job security fears. Turnover continued to be a problem and ran at between 5 and 12 percent per month. Therefore, employee screening and internal training were important issues for firms investing in Mexico.

66   Higher inflation and the government's freeze on wage increases led to a dramatic decline in disposable income after 1994. Further, a slowdown in business activity, brought about by higher interest rates and lower government spending, led many businesses to lay off workers. By the end of 1995, an estimated one million jobs had been lost as a result of the economic crisis sparked by the peso devaluation. As a result, industry groups within Mexico called for new labor laws giving them more freedom to hire and fire employees and increased flexibility to hire part-time rather than full-time workers.

RISKS AND OPPORTUNITIES

67   The peso crisis of 1995 and resulting recession in Mexico left KFC managers with a great deal of uncertainty regarding Mexico's economic and political future. KFC had benefited from economic stability between 1988 and 1994. Inflation was brought down, the peso was relatively stable, labor unrest was relatively calm, and Mexico's new franchise law had enabled KFC to expand into rural areas using franchises rather than company-owned restaurants. By the end of 1995, KFC had built 29 franchises in Mexico. The foreign exchange crisis of 1995 had severe implications for U.S. firms operating in Mexico. The devaluation of the peso resulted in higher inflation and capital flight out of Mexico. Capital flight reduced the supply of capital and led to higher interest rates. In order to reduce inflation, Mexico's government instituted an austerity program that resulted in lower disposable income, higher unemployment, and lower demand for products and services.

68   Another problem was Mexico's failure to reduce restrictions on U.S. and Canadian investment in a timely fashion. Many U.S. firms experienced problems getting required approvals for new ventures from the Mexican government. A good example was United Parcel Service (UPS), which sought government approval to use large trucks for deliveries in Mexico. Approvals were delayed, forcing UPS to use smaller trucks. This put UPS at a competitive disadvantage vis-à-via Mexican companies. In many cases, UPS was forced to subcontract delivery work to Mexican companies that were allowed to use larger, more cost-efficient trucks. Other U.S. companies such as Bell Atlantic and TRW faced similar problems. TRW, which signed a joint venture agreement with a Mexican partner, had to wait 15 months longer than anticipated before the Mexican government released rules on how it could receive credit data from banks. TRW claimed that the Mexican government slowed the approval process in order to placate several large Mexican banks.

69   A final area of concern for KFC was increased political turmoil in Mexico during the last several years. On January 1, 1994, the day NAFTA went into effect, rebels (descendants of the Mayans) rioted in the southern Mexican province of Chiapas on the Guatemalan border. After four days of fighting, Mexican troops had driven the rebels out of several towns earlier seized by the rebels. Around 150—mostly rebels—were killed. The uprising symbolized many of the fears of the poor in Mexico. While ex-president Salinas' economic programs had increased economic growth and wealth in Mexico, many of Mexico's poorest felt that they had not benefited. Many of Mexico's farmers, faced with lower tariffs on imported agricultural goods from the United States, felt that they might be driven out of business because of lower priced imports. Therefore, social unrest among Mexico's Indians, farmers, and the poor could potentially unravel much of the economic success achieved in Mexico during the last five years.

70   Further, ex-president Salinas' hand-picked successor for president was assassinated in early 1994 while campaigning in Tijuana. The assassin was a 23-year-old mechanic and migrant worker believed to be affiliated with a dissident group upset with the PRI's economic reforms. The possible existence of a dissident group raised fears of political violence in the future. The PRI quickly named Ernesto Zedillo, a 42-year-old economist with little political experience, as their new presidential candidate. Zedillo was elected president in December 1994. Political unrest was not limited to Mexican officials and companies. In October 1994, between 30 and 40 masked men attacked a McDonald's restaurant in the tourist section of Mexico City to show their opposition to California's Proposition 187, which would have curtailed benefits to illegal aliens (primarily from Mexico). The men threw cash registers to the floor, cracked them open, smashed windows, overturned tables, and spray-painted slogans on the walls such as "No to Fascism" and "Yankee Go Home."

71   KFC faced a variety of issues in Mexico and Latin America in 1998. Prior to 1995, few restaurants had been opened in South America. However, KFC was now aggressively building new restaurants in the region. KFC halted openings of franchised restaurants in Mexico and all restaurants opened since 1995 were company-owned. KFC was more aggressively building restaurants in South America, which remained largely unpenetrated by KFC through 1995. Of greatest importance was Brazil, where McDonald's had already established a strong market share position. Brazil was Latin America's largest economy and a largely untapped market for KFC. The danger in ignoring Mexico was that a conservative investment strategy could jeopardize its market share lead over McDonald's in a large market where KFC long enjoyed enormous popularity.

CASE 45

R. DAVID THOMAS, ENTREPRENEUR: THE WENDY'S STORY[1]

1   Wendy's International grew from one store to over 1,800 company-owned and franchised outlets in ten short years. Between 1974 and 1979, Wendy's growth was explosive with sales, including company-owned and franchised units, growing 4,200 percent ($24 million to $1 billion). Net income increased 2,091 percent in this period from $1.1 million to $23 million. Earnings per share made substantial gains from $.12 in 1974 to $1.54 in 1979, a 1,283 percent rise. Wendy's grew to a position of being the third-largest fast-food hamburger restaurant chain in the United States, ranking behind Burger King and McDonald's, the leading U.S. hamburger chain.

2   Wendy's entry and amazing growth in the hamburger segment of the fast-food industry shocked the industry and forced competitors within it to realize that their market positions are potentially vulnerable. Wendy's flourished in the face of adversities plaguing the industry. Throughout the 1970's, experts said the fast-food industry was rapidly maturing. Analysts for *The Wall Street Journal*, citing a "competitively saturated fast-food hamburger industry," predicted in the early 1970s that the Wendy's venture would not succeed. As they saw it, market saturation, rising commodity prices, fuel costs, and labor costs were already plaguing the fast-food industry.

3   Clearly unconcerned about such commentary, R. David Thomas pushed Wendy's relentlessly. It opened an average of one restaurant every two days during its first ten years becoming the first restaurant chain in history to top $1 billion in sales in its first 10 years.

HISTORY

4   R. David Thomas had an idea. He knew Americans love hamburgers. If he could develop a hamburger better than those currently offered, he believed he could use it to establish a leadership position in the competitive fast-food hamburger market. A high school dropout that found success as an Army cook, R. David Thomas loved to cook fresh hamburgers. But he detoured into chicken after the Army, where one of his early jobs was helping Mr. Harland Sanders selling chicken recipes and utensils to restaurants in the southeast. Not long after teaming with Kentucky's John Y. Brown, Mr. Sanders became "Colonel Sanders" and KFC was born. R. David Thomas returned to Columbus, Ohio where he became a successful KFC franchisee in the 1960s.

5   In November 1969, Thomas, by now an experienced restaurant operator and veteran Kentucky Fried Chicken franchisee, began to put his idea into reality when he opened Wendy's first unit in downtown Columbus, Ohio. A year later, in November 1970, Wendy's opened its second unit in Columbus, this one with a drive-through pickup window. In August 1972, Wendy's sold L. S. Hartzog the franchise for the Indianapolis, Indiana, market, kicking off Wendy's rapid expansion into the chain hamburger business. Later the same year, Wendy's Management Institute was formed to develop management skills in managers, supervisors, area directors, and franchise owners. After five years, company revenues exceeded $13 million with net income in excess of $1 million. Sales for both company-owned and franchised units topped $24 million for the same period. In June 1975, the 100th Wendy's opened in Louisville, Kentucky. Three months later, Wendy's went public. December 1976 saw Wendy's 500th open in Toronto, Canada. In 1977, Wendy's went national with its first network television commercial, making it the first restaurant chain with less than 1,000 units to mount a national advertising campaign. Eleven months later, Wendy's broke yet another record by opening its 1,000th restaurant in Springfield, Tennessee, within 100 months of opening the first Wendy's in

[1]©2000, Richard Robinson, University of South Carolina.

Columbus. In 1979, Wendy's signed franchise agreements for eight European countries and Japan and opened the first European restaurant, company-owned, in Munich, West Germany. Also 1979 saw test marketing of a limited breakfast menu, a children's menu, and salad bars.

R. DAVID THOMAS' VISION OF A PROFITABLE OPPORTUNITY: THE WENDY'S CONCEPT

The Menu

6   Thomas knew from experience that a limited menu could be a key factor contributing to Wendy's success. The idea was to concentrate on doing only a few things, but to do them better than anyone else. As a result, the aim was to provide the customer with a "Cadillac" hamburger that could be custom-made to meet individual preferences.

7   The basic menu item was the quarter-pound hamburger made of only fresh, 100 percent beef hamburger meat converted into patties daily. This kept Wendy's out of head-on competition with McDonald's and Burger King's 1/10th pound hamburger. If people desired a bigger hamburger, they could order a double (two patties on a bun) or a triple (three patties on a bun). Besides having just one basic menu item, the hamburger, Wendy's also decided to differentiate itself by changing their hamburger's design. Instead of the traditional round patty found in competing fast-food outlets, Wendy's patty was square and sized so its edges would stick out over the edge of the round bun. The unique design alleviated the frequent complaint by most people that they were eating a breadburger. It also made more efficient use of refrigeration space, saving store operators money in the process. Other menu decisions included the following:

- To offer different condiments to the customers—cheese, tomato, catsup, onion, lettuce, mustard, mayonnaise, and relish.
- To provide a unique dairy product, the frosty—a cross between chocolate and vanilla flavors that borders between soft ice cream and a thick milk shake.
- To serve a product that was unique in the fast-food market—-chili.
- To sell french fries because the public expected a hamburger outlet to offer them.

    Chili was an unusually clever menu item. First, it was an adult-oriented item not found on other fast food menus. So an adult could have a hamburger one day and return for something different, chili, the next. Second, chili was made over night—a slow cooking process—using the cooked hamburger meat that was not sold during the day and would otherwise been thrown out or sold to hog farmers. Since meat costs were the largest single part of Wendy's [or any chains] cost of goods sold, using otherwise wasted meat in chili to generate additional revenue provided a "double whammy"—it reduced costs and increased revenue. All fast-food restaurants face a sizable problem with wasted food—burgers in heated racks not sold within 10–15 minutes are typically thrown out or sold at a minimal charge to local hog farmers. And since most hamburger chains use pre-cooked, frozen, round hamburger patties, they cannot recycle it into chili like Wendy's, which uses larger patties of fresh meat cooked on site. The bottomline, then is that Wendy's chili created a strategic cost advantage/margin-increasing advantage in addition to adding a unique, adult-oriented product that other competitors could not easily add without disrupting their current operations and concept.

Facilities

8   Under Thomas's direction, the exterior style and interior decor of all Wendy's restaurants conformed to company specifications. The typical outlet was a freestanding one-story brick building constructed on a 25,000-square-foot site that provided parking for 35 to 45 cars (see Exhibit 1). There were some downtown storefront-type restaurants, which generally adhered to the standard red, yellow, and white decor and design. Most of the freestanding restaurants contained 2,100 square feet, had a cooking area, dining room capacity for 92 persons, and a pickup window for drive-in service (see Exhibit 2).

EXHIBIT 1
Wendy's Typical Site 1—Typical Lot Layout for Freestanding Unit

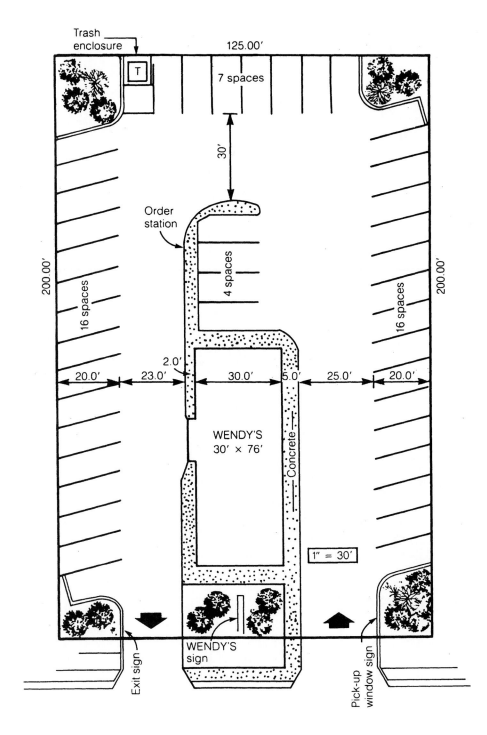

Lot area, 25,000 square feet; building, 2,310 square feet; parking spaces, 43.

EXHIBIT 2
Restaurant Interior Layout

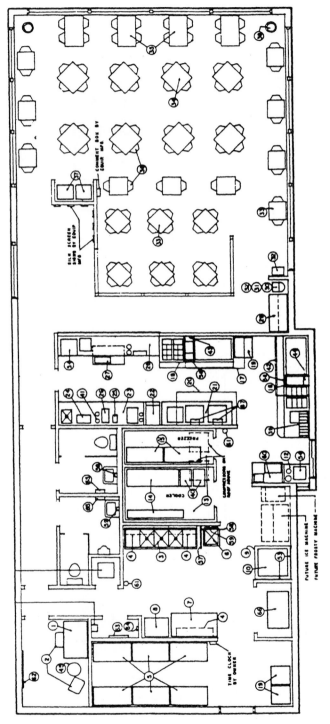

Key:
1. Desk.
2. Chair.
3. Sink unit.
4. Wall shelving.
5. Wall shelving.
6. Sink unit.
7. Work table.
8. Hamburger patty-making machine.
9. Exhaust canopy system.
10. Range top.
11. Open number.
12. Cashier counter assembly.
13. Walk-in cooler/freezer.
14. Wire shelving.
15. Frozen french fry storage platform.
16. Custom cooks counter assembly.
17. Exhaust canopy system.

18. Custom cook.
19. Bun rack.
20. Exhaust canopy system.
21. Custom fry station assembly.
22. Frosty machine.
23. Rear counter assembly.
24. Coffee maker.
25. Tea machine.
26. Hot chocolate machine.
27. Ice and drink machine.
28. Front counter assembly.
29. Condiment station.
30. High chair.
31. Booster chairs.
32. Water fountain.
33. Pedestal tables.
34. Pedestal tables.

35. Pedestal tables.
36. Side chairs.
37. Waste containers.
38. Costumers.
39. Condiment holder.
40. Meat racks.
41. Marshmallow holder.
42. Exhaust canopy system (fire protection).
43. Custom paper holder.
44. Custom paper holder.
45. Floor safe.
46. Litter receptacle.
47. Tiffany-style light fixtures.
48. Carpet.
49. Wall covering.
50. Beads.
51. Installation package.

52. Booster chair hanger.
53. Stainless wall panel.
54. Cash registers.
55. Open number.
56. Bun cabinet.
57. Stainless partition.
58. Towel dispenser.
59. Soap dispenser.
60. Ice and drink machine.
61. Fire extinguishers.
62. Coat hook bar.
63. Broom holder.
64. Hose holder.
65. Hand dryers.
66. Syrup tank rack.
67. French fry computers.

The interior decor featured table tops printed with reproductions of 19th century advertising, Tiffany-styled lamps, bentwood chairs, colorful beads, and carpeting.

9   Generally, the strategy was to build a functionally modern building that would reflect the old-fashioned theme. Another plus for their building design was its flexibility. With only minor changes, they could sell almost any type of food in the building. It would also be possible to change from the Gay 90s theme to any other theme in just a matter of days. But the setting was to be a bit upscale and adult-oriented among fast food outlets.

10   The most unique feature in their building design was the addition of the pickup window, and Wendy's was the first major restaurant chain to successfully implement the use of one. Here, Wendy's was able to gain an advantage because their units could be smaller and at the same time handle the larger amount of business volume generated by using the pickup window. The logic for implementing the use of the pickup window was that people in their cars don't fill up tables or take up a parking space. The result showed that on a square-foot basis, Wendy's units did more business than any other chain.

11   The building design also contributed to what Michael J. Esposito, an investments analyst for Oppenheimer & Company, has called the most impressive part of the company's operation: the delivery system. In a report recommending Wendy's as an investment, Esposito wrote:

> In our judgment, the transaction time (time elapsed from when order is placed to its delivery to the customer) is the lowest in the industry, generally averaging about one minute. Utilizing a grill system where a constant flow of hamburgers is cooked at a relatively low temperature, a worker takes the hamburger off the grill, places it on a bun, adds the condiments ordered by the customer, assembles and wraps the sandwich. Another crew member supplies chili, french fries, beverage, and a frosty dessert, and another reviews the order and releases it to the customer.

The Marketing Strategy

12   In their book, *The Chain-Restaurant Industry*, Earl Sasser and Daryl Wycoff stated:

> The Wendy's strategy was described by one analyst as "selling better hamburgers than McDonald's or Burger King at a cheaper price per ounce." As he commented, it takes no more labor to prepare a large hamburger at a higher price.

13   To support the higher-priced hamburger, Wendy's marketing strategy has been to stress the freshness and quality of their product. The objective of this strategy is to target Wendy's for the world's fastest-growing market segment. By offering a freshly ground, made-to-order hamburger as well as stylish, comfortable decor, Wendy's was aiming squarely at a key segment of the population: young adults with a taste for better food. With the post-World War II babies reaching their 20s and 30s, those young adults have been expanding faster than any other age group. As a result, it is thought that Wendy's success is coming not so much at the expense of the other burger chains but from having selected a special niche in the otherwise crowded market. Most agree that Wendy's basically expanded the market, and statistics from customer surveys bear out the claim. Fully 82 percent of all Wendy's business comes from customers over 25, an unusually old market for any fast-food chain. By contrast, McDonald's generated 35 percent of its revenues from youngsters under 19.

14   Wendy's advertising efforts have emphasized nationwide television advertising to attract this young adult market. Since 1974, Wendy's "Hot 'n' Juicy" advertising theme has been central to this effort. In the late 1970s, with its position established, Wendy's national advertising started focusing on new market segments like dinner after 4 p.m. after family meals on weekends. For some, this theme has sparked considerable attention, particularly a negative reaction to the word "ain't" and the phrase's double negative.[1] Wendy's early "Where's the beef" campaign became an advertising classic which forever distinguished Wendy's from the "bread burger." Since the 1980s, R. David Thomas [Dave] has increasingly been a key, cost-effective figure in Wendy's advertising.

---

[1]An article in *The Wall Street Journal* (July 8, 1980, p. 29) offered another explanation: "Wendy's ads showed diners biting into its hot and juicy hamburgers and then mopping juice from their chins. But some people thought the image projected by the ad was hot and greasy. Many franchises quit advertising, in effect voting no confidence in the company's marketing plan."

Franchising

15   In 1972, Wendy's management made the decision to become a national chain as quickly as possible, which meant growing through franchising. The franchises were awarded on an area basis, rather than single-store franchises. While McDonald's awarded franchises on a site-by-site basis, Wendy's sold whole states or large areas as franchise territories. As a result, Wendy's 10 largest franchise owners operated a total of 406 restaurants by 1979. The franchise agreements were among the most straight-forward in the restaurant industry and are deliberately designed to establish a fair business relationship. They specify the number of units to be opened within a certain time frame, the area to be developed, a technical assistance fee, and a royalty of 4 percent of gross sales. They also stipulate that 4 percent of gross sales be spent for local and national advertising. Wendy's operated no commissaries and sold no food, fixtures, or supplies to franchise owners.

16   To support their growing network of franchised restaurants, Wendy's franchise operations department maintained a staff of 50 franchise area supervisors who are the company's operations advisers to the franchise owners. They are charged with ensuring that Wendy's quality standards are met throughout the entire franchise network.

17   Wendy's also provided the following services to their franchisees:

- Site approval procedures for locations.
- On-site inspection and evaluation by staff representative.
- Counseling in business planning.
- Drawings and specifications for buildings.
- Training for franchisees at Wendy's headquarters.
- Advice on supplies from suppliers selected by Wendy's and assistance in establishing quality-control standards and procedures for supplies.
- Staff representatives to help in the opening of each restaurant.
- Assistance in planning opening promotion and continuing advertising, public relations, and promotion.
- Operations manual with information necessary to operate a Wendy's restaurant.
- Research and development in production and methods of operations.
- Information on policies, developments, and activities by means of bulletins, brochures, reports, and visits of Wendy's representatives.
- Paper-goods standards.
- National and regional meetings.

18   The criteria used by Wendy's for franchise selection is basically simple but strictly adhered to. They look for good proven business ability. The applicant must demonstrate that he or she is interested in making profits and does not mind getting involved. Wendy's did not make their profits by selling goods and services to their franchisees. Their income came from the restaurants' sales volume. Therefore, the franchisee must be able to build sales. While well known national franchises (e.g. Mc-Donalds, Holiday Inns) discouraged or prohibited franchises owning competing brands (e.g. if Mc-Donalds, then no KFC; if Holiday Inns, then no Days Inn), R. David Thomas rejected these industry norms. He reasoned, to create rapid growth via franchising, that he should choose the most experienced restaurant chain builders that he could. He wanted them to have good local supplier contacts, a strong financial capability, ideally to have access to good restaurant operating people, and to understand how franchising worked—the role of franchisor and franchisee, the importance of national advertising, the dependence of each franchise location on another to build and maintain a quality image. Thomas' answer: seek Wendy's franchises among proven, successful builders of other food franchises (e.g. KFC franchises). As his new "entrepreneurial team" in any given territory, they brought restaurant expertise, local area expertise and a capacity to understand the many strengths of Thomas' Wendy's concept if it was developed quickly.

19   Wendy's operates company-owned restaurants in 26 markets around the following cities:

Columbus, Ohio	33	Indianapolis, Indiana	15
Cincinnati, Ohio	20	Dallas/Ft. Worth, Texas	26
Dayton, Ohio	26	Houston, Texas	25
Toledo, Ohio	12	Oklahoma City, Oklahoma	12
Atlanta, Georgia	35	Tulsa, Oklahoma	12
Tampa, Sarasota	22	Memphis, Tennessee	13
St. Petersburg	15	Louisville, Kentucky	14
Clearwater, Florida	4	Syracuse, New York	10
Jacksonville, Florida	20	Harrisburg, Pennsylvania	22
Daytona Beach, Florida	10	Philadelphia, Pennsylvania	20
Detroit, Michigan	6	Virginia Beach, Virginia	15
Portland, Oregon	10	Charleston, West Virginia	14
Reno, Nevada	6	Parkersburg, West Virginia	20
Greensboro, North Carolina	10	Munich, West Germany	2

Other than Detroit, no franchises exist in these markets.

20   At the end of 1979, there were 1,385 franchised restaurants operated by 161 franchise owners in 47 states and 3 foreign countries.

21   In a report to the Securities and Exchange Commission, Wendy's discussed the current state of its franchise program and described the franchise owners' relationship with the company:

> Although franchised areas exist in all states except three, areas of some states remain unfranchised. In addition, most franchise owners have the right to build more units in their franchised areas than had been constructed at December 31, 1979. At that date, no franchise owner had more than 88 stores in operation. Several franchise owners operate restaurants in more than one state.
>
> The rights and franchise offered by the company are contained in two basic documents. A franchise owner first executes a development agreement. This document gives the franchise owner the exclusive right to select proposed sites on which to construct Wendy's Old Fashioned Hamburgers restaurants within a certain geographic area (the franchised area), requires the submission of sites to the company for its acceptance, and, upon acceptance of a proposed site by the company, provides for the execution of a unit franchise agreement with the company to enable the franchise owner to construct, own, and operate a Wendy's Old Fashioned Hamburgers restaurant upon the site. The development agreement provides for the construction and opening of a fixed number of restaurants within the franchised area in accordance with a development or performance schedule. Both the number of restaurants and the development and performance schedules are agreed upon by the franchise owner and the company prior to the execution of the development agreement. The development agreement also grants a right of first refusal to the franchise owner with respect to the construction of any additional restaurants in the franchised area beyond the initially agreed-to number.
>
> The development agreement requires that the franchise owner pay the company a technical assistance fee. The technical assistance fee required by newly executed development agreement is currently $15,000 for each franchise restaurant which the franchise owner has agreed to construct. Under earlier forms of the development agreement or franchise agreements, this fee was either $5,000, $7,500, or $10,000. However, approximately 12 existing franchise owners have the right under certain circumstances to receive additional franchise areas on the basis of the earlier $10,000 fee.
>
> The technical assistance fee is used to defray the cost to the company of providing to its franchise owners site selection assistance; standard construction plans, specifications, and layouts; company review of specific restaurant site plans; initial training in the company's restaurant systems; and such bulletins, brochures, and reports as are from time to time published regarding the company's plans, policies, research, and other business activities.

22   From time to time, during its early years, Wendy's reacquired selective franchised operations. In 1979, the company adopted a rather aggressive approach to franchise acquisition. Of 145 new company-owned operations in 1979 (representing a 50 percent increase during the year), 84 were acquired from franchisees. This major shift to company-owned restaurant growth away from franchised growth reflects the concern for systemwide control of quality as well as the increasing competition

for available locations. Granting large territorial franchises rather than single-outlet franchises was similarly practiced by Burger King in its formative stages. At Burger King, this led to franchise empires that were bigger than parent-company operations. Wendy's emphasis on company-owned growth was intended to avoid the problem that led to Burger King's decline in the late 1960s. At the same time, selling area franchises rather than single sites accelerated Wendy's growth and its ability to attract large, financially strong franchises with proven success in other restaurant concepts.

Finances

23 Wendy's revenues (see Exhibit 3) increased steadily between 1975 and 1980. Net income dropped in 1979 compared to 1978, but Thomas explained:

> During 1979, we were informed by the U.S. Department of Labor that a review of company labor for a three-year period indicated that certain company policies had not been uniformly adhered to, and, as a result, the company was not in full compliance with the Fair Labor Standards Act.
>
> Based on this review and the company's own investigation, we have determined that $3,800,000 should be accrued and charged against 1979 pretax income. Had this charge not been made, 1979 net income would have been $25,096,000, an increase of 8 percent over the $23,215,000 originally reported a year earlier. We believe company labor practices now comply with both company policy and the act, and, in addition, future compliance will not materially affect net income in 1980 and ensuing years.

24 Whether the cost of labor compliance was the only cause of the abrupt slowdown in Wendy's steady increase in revenue and profit is questionable. Several factors suggest that Wendy's, after a decade of rapid growth, was reaching the limits of its current capabilities.

25 The heart of Wendy's success has been its streamlined, limited menu with primary emphasis on a quality hamburger. Since 1977, beef prices have soared, as shown in Exhibit 4. And while Wendy's has responded with tighter controls and a series of price increases just under 15 percent for 1979 alone (see Exhibit 5), this has still contributed to a decline in profitability.

26 Further evidence suggests that Wendy's may have been reaching a plateau in its historical pattern of growth. The average sales per restaurant, which climbed steadily from $230,000 in 1970 to $688,800 in 1978, declined significantly in 1979 at both company-owned and franchised restaurants, as shown in Exhibit 6. The impact on the parent company was felt in every revenue category, as shown in Exhibit 7. Wendy's continued to experience increased retail revenue (company-owned stores) and royalties (from franchises based on a percent of sales) but at a drastically slower rate. And for the first time, Wendy's experienced a decrease in technical assistance (franchise) fees.

27 Other evidence of a slowdown in Wendy's growth can be seen in the rate of new store openings. For the first time in its history, Wendy's experienced a decline in the rate of new store openings, as shown in Exhibit 8.

28 While revenue and profitability growth slowed in 1979, Thomas was confident this was only temporary. Feeling strongly that Wendy's was in a good position to finance continued growth, Thomas offered the following observation:

> While construction money is more difficult to obtain than in the last few years, lines of credit already arranged guarantee financing of 1980 company plans to open 60 or more restaurants. We also anticipate exploring avenues of long-term debt to finance our growth beyond 1980. We believe that with $25 million of long-term debt, exclusive of capitalized lease obligations, and over $100 million in shareholders' equity, we have substantial untapped borrowing power.

Exhibit 9 summarizes Wendy's balance sheet for 1978 and 1979.

WENDY'S FUTURE

29 Addressing Wendy's stockholders in early 1980, R. David Thomas offered the following thoughts about Wendy's first 10 years:

> We are proud to be marking the 10th anniversary of Wendy's International, Inc. Just 10 years ago, in November 1969, we opened the first Wendy's Old Fashioned Hamburgers restaurant in downtown Columbus, Ohio.

EXHIBIT 3

WENDY'S INTERNATIONAL, INCORPORATED
Consolidated Statement of Income
For the Years Ended December 31, 1975–1979

	1979	1978	1977	1976	1975
Revenue:					
Retail operations	$237,753,097	$198,529,130	$130,667,377	$ 71,336,626	$ 35,340,665
Royalties	30,564,613	23,396,211	11,810,277	4,655,432	1,567,008
Technical assistance fees	2,822,500	3,540,000	2,510,000	1,560,000	622,500
Other, principally interest	2,903,261	2,685,909	1,802,691	965,521	246,901
Total revenues	274,043,471	228,151,250	146,790,345	78,517,579	37,777,074
Costs and expenses:					
Cost of sales	146,346,806	113,812,874	72,482,010	40,509,285	19,629,179
Company restaurant operating costs	51,193,050	43,289,285	28,088,460	14,348,150	7,292,391
Department of Labor compliance review	3,800,000				
Salaries, travel, and associated expenses of franchise personnel	4,187,399	3,148,532	1,936,877	1,156,493	622,879
General and administrative expenses	15,741,592	13,292,845	8,191,394	4,137,226	2,581,166
Depreciation and amortization of property and equipment	7,355,818	5,444,092	3,767,259	2,240,215	799,876
Interest	4,357,973	3,771,878	3,215,432	2,583,876	995,410
Total expenses	232,982,638	182,759,506	117,681,432	64,975,245	31,920,901
Income before income taxes	41,060,833	45,391,744	29,108,913	13,542,334	5,856,173
Income taxes:					
Federal:					
Current	15,583,700	18,324,600	12,052,200	5,784,600	2,926,700
Deferred	1,303,200	1,020,800	323,700	(19,600)	(501,900)
	16,886,900	19,345,400	12,375,900	5,765,000	2,424,800
State and local taxes	1,077,500	1,559,700	1,296,200	694,400	298,800
Total income taxes	17,964,400	20,905,100	13,672,100	6,459,400	2,723,600
Net income	$ 23,096,433	$ 24,486,644	$ 15,436,813	$ 7,082,934	$ 3,132,373
Net income per share	$1.54	$1.63	$1.04	$.57	$.29
Weighted average number of common shares outstanding	14,970,526	15,017,708	14,855,503	12,525,294	10,645,694
Dividends per common share	$0.40	$0.14	$0.125	$0.004	$0.001

Source: Wendy's International, Form 10-K, 1979.

Now, after a decade of explosive growth, there are 1,818 Wendy restaurants in 49 states and in Canada, Puerto Rico, Germany, Switzerland and agreements for development of Japan, France, Belgium, Luxembourg, the Netherlands, Switzerland, Spain, Germany, and the United Kingdom. In 1979, our industry was faced with major challenges, such as inflation and energy problems. Higher labor costs and rising beef prices affected Wendy's profitability and depressed profits for our entire industry. The minimum wage, which affects 90 percent of our employees, increased in January 1979 and January 1980. Ground beef prices increased to an average of $1.29 per pound in 1979, 79 percent higher than the 1977 average price. During 1979, we minimized our retail price increases, with the goal of increasing our market share. This strategy, coupled with more aggressive marketing, helped rebuild customer traffic in the latter part of the year. Although holding back on price increases affected our margins, we believe it was appropriate and that margins benefited by our cost efficiencies, especially in purchasing and distribution.

EXHIBIT 4
Yearly Average Meat Price Per Pound for Company-Owned Stores

1969	$0.59	1975	$0.69
1970	0.62	1976	0.72
1971	0.64	1977	0.72
1972	0.67	1978	1.02
1973	0.90	1979	1.29
1974	0.74		

> During 1979, we remained flexible and open to changing customer needs and attitudes, and we continued to take the steps necessary to achieve and support future growth and profitability as we—

- Tested and implemented a highly successful salad bar concept.
- Tested a breakfast concept and other menu items.
- Began development of the European and Japanese markets.
- Initiated a new marketing program designed to increase dinner and weekend business.
- Prepared to open another 250 to 300 Wendy's restaurants systemwide annually.

30   And, setting the tone for Wendy's in the 1980s, Thomas said:

> We are aware, as we enter our second decade, that we have achieved a unique position in a highly competitive industry. It was no less difficult and competitive 10 years ago than it is today, we believe, than it will be 10 years from now. We intend to build further on our achievement of being recognized as a chain of high-quality, quick-service restaurants. We will continue to produce fresh, appealing, high-quality food; price it competitively; and serve it in a clean, attractive setting with employees who are carefully selected, well trained, and responsive to our customers.

31   Similar to the way they questioned R. David Thomas's venture into the hamburger jungle several business writers once again began to question Wendy's future. Illustrative of this is the following article, which appeared in *The Wall Street Journal*:

> Wendy's International, Inc., is making changes it once considered unthinkable.
> Wendy's faced the choice confronting many companies when the initial burst of entrepreneurial brilliance dims: Should it stick with the original concept and be content with a niche in a bigger market, or should it change and attempt to keep growing? Wendy's chose to revamp its operations. It is adding salad bars, chicken and fish sandwiches, and a children's meal to its menu, adopting a new advertising strategy, and considering whether to alter the appearance of its restaurants.
> Some observers predict Wendy's will regret the quick changes. "This is a company that was able to convince a certain segment of the country it had a different taste in hamburgers," says Carl De Biase, an analyst with Sanford C. Bernstein & Co. in New York. "They've achieved their mandate, and anything they do now is just going to screw up the concept."
> But Robert Barney, Wendy's president and chief executive officer, says the company is "in some very difficult times right now." Among the problems: discontented franchise holders and the likelihood that beef prices will rise sharply again in the second half. Barney says Wendy's doesn't even "have the luxury of waiting to see" how each change works before moving to the next one.
> This spring, shortly after the changes began, Thomas resigned as chief executive, saying he wanted more time for public relations work and community affairs. Thomas, who is 47 years old and will continue as chairman, had been closely identified with the old ad campaign and with company resistance to broadening the menu.
> The company has been doing a little better so far this year, and franchisees say they're much more optimistic. The menu changes, they say, were long overdue. "It had been suggested to everyone in the company," says Raymond Schoenbaum, who operates 33 Wendy's outlets in Alabama and Georgia. "But the mentality wouldn't allow menu diversification before. It had to be forced on them."
> Barney concedes that prior to last year "we never did a lot of planning." But that has been remedied, he says, partly with a "research and development department" that will examine new menu prospects.

EXHIBIT 5
Percentage Price Increases for Hamburgers

1/1/77	0.6%	10/22/78	0.15%
3/1/77	0.3	10/29/78	0.10
12/10/77	6.0	12/17/78	3.40
3/19/78	3.0	1/14/79	3.06
4/16/78	2.5	2/25/79	3.60
5/21/78	1.8	4/8/79	0.10
7/23/78	1.2	4/15/79	0.03
10/1/78	1.7	12/16/79	4.45

Not everyone believes that tinkering with the menu will bring back customers and profits. Edward H. Schmitt, president of McDonald's, predicts an image problem for Wendy's and maintains that the company will lose the labor advantage it held over other fast-food outlets. He adds that McDonald's tried and abandoned salad bars. "It's practically a no-profit item," he says, "and it's a high-waste item."

Some franchisees complain that the new children's meal, called Fun Feast, will draw the company into a can't-win competition with McDonald's and Burger King for the children's market, which Wendy's has avoided so far. "Every survey we have says we shouldn't go after that market," a franchisee reports. "Our chairs aren't designed for kids to climb on, and our carpet isn't designed for kids to spill ketchup on."

But Barney insists that Fun Feast isn't intended to attract children. He says Wendy's is trying to remove the adults' reason for not coming to the restaurant. "Where we tested it," he says, "we didn't sell so many of them but we did see an increase in adult traffic."

Wendy's may evolve from a sandwich shop into a more generalized quick-service restaurant that doesn't compete as directly with McDonald's and Burger King. "We're going to be between" McDonald's and quick-service steakhouses, says Schoenbaum, the Georgia and Alabama franchise holder.

To this end, Schoenbaum says, Wendy's will reduce the abundance of plastic fixtures in its restaurants and perhaps cut down on the amount of glass. He says the glass makes Wendy's a pleasant, brightly lit lunch spot but doesn't create a good atmosphere for dinner.

Wendy's officials confirm that they are considering altering the appearance of their restaurants, but they aren't specific. And as for whom Wendy's competes with, Barney says: "We're in competition with anywhere food is served, including the home."[2]

SEARCHING FOR A NEW IDENTITY: 1980–1990

32 Focusing on a long-term growth strategy of continued U.S. penetration, international growth, and concentric diversification into the chicken segment, Wendy's management team reached 4,000 Wendy's restaurants by 1990. Several things have happened, including numerous changes at Wendy's, since 1979. This section provides 29 observations to help you see what happened at Wendy's between 1979 and 1989.

Product/Market Developments

33 The R&D department has helped develop quality products that will help Wendy's growing in the future. The department develops new products within these guidelines:

Any product additions must reinforce their quality image.

They must be profitable.

They must expand a market base.

[2]"Its Vigor Lost, Wendy's Seeks a New Niche," *The Wall Street Journal*, July 8, 1980, p. 29.

EXHIBIT 6
Average Sales per Restaurant

	1979		1978	
	Amount	Percent Change*	Amount	Percent Change*
Company	$624,000	(2.9)%	$624,900	14.3%
Franchise	618,800	(12.4)	706,000	11.7
Systemwide	620,000	(10.0)	688,800	13.0

* Percent increase (or decrease) over the same figure for the previous year.

They must increase frequency of visits.

They must merge easily into their system of operations.

They must help reduce vulnerability to beef price.

34   Wendy's developed and introduced in the 1980s the following products:

The "Garden Spot" Salad Bar and Baked Potatoes for weight-conscious people.

The Chicken Breast Sandwich to respond to high beef price and to provide variety.

The Wendy's Kids' Fun Pack for families with children.

Breakfast to attack McDonald's lack of variety.

35   The core of the strategic role of R&D is to increase sales up to $1 million a year per restaurant. In 1989, the average net sales per domestic restaurant was $789,000, representing a 28 percent increase in 10 years.

Financial

36   Wendy's revenues result primarily from sales by company-operated restaurants. Royalties and technical-assistance fees from franchisees make up the other major source of revenues. In 1989, 91 percent of the $1.07 billion revenues came from retail sales, 7 percent from royalties, and 2 percent from others.

37   With the exception of the buns sold by New Bakery Company of Ohio, Inc., Wendy's does not sell food or supplies to the franchise owners. The New Bakery Company of Ohio, Inc., was acquired by Wendy's in 1981 and now supplies about 1,000 restaurants with buns.

38   Revenues went up to reach a peak in 1986 with $1.15 billion, then decreased to $1.06 billion in 1987 and 1988, and gained 1 percent in 1989 to reach $1.07 billion. After 1979, net income increased steadily until 1985, when it reached $76 million. Wendy's suffered from a loss of $4.6 million the next year, but its profits became positive and increasing again the following years. In 1989, net income was $30.4 million. The dip in net income of 1986 is reflected in the lower pretax profit margin, which dropped from 11.9 percent to 1.3 percent in one year.

39   Out of the capital expenditures in the beginning of the 80s, about 50 percent were for new domestic restaurants, 25 percent for the new subsidiary Sisters and international restaurants, and 25 percent for costs associated with the image-enhancement program, restaurant refurbishing, and computerized registers. After reaching a peak in 1985, with $222 million capital expenditures, Wendy's decreased gradually its investments to $39 million in 1989. In this last year, Wendy's spent $24 million for improvements to existing restaurants and $15 million to others' additions.

40   Exhibit 10 contains additional financial information summarizing Wendy's 1980–1990 results.

Operations

41   Wendy's marketing strategy has been to target the high-quality end of the quick-service market with primary appeal among young middle-age adults, and its philosophy of quality, service, cleanliness, and value was aimed at this key segment of the population.

EXHIBIT 7
Changes in Revenue from 1978 to 1979

	1979		1978	
	Amount*	Percent†	Amount	Percent
Retail operations	$39,224,000	19.8%	$67,862,000	51.9
Royalties	7,168,000	30.6	11,586,000	98.1
Technical assistance fees	(718,000)	(20.3)	1,030,000	41.0
Other, principally interest	(217,000)	(8.1)	883,000	49.0

* Absolute dollar increase (or decrease) over the previous year.
† Percent increase (or decrease) over the previous year.

42   The population of the baby boomers matures. The age range of this segment will be from 35 to 54 years old from 1980 to 1995. Also, currently 50 percent of Wendy's orders are eaten away from the restaurant. Therefore, the maturing population and the increasing demand for convenience and portability will shape Wendy's products in the future.

43   Wendy's is moving its exterior image further away from the brightly colored, plastic fast-food atmosphere with a new, upgraded image, which features copper-colored roof panels and decorative awnings and lightings. The company spent $18 million on remodeling restaurants in 1989.

44   Advertising spending has been increased. Franchise owners, in addition to spending 3 percent of their gross receipts for local advertising and promotions, have increased their contribution to Wendy's National Advertising Program (WNAP) from 1 percent in 1980 to 1.5 percent in 1985, and to 2 percent in 1989. This same year, WNAP spent $55 million on advertising and promotion expenses, a 4 percent increase over 1988 spending levels.

45   Advertising in the fast-food burger chain industry has become more fierce since Burger King launched its now-famous comparative advertising campaign.

46   In the second half of 1985 and into 1986, the company's efforts and advertising were focused on implementing the breakfast program systemwide. During that period, Wendy's major competitors also began to more aggressively advertise their hamburger products. Wendy's began to see some sales erosion in its products and dayparts. As a result, the challenges Wendy's faced were intensified.

47   Management took decisive action in response to these issues. The breakfast program was made optional for franchise owners and retained by the company only where economically viable. Also, the company launched a realignment program in mid-1986, intended to substantially improve its operating and financial performance. The major portion of the plan involved the disposition of all marginal or unprofitable company-operated restaurants, including international restaurants and Sisters as well as domestic restaurants. The company intends to franchise the majority of the domestic restaurants, and the remaining restaurants have been closed.

Franchising

48   Two main thrusts appear to characterize Wendy's franchising emphasis for the 1980s: (1) enhanced operational control and support of domestice franchises and (2) expansion through international locations.

49   The systemwide number of restaurants reached 3,755 in 1989. But as a result of the realignment program, the number of company-owned restaurants kept decreasing from 1986 to 1989, while the number of franchises increased during the same period. However, Wendy's continues to buy franchises from time to time.

50   To stimulate growth, the company announced a unit franchise strategy in the early 1980s. This concept enabled individuals who could not develop a multiunit franchise to join the Wendy's family. To avoid the problem that led Burger King to a decline in the 1960s, Wendy's spends an increasing time in assessing and selecting the franchised locations and managers and also provides the personnel an increasing amount of training. This reflects the concern for systemwide control of quality.

EXHIBIT 8
New Restaurant Openings: 1979 versus 1978

	Company*		Franchise		Systemwide	
	1979	1978	1979	1978	1979	1978
Open at beginning of year	348	271	1,059	634	1,407	905
Opened during the year	71	77	340	425	411	502
Purchased from franchise owners	14	—	(14)	—	—	—
Total open at end of year	433	348	1,385	1,059	1,818	1,407
Average open during year	381	309	1,235	828	1,616	1,137

*Restaurants acquired from franchise owners in poolings of interest have been included since date of opening.

International

51   Wendy's established an international division in 1979, and, by 1989, there were 265 restaurants in foreign countries—87 of them were company-owned. The top 5 international markets and number of restaurants were Canada (131 restaurants), Japan (26), Spain (17), Korea (14), and the Philippines (13).

52   Of the fast-food industry, McDonald's is the best established internationally, with approximately 1,500 units in 32 countries (data of 1983). They are heavily concentrated in Canada, Japan, Australia, and various parts of Europe. It is expecting to develop this international market at a rate of 150 additional units a year. Burger King had in 1983 about 300 units abroad.

53   There are numerous pitfalls and high risks to overseas expansion since, for instance, European per capita spending on "fast-food" is only $3.50 a year, compared to approximately $150 for each American in 1982. Also capital investment—land and buildings—and labor consume a large part of revenues in some countries, such as West Germany. As a matter of fact, after having opened about 30 restaurants in West Germany, Wendy's decided to terminate those operations in 1987.

54   Wendy's strategy in international market is to be flexible in order to be successful in the face of differing eating habits and tastes. It consistently opens new international restaurants but it does not hesitate to terminate any unprofitable operations.

Sisters' Development

55   Thinking that the fast-food burger industry might be over-saturated, Wendy's decided to apply the principles that built its success to other segments of the industry, particularly the one of chicken restaurant industry.

56   Wendy's initially owned 20 percent of Sisters International and, in 1981, exercised its option to purchase then remaining 80 percent. The Sisters' concept, to combine the self-service of the quick-food industry with the full menu and warmth of comfortable dining facilities of the traditional family restaurant, is designed to appeal specifically to the maturing, value-conscious consumer.

57   There were 79 Sisters open at the end of 1985. The company operated 38 of these. However, in 1987, as a result of the realignment program Wendy's sold its subsidiary to SIS CORP, Sisters' largest franchisee for $14.5 million in cash and notes.

Management Reorganization

58   For the first 10 years of its history, Wendy's was guided by an entrepreneurial spirit that gave the company the fastest growth record in the history of this industry. However, with the pressure of soaring beef prices, inflation, and recession, founder and former chairman R. David Thomas, who presently serves as senior chairman of the board, took the first step in 1980, when he recommended to the board that president Robert L. Barney be named chief executive officer. Barney implemented the remainder of the management reorganization program.

EXHIBIT 9

WENDY'S INTERNATIONAL INCORPORATED
Consolidated Balance Sheets
For the Years Ended December 31, 1978, and 1979

	1979	1978
Assets		
Current assets:		
Cash	$ 2,285,180	$ 1,021,957
Short-term investments, at cost, which approximates market, including accrued interest	12,656,352	27,664,531
Accounts receivable	4,902,746	3,248,789
Inventories and other	2,581,528	1,855,313
Total current assets	22,425,806	33,790,590
Property and equipment, at cost Schedule 5:		
Land	30,916,049	23,906,365
Buildings	40,784,581	30,049,552
Leasehold improvements	16,581,947	8,954,392
Restaurant equipment	34,052,952	24,461,860
Other equipment	9,722,666	8,413,363
Construction in progress	1,751,788	2,027,570
Capitalized leases	21,865,829	18,246,427
Total property and equipment before depreciation	155,675,812	116,059,529
Less: Accumulated depreciation and amortization	(20,961,702)	(13,543,473)
Total property and equipment	134,714,110	102,516,056
Cost in excess of net assets acquired, less amortization of $699,410 and $481,162, respectively	8,408,788	5,207,942
Other assets	7,152,131	2,377,648
Total cost over net assets and other assets	15,560,919	7,585,590
Total assets	$172,700,835	$143,892,236
Liabilities and Shareholders' Equity		
Current liabilities:		
Accounts payable, trade	$ 10,174,980	$ 11,666,272
Federal, state, and local income taxes		7,839,586
Accrued expenses:		
Administrative fee		664,770
Salaries and wages	2,368,244	1,970,977
Interest	433,540	369,603
Taxes	1,932,192	1,498,521
Department of Labor compliance review	3,800,000	
Other	1,576,851	739,588
Current portion, term debt, and capitalized lease obligations	3,891,247	2,781,671
Total current liabilities	24,177,054	27,530,988
Term debt, net of current portion	25,097,688	15,308,276
Capital lease obligations, net of current portion	18,707,838	15,130,617
	43,805,526	30,438,893
Deferred technical assistance fees	1,995,000	2,117,500
Deferred federal income taxes	2,027,604	664,300
Shareholders' equity:		
Common stock, $.10 stated value; authorized: 40,000,000 shares; issued and outstanding: 14,882,614 and 14,861,877 shares, respectively	1,488,261	1,486,188
Capital in excess of stated value	34,113,173	33,962,916
Retained earnings	65,094,217	47,691,451
Total shareholders' equity	100,695,651	83,140,555
Total liabilities and shareholders' equity	$172,700,835	$143,892,236

Source: Wendy's International, Form 10-K, 1979.

EXHIBIT 10
Selected Financial Data

WENDY'S INTERNATIONAL, INC. & SUBSIDIARIES

	1990	1989	1988	1987	1986	1985	1984	1983	1982	1981	1980
Operations (in millions)											
Systemwide Wendy's sales	$3,070.3	3,036.1	2,901.6	2,868.9	2,747.2	2,694.8	2,423.0	1,922.9	1,632.4	1,424.2	1,209.3
Retail sales	$ 922.2	973.1	976.6	987.2	1,039.3	1,033.0	877.3	671.6	565.4	450.9	310.1
Revenues	$1,010.9	1,069.7	1,062.6	1,059.8	1,149.7	1,128.6	946.7	728.7	613.1	492.8	348.4
Company restaurant operating profit	$ 115.5	84.1	107.1	81.8	136.6	176.8	166.4	129.6	104.3	76.8	54.4
Income (loss) before income taxes	$ 60.7	36.9	43.8	(11.6)	14.9	134.7	128.4	101.4	80.7	64.7	54.7
Net income (loss)*	$ 39.3	30.4	28.5	4.5	(4.9)	76.2	68.7	55.2	44.1	36.9	30.1
Capital expenditures	$ 41.7	38.9	56.0	73.9	120.3	221.9	153.5	87.4	81.6	74.9	52.6
Financial Position (in millions)											
Total assets	$ 757.9	779.6	777.0	786.2	814.2	853.3	656.1	542.5	485.0	387.4	220.3
Property and equipment, net	$ 569.6	579.6	593.1	610.2	643.8	704.9	518.2	405.4	348.3	291.9	175.6
Long-term obligations	$ 168.1	178.9	192.6	195.4	223.2	235.5	139.0	115.7	128.2	105.6	43.1
Shareholders' equity	$ 446.8	428.9	419.6	412.2	424.7	443.5	364.5	308.3	264.7	201.7	125.6
Per Share Data											
Net income (loss)*	$ .41	.32	.30	.05	(.05)	.82	.75	.61	.51	.46	.40
Dividends	$ .24	.24	.24	.24	.21	.17	.15	.12	.09	.08	.08
Shareholders' equity	$ 4.61	4.44	4.36	4.29	4.45	4.65	3.98	3.40	2.92	2.37	1.68
Market price at year-end	$ 6.38	4.63	5.75	5.63	10.25	13.38	10.00	9.38	6.63	4.25	2.88
Ratios											
Company restaurant operating profit margin	% 12.5	8.6	11.0	8.3	13.1	17.1	19.0	19.3	18.4	17.0	17.5
Pretax profit margin	% 6.0	3.4	4.1	—	1.3	11.9	13.6	13.9	13.2	13.1	15.7
Return on average assets†	% 10.8	7.9	8.5	2.1	4.8	21.7	24.7	23.5	22.7	24.9	31.1
Return on average equity	% 9.0	7.2	6.9	1.1	—	19.3	20.4	19.3	19.5	22.0	26.6
Current	.90	.95	1.00	.75	.81	.44	.56	.69	.81	.61	.54
Debt to equity	% 38	42	46	47	53	53	38	38	48	52	34
Debt to total capitalization	% 27	29	31	32	34	35	28	27	33	34	26

Restaurant Data

Domestic Wendy's open at year-end											
Company	**982**	1,031	1,076	1,114	1,206	1,135	1,014	887	802	734	502
Franchise	**2,454**	2,459	2,445	2,468	2,290	2,106	1,801	1,633	1,503	1,386	1,450
International Wendy's open at year-end											
Company	**88**	87	97	115	129	122	43	35	25	14	4
Franchise	**203**	178	144	119	102	79	134	118	100	95	78
Total Wendy's	**3,727**	3,775	3,762	3,816	3,727	3,442	2,992	2,673	2,430	2,229	2,034
Average net sales per domestic Wendy's restaurant (in thousands)											
Company	**$ 832**	808	793	786	765	850	874	749	687	679	650
Franchise	**$ 803**	781	744	721	748	846	870	769	712	670	634
Total domestic	**$ 811**	789	759	741	754	847	871	762	704	672	638
Other Data											
Weighted average shares outstanding (in thousands)	**96,707**	96,378	96,168	95,783	95,879	92,828	91,903	91,168	87,034	80,990	75,702
Shareholders of record at year-end	**53,000**	55,000	58,000	52,000	48,000	41,000	31,000	25,000	20,000	19,000	18,000
Number of employees at year-end	**35,000**	39,000	42,000	45,000	50,000	48,000	43,000	36,000	29,000	26,000	18,000

* 1990, 1989, and 1987 reflect a $696,000, $.01 per share; $1.6 million, $.01 per share; and a $1 million, $.01 per share extraordinary gain on early extinguishment of debt, respectively; net income in 1989 includes the cumulative effect of change in accounting for income taxes of $5.2 million, $.05 per share.

† Return on average assets is computed using income before income taxes and interest charges.

59   In 1989, James W. Near assumed the functions of CEO, president, and chief operating officer. He replaced Ronald Faye, president from 1980 to 1986, and Barney, former CEO and chairman of the board, who retired in 1989.

60   A new regional structure was also instituted for the Company Operations and Franchising Department, along with the Franchise Advisory Council, in order to increase communication and cooperation between company management and franchisees.

61   The company had 50,000 employees in 1986, but, as part of the realignment program, this number decreased to 35,000 people by 1990.

CASE 46

WENDY'S [B]: RETURNING TO ITS ENTREPRENEURIAL ROOTS?

1   Throughout the 1980s, Wendy's appeared to explore numerous ways to continue growth. Some felt it began to lose focus over the course of these events. By the end of the decade Dave Thomas and the Wendy's management team felt these observations had validity. Perhaps Wendy's had lost its focus. They sought, in a sense, to return Wendy's to its "entrepreneurial roots." This [B] case describes Wendy's strategic program in the 1990s in preparation for the 21st century. Chairman and CEO Gordon Teter gives an overview of Wendy's search for a new entrepreneurial focus when he recently reflected on those deliberations:

2   Seven years ago we decided the Wendy's strategic plan would be to re-focus on four key strategies and to be consistent, yet flexible, in achieving our goals. The validity of our resolve has been borne out by marked success since that time.

        Staying focused on our strategic goals hasn't always been easy. Our fiercely competitive environment became cluttered with discount schemes. Despite the temptation to emulate someone else's game plan, we kept ourselves on our playing field with a strong, balanced strategic plan. Thus far, our steady focus on our long-term goals has proven to be a winner.

        Our average domestic company unit volumes have increased for nine consecutive years. Mainly that is a reflection of consumer satisfaction with our program. It is gratifying to know that they continue to tell us that in the world of quick service, Wendy's is their favorite restaurant, number one in the quality and variety of food on our menu, first in overall satisfaction, and tops in other more specific attributes, such as nutrition.

        When customers visit Wendy's we want to be predictable and familiar yet strive to exceed their expectations. We believe, too, that when customers and employees alike are treated with respect, it creates a strong performance-driven culture and a solid base of people throughout the system.

        Our strategic plan also calls for stepped up Wendy's activity in international markets. We have spent several years strengthening our franchise system as well as restructuring and staffing Wendy's international operations. That work is virtually complete, giving us a strong, dedicated development team. Among their first tasks will be to complete an exciting joint venture in Argentina—a large, local quick-service restaurant chain will join forces with Wendy's to penetrate the Argentine market.

        Argentina could well serve as a gateway to other South American countries, particularly Chile.

        Asia continues to be our strongest overseas market, led by Japan, where our franchisee opened its 50th Wendy's restaurant in 1995.

        The global strategy is exciting and holds tremendous promise. While the Wendy's domestic operation is still the engine that powers the entire system, our goal is for our International Division to become a strong driver of growth.

        No matter what the setting, we are confident we have a strong brand, an equally strong people base, and the focused strategies to build on our success.

WENDY'S CORE [DOMESTIC] STRATEGY: FOCUS ON FOUR BASIS THEMES

3   Since Dave Thomas served his first hamburger thirty years ago, Wendy's has enjoyed a reputation for quality. It is a reputation well earned and justly recognized. For 20 years, surveys by *Restaurants & Institutions* magazines named Wendy's America's favorite (highest quality) quick-service hamburger chain. In addition to being the consumer's restaurant of choice, Wendy's has set its sights on being the "franchisor of choice" and the "employer of choice." Its four-part strategy, which Wendy's initiated around 1990, is designed to help their domestic operation achieve and maintain a vision of Wendy's as a quality leader providing fresh food, fast , in convenient, adult-friendly locations.

4   The first part of Wendy's strategy is to strive to operate its restaurants in a manner that exceeds customer expectations on each visit. They see the key to this being to never underestimate the importance of operational excellence. To achieve this, Wendy's approach to management includes such characteristics as relatively narrow spans of control, heavy investment in training, exacting standards, and incentive compensation systems.

5   Having modern, efficient restaurants also is important in exceeding customer expectations, so Wendy's is making some major changes in its properties. To improve speed of service and convenience for its customers, for example, Wendy's has been adding a second pick-up window for drive-through service. By the end of the decade, virtually all of Wendy's restaurants will have been retrofitted to have two pick-up windows, significantly improving service.

6   In addition, Wendy's is adding drive-through "WenView," an electronic menu board. It has been well received by Wendy's customers because it visually displays what was ordered and the total price, which, Wendy's believes, improves accuracy.

7   Wendy's second theme is to accelerate new store development while strengthening the quality of each Wendy's location. Bottomline, Wendy's seeks to eliminate weaker existing locations or turn around those with higher performance potential. Two examples illustrate this: 1) Wendy's acquisition of a New York competitor and 2) Wendy's franchise "simultaneous equation" program.

• Wendy's aggressively looks for competitor restaurant sites that might be available to buy and convert to Wendy's. In 1995, for example, Wendy's acquired 45 restaurants belonging to a competitor in the New York market. After their conversion to Wendy's, its presence in that market increased by approximately one-third.

• Wendy's aggressively buys back franchisee stores, usually weak performers, then refurbishes and otherwise "fixes" each store. It then resells the store(s) to other franchisees or new franchisees— what Wendy's calls its "simultaneous equation" program—which Wendy's feels has been successful in boosting the health of the system through the buying and selling of restaurants between Wendy's and the franchise community. Where necessary, purchased stores have been remodeled and improved and, in some cases, refranchised. The results of this program in 1991–1997 are summarized in Exhibit A.

8   The third key element of Wendy's domestic strategy is to aggressively increase market penetration by adding new units or what Wendy's calls "special sites"—locations such as retail centers, hospitals and gasoline outlets.

9   Wendy's is particularly focusing on truck stops which will give way to "travel centers" that are inviting to families as they are to truckers. Exxon, BP, Texaco, Shell, Pilot Oil and Petro are among the oil companies that are working with Wendy's to develop these locations. Wendy's seeks to establish 25–50 Wendy's restaurants each year in concert with a service station or "travel center." And Wendy's will also add airport sites on a selective basis.

10   The fourth element of Wendy's new millennium strategy is a marketing strategy of leveraging Wendy's strong quality perception with promotional items positioned at the upper end of the price-quality spectrum. Examples include: Fresh Stuff Pitas, Smoky Bacon Cheeseburger, Monterey Ranch Chicken, Chicken Cordon Blue, and the extremely popular Spicy Chicken Sandwich, which appeared for the third time, doing better each time.

11   Wendy's seeks to balance these check building tactics with a daily, low price approach to providing economical options to its customers through the Super Value menu, combination meals, and a $1.99 Kids' Meal. This approach, Wendy's believes, enables it to compete in an environment in which their competitors have heavily discounted their flagship products. Discounting tends to erode profits and brand equity. Wendy's prefers to avoid discounting and rather to offer value in ways consistent with building the strength of its brand.

12   Wendy's believes that one of its greatest assets is the equity in the "Wendy's" brand. Another is Dave Thomas. Wendy's thoughts about Dave:

   He represents everything that is good about our brand. Consumers can easily identify with Dave Thomas because he is very likable, approachable, very honest, has real integrity, and he is a genuine human being. In our advertising, people can see that and identify with him. Dave Thomas will continue to be our advertising spokesman. Our total advertising awareness ratings approach or surpass those of our two major competitors,

EXHIBIT A

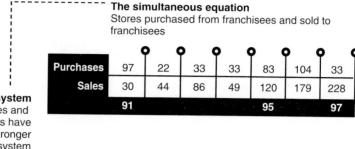

Growing a healthy system
Restaurant purchases and sales with our franchisees have helped us to build a stronger Wendy's system

both of whom dramatically outspend us in terms of media dollars. This speaks to both the effectiveness of the Dave Thomas advertising campaign as well as to the efficiency with which we spend our advertising dollars.

Wendy's Domestic Franchising

13   Wendy's expects 25 to 30 new franchisees each year, with a significant number being minority operators. Of the new franchisees entering the system in the late 1990s, approximately one-third were minority operators. Approximately one-in-four stores were minority-owned by 1998, which is increasing at 16% annually. Wendy's believes this trend is further strengthening and diversifying the system.

14   Wendy's believes it provides a very attractive program for franchisees. Each year Wendy's gets approximately 10,000 inquiries from individuals interested in joining the Wendy's franchise system.

15   To help its franchisees expand with new stores, Wendy's maintains relationships with nine financial institutions that provide financing for new stores, remodeling and other needs. They also have a new program that enables both new and existing franchisees to finance new stores at very favorable rates.

INTERNATIONAL STRATEGY

16   Wendy's international expansion in the 1980s was sporadic and largely unsuccessful. The "catch-22" for Wendy's is the realization that the international arena is perhaps its most untapped growth opportunity. So Wendy's has sought to reconsider its international strategy and improve it for the next century. Wendy's sought to do this via two key initiatives:

1. Put a solid international development team into place, and
2. Enter Canada via a major acquisition of a compatible chain, Tim Hortons coffee/bakery shops.

Building an International Development Team

17   In 1995 Wendy's began building the foundation of its growth strategies by ensuring that it had the support structure required for growth. Wendy's hired several qualified management with food service or international experience, and the obstacles it faced earlier in the 90's began to disappear. They now have what they believe to be a strong organization in the field, with a vice president heading up each of four regional offices: in Honolulu for the Pacific region; in Miami for Latin American operations; in London for the European-Middle East region; and in Toronto for Canadian operations.

EXHIBIT B
International Growth Plan

Latin America/ Caribbean	Canada	Europe/ Middle East	Asia/Pacific
Status			
• Solid presence in the Caribbean	• Strongest penetration of a single country	• United Kingdom stores primarily company operated	• Solid presence in most major markets
• South America entry under way	• Potential to more than double penetration		• Largest opportunity
• 100% franchised and joint ventures	• 50% franchised		• 100% franchised and joint ventures
Priorities			
• Argentina, Puerto Rico, Venezuela, Brazil, Mexico	• Ontario, British Columbia, Alberta	• United Kingdom, Greece, Turkey	• Japan, Indonesia, Philippines
Strategy			
• Joint venture in new countries	• Grow with Company and franchised stores	• Expand franchising in the United Kingdom	• Grow with existing franchisees
• Grow with existing franchisees in the Caribbean and Central America	• Continue development of combination units with Tim Hortons	• Grow with existing franchisees	

18   Each of the regional organizations have marketing, purchasing, operations, engineering, and other key support staff. In addition, training has been shifted to within each region, with satellite training centers in individual locales as needed.

19   Exhibit B summarizes Wendy's international growth plans. Canada was Wendy's largest region, with 245 Wendy's in 1998.

20   There's little question that Asia, Wendy's largest region, will be the immediate growth engineer for international. It started 1998 with 235 sites. Japan, Indonesia, and the Philippines all have large populations and strong or emerging middle classes, and thus give Wendy's confidence that they can support expansion in those areas. These nations are its prime Asian targets. Of all new units planned for Asia, three-fourths of them will be in these three countries. On average, a restaurant approved for development internationally will open a year and a half later. In Japan, however, units open very quickly, so Wendy's expects this market to grow the fastest in number of stores.

21   Latin American development will begin with Argentina, the fourth largest country in the region with a population of more than 33 million and a gross national product that ranks third in South America. Wendy's recently signed an agreement with the owners of an established restaurant chain in the Republic of Argentina for the development of Wendy's restaurants. This arrangement leverages the strength of both entities. Wendy's provides capital for development while its partner provides real estate, local market knowledge and restaurant operating skills.

Tim Hortons—Canada

22   Apart from the scarlet tunics of the Royal Canadian Mounted Police, nothing signifies quality, integrity, and service to Canadian consumers more than the bright, cardinal-red Tim Hortons signs throughout the northern nation. Founded in 1964, it is far and away Canada's largest quick-service restaurant chain offering primarily coffee and fresh baked goods. It is also Canada's overall second largest quick-service restaurant chain. At the end of 1997 there were 1,578 Tim Hortons restaurants, all but 38 of which were franchise operations, and systemwide sales were $771 million.

23   Wendy's and Tim Hortons completed a merger in late 1995. Wendy's agreed to issue 16.45 million common shares in exchange for all of the outstanding shares of Tim Hortons' Canadian parent company. The transaction was treated as a pooling of interests. Wendy's also assumed about $105 million in debt in connection with the transaction.

EXHIBIT C
A Wendy's Milestone

50th Wendy's Opens in Japan

As Wendy's Senior Chairman and Founder Dave Thomas walked into the restaurant on a busy Tokyo street, he noticed an employee polishing the Wendy's sign outside. It sparkled in the bright sun.

Inside he was greeted, as are all customers, with a chorus of "Irasshaymase!" (Welcome!) by the team of well-groomed, smiling young managers and crew people. He looked around; the store was spotless. For Dave Thomas, the 50th Wendy's in Japan was nirvana—the perfect Wendy's.

The restaurant, at 1-27-12 Hamamatsu-cho, is operated by franchisee Wenco Japan, a subsidiary of the Daiei, Inc., one of the world's largest retailers. Wenco opened its first store in Tokyo in 1980 and the 50th, October 2, 1995.

During the opening ceremonies, the store manager personally pledged to his crew and to Wenco President Toshihiko Taniguchi "that we will put all our effort into providing the highest quality, made-to-order, juicy hamburgers and other incomparable food, supplied faster than anybody, thus ensuring our Number One position in the Hamamatsu area."

There's little question the manager felt challenged. Some Wenco Wendy's have the highest sales averages in the system. One Tokyo store averages $94,600 a week, or more than $4.5 million a year.

"This is just a beginning," said Mr. Taniguchi, who expects to have twice as many units open by 1997.

24   Wendy's and Tim Hortons began working together in 1992 when the first Wendy's/Tim Hortons combination restaurant opened June 1 in the Niagara peninsula at Beamsville, Ontario. A day later, it seemed as though the entire town of Montague, P.E.I., turned out to celebrate the grand opening of a second combination unit.

25   At the close of 1997, Wendy's crimson signs had joined Tim Hortons in 48 successful Wendy's/Tim Hortons combination restaurants including the first in the United States in the Minneapolis suburb of Hopkins, Minnesota.

26   Fresh baked products prepared twice a day are vital to the chain's successful marketing mix. Freshness is the key, and it is achieved through "producing stores" equipped with bakeries.

27   The standard Tim Hortons units being built today are primarily free-standing "producing stores" totaling 3,000 square feet. Each includes a bakery capable of supplying fresh baked goods every 12 hours to several satellite Tim Hortons within a defined area. Most of the new stores also have drive-through windows.

28   In addition, Tim Hortons has had considerable success with prefabricated, 500 square foot, drive-through-only units. Satellite units and drive-through only units receive their baked goods from a "producing store" nearby. This concept leverages the capital invested in the kitchens of the larger restaurants.

29   Tim Hortons is proud to say, "We fit in anywhere," pointing out the versatility of the concept, from the Wendy's/Tim Hortons combination stores to the mobile cart that requires only 36 square feet in which to do business. In between are larger kiosks and full-service carts that can easily be placed in high traffic areas. Many of the smaller, modular Tim Hortons adapt well to special sites, such as airport terminals, hospitals and universities. At the University of Western Ontario in London, Ontario, for example, there are 14 Tim Hortons sites of different sizes. At the Calgary International Airport there are six outlets—one "producing store" and five satellites.

30   The largest of the freestanding units, of course, are the Wendy's/Tim Hortons combination restaurants, which average 5,000 square feet. Wendy's and Tim Hortons share a common dining room seating 104, but each has its own food preparation and storage areas and most have a pick-up window for each restaurant. The combination works because approximately 85 percent of Tim Hortons traffic takes place before Wendy's opens or during the afternoon snack hours when Wendy's is less busy. At midday and again at the dinner hour, the heaviest traffic is Wendy's.

31   Throughout the Tim Hortons system, approximately 71 percent of the restaurants are leased or subleased by Tim Hortons to the franchisees. The senior management of Tim Hortons actively participates in the selection of all new restaurant locations.

EXHIBIT D
A Combination that Works

A Canadian franchisee of both Wendy's and Tim Hortons, Danny Murphy found it a natural and successful step to also operate a pair of Wendy's/Tim Hortons combination units in his home province of Prince Edward Island. According to Murphy, "Sales at both Wendy's and Tim Hortons benefit from cross-marketing. Regular customers of one concept are introduced to the other concept at the combination units. Our 5,000 square foot Canadian combination units feature separate kitchens for Wendy's and Tim Hortons, a shared 104 seat dining area, and drive-through windows for both concepts."

Development cost is generally lower for a combination unit than for separate Wendy's and Tim Hortons restaurants. Less land is required, and it is cheaper to build one combined larger building. This means that both concepts can enter areas together that might otherwise be impossible because of high land costs. Also, investment returns can be higher.

Yet another benefit realized at the Wendy's/Tim Hortons combination units is greater employee efficiency and stability. Murphy says he is able to offer eight-hour shifts instead of four, with some employees splitting their shift between Wendy's and Tim Hortons, changing uniforms in between.

The synergy is outstanding considering that more than 60 percent of Tim Hortons' average daily sales occur before 10:30 a.m., when the Wendy's side of the restaurant opens.

32   Over 40 percent of Tim Hortons' sales volume is in coffee—13 million pounds of its special blend last year. Every million pounds of coffee represents about 50 million 7-ounce cups. Ground coffee is also sold in a 13-ounce can at the restaurants as well as in select supermarkets. Coffee is to Tim Hortons what beef is to Wendy's, so coffee price fluctuations are closely watched. After hitting highs in the fall of 1994, prices have declined dramatically.

33   Coffee and other non-perishable goods are distributed from six warehouse distribution centers in Moncton, New Brunswick; Calgary, Alberta; Debert, Nova Scotia; Langley, British Columbia; Kingston, Ontario; and Oakville, Ontario, Tim Hortons' corporate headquarters. The award-winning graphic design, featuring the coffee and a selection of freshly baked products, makes Tim Hortons' trucks rolling billboards on Canadian highways.

34   In the United States donut shops represent only 1.8 percent of traffic share among quick-service restaurants. The category's share is 11 times greater in the Canadian market. The result is that despite a population that is 10 percent of the United States, the donut category is larger in Canada. In 1995 revenues among Canada's donut shops totaled $987.4 million; in the U.S. revenues were almost $192 million less.

35   Tim Hortons leads the coffee and donut segment with 45.1 percent market share. Among all categories of quick-service restaurants, Tim Hortons enjoys the second-largest share of customer traffic with about 7.3 percent of the Canadian market.

36   Tim Hortons enjoys extraordinary loyalty. So devoted are its customers, who are primarily between 25 and 54 years of age, that it is not uncommon for some to visit the restaurant two or more times a day. Tim Hortons is a way of life for many customers, a meeting place, 24 hours a day. Often the staff will spot a "regular" coming in, knowing that customer wants a medium coffee black and an Apple Fritter, and have the order ready by the time the customer reaches the counter.

37   Tim Hortons' systemwide sales growth has averaged more than 20 percent annually in recent years. Buoyed by an annual national television and print advertising budget of more than $25 million, a minimum of 2,000 units in Canada is projected by the year 2000.

38   There is ample room for further development. For example, studies indicate metropolitan Toronto could absorb 100 to 150 Tim Hortons and twice that many in the province of Ontario, which already boasts more than 500 units.

DIVERSITY

39   Wendy's has developed a number of relationships with culturally and ethnically diverse entities, such as the National Minority Supplier Development Council, the Urban League, U.S. Hispanic Chamber of Commerce and the NAACP. We've also had outstanding experiences. *Black Enterprise* Magazine

EXHIBIT E
Seven-Year Selected Financial Data

Operations (in millions)	1998	1997[1]	1996	1995[2]	1994[2]	1993[2]	1992[2] [3]	1991[2]
Systemwide sales								
Wendy's	$5,555	5,226	4,784	4,495	4,227	3,924	3,613	3,224
Tim Hortons	$ 895	772	646	541	440	377	341	308
Retail sales	$1,586	1,652	1,567	1,462	1,366	1,289	1,207	1,039
Revenues	$1,948	2,037	1,897	1,746	1,592	1,482	1,381	1,187
Income before income taxes	$ 242	292	255	165	150	118	104	79
Net income	$ 149	181	156	110	97	81	66	52
Capital expenditures	$ 242	295	307	218	172	137	140	86
Financial Position (in millions)								
Total assets	$1,858	1,990	1,781	1,509	1,215	1,100	1,013	966
Property and equipment, net	$1,290	1,314	1,208	1,007	865	787	745	682
Long-term obligations	$ 246	250	242	337	145	201	234	240
Shareholders' equity	$1,093	1,234	1,057	819	702	624	553	504
Per Share Data								
Net income—diluted	$ 1.13	1.33	1.19	.88	.79	.67	.56	.45
Dividends	$ .24	.24	.24	.24	.24	.24	.24	.24
Shareholders' equity	$ 8.82	9.33	8.16	6.81	5.94	5.33	4.80	4.43
Market price at fiscal year end	$21.81	22.88	20.88	21.25	14.38	17.38	12.63	9.25
Ratios								
Domestic company								
operating profit margin	15.6%	14.8	13.3	15.1	15.7	14.9	14.2	13.3
Pretax profit margin	12.4%	14.3	13.4	9.5	9.4	8.0	7.5	6.7
Return on average assets[4]	14.5%	17.2	17.6	13.6	15.0	13.4	13.1	11.6
Return on average equity	13.0%	15.7	16.6	14.5	14.7	13.8	12.7	10.7
Long-term debt to equity[5]	23%	20	23	41	21	32	42	48
Debt to total capitalization[5]	18%	17	19	29	17	24	30	32
Price to earnings	19%	17	18	24	18	26	23	21
Restaurant Data								
Domestic Wendy's open at year end								
Company		1,073	1,191	1,200	1,168	1,132	1,117	1,080
Franchise		3,502	3,178	2,997	2,826	2,657	2,490	2,408
International Wendy's open at year end								
Company		129	124	111	96	92	91	82
Franchise		503	440	359	321	287	264	234
Total Wendy's		5,207	4,933	4,667	4,411	4,168	3,962	3,804
Tim Hortons		1,578	1,384	1,197	943	721	628	546
Total Units		6,785	6,317	5,864	5,354	4,889	4,590	4,350
Average net sales per domestic								
Wendy's restaurant (in thousands)								
Company		$1,111	1,049	1,014	1,001	978	924	874
Franchise		$1,017	978	974	982	960	907	843
Total domestic		$1,042	998	986	988	966	912	852
Average sales per Tim Hortons								
standard restaurant (in thousands)		$ 730	668	641	623	596	607	621
Other Data								
Diluted shares (in thousands)		140,738	133,684	130,164	128,718	127,377	125,994	115,836
Registered shareholders at year end		92,000	82,000	63,000	57,000	56,000	56,000	53,000
Number of employees at year end		47,000	49,000	47,000	45,000	44,000	43,000	40,000

[1] Before non-recurring charges of $72.7 million pretax ($50.0 million after tax).

[2] Includes special pretax charges of $49.7 million, $28.9 million, $23.3 million, $17.7 million and $17.8 million, for 1995, 1994, 1993, 1992 and 1991, respectively.

[3] Fiscal year 1992 includes 53 weeks.

[4] Return on average assets is computed using income before income taxes and interest charges.

[5] Excludes company-obligated mandatorily redeemable preferred securities.

and the Women's Foodservice Forum named Gordon Teter "Trailblazer of the Year" for building a diverse organization at Wendy's with women and minorities. In 1997 Wendy's increased purchases of goods and services from minority- and female-owned businesses by 15 percent—its sixth consecutive year of increases. By 1999 over 25 percent of Wendy's franchisees were minority or female and minorities and females make up 75 percent of Wendy's workforce and 56.8 percent of its management.

SUPPLIER DIVERSITY

40   An example of Wendy's effort to build a diverse group of partners is the founder and president of its sandwich wrap vendor, Wolf Packaging. Robert Ontiveros founded his company more than 20 years ago and has been an outstanding partner for over three years. Today, Ontiveros' company is Wendy's exclusive sandwich wrap supplier throughout the U.S. and his company ranks 72nd in sales among the nations's top 500 Hispanic-owned businesses. Among his honors, Ontiveros was named Midwest Business Man of the Year in 1991, an award that recognizes business people of Hispanic descent who have achieved outstanding growth for their company, annual sales expansion and civic involvement.

COMMUNITY INVOLVEMENT

41   Wendy's has a diverse community involvement program. For example, Wendy's sponsored the *Black Enterprise* "Kidpreneur Konference" in 1996 and 1997. Children ages four to 17 attended the conference and other events to learn about building a successful business. The older children also learned about writing a business plan, managing finances, and advertising while participating with a franchisee in the Orlando, Fla., market.

THE DAVE THOMAS FOUNDATION FOR ADOPTION

42   Started in 1992, the foundation continues to focus on making the adoption process easier and more affordable while creating awareness and educating the public about the thousands of children waiting to be adopted. Last year it celebrated the passage of landmark legislation and funding for some of the premier adoption projects in the country—all bringing the issue of adoption to national attention. But most gratifying to the trustees of the foundation and Dave was to see how the Wendy's family embraced the adoption cause in 1997. By developing relationships with local adoption agencies, Wendy's restaurants throughout the U.S. and Canada are supporting the foundation with wonderful programs. Company employees and franchisees have created dozens of programs and local public service announcements to bring prospective parents in touch with local agencies to help find children loving, permanent homes. In-store canister programs and other charity events have raised money for adoption organizations and awareness of the adoption cause. In Florida, a statewide in-store canister program generated more than $100,000 last year while thousands of restaurants displayed posters and tray liners during National Adoption Month in November featuring children waiting to be adopted along with the 1-800-TO-ADOPT phone number.

CASE 47

AMERICA ONLINE, INC.

INTRODUCTION

1   America Online (AOL), the market leader in the Internet industry with more than 8 million customers, is fast becoming obsolete. The business of connecting customers to the Internet is becoming more and more competitive. As access gets cheaper and the Internet becomes easier to navigate thanks to web browsers, there is less need for products like AOL. A third of AOL's customers who make up $2/3$ of its revenues, i.e., its most sophisticated customers, will soon outgrow AOL's training wheels like service and move to the less expensive, all you can eat Internet service providers. With falling stock prices and increased competition from software giants like Microsoft, AOL is facing an uncertain future. On top of these concerns AOL is besieged by complaints and lawsuits from angry customers who are unable to log on because of the company's recent capacity problems. AOL management now more than ever needs to develop a short-term strategic objective to confront these problems head on as well as a long term strategic objective that would keep AOL ahead of the competition.

THE INDUSTRY

What Is the Internet?

2   The Internet is a vast computer network that provides customers access to the web. The web is a vast worldwide database of information, and the Internet refers to the hardware and software. The hardware is a giant mass of computers and cables that connects all of the web around the world, and the software is the computer program that makes it easy to navigate the web. The word "Internet" literally means "network of networks."

3   Practically speaking the Internet, also referred to as the Information Superhighway, is composed of people hardware and software. With the proper equipment you can sit at your computer and communicate with someone anyplace in the world as long as that person also has the proper equipment. You can use the Internet to access vast amounts of information, including text, graphics, sound, and video. From your computer you can view works of art in the Vatican Museum, look at a company's annual report, and get up to the second stock prices. You can send e-mail, receive electronic newsletters, and "chat" with others on-line. There are hosts of companies that are scrambling to become Internet providers as more and more people come to rely on all these services.

Global Product

4   The Internet is a truly global product. Information pipelines made of sophisticated fiber optics are being wired around the world, making voice and data traffic faster, cheaper, more reliable and subject to less interference. People from all over the world have access to the same information in a matter of seconds. It is estimated that some 20–30 million computer users populated this global village by mid 1995. The annual rate of growth for worldwide web traffic is 341,000%, reaching approximately 159 countries and more than 400 financial service firms. US supreme court decisions are available on the net in less than one day.

This case was prepared by Bennett A. Nagel and Efram E. Nagel under the direction of Professor Robert J. Mockler of St. John's University.

Who Owns the Internet?

5   The Internet is not owned or funded by any one institution, organization, or government. It does not have a CEO and it is not a commercial service. It is directed by the Internet Society (ISOC) which is composed of volunteers. The ISOC appoints a sub-council, the Internet Architecture Board (IAB), and members of this board work out issues' standards, network resources, network addresses, and so on. Another volunteer group, the Internet Engineering Task Force (IETF), takes care of the day to day issues of Internet operation.

How Did It Originate?

6   In the late 1960s, a group of scientists at the US Department of Defense's Advanced Research Projects Agency (ARPA) wanted to share information with others working on similar research projects, many of whom were government contractors working at large universities. Consequently, ARPAnet was originated. When people at these institutions discovered the enormous utility of a network that linked them with colleagues around the world, the project magnified. The first commercial on-line service, CompuServe, started up in 1969 and was primarily a hangout for computer jocks.

7   In 1986, the National Science Foundation (NSF) created NSFNET to connect super-computer sites around the U.S. It also connected computers at research sites and schools that were near the super-computers. Within two years NSFNET had totally replaced ARPAnet.

8   In 1991, Vice President Al Gore, then a US senator, proposed widening the architecture of NSFNET to include more k–12 schools, community colleges, and 2-year colleges. The resulting legislation expanded NSFNET and renamed it NREN (National Research and Educational Network). This bill also allowed businesses to purchase a part of the network for commercial uses. The mass commercialization of today's Internet is the direct result of this legislation.

Commercial On-Line Services

9   An on-line service is a collection of networked computers that provide content to subscribers. This constitutes the fastest growing segment of the Internet, and almost all now provide access to the Internet. This means that a subscriber can access the Internet from his or her home personal computer. All that is needed is at least 4 megabytes of RAM, a 250 megabyte hard drive, and a 14.4 BPS modem.

10   With a commercial on-line service you would be provided with software that would allow your computer to connect with the Internet provider. Your home computer via the modem would make a local call to the provider which is part of a network that is attached to the Internet. SLIP (Serial Line Interface Protocol) and PPP (Point to Point Protocol) accounts attach your computer to a network of computers that are directly attached. This is the Internet.

11   Once you are connected your provider can give you access to the worldwide web, e-mail, newsgroups, chat rooms and other sites, depending on the provider. The provider would also provide you with customer service that helps you learn what the web has to offer, or problems with billing as well as answers to frequently asked questions (FAQs).

12   Commercial on-line services also have become a media for advertising. Advertisers can select specific demographics and target markets and not only provide information but give users the ability to make purchases on-line.

Who Travels the Web?

13   In January 1994, the Georgia Institute of Technology held the first World Wide Web user survey. Out of 1,300 valid responses, the results indicated the following statistics about the respondents:

- 56% were between the ages of 21 and 30,
- 94% were male,
- 69% were located in North America, and
- 45% described themselves as professionals and 22% as graduate students.

The largest population roaming the web consists of four year campus populations within the United States. The top five worldwide web users by domain are:

- US educational (.edu) with 49%,
- US commercial (.com) with 20%,
- US government (.gov) with 9%,
- United Kingdom (.uk) with 7%, and
- Canada (.ca) with 5%.

Customers

14   Customers for commercial on-line services are divided into three main groups, individuals, businesses and advertisers. The individuals are primarily students who use the Internet for chat with peers and for research. Chat takes place in what are called chat rooms where a person can have a dynamic conversation with a group of about twenty people at a time on a wide range of topics. Rooms are divided by categories and topics. For example there are rooms dedicated to singles, gays, doctors or even people in Miami. A key to success for this is large market share because this gives an individual a larger variety of people to talk to.

15   Research is available through search engines that help you find web pages based on the topic you are interested in. There are web pages covering everything from current news to company information to meteors in outer space and the latest in soap operas. A search engine is software that provides you with a list of sites that contain the key words of the topic you are searching for.

16   The individual customer base consists of anyone with a personal home computer. The Internet is used by this group for e-mail and information as well as on-line transactions.

17   The businesses' customer base uses a commercial on-line service to provide them with what is called an Intranet. An Intranet is a private network that provides a company with the ability to communicate and do business transactions with subsidiaries and suppliers all around the world without giving up privacy and security. They have also been used as "information storefronts" for their employees and customers. For example a bank may let customers access its Intranet to check their account balances or perform other transactions.

18   According to a February 1996 survey of 50 corporations by Forrester Research, just 16% had an Intranet in place at the time of the survey, but some 50% were planning to build one.

19   Advertising is only available to the individual market and promises to be a major source of revenue in the future. Advertisers are wary of the Internet because of the ease with which a user can bypass an ad and how ads can go unnoticed or become bothersome for users because of all the clutter on the screen. Advertisers do, however, see its potential as a means of selectively advertising and because of the desired demographics of consumers on the web. Companies are also now providing transactions on the web. One can sell anything from airplane tickets to books, and this promises to be a major source of revenue for Internet providers who can help companies reach their customers.

Promotion

20   Heavy promotion is essential for attracting new customers. This includes free software giveaways and well-placed commercial advertising. Most companies provide free software for customers to use during a free trial period. This has worked especially well with AOL who drew its millions of customers this way. Internet providers are also spending huge amounts of money for advertising campaigns including commercials during the super-bowl and full page ads in major newspapers and magazines.

Competition

21   The on-line services and Internet markets are highly competitive. The Company believes there are existing competitors, which include commercial on-line services such as CompuServe and Prodigy,

Internet-based services, including the Microsoft Network and Internet service providers, and various national and local independent Internet service providers as well as long distance and regional telephone companies, who are likely to enhance their service offerings. In addition, new competitors, including Internet directory services and various media and telecommunication companies, have entered or announced plans to enter the on-line services and Internet markets, resulting in greater competition for the Company. The competitive environment could have the following effects: require additional pricing programs and increased spending on marketing, content procurement and product development; limit the Company's opportunities to enter into and/or renew agreements with content providers and distribution partners; limit the Company's ability to grow its subscriber base; and result in increased attrition in the Company's subscriber base. Any of the foregoing events could have an impact on revenues and result in an increase in costs as a percentage of revenues.

22   Due to the recent customer dissatisfaction with AOL many competitors are taking advantage of the situation. CompuServe, for example, ran a commercial during the Super Bowl that did not mention AOL by name but played on the concept of dialing up an on-line service and getting only a busy signal. AT&T's head of its Worldnet Internet access service said AT&T has seen the number of its new subscribers double so far this past month. The telecommunications powerhouse will begin test marketing its ads this week, both television and print, which focus on the reliability of AT&T Worldnet. According to a study that compared the chance of being connected during peak hours between AT&T and AOL, Worldnet had a 93.4% success rate, versus 36.7% for AOL.

Pricing

23   Due to the competitive nature of the industry, companies are introducing much more competitive prices including flat rates per month or week. Previously, Internet users were charged by usage, per minute or hour. In February of 1995 AT&T introduced a flat rate of $19.95 for Internet access in order to gain market share. Subsequently, many rivals matched the price even as they doubted they would be able to turn a profit. Many experts say the economics of the Internet dictate that this flat rate will not last. Since the change has occurred there have been backups with all the major Internet providers as people log in once and never log out. Fees are also expected to rise in the future, and telephone companies are searching for ways to increase the fees they charge Internet access providers for using their phone lines. They are lobbying hard to win new "access fees" from Internet firms, much like the fees they charge long-distance companies for routing calls to local Baby Bell customers.

24   Several major firms have already abandoned the $19.95 strategy. Netcom On-Line Communications Services Inc., CompuServe Corp., and now Sprint Corp. all expect to drop the flat rates soon, if they haven't already. While costs vary widely among Internet providers, infrastructure costs alone range from around 80 cents to $1.30 a month. At this rate any customer who goes on-line for more than 20 hours a month has already cut into the company's profits. Moreover, it costs firms another 25 to 30 dollars per hour to provide customer support services. Denny Matteucci, president of interactive services at CompuServe says, "We can't find a way to become profitable at a flat price—and I'm not sure anybody can, we are just not going to spend our marketing dollars going after the mass consumer market where they have price wars and no profits." CompuServe Corp. is now re-focusing on small businesses.

25   MCI Communication Corp., however, aims to keep the flat rates as long as the competitive condition deems it necessary. AT&T Corp. and AOL maintain having no plans to drop the flat rates. Industry insiders predict that big providers will keep the flat-rate deals only until other rivals give up the gimmick. "As the market consolidates, the more powerful players have enough market strength to raise prices and get away with it," says David Goodtree, an analyst at Forrester Research Inc.

AMERICA ON-LINE

Company Background

26   Founded in 1985, America Online, Inc. (NYSE: AOL) is the world's first billion-dollar new media company. The company is headquartered in Dulles, Virginia, with current operations in the United States,

Canada, the United Kingdom, France, and Germany. Expansion into the Japanese market is planned for 1997. Providing vision and leadership, America Online, Inc. has played a leading role in the development of a new medium for information, entertainment, and communication, and will continue to do so far into the future. America Online, Inc. consists of three separate component companies.

AOL Corporation

27   AOL Corporation oversees the operations of three new divisions: AOL Networks, ANS Access, and AOL Studios. The Corporation comprises the core business functions of Finance, Human Resources, Legal Affairs, Corporate Communications, Corporate Development, and Technology. AOL, Inc. is led by Chairman and CEO Steve Case.

AOL Networks

28   AOL Networks includes the flagship AOL service and AOL International Services. The AOL service, which has added more than 3 million members and tripled revenues to more than $1 billion in the last year, is the jewel in the AOL crown. AOL Networks is responsible for extending the AOL brand into the mainstream market, and aggressively developing new revenue streams via interactive marketing programs, advertising and on-line transactions. AOL Networks is led by Robert Pittman, President, formerly managing partner and CEO of Century 21, and co-founder of MTV Networks.

29   The America Online service is the world's most popular Internet on-line service, with over 8 million members worldwide. The service provides subscribers with a variety of interactive features—electronic mail, Internet access, news, sports, weather, financial information and transactions, electronic shopping, and more. The service is charged with creating the unique "AOL experience" through the establishment of technology and media partnerships, marketing, customer service, and product development. With nearly 7 million members worldwide, the AOL Networks business division owns the world's most popular new media business.

ANS Access

30   ANS Access operates the largest and most reliable data communications network in the world. The ANS technical team was actually the architect, designer, and developer of both the hardware and software for the Internet backbone and then managed that backbone in the US for nine years. Today, the network consists of more than 160,000 modems connecting 472 cities in the US and 152 cities internationally. ANS now provides network services to a variety of businesses and operates the AOL network on which the majority of AOL traffic travels. Nearly 85% of the American population can dial into AOLNet on a local number. In addition, AOL GlobalNet, a convenience for AOL members who travel, offers access in approximately 230 additional cities in 83 countries. AOLNet handles approximately six million on-line sessions per day with 140,000 simultaneous users, delivers close to five million e-mail messages to roughly 9.4 million recipients, and processes over 50 million hits to the Web. ANS Access also designs, installs, manages, and maintains nationwide corporate data networks over ANSnet, one of the fastest, largest TCP/IP networks in the world. And there is still additional capacity for further growth, for private AOLs and for other corporate Intranets.

AOL Studios

31   AOL Studios is a new studio system that will develop the most innovative interactive programming for AOL and other distributors. AOL Studios runs AOL's innovative chat (iChatco), games, (INN), local (Digital City), and independent (Greenhouse) programming properties. The AOL Studios division will develop leading-edge technology for broad-band and mid-band distribution; create interactive brands that can be extended into other media properties such as TV and radio; and manage joint ventures with companies including Time-Warner and CapCities/ABC. AOL Studios' Greenhouse property has long been AOL's content development arm, discovering new interactive talents and helping them launch new and innovative content; while AOL Digital Cities has already launched in cities such as Washington DC, Boston, San Francisco, San Diego, and New York, and internationally in London, Edinburgh, and Glasgow. AOL Studios is managed by Ted Leonsis, former president of AOL Services Co.

America On-Line Customers

32   Based on a AOL customer survey, the company found its user breakdown to be as follows:

female: 41%
male: 59%

33   The survey also gave the demographics for AOL customers. Based on these findings they were able to attract more advertisers because of the attractiveness of these demographics to companies. Their customers report:

Other user(s) in household:	56%
Spouses who use the service:	42%
Households who have children:	46%*
Users with children (ages 6–17) in household:	54%
College graduates:	63%**
Use service for both personal and business use:	41%

* vs. U.S. Census: 35%
**vs. U.S. Census: 23%

34   America Online has been having a harder time keeping its customers after they initially subscribe. The retention rates for AOL subscribers who were early in their membership terms is decreasing more than the overall retention rate. The Company believes that factors contributing to these decreases include:

1. competition from an increasing number of service providers;
2. the availability of alternative pricing models from competitors, including unlimited use pricing; and
3. an increase in less-qualified new subscribers as a result of increased direct marketing to the mass consumer audience.

The Company believes that the introduction in July 1996 of the Value Plan and the new version of AOL introduced in late fiscal 1996 address many of the factors that most directly affect retention. In addition, the Company plans to increase spending on programs designed to improve retention both as it relates to increasing trial conversion rates and reducing cancellations among longer-term users.

The average total usage hours per member per month, for AOL subscribers, is expected to increase in the future. The Company believes that the principal factor contributing to this expected increase will be the availability of the Value Plan, which will allow members to spend more time on-line at less cost. Overall average monthly on-line service revenue per AOL subscriber in fiscal 1997 was expected to be comparable to fiscal 1996.

Services and Products

35   America Online offers all the standard services and products but has been stronger than its competitors by being easier to use, more family oriented with exclusive children's sites and sites dedicated to students such as their Academic Assistance Center. This site provides students with on-line help from teachers in chat rooms dedicated to specific subjects.

Revenues

36   About 91% of America Online's revenues come from on-line service revenues. The Company has experienced a significant increase in revenues over the past three years. The higher revenues have been attributed principally to increases in the Company's subscriber base resulting from growth of the on-line services market, aggressive subscriber acquisition marketing and the expansion of its services and content. Additionally, revenues have increased as the average monthly revenue per subscriber has risen during the past three years, primarily as a result of an increase in the average monthly number of paid hours of use per subscriber. The Company's on-line service revenues are generated primarily from subscribers paying a monthly membership fee and hourly charges based on usage in excess of the number of hours of usage provided as part of the monthly fee.

37   The Company's other revenues are generated primarily from the sale of merchandise, data network services, on-line transactions and advertising, marketing and production services, and development and licensing fees. The growth of other revenues is important to the Company's business objectives. In 1996, these other revenues represented approximately 9% of the company's total revenues. Among the Company's business objectives are increasing the subscriber base and changing its business model over time into one in which more revenues and profits are generated from sources other than on-line service revenues, such as merchandise sales, advertising, the provision of data network services, and transaction fees. The Company expects that the growth in other revenues, which generally carry higher margins than on-line service revenues, will provide the Company with the opportunity and flexibility to fund programs designed to grow the subscriber base. If the growth in other revenues does not materialize to the extent the Company expects, there can be no assurance that the Company will be able to meet its business objectives.

38   Advertising has not yet proven to significantly increase revenues for companies that advertise on the web. Despite the attractive demographics of on-line households, the web is not yet a mass medium. Advertisers are suspicious of the web because its interactive capabilities make it easy for consumers to simply bypass an ad. With a very large customer base, AOL hopes to attract more advertisers with exclusive deals and ideal demographic audiences.

Pricing

39   Faced with slumping consumer enthusiasm and increased competition America Online in Dec. 96 unleashed a new pricing structure. AOL moved towards a unique "tiered" pricing, structured to appeal to a broad range of consumers with different interests, needs, and budgets. Members were offered a flat, unlimited use rate of $19.95 per month. Those who chose to pay for their service in advance could opt for a one-year unlimited usage membership for $17.95 per month, or a two-year unlimited membership for $14.95 per month. Consumers who already had Internet service through an ISP could obtain access to AOL content for $9.95 a month, and those who wished to use AOL as an Internet-only provider could do so for only $10 a month. Consumers whose Internet on-line usage is light may join AOL for $4.95 per month for three hours of service, with additional time costing $2.50 an hour. These rates apply 24 hours a day and include the cost of connecting to America Online via a local phone call in the US and Canada.

40   AOL then spent $130 million to add 355,000 new domestic subscribers, or about $366 a head. At less than $20 a month per newcomer, it will take AOL 18 months just to recoup the cost of signing up these customers—if they stick with AOL that long. AOL concedes that it will have to try and raise other revenue from selling on-line ads and from on-line shopping. Robert Pittman, president and chief executive of AOL Networks, says AOL can shoulder the flat fee because, among other reasons, the company's incremental infrastructure costs are currently only at 25 cents an hour, far less than the industry average. AOL can also spread costs over its 8 million customers, more than twice the customer base of its next largest competitor.

41   AOL's new pricing strategy along with its low infrastructure costs have now caught up with them. The rush of new subscribers, along with increased use by its 7 million veteran members, made AOL nearly inaccessible at times. Currently there are class action lawsuits pending against AOL from customers in over 36 states who were not able to access the Internet. One subscriber group hit AOL with a $20 million consumer-fraud lawsuit. Upgrading their networks to handle the increased capacity will cost AOL in excess of $350 million and will take some time.

Availability and Distribution

42   America Online has a $500 million annual marketing budget where consumers can obtain the America Online software and a free trial membership at major software retailers and bookstores, or by calling 1-800-4-ONLINE. In addition, the software has been pre-installed on most leading PCs, including those offered by IBM, Apple, Compaq, AST, Tandy, NEC, and Compudyne.

43   With AOL's move to a flat rate and their successful advertising campaign, AOL is besieged by class action lawsuits from angry customers who receive busy signals when they try to use America Online. This has not only caused a lot of bad press but AOL fears that many current customers will switch to other on-line services.

44   Due to recent capacity issues AOL will need to invest heavily to expand their capacity and avoid new advertising. Ads already in the works will have to carry a disclaimer that users may have problems accessing America Online.

Partnerships

45   America Online is planning a strategic partnership with Barnes & Noble Inc. The partnership with the world's largest bookseller would include large book discounts and immediate delivery of over 400,000 books in stock to AOL's customers. Robert Pittman says the partnership would further strengthen AOL's position as the leader in the retail on-line world and that the service would bring value to AOL's service by bringing members exclusive access to another number one brand, along with unmatched discounts and convenience, and by offering AOL additional opportunities for cross promotion. Len Riggio, chairman and CEO of Barnes and Noble says, we believe this relationship can expand our book market and ultimately bring in millions of new customers who prefer to shop on-line.

46   America Online believes strategic partnerships like this increase the value of their service by providing better transaction availability and hopes to develop more partnerships with other brand name companies.

TOWARD THE FUTURE

Strategic Planning

47   Robert Pittman and his management team at AOL Networks need to outline both a short term and long term plan in order to maintain their position as the industry leader and at the same time remain profitable.

48   In the short run the company needs to pacify angry users and keep them as customers. They need to reduce their marketing expense because it has been too successful, and focus on a pricing strategy that makes sense.

49   In the long run, AOL must learn to balance profitability with market share. They need to maintain their market share and continue to satisfy customers through better service, higher technology, and competitive prices. To do this some managers feel AOL should focus on the small but rapidly growing business segment who are not as price sensitive as the individual. They argue that the business segment is more customer loyal and their user habits are more predictable. Other managers maintain that AOL should continue to focus on the individual market because this is where they have been successful in the past with their user friendly software and their exclusive services. They argue that the individual market also provides a media for advertisers which can be a valuable source of revenue in the future.

LIST OF WORKS CITED

Manly, Lorne. "All in the on-line family." *Folio,* March 1, 1996; v25n3 p. 21.

Galarza, Pablo. "America Onhold." *Financial World,* June 17, 1996; v165n9 pp. 28–32.

Gillin, Paul. "AOL's sellout." *Computerworld,* March 18, 1996; v30n12 p. 36.

Schwartz, Susan. "AOL targets vertical markets with intranet solution." *Insurance and Technology,* July 1996; v21n7 pp. 13–14.

Tedesco, Richard. "AOL lines up alliances." *Broadcasting and Cable,* March 18, 1996; v126n12 p. 54.

Wilder, Clinton. "AOL targets business users." *Information Week,* April 1, 1996; n573 p. 30.

Taylor, Cathy. "AOL reboots ad strategy." *Mediaweek,* July 1, 1996; v6n27 pp. 9–10.

Ramo, Joshua Cooper. "Welcome to the wired world." *Time,* February 3, 1996; v149n5 pp. 30–37.

Wallace, G. David. "The electronic tutor is in." *Business Week,* January 20, 1997, p. 8.

Levy, Steven. "Is AOL out of lines?" *Newsweek,* February 10, 1997, p. 4.

Barret, Amy. "For $19.95 a month, unlimited headaches for AOL." *Business Week,* January 27, 1997, p. 39.

Internet Sites

http://www.
AOL.COM
PRODIGY.COM
COMPUSERV.COM

APPENDIX A: FORM 10-Q, SECURITIES AND EXCHANGE COMMISSION

AMERICA ONLINE, INC. AND SUBSIDIARIES CONSOLIDATED STATEMENTS OF OPERATIONS

(amounts in thousands, except per share data)

Nine months ended March 31, 1996

	1996	1995
Revenues:		
Online service revenues	$688,485	$211,045
Other revenues	70,902	31,390
Total revenues	759,387	242,435
Costs and expenses:		
Cost of revenues	448, 649	142,290
Marketing	145,871	47,856
Product development	35,308	8,664
General and administrative	74,439	24,910
Acquired research and development	16,981	50,335
Amortization of goodwill	5,228	551
Total costs and expenses	726,476	274,606
Income (loss) from operations	32,911	(32,171)
Other income	3,572	2,301
Merger expenses	(848)	(1,710)
Income (loss) before provision for income taxes	35,635	(31,580)
Provision for income taxes	(21,885)	(9,977)
Net income (loss)	$ 13,750	$(41,557)
Earnings (loss) per share:	$ 0.13	$ (0.62)
Weighted average shares outstanding	108,346	67,529

CASE 48

AMAZON.COM

Amazon is the beginning of a completely new way to buy books. . . . It could increase book sales quite dramatically by making it easier for people to find the books they want.

Alberto Vitale,
Chairman, Random House Inc.

1   It is projected that as many as 700 million people worldwide will be using the Internet by the year 2000. The typical Internet user in 1996 was young, affluent, and well educated. The potential size and affluence of this target market has led many observers to coin the phrase the "Internet Gold Rush." Not unlike the California gold rush of 1849 when prospectors lost everything, pickings in the Internet gold rush so far have been extremely limited. Most commercial Web sites—they number in the thousands—generate no revenue and cost upwards of $500,000 a year to maintain and operate. Losses by major corporations are so widespread that Don Logan, CEO of Time Warner, declared publicly that the Time Warner Web site, "Pathfinder," gave a "new definition to the term black hole." Although historically every gold rush has been a net loss, there have always been the successful few who buck the trend and garner extraordinary rewards. This case explores the efforts of one such entrepreneur, Jeffrey Bezos, and his online bookstore—Amazon.com—on the World Wide Web.

2   Amazon.com provides a singular case in which the frequently hyped World Wide Web is actually changing how consumers buy products and services. Not content to just transplant the traditional book retailing format to the World Wide Web, Jeff Bezos, the founder behind Amazon.com, is attempting to transform it through technology that taps the interactive nature of the Internet. At Amazon.com like-minded bibliophiles can meet, discuss books, swap raves and pans, and, most importantly, spend money. Over the past two years, Bezos has quietly built a fast-growing business. His Web site (http://www.amazon.com) has become an underground sensation for thousands of book lovers around the world who spend hours perusing its vast electronic library, reading other customers' amusing online reviews, and ordering books. This case describes how Bezos has managed to build a rapidly growing business on the Internet and the challenges he currently faces as other firms attempt to imitate his model of competition.

COMPANY BACKGROUND

3   In 1994, Jeffrey Bezos, a computer science and electrical engineering graduate from Princeton University, was the youngest senior vice president in the history of D. E. Shaw, a Wall Street-based investment bank. During the summer of that year, one statistic about the Internet caught his imagination—Internet usage was growing at 2,300 percent a year. His reaction: "Anything that's growing that fast is going to be ubiquitous very quickly. It was my wake-up call."

4   He left his job, drew up a list of 20 possible products that could be sold on the Internet, and quickly narrowed the prospects to music and books. Both had a potential advantage for online sale: far too many titles for a single store to stock. He chose books.

There are so many of them! There are 1.5 million English-language books in print, 3 million books in all languages worldwide. This volume defined the opportunity. Consumers keep

This case was prepared by Assistant Professor Suresh Kotha and Emer Dooley of the University of Washington, as the basis for class discussion rather than to illustrate either effective or ineffective handling of an administrative situation. Copyright © Kotha and Dooley. All rights reserved.

demonstrating that they value authoritative selection. The biggest phenomenon in retailing is the big-format store—the "category killer"—whether it's selling books, toys, or music. But the largest physical bookstore in the world has only 175,000 titles. . . . With some 4,200 U.S. publishers and the two biggest booksellers, Barnes & Noble and Borders Group Inc., accounting for less than 12 percent of total sales, there aren't any 800-pound gorillas in book selling.[1]

5   In contrast the music industry had only six major record companies. Because these companies controlled the distribution of records and CDs, they had the potential to lock out a new business threatening the traditional record store format.

6   To start his new venture, Bezos left New York City to move west, either to Boulder, Seattle, or Portland. As he drove west, he refined and fine-tuned his thoughts and his business plan. In doing so, he concluded that Seattle was his final destination. Recalls Bezos:

> It sounds counterintuitive, but physical location is very important for the success of a virtual business. We could have started Amazon.com anywhere. We chose Seattle because it met a rigorous set of criteria. It had to be a place with lots of technical talent. It had to be near a place with large numbers of books. It had to be a nice place to live—great people won't work in places they don't want to live. Finally, it had to be in a small state. In the mail-order business, you have to charge sales tax to customers who live in any state where you have a business presence. It made no sense for us to be in California or New York. . . . Obviously Seattle has a great programming culture. And it's close to Roseburg, Oregon, which has one of the biggest book warehouses in the world.[2]

7   Renting a house in Bellevue, a Seattle suburb, Bezos started work out of his garage. Ironically, he held meetings with prospective employees and suppliers at a nearby Barnes & Noble superstore. He also raised several million dollars from private investors. Operating from a 400-square-foot office in Bellevue, he launched his venture, Amazon.com, on the Internet in July 1995.

8   At first Bezo was concerned that sales would be so slow he wouldn't be able to meet the 10-book minimum that distributors require. Improvising, he combed through a big distributor's catalog and found a book entry he suspected wasn't actually available—an obscure publication about lichen (a thallophytic plant). His plan was simple: if the firm needed three books, it would pad the order with seven copies of the lichen book.

9   As it happened this plan wasn't necessary, as word about the new venture spread quickly across the Internet and sales picked up rapidly. Six weeks after opening, Jeff moved his new firm to a 2,000-square-foot warehouse. Six months later, he moved once again to a 17,000-square-foot building in an industrial neighborhood in Seattle. Estimates for the first year of operations indicate that Amazon.com revenues were about $5 million. These revenues are comparable to a large Barnes & Noble superstore.

THE BOOK PUBLISHING INDUSTRY

10   The United States is the world's largest market for books, with retail sales accounting for about $25.5 billion in 1995. Book publishing traditionally has been one of the oldest and most fragmented industries in the United States, with over 2,500 publishers.[3] Exhibit 1 shows the structure of the U.S. publishing industry.

Publishers

11   Books are sold on a consignment basis, and publishers assume all the risk. They accept returns on unsold books guaranteeing their distributors a 100 percent refund. They provide money and contracts to prospective authors and decide how many copies of the book to print. Typically a "first-run" print for a book can vary from 5,000 to 50,000 copies. However, best-selling authors' first-run prints are generally set at around 300,000 copies.

12   In practice, trade and paperback publishers print far more copies than will be sold. About 25 percent of all books distributed to wholesalers are returned and at times these percentages run as high as

EXHIBIT 1
Book Publishing Market Structure

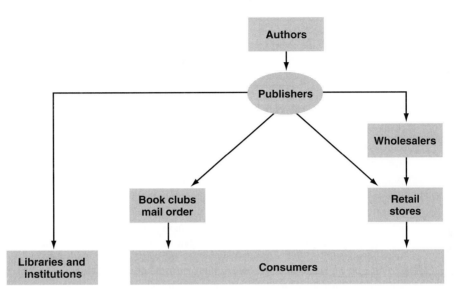

40 percent for mass-market paperbacks. According to industry experts, 20–30 percent for hardcover books returns is considered acceptable, 30–50 percent is considered high, and anything above 50 percent is considered disastrous. Publishers drastically reduce the price after a certain period in a process known as *remaindering* (offering books to discount stores, jobbers, and other vendors). Apart from the material cost of returns and the lost revenue they represent, the industry spends million of dollars each year transporting books back and forth. Profit margins in publishing are driven by book volume, which in turn hinges on the size of each print run. Book publishers generally depend on 10 percent of titles for profit, with 90 percent barely breaking even.[4]

13   The "big three"—Warner Books, Simon & Schuster, and Pearson—accounted for 21 percent of sales. The 20 largest book publishing companies in the United States commanded over 60 percent of all retail sales. Warner Books, a subsidiary of Time Warner, the U.S. entertainment giant, was the largest publisher, with sales of $3.7 billion in 1995. Simon & Schuster, a division of Viacom Corporation, ranked second with sales reaching $2.17 billion. These two leaders are followed by Pearson, a group that owns the *Financial Times,* which recorded sales revenues of $1.75 billion. Exhibit 2 illustrates the margins on a typical hard-cover book.

Wholesalers

14   Books are distributed by wholesalers. Wholesalers take orders from independent booksellers and chains and consolidate them into lot-orders for publishers. Publishers supply wholesalers who in turn supply the thousands of retail bookstores located throughout the country. According to industry estimates, in 1996 wholesalers accounted for almost 30 percent of publishers' sales. Unlike publishing and retailing, wholesalers are highly concentrated with firms such as Ingram Book Co. commanding the major share (50 percent in 1995) of the market. Competition revolves around the speed of delivery and the number of titles stocked. Ingram, for instance, receives more than 70 percent of its orders electronically and offers one-day delivery to about 82 percent of its U.S. customers. In 1994, the average net profit for wholesalers was less than 1.5 percent. This figure was down from the traditional margins of about 2 percent a few years earlier.[5]

15   Technological advances have made warehouse operations more efficient and this in turn has made it possible for wholesalers to provide attractive discounts to retailers. Also, the types of books

EXHIBIT 2
Profit Margins for a "Typical" Book

Book List Price	**$19.95**	
Revenue to publisher (i.e., price paid by wholesaler or bookstore)	$10.37	48% discount off suggested retail price
Manufacturing cost	$ 2.00	Printing, binding, jacket design, composition, typesetting, paper, ink
Publisher overhead	$ 3.00	Marketing, fulfillment
Returns and allowances	$ 3.00	
Author's royalties	$ 2.00	
Total publishing costs	$10.00	
Publisher's operating profit	$ 0.37	Returns amount for 3.7%

wholesalers are supplying to retailers are changing. Increasingly, bookstores are relying on whole-salers for fast-selling titles and less-popular backlist books.[6] However, with the emergence of super-stores, the large retailers, such as Barnes & Noble and Borders Books & Music, are no longer using wholesalers for initial orders of major titles. In 1994, for example, Borders Books & Music bought more than 95 percent of its titles directly from publishers.

Retail Bookstores

16   Retail bookstores, independents, and general retailers accounted for 35 to 40 percent of industry revenues (Exhibit 3). Also 1995 marked the first year in which bookstore chains sold more books than independents.[7] From 1975 to 1995, the number of bookstores in the United States increased from 11,990 to 17,340, and these bookstores accounted for about 21 percent of the total retail book sales. The superstores, the new Goliaths of retailing, such as Barnes & Noble and Borders Books & Music accounted for about 15 percent of all retail sales. Estimates suggest that from 1992 through 1995, superstore bookstore sales grew at a compounded rate of 71 percent while nonsuperstore sales grew at a rate of 4 percent. According to Rick Vanzura of Borders Books & Music: "When one of our super-stores opens up near one of our mall stores, the mall store tends to lose 10 to 15 percent of its sales. But the superstore is doing a lot more business—say, seven times—what the mall store was doing."

17   Experts cautioned that in smaller markets a shakeout was inevitable.[8] Mr. Vlahos, a spokesman for the American Booksellers Association, noted:

> In the three years from 1993 to 1995, 150 to 200 independent-owned bookstores went out of business—50 to 60 in 1996 alone. . . . By contrast in the same period, approximately 450 retail superstore outlets opened, led by Barnes & Noble and the Borders Group, with 348 openings.[9]

18   Independent booksellers believe the growth of superstores may be reaching the saturation point. However, notes Leonard Riggio, the chairman of Barnes & Noble: "We are so far from reaching the saturation point [because] we are in the midst of one of the biggest rollouts in the history of retail." But even as Barnes & Noble and Borders entered city after city, as many as 142 U.S. metropolitan markets still did not have a book superstore. According to Amy Ryan, a Prudential Securities analyst, the current rate of expansion could continue at least through the year 2000. In her opinion, this is because the United States could support about 1,500 such large stores.[10]

Institutions and Libraries

19   There are more than 29,000 private, public, and academic libraries in the United States.[11] Because of its stability and size, this market is crucial to publishers. Because libraries order only what they want,

EXHIBIT 3
Book Sales in 1994 by Various Distribution Channels

Channel	% of Total Sales
Bookstore chains, independents, and general retailers	35–40%
Mail order and book clubs	21
Sales to college bookstores	17
Schools	15
Libraries and other institutions	10

this lowers the overhead costs associated with inventory and return processing, making this market a relatively profitable one for publishers. Moreover, as hardcover trade books have become relatively inexpensive, many readers are borrowing them from libraries rather than purchasing them outright. Industry experts observed that about 95 percent of general titles published in any year sold less than 20,000 copies; of that amount, about 55 percent is purchased by libraries. Libraries also frequently repurchase titles to replace worn-out and stolen books. By doing so, they kept the backlist sales healthy.

Mail Order and Book Clubs

20   The year 1995 witnessed a significant drop in the mail-order book business. This drop in sales was attributed to the growth of large discount-sale retailers. Publishers' book club sales, on the other hand, rose steadily, gaining 9 percent in 1994 and in early 1995. The strong growth in this segment was attributed to the increasing popularity of specialized book clubs which focused on favorite baby-boomer interests such as gardening and computers.

21   The industry sells a variety of books which include: trade, professional, mass market, El-Hi (elementary-high school) and college textbooks, and others. Each of these categories varied in terms of sales, competition, profitability, and volatility (see Exhibits 4 and 5).

22   A survey commissioned by the American Booksellers Association found that some 106 million adults purchased about 456.9 million books in any given quarter. The survey, which looked at book-buying habits of consumers during the calendar year 1994, revealed that 6 in 10 American adults (60 percent) say they purchased at least one book in the last three months. Annually, that corresponds to 1.8 billion books sold, an average of 17 books per book-buying consumer a year. The average amount paid for the three most recent books purchased by consumers in the past 30 days was about $15.

Emergence of "Virtual" Bookstores

23   The two hardest challenges for book selling—physically distributing the right numbers of books to bookstores and getting the word about serious books out to potential readers—are getting a more than trivial assist from the new online technologies.

24   The rapid growth of Internet businesses was spreading to book publishing. According to Larry Daniels, director of information technologies for the National Association of College Stores:

> Booksellers' concern revolves around the potential for publishers to deal directly with consumers and the media on the Internet. . . . The phenomenon could mean the elimination of middlemen such as bookstores.[12]

Moreover, Daniels notes that there is also the potential for publishers to be "disintermediated," because computer-literate writers can now publish and distribute their own works online.

EXHIBIT 4
The Various Product Categories

Trade Books

This segment includes general interest hardcover and paperback books sold to adults and juveniles. Trade books accounted for almost 30 percent of publishers' revenues in 1994. According to an industry group, books sold to adults increased by more than 30 percent between 1991 and 1995. Juvenile book sales, which showed a double-digit growth rate in the late 1980s and early 1990s, however, were much slower at 1.1 percent in 1994. This slow growth was attributed to a decline in the number of popular titles and increased spending by children on toys and games.

In 1995, Random House, Inc., Bantam Doubleday Dell, Simon & Schuster, HarperCollins, and Penguin were some of the leading firms that competed in this product category.

Professional Books

Over 165 million professional books were sold in 1995 accounting for $3.9 billion. Since 1991, professional book sales have grown at a compounded annual rate of 3.0 percent (in units). Legal publishing was the largest segment of the professional books category, with the scientific and technical category in second place. The long-term outlook for this category was good because employment in the medical, legal, scientific, and business professions was expected to grow significantly.

Thomson Corp. was the largest professional books publisher with sales of $1.99 billion. Professional book revenues comprised 3 percent of Thomson's total revenues. Reed Elsevier ranked second with 1994 sales of $1.63 billion and was followed by Wolters Kluwer and Times Mirror with $1.07 billion and $775 million in sales, respectively.

Mass-Market Books

These books are sold primarily through magazine wholesalers and outlets such as newsstands and drugstores. This category includes best-sellers that have shelf lives of about three to six weeks. Although the cost of acquiring the paperback rights to a best-selling hardcover title can cost millions of dollars, the per-unit fixed costs for printing are small because print runs were as large as 500,000. However, when return rates that typically exceed 40 percent are factored in, profit margins are typically less than 12 percent.

The largest mass-market publishers are Random House, Inc., Bantam Doubleday Dell, Simon & Schuster, and HarperCollins.

El-Hi Textbooks

El-Hi or Elementary-High school books accounted for 30 percent of all books sold in 1994. The El-Hi market is driven by state adoption and enrollment levels and the books are sold to school systems on a contract basis. The development of materials for schools is a capital-intensive process that typically takes up to five years for most new programs. Per pupil expenditures as well as the number of students are expected to grow through the year 2000. This implied moderately strong annual growth (about 3 to 4 percent) for El-Hi textbooks through the remainder of the decade.

The big publishers are owned by media conglomerates such as News Corp., Times Mirror, and Paramount. The largest El-Hi publisher is McGraw-Hill, followed by Paramount (the parent company of Prentice Hall and Silver Burdett), Harcourt Brace, and Houghton Mifflin.

College Textbooks

College publishing is the most profitable category. The cost of producing a college text is lower than in the El-Hi market because the texts are typically prepared by university faculty members and used individually. However, the unit sales tend to be small and used textbook sales generally accounted for 20 to 40 percent of total sales. The U.S. Department of Education was forecasting a decline in college enrollments for 1996, and slow growth thereafter. College textbook sales that grew by 4.4 percent in 1995 to 155 million books were expected to decline in the future.

Prentice Hall (owned by Viacom) is the largest college publisher, followed by HB College (owned by Harcourt General), International Thomson, McGraw-Hill, and Irwin (a division of Times Mirror).

25   However, the leading publishing houses are skeptical of electronic book-publishing capabilities and remain uncertain about the Internet's future in the sale of physical books. Despite such skepticism, selling online was a fast-growing phenomenon. A plethora of bookstores are selling books on the Internet. Companies such as Amazon.com, Bookserver, Book Stacks Unlimited, Cbooks Express, Pandora's, and the Internet Bookstore are growing at the self-reported rates of 20 to 35 percent a month. Of the $518 million expected to be sold online in 1996 on the Internet, book sales are a small segment relegated to the "other" category. Total book sales online accounted for less than 1 percent of overall book sales. However, because the amount of money Americans spend on books is projected to reach $31 billion by 2000, selling online is expected to grow further.

EXHIBIT 5
Sales and Profit Margins by Product Category

Product Category	1993 ($m)	1994 ($m)	Profit Margins in 1993, %
Trade books			
Hardcover books for adults	1,069.0	1,187.0	0.6%
Paperback books for adults	586.4	674.5	13.7
Books for juveniles	431.6	439.9	7.7
Bibles, hymnals, and prayer books	45.6	54.7	12.4
Mass-market paperbacks	998.7	1,202.8	3.1
Business, medical, scientific, and technical	813.5	891.6	8.0
El-Hi textbooks and materials	1,977.8	1,836.8	14.9
College textbooks and materials	1,586.7	1,611.3	15.8

Source: *Standard and Poor Industry Surveys,* July 20, 1995.

COMPETING ON THE WORLD WIDE WEB

A Virtual Bookstore

26   Unlike traditional bookstores, there are no bookshelves to browse at Amazon.com. All contact with the company is done either through its Web page (at http://www.amazon.com) or by e-mail. At the firm's Web site, customers can search for a specific book, topic, or author, or they can browse their way through a book catalog featuring 40 subjects. Visitors can also read book reviews from other customers, *The New York Times, Atlantic Monthly,* and Amazon.com's staff. Customers can browse, fill up a virtual shopping basket, and then complete the sale by entering their credit card information or by placing their order online and then phoning in their credit card information.[13] Customer orders are processed immediately. Books in stock (mostly bestsellers) are packaged and mailed the same day. When their order has been shipped, customers are notified immediately by e-mail. Orders for non-bestsellers are placed immediately with the appropriate book publisher by Amazon.com.

27   Shunning the elaborate graphics that clutter so many Web sites, Amazon.com instead loads up its customers with information (see Exhibit 6). For many featured books, it offers capsule descriptions, snippets of reviews, and "self-administered" interviews posted by authors. More importantly, the firm has found a way to use the technology to offer services that a traditional store or catalog can't match. Notes Bezos:

> An Amazon customer can romp through a database of 1.1 million titles (five times the largest superstore's inventory), searching by subject or name. When you select a book, Amazon is programmed to flash other related titles you may also want to buy. If you tell Amazon about favorite authors and topics, it will send you by electronic mail a constant stream of recommendations. You want to know when a book comes out in paperback? Amazon will e-mail that too.[14]

28   Additionally, the firm offers space for readers to post their own reviews and then steps out of the way and lets its customers sell to each other. For example, recently a book called *Sponging: A Guide to Living Off Those You Love* drew a chorus of online raves from customers, one of whom remarked: "This gem is crazy! Flat Out. Hysterical. You'll have a good laugh, but wait! Let me let you in on a lil' secret—it's useful!" This book swiftly made it onto Amazon.com's own best-seller list. Notes Bezos:

> We are trying to make the shopping experience just as fun as going to the bookstore, but there's some things we can't do. I'm not interested in retrofitting the physical bookstore experience in the virtual world. Every few weeks, someone around here asks, 'When are we going to do electronic

EXHIBIT 6
Amazon.com's Web Site as of October 1996

book signings?' We still haven't done them. The experience of book signings works best in the real world.[15]

But he is fast to add:

There are so many things we can do online that can't be done in the real world. We want customers who enter Amazon.com to indicate whether they want to be "visible" or "invisible." If they choose to be "visible," then when they're in the science fiction section, other people will know they're there. People can ask for recommendations—"Read any good books lately?"—or recommend books to others. I'm an outgoing person, but I'd never go into a bookstore and ask a complete stranger to recommend a book. The semi-anonymity of the online environment makes people less inhibited.[16]

29   When asked why people come to the site, Bezos responds:

Bill Gates laid it out in a magazine interview. He said, "I buy all my books at Amazon.com because I'm busy and it's convenient. They have a big selection, and they've been reliable." Those are three of our four core value propositions: convenience, selection, service. The only one he left out is price: we are the broadest discounters in the world in any product category. . . . These value propositions are interrelated, and they all relate to the Web.[17]

At Amazon.com all books are discounted. Bestsellers are sold at a 30 percent discount and the other books at a 10 percent discount. Notes Bezos:

We discount because we have a lower cost structure than physical stores do. We turn our inventory 150 times a year. That's like selling bread in a supermarket. Physical bookstores turn their inventory only 3 or 4 times a year.[18]

30   The firm's small warehouse is used only to stock bestsellers and to consolidate and repack customer orders. Moreover, only after the firm receives a paid customer order does it ask the appropriate publisher to ship the book to Amazon.com. The firm then ships the book to the customer. The firm owns no expensive retail real estate and its operations are largely automated.

31   Industry observers note that although Amazon.com discounts most books, it levies a $3 service charge per order, plus 95 cents per book. And it can take Amazon a week to deliver a book that isn't a bestseller, and even longer for the most esoteric titles. Also, some people don't like providing their credit card number over the Internet.

Virtual Customer Service

32   According to the firm, about 44 percent of the book orders come from repeat customers.[19] To maintain customer interest in Amazon.com, the firm offers two forms of e-mail-based service to its registered customers. "Eyes" is a personal notification service in which customers can register their interests in a particular author or topic. Once registered, they are notified each time a new book by their favorite author or topic is published. "Editor's service" provides editorial comments about featured books via e-mail. Three full-time editors read book reviews, pore over customer orders, and survey current events to select the featured books. These and other freelance editors employed by the firm provide registered users with e-mail updates on the latest and greatest books they've been reading. These services are automated and are available free of charge.

33   According to Bezos, such services are vital for success on the Internet:

Customer service is a critical success factor in any retail business. But it's absolutely make-or-break online. If you make customers unhappy in the physical world, they might each tell 6 friends. If you make customers unhappy on the Internet, they can each tell 6,000 friends with one message to a newsgroup. If you make them really happy, they can tell 6,000 people about that. You want every customer to become an evangelist for you.[20]

34   Additionally, the firm's employees compile a weekly list of the 20 most obscure titles on order, and Bezos awards a prize for the most amusing. Recent entries include: *Training Goldfish Using*

Dolphin Training Techniques, How to Start Your Own Country, and *Life Without Friends.* Amazon.com drums up all these orders through a mix of state-of-the-art software and old-fashioned salesmanship.

Associates Program

35 According to Leslie Koch, vice president of marketing at Amazon.com, the firm is currently growing at the rate of 20–30 percent a month. Part of the reason for this rapid growth is the firm's Associates Program. The program was designed to increase traffic to Amazon.com by creating a referral service from other Web sites to Amazon.com's 1.1 million book catalog. An associates Web site, such as Starchefs—which features cookbook authors—recommends books and makes a link from its Web page to Amazon's catalog page for the books. The associated Web site then earns referral fees for sales generated by these links. Partners receive quarterly referral fee statements and a check for the referral fees earned in that quarter. More than 1,800 sites have already signed up under this program and earn a commission of 8 percent of the value of books bought by the referred customer. Notes Bezos, "[The] Web technology has made it possible to set up microfranchises, and with zero overhead."[21]

Operating Philosophy

36 Unlike traditional bookstores, there are no salespeople at Amazon.com. Moreover, the firm is open for business 24 hours a day and has a global presence. Customers from 66 countries have purchased books from the firm. This list includes Bosnia, where more than 25 U.S. soldiers have placed orders. The firm is devoid of expensive furnishings, and money is spent sparingly. Notes Bezos:

> We made the first four desks we have here ourselves—all our desks are made out of doors and four-by-fours. . . . My monitor stand is a bunch of old phone books. We spend money on the things that matter to our customers and we don't spend money on anything else.[22]

37 According to Leslie Koch, although the firm advertises in print, it spends a substantial amount on Web advertising. According to Jupiter Communications, the firm spent over $340,000 for the first half of 1996 and ranked 34th in Web ad spending. Because Amazon.com is an Internet-only retailer, Web advertising gives it a unique opportunity to track the success of an ad by the number of click-throughs to the store's Web site and the number of Internet surfers who actually purchase something. Industry analysts estimate that between 2 and 3 percent of people who see an ad on the Web will actually click through to see more. Advertising is done mainly in the large-circulation newspapers such as *The Wall Street Journal, The New York Times,* and *San Jose Mercury News,* and on Internet search-engine sites such as Yahoo! and Lycos, the Microsoft Network, and Microsoft's *Slate* magazine. Amazon.com keeps its banner ads simple, with just a few words and a Web address.[23] Recently, the firm has started advertising on CNN.

38 The decision to locate Amazon.com in Seattle appears to be paying off. The firm has been able to attract some Microsoft veterans; for instance, Leslie Koch is a six-year Microsoft veteran. The firm's business development manager, Scott Lipsky, is also from Microsoft, and so is the advertising manager, Jodie de Lyon. See Exhibit 7 for an illustration of how the firm is organized and a brief description of the firm's management.

39 Amazon had 110 employees in October 1996. Of these, 14 employees manage customer support and seven employees attend to marketing. In addition, a few employees manage "content" on the firm's Web site, including such tasks as Web page updating and formatting book reviews for display. The vast majority of the remaining employees work on developing software tools for operating on the Internet. According to Julia King, an executive assistant in marketing, "This is a very driven place. Hours are typically 8 to 8 and many people work weekends. Jeff spends every waking hour on this business." Bezos, for example, lives just a few minutes away, but keeps a sleeping bag in his office for all-nighters.

40 When asked to differentiate this firm from potential rivals, Bezos notes:

> People who just scratch the surface of Amazon.com say—"oh, you sell books on the Web,"—don't understand how hard it is to actually be an electronic merchant. We're not just putting up a

EXHIBIT 7
Amazon.com's Organizational Structure and Top Management

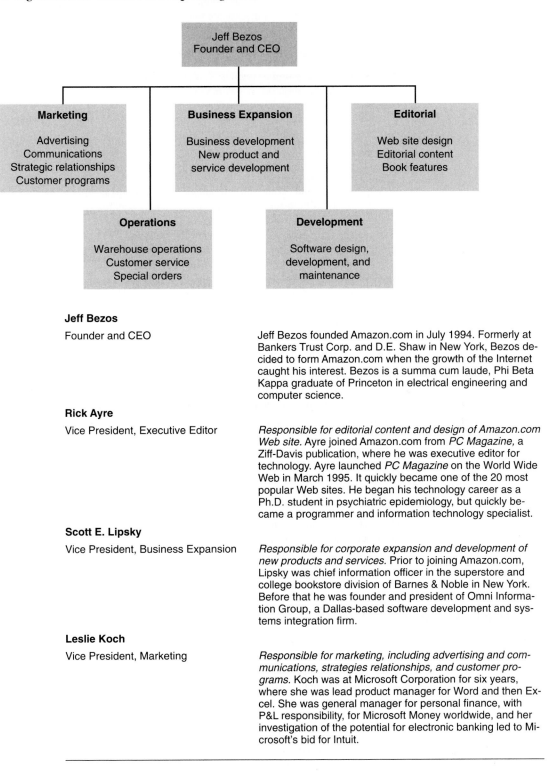

Jeff Bezos

Founder and CEO

Jeff Bezos founded Amazon.com in July 1994. Formerly at Bankers Trust Corp. and D.E. Shaw in New York, Bezos decided to form Amazon.com when the growth of the Internet caught his interest. Bezos is a summa cum laude, Phi Beta Kappa graduate of Princeton in electrical engineering and computer science.

Rick Ayre

Vice President, Executive Editor

Responsible for editorial content and design of Amazon.com Web site. Ayre joined Amazon.com from *PC Magazine,* a Ziff-Davis publication, where he was executive editor for technology. Ayre launched *PC Magazine* on the World Wide Web in March 1995. It quickly became one of the 20 most popular Web sites. He began his technology career as a Ph.D. student in psychiatric epidemiology, but quickly became a programmer and information technology specialist.

Scott E. Lipsky

Vice President, Business Expansion

Responsible for corporate expansion and development of new products and services. Prior to joining Amazon.com, Lipsky was chief information officer in the superstore and college bookstore division of Barnes & Noble in New York. Before that he was founder and president of Omni Information Group, a Dallas-based software development and systems integration firm.

Leslie Koch

Vice President, Marketing

Responsible for marketing, including advertising and communications, strategies relationships, and customer programs. Koch was at Microsoft Corporation for six years, where she was lead product manager for Word and then Excel. She was general manager for personal finance, with P&L responsibility, for Microsoft Money worldwide, and her investigation of the potential for electronic banking led to Microsoft's bid for Intuit.

Web site. We do 90 percent of our customer service by e-mail rather than by telephone. Fourteen of our 110 employees do nothing but answer e-mail from customers. There are very few off-the-shelf tools that help do what we're doing. We've had to develop lots of our own technologies. There are no companies selling software to manage e-mail centers. So we had to develop our own tools. In a way this is good news. There are lots of barriers to entry.[24]

41 In discussing the technical side of the business, Bezos explains:

We have the best programmers, the best servers in the world. We use 64-bit Digital Alpha servers with 500 megabytes of RAM. It's worked very well for us. All of the stuff that actually matters to our customers, we buy the very best.[25]

Explosive Growth

42 Since July 1995 Amazon has doubled in size every 2.4 months.[26] By August 1996, sales were growing at 34 percent a month. Although estimates vary, the company's gross revenue is expected to be around $17 to $19 million for 1996. When the company was founded in 1995, the plan was to be profitable in five years. As of October 1996 the firm claims to have exceeded expectations and has made its business plan more aggressive. According to Bezos: "We're not focused on trying to make the company profitable. If we're profitable any time in the short term, it'll just be an accident."[27]

43 Regardless of the firm's profitability, interest in the new venture remains strong. The firm recently attracted $8 million from Kleiner, Perkins, Caufield & Byers, a venture-capital firm based in Silicon Valley that has funded firms such as Sun Microsystems and Netscape.

44 Bezos is focused on expanding Amazon.com: "In the year 2000, our goal is to be one of the world's leading bookstores. Since the world's leading bookstores are billion-dollar companies, people impute that [this figure is our target]."[28] But he quickly dismisses fears that his firm could ever spell the end of traditional bookstores.

Amazon.com is not going to put bookstores out of business. Barnes & Noble is opening a new superstore every four days. Borders is opening a new superstore every nine days. . . . I still buy half of my books at bookstores. Sometimes I want the book right now, not tomorrow. Sometimes I just like to get out of the office and go to a nice environment. What you're going to see—and it's happening already—is that physical bookstores will become ever-nicer places to be. They are going to have more sofas, better lattes, nicer people working there. Good bookstores are the community centers of the late 20th century. That's the basis on which they're going to compete. There is plenty of room for everyone.[29]

Adds Leslie Koch:

Book sales are stagnating, but we believe we're expanding the market for books. With this new way of selling books on the Web we can expose people to far more books than before. People buy books from us that they won't find in bookstores. And we're growing rapidly in this stagnant market.

CHALLENGES FACING AMAZON.COM

45 Bezos acknowledges that many strategic challenges remain. In particular, two challenges demand his immediate attention. His first concern is to find innovative ways to fruitfully use the massive database his firm has been accumulating about his customers without alienating them. The second more threatening development is the emerging copycat ventures offering books on the Internet.

The "Massive" Database

46 For the past year, Amazon.com has been building a detailed purchasing history and profile of its customers. Notes Alberto Vitale, chairman of Random House, Inc.: "Amazon is creating a database that

EXHIBIT 8
Amazon.com's Customer Bill of Rights

Amazon Bill of Rights claims that as a customer there is:

1. **No obligation.** Eyes & Editors Personal Notification Services are provided free of charge, and you are under no obligation to buy anything.

2. **Unsubscribing.** You can unsubscribe or change your subscriptions at any time.

3. **Privacy.** We do not sell or rent information about our customers. If you would like to make sure we never sell or rent information about you to third parties, just send a blank e-mail message to never@amazon.com.

doesn't exist anywhere else. Book publishers have never had much market data about readers, and some are already salivating for a peek into Amazon's files."[30] Yet customers who buy books from Amazon are assured of privacy by the Amazon Bill of Rights (see Exhibit 8).

47   Bezos is concerned that his customers might be outraged if he turns over this information to other marketers. To him the Web is the ultimate word-of-mouth medium. Still he is considering whether a plan to let publishers offer hand-picked Amazon customers books at discounted prices before their publication date should be implemented.

The Emerging Competition

48   More than half of the Internet's computers reside in the United States, with the rest spread out among connected networks in 100 other countries. Estimates of the number of Internet users (and more importantly the number of potential users) vary widely (see Exhibit 9). The number of businesses joining the Internet has risen dramatically over the past year, and growth hasn't been limited to large corporations (see Exhibit 10 for some leading sites on the Internet). From July 1994 to July 1995, the number of hosts on the Internet rose from 3.2 million to 6.6 million. By the end of the decade, 120 million machines are expected to be linked to the Internet.[31]

49   Every day approximately 150 new businesses come onto the Net, and their total number is estimated to be about 40,000. Most of these companies use the Web as a public relations tool to promote their products and services.[32] More than 35 million Americans now use the Internet—9 million of whom joined just this year. From a commercial perspective, the demographics of Internet and World Wide Web users makes them part of an extremely attractive market segment. The average age of computer users is 39, while the average age of a typical Internet user is 32. About 1 in 10 Internet users (more than 3 million) is under 18 and uses the Internet from home or school. About 64 percent of the Internet users have at least a college degree with a median household income of $60,000.[33]

50   The global Internet market is expected to soar to $23 billion by 2000 (Exhibit 11). Estimates for 1996 indicate that the World Wide Web has attracted more than 100,000 retailers, with some spending more than $1 million each on eye-popping sites. Yet, worldwide retail sales on the Web amounted to only $324 million last year, which averages out to slightly more than $3,000 in sales per retailer.[34] In 1996 about 2.7 million people used the Internet for shopping or to obtain commercial services such as banking or travel information.

51   Recent forecasts suggest that while Internet merchants will sell about $518 million in goods in 1996, online retailing revenues are likely to grow to about $6.6 billion by the end of this century.[35] Notes Bezos:

> We're by far the largest bookseller out there in terms of the number of titles we offer for sale and the services we provide. We are, for all intents and purposes, competing against a vacuum right now. That's not going to last.[36]

52   Bezos's concerns about potential competition are not farfetched. During mid-1996, we witnessed a plethora of virtual bookstores sprouting on the Internet. Exhibit 12 provides a partial list of virtual bookstores on the Internet. Not surprisingly, many of these new virtual bookstores are modeled after Amazon.com. For example, Bookserver was founded with a mere $20,000 by brothers David (26)

EXHIBIT 9
Varying Estimates of Internet Users in 1996

Source	Date	Definition	Users (millions)
Intelliquest	July 1996	U.S. Internet users	35.0
Louis Harris	May 1996	U.S. Internet users	29.0
International Data Corp.	May 1996	WWW surfers	23.5
Computer Intelligence	May 1996	Year-end 1995 (U.S. Internet users)	15.0
Hoffman/Novak	April 1996	U.S. Internet users	16.4
Wall Street Journal	March 1996	North American home/office users	17.6
Morgan Stanley	February 1996	1995 Net/Web users	9.0
Matrix	February 1996	1995 Worldwide Internet users	26.4
Find/SVP	January 1996	U.S. users who use any Internet service except e-mail	9.5

Source: *CyberAtlas,* August 1996.

and Michael (23) Mason and originally operated from their family garage. This firm claims to offer more than a million book titles. Additionally, the firm specializes in finding books for customers. Books are offered in English, German, Dutch, and Spanish at discounts similar to Amazon.com and at half the shipping fees charged by Amazon.com. According to David, the store's sales have increased steadily by about 20 percent a month since founding. This growth has enabled the firm to shift operations from the family garage to a strip mall in Lavergne, Tennessee. Bezos was also concerned about the prospect of new competition from some of high-tech and retailing's mightiest players: a new joint venture between Wal-Mart Stores Inc. and Microsoft Corp., Amazon.com's neighbor in nearby Redmond, Washington.

53   Elliot Bay Books, a Seattle-based independent bookstore, had set up a Web site to establish an Internet presence. Further, a report in the *Seattle Times* indicated that both Barnes & Noble and Borders, the giants in the industry, expect to offer online services in 1997.[37]

54   In response Bezos is considering novel ways to attract new customers and, at the same time, maintain his existing customer base. One of the options under consideration is to customize offerings for each customer. Describes Bezos:

> We want to "redecorate the store" for every customer. We can let people describe their preferences, analyze their past buying patterns, and create a home page specifically for them. If you're a big mystery reader, we can show you the three hottest new mystery novels and highlight one from an author you've bought before. These interactive features are going to be incredibly powerful. And you can't reproduce them in the physical world.[38]

Yet, he is concerned and is searching for ways in which Amazon.com can stay ahead of this emerging competition. Although sales are increasing, he sees this as a continuing challenge:

> Our customers are loyal right up to the point somebody offers them a better service. That's the dimension on which we compete. The goal of Amazon.com has to be to make sure that we are the preeminent brand name associated with online bookselling in the year 2000. I think we have a huge opportunity to build an interactive retailing company beyond books.[39]

55   Paul Hilts, technology editor of *Publishers Weekly,* remains guarded:

> It remains to be seen whether online bookselling will completely transform the industry. Their [Amazon.com] timing was exquisite, and they promoted the heck out of it. Everyone will have their eyes on them to see how it goes.[40]

EXHIBIT 10
Leading Sites on World Wide Web

In a June 1996 survey of 1,100 Web-based businesses, 31 percent claimed to be profitable and 28 percent said that they would be profitable in the next 12 to 24 months. Here are a few of the most prominent Web success stories:

- **Auto-by-Tel.** Founder Peter Ellis claims his car-buying service will turn a profit on $6.5 million in revenue this year.

- **CDnow.** Started in the basement of their parents' home, Jason and Matthew Olim expect to reach $6 million in sales in 1996, triple last year's revenue, while maintaining an 18 percent operating margin.

- **Netscape.** Netscape already sells $1.5 million worth of its products over the Net each month.

- **ONSALE.** This auction house, founded by Jerry Kaplan (of Go fame), is on a $45 million annual run rate.

Source: *ActivMedia*, May 1996, and *Business Week*, 1996.

NOTES

1. "Who's writing the book on web business?" *Fast Company*, October–November, 1996, pp. 132–133.
2. *Fast Company*, October–November, 1996.
3. U.S. Bureau of the Census, 1992.
4. "World book market 'faces further consolidation,' " *Financial Times*, October 2, 1996, p. 16.
5. *Publishers Weekly*, January 1, 1996.
6. Although the best-selling books get the bulk of the attention and marketing dollars, "backlist" books are considered the "bread and butter" of the industry. A backlist is the publishing company's catalog of books that have already appeared in print. Estimates indicated that as much as 25 to 30 percent of a publisher's revenues come from this source. Backlisted books have predictable sales with occasional bumps, such as when a subject matter loses favor with the consumers or when an author dies. Since these books require no editing and little promotion, they are generally profitable. Moreover, print runs are easier to predict, resulting in fewer returns to publishers.
7. *Philadelphia Business Journal*, September 27, 1996.
8. *Publishers Weekly*, March 11, 1996. Superstores, originally confined to big metropolitan areas, were increasingly entering markets with populations of 150,000 or less. Industry estimates indicated that superstores had to make around $200 a square foot to turn a profit. A typical Barnes & Noble superstore needed, for example, $3 to $4 million in sales revenues to break even. Some industry observers questioned whether such cities can support one or more of these mammoth stores and whether superstores in these locations could sell enough books to turn a profit.
9. "A Nonchain Bookstore Bucks the Tide," *The New York Times*, September 8, 1996.
10. Compounding the competition from superstores, many independent booksellers claimed to be unfairly treated by publishers. They claimed that publishers offered bookstore chains better prices and greater promotional support than independents. In response, the American Booksellers Association (ABA) brought an antitrust suit against six publishers, five of which have been settled favorably out of court. The only remaining ABA suit was against Random House, Inc.
11. *Standard and Poors Industry Surveys*, July 20, 1995.
12. *The Christian Science Monitor*, September 18, 1996.
13. When the company first started, only 50 percent of the people were prepared to enter their credit card number on Amazon's Web page. The other half phoned it in. However, within a year this ratio has changed to 80:20.
14. *The Wall Street Journal*, Thursday, May 16, 1996.
15. *Fast Company*, October–November, 1996.
16. *Fast Company*, October–November, 1996.
17. *Fast Company*, October–November, 1996.
18. *Fast Company*, October–November, 1996.
19. "Booked up on the Net," *Seattle Times*, January 5, 1997.
20. *Fast Company*, October–November, 1996.

EXHIBIT 11
Internet Forecast by Market and Product Segments ($ Millions)

Forecast by Market Segment*				1995	2000
Network services (ISPs)				300	5,000
Hardware (routers, modems, computer hardware)				500	2,500
Software (server, applications)				300	4,000
Enabling services (electronic commerce, directory services, Web tracking)				20	1,000
Expertise (system integrators, business consultants)				50	700
Content and activity (online entertainment, information, shopping)				500	10,000
Total market				1,170	23,200

Forecast by Product Segment**	1996	1997	1998	1999	2000
Computer products	$140	$323	$701	$1,228	$2,105
Travel	126	276	572	961	1,579
Entertainment	85	194	420	733	1,250
Apparel	46	89	163	234	322
Gifts/flowers	45	103	222	386	658
Food/drink	39	78	149	227	336
Other	37	75	144	221	329
Total ($M)	518	1,138	2,371	3,990	6,579

*Source: Hambrecht & Quist, December 1995.
**Source: Forrester Research, Inc., May 1996.

21. "Amazon.com forges new sales channel," *Web Week,* August 19, 1996.
22. *Upside,* October 1996.
23. Web advertising is gaining increasing legitimacy. Revenue for advertising on the World Wide Web rose 83 percent to $46.4 million in the second quarter of 1996. The figure is expected to reach $312 million by the end of the year. This amount is still quite small in comparison to the $30 billion spent on television advertising each year.
24. *Fast Company,* October–November, 1996.
25. *Upside,* October 1996.
26. *Financial Times,* October 7, 1996.
27. *Upside,* October 1996.
28. *Upside,* October 1996.
29. *Fast Company,* October–November, 1996.
30. "Reading the market: How a Wall Street whiz found a niche selling books on the Internet," *The Wall Street Journal,* May 16, 1996.
31. Estimates provided by the *Internet Society,* 1996.
32. Statistics from *Internet World,* November 1995 and TDM Software and Consulting.
33. Nielsen Media Research, 1995.
34. Based on data from *International Data Corp. 1996.*
35. *Forrester Research Inc.,* May 1996.
36. *Upside,* October 1996.
37. *Seattle Times,* January 5, 1997.
38. *Fast Company,* October–November, 1996.
39. *Seattle Times,* January 5, 1997.
40. *Seattle Times,* January 5, 1997.

EXHIBIT 12
Partial List of Virtual Bookstores on Web in October 1996

- **Bookserver.** This firm was founded by brothers David and Michael Mason from the family garage in Tennessee. Since its founding, the firm has moved to a mall in Lavergne, Tennessee.
- **CBooks Express.** This Internet startup specializes in technical books and computer-related materials.
- **Pandora's Books Ltd.** This firm features out-of-print science fiction and fantasy books to read when Star Trek reruns can't be found.
- **The Internet Book Shop.** This firm claims that it is the biggest online bookstore in the world with over 912,000 titles. The firm lets you track your order online.
- **MacMillan Information Superlibrary.** This Web site is an attempt to pull together Macmillan's various print, reference, and electronic publishing efforts. Its bookstore, however, carries only 6,000 titles.
- **The Cosmic Web.** This is a nonprofit book center dedicated to circulating "words of inspiration and evolutionary answers that awaken souls to the infinitude of our experience as planetary beings."
- **Dial-A-Book.** This venture focuses on selling books in a downloadable format.
- **Moe's Books.** This firm specializes in used books. The firm searches 1,500 affiliated stores to bring you the used books you're looking for. Customers specify the condition they would like the book to arrive in.

CASE 49

THE US AIRLINE INDUSTRY

INTRODUCTION

1   The Airline Industry is characterized as an oligopoly, that is an industry being dominated by few firms producing similar products—Available Seat Miles (ASM). Prior to 1978, the airlines were highly regulated by the CAB (Civil Aeronautics Board). The CAB was able to dictate ticket prices, route authorities, and barriers to entry or exit. An anti-competitive industry was promoted for decades under the CAB, in which prices were adjusted to meet the rising operating costs of the airlines. Airlines became highly inefficient under regulation, and allowed costs and capacity to soar without regard to profitability. After numerous price increases during the early 1970's, the consumers demanded a more competitive industry—lower prices. Eventually the consumer won, and the Airline Deregulation Act was passed in 1978. This act was designed to promote competition among carriers by increasing efficiency and lowering costs, thus, airlines were forced to charge what the market would bear, not what CAB dictated. Many airlines have prospered, yet many others have failed, during deregulation.

INCREASED COMPETITION

2   Deregulation allowed existing carriers to enter and exit markets freely, charging prices according to demand. As predicted, deregulation spurred an increase in competition and lowered ticket prices on most routes. Airlines began competing in more route segments and exiting unprofitable markets, making room for regional carriers. New low-cost carriers focused on highly profitable niche markets serving point to point, O & D (Origin and Destination) traffic. In contrast, major airlines increased capacity on high demand markets and began establishing hub and spoke systems.

LOW COST CARRIERS

3   The first of the low-cost carriers to introduce a drastically reduced ticket price was People Express Airlines (PEX). As one of the first post-deregulation start-up airlines, it thrived in the east coast markets from its Newark hub—beginning operations in 1980. Operating a fleet of used narrow body aircraft (B727, B737) and employing non-union workers, PEX was able to achieve very low direct operating costs per ASM (available seat mile). PEX was able to operate at a cost per seat mile of less than 6 cents, 50% less than its competition (Delta, USAir). As a result PEX was able to offer its customers low $35 airfares and attract competing airline customers, while still earning a profit. The lucrative times for PEX however did not continue. Like most airline failure scripts, it over-expanded, attempting to expand into major airline territory and compete head-on with well-established airlines. It was competing with too many airlines in too many markets, and lost the battle. Eventually, PEX merged with failing Frontier airlines, in a flawed attempt to expand its market share westward. In actuality, this merger further weakened the carrier as both United and Continental lowered fares to compete in the western region. PEX was finally purchased in 1987 by Continental Airlines (Texas Air), and the Cinderella story had ended.

This case was prepared by Marc Brodbeck, Trans World Airlines, and Richard Robinson, University of South Carolina.

4 Some important lessons were learned from the PEX failure; Airline seats are commodities, and most customers will be attracted to the lowest priced seat. Customers search for the most value for the lowest price, as a result customer service is the key to return customers. Business travelers search for the most value, and are willing to pay a premium ticket price for this service. An airline must attract a sufficient amount of high yield business travelers to sustain a profit, balancing the low yield from discount tickets. The key lesson from PEX is that small niche carriers should not attempt to over-expand without adequate cash reserves—to sustain long fare wars with major carriers in certain markets.

5 Other more successful low-cost carriers also developed during this time, typically in the highly competitive west and southwest region of the US. Former intra-state carrier Southwest Airlines (SWA) began operations from a small hub at Dallas, Love Field. Using a common fleet of Boeing 737's, SWA served secondary markets and smaller downtown airports to attract customers. By using a "keep-it-simple" approach and catering towards the short-haul traveler, SWA was able to operate at very low costs and maintain profitability. Many airlines have attempted to copy the SWA formula, with marginal success.

SATELLITE AIRLINES

6 To combat the encroachment of low-cost airlines into their own market share, major airlines developed satellite airlines. The concept to create a low-cost no-frills airline is a preemptive move to sustain market share in highly competitive markets (Southwestern, Western US). This "airline-within-an-airline" concept was developed initially by Continental Airlines to combat the threat of low-cost airlines in major markets. What developed was CaLite, a low-cost subsidiary of Continental airlines. By using smaller aircraft (B-737, DC-9) and lower wage employees CaLite attempted to compete with dominant carriers on the east coast (Delta, USAir). Learning no pertinent lessons from the previous failures of PEX, CaLite quickly lost market share as customers lost confidence in the safety and reliability of the airline. More recently United Airlines (UAL) initiated a low-cost spin-off airline called U-2 (Shuttle by United) to compete against low-cost carriers in the western US (SWA, West-Pac, Reno). It's initial attempt to compete head-on with SWA was flawed and after a slight restructuring it has found its niche—feeding the UAL hubs at Los Angeles and San Francisco. Similar to the philosophy of United, Delta Airlines began a low-cost airline called Delta Express in 1996 to compete with no-frills airline ValuJet in the southeast US.

7 The success of the satellite airline system is focused on three key concepts; safety, reliability, and customer satisfaction. The customer must believe the carrier is safe, and the airline must perform reliably, "on-time." Both concepts eluded CaLite and led directly to its failure. Customer preference can be gained by providing more hub connection possibilities and frequent flyer miles on the parent carrier. This added value draws customers from low-cost carriers.

HUB AND SPOKE SYSTEM

8 Another development after deregulation was the hub and spoke network system. In order to compete with small low-cost niche carriers, large major airlines needed to establish regional dominance. Hubs are strategically placed airports that serve as transfer points for connecting traffic. They also serve as the origin and destination for passengers traveling to and from the hub city. Flights arrive in banks within the same time frame, off-load passengers and transfer passengers onto flights to their final destinations. This allows the hub airline to serve many more cities and passengers ("multiplier" effect), when compared with point to point service. It also allows the airlines to achieve higher load-factors on flights, by building up passenger loads in large banks. This system was initially developed by Delta and Eastern Airlines in Atlanta. It provides frequent air-service to travelers in the southeast region.

9 Hubs offer great advantages to the dominate carrier—allowing the carrier to feed regional passengers onto its domestic and international flights. This allows the carrier to realize the effects of "economies of scale" by focusing the work-force on processing these banks of flights. By offering more connecting flights into the hub, airlines gain increased marketshare (S-curve theory).

10   Hubs have also created some disadvantages for a carrier—having several banks arriving during the day at 2–3 hour intervals, causes inefficiencies from the work-force during off-peak times. This has brought about the need and increase in part-time employees. Another disadvantage is large banks of aircraft arriving and departing within the same hour can cause air-traffic delays. As the number of runways and airspace at the hub is limited, planes must either be delayed at the gate (gate hold, flow-control) or placed in a holding pattern awaiting landing clearance (arrival sequencing).

11   The keys to a successful hub airport:

- Hub city must support a large percentage of the total passenger traffic at the airport (Origin and Destination traffic, for both domestic and international passengers). Major commercial centers with diversified industry serve as the best hubs (Dallas, Chicago, Atlanta).
- Airport must be able to expand to meet increased passenger demand (large and efficient terminals) and increased air-traffic (addition runways). Increased runway separation to allow for independent approaches and landings.
- Hub region must have favorable weather (minimize flight delays attributed to weather).
- Low airport landing fees (minimize landing fee costs).

FUTURE INDUSTRY TRENDS

12   As the industry continues to evolve into a stable market, trends will continue to occur that will maximize the efficiency of the airline industry. Some predicted trends:

13   Increase by major carriers to outsource short-haul flying (750 nm or less) to regional jet aircraft. The lower direct operating costs (DOC) attainable by flying regional jets (Canadair RJ, EMB-145) will cause large major carriers to transfer unprofitable routes to low cost regionals. These regionals will continue to feed the hub airports from regional secondary markets. This trend has already begun by the acquisition of large numbers of regional jets by Continental, and ComAir (Delta regional).

14   An increase use of small wide body aircraft and narrow body extended range (ER) aircraft to service "thin" long distance domestic (New York–Orange County) and international routes (Denver–Frankfurt). Before the introduction of aircraft such as the Boeing 757-200ER or B767-200ER, long distance flights dictated the use of wide body aircraft (DC-10, B747-200) for performance reasons. As the range of the new narrow body aircraft increases, the possibility for long "thin" routes increases.

15   The US airline industry continues to expand globally as the domestic markets have begun to reach maturity. Areas for large growth include South America and the Asian markets. The industry has begun to stabilize and recover after a 4 year period of heavy losses. Airlines should take caution now to not over-expand and create excess capacity. The stage has been set for low cost carriers and satellite airlines, and they have forever changed the industry.

REGIONAL AIRLINE INDUSTRY

16   In the 1970's the regional airline industry was primarily made up of local commuter airlines serving local cities and connecting outlying communities to metropolitan areas. The typical aircraft used were the Cessna 402, Piper Navajo, and Beech 99. After deregulation, national and major airlines ended service into smaller communities, concentrating on higher yield routes. At this point, smaller commuter airlines began acquiring larger turboprop aircraft and replacing the major airlines on these low yield routes. In the 1980's, commuter airlines grew primarily through industry consolidation and code sharing with larger airlines. Now in the 1990's they have grown into large regional operators serving many cities and operating turbojet aircraft—creating new routes previously not possible without longer range regional jet aircraft.

17   Large regional airlines have grown considerably since deregulation in 1978 and can now be considered small national airlines. For example ComAir "Delta Connection" had gross revenues of

$463 million during 1996, which statistically places it in the national airline category. Frequent service to 501 airports within the U.S. allows regionals to provide hub connect services with national/ major airlines. The top 3 regional airports (ranked by daily departures) in 1995 were DFW— Dallas/Ft. Worth (370 departures), LAX—Los Angeles (342 departures), and CVG—Cincinnati (255 departures). The top regional airports have the common link of being large hubs for the major airline code-sharing partners.

18   After deregulation in 1978, the U.S. government began to subsidize unprofitable routes, which would have otherwise not been served by scheduled airlines. The EAS (Essential Air Service) programs allowed airlines to sustain a profit on these routes. However, in 1996 government cutbacks caused the EAS funds to be cut 55% to $18.4 million. EAS funding is expected to decrease over time to assist in the decrease of federal spending.

19   A major key to growth in the regional airlines was code sharing. These allowed small regional airlines to use the ticket codes of the larger national/ major airlines and create through ticketing. The key to code sharing is that it allows a single ticket source for the customer. It also enables the airlines to coordinate their schedules allowing a smooth transfer of passengers from one airline (regional) to another code sharing partner (national/major).

20   The route structure of regional airlines can be characterized as a hub feed, high frequency structure, with typical leg segments of 200 miles. New niche markets have also been created using regional jets, allowing longer point-to-point service, and bypassing busy hubs.

21   Remarkable growth has occurred in the regional airline industry since deregulation. Consolidation of smaller commuter carriers into larger regional carriers has occurred, as well as the acquisition of larger turboprop, turbojet aircraft. The number of regionals operating has decreased 51% to a total of 124 carriers in 1995. The average trip length has nearly doubled from 121 miles in 1978, to 223 miles in 1995. Finally, regionals in the U.S. carried 57.2 million passengers in 1995, compared to 11.3 million in 1978.

22   The majority of the 2,138 regional aircraft fleet is 19–30 seat turboprop aircraft with an average seat capacity of 24.6. Further growth in the industry demands larger aircraft, including 50–70 regional jet aircraft. Fleet projections by the RAA (Regional Airline Association) for the year 2007, predict the average seat capacity to increase to 35.3 with an additional 842 aircraft. Currently, the most highly utilized regional aircraft is the Swedish manufactured SAAB 340, with a total of 219 in service. The largest portion of new aircraft deliveries between 1995–2004 will be in the 30–40 seat turboprop category.

23   In 1995 the two largest regional airlines (ranked by passenger enplanements) were Simmons Airlines Inc. (American Eagle carrier) and ComAir Inc. (Delta Airlines connection). Simmons is the major hub feed airline for American Airlines at DFW—Dallas/Ft. Worth and ORD—Chicago, serving over 50 cities with 586 flights per day. Simmons carried 4.98 million passengers and operates a fleet of 92 turboprops. ComAir is a major code-sharing partner with Delta Airlines, with hubs in CVG— Cincinnati and MCO—Orlando that operates over 680 flights per day, serving 79 cities. ComAir was the U.S. launch customer for the Canadair Regional Jet, currently utilizing the aircraft on longer point-to-point routes within the U.S. and into Canada.

24   The current issues involving the regionals today are similar to those of the national/major airlines—continued growth in demand and capacity with the further acquisition of larger regional jet aircraft; further development of off peak flights; and direct service on new thin routes that are unprofitable to larger airlines. Labor relation issues are also becoming more common as the pay scales at regional carriers are typically lower than those at the larger carriers. The regional airline members of the RAA oppose any per flight user based fees, which would cause higher operating costs at higher frequency airlines. In addition, to increase the total safety level of all regional carriers, the FAA now requires carriers operating aircraft with more than 9 seats to comply with FAR 121 regulations.

25   The future growth of regional airlines is expected to outpace that of the national and major airlines (+7.5% in passengers per year) with continued industry consolidation by carriers attempting to gain larger market share. The most prevalent trend of regional airlines will be to acquire turbojet aircraft to serve longer, off-peak routes and to provide direct service on new, thin routes.

MAJOR AIRLINES: ADDING CAPACITY FOR 2000 AND BEYOND. WILL HISTORY REPEAT ITSELF?[1]

26 US Airways Group Inc. and United Airlines Inc. are bulking up flights a startling 53% at Washington's Dulles International Airport in the first half of this year. And that explains why U.S. carriers plan to beef up transatlantic capacity more than 10% in 1999, far outstripping the level of demand indicated by anticipated economic growth. All told, the industry expects to expand capacity by 5.6% this year, faster than the previous six years, says analyst Samuel C. Buttrick of PaineWebber Inc. Growth in 2000 should be close to 5% again. That's not massive compared with the 10% peak annual capacity growth in the '80s, but it's far faster than last year's 1.5% increase and 1997's 3.1%.

27 The inevitable result, predict a growing number of skeptics, will be too many seats chasing too few passengers—even taking into account rising estimates of U.S. growth, to around 3%, this year. Planes were more than 70% full on average in 1998. But analysts are bracing for more empty seats and a return to fare wars this year. Susan M. Donofrio of BT Alex. Brown Inc. figures net earnings for the 10 major carriers will fall 17% in 1999, to $4.4 billion, on 4% revenue growth. And that's assuming airlines can push through another fare increase, like the 2% to 4% hike adopted in late January, the first since September, 1997. "There is simply more capacity than is good for the long-term economics of the industry," says American Airlines CEO Donald J. Carty. PaineWebber estimates of that buildup are shown below.

Forecasts of 1999 Capacity Increases

	Systemwide	Domestic	Int'l
American	4.0%	2.5%	7.4%
Continental	8.6	4.0	17.5
Delta	3.5	3.1	5.0
Northwest	9.2	10.0	7.9
Southwest	11.4	11.4	—
United	2.9	4.6	0.0
US Airways	7.8	7.3	12.2

28 Airline analysts could see the buildup coming two years ago. But they didn't foresee the economic turmoil that would hurt demand in Asia and Latin America. Even at home, in the face of stronger-than-expected fourth-quarter economic growth and low fuel prices, the airlines posted flat revenue and falling profits. One reason: Corporations have been curbing travel budgets and balking at sky-high business fares. And the carriers also face growing wage pressures. American pilots, for instance, staged a sickout in early February over wages and other contract issues, forcing the carrier to cancel more than 2,400 flights.

29 Predictably, each carrier with big expansion plans argues that its outsize goal makes strategic sense. Continental Airlines Inc., for one, says attempting an 8.6% increase in capacity this year, after last year's 10.6%, is justified because it underinvested in Newark, Cleveland, and Houston hubs during two bankruptcies. US Airways is expanding its MetroJet operation as a defense against Southwest Airlines Co. on the East Coast.

30 But, warns Carty, "if you have that mentality at four or five carriers, then it gets away from you." American has trimmed its growth plans from 6% to 4% for '99. And despite its buildup at Dulles, United's overall growth this year is expected to be a modest 2.9%, trimmed from 3.6%. "We are all concerned about industry capacity," says Rono Dutta, senior vice-president for planning at UAL Corp., United's parent.

---

[1]This section was adapted from "Airlines May Be Flying in the Face of Reality," *Business Week:* February 22, 1999.

First to Blink?

31   Competition on transatlantic routes may prove particularly intense. U.S. carriers have plans to boost capacity by 15% to 17% this summer. Some are rerouting planes from Asia, where demand remains slack. European carriers are expanding, too, which is likely to lead to deep discounts to fill empty seats in the peak travel season.

32   There is still time—not much—for airlines to scale back. Carriers start to promote summer flights to Europe in February and March. "If we don't see any [cutbacks] by mid-second quarter, we're stuck for this year," says Donofrio. And unless demand weakens considerably, some analysts believe the airlines won't feel the need to change course. After all, even the projected drop in earnings for 1999 makes this a good year by historical standards. But Carty argues that any missteps will badly wound the airlines' credibility on Wall Street. Continental won't risk such a credibility gap, says President Gregory D. Brenneman. "If we see softness, we will stop the growth or even shrink the airline," he vows. "There's nothing sacred to us about the growth if we can't do it profitably." But for now, it looks as if Continental and others are waiting for someone else to blink first. The longer they wait, the better it looks for airline passengers— and the worse for airline profits.

REFERENCES

Regional Airline Association Web site: http://www.raa.org/

Air Transport Association Web site: http://www.air-transport.org/

[This site contains a wide variety of excellent industry statistics.]

An excellent book about the Airline Industry is available: http://www.air-transport.org/handbk/

A quick link to a variety of Airline Industry-related information: http://www.adx.freeservers.com/marclinx.html

MAJOR DOMESTIC AIRLINES VERSUS LOW-FARE AIRLINE ENTREPRENEURS[2]

33   Fifteen years ago, the prospects of low-fare airlines looked ominous for major airlines. Deregulation had allowed these start-ups access into the industry. And every major airline had a variety of short-haul routes which were virtual monopolies that millions of flyers used. Those flyers were already dumbfounded at airline pricing which charged them more for a short flight to a closeby city than they were subsequently charged to fly across the country. So when start-up airlines started popping up offering greatly reduced fares on those short-haul routes, flyers responded favorably in ever increasing numbers. Until, that is, the last few years. During that time, the major airlines have all but owned the skyways to and from the nation's largest cities. A strong economy combined with the 1996 ValuJet Airlines Inc. crash have left consumers less interested in low-fare airlines. And the lack of landing slots in major airports—which are more concentrated than ever in the hands of the big carriers—has made it difficult for startups even to gain entry. The result: The six largest airlines' profits in 1998 jumped 70%, to $4.8 billion. And the new millennium promised more of the same. So what is an airline entrepreneur supposed to do? How might they challenge, successfully, the majors' stranglehold on a capital intensive industry?

The Startup Entrepreneur Response: David Takes On Goliath

34   ValuJet's crash, and the attendant publicity, left virtually all low-fare airlines thin on the ground—and in the air. Aside from nimble Southwest Airlines Co., few challengers have successfully competed

[2]This section is ©1999 The McGraw-Hill Companies Inc. Created and adapted by Richard Robinson, University of South Carolina, using Wendy Zellner, "Metrojet: Will This Short-Hauler Fly?" *Business Week*, June 8, 1998; and David Leonhardt, "ATA: Small Airline, Tricky Flight Plan," *Business Week*, June 22, 1998.

TABLE 1
1987–1997 Summary of Airline Industry Statistics

(in millions, except when noted)

	1987	1988	1989	1990	1991	1992	1993	1994	1995	1996	1997
Traffic—Scheduled Service											
Revenue Passengers Enplaned	447.7	454.6	453.7	465.6	452.3	475.1	488.5	528.8	547.8	581.2	598.9
Revenue Passenger Miles	404,471	423,302	432,714	457,926	447,955	478,554	489,684	519,382	540,656	578,663	605,434
Available Seat Miles	648,721	676,802	684,376	733,375	715,199	752,772	771,641	784,331	807,078	835,071	860,564
Passenger Load Factor (%)	62.3	62.5	63.2	62.4	62.6	63.6	63.5	66.2	67.0	69.3	70.4
Average Passenger Trip Length (miles)	903	931	954	984	990	1,007	1,002	982	987	996	1,011
Freight & Express Ton Miles	8,260	9,632	10,275	10,546	10,225	11,130	11,944	13,792	14,578	15,301	17,959
Aircraft Departures (thousands)	6,581	6,700	6,622	6,924	6,783	7,051	7,245	7,531	8,062	8,230	8,157
Financial											
Passenger Revenues	$44,940	$50,296	$53,802	$58,453	$57,092	$59,828	$63,945	$65,422	$69,594	$75,286	$79,469
Freight & Express Revenues	6,398	7,478	6,893	5,432	5,509	5,916	6,662	7,284	8,616	9,679	10,464
Mail Revenues	923	972	955	970	957	1,184	1,212	1,183	1,266	1,279	1,360
Charter Revenues	1,612	1,698	2,052	2,877	3,717	2,801	3,082	3,548	3,485	3,447	3,553
Total Operating Revenues	56,986	63,749	69,316	76,142	75,158	78,140	84,559	88,313	94,578	101,938	109,535
Total Operating Expenses	54,517	60,312	67,505	78,054	76,943	80,585	83,121	85,600	88,718	95,729	100,924
Operating Profit	2,469	3,437	1,811	(1,912)	(1,785)	(2,444)	1,438	2,713	5,860	6,209	8,611
Interest Expense	1,695	1,846	1,944	1,978	1,777	1,743	2,027	2,347	2,424	1,981	1,749
Net Profit*	593	1,686	128	(3,921)	(1,940)	(4,791)	(2,136)	(344)	2,314	2,804	5,195
Revenue per Passenger Mile (cents)	11.1	11.9	12.4	12.8	12.7	12.5	13.1	12.6	12.9	13.0	13.1
Rate of Return on Investment (%)	7.2	10.8	6.3	(6.0)	(0.5)	(9.3)	(0.4)	5.2	11.9	11.5	14.9
Operating Profit Margin (%)	4.3	5.4	2.6	(2.5)	(2.4)	(3.1)	1.7	3.1	6.2	6.1	7.9
Net Profit Margin (%)	1.0	2.6	0.2	(5.1)	(2.6)	(6.1)	(2.5)	(0.4)	2.4	2.8	4.7
Employees (average full-time equivalent)	457,349	480,553	506,728	545,809	533,565	540,413	537,111	539,759	546,987	564,425	586,509

* Excludes fresh-start accounting extraordinary gains of Continental and Trans World in 1993.
Source: Air Transport Association.

TABLE 2
Load Factors for the Airline Industry: Total, Domestic, and International

Industrywide

Year	Revenue Passenger Miles	Available Seat Miles	Load
1990	457,926,286	733,374,893	62.44
1991	447,954,829	715,199,140	62.63
1992	478,553,708	752,772,435	63.57
1993	489,648,421	771,640,648	63.46
1994	519,381,688	784,330,936	66.22
1995	540,656,211	807,077,839	66.99
1996	578,663,005	835,070,900	69.30
1997	605,434,474	860,563,774	70.35
1998:			
Jan	43,732,331	68,235,516	64.1
Feb	41,017,449	61,941,849	66.2
March	50,108,104	69,182,844	72.4
April	48,944,948	67,749,333	72.2
May	50,510,930	69,499,868	72.7
June	53,093,865	69,374,001	76.5
July	55,782,235	72,940,566	76.5
Aug	55,717,975	72,671,230	76.7
Sept	45,722,436	64,715,192	70.7
Oct	49,575,082	70,804,907	70.0
Nov	46,113,811	67,416,969	68.4
Dec	47,567,567	70,236,502	67.7
TOTAL	587,616,393	824,768,777	71.2

Domestic

Year	Revenue Passenger Miles	Available Seat Miles	Load
1990	340,230,892	563,064,398	60.4
1991	332,565,881	543,637,976	61.1
1992	347,931,400	557,988,917	62.3
1993	354,176,730	571,102,123	62.0
1994	378,990,381	585,437,528	64.7
1995	394,707,883	603,917,402	65.3
1996	425,596,303	626,389,151	67.9
1997	444,655,254	643,650,455	69.0
1998:			
Jan	31,289,757	50,117,186	62.4
Feb	30,159,808	45,803,557	65.8
March	36,875,305	51,298,255	71.9
April	36,028,305	49,705,498	72.5
May	36,360,817	50,446,086	72.1
June	38,391,631	50,412,718	76.2
July	40,457,396	52,805,629	76.6
Aug	40,103,276	52,701,313	76.1
Sept	32,827,070	47,675,079	68.9
Oct	35,969,375	52,090,662	69.1
Nov	33,985,937	49,864,901	68.2
Dec	35,217,610	51,971,400	67.8
TOTAL	427,350,612	604,838,880	70.7

International

Year	Revenue Passenger Miles	Available Seat Miles	Load
1990	117,695,394	170,309,955	69.11
1991	115,388,948	171,561,164	67.26
1992	130,622,308	194,783,518	67.06
1993	135,471,691	200,538,525	67.55
1994	140,391,307	198,893,408	70.59
1995	145,948,328	203,160,437	71.84
1996	153,066,702	208,681,749	73.35
1997	160,779,220	216,913,319	74.12
1998:			
Jan	12,442,574	18,118,330	68.7
Feb	10,857,641	16,138,292	67.3
March	13,232,799	17,884,589	74.0
April	12,916,643	18,043,835	71.6
May	14,150,113	19,053,782	74.3
June	14,702,234	18,961,283	77.5
July	15,324,839	20,134,937	76.1
Aug	15,614,699	19,969,917	78.2
Sept	12,895,366	17,040,113	75.7
Oct	13,605,707	18,714,245	72.7
Nov	12,127,386	17,552,068	69.1
Dec	12,349,957	18,265,102	67.6
TOTAL 1998	160,220,446	219,876,493	72.9

head-to-head on major routes. But in early 1998, American Trans Air Inc., a $783 million Indianapolis-based carrier, set out to do just that. Though it's less than one-tenth the size of $17.4 billion United Airlines Inc., upstart ATA began competing with the industry giant on flights between Chicago and Denver, United's two largest hubs. As if that weren't enough, ATA is also taking on American Airlines Inc. between its top two hubs, Dallas and Chicago. And come July, it will invade New York's LaGuardia Airport.

35   It's a risky strategy. American and United have already started cutting fares in reaction to ATA's moves. But John P. Tague, ATA's 35-year-old chief executive, is nothing if not ambitious: He claims the airline is now "positioned to be the breakout carrier of the '90s." The key, he says, is finding high-fare routes and serving them in a way that minimizes the response of the major carriers. Whether he succeeds or fails, Tague's moves will test Washington's recently declared plans to better police the allegedly anti-competitive practices of the dominant airlines.

Hit Where It Doesn't Hurt Goliath

36   In many ways, ATA's bid is not so different from a host of others who've failed in attempts to take on the majors. It schedules just a few flights a day but to stay off the giants' radar screens, ATA is counting on some important differences. For example, it is focusing its low-frills service on markets such as Chicago, where limited airport space has kept fares high. That way, it hopes to carve out a niche without threatening the majors' lucrative lock on the business travelers who demand plenty of departures, frequent-flier programs, and first-class cabins. "It is a pretty smart strategy," says Morten S. Beyer, president of aviation consulting firm Morten Beyer & Agnew Inc. in McLean, Va.

37   But so far, American and United aren't playing along with Tague's game plan. The two giants already have gone on the offensive. On Feb. 24, weeks after ATA announced it would begin serving Dallas from Midway Airport, Chicago's secondary airport, American said it, too, would resume limited Midway service. American, which flies mostly from O'Hare International Airport, hadn't flown to Dallas from Midway since 1992. American already has matched ATA's three daily flights each way and will add a fourth in July.

38   They're also playing hardball on price. Though ATA offers much cheaper walk-up fares on all routes, both American and United have started matching ATA's low fares on some seats reserved in advance. They recently offered a $180 round-trip fare from Chicago to Dallas, matching ATA's price. Before ATA started flying the route, consumers would have had a hard time flying for less than $300. American's strong response means the Midway-to-Dallas route will be "very much of an uphill battle," for ATA, says Samuel C. Buttrick, Paine Webber's airline analyst. Now, ATA is concentrating on high-priced routes where it can set itself apart with its low fares at Chicago's Midway, which has long been ATA's biggest base.

39   ATA's large planes and lean marketing budget have helped keep the carrier's costs the lowest in the business. It spends 6.1 cents per seat per mile flown, according to Black & Co., a Portland, Ore., investment firm. Compare that with 7.5 cents for Southwest, 9.5 cents for United, and 10.5 cents for American. This low cost structure allows the upstart to beat the major's fares on many flights, and ATA says early bookings are strong.

40   American and United's swift reaction comes despite the Transportation Dept.'s current consideration of a new set of guidelines aimed at curbing predatory behavior by large airlines. What typically kicks off an antitrust investigation, Justice Dept. lawyers say, is the combination of price cuts and added capacity, which can suggest an airline is deliberately losing money to drive out competition. Though American's decision to enter Midway appears to fit this profile, Transportation and Justice Dept. officials decline to say whether they are looking into the situation.

41   The large airlines, including American and United, consistently maintain that they have never broken the law. American says its decision to fly out of Midway had nothing to do with ATA; instead, it came because the route fits well with its Dallas hub. Still, many in the industry are watching ATA's progress closely—and government action may mean the difference between whether ATA survives or succumbs to the majors' pressure like many before it. "The wild card is what impact the new Department of Transportation guidelines will have," says Mark S. Kahan, chief operating officer of Spirit Airlines.

42   ATA's Chicago move would provide an ideal test case for their scrutiny. United and American have long benefited from government limits on the numbers of takeoff and landing slots in Chicago's

> **Selected Major Airlines Trying to Go "Lite"**
>
> ### Metrojet (US Airways)
> Starts June 1 with service between Baltimore and Cleveland, Providence, Fort Lauderdale, and, soon, Manchester, N.H. Matching Southwest fares and one-class service but its costs are higher than Southwest's.
>
> ### Delta Express
> Launched October '96. Now 29 jets serving 19 cities, from Northeast and Midwest to Florida. Offers reserved seating but no first class. Longer-haul flights than Southwest's, and overlaps less than 3% of Southwest's system.
>
> ### Shuttle by United
> Pulled out of several Southwest routes since its '94 startup. Mainly feeds United hubs in Los Angeles and San Francisco. Serves 20 cities with 1st-class and reserved seating. Covers about 5% of Southwest's system.

major airport, O'Hare. Such limits apply to only four U.S. airports and have left Chicago chronically underserved. As a result, tickets cost about 35% above the national average, according to consultant Beyer. Midway, ATA's base, is smaller, but actually closer to downtown, and increasingly popular.

43   But even with higher prices, United and American still have some big advantages. They offer frequent-flier programs, unlike ATA, and back-to-back flights. Flying United from Denver to Chicago means a choice of 15 flights a day; on ATA, if you miss the 3:55 p.m. flight west, you're stuck until 11:25 a.m. the next day.

The Southwest Challenge

44   Employees at Southwest Airlines Co. are beginning to find it commonplace: Major-Lite. When US Airways Group Inc. launches its new low-fare, no-frills MetroJet operation on June 1, it was the fourth time in five years that a major carrier has started an "airline within an airline" to counter low-cost Southwest.

45   Southwest execs say they're ready for battle, but they're hardly quaking. "Not very many facsimiles of Southwest Airlines have been successful since deregulation of the industry," notes CEO Herbert D. Kelleher. Certainly, Delta Express, Shuttle by United, and now defunct Continental Lite have done little to dent Southwest's growth and profitability. The discount brands "are defensive in nature, and Southwest is offensive," says analyst Samuel C. Buttrick of Paine Webber Inc. A summary of those attempts is provided in the box above.

46   Perhaps that's why MetroJet claims it's not aiming to blow Southwest out of the sky. US Airways Inc. Chief Executive Rakesh Gangwal insists the two can coexist—profitably: "We do not view MetroJet as an assault on Southwest Airlines."

47   Maybe not. But MetroJet is clearly an effort to slow Southwest's attack on the East Coast. Starting with Baltimore in 1993, Dallas-based Southwest has spread to Florida, Providence, and soon, Manchester, N.H. For Southwest, which doubled in size in the past five years, to $3.8 billion in annual revenues, most growth opportunities are in the east.

48   That makes Southwest a dangerous challenger to US Airways, a mostly short-haul East Coast carrier with costs 69% above Southwest's. To compete, US Airways has negotiated a new pilot contract for MetroJet, which cuts wage rates by 23%, and a new operating strategy that will increase the use of its aircraft. This, US Airways believes, will dramatically slash Southwest's cost advantage.

49   MetroJet hopes to erase the losses that US Airways suffers in markets where Southwest and other low-fare rivals have brought down fares. A key focus is on flights from the Northeast and Midwest to Florida, where US Airways loses about $100 million a year.

50   Gangwal, an architect of Shuttle by United, takes both comfort and caution from prior airline-within-an-airline efforts. Shuttle, created in 1994, provides lucrative feeds to United's longer flights

from San Francisco and Los Angeles. The subsidiary line "slowed or stopped Southwest's growth on the West Coast, and they moved elsewhere," boasts Shuttle President Amos S. Kazzaz.

51   Indeed, Southwest says its intra-California market share was 49.5% in the third quarter of last year, the latest data available, vs. 52.6% before Shuttle started. Still, Chief Financial Officer Gary C. Kelly notes that Shuttle pulled out of four routes where it competed with Southwest and most of its growth has come at the expense of other carriers.

Trying a Less Confrontational Approach—Leisure Travelers

52   Delta Express, a lower-cost unit of Delta Air Lines Inc., took a less confrontational approach to Southwest. The carrier's flights are generally longer than Southwest's and focus mainly on low-paying leisure travelers flying from the Northeast and Midwest to Florida. Both Delta Express and Southwest claim to be thriving in the markets where they overlap.

53   US Airways, going head-to-head with Southwest on many routes at the same airports, may have it harder. "I don't think they have any chance. I think it's a doomed enterprise," says Michael Roach, president of consultants Roberts, Roach & Associates in Hayward, Calif. Kelleher figures he has a 30% to 40% cost advantage over MetroJet. Gangwal denies the gap is that large and says he'll offset it by attracting business travelers with US Airways' frequent-flier program—soon to be linked with American's—and such amenities as reserved seating.

54   Southwest promises to fight back if need be. But mostly, it's banking on the basics—on-time flights and friendly customer service—that have fueled its success. "At this point, we're not treating this as some kind of all-out war. But we'll be prepared for that if that's what it leads to," vows Southwest's Kelley. Adds Herb Kelleher: "Southwest Airlines first of all does have a very strong balance sheet and lots of liquidity, which gives us the wherewithal to fight battles for a long, long time. It's not as if you can jump on us and expect us to disappear in two weeks. We have by far the lowest operating cost of any airline in the U.S. And we're used to competition. . . . As far as we can tell, it just expanded the market enormously."

Case 50

Southwest Airlines and Herb Kelleher, Entrepreneur

1   Herb Kelleher is dancing in the airplane aisle. It's 8:30 a.m. and he is already bumming cigarettes, cavorting with flight attendants to the music *Flash Dance,* and sipping a screwdriver. The plane lunges left, then right, as its pilot instructs passengers to sway with the movement. Welcome to the zany world of Southwest Airlines.

2   As Southwest Airlines' chief executive officer, Mr. Kelleher finds the image of a maverick very much to his liking. As he recalls, "If we hadn't been mavericks back in 1967 when we started doodling about an intrastate airline, air travel might still be out of reach for millions of people. Instead of using low-fare flights to reach business meetings a couple of hundred miles away in less than an hour, you might have found yourself driving four to five hours to the destination because air travel was too expensive. That's the impact that Southwest is proud to have made upon the airline industry."

3   In 1967, Roland King hired Herb Kelleher, an up-and-coming attorney in San Antonio, to assist in the dismantling of his small commuter air service. The two met one afternoon to discuss a new business venture—one that sounded like King's old business but with a slight twist. Instead of flying to small towns, King envisioned service to the three largest cities in Texas, offering low fares, convenient schedules, and a no-frills approach quite different from the standards of established airlines. Using a bar napkin to further explain he drew a triangle and labeled the corners: Dallas, Houston, and San Antonio. The young attorney questioned King's judgment, but after some homework decided that he too was willing to give it a try.

4   In November 1967, with $500,000 of newly acquired seed capital, Kelleher filed an application with Texas Aeronautics Commission (TAC), asking permission for the proposed airline to serve Dallas, Houston, and San Antonio. During that era, the aviation industry was highly regulated, and starting new airlines or adding routes required proof that such service was needed and that it would be used by the public. "Air Southwest" was granted approval on the merit of its request. However, Braniff, Trans Texas, and Continental quickly challenged TAC's approval and produced a restraining order that banned delivery of Southwest's operating certificate. The bitter legal battle that followed lasted three years. Southwest lost its appeal in local courts and in the State Court of Civil Appeal. Finally, Kelleher won a series of decisions in the Texas State Court that allowed Southwest to begin service with a fleet of three planes. Finally, on June 18, 1971, the first Southwest Air flight took off from Love Field in Dallas headed for Houston.

5   Southwest had won the first battle, but its legal ordeals were far from over. In 1972, the Dallas/Fort Worth Regional Airport Board sued Southwest, hoping to inhibit its operations at Love Field, Dallas's downtown airport. Southwest's fight to remain at Love Field lasted for five years, and the case finally was settled in its favor during January 1977. In a separate legal skirmish, Kelleher campaigned all the way to Washington to establish interstate traffic routes for the airline. Flights from its downtown airfield headquarters were restricted to intrastate flights. However, his aggressive actions resulted in the passing of federal legislation called the Wright Amendment, 1979, which authorized limited interstate service from Love Field to states adjacent to Texas. This granted Southwest interstate routing but limited it to direct destinations no further than one state away.

6   Ironically, these legal ramifications reinforced some key components of Southwest's competitive strategy. For example, in 1973, the battle to keep Love Field drained Southwest (financially) and forced it to sell one of its four operating jets. Management, however, figured the company could still maintain its same routes with three planes and stay on schedule if the aircraft's turnaround ground times were limited to 10 minutes. Competitors were amazed as they watched Southwest's ground

EXHIBIT A

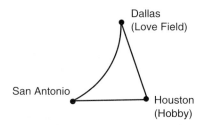

crews service and turn around jets in less than 10 minutes. Rapid turnarounds remain a key part of Southwest's low-cost strategy because of the associated efficiency and low-cost operations.

7   Stemming from its determination to remain at the downtown Dallas field, Southwest earned the critical advantage of convenience for Dallas-bound or departing businesspeople. It continues to utilize downtown airports wherever possible. Although the Wright Amendment restricted Southwest's capacity to compete as an interstate airline, it also forced the company to concentrate on short-haul service: frequent and direct flights. This short-haul strategy is now another key component of Southwest's competitive strategy everywhere that it flies.

8   The 1970s witnessed numerous events that set lasting directions for Southwest's future. In 1973, after only two years of operation, the company experienced its first profitable year. Its common stock was listed on the American Stock Exchange in October 1975, with the ticker symbol "LUV," and the company completed that year with a record load, exceeding 1.1 million passengers. Between 1975 and 1977, the "LUV Line" expanded its web of intrastate service with new destinations to Harligan, Corpus Christi, Austin, Midland Odessa, Lubbock, and El Paso. In 1978, Lamar Muse resigned as CEO, and Herb Kelleher quickly evolved as the new CEO. In the same year, deregulation restructured the U.S. airlines industry, and shortly thereafter Southwest opened its first interstate service to New Orleans, Louisiana.

9   Since deregulation, Southwest has experienced consistent growth and prosperity. Southwest served cities in 15 of the United States, extending from Cleveland, Ohio, to San Francisco, California, by early 1992. It was the seventh largest U.S. carrier, with reported earnings in 1991 of $1.31 billion and 2.6 percent of the nation's air travel market. The company had substantially increased traffic in every route it has opened, and it has spawned economic growth in every downtown airport it has served (estimates credit Hobby Field's reopening with annual benefits of over $1.9 billion to the Houston area economy). In 1992, the U.S. airline industry was decimated by nearly three years of steep losses and was operating with about $7.5 billion of industry red ink. Southwest, however, continued to remain profitable, as it has for all but the first 2 of its 21 operating years. Within the industry, the company has experienced unprecedented success. Exhibit 1 provides a summary of Southwest's financial and operating accomplishments through 1998.

STRATEGY

10   Southwest consistently has favored a low-cost focus strategy since its first flight. The airline is the industry's standard of cheap air travel, typically offering the lowest fares on any of its routes and forcing cheaper rates from competitors whenever it enters a new territory. Believing there was price elasticity in the airline industry, its management felt there were a lot of people who wanted to fly but couldn't because ticket costs were too high. In response, the airline has managed to offer fares averaging only 60–70 percent of those charged by other carriers on similar routes. It has maintained the low-cost strategy and has targeted travelers desiring convenient high-frequency travel between relatively close cities. According to Kelleher, "You can innovate by not doing anything [new] if it's a conscious decision. When other airlines set up hub-and-spoke systems, we continued what we had always been doing. As a consequence, we wound up with a unique market niche: we are the world's

EXHIBIT B

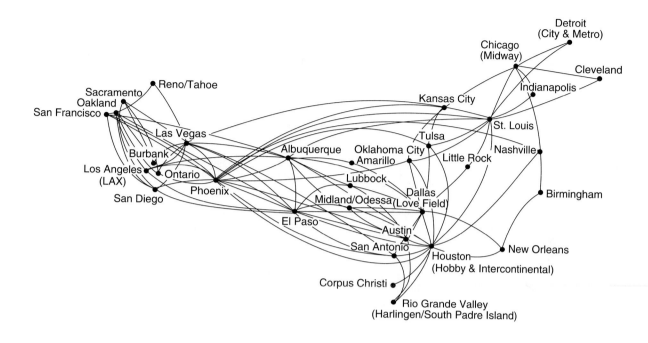

only short-haul, high frequency, point-to-point carrier. Everything about the airline has been adapted to serving that market segment in the most efficient and economical way possible."

11   To support low costs, an airline must operate with peak efficiency. From Southwest's point of view, this means keeping its fleet in the air working rather than spending time on the ground. To shorten total trip time and maximize each plane's air time, Southwest maintains the industry's fastest onground turnaround (unloading, reboarding, and departing the gate) times, sometimes as short as eight and a half minutes. This enables the airline to offer more flights with fewer planes. Not only is its aircraft fleet the youngest and most fuel-efficient in the industry, the fleet is also standardized (utilizing only two types of airplanes), permitting efficiencies in maintenance, training, and spares. Furthermore, Southwest's employees are highly motivated and efficient, creating cost savings both in air and on ground. Selected Southwest operating statistics for 1984–1997 are summarized in Exhibit 1.

12   Southwest steadily has maintained the lowest cost structure in the industry. For example, in 1989, Southwest limited its expenses to only 6.8 cents per available seat mile, compared with an industry average of 10 cents. Southwest has continued to maintain a cost advantage relative to the industry to this day. Comparisons for 1998 with key competitors are shown in Exhibit C. Its low cost structure translates directly into affordable ticket prices and makes the airline a brutal fare war opponent for other airlines. In 1988, Southwest endured $19 flights from Phoenix to Los Angeles as part of a long-standing price war with American West Airlines and eventually drove American West out of this route. During that period, it maintained rock-bottom prices on all its other routes as well (round-trip tickets between Houston and Dallas at that time were a mere $38). Selective Southwest operating expenses for 1984–1998 are summarized in Exhibit 1 and in Exhibit 2. And, on page 50-8, a box insert provides comments by CFO Gary Kelly on how Southwest maintains a low cost advantage.

13   Although Southwest's service is distinctly low-cost, it caters to a distinct market niche. It is a "no-frills" short-haul carrier that does not serve meals on most of its flights, contending that its customers prefer the low fares to typical airline cuisine. Southwest does not arrange connections with other airlines, and passengers must transport their own baggage to recheck them onto connecting airlines. Reserved seating is nonexistent at Southwest, because passengers are seated in the order of their ticket

EXHIBIT 1

Southwest Airlines Co.
Ten-Year Summary

Selected Consolidated Financial Data[1]	1998	1997	1996	1995	1994
(in thousands except per share amounts)					
Operating revenues:					
Passenger	$3,963,781	$3,639,193	$3,269,238	$2,760,756	$2,497,765
Freight	98,500	94,758	80,005	65,825	54,419
Other	101,699	82,870	56,927	46,170	39,749
Total operating revenues	4,163,980	3,816,821	3,406,170	2,872,751	2,591,933
Operating expenses	3,480,369	3,292,585	3,055,335	2,559,220	2,275,224
Operating income	683,611	524,236	350,835	313,531	316,709
Other expenses (income), net	(21,501)	7,280	9,473	8,391	17,186
Income before income taxes	705,112	516,956	341,362	305,140	299,523
Provision for income taxes[3]	271,681	199,184	134,025	122,514	120,192
Net income[3]	$ 433,431	$ 317,772	$ 207,337	$ 182,626	$ 179,331
Net income per share, basic[3]	$ 1.30	$ 1.45	$ .95	$ .85	$ .84
Net income per share, diluted[3]	$ 1.23	$ 1.40	$ .92	$ .82	$ .82
Cash dividends per common share	$.0195	$.03310	$.02932	$.02667	$.02667
Total assets	$4,715,996	$4,246,160	$3,723,479	$3,256,122	$2,823,071
Long-term debt	$ 623,309	$ 628,106	$ 650,226	$ 661,010	$ 583,071
Stockholders' equity	$2,397,918	$2,009,018	$1,648,312	$1,427,318	$1,238,706
Consolidated Financial Ratios[1]					
Return on average total assets	9.7%	8.0%	5.9%	6.0%	6.6%
Return on average stockholders' equity	19.7%	17.4%	13.5%	13.7%	15.6%
Consolidated Operating Statistics[2]					
Revenue passengers carried	52,586,400	50,399,960	49,621,504	44,785,573	42,742,602[9]
RPMs (000s)	31,419,110	28,355,169	27,083,483	23,327,804	21,611,266
ASMs (000s)	47,543,515	44,487,496	40,727,495	36,180,001	32,123,974
Load factor	66.1%	63.7%	66.5%	64.5%	67.3%
Average length of passenger haul	597	563	546	521	506
Trips flown	806,822	786,288	748,634	685,524	624,476
Average passenger fare	$ 75.38	$ 72.21	$ 65.88	$ 61.64	$ 58.44
Passenger revenue yield per RPM	12.62¢	12.84¢	12.07¢	11.83¢	11.56¢
Operating revenue yield per ASM	8.76¢	8.58¢	8.36¢	7.94¢	8.07¢
Operating expenses per ASM	7.32¢	7.40¢	7.50¢	7.07¢	7.08¢
Fuel cost per gallon (average)	45.67¢	62.46¢	65.47¢	55.22¢	53.92¢
Number of employees at yearend	25,844	23,974	22,944	19,933	16,818
Size of fleet at yearend[11]	280	261	243	224	199

(1) The Selected Consolidated Financial Data and Consolidated Financial Ratios for 1992 through 1989 have been restated to include the financial results of Morris Air Corporation (Morris). Years prior to 1989 were immaterial for restatement purposes

(2) Prior to 1993, Morris operated as a charter carrier; therefore, no Morris statistics are included for these years

(3) Pro forma for 1992 through 1989 assuming Morris, an S-Corporation prior to 1993, was taxed at statutory rates

(4) Excludes cumulative effect of accounting changes of $15.3 million ($.07 per share)

(5) Excludes cumulative effect of accounting change of $12.5 million ($.06 per share)

(6) Includes $2.6 million gains on sales of aircraft and $3.1 million from the sale of certain financial assets

(7) Includes $10.8 million gains on sales of aircraft, $5.9 million from the sale of certain financial assets, and $2.3 million from the settlement of a contingency

(8) Includes $5.6 million gains on sales of aircraft and $3.6 million from the sale of certain financial assets

(9) Includes certain estimates for Morris

(10) Excludes merger expenses of $10.8 million

(11) Includes leased aircraft

1993	1992	1991	1990	1989	1988	1984
$2,216,342	$1,623,828	$1,267,897	$1,144,421	$ 973,568	$ 828,343	$519,106
42,897	33,088	26,428	22,196	18,771	14,433	12,115
37,434	146,063	84,961	70,659	65,390	17,658	4,727
2,296,673	1,802,979	1,379,286	1,237,276	1,057,729	860,434	535,948
2,004,700	1,609,175	1,306,675	1,150,015	955,689	774,454	467,451
291,973	193,804	72,611	87,261	102,040	85,980	68,497
32,336	36,361	18,725	6,827[6]	(13,696)[7]	620[8]	649
259,637	157,443	53,886	80,434	115,736	85,360	67,848
105,353	60,058	20,738	29,829	41,231	27,408	18,124
$ 154,284[4]	$ 97,385[5]	$ 33,148	$ 50,605	$ 74,505	$ 57,952	$ 49,724
$ .72[4]	$ .47[5]	$ .17	$ .26	$ .36	$ .27	$ 1.13
$ .70[4]	$ .46[5]	$ .17	$ .26	$ .36	$ .27	$ 1.13
$.02578	$.02355	$.02222	$.02149	$.02073	$.01962	$.0867
$2,576,037	$2,368,856	$1,854,331	$1,480,813	$1,423,298	$1,308,389	$646,244
$ 639,136	$ 735,754	$ 617,434	$ 327,553	$ 354,150	$ 369,541	$153,314
$1,054,019	$ 879,536	$ 635,793	$ 607,294	$ 591,794	$ 567,375	$361,768
6.2%[4]	4.6%[5]	2.0%	3.5%	5.5%	5.1%	8.1%
16.0%[4]	12.9%[5]	5.3%	8.4%	12.9%	10.8%	14.7%
36,955,221[9]	27,839,284	22,669,942	19,830,941	17,958,263	14,876,582	10,697,544
18,827,288	13,787,005	11,296,183	9,958,940	9,281,992	7,676,257	4,669,435
27,511,000	21,366,642	18,491,003	16,411,115	14,796,732	13,309,044	7,983,093
68.4%	64.5%	61.1%	60.7%	62.7%	57.7%	58.5%
509	495	498	502	517	516	436
546,297	438,184	382,752	338,108	304,673	274,859	200,124
$ 59.97	$ 58.33	$ 55.93	$ 57.71	$ 54.21	$ 55.68	$ 48.53
11.77¢	11.78¢	11.22¢	11.49¢	10.49¢	10.79¢	11.12¢
8.35¢	7.89¢	7.10¢	7.23¢	6.86¢	6.47¢	6.71¢
7.25¢[10]	7.03¢	6.76¢	6.73¢	6.20¢	5.82¢	5.86¢
59.15¢	60.82¢	65.69¢	77.89¢	59.46¢	51.37¢	82.44¢
15,175	11,397	9,778	8,620	7,760	6,467	3,934
178	141	124	106	94	85	54

EXHIBIT C

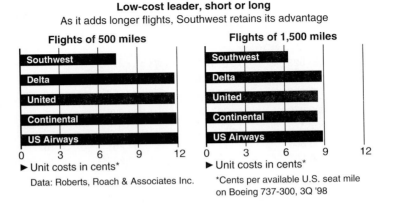

Low-cost leader, short or long
As it adds longer flights, Southwest retains its advantage

Flights of 500 miles — Southwest, Delta, United, Continental, US Airways — Unit costs in cents*
Data: Roberts, Roach & Associates Inc.

Flights of 1,500 miles — Southwest, Delta, United, Continental, US Airways — Unit costs in cents*
*Cents per available U.S. seat mile on Boeing 737-300, 3Q '98

purchases, which are executed at the flight gates. During its early years, Southwest did not use travel agents or a massive (usually leased) reservation system to book its flights.[1] In Southwest's view, computerized reservations systems run up tremendous overhead, and it eliminates premium seating well before departure time. Reserved seating also slows down airplanes during loading, increasing their precious turnaround times.

14   The airline is a "short-haul" carrier, capitalizing on direct routes between major metropolitan areas, with an average flight time of 55 minutes. The short-haul concept, combined with low cost and convenience, was intended to put Southwest's service in direct competition with the automobile as a viable means of transportation. If one can fly between two points in less time and for less expense than driving an automobile, then that person is very likely to leave the car in the garage. In conjunction with the short-haul concept, Southwest's service pattern is point-to-point, as opposed to the hub-and-spoke patterns incorporated by most major carriers. Its goal is to fly people directly to where they want to go, rather than through hubs, and to do so in less time and with less cost than possible in an automobile.

15   Another Southwest feature is the high frequency of flights between any two points. Believing that frequency equates customer convenience, the company lets people fly when they want to fly and not when an airline wants them to fly. For example, Southwest provides the Dallas-Houston route with over 80 flights per day, making it the most heavily served market in the world by any single carrier. The result, Kelleher claims, is that Southwest tends to breed air traffic, with traffic typically doubling on any route within 12 months after his airline begins its service there. The airline's frequent-flyer program is clearly structured to reward travelers for the number of flights they take, rather than their accumulated mileage.

16   Southwest hopes businesspeople will equate their routes with the convenience afforded by a corporate-owned aircraft. According to Kelleher, "You want to leave early—we'll have a flight to get you there at noon. You get through early—we'll have an early flight back. Your meeting runs late— we'll have a late flight back and you can still get home when you're finished." Although this type of scheduling gives Southwest the highest no-show rate of any airline in the nation, management is neither particularly worried about it nor finds it detrimental to the bottom line.

17   To provide additional convenience, Southwest constantly battles tardy departures and strives for a goal of 90 percent on-time schedules. When Kelleher noticed departing passengers dawdling at the airplane's forward closets, he promptly had the forward closets removed from all Southwest's planes. The airline has maintained such high scheduling standards that Department of Transportation

[1]Travel agents typically receive a 10 percent "commission" from airlines for tickets purchased through them. Southwest now uses travel agents, but still handles all reservations "in house" rather than subscribe to expensive outside reservation systems.

EXHIBIT 2
Southwest Operating Expenses

	Years Ended December 31,			
	1998	1997	1996	1995
Operating Expenses:				
Salaries, wages, and benefits	$1,285,942	$1,136,542	$ 999,719	$ 867,984
Fuel and oil	388,348	494,952	484,673	365,670
Maintenance materials and repairs	302,431	256,501	253,521	217,259
Agency commissions	157,766	157,211	140,940	123,380
Aircraft rentals	202,160	201,954	190,663	169,461
Landing fees and other rentals	214,907	203,845	187,600	160,322
Depreciation	225,212	195,568	183,470	156,771
Other operating expenses	703,603	646,012	614,749	498,373
Total operating expenses	3,480,369	3,292,585	3,055,335	2,559,220
Operating Income		524,236	350,835	313,531
Other Expenses (Income):				
Interest expense	56,276	63,454	59,269	58,810
Capitalized interest	(25,588)	(19,779)	(22,267)	(31,371)
Interest income	(31,083)	(36,616)	(25,797)	(20,095)
Nonoperating (gains) losses, net	(21,106)	221	(1,732)	1,047
Total other expenses	(21,501)	7,280	9,473	8,391

statistics have frequently recognized the airline as best in the industry for average on-time performance. It also has consistently maintained an over 99 percent average of flight completion performance (flights that actually arrive at their scheduled destinations). Southwest's unprecedented reputation for fast airport turnarounds is built on the performance typified in Exhibit 3.

18   To compete with automobiles, Southwest realizes that it's not just time in the air that people consider, it's the time it takes to get to the airport, to park the car, and actually to get on the airplane. To further reduce this total travel time, the company serves close-in municipal airports wherever possible. Smaller municipal terminals mean shorter drives to the airport, shorter walks from the parking lot to the ticket counter, and fewer marathon runs to the departure gate. Southwest incorporates quick-ticketing procedures, utilizing cash registers and vending machines, which help reduce ticket purchases to as little as 10 seconds. The tickets themselves resemble sales receipt slips, rather than the higher-cost folders used by other airlines. To insure speedy baggage handling, Southwest has adopted the standard to deliver baggage from aircraft to baggage claim areas within eight minutes.

19   Southwest's management team retains an offensive, competitive posture. They search out markets that are overpriced and underserved, then move in with considerable force. For example, on its top 75 routes, Southwest has captured more than 50 percent of the traffic, while the next carrier averages only 10 percent. "We attack a city with a lot of flights, which is another form of aggression in the airlines industry," states Kelleher. "We won't go in with just one or two flights. We'll go in with 10 or 12. That eats up a lot of airplane capacity, so you can't open a lot of cities. Call it guerrilla warfare against bigger opponents. You hit them with everything you've got in one or two places instead of trying to fight them everywhere."

20   Southwest's management meets competitive and environmental threats head-on, sometimes engaging in court battles and price wars to secure its position. Southwest more than once has faced losing its access to downtown airfields because of excessive noise pollution. Its most serious stand-off was in Dallas, where an influential community group was determined to end its in-town service. Kelleher did not hesitate to confront complainants, in court, with the massive economic benefits

---

SOUTHWEST AIRLINES CO. — FIVE SYMBOLS OF FREEDOM

OUR FARES ARE CONSISTENTLY THE LOWEST, SIMPLEST FARES IN THE DOMESTIC AIRLINE INDUSTRY. BY KEEPING COSTS LOW, WE KEEP OUR FARES LOW. THIS, IN TURN, GIVES CUSTOMERS THE FREEDOM TO FLY.

Southwest is and always has been a very different airline—from the operating strategy we employ to the way we treat our Employees and Customers. But the difference we are most famous for is our ability to generate high profits with low fares. The secret, of course, is low costs, and our operating strategy is a significant ingredient of our low cost formula.

Our operating strategy is unique in the airline industry, and it has, indeed, revolutionized air travel over the last 26 years. We start with a principal focus on the shorthaul traveler, where our average flight time is about an hour. We streamline service to meet the shorthaul traveler's needs. Then, we identify city pairs that can generate substantial amounts of business and leisure traffic with Southwest service.

We offer lots of flights to meet business travelers' demands for schedule convenience and flexibility. We offer low fares that meet all travelers' needs, especially leisure travelers. We specialize in nonstop, not connecting, service. In our experience, this is what Customers want in shorthaul markets. And it is far more cost-efficient than the accepted "hub and spoke" industry standard.

This market focus allows us to be substantially more efficient and productive than the rest of the airline industry. Our aircraft and airport facilities are used continuously throughout the day, maximizing utilization and minimizing ground time. Our aircraft "turn" times at the airport are less than half the industry standard. Therefore, we get lots more use of our aircraft and much lower unit costs.

We also use only one aircraft type, the Boeing 737, in an all-coach configuration. This substantially reduces costs versus the industry due to simplified operations, training, scheduling, and maintenance. Our fleet of 737s is young, safe, comfortable, clean, and perfectly suited for shorthaul flights.

Our fare structure is simple and this means the cost of selling our product is less than industry average. Over 60 percent of our Customers buy travel on Southwest on a ticketless basis—it is easier for our Customers and less expensive for Southwest than a paper ticket. Boarding the aircraft is also fast and efficient.

Finally, and most importantly, we have a Culture that values efficiency, hard work, innovation, and simplicity. Our People have the will and the desire to produce low costs. That's how the low cost producer keeps finding ways to reduce costs further.

"We are a low fare airline by philosophy. When we go into a new market our competitors usually lower their fares. The difference is our fares stay low—whenever and wherever we fly."

Gary C. Kelly, Vice President-Finance, Chief Financial Officer

---

accruing from his transportation activities at Love Field. His arguments convinced the jury, and his airline was allowed to continue its Love Field service. While fare wars frequently have besieged the airline industry, Southwest's low-cost structure, profitability, and aggressive posture have allowed it to consistently outlast and outmaneuver its opponents.

PROMOTIONS

21   Southwest promotions have employed a variety of creative approaches to attract passengers. Early on, the company became synonymous with garish marketing campaigns. Southwest was billed as "Love" airlines, flying from Love Field, serving "love potions" (drinks), "love bites" (peanuts), and

EXHIBIT 3
Anatomy of a 15-Minute Turnaround

7:55	Ground crew chat around gate position.
8:03:30	Ground crew alerted, move to their vehicles.
8:04	Plane begins to pull into gate; crew moves toward plane.
8:04:30	Plane stops; jetway telescopes out; baggage door opens.
8:06:30	Baggage unloaded; refueling and other servicing underway.
8:07	Passengers off plane.
8:08	Boarding call; baggage loading, refueling complete.
8:10	Boarding complete; most of ground crew leaves.
8:15	Jetway retracts.
8:15:30	Pushback from gate.
8:18	Push-back tractor disengages; plane leaves for runway.

On a recent weekday a Southwest Airlines flight arrived at New Orleans from Houston. The scheduled arrival time was 8:00 A.M., and departure for Birmingham, Alabama, was 8:15 A.M. *Forbes* checked the turnaround, half-minute by half-minute.

hiring "lovely" stewardesses. Thinly clad in hot pants and Southwest colors, stewardesses frequently were pictured in the public press, including the cover of *Esquire* and of a Budapest newspaper. The love campaign emphasized Southwest as a fun and caring alternative for regional flyers. "If it hadn't been for the power of that campaign," reflects Kelleher, "it's possible that Southwest might not have survived its early years."

22   Another promotion was the direct response to an aggressive price war waged against Southwest. To compete head-on in Southwest's primary market, Braniff discounted its Dallas-Houston fare to $13, which was exactly one half Southwest's normal $26 fare. Southwest retaliated by running the advertisement, "We're not going to lose you for a lousy $13, so you can fly Southwest for $13, too." But Southwest also offered an alternative: "Or, pay $26 and we'll give you a free bottle of Smirnoff vodka, Canadian whisky, or Wild Turkey bourbon." For about two months, claimed Kelleher, Southwest was one of the biggest liquor distributors in the state of Texas. Forty-five percent of the people flying that route purchased tickets on company accounts and were thrilled to have their company cover the flight cost while taking home free bottles of whiskey. Before closing the campaign, Southwest offered ice buckets as well. Braniff's calculated assault backfired as a result of Southwest's promotion.

23   Other promotions have included "West Fly One, Get One," in which customers flying to any western city on certain days were awarded round-trip tickets to any Southwest destination. The "Sweetheart Pass" awarded free companion trips for any travelers flying three round-trip flights. Southwest's frequent-flyer club offers a variety of bonus awards, including free round trips for every eight round trips flown in one year; and for every 50 round trips flown in a year, a pass is awarded allowing companions to fly free for a year.

24   Some promotions have approached the realm of outrageous. For example, Southwest celebrated its status as official airlines of the Texas and California Sea Worlds by painting three of its Boeing 737s in the distinctive black-and-white markings of Shamu, Sea World's killer whale. Another of its aircraft is painted as an unfurling Texas flag. A 30-second television ad retorted to America West Airline's charge that Southwest passengers were embarrassed to fly on its no-frills flights with "plain" planes. Kelleher appeared on the ad with a brown paper bag over his head as the "Unknown Flyer." His comment, "If you are embarrassed to fly the airline with the fewest customer complaints in the country and with the most convenient schedules to the cities it serves, Southwest will give you this bag." He then lifts the bag from his head and offers it to anyone flying Southwest so they can "hold all the money you'll save by flying with us." The final scene shows Kelleher in a shower of money, grinning at the camera.

CULTURE/KELLEHER

25   Corporate culture at Southwest and the persona of Herb Kelleher are closely intertwined. When asked what was his favorite hobby, Kelleher replied, "My hobby is Southwest Airlines: it really is. There is a lot of talk about stress; but if your vocation is also your avocation, then none of those things apply. I'd much rather spend an evening sitting around talking to some of our people [Southwest's people] than making a trip to Paris." The airline literally epitomizes Kelleher's personality: his irreverence, his spontaneity, his zaniness, his depthless energy, and, most of all, his competitiveness. The airline he helped found and now runs is a direct extension of that personality—Kelleher himself even stars in the company's offbeat commercials.

26   Three themes underlie Southwest's culture: love, fun, and efficiency. Kelleher regards the over 9,000 employees of Southwest as his "lovely and loving family." This feeling is sanctioned among all employees and is especially encouraged in relationships with Southwest customers. For example, a Dallas flight attendant received a company award for befriending Kisha, an 18-month-old customer en route from Amarillo to Dallas for a kidney transplant. During Kisha's hospitalization, Burgess, the flight attendant, ran errands for Kisha's parents, including washing and ironing their clothes. Kelleher beamed while presenting Burgess the award as he described how she had hired a sitter to care for her two children so she could help Kisha.

27   To support a "loving, family" culture, Kelleher knows as many employees by name as possible, and he insists that they refer to him as "Herb" or "Herbie." Herb tells people, at the company's weekly Friday afternoon barbecue, "We've got as many as six members of the family working for us. Why some of our employees have been married to one employee, divorced, and married to two, maybe three others." Employees respond to this warmth with loyalty and dedication. When fuel costs skyrocketed during Iraq's invasion of Kuwait, employees initiated a "Fuel from the Heart" program. As participants, about a third of the 8,600 employees took voluntary deductions from their paychecks to buy aviation fuel for the airline. Kelleher has successfully used his personality to charm workers, earn their trust, and breed leaders throughout the entire organization.

SOUTHWEST AIRLINES CO.—FIVE SYMBOLS OF FREEDOM

TRIPLE CROWN SERVICE IS MORE THAN A SLOGAN, IT IS A BENCHMARK. SOUTHWEST HAS WON FIVE ANNUAL TRIPLE CROWNS—NO. 1 IN ONTIME ARRIVALS, BAGGAGE HANDLING, AND CUSTOMER SATISFACTION.

Southwest Airlines is the only airline that has ever won the annual Triple Crown—#1 in On-time Arrivals, Baggage Handling, and Customer Satisfaction among all major airlines, as published in U.S. Department of Transportation consumer reports.

When Southwest won an unprecedented fourth consecutive annual Triple Crown in 1995, Chairman Herb Kelleher issued his famous "Gimme Five" challenge:

"If you earn a fifth annual Triple Crown, I'll paint the name of every person in this Company on a Boeing 737."

We did. And he did. Behold *Triple Crown One,* a signature salute to the 25,000+ Employees who made this fifth win possible and retired the Triple Crown trophy. True to his word, Herb painted everyone's name onboard this high-flying tribute to our Southwest Spirit.

If Herb gives us yet another challenge, let's just say that he'd better have an extra plane in the hangar and his paintbrush handy.

———

"If there's one thing I've learned about our incredible Southwest employees, it's never give them a challenge unless you're prepared to pay the piper . . . or in this case, paint the plane."

Herbert D. Kelleher
Chairman, President, and
Chief Executive Officer

28   When decorating the new corporate headquarters in Dallas, management declined fancy corporate art for company and employee photographs, print ads, and mannequins dressed in the Southwest uniforms donned over the years. Most of the photographs were from company parties and award ceremonies. The memorabilia is displayed so that a walk through the building displays a 20 year history of the Southwest "family."

29   Community service is part of the company's employee motivation program, because management perceives it to foster a sense of camaraderie. Employees participate in various community service projects, which include cooking dinner once a month at a local Ronald McDonald house, volunteering for Junior Olympics events, and hosting a day at the Muscular Dystrophy Camp. The company is recognized at these events, and participant photos are printed in the company newsletter.

30   Southwest continually encourages its employees to have fun while working at Southwest Air. Kelleher, a frequent Elvis and Roy Orbison impersonator, wants employees to have a meaningful experience at work. At one company picnic before 4,000 workers, he wore a dress, bonnet, and bloomers while singing "Tea for Two" in a duet with his vice president of ground operations. Such behavior is not unusual. The "Southwest Experience" has included flight attendants wearing anything from baggy shorts and wild-print shirts to reindeer or Easter bunny outfits. Safety instructions have been announced in rap, Christmas carols sung over the PA system, and the wrong time announced on purpose. One might have heard the captain announce, "As soon as y'all set both cheeks on your seat, we can get this old bird moving."

31   The philosophy behind this fun focus is that humor rubs off on people. If people are having a good time, they will be back, or want to stay, whether they are customer or employee. In either case, value is created for the airline. As described by the boss, Uncle Herb, "A lot of people think you're not really serious about your business unless you act serious. At Southwest, we understand that it's not necessary to be uptight in order to do something well. We call it professionalism worn lightly. Fun is a stimulant to people. They enjoy their work more and work more productively." For the customer, he says, "What's important is that a customer should get off the plane feeling good: 'I didn't just get from A to B. I had one of the most pleasant experiences I ever had and I'll be back for that reason.'"

32   Southwest runs company contests simply for the fun of it, and prizes might include cash or travel passes. Typical contests are a Halloween costume contest, a Thanksgiving poem contest, or a design contest for the newsletter cover. Each year, the company parking lot is converted to an annual chili cook-off celebration. All these factors create an unusual, enjoyable, yet highly productive culture at the airlines.

33   "Management by fooling around" is the principle adopted by Kelleher to run his airline. For him, that might mean doing a rap video promoting the airline, or it might mean working hands-on with mechanics, baggage handlers, and ticket agents at Love Field, most of whom he knows by name. Or it might mean his wearing jungle-print pajamas or a leprechaun suit on business flights to Houston, and commenting on his employees, "I love their irreverence." Beyond his own commitment to fooling around, he requires that every quarter, every Southwest manager take at least one day to work at some other job—as a gate agent, baggage handler, flight attendant, or even janitor.

34   Every month Kelleher personally hands out "Winning Spirit" awards to employees selected by fellow workers for exemplary performance. For example, one employee was awarded two free airline tickets and a boss's bear hug for returning to a customer a lost purse that contained $800 and several credit cards. This philosophy supports the value that management places on individuality among its workers at all levels of the company. According to Kelleher, individuality produces leadership.

35   To stay in touch with customers, Kelleher and his Vice President for Administration Colleen Barret personally read as many as two hundred letters a week from customers. Kelleher and most employees make it regular practice to interact with customers throughout their exposure to Southwest.

HUMAN RESOURCE MANAGEMENT

36   Underlying Southwest's operational capabilities is an employee relations philosophy aimed at closely linking each employee with the company's short- and long-term goals. Its management feels that mission-oriented employees are more productive. Employees are asked to put out more effort in return for higher pay, yet their efforts go beyond a straight work-harder-for-more-money

arrangement. Their efficiency and commitment allow Southwest to hold down overall costs while paying higher wages. Top management devotes a large part of its time to fostering productive attitudes among employees and to emphasizing direct contact between management and employees. "The front office is there to support the troops, not vice versa," says Kelleher. "We want to know what they need and then supply it."

37   Southwest's primary employee benefit is its profit-sharing plan. Employees collect from this fund only when they leave the company. A stock option plan allows employees to acquire stock at 90 percent of market value via payroll deductions. Other perks include unlimited space-available travel for employees and their families, a flexible health benefit plan, and a 401(k) retirement plan.

38   When a poorly performing year besieged Southwest, the first people to reflect the losses were its corporate officers. "If there's going to be a downside, you should share it," reflects Kelleher. "When we were experiencing hard times [unprofitable year], I went to the board and told them I wanted to cut my salary. I cut all officers' bonuses 10 percent, mine 20 percent." Other employees are moved by such initiatives. When asked about the high productivity of his employees (analysts consider them the most productive in the industry, enabling the airline to minimize its costs), Kelleher replied, "They are that way, because they know we aren't trying to milk them for the bottom line."

39   Southwest looks for special people to staff its vacant positions. "We draft great attitudes," according to Kelleher. "If you don't have a good attitude, we don't want you no matter how skilled you are. We can change skill levels through training. We can't change attitudes. We are fanatics about hiring the right people. We want to give them the latitude to be individuals on their job. We want them to be good-natured and have a good-humored approach to life and to have fun doing their job." In an effort to match employee personalities to those of its customers, Southwest invites its most frequent flyers to both interview and participate in the screening of potential new employees.

40   Unlike many of the airlines created under deregulation, Southwest's employees are unionized. By maintaining a favorable relationship with the unions, management has been able to negotiate flexible work rules for its employees. Relationships throughout the company are cooperative, and people take pride in their organization. For example, since cleaning crews come on board only at the end of each day, flight attendants and pilots often pick up trash left on planes. Employees perceive their airline as an ongoing institution, so they're thinking about its longevity, not its next week.

41   Even though Southwest's work force is 90 percent unionized, its employees own over 14 percent of the company, the highest percentage of any major airline. As of 1991, the average employee age was 34 (among the lowest in the industry), and the average pay was $45,000 per employee (among the industry's highest). Annual turnover was a mere 6 percent (the industry's lowest), and 80 percent of promotions came from within. Annually, over 72,000 people apply for jobs at Southwest. Only 20% will be hired—based on their ability, among other things, to work hard, to have fun, and to be a part of the company's extended family. Employees are consistently aware of their stake in the efficient operations of the company, as evidenced in its rapid turnarounds and high productivity levels.

42   To encourage top-notch performance, management has incorporated employee involvement programs. These programs utilize a suggestion system and a variety of incentives, including cash, merchandise, and travel passes. In the "Together We Make It Great Program" employees work in seven-member teams to create money-saving ideas. These ideas then are studied by a middle- and upper-level management committee, which then forwards the best ideas to departmental managers for approval or disapproval. The committee can override any manager's disapproval; and, even if an idea is not used, the team gets a letter explaining why. The most effective suggestions are printed in the company's newsletter, *Luv Lines*.

43   If an idea is accepted, employee teams receive points, based on the savings that result from the idea. The first year, those whose ideas saved the most money were allowed to trade their points for merchandise in a St. Louis warehouse operated by the incentive firm Maritz, Inc. In years following, winning teams received cash awards, ranging from $150 to $5,000, depending on how much money was saved by the idea. Employees providing ideas that saved company time or made a work process easier, but did not directly save money, were awarded travel passes.

44   Another incentive system is the "Black Bag" program, which encourages baggage handlers to reduce the amount of money having to be spent on lost and damaged baggage. Baggage stations that are at least 15 percent below budget each month receive cash incentives for every employee group working the station. Although each station can spend the money any way it pleases, stations typically spend the money on parties, luncheons, or dinners.

45   Outstanding employees are formally recognized at periodic awards ceremonies. All workers from baggage handlers to ticket agents can participate in the programs and be eligible for awards. At the annual awards banquet, employees are recognized for length of service and awarded plaques for outstanding service to the company or community. The winner of the Founder's Award, Southwest's most prestigious annual award, receives $1,000 cash. Southwest's monthly in-flight magazine, *Spirit,* runs a "Star of the Month" column featuring an outstanding employee chosen from peer nominations and customer recommendations. Management chooses the best examples from its customer mail each month and prints them in the company newsletter, and awards outstanding performers two travel passes, a Winning Spirit pin, and a certificate signed by the president.

46   Management is particularly fond of its pilots and solicits their participation in the evaluation of new aircraft. Kelleher believes that pilots bring technical expertise and pragmatic experience to an evaluation. "You want to make sure that an airplane is acceptable to your pilots in sort of a spiritual way because, if they don't like, it might not fly as well as it should," says Kelleher. "There has got to be a feeling, I think, between the pilot and the airplane like there is between the cowboy and the horse. I wanted to be sure that our pilots were comfortable with the 737-300s. We not only seek the pilot's input on equipment, we seek the pilot's advice on a whole range of questions."

47   Pilots always have been paid on a per-trip basis, rather than hourly. This increases their awareness that the airline must be productive in order to exist. It also is an incentive for them to move things along as fast as possible, consistent with safety regulations. As key members of the airlines industry's first profit-sharing plan, many have benefited handsomely. They know that productivity is the key to maintaining Southwest's low-cost, low-fare niche. The pay-per-trip system gives the pilot a great deal of responsibility and, to a certain extent, the means to control his or her own income.

48   Southwest won first place in the Business Insurance Employee Benefits Communication Awards competition for its unique implementation of a flexible benefits insurance program. In order to lower the $13 million spent on health care during that year, the company opted for a new flexible benefits program, which could save 6 percent of these costs if employee enrollment in the program was 40 percent of the work force or above. Southwest reached that goal within 15 months after the program's implementation kickoff, a remarkable feat. This was done through a series of newspaper and morning news show parodies. Southwest employees found the format less intimidating than typical insurance company booklets that people normally receive but do not read. In conjunction, a humorous 35-minute video on Benefits Plus was aired continuously in high-employee-traffic areas throughout its widely dispersed, 31-city work force. The method was a widely acclaimed success, and the resulting employee participation unprecedented.

FINANCIAL STRATEGY

49   In 1989, Southwest catapulted from a regional to a national carrier, as defined within Department of Transportation categories. To achieve this distinction, its operating revenues exceeded $1 billion for the year. This represented a postderegulation (since 1978) revenue growth of over $900 million. During the same period, the airline industry suffered severe shakeout and massive restructuring. Southwest has coupled its continued growth with an uncanny ability to minimize operating costs. It also has consistently maintained one of the industry's strongest balance sheets (see Exhibit 4), with debt-to-equity ratios typically one-third the industry average. Low-cost operation and favorable debt structures play key roles in Southwest's financial strength.

50   Southwest's low-cost capacity is the core of its financial strategy. Full utilization and standardization of its fleet (on a typical day Southwest planes are in the air 10.56 hours versus an industry average of 8 hours), no-frills operations, and a work force dedicated to low cost and service uniquely position the airline as the industry's premier bargain. Its low-cost operations have allowed Southwest to maintain normal passenger traffic while recent recessions severely deteriorated much of its competitors' business. Its low-cost structure has also allowed Southwest to endure and to conquer rivals in ferocious and long-lasting price wars.

EXHIBIT 4

Southwest Airlines
Consolidated Balance Sheet
(in thousands except share and per share amounts)

	1998	1993	1989
Assets			
Current assets:			
Cash and cash equivalents	$ 378,511	$ 295,571	$ 146,364
Accounts receivable	88,799	70,484	37,951
Inventories of parts and supplies, at cost	50,035	31,707	12,484
Deferred income taxes	20,734	10,475	—
Prepaid expenses and other current assets	36,076	23,787	7,079
Total current assets	574,155	432,024	203,878
Property and equipment, at cost:			
Flight equipment	4,709,059	2,257,809	1,255,076
Ground property and equipment	720,604	329,605	164,362
Deposits on flight equipment purchase contracts	309,356	242,230	137,956
	5,739,019	2,829,644	1,557,394
Less allowance for depreciation	1,601,409	688,280	353,137
	4,137,610	2,141,364	1,204,257
Other assets	4,231	2,649	6,961
Total assets	$4,715,996	$2,576,037	$1,415,096
Liabilities and Stockholders' Equity			
Current liabilities:			
Accounts payable	$ 157,415	$ 94,040	$ 47,986
Accrued liabilities	477,448	265,333	94,816
Air traffic liability	200,078	96,146	32,938
Current maturities of long-term debt	11,996	7,025	3,990
Other current liabilities	3,716	16,068	16,168
Total current liabilities	850,653	478,612	195,898
Long-term debt less current maturities	623,309	639,136	354,147
Deferred income taxes	549,207	183,616	118,395
Deferred gains from sale and leaseback of aircraft	238,412	199,362	157,030
Other deferred liabilities	56,497	21,292	2,310
Commitments and contingencies			
Stockholders' equity:			
Common stock, $1.00 par value: 680,000,000 shares authorized; 221,207,083 shares issued and outstanding in 1997	335,904	142,756	32,254
Capital in excess of par value	89,820	141,168	113,471
Retained earnings	2,044,975	770,095	441,591
Treasury stock at cost: 3,601,121 shares in 1998	(72,781)	—	—
Total stockholders' equity	2,397,918	1,054,019	587,316
Total liabilities and stockholders' equity	$4,715,996	$2,576,037	$1,415,096

51   Southwest employs an aggressive aircraft leasing policy that has helped maintain a favorable reserve of cash and liquid resources. This reserve along with an outstanding debt position has assisted Southwest's survival during adverse economic environments while enhancing its competitive position within the industry. For example, Southwest has been able to expand assertively as circumstances have presented themselves. As new routes and gate facilities became available, the company was able to seize them quickly while other debt-strapped, less-liquid competitors lost these opportunities.

52   Southwest's purchase of Morris Air signified a new direction in its financial strategy. For a price of $129 million in stock, Kelleher picked up Morris' routes to 22 western cities and an airline which operates in a fashion remarkably similar to his own. Morris already employed not only a point-to-point, low-cost service but also the same kind of jets used by Southwest. While Southwest's growth in the past has been internally generated, in this case its expansion is being managed by the issuance of over 3 million new shares of stock. Southwest's only other acquisition was Muse Air, which flopped because of considerable differences between the two carriers' operating styles.

FUTURE

53   Ten years ago Kelleher faced, in front of the Dallas City Council, a citizens' action committee that was determined to drive Southwest from its base of operations at Love Field. The committee's anger stemmed from the obtrusive noise pollution created by Southwest's fleet of jets operating within a heavily congested residential area. Nearly 30,000 people live in housing sections near Love Field that are subjected to unacceptable levels (by federal standards) of aircraft noise. The potential effects include auditory problems, increased blood pressure, narrowed attention spans, and aggravation to the "victims." Kelleher based his counterargument on the economic prosperity that the reopened airport afforded the city, and it won the council's support.

54   Operating in and out of congested populations poses a threat to Southwest's future, particularly where alternative airports exist outside city limits, and particularly as pollution to American citizens becomes a more potent issue. Furthermore, close-in operations are a key element of Southwest's strategy. To a large extent, court decisions are based on past precedents, and so far Southwest has remained within the statutory bounds of precedent. The odds of precedent changing on this thorny issue is anybody's guess.

55   Although Southwest has operated within its niche relatively competition free, its success has attracted the attention of competitors. Attempts to enter this niche have been rather fruitless for other airlines, and Southwest's continued outstanding performance may well depend on its competitors' inability or lack of desire to crack that niche.

56   The airline industry of the 1990s witnessed growing internationalization. Analysts predict that the growth of international travel will exceed that of U.S. domestic travel during the next decade. New destinations will open in the United States for foreign carriers and in foreign nations for U.S. carriers. Many airlines will develop global systems as the incidence of multinational alliance increases. The last decade saw the international revenue passenger miles of several U.S. carriers grew significantly: Delta's increased 448 percent, American's 263 percent, United's 220 percent, and Northwest's 88 percent. In the United States, foreign entities may now own up to 49 percent of a U.S. airline but are still not allowed to control more than a 25-percent voting interest. In a related area, Southwest is well located to capitalize on air transportation needs generated by the expanding economic development in Mexico. And passage of the proposed NAFTA agreement should signal a growing traffic flow between selected U.S. and Mexican destinations.

57   After posing for photos with his finger up his nose and a plastic airplane on his head, irreverent Southwest CEO Herb Kelleher sat down recently with *Business Week*'s Wendy Zellner for some serious talk about Southwest's growth prospects, its move into the New York market, and the possibility of expansion into long-haul service. Here are some excerpts from their conversation:[2]

Q: Some of your competitors believe you've "dug all the shallow holes" and will soon have to choose between high growth and high margins. What's your view on that?

A: I guess we just have a different perspective on life. Southwest Airlines has increased in size very significantly during the course of this decade. At the same time, our margins have improved as we have grown. Our visualization of the future is one that is tremendously promising

---

[2]This section is taken from Wendy Zellner, "We Could Use a Lot More Airplanes Today," ONLINE ORIGINAL from *Business Week:* February 8, 1999, www.businessweek.com, ©1999 The McGraw-Hill Companies.

for Southwest. . . . I think one of the things that may be deceptive is that people look at historic traffic in a given market and they say, "Well, that market isn't big enough for Southwest Airlines to go into." What they fail to realize is we make markets ourselves.

Q: They all realize that now, don't they?

A: They'd like to forget it. Especially our competitors. If you take Providence and Baltimore . . . that was not a city-pair market that airlines were actually gouging and kicking and scratching to get into. We went into it, and in the first year, the traffic increased by 884%.

So when you look at what's left that we're not serving now, you come to the conclusion there are an awful lot of places that we can serve very profitably because the markets will increase by 400-500—800-1,000%. And No. 2, we're obviously expanding a little more rapidly in the longer-haul markets. That is a market segment that has not only not been exhausted but hasn't even been touched by Southwest Airlines.

Our business motivation for doing that is the change in the [federal airline ticket] tax law, which the Big 7 carriers were successful in obtaining from Congress, where they penalized—guess what, big surprise—short-haul, low-fare carriers, namely Southwest Airlines, by putting in a segment fee that gets to 3 dollars in the fall of 2001. Well, the way to offset the enhanced percentage that represents in terms of tax cost is to fly longer-haul, charging bigger fares, and reducing the percentage. . . . It's not a new line of business for us. We don't intend to supplant our traditional niche of high-frequency, short-haul service, but it is a supplement to what we've been doing.

Q: The big guys haven't really responded much to you in long-haul, have they?

A: It's kind of difficult if you're a hub-and-spoke carrier. You have to bust your hub up in order to respond. It's a niche strategy where we're bypassing their hubs in effect. You're flying from Nashville direct to Los Angeles, instead of going through Chicago, St. Louis, or Dallas–Fort Worth airport.

Q: What's the outlook for your profitability this year [1999]?

A: It's very early in the year, but our load factor is very good, our bookings are excellent, fuel prices are low, our yields are very good. I'm not saying necessarily that will prevail for the remainder of the year, but at least we're getting off to a very nice start.

Q: Can you increase capacity at 10% or more a year for the next five years?

A: If the U.S. economy holds up, I would anticipate we could expand along that line for the next five years, and actually right now, in terms of sheer opportunity vs. capacity, we could use a lot more airplanes today. We don't want to overextend ourselves financially. We don't want to injure ourselves culturally, but if you were just looking at opportunities vs. airplanes, we'd be trying to get in all the airplanes we possibly could.

Q: How many markets are left that fit the traditional short-haul, high-frequency, Southwest formula?

A: I can't say. . . . There are a good many. . . . What happens is as you enter new cities you start creating different flows of traffic. . . . It's a pattern. It's not just take a new city here and a new city there, and the two are entirely unrelated to one another.

This year, as an example, we plan to open probably two new cities, possibly three (including already-announced Islip, N.Y.), and 75% of the airplanes we receive will go into service on our existing system. Our existing system presents an enormous demand for additional growth and additional airplanes.

Q: With long-haul flights (over 750 miles) at 20% of your capacity, that's pretty sizable. How big can it get?

A: I'll put it another way for you. Southwest Airlines today operates perhaps 6% to 7% of all the available seat miles furnished in America. What is America's appetite for far lower fares, for far higher quality of customer service? I think it's more than 7%. I think it's more than 14%.

Q: How critical is the long-haul flying to your growth? Wouldn't you have done it without the tax change?

A: No, we wouldn't have. . . . We considered long-haul before this tax bill passed to be something like 750 miles. Now we're flying routes that are 1,900 miles. That's the difference.

Q: How big can long-haul get for you guys as a percentage of your revenue?

A: We're just doing it to alleviate the tax effect on us. We haven't thought further than that.

Q: As you grow more aggressively into longer flying, won't you face a stronger reaction by the bigger carriers?

A: I don't know. Southwest Airlines first of all does have a very strong balance sheet and lots of liquidity, which gives us the wherewithal to fight battles for a long, long time. It's not as if you can jump on us and expect us to disappear in two weeks.

Q: Is USAirways' lower-cost MetroJet unit on the East Coast having any impact on your growth plans or profitability?

A: We haven't changed our growth plans in any way, shape, or form as a consequence of it. We're used to competition. . . . As far as we can tell, it just expanded the market enormously. They are carrying lots of passengers, and we are too. Why should we slow down our expansion in that area of the country?

Q: Is there anything different about your growth in the East than what you've seen elsewhere?

A: It's been bigger on the East Coast. . . . It's the least competitive part of the country in terms of airline service. You have a lot more demand than you have supply.

Q: There are still people who say you have to prove that you can succeed on the East Coast.

A: [Kelleher laughs and recalls when Southwest was first dubbed a "Texas phenomenon," then an "energy belt" company, and a "Sunbelt" airline. He points again to the 884% increase in Baltimore-Providence traffic in the first year.] As if there's some area of the U.S. where people are saying, "Please, dear Lord, no matter what you do, don't give us lower-fare airline service with much better customer service quality because that's not the kind of thing we want here."

Q: Do you see any other low-fare carriers of significance likely to emerge?

A: I just don't see any niches for other carriers to occupy. It's not something I devoutly desire. It's not something I envisioned at the onset of federal deregulation of the airline industry [in 1978]. But it's just what has actually occurred. . . . When you have one airline [Southwest] providing 80% of all the low-fare competition in America, you're pretty much dependent on that airline to have low-fare competition.

CASE 51

SOUTHWEST [B]: A NEW DIRECTION—LONG HAUL FLIGHTS?

1   A shutter recently went through the hearts of American Airline executives in Baltimore and Oakland. Southwest Airlines conducted a Thanksgiving day experiment—their first ever nonstop transcontinental flight from the East Coast to the West Coast. They chose Baltimore to Oakland. The price: $99 one way. The result: a full plane and over half the passengers had never flown Southwest before.

2   Southwest Airlines Co. executives swear that their first nonstop transcontinental flight was a one-time experiment. Chief Executive Herbert D. Kelleher insists there's no immediate plan for more such flights, though he admits "the potentiality is there."

3   That potential isn't lost on anyone tracking Southwest these days—including the American Airlines Inc. spy who flew along on the Baltimore-Oakland trip. Long the most successful purveyor of cut-rate, short-haul flights, Southwest in the past year has sharply stepped up its expansion into longer, nonstop trips on routes such as Baltimore to Las Vegas (2,099 miles) and Austin, Tex., to Los Angeles (1,234 miles). And it's adding one-stop trips through places like Nashville and Kansas City for travel coast-to-coast. The prospect of Southwest going long-haul on a grand scale is "the genie [rivals] always hoped would not come out of the bottle," says analyst Kevin C. Murphy of Morgan Stanley Dean Witter. He believes an even bigger push is likely in the year ahead. "It will really rewrite the economics of the airline industry."

EASTWARD HO?

4   Southwest won't say just how profitable its long-haul routes are. "All I can say is they haven't seemed to drag us down much," says Kelleher. Thanks in part to lower fuel costs, Southwest posted record earnings last year of $433 million, a 36% gain, on 9% higher revenues of $4.2 billion. Its operating margin hit 16.4%, the best since 1981. This year should be even better. The growth in longer flights should help fuel earnings growth of 14%, to $496 million, this year, while profits fall for most of the industry, Murphy estimates. Adds James R. McGlynn, a vice-president at Tom Johnson Investment Management in Oklahoma City: "As they go into more long haul, they should be able to still maintain their margins." His money management firm holds more than 2 million Southwest shares.

5   Certainly, there's still plenty of room for Southwest to expand its traditional short-haul flights. It now flies to 52 cities but has barely scratched the densely populated East Coast, where it first started serving Baltimore in 1993 before moving into Florida, Providence, R.I., and Manchester, N.H. Following its strategy of favoring uncongested secondary airports, Southwest in March will move into New York with service to Islip, Long Island, about 40 miles east of Manhattan. Two other new cities, probably on the East Coast, may come this year. Southwest has done at least as well in building eastern markets as elsewhere: In its first year flying between Baltimore and Providence, traffic soared nearly tenfold.

6   Moreover, because Southwest avoids attacking the bigger carriers head-on, the risks of a sharp price war are low. With nearly 3 million people on Long Island, for instance, Southwest should be successful even if it doesn't lure many Manhattanites. Elsewhere, counterattacks by US Airways' MetroJet, Shuttle by United, and Delta Express could dent Southwest's profitability, but analysts say

that with its lower costs and bulletproof balance sheet, Southwest should prevail. The biggest risk Southwest faces as it moves into longer routes, says one rival airline exec, is outgrowing its roots: "It's very much of a culture issue, how well they can stick to doing what they do well."

7   Southwest downplays any suggestion that it's shifting focus. About 80% of its capacity is still on flights shorter than 750 miles. "We're built for the short-haul markets, and we know that," says Chief Financial Officer Gary C. Kelly. Indeed, the airline's very identity is wrapped up in its underdog tradition—and in the flamboyance of Kelleher, the chain-smoking, Wild Turkey-swilling funnyman who fuels Southwest's legendary esprit de corps. Past stunts include the time Kelleher arm-wrestled another CEO for the rights to an advertising slogan. He lost but still got to keep using the slogan.

A TAX DECISION FOR KELLEHER = A SERIOUS THREAT TO OTHER MAJOR AIRLINES

8   Kelleher claims that Southwest never would have jumped aggressively into routes of 1,000-plus miles if not for changes in the federal ticket tax in 1997 that were pushed by bigger carriers. The new system replaces a percentage tax with one that includes a flat, per-segment fee that hits low-fare carriers harder. But some competitors believe that Southwest would have moved strongly into long hauls anyway. "They've dug all the shallow holes," says Rono J. Dutta, senior vice-president for planning at United Airlines Inc. And he notes that in Southwest's core markets, "they've now got competition" from the majors' low-fare units.

9   On the other hand, Southwest's success on longer routes will put growing pressure on the profits of its bigger competitors. Southwest's cost advantage is built on rapid 20-minute gate turnarounds; an efficient all-Boeing 737 fleet, including new 737-700s that can fly cross-country nonstop; and a more productive workforce. That edge shrinks on longer flights, but it's still significant. Roberts, Roach & Associates Inc., an airline consultant in Hayward, Calif., says Southwest has at least a 59% cost advantage over bigger rivals at flights of 500 miles, and a still husky 35% lead at 1,500 miles. "It's a huge threat," says a rival airline exec.

10   With long-haul flights as a growing part of its arsenal, Southwest has opened a second front in its war on higher-cost rivals. Already, nonstop flights longer than 1,000 miles account for more than 16% of Southwest's capacity, up from 9.5% five years ago, estimates Samuel C. Buttrick, an analyst for Paine Webber Inc. "In the final analysis, Southwest's growth opportunities are bounded by consumer demand for lower fares," he says. As more travelers look for ways to pinch pennies, that demand, long or short, seems almost limitless.

A Long-Haul Flight Southwest Style—What Baltimore-to-Oakland Customers Thought

No reserved seats? No hot meals? No problem, says Dr. Irving Weinberg. "I need to lose weight anyway," cracks the 42-year-old M.D. and president of PEM Technologies, a Bethesda (Md.) medical-equipment company, as we chat aboard a 7:30 a.m. Southwest Airlines flight from Baltimore to Oakland, Calif. Ahead of us loom seven hours of flying, a 25-minute stop in Kansas City, and three servings of snacks. The payoff: a transcontinental ticket that is far cheaper than rivals'.

There are other, less obvious advantages to flying one of Southwest's new no-frills flights cross-country, though. For starters, a noticeable air of congeniality exists among my fellow passengers. It's almost a requirement, since we have to work out things like seat assignments on our own. One passenger lugs aboard a big brown bag of food to share with his seatmates.

Judging by my flight, many who are jumping aboard as Southwest expands into longer routes work for penny-pinching companies that don't want to spring for the sky-high ticket prices big carriers charge for last-minute travel. David Grossweiler, a 30-year-old engineer for Butler Manufacturing Co., booked a flight to his Kansas City headquarters six days ahead. He says other airlines wanted to charge $850, while the Southwest flight was $356. "Five hundred dollars seemed like too much for a small food tray," he says.

But if the food isn't sumptuous, at least we won't starve. Our snack-food banquet begins with a bag of mini-graham crackers and moves on to a ham stick, sesame crackers, a cheese wedge, a NutriGrain Twist, nuts, raisins, and drinks.

Perk Talk

With no movies or music on the flight, many quickly pull out laptops or legal pads. As with all Southwest flights, those who want conversation and leg room sit in "the lounge"—two rows of seats facing each other along the emergency-exit aisle that offers fliers a chance to chat and exchange business cards. There, the discussion soon turns from children and work to the perks we've sacrificed to fly cheaply. Cybelle Lewis, 34, a museum designer for Douglas/Gallagher, an architecture firm in Washington, D.C., complains that she must drive an hour to Baltimore—even though Ronald Reagan National Airport is five miles from her Arlington (Va.) home.

She also laments the loss of first-class pre-boarding and family vacations underwritten with frequent-flier miles. Southwest has a mileage plan, but it flies to destinations such as New Orleans or Albuquerque, not Hawaii or London. Says Lewis with a sigh: "I was a Preferred Plus on US Air."

But that seat-of-the-pants quality is just the ticket for Weinberg. He settles into a lounge seat and is soon raving about Southwest's flexibility on things like carry-on luggage. "I used to carry 200 pounds of equipment," he says. "It was never a problem on Southwest. Other airlines would say, 'That has to go cargo.'"

Weinberg also appreciates the jokes that flight attendants use to spice up announcements. But try as he might this time, Dr. Weinberg can't coax a joke or song out of the crew. "I think they were sleepy," he explains after our flight has finally touched down. Or maybe, after seven hours of passing out peanuts, they're shell-shocked.

The only real glitch: So much trash accumulated during the flight that some of it was inconveniently stowed outside the rest rooms.

Source: Roy Furchott [at 39,000 feet], "Flying on a Discount and Some Pretzels," *Business Week:* February 8, 1999.

CASE 52

VALUJET FLIGHT 592: RESTORING CONFIDENCE IN THE AFTERMATH OF A CATASTROPHIC EVENT

INTRODUCTION

1   Perhaps the name ValuJet spoke to the principles on which the Atlanta-based airline was founded—to provide low fares, every day, everywhere the company's airplanes fly.[1] However, the strategy carved a niche for ValuJet which naysayers believed did not exist. What resulted was the most successful start-up the airline industry had ever witnessed. And that was exactly what ValuJet's four founders envisioned when they launched operations on October 26, 1993. With a total 120 years of airline industry experience, founders Robert Priddy, chairperson and CEO; Maurice Gallagher, vice chairperson and treasurer; Timothy Flynn, director; and Lewis Jordan, president and COO were not newcomers to the industry.

2   These entrepreneur dreamers capitalized on a formula that was all but untested. ". . . Run a low-cost operation that does not fly any single route more than six times a day, charge bargain basement fares, and aim the pitch mostly at leisure travelers."[2] The formula worked. Every quarter since its inception, ValuJet continuously increased its profits, and reported a record $20.7 million net in 1994, its first full year of operation.[3] The profit margin ValuJet maintained since its inception surpassed what similar airlines had taken nearly a decade or more to match. ValuJet's consistent financial performance set a growth and earnings' pace that had not been seen in the airline industry for many years. Its success made believers of many doubters on Wall Street, where ValuJet stock was publicly traded on NASDAQ. "Since going public in June 1994, its shares rocketed from 6¾ to 46½."[4] However, the company suffered a 1996 second-quarter loss of $9.6 million, from 28 cents a share down to 18 cents.[5]

3   Having begun flight operations with two DC-9 jet aircrafts serving Orlando, Tampa, and Jacksonville, the company grew to service 31 destinations in the southeast and midwest. By the celebration of its second anniversary, the company announced that it had placed a $1 billion order for 50 McDonnell Douglas MD-95-30ERS, with options to buy an additional 50 planes. Delivery was expected in 1999.

4   ValuJet seemed to have a dazzling future . . . until tragedy struck on May 11, 1996. On that fateful day, a ValuJet DC-9 en route from Miami to Atlanta plunged into the Florida Everglades, killing all 110 people on board. While final proof of the cause of the crash may bring closure for relatives of the victims, it is likely that many key pieces of evidence will remain lost forever in the swampland. Investigators have theorized that oxygen canisters containing flammable chemicals were most likely the culprit that doomed the 27-year-old plane. Because these canisters were not ordinarily carried on the planes, the theory was further substantiated by the pilot's last transmission to the control tower in Miami, ". . . there's smoke in the cockpit."[6] At the time of this writing, this speculation had not been confirmed.

5   The accident caused widespread concern. Many people wondered whether ValuJet was a safe airline. Others doubted the Federal Aviation Administration's (FAA) ability to create a safe and proper operating environment for air travel. Furthermore, it brought attention to ValuJet's capability to manage a crisis that had devastating implications not only for ValuJet's shareholders and customers, but for the whole industry.

6   Although the order for the MD-95-30ERS had been placed, the status of that order was sidelined. Blemishes on the airline existed but were minimal. Nevertheless, ValuJet had made a commitment to

having its aircraft operated and serviced by highly trained professionals, despite questions about safety and the age of its aircraft.[7]

7   ValuJet was initially structured in a way that went against conventional airline wisdom; it did things differently, but not always successfully. ValuJet entered the market as a bare-necessities airline. Unlike most of its competitors, ValuJet used a ticketless passenger system, no full meal deals, no frequent flyer programs, and no first class or advanced seating. ValuJet also applied a system of strict cost controls to all its operations, spent more efficiently, and passed the savings along to the consumer. The public responded enthusiastically.

8   This case addresses the management challenges that ValuJet faced in attempting first to survive as an organization, and ultimately to restore stakeholder confidence in the aftermath of a catastrophic event. The airline's operations—from maintenance to front office—were subjected to unprecedented scrutiny. ValuJet's stock plummeted, and management's response to those and other challenges would determine the airline's ultimate survival or collapse.

9   Important to ValuJet's survival was leadership's *response* to the crisis. The very principles upon which ValuJet was built and which had fueled its rapid success were now being questioned from practical, ethical, and even realistic perspectives. What did the term "budget carrier" really imply? Had this term become the latest oxymoron?

THE CHALLENGE: DO OR DIE

10   In order to assure its organizational survival, ValuJet had to address three major problems. First, the airline had to regain the trust of the flying public when (and if) it returned to the skies. The second challenge was convincing the FAA and everyone else that ValuJet did not place profits before safety. Third, ValuJet had to maintain its financial stability while its future was decided.

11   Shareholders and the flying public had enjoyed a love affair with ValuJet Airlines. But that relationship was troubled after the crash and ongoing regulatory scrutiny of ValuJet's safety record. Two weeks after the crash, on June 18, 1996, the FAA announced that it was grounding the company's fleet until ValuJet could comply with regulatory concerns. The grounding would certainly cause ValuJet to forgo a significant amount of revenue. Lewis Jordan said, "We're holding up planes for reasons that other carriers wouldn't even think of delaying. We are obviously primarily focused on everything being just right or we don't move."[8]

12   At the time of the crash, many industry experts believed that ValuJet's strongest assets were its balance sheet and its top management. The airline's weaknesses included its relatively short time in existence, the increasing competition in the industry, and the widespread perception that old planes and low paid personnel threatened passenger safety and security.

13   By growing rapidly and creating unprecedented margins, ValuJet wowed Wall Street. The growth strained ValuJet operations, especially during past winters when cancellations and late flights were common. In January and February of 1996, ValuJet suffered several minor incidents, ranging from planes going off runways to broken landing gear. Concerned that ValuJet was not adjusting well to its fast growth, the FAA did an intensive week-long study in February 1996 and instituted a 120-day "special emphasis" program. At that time, ValuJet voluntarily accepted several reforms, ranging from added FAA inspectors to extra crew training.

14   Weeks after the crash, Lewis Jordan knew he must again act quickly and decisively. If the cause of the crash became a clear case of negligence in maintenance or poor training, consultants said the stock price and passenger faith in the carrier would be diminished even further. According to Mike Boyd, head of Aviation Systems Research in Golden, Colorado, most crashes can be cleaned up within a week or two, enabling the bad news to fade from the public's mind within a week. In this case, however, the cleanup took much longer, meaning that ValuJet's name was plastered negatively in the media for an extended period of time. Again the simple yet overwhelming realization . . . restoring public confidence in the airline was going to be difficult.

15   The events following ValuJet's fatal crash were remarkable. The *Atlanta Journal and Constitution* reported that ValuJet had become the most scrutinized airline in aviation history. The media attacked ValuJet because of the crash and because the airline was a low cost, no-frills carrier flying the oldest

fleet of planes of any carrier in the airline industry. These events led to the FAA's decision to ground ValuJet.[9] The decision immediately called public issues management into play.

16   Created for the purposes of making commercial flying safe *and* of promoting airline business, the FAA operated under two, and what many considered conflicting, roles. Robert Wiechowski, an FAA flight-safety inspector for Professional Airways System Specialists, commented in *Business Week*, "The FAA's top brass is in bed with the airlines."[10] Stated more directly, those who needed to be monitored, monitored themselves.

17   The grounding was to be effective until ValuJet met requirements for the FAA to reestablish "airworthiness." The FAA cited ValuJet with maintenance and operational deficiencies while the company's stock plummeted. Wall Street began looking elsewhere for another rising star. The company reported on August 7, 1996, that it lost $9.6 million, or 18 cents a share in its second quarter.[11]

18   According to an article in the *Wall Street Journal* by Holman W. Jenkins, Jr., ". . . USAir had five fatal accidents in five years, killing 231, and nobody talked about yanking its license to fly."[12] The irony of the ValuJet situation was that if the oxygen canisters had been the reason for the accident, it would have been a subcontractor's fault of simply mislabeling the cargo.[13] ValuJet was suffering the consequences directly. Jordan vowed that ValuJet would be back in business.[14] Still, the management team faced a monumental task of regaining the public's trust and re-founding ValuJet as the "Cinderella story" in a very volatile industry.[15]

Confidence Restoration: Transforming ValuJet's Image

19   "We'd better go." Those were the quiet, determined words Jordan spoke upon hearing the news. In an attempt to build teamwork and solidify his company's link to its home city, Atlanta, Jordan along with 27 of his employees was to construct a Habitat for Humanity. "As Jordan was tacking in insulation at about 2:30 that day, the pager on Public Relations Director Marcia Scott's waist trilled. Calling back, Scott turned white: A ValuJet plane in Florida had dropped off radar. Scott did not speak, but Jordan looked at her and recognized trouble. He left the construction site, still wearing his nail apron.[16]

20   Jordan's first and immediate response was to dispatch a ValuJet team to Miami while he remained in Atlanta to organize a care-taking strategy for the family of the victims. It is often in times of a crisis that an individual's true nature is exposed. When that crisis involves loss of life, initial decisions and priorities reflect values and beliefs. In following with his company's stated priorities and with his own personal commitment, the grieving families came first to Jordan.

21   ValuJet's management team initiated the care-taking strategy by assigning one employee to each family. These counselors were to keep families informed of any new developments, helping them with any travel and lodging needs, and assist with their grieving process if appropriate. It was not until the day after the crash that Jordan appeared at the tragic site, confident that what was being done for the families of the victims was as good as could be expected.

22   At this point, Jordan, along with his management team, was intentional about his efforts to be open and candid with the media. His face was seen constantly on local and national television for days following the tragedy. Through interviews, press conferences and even a visit to Capitol Hill, Jordan tirelessly worked at renewing confidence in the troubled airline. "We plan to start all over," Jordan said, "and bring ourselves back as successful, strong, safe, reliable."[17]

23   Although the FAA's decision to ground the airline may have reduced some of the pressure ValuJet's management was experiencing, Jordan's assessment of the decision was that it was "grossly unfair."[18] He vowed to have the airline up and running again in 30 days. The FAA had never completely grounded an airline the size of ValuJet. Many close to the case have said politics (it was an election year) played a major role in the FAA's decision to snip ValuJet's wings.

24   Customers did not immediately abandon ValuJet. Fewer than 10% canceled reservations after the crash. But by May 16, ValuJet's schedule was a shambles as every plane underwent detailed inspection and maintenance. Jordan canceled half of ValuJet's flights indefinitely. And he phoned USAir President and Chief Operating Officer Rakesh Gangwal and asked him to accept ValuJet passengers who were knocked off canceled flights. "Whatever we can do to help," Gangwal told him. The chief executive of another carrier—Jordan won't say who—turned down the same request.[19]

25   A week after the crash, the action had migrated from the command center to executives' offices. Marketing Director Ponder Harrison, who had pulled ValuJet's advertisements off the radio after the crash, began mapping out a postcrash strategy. ValuJet will stick with its "Critter" logo and the "good times, great fares" motto, but like most airlines, it probably will shy away from the safety issue in marketing plans.[20]

26   Meanwhile, Chief Financial Officer Stephen C. Nevin and CEO Robert Priddy reached out to shareholders, bondholders, and lenders. Priddy assured analysts in a May 22 conference call that ValuJet's insurance will cover the accident's costs. And its $254 million in cash, he said, "gives us considerable staying power" even if traffic does not bounce back. One event that may take some heat off ValuJet: SabreTech Inc., the company that supplied oxygen tanks to Flight 592 that may have led to the crash, said on May 21 that it had mislabeled the cargo.[21]

27   Regardless, ValuJet didn't expect to resume a full schedule until year's end. Bottomline, recovery for ValuJet promised to be a long, slow ordeal that would depend on five factors:

1. *The company's ability to financially survive the grounding and comply with FAA standards and regulation.* No one could predict how long the grounding would last. A point of reference, however, was the FAA's grounding of KIWI International Air Lines. After the agency ordered Kiwi to cease operations, the company simply corrected the problems for which it was cited and resumed business within days. Analysts were predicting that it would take weeks for ValuJet to come into compliance with FAA standards because the problems identified by agents were of a systemic nature.

2. *The rate at which the FAA would allow ValuJet to grow—if and when it resumed service.* The management strategies ValuJet used successfully to grow a no-frills, low-cost airline haunted the company. Outside critics accused the company of penny-pinching on safety and maintenance. Jordan contended from the beginning that the airline made safety its highest priority. If and when ValuJet returned to the air, safety would still be at the forefront of operations, according to Jordan, but the level at which the airline grew would be scaled back. Jordan had announced that the airline would restart with fewer planes, fifteen or so versus its original fifty-one.[22]

3. *The willingness of the public to trust ValuJet again.* The ability of management to devise an effective strategy and communicate its strategy to the public would be key to its future success. Many vowed never to fly ValuJet again. However, just as many said they would return to ValuJet once the airline corrected its problems.

4. *The willingness of shareholders to continue to reinvest in ValuJet.* According to the *Atlanta Journal-Constitution* on the rise and fall of ValuJet's stock price, it was reported that on November 27, 1995: Stock hits record high of $34.75. June 18, 1996: Stock hits its record low of $4.50, recovers to close at $6.50, down $3.50."[23] Collectively, ValuJet shareholders lost millions as a result of the FAA's order to cease operations. Many investors lost confidence in ValuJet's ability to recover, and decided to cut their losses and reinvest elsewhere.

5. *Employee motivation.* After the FAA grounded ValuJet, the company was forced to furlough some 4,000 of its workers. ValuJet's management organized a town hall meeting for employees two days following the airline's ceasing operations. This purpose of this meeting was to assist employees in dealing with the loss of work. Only 10 percent of the company's workforce attended the meeting—most in support of their leader, Lewis Jordan.

STAKEHOLDERS' RESPONSE TO THE CRISES

28   ValuJet faced a wide range of responses from critical stakeholders. In order to restore confidence in the troubled airline, the management team had to understand and manage each of those responses. Lee Duffey, president of Duffey Communications in Atlanta, Georgia, commented, ". . . you lose time to think, plan and react when a crisis occurs." (Personal communication, June 11, 1996) After the crash of Flight 592, ValuJet's management team immediately devised a strategy for communicating to the families of the victims, the general public, ValuJet's shareholders, and the media. "The bottom line is that companies should be prepared to show a human side in times of tragedy. Care and concern should be expressed immediately." Duffey continued with three critical questions addressed in times of crisis:

1. Can the disaster be contained within the company? This did not happen with ValuJet because the accident was immediately publicized on national television.
2. Is the crisis of a consumer nature? ValuJet's disaster most definitely was of a consumer nature. All passengers on Flight 592 were killed, and that did not send a positive message to other potential consumers.
3. How visual is the crisis? The ValuJet crash was mysteriously visual. There was a plane crash, but the aircraft shattered into pieces like broken glass and without much of a trace. Furthermore, there were no whole bodies found. (Personal communication, June 11, 1996)

29   Because of the mystery of the crash, the media continued to keep ValuJet in the public eye. Jordan tried to be as forthcoming as he could with information to the media. Numerous press conferences were held to field questions regarding the crash, the safety of the airline's aircraft, and what ValuJet was doing to manage the crisis. Hundreds of news reporters from across the United States converged on Atlanta to tell one of the biggest stories since the trial of O. J. Simpson.

30   Meanwhile, ValuJet's management team upheld its commitment to the care-taking strategy. One week after the crash, ValuJet organized a memorial service in Atlanta for its crew members, passengers, and the families of the victims on Flight 592. Photographs of the ValuJet crew members killed on the flight lined a table in front of the coliseum where the service was held. Hundreds of people filed past the procession to view the photographs and pay their last respects. Seated on the platform were clergy from various denominations, the mother of the pilot, and the father of a young missionary passenger. During the memorial service, Jordan lit a candle in memory of each of the crew members. While the service was a gesture of sorrow and sympathy on the part of ValuJet, the families of the victims struggled to bring closure to the tragedy. About two weeks later, another memorial service was held at the crash site in the Everglades. Family members and friends of the victims were transported to the site, where the mourners laid wreaths, flowers, and stuffed animals in memory of their loved ones.

31   ValuJet's employees' reactions to the crash of Flight 592 were mixed. Some employees left their jobs while others remained and offered their support and confidence in the safety and strength of the airline. Until the grounding, ValuJet continued to pay the salaries of those employees who were sidelined as a result of the altered flight schedule and subsequent loss of business. Some were later forced to seek unemployment assistance from the Labor Department. Flight attendants who had previously worked at ValuJet, and in some cases had been fired with lawsuits pending, spoke negatively about the safety of the airline's aircraft. Because media attention heightened, ValuJet imposed a gag order on its employees. Only Jordan would comment on the crash and anything related to it.

32   In its continued efforts to restore confidence in the airline, ValuJet gave refunds to passengers who canceled their flights following the crash. Also, after the crash, ValuJet voluntarily cut its flight schedule in half. Closer scrutiny by the National Transportation Safety Board (NTSB) and the FAA forced the company to delay and frequently even cancel remaining scheduled flights.

33   To further complicate matters, the FAA's order to ValuJet to cease operations just a month after the crash raised serious questions about the FAA's ability to do its job. Before the crash, ValuJet had been cited by the FAA for serious problems with maintenance, training, and oversight of operations. At the time of the crash, those findings had not yet surfaced with Transportation Secretary and FAA administrator, David Hinson, who repeatedly assured the flying public in national news reports that the airline was safe. The FAA's subsequent change of heart, expressed through its decision to ground ValuJet, left a cloud over its credibility with the public. In an effort to save face in the situation, the FAA announced plans for a restructuring that began with the resignation of longtime Associate Administrator Anthony Broderick. As the "number two man" and unofficial chief of the agency, Broderick oversaw the certification of airlines and "air-worthiness." Broderick believed his move to step down would allow FAA administrators to make the changes necessary to improve public confidence in the agency.[24]

34   Other airlines competitors had already begun to benefit as a result of ValuJet's downfall. Waiting in the wings to come to the rescue of passengers left stranded when ValuJet operations ceased operations were United Airlines, Delta Air Lines, and, to a lesser extent, Southwest Airlines.

Southwest's strategy targeted satellite cities, while ValuJet focused on metropolitan centers. Moreover, ValuJet was a distraction for USAir. Before the tragic crash, ValuJet had begun expanding into Pittsburgh and Charlotte, centers that were considered high-cost hubs for USAir. ValuJet's plan was to further invade USAir territory, taking bargain-hunting passengers under its wings.[25] Still, competitors were scurrying to lure ValuJet passengers who formed a leisure traveler niche which most major airlines had never before targeted.

DESCRIPTION OF THE OPERATING ENVIRONMENT

35   Organizations operate within the context of their internal and external environments. ValuJet was operating in an industry that had been deregulated since 1978. From a marketing perspective, the deregulation removed many of the requirements for establishing an airline. From a safety perspective, the industry's maintenance and safety requirements remained essentially the same. All airlines had to meet the applicable specifications for their types of operations as directed by the FAA's established Federal Aviation Regulations (FARs).

36   Each airline is certified to fly in a particular manner that met the FAA's approval. Each type of certification included a number of programs that the airline could choose to participate in as a carrier. For instance, if an airline elected to carry hazardous cargo as defined by the FAA, then that airline must demonstrate to the FAA that it had an established, documented, and executable hazardous cargo program. Once this program was presented, the FAA could disapprove, approve, or make changes to the program. If approved as written by the airline, those documented procedures were considered federal law. An airline could be found in violation if it were in non-compliance of its own hazardous cargo program or other such programs that the airline actually designed. These regulatory programs increased the cost of doing business in the airline industry. Not following all regulations would basically have led to an airline putting the public's safety in jeopardy or gaining a definite cost advantage.

37   The FAA sometimes gives a new airline reprieve from some regulations for a period of time following its startup. These reprieves were one of the ways that the FAA carried out its two roles. ValuJet received such a reprieve. The reprieve did promote ValuJet's business, but some questioned whether it also ensured the safest possible operation of its airplanes. Because the cost of implementing those regulations based solely on safety was extremely expensive, the dual roles of the FAA placed ValuJet in a compromising position.

38   The FAA's marketing role developed to the point whereby many people claimed that the agency was overlooking the fact that economy airlines were focusing too much on profits at the expense of safety. This focus flew in the face of its other role—that of protecting the traveling public against any potential hazard, no matter how small. It would appear that safety would take precedence over profit. In theory, the position of the FAA was that safety came first. However, the prioritization of these roles now threatened the very existence of the agency itself. The FAA did have a very high success rate of preventing the type of situation they were regulating against, but the fact remained that the FAA is a political body, and economic conditions are influential circumstances within the political arena.

39   ValuJet's leadership was also concerned with restoring public and employee confidence in its equipment. ValuJet chose to operate its route structure with the DC-9 manufactured by the McDonnell Douglas Corporation. The DC-9 had proven performance in the airline industry for approximately 30 years. Most major airlines, at one time or another, flew this airplane successfully, and it was no coincidence that ValuJet chose the DC-9. This aircraft fit perfectly into the company's overall marketing strategy. The intent from inception of the ValuJet idea was to be a low-cost carrier attracting frugal air travelers, as well as travelers who would otherwise either drive or take a bus.

40   The management of ValuJet chose the DC-9 for several reasons. First and foremost, many of these airplanes existed in the used aircraft market during a time when few airlines were purchasing airplanes. No doubt, it was a buyer's market. Second, the DC-9's compact size served ValuJet's targeted route structure very well. The small, simple airplane moved easily into and out of small airfields and had a short turn-around time requiring little human effort and support. Third, choosing only one type of airplane allowed the airline to focus its maintenance on one set of parts and maintenance procedures. ValuJet's rival, Southwest Airlines, found value in operating only one type of airplane for over

25 years. Fourth, the DC-9 offered a two-person cockpit as opposed to a three-person configuration. Most airplanes the age of the DC-9 are configured for three pilots. By allowing for only two pilots, ValuJet met FAA pilot flight duty requirements with the minimum number of personnel.

41   However, one of the drawbacks of the DC-9 was its age. While the older airplanes may have been close to being as safe as newer ones, they required much more attention and resources to ensure safe operations. Many airplanes that were built by such companies as Boeing and McDonnell Douglas were over 35 years old and still flying with few problems. Furthermore, the newer airplanes have the more sophisticated components that probably make them safer than older airplanes. Compared to the DC-9s, newer airplanes are also more fuel efficient. Several technological advancements in the newer airplanes provide increased flexibility in the planes operations, while still keeping safety the highest priority. Features in newer airlines included enhanced computer systems and improved mechanical systems.

DESCRIPTION OF THE FINANCIAL ENVIRONMENT

42   Throughout ValuJet's time of crisis, management maintained confidence in its own financial position. ValuJet could not have been financially healthier prior to the accident. Having posted record profits during the first three years in operation, ValuJet amassed cash liquidity in excess of $254 million. During 1995, ValuJet celebrated outstanding operating margins and consistent increases in operating revenues and net income. For the first three quarters of 1995, ValuJet produced a $48.6 million net profit on revenues of $256.9 million. Net profit margin was 18.9%. In contrast, Southwest Airlines took eight years to produce a $20 million annual net income under equally fierce competitive market conditions. ValuJet surpassed this achievement in its first full year of operation. Following this remarkable financial performance, the Flight 592 tragedy threatened to place the airline under significant financial strain.

43   Because of the uncertainty of the claims against ValuJet, it was too early to tell what effect the crash actually had on the company's bottom line. Before the crash, ValuJet was generating $1.2 million in revenue per day, incurring costs of approximately $1 million. During the imposed grounding by the FAA, the airline was losing approximately $200,000 every day. In addition, the airline faced incurring costs associated with the correction of violations cited by the FAA. These costs lessened ValuJet's cash reserves. Available cash reserves were key to the company's survival while under FAA scrutiny.

44   During this time of crisis, Jordan continually reached out to shareholders to boost confidence in both the company and the stock. Since it began trading on June 28, 1994, ValuJet's stock rose steadily through the end of 1995. It hit an all-time low of $4.50 on June 18, 1996. This low followed a media frenzy of the crash aftermath, FAA investigations and findings, and union worker protests. As a result of the tragedy, ValuJet, Inc. and ValuJet Airlines faced a range of potentially catastrophic legal issues that could financially cripple the fledgling airline.

DESCRIPTION OF THE LEGAL ENVIRONMENT

45   In a related legal issue, three ValuJet shareholders filed suit against the company, claiming they were misled about the safety of the airline. The class action lawsuit filed in late May 1996 alleged that ValuJet issued false statements about airline operations and safety for the purposes of inflating the value of the company's stock.

46   The suit alleged that chairperson Priddy issued published statements that ValuJet's safety record was among the best in the industry. However, nine days before the crash, the FAA issued a report in which ValuJet was singled out as more accident prone than nearly all of its low-cost competitors.

47   ValuJet was now facing possible criminal charges as a result of its transport of oxygen generators, which it was certified to carry. In addition, an investigation was launched that included one of the airline's contractors, SabreTech, Inc. SabreTech was one of the companies responsible for providing maintenance on ValuJet airplanes. It was assumed that SabreTech was responsible for the dispensing,

handling, and transporting of the oxygen generator bottles that were believed to have contributed to or even caused the crash. While ValuJet and SabreTech denied responsibility for shipping the canisters, the Federal Bureau of Investigation (FBI) indicated that criminal charges could be brought if laws were broken.

SUMMARY

48 ValuJet was established in 1993 as a low fare airline that offered a no-frills approach to leisure and business travel. Over three years, the airline grew to serve passengers in cities in the U.S. Southeast and the Midwest. In order to provide its low cost service, ValuJet used older planes that were specifically designed for short flights. This case presented issues surrounding ValuJet's corporate philosophy in its business practices and looked at management techniques used in the face of a crisis. At issue was whether ValuJet cut costs to the extreme and placed an operating profit ahead of passenger safety.

49 The company was still considered a start-up airline after two and one half years of operation, and the FAA apparently overlooked certain procedures that were mandatory for other airlines. ValuJet cut costs wherever possible in order to keep fares low and run a more profitable business. The company outsourced a majority of operations including the maintenance of its older fleet. The company that provided the maintenance service was a reputable organization that also provided some maintenance for one of the "big three" airlines. The crash of Flight 592 may prove to be a symptom of non-procedural handling of hazardous cargo. Human error played a significant role in the mislabeling of the oxygen canisters containing fire spreading chemicals.

50 The cause of Flight 592's crash has remained a mystery much longer than most airline crashes and that keeps ValuJet under the media's relentless scrutiny. The FAA initially reported ValuJet as being a safe airline hours after the crash, but within weeks shut ValuJet down for unsafe operating conditions. The operations of ValuJet had actually been under investigation for several months prior to the crash. ValuJet would be grounded until it could meet the FAA's safe operating standards.

51 Restoring the confidence of the FAA and the flying public was the only way for ValuJet to make a successful comeback and continue its profitable operations. The question remaining was whether or not ValuJet could accomplish the huge task of restoring confidence before it was too late.

EPILOGUE

Early 1998

52 ValuJet, through its wholly owned subsidiaries, AirTran Airlines, Inc. and AirTran Airways, Inc., continued to operate "an affordable, no frills, limited frequency, scheduled airline serving short haul markets primarily in the eastern United States." Prior to June 17, 1996, ValuJet offered service to 30 cities from Atlanta, Washington, D.C. (Dulles Airport), Boston, and Orlando and operated up to 320 flights per peak day with its fleet of 51 aircraft. ValuJet resumed limited operations with service between Atlanta and four other cities as of September 30, 1996, and it continued to work with the FAA since that time to recertify aircraft and expand its flight operations. As of March 6, 1998, the FAA had approved 35 of AirTran Airlines' [original ValuJet operation] DC-9 Series 30 aircraft for flight. In addition, AirTran Airways operates 11 Boeing 737-200 aircraft ("B-737 aircraft"). As of March 1, 1998, ValuJet operated a total of up to 249 flights per day of which 196 flights per day were between Atlanta and 25 other cities and 30 flights per day were between Orlando and 16 cities other than Atlanta. Additional service was offered between Washington, D.C. (Dulles Airport) and Boston and Chicago, between Boston and Philadelphia, and between Knoxville, Tennessee and New York (LaGuardia Airport).

Merger with Airways Corporation

53 ValuJet acquired Airways Corporation ("Airways") on November 17, 1997, through a merger of Airways with and into ValuJet. In anticipation of the merger, the name of ValuJet Airlines was changed

---

A Message from Lewis Jordan, President of ValuJet Airlines
A special flyer sent to personal residences in Atlanta, GA in October, 1996

It gives me great pleasure to inform you that ValuJet and its everyday low fares are back. The Federal Aviation Administration (FAA) and the Department of Transportation (DOT) have fully approved ValuJet's maintenance and safety procedures and the fitness of our organization. Furthermore, the Department of Transportation has favorably cited the extensive qualifications of ValuJet's management team, the airline's strong financial condition, the steps we have taken to strengthen procedures and our cooperative attitude of compliance with all applicable laws and regulations.

Thanks to our dedicated employees and the broad support of the traveling public, ValuJet resumed air service to Orlando, Fort Lauderdale, Tampa and Washington, D.C., on Monday, September 30, 1996. Nonstop service to 12 more cities will be added in the weeks immediately following that date.

While ValuJet's employees and the general public have been steadfast in their support, it is the more than 10 million ValuJet customers who have given us the purpose and resources to continue operations. For that reason, I, on behalf of all ValuJet people, extend my gratitude to each and every one of you. And I want to give you my personal assurance that ValuJet and its employees have done, and will continue to do, everything in our power to provide you with affordable air travel that is comfortable, reliable and—above all—safe. Because while ValuJet was founded on the principle of providing the public with affordable air travel by controlling costs, our most important principle is our commitment to adhering to the highest levels and standards of safety.

We look forward to servicing you soon and often in the years ahead. Thank you for your support.

With warm regards, *Lewis Jordan*

---

to "AirTran Airlines." Upon completion of the merger, ValuJet changed its name to AirTran Holdings, Inc. Airways' operating subsidiary continues to operate under the AirTran Airways name. In January 1998, ValuJet moved its headquarters to Airways' facilities in Orlando, Florida. While ValuJet initially operated AirTran Airlines and AirTran Airways under separate operating certificates, it reserved the right to merge these two operating subsidiaries at a later date.

Strategy

54   In order to return to profitability and resume growth, ValuJet chose to pursue a three-pronged strategy (i) to maintain its traditional cost and value leadership in the markets that it serves, (ii) to reposition its brand image to mitigate the long-term adverse effects of the May 1996 accident and the subsequent suspension of operations, and (iii) to gradually expand capacity as market demand warrants. ValuJet's strategy was predicated on providing a reliable, customer friendly alternative for affordable air transportation. The key element of this approach was the successful repositioning of the product to broaden the base of available traffic. ValuJet changed the name of its ValuJet operating subsidiary to AirTran Airlines and, along with its other operating subsidiary, AirTran Airways, introduced a new business strategy in late 1997 designed to appeal to a broader travel market. The objective of this strategy was to make air travel more attractive to fare conscious business travelers and even more convenient for leisure travelers. The product enhancements included a new corporate livery, a new business class service, featuring two by two seating, pre-assigned seating, and the nationwide distribution of its inventory through travel agents.

55   As part of the product rebranding, ValuJet repainted its DC-9 aircraft with a new livery. ValuJet also repainted Airway's B-737 aircraft in a similar livery. In addition, ValuJet reconfigured its DC-9 aircraft to provide 16 business class seats in each aircraft and reconfigured its B-737 aircraft to provide 12 business class seats in each aircraft.

56   ValuJet's continued its low priced fare structure intended to stimulate new demand for air travel by leisure customers and fare conscious business travelers who would have otherwise not traveled or who would have used ground transportation. ValuJet's fare structure generally defines the pricing in

most markets that ValuJet serves, providing travelers with substantial savings that would not be available in the absence of service by the Company. In addition to advance purchase fares, ValuJet maintains reasonably priced "walk-up" fares that are generally well below similar fares offered by its competitors. ValuJet believes that it has historically generated its own traffic through low fare market stimulation rather than by pursuing the more traditional airline approach of competing for market share with existing carriers.

57   Once ValuJet reestablishes profitability and a favorable brand image, ValuJet intends to pursue a prudent growth strategy. ValuJet entered into a contract with Boeing to purchase 50 new Boeing 717 aircraft ("B-717 aircraft"), to be delivered from 1999 through 2002, with options to purchase an additional 50 aircraft. The B-717 will have 115 seats, consisting of 16 business class seats and 99 coach seats. ValuJet estimates that the B-717 aircraft, which have a slightly larger seating capacity, increased fuel efficiency and lower maintenance costs than ValuJet's DC-9 aircraft, will provide a cost per ASM lower than ValuJet's DC-9 fleet, even after taking into account the aircraft's higher acquisition cost. ValuJet is the "launch" customer of the B-717 aircraft. As the launch customer, ValuJet anticipates that this contract will provide material value in terms of acquisition cost and manufacturer financing assistance. ValuJet determined that the B-717 aircraft offers the optimum balance between operating cost and revenue opportunity.

Impact of Accident and Suspension of Operations

58   On May 11, 1996, ValuJet tragically lost its Flight 592 en route from Miami to Atlanta. The accident resulted in extensive media coverage calling into question the safety of low-fare airlines in general and ValuJet in particular. In response to the accident, the FAA conducted an extraordinary review of ValuJet's operations. Some effects of the accident, ensuing FAA inspections, media coverage and suspension of operations include:

1. ValuJet incurred substantial losses in 1996 and 1997.
2. The expansion of ValuJet's operations is subject to FAA and DOT approval.
3. ValuJet is unable to predict how significantly the accident and suspension of operations will affect load factors and yield or the length of time load factors and yield will be impacted.
4. ValuJet's cost per ASM has increased from 1995 levels.
5. Although ValuJet believes that its insurance will be sufficient to cover all claims arising from the accident, there can be no assurance that all claims will be covered or that the aggregate of all claims will not exceed such insurance limits.
6. Several stockholder lawsuits have been filed against ValuJet and certain of its officers and directors alleging, among other things, violation of federal securities laws. While ValuJet denies that it has violated any of its obligations under the federal securities laws, there can be no assurance that ValuJet will not sustain material liability under such or related lawsuits.
7. Various governmental authorities are conducting investigations of the circumstances surrounding the accident. ValuJet is cooperating with the authorities in connection with these investigations.

Geographic Market

59   ValuJet serves short haul markets (generally under 1,000 miles) primarily from Atlanta and from Orlando offering basic air transportation at affordable fares. The routes served to and from Atlanta range in frequency from two to seven trips per day with some reductions in service on the weekends. The schedules are designed to provide a consistent product for business-oriented travelers and to facilitate connections for passengers traveling through Atlanta. ValuJet also provides nonstop service between Orlando and various cities in the Eastern United States. These routes are served on a daily basis with one round trip per day.

60   ValuJet's markets served from Atlanta are located predominantly in the eastern United States. These markets are attractive to ValuJet due to the concentration of major population centers within relatively short distances from Atlanta, historically high air fares, and the potential for attracting leisure customers who would otherwise use ground transportation. During 1997, the Atlanta Airport was the second busiest airport in the United States, enplaning over 32 million passengers. Additionally, ValuJet offers service to Florida markets as ValuJet believes that more than 20 million people visit the Florida markets by automobile every year from Atlanta and other points in the eastern United States. ValuJet provides direct scheduled passenger air service between Orlando and cities principally in the eastern half of the United States. ValuJet's strategy in developing its route system from Orlando is to serve medium-sized cities from which direct service to Orlando is not typically provided by the major airlines. This strategy involves flying longer stage lengths to medium-sized markets on a low frequency basis.

61   ValuJet offers a range of fares based on advance purchases of 14 days, 7 days, 3 days, and "walk-up" fares. Within the advance purchase fare types, the Company manages the availability of seats by day of week and by flight to maximize revenue on peak travel days. Most of ValuJet's fares are non-refundable, but can be changed prior to departure for a $35 fee. Business class seats are priced at $25 in excess of the full coach fare. ValuJet's fares are always purchased on a one-way basis. ValuJet's fares do not require any minimum, maximum, or day of week (e.g., Saturday night) stay. The Company's fare offerings are in direct contrast to prevalent pricing policies in the industry where there are typically many different price offerings and restrictions for seats on any one flight.

62   ValuJet's published Atlanta fares for non-stop service range from $39 to $99 for one-way travel on a 14 day advance purchase basis and $99 to $169 for one-way travel on a "walk-up" basis. ValuJet's published Orlando fares for non-stop service range from $59 to $99 for one-way travel on a 14 day advance purchase basis and $129 to $189 for one-way travel on a "walk-up" basis. The Company offers fare sales from time to time in order to generate additional traffic. There is recently passed legislation that imposes taxes on domestic airline transportation equal to a per segment flown charge (initially $1.00 to be increased to $3.00 by 2003) plus a percentage of the ticket price (7.5% in 1999). Such taxes will likely have a greater effect on leisure travelers. Since ValuJet relies to a large extent on leisure travelers, such tax increase may affect ValuJet to a greater extent than ValuJet's competitors who rely more heavily on business travelers.

63   On January 11, 1999, Joseph B. Leonard was elected as the Chairman of the Board, President and Chief Executive Officer of AirTran Holdings, Inc. (the "Company"). Mr. Leonard replaced D. Joseph Corr as President and Chief Executive Officer of AirTran and Robert D. Swenson as Chairman of the Board of AirTran. Mr. Corr resigned as President, Chief Executive Officer and as a Director of AirTran effective as of January 11, 1999. Mr. Swenson remains a Director of AirTran.

64   Prior to joining AirTran [ValuJet], Mr. Leonard served in various executive positions for AlliedSignal from 1993 to 1998, his last position being as President and Chief Executive Officer of AlliedSignal's Aerospace Marketing, Sales and Service business unit. Prior to joining Allied-Signal Mr. Leonard worked in various positions at Northwest Airlines, Eastern Airlines, and American Airlines from 1969 to 1993, including roles as chief executive officer/chief operating officer of Eastern Airlines from 1985 to 1990 and as executive vice president of Northwest Airlines from 1990 to 1993.

65   In another development, ValuJet reached an agreement to settle a consolidated, class action lawsuit against ValuJet and certain of its present and former directors and officers. The settlement provides for the dismissal of the consolidated action against all defendants and the establishment of a settlement fund of $2.5 million in cash and $2.5 million in common stock of ValuJet for the class of purchasers of ValuJet's stock during the period from June 9, 1995 through June 17, 1996. The settlement will not have any material effect on ValuJet due to previous accruals for such purposes.

66   "Quarter over quarter, AirTran is showing continued growth," said Leonard. "Now that we have 'rebuilt' the airline to operate more efficiently and effectively, our efforts will be focused on sustained profitability. The systems are in place, and we will move forward, concentrating on the key points of reliability, safety and customer service." "We have much to look forward to," said Leonard. "We believe that in 1999 we will see the results of our reorganization, improved operations, hard work and caring customer service reflected in our bottom line." Leonard pointed out a number of operational and marketing successes achieved in 1998 on which AirTran sought to build in 1999:

- Reconfigured route system to better maximize resources
- Expanded service to key business markets

As of	# Aircraft in Service	# Flights Per Day	# Cities Served
March 1995	27	184	23
June 1995	28	208	24
September 1995	34	228	26
December 1995	42	268	26
March 1996	47	286	28
June 1996	51	0	All service suspended 6/17/96
September 1996	46*	16	Service resumed on 9/30/96 to Atlanta, Fort Lauderdale, Orlando, Tampa, and Washington, D.C.
December 1996	43**	124	18
January 1, 1997	15	124	18
March 31, 1997	24	148	21
June 30, 1997	30	184	24
September 30, 1997	31	200	22
December 31, 1997	44	237	43
March 31, 1998	46	249	38
June 30, 1998	51	281	37
September 30, 1998	50	272	30

* Of which 4 had been approved for service by the FAA.
** Of which 15 had been approved for service by the FAA.

- Roll-out and first flight of the Boeing 717-200, of which AirTran has ordered 50 and expects to begin to take delivery in the fall of 1999
- Completed contracts with the pilot, mechanic, and flight attendant labor unions
- Significant growth in traffic from 1997 to 1998 (year over year and month over month)
- FAA Aviation Maintenance Technician Safety Training Program Special Recognition corporate award for the airline as a whole
- FAA Aviation Maintenance Technician Safety Training Program Diamond Award certificates of excellence for each of AirTran's five maintenance bases
- Introduction of the industry's most innovative frequent flyer reward program
- Installation of business class seating in the airline's entire fleet
- Introduction of direct online booking via the AirTran website
- Initiation of the AirTran Corporate Travel Program

67   "These efforts increased demand for our services and bolstered our status as a leader in providing full service, everyday affordable air travel throughout the southeast, Florida, East Coast and numerous cities in the Northeast and Midwest," he said. "Being recognized as *Entrepreneur* magazine's 1998 Best Domestic Low-Fare Airline," he added, "confirms AirTran's success in rebuilding its operations over the past few years."

NOTES

[1]Woolsey, J. (1995, December). "ValuJet: so far, so good," *Air Transport World*, p. 65.

[2]Lieber, R. B. (1995, November 27). "Turns out this critter can fly," *Fortune Magazine*, pp. 110–12.

[3]Ibid.

[4]Marcial, G. (1995, November 6). "ValuJet soars, but don't bail out," *Business Week*, p. 160.

[5] Ho, Rodney. (1996, August 8). "Grounded ValuJet retains stash of cash," *The Atlanta Journal and Constitution*, p. G1.

[6]Goldberg, D. (1996, May 17). "Smoke is most solid cue in what was likely a fiery end," *The Atlanta Journal and Constitution*, p. A17.

[7]Smith, Bruce. (1995, October 30). "Fuselage Stretch Propelled MD-95," *Aviation Week and Space Technology*, p. 35.

[8]Wall Street Journal News Roundup, file #144 5/24/96 12:23 ID:Dean Witter ValuJet's Job: Prove Low Cost Isn't Risky. Story 0066 (VJET, I/AIR, I/ICS, I/SVC, G/FAA, N/ANL, N/BON, N/COB, N/DJN).

[9]Noman, A., Brannigan, M. (1996, June 18). "ValuJet ceases operations indefinitely," *Wall Street Journal*, p. A3.

[10]Stern, W. (1996, June 10). "Warning! Bogus parts have turned up in commercial jets. Where's the FAA?," *Business Week*, p. 86.

[11]News Brief (1996, August 8). "ValuJet losses," *USA Today*, p. B1.

[12]Jenkins, H. W. (1996, May 21). "Look what lunacy one plane crash kicks up," *Wall Street Journal*, p. A23.

[13]Dahl, J. (1996, May 17). "Airline cargo can carry its own risks," *Wall Street Journal*, p. A2.

[14]Alexander, K. (1996, June 5). "ValuJet president is firm in resolve to rebuild airline," *USA Today*, p. B4.

[15]Brannigan, M., de Lisser, E. (1996, June 19). "ValuJet lays off 4,000 of its workers—Faces major challenges to a comeback," *Wall Street Journal*, p. A3.

[16]Greising, David. (1996, June 3). "Managing tragedy at ValuJet," *Business Week*, p. 40.

[17]McKenna, James. (1966, June 24). "Safety Concerns Ground ValuJet," *Aviation Week and Space Technology*, p. 20.

[18]Ibid.

[19]Greising, David. (1996, June 3). "Managing tragedy at ValuJet," *Business Week*, p. 41.

[20]Ibid.

[21]Ibid.

[22]Velocci, Anthony. (1966, June 24). "ValuJet Future Hinges on Length of Hiatus," *Aviation Week and Space Technology*, p. 27.

[23]Giles, Mark. (1996, June 23). "Safe price for a cheap flight," *The Atlanta Journal and Constitution*, p. B6.

[24]Ott, James. (1996, June 24). "ValuJet grounding shakes industry," *Aviation Week & Space Technology*, p. 23.

[25]McKenna, J. (1996, June 24). "Safety concerns ground ValuJet," *Aviation Week & Space Technology*, p. 27.

CASE 53

TEXTRON INC. AND THE CESSNA 172

1   The situation was not one that promised inevitable success. The corporation had a reputation for state-of-the-art aerospace technologies, yet it was rejuvenating a vintage-1950s product design. The product had become a venerable cash cow in the past, but its rejuvenation was to cost at least $75 million. The market it was aimed at had collapsed by over 95% since its peak in the 1970s, a demise that was accompanied by a serious deterioration in the relevant consumer infrastructure. The product always had, and again was planned to have, some of the dullest performance features in its product class. In recent years much more economical variants had appeared at the low end of its market, and the high end was dominated by much newer technologies. Head-to-head competition would likely be dominated—of all things—by its own established base. A rapidly globalizing economy had changed the nature of competition from an oligopolistic triad of U.S. firms to the inclusion of strong international players, some of which were spilling over from other industries and certain to change the nature of competition. Consumers would surely see the product as, by and large, the same old thing, yet its production would be in a brand new facility, restarted after a ten-year production moratorium, guided by a management philosophy that was wholly new to the division, and would incorporate a solid handful of small but important technological improvements related to the safe operation of the product. Any quality imperfections at all were almost sure to become the subject of catastrophically expensive lawsuits. History showed that just the cost of protecting the firm from product liability claims, when distributed across total production, was a per-unit figure that could easily exceed any competitive selling price.

2   Yet announcement of the product was highly praised by internal corporate management, consumers of the product type, Wall Street, and just about every other interested observer, except of course its probable competition. Not only was market success predicted as certain, but so was market leadership. Could one change in product liability statutes, which supplied immunity only to products at least eighteen years old, possibly have such an impact that the other dismal signs could largely be ignored?

PRODUCT LIABILITY IN GENERAL AVIATION

3   The term "product liability" addresses the issue of who bears risks associated with accidents (Huber & Litan, 1991; Eichenberger, 1994; Stern, 1994; Barnard, 1985; Harrison, 1995; Truitt & Tarry, 1995). In effect, this amounts to determining which party is at fault (and the extent of that responsibility) when a product fails to perform to a required standard or reasonable expectation. In principle, the objectives of liability statutes include the compensation of victims, the deterrence of injuries, the equitable spreading of risks, and the stimulation of safety-related innovation. In an important 1963 case, the Supreme Court of the United States ruled that even if a manufacturer of a product took reasonable care in the production of its goods, and had no prior knowledge that a product was defective in its manufacture or design, the manufacturer was nevertheless responsible, and wholly liable for associated damages. This "strict" interpretation of liability inaugurated a decades-long precedent where more and more types of liability burdens were consistently shifted from consumers to producers.

4   Because of the technological complexity of aircraft, their operating environments, and the egregious injuries that resulted from accidents, product liability expenses became enormous in the general aviation industry after the 1963 decision. Legal defenses became not only difficult, but easy to distort. For example, full compliance with Federal Aviation Administration (FAA) standards became

This case was prepared by Robert N. McGrath, Blaise P. Waguespack, Jr., and George A. Wrigley all of Embry-Riddle Aeronautical University, Department of Aviation Business Administration, Copyright 1996.

understood by precedent to be merely the accomplishment of design and manufacture minimums; i.e., plaintiffs successfully argued that manufacturers that produced to FAA standards were trying to do as *little* as possible. The best efforts of the manufacturers' scientists and engineers, so difficult to understand by lawyers and judges, not to mention juries, were easily assailed.

5   It was sometimes argued that in this environment, innovation was stymied rather than stimulated, since the risks of newness became so much greater than the risks of holding on to the tried-and-true. It was entirely possible, though difficult to show conclusively, that flight safety in general aviation was retarded, not improved, because of the "strict" liability standard. Nevertheless, immediate consumer sovereignty reigned supreme.

6   By the late 1980s the average amount per claimant per occurrence was about $10 million; the average total cost (losses plus defense expenses) became about $530,000. Even though manufacturers won over 80% of cases that went to trial, General Aviation's Big Three asserted that the annual cost incurred from all product liability expenditures was from $70–100,000 *per aircraft delivered.* Consequently, liability insurance expenses skyrocketed, from an industry-wide $24 million in 1978, to $210 million in 1985. The problem became so acute that insurers eventually became reticent to accept this business at all. Quipped one official of Lloyd's of London, "We are quite prepared to insure the risks of aviation, but not the risks of the American legal system." (Truitt & Tarry, 1995: 56) In this environment, Cessna withdrew from the single engine aircraft market altogether, Beech substantially reduced levels of production, and Piper was forced to file for Chapter 11 status.

7   Many industry participants and followers felt that the demise of general aviation manufacturing was principally the result of legal conditions, and responded with eventually-successful attempts to rectify the situation. Lobbies such as the General Aviation Manufacturers Association (GAMA) and the Aircraft Owners and Pilots Association (AOPA) convinced legislators such as Representatives Dan Glickman and Nancy Kassebaum (both Republicans from Kansas) to introduce product liability reform bills. Consumer groups, organized labor, and the Association of Trial Lawyers of America (ATLA) successfully battled these movements for several years, but eventually the General Aviation Revitalization Act of 1994 was signed into law by President Bill Clinton on August 17 of that year (Banks, 1994; *Business Week,* 1995; *Design News,* 1995).

8   The most significant effect of this bill was to relinquish manufacturers from the liability for products more than eighteen years old. This relief to manufacturers might seem benign, but it was seen as a great breakthrough for several reasons. First, since the average age of a general aviation aircraft was more than 28 years, a very substantial window of litigation opportunity was erased. Second, since the most recent surge in production occurred in the late 1970s, more and more general aviation aircraft necessarily would become immune from liability in the near future. Therefore advocates hailed this legislation as the beginning of a renaissance for general aviation aircraft development and manufacturing, and predicted the creation of as many as 25,000 new jobs. Detractors, of course, wailed at the deterioration of consumer sovereignty and, from one side of legal theory, innovation incentive.

THE GENERAL AVIATION INDUSTRY—BACKGROUND

9   The term "General Aviation," like terms used to describe other industries, was not entirely definitive, but had become understood by what it generally included and by what it excluded (Truitt & Tarry, 1995; *FAA Aviation Forecasts,* 1996; *GAMA Report,* 1996). The General Aviation Industry included a light aircraft segment, a business aviation segment, and a regional/charter aircraft segment; it excluded the commercial airlines (with some ambiguities regarding regional/local carriers) and the military. In effect this mostly differentiated private from commercial aviation. On the production side, it clearly distinguished firms like Boeing, Lockheed-Martin, and McDonnell-Douglas from what in effect was the "Big Three" of general aviation: Beech, Cessna, and Piper. During the 1980s, Cessna manufactured about 100,000 general aviation aircraft; Piper manufactured about 50,000, and Beech manufactured about 24,000.

10   More specifically, general aviation aircraft were considered to be single and multi-piston-engine powered fixed wing airplanes weighing less than 12,500 pounds (i.e., "light" aircraft) and some turboprop and jet powered aircraft (i.e., business or executive aircraft). U.S. airframe manufacturers

traditionally dominated this industry, as one would expect in the nation where 75% of all general aviation aircraft had been owned and operated.

11   By the mid-1990s, the industry was a more important component of the American economy than many people appreciated. In a clear economic sense, the production and sale of general aviation aircraft, avionics and many other types of equipment, as well as associated services such as finance, insurance, flight instruction, maintenance, airport services, and so forth, accounted for about $40 billion annually, and employed about 540,000 people with about a $10 billion aggregate payroll. In less quantifiable terms, the industry also served to accommodate various social needs of its 120 million annual consumers that the "market imperfections" of other aviation sectors might otherwise have been economically pressured to leave unresolved, such as the costly transportation of live human organs urgently needed for surgical transplants.

12   Historically, the industry was earmarked by cyclical patterns, tied to the larger national economic picture. For example, aircraft sales plummeted after the economic recessions of 1960, 1970, and 1975, followed by industry recoveries that paralleled recoveries of the national economy as a whole.

13   There have been two major slumps in production. Immediately following the at-large overexpansion of the 1960s (aircraft sales peaked at 15,768 in 1966), only 7,242 aircraft were sold in 1970. More recent developments were even more dramatic. After a recovery of 125% in a six-year period (1977 sales totalled 17,000), and an industry peak of 17,811 aircraft sold in 1979, production then crashed by 95.5%, to a point where only 811 aircraft were sold in 1993, and 444 in 1994. During the same period the number of U.S. manufacturers fell from 29 to 16; meanwhile, elsewhere in the world, the number of manufacturers rose from 15 to 29. In 1980, U.S. manufacturers employed 40,000 people; in 1991, the figure was about 21,580. Whereas U.S. firms traditionally captured 20–30% of the world market in addition to their dominance at home, in 1981 the U.S. became a net importer of general aviation aircraft, and by 1988 net importation of foreign aircraft accounted for $700 million of the larger national trade imbalance. Whereas 3,395 aircraft were exported in 1979, 440 were exported in 1986. Whereas U.S. manufacturers held 100% of home market share in 1980, by the mid-1990s this figure was less than 70%.

INTERPRETATIONS—"WHERE YOU STAND DEPENDS ON WHERE YOU SIT"

14   In 1989, Russell Meyer, President of Cessna, was quoted as saying "I can tell you without equivocation that the sole reason Cessna suspended production of piston aircraft indefinitely was the cost of product liability. I can say with similar candor that Cessna will not build another piston aircraft unless we can somehow reduce the horrendous ongoing cost of product liability" (Horn, 1989:2).

15   There was no question that the demise of the general aviation industry in the United States was coincident with the dynamics associated with the prosecution of product liability claims, in the larger legal framework of extant laws. What was more arguable was the extent to which the coincidences contained a causal element. That is, while some stakeholders viewed product liability dynamics as the smoking gun in the demise of the industry, others saw the product liability issue as only one factor amongst many others, which all seemed partially explanatory.

16   As described earlier, the industry was cyclical, and its fortunes were strongly tied to the national economy as a whole. Here, some observers noted that various oil embargoes and crises, the relatively high inflation rates experienced during the 1970s, and the prolonged periods of recession that occurred during the 1980s, all had negative impacts on the industry. Also in recent decades, disposable incomes generally fell, hurting all industries that depended on these dollars. A growing general skepticism about economic futures had a related impact on the demand for luxuries.

17   Some factors were extended effects of more basic explanations. In addition to the crippling effect of record-high oil prices, costs of maintenance and flight instruction also continued to rise substantially. Elimination of the investment tax credit, in essence, increased the absolute cost of purchasing an airplane. The heyday of production during the boom periods caused a glut during the slow years, creating an aftermarket which competed directly with new aircraft sales. Manufacturers were economically pressured to offer financial arrangements not only to their customers (dealers), but directly to consumers as well, exacerbating their overall cost problems.

EXHIBIT A
Textron's Consolidated Statement of Cash Flows

($000)

	1994	1993
Net Income	379,000	(355,000)
Effect of changes in accounting principles	—	679,000
Depreciation and Amortization	424,000	397,000
Provision for Losses on Receivables	195,000	196,000
Insurance policy liabilities	342,000	309,000
Deferred income taxes	28,000	37,000
Commercial and US government receivables	(27,000)	(2,000)
Changes in inventories	176,000	55,000
Additions to insurance policy acquisition costs	(235,000)	(205,000)
Increase in other assets	(80,000)	(22,000)
Accounts payable	108,000	(50,000)
Accrued liabilities	(11,000)	20,000
Other	1,000	(17,000)
Net cash provided by operating activities	1,300,000	1,042,000
Securities to be available for sale	(220,000)	—
Securities to be held to maturity	(1,497,000)	(1,846,000)
Other purchases	(27,000)	(17,000)
Sales of securities available for sale	205,000	—
Sales of securities held to maturity	173,000	737,000
Mature and calls	768,000	743,000
Proceedings from other investments	42,000	27,000
Finance receivables originated or purchased	(5,011,000)	(4,853,000)
Finance receivables repaid or sold	4,253,000	4,212,000
Cash used in acquisition of business	(139,000)	(905,000)
Proceeds from sale of minor interests	175,000	—
Capital expenditures	(252,000)	(217,000)
Other investing activities	27,000	(15,000)
Net cash used by investing activities	(1,503,000)	(2,134,000)
Short-term debt	485,000	(50,000)
Proceeds from issuance of long-term debt	1,669,000	2,913,000
Principal paid on long-term debt	(1,954,000)	(1,780,000)
Receipts—interest sens insured products	193,000	142,000
Return of balance—interest sens product	(105,000)	(88,000)
Stock options	19,000	34,000
Dividends paid	(110,000)	(98,000)
Net cash provided by financing activities	197,000	1,073,000
Effect of foreign exchange rate change on cash	1,000	—
Net change in cash	(5,000)	(19,000)
Cash at beginning of year	31,000	50,000
Cash at end of year	26,000	31,000

Source: Moody's, 1995.

18   Some parts of the overall explanation were truly idiosyncratic to the industry. For example, American citizens who served in the armed forces during World War II and the Korean conflict, were subsidized under the version of the GI Bill which applied to them, to pursue flight training. A substantial portion of these many thousands of veterans took advantage of this benefit, transforming

EXHIBIT B
Consolidated Textron's Balance Sheet

($000)

	0/01/94	1/02/93
Assets		
Cash	26,000	31,000
Investments	4,764,000	4,152,000
Receivables, net	8,240,000	7,731,000
Inventories	1,488,000	1,648,000
Property, plant & equipment	1,269,000	1,183,000
Unamortized insurance policy acquisition costs	784,000	696,000
Goodwill, net	1,437,000	1,366,000
Other assets	1,650,000	1,559,000
Total assets	19,658,000	18,367,000
Liabilities		
Accounts payable	614,000	489,000
Accrued postretirement benefits	1,033,000	981,000
Other accrued liabilities	2,268,000	2,072,000
Insurance reserves and claims	4,091,000	3,615,000
Textron parent company borrowing group	2,025,000	2,283,000
Finance and insurance subsidiaries	6,847,000	6,440,000
Total debt	8,872,000	8,723,000
Total liabilities	16,878,000	15,879,000
Pfd stk $2.08 cum conv, ser A	9,000	11,000
Pfd stk $1.40 cum conv, ser B	7,000	8,000
Common stock	12,000	11,000
Capital surplus	687,000	661,000
Retained earnings	2,209,000	1,940,000
Other	52,000	52,000
Total	2,872,000	2,579,000
Less cost of treas. shares	92,000	91,000
Total shares equity	2,780,000	2,488,000
Total liabilities and stock equivalents	19,658,000	18,367,000
Book value	$15.08	$12.53

Source: Moody's, 1995.

fundamental skills learned during military service into civilian occupations and hobbies. As time progressed, however, this population aged and fewer and fewer eligible veterans took advantage of the benefit. Meanwhile, change to the GI Bill which applied to younger veterans eliminated the benefit. The net result was far, far fewer general aviation pilots, of both the small-business and recreational variety. And pilots, after all, were obviously the nexus of demand for general aviation airplanes.

19   Technologically, the advent of reliable "kit" airplanes helped gut the low-end part of general aviation aircraft manufacturing. What was once viewed as the purview of backyard eccentrics became legitimized by actions such as the FAA's ever-expanding certification of worthwhile kit models, and by the advocacy of organizations like the Experimental Aircraft Association and the Small Aircraft Manufacturers Association—all which helped change the public's perception of flying as a luxurious hobby (typical kitplanes could be purchased for $45,000 to $80,000).

20   Profit margins on kitplanes were low, however, so the understandable reaction of industry incumbents to these relatively unproven technologies was abandonment of the market they served, in favor of the high-profit, technologically safer, high-end (upscale business) segment. Overall, manufacturers netted over $2 billion in sales in 1990 on sales of 1,144 aircraft; in 1993, sales rose from this figure

EXHIBIT C
General Aviation Active Aircraft by Primary Use (top) and Hours Flown (bottom)

(Both figures in thousands)

Use Category	1994	1993	1992	1991	1990
Corporate	9.7	9.9	9.4	10.0	10.1
	2,548	2,659	2,262	2,617	2,913
Business	25.6	27.8	28.9	31.6	33.1
	3,005	3,345	3,537	4,154	4,417
Personal	100.8	102.1	108.7	115.1	112.6
	8,116	7,938	8,592	9,685	9,276
Instructional	14.6	15.6	16.0	17.9	18.6
	4,156	4,680	5,340	6,141	7,244
Aerial Application	4.2	5.0	5.1	7.0	6.2
	1,210	1,167	1,296	1,911	1,872
Aerial Observation	4.9	4.8	5.6	5.1	4.9
	1,750	1,750	1,730	1,797	1,745
Sight Seeing	1.3	1.6	n/a	n/a	n/a
	323	412	n/a	n/a	n/a
External Load	0.1	0.1	n/a	n/a	n/a
	172	105	n/a	n/a	n/a
Other Work	1.2	1.0	1.7	1.7	1.4
	226	175	343	471	572
Air Taxi	3.9	3.8	4.6	5.5	5.8
	1,670	1,452	2,009	2,241	2,249
Other	4.2	4.2	3.5	3.9	4.1
	640	656	358	473	475
Total	170.6	175.9	183.6	198.5	198.0
	23,866	24,340	25,800	29,497	30,763

Source: FAA Aviation Forecasts.

by about $140 million, but it was on sales of only 964 total aircraft. Here, only about 5% of sales was accounted for by piston powered aircraft; turboprop and jet aircraft dominated.

21   Cessna and Beech particularly profited from this shift in emphasis. Not coincidentally, since Beech had become a subsidiary of Raytheon and Cessna had been acquired by Textron (both technological conglomerates tuned to corporate and military markets), associated decisions to abandon high-risk, low return segments of the general aviation industry seemed only consistent with "bigger pictures" and overall corporate strategies.

22   Some industry observers viewed these events as being the natural symptoms of an industry which had transitioned from a general period of growth to a period of maturity. The "demise" might have been nothing more than an ordinary shakeout, the kind that economists and market analysts often predict. Even if this was true, however, industry incumbents and other stakeholders were apparently determined to not let the industry slip into decline without a fight.

INDUSTRY FUTURE

23   As of 1995, the outlook for the General Aviation Industry was mixed (*U.S. News & World Report,* 1995; *FAA Aviation Forecasts,* 1996; *GAMA Report,* 1996). One of the more important factors was the trend regarding the size and nature of the pilot population. As of January 1, 1995, the total

EXHIBIT D
General Aviation Active Aircraft (top) and Hours Flown (bottom)

(Both figures in thousands)

Aircraft Type	1994	1993	1992	1991	1990
Piston	138.9	147.1	162.1	175.3	175.2
	18,370	19,029	21,251	24,102	25,832
Turboprop	4.2	4.4	4.7	4.9	5.3
	1,106	1,227	1,478	1,513	2,319
Turbojet	4.1	3.9	4.0	4.4	4.1
	1,241	1,165	1,072	1,236	1,396
Fixed wing—Total	147.2	155.3	170.8	184.6	184.5
	20,717	21,421	23,801	26,851	29,546
Rotorcraft	4.4	4.5	5.8	6.3	6.9
	2,006	1,832	2,283	2,757	2,209
Other	6.2	5.2	7.8	7.6	6.6
	424	376	410	459	341
Experimental	12.9	10,9	n/a	n/a	n/a
	718	711	n/a	n/a	n/a
Total	170.6	175.9	183.6	197.8	196.9
	23,866	24,340	25,800	29,497	30,763

Source: FAA Aviation Forecasts.

number of private pilots was 284,236, a modest increase of .2% from the year before but a reversal of a steady decline in the previous five years. The number of student pilots (96,254) fell by a disturbing 7.1%, however, a figure which was below 100,000 for the first time since 1962.

24   On the manufacturing side, there were some signs that production of general aviation aircraft had bottomed out in 1994. New aircraft shipments totalled 980 in 1995, with billings of $3 billion—30.5% higher in one year, attributable to the rising unit value of aircraft. More specifically, 234 turboprop aircraft were shipped (up 15.3% from the year before), 241 jet aircraft were shipped (up 8.1%), and 505 piston aircraft were shipped (up 4.3%). Exports, however, still showed signs of industry deterioration. Only 286 general aviation aircraft were exported in 1995, a one-year decline of 2.4%—billings declined 23.2% to $637.3 million. Exports represented 29.2% of total aircraft shipped and 21.4% of billings, figures which fell 33.8% and 36.4% in one year, respectively.

25   In a larger sense, the total number of "active" aircraft (i.e., the number of aircraft flown at least once during the previous year) indicated continuing decline. The number of active single engine piston aircraft declined in one year (1993 to 1994) from 130,687 to 123,332 (down 5.6%), the number of multi-engine piston aircraft fell from 16,406 to 15,577 (down 5.1%), and the number of turboprop aircraft fell from 4,359 to 4,207 (down 3.5%). However, numbers regarding turbojet, experimental, and "other" categories showed significant improvement. The number of active turbojets increased from 3,859 to 4,073 (up 5.6%), the number of experimental aircraft increased from 10,938 to 12,852 (up 17.5%), and the number of "other" aircraft increased from 5,247 to 6,169 (up 17.6%).

26   The number of hours flown showed a somewhat different pattern than the number of active aircraft. From 1993 to 1994, the number of hours flow in multi-piston aircraft (2.6 million hours) rose 3.6%; the number in turbojet aircraft (1.2 million) rose 6.5%; the number in experimental aircraft (.7 million) rose 1%; and the number in "other" aircraft (.4 million) rose 12.8%. Meanwhile, the number of hours flown in single engine piston aircraft (15.8 million) fell by 4.5%, and the number flown in turboprop aircraft (1.1 million) fell 9.9%. Since most hours were accounted for by flying in single engine piston aircraft (66.1%), total hours flown in general aviation aircraft fell from 24.3 million to 23.9 million hours (down 2% overall).

EXHIBIT E

Active General Aviation and Air Taxi Hours Flown Forecast
(millions)

Aircraft Type	1996	1997	1998	1999	2000	2001	2002	2003	2004	2005	2006
Piston:											
Single Engine	15.3	15.2	15.3	15.5	15.7	15.8	15.9	16.0	16.0	16.1	16.2
Multi-Engine	2.5	2.5	2.6	2.6	2.6	2.6	2.7	2.7	2.7	2.7	2.7
Turboprop	1.1	1.2	1.2	1.2	1.2	1.3	1.3	1.3	1.3	1.4	1.4
Turbojet	1.3	1.3	1.4	1.4	1.4	1.5	1.5	1.5	1.6	1.6	1.6
Rotorcraft:											
Piston	0.3	0.3	0.3	0.3	0.3	0.3	0.3	0.3	0.3	0.3	0.3
Turbine	1.6	1.7	1.7	1.7	1.7	1.7	1.8	1.8	1.8	1.8	1.8
Experimental	0.7	0.8	0.8	0.8	0.8	0.8	0.8	0.8	0.8	0.8	0.9
Other	0.4	0.4	0.4	0.4	0.4	0.5	0.5	0.5	0.5	0.5	0.5
Total	23.2	23.4	23.7	23.9	24.1	24.5	24.8	24.9	25.0	25.2	25.4

Active Pilots by Type of Certificate
(thousands)

Type	1996	1997	1998	1999	2000	2001	2002	2003	2004	2005	2006
Students	95.0	94.6	96.4	98.2	100.1	101.9	103.2	104.7	105.8	106.6	107.4
Balloon	0.2	0.3	0.3	0.3	0.3	0.4	0.4	0.4	0.4	0.5	0.5
Private	280.5	278.4	281.4	284.5	287.6	290.5	292.7	294.8	297.1	299.0	300.5
Commercial	137.3	135.9	137.2	138.6	140.0	140.7	141.4	142.1	142.8	143.6	144.3
Airline	118.6	120.4	122.2	124.3	126.8	129.3	131.3	13.2	134.9	136.6	138.3
Helicopter	8.5	8.5	8.6	8.7	8.8	8.8	8.9	9.0	9.1	9.1	9.2
Glider	8.6	8.7	8.8	8.8	8.9	8.9	9.0	9.0	9.1	9.1	9.2
Total	648.7	646.8	654.9	663.4	672.5	680.5	686.9	693.2	699.2	704.5	709.4

Source: FAA Aviation Forecasts.

27   General aviation aircraft were most often used for personal use. In 1994 personal flying accounted for 34% of total general aviation flying, up an impressive 32.6% from the previous year. The second-most popular use was in instructional flying, which in 1994 accounted for 17.4% of the total, a decline of 11.2% from the previous year. Business and corporate flying (as a combined category, 23.3%) also fell, by 7.5%.

28   The mid-1990s also was a period of general decline in the general aviation industry infrastructure. A subtle but important point was the interaction between the decline in single engine piston aircraft activity and overall industry health. Historically, pilots found their way into the industry through single engine piston aircraft, and progressed from there to more sophisticated technologies. Statistics regarding single engine piston aircraft, therefore, served as a bellwether for long-term industry health. For example, it was probably no coincidence that the flight training and flight instructor infrastructure was also in decline, and many of the physical facilities devoted to training showed obvious signs of encroaching dilapidation.

29   By the mid-1990s the industry and many of its stakeholders had reacted in ways aimed at improving overall industry strength. The Federal government restored some of the subsidization of veterans' flight training programs. A Republican Congress restored the investment tax credit, incentivizing the purchase of general aviation aircraft as well as many other durable goods. The FAA developed a comprehensive plan for industry improvement, consistent with its overall mission of advocating all aviation interests. The plan aimed at improving general aviation's image while reducing some of the regulatory burden that the agency itself imposed. The AOPA launched a project designed to attract 10,000 new student pilots, and largely achieved this goal. The National Business Aircraft Association (NBAA) actively promoted the value-addition that business flying had the potential to

EXHIBIT F
Market Survey Results

Factors that Would Make Survey Targets Much More Interested in Learning to Fly

	Total	Male	Female	Likely Student
Fly at twice speed of driving	44	43	45	48
Weekend adventure	43	41	50	46
Get license in 6 months	42	41	44	46
Available mentors	42	41	44	47
Entertain family/friends	42	41	45	47
Rent for $50/hour	41	37	52	39
Recreational license	34	34	34	37
Make friends	32	30	36	37
Safer than biking	32	31	35	34
Airplane clubs	32	33	31	36
High self-esteem	29	28	32	30
Career	23	24	21	24
Learning cost $3,500	21	20	26	26
Used planes for $30,000	18	18	16	21

Survey Target's Participation in Other Activities

	Total	Male	Female	Likely Student
Bicycling	64	62	70	68
Fishing	59	64	46	61
Boating	55	56	51	64
Golf	40	45	26	44
Backpacking	39	39	37	46
Water skiing	35	38	27	41
Tennis	31	31	32	32
Motorcycling	29	32	19	32
Scuba diving	29	23	18	29
Mountain climbing	21	21	20	24
RV touring	19	18	19	22
Auto racing	18	19	14	17
Skydiving	9	8	9	12
Ballooning	5	4	8	7
Hang gliding	4	4	4	5

Source: GAMA Final Report.

bring to individual firms, under the catchy slogan "No plane, No gain." Expansion of university programs in aviation-related degrees and actual flight training programs expanded significantly.

TEXTRON AND CESSNA

30 Dozens of acquisitions, divestitures, reorganizations and other moves peppered the history of Textron, which could trace its history to the establishment of the Franklin Rayon Corporation in 1928, which became known as Textron American, Inc., in 1955, after a merger with the American Woolen Company and Robbins Mills, Inc. (*Moody's Industrial Manual, 1995*). In subsequent decades, the corporate profile changed greatly and purposively. By the mid-1990s, Textron was known as a high-tech conglomerate, employing about 53,000 people in almost sixty subsidiaries operating in two major business sectors: Manufacturing (in 1994, 70% of total revenues and 53% of total profits) and Financial Services (30% of total revenues and 47% of total profits).

31 Textron was renowned as one of the nation's largest defense contractors (sales to the U.S. government represented 18% of the total revenues) and was also a significant exporter (also 18% of revenues). In the most general sense management's aim was to achieve balanced diversification, so that

the corporation would not be vulnerable to economic cycles, and to establish a dependable bedrock which would allow the pursuit of growth opportunities and advanced technologies.

32   The Manufacturing segments concentrated on the following product types: Aircraft, Automotive, Industrial, and Systems and Components. The Aircraft segment consisted of Bell Helicopter and Cessna. The most exciting program in Bell Helicopter was the continuing development of the V-22 tilt rotor aircraft, many years in development and seemingly always on the verge of landing huge contracts with the U.S. Department of Defense, which would probably help launch much more business on an international scale. Overall, this business segment performed well in both civilian and military markets, adept at marketing its products through its own worldwide sales force as well as through a network of independent representatives. Key success factors were price, financing terms, product performance, reliability, and long-term product support. Bell Helicopter typically accounted for 11–14% of total corporate revenues.

33   Cessna was well-known as the world's largest designer and manufacturer of general aviation aircraft; in particular, Cessna designed and manufactured light and mid-sized business jets and single engine utility turboprop aircraft. Cessna was a fairly recent acquisition, having been purchased on February 28, 1992, from the General Dynamics Corporation for $605 million in cash. Two efforts were particularly exciting: the development of the Citation X, a large business jet scheduled for first delivery in 1996; and the decision to re-start the production of the Cessna models 172, 182, and 206 piston-engine aircraft in brand new manufacturing facilities located in Kansas. In 1994 Cessna delivered about 115 Citation business jets, for sales of about $850 million; sales were projected to top $1 billion by 1996. Similar to the profile of Bell Helicopter, Cessna marketed its products through both its own worldwide sales force and through independent representatives, principally relying on product reliability, product support, and superb brand name recognition. Also like Bell, Cessna was making a very positive contribution to the corporation as a whole, in the most recent years attributable to improved margins, lowered product development expenses, lowered administrative expenses in the establishment of new business, and higher sales.

34   The automotive sector supplied components to automotive original equipment manufacturers (OEMs) and competed on the basis of price, product quality and delivery. Several divisions of the Industrial segment competed similarly in industries less oligopolistic than the automotive sector, competing on the base of price, product quality, product performance, brand name recognition, and delivery. The Systems and Components segment mostly supplied the civilian aerospace and military industries, operating its own sales force and competing on price, reliability, product performance, and product support.

35   Textron's situation and overall philosophy were summarized well in CEO James F. Hardyman's letter to shareholders published in the 1994 annual report:

> Textron's record of consistent growth continued in 1994, as earnings per share increased 14 percent over 1993 and the fourth quarter was our 21st consecutive quarter of year-to-year income improvement . . .
>
> Significantly, we achieved consistent improvement in results over the last five years despite an array of challenges, including cutbacks in defense spending, a slump in the commercial aviation industry and disappointments in the disability insurance business . . .
>
> Our ability to deliver consistent growth stems from Textron's two defining characteristics:
>
> • We are a multi-industry company focused on maximizing the benefits of diversification.
>
> • We are committed to disciplined and aggressive management of our businesses and our business mix . . .
>
> Diversification is a source of strength, providing a foundation that supports growth and enables us to manage risk . . .
>
> Textron's presence in diverse industries helps achieve balance and stability in a variety of economic environments by providing insulation from business and industry cycles. More specifically, we were able to maintain consistent growth in 1994 in part because the growth of our Aircraft, Automotive, Industrial and Finance businesses more than offset the downturns in the Systems and Components segment and Paul Revere's disability insurance business . . .
>
> Finally, Textron's mix of businesses is a unique management resource, providing a depth and breadth of management expertise that is shared throughout our operating units, strengthening the corporation overall. For example, in the JPATS competition to build the new training aircraft for the Air Force and Navy, three of our key Textron divisions shared their significant experience in government contracts with Cessna. This,

combined with Cessna's technical expertise, led to a comprehensive proposal. Our constant search for "best practices" applies our most successful methods for operation to all our businesses . . .

Textron is focused on operations. We believe that long-term objectives are attained by coupling strategically driven planning with an intense concentration on day-to-day execution. Throughout the organization, the management philosophy instills a clear focus on the ultimate goal—building value for shareholders—with execution tailored to the unique characteristics of each of our businesses.

We translate this philosophy into action by relying on four basic principles:

Short and Long-Term Planning. We conduct a continuous, corporatewide strategic planning process centered on setting clear, challenging financial and operating objectives.

Continuous Improvement. We are making major improvements in operations, but we will never be satisfied . . .

Consistent Management. We measure our commitment to building value on a monthly basis. All of our divisions use the measurement of return on invested capital relative to the cost of capital as their standard.

Accountability of Performance. We relentlessly follow up to ensure that goals are achieved . . .

Five key strategies . . . guide our commitment to building value:

Internal Growth. Textron's market-driven businesses create products that meet customer needs for quality, reliability and value . . .

Acquisitions. Our acquisitions strategy targets growth and an increased presence in industrial components manufacturing . . . we are capitalizing on the strengths of our core markets: market leadership, competitive advantage and the ability to generate sustained economic value for our shareholders . . .

Increased International Presence. Geographic diversification is a key element in achieving our growth objectives. Our goal is to increase international sales from about one-fourth of our business to more than one-third by the end of this decade . . .

Restructuring/Redeploying. We are making the tough decisions to bring underperforming businesses up to standard—improving the businesses that can meet our requirements, selling those that do not and managing businesses for cash when divestiture is not appropriate. Over the last five years, we have restructured 11 commercial aerospace and defense businesses—closing or selling 254 plants—to meet profitability goals in the face of continued weakness in the defense and commercial aviation markets . . . We take these steps only when global pressures make them necessary . . .

People/Culture. We are also changing our culture to ensure that it supports our shared values of respect, trust, integrity and the pursuit of excellence . . . we are developing a corporate culture in which every member of the Textron team is constantly finding ways to make us better and faster . . . we are creating a Textron that is recognized for its multi-industry strength, market leadership and consistent growth.

THE CESSNA 172

36   The "original" Cessna 172 was introduced to the general aviation market in 1955; not entirely original even then, since it shared many engineering features and componentry with other Cessna models (Charles, 1996; *Aviation Week,* 1995; Stewart, July, 1995; Stewart, October 1995). Key to its success in the early years was aggressive advertising which presented the plane as being comparable, in ease of operation, to the automobile. It even had features like doors on both sides and a steering wheel-like pilot control yoke, rather than the control sticks that were still ubiquitous at the time. More superficially, interior furnishings and exterior paint jobs emulated the automotive fashions of the day.

37   The first year the Cessna 172 was on the market, it outsold its cash-cow predecessor Cessna 170 by a margin of ten to one, prompting management to discontinue the old model in favor of the new, recognizing it as the company's future in general aviation. (Most significantly, the Cessna 170 was a "taildragger," while the Cessna 172 featured a "tricycle" landing gear configuration.) Virtually no design changes were deemed necessary until 1960, when the tail design was changed to a more swept-back look—a feature incorporated for aerodynamic reasons, but one which was immediately popular for its looks as well. Minor changes occurred about every year thereafter, such as better streamlining (the distinguishing characteristic of the 172B Skyhawk, perhaps the version that most clearly embedded itself in general aviation history), shorter landing gear struts, a wrap-around rear window, electric flaps, a baggage door, a larger fuel tank, and new contours that improved its range.

38   The airplane's original engine was the Continental O-300, very expensive to repair and overhaul and troublesome in terms of its tendency for valve failures and carburetor icing. This engine was

replaced in 1968 by the Lycoming O-320-E2D, a proven design which was instantly popular when installed in the 172. In 1977 another engine change was made, but this time for the worse; the Lycoming O-320-H2AD caused camshaft and valve damage, and was plagued by abrupt engine failures related to the design and operation of oil pumps and accessory drive gears. A product recall in 1977–78 fixed some of these problems, and complete resolution was accomplished in 1981 with the installation of the Lycoming O-320-D2J engine.

39   Little could Cessna's management foresee in 1955 that the 172 would become the world's most popular airplane ever, in the sense that in the ensuing 31 years, some 36,010 individual aircraft would be sold, the largest number of aircraft of any single type of aircraft sold in aviation history. From its introduction to the mid-1980s, models A through P were introduced. By the mid-eighties, however, prospects in the general aviation industry were so dire that Cessna pulled out of the single-engine piston engine product line together.

40   As soon as production ceased, the marketplace missed the Cessna 172. Consumers loved this airplane so much that bodies of hobbyists emerged, focused on keeping the 172 alive. The 172 had become something of a legend in its own time and realm, and owners of the 172 discovered that as long as their airplanes were maintained well, they actually appreciated in value. Simple supply and demand evidenced itself in a very strong "used" market for 172s. Most editions of *Trade-A-Plane*, for example, featured one or two whole pages of advertisements regarding the Cessna 172; asking prices were consistently at bluebook value. Strangely, value was not directly related to age, but was more a function of specific model type. Models sold from 1968 to 1976 were considered outstanding; models from the 1956 to 1967 era were considered to be fair, and models from the 1977 to 1980 era were considered to be terrible, relative to other models of the 172. The airplane's continuing popularity stemmed from its excellent safety record, operating economy, and low maintenance costs. Of course, in terms of performance it was always somewhat ho-hum, being the "family car" of general aviation.

41   Inspired by the 1994 tort reform, Cessna Aircraft Company CEO Russ Meyer (not coincidentally, a key lobbyist in the movement to reform aviation liability statutes) announced in 1994 that Cessna would introduce a new version of the venerable 172. Start-up costs would be about $75 million. The new 172s would be produced by the company's Pawnee division, and manufactured in new facilities located in Independence, Kansas, with first deliveries planned for the summer of 1996 (in 1997, larger single-engined Cessna models 182, 206, and Turbo 206 would also be introduced). The new facility would be about 480,000 square feet, with room for final assembly, painting, flight test, delivery, and market functions. Though this new facility meant an important shift from Cessna's traditional Wichita production site, it also meant lower overhead (first, the Wichita facility produced Cessna's jet aircraft; second, the Independence site would be new both physically and philosophically, being benchmarked against GM's Saturn methods of production) and better local flight testing conditions.

42   Plans called for the eventual manufacture of about 2000 planes per year, 600 in the first year which should garner $300 million (this forecast also assumed the simultaneous sale of 400 Cessna 182s and 250 Cessna 206s per year; international sales were forecast at about 300 Cessna 172s, 200 Cessna 182s, and 250 Cessna 206s per year. College, government, military, and civil patrol orders were expected to account for another 300 Cessna 172s). The new business was expected to swell Cessna's payroll from 6,000 employees to over 7,500. Instant market leadership was expected, and full-scale production margins were expected to be double-digit.

43   The "new" 172 was to not be much different in appearance from the 172 legend, incorporating only a few aerodynamic improvements to reduce drag. The most significant improvements would be changes to the engine which would make it quieter, an electronic ignition with back-up magneto, an all-metal florescent-lit instrument panel, a standard backup instrument vacuum system, a gravity-feed 50-gallon wet wing, improved interior crashworthiness (improved seat tracking and seat adjustment system), a standard step-ladder, handle, toe-step and hand-grip provisions, redesigned cowling fasteners, corrosion-proofing, the addition of more modern avionics (the electronic componentry in airplanes), an improved autopilot, and a "derated" (200 hp to 160 hp) fuel-injected, four cylinder, Lycoming IO-360 engine; the derating would be accomplished by the installation of low-compression pistons and by limiting takeoff power to 2500 rpm.

44   Decisions regarding these changes were based on the thousands upon thousands of hours of operating experience accumulated on previous models and, of course, cost considerations. Meyer estimated that the nonrecurring costs of developing an airplane of this type "from scratch" would have been something like $25 million, through to FAA certification, and would optimistically have taken about three and a half years. Even these assumptions were based on traditional aluminum construction; state-of-the-art airframes partially fabricated of space-age composite materials were only that much more costly, difficult, and time-consuming to produce and certify.

45   Well into 1995, decisions regarding the total configuration of the aircraft and its selling price were still at hand. The effects of a renewed regulatory environment were not entirely foreseeable, and there was still a backlog of hundreds of liability cases which needed clarification and resolution. Even Edward W. Stimpson, president of the General Aviation Manufacturer's Association, admitted "the market's very confused right now."

46   Also, other than the continuing evolution of safety/liability issues, it was also not certain that the industry would return to its relatively stable condition of a Big Three oligopoly, especially with Piper just emerging from Chapter 11 status. The world had changed a great deal since 1986. Firms such as the Commander Aircraft Co. (Bethany, Oklahoma), the French Aerospatiale group, and even Toyota had "invaded," or were poised to invade, what was once fairly secure Big Three territory.

47   Ironically, some of the biggest competition was certain to come from the used market. A Cessna 172 purchased new in the 1970s for $50,000 could typically garner a $75,000 resale price in the 1990s, if its condition was good. Taking inflation into account, and the value addition of improved avionics and other "new" features, it looked as if Cessna's management would need to think in terms of about a $100,000 price tag, just if the new 172 was to compete favorably with its own past success.

REFERENCES

Banks, H. 1994. "Cleared for Takeoff," *Forbes.* September 12: 116–22.

Barnard, T. 1985. "Courts and Crashes: Why $70,000 of an Aircraft's Cost Is for Product Liability Insurance," *Canadian Aviation.* July: 33–35.

Charles, B. 1996. "Something's Coming," *Air Progress.* January: 14–15.

"Clearing a Runway for Planemakers," *Business Week.* March 20, 1995: 94–95.

Eichenberger, J. 1994. "The Day After," *The Aviation Consumer.* October 1: 16–17.

FAA Aviation Forecasts: Fiscal Years 1996–2007. 1996. Washington, D.C.: United States Department of Transportation.

"First 'New' C-172s to Fly in Late 1996," *Aviation Week & Space Technology.* June 5, 1995: 64–65.

"General Aviation Experiences a Rebirth," *Design News.* September 11, 1995: 27–28.

Harrison, K. H. 1995. "Drastic Insurance Rate Hikes Sock It to General Aviation," *Aviation International News.* May 1: 25–28.

Huber, P. W., & R. E. Litan (eds.). 1991. *The Liability Maze.* Washington, D.C.: The Brookings Institute.

Moody's Industrial Manual, 1995. New York: Moody's Investor's Services, Inc.

Revitalizing the Piston-Powered Aircraft Industry: Final Report of the General Aviation Manufacturers Association, March 26, 1996. 1996. Washington, D.C.: General Aviation Manufacturers Association.

Stern, W. M. 1994. "A Wing and a Prayer," *Forbes.* April 25: 42–43.

Stewart, C. 1995. "Restart 172," *Air Progress.* June: 12–13.

Stewart, C. 1995. "Affordable Classic," *Air Progress.* October: 30–43.

"The Takeoff in the Small-Plane Market," *U.S. News and World Report.* August 21, 1995: 50.

Truitt, L. J., & S. E. Tarry. 1995. "The Rise and Fall of General Aviation: Product Liability, Market Structure, and Technological Innovation," *Transportation Journal.* Summer: 52–70.

CASE 54

THE ROCHE GROUP: MAKING THE RIGHT MOVES IN THE COMPETITIVE PHARMACEUTICAL INDUSTRY WITHIN A COMPLEX AND VOLATILE ENVIRONMENT

1   The Roche Group, headquartered in Basel, Switzerland, has made a series of strategic moves since 1986 which were expected to prepare the company for the 21st century: companies have been sold; companies have been bought, and internal alignments have been made to strengthen the company's core businesses.[1]

2   Meanwhile, other global pharmaceutical competitors embarked upon a series of major mergers and acquisitions. These included: the 1996 merger of Ciba-Geigy and Sandoz, two Swiss pharmaceutical companies also located in Basel, to form a new company called Novartis, in a business deal calculated to be worth $48 billion[2]; Glaxo bought out Wellcome in 1995 in what was termed a $14.3 billion takeover[3]; the 1995 merger of Pharmacia, 9th largest drug company in the world, with the Upjohn Company was valued at $13 billion[4]; Merck, Eli Lilly, and SmithKline Beecham, adopting vertical integration strategies, purchased drug wholesalers, paying a combined total of $13 billion[5]; and Rhone-Poulec took over Fisons in 1995 at a cost of $2.9 billion.[6]

3   Industry competitors were being forced to question their product lines, their organization, their mission, and their strategies. Not all major participants in the industry, however, agreed on which course of action was appropriate (see Appendix).

4   Roche management faced two critical issues: (1) was the company keeping pace with consolidation taking place within the industry and (2) should the company explore diversification outside the increasingly competitive pharmaceutical industry?

INTRODUCTION

5   The Roche Group was a leading multinational pharmaceutical company that manufactured, processed, distributed, and marketed its products and services worldwide. Revenues for 1994, derived from the company's four core businesses (pharmaceuticals, vitamins and fine chemicals, flavors and fragrances, and diagnostics) were 14.7 billion Swiss francs, a company record. Although 26.6 percent of the company's property, plant, and equipment were located in Switzerland, only 2 percent of Roche's sales were in Switzerland.[7]

HISTORY OF THE COMPANY

6   Roche was founded in 1896 by Dr. Fritz Hoffmann. The family name of the woman he married was La Roche. At that time it was the custom to add the wife's name to one's business title. Thus, Hoffmann-La Roche.

7   Dr. Hoffmann founded the company because of his faith in a sirolin syrup that he had developed to treat coughs and sneezing. The product was well received and Hoffmann subsequently established subsidiaries in Paris (1903); New York (1905); Vienna, Austria (1907); London, England (1909); St. Petersburg, Russia (1910); and Yokohama, Japan (1911).

8   Roche became a public company in 1919. In 1934, Roche began industrial-scale production of synthetic vitamins. Flavors and fragrances were added in the 1960s and the Diagnostics division was formed in 1968.

This case was prepared by James W. Clinton, University of Northern Colorado; and James W. Camerius, Northern Michigan University.

9   Valium, a tranquilizer drug product used to treat anxiety and nervousness, and introduced in 1963, was the company's first major pharmaceutical success. Another Roche success was Rocephin, an antibacterial, which was introduced in 1982. Rocephin not only has become Roche's top selling pharmaceutical product, but also was the number one hospital injectable product in the world for preventing infection and treating infectious disorders. Rocephin's patent protection was not scheduled to expire until the end of the decade.

A STRATEGIC TRANSITION

10   Between 1986 and 1994, Roche divested most of the acquisitions purchased years earlier and which had been designed to diversify the company's product mix. Selected for divestment were: (1) weak performers (i.e., companies that failed to return what the company considered a satisfactory return on investment), (2) those companies that lacked critical mass, or (3) those companies in which Roche could not build critical mass through acquisitions at reasonable purchase prices. The divestitures were as follows:

1. (1988)   Kontron—manufacturer of instruments and electronics
2. (1989)   Maag—plant protection
3. (1989)   Medi-physics—diagnostics
4. (1992)   Microbiology—diagnostics
5. (1993)   Animal Health—vitamins and chemicals

11   Concurrent with these divestitures, Roche made significant acquisitions and additional investments designed to strengthen its core businesses. Most of Roche's businesses, except for fragrances, were considered, to a large extent, recession-resistant. Roche made the following acquisitions and investments between 1990 and 1994:

1. (1990)   Genentech—biotechnology
2. (1991)   Fritzche, Dodge—flavors and fragrances
3. (1991)   Cetus/Chiron—PCR Technology, diagnostics
4. (1991)   Nicholas—over-the-counter (OTC) medical products
5. (1992)   Compuchem—clinical labs; drug testing
6. (1993)   Fisons—consumer healthcare portion of company
7. (1994)   Syntex—transplant medicine, analgesics, and rheumatology
8. (1994)   Agri-Bio—poultry disease treatments

12   As a result of these divestments and acquisitions, Roche's degree of diversification narrowed. Changes in the company's product mix, as they have evolved between 1986 and 1994, appear in Table 1 below. In the 1980s, Roche also entered into two major strategic alliances: Roche-Glaxo and Roche-Amgen.

13   1. Roche-Glaxo. The largest alliance in the global pharmaceutical industry was initiated in 1983 when Roche agreed to market pharmaceutical manufacturer Glaxo's drug, Zantac, a treatment for ulcers, in the United States.

14   2. Roche-Amgen. Roche and the pharmaceutical manufacturer, Amgen, formed the second largest strategic alliance in the pharmaceutical industry to market Amgen's Neupogen, which was used to reduce the negative effects that may be associated with medical products used to fight cancer. Roche marketed Neupogen in Europe.

15   Roche's subsidiary, Syntex, formed a 50-50 joint venture with Procter & Gamble in 1994 to market the over-the-counter analgesic product Naprosyn under the trade name "Aleve." The company also formed a joint venture with the U.S. conglomerate company, Cargill, to develop a new production process for vitamin E.

16   Roche's geographical distribution of sales, and related assets, capital expenditures, and employees are shown below in Table 2.

TABLE 1
Roche Group: Sales by Business Segment, as a Percent of Sales, 1986, 1990, 1992, and 1994.

Business Segment	Percentage of Total Sales			
	1986	1990	1992	1994
Pharmaceuticals	41.0%	49.7%	53.2%	56.6%
Vitamins/fine chemicals	26.0	24.8	23.7	21.7
Diagnostics	11.0	13.6	12.1	10.8
Fragrances and flavors	11.0	11.0	10.4	10.3
Other	11.0	0.9	0.6	0.6
Totals	100.0	100.0	100.0	100.0

Source: Roche Group, Annual Report, 1994; Roche Presentation to Financial Analysts, May 1995.

RESEARCH AND DEVELOPMENT

17   A global presence was crucial to Roche because of the astronomical cost of pharmaceutical research, and the need to spread research expenses across many markets. To develop a new drug typically required ten years of research and an investment of approximately $300 million. Pharmaceutical companies needed to introduce at least one good product every year to remain profitable and competitive.

18   Areas in which Roche conducted research included: the central nervous system, infectious diseases, oncology and virology, inflammatory and autoimmune diseases, metabolic disorders, cardiovascular diseases, bronchopulmonary, and dermatology. Criteria used by Roche to select research projects were: scientific merit, medical need, market potential, and expected time to market. These criteria, as well as pressures to reduce drug prices and the high cost of R&D have forced the company to focus on innovative drugs that represented therapeutic breakthroughs. Consequently, after Roche and Syntex resources were combined, research efforts were rationalized and concentrated on those which showed the most promise.

19   Roche had five research centers: (1) Nutley, New Jersey; (2) Palo Alto, California; (3) Welwyn, Great Britain; (4) Basel, Switzerland; and (5) Kamakura, Japan. Research was decentralized, among other reasons, to capitalize upon the availability and location of scientific talent.

20   Roche spent 16 percent of total sales on R&D, and 24 percent (the highest in the industry) of its pharmaceutical sales on R&D. It was considered to be a key factor in the company's success. Roche's objectives were to: (1) develop innovative products with long-term patented protection that would lower health care costs and (2) take those new pharmaceutical products to market as quickly as possible. Patents were country specific, i.e., the company was required to apply for a patent in each country in which patent protection, typically fifteen to twenty years, was sought. Roche had over 10,000 patents and patent applications in over one hundred countries.[8]

21   Roche planned to submit for approval six new pharmaceutical products between 1995 and 1997. An additional seven were in late stages of development. New applications were being investigated for existing drugs while research into new drugs continued.

22   Roche developed the drug Vesanoid for use in the treatment of acute leukemia. Vesanoid was considered an "orphan drug" because the target consumer population was small and, as a consequence, R&D costs were not expected to be recovered. Roche was committed to the development of life-saving drugs, as well as those drugs which may show lower returns, but produce medical breakthroughs.

23   A Roche manager estimated that there were no effective treatment drugs for two-thirds of known illnesses.[9] Roche's president has been quoted as saying that pharmaceuticals represent the least saturated market in the world. In other words, there were a vast number of drug products yet to be discovered, which represented significant potential for investigation, research, and development.

TABLE 2
**Roche Group: Sales, Operating Assets Employed, Capital Expenditures, (mil. of Swiss francs)
and Number of Employees, by Geographical Area, 1994**

	Sales	Operating Assets Employed	Capital Expenditures	No. of Employees
Switzerland	301	3,366	308	10,512
European Union	4,041	3,569	285	13,628
Rest of Europe	714	259	27	1,177
Total Europe	5,056	7,194	620	25,317
North America	5,839	9,023	565	24,581
Latin America	1,342	1,087	34	5,452
Asia	1,986	1,407	125	4,643
Africa, Austral., Oceania	525	288	11	1,388
Combined Totals	14,748	18,988	1,355	61,381

Source: Roche Group, Annual Report, 1994

MARKETING AND OPERATIONS

24 The company achieved an annual compound growth rate in sales of 8 percent between 1986 and 1994, which was due primarily to internal growth since sales of acquired businesses only slightly exceeded sales of divested businesses.

25 Roche estimated that by 1995, the company ranked eighth in the world in sales of pharmaceuticals, number one in the sale of pharmaceuticals to hospitals, and number three in sales of over-the-counter (OTC) products in Europe. Roche was estimated to be: the global leader in vitamin sales with a 50 percent market share; the global leader in the sale of carotenoids (pigments appearing in vegetable oils and some animal fats); number two in fragrances and flavors with a market share of 11 percent; and number one (or co-equal) in laboratory services revenues in the United States.

26 Construction projects under way or completed in 1994 included sites in Florence, South Carolina; Basel; Nutley, New Jersey; East Hanover, New Jersey; Singapore; and Fukuroi, Japan.

27 To enhance the company's production facilities, pollution was reduced at the source through either: (a) new or improved process technology or (b) energy conversion to cleaner fuels. In addition, safety and environmental protection audits were conducted throughout the organization at production, pre-mix, and distribution centers.

Pharmaceuticals

Overall

28 Worldwide 1994 sales for pharmaceuticals were 8.3 billion Swiss francs, up 7 percent from 1993 sales of 7.8 billion. This segment's respective subdivisions, i.e., prescription drugs, OTC products, and Genentech, were up 7 percent, unchanged, and up 18 percent. Prescription drugs represented 77 percent of sales; OTC, 13 percent; and Genentech, 10 percent. Acquisition of Syntex and investment in Genentech expanded Roche's global market share in pharmaceuticals.

Genentech

29 The purchase of a majority stake in Genentech (of South San Francisco, California) coincided with a major drop in the value of the United States dollar with respect to the Swiss franc. Roche owned approximately 67 percent of Genentech common stock, up from an initial purchase of 60 percent of the company's stock. Roche deliberately chose not to acquire all the shares of Genentech so that Genentech's scientists and managers would have the opportunity to benefit and profit from increased value

in the shares of stock through the purchase of stock options. To preserve Genentech's very unique research approach, Roche took the further step of placing only three of its executives on the thirteen member Genentech board of directors. Genentech continued to operate as an autonomous company, independent of Roche, and Genentech's stock was traded on the New York Stock Exchange.

30 Genentech's 1994 sales rose 27 percent from year earlier figures, while income, including licensing royalties, rose 25 percent to $795.4 million. Genentech was expected to have a "blockbuster" in Pulmozyme, a medical product used in the treatment of cystic fibrosis, an inherited disease that attacked the lungs. The 1994 annual report also noted that Roche and Genentech were engaged in joint research into cancer and the central nervous system.

Syntex

31 Purchase of Syntex of Palo Alto, California, for approximately $5.3 billion, announced in May 1994, was closed at the end of October 1994. The strength of the Swiss franc, coupled with Roche's healthy balance sheet, enabled the company to purchase Syntex with internally generated funds except for a short-term bridge loan. Approximately $3.0 billion of the purchase price represented goodwill, which Roche charged off directly against retained earnings, contributing to a decline of about 700 million Swiss francs in shareholders' equity. Intangible assets (patents, technology, know-how, trademarks, licenses, etc.) associated with the purchase had an estimated value of 3 billion Swiss francs, which was to be amortized over 15 years. The consolidation of Syntex's staff with that of existing Roche facilities was expected to result in a reduction of 5,000 positions. Roche offered transfers, severance packages, early retirement, and outplacement assistance to those employees affected by the acquisition.

32 A Syntex pharmaceutical product, CellCept, was used in conjunction with organ transplants to assist the body to accept the transplanted organ, kidneys in particular, when the body rejected the organ. CellCept was approved by the FDA in May of 1995.

OTC Sales

33 Roche had not entered the OTC market in the United States (except through the joint venture with Procter & Gamble previously mentioned) and Japan.

Vitamins and Fine Chemicals

34 Sales for this segment in 1994 totaled 3.2 billion Swiss francs, down 2.0 percent from 1993 sales. Sales, however, in terms of local currencies, actually rose 5 percent. Sales by product category were: vitamins, 60 percent; fine chemicals (for use in food, pharmaceuticals, and cosmetics), 23 percent; and carotenoids, 17 percent. Geographical sales were concentrated in Europe, 42 percent, and North America, 31 percent.

35 A beta-carotene plant was built in Freeport, Texas. Several new vitamin forms were introduced. Market growth experienced its best success in the Far East and Latin America. Improvements in processes for the production of vitamin B2 and carotenoids were developed. In addition, the company was building a new technical center in Sisseln, Switzerland, to develop new and improved production technologies. The company also planned to be a major player in the China market by participating in joint ventures and providing technological consultation to keep production costs low.

36 To improve economies of scale in logistics, the division centralized product distribution at four distribution centers. In response to industrial customers forming partnerships to consolidate purchases and increase their buying clout, Roche integrated its Europe, Africa, and Middle East marketing organizations. To address intense competition from low wage countries in Asia, Roche increased productivity through both concentration and expansion of production, improvement of production processes, and development of new markets.

Diagnostics

37 Sales revenues for the Diagnostics division declined 7.1 percent from 1.7 billion Swiss francs in 1993 to 1.6 billion Swiss francs in 1994. Diagnostics' 1994 sales were derived from two businesses: Roche Biomedical Laboratories (63 percent of sales) and Roche Diagnostic Systems (37 percent).

38   The sales decline was attributed primarily to intense competition for market share and government cost controls that forced lower fees for laboratory services. Fees also came under pressure because of the increased buying power of managed care organizations which had been achieved through market consolidation, i.e., the merger of service providers.

39   The 1995 merger of Roche Biomedical Laboratories (RBL) of Burlington, South Carolina (which represented 63 percent of this industry segment's sales), with National Health Laboratories of La Jolla, California, was expected to improve this division's competitive position. The merger created a new company, Laboratory Corporation of America (LabCorp), which was estimated to have a 13 percent market share of independent laboratory revenues, equalling that of co-leader in the field, Met-Path, and moving ahead of SmithKline's 10 percent. The merger joined RBL, whose revenues were derived primarily from the eastern United States with NHL, whose sales were geographically dispersed throughout the U.S. In addition to the assets of RBL, Roche contributed $186.7 million. In return, Roche received a 49.9 percent share of LabCorp and 8.3 million warrants convertible to LabCorp shares in the year 2000.

40   Roche Diagnostic Systems generated revenues through sales in clinical chemistry and drug monitoring, 58 percent; polymerase chain reaction (PCR, in which genetic materials can be copied millions of times over to assist in detecting infectious diseases, cancer, or hereditary disorders), 14 percent; immunochemistry, 16 percent; hematology, 10 percent; and other areas, 2 percent. The company was number one in the industry in PCR technology. The company was number one in the industry in PCR technology. The company recently developed an automated system for laboratory testing of a broad range of diseases which was fast, secure, and efficient. Like other sectors of the health care industry, Diagnostic Systems responded to price pressures from health care regulators by consolidating operations.

Fragrances and Flavors

41   Sales revenues for this industry segment were 1.5 billion Swiss francs in 1994, up 6.2 percent over 1993. Fragrances (used in perfumes, toiletries, cosmetics, soaps and detergents, and household and industrial products) represented 39 percent of sales; flavors (compounds for use in foods, beverages, pharmaceuticals, oral hygiene products, and animal foods), 36 percent; and specialties (which included cosmetic and synthetic fragrance ingredients, natural essences, and sunscreen agents), 25 percent. Sales by region were as follows: Europe, 42 percent; North America, 34 percent; Asia/Pacific, 16 percent; and South America, 8 percent. Research was presently focused on the biology of the skin, natural flavors, and the sense of smell with regard to natural scents.

42   Roche was number two in the industry, behind number one International Fragrances and Flavors. Fragrances and flavors companies, Roure and Givaudan, respectively, formerly separate Roche units, were merged into one division in 1991.

43   As was the case in the other divisions, production was concentrated at fewer facilities to improve productivity. The division also paid special attention to key accounts, and by improving responsiveness to their needs, increased sales to these high volume customers.

MANAGEMENT AND ORGANIZATION

44   A key Roche objective was to be a leader in the industries in which it competed, not necessarily number one but perhaps number two or three. The thrust of the company was to focus on research and innovation, above average profitability in its core businesses, and improved efficiency. The company strongly believed that new drug discoveries would do more to improve health care and contain medical costs than any other alternative since drugs not only were cheaper than other health care methods but also could shorten hospital stays.[10]

45   Roche Holding Ltd. formed in 1989, directly controlled 127 subsidiary units in 55 countries. The seven largest subsidiaries, as reported in the company's 1994 Annual Report, were: (1) F. Hoffmann-La Roche Ltd., Basel; (2) Hoffmann-La Roche Inc., Nutley, New Jersey; (3) Roche S.p.A., Milan, Italy; (4) Hoffmann-La Roche Aktiengesellschaft, Grenzach, Germany; (5) Produits Roche S.A.,

EXHIBIT A
An Illustrative Representation of Roche Group Functions, Divisions, Products, and Subsidiaries

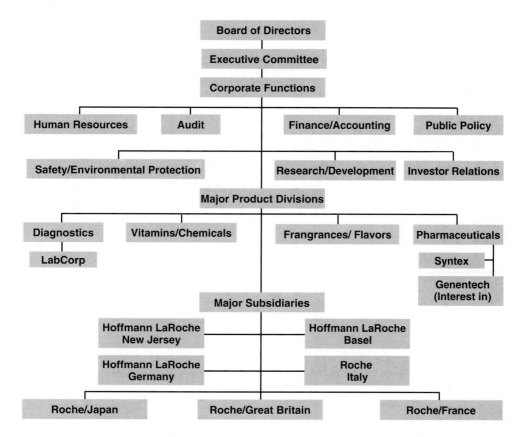

Neuilly-sur-Seine, France and Societe Chimique Roche S.A., Village-Neuf, France; (6) Roche Products Limited, Welwyn, Great Britain; and (7) Nippon Roche K.K., Tokyo, Japan (see Exhibit A).

46   The Roche Group, as described earlier, had four major divisions. Subsidiaries within each division reported to their respective division heads. Changes in organizational alignments were made to decentralize and flatten the organizational structure to speed communications and decision making and encourage management initiative. In keeping with these objectives, in 1990, costs formerly charged off to the corporate headquarters, were assigned to the four major businesses, decentralizing responsibility and decision making.

47   At the corporate level, a functional organization included the following elements: (1) Audit, (2) Finance and Accounting, (3) Human Resources, (4) Investor Relations, (5) Public Policy, (6) Research and Development, and (7) Safety and Environmental Protection. Members of Roche's Board of Directors and Executive Committee are shown below:

Roche Group, Board of Directors:

Mr. Fritz Gerber	Chairman
Dr. Lukas Hoffmann	Vice-Chairman
Dr. Andres F. Leuenberger	Vice-Chairman; Delegate to General Management
Professor Kurt Jenny	
Dr. Armin M. Kessler	
Dr. Henri B. Meier	

Dr. Jakob Oeri

Dr. H. C. Paul Sacher

Professor Werner Stauffacher

Professor Charles Weissmann

Roche Group, Executive Committee:

Mr. Fritz Gerber	Chairman and CEO
Dr. Andres F. Leuenberger	Vice-Chairman
Dr. Henri B. Meier	Finance, accounting
Dr. Markus Altwegg	Pharma Stammhaus Basel, Group informatics
Mr. Jean-Luc Belingard	Diagnostics Division
Dr. Roland Bronnimann	Vitamins, Fine Chemicals Div.
Professor Jurgen Drews	Research and Development
Dr. Franz B. Humer	Pharmaceuticals Division

FINANCE

48   Roche stock was traded on the Zurich, Geneva, and Basel, Switzerland, stock exchanges. American investors could invest in Roche through the U.S. ADR program (American Depository Rights) which were nonvoting stock issued through the Bank of New York (BONY). The ADR program was launched in 1992 with the express purpose of giving U.S. investors easier access to investment in the company. In 1990, to attract international investors, Roche adopted International Accounting Standards (IAS) in the filing of the company's financial reports.

49   After consolidated net income for the Roche Group rose from 2.5 billion Swiss francs (CHF) in 1993 to 2.9 billion CHF in 1994, the market value of Roche's common stock continued to appreciate. (see Exhibit B) In the summer of 1995, Roche's publicly traded stock was valued at slightly more than the combined market value of Swiss competitors Ciba-Geigy and Sandoz, despite the fact that Ciba-Geigy's sales were almost twice those of Roche, reflecting investors' optimistic appraisal of Roche's growth and profit potential. Estimates of the common stock market capitalization of the top pharmaceutical companies in the world, as of July 31, 1995, had Roche on top at $66.9 billion, Merck second at $63.8 billion, Sandoz at $26.4 billion, and Ciba-Geigy at $21 billion.[11]In 1986, reflecting the shift in industry leadership, comparable stock capitalization figures for Roche, Merck, Sandoz, and Ciba were 9 billion Swiss francs, 19 billion, 7 billion, and 13 billion CHF, respectively.

50   Between 1991 and 1995, Roche issued six innovative financial instruments (for a total of about $6 billion). These funds were obtained at an average of 3 percent interest and were then deployed to obtain a yield of 9 percent on investments in marketable securities. The six financial instruments employed by Roche, and the colorful labels assigned to these issues, were as follows:

1. The bull spread—Roche issued $1 billion in bonds at a coupon rate of 3½ percent in 1991. Detachable warrants, which were exercised in 1994, enabled each holder of 100 warrants to receive 10,000 Swiss francs in cash.
2. The knockout—Roche Holdings, Inc. issued bonds with a nominal value of $1.42 billion in 1993, paying an interest rate of 2 3/4 percent. Detachable warrants, exercisable in 1996, entitled the holder of 60 warrants to receive either 6,000 Swiss francs in cash or one nonvoting equity security.
3. Lyon (Liquid Yield Option Notes) I and Lyon II—In 1993, Roche Holdings, Inc. issued $1.42 billion of zero coupon bonds (sold at a discount) that were redeemable in 1988 and 2003 either for cash or American Depositary Shares of Roche Holding Ltd. at a specified conversion rate for each $1,000 of principal.

4. The samurai—In 1994, Roche Financial Management issued bonds, with detachable warrants, valued at 100 billion yen ($1.4 billion) at a coupon rate of 1 percent. The warrants, exercisable in 1998, entitled the holder of 100 warrants to receive one of the following: (a) one non-voting equity security; (b) cash equal to the non-voting equity security prices; or (c) 7,100 Swiss francs in cash.

5 & 6. The "gold option" and the "Helveticus" were two other major bond issues and each returned over $1 billion to Roche under favorable terms.

51   Financial investments made by Roche were significant. At the end of 1994, Roche actively managed marketable securities totaling 13.1 billion Swiss francs—almost the equivalent of the firm's entire investment in long-term assets, and over 62 percent more than the value of the firm's plant and equipment. Liquid funds gave the company the flexibility to invest in operations as opportunities arose, and also enhanced its ability to negotiate a satisfactory price for such investments.

52   Since 98 percent of Roche's sales were outside of Switzerland, the company utilized various strategies to reduce its vulnerability to currency and interest rate risks. These included the purchase of derivative financial instruments, forward exchange contracts, options, and currency swaps.

53   In 1994, Roche's dividend payout ratio remained at around 16 percent. Most of the company's profits were reinvested in the company in the form of R&D and acquisitions. The low payout ratio also limited investors' tax liability and the potential for payment of double taxation. Ceiba-Geigy and Sandoz, Basel's other two major pharmaceutical companies, also had a low payout ratio, but not as low as Roche.

54   Unlike publicly-traded companies in the United States, Roche was not required under Swiss law to maintain records of shareholders. Shares of stock, including non-voting equities, were issued to bearer and for this reason the company did not keep a register of shareholders. Roche was obligated, however, to state in its annual report that the Roche family owned more than 50 percent of the company's common stock.

THE CHALLENGE OF A COMPLEX GLOBAL ENVIRONMENT

55   The rapid and significant changes in the composition and shape of the pharmaceutical industry, together with the dynamics of the environmental sectors that affected the industry, presented the Roche Group and its competitors with major challenges. In the light of recent realignments within the industry and the increasing influence of government, Roche clearly had to reevaluate its organizational structure, product line, and competitive strategies.

APPENDIX: THE GLOBAL PHARMACEUTICAL INDUSTRY

56   The pharmaceutical industry was centuries old and the treatment of diseases had come a long way since the use of herbs and mysterious incantations. Medicine men and "magical" potions from the Dark Ages have been displaced by researchers, scientists, clinicians, and the economies of scale possible through global marketing and manufacture of health care products and services. The pharmaceutical industry was a multi-billion dollar industry that was dominated by a dozen major multinational companies. The industry was also unique in that the Swiss companies Ciba-Geigy, Sandoz, and Roche, three of the world's largest pharmaceutical companies, were each headquartered in Basel, less than a mile away from one another, and each was founded approximately a century earlier to produce and market different, but related, products.

57   Many of the industry's competitors, including both Sandoz and Ceiba-Geigy, were more diversified than Roche, relying upon horizontal diversification to enter manufacturing areas other than pharmaceuticals.

58   A brief overview of a few of Roche's major competitors (Ciba-Geigy Ltd., Sandoz International Ltd., Merck & Co., Inc., the Hoechst Group, and the Glaxo Group Ltd.) appears below. Both these companies and Roche pursued similar strategies in a variety of fields; each company, for example:

EXHIBIT B
Roche Holding Ltd.: Selected Financial Data, 1985–1994

(in millions of Swiss francs)

	1985	1986	1987	1988
Sales	8,940	7,822	7,705	8,690
Depreciation/amortization	498	497	492	538
Research and development	1,196	1,123	1,210	1,419
Net income	452	416	482	642
Cash from operations	—	—	—	—
Long-term assets	5,524	5,509	5,361	5,396
Current assets	7,058	7,344	8,315	9,880
Total assets	12,582	12,853	13,676	15,276
Shareholder's equity	7,954	8,321	8,703	10,075
Minority interests	7	5	5	5
Long-term liabilities	2,649	2,690	2,777	2,768
Current liabilities	1,972	1,837	2,191	2,429
Capital expenditures	542	529	520	652
No. employees end of yr.	45,477	46,513	47,498	49,671
Net income as a % of sales	5.1	5.3	6.3	7.4
Net income as a % of Sh. Equity	5.7	5.0	5.5	6.4
R&D as a % of sales	13.4	14.4	13.8	13.9
Current ratio (as a percent)	357.8	399.8	379.6	406.8
Equity as a % of total assets	63.2	64.7	63.6	66.0
Sales per employee (000 CHF)	197	168	162	175
Number shares outstanding (000)	16	16	16	16
Number non-voting equity securities (000)	61.4	61.4	61.4	61.4
Total shares and non-voting equity securities (000)	77.4	77.4	77.4	77.4
Net income per share and non-voting equity security (CHF)	56	52	60	80
Dividend per share and non-voting equity security (CHF)	12	12	13	14
Total dividends (millions CHF)	100	100	102	161

Source: Roche Group, Annual Report, 1994.

1. Spent heavily on research, which was vital to company growth and profitability;
2. Not only conducted its own research but joined with others to conduct research;
3. Contracted research projects out to specialized companies and leading universities;
4. Established research centers dedicated to specialized areas of inquiry;
5. Formed strategic alliances to manufacture and distribute drug products;
6. Was increasingly aware of the importance of generic (i.e., products whose original patents had expired and now were manufactured by others without payment of royalties to the developer of the patented drug) and over-the-counter (OTC) drug products;
7. Was sensitive to currency exchange rate fluctuations;
8. Cut staff and facilities in selected areas to increase competitiveness and productivity, but also expanded other facilities to achieve economies of scale;
9. Sought new markets in Eastern Europe and the Far East, particularly China;
10. Considered and evaluated acquisition and merger partners while divesting businesses that seemed incompatible with its core businesses;
11. Found its sales and profits coming under increased governmental surveillance and control throughout the world;

EXHIBIT B
concluded

(in millions of Swiss francs)

	1989	1990	1991	1992	1993	1994
	9,814	9,670	11,451	12,953	14,315	14,748
	597	521	822	880	930	979
	1,419	1,444	1,727	1,998	2,269	2,332
	852	948	1,482	1,916	2,478	2,860
	—	1,718	1,980	2,673	2,976	3,120
	5,080	6,937	8,478	9,293	9,522	13,549
	12,200	15,880	16,567	18,290	21,404	22,684
	17,280	22,817	25,045	27,583	30,926	36,233
	11,624	13,243	14,429	16,046	17,914	16,422
	5	446	511	581	625	861
	3,280	5,799	7,029	6,809	7,921	10,034
	2,371	3,329	3,076	4,147	4,466	8,916
	908	907	1,139	1,293	1,407	1,355
	50,203	52,685	55,134	56,335	56,082	61,381
	8.7	9.8	12.9	14.8	17.3	19.4
	7.3	7.2	10.3	11.9	13.8	17.4
	14.5	14.9	15.1	15.4	15.9	15.8
	514.6	477.0	538.6	441.0	479.3	254.4
	67.3	60.0	59.7	60.3	59.9	47.7
	195	184	208	230	255	240
	800	800	1,600	1,600	1,600	1,600
	3,330	3,330	7,026	7,026	7,026	7,026
	4,130	4,130	8,626	8,626	8,626	8,626
	103	115	172	222	287	332
	19	21	28	37	48	55
	157	173	236	312	404	474

12. Increased its degree of decentralization of operations; and

13. Took an active role in minimizing the impact of its facilities upon the environment.

Despite these similarities, however, there were also differences. A few of these differences are noted in the discussion that follows.

Selected Data from Prominent Global Pharmaceutical Competitors

Ciba-Geigy

59   As noted earlier, Ciba-Geigy and Sandoz planned to merge in 1996. Ciba-Geigy sales for 1994 totaled 22.1 billion Swiss francs (CHF), down slightly from 1993 sales of 22.6 billion, whereas net profit rose in 1994 to 1.9 billion from 1.8 billion CHF. Shareholders' equity declined to 15.5 billion CHF in 1994 from 17.1 billion CHF, due primarily to a charge of 2.5 billion in goodwill related to acquisitions against retained earnings, and secondarily to currency translation adjustments. During 1994, Ciba-Geigy acquired a 49.9 percent share of the healthcare company Chiron, and the OTC product line of Rhone-Poulenc Rorer in both the U.S. and Canada. Ciba was engaged in three major

businesses: healthcare, agriculture, and industry (dyes, chemicals, pigments, etc.) whose share of total sales totaled 39.7 percent, 21.7 percent, and 38.6 percent, respectively.[12]

Sandoz

60 Sandoz acquired the Gerber Products Company, the leading U.S. baby food manufacturer, in 1994 for $3.8 billion. Sandoz's chairman believed that this purchase was the most important in the company's history, and would establish nutrition as the company's second core business. The acquisition also was intended to assist the company in reducing its exposure to risks in the pharmaceutical industry associated with increased government controls and price pressures. Like Roche, Sandoz financed most ($2 billion) of its purchase price of Gerber internally, and the remainder with a bridge loan of $1.8 billion.[13]

61 Goodwill associated with the Gerber purchase was written off in 1994 against the stockholders' equity. Sandoz's 1994 sales of 15.9 billion CHF (up 5.1 percent from 1993) were distributed among its divisions as follows: pharmaceuticals, 45 percent; nutrition, 18 percent; chemicals, 14 percent; Agro (crop protection agents), 9 percent; construction and environment, 8 percent; and seeds, 6 percent. The company's pharmaceutical division accounted for 77 percent of total research and development (R&D), which was equal to 17.4 percent of pharmaceutical sales. In January 1994, Sandoz divested one of its chemical division companies, ALPHEN, whose product line did not fit in with the company's other chemical products.

Merck

62 Merck, whose headquarters was at Whitehouse Station, New Jersey, recorded sales of $15 billion in 1994, an increase of 43 percent over 1993 sales, which took into account the company's purchase of Medco Containment Services (for about $6.6 billion) in November, 1993. Without consideration of Medco, sales for Merck rose 7 percent in 1994 above 1993.

63 In 1994, Merck's net income rose 38 percent to $3.0 billion, including Medco, and 12 percent when Medco was excluded. Unlike the Swiss companies which immediately wrote off goodwill resulting from acquisitions, Merck chose to amortize goodwill over a 40-year period, thus preserving growth in its net income. Medco was a pharmacy benefit management company whose mail service pharmacies and retail pharmacy networks dispensed 130 million prescriptions in 1994. One in every seven Americans, 40 million people, were covered by a Medco drug benefit. Merck sales in 1994 were distributed in approximately the following percentages: pharmaceuticals, 62.9 percent; Medco, 27.4 percent; animal health and crop protection, 6.9 percent; and specialty chemicals, 2.8 percent. Early in 1995, Merck sold off its specialty chemical businesses to focus on the other core businesses.[14]

The Hoechst Group

64 Hoechst, of Frankfurt, Germany, was more diversified than most participants in the pharmaceutical industry. Sales were distributed as follows: chemicals, 27 percent; health, 24 percent; fibers, 15 percent; polymers, 14 percent; engineering and technology, 12 percent; and agriculture, 8 percent. The company's 1994 sales totaled 49.6 billion German marks (average 1994 exchange rate was about 1.4 marks per dollar), an increase of 7.8 percent over the prior year. Sales of the health division rose 2.6 percent over the previous year.

65 Germany was the company's largest market for pharmaceutical products. Of total sales, about 60 percent were in Europe, and 30 percent in North America. At the beginning of 1994, Hoechst controlled no more than one percent of the U.S. market for pharmaceutical products. However, later in 1994, Hoechst purchased the U.S. pharmaceutical company Marion Merrell Dow for over $7 billion and Copley, a U.S. generic drugs manufacturer. Hoechst also purchased the U.S. diagnostics firm, Syva, in 1995.[15]

Glaxo-Wellcome

66 Glaxo, whose headquarters was in London, England, increased 1994 sales by 15 percent to 5.7 billion British pounds (1995 average rate of exchange: 1.0 British pound was equivalent to $1.55) over the previous year of 4.9 billion British pounds. Sales in the United States, Europe, and the rest of the world accounted for 43 percent, 35 percent, and 22 percent of sales, respectively. The company's product line consisted entirely of medicines, including ethical (prescribed by a physician) drugs and OTC drugs. Glaxo had subsidiary companies in 70 countries which operated under a decentralized system of management.[16]

67   Manufacturers of OTC drug products, i.e., those that did not require a doctor's prescription and which were frequently used to treat minor illnesses, such as colds and sleeplessness, (which also were treated with prescription drugs) also competed for consumers' heath care dollars. Some OTC manufacturers applied for and received approval from the Food and Drug Administration (FDA) to sell drugs over the counter that previously were sold only by prescription. SmithKline Beecham's Tagamet, a drug used to treat heartburn and acid indigestion, and approved for OTC sale by the FDA in 1995, was an example of such a product.

The Influence of Governments

68   Pharmaceutical companies were under constant pressure to maintain the goodwill of governments so that prescription medicines could be priced at levels that struck a balance between health benefits to patients and economic benefits to the firm that made further drug research feasible. Although the Japanese government, for example, mandated price cuts in prescription drugs, it was believed to be fair in its approval of prices for innovative products that enabled pharmaceutical companies to receive a fair return. "Me too" products that failed to differentiate themselves from previously introduced pharmaceuticals, however, did not obtain very good prices or margins from the Japanese government.

69   Governments in both Europe and Asia placed restrictions upon pharmaceutical manufacturers and health care providers. In Germany, for example, in 1993, the government froze drug prices and placed tight controls on prices for diagnostic services. In Japan, in addition to biennial government-imposed price cuts on pharmaceuticals, hospitals and doctors were under pressure to curtail discretionary drug usage. The French government imposed cost controls on prescription drug prices. The Italian government also prescribed major reductions in prescription drug prices and the amounts reimbursed consumers. These moves by the Italian government led to a decline of 7 percent in the overall Italian market for pharmaceuticals in 1994 (in contrast, Roche Group sales in Italy increased by 3 percent during 1994).[17]

70   In the United States, a universal health care program proposed by the Clinton Administration, was rejected by the Congress in 1994. Subsequently, under pressure to balance the federal budget, the U.S. Congress sought to reduce spending on large government health care programs such as Medicare and Medicaid. The Congress, in turn, applied pressure on medical providers (primarily hospitals, physicians, and health maintenance organizations (HMOs)) and third party providers (administrators of health care programs, such as Blue Cross-Blue Shield) to reduce costs (drug costs were estimated to represent 7.5 percent of total health care costs). HMOs have grown both in size and number and have used their size to negotiate lower prices for drugs and diagnostic services.

71   Economic uncertainty in Latin and South America due to inflation and unemployment and political instability in the Middle East and Africa made it difficult either to negotiate contracts with governments or to successfully market more expensive prescription drug products.

REFERENCES

[1]Interviews with managers of Hoffmann-LaRoche, Basel, Switzerland, June 16, 1995, followed up by numerous telephone calls with the same managers between July and December, 1995.

[2]*Maclean,* March 18, 1996, p. 109.

[3]Ibid.

[4]*Financial World,* November 21, 1995, p. 164.

[5]Weber, Joseph. "Not the Best Prescription for Growth," *Business Week,* October 30, 1995, p. 124.

[6]*Facts on File,* November 2, 1995, p. 55.

[7]The Roche Group, *Annual Report,* 1995.

[8]*The Pocket Roche,* 1993, p. 93.

[9]Interviews, op. cit., June 16, 1995.

[10]Ibid.

[11]*The Wall Street Journal,* October 2, 1995, p. R32.

[12]Ciba-Geigy, *Annual Report,* 1995.

[13]Sandoz, *Annual Report,* 1995.

[14]Merck, *Annual Report,* 1995.

[15]The Hoechst Group, *Annual Report,* 1995.

[16]Glaxo, *Annual Report,* 1995.

[17]Roche Group, *Annual Report,* 1995.

CASE 55

THE "EMERGING" U.S. EDUCATION INDUSTRY: AN ENTREPRENEURIAL FRONTIER?

1   Two short decades ago futurists talked about the coming information age. With its dramatic arrival, internet giddy investors are now looking for the next "age" or "stage" to repeat their investment success. Several futurists say that the "knowledge" age is next, or currently unfolding. This they see as the time when persons armed with information *plus* the understanding of what it means, what to do with it, how to share it, and the research to know how it will evolve—the knowledge merchants—will bring untold value to the information age and build wealth like the computer and software created during the information age.

2   If these notions are accurate, then higher education—U.S. colleges and universities—seem uniquely positioned to exploit this golden, knowledge age. At least, that's what some think should be the case. Lifelong learning, adult education, training, a baby boomlet headed into the college age, internationalization, and distance education—all trends or capabilities traditional colleges and universities should be uniquely positioned to exploit.

3   But something is not right. Colleges and universities, at least the traditional ones, seem to be floundering—caught between tradition, curriculum rigidity, the teach versus research debate, and spiraling costs which they must pass along to their "customers" as governmental funding declines. Some observers believe that the traditional college or university is destined to solely watch as their opportunity for a golden age turns into a nightmare of decline and increasing irrelevance.

4   The complaints are becoming loud and familiar: Primary and secondary schools are flailing about. Colleges and universities are turning out insufficient numbers of graduates for the New Economy. And even when they try, boring unidimensional lecture courses are becoming archaic. Technology is inadequate, course options stale. Yet Corporate America can't keep its employees properly up to speed on technological change. Education may seem to be in crisis and decline, but therein lies opportunity: Scores of entrepreneurs and companies sense a chance to make money by doing better.

5   As a result, the $660 billion education industry is taking on some of the hallmarks of an emerging-growth market, fueled by demographics, technology, and dissatisfaction with the status quo. Well-financed entrepreneurs are spending tens of millions of dollars of their fortunes on education startups or on helping established companies expand. As much as $4 billion in venture capital is looking for deals well beyond the traditional secondary and college markets. Everything is being considered, from educational software to online-learning programs for college students and managers.

6   Financier Michael R. Milken and Oracle Corp. Chairman Lawrence J. Ellison are assembling a "cradle-to-post-retirement" collection of companies under the Knowledge Universe umbrella. "We have a broad vision," says Thomas J. Kalinske, president of Knowledge. "If you start with kids and help them learn faster and better, the chances are that when they are parents they'll have a positive feeling, and later turn to us for continuing education." He says Knowledge Universe has sales of $1 billion to $1.5 billion.

PUBLIC INVESTORS OPEN BUT FINICKY

7   Microsoft Corp. co-founder Paul Allen's Vulcan Ventures Inc. has also invested in a handful of deals, including a corporate training company, Asymetrix Corp., and a series of high school advanced-

©1999 The McGraw-Hill Companies. Created and adapted by Richard Robinson, University of South Carolina, using R. A. Melcher, "Education," *Business Week:* January 11, 1999; and K. H. Hammonds, S. Jackson, G. DeGorge, and K. Morris, "The New University," *Business Week:* December 22, 1997.

NEVER UNDERESTIMATE THE POWER OF THE WEB TO FOSTER DREAMS OF RICHES—THIS TIME, FOR FUZZY-HEADED ACADEMICS. On 3/8/99, the Blackboard.com Web site went live, offering instructors the chance to set up individual Web sites offering online classes, charging whatever they want.

Students can sign up for anything from Cigar 101 to law classes to prep sessions for stock brokers' accreditation exams. Many of the prospective instructors expect to make a good living. Juliana Lutzi, CEO of FIRE Online Training, hopes to get $250 each from as many as 6,000 students from investment-banking houses such as Goldman Sachs, who need to take the brokers' test. The Web site, run by Washington-based online-education company Blackboard, will make money by collecting $100 from each teacher, plus a to-be-determined percentage of tuition. But caveat emptor to students: Blackboard won't screen its instructors. It says the market will do that. "Those most likely to succeed will already have a name," says Chairman Matthew Serbin Pittinsky. Could the Web produce the next Deepak Chopra?

Source: "To Cut Classes, Hit 'Escape', *Business Week:* March 15, 1999.

placement courses for online distribution. "The opportunities are tremendous," says Vulcan President William Savoy.

8   Will a torrent of private-sector money suddenly transform learning? Certainly not overnight. And the public markets, which have gobbled up some three dozen initial public offerings in education in the past few years, quickly anger or turn finicky at the slightest misstep. Case in point: CBT Group PLC, one of the leaders in computer-training software for companies, saw its stock plunge from a peak of nearly 64 to below 7. CBT's tumble affected many other newly public education stocks, sending an important signal. "There has been so much emphasis on education that it has driven some very good companies to tremendous [trading] premiums," says Susan Harman, one of the first education industry investment bankers, now co-president of the new venture firm Core Learning Group LLC. "It reminds me a lot of biotech—there will be blips, and you have to have a long-term perspective."

ARE SOME SECTORS ENTREPRENEURIAL PIPE DREAMS?

9   The education industry will grow by only 5% to 6% this year—but some pieces will grow at nearly triple that pace. Among them are businesses supplying kindergartens through high schools with computers or tutoring. Others likely to grow fast are those delivering specialized college or professional degrees to the growing number of high school graduates or working adults who are seeking education at nontraditional, for-profit schools—such as DeVry Inc. or University of Phoenix Inc. In the $60 billion corporate training market, revenues in the information technology arena should rise nearly 12%, to $10.5 billion, with online delivery up 42%, estimates International Data Corp.

10   The troubled K–12 sector is gaining some interest, although there are plenty of skeptics. Making money by managing primary and secondary schools is "a pipe dream," says NationsBanc Montgomery Securities analyst R. Keith Gay, "but the ancillary opportunities are enormous and non-threatening." Still, The Edison Project has contracts to run 48 schools in 25 cities. And Sylvan Learning Systems Inc. is expanding beyond tutoring centers into on-site coaching in reading, math, and writing in hundreds of public schools. In response to a looming teacher shortage, Sylvan is pushing hard into the training and testing of future educators.

11   The increasing ability of teachers to control so-called supplemental teaching materials—texts or CD-ROMs—is creating yet another new investment area. Now a $2 billion market, supplemental education could grow as much as 9% this year, vs. 4% for traditional textbooks, says Tribune Co. education unit president, Robert Bosau. Tribune plans to boost its sales in this sector, in part by acquisition, from around $325 million to $500 million over the next year.

12   Supplemental education is also attracting the technology-minded. A San Ramon (Calif.) startup, ZapMe! Corp., is putting computer labs with Internet connections into middle and high schools, free of charge. Technology vendors and other corporate sponsors will advertise in corners of the Web pages.

13   In the coming year, there will continue to be new forces driving the market for learning beyond high school. For one thing, the sheer numbers of projected full-time and part-time college students is

fast expanding: From a trough of 2.2 million students in 1992, the total is expected to grow to 3.2 million by 2004. And 44% of those students are now working adults over the age of 24. Companies such as DeVry, Apollo Group Inc. (parent of the University of Phoenix), and ITT Educational Services, which have prospered by providing narrowly focused technical degrees, are all expanding their facilities and course offerings. Sales could jump 18% for the group, to $1.7 billion in '99, estimates NationsBanc.

BREATHLESS RUSH

14   The ability to deliver college and professional certification courses over the Internet is generating an almost breathless rush to the medium, sometimes bringing together for-profit and traditional schools. Sylvan and MCI WorldCom Inc. developed a joint venture, Caliber Learning Network Inc., which they took public last May, with the goal of providing distance learning for professionals in classrooms. So far, Caliber has signed deals with Johns Hopkins University and the Wharton School at the University of Pennsylvania to deliver medical and business courses at sites around the country. But the company is losing money. "There are great growth prospects, but it won't happen overnight," admits Sylvan President Douglas L. Becker.

15   That hasn't stopped plenty of educators from eyeing distance-learning prospects. Kalinske, of Knowledge Universe, hopes to roll out a Knowledge University in the fall of '99, offering professional certificates and, possibly, a master's in business. He's aiming for a program that captures the attention of the busy professional. "You can't just put up endless hours of lectures and note-taking," he says.

16   Corporate trainers are especially keen to go high tech. They're using the Internet and CD-ROMS to teach managers everything from how to use software to the principles of finance and staff diversity. International Data Corp. reckons that technology-delivered training will grow from $1.9 billion in 1998 to $2.7 billion this year and hit $7.8 billion in 2002. "Companies have to live with the fact that, with tight labor forces, they have to train who they have," says Vulcan's Savoy.

17   But the industry is learning it can't take corporate customers for granted. A common problem: Companies don't become repeat buyers of the courses without regular follow-up and, often, in-class teaching and customization. "Too many companies are designing products without regard to the customer's needs and how they'll use them," warns Matthew Feldman, managing director of Learning Insights, which offers CD-ROM finance products. This fast-emerging market has little tolerance for such shortsightedness.

THE COLLEGIATE MARKET

18   On an autumn afternoon on the manicured grounds of the red-brick University of Florida at Gainesville, students stroll under palms and moss-draped oaks. It's a classic collegiate tableau—and completely at odds with the radical vision of the man who presides over the campus from a modest second-story office. It's not that John V. Lombardi wants to destroy what he sees. Quite simply, he has to.

19   As president of the huge state institution, Lombardi contends with a legislature that won't let him raise tuition but has cut university appropriations by 15% since 1991. In response, "we have taken the great leap forward and said: 'Let's pretend we're a corporation,'" Lombardi says. Defying traditional academic notions, departments now vie openly for resources. English professors must demonstrate, in essence, that Chaucer pays the bills using funds as effectively as engineering or business classes. Departments that meet quality and productivity criteria win shares of $2 million in discretionary funding.

20   This isn't a universally popular strategy. Some professors and administrators fear the effects of the new strictures on academic quality. Many hope it is just a president's passing fancy. "Things like this come and go all the time," says John Kraft, dean of the University of Florida's College of Business Administration. Lombardi understands the dissension and skepticism. At institutions like his, he says, "everyone assumes that we'll just keep churning the paper, and it will be business as usual."

EXHIBIT A

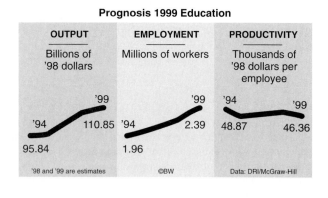

Prognosis 1999 Education

OUTPUT	EMPLOYMENT	PRODUCTIVITY
Billions of '98 dollars	Millions of workers	Thousands of '98 dollars per employee
'94 95.84 → '99 110.85	'94 1.96 → '99 2.39	'94 48.87 → '99 46.36
'98 and '99 are estimates	©BW	Data: DRI/McGraw-Hill

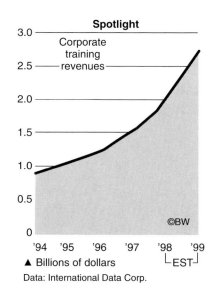

Spotlight

Corporate training revenues

▲ Billions of dollars   └EST┘

©BW

Data: International Data Corp.

21   It isn't—at Florida or at other colleges and universities across the nation. Behind ivied walls and on leafy quadrangles, administrators and professors acknowledge this new reality. Higher education is changing profoundly, retreating from the ideals of liberal arts and the leading-edge research it always has cherished. Instead, it is behaving more like the $250 billion business it has become.

SEEKING FISCAL ACCOUNTABILITY

22   Universities are rethinking the big lecture halls, faculty tenure, discrete academic departments, and other features that have defined traditional institutions for a century. They are designing curriculums more relevant to employers, communities, and students. Schools are pursuing fiscal discipline, forcing accountability on organizations that for decades have expanded as they pleased. And they're wiring the ivory towers, creating with technology more efficient mediums of instruction.

23   Why this transformation, in a system still regarded as unmatched in the world? After all, 62% of Americans today attend college just after high school, testament to the American ideal of a highly educated populace. U.S. universities, moreover, still produce research that extends the bounds of knowledge and feeds innovation in industry.

24   Over the past two decades, though, higher education has failed spectacularly to live within its means. From 1980 to 1994, the most recent year for which Education Dept. data are available, instructional costs per full-time student at private universities increased 48% in real terms; public universities upped research expenses by 35%. In the same time, though, states reduced real, per-student funding to public universities by 22%. In the private sector, students from well-heeled families who could pay full tuition increasingly fled to smaller colleges, taking revenue with them.

25   That has produced an explosion in charges as institutions have sought to close the funding gap. Average annual tuition, room, and board at state universities, after inflation, has jumped 33% since 1976, to $6,349, according to the Education Dept.; at Ivy League and other elite schools, the going rate is $32,000. Schools themselves have eaten some of that increase in the form of "discounting," or student aid, making up in part for a decline in federal grants. But students and their families have borne the brunt: Since 1975, college costs have soared to 20.5% of median household income, up from 14%. "We are pricing ourselves out of Americans' ability to pay," says Thomas H. Kean, Drew University president and a former New Jersey governor.

26   The RAND Corp.'s Council for Aid to Education estimates that mounting college costs, combined with declining real wages—especially among poor families—and growing immigration rates, will create a large class for whom college is utterly out of reach. Given current spending trends and continued pressure on government aid, predicts the council, colleges and universities will see "a catastrophic shortfall in funding"—a $38 billion gap in 2015 in what they require to meet expected student demand. To pay the bills, schools will have to raise tuition or reduce aid—and either action will shut people out.

EMERGING "STRATEGIC GROUPS" WITHIN THE EDUCATION INDUSTRY?

27   Increasingly, then, institutions find themselves grappling with a basic tension between quality and access. As resources grow scarcer, how do they sustain high-level teaching and research at an affordable price? The dilemma cuts to the heart of today's knowledge economy, where more than two-thirds of new jobs require some higher education. Continued productivity gains and economic growth depend on keeping such institutions both accessible and pertinent. "If we're not matching up [students] and educational opportunities well, we're going to lose some productive capacity," says Michael S. McPherson, president of Macalester College in St. Paul, Minn.

28   The innovation on university campuses today attempts to address such concerns. Yet it also is accelerating the evolution of American higher education into what some experts say is a two-tiered entity: one system of exceptionally high quality for those with the means to pay and a second for those without.

29   Robert Zemsky and Susan Shaman of the University of Pennsylvania's Institute for Research on Higher Education found in a study of 1,200 institutions that colleges are sorting themselves into identifiable market segments. "Name-brand" schools provide small classes and well-paid faculty at high prices. A second, more market-savvy group offers convenience and user-friendliness—often catering to students who want quick, cheap degrees to advance their careers. But these schools spend much less on teaching and facilities.

30   Colleges that flourish, argue Zemsky and Shaman, among others, will be those that identify a viable segment of the school population and equip themselves to serve it effectively. This is a provocative concept, given that, for decades, big public universities and small private colleges alike have prospered through breadth, following the models put forth by Harvard University, the University of California, and other top schools. Now, "institutions that don't do well are those that don't develop a real signature in the market," Zemsky says.

31   Rensselaer Polytechnic Institute, which attracts top technical students across the U.S., fits the brand-name category. Like many smaller private schools, however, it must lure enough wealthy students who, by paying the full $27,000 tab, will subsidize poorer classmates. "We concluded we were never going to compete on price, so we had to produce an experience of demonstrably higher quality," says Jack M. Wilson, dean of the faculty.

STUDENT CONVENIENCE

32   Its first-year "studio course," rooted in curricular and physical redesign, was meant to set RPI apart in the marketplace. In new multi-use rooms, built for $100,000 to $150,000 apiece, students face one way to hear a professor's short lecture, swivel around to work on lab equipment or personal-computer programs set up to complement the lesson, then turn again to work in small groups.

33   In an introductory class in circuits, Professor William C. Jennings begins with a short discourse on amplification. Then he turns his 30 students loose to wire and test the equipment behind them, roaming the room to give guidance as needed. Before last year, he lectured for an hour and a half, and students went elsewhere to experiment under a grad student. Students like the merger of two settings. "You don't really know what's going on until you do it yourself," says Melissa Postolowski.

34   RPI can't say yet if students in studios actually learn more; physics students in the new classes tested no higher than those in conventional lectures. But the consolidated design calls for fewer

Cheryl Rowles-Stokes, a 38-year-old working mother of two girls, is nearing completion of a master's in business communication. After slogging through four years of night school to finish a law degree at the University of Denver in 1994, Rowles-Stokes decided that "traditional school was out." So she joined the fast-growing cohort of adults who are distance learners, forsaking the classroom for an Internet-driven program that allows her to learn when and where she wants. "Your classroom is now anywhere your computer is," enthuses Rowles-Stokes, director of human resources at Rifkin & Associates, a Denver cable-management firm.

Distance learning has become far more than the slightly cheesy correspondence courses advertised on matchbook covers. As many as 400,000 students are spending $2 billion on courses provided by both traditional colleges and high-quality private firms, according to consultants Hezel & Associates.

Rowles-Stokes' degree is offered by Jones International University, started by cable-TV entrepreneur Glenn R. Jones. Its 18 professional certificate programs, plus bachelor's and master's degrees in business communications, are delivered to some 700 students who pay $700 for each eight-week class. During her lunch hour or late at night, Rowles-Stokes logs on to the Jones Web site to find out her reading assignments and to participate in online discussion groups. Online learning is not for everyone, she cautions: "You really need self-discipline." And she would steer high school grads away in favor of the social interaction that traditional colleges provide.

Those quibbles aside, Rowles-Stokes couldn't be more pleased with the flexibility of her classes—and their relevance to her work. Rowles-Stokes must design her own Web page to graduate, which she'll use to link Rifkin employees more closely to her human resources department.

Source: "Class Is Where the Computer Is," *Business Week*: January 11, 1999.

---

faculty, freeing professors to create new courses and contribute to revenue-generating projects that, with administrative cuts, have helped reduce the school's $25 million backlog of long-term maintenance and investments by more than half. More important, the changes have created a buzz, and campus visits by prospective applicants are up 49%.

35   Portland State University, alternatively, has positioned itself in the convenience sector by meeting head-on the new demographics of higher education. Traditionally the neglected stepsister of much larger and better-financed state universities, it saw state assistance slip to 49% of its total budget, from 65% in 1991. At the same time, attrition grew among its diverse collection of older, lower-income students, many of whom come ill-prepared academically.

36   Cuts of support staff and middle management saved $3.5 million a year. But PSU also sought to create academic coherence for students who most often had picked courses because they happened to meet at the right time. The answer was University Studies, a program developed with advice from local businesses that hinges on group work and technology. At its heart is Freshman Inquiry, a selection of interdisciplinary, yearlong courses that meet five days a week. Einstein's Universe, for instance, is taught by professors of physics, dance, and history. Students, required to work in groups, discover the theory of relativity but also read and write about the philosophical, historical, and artistic context of Europe in the 1930s. Graduate-student or upper-class mentors help to "model" freshmen who have never confronted serious homework or class participation.

37   For some, the curriculum was a shock. "I expected to be going to lectures and writing 10-page papers," says David Hall, a senior majoring in business and information systems. Faculty, too, had to change stripes, having to confront many students who had never read an entire book. "The attitude used to be that students either could cut it or couldn't," says Susan Hopp, director of student development. More than 80% of students who enrolled last spring in Freshman Inquiry returned for classes this fall—a record.

38   RPI and Portland State, both of which are among six schools recognized by the Pew Charitable Trust for innovative restructuring, are years ahead of most institutions. Many of their peers, by contrast, are just starting to come to terms with the monumental change they will need to survive and compete. In the public sector, especially, that confrontation is proving traumatic.

39   Florida's Lombardi, for one, still is smoothing out his plan's kinks. The university's "bank," whose funding model discourages large classes, initially penalized the college of business for TV teaching, even though TV students test as well as those in conventional classes. English professors

Winners of the Pew Leadership Award, given in 1996 and 1997 to universities and colleges that demonstrate creativity and results in restructuring themselves:

ALVERNO: This Catholic women's college in Milwaukee is the grandmother of reengineering. Its 20-year-old, ability-based curriculum develops competency in communication, analysis, and six other areas.

BABSON: It now stresses interdisciplinary collaboration between once rival business and liberal arts programs. A three-tiered curriculum leads students toward self-directed, independent study.

EASTERN NEW MEXICO: Many of its students are widely dispersed and poorly prepared. The university developed courses for interactive TV and the Internet, using facilitators and peer coaching at 12 remote sites.

MOUNT ST. MARY'S: In inner-city Los Angeles, it established a weekend college for working adults, offered evening classes, and restructured an associate's degree to make graduates more job-ready.

PORTLAND STATE: It wasn't effectively serving its poor, urban students, many of whom dropped out. The answer: an interdisciplinary curriculum that relies on inquiry-based courses and peer mentors.

RENSSELAER POLYTECHNIC: The engineering school reduced the number of courses students take, making each heftier. It came up with "studio classes," combining lecture hall, laboratory, and seminar.

worry that creative writing and other courses requiring very small classes will cost their department funding under a system that strictly measures faculty-student productivity.

RESISTANCE TO CHANGE IN TRADITIONAL COLLEGES AND UNIVERSITIES

40   For now, Florida's faculty is giving Lombardi the benefit of the doubt. In other states, resistance has been fiercer. Faculty at the University of Maine forced Chancellor J. Michael Orenduff to resign in 1995 after he proposed a distinct, accredited institution for satellite-TV learning. Resentment lingers at the University of Illinois four years after reform that, using 25 productivity and performance measures, seeks to rationalize programs and reallocate the savings. Loyola University of Chicago President John J. Piderit sparked an outcry from professors recently by referring to students as "customers."

41   Such protest isn't baseless. Professors and administrators alike are justly concerned about financially motivated strategies that risk eroding quality or reducing education to a pro forma exercise in professional credentialing. Often, though, the angst appears to be a function more of uncertainty with the dramatically shifting terrain. Academics, typically trained at traditional research universities, aren't prepared, for example, to teach in interdisciplinary courses that cross old department lines.

42   Either way, they have little choice but to learn to deal with change, because new competition—unencumbered by tenure, departmental politics, or legislative oversight—is coming fast. The number of corporate "universities," formed by business to offer in-house job-related training, has jumped from 1,000 to 1,400 in five years. Former junk-bond king Michael R. Milken, along with Oracle Corp. CEO Lawrence J. Ellison, has invested $500 million in Knowledge Universe, a for-profit company aiming to capture a $10 billion slice of the education market, from toys to advanced degrees. Its joint venture with Tele-Communications Inc. could provide the backbone for cable-TV distribution of university classes.

43   Cable entrepreneur Glenn R. Jones has created College Connection, offering students Internet access to inexpensive degree programs from 13 institutions including his own, entirely electronic International University. College Connection, with 7,000 students, is growing at 30% a year, says Jones, whose Knowledge TV offers college courses to viewers around the world. This, he says, is a "cyber-university." "Your classroom can be your house, your trailer—anywhere you have a computer."

44   Indeed, much of the convenience segment has been spurred by technology. Using the Net or interactive TV, schools can reach vast numbers of students in many locations at once, with little or no investment in new bricks and mortar. All told, 1.3 million Americans are engaged in some sort of electronic higher education, says researcher InterEd Inc.

45   Does it work? While educators agree that such technology delivers courses to students who otherwise would go without, they worry that electronic coursework is often rudimentary, with little attempt to account for quality or effectiveness and scant opportunities for intimate contact with a professor.

A Niche for Reasonably Priced, Career-Relevant Education?

46   It increasingly appears that many students are prepared to sacrifice traditional collegiate experiences in return for education/training that moves them, particularly working adults, a few more rungs up the career ladder. The University of Phoenix understands this, perhaps better than any school. Its mother campus—basically, two modest office buildings—sits off a traffic circle opposite Phoenix Airport. There are no dormitories, no library stacks, no cafeteria, no labs, no gym. And no kids. The hundreds of students who stream into dozens of spartan meeting rooms each weekday evening for four-hour classes range in age from 23 to 60.

47   With 77 campuses in 13 states, Puerto Rico, and Vancouver, British Columbia, Phoenix' enrollment, 61,000 in 1999, is growing 20% a year—even though it accepts only adults who work full-time and offers classes only at night or online. Students meet twice a week for six weeks per course and get credit for "life experience" toward bachelor's and master's degrees, mostly in business and information technology. Teaching faculty, entirely part-time and tenureless, come from industry and teach from a standardized script. Annual tuition averages $6,500.

48   It may be, as critics call it, McEducation. But students love it. "This way, I finish in the same time as I would if I'd quit my job," says Demario Walton, 24, a Motorola Inc. employee pursuing his MBA. Investors love it, too. Shares of Apollo Group Inc., the university's corporate parent, trade at 23 times their value in 1994. "We will be the first national university," says founder John G. Sperling, a raucous 76-year-old former Merchant Marine and union organizer (with a Cambridge University doctorate) whose stake in Apollo is worth $484 million. "We intend to operate in every major metropolitan area of the U.S."

49   Phoenix thrives so conspicuously because it acknowledges a profoundly changed higher-education market. It and the other new venues stand to win a big share of the surge in college enrollment expected over the next decade as Echo Boomers emerge from high school and as more adults seek continuing education. Many of these students, unable to afford the cost of a full-time program, will start college older, seeking part-time classes that fit into job schedules.

50   Colleges and universities must confront this new competition—and the changing demographics, economics, and technology behind it. And they must adapt rapidly. The great risk is that, having opened its doors to most comers, the huge, centuries-old system will shut people out—sending students instead to nimbler rivals. Milken, Jones, and Sperling will be happy to accommodate.

The Ivy League Response[1]

51   Yale University President Richard C. Levin has for several years mulled what many of his peers have considered for their colleges—running the place more like a business. "We have to manage this institution efficiently," he says. "We can't do everything under the sun." He would like to pare departments that don't serve a strong need and focus on "centers of selective excellence."

52   But Levin's actions haven't matched his ruminations. Yale's restructuring has been limited to modest reductions in administration, consolidation of biology graduate programs, and enrollment cuts at the divinity school. Even those steps galled alumni and professors, who associate Yale's pre-eminence with academic abundance.

---

[1]Adapted from "Meanwhile, The Ivy League Is Rolling in Clover," *Business Week:* December 22, 1997.

EXHIBIT B
Higher Education's Bleak Economics

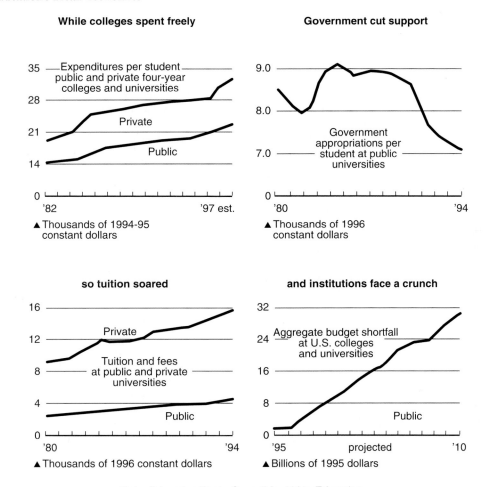

Data: Education Dept., Council for Aid to Education

Surfeit

53   Such is life among the elites. While state universities face plummeting government assistance and smaller private colleges struggle to maintain enrollment, Yale and a few dozen other top-tier institutions still thrive. They attract six or more applicants for every freshman slot—a surfeit that has persisted over the past decade despite annual tuition of more than $20,000. They still guarantee financial aid to everyone who needs it. And they spend liberally to attract star faculty and research grants.

54   These universities remain insulated from market pressures in part because they have established an aura of quality—call it brand strength or snob appeal—that keeps students coming, despite the price. An Ivy League degree doesn't win higher starting salaries than other diplomas, but it does lead more often to top graduate programs and, so, to greater professional attainment. Throw in access to powerful alumni networks, and "the interest of very able people in going to leading institutions has not only remained strong—it has become stronger," says William G. Bowen, president of the Andrew W. Mellon Foundation and ex-president of Princeton University.

55   Indeed, experts believe these schools could charge far more than they do and still draw top students. Yet they don't have to. Most are insulated by coffers bloated by the stock market that spin

off millions in annual operating income. Yale's endowment, swelled by a record $1.7 billion capital drive, is $5 billion. Harvard University, the fund-raising king, has $9 billion.

Public Urgency

56 Such fund-raising feats cushion the effect of ebbing government research assistance. They also reduce universities' reliance on tuition and fees to about 65% of the total budget, compared with 90% or higher at small private schools. So big-endowment institutions can better afford the financial aid that maintains diverse classes even as they plow millions into new technology and upkeep for aging buildings. That perpetuates their reputations as top-drawer academies.

57 This lesson hasn't been lost on big public universities. These days, "we cannot do it just with state support and tuition," says Judith A. Ramaley, president of the University of Vermont, which recently raised $108 million in its first-ever capital campaign. The University of California at Berkeley, ravaged by state cuts, is seeking $1.1 billion in private gifts by 2000; the Universities of Virginia, Illinois, and Michigan all are mounting fund-raising drives to rival the Ivies'.

58 Those urgent campaigns, however, typically have followed radical downsizing and restructuring. Secure in their ivory towers, Yale and its peers generally can afford to eschew such strategies. They know that quality sells—whatever the price.

CASE 56

THE APOLLO GROUP, INC. [UNIVERSITY OF PHOENIX] AND JOHN SPERLING, ENTREPRENEUR

Professor Profit

At 78, **JOHN SPERLING** is Mr. Adult Education. The former San Jose State University prof has built an empire catering to the needs of older students. His Apollo Group, which runs the for-profit **University of Phoenix,** boasts 74,500 students, all over 23. Don't expect ivy-covered towers. Students come to his 119 campuses in 31 states because classes run year-round—at night—and can be finished in six weeks. Over the last two years, earnings have more than doubled, to $46.3 million, on sales up 83%, to $391 million. For the year ending next August, growth should continue at around 30%.

"The Top 25 Executives of the Year," *Business Week:* January 1, 1999.

---

1   Business Week's annual identification of the best business executives around the world identified one educational entrepreneur among those top 25 executives: John Sperling. It was impressive company and a well deserved recognition for an entrepreneur whose foresight has built the largest private university in the U.S. and the largest business school too. More importantly, his early vision has led a trend in higher education that emphasizes educational offerings built around the needs of students, particularly adult students, rather than offerings that emphasized students adapting to various rules and requirements and course offerings built around the institution's needs.

2   John G. Sperling, Ph.D., received his Ph.D. from Cambridge University, an M.A. from the University of California at Berkeley and a B.A. from Reed College. He worked as a professor of Humanities at San Jose State University from 1961 to 1973, where he was the Director of the Right to Read Project and the Director of the NSF Cooperative College-School Science Program in Economics. At various times from 1955 to 1961, Dr. Sperling was a member of the faculties at the University of Maryland, Ohio State University and Northern Illinois University.

3   In 1973 Dr. John Sperling, a Cambridge-educated economist, decided it was time to create an institution of higher education dedicated to serving a very specific population—working adults. For almost 20 years as an academic Dr. Sperling had conducted field-based research in adult education and had heard many working students express the desire to work on degrees but lament the many institutional roadblocks they met. He knew that national demographics would be changing as the population aged and believed that higher education for adults would be a key to a viable economy. He envisioned an "adult-friendly" place that took into account the differences between adults and younger, traditional-aged students. He pictured an institution built around adults' learning styles and life roles. The result was the **University of Phoenix.**[1]

4   The **University of Phoenix** [UOP] recently celebrated its 25th anniversary with more than 61,000 students attending UOP at 77 campuses and learning centers in 17 states, Puerto Rico, and Vancouver, British Columbia. UOP has become the largest and the fastest-growing private educational institution in the United States. It is also the largest business school in the U.S. Still actively involved as Chairman of the Board and CEO of the parent company, The Apollo Group, Sperling's visionary

---

©2000 Richard Robinson, University of South Carolina. Created based on publicly available information provided by The Apollo Group, Inc., SEC filings and selected news organizations.

[1]Professor Elizabeth Pollard, www.smokesig.com.

> The new millennium will continue to see new forces driving the market for learning beyond high school. For one thing, the sheer numbers of projected full-time and part-time college students is fast expanding: From a trough of 2.2 million students in 1992, the total is expected to grow to 3.2 million by 2004. And 44% of those students are now working adults over the age of 24, and expected to reach over 50% of all college students by 2004. Private, for-profit companies in this area will grow at least 18% annually for the foreseeable future exceeding $2 billion in revenue in 2000, estimates NationsBanc.

leadership in the emerging education industry has caught the attention of educators, investors, and business writers around the world.

5   The Apollo Group, Inc. was founded in 1973 in response to a gradual shift in higher education demographics from a student population dominated by youth to one in which approximately half the students are adults and over 80 percent of whom work full-time. Apollo's founder, John Sperling, believed—and events proved him right—that lifelong employment with a single employer would be replaced by lifelong learning and employment with a variety of employers.

6   Lifelong learning, Sperling believed, required an institution dedicated solely to the education of working adults. Today, Apollo Group, Inc., through its subsidiaries, the University of Phoenix, the Institute for Professional Development, the College for Financial Planning, and Western International University, has established itself as a leading provider of higher education programs for working adults by focusing on servicing the needs of the working adult.

7   Apollo has enjoyed continual growth in student enrollments as well as building a strong financial record by having more than doubled its total enrollments and revenues between 1994 and 1998. Apollo Group, looking to continue the growth, completed its initial public offering on December 6, 1994 with a price of $1.63 per share (adjusted for stock splits). The Apollo Group, through its subsidiaries, the University of Phoenix, Inc. ("UOP"), the Institute for Professional Development ("IPD"), the College for Financial Planning Institutes Corporation (the "College"), and Western International University, Inc. ("WIU"), is a leading provider of higher education programs for working adults based on the number of working adults enrolled in its programs. The consolidated enrollment in Apollo's educational programs would make it the largest private institution of higher education in the United States. Apollo currently offers its programs and services at 117 campuses and learning centers in 34 states, Puerto Rico and London, England. Apollo's degree enrollment has increased to approximately 71,400 at August 31, 1998 from approximately 30,200 at August 31, 1994.

8   Based on its degree enrollment of over 53,200 adult students, of which 6,500 were distance education students, UOP is currently one of the largest regionally accredited private universities in the United States and has one of the nation's largest private business schools. UOP has been accredited by the Commission on Institutions of Higher Education of the North Central Association of Colleges and Schools ("NCA") since 1978 and has successfully replicated its teaching/learning model while maintaining educational quality at 70 campuses and learning centers in Arizona, California, Colorado, Florida, Hawaii, Louisiana, Michigan, Nevada, New Mexico, Oklahoma, Oregon, Utah, Washington, and Puerto Rico.

9   UOP has developed specialized systems for student tracking, marketing, faculty recruitment and training and academic quality management. These systems enhance UOP's ability to expand into new markets while still maintaining academic quality. Currently, approximately 56% of UOP's students receive some level of tuition reimbursement from their employers, many of which are Fortune 500 companies. UOP recently won a prestigious quality award based on the well-known Baldrige Award program which recognized UOP as a leader in quality efforts behind its educational services.

10   Apollo's **Institute for Professional Development** [IPD] provides program development and management services under long-term contracts that meet the guidelines of the client institutions' respective regional accrediting associations. IPD provides these services to 20 regionally accredited private colleges and universities at 43 campuses and learning centers in 22 states and shares in the tuition revenues generated from these programs. In addition, IPD has contracted to develop online degree programs for the United States Marine Corp. IPD is able to assist these colleges and universities

---

Apollo Group Inc. Subsidiary, the University of Phoenix, Takes Home Award

PHOENIX—(BUSINESS WIRE)—Jan. 25, 1999—Apollo Group Inc. (Nasdaq: APOL-news) Monday announced that its wholly owned subsidiary, the University of Phoenix has won the Arizona Pioneer Award for Quality.

The Phoenix campus will receive the award at the upcoming Arizona Excellence Conference, sponsored by the Governor's Advisory Council on Quality. According to an article published recently in *The Business Journal,* the University of Phoenix is the first four-year educational institution to win the prize modeled after the prestigious Malcolm Baldrige National Quality Award.

The University of Phoenix competed with 10 organizations for the award based on how their quality systems led to concrete improvements. Arizona Gov. Jane Hull commented, "They (the winners) represent the best of Arizona's public and private sectors. In today's business environment, organizations must have the adaptability and flexibility that are the hallmarks of University of Phoenix and its commitment to lifelong learning."

Dr. John G. Sperling, chairman and chief executive officer, commented, "We are very pleased with this award because it recognizes Apollo's commitment of maintaining high quality standards and excellent customer service."

Apollo Group Inc., through its subsidiaries the University of Phoenix Inc., the Institute for Professional Development, the College for Financial Planning Institutes Corp., and Western International University Inc., is one of the largest providers of higher education programs for working adults in the United States, with total degree-seeking enrollment of approximately 74,500 students. Educational programs and services are currently offered at 119 campuses and learning centers in 34 states and Puerto Rico.

---

in expanding and diversifying their programs for working adults. IPD places a priority on institutions that: (1) are interested in developing or expanding off-campus degree programs for working adults; (2) recognize that working adults require a different teaching/learning model than the 18 to 24 year old student; (3) desire to increase enrollments with a limited investment in institutional capital, and (4) recognize the unmet educational needs of the working adult students in their market. Approximately 16,000 degree-seeking students are currently enrolled in IPD-assisted programs.

11   On September 23, 1997, Apollo acquired the assets and related business operations of the **College for Financial Planning** ["the College"] and related divisions that include the Institute for Wealth Management, the Institute for Retirement Planning, the American Institute for Retirement Planners, Inc., and the Institute for Tax Studies. The adjusted purchase price consisted of $19.4 million in cash, $15.9 million in stock and the assumption of approximately $11.4 million in liabilities. With current enrollments of approximately 750 degree and 23,000 nondegree students, the College is one of the largest U.S. providers of financial planning education programs, including the Certified Financial Planner Professional Education Program.

12   **Western International University** [WIU] currently offers graduate and undergraduate degree programs to approximately 1,300 students and has a total of three campuses and learning enters in Phoenix and Fort Huachuca, Arizona and London, England.

THE EDUCATION MARKET

13   The United States education market may be divided into the following distinct segments: kindergarten through twelfth grade schools ("K–12"), vocational and technical training schools, workplace and consumer training, and degree-granting colleges and universities ("higher education"). Apollo primarily operates in the higher education segment and, with the acquisition of the College and the introduction of other non-degree programs, also operates in the workplace and consumer training

segments. The U.S. Department of Education National Center for Education Statistics ("NCES") estimated that for 1996 (the most recent historical year reported), adults over 24 years of age comprised approximately 6.2 million, or 40.9%, of the 15.2 million students enrolled in higher education programs. Currently, the U.S. Bureau of Census estimates that approximately 75% of students over the age of 24 work while attending school. The NCES estimates that by the year 2003, the number of adult students over the age of 24 will remain approximately the same at 6.1 million, or 40.2%, of the 15.1 million students projected to be enrolled in higher education programs.

14   Apollo believes that the unique needs of working adults include the following:

- Convenient access to a learning environment (including both location and delivery system)
- Degree programs offered by regionally accredited institutions that can be completed in a reasonable amount of time
- Programs that provide knowledge and skills with immediate practical value in the workplace
- Education provided by academically qualified faculty with current practical experience in fields related to the subjects they instruct
- Administrative services designed to accommodate the full-time working adult's schedule
- Recognition of adult students as critical consumers of educational programs and services
- A learning environment characterized by a low student-to-faculty ratio
- Learning resources available electronically to all students regardless of geographical location

15   Apollo also believes that the increasing demand from and the unique requirements of the adult working population represent a significant market opportunity to regionally accredited higher education institutions that can offer programs that meet these unique needs.

16   Most regionally accredited colleges and universities are focused on serving the 18 to 24 year old student market. This focus has resulted in a capital-intensive teaching/learning model that may be characterized by:

(1) A high percentage of full-time tenured faculty with doctoral degrees;
(2) Fully configured library facilities and related full-time staff;
(3) Dormitories, students unions and other significant plant assets to support the needs of younger students and
(4) An emphasis on research and the related staff and facilities.

17   In addition, the majority of accredited colleges and universities continue to provide the bulk of their educational programming from September to mid-December and from mid-January to May. As a result, most full-time faculty members only teach during that limited period of time.

18   While this structure serves the needs of the full-time 18 to 24 year old student, it limits the educational opportunity for working adults who must delay their education for up to five months during these spring, summer and winter breaks. In addition, this structure generally requires working adults to attend one course three times a week, commute to a central site, take work time to complete administrative requirements and, in undergraduate programs, participate passively in an almost exclusively lecture-based learning format primarily focused on a theoretical presentation of the subject matter. For the majority of working adults, earning an undergraduate degree in this manner would take seven to ten years. In recent years, many regionally accredited colleges and universities have begun offering more flexible programs for working adults, although their focus appears to remain on the 18 to 24 year old students.

APOLLO'S BUSINESS STRATEGY

19   Apollo's strategic goal is to become the preferred provider of higher education programs for working adult students and the preferred provider of workplace training to their employers. Apollo is managed as a for-profit corporation in a higher education industry served principally by not-for-profit providers. By design, Apollo treats both its adult students and their employers as its primary customers.

20   Key elements of the Company's business strategy include the following:

- Establish New UOP Campuses and Learning Centers

    UOP plans to add campuses and learning centers throughout the United States, Canada and other foreign markets. New locations are selected based on an analysis of various factors, including the population of working adults in the area, the number of local employers and their educational reimbursement policies and the availability of similar programs offered by other institutions. Campuses consist of classroom and administrative facilities with full student and administrative services. Learning centers differ from campuses in that they consist primarily of classroom facilities with limited on-site administrative staff.

    The timing related to the establishment of new locations and the expansion of programs may vary depending on regulatory requirements and market conditions.

- Establish New IPD Relationships

    IPD plans to enter into additional long-term contracts with private colleges and universities in proximity to metropolitan areas throughout the United States. In general, IPD seeks to establish relationships with colleges and universities located in states where it is difficult for out-of-state accredited institutions to obtain state authorizations. In this way, Apollo is able to optimize its campus-based penetration of potential new markets.

- Expand Educational Programs

    Apollo expects to continue to respond to the changing educational needs of working adults and their employers through the introduction of new undergraduate and graduate degree programs and non-degree programs in business and information technology. UOP received approval in 1998 from the NCA to offer a Doctor of Management degree. This educational program will be the first doctoral degree offered by Apollo. Apollo currently has a full-time staff of over 55 persons involved in its centralized curriculum development process.

    Apollo is also exploring other educational areas, such as the K–12 market, adult remedial education and international opportunities, where it can leverage its educational expertise and/or delivery systems in a cost-effective manner.

- Expand Access to Programs

    Apollo plans to expand its distance education programs and services. Enrollments in distance education degree programs, including Online, have increased to approximately 7,200 in 1998 from approximately 1,600 in 1994. Apollo has started the process of converting many of its non-degree business and financial programs so that they can be delivered through the Internet. Apollo also plans to enhance its distance education delivery systems as new technologies become cost-effective, such as interactive distance education technology.

- International Expansion

    Apollo is conducting ongoing market research in various foreign countries. Apollo has been approved by NCA to begin operations in Canada. The first Canadian campus will be in Vancouver, British Columbia, with classes expected to commence during the second quarter of 1999. The Company is considering international expansion into various European and Latin American markets using the University of Phoenix education model. The Company will continue to monitor and assess the feasibility of expanding its educational program to other international markets.

BUILDING COMPETITIVE ADVANTAGE THROUGH A UNIQUE TEACHING/LEARNING MODEL

21   Apollo's teaching/learning model used by UOP and IPD client institutions was designed for working adults. This model is structured to enable students who are employed full-time to earn their degrees and still meet their personal and professional responsibilities. Students attend weekly classes, averaging 15 students in size, and also meet weekly as part of a three to five person study group. The study group meetings are used for review, work on assigned group projects and preparation for in-class presentations. Courses are designed to facilitate the application of knowledge and skills to the workplace and are taught by faculty members who possess advanced degrees and have an average of

15 years of professional experience in business, industry, government and the professions. In this way, faculty members are able to share their professional knowledge and skills with the students.

22   Apollo's teaching/learning model has the following major characteristics:

Curriculum	The curriculum provides for the achievement of specific educational outcomes that are based on the input from faculty, students and student employers. The curriculum is designed to integrate academic theory and professional practice and the application to the workplace. The standardized curriculum for each degree program is also designed to provide students with specified levels of knowledge and skills regardless of delivery method or location.
Faculty	Faculty applicants must possess an earned master's or doctoral degree from a regionally accredited institution and have a minimum of five years recent professional experience in a field related to the subject matter in which they seek to instruct. To help promote quality delivery of the curriculum, UOP faculty members are required to: (1) complete an initial assessment conducted by staff and faculty; (2) complete a series of certification workshops related to grading, facilitation of the teaching/learning model, oversight of study group activities, adult learning theory, and use of the Internet; (3) participate in ongoing development activities and (4) receive ongoing performance evaluations by students, peer faculty and staff. The results of these evaluations are used to establish developmental plans to improve individual faculty performance and to determine continued eligibility of faculty members to provide instruction.
Interactive Learning	Courses are designed to combine individual and group activity with interaction between and among students and the instructor. The curriculum requires a high level of student participation for purposes of increasing the student's ability to work as part of a team.
Learning Resources	Students and faculty members are provided with electronic and other learning resources for their information needs. Over the past three years, the Company substantially expanded these services, including the addition of research tools available on the Internet. These extensive electronic resources minimize Apollo's need for capital-intensive library facilities and holdings.
Sequential Enrollment	Students enroll in and complete courses sequentially, rather than concurrently, thereby allowing full-time working adults to focus their attention and resources on one subject at a time, thus balancing learning with ongoing personal and professional responsibilities.
Academic Quality	Apollo has developed and operationalized an Academic Quality Management System ("AQMS") that is designed to maintain and improve the quality of programs and academic and student services regardless of the delivery method or location. Included in the AQMS is the Adult Learning Outcomes Assessment which seeks to measure student growth in both the cognitive (subject matter) and affective (educational, personal and professional values) domains.

STRUCTURAL COMPONENTS OF TEACHING/LEARNING MODEL

23   Although adults over 24 years old comprise approximately 40.9% of all higher education enrollments in the United States, the mission of most accredited colleges and universities is to serve 18 to 24 year old students and conduct research. UOP and IPD client institutions acknowledge the differences in educational needs between older and younger students and provide programs and services that allow working adult students to earn their degrees while integrating the process with both their personal and professional lives.

24   Apollo believes that working adults require a different teaching/learning model than is designed for the 18 to 24 year old student. Apollo has found that working adults seek accessibility, curriculum consistency, time and cost effectiveness and learning that has an immediate application to the workplace. Apollo's teaching/learning model differs from the models used by most regionally accredited colleges and universities because it is designed to enable adults to complete an undergraduate degree in four years and a graduate degree in two years while working full-time.

25   The structural components of Apollo's teaching/learning model include:

Accessibility	Apollo offers standardized curriculum that can be accessed through a variety of delivery methods (e.g., campus-based or electronically delivered) that make the educational programs accessible regardless of where the students work and live.
Instructional Costs	While the faculty at most accredited colleges and universities are employed full-time, most of the UOP and IPD client institutions' faculty are part-time. All faculty are academically qualified, are professionally employed and are contracted for instructional services on a course-by-course basis.
Facility Costs	Apollo leases its campus and learning center facilities and rents additional classroom space on a short-term basis to accommodate growth in enrollments, thus keeping the facility portion of its instructional costs variable.
Employed Students	Substantially all of UOP's students are employed full-time and approximately 72% have been employed for nine years or more. This minimizes the need for capital-intensive facilities and services (e.g., dormitories, student unions, food services, personal and employment counseling, health care, sports and entertainment).
Employer Support	Approximately 56% of UOP's students currently receive some level of tuition reimbursement from their employers, many of which are Fortune 500 companies; approximately 46% receive at least half of their tuition and some 23% receive full tuition reimbursement. Apollo develops relationships with key employers for purposes of recruiting students and responding to specific employer needs. This allows Apollo to remain sensitive to the needs and perceptions of employers, while helping both to generate and sustain diverse sources of revenues.

26   The College currently offers text-based self-study programs for students preparing for the Certified Financial Planner designation and other financial-related designations. Apollo plans to offer these same programs in a classroom-based format and also through Internet or Online-based formats. Most of the College's students are employed and over 75% have four or more years of college education.

27   WIU's teaching/learning model has similar characteristics to the teaching/learning model used by UOP and IPD client institutions, including the use of part-time practitioner faculty, standardized curriculum, computerized learning resources and leased facilities. However, WIU provides educational programs in a semester-based format and does not focus extensively on working adult students.

UOP Programs

28   UOP currently offers the following degree programs and related areas of specialization at one or more campuses and learning centers or through its distance education delivery systems:

Degree Programs

Associate of Arts in General Studies
Bachelor of Arts in Management
Bachelor of Science in Business
Bachelor of Science in Nursing
Bachelor of Science in Human Services
Master of Arts in Education
Master of Arts in Organizational Management
Master of Business Administration
Master of Counseling
Master of Science in Nursing
Master of Science in Computer Information Systems

Areas of Specialization

Business
    Accounting
    Administration
    Management
    Marketing
    Project Management

> Computer Info Systems
> > Information Systems
>
> Graduate:
> > Business
> > > Administration
> > > Global Management
> > > Organizational Management
> >
> > Computer Info Systems
> > > Technology Management Information Systems
> >
> > Education
> > > Administration and Supervision
> > > Bilingual-Bicultural
> > > Curriculum and Instruction
> > > Diverse Learner
> > > Educational Counseling
> > > Elementary Education
> > > English as a Second Language
> > > Professional Development for Educators
> > > Special Education
>
> **Nursing**
> > Health Care
> > Women's Health Nurse Practitioner
> > Family Nurse Practitioner
>
> **Counseling**
> > Community Counseling
> > Marriage and Family Therapy
> > Mental Health Counseling
> > Marriage, Family and Child Counseling

29   UOP also offers over 100 professional education programs, including continuing education for teachers, custom training, environmental training and many programs leading to certification in the areas of business, technology and nursing.

30   Undergraduate students may demonstrate and document college level learning gained from experience through an assessment by faculty members (according to the guidelines of the Council for Adult and Experiential Learning ("CAEL")) for the potential award of credit. The average number of credits awarded to the approximately 4,000 UOP undergraduate students who used the process in 1998 was approximately 12 credits of the 120 required to graduate. CAEL reports that over 1,300 regionally accredited colleges and universities currently provide for the assessment mechanism of college level learning gained through experience for the award of credit.

IPD Services

31   IPD offers services to its client institutions including: (1) conducting market research; (2) assisting with curriculum development; (3) developing and executing marketing strategies; (4) marketing and recruiting of students; (5) establishing operational and administrative infrastructures; (6) training of faculty; (7) developing and implementing financial accounting and academic quality management systems; (8) assessing the future needs of adult students; (9) assisting in developing additional degree programs suitable for the adult higher education market and (10) assisting in seeking approval from the respective regional accrediting association for new programs. In consideration for its services, IPD receives a contractual share of tuition revenues from students enrolled in IPD-assisted programs.

32   In order to facilitate the sharing of information related to the operations of their respective programs, the IPD client institutions and UOP formed the Consortium for the Advancement of Adult Higher Education ("CAAHE"). CAAHE meets semiannually to address issues such as the recruitment and training of part-time, professionally employed faculty, employer input in the curriculum development process, assessment of the learning outcomes of adult students and regulatory issues affecting the operation of programs for working adult students. IPD client institutions offer the following programs with IPD assistance:

Degree Programs	No. of IPD Client Institutions
Associate of Arts	1
Associate of Science in Business	8
Bachelor of Arts in Business Administration	2
Bachelor of Arts in Management	1
Bachelor of Business Administration	9
Bachelor of Science in Business Administration	5
Bachelor of Science in Management	11
Bachelor of Science in Management Info Systems	1
Bachelor of Science in Nursing	1
Master of Business Administration	11
Master of Science in Management	6
Master of Science in Health Services Administration	1

The College Programs

33   The College currently offers a Master of Science degree with a concentration in Financial Planning and the following non-degree programs:

Accredited Asset Management Specialist

Certified Financial Planner Professional Education Program

Chartered Financial Analyst Study/Review Program

Chartered Mutual Fund Counselor

Foundations in Financial Planning

Chartered Retirement Plans Specialist

Chartered Retirement Planning Counselor

Accredited Tax Advisor

Accredited Tax Preparer

WIU Programs

34   WIU currently offers the following degree and certificate programs:

Associate of Arts

Bachelor of Science
  Accounting
  Business Administration
  Finance
  Health Systems Management
  Information Systems
  International Business
  Management
  Marketing

Bachelor of Arts
  Administration of Justice
  Behavioral Science

Master of Business Administration
  Finance
  Health Care Management
  International Business
  Management
  Management Information Services
  Marketing

Master of Public Administration

Master of Science
  Accounting
  Information Systems
  Information Systems Engineering

Distance Education Components

35   At August 31, 1998, there were approximately 7,200 degree seeking students utilizing Apollo's distance education delivery systems, approximately 61% of whom are enrolled in Online. Apollo's distance education components consist primarily of the following:

• Online Computer Conferencing

    The Online campus was established by UOP in 1989 to provide group-based, faculty-led instruction through computer-mediated communications. Students can access their Online classes with a computer and modem from anywhere in the world, on schedules that meet their individual needs. Online students work together in small groups of 8 to 13 to engage in class discussion and study group activities that are focused on the same learning outcomes and objectives required in UOP's classroom degree programs. This enables the Online students to enjoy the benefits of a study group, where they can share their regional and cultural differences with each other in the context of their coursework. Students are not required to participate at the same time since the communication method is not asynchronous in nature. Online's degree programs can be accessed through direct-dial or Internet service providers. The same academic quality management standards applied to campus-based programs, including the assessment of student learning outcomes, are applied to programs delivered through Online.

- Directed Study

  Working adult students may also complete individual courses under the direct weekly instructional supervision of a member of the faculty. These directed study programs utilize the same courses, faculty and resources available at UOP campuses. Course assignments are completed in a structured environment that allows the student flexibility with their schedule. Communication with the faculty member is by telephone, e-mail, fax or mail.

- CPE Internet

  Business and investment professionals that require continuing professional education (CPE) as part of their professional certification or for employment requirements may complete individual CPE courses through the Internet utilizing most Internet browsers. These programs are short, interactive courses designed to focus on relevant topics to the students' trade or profession. The students interact primarily with Apollo's web-based software programs with little or no faculty involvement. Apollo plans to convert many of its non-degree programs in business, financial planning and IT to this web-based format in order to provide consumers with an additional delivery option to receive this type of CPE instruction. The College also plans to use this same technology to deliver preparatory work for professional certifications in addition to its text-based self-study delivery methods.

FACULTY

36   UOP's faculty is comprised of approximately 100 full-time faculty and 5,100 part-time faculty. Substantially all faculty are working professionals with earned master's or doctoral degrees and an average of 15 years of experience in business, industry, government or the professions. To help promote quality delivery of the curriculum, UOP faculty members are required to:

   (1) Complete an initial assessment conducted by staff and faculty;
   (2) Complete a series of certification workshops related to grading, facilitation of the teaching/learning model, oversight of study group activities, adult learning theory and use of the Internet;
   (3) Participate in ongoing development activities and
   (4) Receive ongoing performance evaluations by students, peer faculty and staff.

37   The results of these evaluations are used to establish developmental plans to improve individual faculty performance and to determine continued eligibility of faculty members to provide instruction. Most faculty members are recruited as the result of referrals from faculty, students and corporate contacts. All part-time faculty are contracted on a course-by-course basis (generally a five to ten week period).

38   The faculty teaching in IPD-assisted programs are comprised of full-time faculty from the client institution as well as qualified part-time faculty who instruct only in these adult programs. The part-time faculty must be approved by each client institution. IPD makes the AQMS available to its client institutions to evaluate faculty and academic and administrative quality. Apollo believes that both UOP and IPD will continue to be successful in recruiting qualified faculty members.

39   The College's programs are primarily self-study, non-degree programs where there is little or no faculty involvement in the delivery of the programs. However, the College employs approximately 15 full-time faculty who are involved in curriculum development and the instructional design process.

Hughes Network Systems and Apollo Group, Inc. Form Worldwide Distance Learning Company

ONE TOUCH Systems Acquired as Foundation of New Company

Germantown, MD (August 18, 1998)—Hughes Network Systems (HNS) and Apollo Group, Inc. today announced an agreement to form a worldwide, distance-learning company. This company will be the first company to provide a complete end-to-end, satellite-based, distance-learning solution for enterprises, as well as for small office/home office (SOHO) users and consumers. As its first initiative, the new company has agreed to acquire ONE TOUCH Systems, the pioneer and leading supplier of interactive distance learning (IDL) solutions. ONE TOUCH already provides IDL systems to large corporate organizations including Ford Motor Company, Hewlett Packard, J.C. Penney, Oracle, the U.S. Social Security Administration, Prudential Insurance, 3M, and others.

HNS is the world's leading supplier of private satellite networks, as well as high-speed Internet delivery to consumers via its DirecPC™ service. Apollo is one of the largest providers of higher-education programs, certification, and training in the United States. This teaming of the two leading companies in their respective fields—satellite networking and educational content—is unprecedented.

The formation of the new company is expected to be completed within 30 days. Financial terms were not disclosed, however, HNS will hold a majority ownership position in the new company. There will be no change in the management of ONE TOUCH Systems or the location of its corporate headquarters and remote sales offices.

Integrated Product Offering Enables Complete Distance Learning Solutions

"Our company goal is to extend the benefits of satellite technology and communication into larger and new markets," said Pradman Kaul, president of HNS. "We have worked cooperatively with ONE TOUCH in the past to implement distance-learning networks for customers such as Ford. Not only will our existing customers benefit from the new relationship and more integrated solutions, but with the addition of Apollo, we can now offer the world's most complete distance learning solution—from content development to delivery to implementation."

"Network infrastructure limitations have been major obstacles to corporations offering continuing education to their in-house and remote employees," said John Sperling, chairman and CEO of Apollo Group, Inc. "Integrating our educational content and certification with the ONE TOUCH system and Hughes' satellite capability, allows a total, end-to-end solution never before possible. Initial customer response already has been extremely favorable."

"Up until now, ONE TOUCH customers could not go to a single source for educational content, the IDL system, and the network," said Craig A. Conway, president and CEO of ONE TOUCH Systems. "But the key to continuing growth and expansion to new markets is the ability to offer a simple, cost-effective, complete solution including both the network and the educational content. With the combined resources of HNS and Apollo, we are now able to do that."

Customer Benefits   The benefits of a totally integrated IDL approach include lower overall costs, a one-stop IDL solution, easier deployment, and a higher-quality learning experience involving a combination of real-time video, voice, and data. The IDL solutions offered can be deployed in classroom environments, as well as directly to desktop PCs. Classes can be delivered live, or via a soon to be available offline, on-demand mode.

Satellite communications continues to be the most cost-effective way to deliver real-time video, voice, and data simultaneously to hundreds or even thousands of remote locations. With HNS' DirecPC product, high-quality video can now be delivered just as cost effectively, further enhancing the learning experience. And finally, with the introduction of the competencies of Apollo, some of the greatest impediments to an IDL implementation—content and qualified training staff—can be eliminated.

40   WIU's faculty consists of approximately 10 full-time faculty and 170 part-time faculty. WIU's practitioner faculty are working professionals and possess earned master's or doctoral degrees and participate in a selection and training process that is similar to that at UOP.

ACADEMIC ACCOUNTABILITY

41   UOP is one of the first regionally accredited universities in the nation to create and utilize an institutionwide system for the assessment of the educational outcomes of its students. The information generated is employed by UOP to improve the quality of the curriculum, the instruction and the Company's teaching/learning model. UOP's undergraduate and graduate students complete a comprehensive cognitive (core degree subject matter) and affective (educational, personal and professional values) assessment prior to and upon the completion of their core degree requirements.

42   Students at UOP and IPD client institutions evaluate both academic and administrative quality. This evaluation begins with a registration survey and continues with the evaluation of the curriculum, faculty, delivery method, instruction and administrative services upon the conclusion of each course. The evaluation also includes a survey of a random selection of graduates 2–3 years following their graduation. The results provide an ongoing basis for improving the teaching/learning model, selection of educational programs and instructional quality.

ADMISSIONS STANDARDS

43   To gain admission to the undergraduate programs of UOP, WIU and the IPD client institutions, students generally must have a high school diploma or General Equivalency Diploma ("G.E.D.") and satisfy certain minimum grade point average, employment and age requirements. Additional requirements may apply to individual programs. Students in undergraduate programs may petition to be admitted on provisional status if they do not meet certain admission requirements.

44   To gain admission to the graduate programs of UOP, WIU, the College and the IPD client institutions, students generally must have an undergraduate degree from a regionally accredited college or university and satisfy minimum grade point average, work experience and employment requirements. Additional requirements may apply to individual programs. Students in graduate programs may petition to be admitted on provisional status if they do not meet certain admission requirements.

CUSTOMERS

45   Apollo's customers consist of working adult students, colleges and universities, governmental agencies and employers. Following is a percentage breakdown of Apollo's students by the level of program they are seeking, at August 31:

	1998	1997
Degree Programs:		
Master's	30.5%	31.8%
Bachelor's	68.7%	68.1%
Associate	.8%	.1%
Total degree programs	100.0%	100.0%

46   Based on recent student surveys, the average age of UOP students is in the mid-thirties, approximately 55% are women and 45% are men, and the average annual household income is $56,000. Approximately 72% of UOP students have been employed on a full-time basis for nine years or more. The Company believes that the demographics of students enrolled in IPD-assisted programs are similar to those of UOP. The approximate age percentage distribution of incoming UOP students is as follows:

Age	Percentage of Students
25 and under	13%
26 to 33	36%
34 to 45	40%
46 and over	11%
	100%

47   Based on recent student surveys, the average age of students at the College is in the mid-thirties, approximately 32% are women and 68% are men, most are employed and over 75% have four or more years of college education.

48   IPD client institutions have historically consisted of small private colleges; however, IPD also targets larger institutions of higher education that are in need of marketing and curriculum consulting. IPD understands that to develop and manage educational programs for working adult students effectively, these potential client institutions require both capital and operational expertise. In response to these requirements, IPD provides the start-up capital, the curriculum development expertise and the ongoing management in support of the client institutions' provision of quality programs for working adult students. All of the Apollo Companies consider the employers of its students as customers. Many of these employers provide tuition reimbursement programs in order to educate and provide degree opportunities to their employees.

CORPORATE PARTNERSHIPS

49   Apollo works closely with businesses and governmental agencies to meet their specific needs either by modifying existing programs or, in some cases, by developing customized programs. These programs are often held at the employers' offices or on-site at military bases. UOP has also formed educational partnerships with various corporations to provide programs specifically designed for their employees.

MARKETING

50   To generate interest among potential UOP, WIU and IPD client institution students, Apollo engages in a broad range of activities to inform potential students about Apollo's teaching/learning model and the programs offered. These activities include print and broadcast advertising, advertising on Internet service providers, direct mail and informational meetings at targeted organizations. Apollo also attempts to locate its campuses and learning centers near major highways to provide high visibility and easy access. A substantial portion of new UOP and IPD client institution students are referred by alumni, employers and currently enrolled students.

51   Apollo also has Web sites on the Internet World Wide Web (http://www.apollogrp.edu, http://www.uophx.edu, http://www.ipd.org, http://www.wintu.edu, http://www.fp.edu and http://www. mcse.com) that allow electronic access to Company information, product information, research, etc.

52   UOP and WIU advertising is centrally monitored and is directed primarily at local markets in which a campus or learning center is located. IPD client institutions approve and monitor all advertising provided by IPD on their behalf. Direct responses to advertising and direct mail are received, tracked and forwarded promptly to the appropriate enrollment counselors. In addition, all responses are analyzed to provide data for future marketing efforts.

53   The College markets its programs and products primarily through advertising, direct mail, informational meetings, trade shows, and corporate sales efforts with financial service firms. Marketing activity is primarily directed at professionals within the financial services industry. Enrollment advisors are utilized in a comparable fashion to UOP enrollment staff. All marketing activity is tracked to measure effectiveness and to provide information for future activity.

54   Apollo employs over 450 enrollment counselors who make visits and presentations at various organizations and who follow up on leads generated from referrals from customers and advertising efforts. These individuals also pursue direct responses to interest from potential individual students by arranging for interviews either at a UOP, WIU or IPD location or at a prospective student's place of employment. Interviews are designed to establish a prospective student's qualifications, academic background, course interests and professional goals. Student recruiting policies and standards and procedures for hiring and training university representatives are established centrally, but are implemented at the local level through a director of enrollment or marketing at each location.

COMPETITION

55   The higher education market is highly fragmented and competitive with no private or public institution enjoying a significant market share. The Company competes primarily with four-year and two-year degree-granting public and private regionally accredited colleges and universities. Many of these colleges and universities enroll working adults in addition to the traditional 18 to 24 year old students and some have greater financial or personnel resources than Apollo. Apollo expects that these colleges and universities will continue to modify their existing programs to serve working adults more effectively. In addition, many colleges and universities have announced various distance-education initiatives.

56   For its degree programs, Apollo competes primarily at a local and regional level with other regionally accredited colleges and universities based on the quality of academic programs, the accessibility of programs and learning resources available to working adults, the cost of the program, the quality of instruction and the time necessary to earn a degree.

57   In terms of non-degree programs offered by UOP, IPD and WIU, Apollo competes with a variety of business and IT providers, primarily those in the for-profit training sector. Many of these competitors have significantly more market share, longer-term relationships with key vendors and, in some cases, more financial resources. There is no assurance that UOP, IPD and WIU will be able to gain market share in these more competitive non-degree markets to the same extent it has done with its degree programs.

58   The College currently holds a dominant position in the Certified Financial Planning ("CFP") education field. Recently, however, competition is increasing slightly due to a higher number of schools registering CFP curriculum with the Certified Financial Planner Board of Standards, Inc. The College offers all of its programs using the flexibility of its distance education format while the majority of the other competing education programs target local markets using classroom based teaching formats.

59   IPD faces competition from other entities offering higher education curriculum development and management services for adult education programs. The majority of IPD's current competitors provide pre-packaged curriculum or turn-key programs. IPD client institutions, however, face competition from both private and public institutions offering degree and non-degree programs to working adults.

EMPLOYEES

60   At September 30, 1998, Apollo had the following numbers of employees:

	Full-Time	Part-Time	Faculty	Total
Apollo	299	9	—	308
UOP	1,976	98	5,159	7,233
IPD	251	10	—	261
The College	83	4	15	102
WIU	52	11	179	242
Total	2,661	132	5,353	8,146

ACCREDITATION

61 UOP, WIU, the College, and the IPD client institutions are accredited by regional accrediting associations recognized by the DOE. Accreditation provides the basis for: (1) the recognition and acceptance by employers, other higher education institutions and governmental entities of the degrees and credits earned by students; (2) the qualification to participate in Title IV Programs and (3) the qualification for authorization in certain states.

62 UOP was granted accreditation by NCA in 1978. UOP's accreditation was reaffirmed in 1982, 1987, 1992 and 1997. The next focused evaluation visit is scheduled to begin in 1999, and the next NCA reaffirmation visit is scheduled to begin in 2002. IPD-assisted programs offered by the IPD client institutions are evaluated by the client institutions' respective regional accrediting associations either as part of a reaffirmation or focused evaluation visits. Current IPD client institutions are accredited by NCA, Middle States, New England or Southern regional accrediting associations. The College's graduate degree program is accredited by NCA and the Accrediting Commission of the Distance Education and Training Council ("DETC"). NCA and DETC consented to the change of ownership resulting from Apollo's acquisition of the assets and related operations of the College for Financial Planning and related divisions in September 1997. NCA began a scheduled focus-visit for the College in September 1988 which should be completed by the end of the first quarter of 1999. DETC plans to schedule a focus-visit for the College in 2000. WIU was accredited by NCA prior to the acquisition by Apollo and the accreditation was reaffirmed in 1998. WIU's next NCA reaffirmation visit is scheduled to begin in 2005. The withdrawal of accreditation from UOP or certain IPD client institutions would have a material, adverse effect on Apollo.

63 All accrediting agencies recognized by the DOE are required to include certain aspects of Title IV Program compliance in their evaluations of accredited institutions. As a result, all regionally accredited institutions, including UOP, WIU, and IPD client institutions, will be subject to a Title IV Program compliance review as part of accreditation visits.

64 Regional accreditation is accepted nationally as the basis for the recognition of earned credit and degrees for academic purposes, employment, professional licensure and, in some states, for authorization to operate as a degree-granting institution. Under the terms of a reciprocity agreement among the six regional accrediting associations, representatives of each region in which a regionally accredited institution operates participate in the evaluations for reaffirmation of accreditation. The achievement of UOP's and WIU's missions require them to employ academically qualified practitioner faculty that are able to integrate academic theory with current workplace practice. Because of UOP's and WIU's choice to utilize practitioner faculty, they have not sought business school program accreditation of the type found at many institutions whose primary missions are to serve the 18 to 24 year old student and to conduct research.

65 UOP's Bachelor of Science in Nursing ("BSN") program received program accreditation from the National League for Nursing Accrediting Commission ("NLNAC") in 1989. The accreditation was reaffirmed in October 1995. The next NLNAC reaffirmation of the BSN program is scheduled for 2003. The Company believes that the BSN program accreditation is in good standing. The Master of Science in Nursing ("MSN") program earned NLNAC accreditation in 1996. The next NLNAC reaffirmation of the MSN program is scheduled for 2000.

66 UOP's Community Counseling program (Master of Counseling in Community Counseling degree) received initial accreditation for its Phoenix and Tucson campuses from the Council for Accreditation of Counseling and Related Educational Programs in 1995 and the next reaffirmation visit is scheduled for 2002.

67 UOP received approval from the NCA to offer its first doctoral level program in 1998. The first students will be enrolled in the Doctor of Management degree beginning in 1999. The Doctor of Management degree will be offered via distance learning technology with annual two-week residencies in Phoenix throughout their program. The program will be limited to two groups of 30 new students each per year.

STATE AUTHORIZATION

68   UOP currently is authorized to operate in 14 states, Puerto Rico and British Columbia. UOP has held these authorizations for periods ranging from less than one year to twenty years. UOP's NCA accreditation is accepted as evidence of compliance with applicable state regulations in Arizona, Colorado, Louisiana, Michigan, New Mexico, Nevada, Oklahoma, and Utah. Hawaii does not have authorization provisions for regionally accredited degree-granting institutions.

69   California law requires an on-site visit to all out-of-state accredited institutions of higher education every five years to determine if the institution is in compliance with the State of California regulations. All institutions, including UOP, that operate in California and are accredited by a regional accrediting association other than the Western Association of Schools and Colleges are required to be evaluated separately for authorization to operate. UOP was granted its most recent California authorization in 1997 for a period through December 31, 1999.

70   All regionally accredited institutions, including UOP, are required to be evaluated separately for authorization to operate in Puerto Rico. UOP was granted its most recent authorization in Puerto Rico in December 1995 for a period of five years.

71   UOP received a license to operate in Florida in April 1997. In August 1997, UOP received NCA approval to operate in Washington and Oregon and subsequently, has opened campuses in these states. The NCA approved UOP's expansion into British Columbia and Oklahoma in June 1998, and UOP is currently establishing campuses in these locations. UOP is registered with British Columbia's Private Post-Secondary Education Commission and will pursue accreditation through the province of British Columbia after the required one year period of operation. Maryland has also approved UOP's request to establish a new campus, and UOP is currently seeking expansion approval into Maryland from NCA.

72   IPD client institutions possess authorization to operate in all states in which they offer educational programs, which are subject to renewal. The College is currently authorized to operate in Colorado and does not require authorization for its self-study programs that are offered worldwide. WIU is currently authorized to operate in Arizona and London, England.

73   Certain states assert authority to regulate all degree-granting institutions if their educational programs are available to their residents, whether or not the institutions maintain a physical presence within those states. If a state were to establish grounds for asserting authority over telecommunicated learning, UOP may be required to obtain authorization for, or restrict access to, its programs available through Online in those states.

TAX REFORM ACT OF 1997

74   In August 1997, Congress passed the Tax Reform Act of 1997 that added several new tax credits and incentives for students and extended benefits associated with the educational assistance program. The Hope Scholarship Credit provides up to $1,500 tax credit per year per eligible student for tuition expenses in the first two years of postsecondary education in a degree or certificate program. The Lifetime Learning Credit provides up to $1,000 tax credit per year per taxpayer return for tuition expenses for all postsecondary education, including graduate studies. Both of these credits are phased out for taxpayers with modified adjusted gross income between $40,000 and $50,000 ($80,000 and $100,000 for joint returns) and are subject to other restrictions and limitations. The Act also provides for the deduction of interest from gross income on education loans and limited educational IRA's for children under the age of 18. These deductions are also subject to adjusted gross income limitations and other restrictions. These new provisions became effective for the 1998 calendar year, and it is unclear at this time the effect that these additional tax benefits will have on future enrollments.

EMPLOYER TUITION REIMBURSEMENT

75   Many of Apollo's students receive some form of tuition reimbursement from their employers. In certain situations, as defined by the Internal Revenue Code (the "Code"), this tuition assistance qualifies as a deductible business expense when adequately documented by the employer and employee. The Code also provides a safe-harbor provision for an exclusion from wages of up to $5,250 of tuition reimbursement

FINANCIAL INFORMATION

TABLE 1

	Year Ended August 31,				
	1998	**1997**	**1996**	**1995**	**1994**
	(In thousands, except per share amounts)				
Income Statement Data:					
Revenues:					
Tuition and other, net	$384,877	$279,195	$211,247	$161,013	$124,440
Interest income	6,205	4,341	3,028	2,416	280
Total net revenues	391,082	283,536	214,275	163,429	124,720
Costs and expenses:					
Instruction costs and services	232,592	167,720	130,039	102,122	81,313
Selling and promotional	49,035	35,187	27,896	21,016	17,918
General and administrative	33,183	25,648	21,343	18,462	17,194
Total costs and expenses	314,810	228,555	179,278	141,600	116,425
Income before income taxes	76,272	54,981	34,997	21,829	8,295
Provision for income taxes	29,975	21,602	13,605	9,229	3,383
Net income	$ 46,297	$ 33,379	$ 21,392	$ 12,600	$ 4,912
Diluted net income per share	$ .59	$ .43	$ .28	$ .18	$ .10
Diluted weighted average shares outstanding	79,086	77,726	76,763	68,872	50,524
	August 31,				
	1998	**1997**	**1996**	**1995**	**1994**
	(Dollars in thousands)				
Balance Sheet Data:					
Cash, cash equivalents and restricted cash	$ 75,039	$ 78,855	$ 63,267	$ 62,601	$ 12,816
Marketable securities	45,467	41,429	13,273	—	—
Total cash and marketable securities	$120,506	$120,284	$ 76,540	$ 62,601	$ 12,816
Total assets	$305,160	$194,910	$137,850	$102,132	$ 43,638
Current liabilities	$ 95,574	$ 67,394	$ 54,804	$ 45,065	$ 34,890
Long-term liabilities	9,778	3,199	2,432	1,715	1,347
Shareholders' equity	199,808	124,317	80,614	55,352	7,401
Total liabilities and shareholders' equity	$305,160	$194,910	$137,850	$102,132	$ 43,648
Operation Statistics:					
Degree Enrollment at end of period*	71,400	56,200	46,900	36,800	30,200
Number of locations at end of period†	114	96	85	68	60

*Enrollments are defined as students in attendance in a degree program at the end of a period. Average degree enrollments represent the average of the ending degree enrollments for each month in the period. Average degree enrollments were 64,100, 50,500, 41,500, 34,000, and 27,500 for the years ended 1998, 1997, 1996, 1995, and 1994, respectively.

†Includes UOP and WIU campuses and learning centers, IPD client institutions and the College. At September 30, 1998, there were 117 campuses and learning centers.

per year per student under the Educational Assistance Program ("EAP") provision. Although the EAP provision of the Code expired in June 1997, the Tax Reform Act of 1997, which was signed into law in August 1997, extended the EAP until June 2000. The EAP provision does not apply to graduate level programs beginning after June 30, 1996. Employers or employees may still continue to deduct such tuition assistance where it qualifies as a deductible business expense and is adequately documented. The percentage of incoming students with access to employer tuition reimbursement was 56% in 1998.

76   Apollo's revenues, net of student discounts, have increased to $391.1 million in 1998 from $124.7 million in 1994. Average annual degree seeking student enrollments have increased to 64,100 students in 1998 from approximately 27,500 in 1994. Net income has increased to $46.3 million in 1998 from $4.9 million in 1994. At August 31, 1998, 71,400 degree seeking students were enrolled in UOP, WIU, the College and IPD-assisted programs at IPD client institutions.

77   From September 1994 through August 1998, UOP opened 40 campuses and learning centers and IPD established operations at 17 campuses and learning centers with its client institutions. Start-up costs for UOP campuses in new markets average $700,000 to $900,000 per site. These start-up costs are incurred over an 18 to 21 month period, at which time the enrollments at these new campuses average 200 to 300 students. Costs for establishing a learning center in a market currently served by UOP are expected to average $150,000. Start-up costs for IPD contract sites average from $400,000 to $500,000 per site over an 18 to 21 month period, and consist primarily of administrative salaries, marketing and advertising. Start-up costs are expensed as incurred.

78   Approximately 91% of Apollo's net revenues in1998 consist of tuition revenues. Apollo's net revenues also include sales of textbooks, computers and other education-related products, application fees, other student fees, interest and other income. Apollo's net revenues vary from period to period based on several factors that include: (1) the aggregate number of students attending classes; (2) the number of classes held during the period and (3) the weighted average tuition price per credit hour (weighted by program and location). UOP tuition revenues currently represent approximately 87% of consolidated tuition revenues. IPD tuition revenues consist of the contractual share of tuition revenues from students enrolled in IPD assisted programs at IPD client institutions. IPD's contracts with its respective client institutions generally have terms of five to ten years with provisions for renewal.

79   Instruction costs and services at UOP, WIU and the College consist primarily of costs related to the delivery and administration of the Company's educational programs that include faculty compensation, administrative salaries for departments that provide service directly to the students, the costs of educational materials sold, facility leases and other occupancy costs, bad debt expense and depreciation and amortization of property and equipment. UOP and WIU faculty members are contracted with and paid for one course offering at a time. All classroom facilities are leased or, in some cases, are provided by the students' employers at no charge to Apollo. Instruction costs and services at IPD consist primarily of program administration, student services and classroom lease expense. Most of the other instruction costs for IPD-assisted programs, including faculty, financial aid processing and other administrative salaries, are the responsibility of the IPD client institutions.

80   Selling and promotional costs consist primarily of advertising, marketing salaries and other costs related to the selling and promotional functions. These costs are expensed as incurred. General and administrative costs consist primarily of administrative salaries, occupancy costs, depreciation and amortization and other related costs for departments such as Executive management, information systems, corporate accounting, human resources and other departments that do not provide direct services to the Company's students. To the extent possible, Apollo centralizes these services to avoid duplication of effort.

81   JOHN G. SPERLING, Ph.D., is the founder, Chief Executive Officer and Chairman of the Board of Directors of Apollo. Dr. Sperling was also President of Apollo from its inception until February 1998. Prior to his involvement with Apollo, from 1961 to 1973, Dr. Sperling was a professor of Humanities at San Jose State University where he was the Director of the Right to Read Project and the Director of the NSF Cooperative College-School Science Program in Economics. At various times from 1955 to 1961, Dr. Sperling was a member of the faculty at the University of Maryland, Ohio State University and Northern Illinois University. Dr. Sperling received his Ph.D. from Cambridge University, an M.A. from the University of California at Berkeley and a B.A. from Reed College. Dr. Sperling is the father of Peter V. Sperling.

82   TODD S. NELSON has been with Apollo since 1987. Mr. Nelson has been the President of Apollo since February 1998. Mr. Nelson was the Vice President of Apollo from 1994 to February

TABLE 2

| | Year Ended August 31, | | |
	1998	1997	1996
Revenues:			
Tuition and other, net	98.4%	98.5%	98.6%
Interest income	1.5	1.5	1.4
Total net revenues	100.0	100.0	100.0
Costs and expenses:			
Instruction costs and services	59.5	59.1	60.7
Selling and promotional	12.5	12.4	13.0
General and administrative	8.5	9.1	10.0
Total costs and expenses	80.5	80.6	83.7
Income before income taxes	19.5	19.4	16.3
Less provision for income taxes	7.7	7.6	6.3
Net income	11.8%	11.8%	10.0%

1998 and the Executive Vice President of UOP from 1989 to February 1998. From 1987 to 1989, Mr. Nelson was the Director of UOP's Utah campus. From 1985 to 1987, Mr. Nelson was the General Manager at Amembal and Isom, a management training company. From 1984 to 1985, Mr. Nelson was a General Manager for Vickers & Company, a diversified holding company. From 1983 to 1984, Mr. Nelson was a Marketing Director at Summa Corporation, a recreational properties company. Mr. Nelson received an M.B.A. from the University of Nevada at Las Vegas and a B.S. from Brigham Young University. Mr. Nelson was a member of the faculty at University of Nevada at Las Vegas from 1983 to 1984.

83   J. JORGE KLOR DE ALVA, J.D., Ph.D., has been President of UOP and a Senior Vice President of Apollo since February 1998 and has been a director of Apollo since 1991. Dr. Klor de Alva was a Vice President of Business Development of Apollo from 1996 to 1998. Dr. Klor de Alva was a Professor at the University of California at Berkeley from July 1994 until July 1996. From 1989 to 1994, Dr. Klor de Alva was a Professor at Princeton University. From 1984 to 1989, Dr. Klor de Alva was the Director of the Institute for Mesoamerican Studies from 1982 to 1989 and was an Associate Professor at the State University of New York at Albany. From 1971 to 1982, Dr. Klor de Alva served at various times as associate professor, assistant professor or lecturer at San Jose State University and the University of California at Santa Cruz. Dr. Klor de Alva received a B.A. and J.D. from the University of California at Berkeley and a Ph.D. from the University of California at Santa Cruz.

84   JERRY F. NOBLE has been with Apollo since 1981. Mr. Noble has been a Senior Vice President of Apollo since 1987 and the President of IPD since 1984. From 1981 to 1987, Mr. Noble also was the controller of the Company. From 1977 to 1981, Mr. Noble was the corporate accounting manager for Southwest Forest Industries, a forest products company. Mr. Noble received his M.B.A. from UOP and his B.A. from the University of Montana.

85   PETER V. SPERLING has been with Apollo since 1983. Mr. Sperling has been a Senior Vice President since June 1998. Mr. Sperling was the Vice President of Administration from 1992 to June 1998 and has been the Secretary and Treasurer of Apollo since 1988. From 1987 to 1992, Mr. Sperling was the Director of Operations at AEC. From 1983 to 1987, Mr. Sperling was Director of Management Information Service of Apollo. Mr. Sperling received his M.B.A. from UOP and his B.A. from the University of California at Santa Barbara. Mr. Sperling is the son of John G. Sperling.

86   WILLIAM H. GIBBS has been with Apollo since 1980. Mr. Gibbs has been a Senior Vice President of Apollo since 1987 and was the President of UOP from 1987 to February 1998. From 1985 to 1987, Mr. Gibbs was the President of Apollo Education Corporation ("AEC"). From 1980 to 1985, Mr. Gibbs held various positions with Apollo, including Chief Financial Officer and faculty member. From 1975 to 1984, Mr. Gibbs was with the accounting firm of Price Waterhouse and, from 1982 to 1984, served as a management advisory manager. Mr. Gibbs currently serves as the Chairman of the Arizona State Board of Private Post-Secondary Education. Mr. Gibbs received his M.B.A. from the University of Illinois and his B.A. from Arizona State University. Mr. Gibbs is a Certified Public Accountant in the State of Arizona.

TABLE 3

APOLLO GROUP, INC. AND SUBSIDIARIES
Consolidated Balance Sheet
(Dollars in thousands)

	August 31, 1998	August 31, 1997
Assets:		
Current assets:		
Cash and cash equivalents	$52,326	$58,928
Restricted cash	22,713	19,927
Marketable securities	27,538	27,182
Receivables, net	61,282	32,040
Deferred tax assets, net	6,203	2,873
Other current assets	3,945	2,853
Total current assets	174,007	143,803
Property and equipment, net	46,618	25,251
Marketable securities	17,929	14,247
Investment in joint venture	10,807	
Cost in excess of fair value of assets purchased, net	41,398	2,283
Other assets	14,401	9,326
Total assets	$305,160	$194,910
Liabilities and Shareholders' Equity:		
Current liabilities:		
Current portion of long-term liabilities	$333	$295
Accounts payable	9,684	7,714
Accrued liabilities	21,311	11,449
Income taxes payable	1,007	253
Student deposits and current portion of deferred revenue	63,239	47,683
Total current liabilities	95,574	67,394
Deferred tuition revenue, less current portion	4,592	—
Long-term liabilities, less current portion	3,750	2,494
Deferred tax liabilities, net	1,436	705
Commitments and contingencies	—	—
Shareholders' equity:		
Preferred stock, no par value, 1,000,000 shares authorized; none issued	—	—
Class A nonvoting common stock, no par value, 400,000,000 shares authorized; 77,112,000 and 75,614,000 issued and outstanding at August 31, 1998 and 1997, respectively	101	66
Class B voting common stock, no par value, 3,000,000 shares authorized; 512,000 and 548,000 issued and outstanding at August 31, 1998 and 1997, respectively	1	1
Additional paid-in capital	80,677	51,521
Retained earnings	119,029	72,729
Total shareholders' equity	199,808	124,317
Total liabilities and shareholders' equity	$305,160	$194,910

87   KENDA B. GONZALES has been with Apollo since October 1998. Ms. Gonzales is the Chief Financial Officer of Apollo. Prior to joining Apollo, Ms. Gonzales was the Senior Executive Vice President and Chief Financial Officer of UDC Homes, Inc. from 1996. From 1985 to 1996, Ms. Gonzales was the Senior Vice President and Chief Financial Officer of Continental Homes Holding Corp. Ms. Gonzales began her career as a Certified Public Accountant with Peat, Marwick, Mitchell and Company and is a graduate of the University of Oklahoma with a Bachelor of Accountancy.

EXHIBIT A

88   JUNETTE C. WEST has been with Apollo since 1986. Ms. West has been the Vice President-Controller since 1994 and the Chief Accounting Officer since February 1998. Ms. West has held various accounting and finance positions at Apollo from 1986 to 1994. Ms. West received a B.S. in Accounting from Grand Canyon University in Phoenix, Arizona in 1985. Ms. West is a Certified Public Accountant in the State of Arizona.

89   THOMAS C. WEIR has been a director of Apollo since 1983 and is a member of the Audit and Compensation Committees of the Board of Directors of Apollo. During 1994, Mr. Weir became the President of Dependable Nurses, Inc., a provider of temporary nursing services, W.D. Enterprises, Inc., a financial services company and Dependable Personnel, Inc., a provider of temporary clerical personnel. In 1996, Mr. Weir became the President of Dependable Nurses of Phoenix, Inc., a provider of temporary nursing services. In addition, Mr. Weir has been an independent financial consultant since 1990. From 1989 to 1990, Mr. Weir was President of Tucson Electric Power Company. From 1979 to 1987, Mr. Weir was Chairman and Chief Executive Officer of Home Federal Savings & Loan Association, Tucson, Arizona.

90   DINO J. DECONCINI has been a director of Apollo since 1981 and is currently a member of the Audit Committee of the Board of Directors of the Company. Mr. DeConcini is currently Executive Director, Savings Bonds Marketing Office, U.S. Department of the Treasury. From 1979 to 1995, Mr. DeConcini was a shareholder in DeConcini, McDonald, Brammer, Yetwin and Lacy, P.C., Attorneys at Law. From 1993 to 1995, Mr. DeConcini was a Vice President and Senior Associate of Project International Associates, Inc., an international business consulting firm. From 1991 to 1993 and 1980 to 1990, Mr. DeConcini was a Vice President and partner of Paul R. Gibson & Associates, an international business consulting firm.

"Some recent graduate news" . . . From a University of Phoenix Student Newsletter:

- Larry Banks, 1986 BSBA and 1996 MBA/TM graduate, has been promoted to President of DOD Electronics Corporation.
- Linda M. Lambert, 1995 BSN graduate, was named liver and cardiovascular transplant coordinator at Primary Children's Medical Center in Salt Lake City. In July 1996, she was named Pediatric Nurse of the Year, a national honor.
- Jeffery L. Lee, 1993 MBA graduate, has been named President of Profile Products in Salt Lake City.
- Shaun D. Davis, 1995 MAOM graduate has accepted a position as Branch Manager for Industrial Specialists, a specialized division of SOS Staff Services in Salt Lake City.

91   HEDY F. GOVENAR has been a director of Apollo since March of 1997. Ms. Govenar is founder and President of Governmental Advocates, Inc., a lobbying and political consulting firm in Sacramento, California. An active lobbyist with the firm since 1979, she represents a variety of corporate and trade association clients. Ms. Govenar has been a State Assembly appointee to the California Film Commission since 1992. Ms. Govenar received an M.A. from California State University, and a B.A. from UCLA.

92   JOHN R. NORTON III has been a director of Apollo since March of 1997 and is currently a member of the Audit and Compensation Committees of the Board of Directors of Apollo. Mr. Norton founded his own company in 1955 engaged in diversified agriculture including crop production and cattle feeding. He served as the Deputy Secretary of the United States Department of Agriculture in 1985 and 1986. Mr. Norton is also on the Board of Directors of Arizona Public Service Company, AZTAR Corporation, Terra Industries, Inc., Pinnacle West Capital Corporation and Suncor Development Company. He attended Stanford University and the University of Arizona where he received a B.S. in Agriculture in 1950.

Website addresses for the Apollo Group and subsidiary institutions:

Apollo Group Inc., Phoenix
Kenda B. Gonzales, 800/990-APOL
email: kbgonzal@apollogrp.edu
Janess Pasinski, 800/990-APOL (Investors)
email: jmpasins@apollogrp.edu
www.apollogrp.edu
www.uophx.edu
www.ipd.org
www.fp.edu
www.wintu.edu

CASE 57

BILL MOORE, ENTREPRENEUR, AND THE KELLY-MOORE PAINT CO.

1   Kelly-Moore Inc. is a dominant company in the paint industry in the western United States. The paint industry is highly fragmented. While it includes a few large paint manufacturers, the industry is primarily comprised of a number of small-to-medium sized manufacturers, and this pattern is particularly apparent on the west coast of the United States. Kelly-Moore Paint Company started as a partnership between Bill Kelly and Bill Moore in 1945 initially targeting the local Northern California market. Bill Moore assumed complete ownership of the company within five years of its inception after he purchased Bill Kelly's stake in the company. The company has continued to grow since that time. This case examines Bill Moore's entrepreneurial story as the driving force behind the Kelly-Moore Paint Company. That story offers numerous insights future entrepreneurs and strategic managers may find useful.

HUMBLE BEGINNINGS

2   Bill Moore was raised in Hartford, Arkansas, in a middle-class family. His father was a barber who always owned his own shop with several barbers working for him. His grandfather worked in the real estate industry. Bill Moore helped his grandfather during the summers while he was still in college, providing Bill with experiences that would be useful in his initial attempts at being an entrepreneur.

3   Bill Moore attended Georgia Tech with a partial scholarship for playing tennis and he also worked several jobs at Tech over the time he was a student. After Bill graduated from Tech, he moved to Los Angeles and took a job with the National Theatre Supply Company. He was interested in learning about the theater industry to nurture his dream to one day own a chain of theaters. Nine months later he abandoned his theater dream and joined Glidden Paints where he worked as a chemist. After one year, Bill became a paint salesperson for Glidden and worked in that capacity for two more years. As a salesperson, he earned $190 per month as a base salary and a $3,200 bonus his first full year. Bill Moore credits his three years at Glidden for providing him with an insight into the manufacturing and marketing aspects of the paint business. He recognized the large margins associated with manufacturing and marketing paints. Mr. Moore believed then and even now believes that the manufacture of paints is an easy process; it is the marketing of the paint that serves to distinguish the successful companies.

4   While Bill was a Glidden salesman, the United States became directly involved in World War II. Bill knew he would soon join the war effort. So he quit his job at Glidden and invested $3,100 in real estate by purchasing two 5-room houses in Oklahoma. He completed some of the repairs to these properties on his own, such as fixing the electrical systems, vents, etc. He also borrowed money from Prudential Insurance Company to finance the purchase of a 12-unit apartment house for $20,000; he paid $4,000 as a down payment. Bill Moore believes that borrowing money from insurance companies is a more attractive option than borrowing from banks. He believes that banks are always concerned about recovering their investment as quickly as possible; insurance companies on the other hand would rather "keep the money out there with the borrower." He adopted this same philosophy to meet his subsequent financing needs at Kelly-Moore.

5   Mr. Moore, satisfied that his real estate "nest egg" was in place, enlisted in the armed forces and served at sea for two years on a destroyer. He took with him a number of "paint-related" books, and several Harvard Business School cases. After he returned from the war effort, he sold his real estate

holdings. He received $48,000 on his initial investment of $3,100. Bill Moore used this amount to finance his entry into the paint industry.

6   Entrepreneurship often places significant demands on the entrepreneur's social life. It can adversely affect the entrepreneur's relationships with other family members. Bill Moore often describes how his wife, Desiree Moore, was very instrumental in helping the company to survive and grow during the early years. Ms. Moore initially contributed by "managing the books" and invoicing requirements during the first two years of the company. She assisted Bill Moore in the preparation of "*color cards*" every night before their dinner together. She would also accompany him on his rounds every night, delivering paint to the contractors for their use the next day. Most of these deliveries went to the contractor's home since many contractors worked out of their garage. This personal contact also introduced Bill and Desiree to the contractor's spouse, which accelerated business-benefiting social contact.

7   According to Bill Moore, his wife has been extremely helpful as a soundboard for his ideas. He felt this was especially crucial since the company did not have any outside board of directors or advisors. Indeed Desiree remains an active board member today. Bill insists that this be done so that she remains intimately familiar with the overall financial situation at Kelly-Moore—and has for 50+ years.

8   Desiree Moore also enabled Bill to develop strong social ties with his customers, which in turn helped to cement the business relationships with the customers. She was an integral part of socializing with contractors and their spouses as Kelly-Moore grew. As the company has expanded, Bill and Desiree lament that they have been unable to maintain such strong personal relationships with all their customers. This role has now been taken over by the Kelly-Moore salespeople. So, while it is no longer feasible for Bill and Desiree Moore to develop close relationships with each and every customer, their values of providing exceptional customer service to include personal relationships have been institutionalized as a core part of the company's sales effort and the life style of its sales personnel.

9   Several long-time customers (contractors) commented to the case writer that they were drawn to Kelly-Moore because of the honesty they found in Bill Moore and the authenticity they found in the marriage partnership of Bill and Desiree. Bill noted in his review of his early years as an entrepreneur the advice that "marriage, selecting the right person and life partner, is the most important decision in your life. This is particularly true for an aspiring entrepreneur."

SELECTING THE TARGET MARKET

10   Bill Moore's experience at Glidden had familiarized him with the paint industry. He had identified three distinct market segments within the industry. These included (expressed as a percentage of the total market):

Industrial finishes (automobiles, refrigerators, etc.)	50%
Home owners (through various dealer/retailers)	30%
Paint contractors (direct or through dealers)	20%

11   Bill Moore learned from his experience as a salesperson for Glidden that paint dealers [retailers; resellers to homeowners and contractors] handled 80% of all paint sold and they were primarily concerned with "price" so that they could manage their margins and store profit. He saw that they had substantial, often uninformed traffic (buyers) in their stores. As a result, issues of quality were less important than, simply, "how much will you sell me paint" that meets certain categories or minimal specification when dealers made restocking purchases. These dealers needed lower paint costs because they usually chose to locate in better shopping centers and downtown shopping districts close to furniture, home apparel and decorating oriented department stores. These "prime locations" increased fixed costs for dealers, which put pressure on them to manage variable costs [paint and people].

12   Moore also began to believe that the contractor segment presented an intriguing situation. The larger paint companies had chosen not to focus their efforts on this market segment primarily because of credit problems and lower margins. Paint manufacturer's sales personnel preferred to sell to retailers and dealers, who would order larger quantities and be more concerned with price point [which the salesman could control] than quality [which the salesman could not control and which drove the

price up]. Dealer/distributors and independent retail chains found selling to less knowledgeable private consumers was more price than quality driven—so they increasingly sought paint supplies that could improve their price flexibility. Paint contractors were [and are still] typically small businessmen working out of their garage who lived job-to-job, were typically deemed poor credit risks or slow payers, and demanding as customers. Painting contractors tend to make paint-related decisions on their own and are primarily concerned with the quality of the product. They like for it to cover in one coat, without brush marks, and hold its color/appearance for 10 years or more. They were "picky" buyers and viewed as "pains" by many paint dealers and retailers when compared to price-sensitive consumers that knew little about paint quality.

13   Mr. Moore studied the California market and observed that almost all the large cities had two primary paint manufacturers who supplied the contractor segment. However, San Francisco was the only city without any dominant paint manufacturer and hence Mr. Moore decided to initially concentrate his efforts in this market. This decision was consistent with one of Bill's pet philosophies of *"not attempting to race against the fastest person in the world."* He always emphasizes that an entrepreneur should avoid entering the toughest market, especially at the start-up stage since the margins in such markets tend to be extremely small. So Bill entered a market niche and geographic location for that niche where there was less competition. He focused on the smallest segment of the industry, 20%—paint contractors, which was also the most troublesome for current manufacturers and dealers. He avoided competing directly for the other 80% of the market: dealers, retailers, and industrial paints.

14   Kelly-Moore's growth in the contractor segment of the market necessitated that the company cater to the specific needs of this market segment. Mr. Moore was aware that the majority of painting contractors worked out of their garage and were therefore unable to stock large quantities of the input materials. They needed a place where they could go and get whatever raw materials their assignment required. Mr. Moore therefore built huge 10,000 sq. ft. stores to provide one-stop shopping convenience to the contractors. He avoided locating these stores near shopping centers because the rents/leases would be prohibitive for such huge stores. Besides, parking in shopping centers tends to be difficult, and customers would have to lug the heavy paint containers across a significant distance before they got to their trucks. Locating close to interstate highways near suburban enclaves made for easy, quick access with plentiful parking close to most residential job sites.

THE NEW VENTURE TEAM: SOLO, DUO OR TRIO?

15   Bill Moore thought hard about whether or not he should "partner up" or "team" with others to create and build the business he envisioned. He thought about his strengths, personal workstyle, and "weaknesses." His strengths included a strong work ethic, financial acumen, solid sales and marketing experience, and a supportive, talented spouse. He had few personal or family obligations, a modest real estate derived savings, and an adequate credit history based again on his Oklahoma real estate venture, Glidden employment, and his military service. Bill preferred to "call his own shots," make his own decisions, and depend on himself. He understood the fundamentals of paint chemistry and manufacturing, but his experience adapting paint formulas to create quality technical solutions was limited.

16   Bill's conclusion was a need to start the business in partnership with someone that could bring the paint chemistry and manufacturing expertise he lacked. Bill decided to follow up on an inclination and brief discussion he previously had with his boss at Glidden, Bill Kelly, before Moore left to join the Navy. Mr. Kelly had taken a special interest in Bill Moore when Bill worked in his chemistry department. They became close acquaintances while Bill worked for three years at Glidden. Mr. Kelly was a lifetime Glidden employee very familiar with paint chemistry and close to retirement when Bill Moore left for military duty in the Pacific.

17   So Bill Moore returned from military service and decided to use a partnership as a means of establishing his initial foray into the paint industry. This ownership mode enabled him to spread the initial risks typically associated with start-up ventures. Mr. Moore sought to establish his partnership with Bill Kelly who had since retired from Glidden. Kelly agreed to do so. The venture was structured as a 50-50 partnership with each partner investing $9,000. Kelly-Moore Paints' [written] part-

nership agreement had a stipulation wherein Mr. Kelly would sell his share to Mr. Moore after 5 years, at book value. Mr. Kelly agreed to do this because he was 68 yrs. old, was not going to be actively involved in the business, and the entire operation was going to be built by Bill Moore. Mr. Moore believes that this arrangement worked out best since he was able to gain complete control of the business, which he perceives to be crucial for the success of an entrepreneurial business. He does not have much confidence in partnerships, where ownership is shared across more than one person to build a new company, although he quickly recognizes that this is counter to conventional wisdom.

18   Bill Moore likes to tell the story of his experiences with other "co-owners" or "partners" of each of his newly opened retail outlets across California as he began to grow the company. Essentially, Kelly-Moore built a large, modern centralized production facility and then expanded sales by opening up a second, the third and so on retail outlets in different geographic areas to gradually expand their market coverage. Bill Moore reasoned, as he started opening a second and a third retail outlet in new geographic areas, that the effort would be more successful if his store manager in each location had a vested interest in the success of that location—a "piece of the action." Surely, Bill thought, they would be motivated much like him if they were "co-owners" with him developing the store. So, initially, each of these new Kelly-Moore stores was created as a separate corporation with the store-manager holding 49% of the equity, and Bill's [Kelly-Moore] being 51%.

19   To Bill's surprise and regret, this arrangement did not turn out to be very effective from a long-term perspective. The store-managers did a good job at first but they slowly began perceiving themselves as "semi-owners of the business." And, Bill found, "ownership" to Bill Moore meant something very different than it did to these people. According to Mr. Moore, *"ownership creates different attitudes in people"* and this can lead to problems if those attitudes do not coincide with your own. Some of these store-partners were not inclined to put in the required effort, only to become "the richest man in the cemetery." They did not necessarily share Mr. Moore's growth objectives, and were not as excited as he in the continued expansion of the business. Store efficiency slipped and Mr. Moore felt that he was losing control. He therefore bought out these store-partners with the intention to regain complete control of the stores. All future retail outlets were 100% company-owned stores.

20   One former store partner took away his salesmen and clientele and started his own paint store in the same town. That store was critical to Kelly-Moore's operations since it constituted almost 20% of the company's business. Mr. Moore therefore sent his best salesman to that location to regain the lost business. The salesperson was successful in regaining 80% of the business within a period of two years. While this helped to overcome the initial setback, it also sent a strong "signal" to the competition that *"Bill Moore was not going to give up his share of the market without a fight!"* And after completing the last buyback for former "store partners," Bill Moore never entertained the idea of shared ownership again!

IMMEDIATE SUCCESS

21   Kelly-Moore Paint Company started in a very simple way. Bill Moore would call on paint contractors, seeking to get an order for their current or next job. He would get job specifications and special needs, report them back to Bill Kelly who would make up paint that would meet or exceed expectations, and Bill Moore would seek to close the sale. The two would make and mix paint the next day and Bill, along with Desiree, would usually drive to the contractor's home to deliver the paint and leave new paint chips so that the contractor could show future customers. They would repeat the process the next day—Bill selling, Kelly formulating, Kelly and Moore making and mixing, and Bill and Desiree making new chips and delivering paint each evening.

22   Kelly-Moore Paints was successful that first year. The company earned a $32,000 profit in its first nine months of operation. Mr. Moore credits this early success to his decision to focus his attention on the growing San Francisco-San Jose market. Locating his plant in San Carlos gave him an advantage since it was equidistant from both San Francisco and San Jose. Also, there was a surge in construction spending in the Northern California market as a consequence of the pent-up demand in a post-war economy. The paint industry was a direct beneficiary of the growth in the construction business. Since there were no dominant paint manufacturers in the Northern California market, it

provided a start-up company like Kelly-Moore Paints more favorable competitive conditions during its initial years.

QUALITY IS SUPREME

23   One of the things Bill Moore learned during this early phase was how critical paint quality was to a paint contractor. Poor quality paint, even if it "was the right color" selected by a homeowner, often resulted in a paint contractor having to repaint to get coverage or to remove brush marks or for other reasons—potentially losing money because of increased labor cost even if the paint was inexpensive. So Moore repeatedly won new contractor customers once they tried Kelly-Moore paints and they saw first hand the extra quality, thickness, and pigmentation. This in turn led Bill Moore to insist that his employees understand above all else that the core distinctive competence of Kelly-Moore Paints is its utter dedication to provide a product of very high quality. Bill Moore folklore includes this statement employees often recall: "If I can't make a quality paint product and earn a profit, I'll just stop doing that and make mayonnaise instead!" He had recognized that paint contractors are experts at recognizing high quality paint and were not averse to paying a premium for getting a quality product. The contractors were keen on paint quality as it enabled them to satisfy their clients. For instance, contractors are extremely savvy customers with a very low tolerance for paints that leave brush marks. The major paint manufacturers placed a lower emphasis on the contractor segment of the market because it is more expensive to manufacture paints to the specifications of the contractors. However, Mr. Moore was convinced that once the contractors chose his products, the "amateur" (or homeowner) painter would also likely appreciate Kelly-Moore's paint quality and choose it for their painting needs. The paint contractors could therefore generate a secondary demand for his products. Thus, one of the quality indicators of Kelly-Moore paints is that no brush marks are allowed.

24   The Research & Development (R&D) program at Kelly-Moore Paints is geared towards this quality goal. The company now has an annual R&D budget of almost $2.5 million. Since Bill Moore first allocated money for research, and continuing to this day, Kelly-Moore's R&D effort is directed at improving the existing products as opposed to developing new products. According to Mr. Moore, product imitation in the paint industry occurs within about six months and hence a regional company like Kelly-Moore does not have adequate time to recoup its investments in new products. Therefore, Kelly-Moore's product improvement [R&D] efforts are directed towards improving the raw material mix while emphasizing attributes preferred by the customer. Mr. Moore wanted to make this policy explicit because he had observed that sometimes the R&D chemist's preferences did not reflect those of the customer. The chemist's focus was on the ingredients that were used in the paint while the customer's (paint contractor) concern was for the application of the paint. And from the store side, Gene Biddle, manager of the Monterey, California, store, says that Mr. Moore has rejected a number of product ideas over the years which were cost savers but which might have compromised the quality reputation of the paint. "Quality is one attribute of our product on which Mr. Moore has repeatedly made clear that there can be absolutely no compromise" Biddle said.

25   The superior quality of Kelly-Moore paints enables the company to charge a premium for its products, which helps it to be the most profitable firm in the paint industry. The average profit for the industry has been in the range of 2–5% whereas Kelly-Moore Paints has consistently enjoyed profits in the range of 6–10%. Mr. Moore's philosophy has always been to "*make what the buyers want*," and in his case the primary buyer was the painting contractor. Such a dedication to quality has endeared the company to many paint contractors and has resulted in their preferring Kelly-Moore paint in some cases for 40+ years.

26   Kelly-Moore has carried this concern for *what the buyer* [contractor] *wants* beyond just quality. The company has been successful in being customer responsive by asking contractors to articulate their needs. The lunches that the company hosts for contractors are excellent venues for gauging customer needs and for showcasing the new products made and/or marketed by the company. Bill created a unique position, "translator," whose job is to constantly "translate" between contractor/customers, technical, and production. Kelly-Moore now has a translator department to make sure contractor needs shape technical, R&D efforts, and production results. The company's goodwill among the professional contractors enables it to develop a loyalty even among the amateur painters who are referred to the Kelly-Moore brand by the paint contractors. In turn, the company has also provided a number of contractors with referrals to potential clients.

ISO 9000: VALIDATING KELLY-MOORE QUALITY

27   The International Standards Organization (ISO) 9000 label, when awarded to a company's product, is indicative of its consistently superior quality. The ISO establishes standards for manufacturing products to assure customers of high quality products. These standards demand continuous improvements in the production process to achieve this objective. Kelly-Moore paints have always had the reputation among its customers of being high-quality products. Nevertheless, the ISO label awarded to the company in 1995 provided it with an independent, external certification of its products and enabled the company to systematize Mr. Moore's commitment to providing a quality product.

28   Bill Moore has been successful at institutionalizing this dedication to quality within the company right from its inception. The pursuit of ISO 9000 label enabled the company to develop a more formalized approach to this process. The company has also created the position of an environmental safety and quality manager. Mr. Calvin Chung, the person appointed to this post, is responsible for coordinating the implementation of the ISO program in Kelly-Moore, in addition to ensuring that the company's activities are in compliance with environmental and regulatory requirements.

29   Implementation of the ISO 9000 program is more of a bottom-up approach in that employees ensure compliance with the standards by monitoring themselves and others. Employees from each department volunteer as internal auditors for a period of around 3 years and the process is repeated 2–3 times a year. The ISO requires that all quality control equipment (e.g. clocks used in the manufacturing process) must be calibrated accurately. Manuals were prepared documenting even the minutest aspects of the production process. These manuals were prepared by learning and recording all aspects of every production activity in detail and ensuring that all these activities matched standards. The complete ISO process was quite time-consuming taking one full year from the day the program was implemented before Kelly-Moore was awarded the ISO certification. The internal auditors of this program are trained and then certified. Whenever, deviations from the standards occur, Mr. Chung is called in to investigate the problem. There is no penalty imposed on the employee(s) for deviations from the standard. Instead, attempts are first made to retrain the employee concerned, before reassigning him/her. The success of this program is predicated on it being accepted by all the employees. That the commitment to product quality is an integral component of the Kelly-Moore culture has enabled the company to successfully implement the ISO 9000 program.

BUILDING COMPETITIVE ADVANTAGE THROUGH UNIQUE TACTICS AND POLICIES

30   Bill Moore's experience at Glidden had taught him that attacking the bigger competitors head-on would not be the most attractive option. So he crafted three fundamental marketing tactics that attempted to avoid major competition. First, he chose the area between San Francisco and San Jose, California, rather than larger markets like Los Angeles in order to avoid competing with larger manufacturers and national brands. Paint manufacturing then and now is still a fragmented, regionalized industry. So Moore avoided markets that attracted the biggest players because of the population density and opted for a less dense, and somewhat less competitive geographic region but still one with plenty of growth potential. Second, Moore went against industry convention and concluded that marketing his paints through dealer/distributors would not be an effective approach. These dealer/distributors usually had several retail outlets, served as outlets for several brands to include sometimes being the franchised outlet for national brands, and located in large shopping centers or downtown shopping districts close to department stores and other retailers of home apparel and appliances. The fixed costs of such locations were high, causing these dealers to pressure paint manufacturers for better prices. This, in turn, meant paints of lesser quality to meet their pricing needs. Recognizing that his commitment to quality meant lowering his profit potential through dealer/distributor channels, Moore decided to target and go directly to the painting contractor.

31   Third, Moore adopted a somewhat unique marketing strategy to establish his ties in this segment. He selected 5 major paint contractors and contracted with them to buy his product at cost plus 15% margin with the margin being openly allocated as follows:

1%	=	the cash discount offered to the contractor
2%	=	salesman's commission
2%	=	freight costs
10%	=	Kelly-Moore's profit

32   In return, the contractors had to purchase 100% of their paint from Kelly-Moore. He promised them that he would lower his price as the company grew and he was able to enjoy the benefit of economies of scale. He subsequently fulfilled this promise by dropping prices every six months over the next two years, which helped to strengthen his relationship with these leading contractors. Bill believes that this strategy was key in his ability to capture the contractor segment and ultimately the clients of these contractors, i.e., the homeowners, and thousands of other, smaller contractors.

33   In addition to providing a high quality product to the contractors, Kelly-Moore has also provided these contractors with a superior level of service. Bill Moore's dedication to providing the best service was evident beginning in the early days when both he and his wife Desiree personally delivered paint to their customers at night. The couple were also able to develop strong social relationships with their customers during those days. As the company grew, it became increasingly difficult for Mr. or Mrs. Moore to maintain strong social ties with all customers. However, the Kelly-Moore salesperson has been successful in taking over this role and developing similar social relations with the customers. Salespersons are given allowances to cover this type of customer entertainment and they are expected to spend them. The regular sight of salespersons personally delivering paint during the day evidences this superior level service and after they leave the store. It can be seen in other ways. For example, Mr. Moore was also aware that painting contractors tended to start their work early in the morning. To demonstrate his commitment to this market segment, he provided early store hours (from 7 a.m.) along with free coffee for contractors and ample parking. The company has served its contractor customers more than 2.5 million cups of free coffee to date!

34   Once the company had established itself, Bill Moore developed attractive pricing policies that satisfied salespeople as well as contractors. Initially, when salespeople were earning a 5% commission on their sales, they tended to develop an adversarial relationship with the company. Salespeople were offering price discounts to customers so as to inflate their sales figures and thus increase their commissions. Mr. Moore rectified this problem by requiring that the salesperson absorb a portion of any discount. Thus, he developed a pricing policy unique in the industry by offering seven different price lists to the customers wherein the discounts ranged from 2% to 15%. However, for every 5% decrease in price, the company absorbed 3% of the loss and the salesperson incurred the balance of 2%. So this shifted responsibility for pricing discounts directly to each salesperson. They could judge whether a lower commission [absorbing part of the "loss" from a discounted price] was justified by the volume of a customer's purchase and the frequency of purchases or potential future purchases.

35   Also, industry practice in selling to contractors had traditionally made the incentives (price discounts) offered to the contractors directly proportional to the number of product types that they purchased. This resulted in even increasingly complicated systems for pricing decisions for most dealer/distributors which were involving only 20% of their business at best—the small, bothersome contractors. So dealers grew increasingly weary in serving contractors. At the same time, they continued multi-product-centered pricing programs in order to increase the amount these contractors purchased at any one time while also responding to their constant pressure for discount pricing. Mr. Moore had observed during his days as a Glidden salesman and again in the early days of Kelly-Moore that contractors typically purchased only 2-or-3 types of products at a time, and hence he felt he did not have to discount his entire product range to make the sale. He concluded that he could discount items which they might need and which he could afford to sell for less. Yet he also felt he did not need to discount items already selling at a fair price [relative to their quality]. Then, he concluded, the contractor would have multiple purchase and discount pricing options to follow their normal purchase pattern of buying only 2-or-3 items. Furthermore, he thought contractors were fully capable of making this decision if he set reasonable price/quality parameters rather than complicating their decisions and his record keeping by creating elaborate price discount systems. In fact, he

was more concerned with "training" or guiding his salespeople. So Bill Moore simply gave his salespeople a set of pricing schedules for all items and gave them the right to deviate on any two items as long as they followed the "loss-sharing" guidelines described earlier. If they reduced a price, then they reduced their commission. This proved a simple way to merge salespersons' pricing flexibility with contractor buying behavior in a manner that still ensured the company's control and profitability.

36 Another distinct strategy that Kelly-Moore adopted helped it address paint manufacturer/dealers' longstanding hesitancy to give credit to paint contractors. Paint contractors were and are notorious slow payers. It also illustrates Bill Moore's truly creative and unique insight as an entrepreneur and businessperson. Kelly-Moore has never had any credit managers on its payroll. Mr. Moore firmly believes that "*credit is a function of sales*" and hence requires every salesperson to extend his/her own credit terms to the customer. According to Mr. Moore, "the salesperson is the best person to evaluate the creditworthiness of the customer," owing to their proximity to the customer. Besides, Bill Moore created a way to make sure that the salesperson stands to lose if s/he errs in making that judgment. He did this by creating a policy whereby the salesperson has significant latitude making their own decision about extending credit to a contractor customer—it is that salesperson, and their sales manager, who make the credit decision. No one in accounting is involved. By the same token, if that credit proves "bad," or a "slow pay," then the salesperson and sales manager share in the resulting loss along with the company. So, for receivables that go over 30 days, the salesperson takes a 10% loss [10% of the sales amount is deducted from their commission account]; for receivables that go over 60 days and are still not collected, the salesperson takes a 20% loss [20% of the sales amount is deducted from their commission account]. The sales manager in charge of the salesperson also has a stake in this outcome since s/he stands to lose 5% and 10% respectively when the account receivables are 30 days or 60 days past due. This policy has enabled Kelly-Moore to recover at least 30% of its cost from such "bad" sales. Consequently, the need to appoint a separate credit manager is avoided. The results of implementing such a policy were immediate. Credit losses dropped to around 1.5% of sales—far better than the industry average. Mr. Biddle, the Monterey store manager, asserts that this credit system provides an incentive to salespeople to pursue only high quality sales leads so that they can concentrate their efforts on the high volume creditworthy contractors and maximize their earnings.

37 Mr. Moore instituted a sense of *environmental awareness* in the company even before the concept gained widespread popularity. He actively encouraged recycling efforts and provided incentives to the distributors for returning empty cartons. In addition to being "environmental-friendly", it also helped him reduce his costs. Saving costs led Bill Moore to examine what he was spending with transportation of paint ingredients into his plant[s] and distributing paints out to his retail/contractor outlets. He then decided to create KM trucking, Kelly-Moore's own fleet of trucks to pick up supplies and supply its own stores. This allows Kelly-Moore to significantly improve the delivery time and service to its retail/contractor outlets throughout California—an early forerunner of JIT delivery. Assurance of timely delivery gave regional Kelly-Moore salespeople just one more competitive advantage important to their contractor customers. Owning their trucks also reduced Kelly-Moore's transportation costs by being able to pick up supplies to bring back to the manufacturing plant [that would otherwise have been shipped to KM at their expense] and by generating revenue from "backhaul" services—leasing the space in a returning tractor trailer to other businesses needing to send something to the San Francisco or San Jose area when the KM rig was headed that way anyway and would otherwise be empty.

38 The competitive advantages these tactics and policies have generated enable Kelly-Moore to consistently earn returns above the industry average [2–5% industry average; 6–10% at Kelly-Moore]. Kelly-Moore offers its customers a better product, which is also price competitive. Mr. Moore has been able to, in his own words, "run the company with a skinny operation." He has managed to accurately identify and target his market segment, minimize his overhead costs, produce a high quality product, and deliver it to the customer in an economical manner. His salespeople are among the highest paid in the industry, which results in a highly motivated sales-force. The clerks at the company's stores are well trained and hence are able to assist customers in selecting the correct choice of paints to fit their unique needs. These all have added up to a high degree of customer loyalty, and steadily growing repeat business.

LEADERSHIP BILL MOORE STYLE: DAILY INVOLVEMENT IN THE DETAIL

39   Bill Moore has always been involved in day-to-day decisions at Kelly-Moore, even recently as Chairman of the Board and gradually focuses more of his time on other significant activities like creating and managing one of the largest working ranches in Montana. He has always wanted to stay abreast of what was going on in the company and help make or be kept informed about any key decisions relating to Kelly-Moore's operations. According to Desiree Moore, her husband has a knack for the details, which she feels, is crucial. "Most people tend to focus on the bigger picture, but it's the little things that make the difference" says Ms. Moore. Bill asserts that his style of managing has enabled him to develop a comprehensive understanding of all facets of the company and to "*stay on top of things.*" This, he feels, has enabled him to continue to relate with people at all levels and functions within the company. He criticizes the popular business press for only preaching the virtues of delegating authority. He argues that very often there is too much delegation and the owner is ignorant of the state of affairs until things go bad, by which time it is too late. He also believes that if people are left to do things by themselves, their contribution begins to erode over time.

40   Although Mr. Moore has always been the final authority on most major decisions, he would never shy away from accepting input from the firm's employees. He also has no qualms in modifying his decisions if the outcomes do not pan out as anticipated. He has always been willing to suffer the consequences of his mistakes. For instance, he tried to diversify his operations beyond paints (e.g., drywall products) but was willing to back out of such ventures when he realized that his strengths lay primarily in the paint business. He has gone to great efforts in working to nurture Joe Cristiano as his replacement to satisfy himself that Mr. Cristiano will follow suit in his approach to decision-making and employee involvement.

41   Kelly-Moore, Inc. has evolved as a top-down organization with Mr. Moore's personal values indelibly marked on the company. The employees recognize that Mr. Moore has created the company with his hard-work, talent, diligence, and persistence. They have high respect for him because they are confident that he has the customer's basic interests at heart and that he would never ask them to do anything that he has not previously done himself. Indeed, his intimate familiarity with what they each do and his inclination to get involved or ask questions or make suggestions seems to be appreciated, a sort of respectful and informed validation, rather than being seen as intrusive or bothersome or not letting go. They all seem to feel that Mr. Moore will always "take good care of them." For instance, Ms. Larin McGrinn, who has been with the company for more than 35 years asserts that during one of her annual performance reviews Bill unilaterally decided to double her suggested wage because she was willingly doing more than her expected duties. KM employees evidence a strong sense of loyalty to Mr. Moore.

42   Mr. Moore's work ethic has been a source of inspiration to most Kelly-Moore employees. For instance Kelly-Moore's plant manager, Ed Jonsson, and its production supervisor, Bob Smith, affirm that their work habits are modeled after Mr. Moore's. According to Mr. Jonsson, despite being a unionized company, Kelly-Moore's relationship with the union has been extremely amiable owing to the deep respect that the union members have for Mr. Moore. This history of cordial relationship with the union has been further strengthened by the management style of the current CEO, Mr. Joseph Cristiano, who embodies a number of Mr. Moore's characteristics. The company has always avoided emphasizing distinctions between the management cadres and the shop-floor employees.

43   When Mr. Moore was more actively involved in the plant operations, he would often don white coveralls and work alongside the employees on the shop floor. This tradition has also been followed by Mr. Cristiano who during the earthquake of 1989 that hit northern California personally assisted in the clean-up efforts. According to Mr. Jonsson, Mr. Cristiano has been instrumental in creating the right working atmosphere in the company by emphasizing a sense of group camaraderie. Most of the employees assert that Mr. Moore's success in institutionalizing his values within the company will ensure the continuity of the Kelly-Moore culture even after his retirement. These values: making quality products, exceeding customer expectations, doing things that competitors cannot do, building on the company's competitive edge, and taking pride in work.

44   Kelly-Moore has also adopted a promotion-from-within policy. While the current President Joseph Cristiano did not begin his career with Kelly-Moore, he has spent more than ten years as an understudy to Mr. Moore. All employees are treated as professional "partners" jointly dedicated to fulfilling and building the Kelly-Moore reputation and legacy. They prefer frequent, brief and timely performance reviews to the usual formal annual reviews. A number of the managers of the Kelly-Moore stores are women. According to one such manager, Ms. Anne Edwards, female customers are usually happy to see a female manager and prefer to interact with them. Such policies have enabled Kelly-Moore to enjoy extremely low levels of employee turnover. The clerks at the company's stores are well trained and are able to assist customers in selecting the correct choice of paints to fit their needs, especially for the non-professional segment. These services have been valued by the customer and have enabled the company to enjoy a high degree of customer loyalty. And employees feel a part of something important, with career earning opportunities quite promising and professional pride a tangible benefit.

45   Ultimately, creating opportunity for your people requires growth. With growth comes new and more jobs and challenges. Mr. Moore sought to achieve his growth objectives by opening new stores in different territories, albeit in the California market. He considered whether to do this via franchising or using company-owned outlets. Ultimately, Mr. Moore decided that one of the key assets of the company is its reputation. According to Mr. Moore, it may take less than a year to destroy a company's reputation that may have been built over a few decades. He did not have much confidence in the ability of a franchise to safeguard the Kelly-Moore reputation for quality service. He therefore opted to expand his business using company-owned stores. Kelly-Moore has continued to systematically expand via company-owned outlets now located throughout California and other western states.

46   While Mr. Moore found success avoiding the franchising trend, he encountered a major failure along the way. Mr. Moore reasoned that each store needed to be sales driven. So he adopted an approach whereby each new store was opened with the top salesman in that territory as the store manager. However, Mr. Moore found that as store managers they put too much emphasis on the sales function rather than on running the store. So he revised the store organization with a store manager that ran the store—inventory, appearance, accounting, walk-in assistance, ordering, personnel, and security. The top salespeople remained just that—a top salesperson. They retained their aggressive sales commission potential combined with a base salary and also a store bonus participation. The result: no resistance to Moore's change in their compensation structure since their compensation as salesmen exceeded their store managers' take.

47   Mr. Moore also created a compensation plan for the store operators that included a combination of a base salary and bonus pool based on profitability. The distribution of the bonus was such that:

The inside salesmen each retained	1 share
The assistant-manager retained	1 1/2 shares
The store manager retained	2 shares
The bookkeeper retained	1/2 share

48   The bonus was not intended to exceed $100 per month, per share. While Mr. Moore believed in compensating his employees handsomely, he does not like the concept of "profit sharing." He also preferred to minimize the proportion of bonus in the compensation package so as to avoid employee disappointments during unfavorable periods.

49   Mr. Moore was aware that geographical expansion beyond California was imperative if Kelly-Moore intended to achieve its high growth objectives. But, he also recognized the fact that if he opted to expand geographically, it would require him to modify his approach to managing the operations. He perceived that the larger paint companies operating out of the east coast were not as successful on the west coast because they had not yet understood this principle. This was also the reasoning behind his decision to initially establish a foothold in the west coast market.

50   Kelly-Moore first expanded outside California by establishing operations in Texas. Mr. Moore purchased a poorly performing factory in Texas in 1961 and converted it to the Kelly-Moore system (i.e. targeting the paint contractor segment). The Texas factory was able to earn a profit of over a million dollars in its very first year after being taken over by Kelly-Moore. Mr. Moore delegated operational authority for the Texas operations to the General Manager and Sales Manager. Consequently, he was unaware of the subsequent deterioration in performance until after one of the best District Managers in Texas quit the company. Kelly-Moore traditionally has enjoyed extremely low levels of employee turnover. Mr. Moore transferred his best district manager from California to manage the turnaround in the Texas operations.

51   While this person was successful in engineering the turnaround, he became too dominant and somewhat too controlling with his subordinates. Mr. Moore found this to be a characteristic of many of his district managers. Hence, he reconfigured the organizational structure of the company. He created three operating divisions: *sales, store, and accounting*. A vice-president was appointed for each of these three divisions. The personnel in each of the divisions only reported to people above them in their division. So you have each Kelly-Moore store with a store manager, a salesperson(s), and accounting personnel all reporting to a different manager not located at the store. While Mr. Moore admits that this structure tends to create some friction across the divisions, particularly within each store, he believes that it is a small price to pay, especially since this structure enables him to stay informed on every thing that is going on within the company. And while Mr. Moore does admit that he wanted to be able to make all the critical decisions impacting the company, in particular its expansion beyond California, he is also willing to be flexible and modify his decisions if proven wrong or if preceded by better ideas from his people.

52   Mr. Moore does not have much confidence in preparing plans. He uses some simple rules of thumb to select his investments and to evaluate growth aspirations. If the payoff from an investment is within 3 years, he selects the project immediately. If it is within 5 years, he is inclined to accept it. If it takes more than 5 years to recoup an investment, he's likely to give it some consideration. Over the years, Mr. Moore has actively used debt to finance the growth of his companies, to the extent of at times using debt in a 1:1 ratio with equity. However, he prefers to obtain his loans from insurance companies as opposed to from banks. He has a strong understanding of the dynamics of that industry, since a third of his revenue is from his insurance business. According to Mr. Moore, banks are extremely concerned as to when the debtor will pay them back the loan. Insurance companies on the other hand would rather "*keep the money out there*." And in regular business plans or annual budgeting, Bill prefers brevity and minimalism. Sales projections "to better last year" are all that is needed according to Mr. Moore.

53   Bill Moore recommends against expanding a business too rapidly and argues that a number of successful small businesses ran into trouble when they grew too quickly. Expanding the business requires employing more people which in turn makes the control process not only more crucial, but also more difficult. He believes that his approach to growing his business has been successful because he has successfully instituted an excellent audit system within the organization.

FOCUS VERSUS DIVERSIFICATION: WHAT SHOULD WE DO FOR AN ENCORE?

54   Once Bill Moore stabilized the Texas operation and saw it on a steady growth track, he began to contemplate options that would allow him to continue Kelly-Moore's steady growth. Continuing to open new retail/contractor paint outlets in California and Texas provided one answer, but Bill wasn't certain that they alone would satisfy his growth aspirations. He was increasingly convinced that while the paint business he had created was a recipe for continuous growth and opportunity, other opportunities to build a successful revenue stream deserved his scrutiny. In other words, he didn't want to limit his talents, and those of his key people, simply to the paint industry if other opportunities existed. So he began to look more seriously for those opportunities.

55   One of the important ingredients in making paint, mica, created his first chance to diversify Kelly-Moore. He encountered a mica extracting plant in west Texas that was facing some financial difficulty. Bill Moore rationalized that being able to provide his own mica resources would be a good beginning from which to turn around this poorly performing business—not to mention being an obvious cost savings for Kelly-Moore.

56   A few years later, Bill Moore was approached by people that had developed a new type of spraygun for dispersing paint in lieu of using a brush. Sprayguns, if they worked effectively, could cut the time it takes a painter to paint a house by 50 percent or more. So Bill Moore, attracted to the potential synergies between the sprayer and his existing paint business—particularly his growing number of retail outlets—bought the rights to the spraygun design and built a facility to manufacture them.

57   Finally, Moore became intrigued with the home improvement movement as a retailing phenomenon with a future. Why would people just go to a paint store to buy paint when they could go to a
large, warehouse-type store and buy paint along with all the supplies they needed for any kind of
home building or renovation activity? Convinced this could well be the retailing trend that would seriously erode his paint business, Bill Moore entered the business creating a huge Home Depot store
[prior to the Home Depot chain that exists today] in central California that sold every kind of home
building item one would conceivably need. He soon exited at a substantial loss.

58   Bill Moore, reflecting on these ventures, saw key lessons in "these failures we encountered along
the way to building Kelly-Moore. First, I found myself in businesses that we had virtually no real
knowledge to bring to bear. We knew little about mining or about miniature mechanics for sprayguns.
Mica was a commodity. So we had to not only know how to mine effectively and stay competitive
equipment and technology wise, but we had to manage the financial fluctuations encountered when
you sell a commodity worldwide for a variety of manufacturing applications. We soon knew we
were well over our heads and we exited mica at a modest loss. Sprayguns, while they sprayed paint,
were again a technology-based item subject to intense competition and product obsolescence.
Warranty services were intense, and manufacturing precision heavily reliant on numerous outside
vendors of various component parts. Needless to say, success called for expertise far beyond our
knowledge of paint, paint retailing, and paint manufacturing. So we exited this business at a significant cost."

59   Second, they found themselves trying to compete in an exciting new retailing industry, which required financial depth they couldn't match. "Our Home Depot operation was perhaps the biggest mistake. Kelly-Moore profits were cut by two thirds absorbing the losses we encountered trying to
compete in one big store against growing national chains that had huge buying power advantages
over us. So we took a significant loss, ultimately just closing the business, in order to get out of this
one!"

60   Third, according to Mr. Moore, he began to notice that opportunities related to the core paint business began to go begging or unattended simply because the Kelly-Moore management team did not
have the time to invest in them because of the time allocated to the newer outside ventures. In other
words, attractive opportunities were not taken because of the time being wasted on diversification
distractions.

61   Mr. Moore looks back on these lessons and finds one final, overarching entrepreneurial principle.
"FOCUS," he said, "long beyond when you think your growth opportunities are limited or will soon
be! We have continued to create opportunity after opportunity for sales growth and profitability improvement at Kelly-Moore because we are so focused as an organization on the paint business—quality, knowledge, service and convenience. Shedding ourselves of those diversification commitments
and resisting the urge to go down that path again was one of our most important long range decisions
at Kelly-Moore!"

BILL MOORE'S LEGACY: CREATING A LASTING ORGANIZATION AND CULTURE

62   Bill Moore's legacy as an entrepreneur is in large part going to be found in the post-Bill Moore era at
Kelly-Moore. Two ways of viewing that potential legacy are helpful in predicting it. One way is
through looking at what appears on the surface to be a paradox or contradiction in what Bill Moore
claims as a core motivation. Another way, given Kelly-Moore's history as a "top-down" company
under Bill Moore's leadership, is to listen to the thoughts and experiences of Joe Cristiano, Bill's
carefully selected and slowly groomed replacement as Kelly-Moore President. More contradictions
emerge here too.

63   Bill Moore is known to all that know him as a person that speaks his mind, and knows what he
means to say. One of the personal philosophies he is likely to share with someone that asks him about
such things is a very strongly stated notion that he "has no qualms about admitting that one of his key
goals in life was and is to make money." He sees nothing wrong with this goal which for him, upon
reflection, probably emanates out of his experience growing up during the great depression. But, interviewing numerous Kelly-Moore employees about Bill Moore and his "legacy" with the company
one is struck by how very different his lasting impression appears to be. Far from seeing him as

someone dedicated primarily to making money, virtually every employee is quick to recount a "Bill Moore story" that illustrates his dedication to quality, to working hard, to treating others with respect and humility, and absolute commitment to serving paint contractors. Some examples include:

> Bill's commitment to quality of product is ingrained in organization. Bill has always been committed to quality, the ISO certification just systemized Bill's system. All employees are trained on the KM quality system. Quality is the cornerstone of the company. I was surprised and honored to take on the quality certification. ISO requires constant improvement in production through many methods. We must ensure maintenance of historical quality. And I want to impress people with "my" program because of my young age [28] so that their confidence in me is rewarded and so that it reinforces their trust in ambitious young people.

. . . Calvin Chun. Calvin handled quality control for a geo-technical survey firm for a year before coming to Kelly-Moore. Before this he did paint contracting using Kelly-Moore paint during the time he attended San Jose State studying criminal justice. Calvin oversees OSHA and EPA compliance and coordinates Kelly-Moore's ISO 9000-based quality control program. He is 26 years old. Calvin comments further:

> Mr. Cristiano initiated the ISO program's mandate to use all employees in its implementation. He really played a key role in developing the quality program. He is heavily involved in quality system. His philosophy copies Bill's. . . . Being a part of Kelly-Moore is exciting because the company is expanding rapidly and new ideas come from the employees. Bill and Mr. Cristiano regularly solicit and follow employee ideas. My part is to ensure full compliance with regulations and quality. The company sticks to all government requirements and is always concerned with what customer requires.

64   Dave McDonald is an outside Sales Rep for San Carlos, the headquarters retail store location beside the central Kelly-Moore production and corporate facilities. Dave started in 1973 in Kelly-Moore's Colorado division, which started from the purchase of Pro-Mat, a Colorado paint store chain. He started delivering paint, then worked in a Colorado store, then became manager in the Littleton store. In 1977 he came to California on vacation and visited a store, which had no store manager. He expressed interest and was given the job in 1977; and has been in California ever since. His thoughts include:

> All of the people that work directly or indirectly for Bill Moore have high respect for him because he would never ask anyone to do anything that he has not done. He conceived of the company and created the company with a tremendous amount of work. Bill has the customer's basic interest at heart. One day when it was very hot and crowded in the old retail store, one of the customers started to bend his ear because he wanted special service as a contractor. A year later Bill had a contractor store there. Customers love him and respect him. He is the boss. He makes decisions and responds to their needs.

Dave went on to say:

> Bill is very detail-oriented. He not only has the big picture but sees all the components. He is very quality minded. He usually sat in on product meetings, in part to make sure the products were good. "If I can't make a quality paint product and make a profit, I'll just stop doing that and make Mayonnaise" is a famous Bill saying. If it hadn't been paint, it would have been something else. Bill is very energetic, and always on top of things. Secret of Bill's success—he is willing to work harder.

65   Hugh Champeny, assistant sales manager and product coordinator [also called "Translator" within Kelly-Moore]. He determines product line; serves as a key liaison between customers, production and technical personnel. He "translates" between these groups. He has done this for 16 years:

> Part of the success of Kelly-Moore is understanding the business at the corporate level. Kelly-Moore has a shorter line of communication between technical people (corporate level) and customers—less gets lost. Yet Bill also created the "translator" role . . . now a department. This helps make sure they are always focused on having a product that the customer could make money with.
>   "Singleness of purpose," focus primarily on professional painter is our competitive weapon. Companies sometimes scatter their focus. When I came back to CA from Kentucky, I wanted to go to a company that had a good focus. I worked in a paint company in Kentucky.
>   Bill's major contribution to Kelly-Moore: 1) Bill's hard-working dedication—set example for everyone. Did not make a bunch of money and just kicked back. His influence is still in company through Cristiano. 2) His insight into the paint business. 3) Not being afraid to try something. If he made a mistake, he is quick to rectify it. 4) How to do the best job, and how to make most money with resources that you have.

Kelly-Moore appears able to maintain the success ingredients after Bill. It gets harder as the company grows. We must keep the organization lean—not too many levels. We have few levels between sales rep and head office. Bill would say, "keep things simple. Need to keep same focus when growing bigger."

66   John Bacigalupo, Kelly-Moore Treasurer, spent the majority of his work career at Kelly-Moore. He had these thoughts:

Bill Moore was a rare, creative entrepreneur. THINK ABOUT IT: Make your salespeople the credit managers of the company? Come on now! That is unique. Some would say crazy. But Bill Moore's philosophy: "If they sell it, they collect it!" This system was conceived by Bill Moore and it has worked extremely well for over 40 years!

Prior to starting Kelly-Moore, Bill was working for Glidden, where he received less commission than he deserved. Therefore, he created a system at Kelly-Moore wherein a salesmen gets a copy of every invoice. They can keep track of their commissions. And each salesperson also has a written employment contract.

Bill always seemed to have the insight to make decisions a little in advance, e.g., underground tanks were pulled before the problems really started, long-term leases were purchased at good rates.

Impressive number concerning profitability. What produces this? A combination of things: premium pricing because the product is good. Good expense control. Get good values from suppliers. Keep costs down in real estate by good lease arrangements. Do not do a lot of extra seminars and things, which drive costs up.

Offering good product, offering good service. Add teamwork to that. Everyone in the company has that in focus. And decisions are made quickly by the board of directors. The Board had three, now has 5 members: Mr. and Mrs. Moore, daughter—Christine, Steve Ferrari (treasurer), and Cristiano. This insider board works very well for Kelly-Moore. It makes decision-making faster and easier.

I don't see situation in company changing. There are too many people in company that will follow the same philosophy Bill Moore has: know what is going on in all departments, get good sales, watch bottom line, teamwork, quality and service.

67   Gene Biddle, salesman extraordinaire, started with Kelly-Moore in 1961 when he was doing graduate work. Gene was going to be secondary teacher but decided not to because of salaries. He called Bill and made an appointment with him (there were 5 stores at that time), and started full-time in San Francisco. He has known Bill all that time, working throughout CA in various outside sales roles—"some good situations, some bad. I have no regrets. Bill is 'something else to watch in operation.' "

Bill is an individual in total control. He knows every facet of the company, even today. He relates on all levels. He is interesting outside of business. He could share left-handed golf clubs.

Bill is a good poker player. He was always at the "A" poker table at district meetings for the company. He runs the business like poker, "close to vest and knows what's going on." What are the enduring values of Kelly-Moore that Bill established? "Approach business to satisfy painter in field. Ask painter what he needed and then built product. Don't sacrifice quality. Bill wouldn't put name on lower quality products. The company does not cut corners and painters know that. This helps us in the retail business as well."

Bill puts his money in the right place—fair compensation plans for sales force: Compensation to Kelly-Moore sales is one of best in industry. Very generous to sales force:

- choice of region
- in charge of profit level

Originally, sales program built around base salary plus commissions on nets. Multiple system: stages ranking from wholesale down through contractors. Try to keep these as high as possible. Opportunity to go after high volume customers and make more money. Sales rep. sells product and collects money. Sales reps. as good as any credit manager. Share risk with company. Will not last if he does. The system creates time frames to collect, will suffer if still on books at end of year. If salesmen go after sales that aren't that high quality, could hurt them in the end. If they comply with co. standards, then they have no problems.

68   Ed Jonsson, plant manager of Kelly-Moore manufacturing facility, recently completed his 30th year with Kelly-Moore. He started from the bottom in production and has done just about every job in the production/operations side of Kelly-Moore. He said:

Tradition was to make sure customers were happy and to put out a good product. Improved consistency with ISO program.

Bill was always dedicated to the company, inspired employees with his work habits. A lot of people carry the work ethic of Mr. Moore: make sure everything is done before you go home. I spend half of my day in the production area. The work force today requires more leading than before. Spend a lot of time training and in meetings discussing goals. Bill gave us the opportunity for this, and Mr. Cristiano pushes this forward.

69   Kelly-Moore was unionized around 1980 by teamsters and paintmakers unions. Ed became shop steward (9 yrs.) and vice president in the paintmakers local. He then became foreman in Kelly-Moore's paint factory, moving into management and out of the union. He learned one side and then moved to other, and feels that he gets along great with unions now because he worked on both sides. His thoughts:

> Never was a strike. Always work out differences. They respect Mr. Moore and Mr. Cristiano. During the earthquake Mr. Cristiano was down at plant every day cleaning up. Mr. Cristiano gives that feeling of being one group. He learned that employees care about the business. When Bill was still involved in plant activities, everyone in the plant wore white cover-alls. Bill would put his on and come down and work alongside everyone else. He was part of the group.

70   Larain LaGrinn started in 1960. She did general office duties and some production involvement:

> Kelly-Moore is a paint company where we have fun because Mr. Moore wants it that way. Bill is a hands-on boss. He made the company grow through his own efforts. He takes good care of employees and they are loyal to him. What makes it a happy place to be? Owned by Mr. Moore. Employees enjoyed this because Bill was always involved there.
>
> Special memories of the company: everything here because Bill made it special. His son and daughter started out at the bottom as well. Not given special treatment. Mr. Moore was proud of them. This is a great place to work. Bill and Mr. Cristiano listen to input and make changes immediately.

71   Anne Edwards has been the manager at the Seaside store for over two years and has been with the company ten years. Her main tasks as manager in the Kelly-Moore system are customer service, hiring and firing, maintain store operations, keep store looking good.

> I like being the furthest store down the coast, get to spread out business. Diverse base to work with and I grew up in the area over the last 15 years.
>
> Five Kelly-Moore store managers out of 13 in her district are woman managers. Female customers are happy to see a female manager. But I don't feel any different being a woman manager. Kelly-Moore treats employees equal. I have a great future here!
>
> Business volume in my store has been great because of building. It may slow down with closing of the fort. Regardless, I am always looking into ways to improve business on the profit as well as sales side. For example, we have two types of accounts, cash and charge. I discovered that cash accounts were getting contractor's discount even in low volume. Well, we cut those people out of the discount program to improve profitability.

72   Craig Vechue, 28 year old store manager of the San Carlos "fishbowl" store [because it is so close to corporate headquarters], describes his role as "hiring personnel, employee reviews, inventory, overseeing counter operations, and a lot of overseeing customer service." How is the role of a Kelly-Moore store manager different from other competitors?

> We work as a team with our outside sales representatives, and our corporate technical people. Competitors have the same layout we do, but significantly less sales per square foot! We run a better selling operation because we are a team.
>
> Bill Moore's legacy is probably an incredible focus on customer service. He has also an incredible opportunity for young people. I started 8 years ago in San Carlos and was promoted. I worked very hard and learned about paint. After one year as assistant manager, I was promoted again 18 months ago to store manager. Hard work, dedication and attitude leads to promotion . . . the sky is the limit. Many managers at branch offices have come from my store, which I proudly tell every new employee!

73   These observations suggest that while "making money" may be important to Bill Moore, making the best paint available to contractors and providing them with unsurpassed service is a far greater passion and driving force. Money that results is a by-product, a score card. And like the employee comments, a few customers' comments about Bill Moore and Kelly-Moore paint company help illuminate Bill Moore's legacy and priority. Some examples include:

74   Dale Adams has been buying paint primarily from Kelly-Moore for 15 years.

> It's a good paint and good deal for contractors. We know what to expect from the paint. They give you a good price. Degrees of discounts. Each contractor has a certain amount of discount depending on volume. They still

open the company early and have coffees for us contractors. They also have lunch for contractors to show off new products. Nice to have lunch with other contractors and product reps. I've never met Mr. Moore. I deal with Brian Book. Keeps relations on a personal level. Blends professional with personal levels. They treat the customers friendly, which is nice.

75 Fred Courrin has been a Kelly-Moore customer for 10 yrs. in Los Angeles, Tahoe, and now in San Jose: "They have the best products. Kelly-Moore paint is made to cover anything. Like the 550, very durable."

76 Fred Porter works for Macy's of California. He has been a customer since 1958. "My father-in-law, a large contractor, was a personal friend of Bill's and helped him grow the business. Bill called on them personally in those days because they were big customers. Bill tried to go to areas where he could service a few dominant contractors. That was very smart. I'm still using his paint forty years later."

77 Larry Panozzo of Panozzo painters has been in business 6 years. "I started and stayed with Kelly-Moore because of: convenience, good service, good quality paint."

78 Nowhere is Bill Moore's legacy at Kelly-Moore more interesting and revealing than with the story how he has chosen and "trained" his successor, Joe Cristiano. Perhaps the best way to describe this is to listen to Mr. Cristiano's reflections about that experience, about Bill Moore, and about the future of Kelly-Moore. Joseph Cristiano, President of Kelly-Moore, has been with Bill Moore and Kelly-Moore for almost fifteen years now. Joe's thoughts:

I am the legacy bearer at Kelly-Moore. It is a critical part of my job to make sure that the legacy of Bill Moore remains at the heartbeat of this company, in everything that we do. Bill is an incredible person. He spent a lot of time building an organization. He wasn't really out to be a millionaire. As he grew the organization, he spent a lot of time making this the best paint company in the US, not making himself rich. The organization that he left is his legacy—an amazing business system, a quality-committed enterprise, with dedicated people throughout the western United States doing just that happily, efficiently and effectively every day. As the company grew, Bill needed to groom someone to take over responsibilities, particularly in anticipation of his eventual departure from the business. Bill did this. Many companies like Kelly-Moore are turned over to professionals or unskilled family members. Bill had the wisdom to find a professional, experienced manager from the paint industry and then the patience, insight, and perseverance to indoctrinate him into Kelly-Moore culture. That took a long time. Far longer than most founders would be willing to accept. But Bill knows this company, this organization so well; and knows what depth of understanding and appreciation even the best mind must attain to keep it rolling and, more importantly, to avoid interfering with it!

He can now comfortably step aside. No person will change the core values in this company—not even a new President. This decade long process was no doubt the best way to turn the company over—Bill obviously spent considerable time considering how to turn the company over, and, typical of him, made some very wise decisions in how to do that well.

79 A great example of this can be seen in one of the early office assignments Bill gave his newly hired future replacement, someone who left a fine corporate suite in the country's largest paint company to join a closely held and modestly adorned regional paint company. After Cristiano started, Bill called Joe into his office, reassigned their secretary to a closeby office and gave Cristiano the secretary's desk outside Bill's office. Cristiano, the President-to-be, was a little taken back with the thought that he had been assigned simply a secretarial/receptionist desk outside of the boss' office. A far cry from the previous corporate trappings to which he was accustomed, and a seemingly almost insulting waste of his time.

80 Far from that, it was actually a very well thought-out plan: Cristiano would get to know everyone who came into Bill's office and be involved in decisions associated with any and every visitor. So over the course of the year or so that he sat there, Cristiano gained an invaluable exposure to different people, issues, and problems as well as participated in and listened to the rationale behind each and every decision. He saw firsthand how Bill "ran" the company. He was steadily identified as Bill's trusted "aide" because he was always "there" whenever something came up and employees, used to "going to Bill," now gradually began to get used to "going to Bill *and* Joe."

81 About the time Cristiano got comfortable sitting in the secretarial desk and joining each daily happening or decision, Bill changed the cards again. Bill created a new place for Cristiano, telling him not to spend any time in office! Instead, he put Cristiano on the road and told him to go meet all store managers and sales reps and ask questions about improving the company. So for about 6 months, Cristiano spent most of his time outside the headquarters office roaming the western U.S. visiting

Kelly-Moore outlets and plants. He intermittently came back to Bill every couple of weeks and they would discuss ideas. For example, the Reps would say, "we need more money," and Bill would say, "this is why I have this so." Or they would uncover a situation that needed attention; a good idea to implement; and a lot of questions about why things were done as they were.

82   Cristiano's thoughts looking back on these two training approaches:

> Great learning experiences. Unique way to learn the company and to learn Bill's philosophy. Trying to learn Bill's company style was hard. I joined Kelly-Moore after working with the largest paint company in the US (Kelly-Moore was and is the most profitable) and I thought I had all the answers. But Bill's method gave me an opportunity to learn what the Kelly-Moore mystic was all about. It was an incredibly effective way to bring me into the organization; to let me learn, and to let others get to know me and to talk with me and to gradually trust me and trust Bill's comfort with me. It helped make sure that I learned the company they had all created from the ground up, and it helped make sure I listened and that they were comfortable speaking . . . something that Bill has always been a master of at Kelly-Moore.
>
> Large company mentality is much different from small company mentality. I was in charge of the Western U.S. for Sherwin Williams. If a store lease was up for negotiation, I would call a real estate guy [one of our departments or outsourced counsel] to negotiate. When legal problem arose, we would call a lawyer, etc. I never really got into day-to-day operations as Western US vice president at Sherwin Williams. Bill, as entrepreneur, could do everything. He could write a lease or a purchase agreement; by hand. This situation made him a better manager. He could go through a lease himself or would deal with legal problems himself. Bill had designed the equipment and knew all aspects about it. Many managers today just take an overview. Bill had to learn the total business and then do it.
>
> Another huge difference was in financial management. At Kelly-Moore we had very abbreviated budgeting processes; and modest plans. I spent half my time at Sherwin Williams doing these types of things. It took me a couple of years to get used to no elaborate budgeting process at Kelly-Moore. I was used to piles of spreadsheets, etc., but found very little of that here. I was skeptical, but I began to realize how the system worked without all the formality a big company creates. And we eventually have created a five-year plan. But that is interesting too. A big company has a 5-year plan that doesn't change easily, while in Kelly-Moore they could walk down to Bill's office and change plans easily. The flexibility was [and still is] amazing. I like it very much, although it can present challenges as we continue to grow!
>
> Bill is an entrepreneur, and so it worked that way—less formality, quick decisions, seize the opportunity. But it is a different challenge to run a 20-store company than a 145-store, multimillion-dollar company. So we are trying to figure out how to get bigger, but still act like a small company. People enjoy dealing with a small company, but KM wants to grow to provide more opportunities to keep our talented people and attract others. So it is a constant struggle to maintain that "small company feel." Now management takes different techniques. For example, when Bill started the company all the people important to most decisions were close by, but now they could be 2000 miles away. It's harder to motivate these people by telephone than it is in person. The important questions now: Keep core values, grow company, but still react like small company?
>
> Illustration of core values: Value: not get out of niche, selling to contractors. This was simple when they were a small company and they got instant feedback. Now we have to develop mechanisms, to keep this feedback coming. Customer opinion cards now come straight to my office from everywhere. They rate stores on how many good cards or bad cards they get. Good cards get responses from VP's [corporate level]; bad cards are handled by regional managers [each sales territory].

83   Cristiano sees as his key job and challenge maintaining the core values of the company, instilling them throughout the company, as they continue to expand. Cristiano speaks regularly to sales reps, particularly each group of new reps, as often as he can. When he does, he describes these core values that he views as exactly what guided Bill Moore:

1. Absolute honesty and integrity—"can make mistakes, but must be honest, still holds today."
2. Absolute emphasis on product quality and consistency—"see ISO 9000 as evidence of this; Bill has had ISO since he started company."
3. Awesome customer service—"everyone else can be average, but we must be better, as company gets bigger, it is harder to do this, but important today."
4. Bill is never happy with status quo—"if I tell Bill 'our August sales volume is best in history' and he answers 'congratulations, now what are we going to do for September?' Continuous self-correction. When I came from corporate environment, I asked Bill if I should put together formal budget processes, etc. Bill said 'I just want you to do more sales than last year and more profit than last year.' "

5. The people of Kelly-Moore are our strength—"have forgotten this as gotten bigger, but trying to focus on this. If counter workers give customers bad service, it is a big problem. They are at the mercy of the counter person, the lowest paid person in the store, for giving good service. If they have good people, they will do well. They will sometimes replace personnel in unprofitable stores, and that will turn around situation."

84   Cristiano is given the challenge of continuing these values. He finds them his source of flexibility and the chance to do a "his way" version of what Bill Moore did for 50 years. Cristiano feels Bill was able to keep a high level of entrepreneurial involvement in many decisions because he had good people surrounding him. Bill gave people general direction and let them work. They picked up Bill's ideas and then gave them their personal twist. "But," he observes, "sharp people want to be able to do their own thing. It is troublesome today trying to hire bright people and have them do it Bill's, or Joe's way today." So Cristiano "gives people more responsibility and ability to create, but insists that they must operate within Bill's values and organization. As we get bigger, the problem gets bigger. There is only one Bill Moore. Cherish and hold firm to Bill's many good ideas and values. Learn from Bill's mistakes and build the company better and better. Give people more responsibility, is the only way to get good people."

85   Dave McDonald, a longtime employee in sales, captured the essence of how most employees feel and the likely legacy Bill Moore will leave at Kelly-Moore:

> Mr. Moore personifies certain characteristics of successful people. The company must keep those characteristics, or principles, in mind even when Bill leaves. I'm not worried because Bill put an ingrained, indelible stamp on the Kelly-Moore company. There is still commitment to those principles that permeates ever position, person and process within this continually expanding company. And Mr. Cristiano has spent much time with Bill to be able to carry the message and legacy to Bill's satisfaction. It's simple really, an uncompromised commitment to: making quality product, exceeding customer expectations, doing things competitors cannot do, keeping the competitive edge, taking pride in work.

CASE 58

STARBUCKS CORPORATION

1   Starbucks Corporation is a Seattle, Washington-based coffee company. It roasts and sells whole-bean coffees and coffee drinks through a national chain of retail outlets/restaurants. Originally only a seller of packaged, premium, roasted coffees, the bulk of the company's revenue now comes from its coffee bars where people can purchase beverages and pastries in addition to coffee by the pound. Starbucks is credited with changing the way Americans view coffee, and its success has attracted the attention of investors nationwide.

2   Starbucks has consistently been one of the fastest growing companies in the United States with over 1,006 retail outlets in 1996. Over a five-year period starting in 1991, net revenues increased at a compounded annual growth rate of 61 percent. In fiscal 1996, net revenues increased 50 percent to $696 million from $465 million for the same period the previous year (see Exhibit 1). Net earnings rose 61 percent to $42 million from the previous year's $26 million. Sales for Starbucks have been continuing to grow steadily, and the company is still a darling of investors with a PE ratio of 58.

3   To continue to grow at a rapid pace, the firm's senior executives have been considering international expansion. Specifically, they are interested in Japan and other Asian countries, where Starbucks has little or no presence. Japan, the world's third largest coffee consumer after the United States and Germany, represented both a challenge and a huge opportunity to the firm. To explore what changes in Starbucks' strategy were required, and the questions that might arise during expansion, this case looks at the firm's entry strategy into Japan and the nature of issues facing the firm during early 1997.

COMPANY BACKGROUND

4   In 1971, three Seattle entrepreneurs—Jerry Baldwin, Zev Siegl, and Gordon Bowker—started selling whole-bean coffee in Seattle's Pike Place Market. They named their store Starbucks, after the first mate in *Moby Dick*. By 1982, the business had grown to five stores, a small roasting facility, and a wholesale business selling coffee to local restaurants. At the same time, Howard Schultz had been working as vice president of U.S. operations for Hammarplast, a Swedish housewares company in New York, marketing coffee makers to a number of retailers, including Starbucks. Through selling to Starbucks, Schultz was introduced to the three founders, who then recruited him to bring marketing savvy to the company. Schultz, 29 and recently married, was eager to leave New York. He joined Starbucks as manager of retail sales and marketing.

5   A year later, Schultz visited Italy for the first time on a buying trip. As he strolled through the piazzas of Milan one evening, he was inspired by a vision. He noticed that coffee was an integral part of the romantic culture in Italy; Italians start their day at an espresso bar, and later in the day return with their friends. (For a history of the coffeehouse, see Exhibit 2.) There are 200,000 coffee bars in Italy, and about 1,500 in Milan alone. Schultz believed that given the chance, Americans would pay good money for a premium cup of coffee and a stylish, romantic place to enjoy it. Enthusiastic about his idea, Schultz returned to tell Starbucks' owners of his plan for a national chain of cafés stylized on the Italian coffee bar. The owners, however, were less enthusiastic and did not want to be in the restaurant business. Undaunted, Schultz wrote a business plan, videotaped dozens of Italian coffee bars, and began looking for investors. By April 1985, he had opened his first coffee bar, Il Giornale

This case was written by Melissa Schilling and Suresh Kotha, both of the University of Washington. This case was prepared as the basis for class discussion rather than to illustrate either effective or ineffective handling of an administrative situation.

EXHIBIT 1
Selected Financial Data

(in thousands, except earnings per share)

As of and For the Fiscal Year Ended:	Sept 29, 1996 (52 Wks)	Oct 1, 1995 (52 Wks)	Oct 2, 1994 (52 Wks)	Oct 3, 1993 (52 Wks)	Sept 27, 1992 (52 Wks)
Results of Operations Data:					
Net revenues					
Retail	$600,067	$402,655	$248,495	$153,610	$ 89,669
Specialty Sales (Institutional Customers)	78,655	48,143	26,543	15,292	10,143
Direct Response (Mail Order)	17,759	14,415	9,885	6,979	3,385
Total Net Revenues	696,481	465,213	284,923	176,541	103,197
Operating Income	56,993	40,116	23,298	12,618	7,113
Provision for Merger Costs[1]	—	—	3,867	—	—
Gain on Sale of Investment in Noah's[2]	9,218	—	—	—	—
Net Earnings	$ 42,128	$ 26,102	$ 10,206	$ 8,282	$ 4,454
Net Earnings per Common and Common Equivalent Share—Fully Diluted[3]	$ 0.54	$ 0.36	$ 0.17	$ 0.14	$ 0.09
Balance Sheet Data:					
Working Capital	$238,450	$134,304	$ 44,162	$ 42,092	$ 40,142
Total Assets	726,613	468,178	231,421	201,712	91,547
Long-Term Debt (Including Current Portion)	167,980	81,773	80,500	82,100	1,359
Redeemable Preferred Stock	—	—	—	4,944	—
Shareholders' Equity	451,660	312,231	109,898	88,686	76,923

Source: From the consolidated financial statements of the company.

[1]Provision for merger costs reflects expenses related to the merger with The Coffee Connection, Inc., in fiscal 1994.

[2]Gain on sale of investment in Noah's of $9,218 ($5,669 after tax) results from the sale of Noah's New York Bagel, Inc., stock in fiscal 1996.

[3]Earnings per share is based on the weighted average shares outstanding during the period plus, when their effect is dilutive, common stock equivalents consisting of certain shares subject to stock options. Fully diluted earnings per share assumes conversion of the Company's convertible subordinated debentures using the "if converted" method, when such securities are dilutive, with net income adjusted for the after-tax interest expense and amortization applicable to these debentures.

(named after the Italian newspaper), where he served Starbucks coffee. Following Il Giornale's immediate success, Schultz opened a second coffee bar in Seattle and then a third in Vancouver. In 1987, the owners of Starbucks agreed to sell to Schultz for $4 million. The Il Giornale coffee bars took on the name of Starbucks.

6   Convinced that Starbucks would one day be in every neighborhood in America, Schultz focused on expansion. In 1987 he entered Chicago, four years later he opened in Los Angeles, and in 1993 he entered the District of Columbia. Additionally, he hired executives away from corporations such as PepsiCo. At first, the company's losses almost doubled, to $1.2 million from fiscal 1989 to 1990 as overhead and operating expenses ballooned with the expansion. Starbucks lost money for three years running, and the stress was hard on Schultz, but he stuck to his conviction not to "sacrifice long-term integrity and values for short-term profit." [1] In 1991, sales shot up 84 percent, and the company turned profitable. In 1992 Schultz took the firm public at $17 a share.

7   Always believing that market share and name recognition are critical to the company's success, Schultz continued to expand the business rather aggressively. Notes Schultz: "There is no secret sauce here. Anyone can do it." To stop potential copycats, he opened 100 new stores in 1993 and another 145 in 1994. Additionally, he acquired the Coffee Connection, a 25-store Boston chain, in 1994.

EXHIBIT 2
The History of the Coffee House

Coffee made its way up the Arabian peninsula from Yemen 500 years ago. At that time, coffee houses were regularly denounced as "gathering places for men, women and boys of questionable morals, hubs of secular thought, centers of sedition and focal points for such dubious activities as the reading aloud of one's own poetry."

In Turkey and Egypt, coffee houses were meeting places for "plotters and other fomenters of insurrection." In Arabian countries, it was considered improper for a Muslim gentleman to sit at a coffee house—it was deemed a waste of time and somewhat indecent to gather and discuss secular literature, though these activities later became the rage in European coffee houses.

In 17th-century London, coffee houses were suggested as an alternative to the growing use of alcohol. Coffee houses were a very popular place for the masses to gather since in a coffee house, a poor person could keep his seat and not be "bumped" if a wealthier person entered. Coffee houses became known as "penny institutions" where novel ideas were circulated.

Around the turn of the century, espresso was invented in Italy. The name refers to the method of forcing high-pressure water through the coffee grounds, rather than the standard percolation techniques. Espresso and cappuccino rapidly became the preferred beverage of the coffee house; today most Italians and many other Europeans spurn the canned coffee that has been so popular in America.

Sources: *Chicago Tribune,* February 28, 1993; *Los Angeles Times,* December 6, 1992.

8   Everywhere Starbucks has opened, customers have flocked to pay upwards of $1.85 for a cup of coffee (latte). Currently, the firm operates stores in most of the major metropolitan areas in the United States and Canada, including Seattle, New York, Chicago, Boston, Los Angeles, San Francisco, San Diego, Austin, Dallas, Houston, San Antonio, Las Vegas, Philadelphia, Pittsburgh, Cincinnati, Minneapolis, Portland, Atlanta, Baltimore, Washington, D.C., Denver, Toronto, and Vancouver, B.C. Its mail-order business serves customers throughout the United States. Enthusiastic financial analysts predict that Starbucks could top $1 billion by the end of the decade (see Appendix A).

9   In 1996, Starbucks employed approximately 16,600 individuals, including roughly 15,000 in retail stores and regional offices, and the remainder in the firm's administrative, sales, real estate, direct-response, roasting, and warehousing operations. Only five of the firm's stores (located in Vancouver, British Columbia) out of a total of 929 company-operated stores in North America were unionized. Starbucks has never experienced a strike or work stoppage. Management was confident that its relationship with its employees was excellent.

10   Currently the firm is organized as a matrix between functional and product divisions. The firm's functional divisions include Marketing; Supply Chain Operations (manufacturing, distribution, purchasing); Human Resources; Accounting; International; Planning and Finance; Administration (facilities, mail); Communications and Public Affairs; and Merchandising (the group that focuses on product extensions for food and beverages). The firm's product-based divisions include Retail North America (this division accounts for the bulk of the company's business and is split into regional offices spread throughout the United States); Specialty Sales and Wholesale Group (handles large accounts such as restaurants); Direct Response (a division that focuses on mail-order/Internet-related orders); International; and Licensed Concepts Unit. Because of the overlap in these divisions (e.g., Marketing and Retail North America), many employees report to two division heads. Notes Troy Alstead, the company's director of international planning and finance, "We have avoided a hierarchical organization structure, and therefore we have no formal organization chart." Exhibit 3 provides a partial list of Starbucks' top management.

MARKET AND COMPETITION

11   Americans have a reputation for buying the cheapest coffee beans available. Most American coffee buyers have to fight growers to keep them from just showing them the culls. Much of the canned coffee on American supermarket shelves is made from the robusta bean—considered to be the lowest

EXHIBIT 3
Top Management at Starbucks

Howard Schultz is the founder of the company and has been chairman of the board and chief executive officer since its inception in 1985. From 1985 to June 1994, Mr. Schultz was also the company's president . From September 1982 to December 1985, Mr. Schultz was the director of retail operations and marketing for Starbucks Coffee Company, a predecessor to the Company; and from January 1986 to July 1987, he was the chairman of the board, chief executive officer, and president of Il Giornale Coffee Company, a predecessor to the Company.

Orin Smith joined the company in 1990 and has served as president and chief operating officer since June 1994. Prior to June 1994, Mr. Smith served as the company's vice president and chief financial officer and later, as its executive vice president and chief financial officer.

Howard Behar joined the company in 1989 and has served as president of Starbucks International since June 1994. From February 1993 to June 1994, Mr. Behar served as the company's executive vice president, sales and operations. From February 1991 to February 1993, Mr. Behar served as senior vice president, retail operations, and from August 1989 to January 1991, he served as the company's vice president, retail stores.

Scott Bedbury joined Starbucks in June 1995 as senior vice president, marketing. From November 1987 to October 1994, Mr. Bedbury held the position of worldwide director of advertising for Nike, Inc. Prior to joining Nike, Inc., Mr. Bedbury was vice president for Cole and Weber Advertising in Seattle, Washington, which is an affiliate of Ogilvy and Mather.

Michael Casey joined Starbucks in 1995 as senior vice president and chief financial officer. Prior to joining Starbucks, Mr. Casey served as executive vice president and chief financial officer of Family Restaurants, Inc., from its inception in 1986. During his tenure there, he also served as a director from 1986 to 1993, and as president of its El Torito Restaurants, Inc., division from 1988 to 1993.

Vincent Eades joined Starbucks in April 1995 as senior vice president, specialty sales and marketing. From February 1993 to April 1995, Mr. Eades served as a regional sales manager for Hallmark Cards, Inc. From August 1989 to February 1993, Mr. Eades was general manager of the Christmas Celebrations business unit at Hallmark Cards, Inc.

Sharon E. Elliott joined Starbucks in 1994 as senior vice president, human resources. From September 1993 to June 1994, Ms. Elliott served as the corporate director, staffing and development, of Allied Signal Corporation. From July 1987 to August 1993, she held several human resources management positions with Bristol-Myers Squibb, including serving as the director of human resources—corporate staff.

E. R. (Ted) Garcia joined Starbucks in April 1995 as senior vice president, supply chain operations. From May 1993 to April 1995, Mr. Garcia was an executive for Gemini Consulting. From January 1990 until May 1993, he was the vice president of operations strategy for Grand Metropolitan PLC, Food Sector.

Wanda J. Herndon joined Starbucks in July 1995 as vice president, communications and public affairs, and was promoted to senior vice president, communications and public affairs, in November 1996. From February 1990 to June 1995, Ms. Herndon held several communications management positions at Du Pont. Prior to that time, Ms. Herndon held several public affairs and marketing communications positions for Dow Chemical Company.

David M. Olsen joined Starbucks in 1986 and has served as the company's senior vice president, coffee, since September 1991. From November 1987 to September 1991, Mr. Olsen served as its vice president, coffee, and from February 1986 to November 1987, he served as the company's director of training.

Deidra Wager joined Starbucks in 1992 and has served as the company's senior vice president, retail operations, since August 1993. From September 1992 to August 1993, Ms. Wager served as the company's vice president, operation services. From March 1992 to September 1992, she was the company's California regional manager. From September 1988 to March 1992, Ms. Wager held several operations positions with Taco Bell, Inc., including having served as its director of operations systems development.

quality coffee bean with the highest in caffeine content. Japanese, German, and Italian buyers, in contrast, are known for buying the best beans, primarily Arabica. There are many different types and grades of Arabica and robusta beans, though for years Americans have treated them as a generic commodity.[2]

The U.S. Coffee Industry

12   U.S. coffee consumption peaked in 1962. At that time Americans were drinking an average of 3.1 cups per day. However, from the 1960s to the 1980s coffee consumption declined, bottoming out at an average consumption of 1.8 cups per day, or $6.5 billion annually. Over the past decade, coffee demand has been stagnant, with growth only occurring in some of the specialty coffees (see Exhibit 4). Whereas three-fourths of all Americans were regular coffee drinkers in the 1960s, today only half of the U.S. population consumes coffee.[3]

13   There has been a marked consumer trend toward more healthful fare, causing overall coffee consumption to decline. Although the coffee industry had expected decaffeinated coffee brands to increase, decaffeinated sales in the grocery stores have been steadily dropping, making decaffeinated coffee one of the fastest-declining categories in the supermarket.[4] Industry observers note that many consumers are disappointed with the flavor of decaffeinated coffees and have opted to give up coffee entirely. Demand for better-tasting coffees has also hurt the instant coffee market, with sales of instant coffee declining as well. While the instant coffee technology impressed consumers following its introduction in 1939, younger coffee consumers appear to be spurning instants.

Growth of the Gourmet Segment

14   The more faithful coffee drinkers have turned to the gourmet decaffeinated coffees, specialty flavors, and whole-bean coffees. According to the Specialty Coffee Association of America (SCAA), the gourmet coffee segment grew by more than 30 percent each year for the past three years. The SCAA predicts that by 1999 specialty coffee will capture about 30 percent of the market (up from 17 percent in 1988) for combined retail sales of $5 billion. Also by 1999, the number of espresso bars and cafés is expected to grow to more than 10,000, up from 4,500 in 1994 and 1,000 in 1989.

15   Sales of specialty coffee have climbed steadily. For instance, in 1969 the retail sales volume of specialty coffee totaled just under $45 million. However, sales grew to more than $2.0 billion in 1994. During 1994, the specialty coffee segment represented about 19 percent of all coffee sold. This figure was up from 10 percent in 1983. However, by 1996 about 30 percent of all coffee drinkers consumed specialty coffees. This amounted to a customer base of approximately 35 million people in the United States. Today, specialty coffees such as espressos and lattes have become so popular that they are being offered in drive-through cafés and coffee stands throughout many parts of the United States.[5]

16   Some analysts attribute the explosive growth in specialty coffees to the poor economy. They note that as people scale back in other areas, they still need their "minor" indulgences. Although many people cannot afford a luxury car, they can still afford a luxury coffee.[6] Despite this growth, some analysts anticipate trouble on the horizon for the specialty coffee business. As evidence, they cite several indicators. For instance:

- In many markets some of the smaller coffee houses have closed due to excessive competition.
- In Los Angeles, the city council (in response to complaints about rowdy late-night patrons) was considering an ordinance that would require coffee houses open past midnight to obtain a license. This move, suggest analysts, is a sign that the coffee business is maturing.
- The cost of coffee beans is expected to rise in the near future, tightening margins for coffee merchants. Coffee farmers are switching to more profitable fruit and vegetable crops, reducing the world's supply of coffee beans.

Competition for the Gourmet Segment

17   Starbucks faces two main competitive arenas: retail beverage and coffee beans. Starbucks whole-bean coffees compete directly against specialty coffees sold at retail through supermarkets, specialty retailers, and a growing number of specialty coffee stores. According to senior executives at Starbucks, supermarkets pose the greatest competitive challenge in the whole-bean coffee market, in part because supermarkets offer customers the convenience of not having to make a separate trip to "a Starbucks' store." A number of nationwide coffee manufacturers, such as Kraft General Foods, Procter & Gamble, and Nestlé, are distributing premium coffee products in supermarkets, and these

EXHIBIT 4A
U.S. Consumption of Coffee and Other Beverages

	1985	1986	1987	1988	1989	1990	1991	1992	1993	1994	1995
Total Coffee	1.83	1.74	1.76	1.67	1.75	1.73	1.75	na	1.87	na	1.67
By Sex:											
Male	1.91	1.80	1.89	1.86	1.85	1.86	1.92	na	2.11	na	1.81
Female	1.76	1.68	1.64	1.50	1.66	1.60	1.59	na	1.64	na	1.54
By Age:											
10–19 years	0.12	0.09	0.11	0.14	0.11	0.16	0.12	na	0.15	na	0.16
20–29 years	1.24	1.06	0.99	0.94	0.99	0.96	0.83	na	0.89	na	0.69
30–59 years	2.65	2.43	2.56	2.35	2.46	2.34	2.40	na	2.62	na	2.35
60 plus	2.20	2.40	2.18	2.17	2.30	2.32	2.44	na	2.38	na	2.11

Source: National Coffee Association of U.S.A., 1995 Report.
na = not available.

EXHIBIT 4B
U.S. Specialty Coffee Consumption

% of the Population Drinking:	1993	1995	Male*	Female*
Espresso	0.6%	0.9%	0.9%	0.9%
Cappuccino	1.1	1.2	0.7	1.6
Latte	0.5	0.4	0.3	0.5

Source: National Coffee Association of U.S.A., 1995 Report.
*Based on 1995 figures.

EXHIBIT 4C
U.S. Consumption in Gallons

	1990	1991	1992	1993	1994E	1995P
Soft Drinks	47.6	47.8	48	49	50.6	51
Coffee*	26.2	26.6	26.5	25.4	23.4	21.2
Beer	24	23.3	23	22.9	22.6	22.5
Milk	19.4	19.4	19.1	18.9	18.9	18.8
Tea*	7	6.7	6.8	6.9	7.1	7.4
Bottled Water	8	8	8.2	8.8	9.2	9.6
Juices	7.1	7.6	7.1	7	7	7
Powdered Drinks	5.7	5.9	5.8	5.5	5.4	5.3
Wine**	2	1.9	2	1.7	1.7	1.6
Distilled Spirits	1.5	1.4	1.3	1.3	1.3	1.3
Total	148.5	148.6	147.8	147.4	147.2	145.7

Source: John C. Maxwell Jr., *Beverage Industry, Annual Manual* 1995/1997.
*Coffee and tea data are based on a three-year moving average to counterbalance inventory swings, thereby portraying consumption more realistically.
P = Projected, E = Estimates.

products serve as substitutes for Starbucks' coffees. Additionally, regional specialty coffee companies also sell whole-bean coffees in supermarkets.

18   Starbucks' coffee beverages compete directly against all restaurant and beverage outlets that serve coffee and a growing number of espresso stands, carts, and stores. Both the company's whole-bean coffees and its coffee beverages compete indirectly against all other coffees on the market. Starbucks' management believes that its customers choose among retailers primarily on the basis of quality and convenience and, to a lesser extent, on price.

19   Starbucks competes for whole-bean coffee sales with franchise operators and independent specialty coffee stores in both the United States and Canada. There are a number of competing specialty coffee retailers. One specialty coffee retailer that has grown to considerable size is Second Cup, a Canadian franchiser with stores primarily in Canada. In 1996 there were 235 Second Cup stores in Canada. Second Cup also owns Gloria Jean's Coffee Bean and Brother's Gourmet, both franchisers of specialty coffee stores that are primarily located in malls in the United States. Gloria Jean's founded in 1979, operated 249 retail stores with about $125 million in annual sales in 1996. Brother's Gourmet is a Florida-based coffee chain with almost 250 franchisee-owned locations in the Chicago area.

20   Seattle's Best Coffee (SBC) competes fiercely with Starbucks on Starbucks' own turf, Seattle. This firm is following Starbucks' lead in national expansion. However, unlike Starbucks, SBC sells franchise rights to its stores in order to expand rapidly with limited capital. SBC takes advantage of Starbucks' market presence by waiting for Starbucks to invest in consumer education. Then, once customers are familiar with the concept of gourmet coffees, SBC enters that market. In following this approach, the firm has had an easier time finding franchisees. SBC intends to operate 500 stores by 1999.

21   Starbucks also competes with established suppliers in its specialty sales and direct-response (mail-order) businesses, many of which have greater financial and marketing resources than Starbucks. Lately, competition for suitable sites to locate stores has also become intense. Starbucks competes against restaurants, specialty coffee stores, other stores offering coffee stands within them (e.g., bookstores, clothing retailers, kitchenware retailers) and even espresso carts for attractive locations. In many metropolitan areas, a single square block may have four or five different coffee beverage stores. This level of competition prompted Brother's Gourmet Coffee to abandon its 1995 expansion plans after it determined that the market was almost saturated and that Starbucks was already in all of their markets. Finally, the firm also competes for qualified personnel to operate its retail stores.

THE STARBUCKS LEGACY

22   In establishing Starbucks' unique approach to competition, Schultz had four companies in mind as role models: Nordstrom, Home Depot, Microsoft, and Ben & Jerry's. Nordstrom, a national chain of upscale department stores based in Seattle, provided a role model for service and is part of the reason that each employee must receive at least 24 hours of training. Home Depot, the home improvement chain, was Schultz's guideline for managing high growth. Microsoft gave Schultz the inspiration for employee ownership, resulting in Starbucks' innovative Bean Stock Plan. And Ben & Jerry's was his role model for philanthropy; Starbucks sponsors community festivals, donates money to CARE for health and literacy programs in coffee-growing countries, and donates to charity any packages of coffee beans that have been open a week.

23   Schultz's goal is to "Establish Starbucks as the premier purveyor of the finest coffee in the world while maintaining uncompromising principles as we grow." He has since articulated six guiding principles to measure the appropriateness of the firm's decisions (see Exhibit 5).

Securing the Finest Raw Materials

24   Starbucks' coffee quality begins with bean procurement. Although many Americans were raised on a commodity-like coffee composed of Arabica beans mixed with less-expensive filler beans, Starbucks coffee is strictly Arabica, and the company ensures that only the highest-quality beans are used. Dave Olsen, the company's senior vice president and chief coffee procurer, scours mountain trails in

EXHIBIT 5
Starbucks' Mission Statement and Guiding Principles

Mission Statement:

Establish Starbucks as the premier purveyor of the finest coffee in the world while maintaining our uncompromising principles as we grow.

Guiding Principles:

- Provide a great work environment and treat each other with respect and dignity.
- Embrace diversity as an essential component in the way we do business.
- Apply the highest standards of excellence to the purchasing, roasting and fresh delivery of our coffee.
- Develop enthusiastically satisfied customers all of the time.
- Contribute positively to our communities and our environment.
- Recognize that profitability is essential to our future success.

Indonesia, Kenya, Guatemala, and elsewhere in search of Starbucks' premium bean. His standards are demanding and he conducts exacting experiments in order to get the proper balance of flavor, body, and acidity. He tests the coffees by "cupping" them—a process similar to wine tasting that involves inhaling the steam ("the strike" and "breaking the crust"), tasting the coffee, and spitting it out ("aspirating" and "expectorating").[7]

25   From the company's inception, it has worked on developing relationships with the countries from which it buys coffee beans. Traditionally, most of the premium coffee beans were bought by Europeans and Japanese. Olsen has sometimes had to convince coffee growers that it is worth growing premium coffees—especially since American coffee buyers are notorious purchasers of the "dregs" of the coffee beans. In 1992 Starbucks set a new precedent by outbidding European buyers for the exclusive Narino Supremo bean crop.[8] Starbucks collaborated with a mill in the tiny town of Pasto, located on the side of the Volcano Galero. There they set up a special operation to single out the particular Narino Supremo bean, and Starbucks guaranteed to purchase the entire yield. This enabled Starbucks to be the exclusive purveyor of Narino Supremo, purportedly one of the best coffees in the world.[9]

Vertical Integration

26   Roasting of the coffee bean is close to an art form at Starbucks. The company currently operates three roasting and distribution facilities: two in the Seattle area, and one in East Manchester Township, York County, Pennsylvania. In the Seattle area, the company leases approximately 92,000 square feet in one building located in Seattle, Washington, and owns an additional roasting plant and distribution facility of approximately 305,000 square feet in Kent, Washington.

27   Roasters are promoted from within the company and trained for over a year, and it is considered quite an honor to be chosen. The coffee is roasted in a powerful gas-fired drum roaster for 12 to 15 minutes while roasters use their sight, smell, hearing, and computers to judge when beans are perfectly done. The color of the beans is even tested in an Agtron blood-cell analyzer, with the whole batch being discarded if the sample is not deemed perfect.

The Starbucks Experience

28   According to Schultz, "We're not just selling a cup of coffee, we are providing an experience." As Americans reduce their alcohol consumption, Schultz hopes to make coffee bars their new destination. In order to create American coffee enthusiasts with the dedication of their Italian counterparts, Starbucks provides a seductive atmosphere in which to imbibe. Its stores are distinctive and sleek, yet comfortable. Though the size of the stores and their formats vary from small to full-size restaurants, most are modeled after the Italian coffee bars where regulars sit and drink espresso with their friends.

29   Starbucks' stores tend to be located in high-traffic locations such as malls, busy street corners, and even grocery stores. They are well lighted and feature plenty of light cherry wood. Further, sophisticated artwork hangs on the walls. The people who prepare the coffee are referred to as *baristas,* Italian for bartender. And jazz or opera music plays softly in the background. The stores range from 200 to 4,000 square feet, with new units tending to range from 1,500 to 1,700 square feet. In 1995, the average cost of opening a new unit (including equipment, inventory, and leasehold improvements) was about $377,000. The firm employs a staff of over 100 people whose job is to plan, design, and build the unique interiors and displays. The Starbucks' interiors have inspired a slew of imitators.

30   Location choices so far have been easy; Starbucks opens its cafés in those cities where their direct-mail business is strong. By tracking addresses of mail-order customers to find the highest concentration in a city, Starbucks can ensure that its new stores have a ready audience. Although this would normally imply cannibalizing their mail-order sales, mail-order revenues have continued to increase.

31   The packaging of the firm's products is also distinctive. In addition to prepared Italian beverages such as lattes, mochas, and cappuccinos, the retail outlets/restaurants offer coffee by the pound, specialty mugs, and home espresso-making machines. *Biscotti* are available in glass jars on the counter. Many of the firm's stores offer light lunch fare including sandwiches and salads, and an assortment of pastries, bottled waters, and juices. Notes George Reynolds, a former senior vice president for marketing, Starbucks' "goal is to make a powerful aesthetic statement about the quality and integrity of their products, reaffirming through their visual identity the commitment they feel to providing the very best product and service for customers."

32   The company has also developed unique strategies for its products in new markets; for instance, for its passport promotion, customers receive a frequent buyer bonus stamp in their "passport" every time they purchase a half-pound of coffee. Each time a customer buys a different coffee, Starbucks also validates their "World Coffee Tour." Once a customer has collected 10 stamps, he or she receives a free half-pound of coffee. The passport also contains explanations of each type of coffee bean and its country of origin.

33   Despite the attention to store environment and coffee quality, Starbucks' effort at bringing a premium coffee and Italian-style beverage experience to the American market could have been lost on consumers had the company not invested in consumer education. Starbucks' employees spend a good portion of their time instructing customers on Starbucks' global selection of coffee and the different processes by which the beverages are produced. Employees are also encouraged to help customers make decisions about beans, grind, and coffee/espresso machines and to instruct customers on home brewing. Starbucks' consumer education is credited with defining the American espresso market, paving the way for other coffee competitors.[10]

Building a Unique Culture

34   While Starbucks enforces almost fanatical standards about coffee quality and service, the policy at Starbucks toward employees is laid back and supportive. They are encouraged to think of themselves as partners in the business. Schultz believes that happy employees are the key to competitiveness and growth:

> We can't achieve our strategic objectives without a work force of people who are immersed in the same commitment as management. Our only sustainable advantage is the quality of our work force. We're building a national retail company by creating pride in—and a stake in—the outcome of our labor.[11]

35   Schultz is also known for his sensitivity to the well-being of employees. Recently when an employee told Schultz that he had AIDS, Schultz reassured him that he could work as long as he wanted, and when he left, the firm would continue his health insurance. After the employee left the room, Schultz reportedly sat down and wept. He attributes such concern for employees to memories of his father:

> My father struggled a great deal and never made more than $20,000 a year, and his work was never valued, emotionally or physically, by his employer. . . . This was an injustice. . . . I want our employees to know we value them.

36   A recent article on the firm in *Fortune* points out:

> Starbucks has instituted all sorts of mechanisms for its Gen-Xers to communicate with headquarters: E-mail, suggestion cards, regular forums. And it acts quickly on issues that are supposedly important to young kids today, like using recycling bins and improving living conditions in coffee-growing countries. To determine the extent to which Starbucks has truly identified and addressed the inner needs of twentysomethings would require several years and a doctorate. But anecdotally, the company appears to be right on the money.[12]

37   On a practical level, Starbucks promotes an empowered employee culture through employee training, employee benefits programs, and an employee stock ownership plan.

Employee Training

38   Each employee must have at least 24 hours of training. Notes *Fortune:*

> Not unlike the cultural blitz of personal computing, Starbucks has created one of the great marketing stories of recent history, and it's just getting started. The company manages to imprint its obsession with customer service on 20,000 milk-steaming, shot-pulling employees. It turns tattooed kids into managers of $800,000-a-year cafés. It successfully replicates a perfectly creamy caffe latte in stores from Seattle to St. Paul. There is some science involved, and one of its primary labs happens to be Starbucks' employee training program.[13]

39   Classes cover everything from coffee history to a seven-hour workshop called "Brewing the Perfect Cup at Home." This workshop is one of five classes that all employees (called partners) must complete during their first six weeks with the company. This workshop focuses on the need to educate the customer in proper coffeemaking techniques.

40   Store managers (who have gone through facilitation workshops and are certified by the company as trainers) teach the classes. The classes teach the employees to make decisions that will enhance customer satisfaction without requiring manager authorization. For example, if a customer comes into the store complaining about how the beans were ground, the employee is authorized to replace them on the spot. While most restaurants use on-the-job training, Starbucks holds bar classes where employees practice taking orders and preparing beverages in a company training room. This allows employees to hone their skills in a low-stress environment, and also protects Starbucks' quality image by allowing only experienced baristas to serve customers.[14] Reports *Fortune:*

> It's silly, soft-headed stuff, though basically, of course, it's true. Maybe some of it sinks in. Starbucks is a smashing success, thanks in large part to the people who come out of these therapy-like training programs. Annual barista turnover at the company is 60% compared with 140% for hourly workers in the fast-food business. "I don't have a negative thing to say," says Kim Sigelman, who manages the store in Emeryville, California, of her four years with the company. She seems to mean it.[15]

Employee Benefits

41   Starbucks offers its benefits package to both part-time and full-time employees with dependent coverage available. Dependent coverage is also extended to same-sex partners. The package includes medical, dental, vision, and short-term disability insurance, as well as paid vacation, paid holidays, mental health/chemical dependency benefits, an employee assistance program, a 401k savings plan, and a stock option plan. The firm also offers career counseling and product discounts.[16]

42   Schultz believes that without these benefits, people do not feel financially or spiritually tied to their jobs. He argues that stock options and the complete benefits package increase employee loyalty and encourage attentive service to the customer.[17] Notes Bradley Honeycutt, the company's vice president, human resource services and international: "[Our] part-timers are on the front line with our customers. If we treat them right, we feel they will treat (the customers) well."[18] Sharon Elliot, human resources senior vice president, offers another explanation, "Most importantly, this is the right thing to do. It's a basic operating philosophy of our organization."

43   Despite the increased coverage, Starbucks' health care costs are well within the national average, running around $150 per employee per month. This may be due, in part, to the fact that its employees are relatively young, resulting in lower claims. Half of the management at Starbucks is under 50, and retail employees tend to be much younger. Starbucks is betting on the increases in premiums being largely offset by lower training costs due to the lower attrition rate. Comments *Fortune;*

> It has become boilerplate public relations for corporations to boast about how much they value their people. But Starbucks really does treat its partners astonishingly well. The pay—between $6 and $8 an hour—is better than that of most entry-level food service jobs. The company offers health insurance to all employees, even part-timers. . . . Walk into just about any Starbucks, and you'll see that these are fairly soft hands: Some 80% of the partners are white, 85% have some college education beyond high school and the average age is 26.

The Bean Stock Plan

44   Employee turnover is also discouraged by Starbucks' stock option plan, known as the Bean Stock Plan. Implemented in August of 1991, the plan made Starbucks the only private company to offer stock options unilaterally to all employees. After one year, employees may join a 401k plan. There is a vesting period of five years; it starts one year after the option is granted, then vests the employee at 20 percent every year. In addition, every employee receives a new stock-option award each year and a new vesting period begins. This plan required getting an exemption from the Securities and Exchange Commission, since any company with more than 500 shareholders has to report its financial performance publicly—a costly process that reveals valuable information to competitors.

45   The option plan did not go uncontested by the venture capitalists and shareholders on the board. Craig Foley, a director and managing partner of Chancellor Capital Management Inc. (the largest shareholder before the public offering), noted that, "Increasing the shareholders substantially dilutes our interest. We take that very seriously." In the end he and others were won over by a study conducted by the company that revealed the positive relationship between employee ownership and productivity rates, and a scenario analysis of how many employees would be vested. Foley conceded: "The grants are tied to overachieving. If you just come to work and do your job, that isn't as attractive as if you beat the numbers."[19]

46   Since the Bean Stock Plan was put into place, enthusiastic employees have been suggesting ways to save money and increase productivity. The strong company culture has also served as a levy against pilferage: Starbucks' inventory shrinkage is less than half of 1 percent.

47   In 1995, Starbucks demonstrated that its concern for employee welfare extended beyond U.S. borders. After a human rights group leafleted the stores complaining that Guatemalan coffee pickers received less than $3 a day, Starbucks became the first agricultural commodity importer to implement a code for minimal working conditions and pay for foreign subcontractors.[20] The company's guidelines call for overseas suppliers to pay wages and benefits that "address the basic needs of workers and their families" and to only allow child labor when it does not interrupt required education.[21] This move has set a precedent for other importers of agricultural commodities.

Leveraging the Brand

Multiple Channels of Distribution

48   While Starbucks has resisted offering its coffee in grocery stores, it has found a variety of other distribution channels for its products. Besides its stand-alone stores, Starbucks has set up cafés and carts in hospitals, banks, office buildings, supermarkets, and shopping centers. In 1992, Starbucks signed a deal with Nordstrom to serve Starbucks coffee exclusively in all of its stores. Nordstrom also named Starbucks as the exclusive coffee supplier for its restaurants, employee lunchrooms, and catering operations. As of 1992, Nordstrom was operating 62 restaurants and 48 espresso bars. A year later, Barnes & Noble initiated an agreement with Starbucks to implement a "café-in-a-bookshop" plan.

49   Other distribution agreements have included office coffee suppliers, hotels, and airlines. Office coffee is a large segment of the coffee market. Associated Services (an office coffee supplier) provides Starbucks coffee exclusively to the 5,000 northern California businesses it services. Sheraton Hotel has also signed an agreement to serve Starbucks coffee. In 1995, Starbucks signed a deal with United Airlines to provide Starbucks coffee to United's nearly 75 million passengers a year.[22]

50   While Starbucks is the largest and best-known of the coffee-house chains and its presence is very apparent in metropolitan areas, the firm's estimates indicate that only 1 percent of the U.S. population has tried its products. Through these distribution agreements and the new product partnerships it is establishing, Starbucks hopes to capture more of the U.S. market.

Brand Extensions

51   In 1995, Starbucks launched a line of packaged and prepared teas in response to growing demand for tea houses and packaged tea. Tea is a highly profitable beverage for restaurants to sell, costing only 2 to 4 cents a cup to produce.[23]

52   Starbucks coffee is not sold in grocery stores, but its name is making its way onto grocery shelves via a carefully planned series of joint ventures.[24] An agreement with PepsiCo brought a bottled version of Starbucks' Frappuccino (a cold, sweetened coffee drink) to store shelves in August 1996. A similar product released a year before, called Mazagran, was a failure and was pulled from the shelves; however, both Starbucks and PepsiCo had higher hopes for Frappuccino.[25] Starbucks also has an agreement with Washington-based Redhook Ale Brewery to make a product called Double Black Stout, a coffee-flavored stout. In another 50–50 partnership, Dreyers Grand Ice Cream Inc. distributes seven quart-products and two bar-products of Starbucks coffee ice cream.

53   Other company partnerships are designed to form new product associations with coffee. For instance, Starbucks has collaborated with Capitol Records, Inc., to produce two Starbucks jazz CDs, available only in Starbucks stores. Starbucks is also opening tandem units with Bruegger's Bagel Bakeries and bought a minority stake in Noah's New York Bagels in 1995. This minority stake has since been sold.

INTERNATIONAL EXPANSION

54   From the beginning, Schultz has professed a strict growth policy. Although many other coffee houses or espresso bars are franchised, Starbucks owns all of its stores outright with the exception of license agreements in airports.[26] Despite over 300 calls a day from willing investors, Schultz feels it is important to the company's integrity to own its stores. Further, rather than trying to capture all the potential markets as soon as possible, Starbucks goes into a market and tries to completely dominate it before setting its sights on further expansion. As Alstead points out, "Starbucks hopes to achieve the same density in all of its markets that they have achieved in Seattle, Vancouver and Chicago."

55   In 1996, the firm opened 307 stores (including four replacement stores), converted 19 Coffee Connection stores to Starbucks, and closed one store. In 1997, Starbucks intends to open at least 325 new stores and enter at least three major new markets in North America including Phoenix, Arizona, and Miami, Florida. Moreover, Schultz plans to have 2,000 stores by the year 2000.

56   Some analysts believe that the U.S. coffee bar market may be reaching saturation. They point to the fact that there have been some consolidations as bigger players snap up some of the smaller coffee bar competitors.[27] Further, they note that Starbucks' store base is also maturing, leading to a slowdown in the growth of unit volume and firm profitability. Higher coffee costs have also cut into margins, intensifying the competition in what has now become a crowded market. Recognizing this, Starbucks has turned its attention to foreign markets for continued growth. Notes Schultz, "We are looking at the Asia-Pacific region as the focus of our international business."

Expansion into Asian Markets

57   In 1996, Starbucks invested $1.5 million and established a subsidiary called Starbucks Coffee International, Inc. The focus of this subsidiary will be on penetrating the Asia-Pacific region. According to Kathie Lindemann, the director of international operations at Starbucks:

We are not overlooking Europe and South America as areas for future expansion. But, we feel that expanding into these regions is more risky than Asia. The Asia-Pacific region we feel has much more potential for us. It is full of emerging markets. Also consumers' disposable income is increasing as their countries' economies grow. Most important of all, people in these countries are open to Western lifestyles.

58   This international subsidiary consists of 12 managers located primarily in Seattle, Washington. Together these managers are responsible for developing new businesses internationally, financing and planning of international stores, managing international operations and logistics, merchandising in international markets and, finally, training and developing of Starbucks' international managers. Since its establishment, this subsidiary has been responsible for opening Starbucks' coffee houses in Hawaii, Japan, and Singapore.[28]

59   Lindemann, commenting on Starbucks' approach to Asian markets, notes:

At Starbucks we don't like the concept of franchising. Therefore, we decided to work with partners in Japan and other Asian countries. Our approach to international expansion is to focus on the *partnership first, country second.* Partnership is everything in Asia. We rely on the local connection to get everything up and working. The key is finding the right local partners to negotiate local regulations and other issues.

60   When asked to list the criteria by which Starbucks chose partners in Asia, Lindemann highlighted six points:

We look for partners who share our values, culture, and goals about community development. We are trying to align ourselves with people, or companies, with plenty of experience. We are primarily interested in partners who can guide us through the process of starting up in a foreign location. We look for firms with: (1) similar philosophy to ours in terms of shared values, corporate citizenship, and commitment to be in the business for the long haul, (2) multi-unit restaurant experience, (3) financial resources to expand the Starbucks' concept rapidly to prevent imitators, (4) strong real-estate experience with knowledge about how to pick prime real estate locations, (5) knowledge of the retail market, and (6) the availability of the people to commit to our project.

Entry into Japan

61   In October 1995, Starbucks entered into a joint venture with Tokyo-based Sazaby, Inc. This firm was expected to help Starbucks open 12 new stores in Japan by the end of 1997. This joint venture, amounting to 250 million yen ($2.33 million) in capitalization, is equally owned by Starbucks Coffee International and Sazaby. Sazaby, often recognized as a leader in bringing unique goods to the Japanese, operates upscale retail and restaurant chains throughout Japan. Commenting on this joint venture, the president of Starbucks International, Howard Behar, noted:

This powerful strategic alliance, which combines two major lifestyle companies, will provide the Japanese consumer a new and unique specialty coffee experience. . . . We look at this venture as though we're starting all over again, and in many ways, we are.

62   With Sazaby's assistance, the firm opened two stores in Tokyo in September 1996. The first outlet was in Tokyo's posh Ginza shopping district. The Ginza store was planned so that Japanese customers could have the same "Starbucks experience" offered in U.S. stores. The firm's second store was located in Ochanomizu, a student area cluttered with colleges, bookstores, and fast-food restaurants. Starbucks hopes that students and office workers in the neighborhood will come in for a cup of coffee and a light snack. At both stores, customers can eat in the store or take out their purchases.

63   The food-and-drink menus in the firm's Japanese coffee houses are similar to those in the United States. The firm offers 15 types of beverages, snacks such as cookies and sandwiches, coffee beans, and novelty goods such as coffee mugs and T-shirts. The firm's single-shot-short latte costs 280 yen in Tokyo (about $2.50, a price that is roughly 50 cents more than in the United States). According to an August 1996 industry report, a cup of coffee in Tokyo costs about 399 yen, on average, in August 1996.

64   Although the Japanese are not used to Italian-style coffee beverages, Starbucks' executives believe that Japanese consumers are ready to embrace the Starbucks concept.[29] A report in the

EXHIBIT 6
Japan Consumer Preferences*

	1980	1985	1990	1994
Instant Coffee	57.6%	59.2%	50.6%	45.4%
Regular Coffee	33.3%	29.4%	33.1%	37.4%
Canned Coffee	9.1%	11.4%	13.1%	17.3%
Total (Cups per Week)	7.4	9.02	9.52	10.36
Place of Consumption				
Home	55.8%	58.3%	56.6%	54.7%
Coffee Shop	24.6%	11.6%	8.9%	8.0%
Work/School	15.4%	21.8%	23.9%	26.4%
Other	4.2%	8.3%	10.6%	10.9%

Source: *Tea & Coffee Trade Journal,* August 1955.
*Based on a survey from October 20 through November 7, 1994, by the All Japan Coffee Association. The survey reported that men aged between 25–39 years consumed the most coffee at 16 cups per week and girls between 12–17 years consumed the last at 3 cups.

Wall Street Journal suggests that breaking into the Japanese market may not be easy (see Exhibit 6 and Exhibit 7).

> The Japanese haven't developed a taste for espresso drinks like caffe latte and caffe mocha; they drink a lot of instant coffee or ready-to-drink coffee in cans, as well as American-style hot coffee. Moreover, the Japanese coffee market may be saturated with many coffee shops and vending machines serving hot coffees. Coca-Cola alone has more than 80,000 vending machines that sell canned coffee.[30]

65   Similarly, a report in the *Nikkei Weekly* points out:

> Though Japan is the world's third largest coffee consumer, its coffee shops constitute a declining industry, with high operating costs knocking many small operators out of business. In 1992, there were 115,143 coffee shops in Japan, according to the latest government survey available. That figure is nearly 30% less than the peak in 1982.[31]

66   Japan's coffee culture revolves around the *kissaten,* a relatively formal sit-down coffee house. According to the *All Japan Coffee Association,* while U.S. and German consumers consumed 18.1 and 10 million bags, respectively, of coffee in 1994, the Japanese consumed 6.1 million coffee bags (one bag of coffee contains 60 kilograms of coffee beans).

67   Despite the absolute size of the Japanese coffee market, knowledgeable analysts note that Starbucks is likely to face stiff competition and retaliation from well-established players in Japan. Two of Japan's well-established coffee chains are the Doutor Coffee Company and the Pronto Corp.

68   Started in 1980, Doutor Coffee Company is Japan's leading coffee bar chain. In 1996, it had over 466 shops in and around Tokyo. At times, consumers refer to this firm as the McDonald's of coffee houses since it provides a limited menu and emphasizes self-service. In Doutor's shops, seating is limited and counters are provided where customers can stand while they consume their beverages. The focus is on speed of service and quick turnover of customers. The average customer stay in a Doutor Coffee Shop is about 10 minutes, about one-third the stay in a typical *kissaten.* Close to 90 percent of the Doutor's coffee houses are operated by franchisees, while the remaining 10 percent of the shops are operated directly by Doutor. A standard cup of coffee at Doutor costs 180 yen. The firm serves other refreshments, such as juice, sandwiches, and pastries. It is reported that nearly 10 million customers per month visit Doutor coffee houses. The firm has five shops in Ginza, where Starbucks opened its first store.[32]

EXHIBIT 7
Canned Coffee Sales in Japan (US $ Millions)

	Market Share	1991	1992	1993	1994	1995
Coca-Cola	40%	2,718	2,396	2,635	2,899	3,189
UCC	12	653	718	790	869	965
Pokka	11	599	658	724	797	877
Daido	10	544	599	658	724	797
Nestlé	7	381	419	461	507	558
Others	20	1,089	1,198	1,317	1,449	1,594
Total	100	5,445	6,990	6,589	7,248	7,972

Source: *Advertising Age,* 1996.
Notes: Canned coffee accounts for approximately 40% of total beverage sales in Japan, including soft drinks.

69   Pronto Corp. is Japan's second largest coffee bar chain. The firm opened its first shop in Tokyo in 1987. In 1996, it operated over 95 outlets, most of them in Tokyo. The firm's coffee houses serve coffee and light snacks during the day, and at night they switch to neighborhood bar-type operations, serving alcoholic drinks and light meals. At Pronto, a standard cup of coffee costs 160 yen. Reacting to Starbucks' entry into Japan, Seiji Honna, president of Pronto Corp., notes: For the past few years, we've had this nightmare scenario that espresso drinks are going to swallow up Japan's coffee market. . . . And we won't know how to make a good cup of espresso. . . . [And now Starbucks' entry], if they really mean business, I think they'll probably put some of us out of business.[33]

70   But he goes on to comment:

> I don't think that the opening of the first Starbucks store in Japan would immediately be a threat to our business. . . . But Starbucks could become a strong competitor if it is able to gain consumer recognition in the next three years or so. In order to do so, Starbucks will need to have about 30 to 50 stores in the Tokyo area.[34]

Yuji Tsunoda, president of Starbucks Coffee Japan Ltd., indicates that the company intends to have 100 directly owned coffee bars in major Japanese cities in the next five years.

71   According to Kazuo Sunago, an analyst from Japan's leading advertising firm Dentsu Inc., Japanese coffee bars lack the creativity to stop a firm like Starbucks from making inroads in the Japanese coffee market.

> As traditional mom-and-pop coffee shops die off, big chains are looking for more attractive formats. . . . But they are like a dry lake bed—void of new ideas. That's why the whole industry is stirred up about Starbucks.[35]

72   Comments Alstead: "The issue facing Starbucks is how, as we expand geographically and through expanding channels, will we be able to maintain the Starbucks culture."

NOTES

1. *Success,* April 1993.
2. *Chicago Tribune,* July 1, 1993.
3. According to the *Berkeley Wellness Letter,* a newsletter from the University of California, 53 percent of all coffee in the United States is consumed at breakfast. Further, 11 percent of the U.S. population drink decaf coffee, and 10 percent drink instant coffee. Of the people who drink instant coffee, most are over the age of 55.
4. *Wall Street Journal,* February 25, 1993. According to the National Coffee Association, brewed coffee accounted for 85 percent of all coffee consumed in the United States during 1995. This was followed by espresso-based drinks (14 percent) and express coffee (1 percent).

5. Espresso, despite its potent flavor, is lower in caffeine than the canned coffees offered in supermarkets. It is made with Arabica beans that are lower in caffeine content, and the brewing method yields less caffeine per cup.

6. *Wall Street Journal,* February 25,1993.

7. *Sacramento Bee,* April 28, 1993.

8. This Colombian coffee bean crop is very small and grows only in the high regions of the Cordillera mountain range. For years, the Narino beans were guarded zealously by Western Europeans who prized their colorful and complex flavor. It was usually used for upgrading blends. Starbucks was determined to make them available for the first time as a pure varietal. This required breaking Western Europe's monopoly over the beans by convincing the Colombian growers that it intended to use "the best beans for a higher purpose."

9. *Canada Newswire,* March 1, 1993.

10. Though *Consumer Reports* rated Starbucks coffee as burnt and bitter, Starbucks customers felt otherwise, and most of Starbucks' early growth can be attributed to enthusiastic word-of-mouth advertising. The typical Starbucks customer is highly proficient in the science of coffee beans and brewing techniques. The coffee bars even have their own dialect; executives from downtown Seattle businesses line up in force to order "tall-skinny-double mochas" and "2% short no-foam lattes."

11. *Inc.,* January 1993.

12. *Fortune,* December 9, 1996.

13. *Fortune,* December 9, 1996.

14. *Training,* June 1995.

15. *Fortune,* December 9, 1996.

16. The decision to offer benefits even to part-time employees (who represent roughly two-thirds of Starbucks' 10,000 employees) has gained a great deal of attention in the press. According to a Hewitt Associates L.L.C. survey of more than 500 employers, only 25 percent of employers offer medical coverage to employees working less than 20 hours a week. It was difficult to get insurers to sign Starbucks up since they did not understand why Starbucks would want to cover part-timers.

17. *Inc.,* January 1993.

18. *Business Insurance,* March 27, 1995, p. 6.

19. *Inc.,* January 1993.

20. *Wall Street Journal,* April 4, 1995.

21. *Wall Street Journal,* October 23, 1995.

22. In the past, one interesting outlet for Starbucks coffee was Starbucks' deal with Smith Brothers, one of the Northwest's oldest dairies. Smith Brothers used to sell Starbucks coffee on its home delivery routes. The idea for the alliance actually came from the dairy, a supplier for Starbucks. Management at Smith Brothers began to wonder if Starbucks' rapid growth might prompt the company to look for other dairies to supply its milk. A report in the *Seattle Times* (November 6, 1992) noted that Earl Keller, sales manager for Smith Brothers, got the idea that "Maybe if we were a good customer of theirs, it would be more difficult for them to leave us." In 1992, Smith delivered 1,000 pounds of coffee beans a week. The coffee was sold at the same price as in Starbucks' retail stores, and the only complaint has been that Smith does not carry all 30 varieties. The company no longer sells coffee through Smith Brothers.

23. *Nations Restaurant News,* July 10, 1995.

24. According to Troy Alstead, "We are evaluating whether to offer our coffee in grocery stores, and we have done some private labeling of Starbucks coffee for Costco." The Specialty Coffee Association of America predicts that by 1999 supermarkets will account for 63 percent of all coffee sold in America. This will be followed by gourmet stores (14%), mass market (11%), mail order (8.0%) and other (8%).

25. Coke and Nestlé have signed a similar agreement to produce single-serving cold coffee drinks in specialty flavors such as french vanilla, mocha, and café au lait to compete with the Starbucks product.

26. Airports often grant exclusive concessions contracts to a single provider, such as Host Marriott. Because Starbucks wanted to tap these markets, it negotiated licensing arrangements with Marriott to run Starbucks stands in the airports that Marriott has under contract.

27. *Washington Post,* August 1, 1995.

28. The Hawaii entry is based on a joint venture with The MacNaugton Group, a real estate development firm that has been responsible for the successful introduction of several well-known mainland firms such as Sports Authority, Office Max, and Eagle Hardware stores into the Hawaiian Islands. Using this joint venture, the firm plans to develop approximately 30 stores throughout the Hawaiian Islands over the next three to four years. Starbucks' entry into Singapore is based on a licensing agreement with Bonvests Holdings Limited, a firm involved in property and hotel development, investment, related management services, waste management and building maintenance services, food and beverage retailing and marketing of branded luxury products in Singapore. Under this agreement (completed in December 1996), ten Starbucks coffee stores are expected to open within the first 12 to 15 months.

29. *Puget Sound Business Journal,* June 21–27, 1996.
30. *Wall Street Journal,* September 4, 1996.
31. *Nikkei Weekly,* September 23, 1996.
32. According to a report in the *Nihon Keizai Shimbum* (June 18, 1988), Doutor is good at segmenting the coffee market. For instance, the firm has a coffee shop for just about every taste and service level. The low-end shops are located near train stations and busy areas where people are in a hurry. In residential locations, the firm operates Café Colorado where people can sit and chat for a while. The price of coffee in Café Colorado is double that of the firm's inexpensive coffee houses. The firm also caters to more upscale customers via Café Doutor, where the ambiance is more elegant and the coffee price is much higher.
33. According to a report in the *Wall Street Journal,* Honna spent time last year gathering intelligence on Starbucks' method in the United States. He reportedly visited, incognito, more than 20 Starbucks coffee shops along the West Coast.
34. Reuters World Service, August 1, 1996.
35. *Wall Street Journal,* September 4, 1996.

APPENDIX A: STARBUCKS CORPORATION—A BRIEF HISTORY

1971 Starbucks Coffee opens its first store in the Pike Place Market—Seattle, Washington's legendary, open-air farmer's market.

1982 Howard Schultz joins Starbucks as director of retail operations and marketing. Starbucks begins providing coffee to fine restaurants and espresso bars in Seattle.

1983 Schultz travels to Italy, where he's impressed with the popularity of espresso bars. Milan, a city the size of Philadelphia, hosts 1,500 of these bars.

1984 Schultz convinces the original founders of Starbucks to test the coffee bar concept in a new Starbucks store on the corner of 4th and Spring in downtown Seattle. Overwhelmingly successful, this experiment is the genesis for a company that Schultz will found in 1985.

1985 Schultz founds Il Giornale, offering brewed coffee and espresso beverages made from Starbucks coffee beans.

1987 In August, with the backing of local investors, Il Gironale acquires the Seattle assets of Starbucks and changes its name to Starbucks Corporation. The company has fewer than 100 employees and opens its first stores in Chicago and Vancouver, B.C. **Starbucks store total = 17**

1988 Starbucks introduces mail-order catalog, offering mail-order service in all 50 states. **Starbucks store total = 33**

1989 Opens first Portland, Oregon, store in Pioneer Courthouse Square. **Starbucks store total = 55**

1990 Starbucks expands corporate headquarters in Seattle and builds a new roasting plant. **Starbucks store total = 84**

1991 Starbucks opens first stores in Los Angeles, California. Announces Starbucks' commitment to establish a long-term relationship with CARE, the international relief and development organization, and introduces CARE coffee sampler.

Becomes the first U.S. privately owned company in history to offer a stock option program, Bean Stock, that included part-time employees. **Starbucks store total = 116**

1992 Starbucks opens first stores in San Francisco, San Diego, Orange County, and Denver. Specialty Sales and Marketing Division awarded Nordstrom's national coffee account. Completes initial public offering, with common stock being traded on the NASDAQ National Market System. **Starbucks store total = 165**

1993 Opens premier East Coast market: Washington, D.C., Specialty Sales and Marketing Division begins relationship with Barnes & Noble, Inc., as national account. Opens second roasting plant located in Kent, Washington. **Starbucks store total = 275**

1994 Opens first stores in Minneapolis, Boston, New York, Atlanta, Dallas, and Houston. Specialty Sales and Marketing Division awarded ITT/Sheraton Hotel's national coffee account.

The Coffee Connection, Inc., becomes wholly owned subsidiary of Starbucks Corporation in June.

Starbucks announces partnership with Pepsi-Cola to develop ready-to-drink coffee-based beverages.

Completes offering of additional 6,025,000 shares of common stock at $28.50 per share.

Schultz receives Business Enterprise Trust Award recognizing the company's innovative benefits plan. **Starbucks store total = 425**

1995 Starbucks opens first stores in Pittsburgh, Las Vegas, San Antonio, Philadelphia, Cincinnati, Baltimore, and Austin. Specialty Sales and Marketing Division begins relationship with United Airlines.

Starbucks and Redhook Ale Brewery introduced Double BLACK™ STOUT, a new dark roasted malt beer with the aromatic and flavorful addition of coffee.

Acquires minority interest in Noah's New York Bagels, Inc.

Starbucks stores begin serving Frappuccino® blended beverages, a line of low-fat, creamy, iced coffee beverages.

Starbucks opens state-of-the-art roasting facility in York, Pennsylvania, serving East Coast markets.

Announces alliance with Chapters Inc. to operate coffee bars inside Chapters' superstores in Canada.

Announces partnership with Star Markets to open Starbucks retail locations within Star Market stores.

Develops framework for a code of conduct as part of a long-term strategy to improve conditions in coffee origin countries.

Starbucks Coffee International signs agreement with Sazaby, Inc., a Japanese retailer and restaurateur, to form a joint venture partnership that will develop Starbucks retail stores in Japan. The joint venture is called Starbucks Coffee Japan, Ltd.

Forms long-term joint venture with Dreyer's Grand Ice Cream, to develop revolutionary line of coffee ice creams. **Starbucks store total = 676**

1996 Opens first stores in Rhode Island, Idaho, North Carolina, Arizona, Utah, and Toronto, Ontario. Specialty Sales and Marketing Division awarded Westin Hotel's national coffee account.

Starbucks Coffee Japan, Ltd. opens first location outside North America in the Ginza District, Tokyo, Japan. Announces plans to develop 10 to 12 additional stores in the Tokyo metropolitan area over the next 18 months.

Starbucks Coffee International signs agreement forming Coffee Partners Hawaii, which will develop Starbucks retail locations in Hawaii.

First Starbucks store in Honolulu opens at Kalala Mall.

Starbucks Coffee International signs licensing agreement with Bonstar Ptc. Ltd. to open stores in Singapore.

First licensed Singapore location opens in Liat Towers.

Direct Response Division reaches over seven million American Online (AOL) customers through Caffé Starbucks, a marketplace channel store that offers select Starbucks catalog products.

Announces that all Coffee Connection locations in the Boston area will become Starbucks stores during fiscal 1996.

Announces development agreement with three leading digital media companies—Digital Brands, Inc., Watts-Silverstein & Associates and Cyberstruction, Inc.—to develop a wide-ranging online strategy.

Unveils prototype store at Comdex Convention and Trade Show, Las Vegas, with Intel Corp., showcasing some of the technologies Starbucks will be testing in several stores over the next year.

Forms licensing arrangement with ARAMARK Corp. to put licensed Starbucks operators at various locations operated by ARAMARK.

Starbucks and Dreyer's Grand Ice Cream, Inc., introduce six flavors of Starbucks™ ice cream and Starbucks ice cream bars, available in grocery stores across the United States. Starbucks ice cream quickly becomes the number-one brand of coffee ice cream in the United States.

North American Coffee Partnership (between Starbucks and Pepsi-Cola Company) announces a bottled version of Starbucks popular Frappuccino™ blended beverage will be sold in supermarkets, convenience stores, and other retail points of distribution on the West Coast.

Starbucks commemorates the first anniversary of the Blue Note Blend coffee and CD with Blue Note 2, an encore collection of jazz from the Blue Note® Records label. The Blue Note Blend coffee also returns for a limited engagement in the company's coffee lineup.

Celebrates the company's 25th Anniversary with marketing program featuring the art, music, and culture of 1971, the year Starbucks was born. **Current Starbucks store total = 1,100 at year end**

CASE 59

CIRCUS CIRCUS ENTERPRISES, INC.

We possess the resources to accomplish the big projects: the know-how, the financial power and the places to invest. The renovation of our existing projects will soon be behind us, which last year represented the broadest scope of construction ever taken on by a gaming company. Now we are well-positioned to originate new projects. Getting big projects right is the route to future wealth in gaming; big successful projects tend to prove long staying power in our business. When the counting is over, we think our customers and investors will hold the winning hand.

Annual Report, 1997

1   Big projects and a winning hand. Circus Circus does seem to have both. And big projects they are, with huge pink and white striped concrete circus tents, a 600 foot long river boat replica, a giant castle, and a great pyramid. Their latest project, Mandalay Bay, will include a 3,700 room hotel/casino, an 11-acre aquatic environment with beaches, a snorkeling reef, and a swim-up shark exhibit.

2   Circus Circus Enterprises, Inc. (hereafter Circus) describes itself as in the business of entertainment, and has been one of the innovators in the theme resort concept popular in casino gaming. Their areas of operation are the glitzy vacation and convention Meccas of Las Vegas, Reno, and Laughlin, Nevada, as well as other locations in the U.S. and abroad. Historically, Circus' marketing of its products has been called "right out of the bargain basement," and has catered to "low rollers." Circus has continued to broaden its market and now aims more at the middle income gambler and family-oriented vacationers as well as the more upscale traveler and player.

3   Circus was purchased in 1974 for $50,000 as a small and unprofitable casino operation by partners William G. Bennett, an aggressive cost-cutter who ran furniture stores before entering the gaming industry in 1965, and William N. Pennington (see Table 1 for Board of Directors and top managers). The partners were able to rejuvenate Circus with fresh marketing, went public with a stock offering in October 1983, and experienced rapid growth and high profitability over time. Within the five year period between 1993–1997 the average return on invested capital was 16.5 percent and Circus had generated over $1 billion in free cash flow. Today, Circus is one of the major players in the Las Vegas, Laughlin, and Reno markets in terms of square footage of casino space and number of hotel rooms—despite the incredible growth in both markets. For the first time in company history, casino gaming operations in 1997 provided slightly less than one half of total revenues and that trend continued into 1998 (see Table 2). On January 31, 1998, Circus reported a net income of approximately $89.9 million on revenues of $1.35 billion. This was down slightly from 1997's more than $100 million net income on revenues of $1.3 billion. During that same year Circus invested over $585.8 million in capital expenditures and another $663.3 million was invested in fiscal year 1998.

CIRCUS CIRCUS OPERATIONS

4   Circus defines entertainment as pure play and fun, and it goes out of the way to see that customers have plenty of opportunities for both. Each Circus location has a distinctive personality. Circus Circus–Las Vegas is the world of the Big Top, where live circus acts perform free every thirty minutes.

This case was prepared by Professors John K. Ross III, Michael J. Keefe, and Bill J. Middlebrook of Southwest Texas State University. The case was prepared for classroom purposes only, and is not designed to show effective or ineffective handling of administrative situations.

TABLE 1
Directors and Officers of Circus Circus Enterprises, Inc.

Name	Age	Title
Directors		
Clyde T. Turner	59	Chairman of the Board and CEO Circus Circus Enterprises
Michael S. Ensign	59	Vice Chairman of the Board and COO Circus Circus Enterprises
Glen Schaeffer	43	President, CFO Circus Circus Enterprises
William A. Richardson	50	Vice Chairman of the Board and Executive Vice President Circus Circus Enterprises
Richard P. Banis	52	Former President and COO Circus Circus Enterprises
Arthur H. Bilger	44	Former President and COO New World Communications Group International
Richard A. Etter	58	Former Chairman and CEO Bank of America–Nevada
William E. Bannen, M.D.	48	Vice President/Chief Medical Officer Blue Cross Blue Shield of Nevada
Donna B. More	40	Partner, Law Firm of Freeborn & Peters
Michael D. McKee	51	Executive Vice President The Irving Company
Officers		
Clyde T. Turner		Chairman of the Board and Chief Executive Officer
Michael S. Ensign		Vice Chairman of the Board and Chief Operating Officer
Glenn Schaeffer		President, Chief Financial Officer and Treasurer
William A. Richardson		Vice Chairman of the Board and Executive Vice President Circus Circus Enterprises
Tony Alamo		Senior Vice President, Operations
Gregg Solomon		Senior Vice President, Operations
Kurt D. Sullivan		Senior Vice President, Operations
Steve Greathouse		Senior Vice President, Operations
Yvett Landau		Vice President, General Counsel and Secretary
Les Martin		Vice President and Chief Accounting Officer

Source: Annual Report 1998; Proxy Statement May 1, 1998.

Kids may cluster around video games while the adults migrate to nickel slot machines and dollar game tables. Located at the north end of the Vegas strip, Circus Circus–Las Vegas sits on 69 acres of land with 3,744 hotel rooms, shopping areas, two specialty restaurants, a buffet with seating for 1,200, fast food shops, cocktail lounges, video arcades, 109,000 square feet of casino space, and the Grand Slam Canyon, a five-acre glass-enclosed theme park including a four-loop roller coaster. Approximately 384 guests may also stay at nearby Circusland RV Park. For the year ending January 31, 1997, $126.7 million was invested in this property for new rooms and remodeling with another $35.2 million in fiscal year 1998.

5   Luxor, an Egyptian-themed hotel and casino complex, opened on October 15, 1993, when 10,000 people entered to play the 2,245 slot and video poker games and 110 table games in the 120,000-square-foot casino in the hotel atrium (reported to be the world's largest). By the end of the opening weekend 40,000 people per day were visiting the 30-story bronze pyramid that encases the hotel and entertainment facilities.

6   Luxor features a 30-story pyramid and two new 22-story hotel towers including 492 suites and is connected to Excalibur by a climate-controlled skyway with moving walkways. Situated at the south end of the Las Vegas strip on a 64-acre site adjacent to Excalibur, Luxor features a food and entertainment area on three different levels beneath the hotel atrium. The pyramid's hotel rooms can be reached from the four corners of the building by state-of-the-art "inclinators" which travel at a 39-degree angle. Parking is available for nearly 3,200 vehicles, including a covered garage, which contains approximately 1,800 spaces.

TABLE 2

CIRCUS CIRCUS ENTERPRISES, INC.

Sources of Revenues as a Percentage of Net Revenues

	1998	1997	1996	1995
Casinos	46.7%	49.2%	51.2%	52.3%
Food & Beverage	15.9	15.8	15.5	16.2
Hotel	24.4	22.0	21.4	19.9
Other	10.5	11.0	12.2	14.2
Unconsolidated	7.3	6.5	3.5	.5
Less: Complimentary Allowances	4.8	4.5	3.8	3.1

Source: Circus Circus 10-K, January 31, 1995–1998.

7   The Luxor underwent major renovations costing $323.3 million during fiscal 1997 and another $116.5 million in fiscal 1998. The resulting complex contains 4,425 hotel rooms, extensively renovated casino space, an additional 20,000 square feet of convention area, an 800-seat buffet, a series of IMAX attractions, five theme restaurants, seven cocktail lounges, and a variety of specialty shops. Circus expects to draw significant walk-in traffic to the newly refurbished Luxor and is one of the principal components of the Masterplan Mile.

8   Located next to the Luxor, Excalibur is one of the first sights travelers see as they exit interstate highway fifteen (management was confident that the sight of a giant, colorful medieval castle would make a lasting impression on mainstream tourists and vacationing families arriving in Las Vegas). Guests cross a drawbridge, with moat, onto a cobblestone walkway where multicolored spires, turrets and battlements loom above. The castle walls are four 28-story hotel towers containing a total of 4,008 rooms. Inside is a medieval world complete with a Fantasy Faire inhabited by strolling jugglers, fire eaters and acrobats, as well as a Royal Village complete with peasants, serfs, and ladies-in-waiting around medieval theme shops. The 110,000-square-foot casino encompasses 2,442 slot machines, more than 89 game tables, a sports book, and a poker and keno area. There are twelve restaurants, capable of feeding more than 20,000 people daily, and a 1000-seat amphitheater. Excalibur, which opened in June 1990, was built for $294 million and primarily financed with internally generated funds. In the year ending January 31, 1997, Excalibur contributed 23 percent of the organization's revenues, down from 33 percent in 1993. Yet 1997 was a record year, generating the company's highest margins and over $100 million in operating cash flow. In fiscal 1998 Excalibur underwent $25.1 million in renovations and was connected to the Luxor by enclosed, moving walkways.

9   Situated between the two anchors on the Las Vegas strip are two smaller casinos owned and operated by Circus. The Silver City Casino and Slots-A-Fun primarily depend on the foot traffic along the strip for their gambling patrons. Combined, they offer more than 1,202 slot machines and 46 gaming tables on 34,900 square feet of casino floor.

10   Circus owns and operates ten properties in Nevada and one in Mississippi and has a 50 percent ownership in three others (see Table 3).

11   All of Circus' operations do well in the city of Las Vegas. However, Circus Circus 1997 operational earnings for the Luxor and Circus Circus–Las Vegas were off 38 percent from the previous year. Management credits the disruption in services due to renovations for this decline.

12   However, Circus' combined hotel room occupancy rates had remained above 90 percent due, in part, to low room rates ($45 to $69 at Circus Circus–Las Vegas) and popular buffets. Each of the major properties contain large, inexpensive buffets that management believes make staying with Circus more attractive. Yet, recently results show a room occupancy rate of 87.5 percent, due in part to the building boom in Las Vegas.

13   The company's other big-top facility is Circus Circus–Reno. With the addition of Skyway Tower in 1985, this big top now offers a total of 1,605 hotel rooms, 60,600 square feet of casino, a buffet that can seat 700 people, shops, video arcades, cocktail lounges, midway games, and circus acts. Circus–Reno had several marginal years, but has become one of the leaders in the Reno market. Circus anticipates

TABLE 3

CIRCUS CIRCUS ENTERPRISES, INC.
Properties and Percent of Total Revenues

Properties	Percent Revenues			
	1998	1997	1996	1995
Las Vegas				
Circus Circus–Las Vegas	25[1]	24[1]	27[1]	29[1]
Excalibur	21	23	23	25
Luxor	23	17	20	24
Slots-A-Fun and Silver City				
Reno				
Circus Circus–Reno				
Laughlin				
Colorado Bell	12[2]	12[2]	13[2]	16[2]
Edgewater				
Jean, Nevada				
Gold Strike	6[3]	6[3]	4[3]	NA
Nevada Landing				
Henderson, Nevada				
Railroad Pass				
Tunica, Mississippi				
Gold Strike	4	4	5	3
50% ownership:				
Silver Legacy, Reno, Nevada	7.3	6.5[4]	3.5[4]	.5[4]
Monte Carlo, Las Vegas, Nevada				
Grand Victoria Riverboat Casino, Elgin, Illinois				

[1]Combined with revenues from Circus Circus–Reno.
[2]Colorado Bell and Edgewater have been combined.
[3]Gold Strike and Nevada Landing have been combined.
[4]Revenues of unconsolidated affiliates have been combined.
Revenues from Slots-A-Fun and Silver City, management fees, and other income was not separately reported.

that recent remodeling, at a cost of $25.6 million, will increase this property's revenue generating potential.

14   The Colorado Belle and the Edgewater Hotel are located in Laughlin, Nevada, on the banks of the Colorado River, a city 90 miles south of Las Vegas. The Colorado Belle, opened in 1987, features a huge paddle wheel riverboat replica, buffet, cocktail lounges, and shops. The Edgewater, acquired in 1983, has a southwestern motif, a 57,000 square foot casino, a bowling center, buffet, and cocktail lounges. Combined, these two properties contain 2,700 rooms and over 120,000 square feet of casino. These two operations contributed 12 percent of the company's revenues in the year ended January 31, 1997, and again in 1998, down from 21 percent in 1994. The extensive proliferation of casinos throughout the region, primarily on Indian land, and the development of mega-resorts in Las Vegas have seriously eroded outlying markets such as Laughlin.

15   Three properties purchased in 1995 and located in Jean and Henderson, Nevada, represent continuing investments by Circus in outlying markets. The Gold Strike and Nevada Landing service the I-15 market between Las Vegas and southern California. These properties have over 73,000 square feet of casino space, 2,140 slot machines, and 42 gaming tables combined. Each has limited hotel space (1,116 rooms total), and depend heavily on I-15 traffic. The Railroad Pass is considered a local casino and is dependent on Henderson residents as its market. This smaller casino contains only 395 slot machines and 11 gaming tables.

TABLE 4
Selected Financial Information

	FY98	FY97	FY96	FY95	FY94	FY93	FY92	FY91
Earnings per Share	0.40	0.99	1.33	1.59	1.34	2.05	1.84	1.39
Current Ratio	.85	1.17	1.30	1.35	.95	.90	1.14	.88
Total Liabilities/Total Assets	.65	.62	.44	.54	.57	.48	.58	.77
Operating Profit Margin	17.4%	17%	19%	22%	21%	24.4%	24.9%	22.9%

Source: Circus Circus Annual Reports and 10K's, 1991–1998.

16   Gold Strike–Tunica (formally Circus Circus–Tunica) is a dockside casino located in Tunica, Mississippi, opened in 1994 on 24 acres of land along the Mississippi River, approximately 20 miles south of Memphis. In 1997 operating income declined by more than 50 percent due to the increase in competition and lack of hotel rooms. Circus decided to renovate this property and add a 1,200-room tower hotel. Total cost for all remodeling was $119.8 million.

Joint Ventures

17   Circus is currently engaged in three joint ventures through the wholly owned subsidiary Circus Participant. In Las Vegas, Circus joined with Mirage Resorts to build and operate the Monte Carlo, a hotel-casino with 3,002 rooms designed along the lines of the grand casinos of the Mediterranean. It is located on 46 acres (with 600 feet on the Las Vegas strip) between the New York–New York casino and the soon to be completed Bellagio, with all three casinos to be connected by monorail. The Monte Carlo features a 90,000-square-foot casino containing 2,221 slot machines and 95 gaming tables, along with a 550-seat bingo parlor, high-tech arcade rides, restaurants and buffets, a microbrewery, approximately 15,000 square feet of meeting and convention space and a 1,200-seat theater. Opened on June 21, 1996, the Monte Carlo generated $14.6 million as Circus's share in operating income for the first seven months of operation.

18   In Elgin, Illinois, Circus is in a 50 percent partnership with Hyatt Development Corporation in the Grand Victoria. Styled to resemble a Victorian riverboat, this floating casino and land-based entertainment complex includes some 36,000 square feet of casino space, containing 977 slot machines and 56 gaming tables. The adjacent land-based complex contains two movie theaters, a 240-seat buffet, restaurants, and parking for approximately 2,000 vehicles. Built for a total of $112 million, the Grand Victoria returned to Circus $44 million in operating income in 1996.

19   The third joint venture is a 50 percent partnership with Eldorado Limited in the Silver Legacy. Opened in 1995, this casino is located between Circus Circus–Reno and the Eldorado Hotel and Casino on two city blocks in downtown Reno, Nevada. The Silver Legacy has 1,711 hotel rooms, 85,000 square feet of casino, 2,275 slot machines, and 89 gaming tables. Management seems to believe that the Silver Legacy holds promise; however the Reno market is suffering and the opening of the Silver Legacy has cannibalized the Circus Circus–Reno market.

20   Circus engaged in a fourth joint venture to penetrate the Canadian market, but on January 23, 1997, announced they had been bought out by Hilton Hotels Corporation, one of three partners in the venture.

21   Circus has achieved success through an aggressive growth strategy and a corporate structure designed to enhance that growth. A strong cash position, innovative ideas, and attention to cost control have allowed Circus to satisfy the bottom line during a period when competitors were typically taking on large debt obligations to finance new projects (see Tables 4, 5, 6, and 7). Yet the market is changing. Gambling of all kinds has spread across the country; no longer does the average individual need to go to Las Vegas or New Jersey. Instead, gambling can be found as close as the local quick market (lottery), bingo hall, many Indian reservations, the Mississippi River, and others. There are now almost 300 casinos in Las Vegas alone, 60 in Colorado, and 160 in California. In order to maintain a competitive edge, Circus has continued to invest heavily in renovation of existing properties (a strategy common to the entertainment/amusement industry) and continues to develop new projects.

TABLE 5
Twelve-Year Summary (in 000)

	Revenues	Net Income
FY 98	$1,354,487	$89,908
FY 97	1,334,250	100,733
FY 96	1,299,596	128,898
FY 95	1,170,182	136,286
FY 94	954,923	116,189
FY 93	843,025	117,322
FY 92	806,023	103,348
FY 91	692,052	76,292
FY 90	522,376	76,064
FY 89	511,960	81,714
FY 88	458,856	55,900
FY 87	373,967	28,198
FY 86	306,993	37,375

Source: Circus Circus Annual Reports and 10K's, 1986–1998.

New Ventures

22   Circus currently has three new projects planned for opening within the near future. The largest project, named "Mandalay Bay," is scheduled for completion in the first quarter 1999, and is estimated to cost $950 million (excluding land). Circus owns a contiguous mile of the southern end of the Las Vegas strip, which they call their "Masterplan Mile" and which currently contains the Excalibur and Luxor resorts. Located next to the Luxor, Mandalay Bay will aim for the upscale traveler and player and will be styled as a South Seas adventure. The resort will contain a 43-story hotel-casino with over 3,700 rooms and an 11-acre aquatic environment. The aquatic environment will contain a surfing beach, swim-up shark tank, and snorkeling reef. A Four Seasons Hotel with some 400 rooms will complement the remainder of Mandalay Bay. Circus anticipates that the remainder of the Masterplan Mile will eventually be comprised of at least one additional casino resort and a number of stand-alone hotels and amusement centers.

23   Circus also plans three other casino projects, provided all the necessary licenses and agreements can be obtained. In Detroit, Michigan, Circus has combined with the Atwater Casino Group in a joint venture to build a $600 million project. Negotiations with the city to develop the project have been completed, however the remainder of the appropriate licenses will need to be obtained before construction begins.

24   Along the Mississippi Gulf, at the north end of the Bay of St. Louis, Circus plans to construct a casino resort containing 1,500 rooms at an estimated cost of $225 million. Circus has received all necessary permits to begin construction; however, these approvals have been challenged in court, delaying the project.

25   In Atlantic City, Circus has entered into an agreement with Mirage Resorts to develop a 181-acre site in the Marina District. Land title has been transferred to Mirage; however, Mirage has purported to cancel its agreement with Circus. Circus has filed suit against Mirage seeking to enforce the contract, while others have filed suit to stop all development in the area.

26   Most of Circus' projects are being tailored to attract mainstream tourists and family vacationers. However the addition of several joint ventures and the completion of the Masterplan Mile will also attract the more upscale customer.

THE GAMING INDUSTRY

27   By 1997 the gaming industry had captured a large amount of the vacation/leisure time dollars spent in the U.S. Gamblers lost over $44.3 billion on legal wagering in 1995 (up from $29.9 billion in

TABLE 6

CIRCUS CIRCUS ENTERPRISES INC.
Annual Income
Year Ended January 31
(in thousands)

Fiscal Year Ending	1/31/98	1/31/97	1/31/96	1/31/95	1/31/94
Revenues					
Casino	$632,122	$655,902	$664,772	$612,115	$538,813
Rooms	330,644	294,241	278,807	232,346	176,001
Food and Beverage	215,584	210,384	201,385	189,664	152,469
Other	142,407	146,554	158,534	166,295	117,501
Earnings of unconsolidated affiliates	98,977	86,646	45,485	5,459	—
	1,419,734	1,393,727	1,348,983	1,205,879	984,784
Less Complimentary Allowances	(65,247)	(59,477)	(49,387)	(35,697)	(29,861)
Net Revenue	1,354,487	1,334,250	1,299,596	1,170,182	954,923
Costs and Expenses					
Casino	316,902	302,096	275,680	246,416	209,402
Rooms	122,934	116,508	110,362	94,257	78,932
Food and Beverage	199,955	200,722	188,712	177,136	149,267
Other operating expenses	90,187	90,601	92,631	107,297	72,802
General and Administrative	232,536	227,348	215,083	183,175	152,104
Depreciation and Amortization	117,474	95,414	93,938	81,109	58,105
Preopening expense	3,447	—	—	3,012	16,506
Abandonment Loss		48,309	45,148	—	—
	1,083,435	1,080,998	1,021,554	892,402	737,118
Operating Profit before Corporate Expense	271,052	223,252	278,042	277,780	217,805
Corporate Expense	34,552	31,083	26,669	21,773	16,744
Income from Operations	236,500	222,169	251,373	256,007	201,061
Other Income (Expense)					
Interest, Dividends, and Other income (Loss)	9,779	5,077	4,022	225	(683)
Interest income and guarantee fees from unconsolidated affiliate	6,041	6,865	7,517	992	—
Interest Expense	(88,847)	(54,681)	(51,537)	(42,734)	(17,770)
Interest Expense from unconsolidated affiliate	(15,551)	(15,567)	(5,616)	—	—
	(88,578)	(58,306)	(45,614)	(41,517)	(18,453)
Income before Provision for Income Tax	147,922	163,863	205,759	214,490	182,608
Provision for Income Tax	58,014	63,130	76,861	78,204	66,419
Income before Extraordinary Loss		—	—	—	116,189
Extraordinary Loss		—	—	—	—
Net Income	89,908	100,733	128,898	136,286	116,189
Earnings per Share					
Income before Extraordinary Loss	.95	.99	1.33	1.59	1.34
Extraordinary Loss		—	—	—	—
Net Income per Share	.94	.99	1.33	1.59	1.34

Source: Circus Circus Annual Reports and 10K's, 1994–1998.

TABLE 7

CIRCUS CIRCUS ENTERPRISES INC.
Consolidated Balance Sheets
(in thousands)

Assets	1/31/98	1/31/97	1/31/96	1/31/95	1/31/94
Current Assets					
Cash and Cash equivalents	58,631	69,516	$62,704	$53,764	$39,110
Receivables	33,640	34,434	16,527	8,931	8,673
Inventories	22,440	19,371	20,459	22,660	20,057
Prepaid Expenses	20,281	19,951	19,418	20,103	20,062
Deferred Income Tax	7,871	8,577	7,272	5,463	
Total Current	142,863	151,849	124,380	110,921	87,902
Property, Equipment	2,466,848	1,920,032	1,474,684	1,239,062	1,183,164
Other Assets					
Excess of purchase price over fair market value	375,375	385,583	394,518	9,836	10,200
Notes Receivable	1,075	36,443	27,508	68,083	
Investments in unconsolidated affiliates	255,392	214,123	173,270	74,840	
Deferred charges and other assets	21,995	21,081	17,533	9,806	16,658
Total Other	653,837	657,230	612,829	162,565	26,858
Total Assets	3,263,548	2,729,111	2,213,503	1,512,548	1,297,924
Liabilities and Stockholders' Equity					
Current Liabilities					
Current portion of Long-Term Debt	3,071	379	863	106	169
Accounts and Contracts Payable					
Trade	22,103	22,658	16,824	12,102	14,804
Construction	40,670	21,144	—	1,101	13,844
Accrued Liabilities					
Salaries, wages, and vacations	36,107	31,847	30,866	24,946	19,650
Progressive Jackpots	7,511	6,799	8,151	7,447	4,881
Advance room deposits	6,217	7,383	7,517	8,701	6,981
Interest payable	17,828	9,004	3,169	2,331	2,278
Other	33,451	30,554	28,142	25,274	25,648
Income tax payable					3,806
Total Current Liabilities	166,958	129,768	95,532	82,008	92,061
Long-term Debt	1,788,818	1,405,897	715,214	632,652	567,345
Other Liabilities					
Deferred Income Tax	175,934	152,635	148,096	110,776	77,153
Other long-term liabilities	8,089	6,439	9,319	988	1,415
Total other liabilities	184,023	159,074	157,415	111,764	78,568
Total liabilities	2,139,799	1,694,739	968,161	826,424	737,974
Redeemable Preferred Stock		17,631	18,530		
Temporary Equity		44,950			
Commitments and contingent Liabilities					
Stockholders' Equity					
Common Stock	1,893	1,880	1,880	1,607	1,603
Preferred Stock					
Additional paid-in capital	558,658	498,893	527,205	124,960	120,135
Retained earnings	1,074,271	984,363	883,630	754,732	618,446
Treasury Stock	(511,073)	(513,345)	(185,903)	(195,175)	(180,234)
Total Stockholders' Equity	1,123,749	971,791	1,226,812	686,124	559,950
Total Liabilities and Stockholders' Equity	3,263,548	2,729,111	2,213,503	1,512,548	1,297,924

Source: Circus Circus Annual Reports and 10K's, 1994–1998.

1992) including wagers at racetracks, bingo parlors, lotteries, and casinos. This figure does not include dollars spent on lodging, food, transportation, and other related expenditures associated with visits to gaming facilities. Casino gambling accounts for 76 percent of all legal gambling expenditures, far ahead of second place Indian Reservation at 8.9 percent and lotteries at 7.1 percent. The popularity of casino gambling may be credited to a more frequent and somewhat higher payout as compared to lotteries and racetracks; however, as winnings are recycled, the multiplier effect restores a high return to casino operators.

28   Geographic expansion has slowed considerably as no additional states having approved casino type gambling since 1993. Growth has occurred in developed locations, with Las Vegas, Nevada, and Atlantic City, New Jersey, leading the way.

29   Las Vegas remains the largest U.S. gaming market and one of the largest convention markets with more than 100,000 hotel rooms hosting more than 29.6 million visitors in 1996, up 2.2 percent over 1995. Casino operators are building to take advantage of this continued growth. Recent projects include the Monte Carlo ($350 million), New York–New York ($350 million), Bellagio ($1.4 billion), Hilton Hotels ($750 million), and Project Paradise ($800 million). Additionally, Harrah's is adding a 989-room tower and remodeling 500 current rooms, and Caesar's Palace has expansion plans to add 2,000 rooms. Las Vegas hotel and casino capacity is expected to continue to expand with some 12,500 rooms opening within a year, beginning fall of 1998. According to the Las Vegas Convention and Visitor Authority, Las Vegas is a destination market with most visitors planning their trip more than a week in advance (81%), arriving by car (47%) or airplane (42%), and staying in a hotel (72%). Gamblers are typically return visitors (77%), averaging 2.2 trips per year, who like playing the slots (65%).

30   For Atlantic City, besides the geographical separation, the primary differences in the two markets reflect the different types of consumers frequenting these markets. While Las Vegas attracts overnight resort-seeking vacationers, Atlantic City's clientele are predominantly day-trippers traveling by automobile or bus. Gaming revenues are expected to continue to grow, perhaps to $4 billion in 1997 split between 10 casino/hotels currently operating. Growth in the Atlantic City area will be concentrated in the Marina section of town where Mirage Resorts has entered into an agreement with the city to develop 150 acres of the Marina as a destination resort. This development will include a resort wholly owned by Mirage, a casino/hotel developed by Circus, and a complex developed by a joint venture with Mirage and Boyd Corp. Currently in Atlantic City, Donald Trump's gaming empire holds the largest market with Trump's Castle, Trump Plaza and the Taj Mahal (total market share is 30%). The next closest in market share is Caesar's (10.3%), Tropicana and Bally's (9.2% each), and Showboat (9.0%).

31   There remain a number of smaller markets located around the U.S., primarily in Mississippi, Louisiana, Illinois, Missouri, and Indiana. Each state has imposed various restrictions on the development of casino operations within their states. In some cases, for example Illinois where there are only 10 gaming licenses available, this has severely restricted the growth opportunities and hurt revenues. In other states, Mississippi and Louisiana, revenues are up 8 percent and 15 percent, respectively, in riverboat operations. Native American casinos continue to be developed on federally controlled Indian land. These casinos are not publicly held but do tend to be managed by publicly held corporations. Overall these other locations present a mix of opportunities and generally constitute only a small portion of overall gaming revenues.

MAJOR INDUSTRY PLAYERS

32   Over the past several years there have been numerous changes as mergers and acquisitions have reshaped the gaming industry. As of year end 1996, the industry was a combination of corporations ranging from those engaged solely in gaming to multinational conglomerates. The largest competitors, in terms of revenues, combined multiple industries to generate both large revenues and substantial profits (see Table 6). However, those engaged primarily in gaming could also be extremely profitable.

33   Starwood/ITT. In 1996 Hilton began a hostile acquisition attempt of ITT Corporation. As a result of this attempt, ITT has merged with Starwood Lodging Corporation and Starwood Lodging Trust. The resulting corporation is one of the world's largest hotel and gaming corporations, owning the

TABLE 8
Major U.S. Gaming, Lottery, and Pari-mutuel Companies 1996 Revenues and Net Income (in millions)

	1997 Revenues	1997 Income	1996 Revenues	1996 Net Income
Starwood/ITT			$6597.0	$249.0
Hilton Hotels	5316.0	250.0	3940.0	82.0
Harrah's Entertainment	1619.0	99.3	1586.0	98.9
Mirage Resorts	1546.0	207	1358.3	206.0
Circus Circus	1354.4	89.9	1247.0	100.7
Trump Hotel and Casino, Inc.	1399.3	−42.1	976.3	−4.9
MGM Grand	827.5	111.0	804.8	74.5
Aztar	782.3	4.4	777.5	20.6
Int. Game Technology	743.9	137.2	733.5	118.0

Source: Individual companies annual reports and 10K's, 1996.

Sheraton, The Luxury Collection, the Four Points Hotels, Caesar's, as well as communications and educational services. In 1996 ITT hosted approximately 50 million customer nights in locations worldwide. Gaming operations are located in Las Vegas, Atlantic City, Halifax and Sydney (Nova Scotia), Lake Tahoe, Tunica (Mississippi), Lima (Peru), Cairo (Egypt), Canada, and Australia. In 1996 ITT had net income of $249 million on revenues of $6.579 billion. In June 1996, ITT announced plans to join with Planet Hollywood to develop casino/hotels with the Planet Hollywood theme in both Las Vegas and Atlantic City. However, these plans may be deferred as ITT becomes fully integrated into Starwood and management has the opportunity to refocus on the operations of the company.

34   Hilton Hotels owns (as of February 1, 1998) or leases and operates 25 hotels and managed 34 hotels partially or wholly owned by others along with 180 franchised hotels. Eleven of the hotels are also casinos, six of which are located in Nevada, two in Atlantic City, with the other three in Australia and Uruguay. In 1997 Hilton had net income of $250.0 million on $5.31 billion in revenues. Hilton receives some 38 percent of total operating revenues from gaming operations and continues to expand in the market. Recent expansions include the Wild Wild West theme hotel casino in Atlantic City, the completed acquisition of all the assets of Bally's, and construction on a 2,900-room Paris Casino resort located next to Bally's Las Vegas.

35   Harrah's Entertainment, Inc. is primarily engaged in the gaming industry with casino/hotels in Reno, Lake Tahoe, Las Vegas, and Laughlin, Nevada; and in Atlantic City, New Jersey; riverboats in Joliet, Illinois; and Vicksburg and Tunica, Mississippi; Shreveport, Louisiana; and Kansas City, Kansas; two Indian casinos; and one casino in Auckland, New Zealand. In 1997 they operated a total of approximately 774,500 square feet of casino space with 19,835 slot machines and 934 table games. With this and some 8,197 hotel rooms they had a net income of $99.3 million on $1.619 billion in revenues.

36   All of Mirage Resorts, Inc.'s gaming operations are currently located in Nevada. It owns and operates the Golden Nugget–Downtown Las Vegas, the Mirage on the strip in Las Vegas, Treasure Island, and the Golden Nugget–Laughlin. Additionally they are a 50 percent owner of the Monte Carlo with Circus Circus. Net income for Mirage Resorts in 1997 was $207 million on revenues of $1.546 billion. Current expansion plans include the development of the Bellagio in Las Vegas ($1.6 billion estimated cost) and the Beau Rivage in Biloxi, Mississippi ($600 million estimated cost). These two properties would add a total of 265,900 square feet of casino space to the current Mirage inventory and an additional 252 gaming tables and 4,746 slot machines. An additional project is the development of the Marina area in Atlantic City, New Jersey, in partnership with Boyd Gaming.

37   MGM Grand Hotel and Casino is located on approximately 114 acres at the northeast corner of Las Vegas Boulevard across the street from New York–New York Hotel and Casino. The casino is

approximately 171,500 square feet in size, and is one of the largest casinos in the world with 3,669 slot machines and 157 table games. Current plans call for extensive renovation costing $700 million. Through a wholly owned subsidiary, MGM owns and operates the MGM Grand Diamond Beach Hotel and a hotel/casino resort in Darwin, Australia. Additionally, MGM and Primadonna Resorts, Inc. each own 50 percent of the New York–New York Hotel and Casino, a $460 million architecturally distinctive themed destination resort, which opened on January 3, 1997. MGM also intends to construct and operate a destination resort hotel/casino, entertainment and retail facility in Atlantic City on approximately 35 acres of land on the Atlantic City Boardwalk.

THE LEGAL ENVIRONMENT

38   Within the gaming industry all current operators must consider compliance with extensive gaming regulations as a primary concern. Each state or country has its own specific regulations and regulatory boards requiring extensive reporting and licensing requirements. For example, in Las Vegas, Nevada, gambling operations are subject to regulatory control by the Nevada State Gaming Control Board, the Clark County Nevada Gaming and Liquor Licensing Board, and by city government regulations. The laws, regulations, and supervisory procedures of virtually all gaming authorities are based upon public policy primarily concerned with the prevention of unsavory or unsuitable persons from having a direct or indirect involvement with gaming at any time or in any capacity and the establishment and maintenance of responsible accounting practices and procedures. Additional regulations typically cover the maintenance of effective controls over the financial practices of licensees, including the establishment of minimum procedures for internal fiscal affairs and the safeguarding of assets and revenues, providing reliable record keeping and requiring the filing of periodic reports, the prevention of cheating and fraudulent practices, and providing a source of state and local revenues through taxation and licensing fees. Changes in such laws, regulations, and procedures could have an adverse effect on the many gaming operations. All gaming companies must submit detailed operating and financial reports to authorities. Nearly all financial transactions, including loans, leases, and the sale of securities must be reported. Some financial activities are subject to approval by regulatory agencies. As Circus moves into other locations outside of Nevada, they will need to adhere to local regulations.

FUTURE CONSIDERATIONS

39   Circus Circus states that they are "in the business of entertainment, with . . . core strength in casino gaming," and that they intend to focus their efforts in Las Vegas, Atlantic City, and Mississippi. Circus further states that the "future product in gaming, to be sure, is the entertainment resort" (Circus Circus 1997 Annual Report).

40   Circus was one of the innovators of the gaming resort concept and has continued to be a leader in that field. However the mega-entertainment resort industry operates differently than the traditional casino gaming industry. In the past consumers would visit a casino to experience the thrill of gambling. Now they not only gamble, but expect to be dazzled by enormous entertainment complexes that are costing in the billions of dollars to build. The competition has continued to increase at the same time growth rates have been slowing.

41   For years analysts have questioned the ability of the gaming industry to continue high growth in established markets as the industry matures. Through the 1970's and 80's the gaming industry experienced rapid growth. Through the 1990's the industry began to experience a shake out of marginal competitors and consolidation phase. Circus Circus has been successful through this turmoil but now faces the task of maintaining high growth in a more mature industry.

CASE 60

CARNIVAL CORPORATION: 1998

1   Carnival Corporation, in terms of passengers carried, revenues generated, and available capacity, is the largest cruise line in the world and considered the leader and innovator in the cruise travel industry. Given its inauspicious beginnings, Carnival has grown from two converted ocean liners to an organization with two cruise divisions (and a joint venture to operate a third cruise line) and a chain of Alaskan hotels and tour coaches. Corporate revenues for fiscal 1997 reached $2.4 billion with net income from operations of $666 million. And the growth continues with May 1998 revenues up $100 million over the same quarter 1997 to $1.219 billion. Carnival has several "firsts" in the cruise industry, with over one million passengers carried in a single year and the first cruise line to carry five million total passengers by fiscal 1994. Currently, their market share of the cruise travel industry stands at approximately 26% overall.

2   Carnival Corporation CEO and Chairman, Mr. Micky Arison, and Carnival Cruise Lines President, Mr. Bob Dickinson, are prepared to maintain their reputation as the leader and innovator in the industry. They have assembled one of the newest fleets catering to cruisers, with the introduction of several "superliners" built specifically for the Caribbean and Alaskan cruise markets, and expect to invest over $3.0 billion in new ships by the year 2002. Additionally the company has expanded their Holland American Lines fleet to cater to more established cruisers and plans to add three of the new ships to their fleet in the premium cruise segment. Strategically, Carnival Corporation seems to have made the right moves at the right time, sometimes in direct contradiction to industry analysts and cruise trends.

3   Cruise Lines International Association (CLIA), an industry trade group, has traced the growth of the cruise industry for over 25 years. In 1970, approximately 500,000 passengers took cruises for three consecutive nights or more, reaching a peak of 5 million passengers in 1997, an average annual compound growth rate of approximately 8.9% (this growth rate has declined to approximately 2% per year over the period from 1991 to 1995). At the end of 1997, the industry had 136 ships in service with an aggregate berth capacity of 119,000. CLIA estimates that the number of passengers carried in North America increased from 4.6 million in 1996 to 5 million in 1997 or approximately 8.7%. CLIA expects the number of cruise passengers to increase to 5.3 million in 1998; and with new ships to be delivered, the North American market will have roughly 144 vessels with an aggregate capacity of 132,000 berths.

4   Carnival has exceeded the recent industry trends and the growth rate in the number of passengers carried was 11.2% per year over the 1992 to 1996 period. The company's passenger capacity in 1991 was 17,973 berths and had increased to 31,078 at the end of fiscal 1997. Additional capacity will be added with the delivery of several new cruise ships already on order, such as the Elation, which went into service in early 1998, adding 2,040 to the passenger capacity.

5   Even with the growth in the cruise industry, the company believes that cruises represent only 2% of the applicable North American vacation market, defined as persons who travel for leisure purposes on trips of three nights or longer, involving at least one night's stay in a hotel. The Boston Consulting Group, in a 1989 study, estimated that only 5% of persons in the North American target market have taken a cruise for leisure purposes and estimated the market potential to be in excess of $50 billion. Carnival Corporation (1996) believes that only 7% of the North American population has ever cruised. Various cruise operators, including Carnival Corporation, have based their expansion and capital spending programs on the possibility of capturing part of the 93% to 95% of the North American population who have yet to take a cruise vacation.

This case was prepared by Professors Michael J. Keeffe, John K. Ross III, and Bill J. Middlebrook of Southwest Texas State University. The case was prepared for classroom purposes only, and is not designed to show effective or ineffective handling of administrative situations.

THE EVOLUTION OF CRUISING

6   With the replacement of ocean liners by aircraft in the 1960s as the primary means of transoceanic travel, the opportunity for developing the modern cruise industry was created. Ships no longer required to ferry passengers from destination to destination became available to investors with visions of a new vacation alternative to complement the increasing affluence of Americans. Cruising, once the purview of the rich and leisure class, was targeted to the middle class, with service and amenities similar to the grand days of first-class ocean travel.

7   According to Robert Meyers, Editor and Publisher of *Cruise Travel* magazine, the increasing popularity of taking a cruise as a vacation can be traced to two serendipitously timed events. First, television's "Love Boat" series dispelled many myths associated with cruising and depicted people of all ages and backgrounds enjoying the cruise experience. This show was among the top ten shows on television for many years according to Nielsen ratings, and provided extensive publicity for cruise operators. Second, the increasing affluence of Americans and the increased participation of women in the work force gave couples and families more disposable income for discretionary purposes, especially vacations. As the myths were dispelled and disposable income grew, younger couples and families "turned on" to the benefits of cruising as a vacation alternative, creating a large new target market for the cruise product, which accelerated the growth in the number of Americans taking cruises as a vacation.

CARNIVAL HISTORY

8   In 1972 Ted Arison, backed by American Travel Services, Inc. (AITS), purchased an aging ocean liner from Canadian Pacific Empress Lines for $6.5 million. The new AITS subsidiary, Carnival Cruise Line, refurbished the vessel from bow to stern and renamed it the Mardi Gras to capture the party spirit. (Also included in the deal was another ship later renamed the Carnivale.) The company start was not promising, however, as on the first voyage the Mardi Gras, with over 300 invited travel agents aboard, ran aground in Miami Harbor. The ship was slow and guzzled expensive fuel, limiting the number of ports of call and lengthening the minimum stay of passengers on the ship to break-even. Mr. Arison then bought another old ocean vessel from Union Castle Lines to complement the Mardi Gras and the Carnivale and named it the Festivale. To attract customers, Mr. Arison began adding diversions on-board such as planned activities, a casino, nightclubs, discos, and other forms of entertainment designed to enhance the shipboard experience.

9   Carnival lost money for the next three years and in late 1974 Ted Arison bought out the Carnival Cruise subsidiary of AITS, Inc. for $1 cash and the assumption of $5 million in debt. One month later, the Mardi Gras began showing a profit and through the remainder of 1975 operated at more than 100% capacity. (Normal ship capacity is determined by the number of fixed berths available. Ships, like hotels, can operate beyond this fixed capacity by using rollaway beds, Pullmans, and upper bunks.) Ted Arison (then Chairman), along with Bob Dickinson (who was then Vice President of Sales and Marketing) and his son Micky Arison (then President of Carnival), began to alter the current approach to cruise vacations. Carnival went after first-time and younger cruisers with a moderately priced vacation package that included air fare to the port of embarkation and home after the cruise. Per diem rates were very competitive with other vacation packages and Carnival offered passage to multiple exotic Caribbean ports, several meals served daily with premier restaurant service, and all forms of entertainment and activities included in the base fare. The only things not included in the fare were items of a personal nature, liquor purchases, gambling, and tips for the cabin steward, table waiter, and busboy. Carnival continued to add to the shipboard experience with a greater variety of activities, nightclubs, and other forms of entertainment and varied ports of call to increase its attractiveness to potential customers. They were the first modern cruise operator to use multimedia advertising promotions and established the theme of "Fun Ship" cruises, primarily promoting the ship as the destination and ports of call as secondary. Carnival told the public that it was throwing a shipboard party and everyone was invited. Today, the "Fun Ship" theme still permeates all Carnival Cruise ships.

10   Throughout the 1980s, Carnival was able to maintain a growth rate of approximately 30%, about three times that of the industry as a whole, and between 1982 and 1988 its ships sailed with an average of 104% capacity (currently they operate at 104% to 105% capacity, depending on the season). Targeting younger, first-time passengers by promoting the ship as a destination proved to be extremely successful. Carnival's 1987 customer profile showed that 30% of the passengers were between the ages of 25 and 39 with household incomes of $25,000 to $50,000.

11   In 1987, Ted Arison sold 20% of his shares in Carnival Cruise Lines and immediately generated over $400 million for further expansion. In 1988, Carnival acquired the Holland America Line, which had four cruise ships with 4,500 berths. Holland America was positioned to the higher-income travelers with cruise prices averaging 25–35% more than similar Carnival cruises. The deal also included two Holland America subsidiaries, Windstar Sail Cruises and Holland America Westours. This success, and the foresight of management, allowed Carnival to begin an aggressive "superliner" building campaign for their core subsidiary. By 1989, the cruise segments of Carnival Corporation carried over 750,000 passengers in one year, a "first" in the cruise industry.

12   Ted Arison relinquished the role of Chairman to his son Micky in 1990, a time when the explosive growth of the 1980s began to subside. Higher fuel prices and increased airline costs began to affect the industry as a whole, and the Persian Gulf war caused many cruise operators to divert ships from European and Indian ports to the Caribbean area of operations, increasing the number of ships competing directly with Carnival. Carnival's stock price fell from $25 in June of 1990 to $13 late in the year. The company also incurred a $25.5 million loss during fiscal 1990 for the operation of the Crystal Palace Resort and Casino. In 1991 Carnival reached a settlement with the Bahamian government (effective March 1, 1992) to surrender the 672-room Riveria Towers to the Hotel Corporation of the Bahamas in exchange for the cancellation of some debt incurred in constructing and developing the resort. The corporation took a $135 million write-down on the Crystal Palace for that year.

13   The early 1990s, even with industry-wide demand slowing, were still a very exciting time. Carnival took delivery of its first two "superliners": the Fantasy (1990) and the Ecstasy (1991), which were to further penetrate the three- and four-day cruise market and supplement the seven-day market. In early 1991 Carnival took delivery of the third "superliner" Sensation (inaugural sailing November 1, 1993) and later in the year contracted for the fourth "superliner" to be named the Fascination (inaugural sailing 1994).

14   In 1991, Carnival attempted to acquire Premier Cruise Lines, which was then the official cruise line for Walt Disney World in Orlando, Florida, for approximately $372 million. The deal was never consummated since the involved parties could not agree on price. In 1992, Carnival acquired 50% of Seabourn, gaining the cruise operations of K/S Seabourn Cruise Lines, and formed a partnership with Atle Byrnestad. Seabourn serves the ultra-luxury market with destinations in South America, the Mediterranean, Southeast Asia, and the Baltics.

15   The 1993 to 1995 period saw the addition of the "superliner" Imagination for Carnival Cruise Lines and the Ryndam for Holland America Lines. In 1994, the company discontinued operations of Fiestamarina Lines, which attempted to serve Spanish-speaking clientele. Fiestamarina was beset with marketing and operational problems and never reached continuous operations. Many industry analysts and observers were surprised at the failure of Carnival to successfully develop this market. In 1995 Carnival sold a 49% interest in the Epirotiki Line, a Greek cruise operation, for $25 million and purchased $101 million (face amount) of senior secured notes of Kloster Cruise Limited, the parent of competitor Norwegian Cruise Lines, for $81 million. Kloster was having financial difficulties and Carnival could not obtain stock of the company in a negotiated agreement. If Kloster were to fail, Carnival Corporation would be in a good position to acquire some of the assets of Kloster.

16   Carnival Corporation is expanding through internally generated growth as evidenced by the number of new ships on order (see Table 1). Additionally, Carnival seems to be willing to continue with its external expansion through acquisitions if the right opportunity arises.

17   In June 1997, Royal Caribbean made a bid to buy Celebrity Cruise Lines for $500 million and assumption of $800 million in debt. Within a week, Carnival had responded by submitting a counteroffer to Celebrity for $510 million and the assumption of debt, then two days later raising the bid to $525 million. However, Royal Caribbean seems to have had the inside track and announced on June 30, 1997, the final merger arrangements with Celebrity. The resulting company will have 17 ships with approximately 30,000 berths.

TABLE 1
Carnival and Holland America Ships under Construction

Vessel	Expected Delivery	Shipyard	Passenger Capacity*	Cost (millions)
Carnival Cruise Lines				
Elation	03/98	Masa-Yards	2,040	$ 300
Paradise	12/98	Masa-Yards	2,040	300
Carnival Triumph	07/99	Fincantieri	2,640	400
Carnival Victory	08/00	Fincantieri	2,640	430
CCL Newbuild	12/00	Masa-Yards	2,100	375
CCL Newbuild	2001	Masa-Yards	2,100	375
CCL Newbuild	2002	Masa-Yards	2,100	375
Total Carnival Cruise Lines			15,912	$2,437
Holland America Line				
Volendam	06/99	Fincantieri	1,440	274
Zaandam	12/99	Fincantieri	1,440	286
HAL Newbuild	09/00	Fincantieri	1,440	300
Total Holland America Line			4,260	$ 860
Windstar Cruises				
Wind Surf	05/98	Purchase	312	40
Total all Vessels			20,484	$3,337

*In accordance with industry practice all capacities indicated within this table are calculated based on two passengers per cabin even though some cabins can accommodate three or four passengers. 10Q-5/31/98.

18   However, not to be thwarted in their attempts at continued expansion, Carnival announced in June 1997 the purchase of Costa, an Italian cruise company and the largest European cruise line, for $141 million. External expansion continued when on May 28, 1998, Carnival announced the acquisition of Cunard Line for $500 million from Kvaerner ASA. Cunard was then merged with Seabourn Cruise Line (50% owned by Carnival) with Carnival owning 68% of the resulting Cunard Line Limited.

THE CRUISE PRODUCT

19   Ted and Micky Arison envisioned a product where the classical cruise elegance along with modern convenience could be had at a price comparable to land-based vacation packages sold by travel agents. Carnival's all-inclusive package, when compared to resorts or a theme park such as Walt Disney World, often is priced below these destinations, especially when the array of activities, entertainment, and meals is considered.

20   A typical vacation on a Carnival cruise ship starts when the bags are tagged for the ship at the airport. Upon arriving at the port of embarkation, passengers are ferried by air-conditioned buses to the ship for boarding, and luggage is delivered by the cruise ship staff to the passenger's cabin. Waiters dot the ship offering tropical drinks to the backdrop of a Caribbean rhythm, while the cruise staff orients passengers to the various decks, cabins, and public rooms. In a few hours (most ships sail in the early evening), dinner is served in the main dining rooms where wine selection rivals the finest restaurants and the variety of main dishes is designed to suit every palate. Diners can always order double portions if they decide not to save room for the variety of desserts and after-dinner specialties.

21   After dinner, cruisers can choose between many forms of entertainment, including live music, dancing, nightclubs, and a selection of movies; or they can sleep through the midnight buffet until

breakfast. (Most ships have five or more distinct nightclubs.) During the night, a daily program of activities arrives at the passengers' cabins. The biggest decisions to be made for the duration of the vacation will be what to do (or not to do), what to eat and when (usually eight separate serving times not including the 24-hour room service), and when to sleep. Service in all areas from dining to housekeeping is upscale and immediate. The service is so good that a common shipboard joke says that if you leave your bed during the night to visit the head (sea talk for bathroom), your cabin steward will have made the bed and placed chocolates on the pillow by the time you return.

22   After the cruise, passengers are transported back to the airport in air-conditioned buses for the flight home. Representatives of the cruise line are on hand at the airport to help cruisers in meeting their scheduled flights. When all amenities are considered, most vacation packages would be hard pressed to match Carnival's per diem prices that range from $125 to $250 per person/per day, depending on accommodations. (Holland American and Seabourn are higher, averaging $300 per person/per day.) Occasional specials allow for even lower prices and special suite accommodations can be had for an additional payment.

CARNIVAL OPERATIONS

23   Carnival Corporation, headquartered in Miami, is composed of Carnival Cruise Lines; Holland America Lines, which includes Windstar Sail Cruises as a subsidiary; Holland America Westours; Westmark Hotels; Airtours; and the newly created Cunard Line Limited. Carnival Cruise Lines, Inc. is a Panamanian corporation and its subsidiaries are incorporated in Panama, the Netherlands Antilles, the British Virgin Islands, Liberia, and the Bahamas. The ships are subject to inspection by the U.S. Coast Guard for compliance with the Convention for the Safety of Life at Sea (SOLAS), which requires specific structural requirements for safety of passengers at sea, and by the U.S. Public Health Service for sanitary standards. The company is also regulated in some aspects by the Federal Maritime Commission.

24   At its helm, Carnival Corporation is led by CEO and Chairman of the Board Micky Arison and Carnival Cruise Lines President and COO Bob Dickinson. Mr. A. Kirk Lanterman is the President and CEO of the Holland America cruise division, which includes Holland America Westours and Windstar Sail Cruises. (A listing of corporate officers is presented in Exhibit 1.)

25   The company's product positioning stems from its belief that the cruise market is actually comprised of three primary segments with different passengers demographics, passenger characteristics and growth requirements. The three segments are the contemporary, premium, and luxury segments. The contemporary segment is served by Carnival ships for cruises that are seven days or shorter in length and feature a casual ambience. The premium segment, served by Holland America, serves the seven day and longer market and appeals to more affluent consumers. The luxury segment, while considerably smaller than the other segments, caters to experienced cruisers for seven day and longer sailings and is served by Seabourn. Specialty sailing cruises are provided by Windstar Sail Cruises, a subsidiary of Holland America.

26   Corporate structure is built around the "profit center" concept and is updated periodically when needed for control and coordination purposes. The cruise subsidiaries of Carnival give the corporation a presence in most of the major cruise segments and provide for worldwide operations.

27   Carnival has always placed a high priority on marketing in an attempt to promote cruises as an alternative to land-based vacations. It wants customers to know that the ship itself is the destination and the ports of call are important, but secondary, to the cruise experience. Education and the creation of awareness are critical to corporate marketing efforts. Carnival was the first cruise line to successfully break away from traditional print media and use television to reach a broader market. Even though other lines have followed Carnival's lead in selecting promotional media and are near in total advertising expenditures, the organization still leads all cruise competitors in advertising and marketing expenditures.

28   Carnival wants to remain the leader and innovator in the cruise industry and intends to do this with sophisticated promotional efforts and by gaining loyalty from former cruisers, by refurbishing ships, varying activities and ports of call, and being innovative in all aspects of ship operations.

EXHIBIT 1
Corporate Officers of Carnival Corporation

Micky Arison	Howard S. Frank
Chairman of the Board and Chief Executive Officer	Vice Chairman and Chief Operating Officer
Carnival Corporation	Carnival Corporation
Gerald R. Cahill	Roderick K. McLeod
Senior Vice President Finance and CFO	Senior Vice President Marketing
Carnival Corporation	Carnival Corporation
Lowell Zemnick	
Vice President & Treasurer	
Carnival Corporation	
Robert H. Dickinson	Meshulam Zonis
President and COO	Senior Vice President Operations
Carnival Cruise Lines	Carnival Cruise Lines
A. Kirk Lanterman	Peter T. McHugh
Chairman of the Board and CEO	President and COO
Holland America Lines	Holland America Lines

Source: Carnival Corporation, 1998.

Management intends to build on the theme of the ship as a destination given their historical success with this promotional effort. The Company capitalizes and amortizes direct-response advertising and expenses other advertising costs as incurred. Advertising expense totaled $112 million in 1997, $109 million in 1996, $98 million in 1995, and $85 million in 1994.

FINANCIAL PERFORMANCE

29 Carnival retains Price Waterhouse as independent accountants and the Barnett Bank Trust Company–North America as the registrar and stock transfer agent, and their Class A Common stock trades on the New York Stock Exchange under the symbol CCL. In December 1996, Carnival amended the terms of its revolving credit facility primarily to combine two facilities into a single one billion dollar unsecured revolving credit facility due 2001. The borrowing rate on the One Billion Dollar Revolver is a maximum of LIBOR* plus 14 basis points and the facility fee is six basis points. Carnival

*"LIBOR rate" means, for an Interest Period for each LIBOR (London Interbank Offer Rate) Rate Advance comprising part of the same Borrowing, the rate determined by the Agent to be the rate of interest per annum (i) compounded upward to the nearest whole multiple of 1/100 of 1% per annum, appearing on Telerate screen 3750 at 11:00 A.M. (London time) two Business Days before the first day of such Interest Period for a term equal to such Interest Period and in an amount substantially equal to such portion of the Loan, or if the Agent cannot so determine the LIBOR Rate by reference to Telerate screen 3750, then (ii) equal to the average (rounded upward to the nearest whole multiple of 1/100 of 1% per annum, if such average is not such a multiple) of the rate per annum at which deposits in United States Dollars are offered by the principal office of each of the Reference Lenders in London, England to prime banks in the London interbank market at 11:00 A.M. (London time) two Business Days before the first day of such Interest Period for a term equal to such Interest Period and in an amount substantially equal to such portion of the Loan. In the latter case, the LIBOR Rate for

initiated a commercial paper program in October 1996, which is supported by the One Billion Dollar Revolver. As of November 30, 1996, the Company had $307 million outstanding under its commercial paper program and $693 million available for borrowing under the One Billion Dollar Revolver.

30   The consolidated financial statements for Carnival Cruise Lines, Inc. are shown in Exhibits 2 and 3 and selected financial data are presented in Exhibit 4.

31   Customer cruise deposits, which represent unearned revenue, are included in the balance sheet when received and recognized as cruise revenues on completion of the voyage. Customers also are required to pay the full cruise fare (minus deposit) 60 days in advance with the fares being recognized as cruise revenue on completion of the voyage.

32   Property and equipment on the financial statements is stated at cost. Depreciation and amortization are calculated using the straight line method over the following estimated useful lives: vessels 25–30 years, buildings 20–40 years, equipment 2–20 years, and leasehold improvements at the shorter of the "term of the lease" or "related asset life." Goodwill of $275 million resulting from the acquisition of HAL Antillen, N.V. (Holland America Lines) is being amortized using the straight line method over 40 years.

33   During 1995, Carnival received $40 million from the settlement of litigation with Metra Oy, the former parent company of Wartsila Marine Industries, related to losses suffered in connection with the construction of three cruise ships. (Wartsila declared bankruptcy in late 1994.) Of this amount, $14.4 million was recorded as "other income" with the remainder used to pay legal fees and reduce the cost basis of the three ships.

34   On June 25, 1996, Carnival reached an agreement with the trustees of Wartsila and creditors for the bankruptcy that resulted in a cash payment of approximately $80 million. Of the $80 million received, $5 million was used to pay certain costs, $32 million was recorded as other income, and $43 million was used to reduce the cost basis of certain ships that had been affected by the bankruptcy.

35   By May 31, 1998, Carnival had outstanding long-term debt of $1.55 billion with the current portion being $58.45 million. This debt is primarily composed of $306.8 million in commercial paper and a number of unsecured debentures and notes of less than $200 million each at rates ranging from 5.65% to 7.7%.

36   According to the Internal Revenue Code of 1986, Carnival is considered a "controlled foreign corporation (CFC)" since 50% of its stock is held by individuals who are residents of foreign countries and its countries of incorporation exempt shipping operations of U.S. persons from income tax. Because of CFC status, Carnival expects that all of its income (with the exception of U.S. source income from the transportation, hotel, and tour businesses of Holland America) will be exempt from U.S. federal income taxes at the corporate level.

37   The primary financial considerations of importance to Carnival management involve the control of costs, both fixed and variable, for the maintenance of a healthy profit margin. Carnival has the lowest break-even point of any organization in the cruise industry (ships break even at approximately 60% of capacity) due to operational experience and economies of scale. Unfortunately, fixed costs, including depreciation, fuel, insurance, port charges, and crew costs, which represent more than 33% of the company's operating expenses, cannot be significantly reduced in relation to decreases in passenger loads and aggregate passenger ticket revenue. Major expense items are air fares (25–30%), travel agent fees (10%), and labor (13–15%). Increases in these costs could negatively affect the profitability of the organization.

---

an Interest Period shall be determined by the Agent on the basis of applicable rates furnished to and received by the Agent from the Reference Lenders two Business Days before the first day of such Interest Period, subject, however, to the provisions of Section 2.05. If at any time the Agent shall determine that by reason of circumstances affecting the London interbank market (i) adequate and reasonable means do not exist for ascertaining the LIBOR Rate for the succeeding Interest Period or (ii) the making or continuance of any Loan at the LIBOR Rate has become impracticable as a result of a contingency occurring after the date of this Agreement which materially and adversely affects the London interbank market, the Agent shall so notify the Lenders and the Borrower. Failing the availability of the LIBOR Rate, the LIBOR Rate shall mean the Base Rate thereafter in effect from time to time until such time as a LIBOR Rate may be determined by reference to the London interbank market.

EXHIBIT 2

60-8

Carnival Corporation
Consolidated Statements of Operations
[in thousands]

	Six Month Comparison		Years Ended November 30						
	May 31, 1998	May 31, 1997	1997	1996	1995	1994	1993	1992	1991
REVENUES	$1,219,196	$1,117,696	$2,447,468	$2,212,572	$1,998,150	$1,806,016	$1,556,919	$1,473,614	$1,404,704
COSTS AND EXPENSES:									
Operating Expense	669,951	634,622	1,322,669	1,241,269	1,131,113	1,028,475	907,925	865,587	810,317
Selling and Administrative	163,784	156,219	296,533	274,855	248,566	223,272	207,995	194,298	193,316
Depreciation & Amortization	89,266	82,658	167,287	144,987	128,433	110,595	93,333	88,833	85,166
	923,001	493,564	1,786,489	1,661,111	1,508,112	1,362,342	1,209,253	1,148,718	1,088,799
OPERATING INCOME BEFORE AFFILIATED	296,195	244,197	660,979	551,461					
INCOME FROM AFFILIATED	(13,034)	11,694	53,091	45,967					
OPERATING INCOME	283,161	232,503	714,070	597,428	490,038	443,674	347,666	324,896	315,905
OTHER INCOME (EXPENSE):									
Interest Income	5,885	3,382	8,675	18,597	14,403	8,668	11,527	16,946	10,596
Interest Expense, net of capitalized interest	(24,735)	(31,536)	(55,898)	(64,092)	(63,080)	(51,378)	(34,325)	(53,792)	(65,428)
Other Income (expense)	(662)	2,105	5,436	23,414	19,104	(9,146)	(1,201)	2,731	1,746
Income Tax Expense	6,861	6,353	(6,233)	(9,045)	(9,374)	(10,053)	(5,497)	(9,008)	(8,995)
	(12,651)	(19,696)	(48,020)	(31,126)	(38,947)	(61,909)	(29,496)	(43,123)	(62,081)
INCOME BEFORE EXTRAORDINARY ITEM	270,510	212,807	666,050	566,302	451,091	381,765	318,170	281,773	253,824
EXTRAORDINARY ITEM									
Loss on early extinguishment of debt								(5,189)	
DISCONTINUED OPERATIONS									
Hotel Casino Operating Loss									(33,173)
Loss on disposal of Hotel Casino									(135,463)
NET INCOME	$ 270,510	$ 212,807	$ 666,050	$ 566,302	$ 451,091	$ 381,765	$ 318,170	$ 276,584	$ 84,998

Source: 1997 and 1998 10K and 10Qs.

EXHIBIT 3

Carnival Corporation
Consolidated Balance Sheets
[in thousands]

	May 31, 1998	1997	Years Ended November 30 1996	1995	1994	1993	1992
ASSETS							
CURRENT ASSETS							
Cash & Cash Equivalents	$ 120,600	$ 139,989	$ 111,629	$ 53,365	$ 54,105	$ 60,243	$ 115,014
Short-Term Investments	9,414	9,738	12,486	50,395	70,115	88,677	111,048
Accounts Receivable	66,503	57,090	38,109	33,080	20,789	19,310	21,624
Consumable Inventories [Average Cost]	76,226	54,970	53,281	48,820	45,122	37,245	31,618
Prepaid Expenses & Other	102,754	74,238	75,428	70,718	50,318	48,323	32,120
Total Current Assets	375,497	336,025	290,933	256,378	240,449	253,798	311,424
PROPERTY AND EQUIPMENT [at cost]							
Less Accumulated Depreciation & Amortization	5,469,814	4,327,413	4,099,038	3,414,823	3,071,431	2,588,009	1,961,402
OTHER ASSETS							
Goodwill [Less Accumulated Amortization]	403,077	212,607	219,589	226,571	233,553	237,327	244,789
Long-Term Notes Receivable				78,907	76,876	29,136	
Investment in Affiliates & Other Assets	425,715	479,329	430,330	128,808	47,514	21,097	38,439
Net Assets of Discontinued Operations	37,733	71,401	61,998			89,553	89,553
	$6,711,836	$5,426,775	$5,101,888	$4,105,487	$3,669,823	$3,218,920	$2,645,607
LIABILITIES AND SHAREHOLDERS' EQUITY							
CURRENT LIABILITIES:							
Current Portion of Long-Term Debt	$ 58,457	$ 59,620	$ 66,369	$ 72,752	$ 84,644	$ 91,621	$ 97,931
Accounts Payable	187,897	106,783	84,748	90,237	86,750	81,374	71,473
Accrued Liabilities	169,048	154,253	126,511	113,483	114,868	94,830	69,919
Customer Deposits	755,890	420,908	352,698	292,606	257,505	228,153	178,945
Dividends Payable	44,619	44,578	32,416	25,632	21,190	19,763	19,750
Reserve for Discontinued Operations						34,253	36,763
Total Current Liabilities	121,911	786,142	662,742	594,710	564,957	549,994	474,781
LONG-TERM DEBT	1,557,016	1,015,294	1,277,529	1,035,031	1,046,904	916,221	776,600
CONVERTIBLE NOTES			39,103	115,000	115,000	115,000	
OTHER LONG-TERM LIABILITIES	23,907	20,241	91,630	15,873	14,028	10,499	9,381
SHAREHOLDERS' EQUITY:							
Class A Common Stock [1 vote share]	5,949	2,972	2,397	2,298	2,276	2,274	1,136
Class B Common Stock [5 votes share]			550	550	550	550	275
Paid in Capital	871,676	866,097	819,610	594,811	544,947	541,194	539,622
Retained Earnings	2,912,499	2,731,213	2,207,781	1,752,140	1,390,589	1,089,323	850,193
Other	1,799	4,816	546	(4,926)	(9,428)	(6,135)	(6,381)
Total Shareholders' Equity	3,791,923	3,605,098	3,030,884	2,344,873	1,928,934	1,627,206	1,384,845
	$6,711,836	$5,426,775	$5,101,888	$4,105,487	$3,669,823	$3,218,920	$2,645,607

Source: 1997 and 1998 10K and 10Qs.

EXHIBIT 4

Carnival Corporation
Selected Financial Data by Segment
[in thousands]

Years Ended November 30	1997	1996	1995	1994	1993	1992
Revenues						
Cruise	$2,257,567	$2,003,458	$1,800,775	$1,623,069	$1,381,473	$1,292,587
Tour	242,646	263,356	241,909	227,613	214,382	215,194
Intersegment revenues	(52,745)	(54,242)	(44,534)	(44,666)	(38,936)	(34,167)
	2,447,468	2,212,572	1,998,150	1,806,016	1,556,919	1,473,614
Gross Operating Profit						
Cruise	1,072,758	913,880	810,736	726,808	598,642	552,669
Tour	52,041	57,423	56,301	50,733	50,352	55,358
	1,124,799	971,303	867,037	777,541	648,994	608,027
Depreciation & Amortization						
Cruise	157,454	135,694	120,304	101,146	84,228	79,743
Tour	8,862	8,317	8,129	9,449	9,105	9,090
Corporate	971	976				
	167,287	144,987	128,433	110,595	93,333	88,833
Operating Income						
Cruise	656,009	535,814	465,870	425,590	333,392	310,845
Tour	13,262	21,252	24,168	18,084	14,274	23,015
Corporate	44,799	40,362				
	714,070	597,428	490,038	443,674	347,666	333,896
Identifiable Assets						
Cruise	4,744,140	4,514,675	3,967,174	3,531,727	2,995,221	2,415,547
Tour	163,941	150,851	138,313	138,096	134,146	140,507
Discontinued resort and casino	518,694				89,553	89,553
Corporate	5,426,775	436,362				
		5,101,888	4,105,487	3,669,823	3,218,920	2,645,607
Capital Expenditures						
Cruise	414,963	841,871	456,920	587,249	705,196	111,766
Tour	42,507	14,964	8,747	9,963	10,281	11,400
Corporate	40,187	1,810				
	$ 497,657	$ 858,645	$ 465,667	$ 597,212	$ 715,477	$ 123,166

Source: 1997 and 1998 10K and 10Qs.

PRINCIPAL SUBSIDIARIES

Carnival Cruise Line

38   At the end of fiscal 1996, Carnival operated 11 ships with a total berth capacity of 20,332. Carnival operates principally in the Caribbean and has an assortment of ships and ports of call serving the three-, four-, and seven-day cruise markets (see Exhibit 5).

EXHIBIT 5
The Ships of Carnival Corporation

Name	Registry	Built	First in Company	Service Cap*	Gross Tons	Length/ Width	Areas of Operation
Carnival Cruise Lines							
Carnival Destiny	Panama	1996	1997	2,642	101,000	893/116	Caribbean
Inspiration	Panama	1996	1996	2,040	70,367	855/104	Caribbean
Imagination	Panama	1995	1995	2,040	70,367	855/104	Caribbean
Fascination	Panama	1994	1994	2,040	70,367	855/104	Caribbean
Sensation	Panama	1993	1993	2,040	70,367	855/104	Caribbean
Ecstasy	Liberia	1991	1991	2,040	70,367	855/104	Caribbean
Fantasy	Liberia	1990	1990	2,044	70,367	855/104	Bahamas
Celebration	Liberia	1987	1987	1,486	47,262	738/92	Caribbean
Jubilee	Panama	1986	1986	1,486	47,262	738/92	Mexican Riviera
Holiday	Panama	1985	1985	1,452	46,052	727/92	Mexican Riviera
Tropicale	Liberia	1982	1982	1,022	36,674	660/85	Alaska, Caribbean
Total Carnival Ships Capacity 20,332							
Holland America Line							
Veendam	Bahamas	1996	1996	1,266	55,451	720/101	Alaska, Caribbean
Ryndam	Netherlands	1994	1994	1,266	55,451	720/101	Alaska, Caribbean
Maasdam	Netherlands	1993	1993	1,266	55,451	720/101	Europe, Caribbean
Statendam	Netherlands	1993	1993	1,266	55,451	720/101	Alaska, Caribbean
Westerdam	Netherlands	1986	1988	1,494	53,872	798/95	Canada, Caribbean
Noordam	Netherlands	1984	1984	1,214	33,930	704/89	Alaska, Caribbean
Nieuw Amsterdam	Netherlands	1983	1983	1,214	33,930	704/89	Alaska, Caribbean
Rotterdam IV	Netherlands	1997	1997	1,316	62,000	780/106	Alaska, Worldwide
Total HAL Ships Capacity 0,302							
Windstar Cruises							
Wind Spirit	Bahamas	1988	1988	148	5,736	440/52	Caribbean, Mediterranean
Wind Song	Bahamas	1987	1987	148	5,703	440/52	Costa Rica, Tahiti
Wind Star	Bahamas	1986	1986	148	5,703	440/52	Caribbean, Mediterranean
Total Windstar Ships Capacity 444							
Total Capacity 31,078							

*In accordance with industry practice passenger capacity is calculated based on two passengers per cabin even though some cabins can accommodate three or four passengers.

39   Each ship is a floating resort including a full maritime staff, shopkeepers and casino operators, entertainers, and complete hotel staff. Approximately 14% of corporate revenue is generated from shipboard activities such as casino operations, liquor sales, and gift shop items. At various ports-of-call, passengers can also take advantage of tours, shore excursions, and duty-free shopping at their own expense.

40   Shipboard operations are designed to provide maximum entertainment, activities, and service. The size of the company and the similarity in design of the new cruise ships has allowed Carnival to achieve various economies of scale, and management is very cost-conscious.

41   Although the Carnival Cruise Lines division is increasing its presence in the shorter cruise markets, its general marketing strategy is to use three-, four-, or seven-day moderately priced cruises to fit the time and budget constraints of the middle class. Shorter cruises can cost less than $500 per person (depending on accommodations) up to roughly $3,000 per person in a luxury suite on a seven-day cruise, including port charges. (Per diem rates for shorter cruises are slightly higher, on average,

than per diem rates for seven-day cruises.) Average rates per day are approximately $180, excluding gambling, liquor and soft drinks, and items of a personal nature. Guests are expected to tip their cabin steward and waiter at a suggested rate of $3 per person per day, and the bus boy at $1.50 per person per day.

42   Some 99% of all Carnival cruises are sold through travel agents who receive a standard commission of 10% (15% in Florida). Carnival works extensively with travel agents to help promote cruises as an alternative to a Disney or European vacation. In addition to training travel agents from nonaffiliated travel/vacation firms to sell cruises, a special group of employees regularly visit travel agents posing as prospective clients. If the agent recommends a cruise before another vacation option, he or she receives $100. If the travel agent specifies a Carnival cruise before other options, he or she receives $1,000 on the spot. During fiscal 1995, Carnival took reservations from about 29,000 of the approximately 45,000 travel agencies in the U.S. and Canada, and no one travel agency accounted for more than 2% of Carnival revenues.

43   On-board service is labor intensive, employing help from some 51 nations—mostly third world countries—with reasonable returns to employees. For example, waiters on the Jubilee can earn approximately $18,000 to $27,000 per year (base salary and tips), significantly greater than could be earned in their home country for similar employment. Waiters typically work 10 hours per day with approximately one day off per week for a specific contract period (usually 3 to 9 months). Carnival records show that employees remain with the company for approximately eight years and that applicants exceed demand for all cruise positions. Nonetheless, the American Maritime union has cited Carnival (and other cruise operators) several times for exploitation of its crew.

Holland America Lines

44   On January 17, 1989, Carnival acquired all the outstanding stock of HAL Antillen N.V. from Holland America Lines N.V. for $625 million in cash. Carnival financed the purchase through $250 million in retained earnings (cash account) and borrowed the other $375 million from banks at .25% over the prime rate. Carnival received the assets and operations of the Holland America Lines, Westours, Westmark Hotels, and Windstar Sail Cruises. Holland America currently has seven cruise ships with a capacity of 8,795 berths with new ships to be delivered in the future.

45   Founded in 1873, Holland America Lines is an upscale (it charges an average of 25% more than similar Carnival cruises) line with principal destinations in Alaska during the summer months and the Caribbean during the fall and winter, with some worldwide cruises of up to 98 days. Holland America targets an older, more sophisticated cruiser with fewer youth-oriented activities. On Holland America ships, passengers can dance to the sounds of the Big Band era and avoid the discos of Carnival ships. Passengers on Holland America ships enjoy more service (a higher staff-to-passenger ratio than Carnival) and have more cabin and public space per person, and a "no tipping" shipboard policy. Holland America has not enjoyed the spectacular growth of Carnival cruise ships, but has sustained constant growth over the decade of the 1980s and early 1990s with high occupancy. The operation of these ships and the structure of the crew are similar to the Carnival cruise ship model, and the acquisition of the line gave the Carnival Corporation a presence in the Alaskan market where it had none before.

46   Holland America Westours is the largest tour operator in Alaska and the Canadian Rockies and provides vacation synergy with Holland America cruises. The transportation division of Westours includes over 290 motor coaches comprised of the Gray Line of Alaska, the Gray Line of Seattle, Westours motor coaches, and the McKinley Explorer railroad coaches, and three-day boats for tours to glaciers and other points of interest. Carnival management believes that Alaskan cruises and tours should increase in the future due to a number of factors. These include the aging population wanting relaxing vacations with scenic beauty coupled with the fact that Alaska is a U.S. destination.

47   Westmark Hotels consist of 16 hotels in Alaska and the Yukon territories, and also provides synergy with cruise operations and Westours. Westmark is the largest group of hotels in the region providing moderately priced rooms for the vacationer.

48   Windstar Sail Cruises was acquired by Holland America Lines in 1988 and consists of three computer-controlled sailing vessels with a berth capacity of 444. Windstar is very upscale and offers an alternative to traditional cruise liners with a more intimate, activity-oriented cruise. The ships operate primarily in the Mediterranean and the South Pacific, visiting ports not accessible to large cruise ships. Although catering to a small segment of the cruise vacation industry, Windstar helps with Carnival's commitment to participate in all segments of the cruise industry.

Seabourn Cruise Lines

49   In April 1992, the Company acquired 25% of the capital stock of Seabourn. As part of the transaction, the Company also made a subordinated secured ten-year loan of $15 million to Seabourn and a $10 million convertible loan to Seabourn. In December 1995, the $10 million convertible loan was converted by the Company into an additional 25% equity interest in Seabourn.

50   Seabourn targets the luxury market with three vessels providing 200 passengers per ship with all-suite accommodations. Seabourn is considered the "Rolls Royce" of the cruise industry and in 1992 was named the "World's Best Cruise Line" by the prestigious Condé Nast Traveler's Fifth Annual Readers Choice poll. Seabourn cruises the Americas, Europe, Scandinavia, the Mediterranean, and the Far East.

Airtours

51   In April 1996, the Company acquired a 29.5% interest in Airtours for approximately $307 million. Airtours and its subsidiaries is the largest air inclusive tour operator in the world and is publicly traded on the London Stock Exchange. Airtours provides air inclusive packaged holidays to the British, Scandinavian, and North American markets. Airtours provides holidays to approximately 5 million people per year and owns or operates 32 hotels, two cruise ships, and 31 aircraft.

52   Airtours operates 18 aircraft (one additional aircraft is scheduled to enter service in the spring of 1997) exclusively for its U.K. tour operators providing a large proportion of their flying requirements. In addition, Airtours' subsidiary Premiair operates a fleet of 13 aircraft (one additional aircraft is also scheduled to enter service with Premiair in the spring of 1997), which provides most of the flying requirements for Airtours' Scandinavian tour operators.

53   Airtours owns or operates 32 hotels (6,500 rooms), which provide rooms to Airtours' tour operators principally in the Mediterranean and the Canary Islands. In addition, Airtours has a 50% interest in Tenerife Sol, a joint venture with Sol Hotels Group of Spain, which owns and operates three additional hotels in the Canary Islands providing 1,300 rooms.

54   Through its subsidiary Sun Cruises, Airtours owns and operates two cruise ships. Both the 800-berth MS Seawing and the 1,062-berth MS Carousel commenced operations in 1995. Recently, Airtours acquired a third ship, the MS Sundream, which is the sister ship of the MS Carousel. The MS Sundream is expected to commence operations in May 1997. The ships operate in the Mediterranean, the Caribbean, and around the Canary Islands and are booked exclusively by Airtours' tour operators.

Costa Crociere S.p.A.

55   In June 1997, Carnival and Airtours purchased the equity securities of Costa from the Costa family at a cost of approximately $141 million. Costa is headquartered in Italy and is considered Europe's largest cruise line with seven ships and 7,710-passenger capacity. Costa operates primarily in the Mediterranean, Northern Europe, the Caribbean, and South America. The major market for Costa is in southern Europe, mainly Italy, Spain, and France. In January 1998, Costa signed an agreement to construct an eighth ship with a capacity of approximately 2,100 passengers.

Cunard Line

56   Carnival's most recent acquisition has been the Cunard Line, announced on May 28, 1998. Comprised of five ships, the Cunard Line is considered a luxury line with strong brand name recognition. Carnival purchased 50% of Cunard for an estimated $255 million with the other 50% being owned

by Atle Byrnestad. Cunard was immediately merged with Seabourn and the resulting Cunard Cruise Line Limited (68% owned by Carnival) with its now eight ships, will be headed by the former President of Seabourn, Larry Pimentel.

Joint Venture with Hyundai Merchant Marine Co. Ltd.

57   In September 1996, the Carnival and Hyundai Merchant Marine Co. Ltd. signed an agreement to form a 50/50 joint venture to develop the Asian cruise vacation market. Each has contributed $4.8 million as the initial capital of the joint venture. In addition, in November 1996, Carnival sold the cruise ship Tropicale to the joint venture for approximately $95.5 million cash. Carnival then chartered the vessel from the joint venture until the joint venture is ready to begin cruise operations in the Asian market, targeting a start date in or around the spring of 1998. The joint venture borrowed the $95.5 million purchase price from a financial institution and Carnival and HMM each guaranteed 50% of the borrowed funds.

58   This arrangement was, however, short lived as in September 1997, the joint venture was dissolved and the Company repurchased the Tropicale for $93 million.

FUTURE CONSIDERATIONS

59   Carnival's management will have to continue to monitor several strategic factors and issues for the next few years. The industry itself should see further consolidation through mergers and buyouts, and the expansion of the industry could negatively affect the probability of various cruise operators. Another factor of concern to management is how to reach the large North American market, of which only 5% to 7% have ever taken a cruise.

60   With the industry maturing, cruise competitors have become more sophisticated in their marketing efforts and price competition is the norm in most cruise segments. (For a partial listing of major industry competitors, see Exhibit 6.) Royal Caribbean Cruise Lines has also instituted a major shipbuilding program and is successfully challenging Carnival Cruise Lines in the contemporary segment. The announcement of the Walt Disney Company entering the cruise market with two 80,000 ton cruise liners by 1998 should significantly impact the "family" cruise vacation segment.

61   With competition intensifying, industry observers believe the wave of failures, mergers, buyouts, and strategic alliances will increase. Regency Cruises ceased operations on October 29, 1995, and has filed for Chapter 11 bankruptcy. American Family Cruises, a spin-off from Costa Cruise Lines, failed to reach the family market and Carnival's Fiestamarina failed to reach the Spanish-speaking market. EffJohn International sold its Commodore Cruise subsidiary to a group of Miami-based investors, which then chartered one of its two ships to World Explorer Cruises/Semester at Sea. Sun Cruise Lines merged with Epirotiki Cruise Line under the name of Royal Olympic Cruises and Cunard bought the Royal Viking Line and its name from Kloster Cruise Ltd., with one ship of its fleet being transferred to Kloster's Royal Cruise Line. All of these failures, mergers, and buyouts occurred in 1995, which was not an unusual year for changes in the cruise line industry.

62   The increasing industry capacity is also a source of concern to cruise operators. The slow growth in industry demand is occurring during a period when industry berth capacity continues to grow. The entry of Disney and the ships already on order by current operators will increase industry berth capacity by over 10,000 per year for the next three years, a significant increase. (See Table 1 for new ships under construction.) The danger lies in cruise operators using the "price" weapon in their marketing campaigns to fill cabins. If cruise operators cannot make a reasonable return on investment, operating costs will have to be reduced (affecting quality of services) to remain profitable. This will increase the likelihood of further industry acquisitions, mergers, and consolidations. A "worst case" scenario would be the financial failure of weaker lines.

63   Still, Carnival's management believes that demand should increase during the remainder of the 1990s. Considering that only 5% to 7% of the North American market has taken a cruise vacation, reaching more of the North American target market would improve industry profitability. Industry analysts state the problem is that an "assessment of market potential" is only an "educated guess": and what if the current demand figures are reflective of the future?

EXHIBIT 6
Major Industry Competitors

Celebrity Cruises, 5200 Blue Lagoon Drive, Miami, FL 33126
Celebrity Cruises operates four modern cruise ships on four-, seven-, and ten-day cruises to Bermuda, the Caribbean, the Panama Canal, and Alaska. Celebrity attracts first-time cruisers as well as seasoned cruisers. Purchased by Royal Caribbean on July 30, 1997.

Norwegian Cruise Lines, 95 Merrick Way, Coral Gables, FL 33134
Norwegian Cruise Lines (NCL), formerly Norwegian Caribbean Lines, was the first to base a modern fleet of cruise ships in the Port of Miami. It operates 10 modern cruise liners on three-, four-, and seven-day Eastern and Western Caribbean cruises and cruises to Bermuda. A wide variety of activities and entertainment attracts a diverse array of customers. NCL has just completed reconstruction of two ships and is building the Norwegian Sky, a 2,000-passenger ship to be delivered in the summer of 1999.

Disney Cruise Line, 500 South Buena Vista Street, Burbank, CA 91521
Disney has just recently entered the cruise market with the introduction of the Disney Magic and Disney Wonder. Both ships will cater to both children and adults and will feature 875 staterooms each. Each cruise will include a visit to Disney's private island, Castaway Cay. Although Disney currently has only two ships and the cruise portion of Disney is small, its potential for future growth is substantial with over $22 billion in revenues and $1.9 billion net profits in 1997.

Princess Cruises, 10100 Santa Monica Boulevard, Los Angeles, CA 90067
Princess Cruises, with its fleet of nine "Love Boats," offers seven-day and extended cruises to the Caribbean, Alaska, Canada, Africa, the Far East, South America, and Europe. Princess's primary market is the upscale 50-plus experienced traveler, according to Mike Hannan, Senior Vice President for Marketing Services. Princess ships have an ambience best described as casual elegance and are famous for their Italian-style dining rooms and onboard entertainment.

Royal Caribbean Cruise Lines, 1050 Caribbean Way, Miami, FL 33132
RCCL's nine ships have consistently been given high marks by passengers and travel agents over the past twenty-one years. RCCL's ships are built for the contemporary market, are large and modern, and offer three-, four-, and seven-day as well as extended cruises. RCCL prides itself on service and exceptional cuisine. With the purchase of Celebrity, RCCL becomes the largest cruise line in the world with 17 ships and a passenger capacity of over 31,100. Plans include the introduction of six additional ships by the year 2002. In 1997 RCCL had net income of $175 million on revenues of $1.93 billion.

Other Industry Competitors (Partial List)

American Hawaii Cruises	(2 Ships—Hawaiian Islands)
Club Med	(2 Ships—Europe, Caribbean)
Commodore Cruise Line	(1 Ship—Caribbean)
Cunard Line	(8 Ships—Caribbean, Worldwide)
Dolphin Cruise Line	(3 Ships—Caribbean, Bermuda)
Radisson Seven Seas Cruises	(3 Ships—Worldwide)
Royal Olympic Cruises	(6 Ships—Caribbean, Worldwide)
Royal Cruise Line	(4 Ships—Caribbean, Alaska, Worldwide)

Source: Cruise Line International Association, 1996; and company 10Ks and annual reports.

CASE 61

FIAT DRIVES TO CHINA

Let China sleep, for when it wakes, it will shake the world.
—Napoleon

1   Fiat Auto is an operating subsidiary of Fiat S.P.A. Group. It has manufactured, marketed, sold and distributed passenger cars since 1899. Fiat Auto has car factories in several countries all over the world, producing 2,500,000 vehicles a year. One third of the vehicles are sold in Italy, one third in the remainder of Europe and one third in the rest of the world. All vehicles are sold through local distribution networks. Fiat would like to further develop its Globalization Strategy and expand its presence in new foreign markets by increasing its manufacturing of their automobiles in foreign countries.

2   In 1997, the new president of Fiat Auto, Cesare Romiti, during a semi-annual strategic meeting with the management of the company, stated that the near future of Fiat Auto lies in the People's Republic of China. He reached this conclusion after looking at forecasting results derived from several years of research about population growth, economic growth and car market growth in China. He thought that it was time to stop exporting cars from Poland to China and start becoming an active manufacturer in China. This overall decision involved several specific strategic decisions about the company's future. Should Fiat Auto focus only on the Chinese market or should they address the Asian market as well? How should they enter the Chinese market: through a joint venture or through authorized licensees? Should the company, in this new market, launch its newest product or should it manufacture a 1990 successful car model? How should they distribute the product: utilizing and developing local distribution channels or creating their own exclusive distribution network? These are some of the questions that Cesare Romiti's management had to answer in 1997 in order to strategically position the company to succeed in what was becoming an intensely competitive market.

3   In facing these strategic decisions, Fiat's management first had to take steps to overcome its earlier problems in China. It then needed to study the Chinese market with a fresh look to determine Fiat's best strategy for penetrating that market.

THE BACKGROUND

4   Prior to 1997, Fiat had been exporting to China vehicles produced in Poland by authorized licensees. These inferior quality products hurt Fiat's brand name. This was due to low quality parts and inferior assembly car lines. These vehicles, once they were manufactured, were imported into China. When customers in China purchased their vehicles they encountered several problems. When customers' cars would break down, there were difficulties with finding interchangeable parts and with locating sufficient quality service centers. Furthermore, when customers managed to locate these centers they found that personnel lacked not only the appropriate parts, but also the knowledge required to correct the problem. This image of inferior quality was reinforced by the lack of a quality assurance strategy, such as TQM (Total Quality Management). As problems related to Fiat's cars increased, negative public opinion became worse. In short, production in Poland compromised Fiat's brand image. In addition, Fiat's focus was on its overseas operations in South America (Brazil).

5   To remedy Fiat's negative brand image, the company began to export 1980's-style cars into China from Italy. Also, Fiat developed a promotion/advertising campaign in which the company attempted to counter its negative brand image by informing the Chinese market that the previous cars were manufactured in Poland for Fiat and not by Fiat itself. In addition, the company developed a

This case was prepared by Max Herrera and Antonio Mainiero under the direction of Professor Robert J. Mockler of St. John's University.

promotional campaign that emphasized quality and performance of its products. They then commenced negotiations with the State Planning Commission in China, which is the authority for approving new investment in China. It promoted its new design and performance of its new vehicles utilizing the "made in Italy" association with quality.

6   Fiat's assessment of the Chinese market was helped by its prior experience in Indonesia which enabled the company to acquire general information about the Asian culture and market. In fact, Fiat negotiated licensing agreements with local Indonesian manufacturers. These Indonesian companies produced three types of cars, Fiat 126, 127 and 128. The first car, Fiat 126, is a simple practical car ideal for city driving. The third car, Fiat 128, was a sedan produced with 2 or 4 doors. It was the first vehicle which featured a transversal 1100 cubic centimeters engine.

7   Fiat Auto believed that China provided a growing consumer market. This was due to China's increasing GDP which is about 9% yearly. In addition, there is a growing medium level class (17%) with disposable income. Another important characteristic to take into consideration was the fact that purchasing a car in China became the first step for a medium level consumer to improve his poor living standard. Furthermore, a growing number of successful competitors were already present in this market. Therefore, Fiat had decided to enter this market in order to expand its car production and to have the possibility of obtaining more access to the Asian market.

8   In late 1993, the newly created Automotive Industry Bureau (AIB) of the Ministry of Machinery Industry (MMI), replaced the China National Automotive Industry Corporation (CNAIC) in overseeing China's automotive industry. The AIB has responsibility for policy in the automotive industry, but unlike U.S. regulatory bodies, it is also in business. However, China's automotive industry was still under state control in early 1997.

9   The Chinese government, as well as other Asian governments, has facilitated foreign manufacturers' entrance into their country. General Motors, for example, was researching and developing the Asian Car for 1999.[1] This vehicle was intended to be the only car the company manufactured in China, and GM targeted it exclusively at Asian markets. Among the car's features that GM will gear specifically to the Asian market is high clearance and air-conditioning. GM has said that the Asian car will not come with the high-speed tires that it includes as standard equipment on European models.

CHINESE ISSUES

10   In 1997 China was an important market for many reasons. It had a large territory and with 1.2 billion inhabitants, the largest consumer group in the world. Many factors affected success there.

Description of the People's Republic of China.

11   Situated on the western seaboard of the Pacific Ocean north of the equator, the Asian land mass of the People's Republic of China is as large as the whole continent of Europe. Its area is 9,571,300 square kilometers, the distance from north to south being 5,000 kilometers. In 1997, China could be classified into five areas:

- *Western China:* Includes the Tibetan highland and the Xinjiang-Mongolia region. These two areas make up almost 41 percent of China's land mass, and consist largely of deserts and mountains.
- *Northeast China:* Contains the nation's most important industrial centers.
- *North China:* Consists of plains that are intensively cultivated to produce wheat, millet and other crops. The main industrial centers in this region are Beijing, Tangshan and Tianjin. This region has coal, iron ore and ample power supplies.
- *South China:* Includes the basins of Yangtze River and of the West River in Guangdong and Guangxi, and the mountainous coastal provinces of Fujian and Zhejiang. Further downstream at the coast is Shanghai, China's largest city and commercial center, producer of its most

[1]"GM Plans Asian Car for 1999," www.theautochannel.com/news/date/19961203/news02652.html, pp. 1–2.

sophisticated light industrial products, and its most important port. South of the Yangtze, three rivers merge to form the Canton Delta. This is a very densely populated area, with Guangzhou as its main urban center.

- *Southwest China:* Contains the Sichuan Basin, one of the most fertile areas of China. Coal and iron ore deposits have formed the basis of some industrialization, but the fact that the region is separated from the rest of China by difficult terrain has hindered the area's development.

Political Situation

12   After Deng Xiaoping's death in February 19, 1997 it is generally believed that China will experience a change in political control. This change may entail positive or negative consequences. For instance, positive consequences could be the opening of the Chinese market to more foreign investments leading to more money, more technology and international exposure. China would gain economically. On the other hand, negative consequences could be a loss of the old traditional understanding of life. In fact, China would be exposed to westernization which would be perceived as a threat to its ancient culture. However, if political changes were to be gradual and consistent, the reforms implemented by Deng Xiaoping would continue to develop with positive economic results.

Economic Situation

13   In 1976, after Mao's death, Deng Xiaoping and his "reformers" announced plans to modernize four areas (agriculture, science, technology, industry and defense) and to quadruple China's agricultural and industrial output by the year 2000. For the first time, they also acknowledged, at least implicitly, that China could not attain these objectives solely through its own efforts. Rather, modernization would entail substantial inflows of Western science, technology, and possibly even capital. These needs spurred China's decision to "open the door" to the West in late 1978, when formal diplomatic relations with the United States were established after a lapse of 30 years. The 11th Congress of Chinese Communist Party (CCP) proclaimed a need for greater "economic cooperation with other countries on the basis of self-reliance."[2]

14   The Chinese economy is principally a state and collective economy, but has an increasing amount of private and individual ownership. The industrial output of the cooperative and private sector is increasing and now beginning to account for a larger proportion of total output than in the past. The economy is predominantly agricultural and although it has been characterized by centralized planning, administration and control, there is a definite move towards more mixed reforms. A number of rural reforms have also taken place, for example in the enterprise management, pricing system, foreign trade system and in land leasing and securities trading.

15   These reforms resulted in a growth rate averaging 10%+ per year under an increasingly decollectivized economic model (except for heavy industry), allowing individual families to contract for land for farming purposes and villages/counties/individuals to pursue manufacturing. As a matter of fact, the chief growth is in the decollectivized sector accounting for over 50% of China's industrial output in 1995. This has brought about a rising per capita income in China and a huge demand for energy, raw materials, water, land and new products. Presently, it is estimated that 10% of China's population is "middle class" which accounts for 100 million people. "It is this class that attracts the attention of Western firms from Coke to Chrysler."[3]

16   The real boost to foreign investment, however, came with the creation of unique coastal enclaves known as Special Economic Zones (SEZs). "Reminiscent in some ways of the old foreign treaty ports, the SEZs boasted specific administrative and commercial regulations to provide special incentives to foreign investors. In these areas—originally located in Shenzhen, Shantou, Zhuhai, and

---

[2]"China: Polaroid of Shanghai Ltd.," Harvard Business School, p. 3.

[3]Bennet, A. A., "China's Population Growth and Its Economic Boom," www.physics.iast...u/gcp/energy/china. html, pp. 1–12.

Xiamen (Amoy)—corporate taxes were lowered, tax holidays were offered and imported equipment was exempted from customs duties." [4] The regulations that bound foreigners in other parts of China were loosened considerably and bureaucratic interference was kept to a minimum.

17   In October 1983, the State Council designated 14 coastal cities as coastal open cities (COCs). "Like the SEZs, the COCs were given special powers to authorize foreign funded projects, offer state subsidies for technical upgrading, and lower corporate tax rates for joint ventures. Less than two years later, a third type of special zone—an Open Economic Zone, or OEZ—was created to extend these privileges to the delta areas of the Yangtze River, the Pearl River, and the Southern Fujian region. Then in 1988, Hainan Island in the South China Sea was declared a "Super SEZ" and given special authority to attract special foreign business. By mid-1988, the SEZs, COCs and OEZs together covered 130,000 square miles and contained a population of 90 million." [5]

18   The increase of economic growth in these Special Economic Zones has resulted in Shanghai and Shenzhen opening their Stock Exchanges. These cities have flourished to become centers of economic and financial influence. However, in a few months (July 1), Hong Kong will be repatriated to China, becoming its New York. This status is guaranteed by the "Sino-British Joint Declaration" [6], where it states that Hong Kong will establish the Hong Kong Special Administration Region (HKSAR). This provides Hong Kong with a high degree of autonomy enabling it to decide its own economic, financial and trade policies, and to participate in international and trade agreements. This will facilitate Hong Kong's investment in the rest of mainland China.

Infrastructure Limitations

19   Foreign companies must consider the infrastructure present in China. The limitations come about from the lack of infrastructure comparable to that of developed nations.

20   China's transportation and communications systems have not received sufficient investment for development but are now priority sectors. The main means of transporting goods in China is by rail, although inland waterways also play an important part in the transportation network. Roads and highways are still in need of modernization and development, but the construction of superhighways is progressing. Port and harbor development is also a priority in order to cope with an increase in foreign trade. In order to accelerate the modernization of China's transportation networks, it is expected that foreign participation in domestic transportation projects will be encouraged. Therefore, the Chinese government attempted to gather funds and implement strategies to improve the infrastructure network with hopes to facilitate transportation of goods.

Legal Considerations

21   The National People's Congress and its Standing Committee are empowered to exercise legislative power. The State Council is also authorized to adopt administrative regulations and measures in accordance with the Constitution and statutes. At the local level, the people's congresses of the provinces and municipalities directly under the central government may also adopt local regulations, provided they do not contravene the Constitution or contradict the state laws.

22   "The People's Courts are the judicial organs of the state and the judiciary is able to exercise independent power in accordance with the law. The Supreme Court is the highest in the land and is responsible to the National People's Congress and its Standing Committee." [7] It supervises the administration of justice by the local people's court, which is established at different levels and is responsible to the organs of state power that created them. There are also special courts, such as those dealing with military and maritime issues.

---

[4] Polaroid of Shanghai Ltd., *op. cit.*, p. 4.

[5] Ibid., p. 5.

[6] "Hong Kong's Beyond 1997," www.tdc.org.hk/beyond97/after.htm, p. 1.

[7] "General Facts of China," www.xs4all.nl/%7Esv2312/china.html, p. 6.

23   Taxation is an important legal consideration. In 1980 China initiated the concept of tax incentive areas through its Special Economic Zones. These zones were created primarily to attract foreign investment and offer investors tax and other incentives. Tax incentives include preferential tax rates, tax holidays and exemption from tax on certain categories of goods imported into the special incentive areas.

24   There are restrictions in China for new projects due to the decisions made for the next five-year plan, 1996–2000. Therefore, foreign investors must analyze these restrictions to see if they will be allowed access, in general, to China.

Government Trade Policy

25   The State Planning Commission is responsible for drafting China's economic plans. The 20-year plan, which covers the period 1981–2000, provides the guidelines for the country's modernization program. The five-year plans, the first of which was introduced in 1953, establish the targets for each five-year period. Each year, a detailed plan and budget is produced for implementation.

26   The main thrust of China's 1997 economic development policy is "to maintain balanced growth, to avoid the fluctuation of the last decade and to improve the living standards of the people."[8]

27   Foreign enterprises are encouraged to participate in export-oriented projects to help enhance the country's foreign exchange earnings and to improve the balance of trade. Special incentives are granted to foreign companies participating in export-oriented enterprises.

28   Although state-owned enterprises remain the foundation of the Chinese economy, collective enterprises have shown a marked development. The private and individual sectors, while still small, are also developing, although it is likely they will eventually play a greater role than enterprises in the near future. In a recent development, state-owned and collective enterprises have been permitted to operate as joint stock companies or companies limited by shares.

29   With regard to foreign investment enterprises, in an amendment to the "Equity Joint Venture Law"[9] issued in April 1990, the government provided an undertaking not to nationalize or expropriate joint ventures, with expropriation only occurring under special circumstances and with appropriate compensation granted.

30   In 1996, the Chinese government developed a joint venture agreement model with the intention to attract more foreign investment. It facilitated and permitted joint ventures by simplifying the process. It was simplified by eliminating many bureaucratic steps and creating a standard form.

31   In order for the foreign company to be permitted to have a joint venture with one of the "big eight" Chinese car manufacturers, the company must provide detailed information. It would consist of information about the type of vehicle that it would like to produce, the manufacturing process, the environment impact, etc., which the government and the big eight would approve. Regarding the plant location, the government would like the company to locate the plant in one of the Special Economic Zones.

Foreign Trade

32   China's foreign trade is subject to central planning and is conducted principally through the foreign trade corporations, which are under the control of the Ministry of Foreign Trade and Economic Cooperation. Foreign trade has become largely decentralized and a large number of import/export corporations have been authorized to conduct overseas trade.

33   In 1997, China ranked after the United States, E.U., Japan, Hong Kong and Canada as the 6th largest trading nation in the world. Major trading partners include Japan, Hong Kong, the United States, the E.U., Taiwan and South Korea. Principal export items were machinery and electronic products, garments and clothing accessories, textiles, footwear and toys.

34   Due to global economic recovery and China's prudent macro-economic management, the external sector has started to improve since early 1994. With exports and imports growing at respective

[8]Weber, Maria, *Vele Verso La Cina,* ed. Olivares, Milano, December 1996, p. 15.

[9]Ibid., p. 24.

rates of 35 percent and 16 percent, the trade balance switched from a deficit of US$ 1.22 billion in 1994 to a US$ 5.3 billion surplus in 1994. In the first nine months of 1996, China's exports and imports experienced 35 percent and 16.2 percent year on year growth respectively. The trade outlook remained favorable in 1997 following the successful resolution of intellectual property rights disputes between China and the United States.

Overseas Trade Relations

35   China is not currently a member of the General Agreement on Tariffs and Trade (GATT), but is awaiting membership approval. To aid its bid for membership, China has made a number of revisions to its trade system, which include abolishing export subsidies, making the foreign trade corporations responsible for their own profits and losses, abolishing the import adjustment tax and reducing tariffs on certain items.

36   Investment incentives are offered to foreign companies investing in export-oriented enterprises if they are able to meet certain requirements. These are mainly in the form of tax incentives: additional preferential treatments are available if they are located in the designated special investment zones. With the exception foreign investment enterprises are exempt from export duties and consolidated industrial and commercial tax.

37   In order to address the foreign trade imbalance experienced in the mid 1980s, which saw a depletion in China's foreign exchange reserves and a huge trade deficit, China placed severe restrictions on the import of nonessential items and those that competed with domestically manufactured products. As a result, import licenses need to be obtained; heavy duties have been imposed on nonessential items, especially on luxury consumer goods; and access to foreign exchange has been restricted to cut down on foreign exchange spending.

Management and Labor Situation

38   China has a large and inexpensive labor force, the majority of whom are engaged in the agricultural sector. Prior to 1986, when new labor laws came into effect, the work force was highly regulated and individuals were generally assigned to jobs or work units where they remained for life. This system did not help foster an efficient or productive labor force but the situation is now changing and workers have more opportunities to change jobs. There is a shortage of skilled labor in China, which makes it difficult for foreign enterprises to find quality staff. The joint venture law contains provisions for the establishment of labor unions. Although labor is relatively inexpensive in China, many joint ventures offer incentives to attract better qualified staff. For a foreign company doing business in China the cost of maintaining expatriate management is high, as housing, travel, hardship allowances, and other fringe benefits are paid in addition to the basic salary.

39   In order to remedy the situation of lack of skilled labor in China and to avoid the cost of importing qualified staff, it must redesign the curriculum of the Chinese education system. It does not manage to produce thousands of students with undergraduate degrees, as well as lower-level administrative trainees. But, multinationals say most of the students lack the preparation required in modern companies. For instance, Motorola (China) Electronics Ltd., a manufacturing subsidiary of U.S. electronics giant Motorola Inc., says: "I have to teach recruits the most basic management practices such as brainstorming, setting and achieving goals and even what to do when a boss asks them to take on more work than they can handle." [10]

40   China's necessary decision to switch to a market economy has vastly intensified its management problems. In 1996, the government approved more than 84,000 foreign-funded projects with combined investment plans of $111 billion.[11] Those projects alone will require a small army of skilled managers. But an efficient market economy also requires the kind of trained personnel largely missing from the socialist order and the old, largely closed, autocratic China.

[10]"Solving China's Management Crisis," www.asia-inc.com/archive/1994/solving.html, p. 2.

[11]Weber, Maria, op. cit., p. 25.

41   The following are examples of the much needed personnel in China:

- *Lawyers:* The rule of law is the best regulator of dealings between private enterprises. In order to work well, China's new market economy desperately needs expanded, modernized legal mechanisms.
- *Accountants:* For similar reasons, 300,000 accountants will be needed. The Chinese Institute of Certified Public Accountants has only 38,000 members; 80 percent of them are more than 60 years old. In fact, China will need 1 million accountants by the next century based on international standards, according to Eric Li, a senior partner at the Hong Kong accountancy firm Li, Tang, Chen & Co.
- *Foreign experts:* The government announced that in 1997 it would recruit a record 180,000 foreign experts.

42   In efforts to resolve the problem of a lack of qualified personnel, China introduced new programs at its universities. For instance, in 1997 there were 40 M.B.A. programs and they would be about 50 in July, 1997 when Hong Kong will return into the People's Republic of China.[12] All universities are utilizing their resources to expand these programs, as well as to develop and update courses such as international finance and accounting, business law, real-estate management and human-resource management. Enhancement of experienced managers' skills also is being stressed, with most business schools offering part-time executive M.B.A. programs.

Linguistic and Cultural Considerations

43   The linguistic and cultural differences between China and Western countries are so great that in order for foreign companies to be successful in the nation, they must acquire a lot of knowledge and patience necessary to be accepted as a partner in China.

44   Putonghua or Mandarin, is the national language based on the Beijing dialect, though there are numerous other dialects. The principal of these are Cantonese, Shanghainese, Fukienese, and Hakka. The written language, which is ideograph and not phonetic, is uniform, although many of the characters have been simplified.

45   There are several alternative spellings for place names in China. In 1958 the State Council adopted the Chinese Phonetic Alphabet system (Pinyin) for romanizing Chinese names and places. From January 1, 1979 all translated texts of Chinese diplomatic documents and Chinese magazines published in foreign languages have used the new Pinyin system of spelling Chinese names and places. It is an important change that replaces various different spelling systems, including the Wade-Giles (English) and Lessing (German) systems, and is intended to end the confusion that existed for a long time in romancing Chinese.[13]

46   This Pinyin facilitates foreign companies in their negotiations and propositions. It provides a consistent standardized alphabet through which foreign companies and various regional governments can communicate. Whereas in the past, there were various forms of translated contracts, today there are less versions bringing about less confusion. This results in less possibility for litigation. The decrease in confusion decreases the possibility for misinterpretations of official documents. This, in turn, speeds the process and decreases costs associated with drawing up documents.

The Automotive Industry in China

47   The Chinese car market represents an excellent opportunity for foreign investors because the Chinese economy is growing dramatically. Industry guidelines confirm that "the automotive industry will remain one of the most key industries designated to develop China's economy and will be protected from dominance by foreign automotive companies."[14] In addition, the importance of the automotive

---

[12]Ibid., p. 48.

[13]"General Facts of China," *op. cit.,* p. 5.

[14]"Automotive Industry," www.tradecompass . . .rket/China/ISA9506.html, p.2.

industry has been stressed by the Chinese State Planning Commission in the 1996–2000 five-year plan.

48   The Chinese automotive industry has a lack of a rational structure due to the wide diversification of the industry. In 1997, China produced more than 100 models in 125 factories capable of building complete vehicles, with aggregate output of less than one of the U.S. "Big 3".[15] Another 600 factories assemble "specialty vehicles" from parts produced from the over 3000 auto parts manufacturers. Approximately 600 factories assemble or overhaul vehicles and as many as 800 factories manufacture or assemble a small number of buses.

Government Plans for the Automotive Industry

49   The automotive industry's main goal is to attain greater efficiencies of scale in every sector of the automotive industry. However, the rationalization plan is bound to encounter the strong regional forces which are at play in China today. Provincial and municipal governments are important players in the automotive sector and are not likely to want to give up their part of the industry easily.

50   The government would like the auto industry to have the ability to independently develop new products, improve quality, assist the development of lean-burning and alternative-fuel vehicles and develop some focus on export in the future. With the exception of the Tianjin Automobile Industrial Corporation, which produces 60,000 passenger cars a year on a licensing agreement with Daihatsu, a Japanese car manufacturer, all production in any scale and with any real quality has been done with the help of a foreign partner in a joint venture arrangement. As with most investment in China, the foreign partner is expected to contribute money and technology. As overseas companies are lining up to get a piece of the potential world's largest automotive market, the Ministry of Machinery is becoming more and more demanding in the "price of admission" to this market. Companies may find it difficult to negotiate a deal or make a profit in the short-term.

51   China's sedan manufacturing sector, expected to remain an infant industry throughout the 1990s, will be protected for a limited period from competition from foreign built cars. It is also expected that this would be one of the areas for which China would continue to seek protection even if admitted to the World Trade Organization in the near future. Protection consists primarily of high tariffs on imports, and the prohibition of any new joint venture vehicle production. These restrictions do not seem to apply to vans, mini-vans, specialty vehicles, buses, motorcycles or trucks.

52   The plan is for six to seven conglomerates to be formed from the current thirteen existing auto groups. Each is expected to make 300,000 sedans a year, and will receive capitalized state loans and other assistance to reach that goal. By the end of the century, the conglomerates are to be further condensed into three larger ones each making five million vehicles annually, supplying 90 percent of domestic demand. The goal of consolidation is the core of the new policies governing the country's auto industry for the next seven years.

53   No approval will be given to new foreign investment in sedan manufacturing or assembly projects until the implementation of the 1996–2000 five-year plan. After that, approval for such projects will depend on the automotive climate and situation, with priority given to companies that have helped China develop its auto components industry. The Chinese government will also look for foreign partners who are willing to transfer technology and design know-how.

54   The main goals projected for the automotive components, parts and accessories industry are to improve technology and quality, and to develop design capability. The government will encourage foreign investment during the next year in auto component development and manufacturing. The goal is to reduce the current more than 3000 component manufacturers to 30, each making 60 kinds of components.

---

[15]"Big Three Say Target for Auto Export to Japan Has Been Reached,"
www.theautochannel.com/news/date19961203/news02666.html, p.1.

Location Necessities

55   The Chinese government has asked all automotive and component manufacturers to strive for complete localization. Similar to other countries with infant automotive industries, China requires producers to include a minimum amount of local materials and value added work in their final products. However, China's localization goals are far more ambitious than those of other countries.

56   These local content requirements are designed to force assemblers to buy components and raw materials in China, thereby contributing to the development of Chinese industry. However, quality generally drops with localization and the foreign partner of a Sino-foreign joint venture may find start-up costs high.

57   In the past, vehicle assemblers were to reach 40 percent local content by the third year of production, and a local content of 60 percent in the following year. However, the most recently released government report stated that any future manufacturing venture must have a 40 percent local content at the start-up, going to 60 percent the second year, and 80 percent the third.

58   Part of what makes component investment attractive in China is that a vehicle manufacturer or assembler has been able to get 100 percent "local content credit"[16] towards their own localization. In 1997, the industrial policy is looking for components to attain 40 percent local content at the outset, 60 percent local content the second year and 80 percent the third. The goal of government policy is for local content of all components to reach 60 percent by 2000.

59   The percent of local content for major manufacturing components, such as engines, transmissions, and chassis, is determined by the total percentage of local product in that component. Smaller components are considered 100 percent local in content if they are assembled in China.

Passenger Cars

60   With a population of over 1.2 billion, estimates suggest that there were only about 1.6 million motor vehicles in use in China in 1997. About one million of the cars and trucks in use are sedans, of which only a small proportion are owned by individuals. Sedan production currently comprises only 18 percent of the total automotive production (at 230,000 sedans in 1994). By the year 2000, China aims to dedicate half of projected three million unit production to sedans. In 1994, sedans placed third among kinds of vehicles produced in China. In 1995, the sedan took first place accounting for approximately 25 percent of the total market.

61   In spite of the increase in sedan sales in China, commercial vehicles still account for more than 70 percent of sales. As of 1997, the division between passenger cars and commercial vehicles was 35 percent and 65 percent. Some analysts predict a shift from medium trucks to the lighter categories.

Commercial Cars

62   The majority of the more than nine million vehicles in use in China are government-owned either by enterprises, institutions or the military. Private buyers account for only two percent of purchases in China today. According to Beijing press reports, there are only 50,000 private car owners in China, of which 10,000 cars are registered in Beijing. Although this may not seem like much, a mere ten years ago there were only 60 private cars registered in the whole country.

63   As entrepreneurs and businesses become more successful, there will be an ever increasing market for personal cars. Private Chinese citizens have significant personal savings, and their real purchasing power is much higher than their salaries suggest, since housing and medical care are generally provided or subsidized.

64   In the sedan car sector of the automobile industry, demand greatly outweighs supply and individuals wishing to purchase sedans must spend some time on a waiting list. Individuals must compete for cars with the most significant group of vehicle end-users: town enterprises and the taxi and

---

[16]"Automotive Industry," *op. cit.*, p. 4.

tourism industries. This is more interesting when considering that all vehicles are paid for in total with cash, as financing does not yet exist as a method of payment for a vehicle.

Competitive Situation

Domestic Production

65 In 1997, the Chinese automotive industry's domestic production primarily supplied the domestic market, with very few exports.

66 Automobile companies already comprise three of the most productive foreign invested enterprises in China. In descending order they are, Shanghai Volkswagen, Beijing Jeep, and Guangzhou Peugeot.

Imports

67 Imports will continue to play an important role in meeting total market demand in the Chinese automotive sector to fill the gap between domestic production and demand.

68 Competing with the $6000 plus locally produced Jeep 2020 are a surprising number of imported luxury models, especially considering that most officials are prohibited from purchasing luxury cars in recent anti-corruption campaigns. There are dealerships registered in China for Rolls Royce, Ferrari, Mercedes, Jaguar and Cedilla.

Car Companies Market Position and Share

69 In 1997 the average total U.S. market share in the automotive industry was 15 percent, the Japanese and Europeans (including Russia) each had approximately a 45 percent share of the import market. The remaining percent include Korea, Taiwan and Hong Kong.

Major Car Manufacturers Analysis

70 There are several big foreign companies manufacturing in China which are the following:

- *Volkswagen* (Germany) is the leader in sales having established a joint venture in Shanghai with 50% to its Chinese partner. They sell the "Santana," a 4-door hatchback passenger car for customers with high/medium income. Their strengths are: price/quality ratio, mass advertising, a wide distribution network and customer services.
- *Chrysler* (USA) manufactures the "Beijing Jeep" which has been a popular selling vehicle. In 1996 they surpassed 500,000 units of production. They focus on the medium income customers, utilizing mass production and good post-purchase services.
- *Peugeot* (France) has not sold very well due to the fact that the models they offer are considered obsolete and directed only to high income consumers.
- *Daihatsu* (Japan) has conquered the low income market a few years ago with "Charade," a small and inexpensive model. At the moment, they are losing their market share due to the low quality of the product.
- *Suzuki* (Japan) with its "Alto" model. Medium income Chinese consumers consider this model to be very similar to the Fiat "Uno" with respect to price, performance and dimensions. Presently, while sales of the Suzuki "Alto" decreased, Fiat "Uno" sales have increased.
- *Citroen* (France) is also manufacturing in China, producing small cars for medium income consumers. They started operating in China only a few years ago and they are gradually increasing their sales due to a good price policy.

Access to the Chinese Automotive Market

71 In 1992 the U.S. Trade Representative announced an agreement with China on market access for exports to China. Under the agreement, China committed to dismantle its complex system of non-tariff barriers including import license requirements, quotas, and other non-transparent administrative controls or restrictions on importation of U.S. goods. The agreement requires elimination of import barriers beginning 31 December 1992 and continuing until 31 December 1997.

72   Considering the issue of manufacturing vehicles in China, the only alternative that the Government provides to foreign car manufacturing companies, is that of developing a joint venture with a Chinese partner. A joint venture is a combination of two enterprises associated for the purpose of accomplishing a business objective.

73   Those barriers which affect the auto industry were eliminated as of 31 December 1992, and included quotas on auto parts imported by U.S. joint ventures in China required to meet existing needs and production expansion.

74   As of December 1996, import tariffs for gasoline-driven cars with 3 liter and below displacement were reduced from 180 percent to 110 percent. Import tariffs for small cars with over 3 liter displacement and diesel-driven cars with over 2.5 liter displacement were reduced from 220 percent to 150 percent. Many analysts feel this was done as a concession for GATT/WTO entry. However, at the same time, the Chinese government did away with Foreign Exchange Certificates and changed the official exchange rate from 8.7 yuan to the dollars. The effect of this was an approximate 50 percent cost added for the same imports, leaving the price of vehicles approximately the same as before the unification of the two currencies. Despite the high price, the Chinese continue to buy imports and go on major automotive buying missions.

75   In addition to tariffs, imports are also charged value-added and consumption (excise) taxes. These additional charges add substantially to the official tariff rate. China uses this combination of tariffs and additional taxes to clamp down on imports that it views as threatening to its domestic industry.

Distribution

76   Distribution is rudimentary, and vehicles are usually driven to their owners, even if the new owner lives across China. Components seem to make their way around China slowly, but the distribution methods are not well-established.

77   For sales, China does not have a well-established system of independent agents or distributors, and companies may need to use other methods for penetrating China's market. There are a few practices that have been successful, which are the following:

> Use the services of a third country trading company. Many of these trading companies are willing to handle foreign products. Trading companies with offices in China will likely be the most effective.
>
> Use the services of a Hong-Kong based agent or distributor. Many Hong Kong agents and distributors are very active in China and have an extensive network of Chinese contracts.
>
> Establish a representative office in China. This is a good, but expensive way to maintain continued visibility in China.
>
> Establish a technology transfer or licensing relationship with a Chinese partner. Although many companies have engaged in successful technology transfer arrangement with Chinese enterprises, the foreign partner should review carefully intellectual property rights protection which China's legal structure offers.

78   Finally, companies should be aware that, although China has no requirement for countertrade provisions in imports, a foreign company willing to consider countertrade may sometimes gain the competitive edge.

Consumers

79   There exists an opportunity to reach a growing number of consumers in China. This is so because the economy in China is growing which leads to a growing amount of individuals with disposable income. The Chinese market is composed of three different segments: high-end, medium and low-end consumers.

- *High-end consumers* represent only 1% of the entire population. They earn about 600 million Reminbi[18] a year and they prefer to purchase top quality foreign products.[19]

- *The medium level,* which comprises 17.5% of the population, has a monthly income of about $500. They buy moderately priced imported products such as jeans and shoes and can also afford to buy high/medium locally manufactured products such as TV sets, refrigerators, cameras, automobiles and other family-use electric appliances. This is due to the fact that they spend only 5% of their income on basic needs such as housing, transportation and education.

- *The low level,* mainly concentrated in the rural area, makes up the rest of the population: they can only afford to buy domestic manufactured products because their average income never exceeds a top average of $250 a month. Although the above statistics are officially recognized, it is worthwhile to point out that they do not reflect the real state of Chinese consumers because the average pro capita income is significantly affected by several sources of unreported income.

Product

80   The Chinese government is presently pushing the idea of a Chinese "family car" possibly in the hopes of drawing attention away from many luxury cars driven by officials and top executives in the automotive industry. In October 1996, most of the world's automotive manufacturers bid for an opportunity to design and build a "family car" at a Ministry of Machinery industry sponsored show in Beijing. Although many of the companies were not sure if the event was a competition or a display, most participated if for no other reason than to have their small car designs considered should it turn out to have been a competition. Several European companies, including Porsche, designed new cars just for the show.

81   It is indisputable that China has the potential to be the world's largest automotive market. In April 1996, a survey by the Beijing Statistics Bureau suggested that of 1,004 households, 59 percent wanted to buy a car and believed that they would be able to before the year 2010. The number of privately owned cars has skyrocketed within the past decade. As of January 1997 there are 50,000 private cars in China, 10 years ago there was a meager 60. The Chinese government says that it would invest substantially in order to increase production capacity and trim production costs, making Chinese produced cars more affordable for regular families.

82   Both the Chinese industry and the foreign companies are looking to create a low cost car that would become popular with Chinese families. Besides the low price, the car ideally would have low maintenance and service costs and extensive safety and environmental protection features.

83   However, many experts believe that high tariffs on imported components and meager wages will continue to keep the dream of a family car out of reach for most Chinese. Auto experts also say that the Chinese market is too diversified to sustain a single family car. In addition, a car that contains safety and extensive environmental protection features is not likely to be inexpensive.

84   It is also unrealistic to assume that China's infrastructure could sustain a substantial increase of cars. Major cities already face daily traffic jams bordering on gridlock. In addition, there is a distinct lack of parking. For example, in Guangzhou there are 600,000 licensed drivers and 10,000 parking spaces. Perhaps the only thing that has kept this situation under control is that most cars are driven by professional drivers, who can keep moving should there not be anywhere to park. Also, most cars are parked at their work units overnight. Analysts also point out that drivers will not have far to drive considering that all the existing high-speed expressways linked together would not equal the highway length that connects New York to Chicago. The Chinese desire to use foreign capital to build highways through "build-operate-transfer" has not been successful in encouraging much investment in the building of an adequate highway system in China. All of these problems must be solved in order for the dream of a Chinese family car to become a reality.

────────

[18]3 Reminbi are equal to $1.00. Please note that it is not exchanged in the free market. Source by Chinese Embassy in Rome.

[19]Weber, Maria, *op. cit.,* p. 55.

85   To many people, the thought of a large number of privately owned cars in China is unthinkable. Experts say that even if by 2000 China had the car density of Portugal, it would be 120 million. Considering there are about 340 million cars total in use in the world today, the pollution implications alone are staggering.

Promotion

86   Various types of promotional programs are utilized by the car industry that bring about optimal results, several come to mind. The oldest form of promotion is the written form, through newspapers and magazines. This mode of communication is a good source of target consumers because Chinese read very much as seen by their 80% literacy rate. This is an excellent way for advertisers to promote their products because it is a visual instrument in which words and images are combined.

87   Second, through the local and national radio network car manufacturers are able to make the customer aware of their product. It is one of the most powerful instruments of mass communication. This is so because radio is a source of entertainment (music) and information that is easily accessible from anywhere whether on foot, car, or train.

88   In 1997, television is the most important method of communicating messages. It allows car manufacturers to promote their vehicles in an extensive manner. This is so because the viewer not only sees the product but can listen to the message. The Chinese enjoy television because they utilize more of their senses contributing to a more complete reception of information.

Automotive Aftermarket

89   The automotive aftermarket consists of providing auto parts, service centers and replacement of vehicles. Due to the increase in car sales in China, this market is increasing as well. This has brought about new opportunities for car manufacturers in China.

90   In 1997, China's auto aftermarket is currently one of the fastest growing industries and will continue to grow in the next decade. The automotive industry in this fast growing economy is creating a demand for imported and manufactured vehicles. Since the automobile aftermarket is still developing, the market potential is promising.

91   China will replace 400,000 vehicles, in 1997, accounting for 25% of the total demand for auto vehicles in the year. There are 10 million civilian automobiles in use in China, of which 2 million units must be replaced because of age in 1997.[20]

92   There are over 10 million motor vehicles in China, of which 900,000 were imports. Japan has the largest car market share, but European and American market shares are increasing. In 1997, Japanese automakers had set up an extensive system to service and repair their vehicles throughout China.

THE COMPANY

93   Who would have guessed that on July 1, 1899 at the Bricarasio Palace, the birth of one of the world's most renowned car manufacturers was taking place. It occurred when the constitutional act called "Societa' Anonima Fabbrica Italiana Automobili Torino" was signed. There were thirty shareholders with a social capital of 800 thousand lire.

94   They began with the production of thirty exemplary cars of the Fiat 3 1/2 HP model. In 1900, they produced these vehicles at their first factory in Torino. Throughout the years Fiat produced several custom made models.

---

[20] "Automotive Aftermarket," www.tradecompass...rket/China/ISA9505.html.

95   A major change came in 1920 when Fiat's president, Senator Giovanni Agnelli, met with Henry Ford in America. Mr. Agnelli visited Ford's facilities and became convinced that the only real way to reduce prohibitive vehicle costs was to implement Ford's assembly plant strategy.

96   Another change occurred when Giovanni Agnelli, Jr. assumed his father's position as president of Fiat in 1966. He was a man of great stature not only in terms of his 1.80 meters height but also in his capabilities. His charisma allowed him to make the most of his international studies and experiences abroad. He met people from different countries from which he developed a global vision of life. This vision carried over into many aspects of his career. He was particularly concerned about Italy's economic and political environment. His intelligence allowed him to develop many strategies that incorporated his understanding of the relationship between economics and politics. As his business flourished so did his importance in Italy. Again, his charisma facilitated his mediator role in Italy's economic and political arena in 1996. In fact, he was referred to as "the lawyer" because of his capacity to analyze both sides of an issue. Consequently, many Italian and European business leaders look to him for advice.

97   When he took the position of Fiat Group president, he brought with him a new management approach which altered the company's culture. His American education facilitated his innovative strategies concerning engineering, production, and promotion. In fact, this innovative spirit led to Fiat's 124 model becoming the "Automobile of the Year" in 1967. In 1978, these dynamic changes permitted Fiat to introduce incredible innovative car manufacturing techniques. For example, it implemented Robogate, the world's first robotics car assembly system at its Rivalta and at its Cassino plants.

98   The company's continued success led to the creation of Fiat Auto S.p.A. which includes Fiat, Lancia, Alfa Romeo, Autobianchi, Abarth and Ferrari. This allowed Fiat to operate on a world wide level in a more decisive manner because it combined all the resources, financial and technical, that each company offered to their perspective niche markets.

99   In 1995, Fiat introduced Fiat Bravo and Brava. These models, for the first time, were introduced at the same time. They differed in design, dimension, performance and target customer market but were developed from a common engineering model.

100   Exhibit A provides selective financial and operational ratios and statistics as of early 1997. Fiat had 650 million shares outstanding and a dividend yield of 1.28%.

101   In 1997, Fiat Auto was developing major industrial projects all over the world. This company relies on three basic methods: 1) authorizing licensing of production to local manufacturers, 2) establishing joint ventures with local manufacturers, 3) Fiat car production. As for licensing, Fiat has authorized Morocco, Egypt, ex-Yugoslavia, Ecuador, Uruguay, India, Russia, Philippines, Indonesia, Kenya, Zambia, South Africa and Poland. Fiat's joint ventures are in Argentina, Turkey, and Algeria with partners in the production of vehicles. As manufacturing, this company produces cars in Italy, Venezuela, Argentina and Brazil.

102   The company's largest licensing project is in Togliattigrad, Russia where 700,000 units are produced per year. They initiated with the production of Fiat 128, during the 1970s. This company's time spent and experience in Russia has allowed it to familiarize itself with the demands of world expansion. Brazil's production has arrived at 500,000 units produced a year. This success is attributed to Fiat's capability of producing various models in one assembly line. Low labor costs have also contributed to Fiat's achievement. In addition, Fiat's brand image was maintained in this country because of its ability to learn and improve production techniques. Therefore, Fiat's foreign production has required most of their financial and technical resources that would have otherwise been utilized in new markets such as China.

103   Fiat market share value is indicative of the company's success due to its growth strategies. Exhibit B shows that Fiat Auto's car sales were impressive during the fiscal year which ended in December 31, 1996. In Italy, 777,276 units were sold, representing 43.9% of the Italian automobile market share. Moreover, 1,491,219 units were sold in Western Europe, with a market share of 11.3%.

Organizational Structure

104   Fiat Group, S.p.A. has a pyramid hierarchical organizational structure. It is a complex structure because it has various subsidiaries and businesses all over the world. Therefore, Fiat has been growing and expanding in new markets requiring them to alter their organizational structure. The company management staff is primarily composed of the following:

- One Chief Executive Officer (CEO), Cesare Romiti, who develops company strategies.
- Administrative Delegate (Administratore Delegato) who has direct operative contact with the presidents of each subsidiary.
- The presidents of each of the sixteen Fiat Group subsidiaries.
- Managers for each department such as Marketing, Finance and Research & Development in each of the sixteen subsidiaries.

105   During the 1980s and 1990s, Fiat expanded in many ways. This required flexibility on the part of their management. Due to increased intense competition, Research & Development became the most important focus of Fiat. This led to increased investment in researching and developing new technologies in order to create new competitive products and increase sales. The success in Brazil represents this type of focus on developing new competitive markets. In fact, in Brazil, Fiat develops a single assembly line producing five different models. This is a new modular line through which they gained the Brazilian market. These new vehicles, of superior quality, gained consumer acceptance.

Product

106   While Giovanni Agnelli was in his office, sitting in his recliner he began to recall his experiences in China during his trips through Asia. He imagined a Fiat car being purchased by a Chinese family. The idea of developing a family car for China excited him. He convened a meeting with his executives to explore the possibility of producing a family car.

107   The product Fiat Auto was planning to launch in the Chinese market in 1997 as a "family-type car," as defined by Chinese criteria, was the three door hatch back. It would be designed to meet the needs of a medium level standard Chinese family composed of two parents and one child. The "family car" would feature a modern style, good price/quality ratio, high fuel efficiency, low running costs, safety and comfort, handling and interior space. What would differentiate the production of this family-type car would be that it would be manufactured with other models in a modular line, thus utilizing one assembly line. This strategy has been successful for Fiat in Brazil when producing the Palio model, acquiring more than 50% of the Brazilian market share. This allowed the company to not only increase production of several models but to reduce costs. Therefore, Fiat intends to utilize the same strategy, one assembly line for various models in China.

108   Fiat planned to launch other models between 1997 and 2000, such as the five-door Hatch-Back (2 volume car); the Saloon model which is a four-door sedan (3 volume car); the Station Wagon (3 volume car) which is a larger vehicle; and the Pick-up offering a mid-size loading bed. These new models would use the same chassis as the three door hatch back model. In fact, Fiat is planning to adapt the three door hatch back design to meet different customer demands. This would allow Fiat to serve all types of consumers. These models represent an excellent advantage that Fiat would have over its competitors which are the following:

- *Price competitiveness* due to low labor cost and high "local content."[21]
- *High technological performance ratio* due to the fact that this is the newest model designed by Fiat Auto research and development center.

---

[21]Local content implies that there are local manufacturers of interchangeable automobile accessories.

Consumers

109   Fiat Auto's strength was expected to be mainly in the mid-level consumer market. This consumer group is composed of a growing bourgeois class accounting for 17.5% of the Chinese population. Its monthly income was on an average $500 a month. Therefore, the company focused on offering products that these consumers would perceive as price competitive and of high quality performance. However, most consumers perceived Fiat as weak in its post-sale services.

Geographical Market

110   Fiat has many opportunities if it caters to China's many regions. This company would produce cars that focus on mid-level consumers that are concentrated in larger cities. Fiat's strength lies in that their cars meet customer needs of high traffic and unmaintenanced city streets.

Distribution

111   Fiat considers several factors when dealing with physical distribution. It regards the terrain involved when distributing from region to region. While trucking is mainly utilized, it also uses trains to transport their vehicles. Shipping is another option utilized. In addition, distribution channels consist mainly of dealerships. There are dealerships that exclusively sell Fiat vehicles and dealerships that sell their cars as well as other makers' vehicles.

Promotion

112   Promotion must be appealing to the local culture. It must consider the name of the car utilized. In the past, various companies have overlooked this factor which resulted in car names that had negative effects. This, in turn, had serious consequences such as low or no sales. There are some types of promotion programs that would bring about optimal results for Fiat Auto's image. The first consists of special events where consumers have the opportunity to try new models, compare them to others and rate them. In addition, Fiat is a major participant at Car Convention Shows, such as the world renowned Berlin Show, in which it introduces its newly developed models. This serves to solidify a base of Fiat customers. The same type of promotional strategy would be used in China. Fiat would promote its new cars at the Beijing auto show.

TOWARDS THE FUTURE

113   The future for Fiat Auto in the Chinese automotive market is a promising one. The car market in China is growing at a stable rate of 9%. Everyone expects that this trend will continue to grow in the future. However, as time progresses Fiat may encounter some problems that are currently arising. First, Fiat may encounter delays by the central government in Beijing, in approving or rejecting proposals made by them. The company may discover that the delay is due to the conflict between Beijing's goals and commercial viability. For instance, China has demanded that Mercedes split production between factories in two cities hundreds of miles apart. This facilitates China's employment of its citizens in different regions, thus securing political stability.

114   In addition, Fiat's manufacturing may be halted because China lacks an adequate infrastructure. This may lead to increasing taxes and/or registration fees in order to gather funds to improve China's infrastructure. In addition, in order to discourage citizens from purchasing more vehicles car prices will increase. Fiat as well as other car manufacturers will have to deal with production limits imposed by China's central government because pollution and traffic is infesting its major cities. Fiat will have to deal with the problem of regional and central governments' interests. On one hand, regional governments would like to provide employment. On the other hand, Beijing's government observes and would like to prevent further complications association with car production.

115   Most importantly, Fiat will confront already present competitors and their evolving strategies. For instance, General Motors is planning on manufacturing the Asian car. Another problem that Fiat may observe from its competitors is that they are investing a lot of capital without earning profits. For instance, Peugeot has invested a lot of funds without any real profitable return.

116   However, in 1997, a wide range of companies were yearning to enter the Chinese market in anticipation of a flourishing Chinese economy which will lead to China's internal growth in terms of purchasing power. However, this will require some time to achieve. In the meantime, Fiat may commence selling vehicles produced in China to the growing middle level Chinese population. In addition, the company may profit from exporting cars produced in China to other countries.

117   Fiat may, in the future, further expand their Research and Development sector. The company may develop alternative fuel vehicles in order to address China's growing concern about pollution. The development of such vehicles may anticipate other car manufacturers' growth and competition in the alternative fuel car area.

118   In this scenario, it is evident that Fiat may not permit itself to continue as an observer, risking all the time and capital it has invested. The company must develop strategic decisions in order that it may be prepared to challenge all the situations that are growing in the car industry. The first option that Fiat has, is to continue exporting vehicles into China. The other option is to commence production in this country by entering into a joint venture, allowing it to be ready for the real awakening of China. Fiat must also focus on developing the right product for the Chinese market, Asian market or both. This requires that the company take the initiative to research the possibilities and produce the necessary technology. If the new vehicles are produced in China they will be distributed locally through dealerships. However, if they are produced in another country, the cars will be distributed through distribution centers.

119   On February 19, 1997, Deng Xiaoping, China's paramount leader died of respiratory failure as a complication of Parkinson's Disease. He was 92 years old. His death brings about political uncertainty for the world's most populous nation. China finds itself in a transitional phase because it will be led by one of the three possible successors of Deng Xiaoping. However, regardless of which man rises to supreme power, no successor can expect to approach Mr. Deng in standing and authority.

120   Mr. Deng Xiaoping's successor is not well defined. Different news sources such as *The Economist* and *The International Herald Tribune* nominate several possible successors. According to them, power seems to have smoothly passed on to a new team of leaders: Jiang Zemin, Li Peng, and Zhu Rongli. The Communist Party's general secretary, Jiang Zemin is seen as a temporary figurehead. In fact, he lacks the personality and power base to become China's leader. Li Peng enjoys strong support by the conservative Communist party elders but is very unpopular among the people because he was associated with the crushing of the 1989 Tiananmen Square student protest.[22] Mr. Zhu Rongji, Prime Minister, is the occupant of most important job in terms of shaping the Chinese economy. He has a limited power base and his star inextricably is linked to the success of failure of economic reforms.[23]

121   The political implications of this uncertainty of the possible successor to Deng Xiaoping leadership could be the delay of the economic liberation initiated by him. The above mentioned possible successors are linked more to the pre-Deng Communist regime than to be open to Western capitalistic ideology. Most importantly, these three individuals are not seen as leaders by the people when compared to Deng Xiaoping. Furthermore, the uncertainty may freeze the current 1996–2000 five-year plan concerning legislative, economic, infrastructure and distribution reforms.

122   As of February 1997, Fiat has not found an adequate partner in China, however, a joint venture remains the only logical decision for it to manufacture its vehicles there. Perhaps Fiat management must develop a new approach towards negotiating with the Chinese government and the "Big 8" car manufacturers. The new approach would facilitate overcoming linguistic and cultural difficulties that interfere with Fiat growth and success in China.

---

[22]"After Deng," *The Economist,* February 22, 1997, p. 13.

[23]"Deng Xiaoping, Who Transformed China, Dies," *The International Herald Tribune,* February 20, 1997, p. 1.

EXHIBIT A
Ratios and Statistics at a Glance

(as of 02/07/97)

Price $	16.38	EPS (TTM) $	1.27
52 Week High $	18.50	P/E Ratio (TTM)	2.93
52 Week Low $	13.00	Book Value (MRQ) $	NA
3 Month Avg Daily Vol (Mil)	0.03	Price/Book (MRQ)	NA
Beta	−0.18	Sales Per Share (TTM) $	NA
Market Cap (MIL) $	10,742.00	Return on Assets (TTM) %	NA
Shares Outstanding (MIL)	656.00	Return on Equity (TTM) %	NA
Float (Mil)	446.00	Cash Per Share (MRQ) $	NA
Indicated Annual Dividend $	0.21	Current Ratio (MRQ) NM $	
Dividend Yield %	1.28	Total Debt/Equity (MRQ)	NA

Mil = Millions
TTM = Trailing Twelve Months
MRQ = Most Recent Quarter
Source: Fiat Auto S.P.A., "Environmental Sector."

REFERENCES

"After Deng," *The Economist,* February 22, 1997, p. 13.

"AIAL-Special Reports," www.aial.com.hk/siz.html, pp. 1–2.

"Asia Inc. Online—China Business Roundup," www.asia-inc.com/prc-news/970127.htm, pp.1–2.

"Asian Industry Dynamics," www-cmc.sri.co/CIN94/may-jun/article17.html, pp. 1–2.

"Automotive Aftermarket," www.tradecompass...rket/CHINA/ISA9505.html, pp. 1–25.

"Automotive Industry," www.tradecompass...rket/China/ISA9506.html, pp. 1–29.

Bennet, A. A., "China's Population Growth and Its Economic Boom," www.physics.iast...u/gcp/energy/china.html, pp. 1–12.

"Big Three Say Target for Auto Export to Japan Has Been Reached," www.theautochannel.com/news/date19961203/news02666.html, pp. 1–2.

"China Business Focus," www.windowofchina.com/cbfsam.htm, pp. 1–6.

"China: Polaroid of Shanghai Ltd.," Harvard Business School, pp. 4–5.

"China: The Great Awakening," Harvard Business School, pp. 1–19.

"China's Economy Doing Fine," wwwbuildlink.com...politics/96year/124.htm, p. 1.

"Deng Xiaoping, Who Transformed China, Dies," *The International Herald Tribune,* February 20, 1997, p. 1.

"Economic Digest no. 22," www.Ind.cn.net/TEXT/LED/LED22/LED22-05.htm, pp. 1–2.

"Fast Track Action With Top South East Asian Touring Car Drivers," www.macaubiz.net/race96/press4.htm, pp. 1–2.

"Fiat Claims 'No Interest' in Russian Carmaker," www.theautochannel.com/news/dae/19961203/news02668.html, p. 1.

"General Facts of China," www.xs4all.nl/%7Esv2312/china.html, pp. 1–15.

"GM Plans Asian Car for 1999," www.theautochannel.com/news/date/19961203/news02652.html, pp. 1–2.

"Hong Kong's Beyond 1997," www.tdc.org.hk/beyond97/after.htm, pp. 1–2.

"Investment Opportunities and Projects in China," www.xs4all.nl/%7Esv2312/invest.html, pp. 1–2.

Ishihara, Kyoichi, "Internationalization of China's Economy and Relations Among East Asian Economies," www.ide.go.jp/English/Annual/h32500.html, p. 1.

Mockler, Robert J., *Strategic Management—An Integrative Context-Specific Process,* Harringburg: Idea Group Publishing, 1993.

EXHIBIT B
Fiat Auto Car Sales for 1996

(Unofficial)

	Units		Market Share
Italy	772,276		43.9%
Western Europe (EU + Switzerland, Italy included)	1,491,219		11.3
Worldwide	2,282,000		—
Other Market Shares		Brazil	29.3
		Argentina	20.8
		Poland	43.2

"News From China," www.watsonwyatt.com/homepage/chi.htm, pp. 1–3.

"Outline of China's Economic Development in 1994," www.cclink.com/news/china94.html, pp. 1–2.

Qian, Yingyi, and Weingast, Barry R., "China's Transition to Markets—Market Preserving Federalism, Chinese Style," www-hover.staf....u/press/chinatrans.html, p. 1.

"Renault Discussing Joint Venture With Russian Plant," www.theautochannel.com/news/date19961203/news02669.html, p. 1.

"Series Reports of Chinese Industries," www.windowofchina.com/car.htm, pp. 1–2.

"Solving China's Management Crisis," www.asia-inc.com/archive/1994/solving.html, pp. 1–6.

"Trade Compass Library Search Results," www.tradecompass....arysearch.cgi?sum=d3357, p. 1.

Weber, Maria, *Vele Verso La Cina,* Ed. Olivares, Milano Dec. 1996, pp. 7–15.

"Where's That Pot of Gold?" *Business Week,* February 3, 1997, pp. 54 and 58.

CASE 62

AGIP PETROLI ENTERING THE INDIAN MARKET

1   In early 1997, India, together with China, was a rapidly growing market that many multinational companies had entered or were planning to enter in.

2   India's oil market was, in 1995, 1 million metric tonnes (MT) (60% automotive, 40% industrial) and was expected to grow in volume in the industrial sector and in monetary value in the automotive. The share of higher quality products was expected to increase and therefore provide an opportunity for premium brands for companies like Agip.

3   The main alternative entry strategies available to Agip are:

- export products to be sold through local distributors;
- establish a wholly owned company;
- set up a joint venture with an Indian partner.

In addition, should a strategic alliance be selected, Agip management realized that careful attention would need to be paid to how the alliance was structured and managed.

4   A new entrant can mainly use the retailers and workshops channel, which accounts for about 270,000 MT; other channels are almost a monopoly of the Public Sector Companies. As the country is huge and the market highly fragmented, distribution becomes the key factor.

5   In early 1997, the management of Agip Petroli was preparing for a meeting to discuss plans to expand its business. After having expanded worldwide in the past decades, the company was considering how to take advantage of emerging market opportunities in India. Among the issues the top management had to carefully consider were how Agip Petroli should enter India as a foreign company, and how best to take advantage of the resources and capabilities available in the host country.

AGIP PETROLI

Company Overview

6   Agip Petroli, a subsidiary company of ENI (Ente Nazionale Idrocarbui) holding, is a leading supplier, refiner, and distributor of petroleum products in Italy. The company is not only a major competitor in the Italian market; it also plays a substantial role in the international oil market through subsidiaries, branches, joint ventures, and representative offices throughout the world.

History

7   AGIP (Azienda Generale Italiana dei Petroli) was founded by the Italian government in 1926 with the objective of "pursuing all activities relating to the industrial and commercial aspects of petroleum products." The company grew rapidly and was soon engaged not only in oil exploration and refining, but also product distribution.

8   The 1929 depression brought progress to a halt. During the period of autarchy in the thirties, Agip again started to expand and consolidate. In 1945 the government decided to liquidate the company.

This case was prepared by Andrew Cornetti and Paolo Scordino under the direction of Professor Robert J. Mockler of St. John's University.

However, the strong results which rapidly began to emerge from oil and gas exploration induced the government instead to reorganize and recommence operations in all sectors. In 1953, the government established the Italian National Hydrocarbons Corporation, ENI, with Agip as the core company.

9   A period of growth followed for the company in a wide variety of fields: motor vehicles, agriculture, industry, shipping, aviation, domestic heating, and even tourism—with the Agip Motel chain. Meanwhile the company was reinforcing and upgrading its distribution, building service stations offering a wide range of facilities for driver and vehicle alike.

10 The change in conditions in the energy and petroleum markets which occurred in the mid-seventies induced the government to give ENI's Energy Division a broader and more systematic structure so as to enable it to tackle the various phases of the petroleum cycle in a more flexible manner.

11 Agip Petroli was established in 1977 and became sector-head of the ENI Group in 1981. Between 1978 and 1983 Agip Petroli's operations were strongly conditioned not only by market uncertainties but also by the very fact that as a state owned company its definite mission was "to guarantee the country's energy supplies." Moreover it was asked a play a social political role by replacing the various firms that were encountering bad times. Hence, instead of pursuing a policy of expansion in the commercial and production sectors, Agip Petroli had to adopt a strategy of defense and reconversion.

12 After some delays, the long process of reconstruction finally got under way. Industrial and commercial operations were rationalized and throughgoing changes were made in strategies, organization, and entrepreneurial approach. Recovery of economic efficiency was a lengthy struggle, involving a major effort to upgrade technological and organizational aspects of the company, while developing the capacity to operate effectively in very-complex, high-tech sectors. More generally, all this called for the abandonment of the behavioral pattern of a State Company and the adoption of a model based on market efficiency, flexibility, and profitability.

Agip Petroli in the International Markets

13 Agip began its international efforts in the fifties. Its CEO's policy of negotiating direct agreements with producer countries to ensure crude oil supplies led to the decision to allow the company to operate worldwide in the exploration, refining, and distribution sectors. It also led to the establishment of subsidiaries and joint ventures all over the world.

14 In 1997, Agip Petroli operated in the downstream petroleum sector in Italy and abroad, ensuring close integration of the crude-oil supply, refining, and product-marketing system. Supply of crude oil involved complex negotiations with numerous international business interests, long-term purchasing contracts, and spot deals. Supplies originate from fifteen countries, mainly in North Africa and the Middle East. The company had seven refineries processing over 40 million tons per year of crude and feed stock. Its industrial system outside Italy was based on collaboration agreements in Germany and a number of African countries.

15 The organization especially focused on research which is handled by Euron, a subsidiary concerned with studies and experimentation covering all phases of the petroleum cycle. Thanks to the constant revamping of its industrial system, Agip Petroli retains a prime position worldwide as regards refining capacity, advanced technology, prime product yields, and environmental safeguards which enable the company to market high-quality products all over the world.

Products

16 Agip Petroli is one of the few companies in the world operating in all segments of the lubricants cycle, including production and marketing of base oils and finished lubricants for the most varied uses, as well as the recovery and re-refining of used oils. It is also engaged in the design and manufacture of products for rallying and racing on land and sea, as well as the production of LPG and its distribution using cylinders, road tankers, and piped mains systems. In addition, Agip Petroli is one of the first five companies worldwide manufacturing special products such as additives for fuels, lubricants, and solvents.

17   Agip brand lubricants, created in the San Donato Milanese research laboratories, join the excellence of raw materials with continual experimentation and constant cooperation with car manufacturers to provide the guarantees of reliability and safety that drivers all over the world have come to appreciate. In 1969, Agip Petroli was the first European company to introduce a motor oil with a synthetic base, Sint 2000. Since then it has continued its research, providing the market with products increasingly aimed at special requirements like Sint Turbo Diesel for diesel engines and Sint Catalyst for catalytic cars.

18   In early 1997, the goal of the management was to introduce its high-quality products in the huge and fast-growing Indian market. The evaluation of the different alternatives and the final decision was expected to affect the international future of the entire company.

AN INTRODUCTION TO INDIA

19   It was often said, with some justification, that India is not a country but a continent. Almost 900 million people lived within the borders of the world's second most populous nation. Although still predominately a traditional agricultural economy, India was developing rapidly as one of the world's largest industrial powers. The government was pushing through a program of modernization and economic liberalization which aimed to transform India into one of the leading industrial economies by early next century.

20   Although potentially an economic giant, almost two-thirds of the population worked on the land and literacy rates were low; it was estimated by the World Bank that perhaps a third of the world's "absolute poor" lived in India.[1] Nevertheless, it was the marriage of an enormous potential market and the new opportunities for investment which had attracted foreign companies to India in increasing numbers, particularly in the last two years.

Geographical and Cultural Considerations

21   Despite its great size and diversity, India had achieved a notable level of political stability; the governing Congress party was unique in having a national focus, in comparison to the more regional bias of rival parties. The strong lead which the central government had been able to provide had given much impetus to the recent process of economic reform. Nevertheless, any company hoping to develop a role in the Indian market first had to realize that the country was made up of very distinct regions and that individual states or groups of states might be large enough or of sufficiently homogenous character to be treated as separate "national" markets in themselves.

22   India was divided into twenty-five states and seven other Union Territories. State governments had a high degree of autonomy in handling certain activities, including, most notably, local industrial policy. Although English was the most commonly spoken language of the government and business classes there was no "national" language. The country was divided into a great number of local languages and, in many cases, the state boundaries were drawn on linguistic lines. The cultural heritage was rich. Hinduism, Buddhism, Jainism, and Sikhism originated in the North, supplemented much later by Christianity and Islam.

23   Distances between major centers were often considerable and land communications were either slow (by rail) or very poor (by road). Bombay (the main economic center) and New Delhi (the capital) are 1,400 kms apart; an express train covered the distance in 17 hours, and by road the journey could have taken as long. India's physical size was made more daunting by infrastructure deficiencies, which continue to place major constraints on economic growth. Although major investment programs were underway to improve the transport and telecommunications networks, their lack of development was a major constraint on companies operating on a nationwide strategy.

[1]The Economist Intelligence Unit, *Country Report,* 4th quarter 1995.

The Move to a Liberalized Economy

Positive Steps

24   For over forty years after Independence in 1947, the Indian government, guided by the socialist principles of Nehru, pursued an economic policy characterized by central planning and protectionism and an increasing drive towards self-sufficiency.

25   This policy reached its apogee in the 1970s when, for example, the foreign oil companies, which had been dominant, were forced by increasingly restrictive regulations to leave India. A major portion of industry became state-owned and was subjected to strict licensing, labor, and pricing regulations. Free enterprise was not encouraged.

26   By the mid-eighties, it became clear that a controlled economy could not produce the desired results and liberalization measures were first introduced, with the aim of freeing Indian companies from excessive regulations and controls and making the protecting industry more competitive. However, by the time of Rajiv Gandhi's assassination in May 1991, India stood on the brink of a major economic and political crisis.

27   Rajiv Gandhi was succeeded by the current Prime Minister, P. V. Narashima Rao, who immediately set about giving the liberalization process its strongest impetus by the New Economic Policies in July 1991. This set in motion a series of further and continuing reforms of major significance to Indian and foreign companies alike. The main components of the new market conditions are summarized below:

Trade Policy

- Almost all import restrictions have been removed.
- Import licensing has largely been abolished.
- Ceiling rates of import duties were brought down significantly in the 1993 budget from levels which once approached 300% on some goods to an average of 35%. Import rates for priority sectors like petroleum refining have been reduced still further.

Foreign Investment Policy

- Direct foreign investment has been actively encouraged to allow technology transfer and multinational linkage.
- Restrictions on foreign firms entering the industrial sector have been greatly reduced.
- Automatic approval for investments of up to 51% in high priority industries; specific approval for 100% foreign-owned ventures is possible.
- Restrictions on expansion and diversification of companies with majority foreign ownership have been greatly reduced; investors are now allowed to use their own brand names, buy property, open their own branches, and accept deposits.
- Liberal tax and non-tax concessions are available for new investments.
- For approved investments, capital earnings can be freely repatriated subject to normal taxation and exchange control procedures.
- Elimination of manufacturing programs requiring a progressive increase of indigenous content in joint ventures.

Industrial Policy

- Only six industries still reserved solely for the public sector.
- A private sector is evolving rapidly with participation in all other industries permitted; private competition has been particularly encouraged in banking, internal airlines, and telecommunications.
- Major relaxation in the rules allowing branches of foreign trading and manufacturing companies to operate in India.
- Substantial deregulation and simplification of procedures for setting up and operating in business, for example, industrial licensing has been virtually abolished, clearance from the Monopolies

Commission has been dispensed with, and changes have been made to company laws to allow mergers and acquisitions.

- Business taxes substantially reformed.

Foreign Exchange Policy

- Devaluation of the Rupee has allowed for its partial conversion in foreign markets; the exchange rate has been stabilized and a unified exchange rate system has been in place since February 1993.
- Amendments to the Foreign Exchange Regulation Act mean that the importers can pay for goods with foreign exchange bought at the market rate without the permission of the Reserve Bank of India.
- Indian foreign exchange reserves rose from $1 billion to over $20 billion between 1991 and 1994.

The Remaining Obstacles

28   India's progress towards full economic reform had been likened to the slow yet stately progress of an elephant in comparison with the frenetic pace of the other Asian economies, most notably China. Although the implications of reform in India were dramatic, the process they had set in motion was likely to take a number of years before the most far-reaching effects were seen.

29   Widespread reform of the state sector had been avoided, largely to mitigate the catastrophic effects of unemployment in a labor intensive economy. India had no welfare system, but strong trade unions and a number of longstanding labor laws stated that, for example, workers could not be sacked except for serious disciplinary offenses, so loss-making factories could not be closed; anyone leaving a particular job voluntarily had to be replaced; and anybody working for a particular company for ninety days was entitled to a pension for life. Instead, the government sought to improve the competitiveness of the state-owned companies by allowing private operators to set up alongside them.

30   Enormous investment was required in the infrastructure, and particularly transport and telecommunications, if the benefits of the reform process were to be widely distributed. The traditional and hidebound Indian bureaucracy continued to act as a brake on policy directives from above. Thus, while broader issues concerning setting up and managing business had been tackled, more immediate "local issues," for example those concerning premises and setting up telephones, could still take several months to complete.

31   Although there was a large, skilled, and cheap labor force available, levels of literacy were still very low by Western standards; foreign companies were often convinced of an "ethical" need to improve labor conditions with their partner companies in India, particularly in the traditional industries, a policy that could lead to increased investment costs. Cultural differences and the protection afforded by the labor laws had created working habits which differed markedly from the traditional Western work ethic. Foreign companies needed to understand the Indian "way" when examining working practices. Although India had maintained a high degree of political stability over the last four decades, occasional outbursts of tension had proved temporary setbacks to the reform process and disputes between religious factions still formed a threatening backdrop.

LUBRICANT SUPPLY AND DEMAND IN INDIA

The Oil Industry

32   The industry under study was the oil industry, which was mainly divided into *upstream* and *downstream*. *Upstream* included the processes from exploring areas to finding curds, drilling up (the excavation itself), pumping up the crude, and the logistics and the trading of the crude. *Downstream* included all the processes related to the refining of the crude and the commercialization of the oil derivatives. Among these products, the lubricants played an important role. The base oils were the raw material of the lubricant and there were diverse types of bases, classified according to their viscosity and other chemical and physical parameters.

33   The lubricant was a mix of a base oil with additives. According to the percentage of oil base (against a synthetic base which was obtained from non-oil substances) it could be classified as

EXHIBIT A
Demand and Supply Scenario (000 Tonnes)

	1990–91	1991–92	1992–93	1999–2000 est.
Lubricants Demand	892	932	862	1,376
Base Oil Production	552	390	533	827
Imports (Lubs and Base)	340	542	329	549

Source: BTS.

mineral (100% base of oil origin), semi-synthetic, or synthetic (more than 70% of synthetic base). In any case, the three types of lubricant had additives to enhance the lubricant properties.

34   There was another industry which produced lubricants, the petrochemical industry, whose product was synthetic. Lubricants had mainly two uses: automotive (lubricants used in vehicles, e.g., the lubricant used in the charter of the engine) and industrial (used in the industry, e.g., the lubricant used in the axis of a pump). Our project focused on automotive lubricants.

Base Oils and Additives Supply

35   In India, base oils were manufactured in three main refineries (IOC, Hindustan, Madras Refineries). Local production, in spite of extension plans by PSUs and private sector companies, was falling behind demand. In fact almost one third of lubricants were manufactured with imported base oils.

36   Margins of this market were quite high; in fact, prices covered transportation costs from the Mediterranean Sea. Companies like Gulf Oil were currently buying base oils from the Mediterranean and reselling them in India.

37   The two main additives suppliers in India were:

• Lubrizol India LTD

• Indian Additives

Lubrizol was the absolute market leader covering about 80% of the demand. The local base oils provided poor quality, therefore increasing volumes of additives were required to manufacture high quality lubricants. The whole market of additives was estimated around 65,000 MT in 1994.

Lubricants Manufacturers

38   In India about 27 major blending plants and several small plants handled by minor private blenders operated. IOC accounted for almost half of the normal blending capacity, whereas the other PSUs (HPC, BPC, IBP) altogether covered about 30%. Castrol was the biggest private sector blender with four plants and 10% of the capacity.

39   As seen in Exhibit B, there was excess capacity to cover the consumption of new entrants in the next years. As a matter of fact each oil company started its operations blending on third parties' plants as fees were cheap and quality reliable. As soon as the critical mass was reached, foreign oil companies started building their own plants, releasing further blending capacity.

The Automotive Sector

40   Automotive lubricant use in the Indian market made up sixty percent of the lubricant use. Lubricants were used in vehicles such as jeeps, commercial vehicles, passenger cars, tractors, buses, and two- and three-wheelers. While only one Indian in three hundred used a car, one in fifty owned a scooter, moped, motorbike, two- or three-wheeler (see Exhibit C).

41   Of this group, two- and three-wheelers accounted for over seventy percent of vehicles used in India. Cars and jeeps accounted for ten percent of the total vehicle population.

42   The number of vehicles in use in India had been rapidly increasing. Since 1981, the vehicle population had effectively doubled every five years. One explanation for the expansion in vehicle use was an increase in ownership of two-wheeler vehicles. Car ownership, despite tax concessions initiated in

EXHIBIT B
Current and Planned Lubricant Blending Capacity

Plant	1994 Tonnes	Additional Tonnes Planned (1997–98)
IOC	395,000	340,000
Hindustan Petroleum	162,000	105,000
Bharat Petroleum	90,000	75,000
IBP	35,000	50,000
Castrol	86,000	
Tide Water	13,300	
Pennzoil	9,000	
Gulf		75,000
Elf	15,000	
Others	30,000	40,000
TOTAL	835,300	685,000
TOTAL CAPACITY		1,520,000

Source: BMS—Total Research, *Business Opportunities in the Market for Automotive Lubricants in India.*

1993, was still unaffordable to the vast majority of Indians. Thus, given their relatively low cost, two-wheelers promised to capture the disposable income of the growing middle class. The continued growth of the two-wheel vehicle was expected to contribute to the demand for lubricants in India.

43   Medium to heavy commercial vehicle growth was estimated to continue at a lesser rate, while the demand for lighter vehicles widely used to carry a majority of consumer goods in urban and suburban areas was likely to double. The small number of tractors and agricultural vehicles was expected to double by the year 2001. Even though the economy was booming, a car, or commercial vehicle, was still too costly for Indian consumers. Indian vehicle owners tended to keep their vehicles running for as long as possible, hence there were many older model vehicles that consumed lubricants at a much quicker pace than their newer counterparts.

Market Size and Structure

44   **Overall Market Size**   In 1994, the estimated size of the market for automotive lubricants in India was 590,000 tons. This represented a 22% growth in consumption since 1990. The market was worth Rs 29,500 million ($968 million) in 1994 (Exhibit D). This represented a growth in value of 35% since 1990.

45   **The Market Size by Geographic Region**   The largest markets for lubricants were the West (principally Bombay) and North (principally New Delhi) which collectively accounted for almost half of the total market. In general, the lubricant market was largest in regions which had the best developed parcs. Although the West was not the largest region in terms of population (the North, East, and South East were larger), it did have the largest vehicle parc, largely reflecting Bombay's status as the commercial hub of India. Car ownership in the North, East, and South East was approximately half the level in the West, while ownership of two-wheeler and commercial vehicles was also among the highest in India in the West.

46   A high concentration of commercial vehicles, which consume ten times the amount of lubricant per year compared with cars, could also inflate the volume of smaller regions. The North West, for example, had a relatively large commercial vehicle parc and was thus a more important market than its size would have suggested. Despite containing India's second largest city (approximately a fifth of the population in total), the East was a relatively poorly developed market. Vehicle ownership lagged well behind the West and North and the region had been stagnating economically. The South West, and particularly Bangalore, was experiencing rapid economic growth and car ownership was

EXHIBIT C
Vehicle Ownership by Main Regions
(Expressed as no. of inhabitants per vehicle in use)

Region	2/3 Wheels	Cars/Jeeps	CVS	Tractors	Other Vehicles
North West	30	245	294	111	20
North	59	300	719	526	42
North East	148	291	279	2,479	63
Center	59	625	747	703	45
West	34	177	408	767	25
East	146	355	486	1,915	40
South West	48	199	422	1,470	34
South East	54	324	472	2,716	41
All India	57	279	482	683	39

Source: Ministry of Surface Transport (MOST).

second only to the West. The South East was developing less rapidly. Vehicle ownership was similar to the East and Center, although the two stroke market was growing more rapidly. Central India, broadly defined as Madhya Pradesh, but in effect taking up large parts of eastern Maharashtra and Andhra Pradesh, was the least developed market; largely rural, car and commercial vehicle ownership was the lowest in India. Although the smallest region studied, the North East had a relatively large commercial vehicle parc (since rail transport was less well-developed). However, the region was remote, fragmented, and blighted by political instability.[2]

47   **The Market by Product Type** The market was broken down by engine oil, two stroke, and other automotive lubricant products. Monograde engine once dominated the Indian market, but the picture had changed considerably in the last two to three years. Multigrade oils were now the most common engine oil, accounting for 70 percent of the engine oil market. Synthetics and semi-synthetics were very recent introductions and had very limited application for vehicles currently in use.[3]

48   Given the relative size and growth of the two-wheeler market in India, two stroke products had a share of the market considerably in excess of that found in Western markets. Two stroke oil was viewed as a simple "commodity" product by most vehicle owners, with low cost and simplicity of use taking precedence over quality. Consumption per vehicle was, therefore, relatively high. Other lubricants accounted for 17 percent of total lubricant consumption. The largest segment consisted of gear oils, transmission fluids, and brake fluid. Consumption of these products per vehicle in Indian conditions was relatively high; most vehicles had manual gear boxes. The automotive grease market accounted for 27,000 tonnes; again, consumption per vehicle was high, but was gradually falling with the introduction of long life grease.[4]

The Lubricant Automotive Supply

49   Lubricant oil was composed of base oil and additives. In the late 1970s, the government forced the multinational corporations out of India through tax policies aimed at protecting the state owned companies: Indian Oil Corporation, Hindustan Petroleum, Bharat Petroleum, and Indo-Burma Petroleum.

[2]BMS—Total Research, *Business Opportunities in the Market for Automotive Lubricants in India,* Vol. 1, 1995, pp. 80–81.

[3]Ibid., pp. 83–84.

[4]Ibid., p. 85.

EXHIBIT D
Automotive Lubricants Market by Value, 1990–94

Year	Rupee Rs (million)	Dollars ($ million)	% Change
1990	21,820	716	
1991	23,000	754	5.4
1992	24,670	812	7.3
1993	26,740	877	8.4
1994	29,500	968	10.3
% change, 1990–94			35.2

Source: Vehicle manufacturers/BMS—Total Research.

These producers were known as PSUs. Local production of base oils for lubricants had been falling behind demand. The country imported 6,300,000 tons of petroleum products to meet the gap between supply and demand.[5] Almost all base stock for lubricants was manufactured from imported crude oil, and one third of lubricants was manufactured with imported base oils. Due to these supply factors, there was an upward trend in the wholesale price of crude oil and petroleum products. Currently, multinational corporations were collaborating in joint ventures with PSUs.

50   Import tariffs on base oils and finished products had come down forty-three percent. Base oil imports were expected to increase as domestic production fell further behind increasing demand. In 1992 and 1993, petroleum oil and lubricants accounted for twenty-eight percent of India's total imports, making it the largest single imported commodity. After reaching a peak of thirty-four million tons in 1990, production had fallen while the demand had been rising by six to eight percent per annum. Given the relatively poor quality of base oils manufactured in India, significant volumes of additives were required to manufacture high quality lubricants. Eighty percent of additives was produced domestically, the remainder of the supply necessary for lubricants was imported. Recent reductions in import duties promised to create an augmentative effect on additive imports.[6]

Sales Channels

51   Apart from industrial oils, which were sold directly by oil companies or their distributors to customers, the main sales channels were the following:

1. Fuel Stations—There were about 16,000 fuel stations in India and all of them were operated by the public sector companies. Officially only lubricants from the fuel supplier or their joint venture partners (Caltex, Mobil, Shell, and Exxon) were sold through these channels, although unofficially other brands like Castrol were likely to be found in these shops.
2. Retail Outlets—The retailers' channel was known in India as Bazaar, which was basically spares and accessory shops and oil shops. In the whole country there were about 50–100,000 spare shops and about 5–10,000 oil shops. Both types of shops were generally very small and stocked very small quantities.
3. Workshop—This channel consisted of about 6,000 authorized workshops and about 50–70,000 independent service outlets. Most of these outlets serviced two- and three-wheelers. Vehicle owners went to authorized workshops mainly during the warranty, then the loyalty decreased dramatically. However, this segment would have enjoyed some benefits: since more sophisticated and expensive vehicles were being introduced, the quality-concerned population was increasing.

[5]CNR, ENEA, ENEL, ENI, *Rapporto sull'Energia,* Bologna: Il Mulino, 1995.

[6]Dames & Moore International, *Analisi Comparativa del Business Lubrificanti,* January 1995, pp. 152–55.

EXHIBIT E
Market Size by Product Type, 1994

	Volume (000 tonnes)	Volume Share
Engine Oils	**415**	**70.2**
Monograde	125	21.2
Basic SC/CC multi	224	37.9
Standard SF/CD multi	65.5	11.1
High Perf. SG/SH/CE/CF multi	0.5	neg
Synthetics/semi-synthetics	neg	neg
Two Stroke Oil	**72**	**12.2**
Commodity & TA/TB	62	8.5
TC and above	8	2.7
Semi-synthetic/synthetic	2	1.0
Other Lubricants	**102**	**17.0**
Gear oil/transmission fluid	59	10.0
Brake fluid	16	2.7
Grease	27	4.3
TOTAL	589	100

Source: Vehicle manufacturers/BMS—Total Research.

4. Fleets—There had been a huge growth in goods and passenger transport by road as a consequence of the economic boom, although investments were still needed in the infrastructure and in new vehicles. Most of the fleets operated with less than five vehicles and none of them was expected to have their own workshop. Almost 60 percent[7] of the lubricants sold through this channel were bought by State Passengers Fleets which privilege PSUs.

5. Direct Sales—These were the sales performed directly by oil companies or major wholesalers to big customers of which about 50 percent[8] was the oil consumption of the Indian railways supplied almost exclusively by IOC.

FUTURE SUPPLY AND DEMAND IN INDIA

Market Growth

52 The market accounted for about 1 million MT in 1995, of which about 600,000 MT was in the automotive sector only. The Government forecasted about a 1,300,000 MT consumption by the year 2000. Such an increase in volume was mainly due to industrial oils whereas the automotive lubricants were expected to go up in terms of value only.

53 In 2000, the total size of the market for automotive lubricants in India will be an estimated 600,000 tons. Lubricant consumption per vehicle will reduce as new makes with modern specifications are introduced, drain periods increase, and the vehicle parc gets younger. The net result is that although the Indian vehicle parc is expected to increase by at least 40 percent by 2000, the total volume of lubricants consumed will be 6 percent less than at present. Market value will, however, continue to grow as the market for higher quality/higher value lubricants increases, although the growth rate will slow by 2000 as market volume begins to decline.

[7]Source: BMS—Total Research, *Business Opportunities in the Market for Automotive Lubricants in India.*

[8]Source: BMS—Total Research, *Business Opportunities in the Market for Automotive Lubricants in India.*

EXHIBIT F
Estimated Market Growth by Product, 1994–1999

	1994	1995	1996	1997	1998	1999	% change 1994–99
Engine Oils	**415**	**428**	**423**	**414**	**404**	**391**	**−6**
Monograde	125	110	100	95	89	84	−33
Basic SC/CC multi	224	245	241.5	226	207	177	−21
Standard SF/CD multi	65.5	72	79	87	96	106	62
High Perf. SG/SH/CE/CF multi	0.5	1	2	4	8	16	3,100
Synthetics/semi-synthetics	neg	neg	0.5	2	4	8	1,500
Two Stroke Oil	**72**	**72**	**72**	**71**	**69**	**67**	**−7**
Commodity & TA/TB	62	56	51	46	41	36	−42
TC and above	8	12	14	16	18	20	150
Semi-synthetic/synthetic	2	4	7	9	10	11	450
Other Lubricants	**102**	**105**	**103**	**101**	**98**	**95**	**−7**
TOTAL	589	605	598	586	571	553	−6

Source: BTS.

54   The share of the market held by engine oil was forecast to remain steady at approximately 70 percent, although overall consumption of all main lubricant types was going to decline by 6–7 percent (Exhibit F).

55   In the engine oil market, consumption of monograde began to fall again after a recovery during 1994, but there was expected to be a "hard-core" of purchasers to ensure the residual importance of these products. Basic SC multigrades were anticipated to increase in consumption between 1994 and 1995, picking up former monograde users, but then decline in importance gradually, as these grades were in turn substituted by SF quality products. SG/SH quality mineral oils and synthetic/semi-synthetics were going to rapidly increase their consumption over the next five years, but were not going to account for more than 6–10 percent of the market by 1999. SC multigrades was going still to be the predominant product, but SF quality grades have secured almost 30 percent of the engine oil market.

56   The two stroke sector was likely also to change significantly by 1999. Higher quality packaged oils which had less than 15% of the current market were estimated to grow to such an extent that consumption would be almost equal to commodity products by the turn of the century.

57   The largest decline in consumption was estimated to be in regions where the vehicle parc was already high and/or where new vehicle sales would have been greatest—the West, North West, North, and South West. Although the vehicle parc was expected to increase rapidly, these regions represented the best opportunity for higher quality, long drain lubricants. In the East and South East, vehicle ownership was lower than more developed regions and usage of higher quality lubricants was at a lesser level. An above average increase in the number of vehicles, coupled with a less significant fall in lubricant consumption per vehicle, suggested that overall lubricant consumption in these regions would have fallen less dramatically. The North East and Center were likely to continue to be relatively undynamic markets; the vehicle parc was not expected to increase as rapidly as elsewhere and per vehicle consumption was not going to be greatly reduced.

58   Authorized service and repair outlets were the only purchaser channels likely to actually increase consumption of lubricants for the following five years; this would have been a reflection of developments in the vehicle market with many new manufacturers entering the market. Owners of new vehicles were much more likely to use authorized outlets rather than independent mechanics and, with more new vehicles on the road, the independent mechanics might lose some of their traditional, cut-price business.

59   Petrol stations and retail outlets were not expected to suffer a more than average decline in consumption. Petrol stations were going to continue to be the primary source of lubricants, particularly

if higher quality joint venture brands proved successful, although some of their oil change activities were going to be lost to authorized outlets. Retail outlets were expected to continue to be an important source for mechanics and truck owners. Although the number of fleets with workshops was expected to rise slightly and the commercial vehicle parc itself was going to increase, per vehicle consumption was likely to fall by up to 50 percent and the sector itself to shrink in volume, while increasing in value.

The Changing Competitive Scene

60 **Market Shares of Suppliers**   The PSU suppliers (state sector composed of four main companies: Indian Oil Corporation, Hindustan Petroleum, Bharat Petroleum, and Indo-Burmah Petroleum) had been losing market share steadily in the last years, but still retained the largest share of the market, with sales of 413,000 tonnes during 1994 (approximately 70 percent of the market). IOC (Indian Oil Corporation) was the largest single supplier; the Servo brand, accounting for four in every ten liters of lubricants, sold more than the other PSU brands put together (Exhibit G).

61   Castrol, in particular, had benefited from the declining share of the market held by the PSUs and was estimated to be the third-largest supplier, selling 72,000 tonnes during 1994. Castrol had thus moved ahead of Bharat, the third-largest PSU supplier. Castrol sold almost three times as much volume as its nearest sector rival, Tide Water, who had enjoyed a recent revival in sales. Gulf, Pennzoil, and Elf were the only other foreign suppliers to have made significant inroads to date. In total, foreign brands accounted for 16–17 percent of lubricant sales. The remaining 6 percent of the market (35,000 tonnes) was shared between a large number of smaller local manufactures (mainly re-refining used oils) and "bogus" products, whose share of the market was increasing.

62   Exhibit H shows that the PSU suppliers and foreign/private sector suppliers effectively operated in parallel markets at present. The PSU suppliers dominated sales through fuel to fleets and to the railways, and through rural LPG dealers to the agricultural sector. Foreign brands were sold unofficially through fuel stations to a small extent and some fleets had recently switched from sourcing from the PSUs. Foreign and private sector suppliers were predominant in the retail sector and also sold marginally more than the PSU suppliers in the third party service and channel, particularly to authorized outlets.

63 **Projected Market Shares**   It was not possible to estimate market shares over the following five years with any accuracy. The market had suddenly become very competitive, but most of the new entrants had not yet established a solid platform. There was no consensus in the industry itself about the number of suppliers the market could successfully sustain, although there was a widely held opinion that, as the market "shaked down" and prices, in particular, became more stable, a number of the current suppliers were going to leave the marketplace.[9] The main trends to note were:

64   The PSUs had been losing market share for the last three years (industry sources indicate by as much as 14% per annum). This trend was certain to continue; conservative estimates, for example, felt Servo's share of the market was going to dip below 30 percent over the following two or three years.[10] The introduction of joint venture brands was certain to cannibalize sales of higher quality PSU brands which might have otherwise benefited from the growing share of the market regained by PSU brands. Thus, while it was reported that Mobil was going to start by offering equivalent Servo and Mobil brands in the higher quality sector of the market. Bharat Shell was expected, instead, to phase out the Bharat brand name altogether over a period of time. In the past, the PSU brands sought to stave off the competitive threat of Castrol and Gulf in the fleet sector by providing storage facilities for established bulk clients and linking fuel and lubricant sales, thus helping them to keep down their inventories. This had proved a major advantage in retaining market share in this sector, but was dependent to a large degree on the PSU brands holding on to their price advantage.

65   Castrol had been the main beneficiary of the PSUs decline in market share and should have continued to increase market share in the following five years. However, Castrol was facing an unprecedented competitive situation:

[9]Icconol, *Proposal for Joint Venture with Agip Petroli,* 1995.

[10]Escorts, *Lubricant Project,* 1995.

EXHIBIT G
Estimated Market Shares by Volume, 1994

	Volume (−000 tonnes)	Volume Share (%)
IOC	242	41.0
Hindustan	97	16.4
Castrol	72	12.2
Bharat	56	9.5
Tide Water	25	4.2
Gulf	22	3.7
IBP	18	3.0
Pennzoil	10	1.7
Elf	10	1.7
Others (a)	37	6.2
TOTAL	589	100
Approximate non-Indian share		16–17

(a) includes smaller manufactures (often recycled products) and "bogus" products largely sold through spares and accessory shops.

Source: Indian Petroleum & Natural Gas Statistics.

- The PSUs had all adopted, through joint ventures, international brands which competed with Castrol in the "quality" market.
- The sudden influx of new entrants also challenged Castrol's supremacy in the "quality" market and immediately targeted the channels upon which Castrol had based its success (retail outlets and mechanics).[11]

66 Tide Water had shown a marked recovery in recent years and had the advantage of a well-known brand name (Veedol) and an extensive network. The technical collaboration with Mitsubishi had given Tide Water an opportunity to target the tiny but growing high quality sector of the market and the company stated the intention of doubling market share in the following few years.[12]

67 The new entrants that has been most successful to date—Gulf, Elf, and Pennzoil—were not yet selling in sufficient quantities to guarantee a longstanding position in the market, but at least had the advantage of establishing themselves ahead of a flood of more recent entrants. At that time, Gulf looked the most likely to succeed, having a well-recognized brand name (from a former relationship with Petrosil) while the tie-up with Ashok Leyland might prove advantageous. It was far too early to comment on the likely prospects for other new entrants, but, given the planned capacity of the new blending plants, it would have seemed that 15,000 tonnes was the critical mass required to gain a reasonable foothold in the market.[13]

68 The smaller Indian private sector suppliers were likely to keep a toehold on the market and some might even increase their share by specializing in supplying basic quality grades. Despite the entry of foreign competitors, there was optimism among the Indian private sector suppliers. The current import prices of base oil and finished lubricants continued to make local blending and/or filling an attractive proposition (as was going to be the selling of "bogus" products).

69 The PSUs were finding that, as their prices increased, their low-end products were less competitive and they were, in any case, seeking to build up their "quality" profile. The high volume/low margin sales might, therefore, be left to others for as long as re-refined products retained their price

[11]Birla Technical Services, *Lube Refinery Project in India,* 1995, pp. 40–41.

[12]Ibid., p. 42.

[13]Ibid., p. 43.

EXHIBIT H
Market Shares by Main Sector, 1994

	PSU Suppliers	%	Foreign/ Non-PSU	%	Total Volume
Fuel Station (a)	204.6	98	4.0	2	208.6
Retail	52.5	37	91.0	63	143.5
Service/Repair	63.0	48	67.0	52	130.0
Fleets	36.0	88	5.0	12	41.0
Railways	30.0	100	0.0	0	30.0
Other Channels	27.9	76	9.0	24	36.9
TOTAL	414	70	176	30	590

(a) includes joint-venture petrol stations selling foreign brands.

Source: BTS.

advantage. Nevertheless, as the demand for higher quality products gradually increased, many smaller suppliers were going to be driven out of the market.

70   It is important to note that some of the larger private sector Indian companies were optimistic. Motorol (formerly Rinki), for example, was looking at markets outside India and planning lubricant plants in Mauritius, Indonesia, and South Africa, having already transferred technical know-how to a manufacturer in eastern Malaysia.

THE DECISION TO ENTER THE MARKET

71   In order to decide whether and, eventually, how to enter the Indian market, Agip's management focused its attention on all the possible opportunities and threats for a new entrant. On one hand there were some factors which the company could use to its advantage. The market was rapidly growing: industrial oils were growing in terms of volume and automotive oils in terms of value. The private sector was gaining market share in disfavor of public sector. Moreover, more sophisticated models and further vehicle manufacturers were expected to enter the market, thus the demand for higher quality lubricants was expected to grow and premium brands were going to enjoy an advantage. Among sales channels Bazaar market was increasing its share. In this context, retailers and mechanics played a very important role in the purchase decision process; however, they knew very little about lubricants. Providing training was considered to be an advantage.

72   On the other hand, management was aware of the fact that a new entrant had to face several difficult problems. Industrial supply was largely provided by PSUs, best-selling oils were still low-price (and low-margin), and OEM (original equipment manufacturer) approvals were necessary to qualify a new brand. The competition was intense: there were about 60 market players of which about 20 were multinational companies. From the distribution point of view, the fuel stations channel was closed to a new entrant and best distributors had already been taken. Moreover, Bazaar market was highly fragmented so that the average lub consumption per outlet was low.

Entry Strategies

73   Having all this in mind, Agip's management planning team considered several alternatives in several areas. There are several ways to enter a new market for a company. Agip, by the way, took into consideration only the more consistent strategies.

   1. Export products to be sold through distributors. As India is such a big country, it takes at least a distributor for each state (25 plus 7 Union Territories). For Agip Petroli, it could be difficult to handle such a big number of distributors from Europe.

2. Establish a wholly owned company. For Agip Petroli it is risky and costly to build a distribution network nationwide from scratch as the best ones have already been taken by the competitors (mostly Castrol and Elf). Besides, the country is huge and the market is highly fragmented; therefore, it takes a very good knowledge of each factor, including bureaucracy and politics, which is quite difficult to achieve from the beginning as a new entrant.

3. Set up a joint venture with an Indian partner. This alternative could be pursued entering the market through a 50 percent joint venture between Agip and an Indian partner. We took into consideration the following supply policies:

- Importing finished products. Though the import tax has been reduced to 30 percent (down from 80%), all competitors produce locally, thus they can enjoy a cost advantage.

- Local production. Production can be performed on joint venture's own blending plant or on third parties' plants. Third parties' blenders are cheap, reliable, and have enough blending capacity. Furthermore before the critical mass is reached, production at variable costs is at very low risk. However, as volumes increase it gets more difficult to keep quality and production control on third parties' blenders. On the other hand, the construction of a local blending plant requires higher initial investment and risk associated with it.

The Indian Partner

74 Once it had been decided to enter the Indian market through a joint venture, the key factor to success is to find a partner with a distribution network already in place in the automotive market; this partner should be selected within engineering companies, small Indian oil companies, or vehicle producers.

75 One partner under consideration is Escort LTD. Escort was a conglomerate with interests in the areas of agriculture, transportation, construction, and telecommunications with a turnover of US$ 688 million and 22,000 employees in the year 1994. The group is structured in several joint ventures which also manufacture and sell the following items of major interest for Agip:

- Motorcycles—90,000 Rajdoot and 120,000 Yamaha RX-100 in 50 percent joint venture with Yamaha (market share 33%).
- Mopeds—24,000 units of new model Toro (market share 8%).
- Tractors—20,000 Escort tractors and 18,000 in JV with Ford (market share 25%).
- Pistons and Piston-Rings—These products are sold both directly to engine manufacturers (market share 60%) and to the spare-parts market (market share 40%).

76 Escort's sales organization is very capillary and dealers/distributors are at a very high level compared to the country standard, with a good hold on the market. Besides, the link between dealers and Escort is very strong, and Escort can rely on a long time relationship and count on their support for improvements and restyling of the outlets. These dealers are very well located and the look is at western or Japanese standard. Escort also has a strong link with original equipment manufacturers (OEMs) whose approvals are required to qualify a new brand. A market oriented corporate culture, training facilities, and a highly professional management are other features that contributed to choosing Escort as a possible available partner.

77 On the other hand, Escort has no existing know-how for lubricants and no current involvement in the production of cars. In addition, there might be possible overlaps among the sales organizations of the group companies. Agip Petroli therefore has to carefully evaluate all these factors before deciding whether and how to enter the Indian lubricant market.

Joint Venture Structure

78 The company would be a 50 percent joint venture between Agip and an Indian partner. Agip would bring basically the technical know-how and the brand to the deal which was still unknown in India, whereas the Indian partner would provide the distribution network which was the key factor for the success of the venture and of the entire operation.

EXHIBIT I

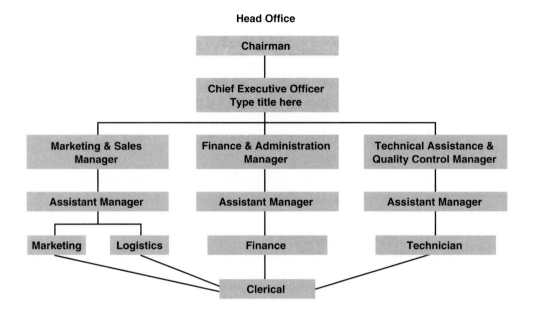

79   As India is such a huge country, we forecasted four regional offices to keep hold of the distributors and promote sales:

North—New Delhi
East—Calcutta
West—Bombay
South—Bangalore

80   The organizational structure required for the short and medium term should be seen in Exhibit I.

DECISION CHART

Kind of decision	Alternative 1	Alternative 2	Alternative 3
Method of Entry	Export Products	Establish a wholly owned company	Joint venture with an Indian partner
Production	Italy	India	India
Distribution	Through local distributors	Build a distribution network	Partner's distribution network
Regions	North and West	North and West	All India

CASE 63

COLGATE-PALMOLIVE ORAL CARE DIVISION IN THE ITALIAN MARKET

1   Colgate is a truly global company serving 5.7 billion people around the world with consumer products that help make their lives healthier, cleaner, and more pleasant. Colgate serves global consumers with products in five major categories: Oral Care, Personal Care, Household Surface Care, Fabric Care, and Pet Nutrition.

2   Its business focus was only in the US until the very early 1900's when the Company began a very aggressive expansion program that led to the establishment of Colgate operations throughout the world. Today, Colgate-Palmolive is an $8.4 billion company, marketing its products in 206 countries and territories. To meet the needs of this vast market, Colgate sets and attains the highest standards for its products. Quality is the hallmark of everything it does. So, too, is consumer value. The Company continually works to understand consumers' changing needs, and then meet those needs with innovative products that are affordable to the greatest number of people.

3   The Oral Care division is concerned with three different kinds of products, Toothpaste, Toothbrushes, and Mouth Rinses. Oral Care is the most profitable category with 26% of Colgate total sales in 1994. Specifically, it accounted for $1972.9 million in 1994 worldwide sales.

4   In Italy, Colgate shares the market with several large competitors such as Unilever, Procter & Gamble, Smithkline Beecham, and Gillette. The future in this country appears complex as well as interesting. In early 1997, Colgate's management faced the problem of how to increase its market share in Italy. In developing a strategy for its Italian business unit, in light of the intense competitive market, Colgate's planners were concerned with answering several questions. How will manufacturers be able to extend their own market shares in a market such as the Italian one which is highly saturated? How can they most effectively communicate the product's characteristics to the consumer? Should they consider other distribution channels?

5   In answering these questions, the planners felt it was necessary to first carefully study the Italian market, especially the strengths and weaknesses of competitors in key to success areas in specific opportunity areas. Within that competitive market framework they then studied the company's comparative position as a first step in developing an overall strategic business unit strategy.

THE INDUSTRY AND COMPETITIVE MARKETS

The Italian market

6   Prior to the case, the Italian oral care market had been growing. The growth was mainly due to consumers' increasing awareness of the oral hygiene importance. The market included three different kinds of products: toothpaste, toothbrushes, and mouth rinses. Italy is not in line with the main European countries in terms of sales, thus, there appear to be very strong growth opportunities.

7   A very important factor in this business is advertising. Advertising has allowed consumers to be aware of the existence of different formulations, demonstrating how important oral hygiene is. The concept of prevention, extendable to toothbrushes and mouth rinses, enabled the beginning of a diversification process and of a specialized supply, and consequently, new items appeared on the shelves of distributors. Between 1980 and 1993, sales of toothpaste, toothbrushes, and mouth rinses grew at incredible levels. In continuation of this trend, the Italian oral care market is expected to continue to grow.

This case was prepared by Allesandro Faccini under the direction of Professor Robert J. Mockler of St. John's University.

Products

8   Three types of products are offered in the oral care industry: toothpaste, toothbrushes, and mouth rinses.

Toothpaste

9   Until 10–15 years ago toothpaste was generally considered as a "soap" to clean teeth. At the same time there were so many different brands that the consumer got confused very easily. In fact, the discriminative factor was still price. In the mid 1980's, Italians began to become aware of the importance of using toothpaste formulated to prevent cavities. Therefore, innovation led to new products on the market. Pastes with grumes represented the first alternative followed by a totally innovative toothpaste made of gel. These were the main innovations, and since then toothpaste became a highly standardized product differing only in color or packaging.

10   In 1993, in the mass-market channel, the toothpaste segment grew by 4.7% in value and by 6.5% in volume. Undoubtedly a good performance, but not as good as it appears if compared to 1990 and 1991 performances when sales in value increased by 16.3% and sales in volume increased by 14.6%. This trend shows that demand developed both in terms of quality and in terms of quantity. Actually the mass market channel is the place where more people purchase toothpaste. The pharmacy is not as important as it was in the past. People purchase specific products in a pharmacy, while toothpaste can be found elsewhere and more cheaply.

Toothbrushes

11   The toothbrush has always been purchased as a support to toothpaste, and only in recent years has it started to be considered as a fundamental instrument for prevention of cavities. Nevertheless, the substitution level is still very low: a toothbrush lasts, on the average, 8 months, whereas dentists suggest changing it every 3 or 4 months. Through an efficient and sensitive advertising campaign, sales in this segment could at least double.

12   Toothbrushes normally sold are the result of a compromise between aesthetics and the functional characteristics that the instrument must have. To this end, leading companies, through their R&D Departments, have tried to develop the best shape in terms of efficiency and practicality. Variations in brushes mainly concern the handle and the upper part. The bristle length, its hardness and layout are varied based on different demands and requests. Generally, toothbrush quality depends on how it is produced and on the raw materials utilized in its production. Natural bristles were very popular for some time in the past and then were substituted with synthetic bristles that offer a high degree of versatility and are cheaper than their natural counterparts. In Italy sales in 1993 were 55 million units for a total amount of Lit120 billion, 80 billion of which were generated from the mass-market distribution channel and the remainder from pharmacies.

Mouth Rinses

13   These products represent a recent innovation in the oral care industry. In Italy a mouth rinse was made for the first time in 1990. Its qualities may be therapeutic or cosmetic. The therapeutic mouth rinse is generally suggested by dentists in cases of gingival problems and is particularly recommended to those people who usually suffer from this specific problem. The cosmetic mouth rinse, on the other hand, can be used daily to have a fresh breath, and no specific recommendations are made.

14   Following the Anglo-Saxon countries example where mouth rinse growth reached incredible levels, the product was shifted from the specialized channel to the mass-market one, where it attained remarkable sales success. A mouth rinse is addressed to younger consumers, who are more sensitive to innovation. As the youngest segment of the oral care market it had the most potential. In 1993, 2,382,000 liters were sold for a total amount of Lit36.2 billion. The mouth rinse market was in a growth stage, therefore, it was expected to grow in the near future.

Customers

15   The Italian consumer was willing to spend growing percentages of his/her budget for personal care to increase or maintain his/her physical and aesthetical well-being. The average net income of Italian people was high enough to allow them to invest part of their budget in purchases of oral hygiene products. Thus, the market was massive.

16   Dividing the Italian people by age groups allowed industry experts to identify people, particularly in the age range of from 13 to 40, as the most important market. Despite the demographic reduction, it is a target market characterized by an increasing consumption propensity, since younger people tended to pay attention to their looks. Specifically, the several groups were divided by product as follows:

Toothpaste

- Under 14. This age group included children who tended not to be interested in cleaning their teeth. For this reason they showed low interest in the toothpaste.
- 14–17. This age group included adolescents who understood the importance of practicing correct oral hygiene. Nevertheless, they still were not particularly attracted by this product, showed a medium interest, and preferred to spend their money in different ways.
- 18–34. This age group was absolutely aware of the magnitude of good oral care. In fact, they were willing to spend more money if they appreciated one product's quality. For this reason, they showed a very high interest in using the toothpaste.
- 35–40. This is an age group in which most of its components were not very attracted by a particular toothpaste, and were driven by price in making their purchases.
- Over 40. This age group included people who do not use this product correctly. They show a low interest for this item and they usually buy the cheapest brands.

Toothbrushes

- Under 14. The real purchasers of this product within this age group were the children's parents. Thus, this was a group in which the interest for this product was very low.
- 14–17. Adolescents were a very heterogeneous group in which some, looking for the best, directly bought the toothbrush; others accepted what their parents used to buy without considering the product features. Generally, this age group showed a medium interest for this product.
- 18–34. Almost all of this age group were aware of the importance of practicing correct oral hygiene. In fact, they were usually informed about the toothbrush characteristics and bought the product that met their needs at that moment. They paid very close attention in their purchases, showing a very high interest for this product.
- 35–40. This age group included people oriented differently towards this product. A few components were highly interested in the toothbrush features paying attention when they bought it. Others considered the price as the only important factor to worry about. Generally, this age group showed a medium interest in purchasing this product.
- Over 40. Most of the people belonging to this age group were no longer interested in purchasing a toothbrush with particular features. They brushed their teeth because they were accustomed to doing it. In general, they showed low interest towards this product.

Mouth Rinses

- Under 14. Like the toothbrush, mouth rinse was usually bought by the children's parents, but in this case children sometimes pushed their parents into buying it because they were attracted by its color, its taste, or simply by the nice little bottle. This age group generally showed a medium interest for this product.
- 14–17. This was an age group particularly attracted by this product because it was considered totally new. For this reason they used it, and showed a quiet high interest for the mouth rinse.
- 18–34. This age group was not only interested in the novelty that this product represented in the Italian market, but also in its characteristics. Therefore, they showed a very high interest towards the mouth rinse.

- 35–40. Very few people within this age group were interested in the mouth rinse characteristics, and they bought it when they had gum problems or when the dentist suggested that they use it. Their interest for this product was low.
- Over 40. Most of the people within this group were not interested at all in this product, even considering it as totally useless. Hence, they showed a very low interest for mouth rinses.

17   Since the 1960's, the consumption of oral care items has been increasing but Italy was not yet at the level at which the English or Americans used these products, mainly with reference to the frequent substitution of the toothbrushes. As for the demand by the diverse age groups, the one that paid the most attention to oral care was the 18–34 group as shown above. Women generally showed more care for the teeth, perhaps due to their consideration of this practice as an aesthetical operation. Moreover, immediately after lunch, most women were at home or were able to carry toothbrush and paste with them.

Promotion

18   Promotion was particularly important in the mass-market of the oral care industry. In Italy in 1993, companies in the oral care industry invested Lit110.4 billion to promote lines and Lit70 billion between January and September 1994, confirming a negative trend started two years earlier. Compared to 1992, investments in promotion decreased by about 5%. This situation showed a reduced interest of the companies towards the promotion tool, since the promotion expenses reached about 18% of total sales. So high investments were due to the presence of particularly aggressive competitors able to make enormous financial efforts.

19   Investing in promotion within this industry was both necessary and extremely binding. In a crowded market like this, convincing the consumer to buy one product instead of another, becoming a part of his/her purchasing habits, was not very easy. In 1993, the most widely used advertising tool was the television. In fact, producers spent Lit87.7 billion in both public and private networks, representing 78% of the total annual budget. The remaining 22% was invested in promotion through newspapers (13%), magazines (6%), radio (2%), and specialized magazines (1%). Analyzing the promotion investments by brand, it came out that a few large manufacturers increased sales because of TV advertising. In 1993, Unilever was the major investor with Lit30 billion, in the second position there was Procter & Gamble with Lit24 billion, and finally Colgate with about Lit16 billion.

20   Bill-postings were totally absent due to the big advertising power of television. However, producers found the television to be the ideal tool because it reached millions of people.

21   In addition to the traditional ways of advertising, other promotion tools were used in the Italian oral care industry, such as sales promotion and personal selling. Sales promotion based on the "three for the price of two" was particularly effective in the oral care market. Also promotions based on a kit including several products like one toothpaste, one toothbrush, and one mouth rinse, were very effective and attracted many consumers. Obviously, initiatives like these could not last for a long time. Their objective was not only to determine a lasting sales increase, but also to withdraw as many consumers as possible from the competitors.

22   Personal selling was a kind of promotion mainly used for pharmacies and independent stores. Sales people were assigned to a certain number of pharmacies or stores within a specific territory and periodically they called on them. Since their salary was mainly based on commissions, sales people were free to make discounts, within a fixed range, based on quantities ordered.

Distribution

23   The distribution channel choice was a very important marketing-mix choice. Several factors were considered to select the right channel such as the product characteristics, consumer behavior, competitors' behavior, and government regulations. Oral care producers, generally, used two main channels: the mass-market (GDO) and the pharmaceutical.

24   The manufacturer that decided to market an oral care product line through the pharmaceutical channel understood the consumer who would have been able to purchase the same product in a big

chain store. Since in a pharmacy the consumer could get personal treatment by specialized personnel, it played a fundamental role in the consumer's final choice. In fact, for this added value the consumer was willing to pay more for the same product. Consequently, the producer pursued higher advantages from the distribution through a specialized channel, despite the higher costs. In the long run, in terms of revenues, it was a profitable choice, because the price per unit in the pharmacy was higher than that of the big chains.

25   On the other hand, the big chains were chosen when the purpose was to increase the company's presence in the mass-market, aiming for an extremely high number of units sold. In the mass-market, companies dealt with important distributors who were able to sell the product at a national level. As for the pharmacy, on the contrary, every single sales point had to be directly contacted. To be present in a big chain was very important for a company, but even more important was how the product was positioned on the shelves. Since the brand loyalty was very low within the oral care industry, a good position on the shelf would be a determinant in consumer purchasing behavior.

26   The following chart provides an overview of several brands' positions, on average, on the shelves of the main Italian chains:

Company	Brand	% of Shelf Space
Colgate-Palmolive	Colgate	16.8
Unilever	Mentadent	15.3
Procter & Gamble	AZ	12.3
Gillette	Oral B	7.0
Smithkline Beecham	Aquafresh	5.5
Ciccarelli	Pasta del Capitano	5.0
Smithkline Beecham	Macleens	3.9
Unilever	Durban's	3.9
Henkel-Cosmetics	Antica Erboristeria	3.0
Stafford-Miller	Sensodyne	1.9
Unilever	Benefit	1.8
Manetti & Roberts	Chlorodont	1.6
Colgate-Palmolive	Defend	1.4
Unilever	Denti in Crescita	1.3
Henkel-Cosmetics	Thera-Med	1.1
Others	—	18.2

Source: GDO 1994.

27   Independent stores represented a very small share of total market sales, and in the near future sales were expected to be constant. The reason was that their prices were higher than those of big chains and many brands were not present in independent stores. Thus, consumers preferred to buy products either at a pharmacy or from a big chain. Independent stores still survived in small towns where big chains did not have sales points, and in mountain villages.

28   In terms of total sales it was obvious how much more important the mass-market was if compared to the specialized retail and independent stores. In a few years the mass-market sales increased from 44.7% in 1989, to 92% in 1994 while the pharmacies channel had only 7%, and independent stores 1%.

29   Multinational companies found it difficult to enter the Italian oral care market. In fact, after the usual market researches to monitor the environment, market regulation, consumer behavior, and so on, they met cultural obstacles. In Italy, unlike the US and the main European countries, big chains, small stores, pharmacies, etc., are not open 24 hours-a-day but have different opening hours depending on the season, except for the big chains that usually open from 9:00 a.m. to 7:30 p.m. This situation limited a lot each company's sales that, moreover, had to face very high personnel costs. These were the main reasons that could be considered as a kind of entry barrier. Nevertheless, the Italian oral care market still remains highly profitable and leading companies fight to gain market share.

Competition

30   The oral care market was characterized by the presence of very large multinationals, such as Procter & Gamble, Unilever, Colgate-Palmolive, Smithkline Beecham, and Gillette. The market was also characterized by a low brand loyalty that consequently led to a continual engagement of the companies with the consumer; it was a competition that involved all marketing choices, they fought over prices, product characteristics, distribution choices, even communication. Investments in advertising were incredibly high, and the market segmentation never ended.

Procter & Gamble

31   Procter & Gamble was born in 1956. It manufactures and markets detersives and soaps, distributes and sells pharmaceutical products, cosmetics, perfumes, hygienic products, and food products. It invests $800 million in R&D every year, and 6000 researchers are engaged all over the world. In 1986 the company acquired the "AZ" brand from Pierrel, and in a few years it has been able to implement this product line and launch three new products: AZ Tartar Control (Paste), AZ Verde (Paste), AZ Tartar Control (Gel). Procter decided to market this product line on the mass-market channel rather than on the pharmacy channel only. Between 1991 and 1992 the company launched two new products of the same line in a "Double Package." This strategic choice was made to meet the needs of consumers who asked for more than one package, and the double package allowed a savings of 20% compared to the single one.

32   P&G's strategy was based on a constant evolution and differentiation of the product to create the most complete product line existing in the market. The odontological research was the starting point of each strategy. The many different products were developed as a consequence of the direct cooperation between the R&D department and the dentists.

Unilever

33   Unilever was born in 1930. It actually operates in 75 countries and has over 300,000 employees in more than 500 subsidiaries. Net sales in 1992 were Lit53,000 billion. 60% of sales came from Europe, 20% from North America, and 20% from other continents. In Italy Unilever in 1992 had 7,700 employees and net sales of Lit4,000 billion.

34   In the oral care market the Company was present with its important division Elida Gibbs which proposed all the typical oral care products, toothpaste, toothbrush, and mouth rinses. In the toothbrush segment Unilever was the absolute leader with 37% market share in volume; 21% market share in the mouth rinse segment; and 28.8% market share in the toothpaste segment. Its brands included Mentadent, Durban's, Benefit, and Pepsodent. Its leadership stemmed from very precise strategic planning based on the combination of different brands positioned at different levels on the market, therefore, not in competition with each other.

THE COMPANY

History

35   Founded in 1806, Colgate-Palmolive Company has been recognized as the global leader in oral care for well over one hundred years. These achievements are possible because Colgate consistently demonstrates superiority in meeting professional and consumer needs for oral care products. More than 40% of toothpaste and 25% of toothbrushes sold around the globe carry the Colgate name. Throughout Colgate's oral care history, the constant goal has been to improve oral health through superior technology and ongoing patient education programs.

36   Colgate provides leadership in establishing and maintaining worldwide oral health education programs. Colgate literally taught many of the world's people how to brush and care for their teeth. Each year, 24 million children in 43 countries take part in Colgate programs. In the US, the "Bright Smiles, Bright Futures" educational programs and materials are designed to help dental professionals and elementary school teachers bring good oral health to the next generation of American children. Today,

Colgate continues to deliver superior products and services that improve the oral health and overall quality of life for consumers everywhere. Colgate achieves continued innovation by linking the health of consumers with the latest research findings and technological advances in dental science. Colgate has long recognized the value of maintaining a firm partnership with the worldwide professional dental community, as well as the wisdom of maintaining a substantial investment in professional education, clinical research, and technology.

37   In 1993, Colgate Oral Pharmaceuticals Inc., a subsidiary of Colgate-Palmolive Company, was created in Canton, Massachusetts. This subsidiary was formed to emphasize the company's commitment to developing innovative therapies specifically for the dental professional. Investing in advanced technology, listening to the profession, and encouraging innovation are key elements of Colgate Oral Pharmaceutical's leadership in professional oral health products.

Company Mission

38   Since the very early 1900's, when the Company began its expansion throughout the world, the mission statement of Colgate was one word—QUALITY. Other objectives for the Italian market included establishing Colgate as a major competitor for contractual manufacturing work, such as government contracts to supply the Italian Army, Air Force, and Navy. Colgate applied its strategic ideal of quality to everything it did. It always made heavy investments in research and development in order to find the right product to meet the consumer needs.

Products

39   Products manufactured by Colgate-Palmolive in the Italian oral care sector consist of two main lines:

- Products addressed to the big distribution and independent stores;
- Products addressed to the specialized channel.

40   Each product line is composed of several sub-lines. The following chart lists the many different products made by Colgate-Palmolive in the Oral Care segment:

Toothpaste	Mouth Rinses	Toothbrushes
Colgate	Plax	Colgate
Defend	Periogard	Zig Zag
Periogard	Chlorodex	Total
Fluorigard		
ABC		
Gel Kam		
Platinum		

41   Colgate Palmolive as a product strategy tends to lengthen the life cycle of each product line in order to attract consumers with different needs and tastes, and to give an image of completeness of the product line. At the same time it adds several variations to some single products, increasing the number of products for every brand. Toothbrushes are offered in different shapes and colors, mouth rinses are offered in the half a liter size only. The segmentation operated by Colgate-Palmolive in the toothpaste market depends on the attitude/interest the consumer has towards oral hygiene practices. This is a factor depending on the education level, the age, and the social and economic level.

Customers

42   In the oral care market, brand loyalty was very low; seldom did consumers buy the same product and the tendency was towards a diversification of the purchase. In this situation, advertising, especially

TABLE 1
Decision Chart

Kind of Decision	Alternative 1	Alternative 2	Alternative 3
Product			
Toothpaste:			
Innovation	New formula with a more effective preventive action	New formula with natural ingredients	New formula with a more effective preventive action
Packaging	New and different packages for high priced and low priced items	One standardized package for each differently priced item	New and different packages for high priced and low priced items
Brand name	Different brand names for items positioned at different price levels	One brand name for all items	Different brand names for items positioned at different price levels
Toothbrush:			
Innovation	New shapes and colors	One standardized shape	New shapes and colors
Bristles	Natural fibers	Synthetic fibers	Synthetic fibers
Mouth Rinse:			
Kind of product	Therapeutic	Cosmetic	Both cosmetic and therapeutic
Size	Different sizes	Half a liter only	Different sizes
Distribution			
Channel	Big chains and independents for low/medium price products and pharmacies for high price (specialized) items	Big chains and independents for low/medium price products and pharmacies for high price (specialized) items	Big chains and independents for low/medium price products and pharmacies for high price (specialized) items
Promotion			
Advertising	Concentrate investments on TV advertising	Advertising on TV, radios, magazines, newspapers	Advertising on TV, radios, newspapers, magazines and bill-postings
Sales Promotion	No investments in sales promotion	Investments in 3×2 sales promotion	No investment in sales promotion

on TV, becomes a central point, absolutely important for the consumer who is also influenced by the packaging. A survey done in 1993 about oral care products shows the consumer is attracted by:

- The packaging (36%)
- The price (26%)
- Their recognition of the product (21%)

43   From this survey the importance of the packaging was underscored. In fact, over the last years it has been experiencing an incredible evolution mainly concerned with the material utilized. It shifted from a metallic tube to a soft plastic one which was lighter, and more manageable. More recently, the dispenser was the most important innovation and consumers found it very attractive which increased

TABLE 2
Market Shares

Toothpaste

Unilever	28.7%	(Mentadent 19%, Durbans 2.9%, Pepsodent 3.7%, Benefit 2.7%)
Colgate-Palmolive	22.3%	(Colgate 19.6%, Defend 2.7%)
Procter & Gamble	18.4%	(Az Verde 7.8%, Az Tartar control 6.4%, Protezione Gengive 3.6%)
Smithkline Beecham	9.7%	(Aquafresh 5.8%, Macleens 3.5%, Iodosan 0.4%)
Farm. Ciccarelli	8.7%	(Pasta del Capitano)
Henkel-Cosmetics	4.5%	(Antica Erboristeria 3.5%, Thera-Med 1%)
Gillette	1.9%	(Oral B)
Manetti & Roberts	1.7%	(Chlorodont)
Stafford-Miller	0.9%	(Sensodyne)
Sodalco	0.4%	(Fresh&Clean)
BYK Gulden	0.1%	(Emoform)

Toothbrushes

Unilever	36.9%	(Mentadent 21.3%; Gibbs 15.6%)
Gillette	14.4%	(Oral B)
Colgate	8.7%	
Procter & Gamble	8%	(Az)
Piave	8%	
Squibb	5%	
Others	19%	

Mouth Rinses

Colgate	52%	(Plax, Actibrush)
Unilever	21%	(Mentadent)
Johnson & Johnson	9%	(Reach)
Gillette	8%	(Oral B Fluorinse)
Sodalco	4%	
Ciccarelli	4%	
Others	2%	

the demand as soon as it was marketed. It is not easy to delineate the classic Colgate consumer's profile due to the low brand loyalty existing in this field. Nevertheless, the 18–34 age group remained Colgate's main target market since this was the group most interested in purchasing oral care products.

TOWARDS THE FUTURE

44 In 1997, the future for Colgate-Palmolive looked just as promising as the recent past had been successful. For the Oral Care segment, characterized by a continual launch of new items, keys to success were distributed in two functional areas: in the R&D department product innovation was the determinant, while in the marketing area a good relationship with the distribution channel was important. In addition, the qualitative standards and the sale price were important but not fundamental.

45 Some executives argued that to keep pace with new trends, the proposal of new items with additional characteristics rather than the usual products always carrying the same features, became critical to success. These innovative products, in the toothpaste segment especially, could present a dramatic increase in the preventive action against the cavities, or they could be natural products. Other managers argued that the innovative engagement had to focus on the packaging, through new shapes, new materials, and graphic variants, while others said that a standardized package could be

considered a true innovation by the consumers. Some other executives argued that a good choice would be to create more products carrying new brand names to be sold in the mass-market channel, trying to copy Unilver's strategy.

46   Because of this new continually changing scenario, brands of leading companies were expected to be forced to be present in a growing number of niche markets. As for the toothpaste segment, Colgate, in order to respond to this market trend, marketed different brands, each one covering a diverse area: Colgate and Defend in the mass-market channel, and the specialized items like Periogard, Fluorigard, Gel Kam, ABC, and Platinum in the pharmaceutical.

47   In Italy Colgate has been known since World War II, therefore, it was considered a traditional brand. Competitors' products were younger and it was easier for them to build the image required by the market in that moment. Actually, the toothpaste market in the mass-market channel is extremely crowded, consequently new opportunities to increase the business come from other segments such as toothbrushes and mouth rinses.

48   In fact, as for the toothbrush market, some managers said that sales within this segment could double, and this could occur through a sensitive advertising campaign aimed at making the consumer aware of the importance of a necessary toothbrush change every 3–4 months, as dentists suggest. Other executives thought the right strategy to pursue would be the aesthetical route through new shapes or even new materials. Some managers argued that, like the toothpaste, a standardized shape for the toothbrush to become "the classic Colgate shape" could represent a good alternative. These alternatives include a very different economic engagement for this segment, and each proposal has to be well evaluated by the top management.

49   As for the mouth rinse segment, some executives argued that Colgate should produce therapeutic rinses only, or just cosmetic rinses. Others said the company had to manufacture both. Some other managers thought the right way would be to offer different sizes as opposed to one.

50   In short, management is considering ways in which Colgate can differentiate itself from its competitors and improve its strategic position in the long run.

Case Index

SUBJECT INDEX